THE NEW INTERPRETER'S® BIBLE

IN TWELVE VOLUMES

VOLUME FIVE

THE NEW INTERPRETER'S® BIBLE

GENERAL ARTICLES
&
INTRODUCTION, COMMENTARY, & REFLECTIONS
FOR EACH BOOK OF THE BIBLE
INCLUDING
THE APOCRYPHAL/DEUTEROCANONICAL BOOKS
IN
TWELVE VOLUMES

VOLUME
V

ABINGDON PRESS
Nashville

THE NEW INTERPRETER'S® BIBLE
VOLUME V

Copyright © 1997 by Abingdon Press

This book is printed on recycled, acid-free paper.

Library of Congress Cataloging-in-Publication Data

The New Interpreter's Bible: general articles & introduction,
  commentary, & reflections for each book of the Bible, including the
  Apocryphal/Deuterocanonical books.
    p. cm.
    Full texts and critical notes of the New International Version and
  the New Revised Standard Version of the Bible in parallel columns.
    Includes bibliographical references.
    ISBN 0-687-27818-X (v. 5: alk. paper)
    1. Bible—Commentaries. 2. Abingdon Press. I. Bible. English.
  New International. 1994. II. Bible. English. New Revised
  Standard. 1994.
  BS491.2.N484   1994
  220.7'7—dc20

                                                                      94-21092
                                                                      CIP

PUBLICATION STAFF

President and Publisher: Neil M. Alexander
Editorial Director: Harriett Jane Olson
Project Director: Jack A. Keller, Jr.
Production Editor: Linda S. Allen
Assistant Editors: Deborah A. Appler
                  Joan M. Shoup
Design Manager: Walter E. Wynne
Designer: J. S. Laughbaum
Copy Processing Manager: Sylvia S. Marlow
Composition Specialist: Kathy M. Harding
Publishing Systems Analyst: Glenn R. Hinton
Prepress Manager: Billy W. Murphy
Prepress Systems Technicians: Thomas E. Mullins
                              J. Calvin Buckner
Director of Production Processes: James E. Leath
Scheduling: Laurene M. Brazzell
            Tracey D. Evans
Print Procurement Coordinator: David M. Sanders

97 98 99 00 01 02 03 04 05 06—10 9 8 7 6 5 4 3 2 1

MANUFACTURED IN THE UNITED STATES OF AMERICA

CONSULTANTS

NEIL M. ALEXANDER
President and Publisher
The United Methodist Publishing House
Nashville, Tennessee

OWEN F. CAMPION
Associate Publisher
Our Sunday Visitor
Huntington, Indiana

MINERVA G. CARCAÑO
Director
Mexican American Program
Perkins School of Theology
Southern Methodist University
Dallas, Texas

V. L. DAUGHTERY, JR.
Pastor
Park Avenue United Methodist Church
Valdosta, Georgia

SHARON NEUFER EMSWILER
Pastor
First United Methodist Church
Rock Island, Illinois

JUAN G. FELICIANO VALERA
Pastor
Iglesia Metodista "Juan Wesley"
Arecibo, Puerto Rico

CELIA BREWER MARSHALL
Lecturer
University of North Carolina at Charlotte
Charlotte, North Carolina

NANCY C. MILLER-HERRON
Attorney and clergy member of the
Tennessee Conference
The United Methodist Church
Dresden, Tennessee

ROBERT C. SCHNASE
Pastor
First United Methodist Church
McAllen, Texas

BILL SHERMAN
Pastor
Woodmont Baptist Church
Nashville, Tennessee

RODNEY T. SMOTHERS
Pastor
Central United Methodist Church
Atlanta, Georgia

WILLIAM D. WATLEY
Pastor
St. James African Methodist Episcopal Church
Newark, New Jersey

TALLULAH FISHER WILLIAMS
Superintendent
Chicago Northwestern District
The United Methodist Church
Chicago, Illinois

SUK-CHONG YU
Pastor
San Francisco Korean United Methodist Church
San Francisco, California

CONTRIBUTORS

ELIZABETH ACHTEMEIER
Adjunct Professor of Bible and Homiletics
Union Theological Seminary in Virginia
Richmond, Virginia
(Presbyterian Church [U.S.A.])
Joel

LESLIE C. ALLEN
Professor of Old Testament
Fuller Theological Seminary
Pasadena, California
(Baptist)
1 & 2 Chronicles

GARY A. ANDERSON
Associate Professor of Religious Studies
University of Virginia
Charlottesville, Virginia
(The Roman Catholic Church)
Introduction to Israelite Religion

DAVID L. BARTLETT
Lantz Professor of Preaching and
Communication
The Divinity School
Yale University
New Haven, Connecticut
(American Baptist Churches in the U.S.A.)
1 Peter

ROBERT A. BENNETT, PH.D.
Cambridge, Massachusetts
(The Episcopal Church)
Zephaniah

ADELE BERLIN
Robert H. Smith Professor of Hebrew Bible
Associate Provost for Faculty Affairs
University of Maryland
College Park, Maryland
Introduction to Hebrew Poetry

BRUCE C. BIRCH
Professor of Old Testament
Wesley Theological Seminary
Washington, DC
(The United Methodist Church)
1 & 2 Samuel

PHYLLIS A. BIRD
Associate Professor of Old Testament
Interpretation
Garrett-Evangelical Theological Seminary
Evanston, Illinois
(The United Methodist Church)
The Authority of the Bible

C. CLIFTON BLACK
Associate Professor of New Testament
Perkins School of Theology
Southern Methodist University
Dallas, Texas
(The United Methodist Church)
1, 2, & 3 John

JOSEPH BLENKINSOPP
John A. O'Brien Professor of Biblical Studies
Department of Theology
University of Notre Dame
Notre Dame, Indiana
(The Roman Catholic Church)
Introduction to the Pentateuch

M. EUGENE BORING
I. Wylie and Elizabeth M. Briscoe Professor of
New Testament
Brite Divinity School
Texas Christian University
Fort Worth, Texas
(Christian Church [Disciples of Christ])
Matthew

ix

WALTER BRUEGGEMANN
William Marcellus McPheeters Professor of Old
Testament
Columbia Theological Seminary
Decatur, Georgia
(United Church of Christ)
Exodus

DAVID G. BUTTRICK
Professor of Homiletics and Liturgics
The Divinity School
Vanderbilt University
Nashville, Tennessee
(United Church of Christ)
The Use of the Bible in Preaching

RONALD E. CLEMENTS
Samuel Davidson Professor of Old Testament
King's College
University of London
London, England
(Baptist Union of Great Britain and Ireland)
Deuteronomy

RICHARD J. CLIFFORD, S.J.
Professor of Old Testament
Weston Jesuit School of Theology
Cambridge, Massachusetts
(The Roman Catholic Church)
Introduction to Wisdom Literature

JOHN J. COLLINS
Professor of Hebrew Bible
The Divinity School
University of Chicago
Chicago, Illinois
(The Roman Catholic Church)
Introduction to Early Jewish Religion

ROBERT B. COOTE
Professor of Old Testament
San Francisco Theological Seminary
San Anselmo, California
(Presbyterian Church [U.S.A.])
Joshua

FRED B. CRADDOCK
Bandy Distinguished Professor of Preaching
and New Testament, Emeritus
Candler School of Theology
Emory University
Atlanta, Georgia
(Christian Church [Disciples of Christ])
Hebrews

TONI CRAVEN
Professor of Hebrew Bible
Brite Divinity School
Texas Christian University
Fort Worth, Texas
(The Roman Catholic Church)
Introduction to Narrative Literature

JAMES L. CRENSHAW
Robert L. Flowers Professor of Old Testament
The Divinity School
Duke University
Durham, North Carolina
(Baptist)
Sirach

KEITH R. CRIM
Pastor
New Concord Presbyterian Church
Concord, Virginia
(Presbyterian Church [U.S.A.])
Modern English Versions of the Bible

R. ALAN CULPEPPER
Dean
The School of Theology
Mercer University
Atlanta, Georgia
(Southern Baptist Convention)
Luke

KATHERYN PFISTERER DARR
Associate Professor of Hebrew Bible
The School of Theology
Boston University
Boston, Massachusetts
(The United Methodist Church)
Ezekiel

ROBERT DORAN
Professor of Religion
Amherst College
Amherst, Massachusetts
1 & 2 Maccabees

THOMAS B. DOZEMAN
Professor of Old Testament
United Theological Seminary
Dayton, Ohio
(Presbyterian Church [U.S.A.])
Numbers

JAMES D. G. DUNN
Lightfoot Professor of Divinity
Department of Theology
University of Durham
Durham, England
(The Methodist Church [Great Britain])
1 & 2 Timothy; Titus

ELDON JAY EPP
Harkness Professor of Biblical Literature
and Chairman of the Department of Religion
Case Western Reserve University
Cleveland, Ohio
(The Episcopal Church)
*Ancient Texts and Versions of the New
Testament*

KATHLEEN ROBERTSON FARMER
Professor of Old Testament
United Theological Seminary
Dayton, Ohio
(The United Methodist Church)
Ruth

CAIN HOPE FELDER
Professor of New Testament Language
and Literature
The School of Divinity
Howard University
Washington, DC
(The United Methodist Church)
Philemon

TERENCE E. FRETHEIM
Professor of Old Testament
Luther Seminary
Saint Paul, Minnesota
(Evangelical Lutheran Church in America)
Genesis

FRANCISCO O. GARCÍA-TRETO
Professor of Religion and Chair of the
Department of Religion
Trinity University
San Antonio, Texas
(Presbyterian Church [U.S.A.])
Nahum

CATHERINE GUNSALUS GONZÁLEZ
Professor of Church History
Columbia Theological Seminary
Decatur, Georgia
(Presbyterian Church [U.S.A.])
*The Use of the Bible in Hymns, Liturgy,
and Education*

JUSTO L. GONZÁLEZ
Adjunct Professor of Church History
Columbia Theological Seminary
Decatur, Georgia
(The United Methodist Church)
*How the Bible Has Been Interpreted in
Christian Tradition*

DONALD E. GOWAN
Robert Cleveland Holland Professor of Old
Testament
Pittsburgh Theological Seminary
Pittsburgh, Pennsylvania
(Presbyterian Church [U.S.A.])
Amos

JUDITH MARIE GUNDRY-VOLF
Assistant Professor of New Testament
Fuller Theological Seminary
Pasadena, California
(Presbyterian Church [U.S.A.])
Ephesians

DANIEL J. HARRINGTON
Professor of New Testament
Weston School of Theology
Cambridge, Massachusetts
(The Roman Catholic Church)
Introduction to the Canon

RICHARD B. HAYS
Associate Professor of New Testament
The Divinity School
Duke University
Durham, North Carolina
(The United Methodist Church)
Galatians

THEODORE HIEBERT
Professor of Old Testament
McCormick Theological
Seminary
Chicago, Illinois
(Mennonite Church)
Habakkuk

CARL R. HOLLADAY
Professor of New Testament
Candler School of Theology
Emory University
Atlanta, Georgia
*Contemporary Methods of Reading the
Bible*

MORNA D. HOOKER
Lady Margaret's Professor of Divinity
The Divinity School
University of Cambridge
Cambridge, England
(The Methodist Church [Great Britain])
Philippians

DAVID C. HOPKINS
Professor of Old Testament
Wesley Theological Seminary
Washington, DC
(United Church of Christ)
Life in Ancient Palestine

DENISE DOMBKOWSKI HOPKINS
Professor of Old Testament
Wesley Theological Seminary
Washington, DC
(United Church of Christ)
Judith

LUKE T. JOHNSON
Robert W. Woodruff Professor of New
Testament and Christian Origins
Candler School of Theology
Emory University
Atlanta, Georgia
(The Roman Catholic Church)
James

WALTER C. KAISER, JR.
Colman Mockler Distinguished Professor
of Old Testament
Gordon-Conwell Theological Seminary
South Hamilton, Massachusetts
(The Evangelical Free Church of America)
Leviticus

LEANDER E. KECK
Winkley Professor of Biblical Theology
The Divinity School
Yale University
New Haven, Connecticut
(Christian Church [Disciples of Christ])
Introduction to The New Interpreter's Bible

CHAN-HIE KIM
Professor of New Testament and Director of
Korean Studies
The School of Theology at Claremont
Claremont, California
(The United Methodist Church)
Reading the Bible as Asian Americans

RALPH W. KLEIN
Dean and Christ Seminary-Seminex Professor of
Old Testament
Lutheran School of Theology at Chicago
Chicago, Illinois
(Evangelical Lutheran Church in America)
Ezra; Nehemiah

MICHAEL KOLARCIK, S.J.
Assistant Professor
Regis College
Toronto, Ontario
Canada
(The Roman Catholic Church)
Book of Wisdom

WILLIAM L. LANE
Paul T. Walls Professor of Wesleyan
and Biblical Studies
Department of Religion
Seattle Pacific University
Seattle, Washington
(Free Methodist Church of North America)
2 Corinthians

ANDREW T. LINCOLN
Department of Biblical Studies
University of Sheffield
Sheffield, England
(The Church of England)
Colossians

J. CLINTON MCCANN, JR.
Evangelical Associate Professor of
Biblical Interpretation
Eden Theological Seminary
St. Louis, Missouri
(Presbyterian Church [U.S.A.])
Psalms

ABRAHAM J. MALHERBE
Buckingham Professor of New Testament
Criticism and Interpretation, Emeritus
The Divinity School
Yale University
New Haven, Connecticut
(Church of Christ)
*The Cultural Context of the New Testament:
The Greco-Roman World*

W. EUGENE MARCH
Dean and Arnold Black Rhodes Professor
of Old Testament
Louisville Presbyterian Theological Seminary
Louisville, Kentucky
(Presbyterian Church [U.S.A.])
Haggai

JAMES EARL MASSEY
Dean Emeritus and
Distinguished Professor-at-Large
The School of Theology
Anderson University
Preacher-in-Residence, Park Place Church
Anderson, Indiana
(Church of God [Anderson, Ind.])
*Reading the Bible from Particular Social
Locations: An Introduction;
Reading the Bible as African Americans*

J. MAXWELL MILLER
Professor of Old Testament
Candler School of Theology
Emory University
Atlanta, Georgia
(The United Methodist Church)
Introduction to the History of Ancient Israel

PATRICK D. MILLER
Charles T. Haley Professor of Old Testament
Theology
Princeton Theological Seminary
Princeton, New Jersey
(Presbyterian Church [U.S.A.])
Jeremiah

FREDERICK J. MURPHY
Professor
Department of Religious Studies
College of the Holy Cross
Worcester, Massachusetts
(The Roman Catholic Church)
Introduction to Apocalyptic Literature

CAROL A. NEWSOM
Associate Professor of Old Testament
Candler School of Theology
Emory University
Atlanta, Georgia
(The Episcopal Church)
Job

GEORGE W. E. NICKELSBURG
Professor of Christian Origins and Early Judaism
School of Religion
University of Iowa
Iowa City, Iowa
(Evangelical Lutheran Church in America)
*The Jewish Context of the New
Testament*

IRENE NOWELL
Associate Professor of Religious Studies
Benedictine College
Atchison, Kansas
(The Roman Catholic Church)
Tobit

KATHLEEN M. O'CONNOR
Professor of Old Testament Language,
Literature, and Exegesis
Columbia Theological Seminary
Decatur, Georgia
(The Roman Catholic Church)
Lamentations

GAIL R. O'DAY
Almar H. Shatford Associate Professor of Homiletics
Candler School of Theology
Emory University
Atlanta, Georgia
(United Church of Christ)
John

BEN C. OLLENBURGER
Professor of Biblical Theology
Associated Mennonite Biblical Seminary
Elkhart, Indiana
(Mennonite Church)
Zechariah

DENNIS T. OLSON
Associate Professor of Old Testament
Princeton Theological Seminary
Princeton, New Jersey
(Evangelical Lutheran Church in America)
Judges

CAROLYN OSIEK
Professor of New Testament
Department of Biblical Languages
and Literature
Catholic Theological Union
Chicago, Illinois
(The Roman Catholic Church)
Reading the Bible as Women

SAMUEL PAGÁN
President
Evangelical Seminary of Puerto Rico
San Juan, Puerto Rico
(Christian Church [Disciples of Christ])
Obadiah

SIMON B. PARKER
Associate Professor of Hebrew Bible and
    Harrell F. Beck Scholar in Hebrew Scripture
The School of Theology
Boston University
Boston, Massachusetts
(The United Methodist Church)
*The Ancient Near Eastern Literary
    Background of the Old Testament*

PHEME PERKINS
Professor of New Testament
Boston College
Chestnut Hill, Massachusetts
(The Roman Catholic Church)
Mark

DAVID L. PETERSEN
Professor of Old Testament
The Iliff School of Theology
Denver, Colorado
(Presbyterian Church [U.S.A.])
Introduction to Prophetic Literature

CHRISTOPHER C. ROWLAND
Dean Ireland's Professor of the Exegesis
    of Holy Scripture
The Queen's College
Oxford, England
(The Church of England)
Revelation

ANTHONY J. SALDARINI
Professor of Biblical Studies
Boston College
Chestnut Hill, Massachusetts
(The Roman Catholic Church)
Baruch; Letter of Jeremiah

J. PAUL SAMPLEY
Professor of New Testament and
    Christian Origins
The School of Theology and The Graduate Division
Boston University
Boston, Massachusetts
(The United Methodist Church)
1 Corinthians

JUDITH E. SANDERSON
Assistant Professor of Hebrew Bible
Department of Theology and Religious Studies
Seattle University
Seattle, Washington
*Ancient Texts and Versions of the Old
    Testament*

EILEEN M. SCHULLER, O.S.U.
Professor
Department of Religious Studies
McMaster University
Hamilton, Ontario
Canada
(The Roman Catholic Church)
Malachi

FERNANDO F. SEGOVIA
Associate Professor of New Testament
    and Early Christianity
The Divinity School
Vanderbilt University
Nashville, Tennessee
(The Roman Catholic Church)
Reading the Bible as Hispanic Americans

CHRISTOPHER R. SEITZ
Associate Professor of Old Testament
The Divinity School
Yale University
New Haven, Connecticut
(The Episcopal Church)
Isaiah 40–66

CHOON-LEONG SEOW
Henry Snyder Gehman Professor of Old Testa-
    ment Language and Literature
Princeton Theological Seminary
Princeton, New Jersey
(Presbyterian Church [U.S.A.])
1 & 2 Kings

MICHAEL A. SIGNER
Abrams Professor of Jewish Thought and
    Culture
Department of Theology
University of Notre Dame
Notre Dame, Indiana
*How the Bible Has Been Interpreted in
    Jewish Tradition*

MOISÉS SILVA
    Professor of New Testament
    Westminster Theological Seminary
    Philadelphia, Pennsylvania
    (The Orthodox Presbyterian Church)
        *Contemporary Theories of Biblical
        Interpretation*

DANIEL J. SIMUNDSON
    Professor of Old Testament
    Luther Seminary
    Saint Paul, Minnesota
    (Evangelical Lutheran Church in America)
        Micah

ABRAHAM SMITH
    Assistant Professor of New Testament
        and Christian Origins
    The School of Theology
    Boston University
    Boston, Massachusetts
    (The National Baptist Convention, USA, Inc.)
        1 & 2 Thessalonians

DANIEL L. SMITH-CHRISTOPHER
    Associate Professor of Theological Studies
    Department of Theology
    Loyola Marymount University
    Los Angeles, California
    (The Society of Friends [Quaker])
        *Daniel; Bel and the Dragon; Prayer of
        Azariah; Susannah*

MARION L. SOARDS
    Professor of New Testament Studies
    Louisville Presbyterian Theological Seminary
    Louisville, Kentucky
    (Presbyterian Church [U.S.A.])
        Acts

ROBERT C. TANNEHILL
    Academic Dean and Harold B. Williams
        Professor of Biblical Studies
    Methodist Theological School in Ohio
    Delaware, Ohio
    (The United Methodist Church)
        The Gospels and Narrative Literature

GEORGE E. TINKER
    Associate Professor of Cross-Cultural Ministries
    The Iliff School of Theology
    Denver, Colorado
    (Evangelical Lutheran Church in America)
        Reading the Bible as Native Americans

W. SIBLEY TOWNER
    The Reverend Archibald McFadyen Professor of
        Biblical Interpretation
    Union Theological Seminary in Virginia
    Richmond, Virginia
    (Presbyterian Church [U.S.A.])
        Ecclesiastes

PHYLLIS TRIBLE
    Baldwin Professor of Sacred Literature
    Union Theological Seminary
    New York, New York
        Jonah

GENE M. TUCKER
    Professor of Old Testament, Emeritus
    Candler School of Theology
    Emory University
    Atlanta, Georgia
    (The United Methodist Church)
        Isaiah 1–39

CHRISTOPHER M. TUCKETT
    Rylands Professor of Biblical Criticism
        and Exegesis
    Faculty of Theology
    University of Manchester
    Manchester, England
    (The Church of England)
        Jesus and the Gospels

RAYMOND C. VAN LEEUWEN
    Professor of Religion and Theology
    Eastern College
    Saint Davids, Pennsylvania
    (Christian Reformed Church in North America)
        Proverbs

ROBERT W. WALL
    Professor of Biblical Studies
    Department of Religion
    Seattle Pacific University
    Seattle, Washington
    (Free Methodist Church of North America)
        Introduction to Epistolary Literature

DUANE F. WATSON
    Associate Professor of New Testament Studies
    Department of Religion and Philosophy
    Malone College
    Canton, Ohio
    (The United Methodist Church)
        2 Peter; Jude

RENITA J. WEEMS
Associate Professor of Hebrew Bible
The Divinity School
Vanderbilt University
Nashville, Tennessee
(African Methodist Episcopal Church)
Song of Songs

SIDNIE WHITE CRAWFORD
Associate Professor of Religious Studies
Department of Religion
Albright College
Reading, Pennsylvania
(The Episcopal Church)
Esther; Additions to Esther

VINCENT L. WIMBUSH
Professor of New Testament and
Christian Origins
Union Theological Seminary
New York, New York
(Progressive National Baptist Convention, Inc.)
*The Ecclesiastical Context of the New
Testament*

N. THOMAS WRIGHT
Dean of Lichfield
Lichfield Cathedral
Staffordshire, England
(The Church of England)
Romans

GALE A. YEE
Associate Professor of Old Testament
Department of Theology
University of Saint Thomas
Saint Paul, Minnesota
(The Roman Catholic Church)
Hosea

FEATURES OF
THE NEW INTERPRETER'S® BIBLE

The general aim of *The New Interpreter's Bible* is to bring the best in contemporary biblical scholarship into the service of the church to enhance preaching, teaching, and study of the Scriptures. To accomplish that general aim, the design of *The New Interpreter's Bible* has been shaped by two controlling principles: (1) form serves function, and (2) maximize ease of use.

General articles provide the reader with concise, up-to-date, balanced introductions and assessments of selected topics. In most cases, a brief bibliography points the way to further exploration of a topic. Many of the general articles are placed in volumes 1 and 8, at the beginning of the coverage of the Old and New Testaments, respectively. Others have been inserted in those volumes where the reader will encounter the corresponding type of literature (e.g., "Introduction to Prophetic Literature" appears in Volume 6 alongside several of the prophetic books).

Coverage of each biblical book begins with an "Introduction" that acquaints the reader with the essential historical, sociocultural, literary, and theological issues necessary to understand the biblical book. A short bibliography and an outline of the biblical book are found at the end of each Introduction. The introductory sections are the only material in *The New Interpreter's Bible* printed in a single wide-column format.

The biblical text is divided into coherent and manageable primary units, which are located within larger sections of Scripture. At the opening discussion of any large section of Scripture, readers will often find material identified as "Overview," which includes remarks applicable to the large section of text. The primary unit of text may be as short as a few verses or as long as a chapter or more. This is the point at which the biblical text itself is reprinted

in *The New Interpreter's Bible*. Dealing with Scripture in terms of these primary units allows discussion of important issues that are overlooked in a verse-by-verse treatment. Each scriptural unit is identified by text citation and a short title.

The full texts and critical notes of the New International Version and the New Revised Standard Version of the Bible are presented in parallel columns for quick reference. (For the Apocryphal/Deuterocanonical works, the NIV is replaced by The New American Bible.) Since every translation is to some extent an interpretation as well, the inclusion of these widely known and influential modern translations provides an easy comparison that in many cases will lead to a better understanding of a passage. Biblical passages are set in a two-column format and placed in green tint-blocks to make it easy to recognize them at a glance. The NAB, NIV, and NRSV material is clearly identified on each page on which the text appears.

Immediately following each biblical text is a section marked "Commentary," which provides an exegetical analysis informed by linguistic, text-critical, historical-critical, literary, social-scientific, and theological methods. The Commentary serves as a reliable, judicious guide through the text, pointing out the critical problems as well as key interpretive issues.

The exegetical approach is "text-centered." That is, the commentators focus primarily on the text in its final form rather than on (a) a meticulous rehearsal of problems of scholarship associated with a text, (b) a thorough reconstruction of the pre-history of the text, or (c) an exhaustive rehearsal of the text's interpretive history. Of course, some attention to scholarly problems, to the pre-history of a text, and to historic interpretations that have shaped streams of tradition is important in particular cases precisely in order to illumine the several levels of meaning in the final form of the text. But the *primary* focus is on the canonical text itself. Moreover, the Commentary not only describes pertinent aspects of the text, but also teaches the reader what to look for in the text so as to develop the reader's own capacity to analyze and interpret the text.

Commentary material runs serially for a few paragraphs or a few pages, depending on what is required by the biblical passage under discussion.

Commentary material is set in a two-column format. Occasional subheads appear in a bold green font. The next level of subdivisions appears as bold black fonts and a third level as black italic fonts. Footnotes are placed at the bottom of the column in which the superscripts appear.

Key words in Hebrew, Aramaic, or Greek are printed in the original-language font, accompanied by a transliteration and a translation or explanation.

Immediately following the Commentary, in most cases, is the section called "Reflections." A detailed exposition growing directly out of the discussion and issues dealt with in the Commentary, the Reflections are geared specifically toward helping those who interpret Scripture in the life of the church by providing "handles" for grasping the significance of Scripture for faith and life today. Recognizing that the text has the capacity to shape the life of the Christian community, this section presents multiple possibilities for preaching and teaching in light of each biblical text. That is, instead of providing the preacher or teacher full illustrations, poems, outlines, and the like, the Reflections offer *several* trajectories of possible interpretation that connect with the situation of the contemporary listeners. Recognizing the power of Scripture to speak anew to diverse situations, not all of the suggested trajectories could be appropriated on any one occasion. Preachers and teachers want some specificity about the implications of the text, but not so much specificity that the work is done for them. The ideas in the Reflections are meant to stimulate the thought of preachers and teachers, not to replace it.

Three-quarter width columns distinguish Reflections materials from biblical text and Commentary.

Occasional excursuses have been inserted in some volumes to address topics of special importance that are best treated apart from the flow of Commentary and Reflections on specific passages. Set in three-quarter width columns, excursuses are identified graphically by a green color bar that runs down the outside margin of the page.

Occasional maps, charts, and illustrations appear throughout the volumes at points where they are most likely to be immediately useful to the reader.

CONTENTS

VOLUME V

INTRODUCTION TO WISDOM LITERATURE

RICHARD J. CLIFFORD, S. J.

DEFINITION OF WISDOM LITERATURE

In biblical studies, "wisdom literature" designates the books of Proverbs, Job, Qohelet (Ecclesiastes), and, in the Apocrypha or deuterocanonical books, Sirach and the Wisdom of Solomon. Other biblical literature is sometimes put under the wisdom umbrella. Tobit in the Apocrypha has been called a sapiential short story because of its concern with the morality of everyday life. The Song of Songs is often included on the grounds that it, like the wisdom books, is "of Solomon" (Cant 1:1). Psalms such as 37, 49, 73, 112, and 127 are aphoristic, or meditate on the problem of the innocent righteous person; but to call them wisdom psalms broadens the category unduly in the opinion of many scholars; moreover, there is no consensus on which psalms belong to the group.

Scholars have occasionally regarded whole sections of the Bible as being influenced by wisdom themes, such as wisdom and life, worldly success resulting from shrewdness, or the inherent consequences of human actions. Genesis 1–11 is indeed concerned with cosmic order and with wisdom and life (esp. chaps. 2–3), but these themes come more from "international" epics like *The Epic of Gilgamesh* and the story of Atrahasis than from wisdom books. Genesis 37–50, detailing Joseph's rise at court through sagacity and skill at interpreting dreams, resembles court tales like Ahiqar and Daniel more than wisdom books. The sophisticated court history (2 Samuel 9–20; 1 Kings 1–2) portrays Yahweh as being hidden in the course of human events, as one finds in the wisdom portrayal, but such a shared perspective is no argument for literary dependence. Finally, some think that Deuteronomy and wisdom literature are related because both were written by the Jerusalem scribal class. Such a view is possible, for these literatures share common vocabulary, and Deuteronomy reckons obedience to Yahweh as wisdom (Deut 4:5-8; 32:6, 21, 28-31). Rather than wisdom books influencing other biblical books, however, it is more likely that wisdom thinking was in the main stream of biblical literary production from whence its style and ideas radiated throughout biblical writings.

Jerome (died 420), in his *Prologue to the Books of Solomon,* attributed the unity of the traditional wisdom books to their connection with Solomon, although he was aware that the connection is loose in some instances. The Christian Bible groups the wisdom books together (with the psalms) after the historical books and before the prophetic books. The Jewish Bible places the wisdom literature in the third section of the Tanakh—the Writings (a miscellaneous collection)—after the Torah and the Prophets.

There are good reasons for grouping the wisdom

books together. First, few of the books except the latest wisdom books, Sirach 44–50 and the book of Wisdom 10–19, say anything about the history of Israel, its major institutions of covenant and kingship, and its great personalities, such as Abraham and Sarah, Moses, and David. The name of Israel's God, Yahweh, does not even occur in Qohelet and the Job dialogues (Job 3–37; Yahweh in Job 12:9 is anomalous). Righteousness in the books is not linked to observance of the law and covenant or to performance of rituals as it is elsewhere in the Bible. Genres and themes of neighboring literatures are far more obvious in the wisdom books than in other sections of the Bible. Second, the books all share a strong didactic tone. The word "wisdom" pervades all the books: forty-two times in Proverbs, eighteen times in Job, twenty-eight times in Qohelet, sixty times in Sirach (σοφία *sophia*), and thirty times in the book of Wisdom; the numbers are much higher if synonyms of "wisdom" are counted. There is persistent attention to wisdom in itself, which makes these biblical books different from their canonical counterparts. The books are, of course, concerned with practical wisdom—knowing how to live well, how to perform one's tasks, and how to understand the secrets of the universe. But the Bible goes beyond specific instances of wisdom to explore the nature of wisdom, its importance and limits, and its relationship to Yahweh.

Within this grouping of canonical wisdom literature, there are considerable differences deriving from the presence of distinct literary genres and from the different meanings of wisdom in antiquity. Proverbs includes the distinct genres of wisdom poem, instruction, and proverb; Job is a dialogue on divine justice set within a narrative; Qohelet is (among other things) a royal pseudo-autobiography; Sirach is a vast compendium of instructions and proverbs; and the book of Wisdom is a philosophical exhortation to a way of life (λόγος προτρεπτικός *logos protreptikos*). Each major genre develops different themes in a distinctive way. The concept of wisdom is not univocal; it may signify aphorisms, instructions for the younger generation, magical knowledge derived from the gods (as in oaths), royal and judicial discernment (as of Solomon), and critical, skeptical inquiry. All of these different concepts are included under the umbrella of ancient wisdom.

Modern interest in wisdom literature has gone through several phases since the foundations of contemporary biblical scholarship were laid in the sixteenth century. Renaissance creativity was based on freeing human activity from connection with ultimate and hierarchical patterns of order. Reformation theology was interested in the God of history rather than in the Author of a static system; human destiny was perceived as the realization of spiritual capacities in time. Given the presuppositions regnant at the dawn of modern historical-critical study of the Bible, it is no wonder that wisdom literature took second place to the study of the Pentateuch, historical and prophetic books, and Psalms. Sapiential writings were regarded by many as derivative, a quasi-philosophical distillation of the law and the prophets. Dependence on the prophets was, in fact, thought to account for two traits of wisdom: the doctrine of retribution and the (alleged) suspicion of cult that surfaces in Prov 15:8: "The sacrifice of the wicked is an/ abomination to the LORD,/ but the prayer of the upright is his delight" (NRSV; cf. Prov 21:27; Eccl 5:1; Heb 4:17). It is important to remind ourselves that this neglect of the wisdom literature is relatively modern and that it reflects neither the outlook of the Bible nor that of many centuries of Jewish and Christian interpretation, which have considered every aspect of the world to have been created for the divine purpose. To regard wisdom literature as a foreign body in the Bible, as some scholars still do, is a hermeneutical decision based on the assumption that the historical and prophetic books are normative for what is genuinely biblical.

Three twentieth-century developments have pushed wisdom books to the forefront of scholarly interest:

First, Hermann Gunkel (1862–1932), applying his new form criticism, proposed that much wisdom literature came from ancient oral models and originated in a particular group in Israel: the sages. Thus was introduced the impulse to search for the social location of the wisdom books, an impulse that has become stronger in recent times. Second, the recovery (beginning in the mid-nineteenth century) of texts comparable to biblical wisdom literature in Egypt and Mesopotamia, civilizations far older than Israel, challenged the old assumption that the biblical wisdom books were late systematizings of traditional teaching in accord with a view of religion as obedience to the law. Third, the theological bias against wisdom books was challenged by prominent scholars, such as Walther Zimmerli and Gerhard von Rad, who found a basis for the theological study of wisdom books in the concepts of creation and cosmic order, which attest that every aspect of God's world is good and worthy of study. Their discernment of wisdom literature's theological value prepared the way for the lively interest it holds today.

WISDOM LITERATURE IN THE ANCIENT NEAR EAST

The title "wisdom literature" has been applied to certain literary genres from Egypt and Mesopotamia. Were it not for the example of the biblical wisdom books, however, the extra-biblical texts probably would not be regarded as constituting a special group. Comparison between these other texts and their biblical counterparts is fruitful, nonetheless, chiefly because the foreign examples illuminate two vitally important topics: literary genres (the set of conventions ruling the work) and the social location of the writers. On these points the Bible provides scant information.

Wisdom texts comprise some of the most ancient literature. Some wisdom genres, such as the instruction and the proverb collection, are attested from the first appearance of *belles lettres* (c. 2600 BCE for Mesopotamia, some two centuries later for Egypt) and continued in use long past the biblical period. The following section surveys Mesopotamian, Egyptian, and Canaanite parallels as they are relevant to the Bible, with particular attention to genres and the social location of the scribes.

Mesopotamia. Many wisdom texts entered the "stream of tradition" of cuneiform literature—i.e., texts controlled and maintained by generations of professional scribes, who copied them as part of their elaborate training. Preserved in temple archives and private collections, the works were widely known and accepted, in other words "canonical." They were widely distributed throughout the East including the Levant, and some of them influenced the Bible.

The oldest genre relevant to the Bible is *instruction*. The *Instructions of Šuruppak* was widely known and is extant in two archaic Sumerian versions dating to 2600–2400 BCE: a "classical" Sumerian version of c. 1800 BCE and two Akkadian translations of c. 1500–1100 BCE.[1] Šuruppak was

king of the last antediluvian city (reminiscent of the biblical Noah) and was endowed with the divine wisdom of that privileged time. The text was used in schools, where students practiced cuneiform writing by copying it. In this collection, the father instructs his son, the customary recipient of ancient instructions. Some scholars believe that the father is a personification of the city of Šuruppak. The advice is not as specific and literal as Egyptian instructions, which are generally imparted through metaphor and indirection. Most of the counsels appear in a twofold structure: a command and a reason—e.g., "Do not go surety for another. They shall seize you." Incidentally, the fact that agricultural concerns are prominent in this and other instructions does not mean that instructions originated with peasants rather than with the scribal class. The productivity of the land was such an abiding concern for all classes of an agrarian society that herds and crops occur often in the sayings of urban scribes. Šuruppak advises even the nobles to do their share at harvest time: "At the time of the harvest, days are precious. Collect like a slave girl, eat like a queen!"

Another well-attested genre was the *proverb collection.* No less than twenty-four collections are attested in Sumerian, though only a few survive in bilingual (Sumerian and Akkadian) translations.[2] A few independent Akkadian examples are extant.[3] Kassite scribes of the late second millennium BCE for some reason did not consider these texts worthy of copying. Biblical proverbs were not directly influenced by Sumerian collections, though there are general similarities in form and content.

Some literary works represent a skeptical and critical spirit for which the *edubba* ("tablet house," Sumerian for "the academy") was renowned. The sufferer in the "Sumerian Job" complains bitterly of his treatment by others and of his fate; the composition ends happily with the god's return.[4] The Babylonian Theodicy of c. 1000 BCE, an acrostic poem of twenty-seven stanzas, each of eleven lines, is a Job-like dialogue between a sufferer and a friend.[5] In one stanza, the protagonist complains of his

---

1. See Bendt Alster, *The Instructions of Šuruppak: A Sumerian Proverb Collection* (Copenhagan: Akademisk Forlag, 1974).

2. B. B. Foster, *Before the Muses: An Anthology of Akkadian Literature,* 2 vols. (Bethesda: CDL, 1993) 1:337-48.

3. *See Ancient Near Eastern Texts Relating to the Old Testament,* ed. James B. Pritchard, 3rd ed. (Princeton, N.J.: Princeton University Press, 1969) 595-96.

4. Ibid., 589-91.

5. Ibid., 601-4; Foster, *Before the Muses,* 2:806-14.

sufferings, and in the next, his friend counters with the conventional pieties: Suffering is the fate of all, justice will ultimately be done, and the gods are remote and inscrutable. Eventually the friend concedes that the righteous poor are vulnerable and unhappy, and the sufferer utters a prayer for divine protection. Another poem, often compared with Job since its partial publication in 1885, is the "Babylonian Job," sometimes cited by its first line: "I will praise the lord of wisdom" (*Ludlul bēl nēmeqi*).[6] The full publication of its first tablet in 1980 shows that it can no longer be used as a parallel to Job, for it is not a treatise on the problem of suffering but a bold proclamation of Marduk as the supplicant god. In the midst of terrible personal anguish, the sufferer rejects his personal god in favor of Marduk. (Marduk had become important in the late second millennium BCE.)

Another Mesopotamian genre only recently recognized as relevant to the Bible is the pseudo-autobiography of a king, in which the king makes a lesson of his life and records it for posterity. Especially relevant to the Bible is the standard version of the *Epic of Gilgamesh* in eleven tablets, apparently completed around the thirteenth century BCE.[7] A didactic purpose was imposed on the Old Babylonian version by a new introduction and conclusion as well as the inclusion of wisdom themes. Gilgamesh's opening and closing speeches in the standard version emphasize not his strength but his experience and knowledge gained through sufferings. The work addresses the reader as "thou" as it instructs. The flood story, which has been added in tablet XI, omits giving a reason for the flood (although the tradition attested in the Atra-hases epic did include a reason) to underline the wisdom theme of the inscrutability of the gods. The plant of life that slips away from the hero instances another wisdom theme: the fragility of life. Qohelet quotes the alewife's advice to Gilgamesh as he seeks immortality "You will not find the eternal life you seek. . . . Go eat your bread with enjoyment. . . . Enjoy life with the wife whom you love" (Old Babylonian version). The book of Proverbs may also draw from Gilgamesh; the goddess Ishtar's false offer of life to the hero seems to have influenced the depiction of Woman Folly's false offer of life to the young man in Prov 5:3-6; 7; and 9:13-18.

Mesopotamian literature reflects the world of the scribes. Despite their various specializations, scribes are described with one term: *ṭupšarru*, "scribe." They wrote the literature and saw to its transmission. Literature was by definition what they copied and kept in libraries. This practice accounts for multiple copies of the limited number of works in the stream of tradition. Scribes had three functions—bureaucrat, poet, and scholar. As bureaucrats, they recorded the intake and outflow of palace goods; as poets, they composed literary works, such as hymns, epics, annals, and inscriptions; as scholars, they recorded and arranged omens and practiced divination. For the writing of literature, the royal court was far more important than was the temple; the latter lost its economic and political importance to the palace at an early period. The king sponsored the cultural establishment as an ongoing part of his responsibility to uphold political and economic order and stability.

In contrast to other societies, Mesopotamian scribes were not *ex officio* connected with sanctuaries or other religious institutions, nor did they operate with a body of normative or "classical" texts. They functioned within the palace organization or, with the economic prosperity of the first millennium BCE, independently, selling their "scholarly" services (omens and divination) to wealthy individuals.

Egypt. Literature comparable to the biblical wisdom books was composed as early as the mid-third millennium in Egypt. Egyptologists include three major genres under the heading of wisdom: *instructions, laments* or *complaints,* and *political propaganda.* The first two, instructions and complaints, are relevant to the Bible. Since instruction is such an abundant source of information on the scribal profession, information on the social context will be provided within the discussion of instructions.

Instruction was a pervasive genre; seventeen examples are extant.[8] The oldest is the *Instruction of Prince Hardjedef* (composed c. 2450–2300 BCE),[9] and the youngest, the *Instruction of Papyrus Insinger* of the first century CE, written in Demotic, the vernacular language.[10] One instruction, that of Ame-

---

6. Foster, *Before the Muses,* 1:308-25.
7. *ANET,* 72-99.

8. Helmut Brunner, *Die Weisheitsbücher der Ägypter: Lehren für das Leben* (Munich: Artemis, 1991).
9. Miriam Lichtheim, *Ancient Egyptian Literature,* 3 vols. (Berkeley: University of California Press, 1973–1980) 1:58-59.
10. Ibid., 3:184-217.

nemope, dating to c. 1100 BCE,[11] has directly influenced Prov 22:17–24:22.

Instructions gave advice to enable the young person to lead a life free of undue difficulties and costly mistakes. Instructions make concrete and pragmatic suggestions rather than hold out abstract ideals to live up to—e.g., Don't lie to a judge, since telling the truth will render the judge benevolent the next time around, and in the long run lies don't work anyway. Such pragmatic counsels provide no indication that Egyptian instructions were secular. On the contrary, they were thoroughly religious. Like other ancient peoples, Egyptians believed that God implanted order (*ma'at*) in the world. Ma'at can be variously translated—"truth," "order," "justice"—and is found in nature (the seasons, fruitfulness) no less than in the human world (civic and social order, laws, right relationships within families and professions, among neighbors, and in relation to the king). In mythology, Ma'at is the daughter of Re, the god of the sun and of justice. She is portrayed as crouching with a feather on her knees or head. Ma'at was not revealed directly to humans, but "read off" the course of the world and communicated through the maxims and exhortations of instructions. To help readers fulfill the demands of *ma'at* in every walk of life was the aim of the instructions. Some scholars see *ma'at* as the model for personified Wisdom in Proverbs, though it must be noted that Wisdom in Proverbs, by her vigorous speeches and pursuit of her lovers, goes far beyond the abstract Egyptian goddess. Finally, the scope of the instruction is the guidance of the individual rather than the reform of society; one accepted the world and lived according to its rhythms.

Some themes of the instructions are explained by their context in Egyptian society. The career of the young person was played out, at least initially, within the *famulus* ("private secretary") system; one entered the household of high officials (mostly of royal blood) who trained their successors in their household. The young person served the great personage, establishing a solid relationship, like Joseph with Potiphar (Gen 39:2) and with Pharaoh (Gen 41:40). Eventually formal classes came to be conducted at the royal court. In that world, fidelity to one's master was important. The apprenticeship context explains exhortations to deliver messages accurately, to avoid

(domestic) quarrels, and to guard against entanglements with women of the household.

In portraying human beings, the instructions use the "heart" as the seat of feeling and, especially, of intelligence. A "hard-hearted" person lacks good sense rather than compassion. Human beings are characterized by a fundamental polarity—the wise person and the fool, the hot and the silent person. Fools do not follow the advice of their "father," or elder, and thus do not act according to *ma'at*. The cleverness of the wise is the result of education, nature, and their own shrewd assessment of people and situations. "Hearing" (in the sense of heeding) is an important verb in the exhortations. Egyptian society was open, allowing poor and ambitious young people to rise to positions of power. Such people needed guide books to success.

Instructions were composed in every period during the three millennia of Egyptian history, and they reflect changes in society. The genre arose with the Egyptian state in the third millennium BCE, when the need to administer vast territories required the king's servants to leave behind their village routine to travel and to respond to situations requiring more than just their personal experience. Instructions of the Old Kingdom (2650–2135 BCE) arose within the court and revolved around the king, but with the decline of the monarchy and the social disorder of the First Intermediate Period (2135–2040 BCE), the instructions turned from royal service to private concerns. With the restoration of monarchy in the Middle Kingdom (2040–1650 BCE), instructions once again stressed loyalty to the king. New Kingdom authors came from all levels of society, for daily business was now conducted by a broad range of people. With the *Instructions of Any* in the Eighteenth Dynasty (c. 1550–1305 BCE), concern for the individual and for the acquiring of inner peace reappears and dominates the genre down to Hellenistic and Roman times. Another reflection of societal change is the way success was interpreted. In the Old Kingdom, when courtiers were the intended readers, success meant getting ahead at court. When the readership became less tied to a particular social class, exhortations became more general and more personal—how to avoid suffering, conflicts, and disappointments in life.

In contrast to the Egyptian principle that artists be anonymous, instructions name their authors, presenting them as real people—kings or prominent

---

11. *ANET,* 421-25; Lichtheim, *Ancient Egyptian Literature,* 2:146-63.

scribes. The authority of instructions, after all, rested on the repute of their writers no less than on their antiquity. Reverence for authority and for antiquity did not, however, prevent critical editing and recasting of the ancient wisdom.

Composing, studying, teaching, and copying texts took place in a kind of academy known as the House of Life, which was usually located near a temple and had a cultic function. Instructions were copied out by school children as they learned the Egyptian script; their frequently faulty copies are often the chief manuscript source for instructions. Instructions were never meant solely to be school texts, however. The addressee in instructions was a "son," a broader term than its English equivalent, one that expressed any close relationship with a younger person—one's child, student, or successor. The texts reveal a high level of personal involvement, for the prestige of the "father" depended on the success of the "son." The instructions were class-specific up to the first millennium, at which time general formulations became more common.

At the end of the third millennium another type of writing appeared: pessimistic and cynical attacks on traditional ways of thinking. The *Admonitions of Ipu-wer,* after a grim recital of the troubles of the land (a common topos), blames the creator-god using the form of dialogue.[12] *The Protests of the Eloquent Peasant* is a confrontation in nine speeches between a peasant and a high official.[13] *A Song of the Harper* urges one to enjoy today for who knows about tomorrow.[14] The *Satire on the Trades* criticizes non-scribal activities to glorify the profession of the scribe.[15] The *Dispute of a Person with His Ba* (i.e., vital force) vividly describes the miseries of life.[16] These works show that scribes in Egypt, as in Mesopotamia, were free to criticize the tradition. One should not regard skeptical works *ipso facto* as the products of alienated or marginalized groups, therefore; they could arise within the scribal guild.

Canaan. The larger context for Israel was in the "Canaanite" culture common to the entire Levant (with local variations). Unfortunately, few wisdom writings survive from this culture. The Ugaritic texts, which provide a northern sampling of Canaanite culture, contain a few didactic texts. Most such texts are Babylonian: the *Counsels of Shube'awilum,*[17] collections of sayings, and a hymn of trust to Marduk (similar to the Babylonian "I will praise the Lord of wisdom"). These and other Babylonian texts appear in the Akkadian language, showing that the Ugaritic scribes read and appreciated Mesopotamian literature. One wisdom text, the book of Ahiqar, originally written in Aramaic around the eighth or seventh century BCE, is possibly of Canaanite origin. The book contains the tale of Ahiqar, an official of the Assyrian king, and a collection of his sayings. The tale is similar to stories of courtiers such as those of Joseph and Daniel, in which the courtier loses his high position at court through the envy of others and then regains it through his patience and sagacity. Ahiqar has some links to the book of Tobit. It is noteworthy that the courtier Ahiqar, who has experienced many things and suffered much, is celebrated as the author of sayings, exhortations, and wisdom poems. Practical wisdom is connected with age and experience.

SOCIAL CONTEXT

Form criticism, from its beginnings in the early twentieth century, has inquired about the origin of literary forms in specific arenas of human life. Recent scholarship, with its consciousness of class interest lurking in literary works, asks even more intensely about the social location of authors and their works.

Who were the authors of the wisdom books, and what social class interest(s) did they promote? Were they scribes on the staff of palace and temple, or teachers in schools? Were they elders of tribes or families inculcating tribal traditions and values onto the younger generation? Unfortunately, the Bible does not provide sufficient information about everyday life to answer these questions with certainty.

The complicated writing systems of Mesopotamia and Egypt virtually ensured that authors of literary works were professional scribes and poets. The scribe in Mesopotamia and Egypt belonged to a well-defined profession. Egypt had its House of Life, and Mesopotamia its tablet house.

Scholars have theorized about two different settings for Israel's wisdom literature: the school (under royal sponsorship) and the tribe. Some scholars, on the basis of foreign examples, suggest that the mon-

---

12. Ibid., 441-44; Lichtheim, *AEL,* 1:159-63.
13. *ANET,* 407-10; Lichtheim, *AEL,* 1:169-8.
14. *ANET,* 467; Lichtheim, *AEL,* 1:194-97.
15. *ANET,* 432-34; Lichtheim, *AEL,* 1:184-92.
16. *ANET,* 407-07; Lichtheim, *AEL,* 1:163-69.

17. B. B. Foster, *Before the Muses: An Anthology of Akkadian Literature,* 2 vols. (Bethesda: CDL, 1993) 332-25.

archy, beginning in the tenth century BCE, built up a skilled or "wise" bureaucracy for the keeping of records and accounts, for diplomatic correspondence with foreign powers (requiring a knowledge of Akkadian and Egyptian), and for composing didactic material. From this circle would have come the authors of the instructions and other wisdom literature. King Solomon was recognized by the historian both for establishing administrative structures and for possessing pre-eminent wisdom (cf. 1 Kings 3; 4:29-34; 11:41). His name is associated with wisdom books (Prov 1:1; 25:1; Eccl 1:12; Cant 1:1; Sir 47:13; Wisdom 7–9).

Proponents of the tribal theory point out that the wisdom books do not mention any class of sages. Noting the strong family and tribal traditions of Israel, they propose that the admonitions and warnings of the wisdom books have their roots in prohibitions laid down by tribal elders that regulated social relations within the tribe. A variant of the tribal theory finds the folk element not so much in the admonitions and warnings as in the sayings and comparisons. The latter arose from real-life experiences of ordinary people; the sayings were made concise and memorable by removing details of their originating situations.

In assessing the origin and context of wisdom writings, indeed of other biblical writings, one must concede some influence from tribal tradition on wisdom material, for the family was a dominant institution in ancient Israel. Nonetheless, it is likely that professional scribes or poets, under the general sponsorship of the king, composed the biblical wisdom books, since all of these books represent genres well known in the ancient literary world. Only people able to read and appreciate such writings could have adopted their conventions with the skill and sophistication so evident in the biblical books. References to rural life and farming cannot be used as evidence for tribal origins, for they reflect almost universal anxiety about crops and herds in the precarious economy of the ancient world. Many Israelites, it is true, were able to read the relatively simple alphabetic Hebrew, and they would have constituted a broad readership; but the authors of the biblical books came from the ranks of professional scribes and sages. Skeptical and critical books like Job and Qohelet could have come from these ranks also, for a critical and skeptical spirit was at home among ancient scribes, as is clear in the

writings from Mesopotamia and Egypt. The author of Qohelet is called a sage, a collector, and a sifter of maxims (Eccl 12:9-11). Ben Sira, in the first quarter of the second century BCE, was a professional sage, though not necessarily in the employ of temple or court. He lauds the profession of scribe (Sir 38:24–39:11) and invites young people to his school (Sir 51:13-30). The role the Israelite sage played is difficult to detail, however. Like the Mesopotamian scribe, some Israelite scribes may have been in the employ of the royal court, whereas others may have been privately employed. African societies, where proverb experts provided the king with appropriate maxims, may offer a valuable analogy. Given the small population of Judah and Jerusalem and the limits on the monarchy (and later to the high priesthood) from tribal loyalty and ancient religious traditions, however, one cannot in simple fashion apply to Israel observations about the scribe in neighboring cultures.

FORMAL CHARACTERISTICS OF WISDOM LITERATURE

Biblical and other ancient literatures were ruled by conventions, far more so than is the case with modern literature. Attention to the major genre and smaller genres or forms of each work as well as to other formal features sheds considerable light on biblical wisdom literature. Genre refers to the kind of literature, the literary species of a complete work, such as comedy, tragedy, biography, law code, or instruction. Unfortunately, ancient Near Eastern authors did not commit their theories of literature to writing, forcing modern readers to infer each text's category.

Discussion of the precise literary forms in each work will be found in each commentary. Only the large-scale genres, those that incorporate smaller genres, will be noted here: instructions, proverb collections, dialogues on divine justice and human suffering, pseudo-autobiographies, and philosophical exhortations to a certain way of life.

Instruction. This widely attested wisdom genre is found in both Egypt and Mesopotamia from the mid-third millennium to the beginning of the common era. Most such writings are Egyptian. Formally, Mesopotamian and Egyptian instructions are of two types: those with a title and main text, and those with a title, prologue, and main text (with subtitles and other divisions). The author is always referred to in the third person, often with titles and epithets. There is always a direct address of the son in the prologue, sometimes also in the body of the work. The main text is made up of units consisting of one to seven lines, the two-line couplet by far the most common. The couplet (also called distich or bicolon) occurs in synonymous, antithetic, or synthetic parallelism, or in balanced phrases. Because early instructions are lengthy and sophisticated, attempts to show historical development from short sayings to long essays, or from simple to complex argumentation or forms, are not persuasive. Instructions always contain proverbs and exhortations.

Proverb Collections. Although proverbs or pithy sayings were part and parcel of all ancient literature, *collections* of proverbs were not always present. Besides sayings, the many Sumerian proverb collections contain anecdotes, extracts from works of literature, short fables, and other unidentifiable material. Some sayings occur in parallel lines, whereas others consist of just one line.

Dialogues on Divine Justice and Human Suffering. From a formal point of view, the Egyptian *Dispute Between a Man and His Ba* (second-millennium BCE) mingles prose, symmetrically structured speech, and lyric poetry. From the same period, *The Protests of the Eloquent Peasant* consists of nine carefully framed petitions in poetic form (with prose explanation) framed by a prose narrative describing the injustice done to the peasant. The whole is shaped and unified by irony and contrast. The Mesopotamian "Sumerian Job" has a brief introduction and ending, between which a sufferer addresses god in a long complaint, using pithy sayings. The Babylonian Theodicy has a remarkably regular structure—twenty-seven stanzas of eleven lines, one stanza for the sufferer's complaints, and one stanza for the friend's notions of divine justice. The argument proceeds with concrete examples of justice and injustice and short sayings rather than with abstract reasoning.

Pseudo-Autobiography. The Akkadian genre of autobiography narrates the great deeds of a hero, drawing morals from them. Related to this form of writing is the genre of royal pseudo-autobiography, narrated partly in the first person, in which legendary and historical elements blend. Both adventures and interactions between characters appear in it.

Philosophical Exhortation. Exhortations to follow a particular philosophy or life of wisdom, known as protreptic in classical Greek and Latin literature, employ a variety of arguments and styles to persuade their audience. Some forms of writing that fall within this genre are the diatribe, in which imaginary opponents are chided, and the (elaborate) comparison. The biblical book of Wisdom is such an exhortation.

Brief Forms. The most pervasive small forms in wisdom literature are the *saying* and the *command* or *prohibition*. The saying is a sentence, usually written in the indicative mode. It can be divided into three types: the proverb, the experiential saying, and the didactic saying. The definition of a proverb is controverted, but the following is widely accepted: a concise statement of an apparent truth that has currency. The word *apparent* is used because a proverb is not always and everywhere true but proven so by context—e.g., "many hands make light work" and "too many cooks spoil the broth" are true according to the situation. *Currency* means that people "use" proverbs; they are not just clever sayings. The experiential saying presents some aspect of reality, "telling it like it is," and lets the hearer or reader draw the practical conclusions from it. The saying, "Some pretend to be rich, yet have nothing;/others pretend to be poor, yet have great wealth" (Prov 13:7 NRSV), is open to further verification or qualification. The didactic saying is more than a statement about reality; it characterizes an action or attitude so as to influence human conduct—e.g., "Those who oppress the poor insult their Maker" (Prov 14:31 NRSV).

The sages can impose their will directly through commands (imperative or jussive mood) and prohibitions. Occasionally a command is placed parallel to a saying, moving the saying from observation to command.

MAIN TEACHINGS OF WISDOM LITERATURE

The theology found within the wisdom books does not add up to a system, for the writers did not have a speculative aim; rather, they sought to instruct the next generation, to solve specific problems, to collect, critique, and hand on ancestral traditions. The central assumption of all the books is that God made the world, an order within which the human race must learn to live. That order was given privileged expression on the day of creation. Through wisdom, human beings can cope with the world and live happy and successful lives. Of great concern to the sages was the consequences of human choices ("retribution") upon individuals and society. Wisdom authors saw human beings as active agents, often dramatizing the moral life as involving two ways: the way of the righteous and the way of the wicked. Experience of life forced the sages to confront that surd in the cosmic system, the problem of evil. The sages recognized wisdom to be more than human ability to master life; it was hidden with God and had to be given to human beings. Attempts to consider wisdom in itself led to the personification of wisdom as a woman. Such are the themes constituting a theology of wisdom.

God. The word for "God"—אלהים (ʾĕlōhîm), יהוה (Yahweh), or one of the several names for God in the Joban dialogues (e.g., "the Almighty" [שׁדי šadday, Job 6:4])—occurs throughout the wisdom books, naming One who creates, sustains the universe, and brings all human acts to completion. Although the wisdom mode of understanding the divine presence differs from that of the historical and prophetic books, it is no less real. Scholarly hypotheses that early wisdom was profane and only later made religious by incorporation into Yahwism have rightly been rejected, for all ancient Near Eastern wisdom presupposed the gods even when gods and worship of gods are not mentioned. Skeptical Qohelet, who avoids the name "Yahweh," mentions "Elohim" four times in twelve chapters. In the monotheism of orthodox Yahwism, according to which the Bible has been edited, there is no order beyond Yahweh's will, unlike neighboring cultures.

Cosmic Order. Wisdom literature assumes that there is a divinely implanted order in the universe, embracing the "natural" and the human worlds. The modern, dichotomous distinction between human beings and nature (deriving largely from Greek thought) was unknown in the ancient Near East. The purposeful activity of a colony of ants is as much an example of order as is the purposeful activity of human beings (see Prov 6:6-11). Job's claim that he, as a righteous man, had not experienced any order in the universe (Job 38:2) is refuted by Yahweh's listing of the activity of the inanimate and animate spheres. Analogies are constantly being drawn between human and non-human beings and activities

(Prov 5:15; 11:28-29; 26:21; 27:17, 21). These dispositions are all "righteous" examples of the way the world works.

Cosmic order was perceived in two basic ways in the ancient Near East: order as the result of divine planning and order as being above and beyond divine plans and powers. In the first perspective, the gods in their wisdom justly reward or punish an individual with success or failure in this life. Coexisting with this view, in an existential contradiction, is the second perspective—a deterministic view according to which the course of one's life is fixed from birth. An Akkadian word illustrates well this notion. Šimtu (Sumerian namtar), inexactly rendered "fate" or "destiny," was "a disposition originating from an agency empowered to act and to dispose, such as the deity, king, or any individual"; it refers to the share of fortune and misfortune that determines the direction and temper of life. Other Mesopotamian vocabulary is even more deterministic; e.g., Akkadian uṣurtu (Sumerian giš ḫur), means "drawing" or "design." These two views of cosmic order reflect diverse, even contradictory, experiences of the world.

Israel's monotheism affected, at least implicitly, this ancient Near Eastern interpretive blend of fate and freedom. Instead of an interplay between unchangeable order and divine decree, the sole God, Yahweh, is consistently portrayed as all-powerful and all-wise, utterly responsive to human actions. Yahweh is not capricious, for there are always reasons for divine action. Cosmic order in the Bible, therefore, must be understood as less absolute than elsewhere in the East; it is associated closely with Yahweh's will (on occasion even personified as Yahweh's word or a female friend).

Creation. Unlike modern scientific concepts of creation, which envision only the physical world (typically in its astral and planetary aspects), ancient cosmogonies narrated the creation and organization of human society within the universe. In all cosmogonies, the gods created the world to benefit themselves; humans were slaves of the gods, their task being to ensure that everything operated for the divine service. Elements of the universe were given their purpose on the day of creation; the origin of a reality was its essence. Thus it is not surprising that cosmogonies were common in the ancient world, narrated to ground or to legitimate realities important to human life, such as the stars, the sun, and the moon, which determined time (especially sacred time), temple, king, and other institutions. Cosmogonies or cosmogonic language appear frequently in the Bible (see Genesis 1–11; Psalms 33; 77; 89; 93; 96–98; 104; Isaiah 40–66; and the wisdom literature).

Each wisdom book devotes considerable attention to creation. Proverbs has two cosmogonies: Prov 3:19-20 and 8:22-31. Job contains many allusions to creation, especially in chaps. 38–41. The opening of Qohelet (Eccl 1:3-11) presents a cosmology grounding the sage's ethical teaching about God and human actions. Sirach treats creation in 16:24–18:14; 39:12-35; and 42:15–43:38. In Sir 16:24–18:14, Yahweh creates the world, determining boundaries and arranging forever all their works that never disobey the divine word (Sir 16:26-28). The created world includes human beings whose obedience is not automatic but is given freely to their creator. Formed with a fixed number of days and with "fear of the Lord" and understanding, they are called to live obediently and worshipfully within the covenant (Sir 17:1-17). A lengthy address to the human race follows the cosmogony: Turn back to your righteous and merciful God (Sir 17:17–18:14). For Ben Sira, the nature and purpose of human beings (including Israel) were fixed at creation. The book of Wisdom develops the parallel between creation and redemption that the books of Genesis and Exodus had already drawn through cross-referencing. According to Wisdom, the world was created as salvific by wisdom (Wis 1:14); the cosmos itself is intrinsically involved in the divine judgment that restores the original righteous order (Wis 19:18-21).

Proverbs 8 and Job 38–41 are worth singling out to show the relation between wisdom and creation. The cosmogony in Prov 8:22-31 legitimates the speech of Woman Wisdom in which she promises her friends life and prosperity. Proverbs 3:19-20 likewise grounds the promise of wisdom in Prov 3:13-18. The full cosmogony in Prov 8:22-31 is structured chiastically:

A Yahweh creates Wisdom in honored first
   place vv. 22-23;
   B Creation "negatively" described vv. 24-28;
   B′ Creation "positively" described vv. 28-
   30a;
A′ Wisdom's intimacy with Yahweh vv. 30b-31.

The final two verses (vv. 30b-31), which come after the actual creating, are crucial for understanding Wisdom's appeal:

and I was daily [his] delight,
     [playing] before him at all times,
[playing] in his inhabited world
     and delighting in the human race. (NRSV)

The chiastic placement of "delight" and "play" makes Wisdom's delighting in Yahweh parallel to Wisdom's delighting in the human race. Just as Wisdom is Yahweh's delight "daily" in v. 30b, so also her friends are to wait at her doors "daily" in v. 34. The intimate relationship between Woman Wisdom and human beings on earth is a reflection of the intimate relationship between Woman Wisdom and Yahweh in heaven. Woman Wisdom might be expected to ground her authority on the fact that she has seen Yahweh create and can communicate to her friends the secrets of how the world works. Yet she bases her authority solely on her intimacy with Yahweh; from the beginning she has been with God. She enables those who love her to know the all-wise God as well.

Proverbs 8 goes a step beyond Prov 3:19-20 by personifying wisdom, which the sages traditionally associated with the divine act of creation and the cosmic order. Now the vivid personification in Proverbs 8 grounds Wisdom's claim that only those who court her will enjoy blessing. The search for wisdom in Proverbs 8 becomes more than performing or avoiding certain actions. Rather, one is to seek Wisdom herself. To court her is to touch a quality of Yahweh the creator, and to enter into a relationship with her is to receive every divine blessing. This cosmogony explains how life may have a more profound meaning; it may be not only life in the sense of enjoyment of health, good name, and family happiness, but also "life with" association with Yahweh.

In Job, creation themes and language are vital to the argument. God's first speech (Job 38:1–40:2) refutes Job's denial of order, and the second (Job 40:6–41:34) refutes his charge of injustice (in the sense of God's being unable to restrain evil). The first speech is a list of created things, showing them to be a mix of the useful, the bizarre, and even the playful. God, it appears, creates not for human beings (Job) but for the divine pleasure, which is inscrutable. The second speech simply describes the two primordial beasts, Behemoth and Leviathan. Any cosmogony based on the combat myth, as it was then current in Canaan, would have told how God defeated the primordial monsters as the first act of creation (cf. Isa 51:9); but in Job they are not defeated, and their cosmic menace and hostility to the human race are actually celebrated by the deity! Rather than destroying them to create an orderly world, Yahweh chooses to let them be (although on a leash). God tells Job that these monsters, the very symbols of evil, are alive and well, and that Job must live in the universe where they roam. Creation language here and elsewhere in Job shows paradoxically that the universe is not orderly as some traditional sages had thought. Yahweh remains, however, the powerful if inscrutable friend of such stalwarts as Job.

Wisdom. The rules or laws structured into the world at creation can be discovered through wisdom. Moreover, these norms can be expressed in artful words and communicated to others. Although wisdom cannot be defined solely as a response to cosmic order, the literature accepts this order. The sages hoped to instruct others about how to live in accord with wisdom (see Proverbs), to investigate scandal in that order—namely, the failure of a righteous person to enjoy appropriate blessings (see Job)—to point out why tradition cannot explain the world or ensure happiness (see Ecclesiastes), to anthologize and arrange ancient wisdom and relate it to Israel's literary heritage (see Sirach), and to locate wisdom in a seemingly unjust world for an audience familiar with the philosophical tradition of middle Platonism (see book of Wisdom).

Wisdom cannot be satisfactorily captured in a single brief definition because it has at least four aspects. First, it is practical, involving knowledge about how the world works so that one can master and enjoy life fully. This aspect of wisdom is expressed well in the French term *savoir-faire,* "to know how to act or do," rather than "to know" in an absolute sense, divorced from action. Practical knowledge can involve judicial activity, as when kings exercise their role as judge. David discerns the true intent of the woman from Tekoa (2 Sam 14:1-24, esp. v. 20), and Solomon shrewdly decides which of the two prostitutes is telling the truth (1 Kgs 3:16-28). It can mean skillful composition of proverbs and songs (1 Kgs 4:32) or cataloging related objects (1 Kgs 4:33). Jewelers and artisans can be

"wise," like the artisans who constructed the tabernacle (Exod 35:30–36:1). More generally, wisdom designates knowing how to live life; human life, as such, is a constant theme in wisdom literature. Most of the sayings in the wisdom books do not give advice but state a thesis about the world. "Hope deferred makes the heart sick,/ but a desire fulfilled is a tree of life" (Prov 13:12 NRSV) is not advice to finish projects for the sake of psychological health; rather, it states the way people ordinarily respond to disappointment and fulfillment of desires. Life is sufficiently regular that the sage can discover its rhythms and formulate them into theses or statements.

Second, human wisdom has limits. Proverbs, which is sometimes regarded as naively optimistic, has as its heroine Woman Wisdom, who from her place with God gives wisdom to those who wait upon her. Proverbs 26:4-5 wittily expresses the limits of wisdom sayings to fit every occasion: "Do not answer fools according to their folly,/ or you will be a fool yourself./ Answer fools according to their folly, or they will be wise in their own eyes" (NRSV). Wisdom in Proverbs involves the careful application of the tradition to individual situations. Job, that legendary wise man, refutes the traditional wisdom of his friends by using his own case; yet, he in turn is refuted by God's description of a vast, complex, and totally theocentric universe. Qohelet poses as the weary king who has seen all in order to put down any claim of wisdom to master life. The moments of life are hidden with God and parceled out to the foolish and the wise alike (Eccl 3:1-15). Ben Sira, though confident in the wisdom project, nonetheless writes long hymns to the divine wisdom (Sir 16:29–18:14; 39:12-35; 42:15–43:33) and pays court to her (Sir 51:13-50). The book of Wisdom focuses on divine wisdom; the model sage (Solomon) desires and prays intensely that it will be given to him (Wisdom 7–9).

The third point develops naturally from the foregoing one: Wisdom generally is both a human task and a divine gift, acquired through experience and obedience *and* given by God. Reconciling divine sovereignty with human freedom may be a major problem in the Western philosophical tradition, but the Bible does not perceive this dual affirmation to be a problem requiring a solution.

Fourth, wisdom in the Bible is itself an object of constant reflection. A major difference between the wisdom books of neighboring cultures and those of

Israel is the constant occurrence of the word "wisdom" (חכמה *ḥokmâ*) in the biblical books. Job 28 declares that wisdom is hidden with God and that the only way to wisdom is fear of the Lord (Job 28:28). Proverbs 1–9 goes further and personifies wisdom as an attractive woman who offers to share with her friends the life she shares with God (Proverbs 8–9). She shares in the divine governance of the world, doing what Yahweh elsewhere is depicted as doing. Sirach 24 identifies wisdom with "the book of the covenant of the Most High God" (Sir 24:23 NRSV), part of Ben Sira's project of incorporating wisdom into the other literature of Israel. In the Wisdom of Solomon, wisdom is closely associated with God and is like an ether permeating the cosmos (Wis 7:22–8:1); wisdom is revealed to human beings after prayer and pursuit (Sir 7:1-22; 8:2–9:18).

Consequences of Human Choice. Because biblical wisdom is so linked to action, the sages were much concerned with the effects of human action on each individual and on the community. The term "retribution" is often used to describe the relation between deed and consequence, but its negative connotation in English (punishment from an external source) makes it an unsatisfactory term to use. The effects of actions, according to the sages, could come from the very actions themselves as well as externally—i.e., directly from God, who sees all. Klaus Koch has emphasized the deed/consequence side of human acts: The deed creates its own effect, that consequences are latent in all significant good and evil actions.[18] The theory is an instance of cosmic order applied to human activity. God acts as "midwife" (Koch's term) to the law. A good example is the parent's warning to their offspring not to join a band of robbers on the grounds that a life of brigandage is inherently self-destructive. The robbers

> lie in wait—to kill themselves!
>   and set an ambush—for their own lives!
> Such is the end of all who are greedy for gain;
>   it takes away the life of its possessors.
> (Prov 1:18 -19 NRSV)

Another example of inherent outcomes is Prov 26:27 (NRSV): "Whoever digs a pit [to trap enemies] will fall into it,/ and a stone will come back on the one who starts it rolling." Inherent outcomes, however, are only one side of human action, for God is depicted as intervening directly: Yahweh "does not let the righteous go hungry,/ but he thwarts the craving of the wicked" (Prov 10:3 NRSV; cf. Prov 15:29; 16:4; 17:15). Job disproves his friends' belief that the deeds of the wicked always come back on them even as God is the ultimate source of Job's undeserved afflictions. The internal and the external perspectives that seem exclusive to modern readers remain valid for the biblical authors.

Doctrine of the Two Ways. The Bible, especially the book of Proverbs, imagines the moral life as presenting two ways, each with an intrinsic dynamism. Sometimes the two ways are explicitly contrasted, as in Woman Wisdom and Woman Folly in Proverbs 1–9 (esp. Prov 4:10-19) and in the persistent contrast in the sayings between the wise or the righteous and the fool or the wicked; Psalm 1 is also a good example of the inherent dynamism of two ways of life. The parental warning that opens Proverbs (1:8-19) envisions the future of the child as a way of life (Prov 1:15) shared with others ("we will all have one purse" [Prov 1:14 NRSV]). The doctrine of the two ways has sometimes been interpreted statically, as if it described a class of people who meticulously observe the law and a class who do not; but this reading is incorrect. The concept is dynamic: There are two ways of living, one blessed and the other cursed, and people are invited to follow the way of the righteous and to avoid the way of the wicked. There is no room for pride or smugness, for one can leave the righteous way at any time. The way of the righteous is protected and guaranteed by God, but people must walk in it—that is, act accordingly. The doctrine is implicit in Job, where the point at issue is the result of righteous living, and also in Ecclesiastes, where, since one cannot fully understand human behavior, Qohelet denies the epistemological basis for the two ways. The book of Wisdom contrasts the wicked (Wis 2:1-24; 4:20–5:23) with the righteous child of God, interpreted individually (Wis 2:12-20; 5:15-16) or corporately as Israel (Wisdom 19). In the Qumran texts and in the New Testament, the notion of two ways is expressed in the concepts of the children of light and the children of darkness.

The Problem of Evil. A skeptical and critical thread runs throughout ancient wisdom literature. The problem of evil was often formulated as a

---

18. Klaus Koch, "Is There a Doctrine of Retribution in the Old Testament?" in *Theodicy in the Old Testament,* ed. James L. Crenshaw (Philadelphia: Fortress, 1983) 57-87.

case—the sufferer who is not aware of having sinned or, conversely, the prosperous scoundrel. Proverbs does not subject the problem of evil to explicit reflection, though it does not necessarily regard its sayings as the ultimate answer to life's mysteries. Job narrates a case of the innocent just person. Qohelet's skepticism and criticism of traditional wisdom attempts to explain inconsistencies in the world. Ben Sira is aware of inexplicable evil in life but simply affirms the divine origin of evil as well as good (Sir 39:12-35), and he insists that God has created all things in pairs, corresponding to the human ability to choose between right and wrong (Sir 15:11-20; 33:7-15). The suffering of the innocent just person is so important in the book of Wisdom that it led to the teaching on immortality as its solution.

Biblical exploration of inexplicable suffering differs from that of Israel's neighbors. In Mesopotamia there was, strictly speaking, no such thing as a righteous sufferer. If one is afflicted without apparent reason, it can only be that one has infringed upon the sovereign order of the gods. This perception continues throughout the history of ancient Mesopotamia:

> In the Old Babylonian period this theology may find expression in a simple confession of bewilderment and ignorance of what one has done, or in the acceptance of one's sinfulness, along with its necessary consequences, as another manifestation of *fragilitas humana* common to all men. Later, one may infer from a clear conscience and a life re-examined and found, according to the known rules, faultless, that the gods hold men to the observance of other rules that he cannot know. To these thoughts one may join a contempt for man as the minion of many moods, a creature that may live gloriously only to die miserably. Or one may make the problem of the mind a problem of the heart, and solve it with reasons of the heart. Instead of wisdom, belief; instead of reflection and argument, a hymn to paradox and contraction. *Credo quia absurdum.* Attitudes and expression change; the theology does not.[19]

Against that background, Job is unique: "An explicit, unyielding declaration of innocence is not found before the book of Job."[20] The Bible's confession of one God, all-wise and all-powerful, makes its exploration of the problem of evil and of the righteous

sufferer more pressing and more poignant than that of neighboring cultures. Who but God is ultimately responsible for whatever happens in the world?

Personification of Wisdom. Israelite wisdom literature attended to wisdom itself alongside pragmatic wisdom. This "theoretical" interest is first clearly visible in Proverbs 1–9 (also in Job 28), where traditional teacher-disciple instructions exhort one not only to proper conduct but also to the acquisition of wisdom, which is portrayed as the source of long life, wealth, honor, and closeness to Yahweh. Although Israel had long singled out divine attributes such as power, love, and fidelity, occasionally even personifying them ("love and faithfulness go before you" [Ps 89:14 NRSV]; "Awake, awake, put on strength,/ O arm of the LORD!" [Isa 51:9 NRSV]), the consistent and vivid personification of wisdom as an attractive woman in Proverbs 1–9; Sirach 24; Bar 3:9–4:4; and Wisdom 7–9 stands on a different level. Wisdom acts and speaks, threatening or promising her audience, exulting in her intimacy and privileged place with Yahweh. For explanation, scholars have adduced venerable parallels such as an alleged Canaanite goddess; Ma'at, the Egyptian goddess of order; or the type scene found in the Mesopotamian Gilgamesh epic, the Canaanite Aqhat epic, and the Greek *Odyssey* (Calypso in Book V and Circe in Book X), in which a goddess offers life to a young hero only to destroy or transform him later on. Although personified Wisdom probably has non-Israelite roots, one must also reckon with influences from the social roles of real women in Israelite history and literary traditions about them—e.g., wife, harlot, wise woman—and with folk literature motifs such as the "sought-for person" (princess/bride).

In Prov 1:10-33 and chap. 8 (the frame for Proverbs 1–9), Wisdom invites the young disciple into a relationship with her, using language of love and courtship that is found also in Song of Songs (seeking and finding amid danger, waiting for the beloved). Her intimacy with Yahweh is the model of her relationship to the disciple; it enables her to give other gifts as well (Prov 8:30-36). Scholars grope for the right term for this presentation of Wisdom in Proverbs. Is it a hypostatization of a divine attribute or of the divinely implanted order in the world, or is it straightforward literary personification? Whatever explanation is adopted, Proverbs provides the primary interpretive context: Wisdom is a symbol of

---

19. W. L. Moran, "Rib Adda: Job at Byblos?" *Biblical and Related Studies Presented to Samuel Iwry* (Winona Lake: Eisenbrauns, 1985) 176-77.

20. Ibid., 177n. 16.

divine presence as well as of revelation; she is closely related to the instruction of the human teacher and to wisdom; a countervoice parodies Wisdom's message (Prov 2:16-19; 5; 6:20-35; 7; 9:13-18); and the quest for her is modeled on human love.

Personified wisdom appears in later books of the Bible as well. Sirach 24 (written c. 180 BCE) develops the link of wisdom and Yahweh and the old question of where wisdom dwells (Job 28) in a narrative in which Wisdom tells how she "came forth from the mouth of the Most High" (Sir 24:3 NRSV) and, at God's command, settled with Israel in Jerusalem (Sir 24:10-12). The author then identifies Wisdom with "the book of the covenant of the Most High God" (Sir 24:23 NRSV). Baruch 3:9–4:4 similarly identifies wisdom with the Torah. Wisdom of Solomon (c. first century BCE) combines the tradition of personified Wisdom living at God's side with Greek philosophical notions to assign a cosmic role to wisdom. The famous twenty-one qualities of Wisdom enumerated in Wis 7:22-23 highlight her pervasive agency in all things. For the influence of Wisdom on early Christian reflection about the cosmic role of Christ, see the section "New Testament" below.

THE CONTINUATION OF WISDOM LITERATURE

Judaism. The wisdom genres of instruction, saying, dialogue, and its themes of the blessed life and of cosmic order continued in the writings of early Judaism. Many literary works of the period used the technique of "relecture"—that is, rereading and recasting the classic texts. In the second century BCE, Sirach 24 rereads Proverbs 8, and Sirach 44–50 rereads the historical books, viewing the great personalities of Israel's history as individuals inspired by wisdom. Baruch 3:9–4:4 rereads Job 28 and Sirach 24, showing how the rulers of nations never found Wisdom, unlike Israel, who finds her in the book of the commandments of the law (Bar 4:1). Wisdom 10–19 interprets the books of Exodus and Numbers in seven great comparisons. *Pirqe 'Abot* (*The Sayings of the Fathers*) is a collection of sayings from the "men of the Great Assembly" (between the late fifth and the third centuries BCE) down to the descendants of Rabbi Judah the Prince in the third century CE. One of the treatises in the Talmud became the object of commentary in *'Abot de Rabbi Nathan.* Its opening sentence places the men of the

Great Assembly in a line from Moses, Joshua, the elders, and the prophets. The wisdom text of the Cairo Geniza, which some date in the first century CE but more likely dates to the early medieval period, continues the old wisdom tradition. Hebrew ethical wills, in which parents hand on to their children their wisdom, draw on traditional wisdom instruction.

The New Testament. Early Christians saw Jesus as a wisdom teacher and employed the tradition of personified wisdom to express his incarnation. Among the various influences on the New Testament was the wisdom teaching of "the Scriptures" (i.e., the Old Testament)—the themes of wisdom hidden with God and revealed to human beings, its identification with divine Spirit, Word, and Law, as well as the forms of instruction and admonition.

Unique among New Testament writings is the Letter of James, for it is an instruction. Although classed among the seven catholic epistles, it is a letter only in its opening address, "James, a slave of God and of the Lord Jesus Christ, to the twelve tribes in the dispersion, greetings" (Jas 1:1 NAB). The rest of the work comprises a series of instructions using the familiar exhortatory verbs (imperatives, jussives), followed by reasons, which are often sayings or proverbs. Old wisdom themes appear: the dangers of an unbridled tongue (James 3; cf. Prov 10:18-21), of presumptuous planning (Jas 4:13-17; cf. Prov 16:1), or of ill-gotten wealth (Jas 5:1-6; cf. Prov 10:2-3). Although commonsensical in the style of the instruction, James nonetheless exalts "wisdom from above" (Jas 3:13-18 NRSV; cf. Jas 1:17), invoking the tradition of wisdom beyond human capacity but graciously given to human beings (see Job 28; Proverbs 8; Sirach 24). In Jas 3:17, wisdom from above is designated by seven qualities, recalling the famous twenty-one qualities of wisdom in Wis 7:22-23. The wisdom instruction does not remain unchanged, however, for it is altered by the addition of prophetic denunciations of the callous rich (Jas 1:27; 2:1-13; 4:1-10; 5:1-6).

Paul's argument against those who are scandalized by the cross (1 Cor 1:17–2:13) employs the traditional wisdom literature contrast between the wise and the foolish as well as that between human wisdom and divine wisdom (see Job 28; Proverbs 8): "For since in the wisdom of God the world did not come to know God through wisdom, it was the will of God through the foolishness of the proclamation to save those who have faith" (1 Cor 1:21 NAB). So harsh is Paul's judgment on the ability of the sage to know Christ that one may question whether this passage singlehandedly eliminated wisdom genres as vehicles for the early Christian message.

Wisdom traditions influenced the putative written source of the synoptic Gospels Matthew and Luke: Q, for *Quelle,* the German word for "source." Most scholars believe that Q emphasized Jesus' teachings rather than his death and resurrection. A few scholars even hypothesize a trajectory of the genre "words of the wise" from early collections of wisdom sayings, such as Proverbs, to gnostic collections of sayings, such as the *Gospel of Thomas* (late first century BCE), with Q falling somewhere in the middle of the trajectory. In its pure form the hypothesis runs into serious problems, for Q at some stage had eschatological statements incompatible with gnostic timelessness and lacking distinctively gnostic sayings. Wisdom themes nonetheless are strong in Q, as is illustrated by Matt 11:27//Luke 10:22: "All things have been handed over to me by my Father. No one knows the Son except the Father, and no one knows the Father except the Son and anyone to whom the Son wishes to reveal him" (NAB). The saying is part of the Jewish (and early Christian) debate about what and where wisdom is. Is it to be identified with the law (Sirach 24), with heavenly mysteries (*1 Enoch* 42:1-3), or with Christ (John 1:1-18; Col 1:15-20)? Is wisdom to be found in the Jerusalem Temple (Sir 24:8-12), everywhere in the cosmos (Wis 7:24-26), in heaven (*1 Enoch* 42:1-3), or in the church (Col 1:18)? Jesus in the text is divine wisdom incarnate, for to know him is to know God, who is wisdom itself. The immediately following verses, "Come to me, all you that are weary and are carrying heavy burdens, and I will give you rest. Take my yoke upon you, and learn from me" (Matt 11:28-29 NRSV), echo Sir 51:23-30, which is an invitation to attend Ben Sira's school and become his disciple. Matthew, therefore, answers the question of the early debate: Wisdom is found in Jesus and in his teaching.

Of all the Gospels, John is the most persistent in regarding Jesus as incarnate wisdom descended from on high to offer human beings light and truth. The Gospel expresses Jesus' heavenly origin by identifying him with personified Wisdom. Just as Woman Wisdom was with God from the beginning, even before the earth (Prov 8:22-23; Sir 24:9; Wis 6:22),

so also Jesus is the Word in the beginning (John 1:1), with God before the world existed (John 17:5). Just as Wisdom teaches human beings heavenly secrets (Job 11:6-7; Wis 9:16-18) and shows them how to walk in the way that leads to life (Prov 2:20-22; 3:13-26; 8:32-35; Sir 4:12) and immortality (Wis 6:18-19), so also Jesus functions as the revealer in John. Jesus speaks in long discourses, as did Woman Wisdom (Prov 1:20-33; 8). Wisdom invites people to partake of her rich banquet, where food and drink symbolize life and closeness to God (Prov 9:2-5; Sir 24:19-21). Jesus does the same: "I am the bread of life. Whoever comes to me will never be hungry, and whoever believes in me will never be thirsty" (John 6:35 NRSV; cf. Prov 9:1-6, 11). Just as Wisdom seeks friends (Prov 1:20-21; 8:1-4; Wis 6:16), so also Jesus recruits followers (John 1:36-38, 43), though an individual might reject Wisdom (Prov 1:24-25; Bar 3:12; *1 Enoch* 42:2) or Jesus (John 8:46; 10:25).

Two early Christian hymns identify Jesus with God's creative Word and with heavenly wisdom: John 1:1-18 and Col 1:15-20. The Greek word λόγος (*logos*, "word") in John 1 has more in common with Old Testament wisdom than with merely a word. Sirach 24:3 ("From the mouth of the Most High I came forth," NAB) and Wis 9:1-2 had already made "wisdom" and "word" parallel. Proverbs 8:22-23 ("The LORD created me at the beginning. . . . Ages ago I was set up . . ." [NRSV]) and Sir 1:1 affirmed that Wisdom comes from God and remains with God forever. The Johannine prologue states that the Word was always with God. Wisdom as an aura of the might of God and pure effusion of the glory of the Almighty (Wis 7:25-26) seems to be echoed in John 1:14, where Jesus is the refulgence of eternal light (cf. Heb 1:1-2). Wisdom 7:22 says that Wisdom is unique (μονογενής *monogenēs*), and the prologue declares that the Word is God's unique (*monogenēs*) son. Wisdom sets up her tent in Sir 24:8, as does Jesus in John 1:14 (ἐσκήνωσεν *eskēnōsen*, "to tent"). In Sir 24:16, Wisdom has "glory" (δόξα *doxa*) and "grace" (χάρις *charis*), as does Jesus in John 1:14.

The hymn about creation in Col 1:15-20 (NAB) applies to Christ the creative role of wisdom:

> He is the image of the invisible God,
> the first born of all creation.
> For in him were created all things in heaven and on
> earth,

He is the head of the body, the church.
He is the beginning, the firstborn from the dead.

He is the beginning, the firstborn from the dead. As in John 1, the hymn combines vocabulary of Genesis 1 with ideas from Proverbs 8 and Wisdom 7 to show that Christ, who created and governs the world, is now redeeming it. Creation and redemption stand in structural parallelism. Colossians 1:15-17 affirms that Christ was the model for the human race (created in the image of God, Gen 1:27-28) and is now the model for all members of the body, the church, and the means by which they are reconciled and exist together.

SUMMARY

The people of the ancient Near East, like people today, were interested in learning how to live optimally in a world they found only partially understandable. They took note of successful and unsuccessful ways of coping with life, stated them memorably, and handed them on to others. They also observed that life is often inexplicable and the lot of human beings to be miserable, and they explored such problems in complaints and dialogues. It was the human task to observe carefully the world the gods had made and to record their observations. Because of this common commitment to attend to the world and its rhythms and laws, there is remarkable continuity among the wisdom literatures of antiquity.

The people of Israel lived in that world and responded to it in literature similar to that of its neighbors. Belief in the sole God, Yahweh, made things different, however. The relation of wisdom to Yahweh had to be explained. The problem of evil was an especially vexing problem, because there were no demons to blame or a fate beyond God; there was only Yahweh, whom they celebrated as all-wise and all-just.

The wisdom books now appear in the Bible, a book of books. In the perennial dialectic of the Bible, the wisdom books "charge" other books and themselves receive a charge from them. They are incor-

porated into a story, which Christians and Jews regard as still ongoing. The wisdom books remind readers that one must take hold of life as both gift and task, that there are many possibilities but also profound limits, and that honest observation and fidelity to one's experience of life can put one in touch with a wondrous order whose source is God. The wisdom books' starting point of everyday experience and honest observations create common ground for Bible readers to engage with other people just as it once did for ancient Israel and its neighbors.

BIBLIOGRAPHY

Ancient Near Eastern Wisdom Literature:

Brunner, H. *Die Weisheitsbücher der Ägypter: Lehren für das Leben.* Munich: Artemis, 1991. Annotated translations of all the extant instructions, with a fine general introduction.

Pritchard, J. B. *Ancient Near Eastern Texts Relating to the Old Testament.* Princeton: Princeton University Press, 1955). Standard translations of many wisdom texts from Egypt and Mesopotamia. Lichtheim (below) is generally preferable for Egyptian texts.

Lambert, W. G. *Babylonian Wisdom Literature.* Oxford: Clarendon, 1960. Authoritative introduction and translations.

Foster, B. B. *Before the Muses: An Anthology of Akkadian Literature.* 2 vols. Bethesda: CDL, 1993.

Lichtheim, Miriam. *Ancient Egyptian Literature.* 3 vols. Berkeley: University of California Press, 1973–1980. Excellent commentary and translation of many wisdom texts.

Biblical Wisdom Literature:

Barré, M. L. " 'Fear of God' and the World View of Wisdom," *BTB* 11 (1981) 41-43. Effective argument that ancient wisdom was always religious, against some recent scholarship.

Murphy, R. *The Forms of Old Testament Literature.* FOTL 13. Grand Rapids: Eerdmans, 1981. Good form-critical analysis of all the wisdom books, with bibliography.

———. *The Tree of Life: An Exploration of Biblical Wisdom Literature.* 2nd ed. Grand Rapids: Eerdmans, 1996. Comprehensive and judicious introduction with annotated bibliography.

The Sage in Israel and the Ancient Near East. Edited by J. G. Gammie and L. G. Perdue. Winona Lake, Wis.: Eisenbrauns, 1990. Essays on biblical and other wisdom books with special attention to their social context.

Smalley, B. *Medieval Exegesis of Wisdom Literature.* Edited by R. Murphy. Atlanta: Scholars Press, 1986. Solid historical studies.

Studies in Ancient Israelite Wisdom. Edited by J. L. Crenshaw. New York: KTAV, 1976. Influential scholarly essays.

Theodicy in the Old Testament. Edited by J. L. Crenshaw. Philadelphia: Fortress, 1983. Essays, some not previously in English, on the problem of God's wisdom and justice in the world.

Vanel, A. "Sagesse," *Supplément au Dictionnaire de la Bible* (1986) 7:4-58. Thorough and recent survey of the major question.

von Rad, G. *Wisdom in Israel.* Nashville: Abingdon, 1972. A seminal work, full of fresh insights, and extremely influential on theological discussion of wisdom literature.

Whybray, R. N. *The Intellectual Tradition in the Old Testament.* BZAW 135. Berlin: de Gruyter, 1974, An argument that the authors of wisdom books were from a class of intellectuals rather than professional sages.

THE BOOK OF PROVERBS

INTRODUCTION, COMMENTARY, AND REFLECTIONS
BY
RAYMOND C. VAN LEEUWEN

THE BOOK OF
PROVERBS

INTRODUCTION

E very human needs wisdom for living, and every healthy society hands its wisdom on to
the next generation. Proverbs is a literary anthology of Israel's traditional wisdom, gathered
from diverse spheres of life. The book's purpose is to help people become wise and godly (1:2-7).
Yet its writers were aware of a hermeneutical circle of living and reading, in which one needs
godly wisdom to get wisdom (2:1-6; 8:9). The book's entry into this circle of life and learning
is generational. In traditional oral cultures, mothers and fathers, teachers and leaders pass on
their own life experience and ancestral wisdom to their "children," both real and figurative
(1:8; 4:3-4; 6:20; 31:1). Proverbs is a literary gathering of such diverse wisdom. Its readers are
invited to walk the path of wisdom and "the fear of the LORD."

Although many readers find Proverbs full of "common sense" with which they can
connect, there are still many difficulties in a book whose world, culture, and language are
ancient and foreign. We often find ourselves listening in on a fragmentary conversation
intended for someone else and filled with hidden assumptions and references. In addition
to the challenges faced by all readers, feminism has made us aware that women face
additional barriers in appropriating the wisdom of Proverbs, because it is addressed to men
and presents women in terms of their relations with men. In the Hebrew of Proverbs, the
word translated "my child" or "children" (NRSV) is invariably literally "my son" (בני *běnî*)
or "sons" (בנים *bānîm*). Presumably, Israelite parents taught daughters as well as sons,
but this book gives no sign thereof. Many readers today find this androcentric focus
objectionable. Moreover, some women declare Proverbs to be oppressive because of its
ancient patriarchal worldview, because it lacks a (nonpatriarchal) woman's voice, and

because of its portrayal of women.[1] It is, perhaps, important to remember that the male focus of Proverbs is a reflection not only of patriarchal culture but also of the book's genre (see below).

Proverbs is a challenge to all modern and postmodern readers whose world and worldviews can make it difficult to connect with aspects of this ancient book. Biblical scholars have shown the naivete of selectively domesticating the Bible to fit present cultural patterns (so that the Bible's own voice is silenced, as we assume it means what we mean), or of attempting to transform the present society into an ancient Israel (so that the particularity of the present culture and society is not taken seriously). Wisdom, however, requires that we see new situations fittingly (see Commentary on 26:1-12). This means seeing not just the different or the particular in a new situation, but also recognizing in it those old fundamental patterns of life described by the sages of Proverbs. Wisdom requires a humble, earnest effort to hear what the other says and a willingness to see our world in the other's terms (18:13).

TITLE AND DATE

The English title "Proverbs" stems from *Proverbia,* the Latin title that Jerome gave the book in the Vulgate. In Hebrew, the book is known by its first word, [שלמה] מָשְׁלֵי (*miš lê* [*š ĕlō mō h*]), "The Proverbs [of Solomon]." *Miš lê* (sg., *māš āl*), however, has a wider range of reference than English "proverb." The word's meaning suggests "comparison," though some think it connotes "mastery" (over life or language). It is used to refer to a variety of oral and literary genres, including not only sayings and admonitions, but also parables, poems, and songs (see Num 21:27; 23:7; Ps 49:5; Isa 14:4; Ezek 17:2; 21:5).

The title "Proverbs of Solomon" is traditional and honorific, for it is clear that Solomon is not the author of the book in its present form (see 25:1; 30:1; 31:1), though some have argued for the origin of sections of the book in the Solomonic court. Solomon is Israel's paradigmatic wise king (1 Kings 3–4; 10). To him the ancients ascribed not only Proverbs, but also the Song of Songs, Ecclesiastes, the book of Wisdom (written in Greek!), and other works. In much the same way, all Psalms are conventionally ascribed to David and all of Israel's laws to Moses. The issue for the ancients was not authorship in the modern sense, but the authority of works written in the "spirit" of the archetypal lawgiver, psalmist, or sage.

Proverbs is a collection of collections, organized and edited with an Israelite character of its own. It was compiled over several centuries and bears the stamp of its diverse origins in the headings of its subcollections and sections (1:1; 10:1; 22:17; 24:23; 25:1; 30:1; 31:1) and in the variety of its materials.

Generally scholars consider the "Solomonic Collections" (10:1–22:16; 25:1–29:27) to be the earliest monarchical sections of the book. Though some have pointed out early ancient Near Eastern parallels to the personification of Wisdom in Proverbs 8,[2] the first nine chapters

---

1. Sharon H. Ringe lists a variety of women's approaches to interpretation of the Bible in her essay "When Women Interpret the Bible," in Carol A. Newsom and Sharon H. Ringe, eds., *The Women's Bible Commentary* (Louisville: Westminster, 1992) 4-5.

2. Christa Kayatz, *Studien zu Proverbien 1–9,* WMANT 22 (Neukirchen-Vluyn: Neukirchener Verlag, 1966); G. von Rad, *Wisdom in Israel* (Nashville: Abingdon, 1972) 143-76.

and the thirty-first chapter are usually dated in the early Persian period, after the return from the Babylonian exile (538 BCE).[3] However, the possibility of a Greek-Hebrew word play in 31:27 (see Commentary) may mean that the final sections of the book were composed after Alexander the Great's conquest of Palestine (332 BCE). The Septuagint (LXX), with its different ordering of the last sections and its pluses and minuses, constitutes in effect another edition of the book. Thus different versions of the book existed during the Hellenistic period.[4]

The nature of this literature makes it extremely difficult to date. Proverbs (sayings and admonitions) refer to the common structures and patterns of human life. Sayings and admonitions are traditional and can preserve wisdom from earlier times in fossilized form (as in English, "Pride *goeth* before a fall"). The problem is made more difficult by the extremely brief scope of the various sayings and admonitions. In addition, there are virtually no historical "hooks" on which to hang a secure date or dates for the whole and its parts. Aside from the references to Solomon (1:1; 10:1) and to Hezekiah (25:1), there are no specific historical references in the book (Lemuel and Agur are otherwise unknown). Proverbs is entirely silent concerning Israel's history of redemption (patriarchal promises, covenants, exodus, law, gift of the land, exile and return—but see 2:21-22; 10:30; 22:28).

This silence does not imply that the various authors of the book had no interest in matters of redemptive history or in other biblical books (see Commentary on 16:5-6; 25:18; 30:4-5). Like most books, Proverbs does not reveal the full range of its authors' concerns. Similarly, the New Testament wisdom book called James bypasses the events of the life of Jesus, a matter that displeased Martin Luther. Such silences in wisdom writings are a function of their genre and purpose, and too much should not be concluded concerning the isolation of the sages from Israel's historical traditions. To borrow a remark on Psalm 119, the sage "so focuses upon *ethos* that he barely notices *mythos,* in this case, the history of redemption."[5] The same holds true for the book's infrequent mention of worship.[6] The clues for dating that remain are the uncertain ones of language, culture, and social location.

SOCIAL LOCATIONS: ORAL AND LITERARY

Like the quest for firm dates, the attempt to establish the social location of the book, its sections, and sayings has proved difficult.[7] Arguments in these matters are especially prone to circular reasoning: One posits a date and social location for a section of the book and then proceeds to explain that section in terms of the proposed location. Neither have scholars always clearly distinguished among (1) the original *sources* of sections and proverbs (whether oral or written); (2) the *persons, processes,* and *places* of literary

3. Claudia V. Camp, *Wisdom and the Feminine in the Book of Proverbs* (Sheffield: JSOT, 1985) 179-208, 233-254.

4. E. Tov, *Textual Criticism of the Hebrew Bible* (Minneapolis: Fortress, 1992) 337.

5. Jon D. Levenson, "The Sources of Torah," in *Ancient Israelite Religion,* Patrick D. Miller, Jr., Paul D. Hanson, and S. Dean McBride, eds. (Philadelphia: Fortress, 1987) 568, 559-74. See J. J. Collins, "Proverbial Wisdom and the Yahwist Vision," *Semeia* 17 (1980) 1-17.

6. See Leo G. Perdue, *Wisdom and Cult* (Missoula: Scholars Press, 1977).

7. R. E. Murphy, "Form Criticism and Wisdom Literature," *CBQ* 31 (1969) 481; J. L. Crenshaw, "Wisdom," in John L. Hayes, ed., *Old Testament Form Criticism* (San Antonio: Trinity University Press, 1974) 236.

collection; (3) editorial *composition*; and (4) the Hebrew book in its final form, embodying all the earlier collections, but reflecting the shape, scope, and purpose of the final editors and ultimately of the Holy Spirit (see Commentary on 30:5-7).[8] These writer-editors have put all their materials together for a new purpose, in which the whole is more than the sum of its parts.

The embodiment of oral traditions in literary works raises problems with which biblical scholars still struggle.[9] A number of scholars have compared sayings and admonitions in Proverbs to oral traditions from Africa to argue that the source of the biblical sayings and admonitions is the Israelite "folk," in family, clan, and village.[10] For R. N. Whybray, many of the sayings reflect the perspective of the Israelite peasant. For them life was hard and difficult, a matter of survival. Yet he notes that chaps. 1–9 and 22:16–24:22 have a more aristocratic social level, as does chap. 31.[11] Others believe that the book reflects the aristocratic world of the royal court. Although the sayings and admonitions of the Solomonic collections appear to arise from a variety of social locations and periods, the royal court remains the most plausible location for their literary compilation (10:1; 25:1; cf. 31:1). Even a scholar such as F. Golka (an advocate of the "folk" origin of proverbs), who claims to show that sayings about the king do not require a courtly origin, assumes that the sayings were collected and redacted in the royal court.[12]

The theory that the book (or its parts) arose from a school setting remains disputed, suffering from a lack of conclusive evidence that Israelite schools existed independently in the pre-exilic period.[13] The probable final editing of the book took place in the early Hellenistic period (after 322 BCE; see Commentary on 31:27). The final editors of Proverbs were among the scribal sages who gave the Hebrew Bible its canonical shape. Parallels to these redactors may be found in literary sages like Ben Sira and the poet-writers of Qumran.[14]

The foregoing uncertainties about dating and social location are partly due to the variety and even contradictory character of sayings gathered in the book. It is likely that differing social groups produced and made use of originally independent sections and that the final author-editors collected, augmented, and edited the parts to provide a complex and diverse compendium of wisdom.[15] One group learns from another, borrowing and adapting its

8. For an astute defense of God's speaking in the diverse texts of Scripture, see N. Wolterstorff, *Divine Discourse: Philosophical Reflections on the Claim That God Speaks* (Cambridge: Cambridge University Press, 1996).

9. Walter J. Ong, *Orality and Literacy: The Technologizing of the Word* (London: Methuen, 1982); Jack Goody, *The Logic of Writing and the Organization of Society* (Cambridge: Cambridge University Press, 1986). For the ancient Near East, see J. Bottero, *Mesopotamia: Writing, Reasoning, and the Gods* (Chicago: University of Chicago Press, 1992) 4, 67-137.

10. Most recently, C. Westermann, *The Roots of Wisdom: The Oldest Proverbs of Israel and Other Peoples* (Louisville: Westminster John Knox, 1995).

11. R. N. Whybray, *Wealth and Poverty in the Book of Proverbs* (Sheffield: JSOT, 1990); and *The Composition of the Book of Proverbs* (Sheffield: JSOT, 1994).

12. Friedemann W. Golka, "Die Königs und Hofsprüche und der Ursprung der Israelitischen Weisheit," *VT* 36 (1986) 13-36, here 13. See Michael V. Fox, "The Social Location of the Book of Proverbs," in Fox et al., eds., *Texts, Temples and Traditions: A Tribute to Menahem Haran* (Winona Lake: Eisenbrauns, 1996) 227-39.

13. See James L. Crenshaw, "Education in Ancient Israel," *JBL* 104 (1985) 601-5; S. Weeks, *Early Israelite Wisdom* (Oxford: Clarendon, 1994) 132-56. Cf. Andre Lemaire, "The Sage in School and Temple," in *The Sage in Israel and the Ancient Near East,* ed. John G. Gammie and Leo G. Perdue (Winona Lake: Eisenbrauns, 1990) 165-81.

14. See R. C. Van Leeuwen, "Scribal Wisdom and Theodicy in the Book of the Twelve," in Leo G. Perdue, et al., eds., *In Search of Wisdom: Essays in Memory of John G. Gammie* (Louisville: Westminster/John Knox, 1993) 31-49.

15. James L. Crenshaw, "The Sage in Proverbs," in Gammie and Perdue, *The Sage in Israel,* 205-16. See also the essays by Camp, Fontaine, Whybray, and Lemaire in the same volume.

wisdom for its own ends. This is entirely in keeping with the amazing mobility of proverbial wisdom. Each group in a society produces its own sayings, some of which become universal. For example, everyone today knows the computer proverb, "Garbage in, garbage out." Proverbs not only cross social boundaries within a society, but they can even cross linguistic and cultural barriers as well.[16] Erasmus domesticated ancient and medieval Latin proverbs in his *Adages.* Western anthropologists and missionaries have collected sayings throughout the world.

When proverbs are contradictory, it is not necessarily a sign of different origins or conflicting worldviews. Proverbs even from a single group or person can be contradictory, because life is complex. In a proverb collection, or in the collective oral memory of a culture, we find a "universe" of wisdom, a world of discourse. The collection is undergirded by a common view of reality, but may be diverse and even contradictory in its particulars. Thus users of proverbs must choose from the diverse sayings and admonitions the one that best "hits the nail on the head." With proverbs, one may say, "If the shoe fits, wear it" (see Commentary on 25:7, 9). Proverb use is always situational.

Another factor is at work in a written compendium of wisdom such as Proverbs. Whether individual units were originally oral or written, their juxtaposition cheek by jowl in a book creates a *literary* context for the reader. Their original oral settings have disappeared; we have only a literary context to clarify their meaning. Often proverbs are juxtaposed in such a way that one "comments" on its neighbor (see Commentary on 17:17-18; 26:4-5). Among these "proverb pairs," the Yahweh sayings are particularly sharp in qualifying their fellows (see Commentary on 18:10-11).

In addition, within each section of Proverbs, certain themes, genres, or patterns are more prominent than in other sections. While the differences among the collections are not absolute, they are significant, for they create typical patterns of emphasis and concern. For example, the contrast between righteous and wicked in chapters 10–15 is typical of the first Solomonic subcollection (chaps. 10–15). It creates an orderly view of reality and justice in which good and bad actions are met with corresponding consequences. In contrast, the second Solomonic subcollection (16:1–22:16) presents a more complex view of acts and consequences. Here the focus on God's freedom and on the king (16:1-15) introduces the notion of limits to human wisdom and of mystery in the divine disposition of events. Here we see that sometimes the righteous suffer while the wicked prosper (see Commentary on 16:8).

A further, crucial aid to interpreting Proverbs is the existence of long-distance literary context, created by repetitions of themes, of phrases, and even of lines and couplets.[17] This literary context is first of all within and among sections of Proverbs itself, but the alert reader will find many connections among Proverbs, the rest of the Bible, and other Jewish and Christian writings (see below, "On Using This Commentary"). Finally, comparative study of ancient Near Eastern and Egyptian cultures greatly enriches our understanding of Proverbs.

---

16. The classic, essential work remains Archer Taylor, *The Proverb* (Cambridge, Mass.: Harvard University Press, 1931; reprint edited by W. Mieder [Bern: Peter Lang, 1985]). See also W. Mieder, *Proverbs Are Never Out of Season: Popular Wisdom in the Modern Age* (New York: Oxford University Press, 1993).

17. Daniel C. Snell, *Twice Told Proverbs and the Composition of the Book of Proverbs* (Winona Lake: Eisenbrauns, 1993).

GENRE AND CONTENT

Proverbs has affinities in genre and content to a long list of Egyptian "instructions" and other ancient Near Eastern works.[18] Indeed, many scholars believe that the section titled "Sayings of the Wise" (22:17–24:22) adapts parts of the Egyptian *Instruction of Amenemope* for its own purposes.[19] The book begins with a brief title, an extended statement of purpose, and a motto: The fear of the Lord is the beginning of knowledge (1:1-7). The remainder of Proverbs 1–9 comprises a series of speeches by parents to a young son. These speeches especially are akin to the Egyptian "instructions" in which a royal father left a testament of wisdom to his heir. A similar medieval Jewish genre is the "Ethical Will." This sort of literature is based on oral "rites of passage." The parent—often portrayed as being on the point of death—gives advice to a son (occasionally a daughter) about to enter the responsibilities of adulthood (see 1 Kgs 2:1-9; Tob 4:1-21; Sir 3:1-16).[20]

Within the book, however, chapters 1–9 have a literary function. Together with chapters 30–31, they form an interpretive "frame" through which to view the small wisdom utterances they enclose. The worldview of these chapters—to change the image—gives the reader lenses through which to read the diverse sayings and admonitions in chapters 10–29. Even when contemplating the minutia of table manners, of farming, or of the law court, all of life expresses "the fear of the LORD"—or lack thereof (1:7; 9:10; 31:30). No aspect of reality is irrelevant to wisdom, because the Lord made all things through wisdom (3:19-20; 8:22-31).

The wisdom of Proverbs requires a knowledge of the common structures and patterns of the world and of human life as ordained by God. Globally, this is presented in the imagery of chaps. 1–9, in which "ways," "women," and "houses" in relation to the young male addressee form a metaphorical system for Wisdom and Folly that communicates the basic character of life in God's world (see Overview on 1–9). On a smaller scale, this is often true of the sayings and admonitions as well (chaps. 10–29). Sayings are often narratives in a nutshell; they distill the manifold patterns of life down to their basic elements. Thus Mario Puzo can expand the insight of Prov 10:21 *b* into an entire novel.[21] The reader familiar with biblical stories will find in them many proverbs "writ large," as the commentary attempts to show.

Wisdom requires reverence for God and a general knowledge of how the world and humans work. Wise folk know the way things "ought to be," and they have a sense of

18. Stuart Weeks, *Early Israelite Wisdom* (Oxford: Clarendon, 1994) 162-89; Miriam Lichtheim, *Ancient Egyptian Literature,* 3 vols. (Berkeley: University of California Press, 1973–80) and *Late Egyptian Wisdom Literature in the International Context* (Freiburg and Göttingen: Vandenhoeck & Ruprecht, 1983).

19. Harold C. Washington, *Wealth and Poverty in the Instruction of Amenemope and the Hebrew Proverbs,* SBLDS 142 (Atlanta: Scholars Press, 1994).

20. See Fox, "The Social Location of the Book of Proverbs," 232. For examples, see *Ancient Near Eastern Texts Relating to the Old Testament,* ed. James B. Pritchard, 3rd ed. (Princeton, N.J.: Princeton University Press, 1969) 412-25, or *AEL* 1:58-80, 134-39; 2:135-63; 3:159-217.

21. Mario Puzo, *Fools Die* (New York: Putnam, 1978).

right and wrong.[22] Wisdom also demands an understanding of concrete situations, of particular institutions and persons with their individuality and quirks (this job, this company, this boss, this employee, this woman or man, this teacher, this country, etc.). Wise people know what the present moment and its constituents require. Wise action and speech are *fitting* (see Commentary on 26:1-12). Consequently, proverbs can be contradictory on verbal and social levels because different sayings apply to different persons, circumstances, and times. The wise person recognizes which is which and acts appropriately. The conceptual adequacy of Proverbs to illumine reality comes only when the rich diversity of proverbs is wisely exploited (see 26:7, 9).

The use of proverbs can be even more complex or subtle than suggested so far. The same proverb can be legitimately used for quite different purposes and to communicate quite different things, depending on who speaks, to whom, and in what way and circumstances. For a disadvantaged poor person to say, "Money talks," has a different meaning than when someone rich and powerful says it.[23] Social location and relations matter.

Even on something so basic as the "act-consequence connection" (the basic wisdom doctrine that people reap what they sow), the book of Proverbs can be contradictory. Its basic teaching (chaps. 1–15) is that right living produces wealth and well-being. Folly and wickedness produce poverty, disgrace, and even death. This is true because God made the world in wisdom, and God is faithful to its principles. But as the book proceeds (chaps. 16–29), we learn that there are exceptions to the general rules of life. Not even the wise can comprehend all the contradictions and mysteries of life, of God and cosmos. The wicked can prosper, especially in a time of chaos, and the righteous can suffer unjustly. (These themes are developed more extensively in Job and Ecclesiastes.) Still, Proverbs insists that it is better to be poor and godly than rich and wicked (see Commentary on 15:16; 16:8). Ultimately Proverbs is a book of faith (1:7), insisting on the reality of God's justice and righteousness, even when experience seems to contradict it (see Hebrews 11).[24] God's justice often remains hidden, since much of life—and God's own self—is beyond human grasping (see Commentary on 16:1-9; 21:30-31).[25]

The bulk of the book is devoted to short, mostly two-line indicative "sayings" or "sentences" of the sort commonly called "proverbs" (esp. 10:1–22:16; 25:1–29:27). A middle section of the book (22:17–24:22) is largely devoted to "admonitions," brief second-person precepts that usually provide reasons or motive clauses for doing or not doing something. These motives can be practical (looking at positive or negative consequences) or explanatory (appealing to the nature of things). Ultimately, and sometimes explicitly, they are theological, rooted in the God

22. Cornelius Plantinga, Jr., *Not the Way It's Supposed to Be: A Breviary of Sin* (Grand Rapids: Eerdmans, 1995) 113-28.

23. Barbara Kirshenblatt-Gimblett, "Toward a Theory of Proverb Meaning," in *The Wisdom of Many: Essays on the Proverb,* W. Mieder and A. Dundes, eds. (New York: Garland, 1981) 111-21; Peter Seitel, "Proverbs: A Social Use of Metaphor," 122-39 in the same volume; Carole R. Fontaine, *The Use of the Traditional Saying in the Old Testament* (Sheffield: JSOT, 1982).

24. R. C. Van Leeuwen, "On Wealth and Poverty: System and Contradiction in Proverbs," *Hebrew Studies* 33 (1992) 25-36.

25. G. von Rad's work remains basic, *Wisdom in Israel* (Nashville: Abingdon, 1972) 97-110.

who made and rules all things wisely. Both genres, sayings and admonitions, appear throughout the book, sometimes embedded in larger structures.

This diversity of sayings and admonitions constitutes one of the main problems in understanding the book (see below, "On Using This Commentary"). A master scholar of world proverbs has declared that "the proverb in a collection is dead," because readers have no direct access to the life situation in which they are used.[26] Proverbs (both sayings and admonitions) are generally short, pithy utterances that require a social and cultural context for us to understand them fully. Proverbs are addressed to particular people in particular situations, and yet, they embody common human truths, recurring patterns in ordinary life. Wisdom applies old truths to new situations, because in a certain sense, "There is nothing new under the sun" (see Matt 13:52). A mother tells a sluggish college student that "the early bird catches the worm." A Nigerian father tells a teenager who hangs out with the wrong crowd that those "who sleep with puppies catch fleas." One child needs to be told, "Look before you leap," another, "She who hesitates is lost."

Proverbs also embody a culture's commitments, contradictions, and myths. Many Americans believe that "money talks" and that "sex sells." Yet we emblazon "In God we trust" on our currency, perhaps to remind ourselves that "money isn't everything." And advertisers fervently exploit our belief that "the sky's the limit"—meaning that for us there are no limits, whether ecological, moral, or divine—to self-gratification.[27]

THEOLOGY

Some scholars believe that the God of Proverbs was a mere variant of the deities in other ancient Near Eastern wisdom writings. An extreme form of this view argues that the God of Proverbs is *not* the God of the rest of the OT.[28] This position, however, presupposes the widespread (and mistaken) belief that the uniqueness of Israel's God had to do with Yahweh's involvement in history; it also entailed a corresponding marginalization of creation.[29] A related position, using the method of tradition history, separates creation of the cosmos from creation of humans, so that the theology of Proverbs 1–9 (cosmos) has little to do with Proverbs 10–29 (humans).[30] This position, however, ignores the actual coexistence of both traditions in Proverbs and the editors' evident intent in chaps. 1–9 to create a cosmic context for understanding the sayings of chaps. 10–29. It is also anachronistic because, unlike the modern West with its separation of nature and culture, ancient Near Eastern anthropologies presuppose cosmologies, which may be largely implicit (as in chaps. 10–29) or explicit (as in

---

26. Wolfgang Mieder, cited by Fontaine, *The Use of the Traditional Saying in the Old Testament,* 54.

27. Alan Dundes, "Folk Ideas as Units of Worldview," *American Journal of Folklore* 84 (1971) 93-103.

28. H. D. Preuss, "Das Gottesbild der älteren Weisheit Israels," *VTS* 23 (1972) 117-45.

29. See H. G. Reventlow, *Problems of Old Testament Theology in the Twentieth Century* (Philadelphia: Fortress, 1985) 59-124; Rolf P. Knierim, "Cosmos and History in Israel's Theology," in *The Task of Old Testament Theology: Substance, Method, and Cases* (Grand Rapids: Eerdmans, 1995) 171-224.

30. P. Doll, *Menschenschöpfung und Weltschöpfung in der alttestamentlichen Weisheit,* SBS 117 (Stuttgart: Verlag Katholisches Bibelwerk, 1985); C. Westermann, *The Roots of Wisdom: The Oldest Proverbs of Israel and Other Peoples* (Louisville: Westminster John Knox, 1995).

chaps. 1–9). On another front, some scholars seek in Lady Wisdom evidence for an Israelite goddess whose existence was suppressed by the monotheistic editors of the book.[31] One's hermeneutical approach to these theological-exegetical questions greatly influences one's reading of the evidence and the conclusions drawn from it. On this point leading scholars are divided. James L. Crenshaw, writing in honor of Roland E. Murphy, put it succinctly: "For me, the crucial issue concerns whether or not ancient sages accepted the world view of Yahwism. Murphy thinks they did; I am not able to accept that position."[32]

Yet, the writer-editors of Proverbs clearly considered the God of wisdom to be Israel's God, Yahweh. This is evident in their almost exclusive reference to God by that name (see Commentary on 1:7; 16:5-6). That there are features common to both Israel's God and the gods of the nations is a theological problem not unique to Proverbs and the wisdom literature.[33] The evidence of Proverbs itself and its inter-textual relations within the larger canon leads one to see these commonalities in the light of the particular grace given to Israel.[34] At the same time, these commonalities, and the cosmic context of Israel's wisdom, lead one to recognize the God of Israel as the wise creator of all things and persons. Thus this commentary will begin with the book as a whole and assume it and the OT are the primary, though not only, literary context for theological interpretation.[35]

ON USING THIS COMMENTARY

Because proverbs presuppose both specific life situations and a larger cultural context to make sense of them, their interpretation can be difficult. Consequently, there is an abundance of cross-references in this commentary; and perhaps more than any other book, Proverbs requires that one pay attention to them. The great German poet Goethe once said of languages that "whoever knows only one, knows none." This saying is all the more true of proverbs. Because the sayings and admonitions are so short, they require some larger context for understanding. For ancient Israelites that larger context came naturally. Their sayings reflected their own culture and experience. Moreover, they used sayings (as do we) to comment on real-life situations. The truth of many sayings is only realized when

---

31. B. Lang, *Wisdom and the Book of Proverbs: An Israelite Goddess Redefined* (New York: Pilgrim, 1986); C. Camp, "Woman Wisdom as Root Metaphor: A Theological Consideration," in *The Listening Heart,* ed. K. G. Hoglund et al. (Sheffield: JSOT, 1987) 45-76.

32. James L. Crenshaw, "Murphy's Axiom: Every Gnomic Saying Needs a Balancing Corrective," in *Urgent Advice and Probing Questions: Collected Writings on Old Testament Wisdom* (Macon, Ga.: Mercer University Press, 1995) 352, 344-54. See Roland E. Murphy, "Wisdom and Yahwism," in *No Famine in the Land,* ed. J. Flanagan and A. Robinson (Missoula: Scholars Press, 1975) 117-26; "Wisdom and Creation," *JBL* 104 (1985) 3-11.

33. Bertil Albrektson, *History and the Gods* (Lund: Gleerup, 1967); J. J. M. Roberts, "The Ancient Near Eastern Environment," in *The Hebrew Bible and Its Modern Interpreters,* Douglas A. Knight and Gene M. Tucker, eds. (Chico, Calif.: Scholars Press, 1985) 75-121.

34. G. von Rad, *Wisdom in Israel* (Nashville: Abingdon, 1972), remains basic. See also L. Bostrom, *The God of the Sages: The Portrayal of God in the Book of Proverbs* (Stockholm: Almquist & Wiksell, 1990); R. E. Clements, *Wisdom in Theology* (Grand Rapids: Eerdmans, 1992.)

35. See Raymond C. Van Leeuwen, "Heuristic Assumptions," in *Context and Meaning in Proverbs 25–27* (Atlanta: Scholars Press, 1988) 29-38; Jon Levenson, *Hebrew Bible, Old Testament, and Historical Criticism: Jews and Christians in Biblical Studies* (Louisville: Westminster/John Knox, 1993) 106-26, 177-79.

they are "fittingly" applied.[36] Unfortunately, we do not have access to these life situations, though certain biblical stories and cross-cultural comparisons can give us some idea of how the Israelites actually used their proverbs.[37]

Consequently, finding the meaning of ancient biblical proverbs can be difficult. Sometimes knowledge of archaeology and ancient Near Eastern cultures and languages can help us. But our main resource is the language of the sayings themselves. Proverbs, in any language, never exist in isolation. One proverb comments on or contrasts with another. Thus proverbs can happily "contradict" each other: "Haste makes waste," but "whoever hesitates is lost." Again, when it comes to marriage and friendships, a recent authoritative study tells us that "birds of a feather flock together."[38] Yet, there are some marriages in which "opposites attract." Indeed, without the latter truth, the sexes would never get together.

Again, for proverbs, "whoever knows only one knows none." One proverb may not fit a situation, but another will. One saying calls for another to qualify it, or for a biblical story to flesh it out. Hence the many cross-references in this commentary. Often a proverb theme will appear more than once. Frequently, the reader will find that the information needed to understand one saying is given in the commentary on another. Hence the frequent appearance of the words in parentheses, "see . . ." or more important, "see Commentary on. . . ." The former reference means that one can find a worthwhile parallel in another proverb or biblical passage. The latter reference means that the comment on another particular passage will provide crucial information for the passage at hand. Brief as proverbs are, no one saying contains the whole truth. Reality is too rich and complex for that.

36. C. E. Carlston, "Proverbs, Maxims, and the Historical Jesus," *JBL* 99 (1980) 87-105.

37. See Carole Fontaine, *The Use of the Traditional Saying in the Old Testament* (Sheffield: JSOT, 1982); Susan Niditch, *Folklore and the Hebrew Bible* (Minneapolis: Fortress, 1993) 67-91; Mieder and Dundes, *The Wisdom of Many.*

38. Robert T. Michael, John H. Gagnon, Edward O. Laumann, Gina Collati, *Sex in America: A Definitive Study* (Boston: Little, Brown, 1994).

BIBLIOGRAPHY

Commentaries:

Alonso-Schökel, L., and J. Vilchez. *Proverbios.* Madrid: Ediciones Cristiandad, 1984. For Americans with facility in Spanish, a valuable commentary with insightful literary observations.

McKane, William. *Proverbs: A New Approach.* OTL. Philadelphia: Westminster, 1970. A long commentary on a short genre, useful in linguistic matters and for international wisdom.

Toy, Crawford H. *The Book of Proverbs.* ICC. New York: Scribner's Sons, 1902. A classic, comprehensive commentary, still valuable for text, language, and insight.

Whybray, R. N. *Proverbs.* NCBC. Grand Rapids: Eerdmans, 1994. Valuable for close attention to problems of translation and for exploring the issue of literary context among the sentences.

Other Works:

Camp, Claudia V. *Wisdom and the Feminine in the Book of Proverbs.* Sheffield: Almond, 1985. A pioneering feminist reading of Proverbs.

Fontaine, Carole R. *Traditional Sayings in the Old Testament.* Sheffield: Almond, 1982. Very useful for the literary portrayal of Israelite proverbs in action, and for introduction to broader (non-biblical) proverbs research.

Mieder, Wolfgang, and Alan Dundes, eds. *The Wisdom of Many: Essays on the Proverb.* New York: Garland, 1981. A collection of essential essays on non-biblical proverbs.

Van Leeuwen, Raymond C. *Context and Meaning in Proverbs 25–27.* Atlanta: Scholars Press, 1988. A study of the problem of literary context in Proverbs.

von Rad, Gerhard. *Wisdom in Israel.* Nashville: Abingdon, 1972. This book remains the most profound theological treatment of Proverbs available.

Washington, Harold C. *Wealth and Poverty in the Instruction of Amenemope and the Hebrew Proverbs.* Atlanta: Scholars Press, 1994.

Weeks, Stuart. *Early Israelite Wisdom.* Oxford: Clarendon, 1994. A recent study of key issues in wisdom and Proverbs, with bibliography.

Whybray, R. N. *The Book of Proverbs: A Survey of Modern Study.* Leiden: Brill, 1995. A valuable overview and bibliography.

———. *The Composition of the Book of Proverbs.* Sheffield: JSOT, 1994.

———. *Wealth and Poverty in the Book of Proverbs.* Sheffield: JSOT, 1990.

Williams, James G. *Those Who Ponder Proverbs.* Sheffield: JSOT, 1981.

OUTLINE OF PROVERBS

I. Proverbs 1:1–9:18, The Parental Legacy: Wisdom's Worldview

    A. 1:1-7, Title and Prologue

    B. 1:8-19, Warning Against Outlaws

    C. 1:20-33, Wisdom's Prophetic Warning

    D. 2:1-22, The Search for Wisdom

    E. 3:1-12, Instruction in the Fear of the Lord

    F. 3:13-35, On Wisdom: Blessing, Creation, Admonitions

    G. 4:1-27, Tradition, Wisdom, and Ways

    H. 5:1-23, Adultery as Folly; Marriage as Wisdom

    I. 6:1-19, Money, Sloth, Good, and Evil

    J. 6:20-35, Teaching Against Adultery

    K. 7:1-27, A Tale of Seduction and Death

    L. 8:1-36, Wisdom's Cosmic Speech

    M. 9:1-18, Two Houses at the End of the Road

PROVERBS 1:1–9:18

THE PARENTAL LEGACY: WISDOM'S WORLDVIEW

OVERVIEW[39]

After a brief prologue (1:1-7), Proverbs 1–9 presents a series of instructions addressed to "my son" by a mother or father (1:8-9). This advice is designed to guide young men as they step into the adult world, with its problems and possibilities (see Reflections on 1:1-7). The instructions form a literary "testament," modeled after oral instructions given at key life transitions. But more than this, they introduce readers to the book's worldview, to its fundamental framework of meaning. The seemingly random and scattered events of life, so richly described in the tiny sayings of chaps. 10–29, are here given an interpretive context. Chapters 1–9 provide a moral map of the world, a portrait of the "universe" as made by God with wisdom (3:19-20; chap. 8).

This divinely ordered cosmos comprises the conditions that make life possible. It provides the arena within which humans find freedom. The writers employ a set of repeated metaphors to create a symbolic representation of reality.[40] The dynamic, purposeful character of life is signaled by good or bad paths and by legitimate or misdirected male desire for women and material goods (1:10-19; 3:9-10). Life is thus a journey whose motive force is a quasi-erotic desire for real or bogus goods, whose end is determined by the "woman" one chooses to love. At the end of the journey, the young man finds a "house." In Wisdom's house there is life (9:1-6), but to cross the "threshold" of the "strange woman" or "Folly" is death (2:16-19; 9:13-18).

These pervasive metaphors illustrate and embody basic reality principles. The proper desire of a young man for his wife (5:16-19) is contrasted to desire for another woman (2:16-19). Love of wife embodies wisdom, but to fulfill one's desire for another is folly. This interplay of literal and metaphorical relationships among men and women, roads and houses, spells out the authors' view of cosmic and human reality (see Commentary on chap. 8). Life is a matter not only of created structures and limits (signaled by God's setting limits to the sea [8:29]), but also of ultimate "loves" for one "woman" or another. When love is misplaced, when one loses direction, when boundaries are violated, when creation's goods are misappropriated, then the good becomes harmful and damage is done. Consequently, wisdom implies love within limits, freedom within form, and life within law.[41]

---

39. See also the section "Genre and Content" in the Introduction.

40. R. C. Van Leeuwen, "Liminality and Worldview in Proverbs 1–9," *Semeia* 50 (1990) 111-44.

41. R. L. Cohn, *The Shape of Sacred Space: Four Biblical Studies,* AAR Studies in Religion 23 (Chico, Calif.: Scholars Press, 1981).

PROVERBS 1:1-7, TITLE AND PROLOGUE

NIV

1 The proverbs of Solomon son of David, king of Israel:

²for attaining wisdom and discipline;
for understanding words of insight;
³for acquiring a disciplined and prudent life,
doing what is right and just and fair;
⁴for giving prudence to the simple,
knowledge and discretion to the young—
⁵let the wise listen and add to their learning,
and let the discerning get guidance—
⁶for understanding proverbs and parables,
the sayings and riddles of the wise.

⁷The fear of the Lord is the beginning of knowledge,
but fools*a* despise wisdom and discipline.

a7 The Hebrew words rendered fool in Proverbs, and often elsewhere in the Old Testament, denote one who is morally deficient.

NRSV

1 The proverbs of Solomon son of David, king of Israel:

² For learning about wisdom and instruction,
for understanding words of insight,
³ for gaining instruction in wise dealing,
righteousness, justice, and equity;
⁴ to teach shrewdness to the simple,
knowledge and prudence to the young—
⁵ let the wise also hear and gain in learning,
and the discerning acquire skill,
⁶ to understand a proverb and a figure,
the words of the wise and their riddles.

⁷ The fear of the Lord is the beginning of knowledge;
fools despise wisdom and instruction.

COMMENTARY

These verses state the pedigree, essence, and purpose of the book called Proverbs. Similar beginnings are found in non-Israelite wisdom books.[42] The prologue also makes clear the primary audience of the book: young, inexperienced males on the threshold of adult life (1:4). Secondarily, the book serves to confirm and increase the wisdom of the wise (1:5).

1:1. The opening verse is the book's title; several subtitles head sections in the book (e.g., 10:1; 22:17; 24:23; 25:1; 30:1; 31:1). The title identifies Solomon as the spiritual fountainhead of the wisdom compiled in Proverbs (cf. 1 Kgs 2:6; 3:3-28; 4:29-34; 10:1-25; Eccl 1:1; Cant 1:1; Wisdom 7–9; Sir 47:12-17). As with the Davidic psalm headings, Prov 1:1 cannot be taken as a simple assertion of authorship in the modern sense. This is clear from the composite character of the book and its subtitles. For example, Hezekiah's men (Prov 25:1) are active some two hundred years after Solomon's death. Whatever

the origins of the book's sayings and sections, the whole now claims the heritage of Solomon, David's son, to whom God gave wisdom and the covenant promises (2 Samuel 7; 1 Kings 3; 10; Psalm 132). The title communicates that this book is endued with the same "spirit of wisdom" that animated Solomon (see Moses and Joshua, Deut 34:9).

"Proverb" (משל *māšāl*; 1:1,6; 10:1; 25:1) can refer to a variety of genres, such as parables, taunt songs, and the like. In Proverbs, it includes several genres. Foremost among these are instructions (mainly chaps. 1–9), admonitions (see esp. 22:17–23:28; 24:1-29), and sayings (esp. 10:1–22:17; 25:1–29:27).

1:2-6. These verses state the book's purpose and primary audience. In a series of purpose clauses (interrupted by 1:5, an editorial link with 9:9), the writer heaps up key wisdom terms that are repeated throughout the book (e.g., 1:3*b* and 2:9; 1:2 and 23:23). The basic concepts conveyed by these terms, however, are often present in proverbial images and actions even when the terms are not used. Proverbs 28:15, for example,

42. See R. Clifford, "Introduction to Wisdom Literature," 1-15 in this volume.

does not mention righteousness, justice, or equity (1:3), but these are nonetheless the standards by which rulers are judged. Moreover, by such key terms the final editors of Proverbs sought to link this wisdom book with key concepts in the Torah (Gen 18:19; Deut 4:5-8; 34:9), the Prophets (Isa 11:1-5; Hos 14:9), and the other Writings, such as Psalms. For example, Ps 99:4 declares that Yahweh "has established *equity*" and done "*justice and righteousness* in Jacob" (see also Psalms 1; 25; 34; 37; 111–112; 119; and the "Solomonic" Psalm 72).

Verse 6 includes in the book's purpose the mastery of the forms, language, and thought patterns of "the wise." Through study of the book, one gains understanding of its sayings. The book itself provides the needed context, since as a book its sayings can be compared and contrasted. The book, however, affords no example of a genuine "riddle," though perhaps the words of Agur provide one (30:1-9). Perhaps the term here refers to any puzzling, thought-provoking utterance (see Hab 2:6) and to the mental effort required to use proverbs rightly (see 26:7).

1:7. This verse is the book's motto and states its theological theme (variants are 9:10; Job 28:28; Ps 111:10; cf. Prov 13:19; 15:33; 16:6, 17; 31:30). Here God and humans, wisdom and folly, knowledge and discipline borne of parental urging are all related in eight packed Hebrew words. To fear Yahweh means to hate evil and turn from it (3:7; 8:13; Job 28:28; cf. Psalm 1). But "fools" disdain wisdom and discipline.

The great phrase "the fear of the LORD" grounds human knowledge and wisdom (cf. 9:10) in humble service of Yahweh. This phrase frames the first section of the book (1:7; 9:10), as well as the whole book (1:7; 31:31). The book of Proverbs is meant to teach humans wisdom. But the fear of the Lord relativizes human wisdom, because the mysterious freedom of God can subvert human plans and purposes (16:1, 9; 19:21; 21:30-31; 27:1). Without the God of Israel, the best human wisdom becomes folly, because God alone holds the world and all outcomes in God's hands (2 Sam 16:15–17:23; 1 Cor 1:18-31, with its OT

quotations). Although this phrase has its origin in the experience of God's numinous majesty (as at Sinai, Deut 4:9-10), it eventually has come to express the total claim of God upon humans and the total life-response of humans to God. In the covenant context of Deuteronomy (a book with wisdom concerns, Deut 4:6) we find:

So now, O Israel, what does the Lord your God require of you? Only to fear the Lord your God, to walk in all his ways, to love him, to serve the Lord your God with all your heart and with all your soul, and to keep the commandments of the Lord . . . for your own well-being. (Deut 10:12-13 NRSV; see also Deut 10:14-20; 8:6; Mic 6:8)

This command succintly elaborates the meaning of fearing God. Similarly, Ps 34:7-14 describes this divine-human relationship (see 1 Pet 3:10-12). On the divine side, the Lord protects and provides for those who fear God (vv. 7-9). On the human side, those who fear God pursue moral good and shun evil (vv. 13-14). This in turn produces enjoyment of life (v. 12). In sum, the fear of Yahweh is not just *worship* (a topic hardly mentioned in Proverbs), but *religion* in the comprehensive sense of life in its entirety devoted to God's service. Here, *all* human activities are undertaken in the light of God's presence and purposes in the world (see Psalms 90; 139; Matt 28:16-20).

With very few exceptions, Proverbs refers to God as "the LORD" (Yahweh), the God who made covenant with Israel and led the people throughout history (cf. Gen 20:11; Eccl 12:13). Proverbs never uses אֵל (ʾēl, "god") and uses אלהים (ʾĕlōhîm, the most common word for "god" or "gods") only three times: 2:5, par. to "fear of the LORD"; 3:4; 25:2. The editors of Proverbs are very consistent in avoiding the suggestion that the God of the sages is any other than Israel's covenant God, Yahweh (see Exod 3:15; 33:18-20; 34:6-7; John 1:14-18). Proverbs has profound similarities to ancient Near Eastern wisdom. Perhaps the consistent use of "Yahweh" was meant to forestall the idea that the God of Proverbs was not Israel's covenant God.

REFLECTIONS

1. The word "beginning" in the book's thematic motto (1:7) contains the hint, to be elaborated throughout the first nine chapters, that life is not static, but a journey whose end is found in its God-centered beginning. One may recall the profound lines from T. S. Eliot's *Four Quartets:*

> What we call the beginning is often the end
> And to make an end is to make a beginning.
> The end is where we start from. . . .
>   We shall not cease from exploration
> And the end of all our exploring
> Will be to arrive where we started
> And know the place for the first time.[43]

The fear of Yahweh is the absolute beginning and foundation of wisdom. On this foundation, the opening verses lay down the great concepts that give order and coherence to the bewildering diversity of insights and admonitions in Proverbs as a whole. Without basic biblical concepts such as righteousness and justice, wisdom and discipline, all of them grounded in the fear of God, we cannot think wisely about life or live it well. These concepts are not random, unrelated ideas but building blocks for a Christian worldview and praxis. Oliver O'Donovan has seen this clearly:

> We will read the Bible seriously only when we use it to guide our thought towards a *comprehensive* moral viewpoint, and not merely to articulate disconnected moral claims. We must look within it not only for moral bricks, but for indications of the order in which the bricks belong together.[44]

It is the function of 1:1-7 (and chaps. 1–9) to point to the order of the many bricks in wisdom's house. Mastery of these fundamental concepts in an often confusing world is the goal of the book's teaching.

2. In Proverbs, faith is not opposed to reason, but constitutes its possibility, its connection to reality.[45] Proverbs 1:7 contradicts an assumption basic to most current worldviews—namely, that knowledge of the real world is independent of the "fear" or "knowledge" of God. This modern assumption is expressed, even in works of biblical scholarship, by a variety of separations of "sacred" and "secular" realms: public vs. private, facts vs. values, science vs. religion, reason vs. faith, "objective" vs. (merely) "subjective."[46] But the critique of modernity in 1:7 is not just a matter of ideas or perspectives. The very patterns, structures, and institutions of our public and private lives have been largely shaped by reason, science, and technique in the service of modern idols such as wealth, power, pleasure, nation, and unbridled individual "freedom." Technology, with its focus on specific outcomes, without consideration of the whole fabric of existence, often does life and creation much harm.[47]

For Proverbs, all of reality is God's reality (cf. 8:22-31) and is subject to God's cosmic order for good (cf. Genesis 1). Although we may legitimately distinguish between worship and secular affairs, for Proverbs, "life is religion." That is, the ordinary affairs of daily life as well as cult and worship are to be lived in service of God and according to God's norms or "ways." Anything else is arrogant folly (1:7*b*). Thus the various "worldly" activities of the "valiant

43. T. S. Eliot, *The Complete Poems and Plays: 1909–1950* (New York: Harcourt, Brace & World, 1952) 144-45.
44. Oliver O'Donovan, *Resurrection and Moral Order* (Grand Rapids: Eerdmans, 1986) 200.
45. Von Rad, *Wisdom in Israel,* 53-73.
46. W. McKane, *Prophets and Wise Men,* SBT 44 (London: SCM, 1965). For critique, see S. Weeks, "Was Early Wisdom Secular?" in *Early Israelite Wisdom* (Oxford: Clarendon, 1994) 57-73.
47. J. Ellul, *The Technological Society* (New York: Random House, 1967).

woman" are not opposed to or separate from her "fear of the LORD," but are its living embodiment (31:10-31; cf. Ruth 3:11).[48]

The great scholar Gerhard von Rad put it well: "Humans are always entirely in the world, yet are always entirely involved with Yahweh."[49] Again, "the experiences of the world were for [Israel] always divine experiences as well, and the experiences of God were for her experiences of the world."[50] (This does not entail erasure of the Creator-creature distinction.) Thus, "folly is practical atheism." Israel was "of the opinion that effective knowledge about God is the only thing that puts a man in a right relationship with the objects of his perception, that it enables him to ask questions more pertinently, to take stock of relationships more effectively and generally to have a better awareness of circumstances."[51]

3. Women are conspicuously absent from the address of Proverbs; they appear mainly in relation to the young males whom it addresses. It thus requires an extra act of interpretive imagination for women to appropriate the wisdom of Proverbs. Yet, Israelite mothers taught wisdom (1:8; 6:20; 31:1), Lady Wisdom is personified as a woman (1:20-33; 8:1-35; 9:1-6), and the human incarnation of wisdom is a "capable woman" (31:10-31). Ultimately, it is our common humanity that enables all who are different to gain wisdom from Proverbs, concerning both ourselves and others who are ethnically, culturally, or personally different from us. Our humanness is more basic than our gender and other differences (Gen 1:27). The same Creator has made us all and placed us in a creation governed by wisdom (Prov 3:19-20; 8:22-31). We modern folk are not ancient Israelites, nor are most modern males courtiers (25:1-7). Wisdom seeks to overcome such differences. In new and different situations, the wise speak and act appropriately because they have learned the common structures and patterns of life (see Commentary on 26:1-12). Wisdom sees the universal through the particular and judges the particular for what it is.

Still, some scholars believe that benefit can be gained from Proverbs 1–9 only by subverting its patriarchal discourse. Carol A. Newsom has written a brilliant essay in this vein.[52] For Newsom, the fundamental opposition in Proverbs 1–9 is male versus female. However, the fundamental opposition in the biblical text is wisdom versus folly, which is not gender specific (see on 2:12-19), though gender relations illustrate it.

In my judgment, several issues are at stake here. Most basic is whether Proverbs 1–9 is merely a patriarchal construct or a revelatory, symbolic representation of reality; whether—despite being subject to the limitations of all human discourse—its metaphors illumine a real order of creation that impinges on humans, to which they are accountable, and within which they may find freedom and life;[53] and, finally, whether God can speak truth about God's own self and reality through the medium of a patriarchal culture.

According to Hebrews, God "spoke in many and various ways" and has finally spoken in Christ, through whom all things were created, and by whose powerful word all things are sustained (Heb 1:1-3). If so, the second, difficult hermeneutical issue lies in distinguishing mere cultural variation from abiding standards for behavior and truth. Clearly, one cannot simply appeal to human behavior (in or out of Scripture) to determine right from wrong, for two reasons. Humans are endowed with an enormous freedom to name and shape created reality (Genesis 2). In addition, humans have an enormous capacity for sin and self-deception. Not

---

48. Al Wolters, "Nature and Grace in the Interpretation of Proverbs 31:10-31, *Calvin Theological Journal* 19 (1984) 153-66.

49. von Rad, *Wisdom in Israel,* 95; Van Leeuwen's translation.

50. Ibid., 62.

51. Ibid., 65, 67-68.

52. C. A. Newsom, "Woman and the Discourse of Patriarchal Wisdom," in *Gender and Difference in Ancient Israel,* ed. Peggy L. Day (Minneapolis: Fortress, 1989) 142-60.

53. For the view of metaphor assumed here, see Janet M. Soskice, *Metaphor and Religious Language* (Oxford: Clarendon, 1985). For a different view, see Sallie McFague, *Metaphorical Theology: Models of God in Religious Language* (Philadelphia: Fortress, 1982).

only do we have difficulty living in harmony with creation, but also we are not at peace with ourselves and our neighbors.

On the one hand, Christians have often erred on the side of self-righteous legalism and moralism by making the boundaries of creation more restrictive than they need be. This stifles God-given creativity and freedom. On the other hand, people today often act as if there are no created norms for culture and society. Our contemporary prejudice against an external, normative order of meaning is profound and pervasive.[54] This is perhaps the most fundamental way in which current worldviews differ from that of Proverbs.

4. The prophets called on sinful men and women to reflect on their relation to God by using the shocking metaphor of Israel as God's unfaithful wife (Hosea 1–3; Jeremiah 3). In a different cultural setting, Ephesians used the metaphor of marriage to illustrate the positive relation of Christ and his church (Eph 5:22-33). In a somewhat similar way, male and female readers of Proverbs 1–9 are challenged to imagine the common human quest for Wisdom in terms of a young man's disciplined search for a good wife, "forsaking," as the wedding liturgy has it, "all others." Admittedly, metaphors are only partial reflections of the realities they point to. Yet these biblical metaphors portray the moral ambiguity of life and the need for fidelity. Humans can be unfaithful, they can choose folly or wisdom, Yahweh or Baal. Proverbs 1–9 invites all humans to love wisdom and eschew folly. The fact that wisdom relates to humankind as woman to man, and that Yahweh relates to Israel as husband to wife, is a metaphoric representation of reality whose depths remain unplumbed.

54. Charles Taylor, *Sources of the Self: The Making of the Modern Identity* (Cambridge, Mass.: Harvard University Press, 1989).

PROVERBS 1:8-19, WARNING AGAINST OUTLAWS

NIV	NRSV
[8]Listen, my son, to your father's instruction 　　and do not forsake your mother's teaching. [9]They will be a garland to grace your head 　　and a chain to adorn your neck. [10]My son, if sinners entice you, 　　do not give in to them. [11]If they say, "Come along with us; 　　let's lie in wait for someone's blood, 　　let's waylay some harmless soul; [12]let's swallow them alive, like the grave,[a] 　　and whole, like those who go down to the 　　　　pit; [13]we will get all sorts of valuable things 　　and fill our houses with plunder; [14]throw in your lot with us, 　　and we will share a common purse"— [15]my son, do not go along with them, 　　do not set foot on their paths; [16]for their feet rush into sin,	[8] Hear, my child, your father's instruction, 　　and do not reject your mother's teaching; [9] for they are a fair garland for your head, 　　and pendants for your neck. [10] My child, if sinners entice you, 　　do not consent. [11] If they say, "Come with us, let us lie in wait 　　　　for blood; 　　let us wantonly ambush the innocent; [12] like Sheol let us swallow them alive 　　and whole, like those who go down to the 　　　　Pit. [13] We shall find all kinds of costly things; 　　we shall fill our houses with booty. [14] Throw in your lot among us; 　　we will all have one purse"— [15] my child, do not walk in their way, 　　keep your foot from their paths; [16] for their feet run to evil, 　　and they hurry to shed blood.

NIV

they are swift to shed blood.
¹⁷How useless to spread a net
    in full view of all the birds!
¹⁸These men lie in wait for their own blood;
    they waylay only themselves!
¹⁹Such is the end of all who go after ill-gotten
    gain;
    it takes away the lives of those who get it.

ª12 Hebrew *Sheol*

NRSV

¹⁷ For in vain is the net baited
    while the bird is looking on;
¹⁸ yet they lie in wait—to kill themselves!
    and set an ambush—for their own lives!
¹⁹ Such is the endª of all who are greedy for gain;
    it takes away the life of its possessors.

ª Gk: Heb *are the ways*

COMMENTARY

The first parental instruction (vv. 8-19) begins with a typical call to listen, followed by a motivating metaphor (vv. 8-9; cf. 6:20-21; Deut 6:4-8). A mother or father addresses a young man on the threshold of adult life (See Overview). "My son" is a literal translation of the Hebrew and better fits the male-oriented focus and symbolism of sexual attraction running through chaps. 1–9 than does the NRSV's "my child." Together with Wisdom's first speech (1:20-33), this instruction establishes several key images and issues in the conflicts of good vs. evil, wisdom vs. folly, which preoccupy Proverbs 1–9.

The instruction proper begins at v. 10 with a warning against joining a murderous gang of "sinners" (חטאים *ḥaṭṭā'îm*; see Ps 1:1) who entice the naive with get-rich-quick schemes based on murder and a community of "honor among thieves" (v. 14). The parent recognizes the need for independent judgment on the part of the youth. Her persuasive speech lays out the options and appeals to the son to make up his own mind. The parent subverts the sinner's invitation (vv. 11-14) by encapsulating it within her own better invitation to wisdom and reality. She sees through wicked arguments, because she has a more comprehensive vision of right and wrong, of acts and consequences, of the way the world works. She appeals to her son to see for himself the way things are. The adolescent is no longer solely under parental influence. There are other voices out there, and he must now choose for himself which voice to listen to, which community to belong to. But in the end, the voice and the reality of cosmic justice

and wisdom (1:20-33; 8) will shatter unreal promises of worldly success.

The sinners' speech is a masterful invitation (cf. 9:4-6, 16-17) to cross the threshold into a community of crime. The concrete invitation is to a roadside ambush (1:11, 16; cf. 4:14-17). This "path" (דרך *derek*, v. 15—a key metaphor throughout chaps. 1–9) leads away from law-abiding society, and its violence marks the threshold the young man must cross to join the gang. Thus would he be incorporated into a society from which, like death, there is no return. In contrast to the segmented society of Proverbs, with its degrees of honor, the company of sinners presents itself as a successful community with egalitarian and utopian claims: share and share alike (vv. 13-14). Unfortunately their offer of equality and wealth is a lie.

Some scholars put this poem in the troubled time of Ezra and Nehemiah (see Introduction).[55] The redactional quotation of Isa 59:7 in Prov 1:16 shows at least that its editing is post-exilic (see also 4:10-19, which the present poem anticipates). This quotation also ties the independent poem in 6:16-19 to its context in Proverbs 1–9 through the near duplicates in 6:17*b*, 18*b* (see also 1:13; 6:31).

In literary terms, this invitation into a community of death finds its parallel in the deadly invitations of the "strange woman" and Woman Folly to cross their thresholds (7:10-27; 9:13-18; see Commentary on 2:12, 16). But the promises of

55. See Claudia V. Camp, *Wisdom and the Feminine in the Book of Proverbs* (Sheffield: JSOT, 1985) 233-54.

sinners are unreal. They promise a wealth that belongs properly to wisdom (1:13; 8:18; 24:4; 31:11*b*), and they seek to gain it by trespassing upon the goods and lives of their neighbors. True life and wealth are found only within the righteous limits set by wisdom. The parent warns the son of the inherent instability of such anti-societies (cf. 24:23-24). While sinners seek abundant life, their ironic end is death because they step outside the conditions of life, like a fish out of water. The sinners, greedy for gain, think to ambush and kill others (Mic 7:2), to swallow them alive, like *Sheol* ("the grave"; cf. 5:5; 7:27; 9:18; 27:20; Num 16:30-33; Isa 5:14; Hab 2:5). Instead, they trap themselves (v. 18). The wickedness of these sinners is revealed as folly. Birds, at least, can see a net spread before them (v. 17), but sinners are blind to the consequences of their own actions.

REFLECTIONS

For some readers, the sinner's invitation to violence may seem far removed from their secure, middle-class world. Indeed, some scholars think the parent's vignette of violence is an exaggerated didactic lesson, "an extreme case" that "cannot be generalized."[56] But to hear the relevance of this text for the human condition, it is necessary to attend to its literal sense. The parent who speaks in 1:10-19 is from the upper stratum of Israelite society. But the problem of evil the parent addresses is universal. Our own century has known two world wars, a flood of smaller ones, and countless terrorist acts both political and private. Violence is a human reality. As M. Scott Peck's analysis of the Mylai massacre in Vietnam has shown, American violence may be a *systemic* problem.[57] It invades all social groups. It implicates even "good people" who are not overtly immoral, because there are no innocent bystanders to societal evil.[58]

The parent of 1:10-19 knows that evil is a real option for the son, that anyone can cross the line from good to evil (cf. Gen 8:21). The parent does not assume that "good families" are innoculated against evil or that godly virtue automatically continues from generation to generation. The speech is brutally realistic about the possibilities that lie before the son.

This dissuasive speech speaks to many situations. Shakespeare used it and Wisdom's prophetic warning (1:20-33) to shape his account of the moral education of young Prince Hal.[59] It would be suitable as well on the lips of a mother on Chicago's South Side today, or of a father to a potential Nazi SS recruit in the 1930s. It could have served a mother of an Israelite lad about to join one of the bloody rival gangs in the days of Abimelech (Judg 9:4, 25, 29). It might serve Christian parents of a bright young son or daughter tempted to join a firm whose profits rest on exploitation of laborers, on destruction of the environment, or on success at the expense of justice and truth.

56. O. Plöger, *Sprüche Salomos,* BK 17 (Neukirchen-Vluyn: Neukirchener Verlag, 1984) 15, 17, 20; cf. B. Lang, *Wisdom and the Book of Proverbs: An Israelite Goddess Redefined* (New York: Pilgrim, 1986) 15.
57. M. Scott Peck, *People of the Lie: The Hope for Healing Human Evil* (New York: Simon and Schuster, 1983) 212-53.
58. See D. Bonhoeffer, *Ethics* (New York: MacMillan, 1965).
59. See Shakespeare *King Henry IV* I.ii.98-100; cf. Prov 1:20-21, 24.

PROVERBS 1:20-33, WISDOM'S PROPHETIC WARNING

NIV

²⁰Wisdom calls aloud in the street,
  she raises her voice in the public squares;
²¹at the head of the noisy streets*a* she cries out,
  in the gateways of the city she makes her speech:

²²"How long will you simple ones*b* love your simple ways?
  How long will mockers delight in mockery
  and fools hate knowledge?
²³If you had responded to my rebuke,
  I would have poured out my heart to you
  and made my thoughts known to you.
²⁴But since you rejected me when I called
  and no one gave heed when I stretched out my hand,
²⁵since you ignored all my advice
  and would not accept my rebuke,
²⁶I in turn will laugh at your disaster;
  I will mock when calamity overtakes you—
²⁷when calamity overtakes you like a storm,
  when disaster sweeps over you like a whirlwind,
  when distress and trouble overwhelm you.

²⁸"Then they will call to me but I will not answer;
  they will look for me but will not find me.
²⁹Since they hated knowledge
  and did not choose to fear the LORD,
³⁰since they would not accept my advice
  and spurned my rebuke,
³¹they will eat the fruit of their ways
  and be filled with the fruit of their schemes.
³²For the waywardness of the simple will kill them,
  and the complacency of fools will destroy them;
³³but whoever listens to me will live in safety
  and be at ease, without fear of harm."

a21 Hebrew; Septuagint / *on the tops of the walls*   *b22* The Hebrew word rendered *simple* in Proverbs generally denotes one without moral direction and inclined to evil.

NRSV

²⁰ Wisdom cries out in the street;
  in the squares she raises her voice.
²¹ At the busiest corner she cries out;
  at the entrance of the city gates she speaks:
²² "How long, O simple ones, will you love being simple?
  How long will scoffers delight in their scoffing
  and fools hate knowledge?
²³ Give heed to my reproof;
  I will pour out my thoughts to you;
  I will make my words known to you.
²⁴ Because I have called and you refused,
  have stretched out my hand and no one heeded,
²⁵ and because you have ignored all my counsel
  and would have none of my reproof,
²⁶ I also will laugh at your calamity;
  I will mock when panic strikes you,
²⁷ when panic strikes you like a storm,
  and your calamity comes like a whirlwind,
  when distress and anguish come upon you.
²⁸ Then they will call upon me, but I will not answer;
  they will seek me diligently, but will not find me.
²⁹ Because they hated knowledge
  and did not choose the fear of the LORD,
³⁰ would have none of my counsel,
  and despised all my reproof,
³¹ therefore they shall eat the fruit of their way
  and be sated with their own devices.
³² For waywardness kills the simple,
  and the complacency of fools destroys them;
³³ but those who listen to me will be secure
  and will live at ease, without dread of disaster."

COMMENTARY

1:20-21. Wisdom's first speech as personified woman begins with a two-verse introduction. In vocabulary and setting, these verses are parallel to 8:1-5 and 9:1-6. This parallelism makes clear that personified wisdom in chaps. 1, 8–9 is the same figure. But it also establishes a contrast over against Dame Folly (9:13-18) and her symbolic counterpart, the "strange woman" (5:3-6, 20; 7:5; cf. 5:15-19). For example, among the verbal echoes are "busiest" or "loud" (המיה *hōmiyyâ*; cf. 7:11; 9:13). These parallel passages (1:20-21; 8:1-5; 9:1-6) thus contribute to the metaphorical equivalence among "house" (15x), "city," and "[woman's] body," all of which one enters through "openings" (פתח *petaḥ*; 1:21; 5:8; 8:3, where "mouth" should not be emended, 34; 9:14), either for good or for ill.

As is common in the symbol systems of many cultures, in Proverbs 1–9, "house," "city," and "body" have cosmic cultural implications (see Commentary on Proverbs 8; 9:1).[60] Via their connection with wisdom and folly, these images represent the world of divine norms for creatures, in contrast to a world of norms violated by human folly and delusion. This symbolic world includes what moderns call nature as well as human history and society. To enter the house/body of folly is a cosmic trip into Sheol, the underworld (see Commentary on 1:12; cf. 5:5; 7:27; 9:18). At stake in Proverbs 1–9 is nothing less than the nature of reality as created by Yahweh. What is such a world like? What are the conditions for living well in it?

1:22-31. Wisdom addresses young men (qualified here as "mockers" and "fools") in the public square, perhaps in contrast to the secret invitation of sinners (v. 14). She also first raises the recurring theme of love and delight, which pervades chaps. 1–9. Humans are responsible for the loves they choose. The body of Wisdom's speech (vv. 22-31) adopts the genre of a prophetic judgment for

purposes of instruction. She speaks to those who have heard her before, but have rejected her (vv. 22, 24; cf. Ps 82:2-7; Jer 23:26-32). One may compare God's mouthpiece, Moses, speaking to Pharaoh after several plagues have already been sent (Exod 10:3-6). Other prophetic motifs here are the reciprocal calling and not being heard (v. 24; cf. v. 28; 21:13; Isa 65:12; 66:4; Mic 3:4), seeking and not finding (v. 28; Amos 8:12; Hos 5:6, 15; cf. Prov 8:17; Matt 7:7-8).[61] But Wisdom speaks for herself. She takes her stand at the center of communal life, in the gates of the city, in the highway. She addresses all humans. No one can claim that he or she has not heard Wisdom's voice, that they did not know (the reasons for this are made clear in Proverbs 8; cf. Ps 19:1-4; Rom 1:18-20; 2:14-15).

1:22-25. These verses function as a prophetic accusation. The "simple" have been hearing Wisdom, but they have not been listening. Indeed, they have rejected her message (cf. Jer 6:19). The translation of vv. 22*b*-23 is problematic. In line with the argument of the passage as prophetic accusation and the grammatical possibilities, it is best to translate, "You refused my reproof; I poured out my thoughts to you; I made known my words to you"[62] (cf. Ps 107:11; Zech 7:8-14).

1:26-28. The consequences of rejecting Wisdom are spelled out: calamity like a storm (v. 27; 10:24-25), accompanied by the laughter of Wisdom, who responds in kind to the mocking young (v. 22; see Deut 28:63; Pss 2:4; 37:13; 59:8). Verse 28 shows that timing in life is essential (Eccl 3:1-8). There are points of no return; when the storm is upon us, it is too late to seek shelter. Moments of decision pass and are gone forever. Timing is all.

1:32-33. The final passage briefly describes the consequences of rejecting and of listening to Wisdom's advice: death or security in life (cf. Jer 17:23, 27).

---

60. Mary Douglas, *Purity and Danger* (London: Routledge and Kegan Paul, 1966) 115; and *Implicit Meanings: Essays in Anthropology* (London: Routledge and Kegan Paul, 1975) 47-59. For house and city building as a repetition of creation, see M. Eliade, *The Myth of the Eternal Return or Cosmos and History* (Princeton: Princeton University Press, 1971).

61. Roland E. Murphy, *Wisdom Literature: Job, Proverbs, Ruth, Canticles, Ecclesiastes, Esther,* FOTL 13 (Grand Rapids: Eerdmans, 1981) 52.

62. R. E. Murphy, "Wisdom and Eros in Proverbs 1–9," *CBQ* 50 (1988) 600-603.

REFLECTIONS

1. Wisdom addresses the paradoxical mixture of naivete and scorn that sometimes afflicts the young and arrogant (cf. 1:29; 5:12; 12:1). When people persist in ignorance, in defiance of Wisdom's teaching, they become culpable. It is not wrong to be young and naive; it is blameworthy, though, to want to stay that way (1:22). There is no hope for "scoffers" and "fools," who "know it all," yet "know what they like" and only "love what they know" (15:12; 26:11-12; 28:26; Isa 5:21)! Sometimes, "I like myself just the way I am" is not a healthy affirmation of self-respect, but a denial that life requires growth and correction from external forces: "When I was a child, I spoke like a child . . . [but now] I put an end to childish ways" (1 Cor 13:11).

2. The laughter of Wisdom is shocking. It is perhaps to be understood as a response to the absurdity of those who flaunt reality, who "spit into the wind" and are puzzled when they get wet. It is also, perhaps, a fierce joy that the goodness of the world order and justice have been vindicated when the wicked reap what they have sown.[63] When a tyrant falls, the people rejoice (11:10; cf. Job 22:19; Isa 14:4-20; Rev 18:20). It is important to note that the persons whom calamity overcomes are themselves responsible for it (1:18). When they refuse to eat Wisdom's fruit (3:18; 8:19), they are stuffed with the "fruit of their [own] way" (1:30-31 NRSV; 14:14; 18:20-21; Isa 3:9-11). Such self-induced calamities befall not just individual persons, but entire nations (Jer 6:16-19; cf. Prov 26:3 LXX). Wisdom is a matter of life and death not just for individuals but for families, corporations, universities, nations, and cultures. They, too, reap what they sow.

63. See Abraham Heschel's classic work on the pathos of God, *The Prophets,* vol. 2 (New York: Harper & Row, 1962).

PROVERBS 2:1-22, THE SEARCH FOR WISDOM

NIV	NRSV

2 My son, if you accept my words
   and store up my commands within you,
²turning your ear to wisdom
   and applying your heart to understanding,
³and if you call out for insight
   and cry aloud for understanding,
⁴and if you look for it as for silver
   and search for it as for hidden treasure,
⁵then you will understand the fear of the LORD
   and find the knowledge of God.
⁶For the LORD gives wisdom,
   and from his mouth come knowledge and
      understanding.
⁷He holds victory in store for the upright,
   he is a shield to those whose walk is
      blameless,
⁸for he guards the course of the just
   and protects the way of his faithful ones.
	2 My child, if you accept my words
	   and treasure up my commandments
	      within you,
	² making your ear attentive to wisdom
	   and inclining your heart to understanding;
	³ if you indeed cry out for insight,
	   and raise your voice for understanding;
	⁴ if you seek it like silver,
	   and search for it as for hidden treasures—
	⁵ then you will understand the fear of the LORD
	   and find the knowledge of God.
	⁶ For the LORD gives wisdom;
	   from his mouth come knowledge and
	      understanding;
	⁷ he stores up sound wisdom for the upright;
	   he is a shield to those who walk blamelessly,
	⁸ guarding the paths of justice
	   and preserving the way of his faithful ones.

NIV

⁹Then you will understand what is right and just
and fair—every good path.
¹⁰For wisdom will enter your heart,
and knowledge will be pleasant to your soul.
¹¹Discretion will protect you,
and understanding will guard you.

¹²Wisdom will save you from the ways of wicked
men,
from men whose words are perverse,
¹³who leave the straight paths
to walk in dark ways,
¹⁴who delight in doing wrong
and rejoice in the perverseness of evil,
¹⁵whose paths are crooked
and who are devious in their ways.

¹⁶It will save you also from the adulteress,
from the wayward wife with her seductive
words,
¹⁷who has left the partner of her youth
and ignored the covenant she made before
God.ᵃ
¹⁸For her house leads down to death
and her paths to the spirits of the dead.
¹⁹None who go to her return
or attain the paths of life.

²⁰Thus you will walk in the ways of good men
and keep to the paths of the righteous.
²¹For the upright will live in the land,
and the blameless will remain in it;
²²but the wicked will be cut off from the land,
and the unfaithful will be torn from it.

ᵃ17 Or *covenant of her God*

NRSV

⁹ Then you will understand righteousness and
justice
and equity, every good path;
¹⁰ for wisdom will come into your heart,
and knowledge will be pleasant to your soul;
¹¹ prudence will watch over you;
and understanding will guard you.

¹² It will save you from the way of evil,
from those who speak perversely,
¹³ who forsake the paths of uprightness
to walk in the ways of darkness,
¹⁴ who rejoice in doing evil
and delight in the perverseness of evil;
¹⁵ those whose paths are crooked,
and who are devious in their ways.

¹⁶ You will be saved from the looseᵃ woman,
from the adulteress with her smooth words,
¹⁷ who forsakes the partner of her youth
and forgets her sacred covenant;
¹⁸ for her wayᵇ leads down to death,
and her paths to the shades;
¹⁹ those who go to her never come back,
nor do they regain the paths of life.

²⁰ Therefore walk in the way of the good,
and keep to the paths of the just.
²¹ For the upright will abide in the land,
and the innocent will remain in it;
²² but the wicked will be cut off from the land,
and the treacherous will be rooted out of it.

ᵃHeb *strange*   ᵇCn: Heb *house*

COMMENTARY

This brilliant poem comprises one elaborate sentence of twenty-two lines, corresponding to the length of the Hebrew alphabet (see 31:10-31).[64] Its sections are marked off by the first and twelfth letters of the Hebrew alphabet, א (*ʾalep*; 2:1, 5, 9) and ל (*lamed*; 2:12, 16, 19). This instruction plays off the speeches by the parent (1:8-19) and by Wisdom (1:20-33), just preceding. It also states the themes that will occupy the parental instructions (excluding the "Insertions" 3:13-20; 6:1-19) until Wisdom herself returns to speak in chap. 8.[65]

The parent speaks in his own voice (v. 1), but urges the son to listen to "Wisdom" and "Understanding" (v. 2; cf. 8:1). The parent thus points beyond himself to wisdom, which (or "who") is

64. See Dennis Pardee, *Ugaritic and Hebrew Poetic Parallelism: A Trial Cut (ʾnt and Proverbs 2)*, SVT 39 (Leiden: Brill, 1988). For a different assessment, see R. N. Whybray, *Proverbs*, NCB (Grand Rapids: Eerdmans, 1994) 49-51.

65. So A. Meinhold, *Die Sprüche*, Zücher Bibelkommentare (Zürich: Theologischer Verlag, 1991) 1:46.

the goal of parental teaching. Through repetition of terms from 1:20-33, the instruction shows that the relationship between humans and Wisdom is reciprocal. In the previous speech, Wisdom "cried out" and "raised her voice" (1:20b-21a; cf. 8:1). Now, in the same words, the son is urged to do the same (v. 3). Wisdom's call to humans is echoed by the call of humans for Wisdom, like lovers seeking each other in the street (Cant 3:1-2 LXX; 5:6; cf. Prov 7:4). The opening verses also play upon the search for treasure. The son is to "treasure up" the words of the father (2:1a; cf. 1:11, 19; 2:7 Hebrew), and to "seek" and "search" for wisdom "like silver" and "hidden treasures" (v. 4), which the Lord "stores up" for the good (v. 7). The search for wisdom begins with mastery of parental "words" and "command-ments" (v. 1).[66] In the poem's second half (vv. 12-22), Wisdom will rescue the young from the parallel evils of wicked men (vv. 12-15) and the "strange" woman (vv. 16-19) who will play such an important role in the symbolism of these chap-ters. The chapter concludes with a call to good-ness and a final promise and warning (vv. 20-22).

2:1-4. The long condition ("My son, if . . . ") has two global outcomes, both governed by wis-dom. The first concerns the son's relation to God ("then," vv. 5-8) and the second his positive relation to humans ("then," vv. 9-11). This sec-ond, principled relation to others is contrasted with two negative relations that Wisdom enables the young to avoid. These dangerous, parallel relations are with "wicked men" (vv. 12-15) and the "strange woman" (vv. 16-19).

2:5-9. The first outcome of the son's search is, somewhat surprisingly, practical insight into "the fear of the LORD" (see Commentary on 1:7). The son will "know" (ידע yāda') God (v. 5). "Knowledge of God" here is not due simply to individual activity or to immediate divine revela-tion. Humans get to know God somewhat as they get to know a language, through interaction with parents and others who speak and act in the ordinary activities of life. As parents relate to God, world, and others, they communicate a certain understanding of God and reality. The child's business is gradually to take responsibility for his

or her life in response to parents, persons, the world, and God.

The quest for wisdom is necessarily a quest for God, for wisdom comes from God (vv. 6-7). Like the prophets, Proverbs 2 resolutely refuses to separate right living from knowledge of God (see Jer 22:13-16; Hos 4:1-3). The poet communicates this by the parallel outcomes in vv. 5 and 9 ("then you will understand . . . "). God's giving of wis-dom, however, is complex. It comes through tradition, teaching, experience, and the disciplined practical learning of how things work in God's world (Isa 28:23-29). God gives wisdom through the ordinary.

God "stores up" (or "hides") "sound wisdom" for the "upright," and protects those who walk with integrity (= "blameless," v. 7). "Sound wis-dom" translates an obscure Hebrew word (תושיה tûšîyâ), which appears in Proverbs only at 2:7; 3:21; 8:14; 18:1. It "denotes clear, proficient thinking in the exercise of power and practical operations." It has connotations of "stability, effi-cacy, confidence, and resilience." It is a "power . . . used in determining a course of action and dealing with difficulties."[67] Such resourceful competence is not automatic, for God ultimately dispenses it. A blameless walk (v. 7) is defined by the "paths of justice," which God's "faithful ones" negotiate, step by step (v. 8). The standard for integrity is justice as determined by God (see 1 Kgs 9:4). Wisdom and justice are inseparable, each being rooted in God's ordering of reality (see Commen-tary on 8:20). God preserves those who walk in tune with God's requirements.

Verse 9 repeats the opening of v. 5 ("then"), thus marking the move from God (vv. 5-8) to humanity, whose existence is subject to the cos-mic-social norms of "righteousness and justice and equity" (v. 9; see 1:3; 8:20).

2:10-11. Wisdom enters the core of one's being or "heart" (see Excursus, "The 'Heart' in the Old Testament," 60-61) and thereby enables right conduct toward God and neighbor. Wisdom here is already personified, and a cluster of parallel terms is used to designate her (cf. 8:1). Among them is the word translated as "prudence" or "discretion" (מזמה mĕzimmâ), which actually is the capacity for private, hidden thought.

---

66. Michael V. Fox, "The Pedagogy of Proverbs 2," *JBL* 113 (1994) 233-43.

67. Michael V. Fox, "Words for Wisdom," *Zeitschrift für Althebräistik* 6 (1993) 149-69, see also 162, 164-65.

It is to be used in keeping your own counsel and thinking for yourself. This power will protect you from the temptations of the wicked man and woman (2:11f.; 5:2f.), because when they try to seduce you to their ways, you will be able to look inward, maintain independence of thought, and stand up to their inveiglements.[68]

When Wisdom enters the son (v. 10), she protects him from two parallel evils, the communal "way of evil" (v. 12; cf. 8:13), represented by "those who speak perversely" or "topsy turvy" (תהפכות *tahpukôt*; see also 1:11-19; 4:14-17; cf. Isa 5:20-21), and "the strange woman" (NRSV margin, vv. 16-19).

2:12-15. The masculine evil is portrayed by the bad path, found first in the parental speech on sinners (1:15-16, 19; cf. 3:31) and developed throughout chaps. 1–9 (the vocabulary for "path" and "way" is the most frequent of any in these chapters, the terms for "wisdom" coming second). The young "choose" their life's path (v. 13) and do not merely fall into them. "Path" here is not simply the course of events in a life, but the religio-ethical manner in which people negotiate the events that come their way. Yet, by just or unjust conduct, we humans also manufacture the events that come to us (1:18, 31-33). Some tread "ways of darkness" (v. 13)—a metaphor developed in 4:19 (cf. 7:9)—in contrast to the sunlit "path of the righteous" (4:18 NRSV; cf. 6:23; Ps 119:105). The wise and the wicked desire contrary pleasures; they delight in opposite paths (vv. 10, 14; cf. 5:18).

2:16-17. This logic of desire (and of forsaking good paths for worse, v. 13) leads naturally to the figure of the "loose woman"/"adulteress" (v. 16). The NRSV and the NIV paraphrase the two parallel terms used to describe the strange woman. Literally she is "strange" and "alien" (זרה *zārâ*; נכרי *nokrî*; see Commentary and Reflections on 5:3, 9-10). The allurements of the strange woman are powerful, but they can be avoided through the deeper and nobler love of wisdom (v. 16). Greater passions displace lesser ones. The "stranger" herself embodies the failure of fidelity, for she "forsakes the partner of her youth"—that is, her husband (v. 17; cf. 4:17). The forsaking of proper sexual love is a problem not only for men

but also for women. This abandonment of proper love entails ignoring her "sacred covenant" (lit., "the covenant of her God"). This reference to "covenant" is unique in the Proverbs. The phrase "of her God" also begs explanation. The closest verbal and conceptual parallel to 2:17 is Mal 2:14-16.[69] The issue there is faithfulness in marriage, with God appearing as witness to the "covenant" between the marriage partners (see Gen 2:24). In other passages, Israel (metaphorically a bride) is bound by a marriage covenant to Yahweh (cf. Jer 3:4; Ezek 16:8; Hos 2:18-20; Mark 10:2-9; Eph 5:21-33). Proverbs 2:17 perhaps alludes to such prophetic use, as well as to the aged folly of Solomon, led into spiritual adultery by his foreign wives to violate his covenant with Yahweh (1 Kgs 11:1, 4, 11).

But the issue in Proverbs is not directly that of breaking a marriage covenant with the Lord, for OT covenant-as-marriage imagery always portrays Yahweh as husband and Israel as wife. In contrast, the portrayal of faithful and unfaithful marriage in Proverbs 1–9 has as its analogue, not Israel's relation to Yahweh or to a foreign god, but humanity's relation to female Wisdom or Folly. In this symbolic context, all humans, male and female alike, are portrayed in the image of young males attracted to females.

Neither is the problem of literal exogamy with "foreign women" (as in the days of Ezra and Nehemiah) the direct concern of these chapters. Here the woman in v. 17 is chastised, not for the foreignness of her religion (as with Solomon's wives), but for ignoring the covenant of "her God" (i.e., Yahweh) through being unfaithful in literal human marriage (with metaphorical repercussions throughout Proverbs 1–9). The poet of Proverbs 1–9 would probably share Ezra's aversion to marriage to foreign women, and his choice of "stranger"/"alien" may allude to that aversion (cf. Ruth 1:16 and Ps 45:10, which honor women who forsake pagan gods for Israelite religion and marriage).[70]

2:18. The Hebrew has a grammatical conflict of gender in verb ("sinks," fem. [שחה *šāḥâ*]) and subject ("her house," masc. [ביתה *bêtāh*]). This

---

68. Ibid., 160. Cf. *Amenemope*, chap. 1 in Miriam Lichtheim, *Ancient Egyptian Literature*, 3 vols. (Berkeley: University of California Press, 1973–80) 2:149.

69. Gordon Paul Hugenberger, *Marriage as a Covenant: A Study of Biblical Law and Ethics Governing Marriage Developed from the Perspective of Malachi*, SVT 52 (Leiden: Brill, 1994) 296-302.
70. Cf. J. Blenkinsopp, "The Social Context of the 'Outsider Woman' in Proverbs 1–9," *Bib* 72 (1991) 473-75.

may be due to the metaphorical equivalence of the strange woman's "body," "pathway," and "house"; to enter one is to enter all (see v. 19). Although she herself is not Sheol (the grave), her body/house/path is the "entrance" (5:8; 9:14; cf. 8:34) to Sheol (7:27; 9:18). There may also be a punning relation between the verb שׁוח (*šûaḥ*, "sink down") and the conventional image of the strange woman as a "pit "(שׁוחה *sûḥâ*, 22:14; cf. 23:27).[71] For the "shades," see 9:18; 21:16; 1 Sam 28:8-19; Isa 14:9; 26:14. Apparently Israel, like its ancient Near Eastern neighbors, pictured the dead as having a shadowy, impotent existence of some sort. There is no real life (Isa 26:14), and thus no praise of God in the gloomy netherworld (Ps 6:5).

2:19. To "go [in] to her" is a phrase with sexual connotations (see 6:29; Judg 15:1), but the activity here symbolizes all irrevocable deeds, from which there is no turning back. This verse echoes the language of sinners in 1:12, but it also reveals the fate of sinners seduced: They are themselves swallowed.

2:20-22. The parental speech ends with a purpose statement and warning. The outcome of pursuing wisdom (vv. 1-4) is a life in the company of "the good" (plural) and "the righteous" (plural, v. 20), in contrast to the deadly path of sinners (1:19). Although each person must walk his or her own path, we humans travel in companies gathered and directed by ultimate loves for either wisdom or folly. Life is not neutral and static, but a movement toward good or ill, however hidden and subtle that may be.[72] This view of the collective nature of the human journey (v. 20) leads to vv. 21-22, which focus on "the land"/"earth" (ארץ *eres*), the place where humans live together.

Connections with Israel's historical traditions are unusual in the wisdom books (cf. 10:30; 22:8; Job 15:18-19). But Prov 2:20-22 seems dependent on traditions concerning the "land": promise to the patriarchs, conquest under Joshua, loss in exile, second exodus in the return from Babylon (Isaiah 40–55). However, these verses do not merely repeat old traditions concerning the land (Deut 8:1, 19-20; 30:11-20; Ps 69:35-36). Rather, they move toward considering the final justice of God over the entire earth (cf. Pss 96:10, 13; 98:7-9). Proverbs 2:21-22 is linked especially with Zech 13:8 and Psalm 37 by vocabulary and by the conviction that evil will be cut off from God's land/earth and that only good will remain (Ps 37:3, 9, 11, 20, 22, 29, 34, 38; Matt 5:5). As with Deuteronomy, where Israel can choose for or against the Lord's covenant, so the choice for wisdom or folly (here for the first time defining the "righteous" and the "wicked") is an ultimate one, a matter of life and death.

---

71. See the Mesopotamian "Dialogue of Pessimism," in *Ancient Near Eastern Texts Relating to the Old Testament,* ed. James B. Pritchard, 3rd ed. (Princeton, N.J.: Princeton University Press, 1969) 438.

72. See M. Scott Peck, *The Road Less Traveled* (New York: Simon & Schuster, 1978).

REFLECTIONS

1. In Prov 2:9, the poet repeats the opening of 2:5, thus moving from God (2:5-8) to humans, who are subject to the cosmic-social norms of righteousness, justice, and equity (2:9-11; see 1:3; 8:20). This move, from the divine to the human and cosmic, is fundamental for biblical faith. The same move will determine the sequence of Proverbs 3. It reflects the fundamental principle that "the fear of the LORD is the beginning of knowledge" (1:7 NRSV). Only when humans "begin" with God in all their thinking and doing does humanity, the world, and all within it fall into harmony (Ps 24:1; Matt 6:33).

Central passages of Scripture follow the same pattern. For example, it determines the order of the Ten Commandments (cf. Matt 22:37-40). Exodus 20:1-7 concerns God; Exod 20:8-11 concerns the sabbath, during which human action is to emulate the divine "rest"); and Exod 20:12-17 concerns right dealing with others. Similarly, the Lord's prayer begins first with God's name, kingdom, and will (Matt 6:9-10), followed by the more obvious human needs for provision, forgiveness of sins, and protection from evil (Matt 6:11-13). Again, Hosea laments the lack of knowing God and documents it by Israel's failure to keep the commandments that concern the neighbor (Hos 4:1-2; see also Hos 6:6). Although there is an order in reality (God before creatures, and creatures "according to their kind,"[73] Genesis 1; Psalm 104; Prov 16:4), God and creation are inseparable, for the world reflects God's glory and righteousness (Pss 19:1; 97:6). Consequently, our relationship to God is manifested in our conduct toward others and toward the creation itself. And our worldly conduct, no matter how moral, eventually goes awry without God: "Fear God and keep the commandments" (see Eccl 12:13).

2. In 2:7-8 God dispenses wisdom to those who are faithful and live wisely. This sort of interactive circle of divine and human synergy is not uncommon in Scripture (cf. 8:9). For example, in Leviticus, the process of sanctifying persons or things (making them "holy") is both a human moral-ritual responsibility and an act of God (Lev 21:8).[74] God gives what humans actively seek, whether for ill or for good (see Commentary on 11:27; Matt 7:7-11). In this respect, gaining God's gift of wisdom is not unlike putting on "the whole armor of God" (Eph 6:10-17 NRSV).

In the same way, wisdom is both a gift of God (2:6) and a human achievement (2:1-4; 4:7; cf. Phil 2:12-13). Its result is personal transformation and the ability to live with integrity, unswayed by various temptations. For example, justice and righteousness (2:9), which can be experienced as external and alien to oneself (cf. Hos 4:1-2), now become "pleasant" (2:10) instead of onerous. This picture of personal transformation may be compared to Jeremiah and Ezekiel. These prophets placed the divine transformation of the human "heart" in a redemptive-historical perspective. After Israel's failure to keep the Sinaitic covenant (Jeremiah 11), God promised to give Israel a new heart that will transform the people and enable them to keep the "new covenant" (Jer 24:7; 31:31-34; 32:37-41; cf. Ezek 36:26-27).[75] These prophetic traditions become the basis for New Testament views of human transformation in the image of Christ (Rom 5:5; 12:2; 2 Cor 4:6, 16). Yet also for Ezekiel, a new heart is not merely a result of divine fiat, but requires human initiative (Ezek 11:18-21; 18:31; cf. Rom 12:1-2).

3. Wisdom "saves" the young from both the evil way of the "bad man" (2:12) and the "strange woman" (2:16). The parallelism of wickedness here is crucial for understanding the metaphorical role of woman in Proverbs 1–9. In Hebrew, Prov 2:12, 16 begin with exactly the same expression, and both male and female use speech to persuade to wrong. For the writer-editors of Proverbs 1–9, good and evil are not primarily a matter of gender. Rather, the writer uses gender relations, in the cultural context of that day, as a primary metaphor for understanding the bipolar attraction humans have for good (i.e., one's spouse, wisdom, and justice in general) or for what seems to be good (i.e., "thy neighbor's wife" or husband, folly, and sin in general). Warnings against adultery in these chapters do function as literal advice to sexually volatile young men. But literal woman and metaphorical woman (Wisdom or Folly) interanimate each other's meaning.

---

73. This phrase should not be identified with medieval concepts of hierarchy. See Oliver O'Donovan, *Resurrection and Moral Order* (Grand Rapids: Eerdmans, 1986) chap. 2.
74. See Gordon J. Wenham, *The Book of Leviticus* (Grand Rapids: Eerdmans, 1979) 22-23.
75. See G. von Rad, *Old Testament Theology* II (New York: Harper & Row, 1965) 211-17.

PROVERBS 3:1-12, INSTRUCTION IN THE FEAR OF THE LORD

NIV

3 My son, do not forget my teaching,
but keep my commands in your heart,
[2] for they will prolong your life many years
and bring you prosperity.

[3] Let love and faithfulness never leave you;
bind them around your neck,
write them on the tablet of your heart.
[4] Then you will win favor and a good name
in the sight of God and man.

[5] Trust in the LORD with all your heart
and lean not on your own understanding;
[6] in all your ways acknowledge him,
and he will make your paths straight.[a]

[7] Do not be wise in your own eyes;
fear the LORD and shun evil.
[8] This will bring health to your body
and nourishment to your bones.

[9] Honor the LORD with your wealth,
with the firstfruits of all your crops;
[10] then your barns will be filled to overflowing,
and your vats will brim over with new wine.

[11] My son, do not despise the LORD's discipline
and do not resent his rebuke,
[12] because the LORD disciplines those he loves,
as a father[b] the son he delights in.

[a]6 Or *will direct your paths*   [b]12 Hebrew; Septuagint / *and he punishes*

NRSV

3 My child, do not forget my
teaching,
but let your heart keep my commandments;
[2] for length of days and years of life
and abundant welfare they will give you.

[3] Do not let loyalty and faithfulness forsake you;
bind them around your neck,
write them on the tablet of your heart.
[4] So you will find favor and good repute
in the sight of God and of people.

[5] Trust in the LORD with all your heart,
and do not rely on your own insight.
[6] In all your ways acknowledge him,
and he will make straight your paths.
[7] Do not be wise in your own eyes;
fear the LORD, and turn away from evil.
[8] It will be a healing for your flesh
and a refreshment for your body.

[9] Honor the LORD with your substance
and with the first fruits of all your produce;
[10] then your barns will be filled with plenty,
and your vats will be bursting with wine.

[11] My child, do not despise the LORD's discipline
or be weary of his reproof,
[12] for the LORD reproves the one he loves,
as a father the son in whom he delights.

COMMENTARY

Proverbs 3, like chaps. 8–9, is composed of three parts: (1) an instruction on the "fear of the LORD" (vv. 1-12); (2) a blessing that praises Wisdom's benefits and role in Creation (vv. 13-20; cf. chap. 8); and (3) an instruction on relations with other people (vv. 21-35). Proverbs 3 is a summary of right human behavior toward God (vv. 1-12) and toward other people (vv. 21-35). Thus these instructions develop the first two themes stated in chapter 2's programmatic instruction. Verses 13-20 add the essential cosmic dimension to these relations, because creation is the arena in which divine and human concerns are played out.

3:1-2. The chapter opens with a negative and positive admonition to keep the parent's "instruction" and "commandments" (see 6:20; 7:2). "Keep . . . in your heart" means both "learn by heart" and "take to heart," in the sense of living out of what is learned, as Jacob and Mary do (Gen 37:11; Luke 2:19). The admonition promises a long and good life ("abundant welfare" שלום *šālôm*]; see 4:10; 6:20-23; cf. Moses' speeches to Israel, Deut 8:1, 18-20; 30:16, 20). The logic that connects admonition and blessing here is similar to the command to honor parents in Deuteronomy with its promise of long life (Deut 5:16; cf. Exod 20:12; Eph 6:2). This extravagant promise of life assumes that the parental teaching faithfully mediates the teaching of Lady Wisdom and thus her rewards (3:16-18; 8:35; 9:10-11; cf. 10:27). The authority of the parental speech defers to Lady Wisdom and is accountable to her cosmic standards. This is not spelled out, but simply assumed in the logic of a promise that only God and Wisdom can fulfill. Behind the parent stands Wisdom, not as authoritarian cudgel, but as reality and reason (see 2:1-4). In a similar but grander vein, even the Mosaic law only reflects cosmic norms imperfectly (Matt 19:3-19; in Sir 24:23, cosmic Wisdom and Mosaic law are identified, but there, too, Wisdom has priority.).

3:3. The first clause of this verse appears to be an editor's elaboration. Grammatically, two readings of "loyalty and faithfulness" are possible. The phrase may continue the promises of v. 2, and the clause may be translated, "loyalty and faithfulness will not forsake you." On this reading, reference is to the essential attributes of Yahweh once revealed on Mt. Sinai (Exod 34:6; Pss 25:10; 57:3; 67:7); "bind them" refers to the instruction and commandments of v. 1 (cf. 6:20-21; 7:1-3; Exod 13:9, 16; Deut 6:6, 8). In ancient Israel, as in orthodox Judaism today, amulets with sacred writing were bound about the neck (1:9; 6:21), thus close to the heart, as spiritual reminders. But writing "on the tablet of your heart" is also metaphorical for memory at the deepest level of one's being (3:1; 7:3; Jer 17:1). What penetrates to the depths of the heart determines one's very character and actions. Thus to transform the heart is transform the person (Jer 31:33; Rom 12:2; 2 Cor 3:3; see Commentary on Prov 4:23). But, more probably, "loyalty and faithfulness" stand as parallels to "instruction" and "commandments" and refer to human attributes that sum up the whole of our religio-ethical life (so NIV and NRSV). Thus in Hos 4:1-3, these two terms summarize the radical and comprehensive nature of Israel's moral-spiritual failure.

3:4. The author spells out the consequences of heeding the previous admonition: divine and human approval. This cliché indicates that one's life meets the standards of God and society. The phrase presupposes that human identity is formed through two fundamental relationships, with God and with other humans (1 Sam 2:26; Luke 2:52; Acts 2:47; Rom 14:18). Ancient Israel was a shame-and-honor culture, in contrast to modern Western societies, which often exercise social control through blame and guilt.[76] In the former, one's status and honor are public matters (see Commentary on 26:1), openly given or taken away by a (hopefully healthy) community. This is in contrast to the self-evaluation of those who trust in themselves (28:6; cf. 18:10-11), who are "wise/good/right in their own eyes," but ignore the perceptions of God and others (3:7; 26:12; cf. 27:2; Judg 17:6; 21:25). Good repute is literally "good sense" (שכל-טוב *śēkel-ṭôb*), which leads to a good reputation (see Commentary on 12:8; 13:15). So the Hebrew says that heeding the admonitions of 3:3 not only leads to social approval, but also enables one to acquire good sense. Matthew Poole, a seventeenth-century divine, commented: "The serious practice of religion is an excellent mean to get a solid understanding of it; as, on the contrary, a vicious life doth exceedingly debase and darken the mind, and keep men from the knowledge of truth."[77]

3:5-8. These verses teach the inner spirit of the "fear of the LORD" (see Commentary on 1:7). Essential is first a total (cf. Deut 4:29; 6:5) trust in the Lord (3:5; 16:20; Ps 37:3), which is contrasted to a self-reliance that trusts in its own insight (28:26), power, and wealth (11:28; Ps 52:7; Jer 9:23-24), quite unaware of human limits. Mighty Sennacherib's attack on Jerusalem (2 Kgs 18:17–19:37) is a tale of King Hezekiah's trust in Yahweh (2 Kgs 18:5, 19-24; 19:10) when no human power could save (Pss 33:16-17; 118:8-9; 146:3). It illustrates most of the issues at stake in Prov 3:5-6 (cf. 29:25).

Literally, "In all your ways know him" (v. 6;

76. See Victor H. Matthews and Don C. Benjamin, *Social World of Ancient Israel: 1250–587* BCE (Peabody, Mass.: Hendrickson, 1993) 142-54.

77. Matthew Poole, *A Commentary on the Holy Bible II* (McLean, Va.: MacDonald, n.d.) 218, on Prov 3:4.

cf. 1 Chr 28:9, of Solomon). "Ways" refers to human conduct in the world in its diversity: our behavior in various activities and circumstances, none excluded (16:2-3). This ordinary world is the arena in which human knowledge of God, or lack thereof, is revealed by human responses to the divine standards of justice and righteousness (1:3; 16:12; Jer 22:13-16; Amos 5:21-24). Knowing and doing justice are not the same as being in relationship with God, but the two are inseparable (28:5, 9).

Verses 7-8 form another admonition with a promissory motive, at the center of the series in vv. 5-10, that lays down the essentials for a God-fearing life. The first precept of v. 7 warns against being "wise in your own eyes." This phrase is used to express one person's subjective evaluation of things in implicit contrast to some other person's evaluation. The "other" must always be kept in mind. The first is usually a positive or negative adjective (good, just, right, wise, evil, wicked). The "other" is sometimes other people (12:15; 28:11), but most important it is some higher judge of what is right or wise (cf. 16:2, 25). Ultimately this judge is the Lord. In Judges, when each person does what is right in his or her own eyes (Judg 17:6; 21:25), it is because there is no king to ensure that what is right in his eyes is done. The human king is in turn accountable to Yahweh, the divine king (cf. 1 Kgs 11:33, 38). Since Yahweh is the creator, Yahweh's view of things is true, the way things are, and to go counter to this view is to flout reality (Isa 5:20-21). The folly of being wise in one's own eyes (3:7; 26:12, 16; 28:11) is parallel to the notion of relying on one's own heart (cf. 3:5), as the proverb pair in 28:25b-26 makes clear.

Verse 7b complements v. 7a. The opposite of overblown self-assurance and pride (see 1 Cor 8:1) is to "fear the Lord, and turn away from evil" (see Commentary on 16:5-6). This positive and negative precept is the sum of a godly and good life (Job 1:1, 8; 28:28; see Commentary on Prov 1:7), for to shun evil is to turn toward God and the good (16:6; Amos 5:4b, 14-15). The issue is a lifelong journey of "conversion" (16:17). Such a mind-set (a Hebrew might say "heart-set"; cf. Pss 57:7; 78:37) promises life and well-being to one's very self, both inner and outer, "body"

("flesh" or perhaps "navel" as the body's center) and "bones" (3:8; 16:24; cf. Isa 66:14; Rom 12:1). Such promises have often been misused by the purveyors of a "health-and-wealth" gospel (see Reflections on 3:11-12). The promise here is more modest and qualified. It means that a godly and good life is a healthy one, one that ought to be a matter of common sense, not wholly unlike Benjamin Franklin's *Poor Richard's Almanac* entry, "Early to bed, early to rise, makes a man healthy, wealthy and wise" (cf. 1 Tim 4:7b-8 and the qualifications in 1 Tim 6:5-10, which set sharp limits on the goal of well-being for its own sake). Well-being and wealth, like the more elusive happiness, when God grants them, are natural by-products of a quest for more ultimate goods.

3:9-10. The text moves naturally from the inner dispositions of the heart (3:1, 3, 5, 7) to the practical "payoff." Money talks, and it shows the heart's true home (Matt 6:21). Our use of world and wealth reveals our true commitments. Specifically, by it we show either honor or scorn to God (14:31; 19:17; 1 Sam 2:29; Dan 11:38). For Israel, this meant that the "first fruits," the first produce of a new harvest and symbolically the best, were dedicated to God alone, sometimes for the use of the priests (Lev 23:10; Num 18:8-15) or for lay folk (Deut 26:1-11).

Such first fruits are part of a symbol system that includes the firstborn of human and beast (Exod 13:1-3, 11-16) because Israel, God's people, has been graciously elevated to the status of God's firstborn (Exod 4:22; Hos 11:1) and first fruits (Jer 2:3). All things and persons belong to God, Israel's creator and redeemer, and the gift of the first fruits and the redemption of the firstborn acknowledges this (Deut 26:1-11). But first fruits/firstborn also are a sign and a promise of the full harvest to come, a matter taken up in New Testament representations of Christ and his people (Matt 2:15; Rom 8:29; Rev 1:5).

Verse 10 presents an abundance of crops and wine as a natural outcome of giving honor to God. There is a sort of natural symmetry between the gifts to God (cf. Num 18:27, 30) and the blessings of barn and vat, which ensue (3:10; cf. Sir 35:9-13). Similar language and thought also appear in Deuteronomy (cf. Deut 15:13-14; 28:8). Proverbs 3:9-10 is one of the few places in the book of Proverbs where cultic language and matters are presented (see 15:8; 28:13; cf. Mal 3:8-12). Worship and liturgy in the narrow sense are not the focus of Proverbs. The book takes Israel's covenant faith as a given (see the section "Theology" in the Introduction). Its particular concern is daily life lived in the presence of God.

3:11-12. The solemn precept and explanatory motive here present a sharp, deliberate contradiction to vv. 9-10. Sometimes those who honor the Lord find their barns empty and their vats dry, so that joy and gladness flee away (cf. Isa 17:10). This alternative, godly, Job-like experience of life sometimes finds an explanation in the loving discipline and reproof of God the parent (cf. 1:7-8; 13:24; 15:5).

REFLECTIONS

1. Proverbs 3:11-12 presents a direct contradiction to glib "health-and-wealth" (sub)versions of the gospel, which appeal to vv. 9-10. Proverbs 3:11-12 shouts "No!" to promises of wealth made by preachers who exploit the naive, the desperate, and those who practice religion as a means of gain. Genuine faith is sometimes called upon to "fear God for nothing" (see Job 1:9-11). On Prov 3:11-12, the best commentaries are Deuteronomy 8 and Hebrews 12. Moses' profound sermon on the wilderness sufferings of Israel provides one explanation of the meaning of human suffering (esp. Deut 8:5), and also warns of the dangers of material prosperity (Deut 8:11-20). Hebrews 12 follows upon the grand story of godly heroes in Hebrews 11, with its litany of human promises kept through faith and suffering, and its litany of divine promises left unfulfilled by God. Then the writer of Hebrews quotes Prov 3:11-12 and encourages readers who also suffer: "Now, discipline always seems painful rather than pleasant at the time, but later it yields the peaceful fruit of righteousness to those who have been trained by it. Therefore lift your drooping hands" (Heb 12:11-12 NRSV).

2. This section also deals with the matter of trust and reliance. Ralph W. Emerson's classic essay "Self-Reliance" established that concept as a basic American virtue. But the Bible presents a paradox. The more one relies on God, the more independent one becomes. Paradoxically, then, it is the most God-dependent persons who are the most independent of external controls and coercion. For the writer of Proverbs to say, "Get understanding, get wisdom" (see 4:7) is not incompatible with "lean not on your own understanding."

Humans have a marvelous capacity to understand and live meaningfully in the world. But life is riddled with evils, mysteries, and troubles beyond human grasping or fixing. Some of these troubles are due to sin, but some are not. There are gaps between what humans expect and what actually happens. More sharply, there are gaps and contradictions between what God promises and what humans receive in life (Hebrews 11). This fact of life is presented but not resolved in the great works of Ecclesiastes and Job (see also Psalm 73). The problem is already present in Proverbs (3:9-12; 16:1, 9; 19:21; 21:30-31; 27:1).[78]

Thus there is no true wisdom without humble recognition of our limits and of God's transcendence (Psalm 131; Jer 9:23-24). God is the ultimate reality with which humans have to deal in the thick of life. The Bible does not present God as a quick and easy answer to human terror, as many would wish. Rather, God's involvement in the mystery of evil renders God mysterious to us, for evil seems to call divine goodness and truth into question. This paradox is powerfully expressed in the contradictory formulations of Genesis, where the evil actions of Joseph's brothers are attributed to God's saving purposes and action: "It was not you who sent me here, but God" (Gen 45:8 NRSV; cf. Gen 50:20).

The consistent biblical answer to this dilemma of life is faith or trust in the One we do not

---

78. See G. von Rad, *Wisdom in Israel* (Nashville: Abingdon, 1972) 97-110; R. C. Van Leeuwen, "Wealth and Poverty: System and Contradiction in Proverbs," *Hebrew Studies* 33 (1992) 25-26.

and cannot fully comprehend (Job 28:28; Eccl 12:13-14). The gospel says that the solution to evil lies mysteriously beyond us; according to the "foolish" wisdom of the cross, it lies with God in Christ (1 Cor 1:18-31; 2 Cor 4:18). Meanwhile, Christians, like ancient Israel, live in hope (Rom 5:1-5), being enjoined to trust and obey where they cannot clearly see. We walk by faith, not by sight (2 Cor 5:7).

3. Walking in the knowledge of God is motivated by the promise that God will "make straight your paths" (3:6*b* NRSV). The use of this phrase in 9:15 suggests that "straight paths" does not necessarily mean a life free from difficulties. It does mean that one's life has a clear direction and goal that a Godward person will attain (11:3, 5; 15:21; cf. 4:25). A divine and human synergy occurs when humans are in tune with God and with God's purposes. Thus Isaiah can tell the Babylonian exiles to "make straight in the desert a highway for our God" (Isa 40:3 NRSV; cf. Prov 15:21). The desert is not a place of abundant life, but the purposes of God and humans may be fulfilled there. The German theologian and martyr Dietrich Bonhoeffer wrote from a prison cell:

> Not everything [evil] that happens is the will of God, yet in the last resort nothing happens without his will (Matthew 10.29), i.e., through every event, however untoward, *there is always a way through to God*.[79]

Abraham set off on a journey, not knowing where he would go, only that God would go with him on the way (Gen 12:1-3; cf. Heb 11:8).

79. Dietrich Bonhoeffer, "Letter of December 18th, 1943," in *Letters and Papers from Prison,* E. Bethge, ed. (London: SCM, 1953) 84; italics added.

PROVERBS 3:13-35, ON WISDOM: BLESSING, CREATION, ADMONITIONS

NIV	NRSV

[13]Blessed is the man who finds wisdom,
    the man who gains understanding,
[14]for she is more profitable than silver
    and yields better returns than gold.
[15]She is more precious than rubies;
    nothing you desire can compare with her.
[16]Long life is in her right hand;
    in her left hand are riches and honor.
[17]Her ways are pleasant ways,
    and all her paths are peace.
[18]She is a tree of life to those who embrace her;
    those who lay hold of her will be blessed.
 	
[19]By wisdom the LORD laid the earth's foundations,
    by understanding he set the heavens in place;
[20]by his knowledge the deeps were divided,
    and the clouds let drop the dew.
[21]My son, preserve sound judgment and
    discernment,
	[13] Happy are those who find wisdom,
	    and those who get understanding,
	[14] for her income is better than silver,
	    and her revenue better than gold.
	[15] She is more precious than jewels,
	    and nothing you desire can compare with her.
	[16] Long life is in her right hand;
	    in her left hand are riches and honor.
	[17] Her ways are ways of pleasantness,
	    and all her paths are peace.
	[18] She is a tree of life to those who lay hold of her;
	    those who hold her fast are called happy.
	
	[19] The LORD by wisdom founded the earth;
	    by understanding he established the heavens;
	[20] by his knowledge the deeps broke open,

NIV

do not let them out of your sight;
22they will be life for you,
an ornament to grace your neck.
23Then you will go on your way in safety,
and your foot will not stumble;
24when you lie down, you will not be afraid;
when you lie down, your sleep will be sweet.
25Have no fear of sudden disaster
or of the ruin that overtakes the wicked,
26for the LORD will be your confidence
and will keep your foot from being snared.

27Do not withhold good from those who deserve it,
when it is in your power to act.
28Do not say to your neighbor,
"Come back later; I'll give it tomorrow"—
when you now have it with you.
29Do not plot harm against your neighbor,
who lives trustfully near you.
30Do not accuse a man for no reason—
when he has done you no harm.
31Do not envy a violent man
or choose any of his ways,
32for the LORD detests a perverse man
but takes the upright into his confidence.
33The LORD's curse is on the house of the wicked,
but he blesses the home of the righteous.
34He mocks proud mockers
but gives grace to the humble.
35The wise inherit honor,
but fools he holds up to shame.

NRSV

and the clouds drop down the dew.

21 My child, do not let these escape from your sight:
keep sound wisdom and prudence,
22 and they will be life for your soul
and adornment for your neck.
23 Then you will walk on your way securely
and your foot will not stumble.
24 If you sit down,[a] you will not be afraid;
when you lie down, your sleep will be sweet.
25 Do not be afraid of sudden panic,
or of the storm that strikes the wicked;
26 for the LORD will be your confidence
and will keep your foot from being caught.

27 Do not withhold good from those to whom it is due,[b]
when it is in your power to do it.
28 Do not say to your neighbor, "Go, and come again,
tomorrow I will give it"—when you have it with you.
29 Do not plan harm against your neighbor
who lives trustingly beside you.
30 Do not quarrel with anyone without cause,
when no harm has been done to you.
31 Do not envy the violent
and do not choose any of their ways;
32 for the perverse are an abomination to the LORD,
but the upright are in his confidence.
33 The LORD's curse is on the house of the wicked,
but he blesses the abode of the righteous.
34 Toward the scorners he is scornful,
but to the humble he shows favor.
35 The wise will inherit honor,
but stubborn fools, disgrace.

aGk: Heb *lie down*   bHeb *from its owners*

COMMENTARY

After the preceding instruction in the fear of the Lord (vv. 1-12), there follow a blessing (vv. 13-18) and a saying on creation (vv. 19-20).

Formally, vv. 13-18 comprise a blessing. (The root אשר [ʾšr, "happy," "blessed"] marks the beginning and end of the section, an inclusio; cf. 8:34.) But the blessing functions here to praise the benefactions of wisdom in hymnic fashion. In vv. 19-20, as in 8:22-31, the role of Wisdom in creation grounds the preceding account of her benefits (3:13-18; 8:1-21). Another instruction follows (vv. 21-35), comprising two parts. The first part (vv. 21-26) is a summary instruction based on the foregoing teaching (vv. 1-20; cf. 7:24-27; 8:32-35). The second part (vv. 27-35) concludes the chapter with six practical admonitions and a divine curse (v. 33), which contrasts with the blessing of vv. 13-18.

3:13-18. The blessedness ("happy" vv. 13, 18; 8:34; Ps 1:1) of those who find wisdom and get understanding is here detailed. This language links this section and its message to chap. 2 and especially to chap. 8. It repeats the search-and-find motif that in Prov 2:2-6 (cf. 8:17*b*; 1:28*b*) entailed the fear of the Lord, a topic treated at length in 3:1-12. The quest for wisdom is inescapably a journey in the presence of God. The vocabulary of v. 13 is also repeated in the beginning and ending of Wisdom's great speech (8:1, 34-35). Again, creation through Wisdom (vv. 19-20) is more fully elaborated in 8:22-31.

The language of v. 13 is also used of the acquisition of a wife, who symbolizes wisdom (18:22; cf. 8:35). Hence, it is not surprising that the language of vv. 13-18 reappears to describe the "capable wife" of Proverbs 31. Her children call her "blessed" (31:28; cf. 3:13, 18; 8:32, 34). The rewards of Wisdom are priceless (vv. 14-15; see 8:11*a*, 19; 16:16; 31:10, 18, with parallel vocabulary), and nothing one might desire is comparable to her (v. 15*b* = 8:11*b*; 31:10). These verbal and thematic parallels create a three-way link among 3:13-20; 8:1-35; and 31:10-31. Through repetition, they forge a long-distance, interactive parallelism among cosmic wisdom and human cultural activities, especially as exemplified in the earthy, life-enriching activity of the "capable woman" (31:10-31).[80]

In Wisdom's hands are long life (vv. 16-17; cf. 3:2; 4:10; Ps 91:16) and riches and honor (v. 16; 8:18). Verse 16 perhaps alludes to Solomon's request for wisdom and God's surprising gift of what Solomon did not ask for (1 Kgs 3:5-14). The

image of Wisdom holding "life" in her hands has an Egyptian counterpart in Ma'at, the goddess of world order and justice, who holds the *ankh* ("life") sign in one hand and the *was* scepter, symbol of wealth and honor, in the other (see Commentary on 8:27).[81] Wisdom's "ways" (v. 17) are pleasant (cf. 2:10; 9:17), "paths of peace."

Within Proverbs 1–9, שׁלום (*šālôm*, "peace and prosperity," appears only here and in 3:2. This repetition suggests that Wisdom's gifts (vv. 16-17) may be gotten through parents (v. 2). Again, "way" and "path" reinforce the theme of life as a journey governed by either Wisdom or Folly.

The "tree of life" (v. 18) is a cosmic image known throughout the ancient Near East. In the Bible, outside of Proverbs, this tree is present only at the beginning and the end of all things, in the Garden of Eden (Gen 2:9; 3:22, 24) and in the city-garden of the new creation, where it bears its fruit in season (cf. Ps 1:3) and its leaves are for the "healing of the nations" (Rev 2:7; 22:2, 14). In Proverbs, the phrase has become a metaphor for the good life offered by Wisdom (3:18; 11:30; 15:4) or even by hope fulfilled (13:12). In the context of vv. 19-20, the cosmic overtones of this image are still active, though the everlasting life of the Garden of Eden is not (Gen 3:22-23). Nonetheless, the human imperative here must not be overlooked; one must "lay hold" of wisdom and "hold her fast." If Wisdom in a fallen world does not afford eternal life, she does offer the best and fullest life humans can possess. One should not wait for the plums to fall from the tree (cf. Eccl 9:10)!

3:19-20. The double naming of Wisdom as "Wisdom" and "Understanding" is repeated from v. 13 (cf. 8:1) and marks a shift from the human (vv. 13-18) to the divine relationship with wisdom. It provides the cosmic warrant for all the blessings just described (vv. 13-18; cf. 8:22-31). The passage has affinities with Ps 104:24 and Jer 10:12. "Earth," "the heavens," and "the deeps" are a tri-part way of summing up the entire creation (cf. Exod 20:4; the opposites, "heavens" and "earth" can also have such a summary function, Gen 1:1). The verbs of v. 19, which are used of God's creating acts (see also Job 38:4; Ps 24:2; Isa 14:32; 45:18), are also used of "found-

80. For the cohesive effect of repetition in distant parallelism, see Dennis Pardee, *Ugaritic and Hebrew Poetic Parallelism: A Trial Cut ('nt and Proverbs 2)*, SVT 39 (Leiden: Brill, 1988).

81. Christa Kayatz, *Studien zu Proverbien 1–9*, WMANT 22 (Neukirchen: Neukirchener Verlag, 1966) 104-5.

ing" and "establishing" a city or a house, whether a domestic domicile or a temple (1 Kgs 6:37; 1 Chr 17:24; Ezra 3:12; Isa 14:32). Building a house is a human echo of God's wise work of creation (see Commentary on 9:1; 24:3-4).[82]

Verse 20 presents another bi-polar figure of the universe, life-giving waters from below and above ("dew"). The "deeps" were divided at creation so that the dry land and the waters were separated into their proper domains (8:29; cf. Gen 1:9; Job 38:8-11; Ps 104:9). This separation of the waters from the dry land represents the cosmic stability of the world, in which potentially destructive and chaotic forces, symbolized by the deeps, are kept harmless, in their proper sphere. But the ongoing order of creation, represented by the waters, also enables life to flourish. In arid Palestine, a water source is a natural symbol of life (10:11; 13:14; 14:27; 16:22; cf. Jer 2:13). Thus for Israel, God's disposal of water was one of the surest signs of divine wisdom. The land is dry; lack of rain in season can bring famine. In the rainless summer months (see Commentary on 26:1), the heavy dew, brought from the Mediterranean by the west wind, can keep crops alive. Thus the cosmic imagery here is not fortuitous, but comports with the imagery of vegetative life from v. 18.

3:21-35. These verses belong together as an instruction that develops the second theme from the programmatic instruction in Proverbs 2:9-11—namely, correct relations with other persons. The return to instruction is signaled by "My son" (v. 21), a general admonition with promissory motivations (vv. 22-26), a series of negative admonitions concerning relations with other people (vv. 27-31), and is concluded by an extended theological grounding of the series (vv. 33-35). The overall pattern of this instruction is thus similar to that of vv. 1-12.

3:21-26. In v. 21, the instruction is something the son must "keep," but in 2:11 prudence and understanding "keep" the son. (For "prudence" [= one's inner thought] see the Commentary on 2:11.) There is a mutuality between wise humans and the cosmic Wisdom they seek and keep (see Commentary on 2:1-4). But what is the relation between the security that comes from keeping "sound wisdom and prudence" (v. 21b, 23-25,

alluding backward to Wisdom's speech in 1:26-27 and forward to 4:19) and the security that Yahweh affords (v. 26; cf. v. 5)? Through human wisdom "your foot will not stumble" (v. 23; cf. Ps 91:12, Hebrew), but Yahweh "will keep your foot from being caught" (v. 26). This parallel suggests that Yahweh stands behind Wisdom, as her ultimate guarantor. Conversely, the unwise and sinners are caught by their own folly (5:21-23; 6:2; 11:6). Yahweh's protection, mediated through wisdom, does not save from that! The focus here is not on the Lord's extraordinary deeds of salvation, but on the ordinary connections between human responsibility and life in the world as ordained and ordered by God.

Verse 22 echoes the imagery of v. 3 (cf. 1:9; 4:9). In Hebrew there is also a double pun that exploits the imagery of the necklace: "they will be life for your soul [throat]" and "adornment [favor] for your neck" (נפש *nepeš* can mean "soul"/"life" and the "throat" that a necklace adorns; see Isa 5:14; Jonah 2:5; חן *ḥēn* means "favor," but can also be a (beautiful) ornament, such as a necklace; cf. Prov 3:4). The security wisdom provides (v. 23) recalls 1:33 and, more broadly, the covenant promises of dwelling in the land (2:21; 10:30; cf. Lev 25:18; Psalm 37; Matt 5:5).

3:27-35. Verses 27-31 are a row of negative admonitions, all beginning with the command, "Do not," an example of anaphora. Verses 28-29 also end with the same Hebrew terms ("with you"/"near you"), an epiphora. The issue in each is not mere advice that may or may not be followed, depending on the situation (cf. 26:4-5). Rather, these admonitions, like the Ten Commandments, lay down basic, non-negotiable rules for dealing with others.

Verses 29-30 are linked to the foregoing by anaphora and the key word "neighbor" (רע *rēaʿ*), and also form a thematic pair in themselves ("Harm" [רעה *rāʿâ*] is a key word that also forms a wordplay with "neighbor" in Hebrew). Verse 29 moves from the withholding of "good" (v. 27) to the active plotting of evil against one's neighbor, where the thought is parent to the crime (Ps 7:14-16). The neighbor, meanwhile, lives in naive security, like the innocent inhabitants of Laish, destroyed by the tribe of Dan (Judg 18:7-10, 27-28). Thus this cluster of admonitions moves

---

82. M. Eliade, *Cosmos and History or the Myth of the Eternal Return* (Princeton: Princeton University Press, 1971).

from sins of omission to those of commission against the neighbor for personal advantage (cf. 1:11-12).

Verse 30 broadens the venue from neighbor to the more inclusive "anyone" (אדם, 'ādām, "human," "man") in a way reminiscent of the contrast between Lev 19:18 ("neighbor") and Lev 19:34 ("stranger"). The focus is on the unjustified "quarrel" or "lawsuit" (ריב, rîb, means both; see Commentary on 25:7b-10).

The summarizing precept (v. 31) and the motive clauses that follow (vv. 32-35) provide depth to the foregoing admonitions. Actions of greed (vv. 28-29) or assault (vv. 29-30) are "ways" of the violent. The violent are immoral persons whose might is their right, who use whatever force they command, whether moral or not, to expand their own kingdom at the expense of their neighbors. The parent's parable on sinners (1:10-19) is only a flagrant example of this human tendency to envy (cf. 4:16-17).

Verses 32-35 give grounds for not envying the violent of v. 31 in a series of contrasts between the good and the bad vis-à-vis their relations to God. A stock series of terms describes the opposed parties. "Perverse" or "devious" (cf. 2:15) people are an "abomination" to God, and thus they are far from God (see Commentary on 11:1). But God is near to the upright, the "straightforward" who partake, almost in prophet-like fashion, in God's inner "counsel"/"council" (סוד sôd means both; cf. Job 15:8; 29:4; Ps 24:14; Jer 23:18; Amos 3:7). The stories of Noah before the flood (Gen 6:9-22) and Abraham before Sodom and Gomorrah (Gen 18:17-19) illustrate Prov 3:32b (cf. John 15:15).

Verse 33 continues the series of motivational oppositions, contrasting "the LORD's curse" with God's "blessing" (10:6-7, 22; cf. Job 42:10-16; Zech 5:3-4). The contrast of blessing and curse in consequence of obedience and disobedience was basic to Israel's covenant relation with Yahweh as spelled out in Deuteronomy (Deut 11:26-28; 27:14–28:68). It is by the Lord's blessing that houses, domestic and dynastic, get built (2 Samuel 7; Psalm 127; Luke 2:4).

God deals with humans in kind (v. 34a; Job 34:11); as we give, so we get. Compare the American proverbs, "What goes around, comes around" and "Violence begets violence." Like is related to like in actions, in consequences, and in relations with God and with other humans (cf. 24:23). Yet God's grace or favor can surprisingly reverse human expectations dimmed by evil in the direction of justice and shalom (v. 34b; cf. 1 Sam 2:4-8; Luke 1:51-55). The logic compressed in v. 34b is laid out more fully in Ps 18:24-27, though there is little overlap of vocabulary (cf. Prov 30:5 with Ps 18:30). God "scorns scorners"—that is, God shows them no respect (for the verb, see 19:28a). The LXX of 3:34 is quoted in James 4:6 and 1 Pet 5:5. The quotation in James follows upon a passage on coveting whose logic is similar to Prov 3:31-34.

Verse 35 appropriately closes the passage with a contrast of "wise" and "fools" who receive "honor"/"wealth" (see Commentary on 11:16) and "disgrace" respectively, rewards appropriate to each life-style. Thus, by giving fitting rewards, God helps the "humble" (v. 34b), while subverting the wrongful attempts of the wicked to get gain at the expense of their neighbor.

REFLECTIONS

1. As so often in Proverbs, 3:13-35 considers life in terms of two antithetical directions: toward God, wisdom, righteousness, and life (3:13-26) or toward sin, folly, and death, with the loss of all the former (3:27-28). The implications are not just individual (though the passage speaks personally), or merely ecclesiastical. They are cosmic in scope (3:19-20; also the tree of life) and social in the broadest sense.

With concrete, albeit negative, examples, 3:27-28 expresses principles of justice essential to any society's health. First, as the Western legal proverb has it, one must give "to each his own." Humans have a general claim on certain things that their humanity entitles them to. Life, food, shelter, and dignity are among the most obvious of these things essential to our humanness.

Each person is unique. But part of that uniqueness stems from membership in families, countries, and various groups. Part of it stems from our roles as workers, clients, students, employers, spouses, and so forth. In short, justice requires not only that individuals receive what is their due simply as human beings, but also that they receive what is theirs as unique individuals who stand in a rich array of relationships. The short admonition of 3:27-28 thus casts a very wide umbrella over human existence. Perhaps no aspect of social and personal life is not touched by it. Wisdom consists in knowing what properly belongs to my neighbor, at the proper time, and in the proper way, by virtue of who he or she is and my relationship to that neighbor.[83] Teachers, for example, owe their students a journey into the truth. This journey should happen in a way pedagogically appropriate to the students' age, development, training, and abilities. Justice (and love) consists of granting what is properly yours to you, *when it is in my power to do it.*

The second principle appears in 3:27*b*. Our actions, also with respect to God, to rulers, and to our neighbor (cf. 3:9; 24:21; Matt 22:21; Rom 13:7-8), are determined both by our ability (3:27*b*-28) and by our responsibility according to the standard of justice (3:27*a*). Justice determines that when I have something that I owe to my neighbor, I am responsible to him or her for it. (In some cases, we may owe good to God or to our neighbor but be unable to meet our obligation.) The present admonition considers a case in which I am able to give good, in which my sphere of influence matches my sphere of responsibility. It is at this point that we may be tempted to deceive ourselves and our neighbor—but not God (3:28; cf. 24:10-12). By committing sins of omission, we neglect to do what is right and deny our responsibility for it. Finally, the disposition of obligations must be timely (3:27*b*-28). While v. 27 refers to one with a claim on you, v. 28 may also refer simply to a neighbor in need who asks for help that you can render, whether that neighbor has any legal claim to it or not (cf. 14:21, 31; Exod 22:25-27; James 4:17; 1 John 3:17-18). There are sins of omission against the command to love one's fellow human beings (Lev 19:18, 34), as the parable of the good Samaritan illustrates (Luke 10:29-37).

2. Proverbs 3:29-30 considers active wrongs instead of sins of omission. Verse 29 discusses the inward malice that comes to the surface in actions that harm a neighbor, whether in violent or legal ways. Quarrels and litigation can be used wrongly to seek personal gain from another who has done you no harm. For instance, a man picks a fight with a newly arrived, confused tourist, while his associate picks the tourist's pocket. But the more common and significant application of this admonition is in the legal arena, where false accusation and irresponsible litigation can do great harm to others, even as they erode the fabric of civility and justice that bind a society together in harmony. In the litigious United States (with 4 percent of the world's population and one-half of the world's lawyers), one would wish this saying were inscribed on the portals of every courthouse and on the hearts of all who enter there.

3. The writer of Proverbs reveals the spiritual source (3:31) of the sins warned against previously (3:27-30); they are rooted in "envy"[84] (see 24:1-2, 19-20; Psalm 37). Beginning with Adam and Eve and their progeny, Cain and Abel (Genesis 3–4), the Bible repeatedly describes humans as being smitten with envy of God and of neighbor. "The grass seems greener on the other side of the fence." We covet what others have (Exod 20:17; cf. Col 3:5; Jas 4:2). And we envy those who have what we have not, even when their goods have been gained by wrong. This is the disease described by Shakespeare:

83. See Aristotle *Nicomachean Ethics* III.i.16, 1111*a;* Oliver O'Donovan, *Resurrection and Moral Order* (Grand Rapids: Eerdmans, 1986).

84. Cornelius Plantinga, Jr., "A Select History of Envy," in *Not the Way It's Supposed to Be: A Breviary of Sin* (Grand Rapids: Eerdmans, 1995) 157-72.

And look upon myself and curse my fate,
Wishing me like to one more rich in hope,
Featured like him, like him with friends possess'd,
Desiring this man's art, and that man's scope,
With what I most enjoy contented least. (Sonnet 29).

PROVERBS 4:1-27, TRADITION, WISDOM, AND WAYS

NIV

4 Listen, my sons, to a father's instruction;
pay attention and gain understanding.
[2]I give you sound learning,
so do not forsake my teaching.
[3]When I was a boy in my father's house,
still tender, and an only child of my mother,
[4]he taught me and said,
"Lay hold of my words with all your heart;
keep my commands and you will live.
[5]Get wisdom, get understanding;
do not forget my words or swerve from them.
[6]Do not forsake wisdom, and she will protect you;
love her, and she will watch over you.
[7]Wisdom is supreme; therefore get wisdom.
Though it cost all you have,[a] get understanding.
[8]Esteem her, and she will exalt you;
embrace her, and she will honor you.
[9]She will set a garland of grace on your head
and present you with a crown of splendor."

[10]Listen, my son, accept what I say,
and the years of your life will be many.
[11]I guide you in the way of wisdom
and lead you along straight paths.
[12]When you walk, your steps will not be hampered;
when you run, you will not stumble.
[13]Hold on to instruction, do not let it go;
guard it well, for it is your life.
[14]Do not set foot on the path of the wicked
or walk in the way of evil men.
[15]Avoid it, do not travel on it;
turn from it and go on your way.
[16]For they cannot sleep till they do evil;
they are robbed of slumber till they make someone fall.
[17]They eat the bread of wickedness

NRSV

4 Listen, children, to a father's instruction,
and be attentive, that you may gain[a] insight;
[2] for I give you good precepts:
do not forsake my teaching.
[3] When I was a son with my father,
tender, and my mother's favorite,
[4] he taught me, and said to me,
"Let your heart hold fast my words;
keep my commandments, and live.
[5] Get wisdom; get insight: do not forget, nor turn away
from the words of my mouth.
[6] Do not forsake her, and she will keep you;
love her, and she will guard you.
[7] The beginning of wisdom is this: Get wisdom,
and whatever else you get, get insight.
[8] Prize her highly, and she will exalt you;
she will honor you if you embrace her.
[9] She will place on your head a fair garland;
she will bestow on you a beautiful crown."

[10] Hear, my child, and accept my words,
that the years of your life may be many.
[11] I have taught you the way of wisdom;
I have led you in the paths of uprightness.
[12] When you walk, your step will not be hampered;
and if you run, you will not stumble.
[13] Keep hold of instruction; do not let go;
guard her, for she is your life.
[14] Do not enter the path of the wicked,
and do not walk in the way of evildoers.
[15] Avoid it; do not go on it;
turn away from it and pass on.
[16] For they cannot sleep unless they have done wrong;

NIV

and drink the wine of violence.
¹⁸The path of the righteous is like the first gleam
of dawn,
    shining ever brighter till the full light of day.
¹⁹But the way of the wicked is like deep darkness;
    they do not know what makes them stumble.

²⁰My son, pay attention to what I say;
    listen closely to my words.
²¹Do not let them out of your sight,
    keep them within your heart;
²²for they are life to those who find them
    and health to a man's whole body.
²³Above all else, guard your heart,
    for it is the wellspring of life.
²⁴Put away perversity from your mouth;
    keep corrupt talk far from your lips.
²⁵Let your eyes look straight ahead,
    fix your gaze directly before you.
²⁶Make level^b paths for your feet
    and take only ways that are firm.
²⁷Do not swerve to the right or the left;
    keep your foot from evil.

a7 Or Whatever else you get   b26 Or Consider the

NRSV

    they are robbed of sleep unless they have
      made someone stumble.
¹⁷ For they eat the bread of wickedness
    and drink the wine of violence.
¹⁸ But the path of the righteous is like the light
    of dawn,
    which shines brighter and brighter until full day.
¹⁹ The way of the wicked is like deep darkness;
    they do not know what they stumble over.
²⁰ My child, be attentive to my words;
    incline your ear to my sayings.
²¹ Do not let them escape from your sight;
    keep them within your heart.
²² For they are life to those who find them,
    and healing to all their flesh.
²³ Keep your heart with all vigilance,
    for from it flow the springs of life.
²⁴ Put away from you crooked speech,
    and put devious talk far from you.
²⁵ Let your eyes look directly forward,
    and your gaze be straight before you.
²⁶ Keep straight the path of your feet,
    and all your ways will be sure.
²⁷ Do not swerve to the right or to the left;
    turn your foot away from evil.

a Heb know

COMMENTARY

4:1-9. These verses present an extended parental invitation to get wisdom, an expansion of the usual introduction to an instruction. Its language is stereotypical, with slight variations (e.g., a plural address). The central theme is tradition itself, the notion that wisdom is something passed on from generation to generation. Israelite culture, strongly traditional and oral in character, revered the aged as treasure houses of wisdom (cf. 8:22-31; 16:31; 20:29; Job 15:7-10).

4:1-4. Wisdom from the past, refined in the crucible of experience, is passed on from parents to children, from teachers to pupils, and from craftspeople to apprentices. This notion has left its traces in the word "learning" (לקח *leqaḥ*, v. 2), which connotes something received from another, something handed on, accepted, and finally made

one's own by the recipient (cf. 1:5; 9:9; 16:21, 23; as verb, 2:1; 4:10; 24:32). The great rabbinic wisdom work *Pirqe 'Abot* ("Sayings of the Fathers") captures this traditional notion of learning by its repeated, "So and so received [the tradition] from so and so." More than any inheritance of wealth and property, parental teaching is to be "treasured" (2:1; 7:1; 10:14; see Commentary on 19:14) and used by the next generation as they make their own way through life. The chain of tradition is made explicit by the father-son-father-son links in vv. 3-4. What the father was taught, with verbal variation, he now adapts and teaches to his own son (v. 4; cf. 2:1; 3:1; 7:2).

Several biblical and ancient Near Eastern scenes portray or allude to the drama of a father (figurative or literal) who, as he approaches death, passes on his wisdom and commands to the next generation. Such transmission may be to the next leader or to a son (Deut 34:9; Josh 1:7-9; 1 Kgs 2:1-9; cf. Luke 1:17; 2 Tim 2:2).[85] The parental wisdom and commands are sometimes explicitly linked with the Mosaic Torah (תורה *tôrâ* means "teaching" or "instruction," and, secondarily, "law."). The language in v. 2*b*, "do not forsake my teaching," resonates with passages on the forsaking of Yahweh's law as received by the ancestors. In Ps 89:30 the concern is with the royal sons in the line of David; in Jer 9:13, it is with Israel generally.

4:5-9. Here is an extended admonition to "get wisdom" first and foremost. The juxtaposition with the foregoing verses (vv. 1-4; cf. v. 5*b*), which urged children to listen to their parent's teaching, is not accidental. The assumption is that the parent, as portrayed in Proverbs, is a faithful mediator of wisdom to the young. But even so, the young are to get wisdom. They are responsible for laying hold of the wisdom offered them. The issue is not the parent's authority and tradition for its own sake, but rather Wisdom herself. All good parental teaching seeks to put children in touch with reality and its norms (cosmic Wisdom) and to engender those habits of the heart and mouth and hands that constitute the good life (human wisdom). Human wisdom is fostered by pointing to Wisdom as something "out there" to be gotten hold of, to be loved, embraced, and prized (vv. 6, 8), like the wife in 5:15-20. Human wisdom is love of reality, of the world, and of its excellent "norms." And those who embrace Wisdom are in turn kept, guarded, and honored by her reality (vv. 6, 8; for the imagery of v. 9, cf. 1:9). The love affair of humans and Wisdom is reciprocal and mutual (see Commentary on 8:17, 31, 35).

4:10-19. These verses provide additional instruction on the theme of the two ways. It begins with the traditional call to listen (v. 10) and contrasts the "way of wisdom" (vv. 11-13) with the "path of the wicked" (vv. 14-17), a negative anti-reality illustrated most vividly in 1:10-19. It concludes with a two-verse summary, again contrasting the two ways, this time in terms of cosmic light and darkness.

85. Leo G. Perdue, "Liminality as a Social Setting for Wisdom Instructions," *ZAW* 93 (1981) 114-26; "The Testament of David and Egyptian Royal Instructions," in *Scripture in Context II: More Essays on the Comparative Method*, W. W. Hallow, J. C. Moyer, and L. G. Perdue, eds. (Winona Lake: Eisenbrauns, 1983) 79-96.

4:10-13. The parent refers beyond herself to Wisdom (v. 11), whose way sets the child free to run the path of life unfettered. Verse 10, with its promise of increased life, suggests that the parent's teaching is a conduit of Wisdom, who, as God's cosmic agent, is the true source of life (cf. 3:16, 18, 22; 4:4, 13, 22; 8:35). Instruction (v. 13) is not a hindrance to freedom but its precondition. ("Instruction" is literally "discipline" [מוסר *mûsār*], which does not here imply punishment, as the term often does in American English). To "keep hold" of "discipline" is like committing oneself to an athlete's regimen of a wise diet, exercise, and training. By limiting themselves in this way, athletes are set free to run in top form and speed, without "stumbling" (4:12; cf. 4:16, 19). The encouragement given here, when compared with the language of 3:6 and Isa 40:30-31, is a reminder that a life of forward momentum is a matter of both wisdom (attained by human effort) and divine grace. Thus the argument emphasizes both the responsibility of the hearer for discipline (v. 13) and the gift-character of Wisdom's way as straight and free of obstacles (vv. 11-12; cf. 2:13; 3:6, 23; 10:9). The feminine pronouns ("her," "she") in v. 13*b* do not refer to "instruction" (which is masculine in Hebrew), but to the feminine "wisdom" of v. 11*a* (cf. 3:16; 4:6; 8:35).

4:14-19. This unit begins with a verbal and thematic echo of 1:10, 15. The "path of the wicked," like the house of the adulterous woman, should not be entered, but avoided. One must "turn away from it and pass on" (v. 15). Similar admonitions and language are applied to the adulterous woman as a symbol of folly (7:25; cf. 2:19; 5:8; 7:8; 9:15-16). For v. 16, see Commentary on 6:4-5. Verse 18, with its image of the rising sun, may be compared to the description of the righteous ruler in 2 Sam 23:4.

Verse 19 suggests that sin is blind, "in the dark" about the path it walks: "They do not know what they stumble over." This not knowing is an essential part of sin. Folly lives unaware of consequences, of what lies ahead in the path chosen (28:22). The young man seduced does not know "it will cost him his life" (7:23 NRSV; cf. 9:18). The adulterous woman wanders from the path of life and joy (cf. Ps 16:11), "and she does not know it" (5:6 NRSV). And those who sin by omission, who deny responsibility for their neighbor, claim, "we did not know. . . ." Meanwhile, God knows it and will "repay all according to their deeds" (24:12 NRSV).

4:20-27. The chapter closes with a short instruction with a call to listen motivated by a promise of life. The positive and negative admonitions that follow are linked by body parts used for good or for ill. Such lists of parts of the body function to convey the unity and diversity of human actions (see 6:12-15, 16-19).

4:20-21. The parent's "words" are to be kept in the "heart," that inner receptacle and fountain of the self (see Excursus, "The 'Heart' in the Old Testament," below). The translation "keep them within your heart" is somewhat misleading, for it might seem as if the teaching were only an inward, private matter, not affecting life. The sense (to anticipate v. 23) is, rather, "memorize" these words (cf. 3:3; 7:3) and set them at the center of your consciousness, so that your life flows from them. In an oral culture, only what is

"known" is remembered.[86] Hence, the tremendous emphasis on remembering the parent's utterances and the memorable, poetic form in which the instructions and, especially, the short sayings are couched. The astounding brevity of these sayings often does not survive translation (see Introduction). "To those who find them" is another phrase that sets the parent's teaching parallel to Wisdom as something that must be sought and "found" (cf. 1:28; 3:13; 8:17, 35; 19:8).

4:22. This verse provides the fundamental, rock-bottom motivation for listening and keeping the parent's words: They bring "life" and "health"/"healing," a common pair stemming from Wisdom (14:30; 15:4; cf. 3:8, 18; 4:10).

4:23. The writer here presupposes the utter importance of the "heart" or the "mind" (see Excursus, "The 'Heart' in the Old Testament," below). Because the heart is the center and wellspring of the self, to guard it is to care for one's very life.

86. Walter J. Ong, *Orality and Literacy: The Technologizing of the Word* (London: Methuen, 1982).

❖   ❖   ❖   ❖

EXCURSUS:
THE "HEART" IN THE OLD TESTAMENT

The Hebrew term for "heart" (לב *lēb* or לבב *lēbāb*), often translated as "mind," is easily misunderstood in English translation. In both languages, the heart can simply be the organ in one's chest. But of greater interest biblically is its metaphorical use for the internal wellspring of the acting self. In the modern West, heart and head are often opposed as the loci of feeling and thinking respectively. But the ancient Hebrews used "heart" comprehensively to indicate the inner person, the "I" that is the locus of a person's will, thought (Prov 16:1, 9; 19:21), and feeling (Prov 14:10, 13; 17:22). Thus all of a person's actions (Prov 15:13; 2 Sam 7:3), especially speech (Prov 16:23), flow from the heart, expressing its content, whether good or bad (Gen 6:5; 8:21; Sir 37:17-18; Matt 12:33-35; 18:18-19). Scripture can use related terms, such as "belly" and "kidneys" (כליות *kĕlāyôt*; Jer 11:20; 17:10) in much the same way as "heart" (cf. John 7:38 NRSV).

Most important, one's basic disposition toward God is a matter of the "heart" (Prov 3:5; 19:3; Deut 6:5; 1 Sam 12:20). Like a deep well, the heart has a hidden depth (Prov 20:5). Its deepest depths, what modern psychologists might call the subconscious or the unconscious, only God can plumb (Prov 25:2-3), though hidden even from the heart's owner and friends: "The heart is devious above all else, and beyond cure—who can understand it? I the LORD test the mind and search the heart" (Jer 17:9-10 NRSV and NIV collated; cf. Prov 21:2; 15:11).

When seeking to replace Saul, the Lord finds in David "a man after his own heart" (1 Sam 13:14 NRSV). But even the seer Samuel is not able to recognize the Lord's chosen, because mortals "look on the outward appearance, but the LORD looks on the heart" (1 Sam 16:7 NRSV). In Proverbs, since the heart is the locus of wisdom, it often stands in metonymy for wisdom: Those who are not wise "lack heart" (Prov 7:7; 10:13). Israel shared the general structure of its anthropology concerning heart and other bodily members with its neighbors. The famous "Memphis Theology" from Egypt illustrates the biblical conception well:

> The sight of the eyes, the hearing of the ears, and the smelling the air by the nose, they report to the heart. It is this which causes every completed (concept) to come forth, and it is the tongue which announces what the heart thinks.[87]

Against this background, we can understand the absolute urgency of the admonition in Prov 4:23: "Above all else, guard your heart" (NIV). This is a fundamental precept, like Socrates' "know thyself"; but it goes beyond Socrates in depth and scope. For Israel, all human hearts are inescapably related to the one Lord, whether in loving service, in uncertain vacillation (1 Kgs 18:21; Ps 86:11), or in grievous rebellion (Prov 19:3). Thus in a prayer that plumbs anthropological depths, the psalmist, wary of personal sin and self-deception, concludes, "Search me, O God, and know my heart" (Ps 139:23 NRSV). Augustine understood the biblical heart well: "Our hearts are restless until they find their rest in thee."[88] And when the prophets anticipate God's final renewal of a wounded and disobedient human race, they do it in terms of the heart, as it is the hidden seed of the new humanity: "A new heart I will give you, and a new spirit I will put within you. . . . I will put my spirit within you, and make you follow my statutes . . . and you shall be my people, and I will be your God" (Ezek 36:26-28 NRSV; cf. Ps 51:7-11; Jer 24:7; 31:33).

Even though the heart can stand in metonymy for the whole person in its "mental," inner aspect (what my heart thinks is what I think), there is in the admonition to guard one's heart an awareness of the mysterious reflexivity that humans possess: I can look at myself and make even my inmost self the object of care, reflection, improvement, and betterment. Some commentators have looked upon guarding the heart (Prov 4:23) as equivalent to keeping it from sin. The admonition is more comprehensive than that, but certainly does not exclude it, as is evident from Prov 4:24.

87. *Ancient Near Eastern Texts Relating to the Old Testament,* ed. James B. Pritchard, 3rd ed. (Princeton, N.J.: Princeton University Press, 1969) 5; cf. Prov 6:12-19.
88. Augustine *Confessions* 1.1.

❖   ❖   ❖   ❖

4:24. The close connection of the heart and the external organs and actions that give expression to it are revealed here. "Crooked speech" is literally a "crooked mouth" (עקשות פה *'iqqĕšût peh*), perhaps the most important part of the wicked person's crooked life-style (2:15; 6:12). "Put away" (הסר *hāsēr*; lit., "turn aside") is part of the larger conversion from evil that fools find so difficult (3:7; 4:27; 13:19; 16:6; cf. Col 3:7-10).

4:25. This verse pictures the single focus required of those who pursue wisdom. The saying does not advocate tunnel vision, which is blind to broad reality. Rather, one's vision must be focused, like a navigator who does not lose sight of the star that guides the ship, lest the course be lost and the ship come to a bad end.

4:26-27. These verses continue the thought of v. 25. One may translate the admonition in v. 26a, "Examine the path of your foot" (author's trans.), since "examine" (פלס *pālas*) is the same verb used in 5:6a, 21b. Compare the psalmist, for whom God's word was a "lamp to my feet and a light to my path" (Ps 119:105 NRSV). The NRSV and the NIV differ in the second line over how to take the verb—as a simple future or as continuing the admonition respectively. Both are grammatically possible. Most commentators go with the NRSV, but the NIV version has the advantage of not interrupting the sequences of precepts. In v. 27, the singleminded pursuit of the right path is reiterated in an image best known from the deuteronomic tradition of not turning aside from the law of God, either to the right or to the left (cf. Josh 1:7).

REFLECTIONS

1. "Tradition," Chesterton wrote, "means giving votes to the most obscure of all classes, our ancestors. It is the democracy of the dead. Tradition refuses to submit to the small and arrogant oligarchy of those who merely happen to be walking about. . . . We will have the dead at our councils."[89]

Human wisdom is a matter of tradition, the knowers passing on what they know to those who need to know, whether in medicine, law, or family. Most of what we do in life is based on what we have observed or have been taught, on what is commonly accepted by our culture and, more narrowly, by the overlapping subcultures and groups to which we belong. Without such cultural common sense, our lives would be reduced to constantly reinventing the wheel. A true "permanent revolution" is unlivable. In spite of massive changes in the modern era, much in life remains traditional, handed down from the past. Culture is inherently, necessarily conservative—as in, "If it ain't broke, don't fix it." The question for a wise society, however, is this: *What* from the past should be retained and conserved? What from our fathers and mothers should we embrace, and what should we reject? Wisdom also asks, By what criteria do we distinguish the ancestral dross from the gold? Labels like "progressive," "conservative," and "liberal" are not helpful here, because they do not tell us what is to be conserved or changed, or why.

Biblical wisdom appeals to creation order and the distilled experience of past generations to provide the insight for meeting new situations. The abiding patterns of reality, including human nature, provide a context, or frame, within which we can recognize the new.

> Wisdom is the perception that every novelty, in its own way, manifests the permanence and stability of the created order, so that, however astonishing and undreamt of it may be, it is not utterly incommensurable with what has gone before. This does not imply a pretense that the unlikeness of the new to the old is unreal. Even unlike things can be seen as part of the same universe if there is an order which embraces them in a relation to one another.[90]

Wisdom is the ability to perceive the new appositely, in terms of something humans have met before. A new scam on the stock market can be recognized by someone who understands the market's principles and processes and remembers the shenanigans of the 1920s and 1980s. The wise, in any area of life, know "there is nothing new under the sun."

Thus the great importance of history and tradition and the pervasive biblical insistence that we remember and not forget the past (Deuteronomy 8; 1 Cor 11:23-26). Through the godly experience and wisdom of the past, we are equipped to recognize the things that matter, the cast of characters, the events and situations that make up the dangers and opportunities of life for good or for ill. None of us lives long enough to experience enough of God, world, and humanity to be adequately equipped without the wisdom of the past.

2. The idea of "two ways" is fundamental to the piety and worldview of both Proverbs and Psalms (see Psalm 1). The sharp polarity of the two ways is a teaching tool parallel to the

---

89. Quoted by Barbara Grizzuti Harrison, "Arguing with the Pope," *Harper's* (April 1994) 56.
90. O'Donovan, *Resurrection and Moral Order*, 189-90.

sharp contrast between "righteous" and "wicked" in Proverbs 10–15. The point is not so much that people can be neatly separated into "good guys" (us) and "bad guys" (them), as in some simple "cops and robbers" film, wholly unaware of the moral ambiguity that runs through every human heart. Rather, we all are constantly placed before choices or "steps" (4:12) that eventually shape paths, patterns, habits, a way of life, a form of culture that settles into character. Like the footpaths that cut across campus greens, such paths are formed over time by the steps of many generations, each person, on a smaller scale, pursuing the goal of wisdom or unwitting folly. The steps we make and the paths we take depend not only on what we have inherited, but also on where we want to go. Paths are also tradition.

3. Traditions can do damage. Traditions are especially powerful among those who assume them as self-evident and ultimate and have no higher norm by which tradition can be corrected and renewed as circumstances change. Thus Mark 7:1-13 may be taken as a sharp critique of the Christian church whenever it elevates tradition above the dynamic word and purposes of God. Traditions also damage those who reject them. Ironically, in this case, tradition limits people's choices to what is *not* the tradition, thereby cutting people off from their roots; the baby gets thrown out with the bath water. This happens not only with individuals, but also with generations (Judg 2:10). Among those who flee from tradition, sometimes the content changes, but the interpersonal processes remain (as when a dogmatic fundamentalist parent raises a dogmatic liberal child, or vice versa). The French say, "The more things change, the more they remain the same." On a larger scale, one may consider the historical continuities and discontinuities of the French Revolution, with its reign of terror and devotion to the goddess of reason. In their wholesale rejection of a flawed Christianity, the revolutionaries were unable to separate the wheat from the chaff. T. S. Eliot once wrote that the surest thing to drive out old evil is new evil.

4. "The beginning of wisdom is this: Get wisdom,/ and whatever else you get, get insight" (4:7 NRSV; cf. 1:7; 9:10). Scripture has a number of statements about "the one thing needful": Love the Lord your God with all your heart, soul, and might (Deut 6:5). Seek first the kingdom of God and his righteousness (Matt 6:33). What does the Lord require of you but to do justice, and to love kindness, and to walk humbly with your God (Mic 6:8). Fear God, and keep his commandments; for that is the whole duty of everyone (Eccl 12:13). Proverbs puts the getting of wisdom first, because wisdom is the key to God's reality (Proverbs 8).

Finally, Christ is the wisdom of God, revealed in the person of Jesus (1 Cor 1:24, 30). Thus the getting of wisdom and the knowing of God in Christ are inseparable, fulfilling the sense of Prov 9:10, "The fear of the LORD is the beginning of wisdom" (NRSV).

5. Proverbs 4:17 represents moral-spiritual activity under the universal figure of food: "bread of wickedness," "wine of violence" (see 30:8-9, 14-15, 20, 22, 25). Leon Kass has shown that "literal" eating itself is a bodily activity that lays bare human nature and its cultural propensities for virtue and vice.[91] For humans, eating is never merely nourishment, no more so than sex is ever merely sex (see 30:20). When we eat, we ingest creation, and this activity speaks more convincingly than can words of our most deeply held commitments concerning creation, God, and human relations. A serious consideration of who in our world eats and who goes hungry is fundamental to a biblical view of justice.[92] A German proverb declares, "What you eat is what you are." Like all proverbs, this one does not tell the whole truth. Yet, what and how we eat reveals who we are and shows that material things are vehicles of spirit. In the profound film *Babette's Feast,* for example, we see culturally shaped creation (food) as a means of grace, reconciling estranged sinners.

---

91. Leon Kass, *The Hungry Soul: Eating and the Perfecting of Our Nature* (New York: Macmillan, 1994).
92. See Rolf P. Knierim, "Food, Land, and Justice," in *The Task of Old Testament Theology: Substance, Method, and Cases* (Grand Rapids: Eerdmans, 1995) 225-43.

Food is everything that nourishes us as persons. Jesus said, "My food [bread] is to do the will of him who sent me" (John 4:34 NRSV). The "capable wife" of Proverbs 31 "does not eat the bread of idleness" (31:27 NRSV). These images represent the nourishment with which humans feed their souls. Our spiritual food and drink (both good and bad) is thus any cultural product that shapes and fills our inward self, whether music, speech, film, literature, advertisements, urban architecture, or the daily experience of commuting in bumper-to-bumper traffic, breathing smog.

The paradoxical tendencies of humans to eat what is not good for them, to eat too much (25:16) or too little, or to covet a neighbor's piece of pie are all signals of human distress and folly, signals of our painful alienation from our bodies, from that personal piece of cosmos that is I and you. What we do with real food, we also do with metaphorical food. Contemporary Americans need only to turn on the TV or radio to be flooded with the "wine of violence" and stuffed with the "bread of wickedness."[93] Christian folk need to turn away from junk food for the soul and cultivate space and time for rumination on "whatever is true . . . honorable . . . just . . . pure . . . pleasing, whatever is commendable, if there is any excellence and if there is anything worthy of praise" (Phil 4:8 NRSV).

6. Proverbs 4:20-21 employs the conventional "call to hear" and begins a sequence of bodily organs that stitch the instruction together. In a certain sense, the ear is obviously for hearing and the eyes for seeing (20:12; cf. Ps 94:9). But hearing and seeing are by no means automatic. Scripture is full of admonitions to hear, because people can choose not to and sometimes are simply unable to (Exod 6:9, 12; Deut 29:4). Alternately, the blind lead the blind (Matt 15:14), and a "foolish and senseless [lit., "heartless"] people . . . have eyes but do not see . . . have ears but do not hear" (Jer 5:21 NRSV; cf. Ps 115:6; Isa 6:9-10; 43:8; Mark 4:9-12). Hearing and seeing, or their lack, are reflexes of an open or recalcitrant "heart" (see Excursus, "The 'Heart' in the Old Testament," 60-61, and the parallelism of 2:2; 18:15). The hymnic confession, "Once I was blind, but now I see," concerns the inner self. Proverbs speaks of a "listening ear" (15:31; 20:12; 25:12), but Solomon, wisest of kings, is given a "listening heart" to judge the people and to distinguish right from wrong (1 Kgs 3:9). Jesus, knowing of resistance to his teaching (Mark 4:9-12), ends his parables in wisdom fashion, "He who has ears to hear, let him hear" (Luke 14:35 NRSV).[94]

7. The world and life are filled with distractions, and "the eye is not satisfied with seeing" (Eccl 1:8 NRSV; cf. Prov 27:20). Jesus made the point more radically, "If your right eye causes you to sin, pluck it out" (Matt 5:29 RSV). The admonition of Proverbs 4:25 is concerned first with avoiding sin, but its message is broader. One must avoid not only sin, but also anything that impedes the path to excellence (Phil 4:8): "The good is the enemy of the excellent." Only those who resolutely "put first things first"[95] gain their goal. But "a fool's eyes wander to the ends of the earth" (17:24 NIV).

93. See Neil Postman, *Amusing Ourselves to Death: Public Discourse in the Age of Show Business* (New York: Penguin, 1985).
94. See David L. Jeffrey, "Ears to Hear," *A Dictionary of Biblical Tradition in English Literature* (Grand Rapids: Eerdmans, 1992) 219-20.
95. Stephen R. Covey, *The Seven Habits of Highly Successful People* (New York: Simon and Schuster, 1989) habit number 3.

PROVERBS 5:1-23, ADULTERY AS FOLLY; MARRIAGE AS WISDOM

NIV

5 My son, pay attention to my wisdom,
   listen well to my words of insight,
[2]that you may maintain discretion
   and your lips may preserve knowledge.
[3]For the lips of an adulteress drip honey,
   and her speech is smoother than oil;
[4]but in the end she is bitter as gall,
   sharp as a double-edged sword.
[5]Her feet go down to death;
   her steps lead straight to the grave.[a]
[6]She gives no thought to the way of life;
   her paths are crooked, but she knows it not.

[7]Now then, my sons, listen to me;
   do not turn aside from what I say.
[8]Keep to a path far from her,
   do not go near the door of her house,
[9]lest you give your best strength to others
   and your years to one who is cruel,
[10]lest strangers feast on your wealth
   and your toil enrich another man's house.
[11]At the end of your life you will groan,
   when your flesh and body are spent.
[12]You will say, "How I hated discipline!
   How my heart spurned correction!
[13]I would not obey my teachers
   or listen to my instructors.
[14]I have come to the brink of utter ruin
   in the midst of the whole assembly."

[15]Drink water from your own cistern,
   running water from your own well.
[16]Should your springs overflow in the streets,
   your streams of water in the public
      squares?
[17]Let them be yours alone,
   never to be shared with strangers.
[18]May your fountain be blessed,
   and may you rejoice in the wife of your youth.
[19]A loving doe, a graceful deer—
   may her breasts satisfy you always,
   may you ever be captivated by her love.
[20]Why be captivated, my son, by an adulteress?
   Why embrace the bosom of another man's
      wife?

NRSV

5 My child, be attentive to my wisdom;
   incline your ear to my understanding,
[2] so that you may hold on to prudence,
   and your lips may guard knowledge.
[3] For the lips of a loose[a] woman drip honey,
   and her speech is smoother than oil;
[4] but in the end she is bitter as wormwood,
   sharp as a two-edged sword.
[5] Her feet go down to death;
   her steps follow the path to Sheol.
[6] She does not keep straight to the path of life;
   her ways wander, and she does not know
      it.

[7] And now, my child,[b] listen to me,
   and do not depart from the words of my
      mouth.
[8] Keep your way far from her,
   and do not go near the door of her house;
[9] or you will give your honor to others,
   and your years to the merciless,
[10] and strangers will take their fill of your wealth,
   and your labors will go to the house of an
      alien;
[11] and at the end of your life you will groan,
   when your flesh and body are consumed,
[12] and you say, "Oh, how I hated discipline,
   and my heart despised reproof!
[13] I did not listen to the voice of my teachers
   or incline my ear to my instructors.
[14] Now I am at the point of utter ruin
   in the public assembly."

[15] Drink water from your own cistern,
   flowing water from your own well.
[16] Should your springs be scattered abroad,
   streams of water in the streets?
[17] Let them be for yourself alone,
   and not for sharing with strangers.
[18] Let your fountain be blessed,
   and rejoice in the wife of your youth,
[19]   a lovely deer, a graceful doe.
   May her breasts satisfy you at all times;
   may you be intoxicated always by her love.

NIV

²¹For a man's ways are in full view of the LORD,
    and he examines all his paths.
²²The evil deeds of a wicked man ensnare him;
    the cords of his sin hold him fast.
²³He will die for lack of discipline,
    led astray by his own great folly.

ᵃ5 Hebrew *Sheol*

NRSV

²⁰ Why should you be intoxicated, my son, by
        another woman
    and embrace the bosom of an adulteress?
²¹ For human ways are under the eyes of the
        LORD,
    and he examines all their paths.
²² The iniquities of the wicked ensnare them,
    and they are caught in the toils of their sin.
²³ They die for lack of discipline,
    and because of their great folly they are lost.

ᵃHeb *strange*   ᵇGk Vg: Heb *children*

COMMENTARY

This parental speech contrasts adultery and marriage as the right and wrong modes of sexual love. The passage functions not only literally, but also as metaphor and illustration within Proverbs 1–9. Literally, we have a warning against adultery and a frank invitation to the erotic delights of married love, expressed in liquid images. Metaphorically, desire for someone who is not one's spouse is similar to the love of Folly, while love of Wisdom is represented by desire and delight in one's spouse. Finally, as illustration, the opposition of adultery to married love concretely shows that sin and folly cross created boundaries, while the play of eros within marriage illustrates freedom within form. Underlying these metaphors is the cosmic principle that God has set good limits to human play and freedom, just as God has set limits to the watery powers of the sea (see Commentary on 8:27-29).

Chapter 5, an instruction, begins with the usual call to hear (vv. 1-2), followed by a warning against the "loose woman" (lit., "strange woman" [זרה *zārâ*], NRSV margin) in vv. 3-14. A contrasting, metaphor-rich invitation to enjoy one's own spouse (vv. 15-19) leads to an appeal to the son to draw his own conclusions from the foregoing (v. 19). Finally, the argument is grounded theologically (vv. 20-23). God's eyes see the course of a person's life. God sees to it that habits have consequences.

5:1-2. The opening verses are a variation on the typical invitation to hear. The pairing of "my wisdom" and "my understanding" is especially

important, for it suggests that the parent's wisdom communicates cosmic wisdom and understanding (8:1, the two terms refer to aspects of one reality). Heeding the parent's wisdom will help the son in "prudence," the capacity for private thought (see Commentary on 2:10-11), and will enable his "lips" to "guard knowledge" (cf. Mal 2:7). This unusual image suggests that the organs of speech are the public guardians of the heart's deep truths. The lips, so to speak, are the border guards that allow thoughts to be released or to remain unspoken (cf. 17:27-28; 18:2; Ps 141:3). The issue here is not duplicity of our inner and outer, private and public selves (on which see 26:22-26). Rather, there are times to keep silent and times to speak (Eccl 3:7). Through their lips, fools and the wise distinguish themselves (15:1-2, 7; 18:6-7).

5:3. This verse uses "lips" as a pivot to shift from the son to the seductress. The verse as a whole is highly sensual, a fact somewhat disguised by the translation "speech" in v. 3*b* (lit., "mouth"/"palate" [חך *ḥēk*], with a pun on "lap"/"bosom" [חיק *ḥêq*]; see 5:20; Deut 28:56; Mic 7:5). One may translate, "her mouth is slicker than olive oil." The imagery is suggestive on several levels. The liquid image of lips dripping honey appears more elaborately in Cant 4:11 (cf. Cant 2:3; 5:13, 16). On one level, it refers to the "smooth talk" or "sweet talk" that flows from the woman's lips (26:28). What she says is easy to swallow; she competes with Wisdom in sweetness (24:13-14). On another level, "lips" and "mouth" evoke the liquid delights and organs of love (see Commentary on 5:15-19; 20:14; 30:20), which turn into a deadly trap when offered by the "strange woman," who is out of bounds (2:16).

The image of honey is especially telling in its ambiguity. It is not quite solid, not quite liquid. It does not hold its shape or stay in place. Its boundaries are not firm. It represents what is sweet and good (16:24; 24:13-14), and also what is addictive and potentially dangerous. To eat too much honey is not good (25:27a). Greedy flies get stuck in it, and it sticks to greedy children. Honey certainly sweetens life. But by itself, it neither makes a square meal nor quenches one's thirst. A satisfied person disdains honey (27:7). It is crucial to take only the honey that is properly yours and only the right amount for you, lest it make you sick (see Commentary on 25:16).

Consider the story of Samson (Judges 13–16), though it employs a symbol system for holiness that is not found in Proverbs. Samson was a Nazirite, separated for divine service. As a holy person, he had forsworn all that is "unclean" (Num 6:1-8). But when he got honey out of the lion's carcass, he crossed the boundary between holy and unclean, for what is dead is especially unclean. The carcass is contagious and will render the honey (good in itself) unclean. In the Samson narrative cycle, this episode mirrors Samson's unfaithfulness in getting his sexual "sweets" from ritually unclean Philistine women. But it also symbolizes Israel's sin in leaving its calling as a holy nation, while seeking its cultural "sweets" from the foreign societies around them. Samson, in language that echoes Gen 3:6, gives some of the unclean honey to his parents, who eat it (Judg 14:9).

Thus v. 3 vividly portrays the reality and the ambiguity of temptation, both to illicit love and to the love of folly, in line with the larger metaphorical system of Proverbs 1–9.

5:4. This verse follows the tale begun in v. 3 to its end. The sweet has become bitter, and slippery softness has become sharp. Literally, "her end" is bitter as wormwood, sharp as a "sword with mouths" (i.e., two-edged sword; Judg 3:16; Ps 149:6). A sword has two edges, or "mouths," that "devour" those it kills (Isa 1:20). The imagery here ironically reverses the devouring roles of deadly male sword and female mouths (literal and

metaphorical). In addition, the language intersects with the "way" imagery pervasive in chaps. 1–9. To enter the "door" of the forbidden woman's body (or "house, 5:8; cf. 8:3, 34; 9:14; Job 31:9-10) is the end of the road called Folly (cf. 14:12; 16:25; 24:13-14). Her body/house is a place of no return on a dead-end street where Sheol swallows fools alive (see Commentary on 1:12; 2:18-19; 7:27; 9:13-18).

5:5-6. The writer makes the connection of wrong woman, ways, and death explicit in these verses. "Her feet" may also be rendered "her legs" (sometimes a euphemism in Hebrew; see 2 Kgs 18:27; Isa 7:20), which themselves "go down to death" even as they lead young men on the same path. Those who walk the path of folly are blind. The woman herself wanders toward death and "does not know it" (see Commentary on 4:19). For "Sheol," see Commentary on 1:12.

5:7-14. The focus turns to the son and spells out the consequences of yielding to seduction by the "stranger" of vv. 3-6. A brief call to hear (v. 7) leads to an admonition (v. 8), followed by an extended account of the negative consequences of not heeding the warning (vv. 9-14). These consequences are both social (vv. 9-10) and psycho-spiritual (vv. 12-14), as the youth becomes remorseful about past actions whose present consequences must be lived with. Hindsight is clearer than foresight. Verse 14 perhaps affords a glimpse of grace.

5:7-8. The parent speaks with profound awareness that the sons are themselves responsible for what they do with his words (see Commentary on 8:9). They can listen, but they can also "depart from the words of [his] mouth" (a contrast to the "mouth" of the temptress). So he appeals to their growing maturity and ability to discern consequences and to take appropriate action.

Verse 8 spells out the required evasive action in the light of the highly visual nature of male sexuality (6:25; Matt 5:27-29): "Keep your way far from her." The father assumes that his son, like any immature male, may be tempted to have sex without love. He advises the son to take responsibility for this weakness (a conflict of biology and humanity) and set his course in another direction. "The door of her house" represents the threshold, the point of entry and no return. This is where one crosses the borderline and enters a new and deadly world (see Commentary on 5:4).

5:9-11. The writer warns of the social and personal consequences of trespassing limits. The "cruel" one may be the outraged husband (cf. 6:34-35) or perhaps Sheol, which devours the dead (1:12). The heaping up of masculine parallels in vv. 9-10 makes the reference indeterminate: "others"//"cruel one" [sing.]//"strangers"//"alien." It is not clear who the others are. Nor is it specified how the personal loss will take place. This open-endedness permits the reader to apply the admonition to his or her own life-world, whatever the circumstances may be. The same open-endedness appears also when the same vague adjectives ("strange"/"alien") are used to describe any woman who is not one's proper sexual partner (2:16; 5:3).

The son who transgresses sexual limits is himself responsible for loss of fortune, health, reputation, and vitality. It is not just that others take and enjoy it (v. 10; cf. Job 31:9-10), but that he foolishly gives to others what is essential to his own existence (cf. 31:3). The terms "honor," "best strength," "wealth," "years," and "labors" are also suggestive of a variety of possibilities, including venereal disease. This latter prospect is explicitly included in v. 11, "when your flesh and body are consumed." This clause, with its traditional components, may also refer literally and metaphorically to a variety of psychosomatic illnesses (cf. Job 33:21; Pss 71:9; 73:26).

5:12-14. These verses conclude this section of the instruction with a future autobiographical speech, in which the (potentially) erring son owns up to his folly. In daring fashion, the parent enters empathetically into the life-world of the son. The rhetorical strategy is hypothetical and dangerous: How does the parent know what might be in the mind of a child, especially in relation to events that are only potential? Wisdom knows that acts have consequences. You reap what you sow. The parent can "know" what the son will experience because the invented speech here reflects the pattern first described by Wisdom herself (1:24-25, 29-31).

In vv. 12-14 the son's folly is first the rejection of community "discipline" and "reproof" (see Commentary on 12:1) as mediated by parents and teachers (vv. 12-13; cf. 3:11-12 of the divine

"parent"). The son's words reflect first on his behavior and conclude with its consequences: near ruin in the community (v. 14).

5:15-19. The instruction here takes a joyful turn, enjoining delight in one's wife, while continuing the warning against the strange woman. As in v. 3, sexuality is portrayed in liquid images. But a sharp contrast exists between the deadly portrait of honey and oil in v. 3 and the life-giving well and waters of married sexuality in vv. 15-19. These verses also repeat the pattern of spending personal honor and goods for "strangers" (vv. 9-10), in the image of "scattering springs . . . abroad" (vv. 16-17).

In this passage, all the water sources mentioned are parallel metaphors for "the wife," as is finally made clear in v. 18. The poem plays on the life-giving and joy-enhancing qualities of water. In arid, hot Palestine (cf. 30:16) water is exceedingly precious. Thus water flowing freely down the street is a disaster (v. 16). Water spilled is life lost.

Palestine is generally arid, especially in the south. In summer rain does not fall; all is hot and dry (26:1). Water is experienced as the very stuff of life and joy. Cisterns are usually carved out of solid rock; they are used to collect and store rain water, either for the community or (as here) for private use. The young husband may drink only from his own "cistern." A well is dug in the ground to tap the aquifer. Once dug, a well might be hotly contested (Gen 26:18-22). Wells, like cisterns and suitable wives, are hard to acquire. Cities and individuals jealously guarded their water sources in order to preserve the life of the community or family in times of war, siege, or drought. The strange woman's "honey" (v. 3) and the sweet "waters" of Lady Folly (9:17) are deadly and produce conflict precisely because they are stolen.

There is a gradual progression in the quality of water sources pictured in vv. 15-16. A cistern stores water and is liable to contamination (though cistern water is better than no water at all).[96] But a well continually receives fresh water from the aquifer and produces running or "living water" (נזלים *nōzĕlîm*). No sensible person would prefer a cistern to a "fountain of living water" (Jer

---

96. See "Water Works," in *Anchor Bible Dictionary,* 6 vols. (New York: Doubleday, 1992).

2:13 NRSV; cf. Cant 4:15). The images continue to grow in clarity and desirability. The "fountains" flow with "streams of water" (v. 16; cf. Ps 46:4; Ezek 47:1-12) and prefigure the fountains made by God (8:24). These sequential, parallel images do not stand in contrast with each other, as if several wives were portrayed. Rather, they cumulatively picture the one wife as a personal source of life, sexual delight, blessing, and fecundity. They also reinforce the parallel of wife and wisdom (cf. "fountain" in 13:14; 14:27). The "springs" of marriage are parallel to the life-giving "springs" of creation (8:24, 29).

Verse 17 makes clear that the water sources in vv. 15-16, 18 do not refer to male fluids (cf. Sir 26:19-21) or to progeny. Some have argued that the shift from singular water sources to plural in this verse indicates a shift in subject. Instead, the plural serves to intensify the notion of abundance found in the wife (the word "water" [מים mayim] itself is plural in Hebrew; cf. "all my springs are in you," said of the Lord in Ps 87:7). As v. 18*b* makes explicit, the water images all refer to the wife (cf. Cant 4:12, 15). A wife is "for her [husband] alone." Sexual exclusivity is basic to human well-being in marriage, family, and society (cf. Exod 20:14). But fidelity is also essential to healthy and joyous sexual love. In the Song of Songs, this point is beautifully made by the joyous refrain, "My beloved is mine and I am his" (Cant 2:16 NRSV; 6:3; cf. Cant 6:9; 7:10; 8:12), by the imagery of "a garden locked, a fountain sealed" (Cant 4:12, 15 NRSV), and by the private vineyard (Cant 8:12).

Verses 16-17 present an implicit picture of retributive correspondence, a sort of poetic justice. The husband's (potential) unfaithfulness is answered by the wife's sexual exploitation, willingly or unwillingly, by "strangers"—that is, those who are alien to the marriage bond and its privileges (cf. v. 10). This sort of correspondence, in which the "punishment fits the crime," appears not only in wisdom literature, but also in other biblical genres (see Job 31:9-10; Amos 7:17).

The "riddle" of the water sources in vv. 15-17 is answered in v. 18 by spelling out the reference as "the wife of your youth." This fountain, when faithfully loved, is blessed—that is, a source of blessing (cf. 3:13, 18, of the man who finds Wisdom; Ps 128:3). The young man is com-

manded to "rejoice" (שמח śāmaḥ) in his wife. The same verb is used of mutual divine and human delight in each other and the good (Ps 104:15, 31; Cant 3:11; see also Commentary on Prov 8:30-31; cf. Isa 62:5).

The image of the beloved wife shifts to that of "a lovely deer, a graceful doe" (v. 19). The use of animal metaphors to portray lovers is universal. Song of Songs 2:8-9 uses similar figures for a male beloved, and Cant 4:5 portrays the young woman's breasts as twin fawns.[97] There is a wordplay in "may her breasts satisfy you." The Hebrew for "breasts" (דד dad) plays on "love" (דוד dôd, 7:18), while "satisfy" (רוה rāwâ) also connotes "drinking one's fill," an echo of the liquid images in vv. 15-18 (see Isa 60:16, where restored Israel "shall suck the breasts of kings" [NRSV]). "Be intoxicated" (שגה śāgâ) generally means "wander," "go astray" as when drunk (20:1; Isa 28:7). This verb links vv. 19, 20, and 23. Here it conveys the unfettered passion of love. Through repetition, however, it creates a contrast between marital and extra-marital love (vv. 19-20) and reinforces the parallel between love out of bounds and folly (v. 23).

5:20-23. These verses draw the moral from the preceding instructions. The language recapitulates earlier moments in the chapter (cf. v. 3 with v. 20; vv. 6, 8 with v. 21; v. 5 with v. 22; vv. 5, 12 with v. 23). In the light of married realities (vv. 15-19), the unreal pleasures of the "stranger" make no sense. So "Why be . . . intoxicated" (lit., "led astray") by "another woman" (lit., "strange" [זרה zārâ])? The rhetorical question invites the son to draw his own conclusions, to "own" the logic of the parental instruction. In view of the divinely approved delights of marital love, wandering is simply folly.

Verse 21 grounds the preceding wisdom in the Lord. God has created all things good, including male and female sexuality (Genesis 1; 2:18-25). But humans are accountable and transparent to their Maker, before whom even the cosmic depths lie open (15:3, 11; 16:2; 24:12; cf. Jer 16:17-18). The Lord judges human actions and ways (cf. 5:6), the myriad acts and steps that comprise a life and its fundamental direction. Finally, the parallel lan-

97. See Othmar Keel, *The Song of Songs* (Minneapolis: Fortress, 1994) 22-29.

guage of 4:26 and 5:21 reveals that divine oversight and human responsibility are correlates.

The principle underlying the example of seduction is summarized in v. 22 (cf. Sir 23:16-21). People get caught in the netlike toils of their own sin, like a spider strangely stuck in the web it has spun (see 1:17-18, 31-32; cf. Job 18:7-10). The juxtaposition of vv. 21 and 22 conveys something of the mystery of God's justice. While God's are the eyes that see, and God is the one with whom we have to do, the working out of human good and evil is generally a mundane, even banal thing (see Commentary on 13:6).

The instruction concludes by returning to basic themes of discipline (self-control and self-denial for a higher good) and the threat of death for one led astray by folly (v. 19).

REFLECTIONS

1. In the Lord's prayer, Christians pray, "lead us not into temptation." With respect to the "strange woman," the parent specifies the human task of avoiding temptation, whatever that may be (5:8). Both the prayer and the task of watching our step are necessary. The ancient Latin proverb says, "Pray and work" (*Ora et labora*). That is, work at what you pray for, knowing that the gift of grace is often the gift of work (Phil 2:13). The particular sins we pray about and work at avoiding vary according to our position and personality. Wise recovering alcoholics avoid bars and go to AA meetings; godly traveling salespersons avoid singles bars; smart gluttons stay away from ice cream parlors; members of Congress who have integrity shun lobbyists with money (see Commentary on 17:23). If the shoe fits, wear it.

2. Chapter 5 again reflects on a person's way. Although life patterns have been traced by the feet of our forebears, each new generation and individual is responsible for making their own way in the world. Cultural or familial traditions and patterns of behavior, like paths, may help or hinder, may lead to weal or to woe. But the responsibility for choosing and the determination to walk the chosen path rest with each new generation. It may be difficult to break out of unhealthy or dysfunctional family paths. But blaming the past does not obviate present responsibility to make our own way as humans.

3. The Lord limits the potentially destructive powers of the sea by keeping its mighty waters within boundaries (8:29; see 2 Esdr 4:13-19). The shore limits the "play" of the waves. But just as when the sea surges onto land as a hurricane or typhoon, great harm is done, so also human sexuality is a great and good power that turns destructive when out of bounds. But within the safety zone of marriage the liquid play of sex is a life-generating, life-enhancing delight (5:15-19). Marriage is not an arbitrary (and thus dispensable) human invention, one of several possibilities for taking care of sexual drives, procreation, and the rearing of the next generation. In the cosmic-social terms of Proverbs 1–9 (cf. Gen 1:27-28; 2:21-24; Matt 19:3-9), marriage is a divine creation that sets the parameters within which human cultural and personal variations may take place. Similarly, the Ten Commandments, which set limits, are basic boundaries within which humans are free to function. Outside those divine, cosmic boundaries, humans cause damage to themselves and to others.

4. Some readers object to the limited portrayal of women in these chapters—either as desirable wife or as desirable temptress in relation to the son whom the parents address.[98] There is also concern that the book seems not to protest against the exploitation of women who may be forced to prostitution by social marginalization or poverty (23:26-28; see Genesis 38).[99] However, it is characteristic of the proverb genre to focus on one aspect of an issue and

98. See C. Osiek, "Reading the Bible as Women," in *The New Interpreter's Bible*, vol. 1 (Nashville: Abingdon, 1994) 181-87.
99. See Carole Fontaine, "Proverbs," in Carol A. Newsom and Sharon H. Ringe, eds., *The Women's Bible Commentary* (Louisville: Westminster, 1992) 146-47.

not treat all. The proverb genre often portrays evils without comment, because the reader is assumed to know they are evil (e.g., 26:20-23). Moreover, the book's appeal to God's defense of the widow, the orphan, and the poor shows that vulnerable women must be provided for and protected from exploitation (15:25; 22:16, 22-23; 23:10-11).

The book's focus on woman as wife/mother or temptress arises largely from its male-oriented symbolism of wisdom and folly, (see Overview to chaps. 1–9). This focus also stems from Israel's commitment to marriage and family as created realities (Gen 2:24), a commitment that some women echo today.[100] Because these chapters are directed at males, the genesis of female prostitution and adultery is largely ignored, except in as much as male behavior makes them possible. If males heeded the parental advice to be faithful in marriage and to avoid illicit liaisons, female prostitution and adultery would obviously cease. The writer is concerned with the damage that male promiscuity can do to family, society, and self. The problem for the writer is to persuade young males not to yield to their promiscuous sexual impulses. In the same manner that dreams of illicit wealth were shattered (1:10-19), the parent exploits adolescent male fantasies of illicit sexual bliss to debunk them (7:10-27). Male sexual desire is a force that needs to be disciplined and set within the context of lifelong commitment and love (5:15-19).

100. See Osiek, "Reading the Bible as Women," 186.

❖   ❖   ❖   ❖

Excursus: Death and the Strange Woman in Proverbs 1–9

Who is the figure in Proverbs 1–9 designated by the parallel terms "strange woman" (אשה זרה *'iššâ zārâ*; NRSV, "loose woman") and "alien" (נכריה *nokriyyâ*; NRSV, "adulteress")?[101] And how are we to understand the constant connection between this woman and death (2:16-19; 5:5-6, 20; 7:5, 22-27; cf. 9:18)?

Compare the meaning of death in Proverbs 1–9 to the paradise story of the first temptation: "Of the tree of the knowledge of good and evil you shall not eat, for in the day that you eat of it you shall die" (Gen 2:17 NRSV). The tree itself, as Eve saw, is simply "good" (Gen 3:6), an echo of "God saw that it was good" in the creation story of Genesis 1. But because God has put the tree "out of bounds" with respect to eating, the good tree becomes a source of disorder and death.[102]

The "strange woman" in Proverbs 1–9 is, in the first instance, "your neighbor's wife" (see Commentary on 6:24, 29). A woman (or man) other than one's spouse, like the fruit in the garden, may be "good . . . a delight to the eyes." But she is not good as a mate for anyone other than her own husband. Her strangeness is a function of the exclusivity of the marriage relation (cf. Jer 3:25, of spiritual "adultery" with "strangers," where the foreignness of the Baals is secondary). In this (sexual) regard, the creator has placed the strange woman off limits, out of bounds. To eat this fruit causes disorder and death (see Reflections on Proverbs 4, number 5). In the second instance, the strange woman is a metaphorical illustration of folly.

The exact (male) semantic counterpart of the "strange woman" is the "strange man" of

101. See R. N. Whybray, *Proverbs*, NCBC (Grand Rapids: Eerdmans, 1994) 72-73 and bibliography.
102. See Richard D. Nelson, *Raising Up a Faithful Priest: Community and Priesthood in Biblical Theology* (Lousiville: Westminster/John Knox, 1994).

Deut 25:5. According to the law of levirate marriage, a widow may not marry a "stranger" (זר איש *'îš zār*)—that is, someone outside the family—but is restricted to the brothers of her dead husband. The strange woman of Proverbs, like the "strange fire" offered by Aaron's sons (Lev 10:1), is something God has not "commanded" or allowed (cf. "illicit fire," Num 3:4 NRSV). Again, only the priests are allowed to touch holy things or to make offerings. With respect to these functions, even fellow Israelites are called "strangers" or "outsiders" (Num 1:51; 16:40[17:5]; 18:4 [זר *zār*, the word used in Proverbs]). This common usage of *zār* in the sense of "another," or of one who stands outside a specific relation, appears also in Prov 27:2 (cf. 6:24; 14:10; 1 Kgs 3:18; Job 19:27). The stereotypical parallel of "strange" and "alien" does not affect this usage of *zār*. God's work, when it is contrary to human expectations, is "strange" and "alien" (Isa 28:24; cf. Prov 27:2).

To step beyond the boundaries of freedom set by God is to attempt the impossible: to live outside the very conditions that make life possible. In the end, humans can no more live outside God's moral order than can the proverbial "fish out of water" live outside God's biotic order. Outside the ordinances of God we find not life but, ultimately, death. Humans have little difficulty seeing this truth in the so-called natural world. We cannot leap off a building, flap our arms, and fly. If we eat poison, we get sick or die. But humans are more easily confused in the moral sphere because of the great freedom God has entrusted to us—freedom to shape culture, language, art, and even created institutions as fundamental as marriage and family in a variety of ways. Nevertheless, a culture that thinks there are no limits to freedom finds itself in the "out of bounds" territory of death and chaos. Death is the ultimate limit to freedom. It drives us to accept reality and to find the good within its limits. It is this truth that Pharaoh was unwilling to learn, when plague after plague confronted him (Exodus 5–11).

The freedom to shape the world and our way in it has thus led to opposite errors. On the one hand, there is legalism, which attempts to prevent evil and ensure life by making laws on top of God's laws, to avoid coming close to sin. Since sex is dangerous, we will forbid dancing. Alcohol is dangerous, so we will forbid drinking. Such an approach to religion has only the appearance of wisdom; it errs when it identifies human conventions with God's will. The apostle Paul condemns it (Col 2:20-23). Much of the New Testament attacks legalism, which reduces religion to morality. Ironically, churches have often made asceticism mandatory rather than voluntary.

The modern age, however, makes an opposite error. As never before, modernity has become aware of freedom, of the human role in social formation, and of the consequent diversity of cultures. But this important insight has been accompanied by the erroneous belief that culture is purely the creation of human ingenuity. The eminent anthropologist Clifford Geertz put it this way: "Believing that . . . man is an animal suspended in webs of significance he himself has spun, I take culture to be those webs."[103] But even spiders need twigs to hang their webs on and flies to come their way and bodies made for spinning. Taken to its conclusion, this view suggests that there are no created limits, that culture is arbitrary, and that everything is permitted as a matter of personal or collective preference—a view advertisers constantly exploit.

This collective tendency rebels against realities that limit human freedom.[104] Often arguments against such a knowable reality, which holds humans accountable, exploit the protean ambiguity dwelling on the margins of language. Yet, though language shapes humans' grasp of reality (Gen 2:19-20), only God orders a reality for Adam to name and to shape (Gen 2:21-23). Consequently, it is possible to shape reality truly or falsely.

---

103. Clifford Geertz, *The Interpretation of Cultures* (New York: Basic Books, 1973) 5. See also Peter L. Berger and Thomas Luckmann, *The Social Construction of Reality: A Treatise in the Sociology of Knowledge* (Garden City, N.Y.: Doubleday, 1966).

104. See Charles Taylor, *Sources of the Self: The Making of Modern Identity* (Cambridge, Mass.: Harvard University Press, 1989); G. von Rad, "The Age of Jeremiah," in *Old Testament Theology* (New York: Harper & Row, 1965) 2:212-17.

PROVERBS 6:1-19, MONEY, SLOTH, GOOD, AND EVIL

NIV

6 My son, if you have put up security for
your neighbor,
  if you have struck hands in pledge for
    another,
[2] if you have been trapped by what you said,
  ensnared by the words of your mouth,
[3] then do this, my son, to free yourself,
  since you have fallen into your neighbor's
    hands:
 Go and humble yourself;
  press your plea with your neighbor!
[4] Allow no sleep to your eyes,
  no slumber to your eyelids.
[5] Free yourself, like a gazelle from the hand of
    the hunter,
  like a bird from the snare of the fowler.

[6] Go to the ant, you sluggard;
  consider its ways and be wise!
[7] It has no commander,
  no overseer or ruler,
[8] yet it stores its provisions in summer
  and gathers its food at harvest.

[9] How long will you lie there, you sluggard?
  When will you get up from your sleep?
[10] A little sleep, a little slumber,
  a little folding of the hands to rest—
[11] and poverty will come on you like a bandit
  and scarcity like an armed man.[a]

[12] A scoundrel and villain,
  who goes about with a corrupt mouth,
[13]   who winks with his eye,
  signals with his feet
  and motions with his fingers,
[14]   who plots evil with deceit in his heart—
  he always stirs up dissension.
[15] Therefore disaster will overtake him in an
    instant;
  he will suddenly be destroyed—without
    remedy.

[16] There are six things the LORD hates,
  seven that are detestable to him:

---

[a] 11 Or *like a vagrant / and scarcity like a beggar*

NRSV

6 My child, if you have given your pledge
  to your neighbor,
  if you have bound yourself to another,[a]
[2] you are snared by the utterance of your lips,[b]
  caught by the words of your mouth.
[3] So do this, my child, and save yourself,
  for you have come into your neighbor's
    power:
  go, hurry,[c] and plead with your neighbor.
[4] Give your eyes no sleep
  and your eyelids no slumber;
[5] save yourself like a gazelle from the hunter,[d]
  like a bird from the hand of the fowler.

[6] Go to the ant, you lazybones;
  consider its ways, and be wise.
[7] Without having any chief
  or officer or ruler,
[8] it prepares its food in summer,
  and gathers its sustenance in harvest.
[9] How long will you lie there, O lazybones?
  When will you rise from your sleep?
[10] A little sleep, a little slumber,
  a little folding of the hands to rest,
[11] and poverty will come upon you like a robber,
  and want, like an armed warrior.

[12] A scoundrel and a villain
  goes around with crooked speech,
[13] winking the eyes, shuffling the feet,
  pointing the fingers,
[14] with perverted mind devising evil,
  continually sowing discord;
[15] on such a one calamity will descend suddenly;
  in a moment, damage beyond repair.

[16] There are six things that the LORD hates,
  seven that are an abomination to him:
[17] haughty eyes, a lying tongue,
  and hands that shed innocent blood,
[18] a heart that devises wicked plans,
  feet that hurry to run to evil,

---

[a] Or *a stranger*   [b] Cn Compare Gk Syr: Heb *the words of your
mouth*   [c] Or *humble yourself*   [d] Cn: Heb *from the hand*

NIV

17   haughty eyes,
        a lying tongue,
        hands that shed innocent blood,
18   a heart that devises wicked schemes,
        feet that are quick to rush into evil,
19   a false witness who pours out lies
        and a man who stirs up dissension among
            brothers.

NRSV

19 a lying witness who testifies falsely,
        and one who sows discord in a family.

COMMENTARY

6:1-5. The focus turns from sexuality to another prime mover in human affairs: money (cf. 1:13-14). This brief instruction advises not to "put up security" for a "neighbor" ("another" [זר zār] here is literally "stranger," the same term used in 5:10, 17). This warning is common in Proverbs (11:15; 17:18; 20:16 = 27:13; 22:26-27). These sayings are not against commerce and for agriculture. Rather, the issue is the wise conduct of fiscal and related affairs. (See Commentary on 11:15 for the image of "striking hands.")

While the exact mechanisms and persons involved in the financial transactions described in Prov 6:1-5 are disputed, the wisdom issues are clear and subtly treated. More is at stake than financial advice. The "son" has put himself at financial and personal risk by making a rash commitment to another. Wisdom requires that the mistakes be corrected, if possible. But at this point it is difficult even to recognize that a mistake has occurred, for negative consequences have not yet occurred. The damage is only potential, though the parent portrays the son as already caught in another's power. Wisdom requires insight into the whole situation: the nature of the investment, the character and reliability of the "neighbor" (see Commentary on 17:17-18), possible future outcomes, and the son's ability to sustain loss (22:27). Without specifying details, the parent has judged the financial transaction a mistake. The son needs to overcome his reluctance to admit error caused by shame ("humble yourself," v. 3), and to overcome the inertia of laziness, perhaps intensified by shame (cf. vv. 4 and 9-10). The mistake concerns poor judgment and a failure to maintain proper personal boundaries; the son has

let himself be engulfed by the agenda and power of another, a "stranger" (see Excursus, "Death and the Strange Woman in Proverbs 1–9," 71-72). While the wicked are "caught" by their own iniquity (5:22), here the son is "caught" by foolish commitments (18:7; cf. 12:13; 24:16; 29:6; Ps 124:7).

Verse 3 urges the hapless son to regain control of his existence from the stranger to whom he has foolishly given it. In relation to others, personal responsibility is essential, as well as a clear sense of the limits of one's own "turf." This entails rejecting what lies outside the limits of our competence (including fiscal competence) and affirming what is properly ours to dispose of.

Verses 4-5 urge fiscal self-redemption. To gain financial control of one's life can be to "save" oneself (v. 5), because control of material goods is life's foundation. Moreover, our heart is where our treasure is (Matt 6:21; see Excursus, "The 'Heart' in the Old Testament," 60-61). Money matters. By denying oneself sleep (v. 4), one may gain soul, self, and life. This image anticipates the discussion of sleep and sloth that follows in vv. 9-10. But it also sets up an ironic contrast with the wicked (4:16), who often seem more shrewd and more zealous in wrongdoing than the righteous in well doing (Luke 16:8; cf. Ps 132:3-6, of David's wish to build the Temple).

6:6-11. This passage is a reproving poem addressed to the "sluggard." The lowly ant serves as a moral example. The admonition is gently humorous but ends with a stern warning. (The LXX version adds a section on the bee as well.) In Hebrew, the word "ant" (נמלה němālâ) is grammatically feminine and singular, a fact obscured by the NRSV and the NIV, which translate "she" as "it." This small detail reveals yet another female symbol of wisdom in Proverbs. The use of the singular is also important, for the example concerns individual responsibility (the collective nature of ant behavior is ignored). Each ant does its own job within the socio-cosmic system. In the biblical world, non-human animals are seen as creatures of God (Genesis 1–2) who inhabit and respond to the same world order that impinges upon humans. Thus their behavior serves as models and analogues for humans (30:24-28; Job 12:7-9; Isa 1:3; Jer 8:6-9). In the prophets, animals are often in better harmony with reality than are humans.

Proverbs devotes three poems to the "sluggard" (6:6-11; 24:30-34; 26:13-16) as well as scattered sayings (10:26; 13:4; 15:19; 19:24 = 26:15; 20:4; 21:25; 22:13; cf. 19:15; 31:27). The topic is clearly important. Sloth is folly by default, for the sluggard avoids the hard work done "in season," which wisdom requires (Eccl 3:1-8; Isa 28:23-29). To imitate the ant's ways makes one wise (6:6), because the ant acts in harmony with the cosmic rhythm of the seasons (6:8). The ant's diligent work is a model for the son of 10:4-5, a saying that repeats the language of 6:8 (cf. 20:4; 30:24-25).

The ant (v. 7) is proactive, a "self-starter." She needs no boss to tell her what has to be done. By being responsible for her task, she blesses her community.

The ant acts in harmony with reality, seen in the rhythm of the seasons (v. 8). Palestine has basically two seasons: the cool, rainy season (roughly October through May) and the warm, dry season, which includes three or four months of no rain at all (see Commentary on 20:4; 26:1). Harvest occurs during the dry season as crops ripen. Thus the ant's actions are not determined by present appearances, whether of bounty or of blight. Rather, she uses the present (harvest with its bounty) to provide for the future and its different circumstances (the rainy season). The ant is not beguiled by present abundance, but uses it for the future. Such a creature lives in faith that the good order of the world will continue (see Gen 8:22) and that present faithfulness will establish a future. The story of Joseph's wise admini-

stration of the abundant and lean years (Genesis 40–45) is a version of Prov 6:6-8 writ large.

Verses 9-11 begin with a warning question, "How long . . . ?" designed to prod the sluggard to wake up. The question throws the responsibility where it belongs, but gives the sluggard freedom to make up his own mind. The question, "When will you rise?" also holds out the option of personal change through action, as if to say, "You need not continue in your present impotence." The question appeals to the sluggard to "come to himself" like the prodigal son (Luke 15:17), but before the damage is done. A word to the wise is sufficient, though fools only learn from hard knocks. Sleep, like sexual desire and ambition for gain, must be kept within its proper limits, lest opportunity fly away and one come to poverty (10:5*b;* 19:15; 20:13). In other words, "Make hay while the sun shines."

Verses 10-11 are a stock couplet (see 24:33-34; cf. Eccl 4:5). It mocks the false security of a "lazy bones" in his bed (see 26:13-14), suddenly overtaken by calamity (see v. 15; 1:27). In contrast, the sleep of the wise is secure (3:24; cf. Pss 3:5-6; 4:8). Verse 11 portrays poverty and want as an armed robber. The Hebrew (אִישׁ מָגֵן *'îš māgēn*) suggests a "highwayman" who appears when least expected (cf. 1:11; Judg 9:25; Matt 24:43) and takes by force what belongs to his victim. Ironically, the sluggard is his own victim.

6:12-19. Verses 12-15 and 16-19 are poems that sketch the inside and outside of human evil. The first poem presents bodily members as "instruments of wickedness" (Rom 6:13), while the second presents sin as what God hates. The diversity in the first list is united by its representation of a single person with a full panoply of evil acts. Verse 15 describes the disastrous consequences of the person's evil. The second poem employs a similarly diverse list of evil deeds, now united by the Lord's opposition to them. The interaction of the two poems is facilitated by repetition and parallelism, especially of the two lists of body parts (cf. 4:20-27). To the bodily members may be added two actions, for a total of seven parallels.[105] The list follows the order of vv. 17-19, which explicitly identify "seven things" abominable to the Lord:

---

105. See L. Alonso-Schökel and J. Vilchez, *Proverbios* (Madrid: Ediciones Cristiandad, 1984) 213-15.

Verses 17-19	Verses 12-14
17*a*, eyes	13*a*, eyes
17*a*, tongue	
(speech organs)	12*b*, mouth
17*b*, hands	13*b*, fingers
18*a*, heart	
devising evil	14*a*, heart devising evil
18*b*, feet	13*a*, feet
19*a*, lying	14*a*, upside-down deceit
19*b*, sowing discord	14*b*, sowing discord

In Hebrew, the "scoundrel" is literally a "man of *belial* [בליעל *běliyya'al*]"; so 1 Sam 25:25 KJV). The precise sense of *belial* is elusive; its significance is best gained contextually.[106] The term appears to have a mythic background in the powers of chaos, death, and Sheol (Ps 18:4-5 ["perdition," NRSV] = 2 Sam 22:5-6; Ps 41:8 ["deadly thing," NRSV]). It is applied to persons who disrupt the social and moral order (1 Sam 25:17, 25). One who neglects the poor is guilty of *belial* (Deut 15:9). Hannah fears she is mistaken for a "daughter of *belial*," when Eli thinks she is drunk in the holy tabernacle (1 Sam 1:16; cf. Lev 10:8). Psalm 101 is a "mirror for princes" in which the righteous king rejects all that is *belial* ("base," Ps 101:3). In several instances, *belial* refers to wrongdoing by legal manipulation. Honest Naboth is "legally" murdered through Jezebel's employment of false witnesses, "sons of *belial*" (1 Kgs 21:10, 13; cf. Prov 19:28). Verses 12-19 deal with legal matters, but are not restricted to them.

"Crooked speech"/"mouth" (also 4:24) heads a list of bodily agents of wrongdoing. Such a mouth is basic equipment for the life journey ("goes about") of a *belial* person. In human affairs, there is nothing more powerful than an open mouth, whether for good or for ill (see Commentary on 18:21; cf. Sir 37:17-18; Jas 3:1-12). Greater violence can be done with the tongue than with the fist (10:11*b*; 12:18; cf. 25:15*b*). The "crooked mouth" twists reality upside-down and inside-out (6:14); it calls "evil good and good evil," it puts "darkness for light and light for darkness" (Isa 5:20 NRSV). "Crooked" is regularly opposed to "integrity" (11:20; 19:1; 28:6).

Wicked magistrates abhor justice and make crooked what is right (Mic 3:9). The speech of Wisdom herself has nothing crooked in it (8:8). But the crooked mouth distorts reality and breaks the implicit covenant that governs our relations with our neighbor.

Three further agents of wrongdoing, "eye," "feet," and "fingers" are listed in v. 13. The actions described seem to be body language, nonverbal communication whose precise character and significance are uncertain. One scholar suggests the reference is to magical acts that damage the neighbor (cf. 10:10; Ps 35:19).[107] These signals probably refer more generally to any gesture that communicates for malevolent purposes. The Hebrew verbs for "shuffling" (מלל *mālal*) and "pointing" (מרה *mōreh*) are wordplays on "speaking" and "instructing" respectively (4:4, 11). In these verses, the agent of evil moves from the mouth (6:12) to the more elusive body language (6:13). With a shrug of the shoulders, one can deny responsibility for what one has said, as if to say, "I said nothing wrong."

Verse 14 is the climax of the first poem, for it gets at the inner source, or "heart," of human evil (see Excursus, "The 'Heart' in the Old Testament," 60-61). *Belial* persons have deceit in their hearts. (In contrast to 12:20, "deceit" (תהפכות *tahpukôt*) here is lit. "things upside-down"; see Commentary on 6:12; 30:21-23.) Their inner disposition distorts reality, like a drunkard who perceives and speaks things upside-down (23:33). Since evil resides in the spiritual core (heart) of such persons, wrong is not incidental, but basic to their character. They do not grow weary in wrongdoing. Their sins are not passive neglect of duty, but the active "devising [of] evil" (see v. 18; Mic 2:1-3).

Verse 15 portrays the sudden demise of the *belial* person in stock terms (cf. 1:26; 3:25; 29:1*b* = 6:15*b*). The calamity without remedy "descends" (יבוא *yābô'*, "comes") like the warrior in 6:11. The persons and mechanisms that underlie this retribution for wickedness are not spelled out. In the monotheistic world picture of Proverbs, the Lord is the ultimate guarantor of justice. If there were any doubt about this, the following poem presents the Lord in fundamental opposition

106. See Nicholas J. Tromp, *Primitive Conceptions of Death and the Nether World in the Old Testament* (Rome: Pontifical Biblical Institute, 1969) 125-28.

107. William McKane, *Proverbs: A New Approach,* OTL (Philadelphia: Westminster, 1970) 325.

to wickedness. The implicit logic here is that of Mic 2:1-3, which portrays the Lord as devising evil in response to those who have first devised wickedness against their neighbors.

Verses 16-19 are an extended numerical saying of the form N/N + 1. This simple pattern of two numbers in sequence is common in the ancient world. It was popular with the ancient Canaanite poets of Ugarit, who wrote nearly a millennium before the editing of Proverbs (cf. 30:15-31; Amos 1:3–2:8).[108] The effect is something like saying, "Not only this, but also that."

Outside of Proverbs, the term "abomination" (תועבה *tô'ēbâ*) is used mostly in connection with Yahweh (see Commentary on 3:32; 11:1). The wisdom writers use it to refer also to human relations. What the Lord hates here is bodily members turned from their good use to the service of wrongdoing.

"Haughty eyes" (v. 17) fail to balance the glory of humankind (God's viceroy over the earth, Psalm 8) with a realistic humility. Similarly, pride was considered the chief of the seven cardinal sins in medieval Christian theology. But lowered eyes before a superior are a universal gesture of shame, modesty, or proper humility. One does not look God in the eye (Exod 33:20, 23; cf. Gen 32:30; John 1:18). Yet humans can "lift up their eyes" to God and expect that God will take them seriously and deal with them kindly (Psalm 123; cf. Ps 61:2-3). In the face of sin and death, and of humanity's limited wisdom and radical dependence on God, supercilious pride is out of place. Humans have difficulty even in understanding their own ways and heart (Jer 17:9-10). But the Lord, who does know human hearts, "brings down haughty eyes" (Ps 18:27; cf. Ps 131:1; Isa 2:11; Jer 23-24; Sir 23:4).

The juxtaposition of "haughty eyes" with a "lying tongue" (also 12:19; 21:6; 26:28) is suggestive. Liars disdain reality, which they misrepresent, and other people as being unworthy of being told the truth. The lying tongue, like a weapon (25:18), damages both the external world and other people, because humans act upon representations of reality embedded in speech. Psalms 64:2-6 and 109:2-19 provide excellent examples

of this evil dynamic at work. False legal accusations (cf. Prov 6:19; Ps 25:18; 1 Kgs 21:8-14) and seemingly pious curses (cf. 26:2; Ps 109:17) against the neighbor are mainstays of verbal evil (cf. also 10:18; 12:22; 17:7).

"Hands that shed innocent blood" (v. 17*b*) parallels "feet that hurry to run to evil" (v. 18*b;* cf. 4:27). Together, these lines are an expansive echo of 1:16. Evil possesses an impulsive energy arising from a crooked will to power, "a heart that devises wicked plans" (see Commentary on 4:23; 6:14). Evil also does wrong to the innocent, who do not deserve it (cf. Ps 109:2-5).

Verse 19*a* is repeated in 14:5*b* (cf. 14:25; 25:18; Exod 20:16; Ps 27:12). While a false witness may appear in any arena of life, its defining setting is the law court. Israelite justice at different times and places was variously administered by local elders, royal officials, and priestly functionaries. But the role of witnesses in establishing guilt and innocence was basic. To prevent false testimony, multiple witnesses were stipulated (Deut 19:15-21). But the sad tale of Naboth's vineyard shows that this legal safeguard did not always succeed, particularly when the powerful and the wicked were in collusion (1 Kgs 21:8-14). A number of tales recount how judicial wisdom is able to expose the false witness (1 Kgs 3:16-28; Susanna).

The various vices listed in vv. 16-19 culminate in "sows discord in a family" (lit., "incites quarrels among brothers"; see 6:14; 16:28). Evil disrupts the natural bonds of society—family, clan, tribe—and the secondary bonds that evolve as society becomes more differentiated. "Quarrels" (מדון *mādôn*) can refer to various sorts of conflict (cf. 21:9, 19, of marital conflict), but the primary reference here is to litigation, that last resort in settling the conflicts generated by human wrongdoing (cf. 26:21). "Brother" (אח *'āḥ*) is a term with a wide range in ancient Hebrew. It refers not only to male siblings but also to extended kinship relations. Thus the naming of Israel's tribes after twelve siblings communicates that all Israelites are brothers (cf. Exod 2:11; Deut 15:12). By extension, "brother" can also refer to persons bound to one another in voluntary associations, ranging from friendship (2 Sam 1:26) to political and economic pacts (1 Kgs 9:13; 20:32-34; Amos 1:9). Yet, (il)legal conflict can also arise among siblings,

---

108. See "The Legend of King Keret," in *Ancient Near Eastern Texts Relating to the Old Testament,* ed. James B. Pritchard, 3rd ed. (Princeton, N.J.: Princeton University Press, 1969) 142-49.

especially in matters of inheritance, as in the stories of Esau and Jacob (Gen 25:19-34; 27:1–28:9; 32:1-17); of Absalom and Amnon, with its bloody repercussions (2 Samuel 13–18); and of the Solomonic accession to the throne (1 Kings 1–2). A fine example of legal conflict over inheritance is found in Hesiod's archaic Greek wisdom book *Works and Days,* which tells the tale of Hesiod's dispute with his brother Perses.

REFLECTIONS

1. Proverbs constantly reminds us that the arena in which wisdom and folly contend is this world, with its goods and powers. According to Proverbs 1–9, the way we use our material resources, particularly our sexuality and our money, reveals either godly wisdom or its lack: "Money talks." The matters in which our spirituality is most commonly manifested are the goods and activities of ordinary life outside of worship (see Commentary on 31:30).

2. Laziness is a subset of folly and the opposite of wisdom. The sluggard is out of tune with the cosmic rhythms of reality. The sluggard does not realize that human existence is historical, that circumstances change, that opportunities pass, and that one must act in the present to ensure one's well-being in the future.

3. The juxtaposition of Prov 6:12-15 and 6:16-19 is significant. It suggests that sin involves a combination of reality-rejection, active malice, and a rejection of the Lord as the creator and master of reality. Scripture portrays several such evil characters. Perhaps the archetypal figure is the pharaoh of Exodus, in his tyrannical persecution of the Israelites, his tenacious refusal to face the reality of the plagues, the "hardening" of his own heart, and his denial of the Lord (Exod 5:2)—all this in spite of plague upon plague designed to make him know who the Lord is (Exodus 5–11). Another is the king of Babylon (Isa 14:4-20). Because such figures are both malicious (Prov 10:12) and at odds with reality, they incite conflict wherever they go (Prov 6:14*b,* 19*b;* 16:28). When they possess great power and position, they wreak devastation on the earth among humans, as Stalin and Hitler in the twentieth century show.

PROVERBS 6:20-35, TEACHING AGAINST ADULTERY

NIV	NRSV

[20]My son, keep your father's commands
    and do not forsake your mother's teaching.
[21]Bind them upon your heart forever;
    fasten them around your neck.
[22]When you walk, they will guide you;
    when you sleep, they will watch over you;
    when you awake, they will speak to you.
[23]For these commands are a lamp,
    this teaching is a light,
  and the corrections of discipline
    are the way to life,
[24]keeping you from the immoral woman,
    from the smooth tongue of the wayward wife.
	[20] My child, keep your father's commandment,
	    and do not forsake your mother's teaching.
	[21] Bind them upon your heart always;
	    tie them around your neck.
	[22] When you walk, they[a] will lead you;
	    when you lie down, they[a] will watch over you;
	    and when you awake, they[a] will talk with you.
	[23] For the commandment is a lamp and the
	    teaching a light,
	    and the reproofs of discipline are the way
	    of life,
	
	[a] Heb *it*

NIV

²⁵Do not lust in your heart after her beauty
  or let her captivate you with her eyes,
²⁶for the prostitute reduces you to a loaf of bread,
  and the adulteress preys upon your very life.
²⁷Can a man scoop fire into his lap
  without his clothes being burned?
²⁸Can a man walk on hot coals
  without his feet being scorched?
²⁹So is he who sleeps with another man's wife;
  no one who touches her will go unpunished.

³⁰Men do not despise a thief if he steals
  to satisfy his hunger when he is starving.
³¹Yet if he is caught, he must pay sevenfold,
  though it costs him all the wealth of his
    house.
³²But a man who commits adultery lacks
    judgment;
  whoever does so destroys himself.
³³Blows and disgrace are his lot,
  and his shame will never be wiped away;
³⁴for jealousy arouses a husband's fury,
  and he will show no mercy when he takes
    revenge.
³⁵He will not accept any compensation;
  he will refuse the bribe, however great it is.

NRSV

²⁴ to preserve you from the wife of another,[a]
  from the smooth tongue of the adulteress.
²⁵ Do not desire her beauty in your heart,
  and do not let her capture you with her
    eyelashes;
²⁶ for a prostitute's fee is only a loaf of bread,[b]
  but the wife of another stalks a man's very
    life.
²⁷ Can fire be carried in the bosom
  without burning one's clothes?
²⁸ Or can one walk on hot coals
  without scorching the feet?
²⁹ So is he who sleeps with his neighbor's wife;
  no one who touches her will go unpunished.
³⁰ Thieves are not despised who steal only
  to satisfy their appetite when they are
    hungry.
³¹ Yet if they are caught, they will pay sevenfold;
  they will forfeit all the goods of their house.
³² But he who commits adultery has no sense;
  he who does it destroys himself.
³³ He will get wounds and dishonor,
  and his disgrace will not be wiped away.
³⁴ For jealousy arouses a husband's fury,
  and he shows no restraint when he takes
    revenge.
³⁵ He will accept no compensation,
  and refuses a bribe no matter how great.

[a] Gk: MT *the evil woman*   [b] Cn Compare Gk Syr Vg Tg: Heb *for because of a harlot to a piece of bread*

COMMENTARY

This section opens with an appeal to keep the parent's "commandment" and "teaching," followed by praise of the same to motivate the appeal. The passage then turns to its specific topic, adultery. The previous section (6:1-19) had provided a kaleidoscopic view of human wickedness; the present section focuses on that sin that, for the author of Proverbs 1–9, symbolizes the essence of human folly: unfaithfulness and the destructive desire for good things "out of bounds." For Proverbs, this sin represents turning away from wisdom to folly.

Undergirding this representation is the insight that wisdom and the Lord are intimately related

(1:7; 9:10). Thus being unfaithful to one's spouse (and so to wisdom) is tantamount to ignoring God and God's ways for humans. The lesson against adultery in vv. 23-35 can stand by itself. But its full import is sensed only within the larger, bipolar metaphoric system concerning opposed ways, women, and houses. The literal teaching on adultery and the larger metaphorical message reinforce each other. This message may be summed up as: freedom within form, life within law, and love within limits.

6:20-23. The instruction begins with an admonition to keep the father's "commandment" and the mother's "teaching." Both parents have the authority and responsibility to instruct young males (31:1). "Commandment" and "teaching" (תורה *tôrâ* can also mean "law") are terms usually associated with Israel's legal traditions. Here they are wisdom terms denoting parental authority to command and to instruct. Yet the passage develops these ambiguous terms in a way that evokes the Decalogue's prohibition against adultery, theft, and coveting (Exod 20:14-15, 17) as well as its admonition to honor one's parents (Exod 20:12; cf. Deut 5:16-21). This implicit appeal to the divine law is strengthened by verbal and conceptual parallels between Prov 6:20-23 and Deut 6:1-9. Proverbs 6:23 also borrows the language of light from Ps 119:105 in praise of the divine law/word (cf. Ps 19:7-8). Thus underlying parental authority in Prov 6:20-35 is an implicit appeal to the divine law given through Moses. This contrasts with the usual grounding of parental teaching in cosmic wisdom (see Commentary on 2:1-22; 3:1-3). In sum, the highly allusive language of 6:20-35 connects its parental wisdom to the Mosaic law (*tôrâ*), which is also Israel's "wisdom" (Deut 4:5-8). Parental authority always has a norm above and beyond itself, to which it must appeal and to which it is accountable. For Proverbs that norm may be cosmic wisdom or, in this case, the "law" of Moses.

Verse 21 uses images of bodily ornamentation similar to those in Deut 6:8 and Prov 3:3. The parent's teaching finds its home in the hidden "heart" (see Excursus, "The 'Heart' in the Old Testament," 60-61), as well as on the "neck," where it is publicly visible in the form of actions. Moreover, this teaching is to be an abiding reality in the son's life, ever present like a wedding band.

Verse 22 exactly parallels Deut 6:7 in its sequence of walking, lying down, waking. The last two terms form a merism—that is, two opposites used to indicate totality. All of life's activities are under the umbrella of the parental/divine teaching. Parental teaching here is personified (cf. 2:11; 4:5-9); "she" guides, watches over, and talks to the son.

Verse 23a is richly ambiguous and allusive. In its context, it picks up "commandment" and "teaching" from v. 20 (caught by the NIV's "these"/"this"). But "teaching" is *tôrâ,* or "law," as well. As it stands, this half verse describes the commandment and teaching in metaphors identi-

cal to Psalm 119's description of the divine word: "Your word is a *lamp* to my feet and a *light* to my path" (Ps 119:105 NRSV, italics added; cf. Ps 19:8). Thus v. 23a helps to evoke the divine *tôrâ* underlying the parental *tôrâ.* Although the parental "law" is a light, it also sets limits on youthful conduct, the "reproofs of discipline" that keep one on the "way of life" (cf. 4:11; 10:17; 15:24; for "way" and "light," see 4:18.).

6:24. The NRSV translation "wife of another" (lit., "neighbor" [רע *rēa'*, whose consonants also can mean "bad," "immoral"]) is preferable to the NIV's "immoral woman" for several reasons. First, the parallel term is "foreign" (NRSV, "adulteress"). Second, the bound grammatical relation of "woman"/"wife" to "neighbor"/"bad" (*rēa'* / רע *ra'*) in every other biblical instance (12 times) refers to the neighbor's wife. Third, vv. 26 and 29 provide the variant "wife of another." Finally, vv. 24-25 allude to the Mosaic command against coveting the neighbor's wife. The adulterous wife of another captures hearts by "smooth talk," by her beauty, and by the silent speech of her eyes (v. 25; cf. Sir 26:9, 11). The use of eye makeup in the ancient Near East is well known through art and archaeological finds of cosmetic palettes and tools. Jezebel prepared for the arrival of Jehu by making up her eyes (2 Kgs 9:30).

6:25. The admonition "Do not desire" ("covet") combines with "neighbor's wife" from v. 24 to form an echo of "Do not covet your neighbor's wife" in the Ten Commandments (Exod 20:17; Deut 5:21). Jesus takes up the phrase "in your heart" when he radicalizes the command against adultery (Matt 5:28).

6:26. The Hebrew of v. 26a is uncertain. The NIV and the NRSV give two possibilities: A prostitute brings one down to poverty (NIV), or she can be had at a small price (NRSV). The verse's point is found in the second line, which employs the logic of "how much more so." If prostitution is costly and damaging, adultery is even more so. Adultery can cost one's life. It is akin to theft, as the next verses (vv. 30-31) indicate.

6:27-29. These verses are a series of rhetorical questions (cf. Amos 3:3-6; 6:12) to suggest the absurdity of adultery and the impossibility of "not getting burned."

6:30-35. Here the writer compares adultery to thievery and spells out the inevitable disaster that awaits the adulterer. But sexual "theft" is a more destructive breach of faith than is the stealing of material goods. Material goods can be restored, but the adulterer "destroys himself" (v. 32; cf. 1 Cor 6:18). An offended husband's jealousy and fury (v. 34; cf. 27:4) will not be placated.

REFLECTIONS

1. Israel's culture is largely oral; without reference books, only what has been kept in memory is truly known. The teaching is so deeply internalized that it becomes part of the inner dialogue that forms the self. Willy-nilly, for better or worse, even today parental discourses make up the inner, authoritative voice with which children must deal, positively or negatively, over the course of a lifetime. But the parental voice presented here is grounded in the divine Word and law.

2. The end of chapter 6 resumes the theme of sexual fidelity in marriage. The writer uses theft of material goods as the foil for speaking of that transgression of limits, that invasion of a neighbor's "turf," which is adultery. As in some forms of "family-systems therapy," the concept of appropriate boundaries is crucial to the worldview and "personview" of Proverbs (see Commentary on Proverbs 8).[109]

This lesson is crucial because self-limitation (discipline) and deliberate acceptance of interpersonal and cosmic limits are basic to biblical wisdom. When humans practice self-discipline in relation to created goods and other persons (sex, food, sleep, exercise, work, play, speech), it promotes self-knowledge, self-mastery, and, paradoxically, freedom. Bonhoeffer saw this clearly in his poem "Stations on the Way to Freedom":

> Self-discipline
> If you set out to seek freedom,
>   you must learn before all things
> Mastery over sense and soul,
>   lest your wayward desirings,
> Lest your undisciplined members
>   lead you now this way, now that way.
> Chaste be your mind and your body,
>   and subject to you and obedient,
> Serving solely to seek their appointed goal and objective.
> None learns the secret of freedom
>   save only by way of control.[110]

Self-denial (to use a NT formulation, Mark 8:34) is an implicit recognition that life must be lived within limits not created by us for purposes not invented by us and that life ends in death. It is fundamental to following Christ, the paradoxical wisdom of God.

3. In this section, the language continues to be directed at males. In addition, for didactic reasons (see Overview on Proverbs 1–9), the roles in which women appear continue to be limited to sexual partner in or out of marriage (see Commentary on 5:15-19; chap. 7). Clearly, this does not exhaust the multiplicity of roles in which women function not only in ancient Israel, but also in the modern world. Some biblical glimpses of role diversity for competent women with authority appear in Prov 31:10-31 and in biblical stories such as those about Deborah, the judge and prophetess (Judges 4–5), and Huldah, the prophetess (2 Kgs 22:14-20).

109. See Harriet G. Lerner, *The Dance of Anger: A Woman's Guide to Changing the Patterns of Intimate Relationships* (New York: Harper & Row, 1985).

110. Reprinted by permission of Simon & Schuster from *Ethics* by Dietrich Bonhoeffer, translated from the German by N. H. Smith. English trans. copyright © 1955 by SCM Press, Ltd. Copyright © 1955 by Macmillan Publishing Company.

According to Carol Meyers, apart from the minority urban population, Israelite life was largely agricultural and did not exhibit significant gender polarization.[111]

In order to balance the male priority in this portion of Scripture, in addition to exploring passages that show women in diverse roles, it is necessary to remember those biblical passages that express mutuality in marriage and sexuality (see Commentary on 31:10-31). The young woman's refrain in the Song of Songs comes to mind: "My beloved is mine and I am his" (Cant 2:16 NRSV; 6:3; 7:10). Again, Paul wrote, "The wife does not have authority over her own body, but the husband does; likewise *the husband does not have authority over his own body, but the wife does*" (1 Cor 7:4 NRSV, italics added; cf. Eph 5:21). Most fundamentally, the creation of male and female in God's image grounds the dignity of both (Gen 1:26-28).

111. Carol L. Meyers, "Everyday Life: Women in the Period of the Hebrew Bible," in Carol A. Newsom and Sharon H. Ringe, eds., *The Women's Bible Commentary* (Louisville: Westminster, 1992) 249-50; see also Myers, *Discovering Eve: Ancient Israelite Women in Context* (New York: Oxford University Press, 1988).

PROVERBS 7:1-27, A TALE OF SEDUCTION AND DEATH

NIV	NRSV

7 My son, keep my words
    and store up my commands within you.
²Keep my commands and you will live;
    guard my teachings as the apple of your eye.
³Bind them on your fingers;
    write them on the tablet of your heart.
⁴Say to wisdom, "You are my sister,"
    and call understanding your kinsman;
⁵they will keep you from the adulteress,
    from the wayward wife with her seductive words.
 	
⁶At the window of my house
    I looked out through the lattice.
⁷I saw among the simple,
    I noticed among the young men,
    a youth who lacked judgment.
⁸He was going down the street near her corner,
    walking along in the direction of her house
⁹at twilight, as the day was fading,
    as the dark of night set in.
 	
¹⁰Then out came a woman to meet him,
    dressed like a prostitute and with crafty intent.
¹¹(She is loud and defiant,
    her feet never stay at home;
¹²now in the street, now in the squares,
    at every corner she lurks.)
	7 My child, keep my words
	    and store up my commandments with you;
	² keep my commandments and live,
	    keep my teachings as the apple of your eye;
	³ bind them on your fingers,
	    write them on the tablet of your heart.
	⁴ Say to wisdom, "You are my sister,"
	    and call insight your intimate friend,
	⁵ that they may keep you from the loose[a] woman,
	    from the adulteress with her smooth words.
	
	⁶ For at the window of my house
	    I looked out through my lattice,
	⁷ and I saw among the simple ones,
	    I observed among the youths,
	    a young man without sense,
	⁸ passing along the street near her corner,
	    taking the road to her house
	⁹ in the twilight, in the evening,
	    at the time of night and darkness.
	
	¹⁰ Then a woman comes toward him,
	    decked out like a prostitute, wily of heart.[b]
	¹¹ She is loud and wayward;
	    her feet do not stay at home;

a Heb *strange*   *b* Meaning of Heb uncertain

NIV

13She took hold of him and kissed him
and with a brazen face she said:

14"I have fellowship offerings*a* at home;
today I fulfilled my vows.

15So I came out to meet you;
I looked for you and have found you!

16I have covered my bed
with colored linens from Egypt.

17I have perfumed my bed
with myrrh, aloes and cinnamon.

18Come, let's drink deep of love till morning;
let's enjoy ourselves with love!

19My husband is not at home;
he has gone on a long journey.

20He took his purse filled with money
and will not be home till full moon."

21With persuasive words she led him astray;
she seduced him with her smooth talk.

22All at once he followed her
like an ox going to the slaughter,
like a deer*b* stepping into a noose*c*

23 till an arrow pierces his liver,
like a bird darting into a snare,
little knowing it will cost him his life.

24Now then, my sons, listen to me;
pay attention to what I say.

25Do not let your heart turn to her ways
or stray into her paths.

26Many are the victims she has brought down;
her slain are a mighty throng.

27Her house is a highway to the grave,*d*
leading down to the chambers of death.

a14 Traditionally *peace offerings*   *b22* Syriac (see also Septuagint);
Hebrew *fool*   *c22* The meaning of the Hebrew for this line is
uncertain.   *d27* Hebrew *Sheol*

NRSV

12 now in the street, now in the squares,
and at every corner she lies in wait.

13 She seizes him and kisses him,
and with impudent face she says to him:

14 "I had to offer sacrifices,
and today I have paid my vows;

15 so now I have come out to meet you,
to seek you eagerly, and I have found you!

16 I have decked my couch with coverings,
colored spreads of Egyptian linen;

17 I have perfumed my bed with myrrh,
aloes, and cinnamon.

18 Come, let us take our fill of love until morning;
let us delight ourselves with love.

19 For my husband is not at home;
he has gone on a long journey.

20 He took a bag of money with him;
he will not come home until full moon."

21 With much seductive speech she persuades
him;
with her smooth talk she compels him.

22 Right away he follows her,
and goes like an ox to the slaughter,
or bounds like a stag toward the trap*a*

23 until an arrow pierces its entrails.
He is like a bird rushing into a snare,
not knowing that it will cost him his life.

24 And now, my children, listen to me,
and be attentive to the words of my mouth.

25 Do not let your hearts turn aside to her ways;
do not stray into her paths.

26 for many are those she has laid low,
and numerous are her victims.

27 Her house is the way to Sheol,
going down to the chambers of death.

a Cn Compare Gk: Meaning of Heb uncertain

COMMENTARY

This exquisitely crafted instruction contains a vivid cautionary tale (vv. 6-23) set within a frame of a parental call to hear (vv. 1-5) and a concluding warning with a call to hear (vv. 24-27; see 8:32-36; 7:24*a* = 8:32*a*). The passage resumes the warning against adultery in the last chapter (6:24-

35). The seductress is juxtaposed to Lady Wisdom (chap. 8) to intensify the double opposition of wisdom/folly and wife/seductress, which pervades chapters 1–9.

The parent quotes the smooth words of a temptress (vv. 14-20) and uses verbal echoes of the first parental speech (1:10-19), which had quoted male tempters (1:11-14). Thus the first and last parental instructions are parallel and form an envelope around the parental speeches. This parallelism suggests again that sin and folly are the issue, not gender per se (see Commentary on 2:12, 16; 4:10-19). The main character in chap. 7 is the adulterous woman, who represents Folly, in contrast to Lady Wisdom in chap. 8. With Proverbs 7, the parental instructions come to an end. The prologue of Proverbs climaxes in Wisdom's own voice (chap. 8) and concludes with the opposed voices of Wisdom and Folly in chap. 9.

7:1-5. Verse 1 parallels the language of Ps 119:11, "I treasure [store up] your word in my heart" (NRSV). The similar expressions concerning the parental and the divine "word" and "commandments" continue the perspective of 6:20-23. The parent's words are not the divine Word, but they are faithful reflections of it and are thus a means of life (v. 2 echoes 4:4). The "binding" imagery of v. 3 appeared earlier (3:3; 6:21) and reflects the practice of binding the law upon one's person. "Fingers" and "heart" (v. 3) denote the external, acting person and the inner, secret self respectively. And while the parent's words echo the law, they are more immediately connected to wisdom and to understanding, which are personified here as the object of love (v. 4). "Sister" and "kinsman" (NIV; see Ruth 2:1; 3:2; Cant 4:9; 5:1; Tob 7:15) are tender terms addressed to a bride or wife.

The urging to "Wisdom" as a "sister"/"bride" and "kinsman" (v. 4), provides the clue that the seductive adulteress in vv. 6-23 functions as more than just a moral object lesson against adultery. The contrast of Wisdom/bride as a love object maintains the bipolar symbol system of the prologue (see Overview on Proverbs 1–9).

Verse 5 states the teaching's purpose, repeating 2:16 and 6:24 with slight variation (cf. 5:3, 20). Again, the repetition reinforces the symbol system. A "slick mouth" is an identifying characteristic of the "strange woman" (2:16; 5:3; 6:24; 7:21). It is probably a mistake to try to establish one, totally consistent identity for the "strange woman" in the prologue.[112] She is something of a composite picture, showing traits of the harlot, of the adulterous wife, and perhaps on occasion even of a literal foreigner, whose husband is a traveling merchant ("Canaanite" can refer to either an original inhabitant of the land or to a "merchant"; cf. 31:24). That she is a cultic prostitute devoted to a goddess of love is too much to conclude from the vows and sacrifices in 7:14. The problem of the worship of foreign cults does not appear as a significant issue in these chapters.

Rather, the common feature in all the appearances of the strange woman is that she is sexually and spiritually out of bounds. This constitutes her "strangeness," her violation of the created order of marriage. A wise "son" will recognize her in any of her guises. Later (v. 21), her seductive words will ironically be described as "teaching" ("persuasive words"), to contrast with parental "teaching" ("learning," 1:5; 4:2; 9:9) on behalf of Wisdom.

7:6-23. 7:6-9. The parent's speech is introduced in stylized autobiographical fashion.[113] The parent, perhaps the mother, watches a disaster in the making from the window of her house. (The LXX, with its third-person feminine verbs, seems to have the seductress looking out of the window. There may be a type-scene of a royal woman looking out of the window; cf. Judg 5:28; 2 Sam 6:16; 2 Kgs 9:30. If a royal type-scene underlies this passage, it may suggest a queen mother; cf. 31:1-9).[114] With symbolic key words, the naive young man is said to take "the road to her house" (v. 8), thus disobeying 4:15. He does so as day becomes night and twilight descends into darkness (v. 9; cf. 4:18-19). In the dark, boundaries are blurred, and people do "not know" what they do (v. 23; see Commentary on 5:6). The implication of these allusive references to earlier teaching is that the young man is naive and lacks sense (lit., "heart"), because he has not taken parental instruction to heart (see Commentary on 4:4).

7:10-13. These verses describe the woman in action, with language that reinforces her symbolic role as foil to Wisdom/wife. She is "loud" (המיה *hōmiyyâ*), a term in Proverbs that appears only of the "foolish woman" (9:13) and of the bustling

112. See Gale Yee, "'I Have Perfumed My Bed with Myrrh': The Foreign Woman ('iššâ zārâh) in Proverbs 1–9," *JSOT* 43 (1989) 53-68.

113. See Tremper Longman III, *Fictional Akkadian Autobiography: A Generic and Comparative Study* (Winona Lake: Eisenbraun's, 1991).

114. McKane improbably suggests Wisdom herself. See William Mckane, *Proverbs: A New Approach,* OTL (Philadelphia: Westminster, 1970) 335-36.

streets where Wisdom speaks (1:21). She goes out to meet the young man as an aggressor, "wily of heart." She wears a "prostitute's" garb. This does not indicate her profession but her crafty purpose (cf. Gen 38:14-15 and below). "Her feet/legs do not stay at home/in her house" (v. 11). The alternate translations are literal. The term for "legs" (רגלים *raglayim*) anticipates the purpose of her roaming, for "legs" is a common euphemism for private parts (Judg 3:24; 2 Kgs 18:27; Isa 7:20). Moreover, that she does not stay in her house, suggests symbolically that she has left the sexual place proper to her as a married woman (see Commentary on 2:18; 5:4; 7:19; Reflections on Proverbs 9 for the symbolism of the "house;" cf. 7:19; 27:8, which are applied to "men"). She bustles about precisely where Wisdom gives her call, precisely where the young husband was warned not to let his waters run: in the street and squares (v. 12; see 1:20; 5:16). She lies in wait, like the robbers of 1:11. Sexually, both men and women are meant to dine at home (see 30:20).

7:14. Her actual words may or may not be false (cf. v. 13 with 21:28-29). She claims to have settled her religious obligations of vows and fellowship offerings, which must take place in a state of ritual purity. This is perhaps an indirect way of communicating her sexual availability (cf. 2 Sam 11:2, 4, where Bathsheba "sanctifies herself from her impurity.") In any case, the irony is great: She has presumably made herself right with God and now is ready to violate her sacred marital covenant through committing adultery (see Commentary on 2:16-19).[115] A "fellowship offering" leads to a feast, for the meat of this sacrifice was eaten and shared. But the issue here is not a sacred meal (the meal takes place after the sacred activities); rather, sex is on her mind. Having paid her "vows" and "sacrifices" means she is free, it seems, to have a feast and a liaison.[116]

7:15-17. Words of flattery to the young fool suggest he is the "only one" she wants. However, "seeking" and "finding" are characteristic of Wisdom, of Folly, and of their respective lovers; humans are in a courtship dialectic with either

one or the other (v. 15; cf. 1:28; 2:4; 3:13; 8:17, 35). Not only does she offer food and sex (cf. 30:20), but also the sort of wealth that belongs properly to Wisdom in the form of exotic foreign furnishings (for the bed, of course) and the perfumes of love (vv. 16-17; cf. 31:21-22, 24; Ps 45:8; Cant 3:6; 4:12-14; 5:1).

7:18-20. The strange woman's language is a twisted echo of the legitimate love delights in 5:19-20, which anticipates chap. 7 by warning of the stranger. With the ancient equivalent of "out of sight, out of mind," she tells the youth that her husband is not in his house but has gone on a long "road," and will not "come into his house" (both dwelling and woman's body, since the verb connotes intercourse) until the new moon (see v. 8; 27:8).

7:21-23. With a series of animal images—ox, stag, bird—the youth on the prowl for a girl heads instead to the slaughter. He had fancied himself a hunter ready to pierce his prey. Instead, he is himself hunted, "pierced," and caught, totally unawares. The animal images convey the youth's loss of his humanity; he has abandoned the wisdom that enables him to be human, to know what he is getting into (v. 23). Sin here is blameworthy folly, a deliberate ignorance of consequences. Although the young man is portrayed as a senseless beast, usually even animals know better (1:17-18: cf. Isa 1:3; Jer 8:6-7).

7:24-27. These verses are a summarizing warning and call to listen. It draws the moral from the cautionary tale: Keep your "heart" (the center of your selfhood) from her "ways." Learn from the victims who have gone before! Her "house" is the way to Sheol, going down to the chambers of death (v. 27).[117] Sheol, then, is a subterranean house whose chambers are filled with death.[118] This conclusion of the parental speeches powerfully draws together the symbols of woman, house, way, and cosmos (Sheol, the underworld) and so prepares the way for Wisdom's cosmic discourse in chap. 8 (cf. 1:12-13; 2:18-19; 5:5, 8; 9:18). At stake in the symbolism of women, ways, and houses is the very structure of the universe

---

115. See Gordon Paul Hugenberger, *Marriage as Covenant: A Study of Biblical Law and Ethics Governing Marriage Developed from the Perspective of Malachi,* SVT 52 (Leiden: Brill, 1994) 296-302.

116. For another view, see K. van der Toorn, "Prostitution (Cultic)," *ABD,* 5:511.

117. The combination of "ways" and "her house" in 7:27a needs no emendation. Cf. Job 38:19-20.

118. For the cosmos as a metaphorical house with chambers, see Commentary on 9:1; 24:3-4; see also Job 9:9; 37:9. The "chamber" is also the place of lovemaking; cf. Judg 15:1; 1 Kgs 1:15; Ps 45:13; cf. also Ps 19:4-5, with its cosmic images (though a different term for "chamber").

itself, a world where life is a journey (way) motivated by love for either Wisdom or Folly, whose end is life or death. The conditions for life in this world are thus: freedom within form, love within limits, and life within law. To try to live outside the (moral) order of existence is to enter the realm of death. The expression "chambers of death" reinforces the imagery of body and house (see Commentary on 18:8; 20:27).

REFLECTIONS

1. In this autobiographical instruction, the parent says, in effect, "This is what I have seen; learn from my observation and experience." The speech is an artistic "fiction," for the parent does not have access to the woman's intimate words or to the outcome of the tryst. Sometimes the literary genre of fiction, as in Ecclesiastes, best tells the truth about reality. The autobiographical form also models the passing on of experience from generation to generation. Those who are older offer the fruits of their living, hearing, remembering, and communal reflection to a younger generation of persons who have not lived long enough to learn for themselves what only life can teach (see Reflections on Proverbs 4).

2. This chapter presents an ancient, archetypal portrait of a *femme fatale* (see Commentary on 11:16). However, Proverbs 7 does not try to make a general statement about women's sexuality. Any attempt to stereotype women based on this specific portrait is mistaken, for Proverbs also portrays the woman as Wisdom and as a capable wife.

The literal point of chap. 7 is that sexually volatile men must learn to master their desires and fantasies, and not be overcome by them. For Proverbs, marriage is the relationship of commitment within which sexual freedom and delight are to be found (5:15-19). The metaphorical point of chap. 7 is that humans should avoid Folly and seek Wisdom instead. Because sexuality is such a powerful force in male experience, it serves in Proverbs as a paradigm for that self-limitation that human beings need in relation to all earthly goods. In New Testament terms, "there is great gain in godliness combined with contentment" (1 Tim 6:6 NRSV).

PROVERBS 8:1-36, WISDOM'S COSMIC SPEECH

NIV	NRSV

8 Does not wisdom call out? Does not understanding raise her voice?
 ²On the heights along the way,
  where the paths meet, she takes her stand;
 ³beside the gates leading into the city,
  at the entrances, she cries aloud:
 ⁴"To you, O men, I call out;
  I raise my voice to all mankind.
 ⁵You who are simple, gain prudence;
  you who are foolish, gain understanding.
 ⁶Listen, for I have worthy things to say;
  I open my lips to speak what is right.
 ⁷My mouth speaks what is true,
  for my lips detest wickedness.
	8 Does not wisdom call,
	  and does not understanding raise her
	   voice?
	 ² On the heights, beside the way,
	  at the crossroads she takes her stand;
	 ³ beside the gates in front of the town,
	  at the entrance of the portals she cries out:
	 ⁴ "To you, O people, I call,
	  and my cry is to all that live.
	 ⁵ O simple ones, learn prudence;
	  acquire intelligence, you who lack it.
	 ⁶ Hear, for I will speak noble things,
	  and from my lips will come what is right;
	 ⁷ for my mouth will utter truth;

NIV

⁸All the words of my mouth are just;
　　none of them is crooked or perverse.
⁹To the discerning all of them are right;
　　they are faultless to those who have
　　　knowledge.
¹⁰Choose my instruction instead of silver,
　　knowledge rather than choice gold,
¹¹for wisdom is more precious than rubies,
　　and nothing you desire can compare with her.
¹²"I, wisdom, dwell together with prudence;
　　I possess knowledge and discretion.
¹³To fear the LORD is to hate evil;
　　I hate pride and arrogance,
　　evil behavior and perverse speech.
¹⁴Counsel and sound judgment are mine;
　　I have understanding and power.
¹⁵By me kings reign
　　and rulers make laws that are just;
¹⁶by me princes govern,
　　and all nobles who rule on earth.ᵃ
¹⁷I love those who love me,
　　and those who seek me find me.
¹⁸With me are riches and honor,
　　enduring wealth and prosperity.
¹⁹My fruit is better than fine gold;
　　what I yield surpasses choice silver.
²⁰I walk in the way of righteousness,
　　along the paths of justice,
²¹bestowing wealth on those who love me
　　and making their treasuries full.

²²"The LORD brought me forth as the first of his
　　works,ᵇ, ᶜ
　　before his deeds of old;
²³I was appointedᵈ from eternity,
　　from the beginning, before the world began.
²⁴When there were no oceans, I was given birth,
　　when there were no springs abounding with
　　　water;
²⁵before the mountains were settled in place,
　　before the hills, I was given birth,
²⁶before he made the earth or its fields
　　or any of the dust of the world.
²⁷I was there when he set the heavens
　　in place,

ᵃ16 Many Hebrew manuscripts and Septuagint; most Hebrew
manuscripts *and nobles—all righteous rulers*　ᵇ22 Or *way;* or
dominion　ᶜ22 Or *The LORD possessed me at the beginning of his
work;* or *The LORD brought me forth at the beginning of his work*
ᵈ23 Or *fashioned*

NRSV

　　wickedness is an abomination to my lips.
⁸ All the words of my mouth are righteous;
　　there is nothing twisted or crooked in them.
⁹ They are all straight to one who understands
　　and right to those who find knowledge.
¹⁰ Take my instruction instead of silver,
　　and knowledge rather than choice gold;
¹¹ for wisdom is better than jewels,
　　and all that you may desire cannot compare
　　　with her.
¹² I, wisdom, live with prudence,ᵃ
　　and I attain knowledge and discretion.
¹³ The fear of the LORD is hatred of evil.
　Pride and arrogance and the way of evil
　　and perverted speech I hate.
¹⁴ I have good advice and sound wisdom;
　　I have insight, I have strength.
¹⁵ By me kings reign,
　　and rulers decree what is just;
¹⁶ by me rulers rule,
　　and nobles, all who govern rightly.
¹⁷ I love those who love me,
　　and those who seek me diligently find me.
¹⁸ Riches and honor are with me,
　　enduring wealth and prosperity.
¹⁹ My fruit is better than gold, even fine gold,
　　and my yield than choice silver.
²⁰ I walk in the way of righteousness,
　　along the paths of justice,
²¹ endowing with wealth those who love me,
　　and filling their treasuries.

²² The LORD created me at the beginningᵇ of his
　　work,ᶜ
　　the first of his acts of long ago.
²³ Ages ago I was set up,
　　at the first, before the beginning of the
　　　earth.
²⁴ When there were no depths I was brought
　　　forth,
　　when there were no springs abounding with
　　　water.
²⁵ Before the mountains had been shaped,
　　before the hills, I was brought forth—
²⁶ when he had not yet made earth and fields,ᵃ
　　or the world's first bits of soil.
²⁷ When he established the heavens, I was there,

ᵃMeaning of Heb uncertain　ᵇOr *me as the beginning*
ᶜHeb *way*

NIV

when he marked out the horizon on the face
of the deep,²⁸when he established the
clouds above
and fixed securely the fountains of the deep,
²⁹when he gave the sea its boundary
so the waters would not overstep his
command,
and when he marked out the foundations of the
earth.
³⁰   Then I was the craftsman at his side.
I was filled with delight day after day,
rejoicing always in his presence,
³¹rejoicing in his whole world
and delighting in mankind.

³²"Now then, my sons, listen to me;
blessed are those who keep my ways.
³³Listen to my instruction and be wise;
do not ignore it.
³⁴Blessed is the man who listens to me,
watching daily at my doors,
waiting at my doorway.
³⁵For whoever finds me finds life
and receives favor from the LORD.
³⁶But whoever fails to find me harms himself;
all who hate me love death."

NRSV

when he drew a circle on the face of the
deep,
²⁸ when he made firm the skies above,
when he established the fountains of the
deep,
²⁹ when he assigned to the sea its limit,
so that the waters might not transgress his
command,
when he marked out the foundations of the
earth,
³⁰   then I was beside him, like a master
worker;ᵃ
and I was daily hisᵇ delight,
rejoicing before him always,
³¹ rejoicing in his inhabited world
and delighting in the human race.

³² "And now, my children, listen to me:
happy are those who keep my ways.
³³ Hear instruction and be wise,
and do not neglect it.
³⁴ Happy is the one who listens to me,
watching daily at my gates,
waiting beside my doors.
³⁵ For whoever finds me finds life
and obtains favor from the LORD;
³⁶ but those who miss me injure themselves;
all who hate me love death."

ᵃAnother reading is *little child*   ᵇGk: Heb lacks *his*

COMMENTARY

The great poem of cosmic Wisdom falls into seven subsections of five verses each. These five-verse units then combine to form the larger structures of the poem:

vv. 1-5, Introduction: Location and Addressees
vv. 6-26, Wisdom's Priceless Virtues
   vv. 6-11, Her Righteous Words
   vv. 12-16, Her Role in Civil Order
   vv. 17-21, Her Gifts for All Who Love Her
vv. 22-31, Wisdom and the Creation of the Cosmos
   vv. 22-26, Her Genesis Before Creation
   vv. 27-36, Her Role in Cosmic Order
vv. 32-36, Final Invitation and Warning

Prov 8:11, in the third person, and 8:13*a* are editorial additions. Prov 8:29*a* is thematic and not an editorial expansion (although the LXX lacks it). Rather, the tricola in 8:29-30 are climactic. Verses 1-5 combines a description of Wisdom's location and her first words, but these establish all humans as her audience. Prov 8:6 then begins with the usual call to hear.

8:1-5. This section presents Wisdom as virtually omnipresent in the human city: on the heights, in the streets, at the crossroads, and especially at the gates. It was at the gate, in ancient cities, that people would come and go, congregate, and conduct the business of life. There, folks could buy and sell, settle disputes, and arrange marriages (vv. 1-3; cf 1:20-21; Ruth 4:1-12). The city gate is the place for justice (Deut 21:19; 2 Sam 15:1-6; cf. Job 29:7-25). Here, the wise "open their mouths" (24:7) and prophets advise kings (1 Kgs 22:10). These "openings" of the city are places of encounter, where life's basic transactions and transitions occur. Here decisions are made and people "enter into" new situations and embark on new journeys. Where thresholds are crossed and the issues of life decided, there Wisdom takes her stand and speaks. But so does Folly (7:11-12; 9:13-15).

Personified wisdom (חכמה ḥokmâ) is more precisely specified by its parallel term, understanding (תבונה tĕbûnâ). "Understanding" designates the practical competence, or know-how, by which actions are accomplished (see Commentary on 3:19-20; 24:3-4).[119] This term anticipates the active role of Lady Wisdom in "building" creation (8:27-31; 3:19; cf. Ps 136:5; Jer 10:12; 51:15; see Commentary on 9:1).

Through its vocabulary and phrases, the poem in Proverbs 8 establishes links with other parts of Proverbs 1–9 and with the book as a whole. Most of the key terms in the densely compacted prologue (1:1-7) reappear, sprinkled throughout Wisdom's speech (8:1-36; cf. 1:4 and 8:12; 1:7 and 8:13a). Such verbal links communicate that the book's teaching is grounded in cosmic wisdom.

The "body" language of vv. 1-3 suggests that "city" also belongs to the metaphorical interaction of "way," woman's "body," woman's "house" (see Commentary on 8:24; 9:1; cf. Ps 127:1), and "cosmos." Both the wise and the foolish women are located in the "openings" of the city or house. So women are not identical with the city or house (or cosmos) but inhabit it and speak from within it. Folly and Wisdom inhabit the same world, and they affect the son's experience of the world for good or for ill, because his relation to the women reflects his relation to reality and its goods. To enter the "doors" of the wrong woman's body or house is to leave the path of life and enter Sheol, the underworld realm of death and damage (see Commentary on 2:18-19; 5:5-6; 7:25-27). On the other hand, to embrace Wisdom is to embrace reality and life (8:17-21, 34-35); her house contains a life-giving feast (9:1-6). In this, too, the

houses reveal the structure of the cosmos, with its places, persons, and activities permitted or forbidden, life-enhancing or stultifying. The women (good or bad) represent the ordered or disordered goods of the cosmos, those that are legitimate and those that are off-limits and deadly.

In its own way, then, this poem continues to play the "intricate game with 'house' and 'way' " so prominent in Proverbs 7.[120] Lady Wisdom is the foil to the seductress of chap. 7, an opposition repeated again in chap. 9. The symbolic equivalences among "city," "woman," and "Wisdom" as cosmic order are now fully operative. The "crossroads" where Wisdom takes her stand is literally "the house of ways" (בית נתיבות bêt nĕtîbôt; cf. 7:27). The heaping up of terms for entrances to the city ("gates," "entrance," "portals") uses words elsewhere used of the openings of the strange woman's body/house. In 8:3 (the NRSV unnecessarily emends the text to read "in front of the town"), the Hebrew actually calls the city gate the "mouth of the town" (פי-קרת pî-qāret; see Commentary on 22:6). "Portals" (פתחים pĕtāḥîm) is literally "openings," a term used for both the entrance into the strange woman's deadly "house" (5:8; see Commentary on 5:4; 9:14; 30:20; cf. 31:26) and the entrance into Wisdom's house of life (8:34-35; cf. Sir 14:22-27).

In sum, the city is the culture-shaped world of humans, a reflection in miniature of the world itself where Lady Wisdom has been active from the beginning (8:22-31), and where she presently speaks to all humans (8:4, 31) in their condition of moral and spiritual ambiguity (8:5; see Commentary on 9:1).[121] Here, as throughout chaps. 1–9, human beings are represented under the figure of young men ready for wife and Wisdom, yet prone to illicit loves. The point is that Wisdom speaks everywhere, to everyone with ears to hear. In this she is much like the mysterious voice of divine origin that "goes out through all the earth" (Ps 19:1-4 NRSV), reveals God's righteousness, and finds expression in Israel's tôrâ (v. 4; cf. Pss

---

119. Michael V. Fox, "Terms for Wisdom," *Zeitschrift für Althebräistik* 6 (1993) 149-69, see esp. 153, 158.

120. Robert Alter, *The Art of Biblical Poetry* (New York: Basic Books, 1985) 60.

121. In house and city building, a person "must create his own world and assume the responsibility of maintaining and renewing it. . . . The house . . . is the universe that man constructs for himself by imitating the paradigmatic creation of the gods, the cosmogony." So M. Eliade, *The Sacred and the Profane: The Nature of Religion* (New York: Harcourt Brace Jovanovich, 1959) 56-57, see also 172-79.

50:6; 97:6; Rom 1:18-20; 2:14-15).[122] Whatever Wisdom is, no one can claim not to have heard her voice. Like the Stoic personification of virtue, "she is open to all, admits all, and invites all."[123] Wisdom, as God's agent, speaks in and through the creation and its creatures, which all give indirect testimony to her norms (cf. Job 12:7-10; Isa 28:23-29; Jer 8:7-9).[124] In contrast to the other speeches in chaps. 1–9, Wisdom specifies her addressees as all humans, but especially naive ("simple") and foolish people, who may yet change (8:3-5; cf. 1:22).

8:6-21. These verses (along with vv. 22-31) are Wisdom's self-presentation. Self-praise seems strange to Westerners today, for whom it seems immodest and naive. But the function of such speech is like a modern résumé, in which people present their qualifications for a position. Not to know Wisdom leaves one open to choosing Folly. Through her self-presentation, Wisdom enables humans to seek and to find the truth about reality, since she herself is its key. Her self-praise is not self-indulgent (as if Wisdom were insecure and needed to boast), but for the benefit of people who need to know her for their own well-being. In similar fashion, the Lord is presented to the defeated exiles in Second Isaiah, to folk who have become uncertain about the identity of the master of the universe (Isa 42:8; 43:14-21, 25; 44:6-8, 24-28; 45:5-7; 51:12-16; cf. Exod 20:1).

There are parallels to Wisdom's self-presentation from other ancient Near Eastern lands. Various Egyptian gods and goddesses engage in self-presentation and self-praise: Re, Isis, Hike (= magic power).[125] Maat, the goddess of world order and justice, presents herself as being present at the beginning of creation, much like Wisdom in Proverbs 8.[126] Characteristic in these self-presentations is the declaration, "I am so and so," or "I am such and such." Examples are also extant from Mesopotamia. One of these is a speech of Gula, wise goddess of healing:

"I am noble, I am lordly, I am splendid and
  sublime.
"My station is on high, I am a woman of
  dignity.
"I excel among goddesses. . . .
"I am the physician, I can save life,
"I carry every herb, I banish illness . . .
"I give health to mankind. . . .
"At a word from me, the feeble one arises.
"I am merciful, [I am] kindly. . . .
"I am a warrior and am skilled through
  experience . . .
"I make decisions, I give commands . . .
"I have mercy on the weak, I enrich the
  destitute,
"I bestow life on the one who reveres
  me.
"I make straight the path of the one who
  seeks after my ways,
"I am the great one, daughter of Anu
  [= the high god].[127]

Yet the speech of Wisdom employs a broader range of utterances than the "I am . . ." formula. These range from first-person action verbs and participles to prepositional phrases such as "by me."

8:6-11. These verses focus on the quality of Wisdom's words. They open the body of Wisdom's speech with the conventional "hear," but the imperative is plural. Cosmic Wisdom's address is universal; her audience is not restricted (v. 4). This section employs key terms from the prologue (1:1-7) to characterize Wisdom's teaching (cf. 8:12 and 1:4; the roots for "justice" and "righteousness" in 1:3 appear in 8:15-16). But vv. 6-10 are not rich in specific allusions to other passages (cf. the praise of divine law in Ps 19:8-11). Yet, the editorial addition of v. 11 links this section to 3:15 and to the virtuous woman in 31:10.

---

122. The juxtaposition of cosmic voice in Ps 19:1-6 with the "law" (Torah) in vv. 7-13 is an early development in traditions that give a cosmic (Wisdom or Word) setting to Israel's Torah (cf. Ps 147:15-20; Sir 24:23; Bar 4:1; John 1:1-3, 14-18; Col 1:5-6, 15-20). See G. von Rad, *Wisdom in Israel* (Nashville: Abingdon, 1972) 53-73, 78, 92, 144-76.

123. Cited by M. Hengel, *Judaism and Hellenism,* vol. 2 (Philadelphia: Fortress, 1974) 98n. 296.

124. Lang calls this the "language of things" and gives a fine Ugaritic example: "I have a tale that I would tell you, a word that I would repeat to you, a tale of trees and a whisper of stones, the sighing of the heavens to the earth, of the oceans to the stars." See B. Lang, *Wisdom and the Book of Proverbs: An Israelite Goddess Redefined* (New York: Pilgrim, 1986). See also *Ancient Near Eastern Texts Relating to the Old Testament,* ed. James B. Prichard, 3rd ed. (Princeton, N.J.: Princeton University Press, 1969)136; cf. Ps 42:8; Hos 2:23.

125. Christa Kayatz, *Studien zu Proverbien 1–9,* WANT 22 (Neukirchen-Vluyn: Neukirchener Verlag, 1966) 86-93.

126. Coffin Text 80, cited in J. Assmann, *Ägypten—Theologie und Frömmigkeit einer frühen Hochkultur* (Stuttgart: Urban, 1984) 211. See also H. Ringgren, *Word and Wisdom: Studies in the Hypostatization of Divine Qualities and Functions in the Ancient Near East* (Lund: Hakan Ohlssons Boktryckeri, 1947) 27.

127. "Gula Hymn of Bullutsa-Rabi," in Benjamin R. Foster, *Before the Muses: An Anthology of Akkadian Literature* (Bethesda, Md.: CDL, 1993) 2:491-99.

This section insists on the verbal character and quality of Wisdom's teaching. Human wisdom is revealed by what people say (13:14; 15:7; 16:23-24). Similarly, Wisdom's words reveal her insights. Wisdom's words mediate God's wisdom for life in the cosmos and are reflected in human language and tradition (see Commentary on 6:20-23; 7:1-3; 30:4-5). Crucial to this poem is the idea that Wisdom speaks in and through the cosmos and its creatures.

The poem accentuates the bodily instruments of speech by repetition and variation: "lips," "palate" ("mouth"), "lips," "mouth" (vv. 6-8). These terms previously appeared as instruments of the strange woman's seduction (see Commentary on 5:3). Although Wisdom's words are "right" (as in Ps 19:8), they are only so "to one who understands . . . to those who find" (v. 9; cf. the Gula hymn above). In the self-presentation of Hammurabi, king of Babylon (c. 1750 BCE), a similar perspective appears:

I, Hammurabi, am the king of justice,
to whom Shamash [god of justice] committed law.
My words are choice; my deeds have no equal;
it is only to the fool that they are empty;
to the wise they stand forth as an object of wonder.[128]

Humans betray a contrariness to Wisdom (and to God, Wisdom's source). Humans can not only recognize and embrace, but also distort, reject, ignore, or rebel against what is right (Ezek 18:25; Amos 5:7, 10). It is as if we need wisdom before wisdom makes sense to us (14:6; 17:16). Wisdom's first speech held human beings responsible for stubbornly rejecting her counsel (1:20-33; cf. Isa 6:9-10; 1 Cor 2:14-16). Here the problem seems to be people who are not so much rebellious but, as it were, tone deaf. Such folk are unable to recognize the good, the true, and the noble when they hear it (cf. Phil 4:8). They are out of tune with reality and the right. Wisdom and goodness make no sense to them. Only those with "ears to hear" actually hear (Matt 10:13-17).

This section concludes with advice to "take my instruction" rather than silver or gold. The editorial v. 11 comments on v. 10 by quoting 3:15. In this way, Proverbs 8 is explicitly linked with the earlier parental instruction on the virtues of cosmic Wisdom. At the same time, v. 11 fore-shadows the human embodiment of Wisdom in the valiant woman of Prov 31:10, at the book's very end.

8:12-16. Here Wisdom presents her indispensable role for civil or social order. In the ancient Near East, kingship was the organizing social principle for every sphere of life.[129] Each verse of this unit begins or ends with a similar-sounding, self-referential pronoun, "I"/"me" (cf. v. 17). The repeated "I"/"me" creates a powerful rhetorical effect of insistent self-assertion. There is no escaping Wisdom in the courts of the high and the mighty. She is the standard and norm for government.

8:13a. The pattern of first-person speech by Wisdom is broken. The verse thus appears to be an editorial addition, designed to link Wisdom to the "fear of the LORD" (see Commentary on 1:7; 9:10). In combining the fear of the Lord with turning from evil, v. 13a has a close parallel in 3:7 and Job 28:28 (cf. Job 1:1, 8; 2:3; Prov 14:16). The remainder of v. 13 expresses Wisdom's hatred of "pride and arrogance" and "evil," to which high and mighty rulers are prone. (In Hebrew, "pride" [גֵּאָה *gēʾâ*] and "arrogance" [גָּאוֹן *gāʾôn*] punningly allude to the height [*gāʾôn*] of the powerful.) Like the Lord, Wisdom hates evil and arrogance (6:16-19; cf. 2:12, 14).

8:14. The way is prepared in this verse for vv. 15-16 as Wisdom claims for herself those qualities that are indispensable for successful government: counsel, sound wisdom (see Commentary on 2:7), and strength. In 21:30-31, these things are subordinate to the Lord or are possessions of the Lord (the word for "sound wisdom" [תּוּשִׁיָּה *tûšiyyâ*] in v. 14 is translated "victory" in 21:31). Here and increasingly in the following verses, Wisdom's closeness to Yahweh is revealed.

8:15-16. When Wisdom says, "By me kings reign," she claims that all royal functions are done in accordance with her authority and gifts. (For these functions of justice and righteousness and the cosmic blessings that attend justice, see Psalm 72 and Isa 11:1-9.) Her words and speech convey these gifts to humans (vv. 1-11). Wisdom is an active agent in creation, including human affairs. The expression "by me" (or "with me") has an exact, albeit negative, counterpart in a hymn to

---

128. *ANET*, 178, italics added.

129. See H. H. Schmid, *Gerechtigkeit als Weltordnung* (Tübingen: Mohr-Siebeck, 1968).

Marduk, the Babylonian creator god who is the counselor among the gods (like his father, Ea).

Without you, Shamash judges no case,
Without you, no verdict is rendered for the land . . .
Without you, the destitute and widow are not cared for.[130]

In the ancient Near East, kings ruled, judged, waged war, protected the weak, and gave laws by means of the authority and gifts of the gods. They mediated divine blessings to the people and ensured peace and prosperity. Thus the great king of Babylon, Hammurabi, could say that he carried out the various functions of kingship:

With the mighty weapon which . . . Inanna entrusted to me,
with the insight [wisdom] that Enki allotted to me,
with the ability that Marduk gave me.[131]

Similarly, in a setting where Yahweh alone was to be worshiped, Wisdom declares that all the kings and rulers of the earth (v. 16*b* NIV) carry out their functions "by/with me"—that is, by using Wisdom's gifts of insight, justice, and state craft according to her cosmic standards, as determined by Yahweh at creation. This cosmic connection with human government is a common presupposition of ancient Near Eastern and biblical thought. In this text it is spelled out by means of a series of wordplays on the thematic Hebrew root חקק (*ḥqq*). Just as the Lord "marked out" (חקק *ḥāqaq*) "the horizon on the face of the deep" and "gave to the sea its boundary" (*ḥāqaq*), and as God "marked out" (*ḥāqaq*) "the foundations of the earth" (vv. 27, 29), so also do human rulers "decree" (*ḥāqaq*) "what is just" (v. 15).[132]

8:17-21. These verses turn to the motif of seeking and finding, in the context of mutual love between Lady Wisdom and her human suitors, portrayed throughout these chapters in the figure

of a young man ready for marriage (see Commentary on 2:1-4, 11-19; 8:35; cf. 4:6, 8; 29:3). This language also recalls the contrary love of the stranger (7:15, 18). Language of love marks the beginning and the end of this section. Wisdom promises her devotees wealth within the path of justice and righteousness (vv. 18-21). That is, the material goods of creation are not acquired by doing violence to others or by cleverly, perhaps even legally, expanding one's own little "kingdom" at the expense of a neighbor or by violating the good order of the creation itself.

8:22-31. This section provides the warrant for the extraordinary claims made by Wisdom in vv. 6-21. The warrant falls into two parts: vv. 22-26 establish her temporal priority before all created things, and vv. 27-31 establish her active presence at God's work of creation.

8:22-26. Verse 22 has inspired much argument over the centuries, because the verb קנה (*qānâ*) bears several meanings. Besides "create" (Gen 14:19, 22; Ps 139:13; Ugaritic cognate) it can also mean "to acquire" and so "to possess." (The NIV's "brought forth" appears to be a meaning derived from the birth imagery of its context, vv. 24*a*, 25*b*; cf. Gen 4:1; but in Ps 139:13 it makes no sense to say, "You brought forth my inward parts."). In v. 22, Wisdom appears to have been created by the Lord, but she exists prior to and on a different plane from all other creatures (see Reflections). Since Wisdom determines cosmic order and addresses human beings concerning that order, she is the prior condition for the existence and functioning of all things.

The temporal priority of Wisdom is crucial because being wise requires knowledge of reality and the events that take place in it, and this can only be gained over time. Events happen in time, and, other than God, only one who has been there from the absolute beginning knows the whole story. Only Wisdom can be completely wise, since she has seen it all from the beginning. In the human realm, only long experience gives insight into human nature and knowledge of individuals. Consequently, much of the Bible comprises narratives that expand our experience of reality beyond what is possible in one brief lifetime. Thus the OT, the only Bible the early church had, can serve to make humans wise (so the Greek) for living (2 Tim 3:15-17). Similarly, many of the

---

130. Benjamin R. Foster, *Before the Muses,* 2:607-8. Shamash is the sun god, the god of justice. Twelve lines begin, "Without you. . . ." The hymn presents a variety of cultural functions that cannot take place without Marduk. Cf. John 1:3, "without him not one thing came into being" (NRSV).

131. Epilogue to the *Code of Hammurabi,* in *ANET,* 178. Inanna is the goddess of love and war; Enki/Ea is the god of wisdom, counselor to the gods; Marduk is the god of Babylon, son of Enki and endowed with Enki's wisdom.

132. Words based on the root חקק (*ḥqq*) appear four times (vv. 15, 27, 29 twice). The effect of this repetition is strengthened by the repetition of the root's sounds in other words in the immediate context: שׁחקים (*šeḥāqîm,* v. 28); משׂחקת (*mĕśaheqet,* vv. 30-31).

short sayings in Proverbs 10–29 may be seen as narratives in a nutshell that compress typical human events into their essence.

Wisdom's priority in time fits with the ancient view that only the old can be wise, for only they have experienced the world and life. They have gone through the "school of hard knocks." Thus wisdom is the province of the old: "The glory of youths is their strength, but the beauty of the aged is their gray hair" (20:29 NRSV, where gray hair symbolizes wisdom; cf. 16:31). Rehoboam's great mistake was to ignore the advice of the wise old counselors, and instead follow his foolish young friends (1 Kgs 12:1-19). In language similar to Prov 8:25, the "friends" of Job attack his claims to wisdom: "Are you the firstborn of the human race? Were you brought forth before the hills?" (Job 15:7 NRSV; cf. Ps 90:2). In the NT, the language of Wisdom's priority and involvement in creation is applied to Christ (Col 1:15-20; cf. John 1:1-3).

8:27-31. The presence of Wisdom at God's primordial creation and ordering of all things is equally important. This means that she not only knows all the particulars and individual quirks revealed in the history of humankind from the beginning, but that she also knows equally the basic structures, components, patterns, and functions of reality (cf. Wis 9:9, 11). These are the constant, unshakeable conditions of human and cosmic existence, within which change and development take place. These regularities of reality (like the separation of sea and dry land and the daily rising of the sun) make life possible. Without knowing the fundamental, normative patterns of reality, no one can evaluate historical change or judge whether rulers indeed "make laws that are just" (8:15). Wisdom's knowledge of the cosmos (including human nature and justice) provides a stable point of reference by which to judge the new things that occur in human history and behavior.

The writer does not arbitrarily or casually describe some of God's cosmic acts. Rather, through the use of terms like "heavens," "deep," "sea," and "earth," the entire universe is depicted as Wisdom's province (vv. 27-29, 31). These words represent the three realms (sky, waters, land) that for the ancients encompassed all of reality (cf. Exod 20:4; Ps 24:1-2). Various key words and images show that the grand ordering of God's cosmos was done in wisdom (3:13-20), and that human society is regulated by similar cosmic principles.

Some examples may show this correlation between the macrocosmos (world) and the microcosmos of human existence. According to v. 27, the Lord established the heavens. An Egyptian parallel shows how loaded such a phrase is with implications for human life, because the cosmic order establishes the human. Othmar Keel describes an Eighteenth Dynasty (1570–1345 BCE) wall painting from west Thebes:

A qualified village elder, or perhaps the owner of the field himself, takes the following oath while holding the *was* scepter: "As surely as the great god endures in the heavens, this boundary stone is properly erected." From ancient times, the *was*-scepter symbolized the immovability of the pillars of the heavens . . . the *was*-scepter held by the person taking the oath may illustrate the stereotyped saying: "I have set such and such a boundary stone as firmly as the heavens are established." . . . The earthly order emulates the heavenly, and like the heavenly, it is guaranteed by the deity.[133]

Israel too believed that God had made firm the structures of heaven and earth. In similar fashion, human structures and boundaries ought to be fair and stable (cf. 15:25; 22:28; 23:10-11; Deut 19:14; 27:17). Just as the cosmic realms are firmly in place, so also should just human boundaries be observed and protected.

Perhaps the most frequent image of God's setting cosmic limits has to do with God's putting a boundary to the chaotic, playful waters of the sea (v. 29). This verse has parallels in the majestic hymn on creation (Ps 104:9), in God's speech from the whirlwind (Job 38:8-11), and in Jeremiah's prophetic word to a "foolish and senseless people" who, unlike the sea, do not know how to stay within God's limits (Jer 5:21-29). In God's economy, all things, including human beings and their various activities, have their proper place and limits. This wisdom principle, grounded in creation thinking, is nicely spelled out in the parable of the war between the sea and the forest in 2 Esdr 4:13-21. In the context of the imagery of

133. O. Keel, *The Symbolism of the Biblical World: Ancient Near Eastern Iconography and the Book of Psalms* (New York: Seabury, 1978) 96. See further, R. C. Van Leeuwen, "Liminality and World View in Proverbs 1–9, *Semeia* 50 (1990) 119. Cf. Jer 31:35-37.

Proverbs 1–9, with its focus on sexual relations, God's limits on the cosmic waters in chap. 8 provide a model for the limits on human sexual "waters" (5:15-20) and on human behavior generally.[134]

The grounding of human order in cosmic order is emphasized in Proverbs 8 also by the repetition of the thematic root *ḥāqaq,* which is used both of God's ordering of the cosmos and of the ordering of human affairs (see Commentary on 8:15-16). Jeremiah 31:35-37 is comparable, where the stable decrees of nature are a standard for God's covenant promises—that is, for the social order and obligations that obtain between Yahweh and Israel.

Verse 30 is famous among exegetes for the uncertainty surrounding the rare word אמון (*ʾāmôn*).[135] The main interpretations are that the word here means (a) "little child" (NRSV margin); (b) "master worker" (cognate with Akkadian *ummānu* and Aramaic *ʾumān*;[136] cf. Cant 7:2; Jer 52:15, with a disputed text); (c) "architect's plan," something like a builder's blueprint for the cosmos (so *Genesis Rabbah* 1.1, identifying Wisdom and Mosaic *tôrâ*); and (d) that the grammar may be read differently, *ʾāmôn,* so that the word refers to God: "Then I was with [God], the master worker."

The first view (a) appeals to Egyptian Maat, the goddess of cosmic and social order, who is portrayed as playing before her father, the creator god Re. This parallel appears to accommodate the apparently strange association among world order, a personal being, and play with delight. Position (c) is simply derived from (b) by way of narrative elaboration: an architect needs plans—i.e., the Torah in its written and oral forms—to build the cosmos. Position (d) has not found wide support.

It seems best to take the *ʾāmôn* of v. 30 in terms of position (b), based on the Akkadian

cognate *ummānu,* but understood in a broader sense than "master worker." The Akkadian word generally means "wise," "expert," "skilled"; it can refer to a wide range of wisdom, practical skill, and expertise. The *ummānu* can be a counselor, adviser, or scribe.[137] The Hebrew term for "wisdom" (חכמה *ḥokmâ*) bears a similar broad semantic range, including the practical skill to make a temple (Exod 31:1-6; 1 Kgs 7:13-14). A first-person speech by Enki (Akkadian Ea), the Sumerian god of wisdom, may illustrate the role of an *ummānu* (or *apkallu,* a related designation that applies to the primordial wise men before the flood).[138] Although the text is in the Sumerian language and does not use the term *ummānu,* its conceptual world fits it precisely and illustrates certain aspects of Proverbs 8.

My father, the king of the universe,
Brought me into existence in the universe,
My ancestor, the king of all the lands,
Gathered together all the "me's," placed the "me's" in my hand....
I brought craftsmanship to my Abzu of Eridu . . .
I am the first born son of An . . .
I am he who brings full prosperity, . . .
I am he who directs justice with the king An on An's dais [i.e., as royal counselor, or *apkallu*].[139]

Just as Enki is the wise counselor of the divine king Anu, who orders the universe and the arts of civilization, so also Proverbs 8 personifies Wisdom as the architect associate of Yahweh at the creation of the world. The *ʾāmôn* in v. 30 is Wisdom personified as the king's architect-adviser, through whom the king puts all things in their proper order and whose decrees of cosmic justice are the standard for human kings and rulers (v. 15).[140] This interpretation accords with pictures

134. Besides the general emphasis of liquids in 5:15-20 and 8:22-29, note the vocabulary common to these two passages: "springs," "waters," "abroad" = "fields" (חוץ *ḥûṣ*, 5:16; 8:26; cf. 1:20; 7:12), "at all times" (5:19, of sexual delight) = "always" (8:30). "Streets" and "squares/abroad" link 5:16 not with chap. 8, but with Wisdom in 1:20 (in contrast to 7:12; cf. 8:1-3).

135. R. B. Y. Scott, "Wisdom in Creation: The *ʾāmôn* of Proverbs VIII 30," *VT* 10 (1960) 213-33.

136. The Aramaic term, like its Akkadian forebear, has a wide semantic range and can refer to a person practicing almost any skill, craft, or profession. In some Palestinian synagogue inscriptions, the word is used of synagogue builders (whether architect, builder, or both is not clear). See Joseph A. Fitzmyer and Daniel J. Harrington, *A Manual of Palestinian Aramaic Texts* (Rome: Pontifical Biblical Institute, 1978) 254-57. In *Targum Neophyti* to Exod 31:5, a cognate term is used for skilled work in metals and precious stones for the tabernacle.

137. See M. Fishbane, *Biblical Interpretation in Ancient Israel* (Oxford: Clarendon, 1985) 26n. 11.

138. The *apkallu* served to "insure the correct functioning of the plans of heaven and earth." After the flood, the role of *apkallu* is subsumed by the *ummānu.* "This is not an easy term to translate since it covers a broad spectrum including 'scribe, scholar, master craftsman, officer.' " J. C. Greenfield, "The Seven Pillars of Wisdom (Prov. 9:1)—A Mistranslation," *JQR* 76 (1985) 15-17.

139. "Enki and the World Order," in S. N. Kramer, *The Sumerians: Their History, Character, and Culture* (Chicago: University of Chicago Press, 1963), 174-83. The Sumerian word *me* designates basic units of world order that apply to and regulate divine and human social institutions and practices. The one who controls the "me's" "fixes the borders, marks off the boundaries" (issues of justice, see the discussion of *ḥāqaq* in the Commentary on 8:15, 29) and takes "charge of the crook, staff, and wand of shepherdship" (= kingship).

140. For the *ummānu* as "royal counselor," see Jean Bottéro, *Mesopotamia: Writing, Reasoning, and the Gods* (Chicago: University of Chicago Press, 1992) 246-49.

elsewhere in the OT where God as king consults the heavenly court in carrying out decisions (esp. Gen 1:26; cf. Deut 32:6b-9; 1 Kgs 22:19-22; Job 1–2; Isa 6:1-9).

This reading of Wisdom in Proverbs 8 has an antecedent in the book of Wisdom, where the human king needs Wisdom's presence both to rule wisely and to build a temple, because "she knows your works and was present when you made the world" (Wis 9:1-12; cf. 8:4). Wisdom 7:21 and 8:6 allude directly to Prov 8:30 and call Wisdom the "fashioner" of the world (which does not exclude God as "fashioner," Wis 13:1; cf. Prov 3:19).

Scholars have often been puzzled by the delight in v. 31, uncertain as to how it might fit with the "architect-adviser" ("master workman") reading of 'āmôn in v. 30. Hence many have taken 'āmôn as a "nursling" who plays before the Lord. This inference is unnecessary, however. A counselor who gives good advice is a source of delight to the one counseled: "Your decrees are my delight, they are my counselors" (Ps 119:24 NRSV). And Israel, pictured as a vineyard created by God's hard work, is called the "garden of his delight" (Isa 5:7 NIV).

In the ancient Near East, building projects, especially cities, palaces, and temples, were a source of delight both in execution and at their completion. Ashurnasirpal II rebuilt the city of Calah "in that wisdom of mine, the knowledge which Ea . . . has bestowed upon me." Its palace was "a palace of joy and (erected with) great ingenuity." In addition to this joy in the process of "creation," there was celebration and feasting upon completion. So Ashurnasirpal, his palace finished, prepared a giant banquet, slaughtered many beasts (listed in detail), and claimed a total of "69,574 invited guests."[141] Again, an inscription of Assyrian king Tukulti-Ninurta I reads: "I built a temple and completed it and set up a dais. Annunita my Lady in joy and happiness I seated on her dais."[142] Similarly, in Jer 30:18-19 and 31:4 the same pattern (and verb) of playful rejoic-

ing after the (re)building of the city appears (cf. Zech 8:5). When Solomon completed the "house" of the Lord (a microcosmic mirror of the universe), a seven- (or fourteen-) day feast was held, and the king sent the people on their way, "joyful and glad in heart" (1 Kgs 8:62-66 NIV).

This move from cosmic construction to joy, delight, and feasting is basic to Proverbs 8 and 9:1-6, which follow a widespread ancient pattern that combines joy in building with celebration at its completion and inauguration. Indeed, this pattern is universal. In 8:21-30, we have the "building" of the cosmos, employing verbs commonly used of human building projects. The joy in 8:30-31 is joy at the construction and completion of the ordered world, including the human world (cf. Job 38:7). In keeping with the cosmic symbolism of "house," the banquet scene in 9:1-6 must also be understood against this background (see Commentary on 9:1).

The above data suggest that the Lord's delight is in Wisdom, but not because of her playful performance as a "little child."[143] Rather, the Lord delights in Wisdom's active role in creation (8:27-29, 31). Ultimately, the arena of Wisdom's delight and rejoicing is the inhabited world of human beings—that is, the completed creation. Wisdom delights in the world of human culture, and to humans she speaks, so that they may live according to the wisdom she imparts (8:3-21, 31-36). The conclusion of creation is delight. This delight arises from creation's goodness, which is celebrated every sabbath (Genesis 1; Exod 20:8-11; 31:7). When God put the creation in order, "all the heavenly beings shouted for joy" (Job 38:7 NRSV; cf. Ps 104:15, 31, 34; Bar 3:34).

8:32-36. The closing section gives a final invitation and warning and prepares the transition to chap. 9, with its banquet scene upon completion of the "house." The reference to Wisdom's "doors" in v. 34 anticipates the metaphor of the two houses, which dominates 9:1-6, 13-18, especially 9:13-14, where the "foolish woman . . . sits at the door of her house" (NRSV). Between the chapters there is implicit movement from waiting (8:34) to entry upon invitation (9:1-6, 13-18; cf. Matt 25:10).

---

141. *ANET,* 558, 560. In the Ugaritic Baal cycle, Kothar wa-Khasis, the wise artisan god, builds Baal's "house" in seven days with fire. Thereupon beasts are slaughtered, guests invited, and the banquet is held (*ANET,* 134).

142. Cited in V. Hurowitz, *I Have Built You an Exalted House: Temple Building in the Bible in Light of Mesopotamian and Northwest Semitic Writings* (Sheffield: JSOT, 1992) 100.

143. See Othmar Keel, *Die Weisheit Spielt vor Gott: Ein ikonographischer Beitrag zur Deutung des měṣaḥăqät in Sprüche 8, 30f.* (Fribourg: Universitätsverlag, 1974).

Conventional wisdom language is used in this sermon. The "blessed" of vv. 34-35 repeats the blessing and love imagery ("seek," "find," "embrace") from 3:11-18. Wisdom is to be sought and found like a wife. The symbolic equivalence of Wisdom and woman/wife is once again reinforced, not only for chaps. 1–9, but for the entire book in its final form as well. Both Wisdom and wife are gifts from God, and to love them faithfully puts one in touch with God (18:22 par. 8:35; 19:14; 31:10-31). This notion of Wisdom as bride is richly developed in Wis 8:2-16.[144] The final line of Proverbs 8 is staggering in its bluntness: "All who hate me love death."

144. See David Winston, *The Wisdom of Solomon*, AB 43 (New York: Doubleday, 1979) 192-96.

REFLECTIONS

1. The identity of personified Wisdom is much debated. Indeed, her metaphorical portrayal should caution against finding a simple referent for the poem. She exists both as a person who speaks and as cosmic reality. Like some other parts of Scripture, this poem is multireferential. One may compare the famous Immanuel prophecy. Christians maintain that, in some profound sense, Jesus is the fulfillment of the Immanuel ("God with us") prophecy in Isa 7:14 (see Matt 1:23). Yet Isaiah's prophecy clearly refers to events and persons in Isaiah's day and was fulfilled some seven hundred years before Christ. Similarly, while Proverbs 8 is background for Christian understandings of Christ as the Wisdom and Word of God, our first task is to understand this female personification of Wisdom in Proverbs; she was present at creation and, abiding in creation, addresses all humans.

Some have thought that Wisdom is a poetic personification of God's attribute of wisdom, by which God created the world (cf. 3:19-20; Ps 104:24; Jer 10:12). Others think the divine attribute of wisdom has here become a hypostasis, or independent personal being, somewhat like an angelic power. Such moves toward personification are common in the ancient Near East, in Second Temple Judaism, and in early Christianity.

Recently, Wisdom (often with the Greek name *Sophia*) has come to play a significant role in feminist theology. An important example is the work of Elizabeth A. Johnson. Appealing to the portrayal of Wisdom in Proverbs, Sirach, Wisdom, and Baruch, Johnson argues that "Sophia is a female personification of God's own being in creative and saving involvement with the world. The chief reason for arriving at this interpretation is the functional equivalence between the deeds of Sophia and those of the biblical God. . . . Sophia is Israel's God in female imagery."[145]

The poem itself, however, clearly distinguishes Wisdom from the Lord, for Wisdom was "created" by God (8:22) and was with God during the process of creation (8:30). Wisdom is intimately associated with Yahweh and is instrumental in creation (3:19-20). However, she is not identified with Yahweh. Wisdom is an independent entity. This association-with distinction has parallels in such expressions as "the angel of the Lord," "the word of the Lord," "the Name (of the Lord)," and "the Presence." These entities express the working or presence of Yahweh in the world and cannot be separated from God's being; and yet they are not identical with it. A remarkable example is the personified divine Word in Wis 18:15-16 (cf. Isa 30:27, of the Name). This passage is a significant parallel to Proverbs 8, because the book of Wisdom understands the Word of God and the Wisdom of God as variant expressions of the same reality.[146] The scene is Israel's exodus from Egypt:

> Your all-powerful word leaped from heaven, from the royal throne,
> into the midst of the land that was doomed,
> a stern warrior

145. Elizabeth A. Johnson, *She Who Is: The Mystery of God in Feminist Theological Discourse* (New York: Crossroad, 1992) 91.
146. Winston, *The Wisdom of Solomon,* 317.

carrying the sharp sword of your authentic command,
and stood and filled all things with death,
and touched heaven while standing on the earth. (Wis 18:15-16 NRSV)

Here the divine Word is portrayed as a personal, independent being that not only carries out the divine will in history, but also has a cosmic scope, touching "heaven while standing on earth" (cf. Sir 24:5, of Wisdom). God's Word is an immanent intermediary between God and creation. Similarly, Wis 8:1-2 strikingly juxtaposes the cosmic and personal aspects of Wisdom. The Word or wisdom of God put the world in order; it pervades the cosmos (cf. Sir 24:3-6; Wis 8:1-2); it regulates human affairs. Thus Wisdom is "in" the creation; she addresses human beings, but is not of the same kind as other created things. G. von Rad put it as follows:

> This wisdom, immanent in creation, was differentiated . . . from the "real" work of creation (wind, springs, sea, mountains, etc.). This ontological separation of the phenomena within creation is the most interesting element. Obviously what the teachers perceived as a "summons from creation," as the "self-evident nature of its order," was not simply identical with the "real" works of creation.[147]

In the NT, Christ, in his cosmic, creative functions, will be described as the Word and the wisdom of God. Many of the attributes of the "Word made flesh" are framed in the cosmic and personal terms of OT Wisdom (cf. John 1:1-3, 10; Col 1:15-20; Heb 1:2-3; 11:3).[148]

2. For Israel, the order of divine creation set limits and determined the norms for human activity. Human culture and society are embedded in the matrix of the world God made, and this matrix was designed to keep humans from folly and to foster goodness. Just as the sea has freedom within the limits marked out by God, so also do humans. This principle is easy to recognize in the physical realm (human beings cannot breathe in outer space); it is much more difficult to recognize the more subtle and complex limits set by God on human moral and cultural behavior.

Whatever cosmic norms there are, their concrete articulation is culturally specific and variable. We experience cosmic norms mediated through human culture. This makes it deceptively easy to imagine that the norms are purely human creations. For example, the norms for good Baroque music and for good jazz are quite different. Human languages also display great variety. And yet, this rich variability should not obscure the created conditions that make music and speech possible. This is, perhaps, easiest to illustrate with languages. They universally conform to certain limits (e.g., phonemic) and fulfill certain functions and patterns (e.g., of topic and comment) required by communication. Although actual speech performance varies greatly in adequacy (as when a baby lisps), our knowledge of language norms enables us to understand what is meant and even to supply what is lacking.[149] Such imperfect speech is different from sinful speech (e.g., lies). Again, marriage and family show wide variation among cultures (even within the Bible), but according to Matt 19:3-9, the norms and ideals for their basic structures and functions are given with creation—norms such as fidelity, lifelong partnership, love and respect, sexual exclusivity (even in polygamous settings), and the rearing of healthy, appropriately socialized children. Needless to say, human beings continually struggle with and fall short of creational ideals for marriage and family, even as articulated within their specific societies. Many of the marriage and family stories in the Bible are profound tales of sin and dysfunction commingled with redemptive grace and growth (e.g., Genesis 12–50; 2 Samuel 11–1 Kings 2; 2 Tim 1:5).

Thus, for human affairs to be conducted wisely, freedom and form, love and limits, vital

---

147. G. von Rad, *Wisdom in Israel* (Nashville: Abingdon, 1972) 171-72; see also 80, 83, 92, 107, 144-76.

148. See Raymond Brown, *The Gospel According to John I–XII,* AB 29 (Garden City, N.Y.: Doubleday, 1966) cxxv.

149. Linguists speak of "performance" (*parole*) and "competence" (*langue*). See John Lyons, *Introduction to Theoretical Linguistics* (Cambridge: Cambridge University Press, 1968) 51-52.

life and cosmic law have to be balanced. Very often in history, the rich and powerful have identified the cultural status quo, which serves them well, with the will of God and the order of creation. So the culturally specific, the culturally relative, and even things unjust have been preached as the very word of God or the structure of the world. Cosmic thinking has often served to defend a tyrannical status quo.[150] Sinful, relative human order is too often identified with divine order. And yet, for better or worse, human order and behavior are always responses to the divine order, from which we can learn. We sometimes gain a sense of how things *ought* to be from critical assessment of what *is*.

To conclude from the imperfection and relativity of human responses that there is no (culturally mediated) cosmic order for behavior can be disastrous:

> For the recognition of universal principles forces man to judge the established order, or what is actual here and now, in the light of the natural . . . order; and what is actual here and now is more likely than not to fall short of the universal and unchangeable norm. The recognition of universal principles thus tends to prevent men from wholeheartedly identifying themselves with, or accepting, the social order that fate has allotted to them.[151]

Any reformation of a status quo needs a higher, stable standard by which to judge it and the changes advocated by the proponents of reformation or revolution, lest new evil replace old evil.[152] The difficult human task is collectively to recognize those genuine boundaries and reality principles that are non-negotiable givens, so that true human freedom and the goods of creation may be preserved.

3. Proverbs 8 is also significant for the role it played in doctrinal controversy over the centuries. In particular, it was central in the controversy between orthodox and Arian Christians in the fourth century CE. Many Christians sought too simply and directly to apply statements in Proverbs 8 to Christ. And in the divergence of Judaism and Christianity, Proverbs 8 also played its role. For Judaism, Wisdom became elaborated as Torah, for Christians as Christ.

This Christian development occurred first in the NT writings that describe Christ in cosmic terms as God's Word or Wisdom (John 1; 1 Cor 1:24, 30; Col 1:15-20; 2:3; cf. Heb 1:1-3). In the fourth-century Arian controversy, a battle raged over the verb in Prov 8:22*a*. It is perhaps best to accept the ambiguity of the verb קנה (*qānâ*) as part of the richness of the text. (In English, the verbs "get" and "beget" display an ambiguity similar to *qānâ*). On the one hand, God has "possessed" Wisdom from the beginning (cf. Prov 8:30). So also humans, in their own fashion, are to acquire and possess or "get" wisdom (the same verb appears in Prov 1:5; 4:5, 7; 16:16; 23:23). But more profoundly, the verb suggests that God has "created" or "formed" Wisdom as the beginning of God's ways, before the other works of creation. (In Gen 1:1 the same word for "beginning" opens the Bible. In Job 40:19, the awesome creature Behemoth is called the "beginning of God's ways" as a prime example of God's wisdom in creation.) Thus the creation of the universe and all creatures in it was undertaken in, by, and through Wisdom (3:19-20; Ps 104:24; Jer 10:12).

Using Prov 8:22-31, the Arian party argued that Christ (as Wisdom) was the first creation of God, the unique creature before all other creatures. But as created, the Arians reasoned, Christ was not God in the same sense as the Father was God. The orthodox party, which defined subsequent Christian dogma through the centuries, preferred to take the verb in Prov 8:22*a* as "possessed," so following the ancient Greek LXX version. Alternately, the orthodox

---

150. But see J. Richard Middleton and W. Brueggemann, "Is Creation Theology Inherently Conservative? A Dialogue with Walter Brueggemann," *HTR* 87 (1994) 257-89.

151. Leo Strauss, *Natural Right and History* (Chicago: University of Chicago Press, 1953) 13-14. On historicism, see also Oliver O'Donovan, *Resurrection and Moral Order* (Grand Rapids: Eerdmans, 1986), and Jon D. Levinson, *The Hebrew Bible, the Old Testament, and Historical Criticism* (Louisville: Westminster/John Knox, 1993).

152. Knierim's essay "Cosmos and History in Israel's Theology" is indispensible here. See Rolf P. Knierim, *The Task of Old Testament Theology: Substance, Method, and Cases* (Grand Rapids: Eerdmans, 1995) 171-224.

took the verb as meaning "to beget," so that Christ was not created but, as in the Nicene Creed of 351 CE, eternally "begotten, not made." Again, conceding the possibility that the verb meant "to create," Athanasius took pains to say that what was created was not Christ per se, but his position as the "first of God's works/ways."[153]

Christian tradition has thus in various ways identified Wisdom in Proverbs 8 and Christ as one. A better move, perhaps, would be to understand Christ as the hidden reality underlying and fulfilling the cosmic and personal imagery of Wisdom in Proverbs 8, without positing a direct one-to-one correspondence in all particulars. This seems to be the New Testament procedure.

In Jewish tradition, the move has been to identify Torah (the written and oral law or teaching given to Moses by God at Mt. Sinai) with Wisdom. The correlation of Torah and cosmic wisdom (or Word) is suggested already in several biblical passages (Deut 4:6-8; Pss 19:1-10; 33:4-9; 119:89-104; 147:15-20). But the explicit equation of Torah and cosmic wisdom is developed later, in Sir 1:4; 24:3, 9; Bar 4:1. By the time of the great rabbinic midrash on Gen 1:1,[154] the opening word(s) of Genesis are made to intersect with Prov 8:22, 30.

4. God's delight in the goodness and order of the created world is variously expressed in the Bible. It provides the background for human enjoyment of the goodness of creation (cf. 1 Tim 4:4). It also contrasts with most worldviews that find evil somehow intrinsic to (some part of) reality. In the creation account of Genesis 1, God repeatedly sees that what God has made is "good," even "very good." The psalmist prays that the Lord may "rejoice in his works," for "in wisdom you have made them all," including Leviathan, which God "formed to frolic" in the sea (Ps 104:31, 24-26). The verb for "frolic" is translated "rejoicing" or "playing" in Prov 8:30.

O'Donovan speaks, in Christian terms, of the love and delight that permeate Proverbs 8:

Classical Christian descriptions of love are often found invoking two other terms which expound its sense: the first is "wisdom," which is the intellectual apprehension of the order of things which discloses how each being stands in relation to each other; the second is "delight," which is affective attention to something simply for what it is and for the fact that it is. Such love is the fruit of God's presence within us, uniting us to the humanity of God in Christ, who cherishes and defends all that God the Father has made and thought.[155]

153. See Jaroslav Pelikan, *The Emergence of the Catholic Tradition (100–600)*, vol. 1 of *The Christian Tradition* (Chicago: University of Chicago Press, 1971) 191-200.
154. *Genesis Rabbah* 1.1. For the text of *Genesis Rabbah*, see Commentary on Proverbs 9:1-18.
155. Oliver O'Donovan, *Resurrection and Moral Order* (Grand Rapids: Eerdmans, 1986) 26.

PROVERBS 9:1-18, TWO HOUSES AT THE END OF THE ROAD

NIV	NRSV

9 Wisdom has built her house;
    she has hewn out its seven pillars.
²She has prepared her meat and mixed her wine;
    she has also set her table.
³She has sent out her maids, and she calls
    from the highest point of the city.
	9 Wisdom has built her house,
	    she has hewn her seven pillars.
	² She has slaughtered her animals, she has mixed her wine,
	    she has also set her table.
	³ She has sent out her servant-girls, she calls

NIV

⁴"Let all who are simple come in here!"
  she says to those who lack judgment.
⁵"Come, eat my food
  and drink the wine I have mixed.
⁶Leave your simple ways and you will live;
  walk in the way of understanding.

⁷"Whoever corrects a mocker invites insult;
  whoever rebukes a wicked man incurs abuse.
⁸Do not rebuke a mocker or he will hate you;
  rebuke a wise man and he will love you.
⁹Instruct a wise man and he will be wiser still;
  teach a righteous man and he will add to his
    learning.

¹⁰"The fear of the Lord is the beginning of
    wisdom,
  and knowledge of the Holy One is
    understanding.
¹¹For through me your days will be many,
  and years will be added to your life.
¹²If you are wise, your wisdom will reward you;
  if you are a mocker, you alone will suffer."

¹³The woman Folly is loud;
  she is undisciplined and without knowledge.
¹⁴She sits at the door of her house,
  on a seat at the highest point of the city,
¹⁵calling out to those who pass by,
  who go straight on their way.
¹⁶"Let all who are simple come in here!"
  she says to those who lack judgment.
¹⁷"Stolen water is sweet;
  food eaten in secret is delicious!"
¹⁸But little do they know that the dead are there,
  that her guests are in the depths of the grave.ᵃ

ᵃ18 Hebrew *Sheol*

NRSV

  from the highest places in the town,
⁴ "You that are simple, turn in here!"
  To those without sense she says,
⁵ "Come, eat of my bread
  and drink of the wine I have mixed.
⁶ Lay aside immaturity,ᵃ and live,
  and walk in the way of insight."

⁷ Whoever corrects a scoffer wins abuse;
  whoever rebukes the wicked gets hurt.
⁸ A scoffer who is rebuked will only hate you;
  the wise, when rebuked, will love you.
⁹ Give instructionᵇ to the wise, and they will
    become wiser still;
  teach the righteous and they will gain in
    learning.
¹⁰ The fear of the Lord is the beginning of wisdom,
  and the knowledge of the Holy One is insight.
¹¹ For by me your days will be multiplied,
  and years will be added to your life.
¹² If you are wise, you are wise for yourself;
  if you scoff, you alone will bear it.

¹³ The foolish woman is loud;
  she is ignorant and knows nothing.
¹⁴ She sits at the door of her house,
  on a seat at the high places of the town,
¹⁵ calling to those who pass by,
  who are going straight on their way,
¹⁶ "You who are simple, turn in here!"
  And to those without sense she says,
¹⁷ "Stolen water is sweet,
  and bread eaten in secret is pleasant."
¹⁸ But they do not know that the deadᶜ are there,
  that her guests are in the depths of Shĕ'ōl.

ᵃOr *simpleness* ᵇHeb lacks *instruction* ᶜHeb *shades*

COMMENTARY

Chapter 9 forms a carefully constructed conclusion to the first nine chapters. It falls into three six-verse sections (A, vv. 1-6; B, vv. 7-12; A', vv. 13-18). Of these, section B, which interrupts the parallel sections A and A', signals that chap. 9 forms an envelope around the nine chapters through its repetition of key phrases from 1:1-7 (1:7 and 9:10 on "the fear of the Lord"; 1:5 and 9:11) and from Wisdom's first speech in 1:20-33 (1:22, 29 and 9:7-8; 1:29 and 9:10). The city scene in sections A and A' also echoes the one in 1:20-21, which strengthens the envelope effect. Through their contrast of Lady Wisdom and Dame Folly, sections A and A' summarize key images and themes in chaps. 1–9: opposed ways, women, and houses. This summary function appears in verbal echoes from earlier passages that reinforce the connection between literal and figurative invitations to wisdom and folly (cf. 5:8 with 9:14; 1:21 with 7:11 and 9:13; 5:6 with 9:13, 17 and 7:23; 4:17 with 9:17). Literal adultery or fidelity (5:18-20; 7:6-27) are now definitively revealed in their metaphorical function as symbols of folly and wisdom. Folly's house of death has been anticipated in the house of the "strange woman" (see Commentary on 2:18; 5:5; 7:27; 9:18). Wisdom's banquet house is the cosmos created in 8:22-29 (see below). Wisdom spoke previously in 1:20-33 and 8:3-36. Folly spoke in the figure of the "strange woman" and the adulteress of 7:14-20.

Although the invitation to banquets is a new element, the fit of chap. 9 within the symbol system of Proverbs 1–9 makes unlikely the older view that sacred prostitution or a fertility cult is being portrayed in 9:13-18 (or in 7:14-20). Indeed, some doubt the reality of sacred prostitution in the ancient Near East.[156] The "house" built by Wisdom is not a temple, nor is her meal sacrificial. Though it has been argued that Wisdom in Proverbs 1–9 was originally an ancient Israelite goddess of learning (disguised by the monotheistic editors of Proverbs), the evidence for this theory is inadequate.[157]

Evidence from Proverbs suggests that its final editors provided clues to the meaning of Wisdom's mysterious house building. They have created a set of parallel passages that present cosmos building in the same terms as house building. A literal translation makes these parallels clear:

A Yahweh *by wisdom* founded the earth,
  B Establishing the heavens *by understanding,*
    C *By his knowledge* the depths were split. (3:19-20)
A *By wisdom* a house *is built,*
  B *By understanding* it is established,
    C And *by knowledge* its chambers are filled (24:3-4)
A *Wisdom has built her house* (9:1)
A *Wisdom of women has built her house*
      D But Folly with her hands tears it down (14:1)

In the first two passages, house building (24:3-4) is parallel to cosmos building (3:19-20). Both God and humans operate by the architectural and practical skill indicated by the trio wisdom-understanding-knowledge (see Commentary on 8:1). This exact sequence of attributes is given by God to the builders of the Mosaic tabernacle and of the divine "house" built by Solomon (Exod 31:3; 35:31; 1 Kgs 7:14). These cultic houses are also microcosmic reflections of the macrocosmic world of God's creation (cf. Ps 78:69). Moreover, both the cosmos and human houses are "established by understanding" (Prov 3:19*b*; 24:3*b*). To the "filling" of the house (24:4*a*), one may compare Ps 104:24, where all the works of the Lord are made "by wisdom," and "the earth is full of [God's] creatures" (employing the same verb). On this reading, "house" (9:1) and "city" (9:3*b*) are concentric microcosmic analogues of the cosmos.

This understanding of Wisdom's house in Prov 9:1-3 as a symbol of the world was anticipated long ago in the Babylonian Talmud. The Talmud explains the purpose of Adam's creation on the eve of sabbath in terms of Proverbs 9. Its purpose was

that he might straightway go in to the banquet. The matter may be compared to a king of flesh and blood who built palaces and furnished them, prepared a banquet, and thereafter brought in the guests. For it is written . . . Wisdom "hath builded her house—this [Wisdom] is the attribute of the Holy One, blessed be He, who created the world by wisdom."[158]

In many cultures, the building of cities and houses is an analogue of cosmos building, and in the OT similar vocabulary is used for all three. The order of the house, whether secular or sacred, should partake of and mirror the wise order employed by the Creator of the cosmos.[159] The parallelism among the texts quoted above shows that this pattern is operative in Proverbs. These texts also underline the fundamental intersection of woman, house, and wisdom or folly, which governs the symbolic world of this book in its

156. See "Prostitution (OT)" and "Prostitution (Cultic)," in *Anchor Bible Dictionary,* 6 vols. (New York: Doubleday, 1992) 5:505-13.

157. See B. Lang, *Wisdom and the Book of Proverbs: An Israelite Goddess Redefined* (New York: Pilgrim, 1986) 90-93.

158. I. Epstein, *The Babylonian Talmud: Seder Nezikin* (London: Soncino, 1935) *Sanh.* 38*a,* 240-41.

159. See M. Eliade, *The Sacred and the Profane: The Nature of Religion* (New York: Harcourt Brace Jovanovich, 1959) 20-65.

final form (see Commentary on 31:10-31). The analogy of house and cosmos was also anticipated in Proverbs 8. After the cosmos is built (8:22-29) we hear of Wisdom's "doors" (8:34)—that is, of her house.

In Proverbs 8, however, Yahweh is the creator of the cosmos, while in Prov 9:1, Wisdom is the builder of the cosmic "house." This sort of dual agency is not uncommon in Scripture (cf. Gen 45:4-8; 50:20; Exod 9:34–10:1; Phil 2:12-13). Furthermore, in various ways God is said to build the Temple, the city, and ordinary houses (Pss 78:69; 127:1; Isa 14:32; cf. Heb 3:3-6). This dual agency in Proverbs 8–9, whereby Wisdom's house building is also the Lord's cosmos building, is nicely captured by the ancient Midrash on Gen 1:1, which identifies Torah with Wisdom:

'āmôn [from Proverbs 8:30] is a *workman* (*uman*). The Torah declares, I was the *working* tool of the Holy One, blessed be He. In human practice, when a mortal king builds a palace, he builds it not with his own skill but with the skill of an *architect*. The *architect* moreover does not build it out of his head, but employs plans and diagrams to know how to arrange the chambers and the wicket doors. Thus God consulted [lit., looked into] the Torah and created the world.[160]

9:1-6. Scholars have been much puzzled over the "seven pillars" of Wisdom's house (v. 1). Over the centuries, the pillars have provoked much fanciful speculation: the seven gifts of the Holy Spirit, the seven liberal arts, the seven churches of Revelation, and so on. Other scholars have simply taken the seven to be a cipher for "many." Archaeologists have found parallels to the seven pillars in the homes of wealthy patricians.[161] In the present cosmic context, however, the pillars are most likely a reference to the "pillars of the earth" (Ps 75:3; cf. 1 Sam 2:8; Job 9:6; 26:11). Perhaps the general symbolic function of the number seven is also operative here. Seven is widely present in the OT as a symbol for completeness, perfection, and fullness. In this passage, seven would refer to the perfection and stability of the creation.

But the seven pillars may also be a case of inner-biblical allusion to Gen 1:1–2:3. Jewish tradition, including the Talmud passage cited above, saw in the seven pillars an allusion to the six-plus-one pattern of creation and celebration (sabbath) in the days of Genesis 1. This may not be as farfetched as it first seems. The text of Proverbs 8–9 appears to be playing with the pattern six plus one equals seven.[162] In vv. 1-6, the preparation of the house and its feast takes six actions (past tense verbs), and the invitation to celebrate in the completed house takes one action, "she calls" (present-continuous verb). In the preceding chapter, the account of creation falls into two connected sections. The first (8:22-26) has six verbs of creation; the second (8:27-29) has six infinitives of creation. These sections are followed by two identical verbs ("I was," 8:30) referring to Wisdom's joyful presence in creation. This creates a verb pattern of twice six plus twice one, equalling twice seven. In 9:7-12, the root for "wisdom" (חכמה *ḥokmâ*) appears six times, in addition to the reference to Wisdom in the phrase "by me" (9:11; patterned after 8:15-16). Significantly, in the disordered world of Folly (9:13-18), there are no patterns of six plus one to be found.

This sequence of building, preparing for a feast, and inviting people to the feast is a common pattern (see Commentary on 8:30-31 for parallels). In contrast to the adulterous feast implied in 7:14-20, this feast is not the by-product of a sacrifice. It is simply an ongoing celebration at the completion of the building of the house (cf. modern "house-warming" parties). Its language is that of a wealthy woman providing a lavish meal.[163] In the Bible, the closest verbal parallels to Wisdom's festal preparations of meat and wine occur in the story of the rich fool Nabal, who refuses to share his feast with deserving David (1 Sam 25:11). Perhaps not so ironically, it is Nabal's wise wife, Abigail, who sends her servants before her and provides David and his troops with a feast (1 Sam 25:18-19).

In contrast to the bustling activity of Lady Wisdom is the inaction of Dame Folly, who sits on her seat, catching those who come by. Wisdom offers meat and wine, but Folly offers bread and

160. H. Freedman, *Midrash Rabbah: Genesis* (London, Soncino: 1951) 1.1, 1; italics added to show words translating the root אמן ('mn).
161. See B. Lang, *Wisdom and the Book of Proverbs: An Israelite Goddess Redefined* (New York: Pilgrim, 1986) 90-93.
162. See U. Cassuto, *A Commentary on the Book of Genesis, Part One: From Adam to Noah* (Jerusalem: Magnes, 1961) 13-15, for the number seven in the verbal patterns of Gen 1:1–2:3.
163. See Claudia V. Camp, *Wisdom and the Feminine in the Book of Proverbs* (Sheffield: Almond, 1985) 271.

water. The metaphorical use of food and drink for moral, sexual, and religious choices is common (Job 20:12-14; Prov 1:31; 4:17; 5:15; 7:18; 20:17; 30:20; Sir 23:17; John 6:35). Wisdom offers her goods without guile. Folly's offer is deceptive; she promises secret delights, but hides death. Wisdom urges from death to life (9:6a) and invites the simple to walk in blessing (the Hebrew puns on "blessed"/"happy" [אשרי 'ašrê] and "walk" [אשרו 'išrû]; cf. 3:13, 18; 8:32, 34).

The double invitation of Wisdom and Folly highlights the ambiguous character of the goods of this world. The poet conveys this ambiguity by using the long-established pattern of similarity between the two women. Especially striking are the identical descriptions of their invitations: " 'You who are simple, turn in here!' And to those without sense she says . . . " (9:4, 16). All sin, all folly, it would seem, are temptations to acquire legitimate created goods (sex, wealth, honor, power) by illegitimate means. The goods of this world are ambiguous; in the wrong context they become problematic. The power of speech is a great good, but its power can bring life or death (8:21; cf. Jas 3:1-12).

9:7-12. This section is an interlude whose presence delays the final contrast between Wisdom and Folly (A and A'). To this point, Proverbs 1–9 has been mainly concerned with presenting the message of Wisdom. The speeches of parents and of Wisdom herself have invited the listener to a banquet of life and have warned about Folly and her counterinvitation to sugarcoated death. Now the author advises wise humans, in the second person (vv. 8-9), concerning the reaction their teaching will provoke in others. Those who are wise and righteous respond to instruction and correction by growing wiser (vv. 8b-9). But scoffers and the wicked hate those who correct and admonish them (vv. 7-8b). Verses 10-11 interrupt this advice with a variation of the book's theme verse on wisdom and the fear of the Lord (see Commentary on 1:7). This is followed by an utterance from Wisdom ("by me"), reminding readers that she offers long life. The section concludes with advice that returns to the contrast between the wise and scoffers (v. 12).

At first glance, this section appears to add little that is new; the passage seems merely repetitive. But this conclusion would mistake its function in the book. Through repetition of key phrases and themes, these verses create links both forward and backward in the final form of Proverbs. In form these verses anticipate the short sayings and admonitions that will predominate in chaps. 10–29. Through parallelism of terms these verses also equate the wise with the righteous, in contrast to the wicked. This equation links the focus on wisdom and folly of chaps. 1–9 with the focus on righteous and wicked, so characteristic of chapters 10–15. Verses 7-12 thus help to connect chaps. 1–9 to the subsequent sentence collections formally and by establishing thematic equivalence. Within chaps. 1–9, Prov 9:11 forms links with Wisdom's speech ("by me" in 8:15-16) and with the parental gift of "years of life" (3:2; 4:10). The envelope function of 9:7-12 with chap. 1 has been discussed above.

9:13-18. The chapter and the book's first major section now conclude. Dame Folly is an explicit contrast to Wisdom in v. 16, even to the point of making an identical invitation (v. 4 = v. 16). But this passage also sums up virtually every theme expressed in Proverbs 1–9 by means of its repetition of key words. In particular, Dame Folly masterfully integrates the portrait of Folly as a seduction to bogus good, in contrast to the genuine good of Wisdom.

REFLECTIONS

1. The food and drink prepared by Lady Wisdom are metaphors for the life-giving gifts of creation (9:6). Her "house" is full, and she offers, in effect, to fill the "house" of her guests (cf. 8:21; 24:4; 27:27; 31:15; cf. 1:13; 17:1; Job 22:18). To enter Wisdom's house is to enter the life-giving center of the cosmos, a Garden of Eden where creation's goods are most intensely present and accessible. Here, the cosmos is in order and humans are in harmony with its life-giving principles. Lady Wisdom is an edenic "tree of life" (3:18; cf. 8:35) whose fruits (or meat and wine) are eagerly to be enjoyed. In Wisdom's house all the goods of creation are to be found, for God made them all "by wisdom" (cf. Ps 104:24). Negatively, to enter Wisdom's house requires that one leave "simpleness" behind. To choose is to lose. But those who give up their foolish self-direction (see 1:22-33) for love of Wisdom, gain genuine life. They continue to walk "in the way of insight" (9:6).

2. Proverbs 9:1-6 shows that the goal of the wise person's path is life in Wisdom's house, in contrast to the deadly house of the strange woman or Folly (9:18; see also 2:18-19). And yet the goal of Wisdom is not something achieved by humans, once for all. Those who enter and feast in Wisdom's house continue to walk "in the way of insight" (9:6). Similarly, one can enter into a marriage and over time travel more deeply into the reality of that relationship. Our ongoing love affair with either Wisdom or Folly gives direction and sets the goal of our life-journey. Over time, we grow in wisdom or folly, according to the ultimate loves and commitments that move us. What we love determines where we are headed, where we end up, and who we become. It determines how we journey (see Commentary on 1:7). Lovers of Wisdom are on the way to Wisdom's banquet house, and they are already in it—a paradox that should not be strange to Christians, who know the gospel paradox of a kingdom that is already and not yet. Augustine captured this insight well in talking of Christ as both the way and the goal of the Christian life: "Thus, though Wisdom was himself our home, he made himself also the way by which we should reach our home."[164]

3. The contrast between Lady Wisdom's house and Dame Folly's house is complex. On the one hand, Wisdom's house designates a world in order, full of life. Folly's house is a world in disorder, descending into Sheol, the realm of death. The fool is free of the very conditions that make life possible. Folly's house represents those things in creation that are out of place, out of bounds, and off limits. Conduct outside Wisdom's limits and order destroys the self and damages others; ultimately it is deadly. Thus food and drink are good, but too much or the wrong type can be harmful (25:16, 27). One cannot really live in Folly's house, for the stolen water and bogus bread she offers are deadly.

On the other hand, Wisdom and Folly inhabit the same cosmos and even the same places in the world. They both make their pitches in the same places (cf. 1:20-21; 7:11-12; 8:2-3; 9:3*b*, 14*b*). Paradoxically, the world that Wisdom has built is also the house where Folly dwells. It is not Folly's house by right but by usurpation. Folly and sin are always parasitic of the good that God by Wisdom has made. Folly takes the goods and destroys their goodness by ripping them from their proper place in the coherence of things. She tears down the ordered human world that Wisdom makes (see Commentary on 14:1). Folly has not built her house; she has stolen it, like the cowbird steals and befouls the songbird's nest.

The identical language in the mouths of Wisdom and Folly (9:6, 16) underscores the parasitic ambiguity of evil. It masquerades as good (Isa 5:20). When humans are tempted, it is by something God created good. But it is a disordered good, because we humans, as Augustine saw it, are driven by disordered loves to disorder reality. Christ, the Wisdom of God, came to set our love right.

---

164. Augustine *De Doctrina Christiana* 1.11.11, cited in David L. Jeffrey, *Dictionary of Biblical Tradition in English Literature* (Grand Rapids: Eerdmans, 1992) 833.

PROVERBS 10:1–22:16

THE FIRST SOLOMONIC
COLLECTION OF SAYINGS

PROVERBS 10:1–15:33, THE ANTITHETICAL
COLLECTION

OVERVIEW

On titles and the divisions of Proverbs, see the Introduction. The first "Solomonic" collection of sayings (10:1–22:16) can be divided into two parts: 10:1–15:33 and 16:1–22:16.

The first part moves from the extended instructions of chaps. 1–9 to the two-line sayings that predominate in the Solomonic collections. Its sayings are with few exceptions antithetical—that is, the parallel lines present topics and comments using a rich interplay of synonymous and contrasting terms. For example, wisdom is contrasted with folly, sloth with diligence, joy with sorrow, so that issues are illuminated from more than one side. In particular, this section pervasively contrasts "righteous" (צדק ṣdq) and "wicked" (רשע rš'). These concepts are active even when the terms are not used, because they are commonly portrayed in concrete words, actions, and images. To move the widow's boundary stone is "wicked," even if that term is not used (15:25; 22:28).

In the book of Proverbs, there is some overlap in meaning between the opposed pairs righteous/wicked and wisdom/folly (which dominated chaps. 1–9), as 10:1-8 shows. In general, righteousness, like wisdom (see Commentary on chaps. 8–9), is a cosmic concept (cf. Pss 50:6; 72:3, 16; 97:6).[165] In the human realm, it carries connotations of social-moral-spiritual-legal right and wrong and is a narrower concept than "wis-

dom" (חכמה ḥokmâ). One can do what is righteous (care for the poor, for example), but do it in an unwise manner. But one cannot be wise without being righteous. There is no way to steal, lie, or murder wisely, because these deeds are wicked and contrary to cosmic-moral order. Wicked deeds are not wise; they produce damage and death; they do not foster goodness and life. In this regard, Proverbs is different from other OT books, because it has shaped its understanding of wisdom and righteousness in terms of the "fear of the LORD" (see Commentary on 1:7). Proverbs would not call wicked Jonadab "very wise," though 2 Sam 13:3 does (perhaps ironically?).

For Proverbs, righteousness is an indispensable but minimal reality requirement. Wisdom includes it, but goes beyond it. The wise do righteous things well, in the best way, in harmony with the requirements of the situation, the time, the persons, and other circumstances. In wisdom, righteous humans exercise their freedom in the best possible way.

Another important feature of Prov 10:1–15:33 is its simplicity with regard to the act/consequence connection. It relentlessly insists that "you reap what you sow." In Proverbs 10–15, good acts predominantly produce good consequences, and bad acts produce bad consequences. This is the ABC of wisdom, the basic rules the young need to live well. Starting with chap. 16, the exceptions to the basic rules of life will appear much more frequently (see Introduction).

165. H. H. Schmid, *Gerechtigkeit als Weltordnung;* "Creation, Righteousness, and Salvation: 'Creation Theology' as the Broad Horizon of Biblical Theology," in Bernhard W. Anderson, ed., *Creation in the Old Testament* (Philadelphia: Fortress, 1984) 102-17.

Proverbs 10:1-8, Introduction to the Antithetical Collection

NIV

10 The proverbs of Solomon:

A wise son brings joy to his father,
but a foolish son grief to his mother.

[2] Ill-gotten treasures are of no value,
but righteousness delivers from death.

[3] The LORD does not let the righteous go hungry
but he thwarts the craving of the wicked.

[4] Lazy hands make a man poor,
but diligent hands bring wealth.

[5] He who gathers crops in summer is a wise son,
but he who sleeps during harvest is a
disgraceful son.

[6] Blessings crown the head of the righteous,
but violence overwhelms the mouth of the
wicked.[a]

[7] The memory of the righteous will be a blessing,
but the name of the wicked will rot.

[8] The wise in heart accept commands,
but a chattering fool comes to ruin.

[a]6 Or *but the mouth of the wicked conceals violence*; also in verse
11

NRSV

10 The proverbs of Solomon.

A wise child makes a glad father,
but a foolish child is a mother's grief.

[2] Treasures gained by wickedness do not profit,
but righteousness delivers from death.

[3] The LORD does not let the righteous go hungry,
but he thwarts the craving of the wicked.

[4] A slack hand causes poverty,
but the hand of the diligent makes rich.

[5] A child who gathers in summer is prudent,
but a child who sleeps in harvest brings
shame.

[6] Blessings are on the head of the righteous,
but the mouth of the wicked conceals
violence.

[7] The memory of the righteous is a blessing,
but the name of the wicked will rot.

[8] The wise of heart will heed commandments,
but a babbling fool will come to ruin.

COMMENTARY

Verses 1-8 form a patterned introduction to the fundamental issues of 10:1–15:33 (see Commentary on 16:1-9, 10-15). Through repeated key words, the introduction sketches the horizon of meaning for the sayings that follow. Many of these terms appear throughout 10:1–15:33, or are elaborated by appropriate images and actions. The concentric pattern of key words is here diagrammed using simplified English forms (in 10:1, 8, the Hebrew terms for "fool" [כסיל *kěsîl*] are different).

A	v. 1,	Wise	Fool
B	vv. 2-3,	Wicked	Righteous
		Righteous	Wicked
C	vv. 4-5,	Illustrations of key terms	
B'	vv. 6-7,	Bless Righteous/	Wicked
		Righteous Bless/	Wicked
A'	v. 8,	Wise	Fool

Verses 1 and 8 frame this introduction with the basic opposition of wisdom and folly; vv. 2-3 and 6-7 introduce the righteous and the wicked; and v. 3 makes explicit the all-encompassing involvement of God in human affairs.[166] Wisdom and ethical order are inseparable from the divine source of order (see Commentary on 1:7). Verses 4-5, at the center of the introduction, focus on human responsibility and on the consequences of human habits and actions, setting them in their cosmic context.

10:1. The opening verse (variant in 15:20; see Commentary on 13:1) assumes that wisdom is a matter of generations. By taking up this insight from chaps. 1–9 (see Commentary on 29:3), the proverb creates a strong link between chaps. 1–9 and the first Solomonic collection. Wisdom is handed down by parents and received (v. 8, "accepted" NIV; cf. 2:1; 4:3) or rejected (13:1) by children. Each generation (and individual) must choose for itself wisdom or folly, and these choices come in terms set by previous generations. Moreover, children's choices can bring joy or sorrow to their parents (cf. 17:21, 25; 19:26; 23:15-16, 22-25; 27:11; 28:7; 29:3, 15; Eccl 2:18-21; Sir 3:1-16). In keeping with the character/consequence schema (humans reap what they regularly sow), v. 1 uses general categories (wise/foolish, parents/son) to focus on specific consequences within the parent-child relationship (cf. v. 5b). This saying is illustrated by the poignant stories of the old priest Eli and his wicked sons (1 Sam 2:12–4:18), of Samuel and his sons (1 Sam 8:1-9), and of King David and his sons Amnon and Absalom (2 Sam 13:21; 18:33).

10:2-3. Verse 2a suggests that wicked wealth is unstable, of no profit in the long run. "Ill-gotten treasures" is a prophetic phrase (Mic 6:10-11; cf. Prov 11:1). But righteous human behavior "delivers" from death (see 11:4), a rescue operation elsewhere ascribed to the Lord (Pss 33:19; 56:13). In later Hebrew, "righteousness" (צדקה *şĕdāqâ*) can refer to "alms" (Sir 16:14; cf. Matt 6:1-4, where "alms" is a specification of "righteousness" in 6:1).

Verse 3 sets up one of the theological problems of wisdom: Does God never let the righteous go hungry (cf. Ps 34:10; 37:25; Matt 6:11)? One

proverb is never adequate to describe all of reality; here we find a statement of God's fundamental and usual mode of dealing with humans. Other sayings (and various Psalms [44; 73], Job, and Ecclesiastes) show that the situation is more complex (see Commentary on Prov 16:8). There is a pun in v. 3b on הוה (*hawwâ*), a word that means both "desire" and "disaster": The Lord "thrusts forward the disaster of the wicked!"

10:4-5. These verses link laziness to poverty and hard work to success, as causes to effects. Again, no one proverb provides a complete picture (see Commentary on 13:23). In this introductory section (as in chaps. 10–15 generally) the ABC's of wisdom are being taught; the exceptions to the rules will come later. Without hard work, there can be no success, and laziness destroys the best of circumstances. The imagery is simple: The "slack hand" and the "diligent hand" each has its consequences. But the image is suggestion rich. "Hand" (יד *yād*) is a standard Hebrew metaphor for power. The proverb says to the young, in effect, that success or failure is in your hands. One must be proactive and take responsibility for one's own existence.[167]

Verse 5 sets the issue of personal responsibility and labor in the context of the created order (see Commentary on Proverbs 8). To be wise and good requires that humans be in touch with reality, that their actions be in tune with the rhythms of the cosmos as well as the nature of individual things (Isa 28:23-29; Rom 1:18-25; 2:14-15). The imagery is drawn from the world of the Palestinian farmer. "Summer" and "harvest" are parallel terms, since the crops ripen, each in its order, during the dry hot months of summer (cf. 26:1). To harvest at the appropriate time is an instance of basic wisdom. This truth—obvious except to the one who ignores it—is built into the fabric of creation itself. The parallel passage in 6:6-11 (cf. 20:4) seeks to teach the sluggard by using the lowly ant as an example of wisdom (on laziness, a subspecies of folly, see 24:30-34; 26:13-16).

10:6-7. The consequences of righteousness and wickedness are generalized in terms of blessing—that is, the divine act of granting success and *shalom* (peace and prosperity) to humans in tune with God and reality. The implicit divine action

---

166. See L. Alonso-Schökel and J. Vilchez, *Proverbios* (Madrid: Ediciones Cristiandad, 1984) 256.

167. See Stephen R. Covey, *The Seven Habits of Highly Successful People* (New York: Simon and Schuster, 1989) 65-94.

in blessing further strengthens the concentric parallel with vv. 2-3. The relation of v. 6*b* to v. 6*a* is difficult to establish; the fit of the repetition in v. 11*b* is more obvious. Perhaps 11:26 provides a solution: The good person receives public blessing while the wicked person conceals his or her ill intentions.[168] (For the NIV translation, cf. Ps 140:9; Hab 2:17.)

10:8. This verse is elliptical; the consequences of heeding commandments are not spelled out, but the ruin that follows unbridled speech is. In the OT, the word for "ruin" (לבט *lābaṭ*) appears only in 10:8, 10 and Hos 4:14, where it is applied to Israel as a people lacking understanding.[169] The nexus of character, acts, and consequences applies not merely to individuals but to nations, societies, and cultures (cf. the LXX reading of 26:3, "a rod for a lawless nation").

168. Alonso-Schökel and Vilchez, *Proverbios,* 261.

169. Cf. the Qumran hymn 1QH 2:19.

REFLECTIONS

1. Proverbs assumes that the wise formation of children is the work of mothers and fathers. It portrays women as authoritative sources of instruction and models of wisdom also for males (cf. Proverbs 1–9; 23:22-25; 31:1). In contemporary North America, however, the work of parenting suffers generally from deficient or absent fathering, with too much of the burden placed on the shoulders of women, whether single mothers or married. Some research suggests that the sons of absent or aloof fathers may more frequently grow up with a "macho," or authoritarian identity, especially in relation to women.[170] More than that, individualistic Americans need to remember that "it takes a village to raise a child."

It should perhaps also be noted that analyses of Israel's patriarchal society need to account for the role of both women and men in maintaining and handing on a worldview and its norms. In addition, the role of Israel's mostly agrarian material culture in limiting gender roles must be given serious consideration, lest the complexities of life be reduced to a play of ideas, as if only male ideas shaped society.[171] This is not to deny wicked male misogyny, violence, and oppression of women past and present. It is, rather, a plea for analysis of a cultural system in which both women and men are responsible, (inter)active agents. One explanation is that women have internalized dominant male attitudes, including "male fear of women."[172] But such an explanation begs explanation. How does this happen? Does it imply bad faith on the part of women in patriarchal cultures? Or is it a function of their status as victims? Does the "elite mother" (perhaps writer) of 31:1-9 experience herself as a victim? Family and cultural dysfunction or health, the frenzy or felicity between the sexes, the war or peace between the generations—these are systemic matters that need to be analyzed and addressed on many levels by divine grace and human labor.[173]

2. Wisdom and folly are not merely intellectual or spiritual qualities; they are inseparable from actions of virtue or vice, as the repetition of key terms in these verses shows. If the good are not wise, their goodness is ineffectual. If the wise are not good and godly, their wisdom is eventually unmasked as folly by the flow of history. For example, the wise but unscrupulous Jonadab sets in motion events that culminate in Absalom's revolt (2 Sam 13:1-22; 14:32-34). It is such overweening "wisdom" that the prophets and the apostle Paul attacked (Isa 5:18-25;

170. See Mary S. Van Leeuwen, *Gender and Grace* (Downers Grove: Inter-Varsity, 1990) 125-63; Samuel Osherson, *Finding Our Fathers: How a Man's Life Is Shaped by His Relationship with His Father* (New York: Fawcett Columbine, 1986).

171. See Carol Myers, "Everyday Life," in Carol A. Newsom and Sharon H. Ringe, eds., *The Women's Bible Commentary* (Louisville: Westminster, 1992) 244-51.

172. Cf. the views of Carol Newsom, "Woman and the Discourse," Carole R. Fontaine, "Proverbs," (on Prov 31:1-9) in *The Women's Bible Commentary,* 151.

173. See Harriet G. Lerner, *The Dance of Anger: A Woman's Guide to Changing the Patterns of Intimate Relationships* (New York: Harper & Row, 1985).

Jer 8:4-12; 1 Cor 1:18-31). The classic narrative of wisdom undone by God's superior judgments is the tale of Ahitophel (2 Sam 16:15–17:23). Indeed, virtually the entire narrative of David's reign, from his sin with Bathsheba until his final decline, may be read as a tale of royal folly, pregnant with disasters narrowly averted, thanks to God's stern covenant mercy (2 Samuel 11–20; 2 Kings 1–2).[174]

174. R. N. Whybray, *The Succession Narrative: A Study of II Sam. 9–20 and 1 Kings 1 and 2,* STB 2nd series 9 (London: SCM 1968).

Proverbs 10:9-32, Sayings on the Antithesis of Good and Evil

NIV	NRSV

[9]The man of integrity walks securely,
    but he who takes crooked paths will be found out.
	[9] Whoever walks in integrity walks securely,
	    but whoever follows perverse ways will be found out.

[10]He who winks maliciously causes grief,
    and a chattering fool comes to ruin.
	[10] Whoever winks the eye causes trouble,
	    but the one who rebukes boldly makes peace.[a]

[11]The mouth of the righteous is a fountain of life,
    but violence overwhelms the mouth of the wicked.
	[11] The mouth of the righteous is a fountain of life,
	    but the mouth of the wicked conceals violence.

[12]Hatred stirs up dissension,
    but love covers over all wrongs.
	[12] Hatred stirs up strife,
	    but love covers all offenses.

[13]Wisdom is found on the lips of the discerning,
    but a rod is for the back of him who lacks judgment.
	[13] On the lips of one who has understanding wisdom is found,
	    but a rod is for the back of one who lacks sense.

[14]Wise men store up knowledge,
    but the mouth of a fool invites ruin.
	[14] The wise lay up knowledge,
	    but the babbling of a fool brings ruin near.

[15]The wealth of the rich is their fortified city,
    but poverty is the ruin of the poor.
	[15] The wealth of the rich is their fortress;
	    the poverty of the poor is their ruin.

[16]The wages of the righteous bring them life,
    but the income of the wicked brings them punishment.
	[16] The wage of the righteous leads to life,
	    the gain of the wicked to sin.

[17]He who heeds discipline shows the way to life,
    but whoever ignores correction leads others astray.
	[17] Whoever heeds instruction is on the path to life,
	    but one who rejects a rebuke goes astray.

[18]He who conceals his hatred has lying lips,
    and whoever spreads slander is a fool.
	[18] Lying lips conceal hatred,
	    and whoever utters slander is a fool.

[19]When words are many, sin is not absent,
    but he who holds his tongue is wise.
	[19] When words are many, transgression is not lacking,
	    but the prudent are restrained in speech.

[20]The tongue of the righteous is choice silver,
    but the heart of the wicked is of little value.
	[20] The tongue of the righteous is choice silver;
	    the mind of the wicked is of little worth.

[21]The lips of the righteous nourish many,
    but fools die for lack of judgment.
	[21] The lips of the righteous feed many,
	    but fools die for lack of sense.

[22]The blessing of the LORD brings wealth,	[22] The blessing of the LORD makes rich, and he adds no sorrow with it.[b]

[a] Gk: Heb *but a babbling fool will come to ruin*   [b] Or *and toil adds nothing to it*

NIV

and he adds no trouble to it.

²³A fool finds pleasure in evil conduct,
but a man of understanding delights in
wisdom.

²⁴What the wicked dreads will overtake him;
what the righteous desire will be granted.

²⁵When the storm has swept by, the wicked are
gone,
but the righteous stand firm forever.

²⁶As vinegar to the teeth and smoke to the eyes,
so is a sluggard to those who send him.

²⁷The fear of the LORD adds length to life,
but the years of the wicked are cut short.

²⁸The prospect of the righteous is joy,
but the hopes of the wicked come to nothing.

²⁹The way of the LORD is a refuge for the
righteous,
but it is the ruin of those who do evil.

³⁰The righteous will never be uprooted,
but the wicked will not remain in the land.

³¹The mouth of the righteous brings forth wisdom,
but a perverse tongue will be cut out.

³²The lips of the righteous know what is fitting,
but the mouth of the wicked only what is
perverse.

NRSV

²³ Doing wrong is like sport to a fool,
but wise conduct is pleasure to a person of
understanding.

²⁴ What the wicked dread will come upon them,
but the desire of the righteous will be
granted.

²⁵ When the tempest passes, the wicked are no
more,
but the righteous are established forever.

²⁶ Like vinegar to the teeth, and smoke to the
eyes,
so are the lazy to their employers.

²⁷ The fear of the LORD prolongs life,
but the years of the wicked will be short.

²⁸ The hope of the righteous ends in gladness,
but the expectation of the wicked comes to
nothing.

²⁹ The way of the LORD is a stronghold for the
upright,
but destruction for evildoers.

³⁰ The righteous will never be removed,
but the wicked will not remain in the land.

³¹ The mouth of the righteous brings forth
wisdom,
but the perverse tongue will be cut off.

³² The lips of the righteous know what is
acceptable,
but the mouth of the wicked what is
perverse.

COMMENTARY

10:9. Psalm 26 elaborates the character of one who "walks in integrity" (see 2:7; 20:7; 28:6, 18; Job 1:1). The psalmist prays that God will deal with him according to his inner and outer, godly integrity (Ps 26:1-3). Such oneness of direction in life ("walk") and unity of character is associated in Psalm 26 with "trusting" the Lord (i.e., finding one's security in God; 26:1-3, 11; Ps 23:4; Isa 33:15-16). The inner and outer person are of one piece (Ps 26:2; cf. Prov 26:23-26, where outward action conceals inner evil). Such integrity is often contrasted with "twistedness" (Prov 11:20; 17:20; 19:1; 28:6). The "twisted" or "crooked" person will eventually be exposed (Prov 26:26). Crookedness, like murder, will out. Since the righteous

psalmist must request God's vindication, the security promised in Prov 10:9*a* is not necessarily the same as a trouble-free, prosperous life.

10:10. "Winks the eye" refers to some secretive, non-verbal communication meant for ill (Prov 6:13; Ps 35:19; Sir 27:22-24). The body and its parts express and are agents of good and ill (Prov 6:17-18; Mark 9:43-48). The Hebrew text of v. 10*b* seems misplaced from v. 8 (NRSV margin), since it breaks the pattern of antithesis in these chapters and the connection between v. 10*a* and v. 10*b* is unclear. Most scholars follow the LXX (e.g., NRSV).

10:11-12. These verses form a proverb pair ("conceals" and "covers" are the same word in

Hebrew [כסה *kāsâ*]; for NIV, see Hab 2:17) and are part of a cluster of verses on good and bad speech (vv. 11-14; see vv. 18-21). Verse 11 contrasts the effects of a righteous or wicked "mouth." "A fountain of life" (see Ps 36:9[10]; Prov 13:14; 14:27; cf. Jer 2:13; 17:13) is a powerful image in hot and dry Palestine, where life is impossible without water (cf. 3:18; 15:4, "tree of life"). The parallels suggest that God and human agents are not to be artificially separated as sources of life (see Ezek 47:1-12; John 4:13-14; 7:37-39). The righteous mouth brings life because wisdom flows from it (see 3:13-18; 10:13, 31; Ps 37:30).

Deceptive speech "conceals violence" (v. 11*b*) against others (v. 18), but ultimately also against oneself. "Here is a double opposition between the righteous and the wicked; first in the contrary effects, the former causeth life, the latter mischief and death; and secondly in the manner of producing them, the righteous doth it by uttering his words, and the wicked doth it by concealing his mind."[175]

Whether concealed (v. 18) or open, hate stirs up conflict (6:14), while love can remove it by covering offenses (in the sense of forgiving them; see Ps 85:3; cf. Prov 11:13; 17:9; Jas 5:20; 1 Pet 4:8) In this sense, one cannot cover one's own sin (28:13; Job 31:33; Ps 32:5). Alternately, "covering" has the sense of "ignoring" as in 12:16.

10:13. "Lacks sense" (חסר-לב *ḥăsar-lēb*) is literally "lacks heart," the central organ of insight and understanding (see Commentary on 26:3.). This idiom occurs 11 times in Proverbs, while the Hebrew for "heart" (לב *lēb*) occurs 99 times (see Excursus, "The 'Heart' in the Old Testament," 60-61).

10:14-15. The mouth has tremendous power for good or for ill, whether to oneself or to others (see 2:1-2; 7:1-3.). Verse 15 is linked to v. 14 by the term "ruin" (חתת *ḥătat*; see 13:3; 18:7). Here wealth and poverty are portrayed as strength and disaster respectively, with no moral or spiritual judgments attached (cf. v. 4). But the picture is more complex, as the proverb pair in 18:10-11 shows (cf. 10:29).

10:16-17. Wage(s) and gain foreground the character/consequence nexus (cf. Paul's "the wages of sin is death," a good wisdom saying [Rom 6:23]). The same Hebrew word can refer to sin proper or to sin's consequences, punishment and ultimately death. The ambiguity ought not to be eliminated, since the wealth of the wicked can embroil them in further wickedness.

Verse 17 is linked to v. 16 by the phrase "to life" (see 6:23; 15:10 and the Overview to Proverbs 1–9 on path imagery). In the expression "Goes astray/leads others astray," the Hebrew verb form is ambiguous, and its causality can be either internal (damage to self, 12:26; cf. Isa 47:10) or external (damage to others; cf. Isa 3:12; Jer 50:6).

10:18. Now begins a second cluster of verses on good and bad speech (vv. 11-14; 11:12-13, 18–21; 26:26). The NRSV and the NIV differ on the grammatical subject of v. 18*a:* "Lying lips" or "He who conceals"; the latter supplies a better antithesis to the second line. Usually, a person's inner character and convictions are expressed in word and deed (1 Sam 24:13; Luke 6:43-45). There is an integrity of the inner and outer person. But the heart is able to conceal its hatred (see 26:23-28, where "enemy" and "hatred" share the same Hebrew root; cf. 2 Sam 13:22). The wise will be aware of this phenomenon and beware. Conversely, honest conflict is better than hidden love (Prov 27:5-6; Lev 19:17-18). In the light of this verse, the young Joseph may have been a fool (Gen 37:2, 5, 9).

10:19. These thoughts continue in the tradition: "All my days I have grown up among the Wise, and I have not found anything better than silence; and not study is the chief thing but action; and whoso makes many words occasions sin."[176] Appropriate, timely expression or restraint of what is in the heart is essential to wisdom (12:23; 15:2; 17:27-28; 18:2; Eccl 5:2-7). Compare the World War II proverb, "Loose lips sink ships."

10:20. Monetary metaphors are here juxtaposed with body parts ("tongue"/"choice silver" vs. "heart"/"little worth") in an attempt to communicate the surpassing worth of righteous speech (cf. 8:19). Even in ancient Israel, "money talks." The connection of heart and organs of speech is once again assumed (see Commentary on v. 18). This verse contains a lovely wordplay on "tongue"

175. Matthew Poole, *A Commentary on the Holy Bible II* (McLean, Va.: MacDonald, n.d.) 2:231.

176. Mishnah tractate *Abot* 1:17; cf. Jas 3:1-12; *APOT* II, 694.

(לשׁון *lāšôn*), because the word also can refer to a tongue-like ingot of gold or silver (cf. Josh 7:21, 24: "bar," "wedge").

10:21. The contrast of life and death is implicit in "feed many" versus "die." But the relationship between the two lines of the saying needs to be determined. "To feed many" employs a verb (lit., "to shepherd" [רעה *rā'â*]; see Psalm 23), which is a metaphor of kingly rule throughout the ancient Near East, including Israel. Psalm 8, however, portrays the democratization of kingship. Thus the righteous here are those persons in various positions of responsible authority (parents, teachers, pastors, rulers, employers, etc.) who care for and nurture their "flock" with wisdom and justice (Jer 3:15; 23:1-6). In the "peaceable kingdom," the wise shepherd is implicitly present (Isa 11:1-9). But fools who "lack heart" (v. 13) will die like errant sheep in spite of "pastoral" nurture (29:19). "A word to the wise is sufficient," but not for fools.

10:22. Verse 22b is ambiguous (see NRSV margin), and this ambiguity has profound theological and practical implications. The way one interprets and contextualizes this proverb may say much about the reader's own world and life view. The NRSV and NIV translations suggest that God grants blessings unadulterated with sorrow or trouble. Yet in the real world even the blessed suffer. One might attempt to escape the problem by suggesting that sorrow comes not from God but from elsewhere. But in the monotheistic OT, this theological move is countered by the prologue of Job 1–2 and many psalms of lament (e.g., Psalms 22; 35; 44), which hold God ultimately responsible for the welfare of the people.

The variation suggested in the margin of the NRSV is preferable, even though it brings its own complications. On the surface, "toil adds nothing" contradicts the wisdom principle that toil produces wealth (10:4; 14:13).

10:23. This verse states a mystery of folly: Its pleasure is to do evil (1:16; 2:14; 15:21; 26:19). It is also a mystery to fools that wisdom may give delight. "Sport," "pleasure," and "delight" are the same word in Hebrew (שׂחק *śāḥaq*), which appears only in the first line and functions elliptically in the second. Just as a primary love determines the character and direction of individuals, groups, and societies (a basic theme of Proverbs 1–9 as

well as of Augustine's *City of God*), so also the "sport" of persons and cultures shapes their character and reveals their ethos.[177] Our tendency toward good or evil depends on what we delight in (2:14; 15:21; 26:19; cf. Matt 6:21).

10:24-25. These verses form a proverb pair (see v. 28). The wicked stand in a love/hate relation with evil. By the evil done to others, they hope to gain personal good. Yet such persons dread that what they do will be done to them, that the punishment will fit the crime (cf. 11:27b; 21:13; Isa 66:3-4; cf. Job 3:15). But since the desire of the righteous conforms to the order of reality and to God's own purposes, it will surely come to be (11:23; Pss 20:4; 21:2; Matt 6:33). It will "be granted" (יתן *yittēn*, used in ellipsis; cf. 12:12, 14; Job 36:6; Ps 121:3), that is, by God.

Verse 25 contrasts righteous and wicked in the context of cosmic imagery (see Commentary on 10:30; Pss 93:1-2; 96:10; Wis 5:14-15). The expansion of this proverb in Jesus' parable suggests that the wicked and the fool are close kin (Matt 7:24-27). "Storm"/"tempest" (associated with God's theophany in judgment, Isa 29:6; 66:15; Nah 1:3) in the first line contrasts with "established"/"stand firm forever" in the second. The latter phrase (lit., "a lasting foundation"), corresponds to declarations concerning the stable foundation of creation itself (Pss 78:69; 104:5; cf. Job 38:4; Ps 24:2; Prov 3:19). But the wicked do not survive the storms of life (cf. 1:27; Job 27:20-21; Ps 73:18-19; but note Prov 25:26 and Job's complaint in Job 21:18).

10:26. This is one of several sayings on the incongruous or unfitting (25:20; 26:1, 6-7; 27:14). Ancient Israel did not possess modern dentistry. Thus vinegar would cause pain to teeth that were broken or decayed. "Employers" (NRSV) is literally "those who send him" (NIV; see 13:17; 25:13). For "fittingness," see Commentary on 26:1-12.

10:27-28. The "fear of the LORD" (1:7), wisdom, and parental teaching are of one piece in their effects (3:1-2, 16; 9:11), the latter two as the objective reality and the first as its subjective appropriation (2:5). As is usual with proverbs, this saying needs to be qualified, for the

177. For a modern Augustinian analysis of history, see E. Rosenstock-Huessey, *Out of Revolution: Autobiography of Western Man* (Norwich, Vt.: Argo, 1969). See also J. Huizinga, *Homo Ludens: A Study of the Play-Element in Culture* (Boston: Beacon, 1950).

life of the righteous is sometimes cut short (Ps 102:24-25). Compare Isa 57:1, which offers one explanation for this phenomenon, and Ps 44:22 and Wis 4:7-20, which offer others. The problem's ultimate resolution requires a developed view of life after death.[178]

Verses 27-28 form a proverb pair on the alternate futures of the righteous and the wicked. Verse 27 concerns the future's objective realization, v. 28 inner expectations for the future, which are realized or not (cf. 10:24; 11:7, 24; Job 8:13; 11:20; Ps 112:10c [= Prov 11:28b]; John 5:45). The sure object of godly hope is joy, though at present the reality may be absent (see Ruth 1:12; Pss 9:18; 33:18; Rom 8:24-25; Heb 11:1). For "comes to nothing" (lit., "perishes"), see Commentary on 11:7.

10:29. "The way of the LORD" occurs only here in Proverbs. Does it refer to God's action or "way" (8:22; Exod 33:3) or to the "way" revealed by God for human conduct? Delitzsch suggests that it is "the way which the God of revelation directs men to walk in [Pss 27:11; 143:8], the way of His precepts [Ps 119:27], His way of salvation [Ps 67:2]."[179] In the NT it appears as "the way of God," (Matt 22:16; Acts 18:25-26) or simply, "the Way" (Acts 9:2; 24:14. In Proverbs, one must also think of the way of Wisdom (cf. 3:17; 4:11; 8:20). Thus revealed religion (including general revelation, as in Proverbs 8) is comfort and protection to those of integrity, but a source of destruction to evildoers (cf. 2 Cor 2:14-16).

Alternately, the verbal parallels between 10:29 and 21:15 suggest that "the way of the LORD" may refer to God's judgments on human conduct. Compare the wisdom saying that concludes Hosea (Hos 14:9) and Isa 55:8-9. Finally, the Hebrew of v. 29a permits the translation, "Yahweh is a fortress to the man whose conduct is blameless" (see 11:20; 13:6).

10:30. This verse has strong thematic and verbal connections to Psalm 37 (esp. Ps 37:9, 11, 22, 27-29; see also Ps 125:1; Prov 10:25; 12:3). Wisdom rarely intersects explicitly with Israel's historical theological concerns: promises to the patriarchs, covenants, exodus, Sinai, and the gift of or exile from the land (but cf. 22:28; Job 15:18-19; 24:2, 18). The possession of the

land (of Canaan), or "earth" (the Hebrew term ארץ ['eres] means both), is here not related to Israel per se (Gen 15:18; 17:8) but to the contrast of "righteous" and "wicked" (see Commentary on 2:21-22; note the condition of obedience in Deut 4:1; 8:1; 25:15; 28:36-37, 49, 64; cf. Jer 7:7; Amos 7:17). Thus this proverb belongs to that matrix of traditions that grows into Israel's and the church's eschatology (Matt 5:5; Rom 4:13). "Will never be removed/uprooted" is literally, "totter," "slip" (25:26: Pss 93:1; 96:10; see Commentary on 12:3). Experience sometimes contradicts this statement (25:26), and past commentators have resolved the tension in various ways. The steadfastness of the righteous may refer to individuals whose fall is only temporary (24:15-16; Ps 34:21-22), to their posterity (Pss 89:29; 102:28), or to the future life.[180] The first two options appear already in the medieval Jewish commentators Rashi and Moses Kimchi.

10:31-32. The final verses are a proverb pair, related by parallelism of speech organs and the opposition of righteous and wicked.

v. 31	Mouth-righteous	Perverse-tongue
v. 32	Lips-righteous	Mouth-wicked
		(perverse)

"Brings forth" (v. 31; cf. 10:11, 21; 15:28) is literally "to bear fruit" (נוב *nûb*; cf. 11:30; 15:4; Ps 92:14). "Perverse" (תהפכה *tahpukâ*; used nine times in Proverbs, and elsewhere only in Deut 32:20) refers to what is "upsidedown," here to speech that inverts and distorts reality (cf. 2:12; 6:14; 8:13; 23:33; Isa 5:20). "Cut off" seems a gruesome image when applied to the tongue (used only here and Ps 12:4). The ancient Assyrians actually tore out the tongues of rebels.[181] But "tongue" is used here in a literary device called synedoche, in which the part stands for the whole (see Gen 9:11; Num 15:31). "Acceptable"/"fitting" (v. 32) is what delights both God and humans (see 8:35; 11:1, 27; 12:22; 14:35; 16:13; Rom 12:1-2; Phil 4:9).

178. F. Delitzsch, "Proverbs," in C.F. Keil and F. Delitzsch, *Commentary on the Old Testament*, vol. 6 (Grand Rapids: Eerdmans, 1975) 226.
179. Ibid., 227.

180. Examples may be found in Matthew Poole, *Synopsis criticorum* (1671) 2:1549. On the conflict of experience and faith, see R. C. Van Leeuwen, "On Wealth and Poverty: System and Contradiction in Proverbs," *Hebrew Studies* 33 (1992).
181. See *Ancient Near Eastern Texts Relating to the Old Testament*, ed. James B. Pritchard, 3rd ed. (Princeton, N.J.: Princeton University Press, 1969) 288.

REFLECTIONS

1. The topics of Proverbs 10 are diverse. What unites this and the following chapters is the relentless opposition of "righteous" and "wicked," good and evil. Every verse (including v. 10 if we follow the LXX) presents an opposition, in one form or another, of good and evil. This polarized world corresponds to the two ways in chapters 1–9. In this world humans have to find their way, and they do so by making and keeping ultimate commitments. Human beings are an ambiguous mixture of good and evil (see 20:9). But this does not erase the fundamental opposition between two directions in life.

2. The chapter also forces us to face up to reality—first, in the sense that there is an objective, created order that sets the terms in which humans are responsible to God, to others, to self, and to creation itself: Sow in season; harvest in season. Human habits and actions, including words, have consequences for which we are accountable. Both folly and sin begin with denial and distortion, with the embracing of irreality.[182] Second, to face up to reality requires that we acknowledge the conflict of good and evil in the world and in ourselves and not try to paper it over. Americans, still enamored of myths of progress, tolerance, and the innate virtue of the United States ("America: love it or leave it"; "My country, right or wrong"), are tempted to ignore internal evil and the tremendous labor and sacrifice that are required to achieve personal or corporate good.

The gospel here is that God has made this world good and, in spite of quirks, quandaries, and sin, it runs with a certain reliability that rewards the wise, the diligent, and the righteous (Gen 8:22). If this were not true, ordinary work, success, love, and life would not be possible.

3. Proverbs 10:22 suggests that a theology that holds that God "does it all" can lead to passivity or to ritual magic (like anointing one's wallet, advocated by some televangelists). This is an abdication of the power and responsibility given to human beings. Yet a secular "untheology" of human achievement also misses reality (Deut 8:17-18), for it neglects the mysterious role of divine blessing (Gen 1:22, 28) in the fecundity of creation and the felicity of life. Human action and divine providence are not in tension (cf. the paradoxical formulation in Gen 45:8). Rather, toil, which has no independent power to add to God's blessing, is nonetheless the means of its realization (Pss 127:1-2; 128:1-6; Phil 2:12-13, a passage pertaining not so much to eternal destiny as to life in this world). For humans, this paradox is resolved in the old Latin proverb, *Ora et labora,* or "Pray and work." Blessing is a grace that does not annul or contradict nature (including human work) but is its ground and sole possibility.[183] The godly worker, having prayed and labored (Ps 90:17), experiences the fruit of labor as a gift (Eccl 3:12-13, 22; 5:18-19).

4. If we consider the cross of Christ in relation to sinful acts and consequences (see Commentary on 10:16), we may say that the cross does not annul this connection, but reroutes the consequence of death to Christ, while releasing his life for humans. A similar logic of grace obtains in OT sacrifice.[184]

---

182. See M. Scott Peck, *People of the Lie* (New York: Simon & Schuster, 1983).
183. The grammar of Prov 10:22a is emphatic, specifying "the blessing of the Lord" as the ultimate source of wealth.
184. See Gordon J. Wenham, *The Book of Leviticus* (Grand Rapids: Eerdmans, 1979) 25-29.

Proverbs 11:1-31, Further Sayings on the Antithesis of Good and Evil

NIV

11 The LORD abhors dishonest scales,
but accurate weights are his delight.

[2] When pride comes, then comes disgrace,
but with humility comes wisdom.

[3] The integrity of the upright guides them,
but the unfaithful are destroyed by their
duplicity.

[4] Wealth is worthless in the day of wrath,
but righteousness delivers from death.

[5] The righteousness of the blameless makes a
straight way for them,
but the wicked are brought down by their
own wickedness.

[6] The righteousness of the upright delivers them,
but the unfaithful are trapped by evil desires.

[7] When a wicked man dies, his hope perishes;
all he expected from his power comes to
nothing.

[8] The righteous man is rescued from trouble,
and it comes on the wicked instead.

[9] With his mouth the godless destroys his
neighbor,
but through knowledge the righteous escape.

[10] When the righteous prosper, the city
rejoices;
when the wicked perish, there are shouts of
joy.

[11] Through the blessing of the upright a city is
exalted,
but by the mouth of the wicked it is
destroyed.

[12] A man who lacks judgment derides his
neighbor,
but a man of understanding holds his tongue.

[13] A gossip betrays a confidence,
but a trustworthy man keeps a secret.

[14] For lack of guidance a nation falls,
but many advisers make victory sure.

[15] He who puts up security for another will surely
suffer,

NRSV

11 A false balance is an abomination to the
LORD,
but an accurate weight is his delight.

[2] When pride comes, then comes disgrace;
but wisdom is with the humble.

[3] The integrity of the upright guides them,
but the crookedness of the treacherous
destroys them.

[4] Riches do not profit in the day of wrath,
but righteousness delivers from death.

[5] The righteousness of the blameless keeps their
ways straight,
but the wicked fall by their own
wickedness.

[6] The righteousness of the upright saves them,
but the treacherous are taken captive by
their schemes.

[7] When the wicked die, their hope perishes,
and the expectation of the godless comes to
nothing.

[8] The righteous are delivered from trouble,
and the wicked get into it instead.

[9] With their mouths the godless would destroy
their neighbors,
but by knowledge the righteous are
delivered.

[10] When it goes well with the righteous, the city
rejoices;
and when the wicked perish, there is
jubilation.

[11] By the blessing of the upright a city is exalted,
but it is overthrown by the mouth of the
wicked.

[12] Whoever belittles another lacks sense,
but an intelligent person remains silent.

[13] A gossip goes about telling secrets,
but one who is trustworthy in spirit keeps
a confidence.

[14] Where there is no guidance, a nation[a] falls,
but in an abundance of counselors there is
safety.

[15] To guarantee loans for a stranger brings trouble,
but there is safety in refusing to do so.

[a] Or an army

115

NIV

but whoever refuses to strike hands in pledge
is safe.

¹⁶A kindhearted woman gains respect,
but ruthless men gain only wealth.

¹⁷A kind man benefits himself,
but a cruel man brings trouble on himself.

¹⁸The wicked man earns deceptive wages,
but he who sows righteousness reaps a sure
reward.

¹⁹The truly righteous man attains life,
but he who pursues evil goes to his death.

²⁰The LORD detests men of perverse heart
but he delights in those whose ways are
blameless.

²¹Be sure of this: The wicked will not go
unpunished,
but those who are righteous will go free.

²²Like a gold ring in a pig's snout
is a beautiful woman who shows no
discretion.

²³The desire of the righteous ends only in good,
but the hope of the wicked only in wrath.

²⁴One man gives freely, yet gains even more;
another withholds unduly, but comes to
poverty.

²⁵A generous man will prosper;
he who refreshes others will himself be
refreshed.

²⁶People curse the man who hoards grain,
but blessing crowns him who is willing to
sell.

²⁷He who seeks good finds goodwill,
but evil comes to him who searches for it.

²⁸Whoever trusts in his riches will fall,
but the righteous will thrive like a green leaf.

²⁹He who brings trouble on his family will inherit
only wind,
and the fool will be servant to the wise.

³⁰The fruit of the righteous is a tree of life,
and he who wins souls is wise.

³¹If the righteous receive their due on earth,
how much more the ungodly and the sinner!

NRSV

¹⁶ A gracious woman gets honor,
but she who hates virtue is covered with
shame.ᵃ
The timid become destitute,ᵇ
but the aggressive gain riches.

¹⁷ Those who are kind reward themselves,
but the cruel do themselves harm.

¹⁸ The wicked earn no real gain,
but those who sow righteousness get a true
reward.

¹⁹ Whoever is steadfast in righteousness will live,
but whoever pursues evil will die.

²⁰ Crooked minds are an abomination to the LORD,
but those of blameless ways are his delight.

²¹ Be assured, the wicked will not go
unpunished,
but those who are righteous will escape.

²² Like a gold ring in a pig's snout
is a beautiful woman without good sense.

²³ The desire of the righteous ends only in good;
the expectation of the wicked in wrath.

²⁴ Some give freely, yet grow all the richer;
others withhold what is due, and only suffer
want.

²⁵ A generous person will be enriched,
and one who gives water will get water.

²⁶ The people curse those who hold back grain,
but a blessing is on the head of those who
sell it.

²⁷ Whoever diligently seeks good seeks favor,
but evil comes to the one who searches for
it.

²⁸ Those who trust in their riches will wither,ᶜ
but the righteous will flourish like green
leaves.

²⁹ Those who trouble their households will
inherit wind,
and the fool will be servant to the wise.

³⁰ The fruit of the righteous is a tree of life,
but violenceᵈ takes lives away.

³¹ If the righteous are repaid on earth,
how much more the wicked and the sinner!

ᵃCompare Gk Syr: Heb lacks *but she . . . shame*   ᵇGk: Heb lacks
The timid . . . destitute   ᶜCn: Heb *fall*   ᵈCn Compare Gk Syr:
Heb *a wise man*

COMMENTARY

11:1. This saying brings righteousness into the marketplace and grounds economic fair play in the good pleasure of Yahweh (see 20:10, 23). Its language echoes Israel's legal codes (Lev 19:35-37; Deut 25:13-16) and the prophetic condemnation of commercial greed and deception (Ezek 45:10; Hos 12:7-8; Amos 8:5; Mic 6:11). Because God "created" commerce, money matters to God (16:11). Abomination/delight is a standard antithesis, referring occasionally to human standards (16:12; 29:27; cf. 13:19), but more usually to Yahweh as the ultimate judge of good and evil (6:16; 11:20, 27). However, besides eleven occurrences in Proverbs, the phrase "abomination to the LORD" appears only in Deuteronomy (8 times, usually of cultic matters; cf. Prov 15:8). Crooked commerce is an "abomination" to the gods also in Egyptian wisdom.[185]

11:2. This verse is a variation on "Pride goes before a fall" (see 15:33b; 18:3, 12 for the form). Our English saying is a condensation of 16:18. Verse 2b associates wisdom with the humble (cf. 13:10), while 22:4 associates humility with the fear of the Lord. Although one should avoid self-praise (27:2; Deut 8:17-18), the requirement here is not for false modesty, but for "sober judgment" of self, including a realistic assessment of both one's gifts and limitations (26:1, 8), with a view to service of God and neighbor (Rom 12:3-8; 1 Cor 12:12-26). God ultimately humbles the proud (1 Sam 2:3; Isa 10:12-19).

11:3. Here the writer describes lives ruled by contrary inner principles: integrity versus unreliable crookedness. Integrity ("blameless," Job 1:1; 9:20-22) is what Job struggles to maintain in the face of calamity and God's apparently unjust silence. Since "practice makes perfect," these principles build character over time. Consistency of character either guides one's journey through thick and thin or destroys one (10:9; 19:3; Rom 5:3-5). As Aristotle said, "We are what we repeatedly do. Excellence, then, is not an act, but a habit." Here "treacherous" is the same as "faithless" (see Commentary on 13:15).

185. See "Amenemope," chaps. 16-17, in Miriam Lichtheim, *Ancient Egyptian Literature,* 3 vols. (Berkeley: University of California Press, 1973-80) 2:156-57.

11:4. Language and thought from the prophetic tradition of the "day of the LORD," when Yahweh judges nations on a cosmic scale (Isa 13:9, 13; Ezek 7:19; Zeph 1:15, 18), are used here (see 16:4; Sir 5:8; 11:18-19). Although the saying does not exclude such a cosmic reference, a focus on people is more typical of Proverbs. This proverb may be applied to the "end" of individuals: Money will not help when death threatens (Ps 49:7-9, 16-20; Luke 12:15-21). At that moment, only one's righteous standing before God will matter (see Ps 49:15, though the sense is uncertain). Thus "death" may refer simply to calamities and mortal threats in the course of life (Ps 33:18-19).

11:5-6. These verses form a proverb pair closely tied to vv. 3-4 ("blameless" and "integrity" translate the same Hebrew root [תמם *tmm*]). In v. 3, integrity guides; in v. 5, righteousness clears one's way (see 3:6; cf. Commentary on 11:31).

Verse 6 forms a pair with v. 5 through verbal, formal, and thematic parallels; and v. 6a is a more general form of v. 4b. Verse 6b contains a wordplay on "desires" (הות *hawwat*; see Commentary on 10:3; Ps 5:10): "the treacherous are trapped in [or by] their [own] chasm/ruin/desires" (see 26:27; Pss 7:15-16; 9:15-16; 38:12; see also Commentary on 13:6). For "treacherous," see Commentary on 11:3; 13:15.

11:7. Death is God's final "no" to evil (cf. v. 23; 10:28). The destructive projects of the wicked perish with them, while Yahweh's purposes continue (Ps 73:18-20; Isa 40:6-8, 22-24). In "Godless" and "from his power," the NIV and NRSV translations chose alternative possibilities for an obscure Hebrew phrase.

11:8. The righteous do not lack for troubles, but God rescues them (Exod 2:23-25; Pss 34:4, 19; 107:2). The saying as a whole, however, implies a more complex narrative of poetic justice. Unlike most sayings, which use generalizing verb forms, v. 8 uses the narrative verb sequence for specific events in the past. Literally, "A righteous person was rescued from trouble, and a wicked one got into it instead." Thus this saying, more clearly than most, is a narrative in a nutshell that summarizes the way God's justice sometimes works (see Sir 10:14). The hanging of wicked Haman on the gallows intended for Mordecai perfectly realizes this proverb (Esth 5:14; 7:10; 9:1-10), as does the story of Daniel in the lions' den (Dan 6:23-24). The parable of Lazarus and the rich man moves the pattern into the realm of the afterlife (Luke 16:25).

11:9-15. 11:9. This passage begins a cluster of sayings exploring the interplay of social and political relations; it also has a backward verbal tie to v. 8 in "delivered." The ancient Greek translation (LXX) intensified the political focus of these verses by translating "neighbor" (vv. 9, 12) as "citizen." The "godless" or "profane" person is one who goes through life ignoring God (Job 8:13; Isa 32:6). But profane persons show their godlessness in dealing with their neighbors. The life-style of the godless reflects the dictum of Dostoyevsky, "If God does not exist, everything is permitted." Strangely, such practical atheism may be masked by "pious" worship (Isa 1:12-17; Jer 22:16; Amos 5:21-24) or even prophetic preaching (Jer 23:15). In this saying, the destructive power of speech (see also 18:21) is contrasted with the ability of righteous knowledge to rescue. The knowledge that saves may include knowledge of God, of oneself, of others, or of a particular situation and the wisdom that applies to it (see Eccl 9:14-15, with its ironic qualification).

11:10-11. These verses form a pair that move us from interpersonal relations (v. 9) to the city as a symbol of political reality in general (see 14:34; Gen 11:1-9). This move suggests that the political realm is founded on the personal and that its health presupposes the vitality and integrity of the latter. Verse 10, like most sayings, is open to various applications. The prosperity of the righteous may refer to their own wealth, by which they promote civic good. It may also refer to the good they do directly for the people. Again, the righteous and the wicked may be ordinary citizens, or those who rule and govern (28:12, 15-16, 28). The good of good people makes the city rejoice, but so does the departure of the wicked, because their destructive power dies with them. The story of Haman and Mordecai illustrates v. 10 well (Esth 3:15; 8:15-17).

The Hebrew for "is exalted" (רום *rûm*, v. 11) may also mean "is built up" in contrast to the "overthrow" or "tearing down" of the city, both physically and as the symbol of the body politic. "Blessing" (ברכה *bĕrākâ*) in this verse displays the same ambiguity as the prosperity of the righteous in v. 10; but "mouth" in v. 11*b* suggests that it refers to the verbal act of blessing. Such blessing functions as a prayer that calls God to act on behalf of the people: "Pray for the peace of Jerusalem" (Ps 122:6 NRSV; see 1 Kgs 8:14, 55; Pss 51:18; 128:5-6; 133:1-3).

11:12-13. These verses form another pair (see Commentary on 10:12, 18; 11:9). For "lacks sense," see Commentary on 10:13. To "belittle" or "deride" one's neighbor is a human impulse that violates the essence of biblical religion (14:31). It is also, in merely practical terms, deeply foolish and counterproductive. The Hebrew word (בוז *bûz*) connotes an attitude that despises (14:21) another human being, for real or imagined flaws and failings.

Verse 13 applies the matter raised in v. 12 to gossip, echoing the law of Lev 19:16 (see Prov 20:19; Jer 6:28; Sir 27:16). This legal parallel opposes gossip to the great command to love the neighbor as oneself, from the heart (Lev 19:16-18; Matt 22:39; Rom 13:9). Several other sayings contrast verbal destruction of the neighbor to wise love, which knows when silence is right (Prov 10:12, 19; 12:16; 17:9; 20:19).

11:14. What follows is one of several sayings on the need for wise counsel, especially in affairs of governance, state craft, and the waging of war (15:22; 20:18; 24:6). "Guidance" refers to the art of steering, of giving direction to things, as God does to clouds pregnant with moisture (Job 37:11-12).

11:15. This saying and related ones concern the obvious danger of being a direct or indirect guarantor of a loan (see Commentary on 6:1-5), especially to a stranger (20:16; 22:26; 27:13). To strike hands is a symbolic action that seals a deal.

11:16. It is difficult to understand the connection between the two lines of the Hebrew text of this verse. The NIV adds "only" to suggest that a "kind-hearted woman" is worth more than the ruthless who only gain wealth (see 22:1, where "favor" is the same word as "kind-hearted"). The NRSV solves the problem by adding to the Hebrew text lines from the Greek (LXX) and Syriac versions. But the Hebrew term for "kind-hearted"/"gracious" (חן *ḥēn*), when referring to a woman, generally means "beauty" (5:19; 31:30; cf. 1:9; 4:9; 17:8; Nah 3:4). Sirach 9:8 uses the identical Hebrew phrase to mean "beautiful woman." "Honor"/"respect" (כבוד *kābôd*) is usually translated "glory," but the term includes "wealth" as well. The saying is probably to be understood as a shrewd observation on beauty (see 11:22) and violence: "A beautiful woman gets 'glory;' ruthless men get wealth." The point of the comparison is that beauty can be the instrument by which a woman gains glory—that is, status, power, wealth, and the splendid symbols thereof (cf. 26:1). In the same way, ruthless/aggressive men find ways to get riches. ("Glory" and "riches" are parallel in 3:16; 8:18; 22:4; see also 1 Kgs 3:13; 1 Chr 29:28.)

11:17. The text implies that our disposition and behavior toward others, for good or for ill, affect our very selves in boomerang-like fashion (see 21:21). The Hebrew uses two different terms for the repeated English "themselves"; the first (נפש *nepeš*), sometimes translated "soul" (Ps 103:1), denotes the whole human person from an inner perspective, as does the second (שאר *šĕ'ēr*) from an outer, or "bodily," perspective. Literally, the verse may read, "The cruel trouble their own flesh" (see v. 29). Here the ethical problem of self-love finds its proportion and resolution. Contrary to the myth of rugged individualism, human solidarity is such that to love or harm others is to do the same to oneself. Moreover, the closer the human bond, the more intense the blessing or bane to the self (see 1 Cor 7:4; Eph 5:28-29).

11:18. Here the writer contrasts deceptive versus true wages earned by the efforts of the wicked and the righteous respectively (see 10:2, 16). "All that glitters is not gold." The contrast here of appearance and reality lends complexity to the basic act-consequence pattern, by providing one explanation of the anomaly of wicked wealth. The fruits of wicked labors may seem impressive, but they cannot be relied upon (Psalms 49; 73), even as one cannot rely on deceptive words. The imagery of sowing and reaping is a basic biblical metaphor for the character-consequence pattern (Job 4:8; Ps 126:5; Prov 22:8; Hos 10:12; 2 Cor 9:6; Gal 6:7). Because sowing and reaping are general patterns (not every seed bears the expected fruit, Jer 12:13; Mic 6:15; Matt 13:3-8, 24-30), the metaphor allows for anomalies and

exceptions to the general rule. Sowing righteousness appears also in Hos 10:12-13 (see Prov 22:8; James 3:18).

11:19-20. Verse 19 has a small uncertainty in its first line. Perhaps "steadfast"/"truly" is a particle ("Thus righteousness . . . ") linking v. 19 to the preceding verse. This saying repeats the basic life issues central to chaps. 10–15. The end (good or evil) one pursues over the course of a lifetime determines the outcome (see Commentary on 11:4-5, 27; see 13:21; 15:9; 21:21). For "abomination"/"delight" (v. 20), see v. 1; for the contrasts "crooked"/"blameless" and "heart"/"way," see Commentary on 10:9.

11:21. The phrase "will not go unpunished" (used 7 times in Prov 6:29; 11:21; 16:5; 17:5; 19:5, 9; 28:20) is one of several that connect wisdom with the great revelation of the name of Yahweh in Exod 34:6-7 (see also Exod 20:7). The phrase affirms the ultimate justice of God, not on the basis of empirical observation, but on the basis of God's nature. Verses 20*a* and 21*a* together find a near duplicate in 16:5.

11:22-23. Ancient Israelite women wore nose rings for beauty and ornament (Gen 24:47; Ezek 16:12), but the shock of a pig's snout bedecked with gold provokes insight. Without good sense, beauty in a wife or woman (the Hebrew means both) is out of place. Beauty and wisdom may combine, as with Abigail (1 Samuel 25) and the heroines in Esther, Susanna, and Judith. But just as wisdom prohibits one from worshiping wealth (23:4-5), so also it cuts short the human tendency to idolize female beauty (31:30). Verse 23 is a variant of 10:28 (on "wrath," see v. 4).

11:24-26. These verses form a trio on economic relations between rich and poor. "Gives freely" (v. 24) is literally "scatters" (מפזר *mĕpazzēr*; see Ps 112:9)—that is, to the needy. The verse plays on a surface paradox that confirms the deeper principle of reaping as one sows. Generosity would seem to diminish one's resources but, in God's economy, brings gain (3:9-10; 19:17). To withhold more than is just, conversely, does not preserve wealth but brings lack. Verse 25 may be seen as an explication of the paradox in v. 24, according to the correspondence of acts and consequences (see 22:9).

Verse 26 completes the trio with a move from alms to commerce (see 11:1). The saying refers to a time of need, when hoarding staples can lead to personal profit at the cost of public starvation. The people's curse and blessing are in effect prayers to God (2 Sam 16:5-12; Prov 26:2), that God right injustice (24:24) or prosper the generous, who sell to the needy though the latter have only their labor to offer. The story of Joseph may serve as a general illustration of the positive second half of this saying (Gen 41:56; 42:6; 47:25; 49:26*b*). For profiteering (and the collapse thereof) in time of famine, see 2 Kgs 6:25; 7:1, 16.

11:27. "Favor" (רצון *rāṣôn*) is happily ambiguous, referring to what pleases God and humans (3:4; 1 Sam 2:26; Luke 2:52) and to the goodwill evoked thereby, though divine favor is infinitely uppermost (8:35; 12:2; 18:22; see 11:1, 20 where "delight" = "favor"). "Evil" (רעה *rā'â*) is unhappily ambiguous, referring to the wrong done by folks in their errant search for good (Gen 3:6), and to the trouble that comes to them instead (10:24*a;* Pss 7:16; 9:16; Sir 27:26-27). Beneath this saying lies the question, "What do I seek?" and the realization that no human has fully arrived (Phil 3:12-16). (The NRSV, with its double "seeks" in v. 27*a* hews closer to the Hebrew than does the NIV.) So the search for "good" and for God are parallel, inseparable, with life and death at stake (v. 19; Amos 5:6, 14-15). For Jesus, such a search is the one thing needful: "Seek first the kingdom of God and His righteousness" (Matt 6:33 NRSV; 7:7).

11:28. Other things being equal, wealth is good (10:15), but without righteousness it is worthless (v. 4; 16:8). To make riches—any sort of human power really—into a source of security is to fall into unreality (18:11; Psalm 49; 1 Tim 6:17) and to separate the fruits from their root (15:20; 28:25; 29:25; Deut 8:17-18; Hos 2:8). Ultimate security and blessing are with God (3:5-8). The thought, antithesis, and botanical imagery of this saying parallel Psalm 1 and Jer 17:5-8 (see also Pss 52:7-8; 92:6-7, 12-14). The variation in translation of "whither" and "fall" perhaps reflects a deliberate pun in the Hebrew.

11:29. Literally, the Hebrew reads, "He who troubles his house," a rather open-ended phrase (= 15:27*a;* for the verb, see Gen 34:30; 1 Sam

14:29; 1 Kgs 18:17). The Hebrew for "house" (בית *bayit*) can mean "house(hold)" as well as "family." One's "house" is an inheritance from one's parents (19:14), to be built up by wisdom, labor, and care (24:3-4, 27). One's "house" is that microcosm of God's greater world for which we are most immediately responsible (see Commentary on 9:1-6). As an ill bird fouls its own nest, so humans can trash their own "house" and thus "inherit the wind"—that is, nothing. The second line suggests a further descent: Fools who fail to exercise responsibility over their own turf will serve the realm of those who do (see 12:24; 14:1, 19; 17:2; and the peculiar development of wisdom themes in Matt 25:14-30; Luke 19:11-27).

11:30. For "tree of life," see Gen 2:9; 3:22; Prov 3:18; 13:12; 15:4. The difficulty of the second line is reflected in the two translations. The rendering by the NIV, with its view to gaining souls for eternal life, has its forerunners in medieval Jewish commentators. The NRSV, however, is aware that to "take lives" (lit., "get/take souls" לקח נפשות *lāqaḥ nĕpāšôt*) in Hebrew often means "to kill" (1:19*b;* Ps 31:13, though the rabbis appeal to Gen 12:5 for a positive sense). Thus the NRSV changes the Hebrew subject to violence. This, however, destroys the text to be explained. A fully satisfactory solution remains to be found.

11:31. It might seem that the righteous here are repaid for their righteousness, while the wicked are repaid for their sins. But on such a reading, the move from minor to major (how much more) remains unexplained. The point is, rather, that since during their life (on earth; see Ps 58:11) even the righteous receive judgment for their sins (Num 20:12; 2 Sam 12:10-12), surely the wicked will as well. (The Greek translation taken over in 1 Pet 4:18 may be a paraphrase in this vein.) Verse 31 thus qualifies a too simplistic reading of the many sayings that, for pedagogical purposes, employ "righteous" and "wicked" as unnuanced, primary character types. (Such agonistic, "heavy" portrayal of types is characteristic of oral cultures.)[186]

---

186. See Walter J. Ong, *Orality and Literacy: The Technologizing of the Word* (New York: Methuen, 1982) 43-45, 69-71.

REFLECTIONS

1. While continuing the antithesis of righteous and wicked, Proverbs 11 introduces a few sayings that are not antithetical (11:7, 16, 22, 25, 29) and presents a richer variety of antitheses. Prominent in this chapter is a turn to the interwoven public arenas of commerce (11:1, 15, 24-26) and the sociopolitical commonweal (11:9-14, 24-26).

It is common for scholars to note in these chapters a straightforward connection between goodness and success and between wickedness and failure. Here, goodness leads to prosperity and badness leads to calamity (see Overview to 10:1–15:33). They further assume that such a simplistic view of acts and consequences must reflect a secure, almost complacent, social setting, perhaps among the scribes of the royal court. But the severity of the calamities (death and destruction, the "day of wrath," the fall of cities and nations) suggests that these sayings have currency even beyond a complacent middle-class world of decency and order.[187]

Whatever their social origin in ancient Israel, the application of these sayings certainly stretches to times of crisis and chaos. Perhaps especially in crisis and chaos it is necessary for the righteous to insist on the reality of justice, of consequences that follow upon good and evil. Such a view of meaning and order in life is grounded in the goodness and justice of the Creator, who calls human beings to account. Such a faith maintains belief in the God of justice, even when it does not experience justice. Such a faith was typical of Israel, as the psalms of lament eloquently attest.

For this American son of Dutch immigrants, the proverb clusters of chapter 11 evoke parental stories of life in the Nazi-occupied Netherlands during World War II. Others will have other tales to tell: of America's inner cities, of Vietnam, of Bosnia, of Ireland, of Rwanda, or of the former Soviet Union. In times of socioeconomic distress or oppression, the distinction of "righteous" and "wicked" becomes more visible, and the fence-sitting majority find it more difficult to maintain their posture of uncommitted respectability. These proverbial observations are also illustrated by Langdon Gilkey's wise first-person account of life in the microcosm of a war-time prison camp. When human goodness costs personal sacrifice, it becomes a rare commodity.[188] Trouble tests the heart's true mettle. In times of crisis and injustice, whispered words become more potent to destroy (Prov 11:9*a*, 11*b*, 13*a*); silence saves lives (Prov 11:12*b*, 13*b*); and shrewd ploys rescue the perishing (Prov 11:89*b*, 14*b*). And when the righteous triumph and the wicked finally fall, there is dancing in the streets (Prov 11:10).

2. To have contempt for other human beings is to insult their Maker (11:12-13; 17:5; see 14:31; 22:2). Although Proverbs does not make the connection, something like the priestly theology of humans' being created in the image of God's glory is operative here (Gen 1:26-28; Psalm 8; Jas 3:9). No doubt "other" people are flawed, weak, poor, and doers of what is despicable. Self-knowledge, however, ought to remind us that we belong to "them" (Prov 20:9). There is a twofold human solidarity that transcends race, sex, class, culture, and any other difference. First, God has made us all of one flesh, in God's image to reflect the glory of God (see Acts 17:26). Second, there is the fragmented solidarity of sin, which prohibits pride and reveals our common need of grace (1 Cor 4:7). It is precisely defective and deficient humans, the failed and the unlovely, who receive God's compassion: "a broken and contrite heart, O God, you will not despise" (Ps 51:17 NRSV; see also Pss 22:24; 102:17; Isa 57:15; Matt 9:13; Rom 5:6-8).

On the practical level, to belittle another person is to damage the bond of common humanity, to sever ourselves from our own flesh. In marriage and family, in corporate and civic life, to belittle the other destroys the ability to continue our common work, whatever that may be.

---

187. See R. N. Whybray, *Wealth and Poverty in the Book of Proverbs* (Sheffield: JSOT, 1990).
188. Langdon Gilkey, *Shantung Compound: The Story of Men and Women Under Pressure* (New York: Harper and Row, 1975).

It is a form of win/lose thinking that ultimately redounds to our own loss. The person I insult, directly or in secret, is unlikely to help me in my time of need. Understanding knows when to hold its tongue (11:12*b;* 10:18-19; 17:27-28).

3. Lurking behind sayings on guidance and counsel (11:14) is the apparatus of the royal court and a variety of counselors on whose wisdom the success or failure of the nation in no small part depends. Before projects can be born in reality they must be conceived in the mind. But such deliberation must be communal, for "two heads are better than one." No one, not even the king, has all the answers, thus the need for counselors. But even the sharpest and shrewdest human wisdom has its limits. The best wisdom of the earthly court may be utterly undone by the contrary plans of the heavenly court (16:1, 9; 19:21; 21:30-31; Isa 29:14-16). Such sayings in Proverbs anticipate the intense discussion of the limitations of human wisdom found in Ecclesiastes and Job. The stories of David and Ahitophel (2 Sam 16:15–17:14) and of Ahab and the prophet Micaiah (1 Kings 22:19-28) illustrate the failure of human wisdom in the face of the divine counsel.

4. The advice implicit in 11:15 has universal validity (like "let the buyer beware"), even though forms of financial risk taking change. It speaks also to a culture of stocks, (junk) bonds, failed savings and loans, and of leveraged buyouts. "The more things change, the more they stay the same." Nonetheless, there are times when it is proper to risk oneself as guarantee (the Hebrew term is not limited to loans) for another, as the Judah and Benjamin episode in the Joseph cycle indicates (Gen 43:9; 44:32-33; John 15:13; see Commentary on Prov 17:17-18).

5. Two sayings concern women and beauty (11:16, 22). In his autobiographical book, *Telling Secrets,* F. Buechner notes how his mother failed to develop character because she was able to trade upon her extraordinary beauty.[189] Proverbs is aware of the goodness and power of beauty and wealth. Yet, it steers us away from evaluating persons (even ourselves) on the basis of wealth or beauty; for human beings, male or female, other attributes are more important (see Commentary on 16:8). Wealth is no ultimate source of security (11:28). In spite of the widespread male idolatry (and fear) of beauty, wisdom does not value women according to mere appearance (11:22; 31:30; 1 Pet 3:3-5*a*). Men too frequently render themselves fools and sinners on account of a woman's beauty (2 Sam 11:2-27; 13:1-21; Prov 7:4-27; Matt 5:27-30). In general, according to social scientists, humans are inclined to attribute intelligence and other virtues to those who are of striking appearance (1 Sam 16:7). If beauty is skin deep, wisdom requires that we look deeper.

6. It is a pervasive biblical principle that people reap what they sow and that the punishment, in the negative instance, will fit the crime (Exod 21:23-25; Pss 7:15-16, 9:15-16; Prov 11:29). The evil folks do will come back to haunt them (1:18-19). The tales of Joseph's wicked brothers (Genesis 37–50) and of David's adultery with Bathsheba and murder of Uriah, her husband (2 Sam 11:2-17) may be considered extended instances of Prov 11:5*b,* 31*b.* Joseph's brothers are caught in the net they wove by selling Joseph to Egypt. And the saddest result of David's sins is his impotence in dealing with the similar sins of his sons Amnon and Absalom, an impotence that enables the latter's revolt and the near loss of David's kingdom. In the end, lusty King David is merely impotent (1 Kings 1). In both these stories, it is only God's grace and purpose that break the fateful chain of consequences for Joseph's brothers and for David (Gen 45:4-8; 50:15-21; 2 Sam 17:14). In the pedagogy of grace, people inclined to be wicked become righteous.

189. F. Buechner, *Telling Secrets: A Memoir* (New York: HarperCollins, 1991) 11-20.

Proverbs 12:1-28, Whoever Loves Discipline Loves Knowledge

NIV

12 Whoever loves discipline loves knowledge,
but he who hates correction is stupid.

2 A good man obtains favor from the LORD,
but the LORD condemns a crafty man.

3 A man cannot be established through wickedness,
but the righteous cannot be uprooted.

4 A wife of noble character is her husband's crown,
but a disgraceful wife is like decay in his bones.

5 The plans of the righteous are just,
but the advice of the wicked is deceitful.

6 The words of the wicked lie in wait for blood,
but the speech of the upright rescues them.

7 Wicked men are overthrown and are no more,
but the house of the righteous stands firm.

8 A man is praised according to his wisdom,
but men with warped minds are despised.

9 Better to be a nobody and yet have a servant
than pretend to be somebody and have no food.

10 A righteous man cares for the needs of his animal,
but the kindest acts of the wicked are cruel.

11 He who works his land will have abundant food,
but he who chases fantasies lacks judgment.

12 The wicked desire the plunder of evil men,
but the root of the righteous flourishes.

13 An evil man is trapped by his sinful talk,
but a righteous man escapes trouble.

14 From the fruit of his lips a man is filled with good things
as surely as the work of his hands rewards him.

15 The way of a fool seems right to him,
but a wise man listens to advice.

16 A fool shows his annoyance at once,
but a prudent man overlooks an insult.

17 A truthful witness gives honest testimony,

NRSV

12 Whoever loves discipline loves knowledge,
but those who hate to be rebuked are stupid.

2 The good obtain favor from the LORD,
but those who devise evil he condemns.

3 No one finds security by wickedness,
but the root of the righteous will never be moved.

4 A good wife is the crown of her husband,
but she who brings shame is like rottenness in his bones.

5 The thoughts of the righteous are just;
the advice of the wicked is treacherous.

6 The words of the wicked are a deadly ambush,
but the speech of the upright delivers them.

7 The wicked are overthrown and are no more,
but the house of the righteous will stand.

8 One is commended for good sense,
but a perverse mind is despised.

9 Better to be despised and have a servant,
than to be self-important and lack food.

10 The righteous know the needs of their animals,
but the mercy of the wicked is cruel.

11 Those who till their land will have plenty of food,
but those who follow worthless pursuits have no sense.

12 The wicked covet the proceeds of wickedness,[a]
but the root of the righteous bears fruit.

13 The evil are ensnared by the transgression of their lips,
but the righteous escape from trouble.

14 From the fruit of the mouth one is filled with good things,
and manual labor has its reward.

15 Fools think their own way is right,
but the wise listen to advice.

16 Fools show their anger at once,
but the prudent ignore an insult.

17 Whoever speaks the truth gives honest evidence,
but a false witness speaks deceitfully.

18 Rash words are like sword thrusts,

a Or covet the catch of the wicked

NIV

but a false witness tells lies.

[18]Reckless words pierce like a sword,
but the tongue of the wise brings healing.

[19]Truthful lips endure forever,
but a lying tongue lasts only a moment.

[20]There is deceit in the hearts of those who plot evil,
but joy for those who promote peace.

[21]No harm befalls the righteous,
but the wicked have their fill of trouble.

[22]The LORD detests lying lips,
but he delights in men who are truthful.

[23]A prudent man keeps his knowledge to himself,
but the heart of fools blurts out folly.

[24]Diligent hands will rule,
but laziness ends in slave labor.

[25]An anxious heart weighs a man down,
but a kind word cheers him up.

[26]A righteous man is cautious in friendship,[a]
but the way of the wicked leads them astray.

[27]The lazy man does not roast[b] his game,
but the diligent man prizes his possessions.

[28]In the way of righteousness there is life;
along that path is immortality.

[a]26 Or *man is a guide to his neighbor*   [b]27 The meaning of the Hebrew for this word is uncertain.

NRSV

but the tongue of the wise brings healing.

[19] Truthful lips endure forever,
but a lying tongue lasts only a moment.

[20] Deceit is in the mind of those who plan evil,
but those who counsel peace have joy.

[21] No harm happens to the righteous,
but the wicked are filled with trouble.

[22] Lying lips are an abomination to the LORD,
but those who act faithfully are his delight.

[23] One who is clever conceals knowledge,
but the mind of a fool[a] broadcasts folly.

[24] The hand of the diligent will rule,
while the lazy will be put to forced labor.

[25] Anxiety weighs down the human heart,
but a good word cheers it up.

[26] The righteous gives good advice to friends,[b]
but the way of the wicked leads astray.

[27] The lazy do not roast[c] their game,
but the diligent obtain precious wealth.[c]

[28] In the path of righteousness there is life,
in walking its path there is no death.

[a]Heb *the heart of fools*   [b]Syr: Meaning of Heb uncertain
[c]Meaning of Heb uncertain

COMMENTARY

12:1. Aristotle begins his *Metaphysics* by observing that all people naturally desire knowledge. He illustrates his point by referring to our "love" of the senses, especially sight, which "best helps us to know things, and reveals many distinctions." Verse 1, however, has a focus characteristic of oral cultures: Wise knowledge comes through verbal interaction with others in the midst of life. Chapters 1–9 explored the theme of rebuke and correction in the figure of Lady Wisdom (1:25, 29-30). In this verse, the focus is on love of discipline (the broader term) and correction as essentials on the road to life (10:17). Paradoxically, discipline is a "station on the way to freedom."[190] In and of itself, our natural inclination is not to love discipline, but to reject and resist it (5:12; 9:7; 13:1, 18). Discipline is difficult, for it requires self-limitation at the behest of another (Heb 12:3-13; cf. Deut 8:5; Prov 3:11-12). But discipline may be loved for its fruit: knowledge. Knowledge makes us human; without it we are mere beasts ("stupid" in 30:2; in Ps 92:6 the term means "beast-like").

12:2. This verse employs language that resonates with key moments in the book. The "good" person receives the Lord's favor or goodwill (11:1,

190. D. Bonhoeffer, *Ethics* (New York: Macmillan, 1965) 15. See also Reflections on Proverbs 6.

27)—that is, life in the bosom of Lady Wisdom (8:35). This finding and receiving has its mundane parallel in the divine gift of a wife (18:22; 19:14). In such a woman, but not in man, the human incarnation of wisdom is manifested (31:10-31).

But God "condemns the crafty." To be crafty is not in itself bad (1:4; 3:21; 8:12). But in this context, the Hebrew word for "crafty" (זמה *zimmâ*) signals those who rely on the devices of their own mind while ignoring God—the ultimate form of unreality (16:9; 19:21). Alternatively, the crafty are those who actively plan evil (24:8; Gen 6:5; 8:21; Eccl 7:29). The psalmist prays that such people be "caught in the schemes they have devised" (Ps 10:2 NRSV). God's justice "condemns" them, providing the model for human judges (17:15; Exod 23:7).

12:3. This verse democratizes a cosmic principle of divine and human kingship (Pss 89:14; 93:1-2; 97:1-2). On pillars such as these the house of Wisdom is built. Whereas the divine and Davidic thrones are "established through righteousness" (16:12 NIV; 25:4-5), this verse asserts the same of humankind in general, but in negative form.

12:4. As noted before, the original audience of Proverbs was male. Thus the possibility of a spouse's being good or bad is portrayed in terms of a good or bad wife. The phrase "a good wife of noble character" appears only three times in the OT (and also Sir 26:2). It receives a full description in the heroic hymn of Prov 31:10-31. Boaz uses it to describe the enterprising young widow, Ruth (Ruth 3:11), whose book immediately follows Proverbs in the Hebrew canon. The phrase seems to lie behind Paul's statement in the NT that a wife is her husband's glory (1 Cor 11:7), for "crown" and "glory" are closely associated (Prov 4:9; 16:31; Isa 28:1, 5; Jer 13:18).

12:5. The righteous and the wicked are here characterized by the thoughts and advice that preoccupy each. The Hebrew word translated as "advice" (תחבלות *taḥbulôt*) more precisely denotes stratagems that steer or govern life and its activities, such as battles (20:11; 24:6; see Commentary on 11:14, "guidance"). "Just" (משפט *mišpāṭ*) is literally "justice"; the mind of the righteous is focused on justice, which is God's basic intention for the descendants of Abraham (Gen 18:19; see Commentary on 21:3).

12:6. The positive and negative powers of speech are contrasted (see Commentary on 12:13; 18:21). The first line continues the thought of v. 5*b* by giving a concrete instance that echoes the invitation to murder in 1:11 (see NIV). The second line varies the language of 11:6.

12:7. The word root of "overthrown" (הפך *hāpak*) is used elsewhere of the destruction of Sodom and Gomorrah (Deut 29:23; Isa 13:19; Jer 49:18; Amos 4:11). On "are no more," see Job's lament that he is treated like the wicked (Job 7:7-10, 21). "House" can refer to a dwelling, to one's turf, or to one's posterity (15:25; 23:10-11). For further discussion, see the Commentary on 10:25; 12:3; 14:11.

12:8. For Israel, praise and life are inseparable partners. Where there is life, there is praise: praise of all things bright and beautiful (see Ps 104:24), praise of persons (31:10-31; 2 Sam 23:8-39; Sir 44:1–50:21), and ultimately praise of the Lord God who made them all (see Psalm 148; Sir 50:22-24). Only with death, in the grave, does praise cease and silence reign (Pss 6:5; 115:17). To use an imperfect anthropological typology,[191] Israel's culture is a shame-and-honor culture, in which persons are publicly affirmed and celebrated for the virtues and well-being they bring to the community, and conversely they are condemned for the havoc they wreak (see Commentary on 3:4; 10:5, 7; 22:1; see also Eccl 7:1). Such praise and blame express the speaker's delight or dismay in the other person and powerfully enforce the community's standards of good and evil upon the recipient of praise or blame. It is foolish to praise oneself (27:2, 21), a thought that provides a link to the next verse.

12:9-11. These verses form a triplet linked by their rootage in the agricultural life on the land. Verse 9 is the first of many better-than sayings that offer paradoxical comparisons that invert conventional judgments of value, especially regarding wealth and poverty (cf. 15:17; 16:8). The laconic Hebrew of v. 9 may be understood several ways. The NIV and the NRSV translations contrast two types of persons. The first are poor peasants, lightly esteemed by society, who have the means and initiative to support themselves. The second also lack social status, for they pretend to have

191. Clifford Geertz, *The Interpretation of Cultures* (New York: Basic Books, 1973) 400-403.

social weight or wealth. Perhaps because they consider themselves to be above working, they go hungry (12:11//28:19; see Commentary on 6:6-11; 20:4). The medieval Jewish commentator Rashi takes this saying as follows: "Better is a person of little account (in his own eyes) who works for himself, than one who honors himself but comes to lack food" (author's paraphrase; see Commentary on 25:6-7). However the saying is taken, it provokes the reader to wrestle with the question of societal versus personal perceptions and with the related problems of self-knowledge and realism about oneself, one's circumstances, and one's legitimate responsibilities (see Commentary on 13:7; 26:1, 12, 16).[192]

Verse 10 uses the Hebrew "know" (ידע *yāda‘*) to convey understanding and insight into as well as care for one's animal (see 27:23). Domestic animals are utterly dependent upon their master's benevolence. They cannot clearly articulate their needs or desires (the Hebrew word often translated "soul" [נפש *nepeš*] also connotes needs and appetites; see 16:26). Yet, the righteous, who are in tune with reality, can read what is "on the mind of" their animals and provide for them. So the righteous hear and answer the voice of those who have no voice (Job 12:7-10). "Cruel mercy" is a deep oxymoron (see Jer 6:23).

Verse 11 (par. 28:19; see also 13:25; 20:13) reflects the world of the small farm, on which life is maintained only by wise, hard work.[193] Wise humans are responsible realists who "work" (lit., "serve" [עבד *‘ābad*]; see Gen 2:15; 1 Kgs 12:7) the turf God gives them (Lev 25:2, 23), whatever that may be, to earn their daily bread (20:13; 30:8-9), the fruit of God's good creation. Those who serve the creation and its creatures are in turn served by it. "Fantasies" (ריקים *rêqîm*) is literally "emptinesses" or "nothings." Not to work with what is ours is to flee the real to chase the unreal. To lack judgment is literally to lack heart, without which one cannot acquire wisdom (17:16; see Pss 51:6; 90:12). The heart, in OT psychology, is the burning center of our humanity from which flow our thoughts, words, and deeds (see Excursus, "The 'Heart' in the Old Testa-

ment," 60-61; see also 10:13). It is thus the deepest home of wisdom, where knowledge of God and the world meet (see Commentary on 1:7).

12:12. The Hebrew of this verse has found no satisfactory explanation. The NRSV and the NIV translations are two of many educated guesses. The saying may mean that the wicked desire a source of security ("stronghold," see 18:10-11) built of evil, but that God grants (10:24; 12:14) security (see v. 3) only to the righteous.

12:13. Verse 13*a*, with its reference to lips, is a more specific variant of 29:6 (see also 1:17-18; 6:2; 12:6; 18:7). It may also be translated literally, "In the transgression of the lips is an evil trap" (see Eccl 9:12). The story of Susanna illustrates both halves of this saying. The two lustful elders are caught by their false testimony, while innocent or righteous (the Hebrew word means both) Susanna escapes death (see Ps 34:17-19). The connection between the verse halves may be this: When people are in trouble, they are tempted to escape their plight through false speech. But such speech is itself a deadly trap, because it distorts reality. Sinful speech may move one from the frying pan into the fire.

12:14. In 15:4, the tongue is a "tree of life," presumably for others who can pluck its healing fruit or leaves (Rev 22:2). In this verse (see also 13:2; 18:20; Isa 3:9-11), our deeds affect not only others but also ourselves (see Commentary on 11:17), we are sated with the "fruit" of our own speech. This saying focuses on good eating and thus implies good fruit. But the more general form of the saying in 18:20 suggests that the produce of mouth and hands may be either good or evil (18:21), because good and evil each bears its own fruit. The NRSV and NIV translations convey a natural sequence of act and consequence. But one of the two traditions preserved in the Hebrew text, the *Qere*, implies that God is the one who rewards human works (see Commentary on 10:24; 12:12). Theologically, this ought not to be an either/or, for God's mysterious hand is present in the processes of the world God has made (Pss 7:11-16; 9:15-16).

12:15-16. These verses concern the fool. Verse 15 is a more specific variant of 16:2 and 21:2 (see also 14:12; 16:25). Literally, "The way of a fool is right in his own eyes." The Hebrew expression "X in the eyes of P" denotes a subjec-

192. See "Discipline" in M. Scott Peck, *The Road Less Traveled* (New York: Simon and Schuster, 1978).

193. See R. N. Whybray, *Wealth and Poverty in the Book of Proverbs* (Sheffield: JSOT, 1990).

tive perception that is implicitly in contrast to the judgment of some other, "X in the eyes of Q." This "other" may be human, as here and in 28:11, but most important it can be God, the ultimate judge of right and wrong, of wisdom and folly. When in Judges each person does what is right in his or her own eyes (Judg 17:6; 21:25), the narrative shows that these people are actually doing "evil in the eyes of the Lord" (see, e.g., Judg 2:11; 3:7; 4:1). In the monarchy, the human king is to do what is right in the eyes of the divine king (1 Kgs 11:33, 38; see Prov 25:2-3). In v. 15, fools are individualists, satisfied with their lives, because they are satisfied with their own standards. Wise persons know the limits of their own understanding and listen to the wise (15:12, 22). Fools, however, do what is right in their own eyes even when they consult others, because they listen only to people like themselves (1 Kgs 12:1-16; see Commentary on 3:7; 26:12).

Fools lack self-control when provoked. Yet wounded rage is impotent; it shows the opponent's power, and it lends credence to an insult. Inner strength and wisdom are needed to refrain from expressing self-defeating emotions. The ability to keep silent often distinguishes the prudent from the foolish (12:23; 13:16; 18:2), but not always (17:27-28)! There may be more than one reason for covering over personal injury (10:12).

12:17. This verse moves speech into the legal arena (see 6:19; 14:5, 25; 19:5, 9, 28; 21:28; 25:18). In predominantly oral cultures, legal disputes and criminal cases are decided primarily through the testimony of witnesses (Deut 17:6; 19:15-18; 1 Kgs 21:8-14; Matt 26:57-66). Matthew 18:16 applies this principle to life in the church, where "honest testimony" is literally "righteousness"—that is, testimony in harmony with reality. The frequency of this topic in Proverbs reflects its tremendous importance; in the law court, truth and falsity can rescue or kill (see Commentary on 25:18, which links this insight to the Ten Commandments).

12:18. "Reckless words" may occur in any setting: in the making of vows (Lev 5:4), or in a fit of rage (Num 20:10; Ps 106:33). The tragic story of Jephthah and his daughter illustrates the rash vow (Judges 11), as does the nearly tragic tale of Saul and Jonathan (1 Sam 14:24-45). Once a word has been uttered, it cannot be called back.

At v. 18, the juxtaposition of v. 17 and the parallel in 25:18 underscore the deadly power of words in the law court. The tongue can cut like a sword (Pss 57:4; 64:3-4; the Hebrew term חרב [ḥereb] covers both the long sword used in war and the dagger, the most dangerous and intimate weapon known to the ancients [see Judg 3:16-23].) But the wise tongue heals wounded persons (15:4; 16:24) and broken communities (15:1), a fact that underscores again the ambiguity of the Hebrew (see Commentary on 12:14; cf. Jas 3:1-12).

12:19. This verse contains observations similar to vv. 3, 7, but continues the present focus on speech. "Lips" and "tongue" stand for those who speak. They endure, or not, because their words do, or do not, reflect reality. What goes counter to reality is shattered by it in a moment, like a ship on the rocks. In Hebrew, "only a moment" (עד-ארגיעה ʿad-ʾargîʿâ) contains a nice pun on the word for "witness" (עד ʿēd, v. 17), suggesting that a liar will be a short-lived witness.

12:20. Those who plan evil (see 6:14; 14:22) do so in their heart, the hidden center of the human person (see Excursus, "The 'Heart' in the Old Testament," 60-61). The heart's deceit includes self-deception (Jer 17:9-10) as well as distortion of reality. It bears unreliable fruit in the real world (Job 4:8; "plan" and "plow" are the same Hebrew verb). Similarly, the joy of those who "counsel peace" (see 12:22; Ps 120:6-7) may be internal or external, when their advice is enacted (21:15).

12:21. This verse is typical of Proverbs 10–15 (see Overview to Prov 10:1–15:33; see also Pss 32:10; 91:10; Sir 33:1a): good leads to good, and bad leads to bad. The rhetorical force of the verse is to encourage and remind readers of the basic pattern of good and evil consequences in the world (see Commentary on 10:3).

12:22. The psalmist prays for deliverance from lying lips, whose power to hurt are like weapons of war (v. 20; 25:18; Ps 120:2, 4). Those who act faithfully are literally those "who do truth." Although speech can be deadly, this saying moves from negative words to positive deeds backed respectively by the power of God's abomination or delight (see Commentary on 11:1; Zech 8:16-17). This contrast of word and deed parallels James's opposition between hearing and doing the word of truth (Jas 1:22-23, 25; see *m. 'Abot* 1:15, 17).

12:23. This verse is a companion to 10:18; 11:13; 12:16; and 13:16. Concealing and revealing are highly complex and ambiguous actions, whose good or evil, wisdom or folly is highly dependent upon the motives, persons, matters, and circumstances in question. Here, as in 13:16, the wise act with knowledge (keeping silence is such an action), while fools involuntarily reveal their folly. When Saul begins to lose his royal wisdom, he reveals every matter to his son Jonathan (1 Sam 20:2; see Commentary on Prov 25:2-3).

12:24. Although the inertia of institutions and social systems is massive, social status is not simply static (see Commentary on 10:4; 17:2; 30:21-23). Character and drive, or lack of same, can elevate or lower one socially. Sayings such as this one criticize passive proponents of the status quo (see 17:2; 22:29). The indolent rich should not expect to enjoy power forever, nor are the diligent poor doomed to perpetual poverty. This general point is given a political edge in v. 24. "Rule" and "forced labor" refer to the opposite extremes of political power. The NIV's "slave labor" is misleading. The reference is to an ancient form of taxation in the form of obligatory labor, or corvee, required of citizens or subject peoples (see Judg 1:28-30; 1 Sam 8:10-18; 1 Kgs 5:13-17; 15:22; Isa 31:8). Yet, the human diligence that gains lordship does so only in the context of God's direction of history. This larger lesson is sung by Hannah and Mary (1 Sam 2:2-10; Luke 1:46-55; see also Pss 90:17; 127:1-2).

12:25. The NIV and NRSV translations of this verse concern a common human experience (see 15:30*b*; 25:13, 25; Gen 45:25-28; Ps 94:19). But the Hebrew grammar of this psychologically profound verse is not completely clear. Following rabbinic traditions, it may be translated, "A man tries to suppress the care in his heart, but a good word turns the care to joy."

12:26-28. Verse 26*a* begins a series of obscure verses. The NRSV and NIV margins follow the ancient Syriac translation of v. 26. The hiphil verb form may be more closely rendered, "The righteous help their neighbors find [their own way], but. . . . " This reading makes a clear antithesis with the second line. (For the contrasting way of the righteous and the way of the wicked, see Commentary on 1:15.)

Verse 27 concerns the contrast of "lazy" and "diligent" (6:6-11; 12:24). The sense seems to be that, even when food is brought home, the sluggard is too lazy to take advantage of what he or she has gotten (see 26:15). The NRSV and the NIV share a common understanding of v. 28*b*, but the NIV's "immortality" is an unlikely interpretation of the Hebrew (אל-מות *'al-māwet*), rendered more literally by the NRSV as "no death." Immortality is improbable in Proverbs, since the teaching of resurrection (Dan 12:1-3) is very rare in the OT and does not become widespread until the last two centuries BCE. This saying renders in positive terms the thought of 10:2*b*; 11:4*b*.

REFLECTIONS

1. A frequent, sometimes implicit, metaphor for humans (both male and female) in the OT is that of a democratized kingship in service of Yahweh the great king. All human beings (collectively and individually) have a limited sovereignty and accountable freedom over the little "kingdom" that God has given to each (e.g., body, mind, land, wealth, relationships; see 12:11; Gen 1:26-28; Psalm 8). This view comes to the surface, from time to time, in the language of Proverbs. For example, humans are not "established through wickedness" (12:3). This proverb uses the vocabulary of kingship in a negative, antithetical way. Positively, a king's throne "is established through righteousness" (16:12 NIV; see Commentary on 16:12). Humanity's royal freedom is limited by the constraints of righteousness, service of God, and the good of creation. Outside these constraints is the unstable realm of wickedness. Like the tree of Psalm 1, the righteous person is rooted in the creation and will never be moved, a phrase that also has a cosmic backdrop (see Commentary on 10:25, 30).

2. A considerable cultural gap separates us from 12:4, whether we are inclined to affirm the saying as supporting family values or to reject it as hopelessly patriarchal. On the one hand, the "good wife" (lit., "woman of valor") is not a mere domestic housewife who finds her identity through her husband and who leads a mainly private existence at home, excluded from the public business of life. This is clear from the stories of a variety of public women in the Bible (see Judges 4–5; Ruth; Prov 31:1, 10-31), and from powerful queen mothers, such as Bathsheba (1 Kings 1). On the other hand, there is in this saying a profound sense of the mutuality of husband and wife, of their being one flesh (see Commentary on 11:17). This saying runs counter to modern perspectives that conceive of human existence in individualistic fashion.

3. The "mercy of the wicked is cruel" (12:10), because they do not "know" or "listen" to their animals. What applies to the relation between humans and animals applies so much more to the relation between wealthy, powerful people and their neighbors (14:31) who are needy, dependent, or marginalized (19:17; 1 Cor 9:9-10). The kind deeds of the wicked may be cruel because they arise from self-interest imposed on the other, who has not been truly heard or known. There are also those who are cruel simply because they are cruel. Bonhoeffer, his insight honed by the Holocaust, says that the bad deeds of a good person are better than the good deeds of the wicked.[194]

4. The "good word" that cheers a human heart is spoken by another (12:24). Although there is something inscrutably single about the human heart (14:10), words can join person to person, so that the solitary heart is made whole (12:18; 15:4 NIV; 16:24). There is more. We are also bearers of the divine Word, which heals (Ps 107:19-20; Wis 16:12; Luke 7:7; 9:2, 6; Acts 9:34). "A Christian needs another Christian who speaks God's Word to him. . . . The Christ in his own heart is weaker than the Christ in the word of his brother; his own heart is uncertain, his brother's is sure."[195]

194. D. Bonhoeffer, *Ethics* (New York: Macmillan, 1965) 64-65.
195. D. Bonhoeffer, *Life Together* (London: SCM, 1954) 12.

Proverbs 13:1-25, On Listening to Wise Counsel

NIV

13 A wise son heeds his father's instruction,
   but a mocker does not listen to rebuke.

[2]From the fruit of his lips a man enjoys good things,
   but the unfaithful have a craving for violence.

[3]He who guards his lips guards his life,
   but he who speaks rashly will come to ruin.

[4]The sluggard craves and gets nothing,
   but the desires of the diligent are fully satisfied.

[5]The righteous hate what is false,
   but the wicked bring shame and disgrace.

[6]Righteousness guards the man of integrity,
   but wickedness overthrows the sinner.

NRSV

13 A wise child loves discipline,[a]
   but a scoffer does not listen to rebuke.

[2] From the fruit of their words good persons eat good things,
   but the desire of the treacherous is for wrongdoing.

[3] Those who guard their mouths preserve their lives;
   those who open wide their lips come to ruin.

[4] The appetite of the lazy craves, and gets nothing,
   while the appetite of the diligent is richly supplied.

[5] The righteous hate falsehood,

[a]Cn: Heb *A wise child the discipline of his father*

NIV

⁷One man pretends to be rich, yet has nothing;
    another pretends to be poor, yet has great
        wealth.

⁸A man's riches may ransom his life,
    but a poor man hears no threat.

⁹The light of the righteous shines brightly,
    but the lamp of the wicked is snuffed out.

¹⁰Pride only breeds quarrels,
    but wisdom is found in those who take
        advice.

¹¹Dishonest money dwindles away,
    but he who gathers money little by little
        makes it grow.

¹²Hope deferred makes the heart sick,
    but a longing fulfilled is a tree of life.

¹³He who scorns instruction will pay for it,
    but he who respects a command is rewarded.

¹⁴The teaching of the wise is a fountain of life,
    turning a man from the snares of death.

¹⁵Good understanding wins favor,
    but the way of the unfaithful is hard.ᵃ

¹⁶Every prudent man acts out of knowledge,
    but a fool exposes his folly.

¹⁷A wicked messenger falls into trouble,
    but a trustworthy envoy brings healing.

¹⁸He who ignores discipline comes to poverty and
        shame,
    but whoever heeds correction is honored.

¹⁹A longing fulfilled is sweet to the soul,
    but fools detest turning from evil.

²⁰He who walks with the wise grows wise,
    but a companion of fools suffers harm.

²¹Misfortune pursues the sinner,
    but prosperity is the reward of the righteous.

²²A good man leaves an inheritance for his
        children's children,
    but a sinner's wealth is stored up for the
        righteous.

²³A poor man's field may produce abundant food,
    but injustice sweeps it away.

²⁴He who spares the rod hates his son,
    but he who loves him is careful to discipline him.

ᵃ15 Or *unfaithful does not endure*

NRSV

    but the wicked act shamefully and
        disgracefully.

⁶ Righteousness guards one whose way is
        upright,
    but sin overthrows the wicked.

⁷ Some pretend to be rich, yet have nothing;
    others pretend to be poor, yet have great
        wealth.

⁸ Wealth is a ransom for a person's life,
    but the poor get no threats.

⁹ The light of the righteous rejoices,
    but the lamp of the wicked goes out.

¹⁰ By insolence the heedless make strife,
    but wisdom is with those who take advice.

¹¹ Wealth hastily gottenᵃ will dwindle,
    but those who gather little by little will
        increase it.

¹² Hope deferred makes the heart sick,
    but a desire fulfilled is a tree of life.

¹³ Those who despise the word bring destruction
        on themselves,
    but those who respect the commandment
        will be rewarded.

¹⁴ The teaching of the wise is a fountain of life,
    so that one may avoid the snares of death.

¹⁵ Good sense wins favor,
    but the way of the faithless is their ruin.ᵇ

¹⁶ The clever do all things intelligently,
    but the fool displays folly.

¹⁷ A bad messenger brings trouble,
    but a faithful envoy, healing.

¹⁸ Poverty and disgrace are for the one who
        ignores instruction,
    but one who heeds reproof is honored.

¹⁹ A desire realized is sweet to the soul,
    but to turn away from evil is an abomination
        to fools.

²⁰ Whoever walks with the wise becomes wise,
    but the companion of fools suffers harm.

²¹ Misfortune pursues sinners,
    but prosperity rewards the righteous.

²² The good leave an inheritance to their
        children's children,
    but the sinner's wealth is laid up for the
        righteous.

²³ The field of the poor may yield much food,

ᵃGk Vg: Heb *from vanity*   ᵇCn Compare Gk Syr Vg Tg: Heb *is
enduring*

NIV

25The righteous eat to their hearts' content,
  but the stomach of the wicked goes hungry.

NRSV

but it is swept away through injustice.
24 Those who spare the rod hate their children,
  but those who love them are diligent to
    discipline them.
25 The righteous have enough to satisfy their
    appetite,
  but the belly of the wicked is empty.

COMMENTARY

13:1-4. These verses are bound together in several ways. Actions and organs of speaking and hearing link vv. 1-3. The Hebrew catchword נפשׁ (*nepeš,* "craving," "life," "craves," "desires") connects vv. 2-4, appearing twice in v. 4. Verse 3 follows logically upon v. 2, a connection reinforced by the repetition of "mouth" (פה *peh;* "lips," NIV). Verses 2 and 4 are linked by "craving" and "desire," negated or fulfilled.

The NIV best construes the Hebrew of v. 1, taking the "listen" in v. 1*b* as double duty ("heeds"). The saying reinforces the pattern of parental training or discipline presupposed or expressed throughout chaps. 1–9 and in the sayings (see Commentary on 10:1; 12:1).

Proverbs 12:14 is a near duplicate of 13:2*a* (also 18:20). Here the bodily imagery of eating and desire forms an elaborate conceit over both lines. One's mouth (NIV, "lips"), like a "tree of life," produces the very fruit one eats with the mouth and is nourished (see 3:18; 11:30*a;* 15:4). That is, speech that nourishes others (10:21) produces good social consequences for the speaker. But the treacherous cannot be relied upon to keep their word (Jer 3:20); their speech destroys their neighbor (11:9). They have an inner appetite for destruction (see Commentary on 10:11). "Craving" can also refer to the inner self, which chooses to move from desire to action (6:30). In 16:26, *nepeš* is parallel to "mouth."

Verse 3 follows logically upon v. 2. Since speech bears good or bad fruit, the organs of speech must be carefully controlled (10:19; 17:27-28). But v. 3 raises the stakes: Speech is a matter of life and death (18:21). Each person possesses and must take responsibility for these powerful organs, by which we harm or help ourselves, first

of all. But words knit us to others. So the thought may be broadened to the societal sphere, as suggested by the World War II saying, "Loose lips sink ships." Proverbs 21:23 expands on 13:3*a.*

The sluggard's desire is frustrated because he or she does not do what reality requires (v. 4; see 21:25-26). A lazy person becomes heartsick because of unrealized dreams (v. 12). Such lives are botched by sins of omission. As often, the issue here is taking responsibility for one's own turf—whatever that may be—and working it in season (see Commentary on 6:6-11; see Reflections on Proverbs 12). But those who work hard are satisfied when they reap what they sow. The saying, "God helps them that help themselves," is not far from the mark. Nor is "make hay while the sun shines."

13:5. The NRSV and the NIV differ on the rendering of the hiphil verbs in v. 5*a;* the NIV, with a causative sense, seems closer to the mark (see 10:5; 19:26). The wicked may bring shame or odium onto others by the false word or deed (דבר [*dābār*] can refer to both) that the righteous hate (see 8:13; Pss 101:7; 119:163).

13:6. Righteousness and wickedness are personified as agents that hold sway over someone's existence, guarding or overthrowing the one under their power (see 5:22; 11:3-6; 19:3). In 22:12 these functions are ascribed to God, using the same verbs (see also 21:12).

13:7-8. These verses are linked by Hebrew roots for "rich" (עשׁר *ʿāšar*) and "poor" (רושׁ *rûš*). Their meaning may also be connected. Verse 7 is wonderfully ambiguous. Literally, it reads, "One makes himself rich, yet nothing at all; another makes himself poor, yet great wealth." Thus the saying may deal with deception of self and of others (see 12:9) or the contrast between what is and what appears. There are some who think themselves rich and do not know their poverty (Rev 3:17-18). Others are too blind to work with what they have, letting it lie useless and barren (Luke 19:11-27). Again, the saying may refer to one who began with nothing but became wealthy. Or it may refer to a greedy person who becomes rich, yet in the end has nothing (Luke 12:13-21). This paradoxical saying would then be parallel to 11:24 (see Ps 112:9). Finally, there is the Christian paradox of rich poverty, which we find in both Christ and Paul (2 Cor 6:10; 8:9).

How to link the two lines of the saying in v. 8 is difficult. Verse 8*b* is identical to v. 1*b*, except for the substitution of "poor" for "scoffer" (lit., "The poor does not hear rebuke"). The rich are subject to criminal threats where the issue is "Your money or your life!" (1:11-13). But the poor do not hear such threats, for they have nothing to give. If this interpretation is correct, then v. 1*b* and v. 2*b* bear different meanings because of their changed context. Elsewhere, גערה (gĕ'ārâ) refers consistently to a rebuke by which one sets constraints on another. Here the sense would be extended to include a threat of death. The Torah allows for ransom for life (Exod 30:12), but forbids it in the case of deliberate murder (Num 35:31). In the ultimate sense of the death all humans die, wealth affords no ransom, so as to buy God off (Ps 49:7-9). But one may ask if Ps 49:15 holds open the possibility that God will provide a ransom to redeem human life (Matt 20:28).

13:9. Verse 9*b* is repeated in 24:20 (see also 20:20; Job 18:5-6; Ps 38:10), while the thought of v. 9*a* is close to 15:30. Light is a metaphor for life, vitality, and goodness; its natural companion is joy (4:18; Ps 19:5; Eccl 11:7-8). The Lord is the ultimate source of light as life (29:13; Ezra 9:8; Pss 18:28; 27:1; 36:9). To lose the light of the eyes is to lose vitality, joy, even life itself (Ps 38:10).

13:10-11. The Hebrew of v. 10*a* is not entirely clear (see Commentary on 11:2; 12:15). Several scholars read, "An empty [of no account] person creates conflict by pride." The translations of v. 11 are unclear on the sense of the Hebrew behind "from vanity" (NRSV suggests the word can connote "nothing") and the versions reflect a variety of textual options or emendations (see 20:21; 21:6; 28:22). But in the economic realm, the ideas of haste, easy money, something for nothing, and what is dishonest are not unrelated. When we speak of get-rich-quick schemes, fraud and deceit come to mind. It appears these associations also existed for the ancients. The proverb states a paradox of the sort "slow and steady wins the race," and the tortoise outruns the hare. Limits are set to clever greed here, and the homely truth that connects steady work and success is affirmed.

13:12-19. Verse 12 and v. 19 form an envelope construction around vv. 13-14, 18 (on instruction), which in turn envelope vv. 15-17 (examples of successful or failed instruction?). Thus vv. 12-19 form a relatively patterned cluster of sayings.

13:12. This verse may provide an implicit, paradoxical contrast to v. 11 concerning the quick or slow realization of human aspirations. Verse 11 suggests that the slow and steady pursuit of a good goal wins the race. But hope delayed can crush the spirit. Verse 12, however, does not specify the type or moral quality of hope in question, a matter taken up in v. 19.

13:13-14. These verses are a proverb pair. Scholars quibble over whether v. 13 refers to a divine or a human word and command (see 2:6; 6:20; 16:20; Deut 30:11-15). A contextual reading of the proverb pair suggests the topic is human instruction ("teaching of the wise") of the sort found in Proverbs (3:1-2; 7:15). Yet the ambiguity of "word" and "command" should be maintained. Divine imperatives are mediated through humans, whether by Moses on Sinai or by wise generations of parents and teachers (Deut 4:6, 9; 6:6-9; 30:11-20; 32:46-47). Such "teaching" (תורה tôrâ; 6:23; 28:4, 7, 9; 29:18) has life-and-death consequences, depending on its reception by the next generation (for "despise," see 1:7-8, 29-33; 23:9). The biblical tradition that understands Mosaic Torah ("law") as an expression of wisdom (Deut 4:6) is explicitly developed in Sir 24:23; 45:5. Proverbs 14:27 is identical to 13:14 but has "the fear of the LORD" (see also 19:23) for "the teaching of the wise" (see Commentary on 2:1-5; "fountain of life," 10:11*a;* 16:22*a;* Ps 36:9).

13:15. "Good sense" has connotations of general human competence and excellence, which produces success and earns one honor (see Commentary on 12:8). The decisive Abigail is a "woman of good sense" (1 Sam 25:3). But the way of the faithless or treacherous (cf. 11:3, 6) is to speak and act in ways that betray basic human commitments in marriage (Exod 21:8; Jer 3:20; 9:2), in business, or in politics (Judg 9:23). Like a brook that runs dry (Job 6:15), they cannot be relied upon (25:19). The final word, "ruin"/"hard" (איתן 'ēṭān) is uncertain, as reflected in the NIV and NRSV translations.

13:16. The NIV attaches "all"/"every" to the subject of the sentence (which is grammatically more plausible), while the NRSV makes it the verb object (see Commentary on 12:23; 15:2; 18:2; 29:11.) "Out of Knowledge" (lit., "by/with knowledge") is parallel to "by/with wisdom" (see 3:19-20; 9:1; 14:1; 24:3-4; Ps 104:24). These parallels suggest that wise humans imitate not only God but also Wisdom by acting according to knowledge. But fools broadcast folly (17:12; 26:4-5), because that is what is in them (Luke 6:43-45).

13:17. In the ancient Near East, messengers possessed an important role scarcely comprehensible to modern people. Messengers could belong to the highest social strata, such as members of the royal family or court. They might function as ambassadors and conveyors (with armed guards) of large sums of tribute. Prophets functioned as royal messengers from the heavenly court to the earthly one (1 Kgs 22:13-23; Isa 6:1-8; 7:3). But messengers could also be go-betweens for common folk. Messengers generally possessed considerable responsibility and freedom in representing the mission of their (absent) senders. They might bring news good and bad, reports accurate or false, or even misstate their master's intentions. Thus messengers variously made their senders and hearers glad or sad (10:26; 22:21; 25:13, 25; 26:6). One of the models of the Christian life is that of the messenger as well (Matt 28:18-20; John 20:21; 2 Cor 5:18-21). The NRSV repoints the vowels of v. 17a to make the antithetical parallel with v. 17b more symmetrical. The NIV translates the traditional medieval (MT) pointing.

13:18. In Hebrew, this proverb begins with "poverty and disgrace" and ends with "honored," a root (כבד kbd) that connotes "wealth" (see Commentary on 5:10-12; 11:16; 13:13-14; 15:32). This opposition concerns not only social status in the community, but also the substance of a person, which may or may not find social recognition (16:8; 19:1; 28:6; Eccl 8:14; 9:13-16). The public and private sides of disgrace and honor find subtle expression in a common Hebrew word-play on "light" and "heavy," implicit in "disgrace" versus "honored" (roots קלל [qll] and כבד [kbd]; e.g., 3:35; Job 40:2; Isa 3:5; Hos 4:7; Hab 2:16; Sir 3:6-12). The paradox is that the path to becoming a human of "weight" begins by submitting to the formative discipline of another self. Character formation requires parents, teachers, and mentors who know what makes a solid person and how to help others become solid people (see Commentary on 12:1).

13:19. As noted earlier, this verse is a subtle companion to v. 12. A longing satisfied is certainly sweet, at least initially (9:17; 20:17). "Soul" (נפש nepeš) here has the sense of "appetite" (see Commentary on 16:24). Longings generally seek some limited good (cf. 4:5, 7; Matt 6:33), but this good may not be good for me (see Gen 1:31; 3:6).

13:20. This verse follows naturally upon the teaching of vv. 13-14, 18. Human beings are social creatures. Our self-identity and fate are profoundly shaped by our fellow travelers (see Commentary on 14:7). Even more, our formation is influenced by the communities and families that laid down the paths, traditions, and modes of being we grow into and then travel in, happily or brokenly, consciously or blindly, willingly or rebelliously. To turn from a bad path is very difficult (v. 19). Indeed, grace may be defined as the gift that makes such turnabouts possible (Eph 2:1-10; Phil 2:12-13).

13:21-22. These verses form a proverb pair, linked by the repetition of "righteous" and by a chiasm (in Hebrew) of the first and last words of each line: sinners/good/good/sinners. People are sometimes portrayed as pursuing good or ill (15:9; 21:21; Pss 34:15; 38:20; 119:150). What people chase generally comes to them (see Commentary on 10:24; 11:19, 27; 28:19). This ought to give sinners pause, but often it does not (vv. 19-20). Verse 21, however, personifies misfortune (רעה rā'â, a general term for "evil," "trouble") as hunting down sinners (see Sir 27:10). Psalm 23:6 is similar, but positive: "goodness and mercy will pursue me." The underlying conception is that good and evil are active powers in God's world. These cosmic, moral realities pursue humans whose actions correspond to them, as lovers rush to meet each other. We find what we love, and it finds us. Again, Wisdom or Folly and humans, good or bad, mutually call out and seek each other (see 1:24; 2:2-3; 7:15; 8:17, 35; 9:3, 14). In a different context, Paul personifies sin as an active cosmic, spiritual power (Rom 7:7-11, 14). Verse 21*b* has no explicit subject. It is perhaps best to take Yahweh as the implicit subject: "The Lord recompenses the righteous with (the consequences of their own) good" (so the medieval Rabbi Moses Kimchi; see Commentary on 10:24; 12:12, 14). If this is correct, Yahweh appears as the hidden agent behind the character-consequence schema (see Reflections no. 2 below).

Verse 22 (see 28:8) extends the act-character-consequence schema of v. 21 to reflect on God's faithfulness over generations. Eventually good is passed on to children's children; and in unexpected ways the good inherit what sinners wrongly took or used (11:8; 28:8; Job 27:13-17; Eccl 2:26; cf. Eccl 6:2; Sir 11:18-19). There is a fine wordplay in "stored up" (צפן *ṣāpan*), for the Hebrew connotes what is "hidden," as in buried treasure that comes to light for those who least expect it (Matt 13:14). Verse 22 thus provides one solution to apparent failures in the pattern of retribution: Things will be made right in the generations to come (14:26; 20:7). Israel did not think in merely individualistic terms. Proverbs

2:20-22 develops this theme in the direction of a cosmic, eschatological hope.

13:23. The Hebrew of this verse is difficult and susceptible to various readings. The NRSV and the NIV understanding of the verse seems most likely (see v. 25). Through hard work and God's blessing, the "freshly broken field" (ניר *nîr* ; Jer 4:3; Hos 10:12; *m. ʾAbot* 3:9) of the poor produces abundant food. But injustice (see 16:8; Jer 17:11; 22:13; Ezek 22:29) robs the poor of the fruits of their land and labor. This scenario violates the principles of justice expressed in the Law (Leviticus 25) and the Prophets (Isa 5:7-8; Amos 8:4-6; Mic 2:1-2; 3:1-3).

13:24. This verse (see Commentary on 22:15; 23:13-14) comes from an ancient Near Eastern culture that recognized the human inclination toward sin and folly, and used physical discipline as a means to keep older children, fools, and wrongdoers from destructive paths (Deut 25:1-3). In Egyptian, the word for "education" was accompanied by the hieroglyph of a striking man or arm (see Prov 17:10; 19:18; 29:15, 17; Sir 30:1-2, 11-13.

13:25. Verse 23 is linked to this verse by root and sound repetition (אכל *ʾkl*), and by implicit contradiction, if the interpretation of v. 23 is correct (see Commentary on 10:3). Instead of promising wealth to the righteous, v. 25 modestly suggests that they will have enough to eat (see Commentary on 30:8). The wicked come to lack because their life-style runs counter to the good order of creation (see Commentary on 10:4-5).

REFLECTIONS

1. The implied author of the book speaks in the voice of an inspired parent (13:1). This construction functions as an ideal that defines the office of parent: to pass on wisdom and life to the next generation (Gen 18:19; Deut 6:4-7), who then become responsible for their use of the tradition (Ezek 18:1-32). Only a know-it-all scoffer rejects wise parental reprimands. Yet this ideal, which governs the shape of Proverbs, is susceptible to authoritarian misuse (see Commentary on 13:24; 23:13-14), for Proverbs never explicitly portrays a parent as being in the wrong (see Commentary on 29:15). In the light of widespread familial dysfunction and abuse, Paul's corrective to an authoritarian reading of these sayings must be heard: "Fathers, do not provoke your children to anger, but bring them up in the discipline and instruction of the Lord" (Eph 6:4; Col 3:21). Discipline aims at hope (19:18) and freedom (see Reflections on Proverbs 6).

2. Israel saw the act-character-consequence schema both as a natural pattern in life and as the work of God's justice (see Commentary on 13:6). We moderns tend to exclude the divine mystery from history, leaving only natural connections between acts and consequences. But ancient Israel saw God as the hidden actor even in the mundane (see Commentary on 5:22). The parallelism of Ps 9:15-16 (see also Ps 7:15-16) perhaps expresses the mysterious presence of God in ordinary consequences most clearly:

The nations have sunk in the pit that they made

The LORD . . . has executed judgment;
the wicked are snared in the work of their own hands. (NRSV)

3. Arrogance produces conflict (13:10), because the inflation of one ego occurs at the expense of the dignity and worth of others, who naturally fight back to protect themselves. *All* people possess worth as God's creatures (14:31; 29:13), and we instinctively react against whatever diminishes that worth. When both parties are arrogant, the conflict is all the worse. But the wise know the limits of their own insight and that "two heads are better than one" (see Commentary on 11:14; 12:15; 21:30-31; 26:12). Genuine wisdom is not egotistically independent but realistically inter-dependent.

4. Human beings become sick at the core of their being (heart) when hope suffers delay (13:12*a*). But with desire fulfilled, life flourishes as in paradise (see Commentary on 3:18). When the Lord fails to deliver Israel out of Egypt quickly, the people stop believing Moses, "because of their broken spirit and their cruel slavery" (Exod 6:9 NRSV). The Scriptures are filled with the cries of people, sick at heart, who ask, "How long, O Lord?" (e.g., Pss 13:1; 35:17; 74:10; 89:46; Hab 1:2; Rev 6:10). Biblical faith constantly struggles with the tension between what is promised and hoped for, but not yet come. We walk by faith and not always by sight (see Hebrews 11).

5. Humans naturally delight in legitimate goods (13:19). But goods wrongly attained or used turn bad, like cream that sours. Yet fools hate to give up such evils. The mysterious addiction of fools to evil is perhaps explained by evil's parasitic dependence on the good. Gradually the acids of folly transform good into something corrupt, even as they erode the fool's awareness of the difference. So it is that fools delight in vomit (26:11). To turn from evil is basic to wisdom because it sets one's path and life in a new direction (3:7; Job 28:28; cf. Amos 5:14-15). It is an act of conversion of the sort required by incarnate Wisdom (Luke 5:27-28; 9:57-62).

6. Agricultural injustice (13:23) is still common today, for example, in tropical lands in which coffee or bananas are grown for export to the United States. But the saying may be applied wherever greed, wealth, and power deprive others of opportunity, labor, or the fruits thereof. Americans need not look abroad.

7. The imagery of 13:24 makes it offensive to many. Today, violent parents and child abuse are commonly reported in news media, so that any form of corporal punishment seems repugnant and wrong in principle (see Commentary on 17:10). The deeper issue in this proverb is the paradox of "tough love," both in the family and in society. Parents may be compelled by love to be severe with a child "for the child's own good" (see 3:11-12; Deut 8:5; Heb 12:5-11). If human nature has been distorted by sin, to let a child do as it pleases is no kindness. To let a child grow up with no sense of boundaries or consequences is cruel. It seems better to spank the hand of a headstrong toddler than to allow him or her to burn a hand by touching a boiling pot. Discernment and wise love are crucial here; the same slap may be abusive in one case (with a particular child) and not in another.

In society, one of the functions of punishment is to redress wrongs justly. An ancient Israelite might consider our contemporary practice of incarceration more dehumanizing and unjust than the momentary, painful humiliation of a caning. Prison deprives people of the responsible freedom that is essential to their humanity. Bonhoeffer, during his long confinement in Hitler's Tegel prison, noted that Israel did not use imprisonment as punishment. He observed that imprisonment over the long term was utterly demoralizing, especially for the young. Instead, Bonhoeffer sought to make the punishment fit the crime.[196] A judicial caning (of one who assaulted another, for example) might permit the offender to resume life in society as God's image, rather than wasting life in confinement. C. S. Lewis argued that by appropriate punishment government honors the image of God in a person—that is, their capacity as responsible agents. When legitimate authority fails to punish, we treat wrongdoers as less than human. This problem today is made more complex by theories concerning rehabilitation, as opposed to punishment of wrongdoers,[197] and by the inhumane conditions in American prisons. This matter bears communal reflection in America, with its burgeoning prison population.

196. D. Bonhoeffer, *Letters and Papers from Prison* (New York: Macmillan, 1972) 134, 164, letters of 20 November and 15 December 1943.
197. See C. S. Lewis, "The Humanitarian Theory of Punishment," in *God in the Dock* (Grand Rapids: Eerdmans, 1970) 287-300.

Proverbs 14:1-35, The Wise Woman Builds Her House

NIV

14 The wise woman builds her house,
but with her own hands the foolish one tears hers down.

2He whose walk is upright fears the LORD,
but he whose ways are devious despises him.

3A fool's talk brings a rod to his back,
but the lips of the wise protect them.

4Where there are no oxen, the manger is empty,
but from the strength of an ox comes an abundant harvest.

5A truthful witness does not deceive,
but a false witness pours out lies.

6The mocker seeks wisdom and finds none,
but knowledge comes easily to the discerning.

7Stay away from a foolish man,
for you will not find knowledge on his lips.

8The wisdom of the prudent is to give thought to their ways,
but the folly of fools is deception.

9Fools mock at making amends for sin,
but goodwill is found among the upright.

10Each heart knows its own bitterness,
and no one else can share its joy.

11The house of the wicked will be destroyed,
but the tent of the upright will flourish.

NRSV

14 The wise woman[a] builds her house,
but the foolish tears it down with her own hands.

2 Those who walk uprightly fear the LORD,
but one who is devious in conduct despises him.

3 The talk of fools is a rod for their backs,[b]
but the lips of the wise preserve them.

4 Where there are no oxen, there is no grain;
abundant crops come by the strength of the ox.

5 A faithful witness does not lie,
but a false witness breathes out lies.

6 A scoffer seeks wisdom in vain,
but knowledge is easy for one who understands.

7 Leave the presence of a fool,
for there you do not find words of knowledge.

8 It is the wisdom of the clever to understand where they go,
but the folly of fools misleads.

9 Fools mock at the guilt offering,[c]
but the upright enjoy God's favor.

10 The heart knows its own bitterness,
and no stranger shares its joy.

11 The house of the wicked is destroyed,

a Heb *Wisdom of women*   b Cn: Heb *a rod of pride*   c Meaning of Heb uncertain

NIV

¹²There is a way that seems right to a man,
    but in the end it leads to death.

¹³Even in laughter the heart may ache,
    and joy may end in grief.

¹⁴The faithless will be fully repaid for their ways,
    and the good man rewarded for his.

¹⁵A simple man believes anything,
    but a prudent man gives thought to his steps.

¹⁶A wise man fears the LORD and shuns evil,
    but a fool is hotheaded and reckless.

¹⁷A quick-tempered man does foolish things,
    and a crafty man is hated.

¹⁸The simple inherit folly,
    but the prudent are crowned with knowledge.

¹⁹Evil men will bow down in the presence of the good,
    and the wicked at the gates of the righteous.

²⁰The poor are shunned even by their neighbors,
    but the rich have many friends.

²¹He who despises his neighbor sins,
    but blessed is he who is kind to the needy.

²²Do not those who plot evil go astray?
    But those who plan what is good find^a love
        and faithfulness.

²³All hard work brings a profit,
    but mere talk leads only to poverty.

²⁴The wealth of the wise is their crown,
    but the folly of fools yields folly.

²⁵A truthful witness saves lives,
    but a false witness is deceitful.

²⁶He who fears the LORD has a secure fortress,
    and for his children it will be a refuge.

²⁷The fear of the LORD is a fountain of life,
    turning a man from the snares of death.

²⁸A large population is a king's glory,
    but without subjects a prince is ruined.

²⁹A patient man has great understanding,
    but a quick-tempered man displays folly.

³⁰A heart at peace gives life to the body,
    but envy rots the bones.

³¹He who oppresses the poor shows contempt for
        their Maker,

ª22 Or show

NRSV

    but the tent of the upright flourishes.

¹² There is a way that seems right to a person,
    but its end is the way to death.^a

¹³ Even in laughter the heart is sad,
    and the end of joy is grief.

¹⁴ The perverse get what their ways deserve,
    and the good, what their deeds deserve.^b

¹⁵ The simple believe everything,
    but the clever consider their steps.

¹⁶ The wise are cautious and turn away from evil,
    but the fool throws off restraint and is
        careless.

¹⁷ One who is quick-tempered acts foolishly,
    and the schemer is hated.

¹⁸ The simple are adorned with^c folly,
    but the clever are crowned with knowledge.

¹⁹ The evil bow down before the good,
    the wicked at the gates of the righteous.

²⁰ The poor are disliked even by their neighbors,
    but the rich have many friends.

²¹ Those who despise their neighbors are sinners,
    but happy are those who are kind to the
        poor.

²² Do they not err that plan evil?
    Those who plan good find loyalty and
        faithfulness.

²³ In all toil there is profit,
    but mere talk leads only to poverty.

²⁴ The crown of the wise is their wisdom,^d
    but folly is the garland^e of fools.

²⁵ A truthful witness saves lives,
    but one who utters lies is a betrayer.

²⁶ In the fear of the LORD one has strong
        confidence,
    and one's children will have a refuge.

²⁷ The fear of the LORD is a fountain of life,
    so that one may avoid the snares of death.

²⁸ The glory of a king is a multitude of people;
    without people a prince is ruined.

²⁹ Whoever is slow to anger has great
        understanding,
    but one who has a hasty temper exalts folly.

³⁰ A tranquil mind gives life to the flesh,
    but passion makes the bones rot.

³¹ Those who oppress the poor insult their
        Maker,

ª Heb *ways of death*   ^b Cn: Heb *from upon him*   ^c Or *inherit*
^d Cn Compare Gk: Heb *riches*   ^e Cn: Heb *is the folly*

NIV

but whoever is kind to the needy honors God.

³²When calamity comes, the wicked are brought down,
but even in death the righteous have a refuge.

³³Wisdom reposes in the heart of the discerning
and even among fools she lets herself be known.^a

³⁴Righteousness exalts a nation,
but sin is a disgrace to any people.

³⁵A king delights in a wise servant,
but a shameful servant incurs his wrath.

^a33 Hebrew; Septuagint and Syriac / *but in the heart of fools she is not known*

NRSV

but those who are kind to the needy honor him.

³² The wicked are overthrown by their evildoing,
but the righteous find a refuge in their integrity.^a

³³ Wisdom is at home in the mind of one who has understanding,
but it is not^b known in the heart of fools.

³⁴ Righteousness exalts a nation,
but sin is a reproach to any people.

³⁵ A servant who deals wisely has the king's favor,
but his wrath falls on one who acts shamefully.

^aGk Syr: Heb *in their death*   ^bGk Syr: Heb lacks *not*

COMMENTARY

14:1. Verse 1*a* has a difficult text. Its consonants are identical to 9:1*a* except for the addition "of women." Underlying this verse we may assume an original saying: "Wisdom has built her house, but Folly tears it down with her own hands." This earlier version of v. 1 would be a concise statement of Folly's negative relation to Wisdom's good work of cosmic house building. Folly reduces the house to chaos by the works of her hands (11:11). Folly tears down the house built by Wisdom, not her own house (with NRSV, against NIV; see 11:11, of a city).

The difficulty in this verse is the addition "of women." "Wisdom of women builds her house" (NRSV margin). The sense is that womanly wisdom builds her house.[198] Since "of women" is an editorial expansion of 9:1*a*, it seems best to seek an explanation in terms of the editing of the book as a whole. The addition "of women" creates a distinction between human wisdom and cosmic wisdom as personified in 8:1 and 9:1. Proverbs 14:1 now well suits its context among the small sayings that characterize chaps. 10–29. Here the focus is not cosmology but anthropology. The point of this shift is that human wisdom imitates the divine creative Wisdom.

198. A genitive of genus. See Bruce K. Waltke and M. O'Connor, *An Introduction to Biblical Hebrew Syntax* (Winona Lake: Eisenbrauns, 1990) 153, ¶9.5.3i. See also Prov 14:8; 15:20.

In a similar vein, v. 1*a* anticipates 24:3-4. As allusions to 9:1, these passages represent humans as being engaged in the imitation of Wisdom. Elsewhere Scripture presents humans as being made in God's image and assumes human life in manifold ways to be the imitation of God. A well-known example of this pattern is the motivation for sabbath rest, based on God's rest from the work of creation (Exod 20:11; Eph 5:11; 1 Thess 1:6).

There is dispute as to the meaning of "house" in this verse, based on the idea that Israelite women were not literal house builders. (In truth we know little about who built houses in ancient Israel.) The Hebrew term for "house" (בַּיִת *bayit*) is very broad in its referential range. It can refer to buildings as varied as a temple, a palace, or a peasant dwelling. It can also refer to a family, a dynasty, or a household. Thus women can be said to "build a house" by bearing children (Ruth 4:11; see Exod 1:20-21, where "family" = "house"). The "capable woman" oversees the well-being and provision of her house (31:15, 21, 27). When David wishes to build the Lord a house (temple) the Lord counters with the promise of a lasting Davidic dynasty, or house (2 Samuel 7; Luke 2:4). Yet the folly endemic in the Davidic house, beginning with David's adultery and the murder of Uriah, nearly tears his royal house to the ground.

In general, the building of houses and cities apart from God is labor in vain (Psalm 127).

14:2. This verse is composed of two nominal clauses, where the subjects and predicates are noun phrases simply juxtaposed as follows (in a literal rendering):

A One walking uprightly
  B One fearing the Lord
A' But one twisted in his ways
  B' One despising him (i.e., the Lord]

In each clause it must be determined whether A or B is predicate or subject. The NRSV and the NIV both take the A lines as subjects in their clauses. But there is reason to think that the predicate phrase precedes in A, so that we may translate: "One who fears the Lord walks uprightly" (see 10:9; 20:7). There may be grammatical reasons for this rendering,[199] but there are also logical grounds. Not everyone who "walks uprightly" fears the Lord; even those who do not know Israel's God can do good deeds. The implication is that those who fear the Lord will live uprightly (see Commentary on 1:7) and that an unjust life gives the lie to claims of fearing the Lord.

With the second half-verse the order of predication is not so clear, again for grammatical and logical reasons. One cannot be a person of consistently twisted behavior and genuinely fear the Lord. In the long run, the two are mutually exclusive, though all humans suffer from varying degrees of inconsistency in the implementation of their basic beliefs and commitments (consider David and Bathsheba, and Peter at Jesus' trial). Conversely, one cannot despise the Lord and not end up a person of twisted and devious behavior.

14:3. Both the NIV and the NRSV follow a conjecture in v. 3a (see 10:13; 26:3b); the Hebrew is literally, "In a fool's mouth is a shoot of pride." The word for "shoot" (חמר *ḥōṭer*) appears only here and in Isa 11:1, "A shoot shall spring up." The sense of the original is perhaps that a fool's speech "sprouts" arrogance and that this "fruit of the mouth" (12:14; 18:20-21) typifies some sorts of folly. Speech is frequently the instrument and revealer of human pride. God and

Wisdom are opposed to human arrogance (8:13; 15:25; 16:5), so that pride goes before a fall (16:18). On the other hand, v. 3b declares that their speech protects the wise.

14:4. The first line of this verse is uncertain. The NIV and the NRSV express one option in which v. 4a and v. 4b are two sides of the same coin. Another likely reading of the Hebrew is, "Without oxen there is [only] a crib of grain." That is, you either have oxen who constantly eat up the grain in the crib, or you have a crib full of grain, but no oxen whose work in the field both fills the crib and feeds the household. If this reading is right, v. 4a is an either/or saying, like, "You can't have your cake and eat it too." In any case, the saying underscores the mutuality of humans and their domesticated beasts. In God's creation, the earth, animals, and humans are part of one vast fabric (Psalms 8; 104). Wise humans care for the creatures that God has placed in their care, for the good of both (12:10; 27:23-27).

14:5. This verse seems tautological. Does it say more than "honest folk don't lie, but liars do"? Tautological sayings convey more than their literal meaning, as in "business is business" (see Commentary on 14:24). Perhaps the point of this verse is that it is the way things are, and wise persons (including judges) will accordingly distinguish truth tellers from liars (1 Kgs 3:16-28). Verse 5b duplicates the first line of 6:19 from the catalogue of things the Lord hates (see 19:5, 9). "False witness" is an expression based in Israel's legal traditions and principles (Exod 20:16; Deut 19:18; see also Commentary on 12:17; 14:25).

14:6. The writer distinguishes two types of persons in this verse. Mockers figured prominently in 9:7-12. Because they do not accept correction (15:12), their seeking for wisdom is not genuine. In wisdom and religion, people generally find what they truly seek (11:27; Matt 7:8). Mockers like the idea of having wisdom but are not willing to pay the price of discipline and submission to the educational authority of another. The mocker is like the fool who lacks the capacity for wisdom (17:16). Like the lazybones, who seek for food without result (13:4; 20:4), so the actions of mockers undermines their search for knowledge. For "one who understands," however, learning comes naturally (8:9).

14:7. An exception, this verse is an admoni-

---

199. See ibid.¶ 8.4.2.

tion in the midst of the sayings that dominate chaps. 10–15. The advice is common sense: Do not keep company with fools because the knowledge you need cannot be found with them. Proverbs 13:20a provides the positive corollary: One becomes wise by joining others already en route to wisdom.

14:8. The clever have a certain practical wisdom that knows what it is up to, considers well the path to take, and understands the consequences of taking it (vv. 14-15; 22:3). "Clever(ness)" (ערום 'ārûm; the NIV's "prudent" is moralizing) is the talent for devising and using adroit and wily tactics in the attaining of one's goals, whatever these may be."[200] It is something approved by Wisdom herself (1:4; 8:12), but like many good things it is susceptible to corruption (Gen 3:1). Implicit here is the notion that humans are responsible for their lives, their choices, and their actions. The wise use their brains and their resources. They set goals, work hard, and, "weather permitting," they achieve them like a fine harvest. They succeed because their way accords with reality (see Commentary on 10:4-5 and Overview on Proverbs 1:1–9:18). On the other hand, the folly (the same term personified in v. 1) of fools has skewed perceptions of reality, whether of the world, of others, or of self. The deceit may be deliberate and perverse. It may be unconscious, the product of a general moral-spiritual blindness. What looks good to a fool is not actually good (12:15; 14:12 articulates a different point). Yet the best human wisdom can fall short (see Commentary on 20:24; 21:29-31).

14:9. A satisfactory explanation of the Hebrew of this verse has not yet been found. The NIV and the NRSV present conjectural translations. Literally it reads, "Fools [plural] mocks [singular] guilt; and between upright persons is favor." If God is the implicit subject (see NRSV), one might translate, "God mocks fools [with] guilt, but between upright persons is [divine] favor."

14:10. No description of human solitude is more exact or penetrating (see Commentary on 13:12; 14:13). In our inmost self, we are single (see Excursus, "The 'Heart' in the Old Testament," 60-61; 1 Cor 2:11; Rev 2:17). In this solitude we suffer, but it is also a sacred preserve,

a garden of the self, where others cannot intrude. The topic of this proverb is not the contrary emotions of joy and bitterness (see 1 Sam 1:10; 2 Kgs 4:27), nor is it a pre-modern statement of existential isolation. The topic is the self-reflective singleness of the heart in all circumstances. The opposition of joy and sorrow is a cipher (merismus—two opposites used to express totality) for the entire spectrum of human emotions. While bitterness is often a lonely state (Ruth 1:11-13, 20-21), joy makes obvious claims on community. Gladness invites others to join in (Ps 122:1; Luke 15:6, 9, 23). But this verse says that even in gladness—perhaps surrounded by revelers—the heart is alone. No matter how close humans come to knowing one another, even in the one flesh that is marriage, we remain individual persons, unique centers of consciousness and responsibility, each with his or her own hiddenness. In its depths, this hiddenness lies open only to God (15:11; 17:3; 1 Sam 16:7; Ps 44:21; Jer 17:9-10). This saying is not a denial of human community (see Commentary on 13:20; 14:7), but a statement of its limits. The admonition of the apostle Paul to those who are one body remains valid, "Rejoice with those who rejoice, weep with those who weep" (Rom 12:15 NRSV, from Sir 7:34-36). Verse 10a does not tell us what to do with the heart's bitterness. The psalmist shows a way in the prayer, "Search me, O God, and know my heart" (Ps 139:23 NRSV). Similarly, the old spiritual that laments, "Nobody knows the troubles I seen" continues with "nobody knows, but Jesus." This move from solitude toward God is beautifully captured in the story of Hannah. In "bitterness of soul" she prays, and God hears her (1 Sam 1:10-15).

14:11. With a lovely irony, this saying moves from the destruction of the well-built house (14:1; 24:3-4) to the abiding fruitfulness of the more fragile tent. As usual in chaps. 10–15, there is a sure declaration of the consequences of good and evil. Here the character-consequence connection is extended beyond the individual to include family and clan ("house"). The imagery of humans as fruitful plants (or gardens) is common but profound (11:28; Pss 1:3; 92:12-15; Isa 5:1-7; Jer 17:8; John 15:1-17; see also 3:33; 12:3, 7, 12).

14:12. Parallel to 16:25, this verse is similar to 12:15 but says something different from that

---

200. Michael V. Fox, "Words for Wisdom," *Zeitschrift für Althebräistik* 6 (1993) 158.

passage. In 12:15, it is understandable that a fool considers a path to be right, though it is not. Fools and sinners deceive themselves, misread reality (21:2), and ignore consequences (14:15-16; Ps 73:17-20). However, in itself, abstracted from its literary context, v. 12 refers to any person, not necessarily godless or foolish, who considers a way to go. "The best laid schemes o' mice an' men/ Gang aft a-gley." The outcome of any human venture is uncertain. The reasons why are various: the limits of human knowledge and power, the destructive power of self-deception, the sometimes absurd combination of events, and ultimately the inscrutable workings of providence (see Commentary on 16:1-9; 21:30-31). The sharpest examination of human limits and the inscrutability of things occurs in Ecclesiastes and Job. In view of the different literary context of 14:12 and 16:25, it is probable that this saying's radical possibilities are not intended in chap. 14 (vv. 8, 11, 14-15). That awaits its second appearance, where Prov 16–22:16 explores the problem of limits and the absurd (see Introduction).

14:13. Like v. 12, this verse has an unexpected, paradoxical end in view. Both the NIV and the NRSV translations are grammatically possible. But the NRSV better reflects the nature of proverbs: to state something sharply in universal terms and to leave the application to the user. The more absolute form (NRSV) provokes deeper and broader reflection; it makes the proverb maximally versatile. Since humans die, joy inevitably ends in grief (see 27:1). The party always ends; acts of love cease. Because we are creatures with a limited future and are conscious of it, "even in laughter the heart is sad." Operative here is the gap that can exist, whether purposely or unconsciously, between our inner selves and our outer persona (see Commentary on 26:23-26). Ecclesiastes 7:1-5 appears to further develop implications of this saying. Less ultimate observations also lie at hand: Even in an exuberant allegro, Mozart's music is borne along on an undercurrent of sadness.

14:14. The NRSV correctly translates this verse according to a root and sense found in Isa 3:10-11 and Hos 12:2. "Perverse" is literally "a backslider in heart" (סוג לב *sûg lēb*) and continues the focus of these verses on the human heart. It is another expression of the theme of character

(here at the deepest level) and consequences in human life (see v. 12 and the common term "way"). Related sayings include 1:31; 12:11, 14; 22:8; and Job 4:8. Psalm 44:17-19 provides a paradoxical exception to this consequential rule. Although exceptions occur, one should not base one's life on them.

14:15. This saying is paired with the next through a contrast of careless confidence and appropriate caution or fear. The young, in contrast to the prudent (v. 18), are gullible because they have no experience to judge words, persons, and situations. One purpose of Proverbs is to give the young vicarious experience, and thus to make the simple prudent (1:4; 9:4-6). Several scenes from the prologue illustrate this saying (4:14-15; 7:7-8; see also 14:8, 12; 16:9; 22:3; 26:25).

14:16. The first line of this verse is probably elliptical (lit., "the wise one fears"), so that the NIV translation, which adds "the LORD," captures the sense on the analogy of 3:7 and Job 28:28, which also links "fear of the LORD" with "turning from evil" (see 8:13; 13:19; 16:6, 17). The NRSV reading remains on the horizontal plane, by contrasting caution with heedless folly. Verse 16*b* is also ambiguous. The fool either gets angry or out of line ("throws off restraint"), or perhaps gets involved with trouble ("evil," v. 16*a*; see LXX and Syriac, with an inversion of consonants; see also Commentary on 26:17). Fools are careless, because they are groundlessly confident (lit., "trust," as in 28:26). In 3:5 "trust" refers to confident trust in God. Here it forms a parallel with "believes" (v. 15*a*).

14:17. "Quick-tempered" is literally "quick to anger" (קצר-אפים *qĕṣar-ʾappayim*), the opposite of "slow to anger" or "patient" (v. 29; 25:15). Verse 17*a* states a common human failing. Of themselves, emotions are morally neutral. Their value is in reflecting the personal significance of things for us, whether good or ill. Their limitation is that they possess neither wisdom nor restraint, since that is not their function. Emotions present information that may need responsible consideration and restraint (11:12; 17:27). Overly hasty, intemperate reactions to others do damage, because, without reflection, angry people do foolish things they later regret. On the other hand, the schemer who masters feelings while inwardly plotting personal advantage is eventually hated (see 12:2).

14:18. Here the writer returns to the opposition of the simple and the clever (v. 15). Verses 15-18 illustrate aspects of this contrast with alternative vocabulary. The NRSV emends the text of v. 18*a*, but its reading appears in no ancient version and is unnecessary; the NIV better reflects the Hebrew. The two lines are connected in that both folly and kingship ("a crown") are passed on in families; the first to shame, the latter to honor (see 3:35; 19:14; 28:10). Abstract qualities can be metaphorically worn as clothing (1:9; Ps 73:6)—i.e., "He wears his heart on his sleeve." Ancient kings were expected to be wise and knowledgeable; the proverb slyly suggests a royal dignity for all who are "crowned with knowledge" (see Commentary on 14:24; cf. Psalm 8).

14:19-24. This section of Proverbs 14 is a cluster of sayings about relations among people who differ morally or socioeconomically.

14:19. This verse is a didactic saying about the superiority of goodness over evil. The lesson is made concrete and visible in the oriental images of a person bowing down before a superior or begging at the gate of the prosperous (see Lazarus in Luke 16:19-31, a story of reversal).

14:20-21. These verses form a proverb pair within vv. 19-24; v. 21 comes as a sharp qualification after the bluntly realistic observation in v. 20. That the poor are disdained ("hated") is a sorry commentary on humankind. People seem to shun those who reflect the fragility of the human condition to them. If the evil of poverty is located in the other, we can distance ourselves from it (Luke 10:29-37; 16:19-21, 25). That people curry favor with the rich, the beautiful, and the powerful—those who seem to possess life to the full—is a converse comment on the drive to seek security and life on the horizontal human plane rather than in God (see 18:10-11; 22:16; Psalms 49; 62:9-10; 146:3-4). Ultimately, human differences are merely relative. They are leveled by that judgment of God that is death (Job 3:13-19; Isa 14:10-11). Verse 21*a* bluntly condemns the behavior of v. 20*a* as sin. It is also stupidity (11:12), because the Lord, who made all, is compassionate to all and will not tolerate cruelty (14:31; 17:5; 22:2; 29:13-14). Verse 21*b* may be compared with Ps 41:1-2. The verb "is kind" (חנן *ḥānan*) here refers to humans, but is one of the basic attributes of the Lord ("merciful" in Exod 34:6). In this

regard, good people practice the imitation of God (19:17; 21:10*b*; 28:8; see "merciful" in the twin Psalms 111:4 and 112:4; Matt 5:7). The wisdom of these sayings was also found outside of Israel:

God prefers him who honors the poor
To him who worships the wealthy.[201]

14:22. Like v. 21, this verse borrows key terms ("kind," "love." and "faithfulness") from the list of divine attributes found in Exod 34:6 (and repeatedly in the OT; e.g., Num 14:18; Neh 9:17; Pss 86:15; 103:8; Joel 2:13; Jonah 4:2; John 1:14, 17; see Commentary on 16:5-6). Those who plan evil (3:34; 6:14; 12:20; the verb is used of a smith's work of shaping metals) are opposed to those who plan good (only here); this opposition echoes the contrast of good and evil in v. 19. The relation of love and faithfulness to those who plan good is not spelled out. Grammatically, the phrases are simply juxtaposed in a non-verbal sentence. One might supply, "Those who plan good do love and faithfulness." But the NIV and the NRSV translations may also be followed; they suggest that God's love and kindness come to those who plan good (see Commentary on 3:3-4).

14:23. This verse repeats the common theme that hard work and success or sloth and failure are connected as acts are to consequences (see Commentary on 10:4-5). For theological issues connected with this verse, see Commentary on 10:22. Sloth is here nicely pictured as mere talk (lit., "a word of the lips"). In other words, "all talk and no action."

14:24. The NRSV of v. 24*a* follows the LXX, though πανοῦργος (*panourgos*) reflects the Hebrew word for "cleverness" (ערמה *'ormâ*) rather than the usual term for "wisdom" (חכמה *ḥokmâ*). The NIV translates the Hebrew with the sense that wealth is a consequence, or "crown," of wisdom (see 3:16; 8:18; 12:4; 16:31; 17:6; 1 Kgs 3:13). In v. 24*b* the Hebrew reads, "the stupidity of fools is stupidity" (see 16:22*b*). This seems too tautological and produced a variety of translations already in ancient times (see Commentary on 14:5). The NIV adds "yields," while the NRSV, with many commentators, slightly emends "folly"

201. *Amenemope*, chap. 28, in Miriam Lichtheim, *Ancient Egyptian Literature*, 3 vols. (Berkeley: University of California Press, 1973–80) 2:161. Cf. Prov 22:16.

(אולת ʾiwwelet, the same word used for "stupidity" above) to get "garland" (ולית wĕliwyat) as a parallel to "crown," as in 4:9. Perhaps the tautology is to be retained; while wisdom produces a crown, stupidity is and remains merely stupidity. Such utterances appear elsewhere and require some context, either social or literary (like the first contrasting line) to make them work. Note the ancient proverb, "An ape's an ape, a varlet's a varlet, though they be clad in silk or scarlet."

14:25. This verse is one of a number of sayings on true and false witnesses (see Commentary on 12:17; 14:5). These sayings have nearly interchangeable parts (e.g., 12:17*b* and 14:25*b*) and do not produce startling insights. Their frequency, however, is a reminder of the great importance of justice and of the significance of witnesses in legal and criminal procedures.

14:26-27. These verses are a pair of sayings on the fear of the Lord (see Commentary on 1:7; 14:2). Verse 26 has strong links with the theology of the psalter, which also combines "the fear of the Lord," trust/confidence, and "refuge." Psalm 25 combines all these themes from v. 26 and includes the believer's children (Pss 25:2, 12-14, 20; 34:8-9, 11, 22). The God-fearing pass on the faith to their children by example and by precept (see 20:7; Exod 20:6; Deut 6:2). The theme of refuge is important in the editing of the psalter (see Pss 2:12; 37:40).[202] In the psalms, as in Proverbs, the root בטח (*bṭḥ*) regularly expresses ultimate trust or confidence, either in God or in human beings (Pss 26:1; 37:2, 40 ["refuge"]; 40:3-4; 56:3-4, 11; see Prov 3:5; 11:28 18:10-11; 28:25-26).

Verse 27 moves to a different metaphor for the fear of the Lord. It is a "fountain of life," because through it one is connected with the Lord who, indeed, is that fountain (10:27; 19:23; Ps 36:9; Jer 2:13). Elsewhere in Proverbs, the wise themselves are such a fountain of life. This logic of derivation, whereby humans mediate divine goodness, is a common one in Proverbs and elsewhere (see Commentary on 10:11). Proverbs 13:14 is nearly identical to 14:27, except that teaching of the wise takes the place of fear of the Lord. It is impossible to say that one of these two sayings

has temporal priority over the other. In Ps 34:11, the fear of the Lord is something that can be taught (see Prov 2:5; 15:33).

14:28. The first of many references to a king in the saying collections (roughly chaps. 10–29), this verse follows upon a Yahweh saying, thus presenting a frequent and important linkage in Proverbs (20:26-28; 21:1-4; 22:11-12; 25:2-7; 29:12-14; see Commentary on 15:33; 16:1-15).[203] Proverbs 25:2-3 in particular links "the glory of a king" with Yahweh's glory.

In Judah, kingship or government had its ultimate basis in the rule of Yahweh (see Commentary on 16:12). Large kingdoms (and their rulers) have more glory and power than do small ones. This fact plays a role in David's proud desire to number his populace and in his general Joab's response, " 'May the LORD your God increase the number of the people a hundredfold. . . . But why does my lord the king want to do this?' " (2 Sam 24:3 NRSV). The saying may also imply, conversely, that the glory of a king does not consist in the splendor of his court, in his army, or in his wealth, but only in the well-being of the ordinary citizens whose care, justice, and prosperity are his responsibility (Psalm 72).[204] Except for brief moments in its history, as under David and Solomon, Judah (Israel) was a very small kingdom. The amazing impetus toward universal claims to sovereignty in Judean royal theology has its basis in the universal scope of Yahweh's kingdom (see, e.g., Pss 2:8; 18:43; 22:27-28; 72:11, 17; 103:19; 145:11-13; Luke 1:33; 4:5).

14:29-30. These verses reflect on the damage unrestrained emotions can do. Verse 29 provides an antithesis to v. 17*a* and complements its reflections on being quick to anger (see Commentary on 15:18 for "slow to anger"). The principle of self-restraint is not unique to Israel. It is a commonplace, for example, in the ancient Egyptian contrast of the "heated man" and the "silent" one, which runs throughout the *Instruction of Amenemope*.[205] Wisdom about the human condition is not restricted to Israel or the church.

202. Gerald T. Sheppard, " 'Blessed Are Those Who Take Refuge in Him' (Psa. 2:11, Biblical Criticism and Deconstruction," *Religion and Intellectual Life* 5 (1988) 57-66.

203. See R. N. Whybray, *Proverbs,* NCBC (Grand Rapids: Eerdmans, 1994) 221.

204. See L. Alonso-Schökel and J. Vilchez, *Proverbios* (Madrid: Ediciones Cristiandad, 1984) 323.

205. Lichtheim, *AEL,* 2:146-43. See esp. chap. 4, (150-51), with its contrast of two trees, as in Psalm 1.

While v. 29 considers the social consequences of emotional restraint and excess, v. 30 looks at the impact of inner emotional life on a person's bodily well-being (15:4, 13; 17:22). In this area, too, "the springs of life" flow from the heart ("mind," 4:23). For "envy"/"passion" see Commentary on 27:4. Because of the intimate connection of husband and wife, a difficult spouse can also be a "rottenness in the bones" (12:4). "Flesh" and "bones" together are a conventional way to express the whole, bodily existence of a person (4:22; 16:24). Today the insight of v. 30 is expressed in terms of psychosomatic illness, though the implicit anthropologies underlying modern theories and the biblical observation may be different.

14:31. The fundamental principle of kindness to the weak and vulnerable is emphasized in Israel's wisdom writings, in its laws, and by its prophets (see 17:5). It was also affirmed by Israel's neighbors. The Babylonian king Hammurabi, famous for his law code, claimed "to cause justice to prevail in the land, to destroy the wicked and the evil, that the strong might not oppress the weak . . . that justice might be dealt the orphan [and] the widow."[206] For Israel, this principle rested in the compassionate ("kind") nature of God, who made humans (see Commentary on 14:21; Exod 22:27; Sir 18:13; Matt 9:36; Luke 7:13; 10:33). Such proverbs are deepened by awareness that human beings are made in God's image (Gen 1:26). Thus to accord the needy their dignity as human beings is indirectly to honor God, whose representatives on earth the poor are—along with all humans (see Reflections on 15:25). In this verse, the intimate bond between the needy and God is emphasized; the Lord is his Maker (Hebrew singular), and each poor person can claim God's special protection (22:22-23; 23:10-11).

14:32. The NRSV clearly renders v. 32a, but it is inexactly translated by the NIV. The thought is a common one, that people reap what they sow and that the wrongdoing of sinners does damage to them (see Commentary on 13:6; 26:27). The second line is textually difficult. The NRSV trans-

lation, "in their [his] integrity," is based on the ancient LXX and Syriac versions, which read an inversion of two consonants (metathesis) where the MT has "in his death." But never does the verb "find refuge" (חסה ḥāsâ) have an abstraction like "integrity" as its object. Indeed, the verb actually means "to seek refuge" in or under something, and not "to find."[207] It makes no sense to say that the righteous seek a refuge in the death of the wicked (which is what a literal translation of the MT requires; the NIV without reason omits the pronoun referring to the wicked in both lines. The attempt to find a reference to life beyond death ["refuge"] is unwarranted here). In the OT, by far the most common object of "to seek a refuge (in)" is the Lord (30:5; Ps 2:12). The verb never appears without a preposition ("in" or "under") except here and in Ps 17:7, which is textually suspect (see the LXX). In Ps 64:10, "the righteous rejoice in the LORD and take refuge in him" (NRSV). Something of this sort is to be expected in v. 32b. By a slight emendation the following translation is possible, "and the righteous person seeks refuge in him [the Lord], when he [the wicked] dies."[208] The elements of this non-antithetical proverb would then have an illustration in David's song of thanksgiving (2 Sam 22:1-3, 21-22, 38-43).

14:33. The MT of the second line appears to lack a word. The NRSV supplies "not" (following the LXX and the Syriac). The Targum adds "stupidity" as the subject of "is known." One scholar suggests translating the second line as a question, "But can it [wisdom] be known in the inner being of fools?"[209] The NIV translation presupposes the idea that Wisdom speaks to all people alike (see Commentary on 8:1-5), although "among fools" is more probably "in the inner being of fools," parallel to "in the heart of one" (cf. 15:31). Egyptian wisdom also recognized that insight could be found in unexpected places:

Don't be proud of your knowledge,
Consult the ignorant and the wise . . .
Good speech is more hidden than
greenstone

---

206. *Ancient Near Eastern Texts Relating to the Old Testament,* ed. James B. Pritchard, 3rd ed. (Princeton, N.J.: Princeton University Press, 1969) 164, 178. See also "Amenemope," chap. 25 in Lichtheim, *AEL,* 2:160.

207. William McKane, *Proverbs: A New Approach,* OTL (Philadelphia: Westminster, 1970) 475.

208. Reading צדיק במותו בו וחסה (*wĕḥōseh bô bĕmôtô ṣaddîq*) with haplography of ב (*b*) and consequent loss of ו (*w*). The antecedent for "in him" may be found in the previous saying, "his Maker."

209. A. Meinhold, *Die Sprüche*, Zücher Bibelkommentare (Zürich: Theologischer Verlag, 1991) 1:242.

Yet may be found among maids at the grind-stones.[210]

But the paradox is that the untutored maids are actually wise, not fools, as in the NIV. The ancient solution followed by the NRSV seems best to capture the sense of the saying. Wisdom finds a home in some hearts, but is a stranger in others.

14:34. The focus turns to concern for the moral-spiritual character of the largest of human social-cultural units: the nation. Although Proverbs speaks mostly to (young male) individuals, its principles can be applied to other persons and to groups (see also 11:10-11, 14).

14:35. This verse is another royal saying (see 19:10; 30:22), its position after v. 34 is significant, for the king is the moral-spiritual heart of the nation. In Israel, "servant" and "slave" (both עבד *'ebed*) is a fluid term, having multiple references, depending on social location (see Commentary on

210. *Ptahhotep*, chap. 1., in Lichtheim, *AEL,* 1:63.

25:2-3). Thus a servant of the king may be a nobleman or a relative in the king's court, while a small landowner's servant may share in his poverty. The servant is responsible to the king for loyalty, obedience, and for specific functions within an office (soldier, administrator, etc.). In North American culture, an egalitarian ethos often obscures or fails to illuminate necessary inequalities in specific, limited social relations: employers and employees, teachers and students, the commander in chief and the armed forces, magistrates and citizens. Verse 35 looks candidly upon one such relationship and suggests that the king's well-being depends on the quality of his servants, in whom he either delights or is angry, as the case may be (see 10:1, 5; 16:13; 17:2). The king's ability to carry out the weighty tasks of his office depends largely on the quality of his servants. Reciprocally, a king's disposition can bring good or ill upon his servants (16:15; 19:12).

REFLECTIONS

1. The saying "The proof of the pudding is in the eating" also applies to faith (14:2; Jas 2:14-26). True godliness is incompatible with an unjust life-style. The same religious logic animates the opening of Psalm 128: "Blessed are all who fear the LORD, who walk in his ways." Fearing the Lord entails a just walk.

One's relationship to God and one's behavior are two sides of the same coin. The practice of life is not indifferent to religion, for God is not indifferent to the practice of life. On this, the writers of the wisdom literature and the prophets agree. Indeed, daily life is the practice of religion in things ordinary, in contrast to the practice of religion in divine worship. God is the creator and Lord of all things, and our disposal of all things is inextricably related to our disposition toward God.

2. Proverbs assumes that human beings are shaped by the company they keep and by the common goals and way of life they share with others (14:7). Thus, when God renews the people, they will have "one heart and one way" (Jer 32:39 NRSV). Shared commitments animate a people in a common way of life and create communities, some good, some bad. This insight also leaps forth from the beginning of Psalm 1: Blessed are those who do not become increasingly enmeshed (walk, stand, sit) in the company of the wicked (see 1 Cor 15:33). The question of individual identity is always also a question of community, from family and church, school and business, all the way up to nation and state. Communities create the paths we walk.

3. In the ultimate order of things, goodness and right prevail over wickedness and wrong (14:19). For Proverbs, the most important difference among persons concerns not their wealth or social status, but their moral-religious character (see Commentary on 14:21). The young need to learn these patterns of reality lest they try to build a life based on those inverted instances where wickedness overturns good (see Commentary on 25:26). Similar in function are the American proverbs "crime doesn't pay" and "honesty is the best policy." Such principles are ultimately moral and spiritual convictions about God and reality. Good folk commit themselves to such principles even when temporal evidence seems to contradict them. They do good because it is good.

4. All human groups, whatever their size, can be characterized in terms of their spiritual-moral behavior (14:33). In the bare-bones language of Proverbs, such behavior is simply righteousness or sin. The Hebrew word for "righteousness" is closely associated with Yahweh (Ps 72:1-4). Yet, since the Lord is creator of the universe (3:19-20), this saying applies not just to Israel, but to all nations, which are subject to God's standards for human conduct (Amos 1:3–2:16). A nation is a unit, a body politic. But in a nation as large and diverse as the United States, good and moral people are easily tempted to distance themselves from segments of the nation they consider violent or sinful. About this problem, M. Scott Peck wrote:

> Any group will remain inevitably potentially conscienceless and evil until such time as each and every individual holds himself or herself directly responsible for the behavior of the whole group—the organism—of which he or she is a part. We have not yet begun to arrive at that point.[211]

211. M. Scott Peck, *People of the Lie: The Hope for Healing Human Evil* (New York: Simon and Schuster, 1983) 218.

Proverbs 15:1-33, The End of the Antithetical Collection

NIV	NRSV
15 A gentle answer turns away wrath, but a harsh word stirs up anger.	**15** A soft answer turns away wrath, but a harsh word stirs up anger.
²The tongue of the wise commends knowledge, but the mouth of the fool gushes folly.	² The tongue of the wise dispenses knowledge,[a] but the mouths of fools pour out folly.
³The eyes of the LORD are everywhere, keeping watch on the wicked and the good.	³ The eyes of the LORD are in every place, keeping watch on the evil and the good.
⁴The tongue that brings healing is a tree of life, but a deceitful tongue crushes the spirit.	⁴ A gentle tongue is a tree of life, but perverseness in it breaks the spirit.
⁵A fool spurns his father's discipline, but whoever heeds correction shows prudence.	⁵ A fool despises a parent's instruction, but the one who heeds admonition is prudent.
⁶The house of the righteous contains great treasure, but the income of the wicked brings them trouble.	⁶ In the house of the righteous there is much treasure, but trouble befalls the income of the wicked.
⁷The lips of the wise spread knowledge; not so the hearts of fools.	⁷ The lips of the wise spread knowledge; not so the minds of fools.
⁸The LORD detests the sacrifice of the wicked, but the prayer of the upright pleases him.	⁸ The sacrifice of the wicked is an abomination to the LORD, but the prayer of the upright is his delight.
⁹The LORD detests the way of the wicked but he loves those who pursue righteousness.	⁹ The way of the wicked is an abomination to the LORD, but he loves the one who pursues righteousness.
¹⁰Stern discipline awaits him who leaves the path;	

a Cn: Heb *makes knowledge good*

NIV

he who hates correction will die.

¹¹Death and Destruction*ᵃ lie open before the
  LORD—
  how much more the hearts of men!

¹²A mocker resents correction;
  he will not consult the wise.

¹³A happy heart makes the face cheerful,
  but heartache crushes the spirit.

¹⁴The discerning heart seeks knowledge,
  but the mouth of a fool feeds on folly.

¹⁵All the days of the oppressed are wretched,
  but the cheerful heart has a continual feast.

¹⁶Better a little with the fear of the LORD
  than great wealth with turmoil.

¹⁷Better a meal of vegetables where there is love
  than a fattened calf with hatred.

¹⁸A hot-tempered man stirs up dissension,
  but a patient man calms a quarrel.

¹⁹The way of the sluggard is blocked with thorns,
  but the path of the upright is a highway.

²⁰A wise son brings joy to his father,
  but a foolish man despises his mother.

²¹Folly delights a man who lacks judgment,
  but a man of understanding keeps a straight
    course.

²²Plans fail for lack of counsel,
  but with many advisers they succeed.

²³A man finds joy in giving an apt reply—
  and how good is a timely word!

²⁴The path of life leads upward for the wise
  to keep him from going down to the grave.*ᵇ

²⁵The LORD tears down the proud man's house
  but he keeps the widow's boundaries intact.

²⁶The LORD detests the thoughts of the wicked,
  but those of the pure are pleasing to him.

²⁷A greedy man brings trouble to his family,
  but he who hates bribes will live.

²⁸The heart of the righteous weighs its answers,
  but the mouth of the wicked gushes evil.

²⁹The LORD is far from the wicked
  but he hears the prayer of the righteous.

ᵃ11 Hebrew *Sheol and Abaddon*   ᵇ24 Hebrew *Sheol*

NRSV

¹⁰ There is severe discipline for one who forsakes
    the way,
  but one who hates a rebuke will die.

¹¹ Sheol and Abaddon lie open before the LORD,
  how much more human hearts!

¹² Scoffers do not like to be rebuked;
  they will not go to the wise.

¹³ A glad heart makes a cheerful countenance,
  but by sorrow of heart the spirit is broken.

¹⁴ The mind of one who has understanding seeks
    knowledge,
  but the mouths of fools feed on folly.

¹⁵ All the days of the poor are hard,
  but a cheerful heart has a continual feast.

¹⁶ Better is a little with the fear of the LORD
  than great treasure and trouble with it.

¹⁷ Better is a dinner of vegetables where love is
  than a fatted ox and hatred with it.

¹⁸ Those who are hot-tempered stir up strife,
  but those who are slow to anger calm
    contention.

¹⁹ The way of the lazy is overgrown with thorns,
  but the path of the upright is a level
    highway.

²⁰ A wise child makes a glad father,
  but the foolish despise their mothers.

²¹ Folly is a joy to one who has no sense,
  but a person of understanding walks straight
    ahead.

²² Without counsel, plans go wrong,
  but with many advisers they succeed.

²³ To make an apt answer is a joy to anyone,
  and a word in season, how good it is!

²⁴ For the wise the path of life leads upward,
  in order to avoid Sheol below.

²⁵ The LORD tears down the house of the proud,
  but maintains the widow's boundaries.

²⁶ Evil plans are an abomination to the LORD,
  but gracious words are pure.

²⁷ Those who are greedy for unjust gain make
    trouble for their households,
  but those who hate bribes will live.

²⁸ The mind of the righteous ponders how to
    answer,
  but the mouth of the wicked pours out evil.

²⁹ The LORD is far from the wicked,
  but he hears the prayer of the righteous.

³⁰ The light of the eyes rejoices the heart,

NIV

³⁰A cheerful look brings joy to the heart,
  and good news gives health to the bones.

³¹He who listens to a life-giving rebuke
  will be at home among the wise.

³²He who ignores discipline despises himself,
  but whoever heeds correction gains
    understanding.

³³The fear of the LORD teaches a man wisdom,ᶜ
  and humility comes before honor.

ᶜ33 Or *Wisdom teaches the fear of the* LORD

NRSV

  and good news refreshes the body.
³¹ The ear that heeds wholesome admonition
    will lodge among the wise.
³² Those who ignore instruction despise
    themselves,
  but those who heed admonition gain
    understanding.
³³ The fear of the LORD is instruction in wisdom,
  and humility goes before honor.

COMMENTARY

Proverbs 15 concludes the first Solomonic sub-collection (10:1–15:33), and its distribution of sayings creates a number of significant relations with other chapters. Several sayings here echo elements of Proverbs 10, creating a verbal and thematic envelope to mark off the first Solomonic sub-collection (cf. 10:1 and 15:5, 20; 10:2-3 and 15:6, 16-17; 10:17 and 15:5, 10, 12, 31-32; 10:27 and 15:33). The sayings on heeding rebuke (15:5, 10, 12, 31-32) also connect with the redactional section 9:7-12 and embody principles running throughout chaps. 1–9. Proverbs 15 also frequently mentions the Lord (vv. 3, 8-9, 11, 16, 25-26, 29, 33), thus anticipating the series of Yahweh sayings that opens the second Solomonic sub-collection (16:1–22:16).

15:1-2. Verse 1 simply observes human interaction, with the intent that people use its twofold insight (on speech, see 15:23, 28; 25:11-12, 15). A harsh word is one that causes another person pain (see "sorrow," 10:22; Gen 3:16), but may also embody the speaker's pain, just as a gentle answer embodies the speaker's calm and healing presence (12:18; 14:29; 15:4, 18).

Verse 2 follows naturally upon v. 1. Wisdom not only speaks in the proper manner (v. 28), but also delivers the insight and know-how that a particular situation, task, or problem needs (10:31; 13:16; 15:7; see Commentary on 24:3-4).

15:3. This verse states a fundamental precept of biblical thought, that the Lord knows all things, including the human heart (see Excursus, "The 'Heart' in the Old Testament," 60-61), and that

God is especially concerned with human good and evil, which God judges as King of the universe (v. 11; 16:2; 17:3; Ps 7:9; Jer 17:9-10; Rev 2:23). Whereas systematic theology speaks abstractly of divine omniscience, the Bible uses concrete images or metaphors like "the eyes of the LORD" (2 Chr 16:9 NRSV; Job 31:4; Ps 139; Jer 16:17; see Heb 4:13).

15:4. Here the text picks up from vv. 1-2. The NRSV rendering "gentle" translates the same adjective (מרפא *marpēʾ*) as "tranquil" in 14:30; its root connotes "health." The NIV translation "that brings healing" understands "healthy" in a causative sense; right speech restores hurt, damaged relationships (as in 12:18; see 10:11; 13:17; 16:24). Each translation captures a nuance of the original. For "tree of life," see Commentary on 3:18; such trees bring healing (Ezek 47:12; Rev 22:2). The opposite situation is a tongue whose talk is "twisted." Such perverseness in speech distorts reality and causes damage (11:3; 19:13 uses the same root), in this case despair in another's inmost being (see v. 13; Ps 51:17; Isa 65:14). The psalmists pray against enemies who do damage with their tongues (Pss 5:9; 12:1-4; 73:8-9).

15:5. People are known by what they love and by what they disdain (1:7). A fool rejects parental discipline and thus is cut off from the chain of tradition and from Wisdom herself (1:30; see Commentary on 10:1; 15:12, 20, 31). The ability to accept criticism, however, marks one who will grow and succeed (9:7-9). "Is prudent"

(ערם 'ārûm) is more accurately "become clever," in the sense of someone able to work out solutions to life's problems.

15:6. The main theme of chaps. 10–15 continues: Righteousness leads to well-being, and wickedness to trouble (10:2, 16; 15:25). "Treasure" (חסן hōsen) indicates what is stored over time (Isa 23:18 uses this root), while "income" (תבואה tĕbû'â) suggests the precarious character of existence based on earnings or produce. Job raises objections to the facile application of this saying (Job 21:7-26), but it is already qualified within Proverbs, especially in the next Solomonic sub-collection (see Commentary on 16:8).

15:7. This verse is a variant of v. 2, using the frequent connection of "heart" and organs of speech (see Commentary on 16:1, 9). The second line may also be rendered, "the hearts of fools are not steadfast [or "right"]" (see 11:19 NRSV; 28:2, "order").

15:8-10. Verses 8-9 form a proverb pair, linked by the contrast of divine "abomination" and "delight"/"love" (see Commentary on 11:1). The first saying is one of very few that mention the essential acts of worship: prayer and sacrifice (v. 29; 21:3, 27; 28:9, 13). Proverbs assumes the ordinary practice of worship in Israel, but does not elaborate upon it. The book also ignores Israel's history with God. These omissions are a matter of the genre and function of wisdom sayings and admonitions (see Introduction). A sacrifice (something costly and ordinarily pleasing, 3:9-10; Lev 12:8) is rendered repugnant to God because wickedness pollutes the holy gift (see Commentary on 21:3, 27).[212] By contrast, a mere prayer of the upright, which involves no material cost, pleases God. The Hebrew word for "prayer" (תפלה tĕpillâ) is used of the Davidic psalms, which are predominantly laments requesting divine help (Ps 72:20). The juxtaposition of v. 9 to v. 8 shows that sacrifice and prayer do not please the Lord, unless one also "pursues righteousness" (see Matt 6:33). As in chaps. 1–9, what one loves and pursues determines the character of one's life journey (11:19). Thus, without righteousness, one has neither God nor wisdom (8:20). Indeed, God desires righteousness in ordinary life more than

worship or personal piety (see Commentary on 21:3; 28:9). On this point, the sages and the prophets agreed (1 Sam 15:22-23; Ps 50:7-23; Isa 1:10-17; Amos 5:21-24).

Verse 10 is linked to v. 9 by the words "way" and "path" and by the standard opposition of "love" and "hate." These connections suggest that an abomination leads to severe discipline and ultimately death. The appearance of Sheol and God as judge in v. 11 confirms this movement of thought. Verse 10 is ambiguous and can be taken several ways. Some suggest that discipline seems bad to one who leaves the path (of "right" or "life"; 2:13; 10:17; see Commentary on 8:9). This reading lessens the connection of the two lines. Alternatively, "severe discipline" is parallel to "will die" (so NIV, without the adversative "but"), thus portraying death as the Lord's ultimate device of corrective instruction. Such a pattern of education through death and disaster appears in the plagues of Exodus, with their repeated purpose, "that you may know . . . the LORD" (Exod 10:2 NRSV; cf. Exod 7:3-5; 18:11). Resistance to "rebuke" (or "reproof") typifies those who spurn Wisdom (1:25, 30; 15:5), as does the consequence of death (1:32).

15:11. This verse resonates with v. 3. The God who knows the depths of the cosmos, for whom the mysteries of the underworld lie exposed, has no difficulty in knowing human hearts. Sheol and Abaddon ("Destruction") are a hendiadys (two nouns describing one referent) for the realm of death (27:20; Job 26:6; 28:22) The cosmic scope of divine knowledge appears in Amos 9:2-4, but Psalm 139 most magnificently displays God's knowledge of the cosmos and of the human heart.

15:12. This verse has close affinities with vv. 5 and 10*b* and with 9:7-8. Literally, the first line reads, "Mockers do not love the one who rebukes them." Scoffers do not love those whose criticisms require them to mend their ways. This hatred of correction is most pernicious when it enters the law courts, where the lives of ordinary people can be destroyed (Amos 5:10). The conflict of good and evil entails conflict between persons and determines the company we keep (see Commentary on 14:7; 13:20; see Reflections on Proverbs 28–29).

15:13-17. These verses are stitched together

212. See Richard D. Nelson, *Raising Up a Faithful Priest: Community and Priesthood in Biblical Theology* (Louisville: Westminster/John Knox, 1993) 17-38, 55-82.

by word repetitions. Verses 13-14 are a proverb pair, each beginning with "heart" ("mind" [לֵב *lēb*]); this proverb pair is similar to 18:14-15. Verse 15 seems to have a pivot function, for it contains the word "heart" (looking back) and also "good"/"better," a Hebrew term that begins the next two sayings (the root appears in v. 13). Finally, vv. 16-17 conclude with the phrase "with it."

Verse 13 finds a near duplicate in 17:22 and is the basis for Sir 13:25-26 (see 14:30; 15:4). What is in one's heart will come to the surface, where it can be seen (v. 13*a*). The relation of the heart and the spirit in v. 13*b* is puzzling because both refer to closely related inner capacities. The word "spirit" (רוּחַ *rûaḥ*) also means "wind" and connotes the wind's force and energy. Here it seems best to take "spirit" in the sense of one's vital powers, the inner energy and drive by which a person succeeds in life (see 18:14). A troubled heart quenches the spirit, so that one's vital energy cannot flow. The logic of v. 13*b* implies that the heart is the more profound and abiding dimension of a person; it affects the spirit, which, like wind, comes and goes (John 3:8). Conversely, the advent of spirit brings life and power to the heart.[213] The transitory character of wind/spirit is typical of OT usage (Judg 3:10; Job 34:14-15; Ps 104:29; see Acts 1:8).[214] Without the movement of spirit, life ceases.

The discerning heart (v. 14) has a drive to know (see Commentary on 10:14; 12:1; 18:15), but God does not give such a heart to all (Deut 29:3-4; 1 Kgs 3:9, 12). The mouth of a fool "feeds on" folly like a sheep feeds on grass (the verb is a shepherding term). The wise and the foolish appear to seek and pasture on different mental and spiritual food. Less plausible is the view that the verbs are doubly transitive: The wise shepherd seeks out good pasture for the sheep, but fools feed the sheep folly.[215] In the metaphor, "heart" and especially "mouth" correspond better to sheep than to shepherd (see 18:15*b*).

Verse 15 (see v. 13) begins a series of three paradoxical sayings connected by themes of wealth and poverty, contentment, and the truly "good" (a key word, "good" and "better" [טוֹב *ṭôb*] are the same in Hebrew). The inner person can overcome external circumstances, a paradox powerfully expressed by Paul in a vision of divine grace (see 2 Cor 4:6-10, 16-18).

A paradoxical proverb pair on wealth and poverty follows (vv. 16-17; 16:8; 27:8).[216] Ordinarily, the fatted oxen are good; they are included in wise Solomon's provisions (14:4; 1 Kgs 4:23). But without godliness, the goods of this world become disordered; they exist in turmoil—a reference to troubled and unjust personal and social relations (Ezek 22:5; Amos 3:9). Verses 16-17 are parallel and interpret each other. Verse 16 is not a pious overlay, commenting on the secular proverb in v. 17. Rather, v. 17 portrays the fear of the Lord, or its lack, with vivid images: a plate of greens or a fatted ox, seasoned with love or hate. This picture of contrasting meals shows that the ordinary affairs of life are not apart from good or bad religion, but are their living manifestation (see Commentary on 31:30).

15:18. The idea of troubled relations, implicit in the contrast of "love" and "hate" in v. 17 (see 10:12), is the focus of this verse. It contrasts the hot-tempered person (lit., "angry man") with one slow to anger (see Sir 28:8-12). Each of these types has a characteristic effect on social relations; the first brings conflict (6:14, 19; 22:10; 29:22); the second brings peace and cooperation because slowness gives one freedom to think before speaking or acting (v. 28). Thus one's words and deeds can heal rather than hurt (vv. 1, 4; 17:27; 25:15). Such persons control their spirit or passion (16:32; Eccl 7:8-9). Mastery of emotions is essential to wisdom (19:11; 25:28). While the phrase "slow to anger" is at home in wisdom (14:29; 16:32; 25:15), its most striking use is in the series of attributes that describe the essential character of Yahweh (Exod 34:6-7; see Commentary on 14:21-22).

15:19. This verse presents a variation on the theme of the two ways (see Overview to Prov 1:1–9:18). The parallelism opposes the sluggard to the upright. This unusual pairing suggests that

213. See Knierim, "The Spirituality of the Old Testament," in *The Task of Old Testament Theology: Substance, Method, and Cases* (Grand Rapids: Eerdmans, 1995) 269-97.

214. See H. W. Wolf, *Anthropology of the Old Testament* (Philadelphia: Fortress, 1974) 32-39.

215. R. N. Whybray, *Proverbs,* NCB (Grand Rapids: Eerdmans, 1994) 230.

216. See *Amenemope* IX, 5–8, in Miriam Lichtheim, *Ancient Egyptian Literature,* 3 vols. (Berkeley: University of California Press, 1973–80) 2:152.

there is moral deficiency in laziness but wise virtue in diligence (see Commentary on 6:6-11). How the sluggard's way is "blocked with thorns" (lit., "like a thorn hedge") is not clear. Perhaps they imagine obstacles to possible undertakings (see 22:13). Alternatively, the sluggard's way is in fact overgrown with obstacles because the work needed to make a clear path ("highway") has not been done (see 24:31; Isa 40:3-4).

15:20. This is a variant of 10:1. Its appearance near the end of the first Solomonic collection contributes to the envelope structure of this subsection (see Commentary on 9:10). To "despise" a parent was a heinous crime in Israel (20:20; 30:11, 17; Deut 21:18-21; 27:16; Ezek 22:7). The deficient character of a foolish man (see 21:20) seems rooted in his failure to honor his parents by heeding their advice and instruction about life (1:8; 12:1; 13:1; Deut 5:16).

15:21. This verse repeats the root שׂמח (*śmḥ*, "joy," "glad," "delights") from v. 20, but in a different context (see v. 23). Here something is desperately wrong: Folly is pleasure to one who lacks heart (see Commentary on 10:13). But one with discernment walks by (v. 21*b*). This thought reflects the imagery of Proverbs 1–9, where the wise walk by the seductions of Folly and the strange woman (see 4:25-27).

15:22. For a discussion of the themes of this verse, see the Commentary on 11:14; 14:7 (see also Tob 4:18).

15:23. This is one of many sayings on speech. An answer suggests the dialogical character of speech in community (see vv. 1, 28; 18:21; 24:26; 25:11). A comparative reading of the lines seems unlikely (people may be self-satisfied with their talk, but much better is speech that fits the occasion). The NIV and the NRSV supply "apt," which is not in the Hebrew, apparently reading v. 23*a* in the light of v. 23*b*. There is "joy" in speech that fits the moment (see Commentary on 26:1-12; Eccl 3:1-8). Proverbs themselves, in their verbal artistry and apt use, exemplify this point.

15:24. The "upward . . . path of life" is not an ascent to heaven (cf. Isa 14:13-15; see also Prov 12:28; 15:25), but simply employs the common Israelite imagery of high and low to contrast the goodness of an abundant life with the grave tendency of foolish humans toward Sheol or death (see Reflections on Proverbs 5). A similar use of

the expressions "upward" and "below" appears in Deut 28:13, 43, where the Israelites have success or failure depending on their obedience to the law. In other words, "Onward and upward!" (See 2:18-19; 5:6; 7:27; 10:17.)

15:25. God gives judgment against the proud and justice for the widow (see Commentary on 22:28; 23:10-11). Wisdom's opposition to pride is rooted in its understanding of humility and the fear of the Lord—notions that conclude this chapter (v. 33; see 16:18-19). Oppression is a form of pride that is especially incompatible with godliness (14:31). The widow represents all those who are vulnerable to the arrogant wicked. Similar thoughts are found in the law (Exod 22:22-24), in the prophets (Isa 5:8-10; Hos 5:10), in historical literature (1 Sam 2:1-10; Luke 1:46-55), and in Psalms (Pss 75:6-7; 113:5-8). Several of such passages use the high/low imagery of v. 24 (Isa 2:12-17).

15:26. "Evil plans" or "thoughts" (12:5; see 24:8) run counter to God's nature and purposes for reality. The source of such plans is the heart (6:18; 15:21; see Excursus, "The 'Heart' in the Old Testament," 60-61). Verse 26*b* forms a puzzling contrast to v. 26*a*. The NIV avoids the problem by translating the Greek from the LXX rather than the Hebrew. Inner plans and outer speech ("words"), however, are often contrasted (vv. 14, 28; 26:23-25), as are various expressions for good and evil. "Pleasant" or "gracious" words stand in opposition to "evil plans," and "abomination" is opposed to what is pure and pleasing in the Lord's eyes (for "abomination," see Commentary on 11:1; see also Commentary on 22:11; cf. Hab 1:13). The root for "gracious" or "pleasant" (נעם *n' m*) is related to what is good (Gen 49:15; Job 36:11) and lovely (Cant 1:16; 7:6). Thus Wisdom's ways are pleasant (3:17), and the attributes of "gracious"/"pleasant" words are associated with wisdom (16:24; 24:13-14). The "words" ("promises") of the Lord are pure (Ps 12:6).

15:27. This verse refers to Israel's judicial system, in which the gift (here translated "bribe") was considered compensation for services rendered (18:16) or for damages (6:35). But the practice was easily corrupted, as greedy judges or witnesses accepted bribes in exchange for rendering unjust verdicts or testimony favoring the rich

(28:16; Exod 23:6-8). Sometimes Proverbs condemns the gift or bribe, sometimes it simply observes its power (18:16; 19:6; 21:14; see Eccl 7:7; cf. the related term for "bribe" [שחד *šōḥad*], 6:35; 17:8, 23; 21:14). Ezekiel 22:12-13 connects greed "for unjust/dishonest gain" with ignoring God, a matter that God will judge (see 1:19). Such persons damage themselves and their households (see Commentary on 11:29). This contrasts with the promise, also found in the law, that the judge who rejects bribes will live (28:16; Deut 16:19-20). The phrase "to hate bribes" also appears in the law (Exod 18:21; see Reflection number 1 on Proverbs 18).

15:28-32. These verses comprise a cluster of sayings closely linked by word repetitions and themes of speaking and hearing: ear and eye, heart and mouth. Verses 28-29 contrast the speech of righteous and wicked people toward others and toward God (see 10:31-32). Verses 29-32 are linked by the root for "hear" (שמע *šm'*, also "news," as in "something heard," in v. 30).

15:28. The righteous consider how to answer fittingly (but see Commentary on 16:1; 26:4-5). This inner capacity to reflect, rather than to react emotionally, defines the wise person and produces the sort of speech described in vv. 1*a*, 2*a*, and 23*a*. Compare the folk advice to "count to ten" before responding to an affront (see 15:18; 19:11). A malicious mouth, however, "pours out" harmful words like unrestrained waters (17:14; 19:28; see also 1:23). "Evil" here is plural—"evil things"—perhaps because the behavior and speech of the wicked are not one sort of evil, but diverse. "Heart" and "mouth" are emblems of the inner and outer person (see Commentary on 15:14, 26); what is on the inside will come out (1 Sam 24:13).

15:29. Implicit in prayer and other forms of worship is the spatial image of nearness to God. It is ironic that even when the wicked "come near" in prayer, God is "far" from them (see v. 8; 28:9; Isa 1:15; 29:13). Distance implies the absence of God's loving help and blessing (Pss 22:1, 11; 35:22; 71:12).

15:30. Once again the contrast of the inner and outer person appears. Here, two of the sense organs, eyes and ears, are gateways for light and good news (25:25; see also 12:25) as vivifying influences from the outer world upon the inner person ("heart" and "bones" are in synecdoche for the "body" in its inner aspects). "Light" is a metaphor for life and joy (4:18; Pss 38:10; 97:11) and, naturally, is associated with righteousness (13:9; Matt 6:22-23). For Israel, the laws of God make the heart rejoice and enlighten the eyes (Ps 19:8-9). Yet the Lord gives light to the eyes of both the rich and the poor, the oppressor and the victim (29:13). However, until the early modern period, the eyes were generally pictured as having and emitting their own light, like a lamp (see 13:9; Matt 6:22-23).[217] Wine, another external influence, also gladdens or "rejoices the heart" (Ps 104:15). One's inner self influences one's outer, bodily being (v. 13), but the world and external body also influence the soul.

15:31-32. These verses reflect on the heart and the ears as organs that receive or reject discipline and correction (see Commentary on 12:1; 4:20, 23; 25:12). The latter action is literally to reject or to despise oneself, or "life" (נפש *nepeš*). In antithetical contrast is v. 31*b*: To gain understanding is literally to "gain "heart" (לב *lēb*)—the vital, wise center of life and selfhood (cf. "keeping oneself/life" in 16:17). In Israel's highly oral culture, the organs of understanding and wisdom were the heart, mouth, lips, eyes, and ears (see Rom 10:5-17 for a NT discourse that assumes much the same view, even while it speaks of Moses' writing).

15:33. This verse appears to be a redactional conclusion to the first Solomonic sub-collection (10:1–15:33). Its first line derives its vocabulary entirely from the book's motto in 1:7 (see NRSV; the NIV is very free), so as to link "the fear of the LORD" inseparably to the instruction and wisdom the book teaches. These key words were anticipated in vv. 31-32. Verse 33*b* is derived from 18:12*b*. Reverence for God gives a person a proper sense of self, of realistic humility (16:18-19; see Commentary on 11:2, which uses a different term to the same effect). This verse sets the anthropological stage for the contrast of human limits and divine freedom, which opens the next Solomonic sub-collection (16:1-9).

---

217. W. D. Davies and Dale C. Allison, *The Gospel According to Saint Matthew I,* ICC (Edinburgh: T. & T. Clark, 1988) 635-37.

REFLECTIONS

1. To put Prov 15:1 into practice is difficult because human emotions naturally react to anger and pain in kind. Emotions themselves know no morality; they just are. The way we deal with our emotions, however, is a moral-social issue, because human beings are more than their feelings. Harsh words reveal a lack of self-discipline, a failure of boundaries (25:28).

Another difficulty in practicing Prov 15:1 stems from distorted views concerning genuine strength versus perceived weakness (16:32). In this category are some macho views of manhood. Such styles of masculinity, in whatever cultural context, may plaster over insecurity and inner weakness. They disrupt human relations, often to the detriment of both parties. The story of Rehoboam's harsh answer to the northern tribes, with its disastrous consequences, illustrates this problem (1 Kgs 12:1-16; see also Prov 20:29). But Gideon's proverbial response to angry Ephraim brings peace (Judg 8:1-3). Again, Nabal's harsh words stir up David's wrath (1 Sam 25:10-13), while Abigail's gentle answer deflects it (2 Sam 25:23-31). Abigail's story illustrates the divine origin of wise speech (2 Sam 25:32-35, 39), as does Prov 16:1.

2. The two halves of Prov 15:15 qualify each other in paradoxical fashion. A central task of the king (and of government today) is to do justice by defending the rights of the poor (see Commentary on 29:14; 31:8-9). Poverty or affliction can render every day a bad day and can crush those made in God's image. Thus Scripture consistently looks upon poverty as an evil thing, with negative spiritual consequences. For example, when Israel is overwhelmed by oppression, the people cannot believe God's good news of grace and liberation (Exod 6:9). Those in prosperity should not glibly underestimate the constraints that hobble the poor (see Commentary on 15:13). And yet, there are rare people whose inner disposition, a cheerful heart, renders them always content. The rich person is defined in *m. 'Abot* 4:1 as one "happy with his lot."[218] Because of his existence in Christ and the effect this has on his inner being, the apostle Paul could say he had learned to be content in all circumstances (Phil 4:11-13; see also 2 Cor 4:6-10, 16-18). Most people, including self-professed Christians, fall short of this transcendent goal.

3. Better-than sayings (15:16-17; see 16:8) set conventional understandings of wealth and poverty on their head. They do not deny the goodness of wealth, but they relativize goods by placing them beneath the fear of the Lord. The mutual realities of wisdom, righteousness, and the fear of the Lord are the indispensable foundations of a good life, even if—contrary to usual expectations—they entail suffering or self-limitation. The first better-than sayings in the book stated that wisdom was better than wealth (8:11, 19). Proverbs 15:16-17 is the first of a number of comparative sayings (mostly found in 16:1–22:16) that assert that the fear of the Lord and its moral-spiritual concomitants are better than good things obtained or held without righteousness. These proverbs undermine simplistic readings of Proverbs that say that the book is unrealistic in its portrayal of the causal connections linking virtue to wealth and vice to poverty. In normal circumstances, these connections of acts and consequences hold true—and life would be impossible without them. But in a broken world where injustice and the absurd can prevail, faith persists in belief and obedience even when its rewards remain unseen (Heb 11:1). Christians walk by faith, not by sight, and our conduct must show this. Faith (represented here by "love" and the "fear of the LORD") can transform a "meal of vegetables" into a "continual feast" (15:15).

4. Human delight in the wrong is a grievous mystery (15:21; see 10:23), but the imagery of the strange woman as Folly in Proverbs 1–9 may render it somewhat less mysterious. Sin

---

218. R. H. Charles, *The Apocrypha and Pseudepigrapha of the Old Testament* (Oxford: Clarendon, 1913) 2:703.

and folly always tempt us with some created good. If sin did not offer the semblance of good, people would not be tempted. But Folly's goods are distorted and dangerous, because they are gotten at the expense of other goods and of the comprehensive good of cosmic order, or righteousness (see Commentary on 15:17-18). The consequences of sin are disastrous, "in folly ripe, in reason rotten." Those with understanding recognize such pleasures for what they are and proceed straight on their way (see 11:5a). Proverbs 3:6 sees the ability to walk such a straight path as a gift rooted in one's relation to God. The ability to say no to pleasant follies is rooted in commitment to that one great good that gives direction to one's life and places all lesser goods in their proper place (see Matt 6:33).

5. To consult others is not necessarily "a mark of conservative society which mistrusts individual initiative" (see 15:22).[219] Rather, it is an acknowledgment that no one has enough wisdom even for his or her own life. This saying is all the more striking because of the strong social relations in which ancient Israelites existed. If the Israelites needed such advice, how much more do we modern individualists! The problem is not merely our individualist mind-set (see Commentary on 14:10). The structures and patterns of our lives conspire to isolate us. In contemporary society, the automobile dismantles neighborhoods and mass media isolate even family members from one another; when the TV is on, who really talks? Paradoxically, the media create a bogus sense of community and shared values,[220] even as they alienate us from those closest to us.

In such a life-world, Christians (and people in general) need to create places and naturally recurring situations in which families and neighborhoods can seek and share counsel (15:22) within genuine communities based on common commitments. This goal may also require that citizens work creatively to change the shape of neighborhoods, the architecture of cities, and the patterns of our commuter lives. (Is not "freeway" an oxymoron?) Since God created us as bodies in a physical world, these issues, too, are concerns of biblical wisdom and obedience. The shape of our life-world should not be dictated by commercial interests and technological forces; it should be based on wise, responsible public counsel and action.

6. The idea of boundaries (15:25) is fundamental to Israel's understanding of justice. Justice is rooted in cosmic order and reflects it (see Commentary on 8:27). The law stipulates that boundary markers (usually heavy stones) may not be moved (Deut 19:14; 27:17; Prov 22:28). In agrarian Israel, a family's land was necessary for survival, but also for its collective, familial, and personal identity as God's royal vassal(s). Thus the land was central to Israel's covenant role as God's servant (Lev 25:38, 55). To steal land—by means legal or illegal—was to steal the foundation of a family's humanity, because human beings—Israel and the church included—serve God in and with the fruitful earth God created. By exercising responsible stewardship over that earth, we represent God as servant-kings (Gen 1:26-28; Psalm 8).

To each of these servant-kings (men and women), the Lord has given a little kingdom, a bit of turf, with which to serve God. The psalmist responds to this reality with gladness, linking the oath of loyalty to Yahweh to delight in his portion of land:

> I say to the LORD, "You are my Lord;
> I have no good thing apart from."
>
> .   .   .   .   .   .
>
> The LORD is my chosen portion and my cup;
>   you hold my lot.
> The boundary lines have fallen for me

219. Whybray, *Proverbs,* 233.
220. See Neil Postman, *Amusing Ourselves to Death: Public Discourse in the Age of Show Business* (New York: Penguin, 1985); and Robert N. Bellah et al., *Habits of the Heart: Individualism and Commitment in American Life* (Berkeley: University of California Press, 1985) 279-81.

in pleasant places;
I have a goodly heritage. (Ps 16:2, 5-6 NRSV)[221]

To trespass on our neighbor's God-given kingdom, to violate boundaries, is to violate the righteousness that God's kingdom on earth demands (Matt 6:10, 33). On a personal level, it attacks our neighbor's status as God's image (see Commentary on 14:31).

In the United States, most people do not farm the land. In our world, the boundaries that get violated are not made of stone and dirt. For us, Prov 15:25 must be applied, for example, to the boundaries that concern bodies, emotions, jobs, reputation, and the natural limits of earth's environment. Proverbs 15:25 and related sayings (22:28; 23:10-11) may also speak to the way in which modern commerce and technology invade and trample upon other spheres of life for their own narrow purposes. Wealth and power can invade and subvert politics, democratic processes, and criminal and civic justice. Overweening commercial interests can do violence to the integrity, variety, and quality of sports, arts, and entertainment and to the communication of truth by the mass media.[222] Education also can be subverted when learning and research serve what President Dwight Eisenhower termed the military-industrial complex. The drive to maximize profits needs to stay within the cosmic limits of justice, where every creature and human function has its proper space to flourish. When boundaries are trampled, damage is done (see Commentary on Proverbs 8).

Job, in his extreme situation, complains that God is not judging those who violate boundaries in their drive for wealth and power (Job 24:2). But Isa 1:23-28 declares that God will act against those who do not vindicate the widow and the orphan (see 23:10-11). Eventually, God will straighten out all violated boundaries, because the integrity of the divine name and kingdom require it.

7. Proverbs, like the law and the prophets, insists on God's fundamental passion for justice and equity among humans at law (Prov 15:27; see Isa 1:23-24; 5:23; 10:1-4; Amos 5:12; Mic 3:11; 7:3). The doing of impartial justice is a way in which Israel imitates its maker (Deut 10:17-18). The sometimes subtle, sometimes blatant influence of money on the practice of justice and on the conduct of legislators, lawyers, and judges is also a prominent reality in our time. It is often taken for granted as just the way things are done. Jews and Christians who claim biblical roots for their ethics should not tolerate it, because these are not sectarian issues. They are universally human.

221. See J. Clinton McCann, Commentary on Psalms, in *The New Interpreter's Bible,* vol. 4 (Nashville: Abingdon, 1996) 736-37.
222. See Neil Postman, *Technopoly: The Surrender of Culture to Technology* (New York: Knopf, 1992).

PROVERBS 16:1–22:16, THE ROYAL COLLECTION

Proverbs 16:1-33, Introduction to the Royal Collection

NIV	NRSV
16 To man belong the plans of the heart, but from the LORD comes the reply of the tongue.	**16** The plans of the mind belong to mortals, but the answer of the tongue is from the LORD.
[2]All a man's ways seem innocent to him,	[2] All one's ways may be pure in one's own eyes, but the LORD weighs the spirit.

NIV

but motives are weighed by the LORD.

³Commit to the LORD whatever you do,
and your plans will succeed.

⁴The LORD works out everything for his own
ends—
even the wicked for a day of disaster.

⁵The LORD detests all the proud of heart.
Be sure of this: They will not go unpunished.

⁶Through love and faithfulness sin is atoned for;
through the fear of the LORD a man avoids
evil.

⁷When a man's ways are pleasing to the LORD,
he makes even his enemies live at peace with
him.

⁸Better a little with righteousness
than much gain with injustice.

⁹In his heart a man plans his course,
but the LORD determines his steps.

¹⁰The lips of a king speak as an oracle,
and his mouth should not betray justice.

¹¹Honest scales and balances are from the LORD;
all the weights in the bag are of his making.

¹²Kings detest wrongdoing,
for a throne is established through
righteousness.

¹³Kings take pleasure in honest lips;
they value a man who speaks the truth.

¹⁴A king's wrath is a messenger of death,
but a wise man will appease it.

¹⁵When a king's face brightens, it means life;
his favor is like a rain cloud in spring.

¹⁶How much better to get wisdom than gold,
to choose understanding rather than silver!

¹⁷The highway of the upright avoids evil;
he who guards his way guards his life.

¹⁸Pride goes before destruction,
a haughty spirit before a fall.

¹⁹Better to be lowly in spirit and among the
oppressed
than to share plunder with the proud.

²⁰Whoever gives heed to instruction prospers,
and blessed is he who trusts in the LORD.

²¹The wise in heart are called discerning,

NRSV

³ Commit your work to the LORD,
and your plans will be established.

⁴ The LORD has made everything for its purpose,
even the wicked for the day of trouble.

⁵ All those who are arrogant are an abomination
to the LORD;
be assured, they will not go unpunished.

⁶ By loyalty and faithfulness iniquity is atoned
for,
and by the fear of the LORD one avoids evil.

⁷ When the ways of people please the LORD,
he causes even their enemies to be at peace
with them.

⁸ Better is a little with righteousness
than large income with injustice.

⁹ The human mind plans the way,
but the LORD directs the steps.

¹⁰ Inspired decisions are on the lips of a king;
his mouth does not sin in judgment.

¹¹ Honest balances and scales are the LORD's;
all the weights in the bag are his work.

¹² It is an abomination to kings to do evil,
for the throne is established by
righteousness.

¹³ Righteous lips are the delight of a king,
and he loves those who speak what is right.

¹⁴ A king's wrath is a messenger of death,
and whoever is wise will appease it.

¹⁵ In the light of a king's face there is life,
and his favor is like the clouds that bring
the spring rain.

¹⁶ How much better to get wisdom than gold!
To get understanding is to be chosen rather
than silver.

¹⁷ The highway of the upright avoids evil;
those who guard their way preserve their
lives.

¹⁸ Pride goes before destruction,
and a haughty spirit before a fall.

¹⁹ It is better to be of a lowly spirit among the
poor
than to divide the spoil with the proud.

²⁰ Those who are attentive to a matter will
prosper,
and happy are those who trust in the LORD.

²¹ The wise of heart is called perceptive,
and pleasant speech increases
persuasiveness.

NIV

and pleasant words promote instruction.[a]

²²Understanding is a fountain of life to those who have it,
but folly brings punishment to fools.

²³A wise man's heart guides his mouth,
and his lips promote instruction.[b]

²⁴Pleasant words are a honeycomb,
sweet to the soul and healing to the bones.

²⁵There is a way that seems right to a man,
but in the end it leads to death.

²⁶The laborer's appetite works for him;
his hunger drives him on.

²⁷A scoundrel plots evil,
and his speech is like a scorching fire.

²⁸A perverse man stirs up dissension,
and a gossip separates close friends.

²⁹A violent man entices his neighbor
and leads him down a path that is not good.

³⁰He who winks with his eye is plotting perversity;
he who purses his lips is bent on evil.

³¹Gray hair is a crown of splendor;
it is attained by a righteous life.

³²Better a patient man than a warrior,
a man who controls his temper than one who takes a city.

³³The lot is cast into the lap,
but its every decision is from the LORD.

a21 Or *words make a man persuasive*   b23 Or *mouth / and makes his lips persuasive*

NRSV

²² Wisdom is a fountain of life to one who has it,
but folly is the punishment of fools.

²³ The mind of the wise makes their speech judicious,
and adds persuasiveness to their lips.

²⁴ Pleasant words are like a honeycomb,
sweetness to the soul and health to the body.

²⁵ Sometimes there is a way that seems to be right,
but in the end it is the way to death.

²⁶ The appetite of workers works for them;
their hunger urges them on.

²⁷ Scoundrels concoct evil,
and their speech is like a scorching fire.

²⁸ A perverse person spreads strife,
and a whisperer separates close friends.

²⁹ The violent entice their neighbors,
and lead them in a way that is not good.

³⁰ One who winks the eyes plans[a] perverse things;
one who compresses the lips brings evil to pass.

³¹ Gray hair is a crown of glory;
it is gained in a righteous life.

³² One who is slow to anger is better than the mighty,
and one whose temper is controlled than one who captures a city.

³³ The lot is cast into the lap,
but the decision is the LORD's alone.

a Gk Syr Vg Tg: Heb *to plan*

COMMENTARY

16:1-15. These verses, which introduce the second Solomonic sub-collection, occur just before the physical center of the book (16:17, according to the MT verse count). It is the lengthiest cluster of sayings on God (and king) in the book. This section exhibits more redactional care in its composition than do many other sections of Proverbs, where themes and poetic patterns are not so tightly organized, especially at such length (but see 26:1-12). This section of the book may have

been one of the last to be edited in the Masoretic tradition, for the ancient LXX translation presents 16:6-9 MT interspersed among verses in 15:27-30, omits 16:1, 3 MT, and has significant differences in the verses that do correspond. A different Hebrew text underlies the LXX translation of 16:1-9.

In the MT, vv. 1-9 are filled with repeated sounds, words, and phrases that reinforce the coherence of the whole. The initial words of vv.

2-4, for example, are כל/גל/כל (*kol/gōl/kōl*) with another *kol* appearing in the first line of v. 5.

Verses 10-15 focus on the king as the earthly administrator and agent of God's righteous rule. In Israelite thought, as throughout the ancient Near East, God and king are closely linked (24:21; 1 Kgs 21:10, 13), although Israel's Lord set a particular covenantal stamp upon the God-(Davidic)king relationship (2 Samuel 7; Psalm 132). Both God and king are agents of justice (16:10, 33). Both God and king abominate wickedness (15:9; 16:12). There is as well a social hierarchy of God, king, and subjects (see Commentary on 25:1-3).

16:1. Verses 1 and 9 provide the theological frame and theme for the tightly knit cluster in vv. 1-9 (see v. 33; 19:14, 21; 20:24; 21:30-31). The human heart makes "arrangements" or "plans" that are ordinarily expressed in action or speech (see Commentary on 15:13). Earlier proverbs had given counsel about the different sorts of answers that wise or foolish folk make (see Commentary on 15:1, 23, 28; see also Sir 33:4). But here the presence of God is revealed precisely where humans believe themselves most in control: "Man proposes, and God disposes."

16:2. Deity and humanity are contrasted, setting an individual's self-deception (not just ignorance) against God's unerring evaluation of the evanescent "spirits" of us all (see Commentary on 15:13; see also 17:3; 21:2; 24:12). On the contrast between divine and human perception, see Commentary on 14:12 (see also 15:3, 11; 21:2; 24:12).

16:3. This verse seems to reverse normal causal sequence. We—the reader is directly addressed—may commit our plans to the One who knows our ways and expect that God will establish our works (see 3:6; Ps 90:17). But this verse reverses the order of "plans" and "works" (see 4:26*b*). Why? Perhaps the logic is like that of Psalm 127. Even our works (which naturally embody our plans) will fail unless the Lord is at work to make them efficacious (v. 1). "Commit" (lit., "roll") translates an idiomatic metaphor found also in Pss 22:8; 37:5; Sir 7:17 (MS A). One might translate, "Turn your works over to the Lord" (see Ps 55:22; 1 Pet 5:7). The ancient versions repointed the verb "commit" (גל *gōl*, from the root גלל *gll*) as "reveal" (גל *gal*, from

the root גלה *glh*); what this might mean is uncertain.

16:4. The direct objects and object phrases in v. 4*a* are ambiguous and may be translated several ways:

The Lord makes everything/all for its purpose
The Lord makes everyone for his purpose
The Lord makes everything/one for his purpose
The Lord makes everything/one to answer him

The NIV's "works out everything" is patterned after Rom 8:28 and seems designed to ward off the misreading that God, who creates wicked persons, must be culpable for their wickedness (see Eccl 7:29). The first three translations all make good sense. Less likely is the fourth translation, which would mean that all creatures (Psalms 19; 148), but especially humans, are created to answer or respond to God. Rashi, however, took this to mean that all things are created to praise God (referring to Ps 147:7 with the same Hebrew root) or to "bear witness" to God. Even the wicked will give their account to God in a way that vindicates God's goodness and justice. Jeremiah confesses that God is his refuge in the "day of disaster" and prays that it come upon his persecutors as their just deserts (Jer 17:17-18).

16:5-6. To be "proud [lit., "high"] of heart" is an "abomination" (see Commentary on 11:1) because it renders one incapable of that fear of the Lord that causes one to "turn from evil" (see Commentary on 3:7; 16:17). It connotes a lack of realism about oneself and one's place in the world, vis-à-vis God (17:12; 18:12; 2 Chr 26:5; 32:25; Ps 131:1; Ezek 28:2, 17). Deuteronomy 8 provides a good example of such self-deception. When one's "heart is lifted up" (Deut 8:14 KJV), one forgets God and says, "My power and the might of my own hand have gotten me this wealth" (Deut 8:17 NRSV; see Commentary on 11:2).

Some scholars wonder whether "loyalty" and "faithfulness" (v. 6) refer to divine or human actions (see Commentary on 3:3; 14:21-22; 15:18). It appears that they refer to God in this passage, for vv. 5b-6a contain clustered terminology drawn from Exod 34:6-7, the central biblical description of the name Yahweh. This list of divine attributes conveys the mysterious union of God's justice and compassion (see Exod 20:5-7), which chap. 16 places in the context of God's inscrutable freedom. Allusions to this list of divine attributes play a significant role in various biblical books and in an ancient Israelite inscription. The relevant expressions here are "will not go unpunished" (see 6:29; 11:21; 17:5; 19:5, 9; 28:20), "love" and "faithfulness" (see 3:3; 14:22; 20:28), and "iniquity [is atoned for]." Several texts combine the verb for "atone" (כפר *kipper*, which does not appear in Exod 34:6-7) with "iniquity." Psalm 78:38 describes Yahweh as compassionate—the first epithet from Exod 34:6—and as one who "atones iniquity." Moreover, two parallel verses in the golden-calf story show that the verb for "atone" in Prov 16:6 (see also 16:14b) is a substitute for "forgive" in Exod 34:6 (see also Exod 32:30, 32). The allusions to Exod 34:6-7 at the heart of Prov 16:1-9 remind the reader that Yahweh, the God of Proverbs, is both merciful and just. God's actions and judgments are grounded in the attributes revealed in God's name, "Yahweh" (see Sir 2:11; 5:4-7). The God of the wise is the same Yahweh known in the Prophets, the Psalms, and revealed in the narratives of Israel's salvation history.[223] That "one avoids evil" (lit., "turns from evil") through the "fear of the LORD" is obvious, else one's religion is not genuine (see Commentary on 1:7; 3:7b; 14:16).

16:7. What is pleasing to the Lord (root רצה *rāṣâ* appears as a noun "delight"/"favor" in vv. 13, 15) is the opposite of an abomination (vv. 5, 12; see Commentary on 11:1). This vocabulary links God and king in vv. 1-15 (see v. 8). God's power to bring peace between enemies is frequently recounted, and it is presupposed in some places where it is not explicitly mentioned (Gen 26:26-32; 2 Sam 10:12, 19; 1 Kgs 8:50). Enemies may also be pacified through conquest (Ps 110:1;

Luke 20:43). Ultimately, God makes peace with and for human enemies (Rom 5:1, 10).

16:8. Verses 8a and 16a are near duplicates, alternating "righteousness" for "the fear of the LORD" respectively. These two expressions describe two inseparable, though distinct, aspects of one religious mode of human existence. This close relation of righteousness and reverence for Yahweh and the paradoxical character of v. 8 mean that this verse properly belongs in its present context, though Yahweh is not mentioned. It also anticipates the frequent mention of justice or righteousness in vv. 10-13, further tying the passages on Yahweh and the king closely together (see v. 7). To be righteous is to live in harmony with the righteous order that God has established in the cosmos. It also means that one's relationships with the earth, with other creatures, and with other people are as they ought to be. But such righteousness is inseparable from a right relation ("fear of the LORD") to the God who made, cares for, and judges all things wisely and rightly (3:19-20; 8:22-31; 16:14; Psalms 93–99; 104:24). Engagement with God is what sets humans in a right relation to this world and all that is in it (see Psalms 24; 119; 147). Verse 8 and related better-than proverbs state in a newly radical way the old truth that wisdom is better than wealth (see Commentary on 15:16). When wealth is a product of injustice (13:23), it becomes precarious and unstable (10:2; 11:4). The disordering of God's world, represented by wealth with wickedness or righteousness with little, will not forever endure (1 Sam 2:3-10; Ps 37:16-17; Luke 1:51-53). In the meantime, faith maintains its lived commitment to righteousness, even when the fruits of righteousness are not visible (Heb 11:39).

16:9. This verse is conceptually and verbally linked to v. 1 (see also v. 3); the two verses form an envelope around the theological themes of divine sovereignty and freedom in this passage. "Way" (דרך *derek*) here picks up a key idea from Proverbs 1–9: Life is a journey undertaken step by step, day by day, until we reach our goal. To plan our way is to take the long view of things; we plan a journey to accomplish something significant (Jas 4:13-16). But v. 9 presents a fine irony: God is master of things big and small, immediate and eternal. God makes secure each tiny, cumulative step, out of which a long journey

223. Michael Fishbane, *Biblical Interpretation in Ancient Israel* (Oxford: Clarendon, 1985) 347n. 80; J. Clinton McCann, Jr., *A Theological Introduction to the Book of Psalms* (Nashville: Abingdon, 1993) 54-55n. 9; R. C. Van Leeuwen, "Scribal Wisdom and Theodicy in the Book of the Twelve," in *In Search of Wisdom: Essays in Memory of John G. Gammie*, ed. Leo G. Perdue et al. (Louisville: Westminster/John Knox, 1993) 31-49. See, however, J. L. Crenshaw, "The Concept of God in Israelite Wisdom," in ibid., 1-18.

is made (Pss 66:9; 91:11-12; 121:3). Conversely, one false step, one slip, and all a person's grand plans can come to naught (27:1). In combination with 20:24, this proverb appears in the dark anthropological reflections of Jer 10:23 and the Qumran texts.

> I belong to evil humankind
> to the assembly of wicked flesh . . .
> For to man (does not belong) his path,
> nor to a human being the steadying of his
> step.[224]

16:10. The meaning of this verse is disputed. The root of "oracle" (קסם *qsm*) is elsewhere in the Old Testament translated "divination," a Gentile and Israelite practice generally disapproved of (Deut 18:10; 1 Sam 6:2; 28:8)—perhaps because prophecy became the means of divine revelation during the monarchy. But here *qesem* has a positive sense, seeming to suggest that the king's judgments are indisputable, endowed with God's wisdom (so NRSV's "inspired decisions" and the indicative "does not sin" in v. 10*b*; see 1 Kgs 3:9, 12, 28; Ps 72:1). Josephus asserts that the Hasmonean John Hyrcanus possessed not only the offices of ruler and high priest, but also a reliable prophetic gift.[225] However, in 2 Sam 14:17, 20, where the wise woman of Tekoa suggests the king is infallible, "like the angel of God, discerning good and evil" (NRSV), her irony is great (see Prov 29:26), because she has just shown how fallible the king's judgment has become. Often Israel's kings were less than Solomonic in their judgments. The NIV seeks to solve the problem by translating the verb in v. 10*b* modally, "should not betray." In this reading, the saying does not express what necessarily is, but what ought to be, since the king is God's representative for justice (8:15-16; 16:12; 25:5; 29:4; Psalm 72). Perhaps the best solution is to take seriously the idea of divination in *qesem*. Apparently, this word of itself is religiously neutral (even though most biblical occurrences put it in a negative context). It is here used to refer to a legitimate means of consulting God, such as with the Urim and Thummim. Then the sense is as follows: In a judicial case, when the king's lips report a divine judg-

224. 1QS XI:10-13, in F. G. Martínez, *The Dead Sea Scrolls Translated* 2nd ed. (Grand Rapids: Eerdmans, 1996) 18-19, 323. See also 1QH VII [= XV], 12-17.

225. Josephus *Antiquities of the Jews* XIII.299-300.

ment (conveyed by the casting of lots or some other device), his judgments do not err (see v. 33). An example is Saul's use of the lot in determining his son Jonathan as the one who violated the royal curse (1 Sam 14:37-42; see Josh 7:13-20).

16:11. The only proverb in vv. 10-15 that does not mention the king, v. 11 continues the mixture of divine and human work (v. 3) that runs throughout the two parts of vv. 1-15. The insertion of this Yahweh proverb among the royal sayings sets limits to the mighty powers of the king. In human terms, weights and measures are the king's responsibility; he must ensure that they are honest and consistent throughout the land (2 Sam 14:26). But the norms and practice of economic justice are a creation of God, even though they are carried out by humans (see Commentary on 11:1; Sir 42:4, 7). Economics is a particular, important instance of the broader principle that the world of human culture is a divine creation, placing human freedom within divine limits of justice and righteousness (see Commentary on 8:15-16; cf. Ps 33:4-5). The Hebrew word for "honest" (משפט *mišpāṭ*, or "justice") links vv. 8, 10-11; the closely related root for "righteous(ness)" (צדיק *ṣaddîq*) further links vv. 8, 12-13.

16:12-13. These verses comprise a proverb pair, linked in Hebrew by the initial opposition of "abomination of kings" versus "delight of kings" (see Commentary on v. 7; see also 14:35) and the stereotypical opposition of "wickedness" ("evil") and "righteousness" at the end of the first lines of these verses. Yahweh's justice (v. 11) is followed by the king's. The NRSV's "to do evil" better captures the ambiguity of the Hebrew in v. 12*a*. While it is obvious that for others to do evil is an abomination for kings (the primary point of the saying), it is also an abomination for kings themselves to do evil—a pattern abundant in Judah's and Israel's history. The ground for this pronouncement follows: righteousness establishes the "throne" (place of justice). In Egypt this principle was visually represented by the placement of the hieroglyph for *Maat* (cosmic order, justice = "righteousness") under the pharaoh's throne. This is one of the most basic principles of Judean kingship, for as agent of justice, the Davidic king imitates Yahweh, the heavenly king. The same terms describe Yahweh's throne and the earthly king's throne (Pss 9:4, 7-8; 89:14; 97:2; see Commentary on Prov 12:3; 20:8; 25:5).

Verse 13 flows from v. 12 because the speech the king "loves" is naturally understood as "honest" ("righteous") testimony in cases of law or justice. In this way also the king imitates Yahweh, the divine king (see 12:22).

16:14-15. The section on the king concludes with another proverb pair, which follows naturally upon the preceding one. Verse 14 presents death as a judicial consequence of what the king detests in v. 12 (see 25:4-5; 1 Kgs 2:24-46). Verse 15 portrays the life-giving favor of the king in terms of light from his face and the gracious clouds that bring spring rain, thus ensuring a fruitful summer harvest (see 19:12; 20:2; Jer 5:24; Hos 6:3). Once again the king's power to do good or ill reflects prerogatives of the heavenly king, Yahweh (negatively, see 2 Kgs 6:32-33; Ps 78:49-50; positively, see Num 6:25; Pss 4:6; 44:3; 89:15). The wise person in v. 14b appeases the king's wrath; the verb here is the same translated "atone" in v. 6. Once again the parallelism of God and king is reinforced.

16:16-17. The medieval Jewish scribes marked v. 17 as the middle verse in the book of Proverbs. Verse 16 appears to be an editorial link to themes from chaps. 1–9. Proverbs 3:13-14; 4:5, 7; and 8:10-11, 19 supply most of its vocabulary and ideas (see Commentary on 3:13-18; 8:11). The effect is to link the center of the book (which is also near the center of the Solomonic subsections, 10:1–15:33 and 16:1–22:16) to chaps. 1–9 as the book's hermeneutical prologue with its pervasive instruction to "get wisdom."

Verse 17 picks up the symbolism of life as a journey, which pervades Proverbs 1–9 (see Overview to Prov 1:1–9:18). Proverbs 15:19b provides the clue to the unique expression "highway of the upright." In Hebrew, the predicate "avoids evil" is an infinitive phrase, "to turn from evil." This predicate is ambiguous, as is its relation to the upright's highway. The word translated "evil" (רע rā ') can indicate greater or lesser trouble (13:14; 14:27), which would fit this verse's connection with 15:19b. To paraphrase v. 17a in this sense, "the leveled road of the upright is a highway that avoids trouble." This goes nicely with v. 17b: The upright take good care of the path that is their

life's journey, and thus they preserve themselves (for "guard" used in the sense of "take good care of," see 27:18; Job 27:18; Isa 27:3). But more often to avoid evil in Proverbs refers to turning from what is ethically wrong, an action that befits the fear of the Lord (3:7; 16:6; the related idea, "to hate evil," is uniquely connected with the fear of Yahweh in 8:13). To paraphrase, "to turn from wrongdoing is a crucial means by which the leveled road of the upright is created and guarded." By turning from wrongdoing in this sense, the upright preserve the integrity of their life-journey and of themselves (נפשׁ nepeš connotes both "life" and "self"; see 19:16; 22:5). For the "upright," there is a dual, divine-human agency to guarding one's way (see 2:6-8; 16:9).

16:18-19. These verses form a proverb pair, for which 25:6-7 provides a concrete illustration. Proverbs 18:12a is a condensed variant of v. 18. The contrast of pride and humility is conveyed in the imagery of high and low: a "haughty spirit" versus "a lowly spirit" (see Commentary on v. 5). "Poor in spirit" conveys a similar idea (Matt 5:3). The Lord has little tolerance for the proud (3:34; 15:25). Thus proper humility is a matter not only of human relations, but also of godly wisdom. It is the only realistic posture in a world that we do not ultimately control, though we remain responsible agents (see Commentary on 6:17; 11:2; 15:33; 16:1-9; 26:12). "To share the plunder" usually has a military context (Exod 15:9; but see 1:13; 31:11). The Hebrew terms for "pride" and "proud" (גאון gā 'ôn) provide another link between this section of chap. 16 and chap. 8 (8:13, "pride" and "arrogance").

16:20-24. These verses are intensely intertwined thematically and verbally, and they possess a certain logic concerning wisdom communicated by speech. One must first hear a "word" and trust God (v. 20) before one is recognized as wise in heart and speech (vv. 21, 23). The root שׂכל (śkl, "to have insight or understanding") is a key word uniting vv. 20 and 22-23. It suggests that understanding is a "fountain of life" (v. 22; see 10:11) not just to those who have it, but also to those who hear it through the medium of wise speech (vv. 20, 21-24; see 10:11; 13:14). The seemingly unrelated v. 22b (lit., "but the instruction of fools is folly"), then, finds its place as a negative contrast to wise speech (see Commentary on 14:24).

16:20. In v. 20*a,* the NIV and NRSV translations are interpretations of a deceptively simple Hebrew text. The somewhat literal KJV reads, "He that handleth a matter wisely shall find good." This interpretation joins wise conduct of human affairs with trusting God. But "matter" translates דבר (*dābār,* also "word," "thing"). Thus v. 20*a* may also refer to paying proper attention to a spoken word that refers to some significant matter, perhaps a legal case (see 18:13*a,* 17; 25:2). In v. 20, however, *dābār* more naturally refers to God's Word, since this makes better sense of the whole proverb and its literary context. This reading joins obedience to God (v. 20*a*) with trust in God (v. 20*b*). Giving heed to a word is never merely cognitive; it entails obedience, as in 1 Sam 3:9-10. While the word may be from a wisdom teacher (so NIV's "instruction"), *dābār* in Proverbs by itself never clearly conveys this (see Commentary on 13:13, the only parallel). In keeping with the elliptical style of Proverbs, Yahweh, who is implicit in v. 20*a,* becomes explicit in v. 20*b.* The Lord blesses the persons who trust in the Lord (a variant of 3:5; see 28:25, 29; 29:25). The phrase "shall find good" (not "will prosper") is also used of those who find a good wife (18:22), which in turn is parallel to the "blessed" activity of finding Wisdom as wife (see Commentary on 3:13; 8:35; 19:8; 31:10). Such verbal links further strengthen the ties connecting chaps. 3; 8; and 16.

16:21-23. In Hebrew, vv. 21 and 23 exhibit verbal/thematic repetitions in their beginnings ("heart"/"wise," in chiastic sequence; see 10:8) and endings ("lips"/"promotes instruction"). Pleasant speech is literally "sweetness of the lips." "Sweetness" as a metaphor for wise, persuasive speech is common and links vv. 21 and 24 (see 24:13; 27:9?). Compare the American proverb, "You catch more flies with honey than with vinegar." The expressions "wise," "promotes instruction" (= "add . . . learning"), and "discerning" all appear in 1:5, of which 16:21 may be an editorial echo (see 9:9).

16:24. In Proverbs, honey and sweetness are significant symbols of true or bogus wisdom and of the verbal or nonverbal packaging in which they come (see Commentary on 5:3; 9:17; 16:21; 24:13; 25:16, 27). "Soul" (נפש *nepeš*) is also "appetite" (as in 13:19; 16:26), "life," or "person" (for "health to the body" see 3:8; 4:22; 14:30;

15:4, 30; "pleasant words" appears in 15:26, but not in 16:21, contrary to the translations).

16:25. For details on this verse, see the Commentary on Prov 14:12; 16:2.

16:26. The NIV and the NRSV provide a straightforward translation of this verse, although the Hebrew is not entirely certain. The need to eat drives one to work (Eccl 6:7; 2 Thess 3:10).

16:27-30. These verses form a group of sayings on negative speech as being destructive of community (v. 28*a;* see 6:14, 19; 17:9). In its terminology and ideas, it has many connections with the two catalogues of vice in 6:12-15, 16-19. Verses 27-29 all begin with איש (*'îš*), "a man of. . . . " The form of v. 30 is different, but reveals some signals by which the wicked are known (see 6:13). In v. 27, for the term "scoundrel" (see Commentary on 6:12). For "the violent" who verbally entice their neighbor into a wicked way (v. 29), see Commentary on 1:10, 15.

16:31. Gray hair was a symbol of wisdom throughout the ancient Near East. Traditional cultures believe that only those persons with abundant life experience can be wise (see Commentary on 8:22-31; 20:29). But the sages were also aware that "there's no fool like an old fool." Thus they add that such wisdom is gained only through a righteous life (lit., "way of righteousness"). The image of the way once again suggests that only through the consistent, persistent long haul is a life crowned with glory and wisdom. Yet, from another perspective, such a crown is a gift (4:9).

16:32. This verse is a better-than saying that subtly praises the quiet, inner mastery of oneself over the more macho public conquest of the warrior-hero. Without the disciplined, wise conquest of oneself, mastery of the external world and its problems—in any area and of every sort—is not possible. The self can be an unruly city inhabited by rebellious feelings that disturb its effective integrity and destroy its self-preserving boundaries (see Commentary on 25:28). Proverbs 24:5-6 and Eccl 9:13-18 take the contrast of might and wisdom in different directions. For "slow to anger," see Commentary on 15:18; 25:15.

16:33. The chapter ends with a return to the theme of its beginning: the mystery of divine sovereignty in the midst of human plans and actions (see esp. Commentary on 16:1, 9). For the "lot" as a means of reaching decisions, see

Commentary on 16:10; 18:18. The practice was apparently common in various contexts in which human powers of discrimination and decision were inadequate (see Exod 28:30-31; Lev 16:8-10; Jonah 1:7).

REFLECTIONS

1. Proverbs 16:1-9 focuses on the Lord in a way that sets radical limits to human wisdom. The juxtaposition of these sayings generates a theological dialectic whose sense is greater than that of the individual sayings. To this point the book has largely focused on the ABC's of wisdom: the nature of the world, the need to fear the Lord, the nexus of acts and consequences, and the conflict of wise and foolish, wicked and righteous. But the focus on Yahweh in 16:1-9 marks a shift in pedagogy and profundity that makes the wisdom of Proverbs as a whole more rich—and difficult. Here the book begins to develop a theological depth and complexity it has not possessed to this point. In God's freedom and sovereignty, human wisdom—for all its goodness and indispensability—finds its radical limits.[226] In the mystery of world and human-kind, the sages encountered the mystery of God, who answers finally to no one else. God is not answerable to us humans, nor subject to our manipulations and theological demands (cf. Rom 3:3-8; 11:33-36).

Consequently, in this second Solomonic sub-collection the reader begins to encounter the exceptions to the rules of acts and consequences laid out so simply in chaps. 10–15. Far from providing a warrant for a health-and-wealth gospel, these chapters show that sometimes the wicked prosper and the righteous suffer, contrary to all normal expectations.[227] Here it becomes clear that even believers do not have God or reality figured out. Thus the fear of the Lord (see 1:7; 3:5-8) is here coupled with humility and discipline (see Commentary on 15:33). This section calls for obedient faith without presumptuous arrogance.

2. We are responsible for the plans of our hearts, for the steps we take, and for the answers on our tongue (16:1, 9). And so, at first glance, the route from inner heart to outer speech and action seems direct and unproblematic to us. Yet God is sovereignly present even here (see 21:1). This mysterious reality comes to the fore in two opposite ways. On the one hand, being overly confident in human outcomes can be unexpectedly subverted by an unintended slip. Here, to our dismay, the limits of our control over even our inner and outer selves may be painfully evident (cf. Jas 3:1-12; Excursus, "The 'Heart' in the Old Testament," 60-61).

On the other hand, sometimes persons in situations of great moment or difficulty are graced to speak more wisely and bravely than they or others could imagine (see Matt 10:19-20). Of this phenomenon and proverb, von Rad writes that

> the road from . . . plans to the . . . appropriate word . . . "at the right time," is a long one and much can happen in the meantime which is outside [human] control. But God is there precisely in this incalculable element, and at a single stroke which you have scarcely noticed, he has taken the whole affair out of your hands.[228]

3. Human self-delusion about what is pure (16:2; 20:11; 21:8) ranges over every area of our lives, but what looks good to us is not necessarily so in God's eyes (see Commentary on 3:7-8). Proverbs 16:2 does not portray the arrogant evil of those who plot wrong and imagine God does not see it (Ps 64:68). Rather, this is the deception of hypocrites, who sense the requirement of purity, but deceive themselves about their conformity to it (20:9)—hypocrisy

---

226. Von Rad's chapter on "The Limits of Wisdom" remains indispensable. See G. von Rad, *Wisdom in Israel* (Nashville: Abingdon, 1972) 97-110.
227. On this theme, see R. C. Van Leeuwen, "On Wealth and Poverty: System and Contradiction in Proverbs," *Hebrew Studies* 33 (1992).
228. Von Rad, *Wisdom in Israel*, 100.

being the homage vice pays to virtue. The story of David's anointing sharply reveals the absolute superiority of divine over human perceptions (1 Sam 16:6-7; 17:28). The apostle Paul applies the principle of 16:2 to himself (1 Cor 4:3-5).

4. When God works good through wicked persons, the wickedness is theirs and the goodness God's (16:4). All creatures, wicked persons included, have their ground of being and goal in God alone. Having made them, God takes them up into the unfathomable divine plan and makes them subservient to good ends (Gen 45:4-8; 50:20; Exod 9:16; Eph 1:5-11). In a similar vein, God has made the poor, a fact that points to their dignity, while leaving the causality of their poverty unspecified (22:2; 29:13). When Isa 45:7 says that God makes peace and creates evil ("evil" = "trouble" in Prov 16:4; see Amos 3:6), it is to make God's justice known (Isa 45:6; Ezek 38:22-23). The mysterious thought of Prov 16:4 plays an important role in early Judaism and Christianity alike. It provides a base for reflection on the justice of God, especially when painful history renders God's justice difficult to believe. Sometimes the approach is to develop a rational theodicy. The Jewish sage Sirach develops such a theodicy based partly on this verse (Sir 39:16-35; see Sir 33:7-15). Ecclesiastes 7:13-14 insists on human limits, but the hymns of the Qumran community develop Prov 16:4 in the direction of an earnest double predestination: The righteous are predestined to life, but

> the wicked you have created for the time of wrath,
> from the womb you have predestined them for the day of annihilation.
> For they walk on paths that are not good,
> they reject your covenant
>
> .   .   .   .
>
> Instead they choose what you hate.[229]

Paul also wrestles with the mystery of 16:4 in Rom 9:19-24, and this leads him, eventually, to the great doxology of Rom 11:33-36.

229. 1QH 7[15]:21-23, in Martínez, *The Dead Sea Scrolls Translated*, 323.

Proverbs 17:1-28, Better a Dry Crust with Peace and Quiet

NIV	NRSV
17 Better a dry crust with peace and quiet than a house full of feasting,[a] with strife.	**17** Better is a dry morsel with quiet than a house full of feasting with strife.
[2] A wise servant will rule over a disgraceful son, and will share the inheritance as one of the brothers.	[2] A slave who deals wisely will rule over a child who acts shamefully, and will share the inheritance as one of the family.
[3] The crucible for silver and the furnace for gold, but the LORD tests the heart.	[3] The crucible is for silver, and the furnace is for gold, but the LORD tests the heart.
[4] A wicked man listens to evil lips; a liar pays attention to a malicious tongue.	[4] An evildoer listens to wicked lips; and a liar gives heed to a mischievous tongue.
[5] He who mocks the poor shows contempt for their Maker; whoever gloats over disaster will not go unpunished.	[5] Those who mock the poor insult their Maker; those who are glad at calamity will not go unpunished.
	[6] Grandchildren are the crown of the aged, and the glory of children is their parents.

a1 Hebrew *sacrifices*

NIV

⁶Children's children are a crown to the aged,
  and parents are the pride of their children.

⁷Arrogant^a lips are unsuited to a fool—
  how much worse lying lips to a ruler!

⁸A bribe is a charm to the one who gives it;
  wherever he turns, he succeeds.

⁹He who covers over an offense promotes love,
  but whoever repeats the matter separates
  close friends.

¹⁰A rebuke impresses a man of discernment
  more than a hundred lashes a fool.

¹¹An evil man is bent only on rebellion;
  a merciless official will be sent against him.

¹²Better to meet a bear robbed of her cubs
  than a fool in his folly.

¹³If a man pays back evil for good,
  evil will never leave his house.

¹⁴Starting a quarrel is like breaching a dam;
  so drop the matter before a dispute breaks
  out.

¹⁵Acquitting the guilty and condemning the
  innocent—
  the LORD detests them both.

¹⁶Of what use is money in the hand of a fool,
  since he has no desire to get wisdom?

¹⁷A friend loves at all times,
  and a brother is born for adversity.

¹⁸A man lacking in judgment strikes hands in
  pledge
  and puts up security for his neighbor.

¹⁹He who loves a quarrel loves sin;
  he who builds a high gate invites destruction.

²⁰A man of perverse heart does not prosper;
  he whose tongue is deceitful falls into trouble.

²¹To have a fool for a son brings grief;
  there is no joy for the father of a fool.

²²A cheerful heart is good medicine,
  but a crushed spirit dries up the bones.

²³A wicked man accepts a bribe in secret
  to pervert the course of justice.

²⁴A discerning man keeps wisdom in view,

^a7 Or *Eloquent*

NRSV

⁷ Fine speech is not becoming to a fool;
  still less is false speech to a ruler.^a

⁸ A bribe is like a magic stone in the eyes of
  those who give it;
  wherever they turn they prosper.

⁹ One who forgives an affront fosters friendship,
  but one who dwells on disputes will alienate
  a friend.

¹⁰ A rebuke strikes deeper into a discerning
  person
  than a hundred blows into a fool.

¹¹ Evil people seek only rebellion,
  but a cruel messenger will be sent against
  them.

¹² Better to meet a she-bear robbed of its cubs
  than to confront a fool immersed in folly.

¹³ Evil will not depart from the house
  of one who returns evil for good.

¹⁴ The beginning of strife is like letting out water;
  so stop before the quarrel breaks out.

¹⁵ One who justifies the wicked and one who
  condemns the righteous
  are both alike an abomination to the LORD.

¹⁶ Why should fools have a price in hand
  to buy wisdom, when they have no mind
  to learn?

¹⁷ A friend loves at all times,
  and kinsfolk are born to share adversity.

¹⁸ It is senseless to give a pledge,
  to become surety for a neighbor.

¹⁹ One who loves transgression loves strife;
  one who builds a high threshold invites
  broken bones.

²⁰ The crooked of mind do not prosper,
  and the perverse of tongue fall into calamity.

²¹ The one who begets a fool gets trouble;
  the parent of a fool has no joy.

²² A cheerful heart is a good medicine,
  but a downcast spirit dries up the bones.

²³ The wicked accept a concealed bribe
  to pervert the ways of justice.

²⁴ The discerning person looks to wisdom,
  but the eyes of a fool to the ends of the
  earth.

²⁵ Foolish children are a grief to their father
  and bitterness to her who bore them.

²⁶ To impose a fine on the innocent is not right,

^aOr *a noble person*

NIV

but a fool's eyes wander to the ends of the earth.

25A foolish son brings grief to his father
and bitterness to the one who bore him.

26It is not good to punish an innocent man,
or to flog officials for their integrity.

27A man of knowledge uses words with restraint,
and a man of understanding is even-tempered.

28Even a fool is thought wise if he keeps silent,
and discerning if he holds his tongue.

NRSV

or to flog the noble for their integrity.
27 One who spares words is knowledgeable;
one who is cool in spirit has understanding.
28 Even fools who keep silent are considered wise;
when they close their lips, they are deemed intelligent.

COMMENTARY

17:1. This chapter opens with a better-than saying (see Commentary on 15:16-17). In a family or "house," amiable relations are more important than bounty (15:17). The troubled history of David's house amply displays the insufficiency of bounty (2 Sam 13–19; 1 Kgs 1–2). In the subsistence economy of Israelite peasants, this proverb has a sharpness and depth that may escape affluent readers. The morsel of bread is dry because there is no sauce or olive oil to dip it into (19:24). "Feasting with strife" is literally "sacrifices of conflict" (ריב *rîb*). The principal occasions for eating meat were religious festivals or ceremonies at which sacrifices were offered and then consumed. Only the wealthy could afford abundant ("a house full," see 1:13) sacrifices of meat (see Deut 12:7; 1 Sam 9:12-13, 22-24; 20:6, 29). The picture is of a "religious," wealthy household in which public piety is married to internecine conflict—a topic taken up in the next verse. Perhaps the religious activity and conspicuous consumption are a cover for family dysfunction.

17:2. Like v. 1, this verse subverts ordinary Israelite expectations about family values. It asserts that wisdom is a higher good that reverses the usual evaluation of son over slave. At the same time, it reaffirms the family virtues by implying that sons must measure up to certain standards. (In Israel, women generally did not inherit property, but see Num 27:1-11; 36:1-12). It does this by calling the servant "wise" (see Commentary on 16:20-24) and the son "disgraceful," perhaps

because of laziness, as in 10:5 (see also 12:24). Ordinarily, it would be considered outrageous for a social inferior from outside the family to take a son's place. Thus 19:10*b* and 30:21-23 object to the idea that a servant (see Commentary on 14:35; 22:7) will rule.

17:3. Verse 3*a* is identical to 27:21*a*. Precious metals are tested and purified through smelting and pouring off dross. The process is used here as an image of God's knowing, and perhaps refining, the quality or purity of the human heart (see Excursus, "The 'Heart' in the Old Testament," 60-61). For God's knowledge of the inner person, see Commentary on 15:11; 16:2; 20:27; 21:2; 24:12. This (divine) testing may work through human agency (27:21).

17:4. This verse may be compared to the portrait of the wicked in Ps 52:1-4. Even the wicked, whether king or commoner, are known and shaped by the company they keep (see Commentary on 14:7; 29:12; see also Ps 101:5, 7). Our character determines to whom we listen and is in turn determined by those to whom we listen. This circle can be either vicious or virtuous (13:20). Speech is the instrument that shapes good or bad community (see v. 7).

17:5. The writer condemns malicious laughter at a poor person as a mockery of God (see Commentary on 14:31). The laughter of Wisdom at calamity is different (see Commentary on 1:26-27). Verse 5*b* expands the thought to condemn any joy at another person's misery.

17:6. This verse expresses the generational and familial perspective of biblical thinking (see Commentary on 13:22; 27:10-11; see also Psalms 127–128). Three generations are joined in a chain of fathers and sons (so the patriarchal Hebrew) in which one link finds its "glory" and "crown" in another (these terms are joined in 16:31). This picture of an unbroken family, lasting over the generations, contrasts with the sad collapse of family seen in vv. 1-2.

17:7. This verse is one of three sayings on things unbecoming or not fitting (see 19:10; 26:1; for things not good, see 17:26; 18:5; 19:2; 20:23; 25:27; 28:21). The principle of fittingness is basic to wisdom (see Commentary on 26:1-12). "Fool" here translates a term used infrequently in Proverbs, נבל (nābāl; elsewhere in Proverbs only 17:21; 30:22; see 1 Sam 25:25; Job 30:8). Whybray states that the term denotes someone who "takes a negative stance in every area of life, contributes nothing . . . gives no help, respects nothing, is a nothing, and who ought therefore to be excluded from normal society."[230]

"Fine speech" (not "arrogant lips"), which does good to others, is simply out of character for such a person. Even more unfitting is that a ruler (or "person of noble character"; see v. 26) should lie, because the lies of the powerful, especially when they are trusted, do all the more damage (see Ps 120:2). Conversely, those in power should not listen to lies, no matter how persuasive (see v. 4; 12:22; 15:4; 29:12). The famous opening of Socrates' defense is a masterful illustration of this saying.[231]

17:8. Bribes are regularly condemned in the OT as a means of perverting justice (see Commentary on 15:27; 17:23). The parallelism in 21:14 shows that the line between what is a bribe and a legitimate gift could be difficult to draw. This verse, however, seems ironic, because the bribe's success is assessed in terms of the briber's opinion—which could be quite wrong (for "in the eyes of," see Commentary on 12:15). So, while this saying may simply observe bribery in action, its more likely target is human blindness that does not see God, who "takes no bribe" (Deut 10:17 NRSV).

230. R. N. Whybray, *Proverbs,* NCB (Grand Rapids: Eerdmans, 1994) 255-56.
231. See Plato *Apology.*

17:9. This verse is one of a group of sayings about love or hate covering or revealing things, rightly or wrongly, foolishly or wisely (see also 10:12, 18; 11:13; 12:16, 23). Whether revealing or covering something (also in the sense of forgiving or passing over; see 19:11), what is right or wrong depends on motive (love or hate), on what fits the concrete situation (26:1-12), and on the results: social strife or harmony. To "repeat a matter" is gossip that disrupts friendship (16:28).

17:10. "A word to the wise is sufficient" implies that many words are not enough for a fool. Some people learn only from painful experience, the "school of hard knocks" (see Commentary on 19:29; 26:3-5). The second line is hyperbole, since the law forbids more than forty lashes, lest a person be demeaned (Deut 25:3; 2 Cor 11:24). The fool here is one who is self-satisfied, verging on "wise in one's own eyes" (26:12). Because they "know it all," such persons resist correction and admonition (13:1; 15:10, 12, 31-32). For the problem of corporal punishment, see Commentary on 13:24 and 23:13-14.

17:11-15. A section concerning situations of conflict begins (implicitly) and ends (explicitly) with the mysterious judgment of God operating in and through human conflict. Verse 15 is a particular (legal) instance of the inversion of right and wrong, stated more broadly in v. 13 (see Isa 5:20, 23).

17:11. The word translated "rebellion" (מרי mĕrî) consistently refers to defiance of God, as in 1 Sam 15:23 (cf. Isa 30:9; Ezek 2:8; 44:6). Since the Creator defines good and evil, wrongdoers necessarily set themselves in opposition to God. Sin is not simply moral disorder; it is rebellion against the Creator. The second line refers vaguely to God's judgment against rebels, much on the political model of 16:4 (see Ps 78:49, where "angel" = "messenger").

17:12. "A bear robbed of her cubs" is a proverbial expression for a bitterly angry and dangerous enemy (2 Sam 17:8; Hos 13:8). The proverb is ironic and playful; to meet a fool is even worse. But the hyperbole suggests that the quiet, often unnoticed, damage done to people by fools can be more hurtful than the spectacular calamities that make the headlines. There may be a connection between vv. 11 and 12. In 2 Kgs 2:23-24, bears are sent in judgment, one might say as cruel messengers from God. For the damage done by fools, see 1:32; 10:1; 13:20; 17:21; 18:6-7; 26:6.

17:13. Returning evil for good is an outrageous inversion of the way things should be (Ps 109:5; Jer 18:20). David rages that Nabal (see Commentary on 17:7) has returned him evil for good, and David wrongly plans to get revenge (1 Sam 25:21; cf. 1 Sam 24:17). Eventually God vindicates David and judges Nabal and Saul, Nabal's royal counterpart (see Prov 20:22; 25:21-22; Lev 19:17-18). Joseph makes the same accusation against his brothers (Gen 44:4), but in his story grace breaks through the reproductive cycle of evil begetting evil. Even with grace, repentance, and forgiveness, a certain amount of trouble gets passed on through the generations of a family or house (2 Sam 12:7-12).

17:14. A quarrel is best stopped before it has begun. Once water has broken the dam, you cannot put it back in.

17:15. This verse provides a significant example of the difficulty of translating OT terms into English. The roots usually translated "righteous" (צדק *ṣdq*) and "wicked" (רשע *rš'*), when used in a legal context as here, refer to the innocent and the guilty. Similarly, the verbs "justifies" (מצדיק *maṣdîq*) and "condemns" (מרשיע *maršîa'*)—which tend to have theological connotations for Protestant NT readers—translate the same roots as "innocent"/"righteous" and "wicked"/"guilty" respectively; the NRSV obscures the forensic context, as the NIV does not. Judges who invert justice (18:5; Exod 23:6-8; Deut 25:1; Isa 5:23) are an abomination to God (see Commentary on 11:1).

17:16. It is implied here that wisdom was taught by paid teachers, though the practice is not attested in Israel before Ben Sira in Hellenistic times. The matter is uncertain, for the proverb itself may be as late as the Hellenistic period, or it may use the image of purchasing as a metaphor (see Isa 55:1-3). It seems unlikely, however, that monarchical Israel, with its highly sophisticated literature, should lack paid teachers (see Mic 3:11, where the priests teach for pay but should not). The main point is that money cannot buy wisdom, if a person lacks the intellectual-spiritual equipment to get it (lit., "heart"; see 16:16; 19:8; 23:23; 24:7).

17:17-18. These verses are a proverb pair whose connection in English is obscured because the same Hebrew word (רע *rēa'*) is translated "friend" in v. 17, but "neighbor" in v. 18. The determination of *rēa'* in v. 17 by the definite article "the friend" strengthens the connection between the verses, since *rēa'* in v. 18 is also definite. The definiteness shows the closeness of the relationship in each case).[232] Together the sayings communicate more than they would individually.

The true character of love is revealed by its constancy over time, but especially by its conduct in adversity (v. 9). The *rēa'* in v. 17 is compared to a brother who is obligated to his siblings by birth. Alternately, "brother" is a metaphor for a friend who has become like family. The friendship of David and Jonathan is an example (1 Sam 18:1-4; 2 Sam 1:26). While people are given their siblings, they choose their friends. Yet some friends reveal more of faithful love than siblings do (18:24*b*; 27:10). Such persons are not "fair-weather friends."

Verse 18, however, shows that the *rēa'* (true "friend" or greedy "neighbor"?) is an ambiguous relation (see 14:20; 19:4, 6-7). To one you can entrust your life; to the other you should not trust your cash (19:4). Wise persons know what sort of *rēa'* they are dealing with and act accordingly. On putting up security for one's neighbor/friend, see Commentary on 6:1-5.

17:19. The translation of this verse is obscure because the expression "to make one's opening/door high" is not understood. The NRSV is somewhat loose; the door/opening is not a threshold, and "bones" is not in the Hebrew. This translation interprets the metaphor: If you raise your threshold too high, people will trip over it and get hurt. On this reading, the wicked intentionally set up obstacles that create conflict in relationships. The NIV is straightforward, but also obscure. Some think the "high gate" is a metaphor for pride (see Commentary on 16:5, 18). Finally the "opening" may refer to a (proud) mouth (see 1 Sam 2:3; Mic 7:5). The matter remains uncertain. Verse 19*a* simply juxtaposes "one loving

---

232. The definite article in 17:17 virtually functions as a possessive, "one's friend" rather than "a friend." See Bruce K. Waltke and M. O'Connor, *An Introduction to Biblical Hebrew Syntax* (Winona Lake: Eisenbrauns, 1990) 243,¶13.5.1e.

transgression" and "one loving strife." Thus the ambiguity reflected in the NIV's and the NRSV's inversion of subjects and predicates. Some people love to stir up trouble (10:12).

17:20. The "crooked of heart" (cf. v. 10) are an abomination to God (11:20). The phrase "will not prosper" is literally, "will not find good" (see Commentary on 16:20). The person here portrayed is also twisted in tongue, the heart's outer expression. The two lines express a simple character-consequence connection. But v. 20b is ambiguous; it may be translated, "one perverted by his tongue [i.e., of the crooked of heart; see 21:6] will fall into trouble." This makes the saying more complex: the speech of one crooked person twists another to make him or her fall.

17:21-22. Like v. 25, v. 21 is a variant, perhaps editorial, on 10:1. "Fool" in v. 21b translates נבל (nābāl; see Commentary on 17:7).

Verse 22 is closely parallel to 15:13 (see also 14:30). The first lines are identical, except here the uncertain word גהה (gēhâ) replaces "face" in 15:27a. The word possibly refers to a body part, like the face. The NRSV translation, "is good medicine," relates the word to a rare verb, "to heal," used in Hos 5:13. "Bone" (singular) refers to the inner person, deprived of the vital juices of the spirit.

17:23. This verse portrays the blatant corruption of justice (see 1 Kgs 21:8-14, where bribery of witnesses is to be assumed). The problem is not that there is a bribe (or "gift," 15:27), but that it is concealed—that is, it does not conform to public standards concerning just and appropriate payment for services rendered. Such sayings show that proverbial wisdom is in harmony with Israel's legal and prophetic traditions concerning justice (18:5; 21:14; Exod 23:6-8; Deut 16:18-20). For the "bribe," see Commentary on 15:27; 17:8.

17:24. Wisdom is near to one who is discerning, but distant and inaccessible for the fool who seeks it at "the ends of the earth" (see Commentary on 8:9; 14:6; Deut 30:11-13). The first line of the verse may be translated, "Wisdom is in front of the discerning person."

17:25. For discussion of this verse, see the Commentary on Prov 10:1; 17:21.

17:26. Again the inversion of good and evil is given attention here, specifically in the crucial arena of justice (v. 15). It is one of several sayings using the predicate "not good" (see Commentary on 17:7). The proverb does not explain why these things are not good, but assumes it is obvious. It is wrong to "punish" or "fine" (see 21:11; 22:3) an innocent person (see Commentary on 17:13, 15). Similarly, to flog officials (see 8:16) or persons of "noble" character is wicked, especially when they are flogged for their integrity (properly, "uprightness"). The Hebrew term for "noble" (נדיבים nĕdîbîm) has somewhat the range of the English (see v. 7; 19:6; Isa 32:5-8).

17:27-28. These verses are a proverb pair on the complex relationship between wisdom and folly, speech and silence. The ability to refrain from speech, to speak only with deliberation, is an indispensable aspect of wisdom (see Commentary on 15:28; 10:18-19). Job wishes his false comforters would show their wisdom by keeping silent (Job 13:5). But silence is only a sign of wisdom; even fools can fake it. Yet there may be some gentle, pedagogical irony here: If you are a fool, at least act wise by keeping silent—though it may be difficult (18:2). Others will consider you wise, and, curiously, in recognizing your own personal limitations, you will have made a crucial step on the road to wisdom (see Commentary on 15:33; 16:18-19).

REFLECTIONS

1. In contrast to American individualism, in which individuals choose to join groups, or leave them,[233] the Israelites believed that families are an inescapable given, prior to and more lasting than the individual.[234] In this regard, Americans are profoundly at odds with the biblical

233. Robert N. Bellah, et al., *Habits of the Heart: Individualism and Commitment in American Life* (Berkeley: University of California: 1985) 142-95, esp. 167; and *Individualism and Commitment in American Life: Readings on the Themes of Habits of the Heart* (New York: Harper & Row, 1987).

234. The standard, highly illuminating work on this general topic is Harry C. Triandis, *Individualism and Collectivism* (Boulder, Col.: Westview, 1995).

worldview, often without being aware of it. Our individualism is like a blinder that obscures the critical light the Bible sheds on our society. If we can discard our cultural blinders and learn from ancient Israel, we might see our own society more critically and seek to change ourselves and it for the better.

Proverbs, and the Bible generally, understand family differently and more profoundly than is possible with individualistic assumptions. From Scripture we learn that even when we flee from our families, or are divorced by them, we take them with us—as the Jacob and Joseph stories so profoundly show (Genesis 26–50). In the beginning, we get our identity, even our language, in and through family. In the course of life, we inevitably find and mold that identity in terms of those relations.

Yet, from within Israel's collectivist culture, Prov 17:2 asserts that there are realities more basic than family. Wisdom, godliness, and divine grace can override such natural relations. The stories that exemplify 17:2 often concern women. Rahab and Ruth are wise outsiders who enter the Israelite family at its messianic, Davidic center (Joshua 2; 6:17-25; Ruth 4:13-22; Matt 1:5; Jas 2:25). Grace regularly promotes younger brothers over their elders: Abel, Isaac, Jacob, David, and the nation Israel over its international older "sibling," Egypt (Exod 4:22-23). And grace can break the power of canceled sin that binds one generation to another (see Exod 34:6-7).

In a wisdom speech equally as sharp as Prov 17:2, Jesus insists that discipleship is greater than family (Mark 3:31-34). For Paul, Christians are slaves who have become heirs and children of God by adoptive grace (Gal 3:26–4:7). Christians should thus neither underestimate nor overvalue the importance of the family. Individualistic Americans need to repent of their neglect of family. But for those whose families have been instruments of violence and abuse, the good news is that grace makes us members of God's family, even as it makes us new persons (Rom 12:2).

2. Do those who mock the less fortunate (17:5*a*) imagine that they themselves are immune to woe (Psalms 49; 73:4-9)? Rich and poor, good and bad, black and white, we all share one Maker and die one death (22:2; 29:13). Joy at another's calamity (17:5*b*), what Germans call *Schadenfreude,* is a twisted child of envy. It is not even covetousness, which desires another's goods, hoping that "if you lose, I win." Envy simply takes pleasure in another person's ill fortune.[235] Against such sins, Prov 17:5 levels the same warning as given elsewhere against godless pride and blasphemy: It will not go unpunished (see Commentary on 16:5-6; Deut 5:11).

235. See Cornelius Plantinga, Jr., *Not the Way It's Supposed to Be: A Breviary of Sin* (Grand Rapids: Eerdmans, 1995) 157-72.

Proverbs 18:1-24, A Fool Takes No Pleasure in Understanding

NIV	NRSV
18 An unfriendly man pursues selfish ends; he defies all sound judgment.	**18** The one who lives alone is self-indulgent, showing contempt for all who have sound judgment.[a]
[2] A fool finds no pleasure in understanding but delights in airing his own opinions.	[2] A fool takes no pleasure in understanding, but only in expressing personal opinion.
[3] When wickedness comes, so does contempt, and with shame comes disgrace.	[3] When wickedness comes, contempt comes also;
[4] The words of a man's mouth are deep waters,	*a* Meaning of Heb uncertain

NIV

but the fountain of wisdom is a bubbling brook.

⁵It is not good to be partial to the wicked
or to deprive the innocent of justice.

⁶A fool's lips bring him strife,
and his mouth invites a beating.

⁷A fool's mouth is his undoing,
and his lips are a snare to his soul.

⁸The words of a gossip are like choice morsels;
they go down to a man's inmost parts.

⁹One who is slack in his work
is brother to one who destroys.

¹⁰The name of the LORD is a strong tower;
the righteous run to it and are safe.

¹¹The wealth of the rich is their fortified city;
they imagine it an unscalable wall.

¹²Before his downfall a man's heart is proud,
but humility comes before honor.

¹³He who answers before listening—
that is his folly and his shame.

¹⁴A man's spirit sustains him in sickness,
but a crushed spirit who can bear?

¹⁵The heart of the discerning acquires knowledge;
the ears of the wise seek it out.

¹⁶A gift opens the way for the giver
and ushers him into the presence of the great.

¹⁷The first to present his case seems right,
till another comes forward and questions him.

¹⁸Casting the lot settles disputes
and keeps strong opponents apart.

¹⁹An offended brother is more unyielding than a fortified city,
and disputes are like the barred gates of a citadel.

²⁰From the fruit of his mouth a man's stomach is filled;
with the harvest from his lips he is satisfied.

²¹The tongue has the power of life and death,
and those who love it will eat its fruit.

²²He who finds a wife finds what is good
and receives favor from the LORD.

²³A poor man pleads for mercy,
but a rich man answers harshly.

NRSV

and with dishonor comes disgrace.

⁴ The words of the mouth are deep waters;
the fountain of wisdom is a gushing stream.

⁵ It is not right to be partial to the guilty,
or to subvert the innocent in judgment.

⁶ A fool's lips bring strife,
and a fool's mouth invites a flogging.

⁷ The mouths of fools are their ruin,
and their lips a snare to themselves.

⁸ The words of a whisperer are like delicious morsels;
they go down into the inner parts of the body.

⁹ One who is slack in work
is close kin to a vandal.

¹⁰ The name of the LORD is a strong tower;
the righteous run into it and are safe.

¹¹ The wealth of the rich is their strong city;
in their imagination it is like a high wall.

¹² Before destruction one's heart is haughty,
but humility goes before honor.

¹³ If one gives answer before hearing,
it is folly and shame.

¹⁴ The human spirit will endure sickness;
but a broken spirit—who can bear?

¹⁵ An intelligent mind acquires knowledge,
and the ear of the wise seeks knowledge.

¹⁶ A gift opens doors;
it gives access to the great.

¹⁷ The one who first states a case seems right,
until the other comes and cross-examines.

¹⁸ Casting the lot puts an end to disputes
and decides between powerful contenders.

¹⁹ An ally offended is stronger than a city;ᵃ
such quarreling is like the bars of a castle.

²⁰ From the fruit of the mouth one's stomach is satisfied;
the yield of the lips brings satisfaction.

²¹ Death and life are in the power of the tongue,
and those who love it will eat its fruits.

²² He who finds a wife finds a good thing,
and obtains favor from the LORD.

²³ The poor use entreaties,
but the rich answer roughly.

²⁴ Someᵇ friends play at friendshipᵇ
but a true friend sticks closer than one's nearest kin.

ᵃGk Syr Vg Tg: Meaning of Heb uncertain   ᵇSyr Tg: Heb *A man of*

NIV

²⁴A man of many companions may come to ruin,
but there is a friend who sticks closer than a
brother.

COMMENTARY

18:1-2. These opening verses are a proverb pair that appear to build on an implicit contrast between an isolated (and therefore foolish) individual and the wisdom that can be gained only in community. The meaning of v. 1 is not wholly certain because some of its terms are obscure. Its subject is literally, "one separated" (see the verb in 16:28b; 17:9b; 19:4b), probably from one's proper companions. Rabbi Hillel, a contemporary of Jesus, counseled against separating oneself from the community.²³⁶ Rashi compared it to Lot's separating himself from Abraham to live in Sodom. One may translate, "One who is alienated seeks his own desire; he breaks out [17:14; 20:3] against competent [communal] planning" (for "sound judgment" [תושיה *tûšîyâ*] see Commentary on 2:7; for "counselors," see Commentary on 11:14).

Verse 2 continues the topic of one who resists communal wisdom and is further linked to v. 1 by a wordplay between יתגלע (*yitgallā'*, "defies," "breaks out against") and התגלות (*hitgallôt*, "expressing"). The fool "knows it all" and takes no pleasure in the "understanding" of others, but merely lays bare his own heart or personal opinion. In Hebrew, the irony of this is laughable, because a fool is one who lacks heart—that is, the capacity for understanding (see 11:12).

18:3. This verse is near in form and theme to 11:2. When one thing comes, another follows; the pairs are inseparable. The connection of "wickedness" and "contempt" in v. 3a is suggestive. Wickedness entails a devaluation of some created good or creature, even of other persons (11:12; 14:21, 31). Wickedness fails to love and value what God made good and still loves (Gen 1:31; John 3:16). But v. 3b seems to point the proverb in a different direction, though its sense is uncertain. The terms "dishonor" and "disgrace" are so similar as to obscure the point of their connection. Is it because one dishonors another

236. See *m. 'Abot* 2:5.

that one receives disgrace from society (see 6:33; 9:7)? Then also the first line may be understood differently. When one is wicked, then one earns and receives contempt from others (see Commentary on 12:8; 13:18; 26:1, concerning honor and shame in Israel's culture).

18:4. This verse may be read in two ways. The first line conveys the inscrutability of human words, as expressing the hidden depths of the human heart (see 20:5; 21:1; 25:3). This is somewhat paradoxical, because words would seem to be on the surface and open to all. The depth dimensions of words and persons is at least partially susceptible to human understanding (20:5b), but ultimately only God knows the heart behind the words (16:2; 17:3). Verse 4b may be read as a nominal, somewhat independent sentence: "A fountain of wisdom is a flowing stream." But more likely is that "fountain of wisdom" qualifies the "mouth" of one whose words are "deep waters" (see 10:11; Sir 21:13). Through the opening of the mouth, the waters flow to enrich others. Such a wise person emulates Lady Wisdom, who "pours out" her spirit and words (1:23) for listeners. Similar imagery is taken up in John, where believers, through the Spirit, also become a source of "waters" (John 7:38-39).

18:5. This verse is a "not good" saying (see Commentary on 17:7). The perversion of justice in the law courts violates the fundamental principles of 17:13a, 15 (see Commentary on 17:23, 26; 24:23; 28:21). The idiom "to be partial" (שאת פני *śĕ'ēt pĕnê*) is literally, "to raise the face," as when a supplicant, head bowed to the ground, is given permission to rise (see 6:35; Mal 1:8; 2:9). People are prone to dispense preferential treatment to persons who impress them by wealth, class, or beauty (see Commentary on 11:26). But personal advantage, like a bribe, can also be a powerful persuader. Partiality is forbidden in the law (Lev 19:15; Deut 1:17; 16:19; see also 1 Sam 8:3; Sir 42:1-2; Jas 2:1-7). Partial judges set themselves on the side of the wicked and against the innocent. But impartial judges mirror the Creator (Deut 10:17; Sir 35:12-13; Acts 10:34; Rom 2:11).

18:6-7. A proverb pair concerning the trouble that fools get into by talking is the focus of these verses (see also 26:1-12) . There is a chiasmus of speech organs setting off the two verses: lips/mouth/mouth/lips. Unconsidered speech creates social conflict and calls for punishment. A fool's mouth is his or her downfall, the lips a dangerous trap (see Commentary on 12:13; 20:25; for נפש [nepeš], see Commentary on 16:17; cf. 1:18). The mouths of fools are their own worst enemy.

18:8. Gossip is like junk food (see 16:28), delicious to taste before it settles inside to do its destructive work (16:28; 26:20, 22). It ought to give both the gossiper and the listener pause that God searches everyone's inmost being (lit., "all the rooms of the belly," 20:27). The image of the body as a house with rooms is used in chaps. 1–9 in connection with the "strange woman" (see 7:27). The prophets "eat" and digest God's words before speaking them to the people (Jer 15:16; Ezek 2:8-3:3; Rev 10:9-10; see Prov 18:20).

18:9. The NIV offers a more literal translation than does the NRSV. This is strong condemnation of laziness, because in a subsistence agrarian society, laziness can mean hunger (see Commentary on 10:4-5; 12:11; 28:19). But just as "strike while the iron is hot" speaks far beyond the blacksmith's shop, so also this saying speaks to many situations (see 22:29). It presupposes that humans are to work and do good with the gifts given them. Not to do so makes a person one who destroys (see 28:24).

18:10-11. The text shifts to a proverb pair that relativizes wealth as a source of security, in contrast to trust in God's name (see also v. 12). The imagery in both verses is taken from the military world of civil defense. In 10:15, which has the same first line as 18:11, wealth appears simply as a "strong city." Wealth does provide a certain level of security. But the security of wealth and power (21:22) is not ultimate—as anyone with a life-threatening illness knows. Verse 10 speaks of Yahweh's name (see Commentary on 16:5-6) as a "strong tower" to which the righteous runs and are safe. But "safe" is literally "high"

(נשגב nisgāb), the same word used of the rich person's "high wall." In case of enemy attack, folk retreat to the city, whose elevated location and secure walls place them "high" above danger (see Pss 61:2-3, 5, 7-8; 91:14b). Thus the proverb pair contrasts trust in God (see 14:26a; 28:25-26; 29:25-26) with a false security based on wealth (Luke 12:15-34). A high wall can be breached (Isa 30:12-14). Thus the security of wealth is only apparent, in contrast to the absolute security of trust in Yahweh's gracious name. The illusory character of the rich person's wealth becomes apparent only in the last line of the proverb pair: Wealth is like a high wall of defense only "in their imagination" (the Hebrew phrase is best taken in this sense; see Ps 73:7). Job as well declares that he has not made wealth his trust (Job 31:24-25).

18:12. Verse 12a is a condensed parallel to 16:18, while v. 12b duplicates 15:33b (see Commentary on those verses). Perhaps the saying in its present context is a backward comment on the fate of one trusting in riches (v. 11) and a forward comment on the arrogance of answering without first listening (v. 13).

18:13. The original reference of this saying may have been to legal proceedings (see Commentary on 18:17). In ancient Israel, as in contemporary United States, a court case is a "hearing" (see Sir 11:7-9). But the issue applies to all human relationships. One of Covey's seven habits of highly effective people is, "Seek first to understand, then to be understood."[237]

18:14-15. These verses seem to be a proverb pair that, like 15:13-14, moves from psychosomatic concerns to a focus on the heart as an organ of knowing. Verse 14 is one of several psychological sayings showing profound awareness of the interrelation of the human spirit (or heart) and bodily well-being. Verse 14b intensifies v. 14a. Bodily sickness is a hard, but not impossible, burden for a healthy spirit. A broken spirit, however, can seem impossible to bear (see Commentary on 15:13; 17:22 for this expression; Ps 51:17 uses a different Hebrew adjective for "broken"). "Who can bear" is a rhetorical question that expects the answer, "No one" (see 27:3-4). Physical maladies can stem from a sick spirit, and the spirit shows in a body weighed down as if by an

---

237. Stephen R. Covey, *The Seven Habits of Highly Effective People* (New York: Simon and Schuster, 1989) 236-60.

invisible burden. Although Hans Selye coined the term "stress" in relation to such "psychosomatic" phenomena, the concept is ancient (see Commentary on 13:12, 19).[238]

The two lines of v. 15 are variants of 15:14*a*. The chief means by which the wise gain knowledge in an oral culture is the listening ear (see 4:20; 20:12; 25:12). In the cognate language of Assyria and Babylon (Akkadian) one of the terms for "wisdom," *uznu,* simply means "ear." Jesus' admonition that those who have ears to hear should hear, stands in this broad wisdom tradition. Also in legal matters, hearing is essential (vv. 13, 17). The didactic language here echoes the introduction (1:5) and may be a sign of pedagogical editing.

18:16-17. A proverb pair whose verses implicitly comment on each other comprise this saying (see 19:6). Verse 17 follows a proverb on the power of gifts. The juxtaposition of vv. 16-17 implies that a wealthy person's gift ought not to distort the free, due process of law (see 28:11).

In pre-industrial societies such as ancient Israel, gifts played a major role in the general exchange of goods and services.[239] The land of Canaan itself was a royal gift of Yahweh to Abraham and his descendants (e.g., Gen 12:7). Gifts were used in social interactions of almost every sort, from legal transactions (Prov 15:27), to prophetic consultation (1 Sam 9:7), to marriage arrangements (Gen 34:12; Exod 22:16-17; 1 Sam 18:20-27), and the acquisition of a burial plot (Genesis 23, where the verbs translated as "sell" or "pay" are נתן [*nātan*], "give"). A person who did not give the appropriate promised gift would be condemned (25:14). A gift could also mean access to persons of power (v. 16). This use of the "gift" was especially prone to corruption. Hence, Israel's prophets and sages had to warn against the danger of corrupt gift-giving (see Commentary on 15:27; 17:8, 23).

In legal proceedings, what seemed true on one person's testimony may be exposed as false by the other's cross examination (v. 17). A case should not be judged after hearing only one side (see Commentary on 18:13). When David fled Jerusalem and Absalom's army, David unjustly con-

demned Mephibosheth on the word of Ziba alone (see Deut 19:15-21). This is one of several instances where David failed to act wisely and justly as royal judge (2 Sam 16:1-4; 19:24-30; see Commentary on 16:12; 25:2-5).

18:18. This saying continues the legal topic. For Israel, the ultimate decider of obscure cases was the "lot" (see Commentary on 16:10, 33). Perhaps the lot was used when the arguments of each side seemed equally matched. Like a referee in a boxing match, the lot separates the combatants. When powerful persons contend at law or other matters, much damage can be done to property and to the innocent bystanders who are associated with the powerful.

18:19. The Hebrew grammar of this verse has received no satisfactory explanation, even though many of its words appear in the surrounding verses, and all of them are well known. The saying is either extremely elliptical or corrupt. The general sense seems to be that it is more difficult to win over a brother offended or "sinned against" (the sense supplied by the KJV) than it is to conquer a strong city. One cannot gain entrance because quarrels create barriers like a barred door.

18:20-22. In its present context, v. 20 introduces a trio of related sayings that all begin with the same letter. Verses 20-21 concern the metaphorical fruit of speech organs, and vv. 21-22 are linked by images of women and Wisdom that recall chaps. 1–9. Verse 21 discusses the ambiguous "tongue" in terms that echo the love of Wisdom and Folly (see Overview on Proverbs 1:1–9:18). Verse 22 explicitly echoes 8:35, reaffirming the wife as a symbol and, as it were, the incarnation of Lady Wisdom.

Verse 20 is a near duplicate and expansion of 12:14*a* and 13:2*a*. "To be filled" or "satisfied" (שבע *śābaʿ*) both translate the same Hebrew word, and the object of filling can be negative or positive (see 1:31; 14:14; 18:21). The imagery is playful and punning, as if one can eat words that then go down into the belly (see Commentary on 18:8).

Verse 21 takes up the image of fruit produced by the organs of speech from v. 20 (see Sir 37:17-24). Here, however, the imagery suddenly becomes complex and allusive. The tongue is portrayed as a woman (it is feminine in Hebrew) who has male lovers—a thought that anticipates

238. See Hans Selye, *The Stress of Life* (New York: McGraw-Hill, 1976).

239. See Marcel Mauss, *The Gift: Forms and Functions of Exchange in Archaic Societies* (New York: Norton, 1967).

finding a wife in v. 22. But love of the tongue can entail either life or death—just as love of a woman does in Proverbs 1–9 (see 2:18-19; 4:6; 5:19; 8:17, 35-36). Literally, the verse reads, "Death and life are in the hand of the tongue, her lovers will eat her fruit" (see 8:19; 31:16*b* concerning the fruit of Lady Wisdom and of the capable woman).[240]

Verse 22 is crucial to the interacting theme of woman and wisdom in the book (see Commentary on 8:35; see also 3:13; 19:8*b*, 14; 31:10-31). The affirmation of ordinary life, including marriage, is essential to a biblical view of God as Creator and of the creation as good. Proverbs throughout addresses young men and here considers a wife from a male perspective. But the affirmation of a spouse as divine gift may apply equally to wives. In its present masculine form, however, the saying may combat perennial male tendencies to deny the importance that wives have their husbands' weal or woe (12:4; 19:13: 21:9; Sir 26:1-4, 13-18).[241]

18:23. This saying presents a sharp portrayal of the power difference between rich and poor and of the temptation to arrogance that comes with wealth (see Commentary on 11:24; 14:31; 18:10; 22:7). The poor person who pleads for mercy is likely to be rejected by the rich, but God hears such pleas (Pss 28:2, 6; 116:1). Humans may separate themselves from the misfortunate, thus ignoring their common existence as God's creatures (22:2; 29:13). There is a sharp judgment for such people, a *lex talionis,* in which the punishment fits the crime (21:13).

18:24. The Hebrew of v. 24*b* is clear (see Commentary on 17:17; 18:19), but v. 24*a* is open to a stunning number of readings, reflected in the variety of translations it has occasioned. These possibilities reflect linguistic ambiguity in the original: "There are friends who mutually harm one another." "A man of *many* friends comes to harm" (see NIV; see also 19:4). "There are friends who *merely* chatter." "There are friends who are *merely* friends" (see 22:24). The final reading is perhaps correct (see NRSV). There seems to be a contrast between the appearance and the reality of friendship, but it is difficult to say more than this (for "friend," see Commentary on 17:17-18). In 12:9 and 13:7 hithpael verb forms generate similar ambiguities, though without the added problem of an obscure root.

240. For a different view, see Claudia V. Camp, "Woman Wisdom as Root Metaphor: A Theological Consideration," in Kenneth G. Hoglund et al., eds., *The Listening Heart* (Sheffield: JSOT, 1987) 45-76, esp. 52-53.
241. See Frank S. Pittman's wise book, *Man Enough: Fathers, Sons, and the Search for Masculinity* (New York: G. P. Putnam's Sons, 1993).

REFLECTIONS

1. On occasion, a biblical concept or practice that seems obvious and familiar to us may conceal something foreign. The "gift" is such a concept (18:16). Gifts in ancient societies had more than a merely personal function—unlike capitalist societies where most exchange of goods and services is purely economic. As in the United States, in ancient Israel gifts were used to establish and cement relationships. But unlike the United States, for Israel most exchanges of goods and services bore a "gift" character (see Commentary on 18:16). As a gift, any economic transaction would entail a multifaceted personal relationship of mutual moral and spiritual obligations in a context of community standards.

In our society, however, the ordinary exchange of goods and services has largely lost the biblical sense of mutual personal obligation attached to gift giving. Economic exchange has been rationalized and made impersonal by money, mail, telemarketing, and credit cards. Both buyers and sellers suffer from lack of trust, because transactions are not based on personal relationships. "Let the buyer beware" is an ancient Latin proverb, but it seems ever more relevant today. On the other hand, a real estate agent's proverb in the Philadelphia area complains, "Buyers are liars." Without mutual trust grounded in personal relationships, there is little sense of obligation to fair play and fair dealing. Employers and employees also view their relation in purely economic terms. "To downsize" is a new verb that connotes a company's abandoning employees to their fates. The fiscal "bottom line" and "maximization of profits" devour other human values.

A biblical answer to such problems is not quick and easy. At the very least, it requires that Christians begin to think hard about the implications of biblical faith for shaping community that is more than just a Sunday thing. The obstacles to such community in a highly mobile, TV-saturated, technologized society are immense. But a beginning might be made by striving to deal with all people in the light of their divine creation, dignity, and calling (see Commentary on 14:31; 15:25).

If most economic transactions in our society have become rationalized and impersonal, the converse problem of distorted gift giving has grown to extraordinary proportions. The use of the gift as a means of unjust access to the great and the powerful is a constant feature of our national life. Political access and influence are purchased by wealthy individuals and by powerful corporations whose lobbyists exert undue influence on the legislative process.

The gift as problem is evident in the persistent unwillingness of our legislators to enact genuine campaign finance reform. It is evident in the way that wealthy lobbies manage to subvert legislative action for the common good, while socially harmful or unjust favors are granted to special interest groups of dubious merit. The giving of gifts, without the moral restraints, can do much to undermine a just and democratic society.

Enactment of appropriate legislation is obviously needed. But the solution to such problems cannot be achieved by legal means alone. It requires a turn from mammon to God, from evil to good (Amos 5:6, 14-15). It requires a spiritually and morally healthy humanity such as only God can make (Jer 31:31-34; Ezek 36:25-32; see 2 Corinthians 3–5). This reality may not happen for our nation, but it does define the new humanity in Christ, which is light and salt to the world (Matt 5:13-16; John 8:12).

2. Like the prophets, Proverbs has a persistent concern for righteousness and justice, not only in personal life, but also in the public arena of the law court (18:5, 17). The modern relegation of religion to the private and personal would have been incomprehensible and abhorrent to ancient Israel's prophets and sages. Public justice and righteousness are integral expressions of the "fear of the LORD" (1:3*b*, 7; Jer 22:13-17). For America, with its millions of Christians, this means that claims of biblical piety and godliness are empty unless they bear fruit in collective Christian action for equity between rich and poor, and among races and ethnic groups in our criminal justice system (see Commentary on 13:24).[242]

242. See Dan Van Ness, *Crime and Its Victims* (Downers Grove: Inter-Varsity, 1986); Donald Smarto, ed., *Setting the Captive Free: Relevant Ideas in Criminal Justice and Prison Ministry* (Grand Rapids: Baker, 1993).

Proverbs 19:1-29, Better a Poor Man Whose Walk Is Blameless

NIV	NRSV
19 Better a poor man whose walk is blameless than a fool whose lips are perverse.	**19** Better the poor walking in integrity than one perverse of speech who is a fool.
²It is not good to have zeal without knowledge, nor to be hasty and miss the way.	² Desire without knowledge is not good, and one who moves too hurriedly misses the way.
³A man's own folly ruins his life, yet his heart rages against the LORD.	³ One's own folly leads to ruin, yet the heart rages against the LORD.
⁴Wealth brings many friends, but a poor man's friend deserts him.	⁴ Wealth brings many friends, but the poor are left friendless.

NIV

⁵A false witness will not go unpunished,
   and he who pours out lies will not go free.

⁶Many curry favor with a ruler,
   and everyone is the friend of a man who gives
      gifts.

⁷A poor man is shunned by all his relatives—
   how much more do his friends avoid him!
Though he pursues them with pleading,
   they are nowhere to be found.ᵃ

⁸He who gets wisdom loves his own soul;
   he who cherishes understanding prospers.

⁹A false witness will not go unpunished,
   and he who pours out lies will perish.

¹⁰It is not fitting for a fool to live in luxury—
   how much worse for a slave to rule over
      princes!

¹¹A man's wisdom gives him patience;
   it is to his glory to overlook an offense.

¹²A king's rage is like the roar of a lion,
   but his favor is like dew on the grass.

¹³A foolish son is his father's ruin,
   and a quarrelsome wife is like a constant
      dripping.

¹⁴Houses and wealth are inherited from parents,
   but a prudent wife is from the LORD.

¹⁵Laziness brings on deep sleep,
   and the shiftless man goes hungry.

¹⁶He who obeys instructions guards his life,
   but he who is contemptuous of his ways will die.

¹⁷He who is kind to the poor lends to the LORD,
   and he will reward him for what he has done.

¹⁸Discipline your son, for in that there is hope;
   do not be a willing party to his death.

¹⁹A hot-tempered man must pay the penalty;
   if you rescue him, you will have to do it again.

²⁰Listen to advice and accept instruction,
   and in the end you will be wise.

²¹Many are the plans in a man's heart,
   but it is the LORD's purpose that prevails.

²²What a man desires is unfailing loveᵇ;
   better to be poor than a liar.

ᵃ7 The meaning of the Hebrew for this sentence is uncertain.
ᵇ22 Or A man's greed is his shame

NRSV

⁵ A false witness will not go unpunished,
   and a liar will not escape.
⁶ Many seek the favor of the generous,
   and everyone is a friend to a giver of gifts.
⁷ If the poor are hated even by their kin,
   how much more are they shunned by
      their friends!
When they call after them, they are not there.ᵃ
⁸ To get wisdom is to love oneself;
   to keep understanding is to prosper.
⁹ A false witness will not go unpunished,
   and the liar will perish.
¹⁰ It is not fitting for a fool to live in luxury,
   much less for a slave to rule over princes.
¹¹ Those with good sense are slow to anger,
   and it is their glory to overlook an offense.
¹² A king's anger is like the growling of a lion,
   but his favor is like dew on the grass.
¹³ A stupid child is ruin to a father,
   and a wife's quarreling is a continual
      dripping of rain.
¹⁴ House and wealth are inherited from parents,
   but a prudent wife is from the LORD.
¹⁵ Laziness brings on deep sleep;
   an idle person will suffer hunger.
¹⁶ Those who keep the commandment will live;
   those who are heedless of their ways will
      die.
¹⁷ Whoever is kind to the poor lends to the LORD,
   and will be repaid in full.
¹⁸ Discipline your children while there is hope;
   do not set your heart on their destruction.
¹⁹ A violent tempered person will pay the penalty;
   if you effect a rescue, you will only have to
      do it again.ᵃ
²⁰ Listen to advice and accept instruction,
   that you may gain wisdom for the future.
²¹ The human mind may devise many plans,
   but it is the purpose of the LORD that will
      be established.
²² What is desirable in a person is loyalty,
   and it is better to be poor than a liar.
²³ The fear of the LORD is life indeed;
   filled with it one rests secure
      and suffers no harm.
²⁴ The lazy person buries a hand in the dish,
   and will not even bring it back to the mouth.

ᵃMeaning of Heb uncertain

NIV

²³The fear of the LORD leads to life:
  Then one rests content, untouched by
    trouble.

²⁴The sluggard buries his hand in the dish;
  he will not even bring it back to his mouth!

²⁵Flog a mocker, and the simple will learn
    prudence;
  rebuke a discerning man, and he will gain
    knowledge.

²⁶He who robs his father and drives out his
    mother
  is a son who brings shame and disgrace.

²⁷Stop listening to instruction, my son,
  and you will stray from the words of
    knowledge.

²⁸A corrupt witness mocks at justice,
  and the mouth of the wicked gulps down evil.

²⁹Penalties are prepared for mockers,
  and beatings for the backs of fools.

NRSV

²⁵ Strike a scoffer, and the simple will learn
    prudence;
  reprove the intelligent, and they will gain
    knowledge.
²⁶ Those who do violence to their father and
    chase away their mother
  are children who cause shame and bring
    reproach.
²⁷ Cease straying, my child, from the words of
    knowledge,
  in order that you may hear instruction.
²⁸ A worthless witness mocks at justice,
  and the mouth of the wicked devours
    iniquity.
²⁹ Condemnation is ready for scoffers,
  and flogging for the backs of fools.

COMMENTARY

19:1-3. Each of these proverbs uses imagery of "way" or locomotion. Verse 3 may be a radical instance of the general problem put in v. 2.

Verse 1 is a better-than saying that inverts ordinary valuations of wealth and poverty (see Commentary on 15:16; 16:8). It is almost identical to 28:6, with two differences. Verse 1*b* presents a person who is perverse in regard to the lips (see 8:8; 17:20; 19:5, 9) while 28:6*b* has one perverse in regard to "double ways." For "perverse" and "integrity," see Commentary on 10:9. "Lips" and "ways" each represents action in the world. The more general term "way" designates one's life conduct; it includes "lips" as a specific form of conduct. Proverbs 28:6*b* seems to provide a more natural (and obvious) contrast to the poor person in 19:1*a* (see 18:23; 19:7). Thus the ancient Syriac version and some commentators emend "fool" in v. 1*b* to the "rich" of 28:6*b*, but this is probably hypercritical. That the fool here must be rich is an obvious expectation, which the proverb subverts. The substitution of "fool" for the obvious term "rich" creates in the hearer's

mind an implicit comment: Yes, there are rich fools, though one does not always say so out loud (see 28:11).

"Zeal" and "desire" (v. 2) translate נֶפֶשׁ (*nepeš*; see Commentary on 13:4, 19; 16:24; 19:15). Desire drives one to activity (16:26), but without considered reflection, even well-intentioned, "spiritually" driven activism can be harmful rather than helpful. Those whose "feet are hasty" (see 1:16) miss the way or sin (חוֹטֵא *ḥôṭēʾ* means both; see 8:36; the words "the way" are not in the Hebrew). For "not good," see Commentary on 17:7, 26.

Verse 3 may be a radical instance of v. 2. Literally, it reads, "A man's folly subverts his way, and his heart rages against Yahweh." Folly and sin are cognitive as well as practical dysfunctions. It is an error in thought to shift blame, but the practice is as old as the primeval pair (Gen 3:12-13). Human beings ruin (11:3 has the same root) their own lives but get angry at God.

19:4. The topic of human relations resumes, especially friendships, as they are affected by wealth and poverty (see 18:23-24; 19:1). Modern folk may be culturally disposed to read this saying cynically: "Money talks," and all that counts is "the bottom line," even in human relationships. But the matter was more complicated in ancient Israel. The exchange of gifts cemented relationships and communicated mutual respect and fulfilled moral obligation (see Reflections on 18:1-24). The gifts of the wealthy can be a means by which goods and services are redistributed, so that society benefits. Thus, on special occasions, the king gave gifts to the people (see 2 Sam 6:19; Eph 4:7-13).

19:5. This verse is one of several sayings, whose lines are near duplicates, against bearing false witness (6:19; 12:17; 14:5, 25; 19:9; 21:28). The topic was an important one in Israel's oral culture, in which false testimony could do great damage (25:18). For "will not go unpunished," see Commentary on 16:5.

19:6-7. These verses are an antithetical proverb pair, presenting opposite sides of one social reality (see v. 4). The effects of wealth and poverty on human relationships is presented in terms of nearness and distance. The phrase "to seek favor" is literally, "to seek the face of someone" (יְחַלּוּ פְנֵי *yĕḥallû pĕnê*)—that is, to come close to someone. It is often used with reference to God as the ultimate benefactor of humans (Pss 24:6; 27:8). The face represents the main organ through which humans (and God) communicate the character of their relationship to others (see Num 6:25-26). Thus "curry favor" may be too negative in its connotations. For "generous" (NRSV)/"ruler" (NIV) see Commentary on 17:7, 26. In contrast, people distance themselves from a poor person (v. 7b; see v. 4b and related verses): "Nobody knows you when you're down and out." Even relatives (lit., "brothers") shun (lit., "hate" [שֵׂנֵא *śānē'*], but the Hebrew has a broader range than the English term) their poor sibling. This may be a form of shaming that seeks to reform the lazy (see Commentary on 10:1, 5; 12:8; 17:2) or is simply a neglect of family responsibility to take care of their own (17:17). Translation of v. 7c (two lines in NIV) is uncertain.

19:8. A literal translation brings to light important verbal links with key ideas in Proverbs: "He who gets heart loves himself; he who keeps understanding tends to find good." "Getting heart"

is the same as getting wisdom (see 4:5; 16:16), for the heart is the organ of wisdom (see Excursus, "The 'Heart' in the Old Testament," 60-61). The ideas of love and "finding good" connect v. 8 with the themes of love for Wisdom/wife and "finding good" (see Commentary on 8:17, 35; 18:22). "Understanding" (תְּבוּנָה *tĕbûnâ*) is a parallel term for Lady Wisdom (5:1; 8:1). When the young male addressee of the book "keeps" or "cares" for her, then good ensues, because she in turn watches over or guards him (see 4:5-6). To love oneself is to love one's נֶפֶשׁ (*nepeš*; see Commentary on 16:17; cf. 13:3; 15:32; 16:17; 19:16). Self-love here appears in its appropriate sense: wise regard, respect, and responsibility for oneself as God's creature.

19:9. This verse is nearly identical to v. 5, but v. 9b shares the predicate of 21:28a. Repetition indicates the importance of the topic of false witness.

19:10. Essential to wisdom is a sense of propriety, of "fittingness" (see Commentary on 17:7; 26:1-12). This verse presents a world upside-down, where social order is inverted and people possess things not fitting to them (see Commentary on 17:2; 20:22; 29:2; see also Eccl 10:6-7). This saying has an anti-revolutionary thrust, as does 30:21-23 (but see Commentary on 17:2).

19:11. This verse belongs to those sayings that insist on the human capacity to reflect before responding to a stimulus (see Commentary on 15:28). "To overlook" (lit., "to pass over" [עָבַר *'ābar*]) an offense is akin to the covering of offenses that love does (see Commentary on 10:12; 17:9). More than this, being slow to anger and "passing over offenses" are characteristics of Yahweh (see Mic 7:18, which is based on Exod 34:6-7; cf. Joseph as a quasi-king in Gen 50:17). The person who so acts imitates the goodness of God (see Commentary on 15:18). This is a form of "glory" or "splendor," such as God and kings possess. Thus this saying implicitly comments on the next. Both sayings concern anger as a response to offense, but the perspective of the first saying may be seen as a guide to the king in dealing with wrong.

19:12. The first line of the verse is a near parallel of 20:2, which also compares the king to a roaring lion (the NRSV translates the same Hebrew differently in each case). Verse 12b is a variant of 16:15*b*, and 16:14-15 develop the contrast of the king's wrath and favor in a different direction. Morning dew in dry Palestine was an important source of moisture for plants. While a king's wrath could wrongly harm the innocent, the reference here (like the life-giving dew) may be a positive one. As a judge, the king's anger removes the wicked (see Commentary on 25:4-5). David's anger at the rich man in Nathan's parable is an ironic example of judgment gone awry (2 Sam 12:5-6).

19:13-15. These independent proverbs are cunningly juxtaposed around the topic of family relations. The three sayings are rife with vocabulary that echoes the introduction to the antithetical collection (10:1-5, "foolish son, craving/ruin"; see Commentary on 10:3*b*, "father," "hunger," "prudent," "sleep," "slack," "person," "appetite" [*nepeš*, untranslated in 10:3; see 19:15]). There is also a playful contrast between positive wet weather (dew, v. 12) and the negative dripping of constant rain (v. 13).

Verse 13 combines the calamity of a foolish son (see Commentary on 10:1; Eccl 2:18-21) with that of a quarrelsome wife (see Commentary on 27:15, an expansion of 19:13*b*). In the male-oriented address of Proverbs, the father-son relation and the husband-wife relation are the family connections most important for well-being.[243] These relations could be sources of great good or distress. Wives can embody not only wisdom (see Commentary on 8:35; 12:4; 18:22; 31:10-31), but also chaos (21:9, 19; 25:24; 27:15). The "dripping" may refer to a perpetually leaking roof (see 27:15; Eccl 10:18).

Israel conceived of life in terms of family and land—that is, generations of family, in cosmic space, extended through time. Thus v. 14 is a significant deepening of and contrast to v. 13. The transition of possessions and land—whether much or little—from father to son occurs in predictable fashion (v. 14*a*). But the greatest source of male happiness is God's gift of a "prudent wife" v. 14*b* (see 18:22; her opposite appears in 12:4*b*; 10:5 applies the same contrast to sons). For the mysterious, yet non-coercive presence of God in all human activity, see Commentary on 16:1, 9, 33; 19:21.

243. See Frank S. Pittman, *Man Enough: Fathers, Sons, and the Search for Masculinity* (New York: G. P. Putnam's Sons, 1993).

Verse 15 may possess an implicit connection with the foregoing proverb pair through the association of "deep sleep" with the implicit laziness of the foolish son (opposite of "prudent") who sleeps in harvest (10:5; see also 10:1). The threat of hunger also appears in 10:3. Sleep as a deterrent to energetic, successful work gives rise to such sayings as, "The early bird gets the worm" and "Rise and shine!"

19:16. This verse is similar in form and thought to v. 8. There the focus was on keeping wisdom and understanding, here, literally, "He who keeps the commandment keeps his life" (*nepeš*). The commandment may be parental (4:4; 7:2), but in the background looms the commandment of God as the ultimate standard of good and evil (see Commentary on 6:20-23; 13:13). Some scholars see v. 16*b* as damaged and emend "his ways" to correspond to "word" in 13:13 ("those who despise the word will die"). The change is unnecessary and is not supported by the ancient versions. God's Word and "ways" (for humans to live) correspond (see the use of "ways" in Ps 25:4-10; Mic 4:2). This reading supposes that the possessive pronoun "his" refers to Yahweh (implicit in "commandment"? Cf. "despises him" in 14:2, though there "his ways" refers to a person's conduct). Alternately, we must attend to our own ways, though the threat of death seems an extreme punishment for failure to do so. Moreover, to "despise one's own ways" seems too strong an expression to indicate merely being heedless of one's conduct (see 1:7*b;* 14:2).

19:17. This verse is one of many sayings that directly relate one's treatment of the poor to one's relationship with God (see Commentary on 14:21, 31; 21:10; 28:8). The present saying provides a theological explanation for the mystery of profitable generosity (11:24; see also 3:9-10). Its logic (a gift to the poor is a loan to God) underlies Jesus' saying that "whatever you did for the least of these . . . you did for me" (Matt 25:40). This saying may be an example of keeping the commandment (v. 16; see Deut 15:4-6).

19:18-20. These verses form a cluster of three admonitions, an unusual occurrence in these Solomonic sayings. Verse 18 is advice to a father; v. 19 confirms the need for discipline and for not protecting people from the consequences of their actions; v. 20 then gives advice to young persons to receive (parental) advice (see Commentary on 11:14; 15:22) and instruction (the root [יסר *ysr*] is translated "discipline" in v. 18). Thus both parent and child are addressed as partners in the instructional process.

Verse 18*a* concerns the timeliness of instruction and discipline (see Commentary on 13:24; 17:10; 23:13). In this, as in all activities, there is a fitting or right time (Eccl 3:1-8). Developmental biology and psychology have become aware of critical periods in which certain developmental tasks must occur. Once the phase has passed for developing a language-specific accent, for example, it is gone and the opportunity does not return. It is too late. The adage "as the twig is bent, so grows the tree" conveys a similar idea of timely formation of a child's mind and character. Verse 18*b* is not so clear. It may mean, "Do not pay attention to his [a son is meant] moaning" (see TNK, המיתו *hem-yatô*; see also Isa 14:11) or "Do not set your heart on his death" (המיתו *hămîtô*), perhaps by letting him continue on a deadly way (see 23:13-14). The saying may also refer to the legal process described in Deut 21:18-21, which does eventuate in death, though the implementation of this law is dubious (see 30:17). A few scholars believe that v. 18*b* literally warns against beating a child to death. Most who accept the second translation, however, see it as typical proverbial hyperbole, meaning "do not chastise him excessively."[244] Deuteronomy sets limits on paternal authority to harm a child (see Deut 21:18-21, which requires communal judgment). In contrast, the Roman *pater familias* did have life-and-death power over his children.

Verse 19 begins as a saying but ends as an admonition. Though v. 19*b* is obscure in Hebrew, the NIV and the NRSV reflect the most natural reading of it. It appears to be a warning against enmeshment in another person's dysfunctional life. When one person prevents another from bearing the consequences of his or her own actions, one actually interferes with the act-consequence sequence, and so keeps the person "great of anger" *Qere*), from becoming responsible for his or her own actions. That one must engage in the process again shows that it does not work; it only prolongs the problem. Ironically, the person who

"rescues" another is now caught in the unhealthy dynamics of another person's life; you will have to do it again.

The admonition in v. 20 has affinities with counsel to become wise in chaps. 1–9, but some of its elements and its formulation are new. "Listen to advice" has a near parallel only in 12:15*b;* the term "accept" (instruction) occurs only here in Proverbs, and the formulation of the purpose clause after imperatives is also unique. "In the end" is literally, "in your end," an expression found otherwise only in 5:11, but with near parallels in 23:18; 24:14. "The end" may refer to a person's death (5:4-5), but also, as here, to a less ultimate outcome of a specific course of action ("future").

19:21. This verse comments on v. 20 through a play on the double meaning of the word "advice"/"purpose" (עצה *ʿēṣâ*). God's purpose overrides all human advice and planning, even that of wise parents (see Commentary on 16:1, 9, 33; 21:30-31).

19:22. The difficulty of v. 22*a* is reflected in the differing translations. Literally, it is, "A man's desire is his kindness/shame." The last two terms reflect two homonyms in Hebrew. חסד (*ḥesed*) frequently means "kindness" (see 16:6). But *ḥesed* is used twice to mean "shame" or "disgrace" (14:34; Lev 20:17; cf. Prov 25:10). This is the probable sense here. One should probably translate according to the NIV margin. Excessive desire (18:1) is shameful, so it is better to be poor than corrupt (see Commentary on 19:1; 28:6; 30:8). The NIV text is also possible, but less likely.

19:23. Verse 23*a* is a conventional declaration concerning "the fear of the LORD" (see Commentary on 1:7; 14:27). Verse 23*b* is less clear, and translators grasp its sense through its relation to the first line of the verse, by filling in the gaps. The general thought seems to be that with a genuine relation to God, one is content, gains security, and avoids trouble (see 16:6*b*).

19:24. This saying has a close variant in 26:15 (see Commentary on 6:6-11; 26:13-16). The comical picture is based on the Eastern custom of dipping bread into a dish of oil or "soup." There is food to be had, but the sluggard is too lazy—or sleepy—to profit from it. Even when sluggards desire what is before them, they remain unsatisfied (v. 15).

244. See R. N. Whybray, *Proverbs,* NCB (Grand Rapids: Eerdmans, 1994) 283.

19:25. This saying is reminiscent of 9:7-9 (see 21:11). To discipline mockers through corporal punishment (19:29; 26:3) may not help them, because they are too stubborn to learn. But the simple can learn from such an object lesson and gain some "street smarts" (see 1:4; 14:15). Verse 25b is literally, "He who rebukes a discerning man (he) understands knowledge." That is, the subject of "understands knowledge" may be either the one who rebukes or the discerning person who is rebuked. In the first reading, rebukers understand knowledge because they do not waste time verbally rebuking a mocker (see 9:7-8; see Commentary on 19:19). In the second reading, the wise get wiser; to those who have, more is given (1:5; Matt 13:12). The punishment of mockers is taken up in vv. 28-29.

19:26. Israel's shame-and-honor culture (see Commentary on 12:8; 13:18) had as one of its most significant expressions the principle—fundamental to all ancient cultures—of honoring one's parents (10:1, 5; Exod 20:12). This principle is implied through portrayal of its violation, through violence (not robbery) done to parents (see 20:20; 28:24; 30:11). For "cause shame and bring reproach," compare the intransitive translation in 13:5.

19:27. Unusual in its construction, this verse has given rise to many conjectural emendations. The form is an admonition with a result clause addressed to "my son," which occurs nowhere else in 10:1–22:16, but is typical of chaps. 1–9 (see Commentary on 19:18-20). The NRSV, following Rashi's old suggestion, inverts part of the two lines to get its translation. The NIV takes the two lines as given, but reads the admonition in v. 27a as though it were a protasis, "If you stop listening . . ." followed by v. 27b as the apodosis, or result clause. Some take the admonition ("Stop listening to instruction") as ironic (see 1 Kgs 2:22; Amos 4:4). The verse remains uncertain.

19:28-29. A "worthless witness" is a *belial* witness (עד בליעל *'ēd bĕliyya'al*; see Commentary on 6:12; 16:27; 1 Kgs 21:10), on which "devour" (lit., "swallow" [בלע *bāla'*]) makes a pun. The mouth can pour out things good and bad, but figuratively it also eats them (see Commentary on 18:8). Compare our sayings, "She swallowed it, hook, line, and sinker," or "He really ate it up," used of untruth or gossip. "Mock/mocker" appears in vv. 25, 28-29 as a key word (see 9:7-12) and also creates a link with the next chapter (20:1).

In v. 29, the threat of punishment for mockers is juxtaposed as a warning to the false witness in v. 28 who "mocks" at justice. Literally, "Judgments [שפטים *šĕpāṭîm*] are prepared," unless the word is a dialectical variant of "rods" (so that the פ [*p*] of "judgments" equals the ב [*b*] of שבטים [*šĕbāṭîm*, "rods"]), which would make a good parallel to v. 29b (see 10:3; 26:3). In v. 25 also the mocker is punished by striking.

REFLECTIONS

1. Spirit, zeal, and desire for good things are no substitute for careful analysis and understanding of reality (19:2; see Commentary on 1:7; 12:1). This is also a central thrust of Mark Noll's *The Scandal of the Evangelical Mind*.[245] Too often, says Noll, evangelical Christianity in North America has been characterized by a simplistic activism that shows zeal without a regard for reality and manifests action without insight into the complexities of life. But activism without reflection or knowledge is not unique to evangelicals; it defines a broad stream in North American culture and human nature in general.[246] We fail to look before we leap. We make haste and waste. We want answers and action before we have understood the questions. We often fail to see issues in terms of a comprehensive biblical worldview, and thus we fail to consider the cosmic-social inter-relatedness and implications of things.[247] Too often we are indifferent to the truth, because we are unwilling to suffer for the sake of truth, both in the gaining of it and in the living out of its consequences.

245. Mark Noll, *The Scandal of the Evangelical Mind* (Grand Rapids: Eerdmans, 1993).
246. Richard Hofstader, *Anti-Intellectualism in American Life* (New York: Knopf, 1963).
247. See Oliver O'Donovan, *Resurrection and Moral Order* (Grand Rapids: Eerdmans, 1986); Brian J. Walsh and J. Richard Middleton, *The Transforming Vision: Shaping a Christian World View* (Downers Grove: Inter-Varsity, 1984); Albert M. Wolters, *Creation Regained: Biblical Basics for a Reformational Worldview* (Grand Rapids: Eerdmans, 1988). Walsh and Middleton provide an extensive bibliography.

Exacerbating these problems is the (understandable) rift between ordinary Christians and mainstream North American intellectual culture.[248] The problem is also manifested in the quality and scope of books read by educated Christians and in the often weak financial support of Christian colleges and seminaries.

The wisdom literature insists that God's human servants develop their intellects and use them in every aspect of life, so that—to speak in New Testament terms—we may "destroy arguments and every proud obstacle raised up against the knowledge of God, and . . . take every thought captive to obey Christ" (2 Cor 10:4-5 NRSV). Paul's great discourse on Christ as the Wisdom of God is not intended to support anti-intellectualism, otherworldly pietism, or fundamentalism (inasmuch as it continues nineteenth-century scientism).[249] Rather, it intends that every human thought, action, and institution be converted from foolish rebellion (disguised as "wisdom") and so be made subject to the mind of Christ (1 Cor 1:18–2:16).

2. To drive out one's mother is particularly heinous (19:26), since she is a defenseless widow (object of God's special concern, 15:25). In Israel, a mother would reside with a son only upon the death of her husband. Shakespeare's *King Lear* provides a pre-modern instance of driving out a parent. This issue has become exceedingly difficult in modern, technological societies in which the medical and personal care of the aged is often beyond the capacity of a nuclear family. The basic principles of 19:26 still hold, but wisdom for their implementation has become more difficult to obtain, given the rapid changes in society and medical technology.

248. See George M. Marsden, *The Soul of the American University* (New York: Oxford University Press, 1994).
249. George M. Marsden, *Fundamentalism and American Culture* (New York: Oxford University Press, 1980).

Proverbs 20:1-30, Wine Is a Mocker, Strong Drink a Brawler

NIV

20 Wine is a mocker and beer a brawler;
whoever is led astray by them is not wise.

²A king's wrath is like the roar of a lion;
he who angers him forfeits his life.

³It is to a man's honor to avoid strife,
but every fool is quick to quarrel.

⁴A sluggard does not plow in season;
so at harvest time he looks but finds nothing.

⁵The purposes of a man's heart are deep waters,
but a man of understanding draws them out.

⁶Many a man claims to have unfailing love,
but a faithful man who can find?

⁷The righteous man leads a blameless life;
blessed are his children after him.

⁸When a king sits on his throne to judge,
he winnows out all evil with his eyes.

⁹Who can say, "I have kept my heart pure;
I am clean and without sin"?

¹⁰Differing weights and differing measures—

NRSV

20 Wine is a mocker, strong drink a brawler,
and whoever is led astray by it is not wise.

² The dread anger of a king is like the growling of a lion;
anyone who provokes him to anger forfeits life itself.

³ It is honorable to refrain from strife,
but every fool is quick to quarrel.

⁴ The lazy person does not plow in season;
harvest comes, and there is nothing to be found.

⁵ The purposes in the human mind are like deep water,
but the intelligent will draw them out.

⁶ Many proclaim themselves loyal,
but who can find one worthy of trust?

⁷ The righteous walk in integrity—
happy are the children who follow them!

⁸ A king who sits on the throne of judgment
winnows all evil with his eyes.

⁹ Who can say, "I have made my heart clean;
I am pure from my sin"?

NIV

the Lord detests them both.

11 Even a child is known by his actions,
by whether his conduct is pure and right.

12 Ears that hear and eyes that see—
the Lord has made them both.

13 Do not love sleep or you will grow poor;
stay awake and you will have food to spare.

14 "It's no good, it's no good!" says the buyer;
then off he goes and boasts about his purchase.

15 Gold there is, and rubies in abundance,
but lips that speak knowledge are a rare jewel.

16 Take the garment of one who puts up security
for a stranger;
hold it in pledge if he does it for a wayward woman.

17 Food gained by fraud tastes sweet to a man,
but he ends up with a mouth full of gravel.

18 Make plans by seeking advice;
if you wage war, obtain guidance.

19 A gossip betrays a confidence;
so avoid a man who talks too much.

20 If a man curses his father or mother,
his lamp will be snuffed out in pitch darkness.

21 An inheritance quickly gained at the beginning
will not be blessed at the end.

22 Do not say, "I'll pay you back for this wrong!"
Wait for the Lord, and he will deliver you.

23 The Lord detests differing weights,
and dishonest scales do not please him.

24 A man's steps are directed by the Lord.
How then can anyone understand his own way?

25 It is a trap for a man to dedicate something rashly
and only later to consider his vows.

26 A wise king winnows out the wicked;
he drives the threshing wheel over them.

27 The lamp of the Lord searches the spirit of a man[a];
it searches out his inmost being.

28 Love and faithfulness keep a king safe;
through love his throne is made secure.

29 The glory of young men is their strength,
gray hair the splendor of the old.

30 Blows and wounds cleanse away evil,
and beatings purge the inmost being.

a27 Or *The spirit of man is the Lord's lamp*

NRSV

10 Diverse weights and diverse measures
are both alike an abomination to the Lord.

11 Even children make themselves known by
their acts,
by whether what they do is pure and right.

12 The hearing ear and the seeing eye—
the Lord has made them both.

13 Do not love sleep, or else you will come to
poverty;
open your eyes, and you will have plenty of
bread.

14 "Bad, bad," says the buyer,
then goes away and boasts.

15 There is gold, and abundance of costly stones;
but the lips informed by knowledge are a
precious jewel.

16 Take the garment of one who has given surety
for a stranger;
seize the pledge given as surety for foreigners.

17 Bread gained by deceit is sweet,
but afterward the mouth will be full of gravel.

18 Plans are established by taking advice;
wage war by following wise guidance.

19 A gossip reveals secrets;
therefore do not associate with a babbler.

20 If you curse father or mother,
your lamp will go out in utter darkness.

21 An estate quickly acquired in the beginning
will not be blessed in the end.

22 Do not say, "I will repay evil";
wait for the Lord, and he will help you.

23 Differing weights are an abomination to the Lord,
and false scales are not good.

24 All our steps are ordered by the Lord;
how then can we understand our own ways?

25 It is a snare for one to say rashly, "It is holy,"
and begin to reflect only after making a vow.

26 A wise king winnows the wicked,
and drives the wheel over them.

27 The human spirit is the lamp of the Lord,
searching every inmost part.

28 Loyalty and faithfulness preserve the king,
and his throne is upheld by righteousness.[a]

29 The glory of youths is their strength,
but the beauty of the aged is their gray hair.

30 Blows that wound cleanse away evil;
beatings make clean the innermost parts.

a Gk: Heb *loyalty*

COMMENTARY

20:1. The opening saying takes up the word "mocker" from 19:28-29 to personify wine and beer as bad company and destroyers of wisdom (see Commentary on 23:19-2, 29-35; 31:4-5). Strong drink is also a "brawler" (המה *hmh*), the root used to describe the seductive or foolish woman (7:11; 9:13). In 1:21 the root describes the tumultuous city where Wisdom's cry goes unheeded. This connection of crazy-making drink and Woman Folly is strengthened by their common effect on young males: They both tempt young men to be led astray (see Deut 27:18; Isa 28:7) or intoxicated (שגה *šāgâ*; see 5:19, positively of one's wife; 5:20,–23, negatively of the strange woman). Alcoholic and sexual intoxication—except within the passionate bonds of marriage—rob one of wisdom. That is, those drunk with wine or lust cannot discriminate the limits of creation and conduct (cf. Lev 10:8-11). Lemuel's mother makes a similar association of drinking and lust for women (see Commentary on 31:3-5). These verbal links suggest that this verse is part of the thematic, final editing of the book.

20:2. Verse 2*a* is a variant of 19:12, but v. 2*b* offers indirect advice about not rousing the king's anger (see Commentary on 14:35; 16:14-15). This advice speaks to all situations where a powerful person has the ability to damage a weaker one (though it does not always succeed, 18:23). For instance, young offenders had best not sass the judge presiding over their drug trial. For the expression "angers him" see Commentary on 14:16*b*, where the verb is translated differently. "Forfeit life" is literally "miss life" (חוטא נפשו *ḥôṭē' napšô*) as in "miss me" (8:36 NRSV).

20:3. See 17:14 on stopping a quarrel before it starts, and 15:18 on the qualities of a person who stills a quarrel. For honor and shame in Israel's culture, see Commentary on 12:8; 13:18; 26:1. For the verb here translated as "quick to quarrel," see 18:1 ("defies" or "break" out in 17:14).

20:4. Agricultural life, lived in harmony with the cosmic order of seasons, is a model of wisdom. "In season" is literally, "in late fall" (חרף *ḥōrep*)—that is, the cooler, rainy season when one plows and sows in order to reap in the summer harvest time. This saying varies the act-consequence idea of reaping what one sows. Its focus, however, is on the crucial timing of actions. The famous Gezer calendar shows that each season had its appropriate tasks.[250] On the sluggard, see Commentary on 6:6-11; 10:4-5; 13:4.

20:5. Traditionally, what is in the king's heart is too deep for humans to search out (25:3), but no heart is hidden from God (15:11; 21:1; see Excursus, "The 'Heart' in the Old Testament," 60-61, and 18:4 for "deep waters"). Wise persons can bring to the surface what others have in mind, even when there are attempts at concealment (28:11). The image is of a well into which one descends in order to get life-giving water (see Commentary on 10:11; 13:14). Often in ancient cities (Megiddo is a good example) there is a long stairway carved through rock in order to get down to the protected well at the base of the city mound. No little effort was required to go down, get the water, and carry it back up to the surface for use.

20:6. This verse shows how little humans heed the wisdom of 27:2. It also should make honest folk cautious (see Commentary on 17:17-18) about those who proclaim their reliable love, or חסד (*ḥesed*), a word often associated with faithfulness (see Commentary on 16:5-6). The Lord approves faithful, or "reliable," persons (12:24), and this quality is especially important in witnesses (12:17; 14:5) and messengers (13:17). "Who can find?" is a rhetorical question to express rarity. The idiom expects a negative answer, "no one" or "hardly anyone" (see 31:10).

20:7. For "walk in integrity," see Commentary on 10:9 (see also 19:1). Verse 7*b* again embodies the connection of the generations so basic to biblical thought. This is often conveyed by the word "son" (בן *bēn*), which occurs sixty times in Proverbs (see Commentary on 10:1; 13:22; 14:26; 17:6). Good begets good and is blessed (see Commentary on 3:13) from one generation to the next.

---

250. *Ancient Near Eastern Texts Relating to the Old Testament*, ed. James B. Pritchard, 3rd ed. (Princeton, N.J.: Princeton University Press, 1969) 320; R. de Vaux, *Ancient Israel* (New York: McGraw-Hill, 1961) 1:184.

20:8. The throne (1 Kgs 7:7; Ps 122:5; Isa 16:5) symbolizes the most basic function of kingship: the doing of justice (2 Sam 15:2-4). Justice had an external aspect, the military and diplomatic defense of the nation, as well as a domestic one. In Israel, the latter function entailed the defense of the poor and the needy (28:15; 29:14; 31:8-9; see Psalm 72) and the removal or punishment of the wicked according to the norm of righteousness (16:12; 19:26; 25:4-5). In 2 Samuel 8–9 (cf. Prov 8:15), David is portrayed as a good and wise king who secures the national boundaries against enemies and shows kindness to the crippled Mephibosheth, a survivor from the house of Saul. This saying has "leap-frog" connections (where two or more related verses are separated by intermediate verses) with vv. 10, 12; there also Yahweh appears as judge and creator.

20:9. Set between a proverb on royal judgment and another on divine standards, this verse is a reminder of the universality of sin (see Gen 6:5; 8:21; Psalms 14; 32; 51:5; Jer 17:9-10; Rom 3:9-19). "Who can say . . . ?" expects the answer, "No one."

20:10. Verses 10 and 23 are variants of the same saying and are closely related to 11:1. The repetition of such sayings reinforces God's deep concern for integrity and fair play in matters of money and commerce (Deut 25:13-16; Amos 8:5). Often the use of money and material goods is the best indicator of the operative beliefs of a culture or a person. "Faith without works is dead"; that is, only those beliefs that shape everyday life are genuine (Jas 2:17, 20; 5:1-6l see Commentary on 20:12).

20:11. Along with the NIV and the NRSV, another possible translation of this text (based on another meaning of the root נכר *nkr*) is "A child may be dissembling in his behavior/ Even though his actions are blameless and proper" (TNK; see 26:24*a*). For the vocabulary of v. 11*b*, see 21:8*b*.

20:12. In the sayings of chaps. 10–29, Yahweh often appears as the Creator of humans (14:31; 17:5; 22:2; 29:13), in contrast to chaps. 1–9 where, God appears mainly as Creator of the cosmos—including human beings (3:19-20; 8:22-31). The "hearing ear" is the basic organ through which wisdom enters the heart (see Commentary on 15:31; 25:12; see also 2:2; 18:15). But the "seeing eye" is not portrayed as an organ for

getting wisdom. It is much more ambiguous, often representing mere perception or self-deception (see Commentary on 3:7; 26:12). The fool's eyes and ears do not function rightly (17:24; 23:9). That God creates these organs means that God holds humans accountable for their use (Exod 4:10-16; Ps 94:8-9). The Exodus passage reflects mutual divine-human involvement in speech (see Commentary on 16:1). The ending, "them both," links this verse to v. 10.

20:13. This saying has a catch-word link to the "eyes" of v. 12 (and v. 8?). The contrast of sloth and industry is a particular case of the opposition between folly and wisdom (see Commentary on 6:6-11; 19:15). Proverbs 12:11 and 30:22*b* use similar Hebrew expressions for "plenty of bread." Psalm 127:2 provides an important qualification to this saying: Without God's blessing even sleepless labor profits not.

20:14. Here the NRSV better catches the pithy sharpness, though not the poetic genius, of the Hebrew—an ironic observation on devious behavior in the business of buying and selling. In ancient Israel, as in many non-Western countries today, most transactions were achieved through bargaining over the price of goods. The bargaining ritual was well-known to both buyer and seller. The buyer offers a low initial price, and the seller asks for a higher one. Usually a satisfactory compromise is then reached. Here the buyer condemns a deal as bad, only to boast afterward. Although the issues are judicial rather than commercial, Abraham's negotiating with God for Sodom and Gommorah is a strangely inverted example of negotiating a "price." A gracious God keeps accepting lower offers from Abraham (Gen 18:22-33)!

20:15. Like v. 14, this verse concerns the value of things. Taken together, the two sayings present an ironic contrast between the goods for which one haggles and priceless wisdom (see 3:15; 8:10-11). This verse praises the value of lips as an instrument of wisdom (see 25:11-12). They are not so much a precious jewel but "instruments" or "vessels."

20:16. The NIV follows the MT vowel pointing of this verse and introduces the "strange woman" from Proverbs 1–9 (see 27:13, which is nearly identical). The NRSV translates the *Ketib*, or consonantal text, moving the parallelism from masculine singular "stranger" to masculine plural "foreigners." These words may simply refer to a second party, "another" (see 27:2), with a hint that they are not known well to the guarantor (see Commentary on 17:18) The *Ketib* is probably original here, and its warning echoes common advice (see Commentary on 6:1-5; 11:15). A person's cloak could be taken as surety for a debt, but the law placed restrictions on the practice (Deut 24:10-13, 17; Amos 2:8; see Prov 22:26-27). The admonition to take is probably pedagogical irony, the real target of the saying being one who foolishly gives security for a loan.

20:17. This verse is linked to v. 16 by wordplay on "security"/"sweet." The verbal connection suggests that someone can be enticed by a "sweet deal" but has in fact swallowed a bad deal. "Bread gained by deceit" is literally "deceptive bread" (cf. 23:3). Only afterward is the true nature of the "meal" evident (see 9:17). Job 20:12-23 is a baroque elaboration of the metaphor of swallowing something bad that seems initially sweet. Similarly, the "deceptive bread" of this verse should not be limited to bad business deals or to ill-gotten gain, but may refer to any wickedness or deception that someone "swallows" (see 4:17; 18:8; for "gravel," see Lam 3:16).

20:18. The interest unexpectedly turns to advice appropriate for a king, who is militarily responsible for the integrity of the nation's borders (see Commentary on 11:14; 15:22). Proverbs 24:6 provides a near parallel.

20:19. Another admonition, this verse picks up themes encountered earlier (see Commentary on 11:13*a,* a variant of 20:19*a;* see also 25:9). The principle that humans are shaped by the company they keep (14:7) is given a specific focus here. One should not keep company with gossips and slanderers. It is ironic to associate with those whose speech destroys community (18:8).

20:20. The honoring of parents is a fundamental obligation in ancient cultures (see Commentary on 19:26; Exod 21:17; Lev 20:9). The opposite of honoring parents (כבד *kābēd*) is cursing them (קלל *qālal*; see Commentary on 26:2), a term that also connotes treating them with contempt (see Sir 3:1-16). The punishment of having one's lamp snuffed out befits the wicked (13:9). But there may be a wordplay here, since "lamp" is used as a stereotyped metaphor for the continuance of a

family (1 Kgs 11:36; 15:4; 2 Kgs 8:19). If this reading is correct, then the punishment fits the crime. Those who dishonor the parents who gave them the light of life may have their own line extinguished (see 2 Sam 18:14-18). When Eli "honors" his sons rather than God, this inversion of honor receives a similar judgment (1 Sam 2:29-31, 34).

20:21. Ordinarily an inheritance is not gained through activity but as a parental legacy (19:14). This verse may refer to anyone who wrongfully acquires (*Ketib*) the familial land of another. Ahab's acquisition of Naboth's vineyard is the classic case (see Leviticus 25; 1 Kings 21; Isa 5:8-9). Alternatively, the saying refers to sons who hasten the demise of their parents to get the inheritance. If so, vv. 20-21 form an editorial proverb pair that mutually reinforce each other. The manner in which the inheritance is "quickly gained" (*Qere*) is not spelled out (see 13:11; 28:22).

20:22. This admonition to wait patiently for Yahweh provides the theological foundation for vv. 20-21, because God is the ultimate source of justice (see Commentary on 24:29; see also Deut 32:35-36; Psalms 27; 37). The intent of this verse is not pacifist or anti-judicial, since divine authority for international and domestic justice devolves on human officials appointed to those tasks (Psalm 72; Rom 13:1-7). Rather, it warns victims against arbitrarily taking justice into their own hands (see Lev 19:17-18). David is a model of this principle when he refuses to kill Saul, though he narrowly escapes violating it in the case of Nabal (1 Samuel 24–26). This verse also encourages victims of crime, when human justice fails them (see 29:26; for NT allusions, see Matt 5:38-39; Rom 12:17; 1 Thess 5:15).

20:23-24. These verses are variants of other sayings within Proverbs. The present location of v. 23, a variant of v. 10, reinforces the theme of Yahweh's justice in vv. 20-22. Verse 24 is a variation on themes from 16:1-9 (see also Ps 37:23*a,* a duplicate of v. 24*a*). There are limits to human understanding, even of one's own life journey (see Commentary on 27:1; cf. 14:8). Proverbs presents a paradox by insisting on the importance of human wisdom and responsibility (see Commentary on 21:29) even as it insists that God's guidance of life is beyond human understanding or control. This paradox is essential to the book of Proverbs and to biblical faith. Jeremiah bitterly alludes to a form of this proverb (Jer 10:23; see also Jer 9:12, 23; 17:9-10).

20:25. Here the writer portrays the evil of inattention to God and the created world. To declare something holy is to dedicate it voluntarily, on oath, as a gift to God (the verb is rare, but its general sense seems clear). Such gifts could be animals, money, land, or other property (Lev 27:9-25). Oaths were often made in thanks to God for rescue from trouble (Gen 28:20-22; Jonah 1:16; 2:9). But to do so casually or hastily is a form of taking the Lord's name in vain, of not taking God seriously enough, as if God would not call one to account (Exod 20:7; Lev 19:12; Num 30:2; Deut 23:21-23; Eccl 5:1-6). Such vows are also a form of inattention to (or of self-deception about) the created world, for the use of whose goods we are responsible. To offer God what we cannot pay thus dishonors God and devalues the world entrusted to our care. In the Gospels, Jesus repeatedly discusses the games that people play with vows and other obligations to God (Matt 5:33-37; 15:3-9; 23:16-24). Money talks, also, in its religious deposition.

20:26. This verse is tied to v. 8 and the judicial image of winnowing (lit., "scattering"), by which the righteous and the wicked, like wheat and chaff, are separated (see 25:4-5 for a different image). The image of v. 26*b*, however, is disputed. The NIV supplies "threshing" (not in Hebrew) to explain the metaphor of the wheel. This is probably correct. Various mechanical means were used to separate the husk from the kernel, depending on the nature of the grain (Isa 28:27-28). Verse 26*a* is a summary statement of the process, focused on its conclusion. Verse 26*b* sharpens the severity of judgment with the image of the threshing wheel, though temporally that action precedes winnowing.

20:27. Literally, the Hebrew reads, "The breath of man is Yahweh's lamp,/ searching all the rooms of the belly." Verse 27*a* is a nominal sentence (without a verb) so that either phrase could be subject or predicate. The NIV understands the verb from v. 27*b* to govern v. 27*a* (a double-duty construction). This reading is possible but improbable, and it obscures the suggestive richness of the proverb's imagery. The NIV re-

flects the common thought that God searches and knows the inmost being of persons (see 15:11; 16:2; 17:3; 18:8 for this phrase). Human breath is given by God at creation and taken away at death (Gen 2:7; 1 Kgs 17:17; Isa 42:5). "Breath" (נשמה *nĕšāmâ*), however, "is not only the principle of life . . . but also the principle of wisdom" (Job 26:4; 32:8, 18; see 20:3).[251] In this regard, "breath" is similar to "spirit" (רוח *rûaḥ*; see 1:23). Breath typically goes in and comes out of a person, giving life; but it also comes out as wisdom and words. Lamps give light for seeing and searching. But light is also a symbol of life (6:23; 13:9; 16:15; 20:20; 29:13). The imagery of lamp and breath thus communicate a person's possession of and responsibility for the life and self-reflective insight that God gives. As often in the second Solomonic sub-collection, God is present in the inmost being and actions of persons (see Commentary on 16:1, 9; 21:1). The proverb thus suggests both God's knowledge of humans and human self-knowledge as a gift of God, not either one or the other.

20:28. Verse 28*a* parallels the prayer in Ps 61:8. Love and faithfulness are gifts from God to the king (see Ps 89:33), which the king displays in his own rule (see Commentary on 3:3). Verse 28*b* is a variant of 16:12*b*, with "kindness" in place of "righteousness" (the NRSV translates the LXX).

20:29. This text presents a profound contrast between the characteristic virtues of youth and age. Gray hair is a symbol of wisdom, since only the old have experienced enough reality to be wise (see Commentary on 16:31; Sir 25:3-6). Rehoboam sins against this wisdom principle when he listens to the advice of the young men and ignores the wise old advisers associated with his father, Solomon. This folly costs him the ten northern tribes (1 Kgs 12:6-20).

20:30. Details of this verse are uncertain, but the NIV and the NRSV seem to capture its general sense. Corporal discipline was seen as a means to correct wrongdoers and errant youths. "Evil" in v. 30*a* may be a word for (inner) "thoughts" (see 17:10; 23:13; Ps 139:2, 17). The external discipline of the body affects the inmost being (see Commentary on 20:27).

251. E. Dhorme, *A Commentary on the Book of Job* (Nashville: Thomas Nelson, 1984) 378.

REFLECTIONS

1. Israelite society was often sinfully violent and brutal, as the inter-tribal wars, the conflict between David and Saul, and the separation of northern and southern kingdoms demonstrate. And yet it promoted an ethos of civility, community harmony, cordiality in personal relations, and the avoidance of conflict. These qualities are related to Israel's deep sense of honor and shame (see Commentary on 20:3). Perhaps ancient Israel is closer to Japanese culture and history in these matters than it is to that of the United States. Americans seem to tolerate an ethos of violence fed by the mass media, and too often lack healthy restraint in personal relations. Lack of shame and proper personal boundaries in our society is regularly exposed on television talk shows.

In this context, one of the tasks of the church is to become a counterculture that fosters a biblical sense of the nobility and dignity of persons—without being naive about sin (see Reflections on 15:25). The issue is that we are called to be in the world but not *of* it (John 15:19; 17:6-19), and that we are not to be conformed to this world but renewed by the Word and Spirit of God (Rom 12:1-2).

This task requires that ordinary Christians commit themselves to being shaped by Scripture and Christian wisdom in their daily life (see Phil 4:8-9). Conversely, it requires that Christians be willing to discipline their use of entertainment media. It especially requires that children be provided healthy (not boring!) alternatives to the spiritual trash that panders to them in some television programs (see Commentary on 22:6). It requires that the "body of Christ" be an extended family that helps overstressed parents to rear their children (see Reflections on 15:22).

2. Proverbs 20:9 is a corrective to those who believe that they can maintain their own purity in evil times (see Commentary on 16:2; 26:5-6), while implicitly relegating others to the ranks of the impure and sinful.[252] We are morally ambiguous creatures, and inevitably we are implicated in society's immorality. None of us will be whole until Christ makes humanity whole. Nor can we be pure or fully redeemed until the creation itself is pure and redeemed (Rom 8:18-25). In the meantime, righteous and wicked, pure and impure are standards of judgment to which people more or less conform. A person is only relatively one or relatively the other. The line between wisdom and folly, good and bad, cuts through the heart of us all. What matters is that one is on the road of progressive righteousness and wisdom (see chaps. 1–9). In addition, terms such as "righteous" and "wicked" (see Commentary on 17:15) are often applied to very limited matters.[253] In a criminal case, for example, the thief is called "wicked" or "guilty," and the falsely accused is called "righteous" or "innocent," only with regard to the particular matter at hand. Unfortunately, a person who is righteous or pure in one area may be wicked in another (see Jas 2:8-13).

3. Parents sometimes note that a child's character is present at a very early age (20:11). Ancient Greece and Rome sometimes saw character (and class) as a lifelong, immutable given. Ancient Israel had a more complex view. The Israelites recognized that character in many respects was something given. Yet they also recognized that persons can change morally and spiritually, either for better or for worse.[254] Many of the biblical stories recount the growth, or decline, of such people as Abraham, Saul, David, and Esther. One of the factors in character development is early training (22:6). Another is collective and personal discipline (13:24). But undergirding all our attempts to improve ourselves and our world is the power of divine grace

---

252. See D. Bonhoeffer, *Ethics* (New York: Macmillan, 1965) 67.
253. See John Lyons, *Introduction to Theoretical Linguistics* (Cambridge: Cambridge University Press, 1969) 465-66.
254. See Erich Auerbach, *Mimesis: The Representation of Reality in Western Literature* (Garden City, N.Y.: Doubleday, 1957).

(Gen 39:2-3, 5, 21, 23; 1 Cor 1:26-31; Phil 2:12-13), which can mold ordinary people and families into great ones.

In this fact lies the immediate hope and joy of biblical salvation for all who struggle with woundedness and imperfection. We are all the victims of others, and we are all victims of our own sin. At a certain point the allocation of guilt and blame becomes a futile exercise. The gospel—in both the Old and the New Testaments—urges us to become responsible for our own life journey (1:10-19; see also Reflections on Proverbs 9), to lay hold of divine grace and forgiveness (28:13-14), to join with like-minded Christians, and to press forward knowing that we do not have to remain helplessly stuck in our misery (Phil 3:10-17, 20-21).

4. Kings and rulers need wise counsel in the event of war (20:18). But this admonition applies to any struggle or conflict in human life. Humans need counsel especially when things are difficult. Those affected by a situation may be least able to see the whole picture or to think clearly about it. Jesus applies the metaphor of Prov 20:18 to counting the cost of discipleship (Luke 14:31-33; for the limits of this saying, see Commentary on 21:30-31).

Proverbs 21:1-31, All Deeds Are Right in the Sight of the Doer, but the Lord Weighs the Heart

NIV

21 The king's heart is in the hand of the LORD;
he directs it like a watercourse wherever he pleases.

²All a man's ways seem right to him,
but the LORD weighs the heart.

³To do what is right and just
is more acceptable to the LORD than sacrifice.

⁴Haughty eyes and a proud heart,
the lamp of the wicked, are sin!

⁵The plans of the diligent lead to profit
as surely as haste leads to poverty.

⁶A fortune made by a lying tongue
is a fleeting vapor and a deadly snare.[a]

⁷The violence of the wicked will drag them away,
for they refuse to do what is right.

⁸The way of the guilty is devious,
but the conduct of the innocent is upright.

⁹Better to live on a corner of the roof
than share a house with a quarrelsome wife.

¹⁰The wicked man craves evil;
his neighbor gets no mercy from him.

ᵃ6 Some Hebrew manuscripts, Septuagint and Vulgate; most Hebrew manuscripts *vapor for those who seek death*

NRSV

21 The king's heart is a stream of water in the hand of the LORD;
he turns it wherever he will.

² All deeds are right in the sight of the doer,
but the LORD weighs the heart.

³ To do righteousness and justice
is more acceptable to the LORD than sacrifice.

⁴ Haughty eyes and a proud heart—
the lamp of the wicked—are sin.

⁵ The plans of the diligent lead surely to abundance,
but everyone who is hasty comes only to want.

⁶ The getting of treasures by a lying tongue
is a fleeting vapor and a snare[a] of death.

⁷ The violence of the wicked will sweep them away,
because they refuse to do what is just.

⁸ The way of the guilty is crooked,
but the conduct of the pure is right.

⁹ It is better to live in a corner of the housetop
than in a house shared with a contentious wife.

¹⁰ The souls of the wicked desire evil;
their neighbors find no mercy in their eyes.

ᵃ Gk: Heb *seekers*

NIV

¹¹When a mocker is punished, the simple gain
wisdom;
when a wise man is instructed, he gets
knowledge.

¹²The Righteous One^a takes note of the house of
the wicked
and brings the wicked to ruin.

¹³If a man shuts his ears to the cry of the poor,
he too will cry out and not be answered.

¹⁴A gift given in secret soothes anger,
and a bribe concealed in the cloak pacifies
great wrath.

¹⁵When justice is done, it brings joy to the
righteous
but terror to evildoers.

¹⁶A man who strays from the path of
understanding
comes to rest in the company of the dead.

¹⁷He who loves pleasure will become poor;
whoever loves wine and oil will never be rich.

¹⁸The wicked become a ransom for the righteous,
and the unfaithful for the upright.

¹⁹Better to live in a desert
than with a quarrelsome and ill-tempered
wife.

²⁰In the house of the wise are stores of choice
food and oil,
but a foolish man devours all he has.

²¹He who pursues righteousness and love
finds life, prosperity^b and honor.

²²A wise man attacks the city of the mighty
and pulls down the stronghold in which they
trust.

²³He who guards his mouth and his tongue
keeps himself from calamity.

²⁴The proud and arrogant man—"Mocker" is his
name;
he behaves with overweening pride.

²⁵The sluggard's craving will be the death of him,
because his hands refuse to work.

²⁶All day long he craves for more,
but the righteous give without sparing.

^a12 Or *The righteous man*   ^b21 Or *righteousness*

NRSV

¹¹ When a scoffer is punished, the simple become
wiser;
when the wise are instructed, they increase
in knowledge.

¹² The Righteous One observes the house of the
wicked;
he casts the wicked down to ruin.

¹³ If you close your ear to the cry of the poor,
you will cry out and not be heard.

¹⁴ A gift in secret averts anger;
and a concealed bribe in the bosom, strong
wrath.

¹⁵ When justice is done, it is a joy to the
righteous,
but dismay to evildoers.

¹⁶ Whoever wanders from the way of
understanding
will rest in the assembly of the dead.

¹⁷ Whoever loves pleasure will suffer want;
whoever loves wine and oil will not be rich.

¹⁸ The wicked is a ransom for the righteous,
and the faithless for the upright.

¹⁹ It is better to live in a desert land
than with a contentious and fretful wife.

²⁰ Precious treasure remains^a in the house of the
wise,
but the fool devours it.

²¹ Whoever pursues righteousness and kindness
will find life^b and honor.

²² One wise person went up against a city of
warriors
and brought down the stronghold in which
they trusted.

²³ To watch over mouth and tongue
is to keep out of trouble.

²⁴ The proud, haughty person, named "Scoffer,"
acts with arrogant pride.

²⁵ The craving of the lazy person is fatal,
for lazy hands refuse to labor.

²⁶ All day long the wicked covet,^c
but the righteous give and do not hold back.

²⁷ The sacrifice of the wicked is an abomination;
how much more when brought with evil intent.

²⁸ A false witness will perish,
but a good listener will testify successfully.

²⁹ The wicked put on a bold face,

^aGk: Heb *and oil*   ^bGk: Heb *life and righteousness*   ^cGk: Heb
all day long one covets covetously

NIV

²⁷The sacrifice of the wicked is detestable—
how much more so when brought with evil intent!

²⁸A false witness will perish,
and whoever listens to him will be destroyed
forever.ᵃ

²⁹A wicked man puts up a bold front,
but an upright man gives thought to his ways.

³⁰There is no wisdom, no insight, no plan
that can succeed against the LORD.

³¹The horse is made ready for the day of battle,
but victory rests with the LORD.

ᵃ28 Or / but the words of an obedient man will live on

NRSV

but the upright give thought toᵃ their ways.

³⁰ No wisdom, no understanding, no counsel,
can avail against the LORD.

³¹ The horse is made ready for the day of battle,
but the victory belongs to the LORD.

ᵃAnother reading is *establish*

COMMENTARY

21:1. In arid Palestine, irrigation channels can make the desert bloom (see Isa 32:2, of righteous rulers). Here the image portrays God's inscrutable mastery of the king, who otherwise appears uniquely superior to other people. This saying asserts God's mysterious sovereignty precisely where humans are most free and potent, in the thoughts of their "heart" (see Excursus, "The 'Heart' in the Old Testament," 60-61). The king is cited as that person who is most able to claim such power and freedom (see Commentary on 20:5; 25:2-3).

21:2. This verse is a variant of 16:2, and its repetition suggests—as does the dialectic of Yahweh and royal sayings throughout 20:22–21:4—a close affinity between 16:1-15 (on Yahweh and the king) and this verse. It links with the "heart" of the preceding verse.

21:3. Although it does not mention the king, the similarity of v. 3*a* and 16:12*a* (as opposites) also reinforces the connection of this passage and 16:1-15. This saying does not reject sacrifice as such, but worship by the wicked (15:8-9).

21:4. "Haughty eyes" (see Commentary on 6:17; 30:13) go naturally with a "proud heart" (lit., "broad heart"; see 28:25*a*; Ps 101:5) as "the lamp of the wicked" (see Commentary on 15:30; cf. Matt 6:22-23). These stand in implicit contrast to "the lamp of the LORD," which searches humans (see Commentary on 20:27 for the double sense of "lamp" as "life" and "wisdom"). In the case of

the wicked, their "lamp"—including their "wisdom"—is sin (see 26:12; Isa 5:20-23). Such lamps are doomed to being extinguished (13:9; 20:20). The above understanding may resolve the disputed question as to the relation of the two verse halves.

21:5-6. Together these verses consider opposite ways of getting—or losing—material goods. Verse 5 contrasts the diligent (see Commentary on 10:4-5; 12:24), who make plans, with the hasty, who presumably do not. The former get gain ("profit" should be taken in a broad sense, for agrarian Israel was not a society with capital investments in the modern sense), while haste leads to want or lack (cf. 13:11; 14:23). A farmer's success does not come quickly. The verb for "haste" (אץ *ʾāṣ*) does not have moral connotations per se (see Josh 10:13), but haste in human affairs generally is negative. In monetary matters, haste connotes greed (28:20; cf. 11:24), and haste in speech connotes a lack of reflection (29:20; see Commentary on 15:28; 19:2). One might say that "haste makes waste," or "make haste slowly," or "look before you leap."

Verse 6 describes an evil means of getting rich, "a lying tongue." Treasures gained through deception stand under God's judgment (10:2). Verse 6*b* is textually problematic, as reflected in the NIV and NRSV notes. The solutions suggested rest on emendation and the ancient versions, but remain uncertain.

21:7. The wicked do the opposite of the righteous (see vv. 3, 15) as a matter of deliberate choice ("because they refuse" is an explanatory clause, as in v. 25; see also 2:14). Violence (24:2) begets violence, and the wicked are carried away by it, like fish in a net (see Hab 1:15). As we do to others, so it will happen to us (1:17-19; 11:6*b*). Similar is the saying that those who "take the sword will perish by the sword" (Matt 26:52 NRSV).

21:8. The NRSV and the NIV take the uncertain and unique word זר (*wāzār*) to be cognate with an Arabic word meaning "to be laden with guilt." But this is uncertain. Two ancient versions (Syriac and Vulgate; see also Targum) take the word as the copula *w* ("and") plus *zār,* "strange." Then the saying may be rendered, "Confused is the way of a man and strange,/ but the pure—his work is right." Somewhat along these lines, the TNK translates, "The way of a man may be tortuous and strange,/ Though his actions are blameless and proper." But rendering "blameless and proper" as a coordinate predicate requires the insertion of the copula. There is no wholly satisfactory solution here.

21:9. A duplicate of 25:24 and one of several on the "quarrelsome wife" (v. 19; 27:15; cf. 19:13), this saying has a humorous edge and assumes that relations with a spouse profoundly affect one for good or for ill (see Commentary on 11:17; 12:4). The image is of a hut on a flat roof where one is exposed to the elements—whether rain or withering sirocco winds. A house "shared" may be correct (so LXX and Vg). Or the word may mean a "noisy house."[255] The point is that one is better exposed to nature than to a wife's "storms" (see 27:15). These sayings provide exceptions to the basic perspective in this male-oriented book that a wife is a divine gift to a man (5:15-20; 12:4; 18:22; 31:10-31; see Gen 2:18).

21:10. People may be known by their appetites and desires, by their choices and ultimate loves (see 1:16, 28-29; 4:16-17; 8:17, 35). The soul, an organ of appetite (16:24, 26), wants what it wants, even if other people are injured, because addictive desire tolerates no obstacles to its gratification (for the opposite virtue—kindness or mercy, see 14:21, 31; 19:17; 28:8). The story of

255. Taking חבר (*ḥbr*) as cognate with Akkadian *habrum,* "noisy."

Amnon's rape of Tamar illustrates the proverb in the sexual arena (2 Samuel 13). The Hebrew of this verse makes a sad wordplay; orthographically both "evil" (רע *rā'*) and "neighbor" (רע *rēa'*) are רע (*r'*). Verses 12-13 provide theological perspective on this verse (see Commentary on 12:10).

21:11-12. Either the "simple" and the "wise" are contrasted in their mode of learning (v. 11), or the simple learn both by observing the fate of mockers and by heeding the instruction of the wise (see 1:4-5; 19:25). In Hebrew, "observes" (משכיל *maśkîl,* v. 12) picks up the word for "instructs" in v. 11. The words "wicked" and "evil" (רשע *rāšā'* and רע *ra'*) also link v. 12 to v. 10, on which it offers theological comment. Both the NIV and the NRSV take "righteous" as referring to Yahweh, on the ground that God is the judge of the wicked (see 22:12, where "overthrow" and "cast down" translate the same verb). While God is often described as righteous, the use of the term as a title is disputed.

21:13. This saying is a sharp warning against active indifference toward the unfortunate (see v. 10; 3:27-28; 18:23; 24:11-12). The not-hearing is willful, since the culprit shuts his ears (see 28:27). The not-being-heard is a classic example of the *lex talionis:* as people do, so it happens to them (see Commentary on 21:7; see also Jas 2:13). The hidden agent of justice is God (see 1:28; Isa 58:9; 65:12, 24; Mic 3:4; and Job's complaint in Job 19:7). When humans ignore the cry of the desperate, God hears them (Exod 22:22-24). People who are not gracious to the needy have no part in God's love (see Commentary on 19:17; 1 John 3:17).

21:14. The practice of making a concealed bribe is somewhat like a modern out-of-court settlement. The gift takes care of a problem without public exposure and embarrassment (see 6:35, where the practice fails; cf. 15:27; 17:8, 23; 18:16; 19:6).

21:15. The NIV and the the NRSV take the doing of justice passively ("When justice is done"), so that the righteous have joy as mere observers. But a better reading is that they take pleasure in doing justice themselves (see Commentary on 20:23; cf., negatively, 2:14). With respect to justice, people do what corresponds to their character (see vv. 3, 7, 10).

21:16. This verse says in few words what is

developed at length in chaps. 1–9 (see Commentary on 2:18; 7:25-27; 9:18; see also 4:14-19, where the way of righteousness leads to life).

21:17. This saying is an ancient parallel to "You can't have your cake and eat it too." Wine and oil go with festivity and joy (Judg 9:9, 13; Ps 104:15; Eccl 9:7-8). Oil is used cosmetically for adornment and to soothe dry skin. Later, vv. 20-21 will assert that wisdom and righteousness, which include hard work, are the way to abundance (see 10:4-5).

21:18. Isaiah 43:3 affords a parallel to this puzzling verse. The sense seems to be that justice is achieved by a reversal of positions (see Commentary on 11:8; cf. 1 Sam 2:2-10; Luke 1:51-53), but the meaning of "ransom" (כפר *kōper*) remains puzzling. Its usual sense is a substitute payment for punishment when one is guilty (see 6:35; 13:8; Exod 21:30; in 1 Sam 12:3, it refers to a judicial bribe). Scholars question why the righteous should need a ransom. On the other hand, Psalm 49 states both that no person can by a ransom evade death and that "God will redeem my life from the power of Sheol" (Ps 49:7-9, 15, paraphrase of NIV and NRSV).

21:19. Verse 9 is a variant of this verse. Here the desert is the place of disorder and drought where life is not possible (Deut 32:10). The contrast of the dry desert and the promised cultivated land, with its life and water, is fundamental to Israelite thought and experience (Deut 8:2, 7-10, 15-16).

21:20-21. Oil is a symbol of wealth and luxury, and the link with v. 17 creates an evident contrast of life-styles. The message of these verses is similar to "seek first [God's] kingdom and his righteousness, and all these things will be given to you as well" (Matt 6:33 NIV). Because the world is ordered according to wisdom and righteousness, to pursue them sets one in a right relation with material things (see 8:18; 11:19). The wise and the fool differ in their disposal of goods; one gathers, and the other squanders (cf. 14:1). The NRSV's "remains" only partly follows the Greek (it omits "mouth"). The NIV supplies "food," which is lacking in Hebrew (see 8:21; 10:2; 21:6).

21:22. Unlike most proverbs, which generalize, this saying is a miniature narrative in the past tense (so NRSV; cf. NIV). Ecclesiastes 9:13-16 provides a similar narrative. Wisdom is more powerful than strength of arms (8:14; 16:32; 20:18; 24:5) and than fortified walls in which people trust (18:10-11). Perhaps David's conquest of the well-defended city of Jerusalem by the stratagem of climbing up the water shaft reflects such wisdom (2 Sam 5:8). A modern equivalent of this verse may be "The pen is mightier than the sword." "Warriors" better reflects the Hebrew (גברים *gibbōrîm*) than does "the mighty," however.

21:23-24. Verse 23 is an expansion of 13:3*a* and 18:21. Although the syntax of v. 24 is difficult to determine, its general sense is clear. The Hebrew heaps up expressions for pride and arrogance to define the essential character or name of the mocker (see 9:7-12). Such heaping up of terms is not tautology (a logical problem), but a rhetorical means of intensification, as in "boys will be boys." See Sir 10:6-18 for an expansion of the theme of this verse.

21:25-26. Since v. 26*a* lacks a subject of its own, it seems best to take it as continuation of v. 25 (NIV). The NRSV partially follows the expansive LXX text of v. 26: "An impious person craves bad cravings all the day." The sluggard desires but does not work (v. 17; see also 6:6-11). The contrast with the righteous person is indirect. While the sluggard is consumed with unfulfilled desire, the righteous person (who is implicitly wise and diligent) has enough to share generously (see Commentary on 11:24 within the cluster 11:23-25; 28:27).

21:27. Verse 27*a* is a near duplicate of 15:8*a* (Yahweh is implicit, not explicit). Worship without a corresponding righteous life is execrable to God (see Commentary on 21:3). But v. 27*b* takes the saying in a different direction. With an obvious how-much-more logic, it exposes the internal mental hypocrisy of such sacrifice, which thinks it can buy God off. "Evil intent" is here the internal scheming (see 24:9*a*) of those whose secret thoughts belie the apparent meaning of their deeds. The same word for that expression (זמה *zimmâ*) is misleadingly translated "evil conduct" and "wrong" in 10:23.

21:28. Verse 28*a* expresses a common thought (19:5, 9). Some argue a double sense for "perish"—that the testimony of a liar will not succeed, while honest testimony will endure. Verse 28*b* may refer to the judge (lit., "the man who hears") in a judicial hearing, rather than to someone who listens well (see Commentary on 25:10). Several suggestions for an alternative translation of the predicate in v. 28*b* have been made (e.g., "will have descendants," and the NIV's "will be destroyed") to provide a contrast with "perish," but this appears unnecessary. The sense may be that the "one who listens" will speak (as witness or judge) with enduring consequences and will thus "have the last word." The NIV margin takes "listen" in the sense of "obey," thus following the Vg. Verse 28*b* is not certain.

21:29. Like the seductress of 7:13, "a wicked man [masc. sing.] puts on a bold face." In v. 29*b*, both translations follow the *Qere* (MT) correction of the traditional verb, "gives thought to [or understands] his way(s)" (see Commentary on 14:8). This same verb (בין *bîn*) also occurs in 20:24, which asks, "How can anyone understand his way?" The *Ketib* (or received) text has "establishes his ways," which creates a link with the important verse 16:9 (see 4:25-27). "Way(s)" is another *Qere/Ketib* variation, of which the singular seems preferable. If the *Qere* reading is followed, then vv. 30-31 appear to set limits on even the planning of the upright (v. 29*b*), much in line with 16:1-9. The relationship and contrast between vv. 29*a* and 29*b* are not certain. They may refer to "putting on a mask" of duplicity in contrast to having a straightforward life plan.

21:30-31. This profound couplet insists that ultimately only God's wisdom and purposes prevail, even though the book of Proverbs seeks to train young and old to get wisdom and live by it (see Commentary on 19:21; 20:18; 24:6). Yet there is no contradiction, for an essential part of wisdom is knowing one's limits and facing up to reality. Because people are limited in wisdom and power, the beginning of human wisdom is necessarily the fear of the Lord, who alone has ultimate wisdom (see 1:7; 3:5-8, 19-20; 8). Verse 30 does not merely have in view wisdom that opposes God, as suggested by the translation "against the LORD." Rather, the Hebrew expression is more general, meaning "before" or "over against." Its purpose is simply to contrast human wisdom, whether good or bad, with God's. Verse 31 uses the proud imagery of war horses, a technological innovation that gave surpassing advantage to those armies that had cavalry units.

REFLECTIONS

1. Proverbs makes no attempt to explain the paradox of divine mastery and responsible human freedom (see 21:1; Phil 2:12-13). Several stories illustrate the issues of this saying. In Genesis, Joseph's brothers plan and execute evil against Joseph for their own purposes, but their actions ultimately serve God's good purposes of salvation (see the paradoxical formulations concerning "who did it" in Gen 45:5-8; 50:19-21). In other cases, Yahweh "hardens" Pharaoh's self-hardened heart (Exodus 5–11) and ordains that Absalom choose the wrong counsel against David (2 Sam 15:31; 16:23; 17:14). Proverbs 21:1 again raises the issues of 16:1, 9 and 20:27. Its main thrust, however, is positive, because irrigation waters, like royal wisdom, cause the land and the people to flourish (see 18:4).

Practically, 21:1 gives hope to those who pray for rulers and all in positions of authority (1 Tim 2:1-8)—hope that God will guide and move them to act in wisdom for the common good. In evil times, this proverb may comfort those whose lives are afflicted by capricious tyrants or cruel magistrates. The Lord can indeed turn the hearts of the wicked to do what is right, thereby working God's own good purposes even when human beings intend evil.

Yet in our reflection on the genocidal "ethnic cleansing" perpetrated by the Nazis, by the warring factions in Bosnia, by the Khmer Rouge in Cambodia, by Amin in Uganda, and by opposing sides in Rwanda and Zaire, we ask the anguished question, Why has God not made good the hearts of the mighty and the common folk alike? "Why, O LORD, do you make us / stray from your ways / and harden our heart, so that / we do not fear you?" (Isa 63:17

NRSV). Perhaps the most terrible judgments of God are those in which God confirms the hardness of human hearts and leaves us to our own devices:

> Surely the arm of the LORD is not too short to save,
>   nor his ear too dull to hear.
> But your iniquities have separated
>   you from your God;
> your sins have hidden his face from you,
>   so that he will not hear. (Isa 59:1-2 NIV)

2. "To do righteousness and justice" (21:3) is God's basic requirement for Israel and its king and for humans in general (see 15:9; Gen 18:19; Ps 119:121; Amos 5:24; Matt 5:6, 10; 6:33; 1 Pet 3:13).[256] This the wicked refuse to do (21:7, 15). The prophets also insist that worship or sacrifice without justice is not pleasing to God (1 Sam 15:22-23; Isa 1:11-17; Hos 6:6; Mic 6:6-8). The basis for this is that Yahweh is Creator and Lord of every inch of reality, which God made in wisdom and righteousness.

3. Not only does Proverbs warn Israel of the limits to human wisdom, but it also warns against overconfidence in power and technology (21:30-31). Israel was repeatedly warned not to rely on horses, just as modern nations might be warned not to trust in military technology (see Pss 20:6-9; 33:16-17; Isa 30:15-16; 31:1-3). Deuteronomy forbade the king to acquire horses (17:16). The theological basis for these warnings about human limits and against arrogance is that the outcome of events, sometimes counter to the odds, rests with Yahweh (see 16:33; 29:26). This is also the theological point of the narrative of David and Goliath (1 Sam 17:37, 45-47), of Deut 20:14, of Gideon's radically reduced band of warriors (Judg 7:1-23), and of the fall of Jericho without human military action (Joshua 6). This proverb couplet and such stories can encourage God's people in adverse circumstances of any kind, even as they humble arrogant self-confidence.

256. See Moshe Weinfeld, *Social Justice in Ancient Israel and in the Ancient Near East* (Minneapolis: Fortress, 1995).

Proverbs 22:1-16, The Royal Collection Concluded

NIV

22 A good name is more desirable than great riches;
  to be esteemed is better than silver or gold.

[2]Rich and poor have this in common:
  The LORD is the Maker of them all.

[3]A prudent man sees danger and takes refuge,
  but the simple keep going and suffer for it.

[4]Humility and the fear of the LORD
  bring wealth and honor and life.

[5]In the paths of the wicked lie thorns and snares,
  but he who guards his soul stays far from them.

[6]Train[a] a child in the way he should go,
  and when he is old he will not turn from it.

[a]6 Or *Start*

NRSV

22 A good name is to be chosen rather than great riches,
  and favor is better than silver or gold.

[2] The rich and the poor have this in common:
  the LORD is the maker of them all.

[3] The clever see danger and hide;
  but the simple go on, and suffer for it.

[4] The reward for humility and fear of the LORD
  is riches and honor and life.

[5] Thorns and snares are in the way of the perverse;
  the cautious will keep far from them.

[6] Train children in the right way,
  and when old, they will not stray.

[7] The rich rule over the poor,
  and the borrower is the slave of the lender.

[8] Whoever sows injustice will reap calamity,

NIV

⁷The rich rule over the poor,
　and the borrower is servant to the lender.

⁸He who sows wickedness reaps trouble,
　and the rod of his fury will be destroyed.

⁹A generous man will himself be blessed,
　for he shares his food with the poor.

¹⁰Drive out the mocker, and out goes strife;
　quarrels and insults are ended.

¹¹He who loves a pure heart and whose speech
　is gracious
　will have the king for his friend.

¹²The eyes of the LORD keep watch over
　knowledge,
　but he frustrates the words of the unfaithful.

¹³The sluggard says, "There is a lion outside!"
　or, "I will be murdered in the streets!"

¹⁴The mouth of an adulteress is a deep pit;
　he who is under the LORD's wrath will fall
　into it.

¹⁵Folly is bound up in the heart of a child,
　but the rod of discipline will drive it far from
　him.

¹⁶He who oppresses the poor to increase his
　wealth
　and he who gives gifts to the rich—both come
　to poverty.

NRSV

　and the rod of anger will fail.

⁹ Those who are generous are blessed,
　for they share their bread with the poor.

¹⁰ Drive out a scoffer, and strife goes out;
　quarreling and abuse will cease.

¹¹ Those who love a pure heart and are gracious
　in speech
　will have the king as a friend.

¹² The eyes of the LORD keep watch over
　knowledge,
　but he overthrows the words of the faithless.

¹³ The lazy person says, "There is a lion outside!
　I shall be killed in the streets!"

¹⁴ The mouth of a loose[a] woman is a deep pit;
　he with whom the LORD is angry falls into
　it.

¹⁵ Folly is bound up in the heart of a boy,
　but the rod of discipline drives it far away.

¹⁶ Oppressing the poor in order to enrich oneself,
　and giving to the rich, will lead only to loss.

[a]Heb *strange*

COMMENTARY

22:1. The NIV and the NRSV follow most ancient versions in adding "good" to "name." But "name" includes reputation, as in "let us make a name for ourselves" (Gen 11:4; see also Gen 6:4, lit., "men of name"; 2 Sam 23:22). Israel was an honor-and-shame culture, and one's name meant personal identity as it was recognized and respected (or not) in the community (see Commentary on 12:8; 13:18; 26:1). Usually—but not always—wealth is linked with wisdom, goodness, and honor (see 8:16; 22:4; see Commentary on 11:16 for a contrary case). This better-than saying (see Commentary on 15:16; 16:8) limits the status of wealth by placing wisdom and righteousness above it. To find favor or grace with someone is

to be a *persona grata,* accepted and esteemed (3:4; 28:23; cf. 13:15; 1 Sam 2:26; Luke 2:52). Ecclesiastes puts the worth of a name in the context of death, believing—in contrast to others—that even one's name does not remain (Eccl 2:16; 7:1, "good" is again added to the text; 9:5; Sir 41:11-13).

22:2. Several sayings focus on Yahweh as Creator of persons, not at the beginning of time, but in their present concreteness, especially as "rich" or "poor" (see Commentary on 14:31; 17:5; 29:13; see also Job 34:19; Sir 11:14). The intent is to qualify and mitigate the social and economic divisions that humans are prone to make so much of, thereby denying the humanity that binds them to one another and to their Maker. The saying has a prophetic edge to it, implicitly calling for socioeconomic justice.

22:3. Proverbs 27:12 is a variant of this verse. A crucial part of wisdom is the ability to see what is coming before it arrives. Like 14:15, 18, this saying contrasts the naive or simple, who have little life experience, with the clever, who do (see Commentary on 14:8). It takes the form of a past tense narrative, which is obscured by the English translations (see Commentary on 21:22). Literally, the Hebrew reads, "A clever man [masc. sing.] saw trouble and hid, but the simple [pl.] continued on and suffered."

22:4. The Hebrew word underlying "reward" (עקב *ʿēqeb*) has the sense of "consequence" (cf. the paraphrase in NIV). Verse 4*a* lacks the word for "and," which the translations add. Thus several ancient versions include "the fear of the LORD" among the consequences of humility. But humility and reverence for Yahweh naturally go together in the realism that is essential for true wisdom (see Commentary on 11:2; 15:33; 18:12). Contrary to views that expect godliness to produce only suffering, this saying asserts that godly humility leads to well-being (see 3:13-20; 8:18). The underlying logic is that wisdom puts one in harmony with reality. This proverb should neither be absolutized (as in a prosperity gospel, which says, "God wants you to be rich"), nor should the creational benefits of a realistic godliness be minimized (see Commentary on 10:3; 16:8).

22:5. The Hebrew word translated "thorns" (צנים *ṣinnîm*) is obscure and odd in combination with "snares." The Syriac version and the Targum take the Hebrew term to mean "net" or "trap," which forms a better parallel to "snares." The general sense is clear, however, with a return to the common image of life as a positive or negative journey. For "perverse" as "twisted," see Commentary on 10:9. "Cautious" (שומר נפשו *šōmēr napšô*) is literally, "one who guards his life" (see Commentary on 16:17, 24; 19:16).

22:6. This verse is linked to v. 5 by the key word "way" (דרך *derek*). As translated, this admonition's concern for training the young is like that in 19:18; 29:17; and throughout the book. The verse may have a slightly different focus, however. The root for "train up" (חנך *ḥnk*) is always used in biblical Hebrew and Aramaic for

the dedication or initial use of a house or temple (Deut 20:5; 1 Kgs 8:63 = 2 Chr 7:5; see also the related nouns). This suggests that the verb in v. 6*a* refers to a rite of passage (such as the later Bar-Mitzvah celebration) through which an adolescent gains adult status. Hildebrand argues that the child (נער *naʿar*) is primarily a social classification ("a squire"), designating a person attendant on someone of high social status. This is less certain, for the term can connote both "servant" and "youth." "The way he should go" is literally "according to his way"—a phrase that may mean "in the way that is appropriate to his status." In any case, this proverb should not be used to induce guilt in good parents who have errant children. Proverbs are not absolute promises (see Commentary on 10:3).

22:7. This verse is a straightforward observation on the fundamental effect that credit and debt have on relationships, using the metaphors of political rule and servitude (see Commentary on 14:20; 12:24; 17:2; 18:23; but see the reversal in 28:11). The saying may be used to warn against going into debt (see Commentary on 6:1-5). The poor could sell themselves into servitude in order to provide for themselves and their families (Exod 21:2-7; Neh 5:5).

22:8. This proverb applies the rule of sowing and reaping to the moral and spiritual realms (see Job 4:8; Hos 8:7; 10:13; Gal 6:7-10; see also Commentary on 22:9). Its present placement creates a warning against the potential for abusive rulership inherent in the power of wealth, as described in v. 7. Verse 8*b* is much like Isa 14:5-6, where Yahweh puts an end to the tyrannical "rod" of the king of Babylon (see Habakkuk 2). The saying also offers comfort to the oppressed, assuring them of God's justice. "Rod" (שבט *šēbeṭ*) is a metaphor for rulership (see v. 7), not of punishment, as it is usually used in Proverbs (see 10:13; 26:3). "Fury" (עברה *ʿebrâ*) may also connote "excess." The NRSV omits the pronoun "his," thus obscuring the connection between the two lines (see NIV).

22:9. This verse forms a clear contrast to the two previous verses. "Generous" (טוב-עין *ṭôb-ʿayin*) is literally "good of eye," an idiom whose opposite, "stingy," is "bad of eye" (23:6; 28:22; Deut 15:9; Matt 20:15 margin). The saying appears related to Deut 15:9-11, which forbids stinginess and commands generosity, promising the latter will be blessed by God (see 11:26; 14:21; 19:17; Sir 7:32). The NT (2 Cor 9:6-10) combines the teaching of this verse with the imagery of sowing and reaping, found in v. 8.

22:10. The mocker is arrogant, cynical, and "knows it all" (see 9:7-12; 21:24). Similar to this admonition is the idea that without kindling a fire goes out (see 26:20-21). "Quarrel" refers to litigation, but is not restricted to it. At times the Israelite community, including small local groups such as villages, excluded wrongdoers (see Commentary on 25:4-5) in order to preserve the well-being and integrity of the sociospiritual group—as did the early church (1 Cor 5:1-13; see Deut 7:17). In a morally clouded situation, Sarah uses the same imperative, "drive out," when she tells Abraham to send Hagar and Ishmael away (Gen 21:10). The matter of boundary definition, of inclusion and exclusion, is always difficult. Yet it is crucial, for without it no group, even the family of God, can have identity with integrity.

22:11. The Hebrew grammar of this verse is difficult. Underlying the NIV and NRSV translations is a literal understanding: "He who loves purity of heart [or "one pure of heart"]/ whose lips are grace, his friend is the king." A parallel thought can be found in 16:13. Psalm 101 documents the sort of persons who are and who are not acceptable in the court of a righteous king. Some translators (following the LXX and the Syriac) supply "God" as the subject of "loves," but this makes the difficulties even greater. Others follow Rashi and make "king" from v. 11*b* the subject of v. 11*a*.

22:12. The "knowledge" in question is that which a judge needs in order to effect justice in the land (see 1 Sam 2:3; see also Commentary on 15:3; 21:12).

22:13. This verse has a near duplicate in 26:13, but unlike that version of the saying, the present verse possesses a wonderful word music that imitates the sound of tearing, as the sluggard imagines being torn limb from limb. Note especially the *r, ḥ,* and *ṣ* sounds in the words for "lion, outside," and "murdered!" For the "sluggard," see Commentary on 6:6-11.

22:14. This verse brings the reader back to the world of the strange woman of chaps. 1–9 (see Commentary on 2:16-19). The image of woman as a well of water is positive in 5:15-20. Here it is used negatively, as a hole one may fall into. The same idea appears in the Babylonian *Dialogue of Pessimism.*[257] New in this saying is the thought that such a woman might be an instrument of God's wrath.

22:15. The word "boy" is the same as in v. 6*a* and 23:13 ("child"); the reference is probably to an adolescent or servant. The saying is not a statement of universal youthful depravity, with beating as the remedy of choice for adolescents. The proverb is probably best taken as a conditional sentence, "If folly is bound up in the heart of a boy, then the rod of discipline will drive it far from him." (Cf. 23:13-14 and see Reflections on 13:24 concerning corporal punishment.)

22:16. The end of the first Solomonic subcollection attacks that evil wherein "the rich get richer and the poor get poorer." The needy are made by God and receive God's jealous care and protection (see Commentary on 14:31; 17:5; 22:2). Verse 16*b* attacks the giving of wealth to those who already have it. This act is not fitting, like "carrying coals to Newcastle" (see 26:1-3).

257. W. Lambert, *Babylonian Wisdom Literature* (Oxford: Clarendon, 1960) 147.

REFLECTIONS

1. Proverbs 22:7 speaks of the profound effect debtor and creditor status has on personal relations. Even in the United States—which is deeply committed to the myth of individual freedom and equality—economic status greatly determines one's freedom and class and the degree to which equality under law is actually available. The proverb makes no moral pronouncements; it simply observes a fact of life. Yet, Israel's law consistently forbade lenders from taking interest from the poor (see Commentary on 28:8). By implication, 22:7 in its biblical context sharply condemns one of today's common banking practices. When banks charge usurious interest rates on their freely offered credit cards—while knowing that generally the financially vulnerable are driven to amass credit-card debt—they offend the God who cares for the poor (14:31; 22:9, 16).

Perhaps this proverb applies also to international relations, a possibility that time will answer for America. In the 1980s, the United States went from being the world's largest creditor nation to being the largest debtor nation. Wealthy America may become a "servant" to its international creditors, its freedom to act in international affairs compromised by its financial obligations (see Commentary on 6:1-5). This issue is of even greater moment for poor, developing nations with large foreign debts. Often cash crops for export (coffee, cocoa, opium poppies, and the coca leaf used to make cocaine) are grown instead of foodstuffs desperately needed by the native population. The Lord of the nations also judges nations that exploit those weaker than themselves.

2. Wealth gained by wronging, oppressing, or taking advantage of the poor stands under God's condemnation. In ancient Israel, this happened when the wealthy bought up—and kept—the land of the destitute, so depriving them of their heritage in the land of promise (Leviticus 25; Isa 5:8-10; see Reflections on 15:25). But Proverbs also condemns giving to the rich (22:16). On planet Earth, where resources are limited, the excessive increase of goods for some means loss for many others, both domestically and internationally. This happens when damage to human beings and to the environment results from the manufacture and use of earth-destructive technological products.[258] It happens when executives are paid exorbitant sums as their companies downsize, merge through debt-increasing buyouts, and overwork their remaining employees. It happens when jobs are shipped to sweatshops hidden in inner cities or overseas. It happens when a country's tax code and other laws promote a massive shift of wealth from ordinary people to the nation's richest inhabitants. We expand our little kingdoms at the expense of our neighbors and at the expense of the natural kingdoms—plant, animal, and mineral. Thus we disrupt the righteous order of God's kingdom's coming on earth (Matt 6:10). This we do to our own peril. In the long run, such activities lead to the opposite of what they are intend to do, to loss instead of to gain.

258. See Lester Brown et al., *The State of the World* (Washington: The Worldwatch Institute, published annually); Loren Wilkinson et al., *Earthkeeping in the 90's* (Grand Rapids: Eerdmans, 1991); H. Paul Santmire, *The Travail of Nature: The Ambiguous Ecological Promise of Christian Theology* (Philadelphia: Fortress, 1985).

THE SAYINGS OF THE WISE

OVERVIEW

When the Egyptian *Instruction of Amenemope* was discovered in the 1920s, the study of Israelite wisdom was revitalized. The present section of Proverbs (esp. 22:17–23:11) appeared to be dependent upon that Egyptian work. Though contrary theories exist (that the Egyptian and Israelite works each borrowed from an earlier work, or that the Egyptian work borrowed from the biblical Proverbs), most scholars believe that this section of Proverbs shows a creative use of *Amenemope,* a work written late in the second millennium BCE.[259]

The "Sayings of the Wise" are generally admonitions, brief positive or negative precepts followed by positive or negative motive clauses that provide reasons for obeying the precepts. The admonitions are much briefer than the long instructions in chaps. 1–9, and also much more diverse in the topics of their advice. The reader is addressed directly in the second person, implying that one cannot be an uninvolved observer of wisdom (as if its teaching pertained to someone else), but must make a personal response to wisdom's demands.

259. See Glendon Bryce, *A Legacy of Wisdom* (Lewisburg: Bucknell University Press, 1979); Harold C. Washington, *Wealth and Poverty in the Instruction of Amenemope and the Hebrew Proverbs,* SBLDS 142 (Atlanta: Scholars Press, 1994); cf. R. N. Whybray, *Wealth and Poverty in the Book of Proverbs* (Sheffield: JSOT, 1990).

PROVERBS 22:17–23:35, LISTEN TO THE SAYINGS OF THE WISE

NIV	NRSV

[17]Pay attention and listen to the sayings of the wise;
    apply your heart to what I teach,
[18]for it is pleasing when you keep them in your heart
    and have all of them ready on your lips.
[19]So that your trust may be in the LORD,
    I teach you today, even you.
[20]Have I not written thirty[a] sayings for you,
    sayings of counsel and knowledge,
[21]teaching you true and reliable words,
    so that you can give sound answers
    to him who sent you?
 	
[22]Do not exploit the poor because they are poor
	[17] The words of the wise:
	
	    Incline your ear and hear my words,[a]
	        and apply your mind to my teaching;
	[18] for it will be pleasant if you keep them within you,
	        if all of them are ready on your lips.
	[19] So that your trust may be in the LORD,
	        I have made them known to you
	            today—yes, to you.
	[20] Have I not written for you thirty sayings
	        of admonition and knowledge,
	[21] to show you what is right and true,

[a]20 Or *not formerly written;* or *not written excellent*	[a]Cn Compare Gk: Heb *Incline your ear, and hear the words of the wise*

NIV

and do not crush the needy in court,
[23]for the LORD will take up their case
and will plunder those who plunder them.

[24]Do not make friends with a hot-tempered man,
do not associate with one easily angered,
[25]or you may learn his ways
and get yourself ensnared.

[26]Do not be a man who strikes hands in pledge
or puts up security for debts;
[27]if you lack the means to pay,
your very bed will be snatched from under you.

[28]Do not move an ancient boundary stone
set up by your forefathers.

[29]Do you see a man skilled in his work?
He will serve before kings;
he will not serve before obscure men.

23 When you sit to dine with a ruler,
note well what[a] is before you,
[2]and put a knife to your throat
if you are given to gluttony.
[3]Do not crave his delicacies,
for that food is deceptive.

[4]Do not wear yourself out to get rich;
have the wisdom to show restraint.
[5]Cast but a glance at riches, and they are gone,
for they will surely sprout wings
and fly off to the sky like an eagle.

[6]Do not eat the food of a stingy man,
do not crave his delicacies;
[7]for he is the kind of man
who is always thinking about the cost.[b]
"Eat and drink," he says to you,
but his heart is not with you.
[8]You will vomit up the little you have eaten
and will have wasted your compliments.

[9]Do not speak to a fool,
for he will scorn the wisdom of your words.

[10]Do not move an ancient boundary stone
or encroach on the fields of the fatherless,
[11]for their Defender is strong;
he will take up their case against you.

[12]Apply your heart to instruction
and your ears to words of knowledge.

a1 Or who   b7 Or for as he thinks within himself, / so he is; or for as he puts on a feast, / so he is

NRSV

so that you may give a true answer to those
who sent you?

[22] Do not rob the poor because they are poor,
or crush the afflicted at the gate;
[23] for the LORD pleads their cause
and despoils of life those who despoil them.
[24] Make no friends with those given to anger,
and do not associate with hotheads,
[25] or you may learn their ways
and entangle yourself in a snare.
[26] Do not be one of those who give pledges,
who become surety for debts.
[27] If you have nothing with which to pay,
why should your bed be taken from under
you?
[28] Do not remove the ancient landmark
that your ancestors set up.
[29] Do you see those who are skillful in their
work?
They will serve kings;
they will not serve common people.

23 When you sit down to eat with a ruler,
observe carefully what[a] is before you,
[2] and put a knife to your throat
if you have a big appetite.
[3] Do not desire the ruler's[b] delicacies,
for they are deceptive food.
[4] Do not wear yourself out to get rich;
be wise enough to desist.
[5] When your eyes light upon it, it is gone;
for suddenly it takes wings to itself,
flying like an eagle toward heaven.
[6] Do not eat the bread of the stingy;
do not desire their delicacies;
[7] for like a hair in the throat, so are they.[c]
"Eat and drink!" they say to you;
but they do not mean it.
[8] You will vomit up the little you have eaten,
and you will waste your pleasant words.
[9] Do not speak in the hearing of a fool,
who will only despise the wisdom of your words.
[10] Do not remove an ancient landmark
or encroach on the fields of orphans,
[11] for their redeemer is strong;
he will plead their cause against you.

aOr who   bHeb his   cMeaning of Heb uncertain

NIV

¹³Do not withhold discipline from a child;
 if you punish him with the rod, he will not
  die.
¹⁴Punish him with the rod
 and save his soul from death.*^a*

¹⁵My son, if your heart is wise,
 then my heart will be glad;
¹⁶my inmost being will rejoice
 when your lips speak what is right.

¹⁷Do not let your heart envy sinners,
 but always be zealous for the fear of the LORD.
¹⁸There is surely a future hope for you,
 and your hope will not be cut off.

¹⁹Listen, my son, and be wise,
 and keep your heart on the right path.
²⁰Do not join those who drink too much wine
 or gorge themselves on meat,
²¹for drunkards and gluttons become poor,
 and drowsiness clothes them in rags.

²²Listen to your father, who gave you life,
 and do not despise your mother when she is
  old.
²³Buy the truth and do not sell it;
 get wisdom, discipline and understanding.
²⁴The father of a righteous man has great joy;
 he who has a wise son delights in him.
²⁵May your father and mother be glad;
 may she who gave you birth rejoice!

²⁶My son, give me your heart
 and let your eyes keep to my ways,
²⁷for a prostitute is a deep pit
 and a wayward wife is a narrow well.
²⁸Like a bandit she lies in wait,
 and multiplies the unfaithful among men.

²⁹Who has woe? Who has sorrow?
 Who has strife? Who has complaints?
 Who has needless bruises? Who has bloodshot
  eyes?
³⁰Those who linger over wine,
 who go to sample bowls of mixed wine.
³¹Do not gaze at wine when it is red,
 when it sparkles in the cup,
 when it goes down smoothly!
³²In the end it bites like a snake
 and poisons like a viper.

a14 Hebrew Sheol

NRSV

¹² Apply your mind to instruction
 and your ear to words of knowledge.
¹³ Do not withhold discipline from your children;
 if you beat them with a rod, they will not
  die.
¹⁴ If you beat them with the rod,
 you will save their lives from Sheol.
¹⁵ My child, if your heart is wise,
 my heart too will be glad.
¹⁶ My soul will rejoice
 when your lips speak what is right.
¹⁷ Do not let your heart envy sinners,
 but always continue in the fear of the LORD.
¹⁸ Surely there is a future,
 and your hope will not be cut off.

¹⁹ Hear, my child, and be wise,
 and direct your mind in the way.
²⁰ Do not be among winebibbers,
 or among gluttonous eaters of meat;
²¹ for the drunkard and the glutton will come to
  poverty,
 and drowsiness will clothe them with rags.

²² Listen to your father who begot you,
 and do not despise your mother when she
  is old.
²³ Buy truth, and do not sell it;
 buy wisdom, instruction, and
  understanding.
²⁴ The father of the righteous will greatly rejoice;
 he who begets a wise son will be glad in
  him.
²⁵ Let your father and mother be glad;
 let her who bore you rejoice.

²⁶ My child, give me your heart,
 and let your eyes observe*^a* my ways.
²⁷ For a prostitute is a deep pit;
 an adulteress*^b* is a narrow well.
²⁸ She lies in wait like a robber
 and increases the number of the faithless.

²⁹ Who has woe? Who has sorrow?
 Who has strife? Who has complaining?
 Who has wounds without cause?
 Who has redness of eyes?
³⁰ Those who linger late over wine,

a Another reading is delight in   *b Heb an alien woman*

NIV

[33]Your eyes will see strange sights
and your mind imagine confusing things.
[34]You will be like one sleeping on the high seas,
lying on top of the rigging.
[35]"They hit me," you will say, "but I'm not hurt!
They beat me, but I don't feel it!
When will I wake up
so I can find another drink?"

NRSV

those who keep trying mixed wines.
[31] Do not look at wine when it is red,
when it sparkles in the cup
and goes down smoothly.
[32] At the last it bites like a serpent,
and stings like an adder.
[33] Your eyes will see strange things,
and your mind utter perverse things.
[34] You will be like one who lies down in the
midst of the sea,
like one who lies on the top of a mast.[a]
[35] "They struck me," you will say,[b] "but I was
not hurt;
they beat me, but I did not feel it.
When shall I awake?
I will seek another drink."

[a]Meaning of Heb uncertain   [b]Gk Syr Vg Tg: Heb lacks *you will
say*

COMMENTARY

22:17-21. These verses are an extended invitation to hear, opening a series of admonitions, much like an ancient Egyptian *seboyet,* or "instruction," and like the instructions of Proverbs 1–9. It is strongly personal in its address ("yes—to you," 22:19) and makes rare mention of the written, and not merely oral, character of the instruction (v. 20). The text offers many difficulties. "Words of the Wise" has been identified as a title (cf. 24:23*a*). It is actually embedded in the call to hear (as in NIV). The NRSV has rearranged the text to identify the phrase as a title. "In your heart" is literally "in your belly," an image also found in Egyptian wisdom literature (see Commentary on 18:8). "Ready on your lips" means that what is internal will come to expression in action and speech (see Excursus, "The 'Heart' in the Old Testament," 60-61). Verse 19*a* reminds readers that wisdom is based on trust of Yahweh (see 1:7) and that the book's purpose is to foster such trust, even in mundane aspects of life.

Verse 20 contains one of the most discussed words in the book (see NIV margin). The *Ketib* (reading implied by the consonantal text) has שלשום (*šilšôm*), "formerly," an idiom developed from "three" days ago, and the *Qere* (the MT's preferred reading) has שלשים (*šālišîm*), "officers," which does not make sense. The ancient versions understood the word to mean "in three ways" (LXX, Vg) or "three times" (Syriac, Targum). The latter reading is close to the *Ketib's* "formerly." Since the discovery of Amenemope's "Thirty Chapters," many commentators have emended the word to "thirty" (שלושים *šělôšîm*) and have taken it to refer to "thirty sayings" (see Overview). This too is problematic, because the thirty sayings cannot be clearly identified.

"True answer" (v. 21) may have the sense of a "reliable answer." "To him who sent [you]" is a stereotypical expression for someone who employs a messenger (see 10:26; 25:13; 26:6). This mode of speech was still current in Jesus' day (John 1:22).

22:22-23. The first in a series of admonitions, these verses have a negative precept (v. 22) followed by a theological motive (v. 23; cf. Exod 22:22-27). Warnings against robbing or otherwise harming the poor are common to Israel's laws, prophets, and wisdom writings (see Commentary on 14:31; 22:16; Deut 24:14-15, 17-22; Amos 5:11-12; 8:4-6). The wicked "crush the afflicted" (or "needy") at the gate. The city gate is the place where public business, including justice, is done (see Commentary on 8:1-3; Amos 5:12). The widow and the orphan are the archetypal representatives of all poor and disadvantaged people, whose ultimate defender is God (see Commentary on 15:25; 22:28; 23:10-11). Yahweh contends for the poor, especially when legitimate authorities fail in their duty to do so (see Isa 1:23; "pleads their cause" = "fights their fight," often used in the legal sense of vindicating a person in court; see also 23:11; 1 Sam 24:15; Mic 7:9). Verse 23*b* uses a rare verb (קבע *qāba'*, "despoil," "plunder"), otherwise only in Mal 3:8. Its repetition indicates that the Lord will do to the wrongdoers as they have done to others, and more (*lex talionis*). The NRSV captures the severity of God's judgment better than does the NIV, for God "despoils" the oppressors of their "life" (נפש *nepeš*; see Commentary on 16:17).

22:24-25. This unit is another two-verse admonition with negative precepts and motive clauses. The admonition parallels the logic of the first parental address (1:10-19) by warning against bad company (see Commentary on 14:7), specifically angry persons (see 15:18; 27:4; 29:22), lest one accommodate oneself to "their ways" and suffer the consequences (see 1:19). Those consequences are deadly, for *nepeš* is the final word of the admonition, although neither the NIV nor the NRSV translate it thus.

22:26-27. These verses form another negative admonition with a precept and, unusually, a rhetorical question (see NRSV), preceded by a condition, as a motive clause. See the Commentary on 6:1-5 for the general warning against giving surety for a debt (see also 11:15; 17:18; 20:16). The present admonition clarifies that one should not venture capital or goods beyond one's ability to pay—advice still valuable in our credit-driven society. The snatching of one's bed is probably humorous exaggeration, as if the foolish creditor was caught sleeping, literally and figuratively. Entering a debtor's house to get a pledge is forbidden in Deut 24:10.

22:28. In a culture without modern surveying techniques and records, the displacement of ancient boundary markers was a way of robbing others of the land given by God to each of Israel's families (see Deut 19:14, on which this saying may depend). Also Israel's neighbors took very

seriously the sanctity of boundary markers, whether of persons and families or of nations and city-states. To violate boundaries was an offense against divinely established order (see Commentary on 8:27-29).[260] This proverb is aware that placing boundary stones was human work ("set up by your forefathers"). Yet the historically established social order—though human and flawed—was seen as a work of God, inasmuch as it protected the weak and powerless and fostered justice and righteousness. For the sake of the vulnerable, boundary markers come under God's protection (see Commentary on 15:25; 23:10-11). The archetypal story of the violation of ancestral land is Ahab's bloody appropriation of Naboth's vineyard (1 Kings 21).

22:29. This verse breaks the series of negative admonitions. It is a second-person rhetorical question that begins, "Have you seen . . . ?" (see 24:32; 26:12; 29:20). The question's purpose is to involve readers in the observation so that they may appropriate the lesson personally. A pun on "his work" (מלאכתו *měla'ktô*) and "kings" (מלכים *mělākîm*) uses the closeness of sounds to reinforce the closeness of the skilled person to the king. "Work" is used of God's creation in Gen 2:2 and can refer to a variety of arts, crafts, and activities. Ezra is described as a "scribe skilled in the law of Moses" (Ezra 7:6; see Ps 45:1, apparently a standard phrase for a skilled scribe).[261] In Isa 16:5, the Davidic king is skilled, or "zealous," for justice. "Serve" is literally "stand before," an idiom describing the privilege of being present in court (see 25:5). Verse 29*c* is unusual, but its sense as translated seems satisfactory. This saying uses the general opposition between good and bad traits in human undertakings: diligent/skilled/competent versus lazy/inept/incompetent. Wisdom is concerned not with piety alone, but with responsible excellence in all of God's creation. The opposite of this saying appears in 18:9, and similar thoughts appear in chap. 30 of *The Instruction of Amenemope* (see Overview).

23:1-3. This section continues the theme of interaction with rulers or kings. This admonition is addressed to one who is of high enough status

---

260. See O. Keel, *The Symbolism of the Biblical World: Ancient Near Eastern Iconography and the Book of Psalms* (New York: Seabury, 1978) 96-100.
261. But see William McKane, *Prophets and Wise Men* (London: SCM, 1965) 28-36.

to eat at the ruler's table. It urges alert observation and conduct appropriate to one's situation, especially restraint of appetite. The ruler presumably observes bodily greed and intemperance in subordinates as indicators of similar failings in other, more important matters. "What is before you" may also be "who is before you." A knife to the throat is apparently a proverbial expression for curbing one's appetite.

23:4-5. These verses are a humorous but pointed warning against wearing oneself out in the pursuit of uncertain wealth, which might sprout wings and fly away! Though the topic is different from 22:1-3, both admonitions concern setting limits to the greedy pursuit of good things (like food or wealth). At a certain point they become harmful and damage other goods, such as one's place in court or the well-being of one's family. This point is made more somberly in Eccl 4:7-8 and 5:13-17; Eccl 5:18-20 as well provides some counsel of joy, nonetheless. The image of wealth as birds in flight appears in "Amenemope" (chap. 7).[262] It is found already in the early second millennium BCE, "Possessions are sparrows in flight which can find no place to alight" (see Commentary on 26:2).[263]

23:6-8. These verses are similar to vv. 1-3, and the two admonitions share a line (v. 3*a* = 6*b*); but the circumstances are different. The host is not a ruler scrutinizing a would-be courtier, but one who is stingy (lit., "bad of eye"; see Commentary on 22:9; 28:22). Although "bad of eye" is an idiom for "selfish," the literal connotation of "bad" is also at work here, for the host (masc.) is not well intentioned toward his guest. What he says in friendly fashion and what he thinks in his heart are not the same; he is duplicitous (see Commentary on 26:23-25).[264] Perhaps Simon, who invited Jesus to dinner with bad motives, is an example of such a host (Luke 7:39-48). Saul's malevolent wish to have David at table in order to kill him is another example (1 Sam 20:24-34). God complains about people who "honor me with their lips, while their hearts are far from me" (Isa 29:14).

Verse 7*a* is highly uncertain. The NRSV takes

it in relation to the vomiting reaction in 22:8*a*, "a hair in the throat" ("hair," שֵׂעָר *sēʿār*). This also reinforces the connection with "Amenemope," chap. 11: "A poor man's goods are a block in the throat,/ It makes the gullet vomit."[265] What seemed tasty has a bad consequence. The NIV paraphrases a rare verb (שָׁעַר *šāʿar*, "to calculate") to refer to the host, who thinks more of expenses than of people. The NIV's first marginal note offers an alternate, traditional reading of the same verb. The meaning of the line is uncertain, but the sense of the whole admonition is fairly clear (cf. Sir 13:8-13).

23:9. This verse belongs with 26:1-12, which gives advice on dealing with fools. The refusal to listen to wisdom from others is a defining characteristic of folly (see Commentary on 26:4-5).

23:10-11. This saying duplicates 22:28*a* before it fills out the thought with a reference to orphans and a theological motive clause. God "fights the fight" of the poor, and here their redeemer does the same for orphans ("plead their cause"; see Commentary on 22:23). The entire motive clause has a parallel in Jer 50:34, but see Job's complaint in Job 24:2-12. The topic is similar to "Amenemope" 6, which refers to a widow's boundary marker. Accordingly, some scholars have emended "ancient" to "of a widow." This makes a good parallel to "orphan," but the MT makes good sense as it is, and there are no ancient textual variants.

23:12-35. The remainder of Proverbs 23 introduces a minor subsection (23:12-28), followed by an extended riddle about drinking (vv. 29-35). The section of close parallels to "Amenemope" has ended with the preceding verse. The present subsection repeatedly focuses on the parent-son relation in a way that echoes chaps. 1–9. The stereotyped vocabulary of v. 12 is entirely borrowed from those chapters. These factors suggest the hand of a redactor working to integrate the book as a whole. The poem on drinking is anticipated in vv. 15-16.

23:12-14. These admonitions belong together as an introduction to the minor subsection of vv. 12-28. Verse 12 advises a son to yield himself to discipline (see chaps. 1–9; see also 23:15, 26). Verses 13-14 give corresponding advice to a father

262. Miriam Lichtheim, *Ancient Egyptian Literature,* 3 vols. (Berkeley: University of California Press, 1973–80) 2:152.

263. R. N. Whybray, *Proverbs,* NCB (Grand Rapids: Eerdmans, 1994) 333.

264. Cf. *The Instruction of Ani* 8:11-14 in Lichtheim, *AEL,* 2:142.

265. Ibid., 2:154-55.

(second-person masc.) not to withhold discipline from his son (see Commentary on 13:24; 19:18). Verses 15-28 then provide a composite representation of speech fragments, portraying key themes in parental discipline.

Verses 13-14 reflect Israel's view of corporal punishment, which is different from that of modern Americans. For some, however, "spare the rod and spoil the child" remains a self-evident proverb (see Commentary on 13:24). The admonition seems to have an ironic motive clause that says that a properly restrained parental lashing does no harm. Instead, it does the youth good in the end, keeping him (masc.) from Sheol (see 7:25-27). Perhaps similar is our advice to a child reluctant to take bitter medicine, "Come now, it's not going to kill you!" This motive clause expresses a typical ancient Near Eastern idea (see the Aramaic *Words of Ahikar* and the later Egyptian Papyrus Insinger).[266] On the other hand, Exod 21:20-21 contains a law concerning a beating that turned deadly (see Commentary on Prov 19:18).[267]

23:15-16. The four lines of these two verses form a chiastic (ABB′A′) pattern of condition, two consequences, and a parallel condition, concerning parental joy in the wise son (in Proverbs, the term is gender specific; see the Overview on Proverbs 1:1–9:18; for this theme, see Commentary on 10:1). The son will speak what is right (מישרים *mêšārîm*; "equity" in 1:3; 2:9)—a standard of goodness that is established by God (Ps 99:4). Moreover, when the son's lips speak what is right, he imitates Lady Wisdom (8:6; cf. 16:13; Isa 33:15; see also 23:19).

23:17-18. These verses comprise an admonition with a negative and positive precept followed by motive clauses promising a future. They also echo chaps. 1–9, urging the fear of the Lord (1:7; see 24:21) and warning against envy of sinners (1:10-19; 3:31). The language and topics anticipate 24:1, 14, 19-20 and parallel Ps 37:1, 37-38. A more complex dismay at the prosperity of sinners comes to expression in Psalm 73 and Job 21. The motive clauses promise a future and hope for those who fear the Lord (the afterlife is not

in view here; see 19:20). Because ancient Israel thought collectively and in terms of generations yet to come, such hope may well apply to future generations and not just to individual persons.

23:19-21. The call to hear (v. 19) returns to the parent-son relationship of vv. 15-16. It insists on honoring both mother and father (see Commentary on 19:26; 23:22). This is fleshed out by a warning against failing to observe wise limits in eating and drinking (see vv. 1-3). Drowsiness is the natural consequence of overindulgence, and it is a typical problem for the lazy (see 6:9-11). The admonition uses language, perhaps conventional (28:7), that is found also in Deut 21:20, where a rebellious son is liable to stoning by the covenant community (see Commentary on 19:18). Here, however, the threat is poverty. Concerning drinking, see the Commentary on 20:1; 23:29-35; 31:4-5.

23:22-25. These verses continue the theme of parent-son relations with an extended admonition to listen, get wisdom (see 4:5, 7; 17:16), and so give joy to one's father and mother (see Commentary on 10:1; 17:21; 23:15-16). The parallelism of "righteous" and "wise son" in v. 24 echoes the larger parallelism of the two categories in the first two major sections of the book.

23:26-28. This section contains an implicit contrast between dedication to the father's wisdom and to a prostitute (perhaps "strange woman"; see the LXX) or alien woman (so NRSV margin). The latter term appears regularly in chaps. 1–9 in parallel to the "strange woman" (see Excursus, "Death and the Strange Woman in Proverbs 1–9," 71-72). Thus, like Wisdom in 2:16, the father's wisdom here saves the son from an out-of-bounds woman who symbolizes folly incarnate. "Deep pit" is a conventional ancient Near Eastern slur for a (bad) woman (see Commentary on 22:14). But "pit" also suggests the underworld (Sheol), to which the strange woman's house leads (2:18; 5:5; 7:27). Some commentators wonder how she can add to the number of the faithless. Perhaps she does so in the same manner that the invitation of sinners can add to their number (1:10-19). The request that the son give his heart in v. 26 is perhaps the most intimate address of a parent to a son in the book (see Excursus, The 'Heart' in the Old Testament," 60-61). As often, the inner life ("heart")

266. *Ancient Near Eastern Texts Relating to the Old Testament,* ed. James B. Pritchard, 3rd ed. (Princeton, N.J.: Princeton University Press, 1969) 428; Lichtheim, *AEL,* 3:192.

267. See W. Brueggeman's commentary on this law in *The New Interpreter's Bible,* vol. 1 (Nashville: Abingdon, 1994) 863-64.

has its counterpart in one's conduct, which is to be patterned after the father's ways.

23:29-35. These verses form an extended humorous riddle-poem on drinking. It begins with a series of six questions (v. 29), followed by an answer (v. 30) and a negative admonition (v. 31), with explanatory motive clauses describing the effects of drinking (vv. 32-34), and it concludes with a speech by the addict, who wakes from a stupor only to seek another drink (see Commen-

tary on 23:20-21; 26:9; 31:4-5). While some of the details of the poem are obscure or multivalent, the thrust of the whole is clear.[268] In v. 33 the ancient versions take the feminine plural ("strange things") to refer to strange women (Vg; LXX and Syriac have singular; see Commentary on 23:27-28). The meaning v. 34 is highly uncertain.

268. See Wilfred G. E. Watson, *Classical Hebrew Poetry: A Guide to Its Techniques* (Sheffield: JSOT, 1984) 20-30.

REFLECTIONS

1. The status and importance of the messenger in Israel and the rest of the ancient Near East cannot be exaggerated (22:21; cf. 25:13; 26:6). There was no postal service or instant communication. Thus messengers had to be trustworthy, since they often conveyed money and goods. They also had to be able to speak and negotiate on behalf of the sender, since the sender could not be consulted, being at some distance away. Consequently, the messenger had to have sufficient rank, integrity, and wisdom to represent the sender, much like an ambassador today. If the sender were a king, the messenger would be a high courtier, perhaps a member of the royal family. In Israel, prophets functioned as ambassadors from the heavenly court of Yahweh to the earthly court of a human king. In the New Testament, Christ is the one "sent" from the Father; he in turn "sends" his followers into the world (e.g., John 3:17, 34; 17:18-25; 20:21); and apostles are literally "sent" as ambassadors of Christ.

Christians are sent into this world as God's messengers, commissioned to act on God's behalf and to carry out God's purposes in this world (2 Cor 5:16-21). Christian existence is thus a responsible existence, requiring that we be ready to give "a sound answer to him who sent [us]" (22:21).

2. To modern minds, instruction on etiquette may seem out of place in a book on godly wisdom (23:1-3). But even table manners and food are part of the overall order of things, connecting us to the physical world that sustains us, connecting various people to one another, and giving expression to their varied relationships. Who sits where, for instance, is of great importance, for it usually suggests hierarchy, even in an egalitarian society (see Commentary on 25:6-7).

The life of the Christian community, therefore, will not be fully "Christian" until our entire life-style is shaped in harmony with God's order for creation and consciously dedicated to honor and serve the Lord. In the end, nothing, even table manners, is indifferent to the service of God, even though God gives us servants immense freedom to shape cuisine and culture in various ways (see Reflection number 2 at Proverbs 8:1-36).

PROVERBS 24:1-22, SAYINGS OF THE WISE CONCLUDED

NIV

24 Do not envy wicked men,
do not desire their company;
[2] for their hearts plot violence,
and their lips talk about making trouble.

[3] By wisdom a house is built,
and through understanding it is established;
[4] through knowledge its rooms are filled
with rare and beautiful treasures.

[5] A wise man has great power,
and a man of knowledge increases strength;
[6] for waging war you need guidance,
and for victory many advisers.

[7] Wisdom is too high for a fool;
in the assembly at the gate he has nothing to
say.

[8] He who plots evil
will be known as a schemer.
[9] The schemes of folly are sin,
and men detest a mocker.

[10] If you falter in times of trouble,
how small is your strength!

[11] Rescue those being led away to death;
hold back those staggering toward slaughter.
[12] If you say, "But we knew nothing about this,"
does not he who weighs the heart perceive
it?
Does not he who guards your life know it?
Will he not repay each person according to
what he has done?

[13] Eat honey, my son, for it is good;
honey from the comb is sweet to your taste.
[14] Know also that wisdom is sweet to your soul;
if you find it, there is a future hope for you,
and your hope will not be cut off.

[15] Do not lie in wait like an outlaw against a
righteous man's house,
do not raid his dwelling place;
[16] for though a righteous man falls seven times, he
rises again,
but the wicked are brought down by calamity.

[17] Do not gloat when your enemy falls;

NRSV

24 Do not envy the wicked,
nor desire to be with them;
[2] for their minds devise violence,
and their lips talk of mischief.

[3] By wisdom a house is built,
and by understanding it is established;
[4] by knowledge the rooms are filled
with all precious and pleasant riches.
[5] Wise warriors are mightier than strong ones,[a]
and those who have knowledge than those
who have strength;
[6] for by wise guidance you can wage your war,
and in abundance of counselors there is
victory.
[7] Wisdom is too high for fools;
in the gate they do not open their mouths.

[8] Whoever plans to do evil
will be called a mischief-maker.
[9] The devising of folly is sin,
and the scoffer is an abomination to all.

[10] If you faint in the day of adversity,
your strength being small;
[11] if you hold back from rescuing those taken
away to death,
those who go staggering to the slaughter;
[12] if you say, "Look, we did not know this"—
does not he who weighs the heart perceive
it?
Does not he who keeps watch over your soul
know it?
And will he not repay all according to their
deeds?

[13] My child, eat honey, for it is good,
and the drippings of the honeycomb are
sweet to your taste.
[14] Know that wisdom is such to your soul;
if you find it, you will find a future,
and your hope will not be cut off.

[a] Gk Compare Syr Tg: Heb *A wise man is strength*

209

NIV

when he stumbles, do not let your heart
rejoice,
[18]or the LORD will see and disapprove
and turn his wrath away from him.

[19]Do not fret because of evil men
or be envious of the wicked,
[20]for the evil man has no future hope,
and the lamp of the wicked will be snuffed
out.

[21]Fear the LORD and the king, my son,
and do not join with the rebellious,
[22]for those two will send sudden destruction upon
them,
and who knows what calamities they can
bring?

NRSV

[15] Do not lie in wait like an outlaw against the
home of the righteous;
do no violence to the place where the
righteous live;
[16] for though they fall seven times, they will rise
again;
but the wicked are overthrown by calamity.

[17] Do not rejoice when your enemies fall,
and do not let your heart be glad when they
stumble,
[18] or else the LORD will see it and be displeased,
and turn away his anger from them.

[19] Do not fret because of evildoers.
Do not envy the wicked;
[20] for the evil have no future;
the lamp of the wicked will go out.

[21] My child, fear the LORD and the king,
and do not disobey either of them;[a]
[22] for disaster comes from them suddenly,
and who knows the ruin that both can
bring?

[a]Gk: Heb *do not associate with those who change*

COMMENTARY

24:1-2. This admonition echoes 23:17 and anticipates 24:19-20, all warning against envy of the wicked, presumably because of their success (see also 3:31-32). The function of these admonitions is to strengthen and encourage godly persons to remain faithful to God and to what is good in times of adversity. On "nor desire to be with them," see Commentary on 1:10-19; 14:7. What is in the heart comes to expression on the lips (see Commentary on 4:23).

24:3-4. These verses begin a series of third-person sentences that, for the most part, abandon the second-person address of the admonitions (but see v. 6*a*). On the surface this is a straightforward, four-line saying about building with wisdom. But it uses the language of creation, in which God and Wisdom build the cosmos like a house. The point is that human enterprises should take place in harmony with the order of the cosmos laid

down by God through Wisdom. For this larger conception and the parallels in language, see the Commentary on 9:1-3 and 14:1. This saying also is connected verbally with the parent's opening speech, though this is obscured in the English translations. Sinners promise a house filled with all kinds of costly things (1:13). Identical Hebrew terms for "all precious" and "riches" are used in these verses. Thus a contrast is once again suggested between two ways to achieve prosperity (see Sir 1:17).

24:5-6. Verse 5 is uncertain, though its general point about wisdom's being superior to or essential to strength seems clear. While the superiority of wisdom and righteousness to wealth is often asserted (15:16; 16:18), occasionally their superiority to strength and power is declared (16:32; 20:29; 21:22; Sir 40:25-26). Wisdom gives guidance to strength, and in war that means the taking of counsel (see Commentary on 11:14; 20:18; Eccl 9:18; Sir 37:16). Yet there are radical limits to human wisdom, counsel, and strength (see Commentary on 21:30-31). Verse 6*a* slips back into second-person address.

24:7-9. The final verses in the series that began with vv. 3-4 are a loose cluster of sayings on folly and sin. Wisdom is beyond the capacity of a fool (see Commentary on 17:16), just as the mysteries of God are beyond human capacity (see Commentary on 25:2; Psalm 131). For "in the gate," see Commentary on 8:1-3 (see also 31:23). "Open one's mouth"—that is, with something worth saying—is used of the king and of the capable woman in 31:8-9, 26. Verse 8 has language similar to Ps 21:11, where "those who devise evil" come under God's judgment (see Commentary on Prov 12:2, where "mischief-maker"/"crafty" translates a parallel expression). The NIV translates זמה (*zimmâ*) as "schemer" and "schemes" to capture the root repetition linking vv. 8-9, while "folly" is repeated from v. 7. The line between mere folly and sin is a theoretical one. The two can be distinguished but are practically inseparable because folly generally entails a refusal to recognize one's limits, or reality in general. This pride is tantamount to sin.[269] The character of such persons is recognized by the community, which names the evil. Usually bad things are an abomination to God (see Commentary on 11:1), but here the mocker (3:34; 13:1; 14:6; 15:12; 22:10) offends the sensibility common to humans.

24:10-12. Verse 10 introduces this passage with a conditional sentence applying the admonition to difficult times. There is a pun linking "trouble" (צרה *ṣārâ*) and "small" (צר *ṣar*). In such situations great strength and courage are needed to do what is right (see Reflections on Proverbs 11:1-31). Verse 11 begins with an imperative (so NIV). The syntax of the admonition is difficult. It may be taken as an anacolouthon, or interrupted syntax. It may be translated, "Rescue those being taken away to death . . . if you hold back (from helping), if you say, 'Look we did not know this.' " The person "taken away to death" is not specified.

24:13-14. This admonition to eat honey is a figure for getting wisdom. For the ambiguity of

---

269. See Cornelius Plantinga, Jr., *Not the Way It's Supposed to Be: A Breviary of Sin* (Grand Rapids: Eerdmans, 1995) 113-28.

"honey," see Commentary on 5:3. Here it symbolizes wisdom (see 16:24), as the good that consists (among other things) in knowing the right proportion, the proper limits of things (see Commentary on the related admonition in 25:16-17). Honey is good, but eating too much honey is not good (25:27)! "Find" (מצא *māṣā'*) is a key word in the book's final form, but especially in chaps. 1–9. It is regularly used of finding a wife or wisdom (1:21; 3:13; 8:17, 35; 18:22; 31:10) or good (16:20; 17:20; 18:22). Finding honey or wisdom means finding a future and hope (see Commentary on the parallel in 23:18; see also 24:19-20). This thought appears to be an editorial variant of the idea that finding Wisdom is tantamount to finding life, the theme of chaps. 1–9 (e.g., 3:18; 8:35; 9:11). There is probably also here an awareness that the good (honey or wisdom or "wife") that humans find is specific to them. It is something I have found and not another; it is proper to me. Part of wisdom is joy and contentment with the specific "honey" that we find in life (cf. 5:3; 9:17). This idea is fundamental to Ecclesiastes' insistence on joy in one's lot, even amid life's difficulties (Eccl 5:18-20; 9:7-10).

24:15-16. These verses form an admonition against attacking the righteous (see 1:11; 23:10-11). Its point is in the motive clause: Although the righteous are not free from troubles, even though they fall again and again, they get up and go on (Ps 20:7-8). The wicked, however, are brought down (lit., they stumble and fall), like the wicked in 4:12, 16, 19 (see also 24:17). The underlying premise is that God rewards people according to their deeds (see vv. 12, 29).

24:17-18. These verses are linked to vv. 15-16 by the catch words "fall" and "stumble," and they qualify that admonition. When one's enemy suffers God's just anger, one must not gloat (see 17:5; Job 31:29). This is what the wicked do (Ps 35:15-16). The righteous, who depend on God, must not become smug. A further step on this dangerous path is to take God's justice into one's own hands (see Commentary on 20:22; 24:29). Such sayings move in the direction of loving one's enemy (see 25:21-22; Exod 23:4-5; Matt 5:43-48). The motive clause (v. 18) has caused some consternation. It seems to say that one may hope for God's wrath on one's enemies, in apparent contradiction to the warning in v. 17. But the issue is leaving something to God's justice, the righting of wrongs (for which one may legitimately hope; see 2 Tim 4:14), as opposed to presuming self-righteous superiority. If one sins against an enemy in this matter, then both are subject to God's judgment—or mercy. The psalmists and the sages were aware that they themselves could move from righteousness and wisdom to folly and sin (Pss 19:12-13 NIV; 139:23-24; Prov 26:5-6).

24:19-20. The focus returns to the topic of fretting and envying evildoers (see Commentary on 23:17-19; 24:1-2). Once again the motivating concern is a "future" (אחרית 'aḥărît) or lack thereof

(23:18, 32; 24:14, 20), a term that appears several times in this subsection of Proverbs. On a lamp's being put out, see Commentary on 13:9 and 20:20.

24:21-22. This admonition concludes this subsection of the book. The reading of v. 21*b* is uncertain. The NRSV margin gives a literal translation, whose sense the NIV also follows, interpreting "those who change" as "rebellious" persons who foment insurrection. The NRSV text follows the LXX. In v. 22 the two translations solve the grammar in different ways, but the sense is not significantly changed. (See Reflections at 24:23-24.)

PROVERBS 24:23-34, AN APPENDIX: MORE SAYINGS OF THE WISE

NIV	NRSV
23These also are sayings of the wise:	23 These also are sayings of the wise:
To show partiality in judging is not good:	
	Partiality in judging is not good.
24Whoever says to the guilty, "You are innocent"—	24 Whoever says to the wicked, "You are innocent,"
peoples will curse him and nations denounce him.	will be cursed by peoples, abhorred by nations;
25But it will go well with those who convict the guilty,	25 but those who rebuke the wicked will have delight,
and rich blessing will come upon them.	and a good blessing will come upon them.
26An honest answer is like a kiss on the lips.	26 One who gives an honest answer gives a kiss on the lips.
27Finish your outdoor work and get your fields ready; after that, build your house.	27 Prepare your work outside, get everything ready for you in the field; and after that build your house.
28Do not testify against your neighbor without cause, or use your lips to deceive.	28 Do not be a witness against your neighbor without cause, and do not deceive with your lips.
29Do not say, "I'll do to him as he has done to me; I'll pay that man back for what he did."	29 Do not say, "I will do to others as they have done to me; I will pay them back for what they have done."
30I went past the field of the sluggard, past the vineyard of the man who lacks judgment;	30 I passed by the field of one who was lazy, by the vineyard of a stupid person;
31thorns had come up everywhere, the ground was covered with weeds,	

NIV

and the stone wall was in ruins.
32I applied my heart to what I observed
  and learned a lesson from what I saw:
33A little sleep, a little slumber,
  a little folding of the hands to rest—
34and poverty will come on you like a bandit
  and scarcity like an armed man.*

*34 Or *like a vagrant / and scarcity like a beggar*

NRSV

31 and see, it was all overgrown with thorns;
  the ground was covered with nettles,
  and its stone wall was broken down.
32 Then I saw and considered it;
  I looked and received instruction.
33 A little sleep, a little slumber,
  a little folding of the hands to rest,
34 and poverty will come upon you like a robber,
  and want, like an armed warrior.

COMMENTARY

24:23-25. Verse 23*a* is an editorial heading, introducing this brief section as an appendix to the larger "Sayings of the Wise" (22:17–24:22). In the LXX this section comes after 30:14, a bit of evidence for the book's obscure process of growth. It consists mostly of admonitions, concluded by a didactic poem on the sluggard (see 27:23-27, another poem concluding a subunit).

Verses 23-25 are an expanded "not-good" saying against partiality in the law court (see Commentary on 18:5; 28:21*a* is a near duplicate of 24:23*b*). The language is legal (Deut 1:17; 16:19). In 17:15 the inversion of justice (pronouncing the guilty innocent and vice versa) is an abomination to the Lord. Here peoples and nations curse the unjust magistrate, because perverted justice hurts ordinary people. The unusual reference to "nations" reflects the universal recognition of basic standards for justice, something all ancient Near Eastern kings claimed to provide. With the advent of the monarchy in Israel, the responsibility for justice shifted to rest ultimately with the king (see 2 Sam 15:1-6). In Israel's long history, town elders or priests were variously the agents of justice as well.[270] A curse is essentially a prayer to God to do justice when human institutions—and those responsible for them—fail to provide it (see Commentary on 26:2). The just magistrate receives blessing (the opposite of a curse). Although God is not mentioned, the deity is the implicit source of "rich blessing," a phrase that appears in a prayer for the king (Ps 21:4).

24:26. This verse may be related to the judi-

cial speech of vv. 23-25, but the saying's general character suggests its independent origin. It plays on the role of lips in good speech. An explicit reference to kissing the lips appears nowhere else in the OT, but is implied in Cant 4:11; 5:13. Its use here may be an idiom that is no longer understood (cf. the obscure Hebrew of Gen 41:40, which refers to kissing the mouth; see Job 31:27 for a different idiom). Nonetheless, it suggests the dialogical, give-and-take character of speech. It has been argued that the verb here refers instead to sealing or silencing lips.[271] In that case, the point is that honest speech has the last word. "Give an . . . answer" is a standard expression (see 18:13; 22:21; 27:11; Ps 119:42); Wisdom's words are also honest (8:9).

24:27. Related to vv. 3-4, this admonition has no motive clause, but it argues for right (temporal) order in major life undertakings. Agriculture was the basis of ancient life, in which most of society was actively involved. The procuring of food comes prior to getting a shelter of one's own. A similar logic appears in the Egyptian *Instruction of Any.*[272] The advice is agrarian (see 12:11; 24:30-34), but the principle of setting and accomplishing right priorities applies anywhere.

24:28. This verse is one of many warnings against false testimony in court (14:5; 19:5; 25:18). "Without cause" means that the object of the testimony is innocent (see Commentary on 26:2; cf. 3:30).

24:29. Some commentators wish to take this

270. For basic data, see R. de Vaux, *Ancient Israel* (New York: McGraw-Hill, 1961) 1:150-57.

271. J. M. Cohen, "An Unrecognized Connotation of *nsq peh* with Special Reference to Three Biblical Occurrences," *VT* 32 (1982) 418-24.
272. Lichtheim, *AEL*, 2:139

verse with the preceding one, so that "neighbor" provides an antecedent to "him." More probably, it is an independent admonition (see Commentary on 20:22; 24:17-18). The statement (lit.) "I will pay him back according to his deed" shows a human arrogating a prerogative that is God's (v. 12; Rom 2:6; 12:19).

24:30-34. This saying is a first-person didactic narrative that appeals to personal observation to make its point (see 4:3-9; 7:6-23; Ps 37:25-26, 35-36; Eccl 1:12). The topic of the sluggard is a regular one in Proverbs (see Commentary on 6:6-11; 10:4-5). The narrator's conclusion, drawn from observing the sluggard's farm, is a conventional one borrowed from 6:10-11. Extended poems on the sluggard thus link chaps. 1–9, the present "Sayings of the Wise," and the second Solomonic sub-collection (26:13-16). In addition are the numerous sayings scattered about the first Solomonic sub-collection. The extended poem gives closure to the present sub-collection. This lesson on the gone-to-ruin property of the sluggard forms a sharp contrast to houses built wisely (24:3-4, 27).

REFLECTIONS

1. The true test of a person's strength or mettle is adversity; almost everyone can survive the good times (24:10-12). This principle also applies to families, to social groups and institutions, and to nations. Even when taken literally, this admonition invites wide application. It may refer to victims of theft (see 1:11-12, 16) or to any situation where one is called upon to help a neighbor in trouble (see Commentary on 21:13). Those in a position to help in difficult, dangerous circumstances are tempted to deny reality in several respects. They may deny that innocent people are in danger of harm or death. They may deny that they are responsible for rescuing others who cannot help themselves. Some people think that any potential danger to self or family frees them from moral obligation to do good. This view, in thought and deed, entails the moral and spiritual collapse of a society. It stands under the judgment of the One who sees through human self-deception and denial of reality (see Commentary on 16:2; 21:2). God knows even when we deny that we know. God appears here as a just judge who repays people "according to their deeds" (see the prayer in Ps 28:4; see also Matt 16:27; Rom 2:6). In the United States the infamous case of Kitty Genovese, who was assaulted and left to die on a sidewalk in New York City while her neighbors listened and did nothing, comes to mind. In our time, the complicity of ordinary people in the mass murders during World War II is the ultimate example of the banal brutality of sins of omission.[273]

2. In several key passages, Proverbs associates God and the king (16:1-15; 24:21-22; 25:2-5). The underlying premise is that human governments are ordained by God to be earthly agents in doing justice and righteousness (Ps 72; Rom 13:1-8; 1 Tim 3:1-3; Titus 3:1; 1 Pet 2:13-17; see also Commentary on Prov 21:3). Thus honor is their due. To give honor or respect is the opposite of cursing God or a ruler (Exod 22:28). Yet, a government is not God; its authority is sharply limited to its task and is subject to God's standards for right government (see Reflection 1 on Proverbs 28:1–29:27).

273. For a retelling of Kitty Genovese's story, see Plantinga, *Not the Way It's Supposed to Be*, 182-84, a chapter on "flight" from responsibility.

PROVERBS 25:1–29:27

THE SECOND SOLOMONIC COLLECTION OF SAYINGS

OVERVIEW

The second Solomonic collection[274] begins with an editorial heading that echoes 1:1 and 10:1 and shares stylistic features with 24:23. Scholars generally recognize two main subunits in this collection (chaps. 25–27 and 28–29), as they do in the first Solomonic collection (chaps. 10–15; 16:1–22:16). The last two chapters of the second collection display a special interest in the king and justice. This section has been called "a mirror for princes," because it reflects the standards and behaviors proper to royalty. The collection begins with attention to God, king, and court/subjects (25:1-7), followed by sayings on speech and social conflict of various sorts (25:8-15). The

address of 25:2-7, if not the whole chapter, is to the young men of the royal court. The last half of the chapter (25:16-27; 25:28 seems isolated) is concerned with conflict and strife brought about by wickedness or the failure of wisdom. These are the problems the king, his court, and all people must handle with wisdom and justice. The collection on the "fool" (26:1-12) explores the wisdom theme of fittingness. A subunit on the sluggard follows (26:13-16), and chap. 26 ends with a return to the theme of conflict (26:17-28). Chapter 27 consists of miscellaneous sayings and concludes with a monitory poem on farming (27:23-27). Like the poem in 24:30-34, this one serves to close off a subunit of the book.

274. For a fuller account, see Raymond C. Van Leeuwen, *Context and Meaning in Proverbs 25–27* (Atlanta: Scholars Press, 1988).

PROVERBS 25:1–27:27, ON THE COURT, FOOLS, AND FRIENDS

Proverbs 25:1-28, On God, King, Court, and Conflict

NIV	NRSV
25 These are more proverbs of Solomon, copied by the men of Hezekiah king of Judah:	**25** These are other proverbs of Solomon that the officials of King Hezekiah of Judah copied.
[2] It is the glory of God to conceal a matter; to search out a matter is the glory of kings.	[2] It is the glory of God to conceal things, but the glory of kings is to search things out.
[3] As the heavens are high and the earth is deep, so the hearts of kings are unsearchable.	[3] Like the heavens for height, like the earth for depth, so the mind of kings is unsearchable.
[4] Remove the dross from the silver, and out comes material for[a] the silversmith;	[4] Take away the dross from the silver, and the smith has material for a vessel;
[5] remove the wicked from the king's presence, and his throne will be established through righteousness.	[5] take away the wicked from the presence of the king,

a4 Or *comes a vessel from*

NIV

⁶Do not exalt yourself in the king's presence,
  and do not claim a place among great men;
⁷it is better for him to say to you, "Come up
    here,"
  than for him to humiliate you before a
    nobleman.

What you have seen with your eyes
⁸ do not bring*ᵇ* hastily to court,
for what will you do in the end
  if your neighbor puts you to shame?

⁹If you argue your case with a neighbor,
  do not betray another man's confidence,
¹⁰or he who hears it may shame you
  and you will never lose your bad reputation.

¹¹A word aptly spoken
  is like apples of gold in settings of silver.

¹²Like an earring of gold or an ornament of fine
    gold
  is a wise man's rebuke to a listening ear.

¹³Like the coolness of snow at harvest time
  is a trustworthy messenger to those who send
    him;
  he refreshes the spirit of his masters.

¹⁴Like clouds and wind without rain
  is a man who boasts of gifts he does not give.

¹⁵Through patience a ruler can be persuaded,
  and a gentle tongue can break a bone.

¹⁶If you find honey, eat just enough—
  too much of it, and you will vomit.

¹⁷Seldom set foot in your neighbor's house—
  too much of you, and he will hate you.

¹⁸Like a club or a sword or a sharp arrow
  is the man who gives false testimony against
    his neighbor.

¹⁹Like a bad tooth or a lame foot
  is reliance on the unfaithful in times of
    trouble.

²⁰Like one who takes away a garment on a cold
    day,
  or like vinegar poured on soda,
  is one who sings songs to a heavy heart.

²¹If your enemy is hungry, give him food to eat;
  if he is thirsty, give him water to drink.

ᵇ7,8 Or nobleman / on whom you had set your eyes. / ⁸ Do not go

NRSV

and his throne will be established in
    righteousness.
⁶ Do not put yourself forward in the king's
    presence
  or stand in the place of the great;
⁷ for it is better to be told, "Come up here,"
  than to be put lower in the presence of a
    noble.

What your eyes have seen
⁸ do not hastily bring into court;
for*ᵃ* what will you do in the end,
  when your neighbor puts you to shame?

⁹ Argue your case with your neighbor directly,
  and do not disclose another's secret;
¹⁰ or else someone who hears you will bring
    shame upon you,
  and your ill repute will have no end.

¹¹ A word fitly spoken
  is like apples of gold in a setting of silver.

¹² Like a gold ring or an ornament of gold
  is a wise rebuke to a listening ear.

¹³ Like the cold of snow in the time of harvest
  are faithful messengers to those who send
    them;
  they refresh the spirit of their masters.

¹⁴ Like clouds and wind without rain
  is one who boasts of a gift never given.

¹⁵ With patience a ruler may be persuaded,
  and a soft tongue can break bones.

¹⁶ If you have found honey, eat only enough for you,
  or else, having too much, you will vomit it.

¹⁷ Let your foot be seldom in your neighbor's
    house,
  otherwise the neighbor will become weary
    of you and hate you.

¹⁸ Like a war club, a sword, or a sharp arrow
  is one who bears false witness against a
    neighbor.

¹⁹ Like a bad tooth or a lame foot
  is trust in a faithless person in time of trouble.

²⁰ Like vinegar on a wound*ᵇ*
  is one who sings songs to a heavy heart.
  Like a moth in clothing or a worm in wood,
  sorrow gnaws at the human heart.*ᶜ*

*ᵃCn: Heb or else   ᵇGk: Heb Like one who takes off a garment
on a cold day, like vinegar on lye   ᶜGk Syr Tg: Heb lacks Like a
moth... human heart*

NIV

22In doing this, you will heap burning coals on
his head,
and the LORD will reward you.

23As a north wind brings rain,
so a sly tongue brings angry looks.

24Better to live on a corner of the roof
than share a house with a quarrelsome wife.

25Like cold water to a weary soul
is good news from a distant land.

26Like a muddied spring or a polluted well
is a righteous man who gives way to the
wicked.

27It is not good to eat too much honey,
nor is it honorable to seek one's own honor.

28Like a city whose walls are broken down
is a man who lacks self-control.

NRSV

21 If your enemies are hungry, give them bread
to eat;
and if they are thirsty, give them water to
drink;
22 for you will heap coals of fire on their heads,
and the LORD will reward you.
23 The north wind produces rain,
and a backbiting tongue, angry looks.
24 It is better to live in a corner of the housetop
than in a house shared with a contentious
wife.
25 Like cold water to a thirsty soul,
so is good news from a far country.
26 Like a muddied spring or a polluted fountain
are the righteous who give way before the
wicked.
27 It is not good to eat much honey,
or to seek honor on top of honor.
28 Like a city breached, without walls,
is one who lacks self-control.

COMMENTARY

25:1. The chapter opens with an editorial heading. It locates the work of proverb collection (as opposed to proverb creation) in the royal court of Hezekiah (c. 728–700 BCE), who was sometimes seen as a second Solomon (2 Kgs 18:1–20:21; 2 Chr 29:1–32:33; Sir 48:17-23). Although questions have been raised about the historicity of the heading,[275] there seems no reason to doubt it (see Introduction). The exact meaning of the term translated as "copied" (עתק '*tq*) is not known ("transcribed" or "transmitted"?).[276] Most probably it refers to the work of editing and arranging sayings and admonitions.

25:2-3. These verses are linked by repetition of "(un)search(able)"; together they show not only the close relation of God and king, but also the ultimate difference between them. There is a hierarchy of social position: God inscrutably above all, the king, and then the rest of society (see the subsequent sayings). God can both reveal and

conceal (Deut 29:29), and humanity, led by the king, searches out what God has hidden in reality. The verb "search" (חקר *ḥāqar*) may refer to the king's judicial function of bringing to light the truth in criminal cases (18:17; 1 Kgs 3:28). The hiddenness of the king's heart is compared to the far reaches of the cosmos. Elsewhere the expression "unsearchable" is used only of God and the vast creation (Job 5:9; 9:10; Ps 145:3; Isa 40:28; cf. Job 11:7-10).

25:4-5. These verses form another pair, depicting the king as a judge who removes the wicked to ensure the nation's stability and integrity (see Commentary on 29:4).[277] If the "things" the king searches out in 25:2 refer to judicial matters, then there is a natural flow from vv. 2-3 to vv. 4-5. Verse 4 provides a metaphor for the process of cleansing society and making government stable, like a well-built throne. When a metal is smelted, its impurities rise to the surface, are poured off, and the remaining purified metal is poured into a mold to make a vessel or "im-

---

275. See, Michael Carasik, "Who Were the 'Men of Hezekiah' (Proverbs xxv 1)?" *VT* 44 (1994) 289-300.

276. See M. Fishbane, *Biblical Interpretation in Ancient Israel* (Oxford: Clarendon, 1985) 33.

277. Cf. the Babylonian "Advice to a Prince," in W. Lambert, *Babylonian Wisdom Literature* (Oxford: Clarendon, 1960) 113-15.

plement" (כלי *kĕlî*) for the smith. The wicked are like the impure dross (see Isa 1:21-26; Jer 6:27-30). When the wicked are removed from the king's court (from his presence, the center of national power), "his throne will be established in righteousness." The three key Hebrew words in this clause are central to the royal creation theology of the Davidic house (see Commentary on 16:12). This proverb pair is not addressed to members of the court, but speaks to the duty of the king. Perhaps the best example of this proverb pair is the "wisdom" (1 Kgs 2:6, 9) of young King Solomon in removing those who would undermine the stability of his kingdom. This is not seen by the biblical writers as negative, but as the proper way to "establish" the kingdom (1 Kgs 2:12, 46).[278]

25:6-7b. This unit is an admonition addressed to young members of the court, jockeying for position and status (see 18:16; 19:6; 22:29; Sir 7:4-7; 11:1). It is tied to the previous pair of sayings by the phrase "the king's presence." The expressions "place of the great" and "the presence of a noble" do not refer to different locations, but are parallel designations of the court.

25:7c-10. While the preceding admonition used horizontal and vertical spatial images to convey movement up and down socially, now follow two admonitions linked by a concern for legal disputes among equals. Perhaps the connection is that success in legal disputes can lead to social or political advancement (see 2 Sam 15:2-7). There is also a movement from "seeing" in the first admonition to "hearing" in the second. Both admonitions concern wrongly bringing something hidden (whether seen or heard) out into the open. The avoidance of frivolous lawsuits was already in the ancient Near East a conventional wisdom topic. In vv. 7c-8, the warning is against becoming unnecessarily involved in a dispute that is really not one's business (see Commentary on 26:17; 27:8). This is a form of ignoring proper boundaries, of being enmeshed with another person's affairs. The negative conclusion of the case (see 18:17) suggests that one may not understand what one has merely seen; appearances can be

deceiving, especially if one is not closely acquainted with a situation. Proverbs 20:3 makes a more general warning against hasty litigation (cf. 24:28).

Verses 9-10, by contrast, suggest that if one must be in a dispute, it should be one's own legitimate concern (the NRSV's "directly" is puzzling and is not in the Hebrew; for the legal idiom, see 22:23; 23:11; Ps 43:1). Nor should it entail the unnecessary exposure of what is best kept private, an act typical of gossips (see Commentary on 11:13; 20:19; cf. Matt 18:15). "Your ill repute will have no end" is literally, "the accusation against you does not return (to your accuser)"; cf. Isa 55:11 for the "word" that does not "return" to God "empty" but has its intended effect). "One who hears" may refer to a judge, similar to the modern practice in which a court case is a hearing.

25:11-12. These verses are two artfully constructed sayings that compare fine speech to well-crafted jewelry. In v. 11, the translations have reversed the order of the two lines; in Hebrew the imagery comes first, then comes the reference to speech. "Apples" (תפוח *tappûaḥ*) refers to some kind of fruit, but not the apple we are familiar with. A likely candidate is the apricot, which has a golden color (Cant 2:3, 5; Joel 1:12). "A word . . . spoken" may refer to a judicial decision. "Fitly" (על-אפניו *'al-'opnāyw*) is uncertain, perhaps literally, "upon its *turning*" (if the word is related to "wheel"). Some think it means "according to circumstances" and thus "fitly." Others relate it to an Arabic word for "time," thus a word spoken "at the right time" (see 15:23). The intent remains uncertain.

Verse 12 is delightfully clever, for the gold ring (11:22) hangs, as it were, "on a listening ear" (see 20:12). There is art in wise reproof (27:5), and also in serious listening (12:15; 15:31-32)! In keeping with the apparent judicial background of the preceding admonitions, however, the participle translated "a wise man's rebuke" is literally, "a wise *reprover.*" This may be a technical legal term referring to an arbiter or judge, as in Amos 5:10: "They hate *the arbiter* in the gate, and detest him whose plea is just" (TNK).

25:13-14. These verses are linked by weather images. In v. 13, a person of lower social status wins favor from a superior; in v. 14, the failure

---

278. P. Kyle McCarter, Jr., " 'Plots, True or False' the Succession Narrative as Court Apologetic," *Int* 35 (1981) 355-67; Leo G. Perdue, "Liminality as a Social Setting for Wisdom Instructions," *ZAW* 93 (1981) 114-26.

to deliver what is promised leads to loss of face, or worse, with respect to equals or superiors.

Faithful messengers give relief to their masters (v. 13), who in some way are stressed as if by summer heat (see Commentary on 25:25; 26:1). In Israel and in the ancient Near East in general, messengers were of a status commensurate with those who sent them (see Commentary on 13:17; 22:21). The imagery of cold snow in the hot harvest time may be based on the practice of runners bringing down compacted snow or ice from the mountains to cool the wealthy.[279] For "refreshes the spirit" (נפש *nepeš*, "soul" or "throat"), see Commentary on 16:24 (cf. Exod 31:17; Pss 19:8; 23:3*a* for the idiom).

In v. 14, the clouds do not deliver what they promise: rain for the thirsty ground (cf. 25:23; Jude 12). A literal illustration appears in the Elijah cycle. After a long drought, Elijah sends his servant to look for a cloud as a harbinger of rain (1 Kgs 18:41-45). Worse is a person who does not give what is promised (see Commentary on 18:16, where a gift is the means for access into the circle of "the great"; cf. 25:6).

25:15. The thought returns to one's relation to a ruler, the ultimate social superior (see "king" and "the great" in vv. 2-7), and to the sort of behavior that will move them favorably (see 16:13-16). Patience is a variant of "slow to anger" (see Commentary on 15:18). In the delightful oxymoron of v. 15*b*, the softest organ, the tongue, breaks the hardest organ, the bone.[280] The NIV's "gentle" translates the word for "soft" as in 15:1. Sirach 28:17-18 moves this saying in the direction of the English expression, "The pen is mightier than the sword" (see Ps 55:21). That brains are better than brawn is a recurrent theme in Proverbs (see Commentary on 16:32; 20:29; 21:22).

25:16-17. These verses warn against good social relations going bad. Finding and stuffing oneself with too much honey is compared with presenting oneself too often at a neighbor's door. Both are failures to recognize proper limits to behaviors that are perfectly good in themselves.

Too much of a good thing makes one sick. It is possible to wear out one's welcome. The repeated phrase "too much of" in the NIV nicely captures the Hebrew parallelism of the two admonitions. For the symbolism of honey, see Commentary on 5:3 (see also 24:13; 25:27).

25:18. This verse contains an allusion to the "ten words" as found in Exod 20:16. A false witness in a court procedure can initiate the judicial process as an accuser or join it once begun (see Commentary on 6:19; cf. 1 Kgs 21:13). For honesty in testimony, see the Commentary on 12:17; 14:5. The weapon images convey the deadly force of lying words (see 26:18; Pss 57:4; 120:3-4).

25:19. The tooth is one that breaks, and the foot is one that shakes or "slips" (מעד *m'd*). Humans depend on "reliable" body parts. A healthy society is also interdependent, in that each member must play his or her role reliably, especially in times of crisis. The story of Hezekiah under Assyrian attack uses the same root for "trust" and "reliable" (בטח *bṭḥ*) as a thematic key word (see 2 Kgs 18:20-24; 19:10).

25:20. This verse is difficult. It appears to portray things or actions that do not "fit" their object in character or in time (see Commentary on 26:1-3; cf. 10:26; 27:14). The saying is not a simile ("like" does not appear in Hebrew); the metaphorical images are simply juxtaposed to the point of the saying in the last line (so also in vv. 18-19). The NRSV largely follows the versions, but the shorter Hebrew text can stand. On a cold day one's body should not be exposed, nor should acidic vinegar be poured on a wound (reading נתר [*nāter*] after Arabic *natratu*).[281] Wounds were soothed with oil or balm (Isa 1:6). The NIV translation, "vinegar poured on soda," provides a simple example of incompatibility. These images of pain (or of unfittingness) show the damage done by inappropriate levity to a sad or heavy heart (see Isa 40:2). Sirach 22:6*a* provides a parallel, "Like music in time of mourning is ill-timed conversation" (NRSV). Similarly, an Assyrian hymn to the god Shamash ends with the following curse, "May his string-playing be painful to people,/ May his joyful songs be the prick of a thorn."[282]

279. B. Lang, "Vorläufer von Speiseeis in Bibel und Orient. Eine Untersuchung von Spr 25,13," in *Mélanges bibliques et orientaux en l'honneur de M. Henri Cazelles,* ed. A. Caquot and M. Delcor (Neukirchen-Vluyn: Neukirchener Verlag, 1981) 218-32.

280. A similar image appears in *Ahiqar* 105-106, in *Ancient Near Eastern Texts Relating to the Old Testament,* ed. James B. Pritchard, 3rd ed. (Princeton, N.J.: Princeton University Press, 1969) 429.

281. William McKane, *Proverbs: A New Approach,* OTL (Philadelphia: Westminster, 1970) 588-89.

282. Benjamin R. Foster, *Before the Muses: An Anthology of Akkadian Literature* (Bethesda, Md.: CDL, 1993) 2:726.

25:21-22. In effect, the concrete terms of v. 21 tell the reader to love not only neighbor and stranger, but also one's enemy (cf. Lev 19:18, 34; Matt 5:43-48). The law in Exod 23:4-5 embodies a similar principle (cf. Deut 22:1-4; see Sir 28:1-7). There are further parallels to this principle in ancient Near Eastern writings.[283] Unfortunately, the expression "heap burning coals on his head" remains obscure. Its use in 2 Esdr 16:53 suggests God's punishment of the sinner. A modern suggestion compares an Egyptian rite of contrition, but this has no known resonance in Israelite culture. Another (unlikely) suggestion is to translate, "then you will be snatching coals (from) upon his head." That is, the water you give relieves your enemy of heat, and God will reward you. Another is that the fiery coals represents the red-faced shame of your enemy in response to your kindness.[284] David's encounter with wicked Saul illustrates both the attitude required of the righteous and the theological point of this admonition (1 Sam 24:8-22). The apostle Paul quotes this text in the context of arguing love ("overcome evil with good") and leaving vengeance to God (Rom 12:20; see Commentary on Prov 20:22; 24:17-18). God takes note of those who do good and right wrongs.

25:23-24. Both of these sayings concern bad relations and may have a subtle link in imagery. There is bad weather in v. 23; in v. 24 the husband on the roof is exposed to bad weather (see Commentary on 27:15-16). There is a problem in v. 23, in that rain generally does not come from the north. The solution may lie in a pun. "North wind" can also be read as "hidden wind," and "sly tongue" is literally a "secret tongue." Thus rain storms and emotional storms can both arise from unexpected (hidden or secret) sources (see Job 38:22-23).

Verse 24 appears several times with minor variations (see Commentary on 21:9, 19). One may compare the humorous story in which Socrates' wife, Xanthippe, gave him a scolding and then doused him with water. Socrates remarked

that after the thunder comes the rain. Apparently exposure to the elements was considered better than exposure to the storms of a tempestuous wife. The remarks in Proverbs about a quarrelsome wife are tempered by its pervasive affirmation of the wife as wisdom (see Commentary on 31:10-31); moreover, these remarks are mild in comparison to the misogyny of Sirach (see Sir 25:13-26).

25:25-26. These verses are linked by water images, one positive, one negative. Both sayings presuppose the hot and dry climate of Palestine, where drinkable water is a precious, even life-saving, commodity (see Commentary on 5:15-19). Good news (see 12:25; 15:30) from afar is like water that restores a person worn out by thirst (see Commentary on 25:13). נפשׁ (nepeš, "soul") may suggest "throat" here and in v. 13. When David is in distress he longs for water from his ancestral spring, and his mighty men get him some (2 Sam 23:13-17).

Verse 26 expresses an inversion of the way things ought to be. The "wicked" or "guilty" succeed at the expense of the righteous or innocent. This saying contradicts the truth claim of 10:30, which says that the righteous shall never be moved (see Commentary on 10:30; 12:3; cf. 10:3; Ps 55:22). Things in this world do not always work out justly. The image is of cattle who so trample and befoul a watering place that one cannot drink from it. Something good and essential has been ruined so that the spiritual and social "waters" necessary for communal well-being are polluted and undrinkable. Without divine and human justice, the fountains of life are corrupted.

25:27. Verse 27a is related by theme and verbal repetition to v. 16, as is v. 27b to v. 2. These links, and the reversed repetition of "righteous" and "wicked" in vv. 5 and 26, appear to create a double envelope around vv. 2-27. The sense of v. 27a is straightforward (see Commentary on 25:16). But v. 27b is extremely difficult. Literally it reads, "and to seek/search for their glory is glory," or "is not glory," if the negative in v. 27a does double duty. A shifting of consonants and a repointing of vowels permits the translation, "and to seek difficult things is [no] glory." If this is correct, then the meaning has to do with accepting one's limits (see Psalm 131; Sir 3:21-22; 2 Esdr 4).

25:28. The concluding verse is similar in

283. See *Amenemope* 5, 1-6 and "Papyrus Insinger" 23, 6, in Miriam Lichtheim, *Ancient Egyptian Literature,* 3 vols. (Berkeley: University of California Press, 1973–80) 2:150 and 3:203, respectively. See also "Counsels of Wisdom" 41-48, in Lambert, *Babylonian Wisdom,* 101.

284. See R. C. Van Leeuwen, "On Wealth and Poverty: System and Contradiction in Proverbs," *Hebrew Studies* 33 (1992) 60; A. Meinhold, *Die Sprüche,* Zücher Bibelkommentare (Zürich: Theologischer Verlag, 1991) 2:430.

theme and imagery to 16:32 (cf. 14:29; 17:27). Wisdom is superior to strength; lack of self-control leaves one exposed and without defense (cf. 10:15; 18:10-11).

REFLECTIONS

1. The OT often uses spatial images to convey aspects of the human condition. The imagery of high and low is used frequently in the psalms to indicate security and well-being or, alternatively, misery and calamity (Pss 18:16; 27:5; 30:1, 3, 9; 36:12; 38:6; 40:2; 130:1; see Commentary on Prov 18:10-11). God, who dwells on high, lifts up the lowly and brings down the high and mighty (1 Sam 2:6-8; Isa 2:12-17; 5:15-16; 6:1; Luke 1:52). In Proverbs 25, the inscrutable glory of God and king are conveyed by cosmic height and depth (25:2-3).

Spatial imagery also conveys social position and boundaries. Wisdom at court, or anywhere, requires a recognition of social limits and propriety. This includes self-knowledge (What is my proper place and function in the scheme of things?) and awareness that powerful others also form judgments about who we are. When the one judging us is God, a human ruler, or an employer, realistic humility is called for (see Commentary on 11:2; 16:18-19; 29:23). Jesus expands the admonition of 25:6-7 into a parable on choosing places of honor at table (Luke 14:7-11). Israel's shame-and-honor culture (see Commentary on 12:8; 13:18) made explicit social dynamics that are often present but are obscured in our more egalitarian culture.

2. Proverbs 25:2-10 concerns the social scale in ancient Israel, especially in the royal court, Israel's center of power (like America's Washington, D.C., and New York City). It looks at where people, both good and bad, fit into the "pecking order" and the things they do to climb higher or descend lower on the social ladder. Where there is social mobility, there are also social conflict and competition. People can use litigation and conflict to further their own ends. The restraints that Proverbs here puts on social climbing through devious means and on unwarranted litigation speak a word of caution to our litigious and contentious culture.

3. When body parts crumble, we get hurt (25:19). If those we depend on prove unreliable in times of trouble (see Commentary on 24:10), we are especially vulnerable to injury. Proverbs 25:19 has wide application, from marriage and family in times of personal or cultural crisis to business and military in times of economic distress or war. Given the interdependence of human communities, much depends on mutual reliability and warranted trust. Whether in the body politic or in the church as a body (Rom 12:3-8; 1 Cor 12:12-30), we need one another. Individualistic persons need to reflect on this fact. Christians especially must strive to build a society that raises reliable persons, deeply aware of their role and importance in the community. While this saying focuses on the need for reliable people in times of crisis, we must nevertheless rely wholly on God in times ordinary and extraordinary (see Commentary on 3:5; 16:20; 28:25*b*).

Proverbs 26:1-28, On Fools and Fittingness

NIV	NRSV

26 Like snow in summer or rain in harvest,
     honor is not fitting for a fool.
 ²Like a fluttering sparrow or a darting swallow,
     an undeserved curse does not come to rest.
	26 Like snow in summer or rain in harvest,
	     so honor is not fitting for a fool.
	 ² Like a sparrow in its flitting, like a swallow in
	     its flying,
	     an undeserved curse goes nowhere.

NIV

3A whip for the horse, a halter for the donkey,
and a rod for the backs of fools!

4Do not answer a fool according to his folly,
or you will be like him yourself.

5Answer a fool according to his folly,
or he will be wise in his own eyes.

6Like cutting off one's feet or drinking violence
is the sending of a message by the hand of a
fool.

7Like a lame man's legs that hang limp
is a proverb in the mouth of a fool.

8Like tying a stone in a sling
is the giving of honor to a fool.

9Like a thornbush in a drunkard's hand
is a proverb in the mouth of a fool.

10Like an archer who wounds at random
is he who hires a fool or any passer-by.

11As a dog returns to its vomit,
so a fool repeats his folly.

12Do you see a man wise in his own eyes?
There is more hope for a fool than for him.

13The sluggard says, "There is a lion in the road,
a fierce lion roaming the streets!"

14As a door turns on its hinges,
so a sluggard turns on his bed.

15The sluggard buries his hand in the dish;
he is too lazy to bring it back to his mouth.

16The sluggard is wiser in his own eyes
than seven men who answer discreetly.

17Like one who seizes a dog by the ears
is a passer-by who meddles in a quarrel not
his own.

18Like a madman shooting
firebrands or deadly arrows

19is a man who deceives his neighbor
and says, "I was only joking!"

20Without wood a fire goes out;
without gossip a quarrel dies down.

21As charcoal to embers and as wood to fire,
so is a quarrelsome man for kindling strife.

22The words of a gossip are like choice morsels;
they go down to a man's inmost parts.

NRSV

3 A whip for the horse, a bridle for the donkey,
and a rod for the back of fools.

4 Do not answer fools according to their folly,
or you will be a fool yourself.

5 Answer fools according to their folly,
or they will be wise in their own eyes.

6 It is like cutting off one's foot and drinking
down violence,
to send a message by a fool.

7 The legs of a disabled person hang limp;
so does a proverb in the mouth of a fool.

8 It is like binding a stone in a sling
to give honor to a fool.

9 Like a thornbush brandished by the hand of a
drunkard
is a proverb in the mouth of a fool.

10 Like an archer who wounds everybody
is one who hires a passing fool or drunkard.[a]

11 Like a dog that returns to its vomit
is a fool who reverts to his folly.

12 Do you see persons wise in their own eyes?
There is more hope for fools than for them.

13 The lazy person says, "There is a lion in the
road!
There is a lion in the streets!"

14 As a door turns on its hinges,
so does a lazy person in bed.

15 The lazy person buries a hand in the dish,
and is too tired to bring it back to the
mouth.

16 The lazy person is wiser in self-esteem
than seven who can answer discreetly.

17 Like somebody who takes a passing dog by the
ears
is one who meddles in the quarrel of
another.

18 Like a maniac who shoots deadly firebrands
and arrows,

19 so is one who deceives a neighbor
and says, "I am only joking!"

20 For lack of wood the fire goes out,
and where there is no whisperer, quarreling
ceases.

21 As charcoal is to hot embers and wood to fire,
so is a quarrelsome person for kindling strife.

aMeaning of Heb uncertain

NIV

²³Like a coating of glaze*a* over earthenware
  are fervent lips with an evil heart.

²⁴A malicious man disguises himself with his lips,
  but in his heart he harbors deceit.

²⁵Though his speech is charming, do not believe
  him,
  for seven abominations fill his heart.

²⁶His malice may be concealed by deception,
  but his wickedness will be exposed in the
  assembly.

²⁷If a man digs a pit, he will fall into it;
  if a man rolls a stone, it will roll back on him.

²⁸A lying tongue hates those it hurts,
  and a flattering mouth works ruin.

*a23 With a different word division of the Hebrew; Masoretic Text of
silver dross*

NRSV

²² The words of a whisperer are like delicious
    morsels;
  they go down into the inner parts of the
    body.

²³ Like the glaze*a* covering an earthen vessel
  are smooth*b* lips with an evil heart.

²⁴ An enemy dissembles in speaking
  while harboring deceit within;

²⁵ when an enemy speaks graciously, do not
    believe it,
  for there are seven abominations concealed
    within;

²⁶ though hatred is covered with guile,
  the enemy's wickedness will be exposed in
    the assembly.

²⁷ Whoever digs a pit will fall into it,
  and a stone will come back on the one who
    starts it rolling.

²⁸ A lying tongue hates its victims,
  and a flattering mouth works ruin.

a Cn: Heb silver of dross   *b Gk: Heb burning*

COMMENTARY

The coherence of this passage is evident from the appearance of "fool" (כסיל *kĕsîl*) in every verse but the second. On a deeper level, the passage uses the problem of interaction with fools to teach about the need to properly "read" other people, situations, and even oneself (v. 12). In doing so, it also teaches about the nature of proverbs and their use (vv. 7, 9). Wise interpretation of proverbs, of persons, and of circumstances should lead to fitting relations and actions in every area of life. The passage also shows a structural unity in the regular construction of its sayings (vv. 4-5 are admonitions). The sayings present similes or metaphors in the first line that are figurative comments on the topics (usually concerning a fool) in the second line. (The translations in vv. 6-7, 9-10 turn metaphors into similes with "like"). In vv. 6-11, the B lines alternately present unfitting actions in relation to fools (26:6, 8, 10) or unfitting actions committed by fools (26:7, 9, 11). More precisely, the first group (vv. 6, 8, 10) provides instances of honor or position being given to a fool, as v. 8 spells out. Verse 12

concludes the whole with a saying that has an important relation to other passages in the book.

26:1-3. These verses introduce the theme of fittingness. The first two verses are similes, but the third follows the same pattern of two images followed by the saying's true (human) topic. In each image and topic, the point of comparison is whether two related things "fit."

26:1. Palestine has a warm, dry climate with fall and spring rains. The summer (also the time of harvest) is hot and dry. Rain at that time is such an anomaly that it is a frightful inversion of the cosmic order, a world upside-down (see Commentary on 30:21-23; 1 Sam 12:16-18). It is not fitting (see 17:7; 19:10; Sir 10:18; 14:3; 15:9). Rain in harvesttime is not only an anomaly, but it can also do damage by destroying crops or rotting them. Similarly, the proper order of things is inverted when a fool receives honor (כבוד *kābôd,* "glory" in 25:2, 27).

26:2. At first glance, the saying does not seem to fit its context, because it lacks the key word "fool." Yet it has the same structure as vv. 1, 3, and fittingness is its implicit theme. In v. 1, something good (honor) was given to someone bad (a fool). In v. 2, an inversion takes place. Something bad (a curse) is given to someone good (an innocent person). In v. 3, finally, something bad (a rod) is fittingly given to someone bad (a fool). The person who is cursed here is innocent because the curse was undeserved (lit., "cause-less"). In the same way that a bird does not "come to rest" as long as it flies, a curse will not "stick" to an innocent person (see Commentary on 23:4-5). A curse is implicitly a prayer that God will right wrongs, when human justice fails (11:26; 24:24). God does not honor unjustified prayers— that is, when they do not "fit" their object (Ps 109:17, 28).

26:3. In the third instance, things "fit" their objects. For corporal punishment, see Commentary on 13:24; 17:10. This verse is more compact than vv. 1-2 and imitates a beating rhythm when recited in Hebrew. Fools do not learn from reason and advice, hence the comparison with stubborn animals (cf. Ps 32:8-10; Jas 3:3). This saying leads directly into the next verse, an admonition that draws a logical conclusion from the stubbornness of the fool.

26:4-5. These verses are a contradictory pair of admonitions that present the problem of fittingness in the most radical way. The contradiction of these verses nearly kept Proverbs out of the Jewish canon of biblical books, but the Talmud argued that the admonitions refer to different matters.[285] The solution to the contradiction does lie in this direction: Wisdom does not always mean doing the same thing, even in superficially similar circumstances. Yet the juxtaposition of these admonitions drives one to reflect on the limits of human wisdom, for no clue is given to help the reader identify which fool should be ignored and which spoken to. Of two viable courses of action, we do not always know which is "fitting." The first verse of the pair gives the standard "majority" advice for handling fools (see 23:9; Matt 7:6). Since they do not listen (v. 3), and since they are attached to their folly (v. 11; see 13:19), to join them in discussion is to be dragged down to their level and to allow them to dictate the terms of the debate. Thus one becomes like them.

Verse 5 gives "minority" advice: "Answer a fool," because sometimes to leave self-deluded fools unanswered does greater damage than would exposing their folly. The practical difficulty of vv. 4-5 is knowing whether to speak or to be silent when confronted by a fool. There is, indeed, "a time to be silent and a time to speak" (Eccl 3:7 NIV). Wisdom is a matter of fittingness and timing. But here, no clues are given for making the right decision. This general problem is explored more extensively in the Babylonian *Dialogue of Pessimism,* in which a wise but cynical slave offers equally plausible reasons to his master for doing or not doing a variety of actions.[286] While the "Dialogue" concludes in pessimism, Proverbs arrives at a different outcome (see Commentary on v. 12, "wise in his own eyes").

26:6. A person in authority sends someone on a mission for which that person is not suited (see Commentary on 26:1, 8; 25:13, 25). The lack of diligence (10:26) or competence for the job renders the person—and his or her employer—a fool. The images of v. 6a are ironic; instead of the messenger's being an extra pair of feet for the master, the failed job in effect cuts the master's feet off. The drinking of violence is an unusual image (see 4:17), but it suggests that senders of fools harm themselves.

26:7. Here the writer shows that knowledge of proverbs does not automatically make one wise (see Commentary on 26:9; cf. Sir 20:18-20). Good proverbs can be put to a lame, ineffectual use. The wise make proverbs, and fools repeat them.

26:8. The imagery of v. 8a has not received a satisfactory explanation, but v. 8b, which is the verse's true topic, is a variant of v. 1. Thus by repetition it emphasizes the theme that holds this passage together. Giving honor to a fool is illustrated concretely in vv. 6, 10.

26:9. This verse repeats v. 7b, but changes the figurative comment in v. 9a, which is not entirely clear. Literally it reads, "A thorn(bush) goes up [עלה 'ālâ] in(to) the hand of a drunkard." The NRSV suggests that the drunkard brandishes a thornbush (or "hook" [חוח ḥôaḥ]; see Job 41:2[40:26]), but "brandished" seems a far-fetched rendering of "goes up." The Hebrew may mean that the thorns do damage to the drunkard's hand

---

285. See *m. Sabb.* 30b.

286. W. Lambert, *Babylonian Wisdom Literature* (Oxford: Clarendon, 1960) 139-49; *ANET,* 600-601.

(see the more ambiguous NIV). In any case, dangerous implements are not fitting in the hands of one robbed of reason by drink. In contemporary terms, "If you drink, don't drive."

26:10. This verse is textually corrupt, but the NRSV offers a plausible solution, based on slight emendation. To hire a drunkard (a link with v. 9) or someone otherwise unfit for a task does damage, sometimes deadly damage, in society. Similarly, in North American society, granting the privilege or "honor" (see Commentary on v. 1) of driving to those who drink kills tens of thousands of people every year.

26:11. There is a certain sharp humor here, based on acute observation of both humans and animals. The wise learn from their mistakes, but fools do not.

26:12. An ironic close to this section on fools and fittingness, the direct question of v. 12*a* (see 22:29) forces the reader to become personally involved in the issues of the passage. The saying is linked conceptually and verbally to vv. 4-5. There, the reader was in danger of becoming a fool (v. 4), and the fool was in danger of "being wise in his own eyes" (v. 5). This verse sharpens the point by explicitly raising the problem of self-perception as opposed to perception of the other. Those who consider themselves wise are worse than fools, because they think they are superior. They do not recognize their own limits, the fragility of human goodness, or the limits that relativize all human wisdom. The insoluble contradiction of vv. 4-5 is designed to promote awareness of these limits and to inculcate proper humility. In the larger context of Proverbs, the repetition of the phrase "wise in his own eyes" (see 26:5, 16) should drive readers to ultimate trust in the Lord rather than in themselves (see Commentary on 3:5-8; 28:25-26). The idiom "X in the eyes of P" denotes a person's subjective valuation of something, in contrast to someone *else's* valuation. The X slot in the idiom can be variously filled with terms like "good," "right," "wise," "bad," "great," or "pure" (see 12:15; 16:2; 28:11; 30:12). What ultimately matters is how things appear in God's eyes (e.g., Deut 4:25), rather than how things seem in merely human eyes (Judg 17:6; 21:25).

26:13-16. These verses comprise a short collection of sayings on the sluggard, a subclass of fool. It is related to vv. 1-12, for both sections use repetition of a key word and end with a comparative observation about being wise in one's own eyes. The sentences on the sluggard can exist independently (19:24 and 26:15 are near duplicates, as are 22:13 and 26:13), but their conjunction makes a larger, more humorous statement (see Commentary on 6:6-11; 24:30-34). In v. 13, the sluggard cannot get out of the house; in the next verse he (the Hebrew is masc.) cannot even make it out of bed; in the third, all the tossing and turning in bed has made him too weary to eat. He turns like a door tied to its hinges, but he will not open the door, for fear a lion might be walking the street. Yet, he thinks himself wiser than seven who can render a commonsense account of things. Thus he places himself under the judgment of v. 12. The seven may be an allusion to the proverbial seven wise men of antiquity. Laziness can thwart talent, position, wealth, and power. Sluggards stand in need of wisdom (6:6); in contrast to the wise son (10:4-5), they do not obey the order of the seasons (6:6; 20:4) but reject reality (22:13; 26:13). In vv. 6, 12, and 16 (see also 10:26), "fool" and "sluggard" occupy similar semantic positions.

26:17-28. The remainder of the chapter may be divided into four groups of three verses. The section as a whole concerns conflict between neighbors and the behaviors and characters that underlie conflict. Deceit and the duplicity that can exist between the outer and the inner person receive special attention.

26:17-19. The section begins with a vivid, commonsense reminder of what happens when one gets involved in fights that are not one's own (see Commentary on 25:9). One might, so to speak, get bitten. The implicit advice is obvious, yet people are notorious for simultaneously diffusing their energies in the business of others while neglecting their own responsibilities. The next two verses compare lying speech to deadly weapons, much in the manner of 25:18. The claim that a damaging lie was only a jest adds insult to injury.

26:20-22. These verses continue reflection on the power of words to create conflict, but begins this passage's movement toward exposing the inner malice that is the source of deception. The word "whisperer" translates a root (רגן *rgn*) that includes malicious gossip, but goes beyond it. The word suggests a wrongful verbal attempt to damage the rights, reputation, or authority of another in order to achieve one's own ends (see 16:28; 18:8; Deut 1:27; Ps 106:25; Isa 29:24). Falsehood, slander, gossip, distortion of reality—these are the fuel of interpersonal conflagration. Verse 21 accents the parallel of "fire" and "quarrelsome person" with a pun (אִשׁ־אִישׁ 'ēš-'îš). Verse 22 continues the topic of the whisperer, but moves it toward the next trio of verses, with their focus on the hidden, inner dimensions of conflict (see Commentary on the duplicate in 18:8).

26:23-25. The contrast between the (hidden) inner and the (visible) outer person is basic to biblical wisdom. Here it appears in the contrast respectively of lips/lips/speech with heart/within/heart (so the Hebrew; see Excursus, "The 'Heart' in the Old Testament," 60-61).

The "glaze" (v. 23; this translation is based on a putative Ugaritic cognate to an otherwise unknown Hebrew word) is literally "silver dross," which suggests that the shiny surface of the pot is itself corrupt: "All that glitters is not gold." In any case, the gloss on the pot shows the superficiality and malice of "fervent" (lit., "burning" דֹּלְקִים dōlĕqîm; see 16:27) lips disguising a corrupt heart. (The NRSV's smooth is an unnecessary emendation similar to "flattering" in v. 26). Enemies use the power of speech to hide their true intentions and character (see 6:14; 12:20; 26:26;

Ps 62:4; Jer 9:8). Wise folk see through the facade of hypocrisy, withhold trust, and do not take liars at face value. For "seven abominations," see Commentary on 11:1 (cf. Matt 12:45).

26:26-28. These verses expose inner hatred as the source of duplicitous, hurtful behavior (see Commentary on 10:12, 18), but affirm the act-consequence scheme of just recompense. Verse 27 uses traditional images to show that "what goes around, comes around" (see Eccl 10:8; Sir 27:25-26, 29). The psalms make clear that when people (individuals or nations) dig a hole to harm others and fall into it themselves, God's justice is at work (Pss 7:15-16; 9:15-16; 35:7-8). The image of the rolling stone suggests that things we set in motion assume a life of their own, beyond our control. The logic of the three conjoined verses is much like Ps 28:3-5. Our translations correctly see that v. 26 is connected with v. 25, but provide verbal connectors that are stronger than the Hebrew warrants. Verse 28 is linguistically difficult; the NIV comes close to a viable literal rendering of the Hebrew. "Those it hurts" is literally "those it crushes."[287] In line with the logic of v. 27, v. 28*b* may mean that "a slick mouth works its own ruin." "Flattering" (חלק ḥālāq) is literally "slick" or "smooth," with connotations of falsity.

---

287. See Raymond C. Van Leeuwen, *Context and Meaning in Proverbs 25–27* (Atlanta: Scholars Press, 1988) 112n. 5.

REFLECTIONS

1. "Honor" (or "glory") designates one's place in society (26:1, 8). It encompasses such things as power, authority, position, office, prerogatives, and even wealth (see Commentary on 11:16; 12:8; and on 13:18 for honor and shame). God (Mal 1:6), kings (Ps 21:6), rulers (Gen 45:13), as well as ordinary men and women—all have a glory that is proper to them (3:35; 11:16; 15:33; 18:12; 20:3; 27:18; 29:23; Sir 10:23-24, 27-31). Paul even argues, on the basis of the diversity of "kinds" in God's original creation, that in the age to come each person and creature will have a glory proper to it (1 Cor 15:35-49).[288]

Proverbs 26:1 is an ancient version of the "Peter Principle," in which persons are promoted to their level of incompetence. When persons who are not gifted, trained, or "fit" for a particular position of power, responsibility, and authority are nonetheless given that position, damage results (see 26:6, 8, 10).[289] This is true of musicians without a sense of pitch, of basketball

---

288. See Raymond C. Van Leeuwen, "Christ's Resurrection and the Creation's Vindication," in Calvin B. DeWitt, ed., *The Environment and the Christian* (Grand Rapids: Baker, 1991) 57-71.

289. See "Ankhsheshonq" 5.1, in Miriam Lichtheim, *Ancient Egyptian Literature,* 3 vols. (Berkeley: University of California Press, 1973–80) 3:163-64.

players without depth perception, and of preachers without faith or morals. The principle of giving honor only to those to whom honor is due (Rom 13:7) is especially crucial in the sphere of government (Prov 29:1, 12; Eccl 4:13; 10:5-7). The allocation of honor (including wealth) is a key indicator of a society's true values. When a society showers wealth and adulation on sports figures and entertainment celebrities without morals and underpays those who educate their children, something is desperately wrong with that society's value system. Proverbs 26:1 implies that Christians must respect the diversity of gifts in the body of Christ and in society at large. But it also condemns us for giving glory to fools.

2. Proverbs 26:7, 9 raises the problem of practical hermeneutics or interpretation. It is not enough to read and understand proverbs rightly. One must also rightly "read" life situations, persons, and events in order to use the sayings fittingly. A proverb's wisdom is useless unless it is used at the right time, in the right way, with regard to persons and circumstances that correspond to the saying. When this happens, a situation or problem is suddenly illuminated. The wise have a sense of appropriate context, of what times and circumstances require (Eccl 3:1-8).

This wisdom principle may be applied more broadly to the problem of biblical interpretation. An old adage says that "the devil can quote Scripture for his own ends." Because Scripture presents the most varied circumstances and situations over a great span of cultures and history, one cannot simply pick and choose from the Bible as one pleases. The reader of the Bible needs a sense of the whole—and of the parts. Only a knowledge of the "whole counsel of God" can enable the church to recognize and understand its present circumstances in the light of the appropriate biblical analogies and principles. God's word to discouraged slaves in Egypt, for example, may not fit white male, tenured, well-paid academics.

Proverbs 26:1-12 requires that readers interpret the text, themselves, others, and their present world rightly. But it is not true, as some postmodern folk suggest, that everything is interpretation. There can be quite different, equally valid performances of a Beethoven sonata with regard to tempo, dynamics, phrasing, room acoustics, etc. Yet, if Beethoven wrote G sharp, it is not interpretation to play F sharp! It is simply wrong. On the other hand, some interpretations can be note perfect—but all wrong, because the reading does not "fit" the composer's style or "spirit," however difficult that may be to explain. Of jazz, they say, "It don't mean a thing if it ain't got that swing."

The all too human conflict of interpretations often arises regarding situations that are ambiguous (26:4-5), that lie on the fringes and margins of things. The conflict also arises when human action or insight requires that we have a right sense of both the whole (a worldview, if you will) and the particulars that lie before us. Wisdom requires that we see reality rightly regarding both the overall patterns of existence and the individual circumstances before us, for which we are responsible.

Wisdom and valid interpretation can be distinguished from their opposites. Yet Proverbs insists that human wisdom is not omniscient (26:4-5, 12). None of us transcends reality, to "know it all" from above. We see the world only from below, from that small place where we stand, and our vision is blurred by sin and finitude. Thus, as Calvin argued, we need Scripture as the lens through which we can clearly see the difference between non-negotiable boundaries and truths of reality (G sharp, not F sharp; Yahweh, not Baal) and those legitimate areas of interpretation where wisdom and insight are called into play.

Proverbs 27:1-22, On Friendship and Paradox

NIV

27 Do not boast about tomorrow,
for you do not know what a day may bring
forth.

2 Let another praise you, and not your own mouth;
someone else, and not your own lips.

3 Stone is heavy and sand a burden,
but provocation by a fool is heavier than both.

4 Anger is cruel and fury overwhelming,
but who can stand before jealousy?

5 Better is open rebuke
than hidden love.

6 Wounds from a friend can be trusted,
but an enemy multiplies kisses.

7 He who is full loathes honey,
but to the hungry even what is bitter tastes
sweet.

8 Like a bird that strays from its nest
is a man who strays from his home.

9 Perfume and incense bring joy to the heart,
and the pleasantness of one's friend springs
from his earnest counsel.

10 Do not forsake your friend and the friend of
your father,
and do not go to your brother's house when
disaster strikes you—
better a neighbor nearby than a brother far
away.

11 Be wise, my son, and bring joy to my heart;
then I can answer anyone who treats me with
contempt.

12 The prudent see danger and take refuge,
but the simple keep going and suffer for it.

13 Take the garment of one who puts up security
for a stranger;
hold it in pledge if he does it for a wayward
woman.

14 If a man loudly blesses his neighbor early in the
morning,
it will be taken as a curse.

15 A quarrelsome wife is like
a constant dripping on a rainy day;

NRSV

27 Do not boast about tomorrow,
for you do not know what a day may bring.

2 Let another praise you, and not your own
mouth—
a stranger, and not your own lips.

3 A stone is heavy, and sand is weighty,
but a fool's provocation is heavier than both.

4 Wrath is cruel, anger is overwhelming,
but who is able to stand before jealousy?

5 Better is open rebuke
than hidden love.

6 Well meant are the wounds a friend inflicts,
but profuse are the kisses of an enemy.

7 The sated appetite spurns honey,
but to a ravenous appetite even the bitter is
sweet.

8 Like a bird that strays from its nest
is one who strays from home.

9 Perfume and incense make the heart glad,
but the soul is torn by trouble.[a]

10 Do not forsake your friend or the friend of
your parent;
do not go to the house of your kindred in
the day of your calamity.
Better is a neighbor who is nearby
than kindred who are far away.

11 Be wise, my child, and make my heart glad,
so that I may answer whoever reproaches
me.

12 The clever see danger and hide;
but the simple go on, and suffer for it.

13 Take the garment of one who has given surety
for a stranger;
seize the pledge given as surety for foreigners.[b]

14 Whoever blesses a neighbor with a loud voice,
rising early in the morning,
will be counted as cursing.

15 A continual dripping on a rainy day
and a contentious wife are alike;

16 to restrain her is to restrain the wind
or to grasp oil in the right hand.[c]

17 Iron sharpens iron,
and one person sharpens the wits[d] of another.

[a] Gk: Heb *the sweetness of a friend is better than one's own counsel*   [b] Vg and 20.16: Heb *for a foreign woman*   [c] Meaning of
Heb uncertain   [d] Heb *face*

NIV

[16]restraining her is like restraining the wind
or grasping oil with the hand.

[17]As iron sharpens iron,
so one man sharpens another.

[18]He who tends a fig tree will eat its fruit,
and he who looks after his master will be
honored.

[19]As water reflects a face,
so a man's heart reflects the man.

[20]Death and Destruction[a] are never satisfied,
and neither are the eyes of man.

[21]The crucible for silver and the furnace for gold,
but man is tested by the praise he receives.

[22]Though you grind a fool in a mortar,
grinding him like grain with a pestle,
you will not remove his folly from him.

[a]20 Hebrew *Sheol and Abaddon*

NRSV

[18] Anyone who tends a fig tree will eat its fruit,
and anyone who takes care of a master will
be honored.

[19] Just as water reflects the face,
so one human heart reflects another.

[20] Sheol and Abaddon are never satisfied,
and human eyes are never satisfied.

[21] The crucible is for silver, and the furnace is
for gold,
so a person is tested[a] by being praised.

[22] Crush a fool in a mortar with a pestle
along with crushed grain,
but the folly will not be driven out.

[a]Heb lacks *is tested*

COMMENTARY

The twenty-two proverbs here gathered are the last in the first half of the Hezekian collection (see Commentary on 25:1), and they have much the character of a proverb miscellany. Two topics do receive emphasis, however: friendship and paradoxical twists in human relations. The proverbs of this section are generally joined as pairs, but in some instances they are connected in "leap-frog" or "plaited" fashion, with one saying linked to the second saying following (see also Proverbs 29). The poem in 27:23-27 rounds off the sub-collection; compare the poems in 23:29-35; 24:30-34; and 31:10-31, which ends the entire book.

27:1-2. These verses are linked by a common term; in Hebrew, "praise" and "boast" are the same word (הלל *hālal*). Verse 1 sounds much like Ecclesiastes, with its pervasive focus on the limits of human life and knowledge. The advice (an admonition with motive) is obvious and has parallels in many societies. For instance, "Don't count your chickens before they hatch." Yet we frequently ignore such obvious common sense. The proverb in 1 Kgs 20:11, with its surrounding narrative, gives similar advice in the context of

preparing for battle: "One who puts on armor should not brag like one who takes it off" (NRSV). Confidence regarding the future must be realistic, modest, and grounded in the fear of the Lord (31:25, 30; see Commentary on 20:24). Only God is master of the future (16:1, 9; Jas 4:13-17). Thus Jeremiah urges the wise, the mighty, and the rich to boast only in knowing Yahweh (Jer 9:23-24; for "knowing" God, see Jer 22:13-16).

Verse 2 is another "obvious" admonition. It, too, is routinely ignored by people who may be insecure, feel undervalued, or are vain and proud—perhaps all at the same time. This admonition gives no grounds for the advice, but a little observation shows how much people resent others who are "full of themselves" or who "toot their own horn." Self-praise is generally counterproductive. On the other hand, some Christian bodies fail to affirm their various, diverse members, perhaps for fear of "making" others proud (see Commentary on 12:8). In such communities mutual praise grows silent and unity of spirit flags. The words here for "another" and "stranger" also describe the "strange" or "foreign" woman (see 2:16 and Reflections at 5:1-23).

27:3-4. Another pair, these verses are linked in form and in presenting a crescendo of emotions culminating in jealousy as the most unbearable (see Gen 49:7). The images of v. 3 generate a paradox: Heavier for humans than stone or sand is the "immaterial" burden of a fool's provocation (see Job 6:2-3; Sir 22:14-15). "Provocation" can also refer to "anger" (see v. 4) and to "grief," such as what a foolish youth can give parents (17:25; see 21:19). In v. 4, "jealousy" arises out of an offended, properly exclusive love's being violated (6:34; see 14:30). The rhetorical question, "Who can stand?" expects the answer, "No one."

27:5-6. These verses are a pair of paradoxes on the "tough love" that is sometimes required in faithful relationships. The pair is linked by repetition of the root for "love" (אהב ʾāhēb, "friend" in v. 6), so that v. 6 comments on the paradox of v. 5. The word translated "profuse" or "multiplies" (עתר ʿātar) is uncertain, but may mean "excessive" in the transferred sense of "false."[290] Kisses from an enemy are the ultimate betrayal (Matt 26:48-50).

27:7-8. Although v. 7 at first glance appears isolated, it shares an alliterative use of נ (n) with v. 8 and continues the sequence of paradoxes. In juxtaposition with v. 8, there may be an allusion here to honey as an erotic metaphor for the "strange" or "foreign woman," whose end is "bitter" (see Commentary on 5:3-4; 9:17; 24:13-14). If this is correct, then vv. 7-8 have been paired editorially (note also the mention of jealousy, love, and kisses in vv. 4-6 and of the foreign woman in v. 13b [NRSV margin]; cf. 6:32-34; 7:13, 18). The satisfied husband is content and does not wander like an errant bird from the nest (see 7:19). People controlled by lust or hunger cannot or do not discriminate.

Verse 7 can also stand independently as an astute observation into human behavior and as a suggestive metaphor with many applications: "Appetite is the best pickle," and "Hunger is the best cook." In contrast, the wealthy may have a spoiled appetite. At a deeper level, the inversion of "bitter" and "sweet" serves as a metaphor for moral and spiritual confusion. The wise should be able to tell the two apart, because they know the

proper order of things (Isa 5:20-23). In extreme cases, as survivors of war and famine know, all-consuming hunger can utterly confuse human judgments of what is right and what is wrong (see 2 Kgs 6:24-31).

When read as an independent saying, v. 8 evinces a profound regard for human roots in place and history. It has a parallel in Isa 16:2-3, which refers to the homelessness of exile ("home" here is lit., "place").

27:9-10. These verses form a pair linked by the key word "friend" (רע rēaʿ). The LXX adds "wine" to those things that make the heart glad (see 27:11; Ps 104:15). Wisdom also knows, however, that too much love of good things is folly (see 21:17). The Hebrew of v. 9b (ומתק רעהו מעצת-נפש ûmeteq rēʿēhû mēʾăṣat-nāpeš) is notoriously difficult. The NRSV thus opts to translate the LXX, which provides a good antithesis to v. 9a. There are good reasons for attempting to make sense of the Hebrew, however. The image of sweetness has already appeared in v. 7, in collocation with "appetite"/"soul"/"person" (נפש nepeš), a combination also appearing in v. 9b. Verse 9b, as noted, is also tied to v. 10 through repetition of "friend" (for this term, see Commentary on 17:17-18). The Hebrew may be translated either as in the NIV or as "a friend's sweetness (gladdens) more than one's own counsel," with the verb from v. 9a doing double duty.[291] On this reading, "sweetness" refers to a quality of speech or counsel (see 16:21, 24; 24:13-14; Ps 55:14). Some suggest that "sweetness" (מתק meteq) actually means "counsel." Thus, "a friend's counsel [with a pun on "sweetness"] is better than one's own advice"—"two heads are better than one." The line remains uncertain.

Verse 10 is an admonition that insists on solidarity both in the extended family and among friends and neighbors (see Commentary on 17:17-18). Although siblings are one's most natural allies, one needs to avoid overreliance on them or (in the extended sense of "brother") on clan and covenant partners (see 25:16-17). The somewhat unusual addition of a third line (see 25:13) sharpens the point that family alone is not enough for well-being. It observes realistically that a dis-

---

290. Nahum M. Waldman, "A Note on Excessive Speech and Falsehood," *JQR* (1976–77) 142-45.

291. See Raymond C. Van Leeuwen, *Context and Meaning in Proverbs 25–27* (Atlanta: Scholars Press, 1988) 124.

tant brother can do less good than a close neighbor, a thought that partially corroborates the earlier observation on wandering from one's "place" (v. 8).

27:11. This verse concludes the first half of the twenty-two verses (see Commentary on 23:15). Like v. 10, it is an admonition, addressed to "my son" and urging him to be wise (see Commentary on 10:1). For the expression "makes the heart glad," see Commentary on 27:9. The admonition reflects an intense sense of family solidarity and the mutual pride of the generations in one another (see 17:6). In Israel's patriarchal honor-and-shame culture, one needed to be able to answer those who sought to bring shame on the family (for the idiom, see Ps 119:42). Thus the honor of a "father's house" is preserved.

27:12-13. With minuscule variations, v. 12 duplicates 22:3, and v. 13, another admonition, repeats 20:16. Together these verses may partially spell out what the parent in v. 11 understands a wise son to be. A son who does not look ahead (v. 12) is likely to end up in the predicament described in v. 13. The variant in v. 13*b* refers to the foreign woman, which may be an editorial attempt to connect this passage with chaps. 1–9.

27:14. The focus turns from the "stranger" (v. 13) back to the "neighbor" of v. 10. It portrays a humorous failure of fittingness (see Commentary on 25:20; 26:1-12), where a blessing is received as if it were a curse, because it is delivered at the wrong time ("early in the morning," perhaps a gloss, but see Sir 22:6) or in the wrong manner ("with a loud voice").

27:15-16. Verse 15 is related to a number of sayings on the quarrelsome wife (see Commentary on 21:9, 19; 25:24), and the entire verse is an expansion of 19:13*b* (see vv. 12-13, which are also variants of other sayings). Verse 16, however, has not been satisfactorily explained, though its connection with v. 15 is patent.

27:17. This verse is another saying on friendship, with a leap-frog link to v. 19. The saying is simple and profound with its metallurgical metaphor of sharpening (the translations assume minor repointing of the verbs). "The wits of another" is literally "the face of his friend" (רֵעַ *rēaʿ*; see Commentary on 27:9-10). "Face" is puzzling, but it may be explained as a continuation of the metaphor of sharpening, since the working edge of a sword or knife is called its "face" (Eccl 10:10;

Ezek 21:21).[292] Another solution is to presume a different root for the second verb and translate, "one man makes the face of his friend glad" (cf. 15:13*a* for a similar idiom).[293] But this damages the parallel and point of the sharpening metaphor.

27:18. The writer assumes that every person has an honor or glory appropriate to his or her calling, no matter how humble, and that faithful service receives its reward. Often this is an increase in status and responsibility, as in the well-known stories of Joseph and Daniel in foreign courts. See the Commentary on 26:1 for the meaning of "honor" and its social misapplication.

27:19. This saying is a somewhat cryptic, non-verbal sentence; lit., "as water, the face to the face, so the man's heart to the man." The translators have supplied "reflects," assuming that it or something similar is implicit. The translations of v. 19*b* reveal the major interpretive problem in the verse. Does a man's heart (see Excursus, "The 'Heart' in the Old Testament," 60-61) reflect the man (הָאָדָם *hāʾādām*) to himself (NIV)? On this reading, one comes to self-knowledge by internal self-examination. Or does one heart reflect another person's heart (NRSV)? The latter reading is preferable, because it reinforces the link in form and meaning with v. 17 and the theme of friendship, which dominates this section.

27:20. This verse is simple but deep. For "Sheol" and "Abaddon" see Commentary on 15:11. The grave is never satisfied or filled with the generations of the dead; it never says, "Enough" (30:15*b*-16).

27:21-22. Both sayings concern the possibility of personal refinement. Verse 21 forms an envelope on "praise"/"boasting" with vv. 1-2 (see also 12:8; 31:30). It uses a metallurgical image to portray the process by which persons are tested. Verse 21*a* is a duplicate of 17:3, but v. 21*b* heads in another direction. The thought seems to be that praise is a test of a person's mettle. Will it "go to one's head," or will the person remain even-keeled with realistic self-assessment (11:2)? Verse 22 uses the image of a mortar and a pestle to show the impossibility of separating fools from their folly.

292. R. N. Whybray, *Proverbs*, NCB (Grand Rapids: Eerdmans, 1994) 384.
293. A. Meinhold, *Die Sprüche*, Zücher Bibelkommentare (Zürich: Theologscher Verlag, 1991) 2:455.

REFLECTIONS

1. "Open rebuke" may be the means by which a true friend wounds a loved one, as a surgeon wounds a patient to do good in the end (27:5-6; see 28:23; Deut 8:16). Rebuke can be given and received in a spirit of wisdom (13:18; 15:31-32; 25:12). Though painful, it is better than hidden love, which remains useless, like some treasure buried in a field (Matt 13:44; 25:25). It is not just the thought that counts. Rather, if actions speak louder than words, then they speak immeasurably louder than mere thoughts. Love must manifest itself in wise, appropriate action, because we humans are embodied creatures, made of earth and air. To assert that only one's heart or soul matters is a form of gnosticism that devalues God's good creation. It is true that Paul championed faith without works, but he did so only to assert the indispensability and sufficiency of grace. Nonetheless, Paul also insisted on faith with works, endurance based in hope, and love that labors and suffers in concrete, visible ways (1 Thess 1:3; cf. Rom 5:1-5). The paradox of Prov 27:5-6 is explored in Shakespeare's great tragedy *King Lear.* Though even his fool knows better, Lear prefers false flattery to Cordelia's silent, but honest, love.

2. To stray or wander away can have a variety of causes (27:8; Sir 29:18-28; 39:4). In the biblical story, Cain is the first to wander the earth (Gen 4:12-16). Cut off from the roots that nourish us (geography, family, nation, culture, and community), we are diminished. In these realities, we find our home, our work, our vocation, our blessing. The rootlessness of modern life is an affliction all the more acute because we often suffer it unawares and confuse it with freedom. And yet, Abraham left his home to find a new home, a new city whose maker and builder was God (Gen 12:1-3; Heb 11:8-10). A basic tension of human life is that we are earthlings, made from the earth (Gen 2:7); and yet we have no abiding home here, until all things will be made new in a new creation in which "righteousness is at home" (2 Pet 3:13).

3. Friendship is a major concern of Proverbs 27. Verse 17 focuses on the sharpening effect friends have on one another, presumably because they are not afraid to exercise tough love (27:5-6). Verse 19 treats a related aspect of friendship, the mutuality of self-knowledge and knowledge of the other. We know ourselves as we know, and are known by, others. The self refracted through another self becomes richer and is more clearly seen. Through such a dialectic of personal knowledge, two souls can be knit together in love (1 Sam 18:1-4). In another cultural setting, Aristotle observed that the good person relates to a friend as to oneself, for a friend is "another self."[294] This mutuality of hearts and souls should not be restricted to voluntary friendship. It is utterly essential to the state of being one flesh in marriage. On a much larger scale, when God renews the chosen people, they will be given "one heart and one way" (Jer 32:39 NRSV).

4. The comparison of Sheol to the insatiable human eye (27:20) should give pause on two counts. The Preacher says that the eye is never satisfied with riches (Eccl 4:8; see 1:8), even though death is inescapable. More than that, it is as if the eye feeds on death, and this may be the main point. The "lust of the eyes" (1 John 2:16 NKJV) turns the good things of creation into something deadly to the self. Advertising in our industrial-capitalistic society ceaselessly stimulates visual desire and promotes unwearying covetousness of things and persons (as objects for sex or control). Delitzsch quotes an old Arab proverb, "Nothing fills the eyes of man but at last the dust of the grave."[295]

294. Aristotle *Nicomachean Ethics,* 1166a30.

295. F. Delitzsch, *Proverbs,* in C. F. Keil and F. Delitzsch, *Commentary on the Old Testament,* vol. 6 (Grand Rapids: Eerdmans, 1975) 216.

Proverbs 27:23-27, On Tending One's Flocks

NIV	NRSV
[23] Be sure you know the condition of your flocks, give careful attention to your herds; [24] for riches do not endure forever, and a crown is not secure for all generations. [25] When the hay is removed and new growth appears and the grass from the hills is gathered in, [26] the lambs will provide you with clothing, and the goats with the price of a field. [27] You will have plenty of goats' milk to feed you and your family and to nourish your servant girls.	[23] Know well the condition of your flocks, and give attention to your herds; [24] for riches do not last forever, nor a crown for all generations. [25] When the grass is gone, and new growth appears, and the herbage of the mountains is gathered, [26] the lambs will provide your clothing, and the goats the price of a field; [27] there will be enough goats' milk for your food, for the food of your household and nourishment for your servant-girls.

COMMENTARY

This brief poem may be read in a straightforward fashion as an exhortation to care for one's flocks and to work hard in the fields, with the reward of good provision for family and household (cf. 24:30-34). Yet, sayings and admonitions are designed for application beyond their ostensive reference, as the agricultural proverb in v. 18b shows. (Cf. also the wisdom poem in Isa 28:23-29, which uses agricultural imagery to illustrate Yahweh's fitting action in history.) Several factors suggest that this poem has a royal reference in its present context. In particular, the reference in v. 24b to a crown (often emended to "treasure") implies an oblique address to the king or ruler as metaphorical "shepherd" of the people.[296] The metaphor of the king as shepherd was widespread in the ancient world, including Israel (cf. Psalm

23). Also, the poem's setting in the Hezekian collection naturally connects it with the royal concerns of 25:1-15 and of chaps. 28–29. Moreover, the references to riches, servants, and the purchase of a field all convey a social setting at the upper reaches of society (as does the related poem in 31:10-31).

A good shepherd knows the condition (lit., "face" in the sense of "appearance") or "soul" of his animals and cares for them appropriately (see Commentary on 12:10; the LXX supplies "soul" in v. 23). Such diligence leads to the well-being of all that belongs to the shepherd. Finally, the poem's general interest in domestic economy and the close relation of v. 27b to 31:15b suggest that there may be a redactional relation between these two poems. In this regard, it is striking that "servant girls" appears only in v. 27 and in 9:3 and 31:15.

296. Raymond C. Van Leeuwen, *Context and Meaning in Proverbs 25–27* (Atlanta: Scholars Press, 1988) 131-43. Cf. Bruce V. Malchow, "A Manual for Future Monarchs," *CBQ* 47 (1985) 238-45, esp. 243-45.

REFLECTIONS

Whether applied to a landholder or to a ruler, this little poem (27:23-27) reminds all people that God has given them a quasi-royal responsibility for a bit of this earth (see Reflections at 15:1-33). Our stewardship requires that we know intimately those things, creatures, and persons entrusted to our care (27:23). Governments need to understand the people, the land, and justice. Teachers need to know and love their students and their subjects. Workers and artists need to know their materials and their craft. Pastors ("shepherds" in the religious sense!) also need to know and tend their "flocks." Those in authority should not exercise power for their own glory or ego, but for the good of those persons and things entrusted to them. The quiet warning of this poem is that those who abuse their little kingdoms lose them (27:24), but those who work the earth with wisdom (note the rhythm of the seasons, 27:25; see also Commentary on 10:4-5) enjoy its fruits (27:26-27).

PROVERBS 28:1–29:27, ON JUSTICE AND TORAH

OVERVIEW

Scholars have long seen that the second Solomonic collection (Proverbs 25–29) falls into two parts, with the poem in 27:23-27 marking the divide. While the poem has often been seen as the conclusion to chaps. 25–27, which began with a focus on kingship, some have argued that it introduces chaps. 28–29 as "A Manual for Future Monarchs." What is clear is that these chapters represent a return to the antithetical proverb style of chaps. 10–15, with a similar emphasis on the opposition of "righteous" and "wicked." As Malchow has shown, the thematic character of this opposition in the sub-collection is apparent from the close linkage in thought and vocabulary in four significant verses where it occurs (28:12, 28; 29:2, 16).[297] In addition, the rhetorically important beginning and end of the sub-collection (28:1; 29:27) also employ this opposition. Although 29:7 stands outside the central group of four, it shares their opposition of "righteous" and "wicked" (here singular) and the pervasive concern in these chapters for just rule. Although the two key words are not often repeated, the various characters that appear in these chapters embody the two opposed life-styles.

Another repeated thematic term is תורה (*tôrâ*). While the word in wisdom contexts often refers to the "instruction" or "teaching" of the wise (1:8; 3:1; 4:2; 7:2), it is also used of God's "instruction." In chaps. 28–29, *tôrâ* always appears in the

absolute form (28:4 twice, 7, 9; 29:18), without specifying whose teaching it is (see Commentary on 6:23, the only other absolute occurrence of *tôrâ* in Proverbs). While teaching is no doubt mediated by humans, it is likely that the primary reference here is to God's instruction or law, as the NIV and the NRSV translations consistently render it (see Commentary on 28:9). God's law includes the Mosaic law (Genesis–Deuteronomy), but is not limited to it. It should be remembered that the Mosaic books contain not only guidance for moral living and Israelite worship, but also stories that instruct us concerning the gracious character of God and the purpose of human life—as Paul recognized (1 Cor 10:1-13). Though the explicit use of the Mosaic books in Proverbs is not frequent, occurrences should not be ignored (e.g., see Commentary on 16:4-5; 17:15; 18:5; 25:18; 28:8; perhaps 28:1). In a wider sense, *tôrâ* refers to all of God's instruction, grounded in creation and discovered in history, however such instruction is mediated (see Isa 28:23-28; and the Torah piety of the Psalms, esp. 1; 19; 119; cf. Sir 24:23).[298] Thus Proverbs 28–29 distinguish righteous and wicked, teach pious obedience to God's instruction, and urge justice among citizens and rulers. In short, they contain the key elements necessary for a healthy society.

---

297. See Malchow, "A Manual for Future Monarchs," and Meinhold, *Die Sprüche,* 2:464-65.

298. See Jon D. Levenson, "The Sources of Torah," in *Ancient Israelite Religion,* Patrick D. Miller, Jr., Paul D. Hanson, and S. Dean McBride, eds. (Philadelphia: Fortress, 1987); J. Clinton McCann, Jr., Commentary on the Book of Psalms, in *The New Interpreter's Bible,* vol. 4 (Nashville: Abingdon, 1996) 659-72, and 684 on Ps 1:2.

Proverbs 28:1-28, Torah, the Righteous, and the Wicked

NIV

28 The wicked man flees though no one
    pursues,
    but the righteous are as bold as a lion.

2 When a country is rebellious, it has many rulers,
    but a man of understanding and knowledge
        maintains order.

3 A ruler*a* who oppresses the poor
    is like a driving rain that leaves no crops.

4 Those who forsake the law praise the wicked,
    but those who keep the law resist them.

5 Evil men do not understand justice,
    but those who seek the LORD understand it
        fully.

6 Better a poor man whose walk is blameless
    than a rich man whose ways are perverse.

7 He who keeps the law is a discerning son,
    but a companion of gluttons disgraces his
        father.

8 He who increases his wealth by exorbitant
        interest
    amasses it for another, who will be kind to
        the poor.

9 If anyone turns a deaf ear to the law,
    even his prayers are detestable.

10 He who leads the upright along an evil path
    will fall into his own trap,
    but the blameless will receive a good
        inheritance.

11 A rich man may be wise in his own eyes,
    but a poor man who has discernment sees
        through him.

12 When the righteous triumph, there is great
        elation;
    but when the wicked rise to power, men go
        into hiding.

13 He who conceals his sins does not prosper,
    but whoever confesses and renounces them
        finds mercy.

14 Blessed is the man who always fears the LORD,
    but he who hardens his heart falls into trouble.

a3 Or A poor man

NRSV

28 The wicked flee when no one
    pursues,
    but the righteous are as bold as a lion.

2 When a land rebels
    it has many rulers;
    but with an intelligent ruler
        there is lasting order.*a*

3 A ruler*b* who oppresses the poor
    is a beating rain that leaves no food.

4 Those who forsake the law praise the wicked,
    but those who keep the law struggle against
        them.

5 The evil do not understand justice,
    but those who seek the LORD understand it
        completely.

6 Better to be poor and walk in integrity
    than to be crooked in one's ways even
        though rich.

7 Those who keep the law are wise children,
    but companions of gluttons shame their
        parents.

8 One who augments wealth by exorbitant
        interest
    gathers it for another who is kind to the
        poor.

9 When one will not listen to the law,
    even one's prayers are an abomination.

10 Those who mislead the upright into evil ways
    will fall into pits of their own making,
    but the blameless will have a goodly
        inheritance.

11 The rich is wise in self-esteem,
    but an intelligent poor person sees through
        the pose.

12 When the righteous triumph, there is great
        glory,
    but when the wicked prevail, people go into
        hiding.

13 No one who conceals transgressions will prosper,
    but one who confesses and forsakes them
        will obtain mercy.

14 Happy is the one who is never without fear,
    but one who is hard-hearted will fall into
        calamity.

a Meaning of Heb uncertain   b Cn: Heb A poor person

NIV

15Like a roaring lion or a charging bear
 is a wicked man ruling over a helpless people.

16A tyrannical ruler lacks judgment,
 but he who hates ill-gotten gain will enjoy a
  long life.

17A man tormented by the guilt of murder
 will be a fugitive till death;
 let no one support him.

18He whose walk is blameless is kept safe,
 but he whose ways are perverse will suddenly
  fall.

19He who works his land will have abundant food,
 but the one who chases fantasies will have
  his fill of poverty.

20A faithful man will be richly blessed,
 but one eager to get rich will not go
  unpunished.

21To show partiality is not good—
 yet a man will do wrong for a piece of bread.

22A stingy man is eager to get rich
 and is unaware that poverty awaits him.

23He who rebukes a man will in the end gain
  more favor
 than he who has a flattering tongue.

24He who robs his father or mother
 and says, "It's not wrong"—
 he is partner to him who destroys.

25A greedy man stirs up dissension,
 but he who trusts in the LORD will prosper.

26He who trusts in himself is a fool,
 but he who walks in wisdom is kept safe.

27He who gives to the poor will lack nothing,
 but he who closes his eyes to them receives
  many curses.

28When the wicked rise to power, people go into
  hiding;
 but when the wicked perish, the righteous
  thrive.

NRSV

15 Like a roaring lion or a charging bear
 is a wicked ruler over a poor people.

16 A ruler who lacks understanding is a cruel
  oppressor;
 but one who hates unjust gain will enjoy a
  long life.

17 If someone is burdened with the blood of
  another,
 let that killer be a fugitive until death;
 let no one offer assistance.

18 One who walks in integrity will be safe,
 but whoever follows crooked ways will fall
  into the Pit.a

19 Anyone who tills the land will have plenty of
  bread,
 but one who follows worthless pursuits will
  have plenty of poverty.

20 The faithful will abound with blessings,
 but one who is in a hurry to be rich will
  not go unpunished.

21 To show partiality is not good—
 yet for a piece of bread a person may do
  wrong.

22 The miser is in a hurry to get rich
 and does not know that loss is sure to come.

23 Whoever rebukes a person will afterward find
  more favor
 than one who flatters with the tongue.

24 Anyone who robs father or mother
 and says, "That is no crime,"
 is partner to a thug.

25 The greedy person stirs up strife,
 but whoever trusts in the LORD will be
  enriched.

26 Those who trust in their own wits are fools;
 but those who walk in wisdom come
  through safely.

27 Whoever gives to the poor will lack nothing,
 but one who turns a blind eye will get many
  a curse.

28 When the wicked prevail, people go into
  hiding;
 but when they perish, the righteous
  increase.

aSyr: Heb *fall all at once*

COMMENTARY

28:1. The wicked person is out of touch with reality, just as fools and sluggards are (17:16, 24; 26:11, 13). Verse 1*a* may allude to Lev 26:17, 36, where God's face is set against wicked Israel: "you will flee even when no one is pursuing you. . . . I will make their hearts so fearful . . . that the sound of a windblown leaf will put them to flight." This suggests that beneath the bold facade of wickedness stirs an uneasy conscience. Even the wicked have a suppressed awareness of divinely ordained right and wrong and the consequences of each (cf. Rom 1:18-20; 2:12-15). "Are bold" is better translated as "are confident." This confidence is based on trust (the usual translation of the verb בטח *bāṭaḥ*) in the Lord and God's Word (see Commentary on 3:5; 16:20; 28:25-26). The lion is the "king of beasts" who has no need to fear (19:12; 30:29-30). On the opposition of "wicked" and "righteous," see Commentary on 17:15.

28:2. "Rulers" translates a term (שׂר *śar*) that can refer to a variety of government officials, from judge to general to prince. Cohen cites a proverbial Arabic curse, "May God make your sheiks many!"[299] The saying is one of several that explore the well-being of the body politic and the correlation between authorities and those subject to them (vv. 12, 28; 29:2, 4). Land (ארץ *'ereṣ*) is the created environment for society; here it includes the people who live on it (29:4; 30:21; Amos 7:10). The moral-religious health of the people has an impact on the natural order (Jer 3:1; Joel 3:18-20; Amos 1:2).[300] In Hosea's day in the rebellious north, rulers were multiplied in serial fashion, through murder (Hos 4:2-3; 7:3-7; 8:4). Verse 2*b* is unclear; the NIV gives a fairly literal translation, taking כן (*kēn*) in the infrequent sense of "order" or "right" (see Commentary on 15:7).

28:3. This verse is clear and direct; it gives

the converse of Psalm 72. The word "ruler" here (רשׁ *rāš*) is different from that in v. 2, and it requires a repointing of the consonants that otherwise mean "poor." Scholars generally make this minor emendation to fit with v. 2, because the Bible does not emphasize that the poor can oppress one another. Yet city life all over shows that the poor can prey on the poor. A driving rain can destroy the grain (cf. 26:1).

28:4-5. Here the absolute use of *tôrâ* ("law" or "teaching") appears twice to announce another thematic key word in this subsection (see Overview and Commentary on 6:20-23). The search for Yahweh in v. 5 reminds the reader that the norms for human existence cannot be separated from God (cf. v. 9). These verses divide humanity into two camps: those who seek God and those who do not. This human division is most clearly manifested in the responses people make to the divine law. Some obediently keep it; some forsake and reject it; some seek God and understand justice (see 1 Cor 2:14-16); but others oppress the poor (v. 3). In lawless times, love becomes difficult to maintain (Matt 24:12), and the conflict between the godly and the lawless becomes more evident (v. 4*b;* see Reflections on Proverbs 11:1-31). In his catalogue of sins, Paul takes up the idea that the lawless praise the wicked (Rom 1:32).

Although rulers are not mentioned, the saying in v. 5 has obvious relevance to them (see vv. 2-3). Without justice in human relations and society, there is no true knowledge of God (see 29:7; Jer 22:13-16). Conversely, to seek God without seeking social justice is an exercise in bad faith (Amos 5:46, 14-15).

28:6. This verse is a variant of 19:1. The repetition of the consonants רשׁ (*rš*) in vv. 3-6 (inverted in v. 5) links this verse to its context. This repetition also emphasizes the words "poor" and "wicked," since both words begin with these same consonants. The rich may be tempted to misunderstand justice and so to be crooked in their ways (see Mark 10:25). For the paradoxical situations in which poverty is "better than" wealth, see Commentary on 16:8. "Whose ways are perverse" (see 10:9) is literally, "perverse (in

299. A. Cohen, *Proverbs: Hebrew Text and English Translation with Introduction and Commentary, The Soncino Bible* (London: Soncino, 1945) 185-86.

300. See H. H. Schmid, "Creation, Righteousness, and Salvation: 'Creation Theology' as the Broad Horizon of Biblical Theology," in B. W. Anderson, ed., *Creation in the Old Testament* (Philadephia: Fortress, 1984) 102-17; Ronald A. Simkins, *Creator and Creation: Nature in the Worldview of Ancient Israel* (Peabody, Mass.: Hendrickson, 1994); Rolf P. Knierim, "Cosmos and History in Israel's Theology," in *The Task of Old Testament Theology: Substance, Method, and Cases* (Grand Rapids: Eerdmans, 1995).

regard to) double ways." The dual form is unusual, but see Commentary on 28:18 (see also Sir 2:12, "the sinner who walks along two ways"). In contrast to integrity or unity of heart (Ps 86:11), the Israelites recognized the duplicity of the "double heart" (Ps 12:2) and of limping along a conflicted path of double opinions (1 Kgs 18:21).[301]

28:7. This verse reinforces v. 4 on keeping God's law (see Eccl 12:13) and returns to the theme of the wise or "discerning" son, the opposite of the one who "brings shame" (see Commentary on 10:1, 5, 8). Loose living of various sorts is a perennial theme in wisdom literature of many cultures (see 29:3; Luke 15:13). For the powerful effect of "the company we keep," see Commentary on 13:20.

28:8-9. These verses form a proverb pair. Verse 8 is a clear reference to a consistent biblical legal principle that forbids lending at interest to a fellow Israelite (Exod 22:24; Lev 25:36-37; Deut 23:20; Ps 15:5; Ezek 18:8; 22:12).[302] By translating the Hebrew hendiadys ("interest and increase") as exorbitant interest, the NIV and the NRSV obscure the sociocultural gap between Israel's pre-industrial economy and our modern system of capital investment. The hendiadys apparently refers to interest on money or material goods, such as grain or oil. The OT unanimously forbids lending at interest, in order to protect the poor from exploitation and hunger. This fact led to an intense hermeneutical discussion in the Reformation period, as capital loaned at interest became necessary for economic development. Recognizing that he lived in a social situation different from that of ancient Israel, John Calvin grudgingly allowed the necessity of lending at interest, but strongly warned against using it to take advantage of the needy.[303] Ezekiel 22:12 includes taking interest in a list of major sins that show that the people have forgotten God, because they do what is displeasing to God. The one who is kind to the poor pleases God, imitates God, and receives a reward (see 13:22; 14:31; 19:17; cf. Pss 111:4-5; 112:4-5).

Verse 9 follows upon v. 8 (with its legal language) to remind the reader that piety without kindness to the poor is hated by God and repudiated in the law. For the logic of the verse, see Commentary on 15:8.

28:10. This verse employs the infrequent triplet form (see 25:13), the third line supplying an antithesis. Its warning against leading others astray is varied in the wisdom teaching of Jesus (Matt 5:19; Luke 17:1-2). The image of falling into the pit one has made is a proverbial expression of poetic justice (see Commentary on 26:27).

28:11. "Rich" and "poor" are contrasted, to the latter's advantage (see Commentary on 16:8), because the poor person has discernment, while the rich person may mistakenly think that wealth automatically confers wisdom (see Commentary on 18:10-11; 26:12). A slang saying also expresses the common assumption that associates wealth and wisdom: "If you're so smart, why aren't you rich?" "Sees through [one]" translates the same verb (חקר *ḥāqar*) used in 18:17*b* and 25:2*b* for "to search" (something or someone) out.

28:12. This is the first of several thematic sayings on the weal or woe of the body politic in relation to the rising or falling of the righteous or the wicked (see Overview; 28:28; 29:2, 16). That righteous folk go into hiding when the wicked rise to power has been a common occurrence throughout history, from the time of Abimelech (Judg 9:5) to the present day. Verse 12*a* is literally, "When the righteous rejoice," presumably in response to the defeat of wicked enemies or some other good (see Commentary on 11:10; cf. Ps 68:1-4).

28:13-14. These verses are probably best understood as a couplet, for together they echo vocabulary and themes from Psalm 32, a psalm that ends in a wisdom instruction. As the second of the church's seven "penitential psalms," Psalm 32 (see also Psalms 6; 38; 51; 102; 130; 143) may also be the best OT commentary on these two verses (see also 1 John 1:5-10). Verse 13 contrasts covering up sin—something Job claims not to have done (Job 31:33)—with confessing and forsaking it, and so receiving mercy. One is to understand that such mercy comes from the One whose name is "merciful and gracious . . . forgiving iniquity and transgression and sin" (Exod 34:6-7). Verse 14 pronounces a blessing on the

301. See L. Alonso-Schökel and J. Vilchez, *Proverbios* (Madrid: Ediciones Cristiandad, 1984) 485.

302. See John I. Durham, *Exodus,* WBC 3 (Waco, Tex.: Word, 1987) 329; P. C. Craigie, *The Book of Deuteronomy,* NICOT (Grand Rapids: Eerdmans, 1976) 302-3; Moshe Greenberg, *Ezekiel 1–20,* AB 22 (Garden City, N.Y.: Doubleday, 1983) 330.

303. See John Calvin, *Commentary on Exodus* 22:25. Calvin's treatment is a masterful demonstration of the inadequacy of literalistic interpretation.

one who always fears; the NIV rightly supplies "the LORD" as the implicit object of fear (see Commentary on 1:7, though 28:14 uses a different root for "fear"). One of the patriarchal names of Israel's God is "the Fear of Isaac" (Gen 31:42). Pharaoh is the classic example of one who stubbornly "hardens his heart" (and has it hardened—a variety of verbs are used), thus buying for himself and his people the trouble of the plagues (Exod 7:3; 9:34; cf. Ps 95:8). In contrast to "hard hearted," the Hebrew idioms of the "hard heart" and the "stiff neck" do not mean cruelty or lack of kindness, but instead "stubbornness," especially against God (29:1; cf. Ps 95:8). A corollary of the hard heart is trust in one's own heart (v. 26).

28:15-16. These verses illustrate v. 12*b* and juxtapose the wicked ruler and the ruler without sense; both treat their subjects cruelly, the first by malice, the second by incompetence (see Commentary on 26:1). The lion and the bear are powerful and dangerous animals (17:12; 22:13), fitting images for rulers, whether good or evil (see 19:12; Dan 7:1-8). In v. 15*b*, the adjective "poor"/"helpless" (דל *dal*) also connotes the powerlessness that attends poverty. Israelite rulers were responsible for justice, the righting of wrongs (2 Sam 14:4-11; 15:1-6). They especially were required to do justice for the poor, who have no earthly defender (see 22:22-23; 23:10-11; 29:4, 14; Psalm 72). For this purpose, God has given these rulers authority and power, and they are accountable to God in their exercise of that power (see Wis 6:1-9; Rom 13:1-7). For "who hates unjust gain," see Commentary on 15:27.

28:17. Translation of this verse is obscure. Literally, it reads, "If a man is oppressed by life blood, let him [or "he will"] flee to the pit. Do not hold him back [or "support him"]." It is linked to the verses on either side by repetition of the root עשק (*'šq*, "oppress," "do wrong to"). Since the use here of "oppressed" is unique, the NIV and the NRSV give it an extended meaning, "burdened," though this is uncertain. The idea is that one guilty of murder ("blood," see 1:10-19; 12:6; Gen 9:6; Sir 34:21-22) will be "oppressed" by anxiety (see Commentary on 28:1; cf. Job 20:25; Isa 38:14). The verb in v. 17*b* (תמך *tāmak*) can mean either "support" or "hold back."

28:18. Verse 18*b* reads literally, "One twisted (with regard to) double ways will fall by one (of

them)." "Pit" is a variant reading of "one," based on the Syriac (see Commentary on 10:9; 19:1; 28:6).

28:19. But for its ending, this verse is a duplication of 12:11. Note the implicit contrast with v. 20.

28:20. In an agrarian context, the contrast of a faithful person and one "in a hurry to get rich" (see 29:22) implies that haste in acquiring wealth involves skullduggery, unlike the honest work of the diligent farmer (v. 19). "Blessing" is often associated with fertility of land, animals, and humans (see 10:3-7; Gen 1:22, 28).[304] While Proverbs warns against the too zealous pursuit of wealth (13:11; 20:21; 23:4-5), it also notes that wealth can be a blessing from God (10:22).

28:21. Verse 21*b* is perhaps hyperbole designed to show how little it takes to get a person to sin. The saying refers to bribery (see Commentary on 17:23), and it fits well between vv. 20 and 22 as an example of getting money too hastily (see Commentary on 18:5; 24:23).

28:22. The "miserly" person is literally "bad of eye," apparently an idiom for a greedy person (see Commentary on 23:6). For the idea that the wicked do not know the consequences of their actions, see 7:23; 9:13, 18. In a more comprehensive way, Ecclesiastes develops the limits of all human knowledge as a major theme (see Prov 27:1; see also Commentary on 13:4; 20:21).

28:23. This verse should be compared to 9:8; 19:25; and 27:5-6. The emphasis is on the difference time makes. At first the pain of reproof may provoke a negative reaction. Its good results may appear only later. For "flattery," see Commentary on 7:5; 29:5.

28:24. In Israel, an adult male who took what belonged to his parents—when they were no longer able to defend themselves—might claim that there was no sin involved. After all, what is theirs is (eventually) his by right of inheritance (19:14). In this case, a sinful rationalization ignores the role of time and circumstance in determining what is right. A similar violation of this principle appears in the prodigal son's wish to have his inheritance before his father has died (Luke 15:11-32).[305] Such actions stand under the

304. C. Westermann, *Blessing in the Bible and the Life of the Church* (Philadephia: Fortress, 1978).

305. See Kenneth E. Bailey, *Poet and Peasant & Through Peasant Eyes* (Grand Rapids: Eerdmans, 1976/1987) 158-206.

judgment of 19:26 and 20:21. The teaching of Jesus in Mark 7:10-13 also deals with a hypocritical avoidance of obligation to parents. "One who destroys" is more accurate than "a thug" (see 18:9*b*).

28:25-26. This proverb pair is linked by the middle lines, which contrast one who "trusts in the Lord" with one who trusts in oneself (lit., "in his own heart"). The latter trust is a form of being "wise in one's own eyes" (26:12; 28:11). For the concepts here, see Commentary on 1:7; 3:5-8; and Excursus, "The 'Heart' in the Old Testament," 60-61. The antithetical structure of the sayings implies that those who trust in God will not be greedy (see 28:20, 22, 24). Trust in God frees people from the compulsive drive to find security in material goods and power. Acquisitive greed causes conflict, because it robs the neighbor's little "kingdom" (23:10-11) in its anxious drive to expand its own. Literally, the greedy are "wide of throat/appetite"; like Sheol, they are ready to swallow up their neighbors whole (see 1:12). Paradoxically, those who trust in God are enriched (lit., "made fat," v. 25*b*, a symbol of well-being in the subsistence world of the ancient Near East; cf. 11:25; 16:20). Trust and "walking in wisdom" (or "integrity") go together and have similar results (see v. 18*a*; 29:25*b*).

28:27. The paradox of giving to the poor and having no lack is characteristic of one whose trust is in God (v. 25; see Commentary on 11:24; 22:16). Turning a blind eye is akin to shutting one's ear to the cry of the poor (see Commentary on 21:13).

28:28. This verse (with v. 12; 29:2, 16) is thematic for chaps. 28–29 (see Overview). Verse 28*b* is a variant of v. 12*b*. In the present verse, a pun between "people" (אדם *ʾādām*) and "they perish" (אבדם *ʾobdām*) links the two lines and accents human mortality. This verse, with its thematic companions, links the weal or woe of common people and society to the ascendancy of the righteous or the wicked respectively. The righteous increase in the sense that they thrive, "as do plants, when the worms, caterpillars, and the like are destroyed."[306] (See Reflections at Proverbs 29:1-27.)

---

306. F. Delitzsch, "Proverbs," in C.F. Keil and F. Delitzsch, *Commentary on the Old Testament,* vol. 6 (Grand Rapids: Eerdmans, 1975) 240.

Proverbs 29:1-27, More on Torah, the Righteous, and the Wicked

NIV	NRSV
29 A man who remains stiff-necked after many rebukes will suddenly be destroyed—without remedy.	**29** One who is often reproved, yet remains stubborn, will suddenly be broken beyond healing.
²When the righteous thrive, the people rejoice; when the wicked rule, the people groan.	² When the righteous are in authority, the people rejoice; but when the wicked rule, the people groan.
³A man who loves wisdom brings joy to his father, but a companion of prostitutes squanders his wealth.	³ A child who loves wisdom makes a parent glad, but to keep company with prostitutes is to squander one's substance.
⁴By justice a king gives a country stability, but one who is greedy for bribes tears it down.	⁴ By justice a king gives stability to the land, but one who makes heavy exactions ruins it.
⁵Whoever flatters his neighbor is spreading a net for his feet.	⁵ Whoever flatters a neighbor is spreading a net for the neighbor's feet.
⁶An evil man is snared by his own sin, but a righteous one can sing and be glad.	⁶ In the transgression of the evil there is a snare, but the righteous sing and rejoice.
	⁷ The righteous know the rights of the poor;

NIV

⁷The righteous care about justice for the poor,
  but the wicked have no such concern.

⁸Mockers stir up a city,
  but wise men turn away anger.

⁹If a wise man goes to court with a fool,
  the fool rages and scoffs, and there is no
    peace.

¹⁰Bloodthirsty men hate a man of integrity
  and seek to kill the upright.

¹¹A fool gives full vent to his anger,
  but a wise man keeps himself under control.

¹²If a ruler listens to lies,
  all his officials become wicked.

¹³The poor man and the oppressor have this in
    common:
  The LORD gives sight to the eyes of both.

¹⁴If a king judges the poor with fairness,
  his throne will always be secure.

¹⁵The rod of correction imparts wisdom,
  but a child left to himself disgraces his
    mother.

¹⁶When the wicked thrive, so does sin,
  but the righteous will see their downfall.

¹⁷Discipline your son, and he will give you peace;
  he will bring delight to your soul.

¹⁸Where there is no revelation, the people cast off
    restraint;
  but blessed is he who keeps the law.

¹⁹A servant cannot be corrected by mere words;
  though he understands, he will not respond.

²⁰Do you see a man who speaks in haste?
  There is more hope for a fool than for him.

²¹If a man pampers his servant from youth,
  he will bring grief[a] in the end.

²²An angry man stirs up dissension,
  and a hot-tempered one commits many sins.

²³A man's pride brings him low,
  but a man of lowly spirit gains honor.

²⁴The accomplice of a thief is his own enemy;
  he is put under oath and dare not testify.

²⁵Fear of man will prove to be a snare,

a21 The meaning of the Hebrew for this word is uncertain.

NRSV

  the wicked have no such understanding.
⁸ Scoffers set a city aflame,
  but the wise turn away wrath.
⁹ If the wise go to law with fools,
  there is ranting and ridicule without relief.
¹⁰ The bloodthirsty hate the blameless,
  and they seek the life of the upright.
¹¹ A fool gives full vent to anger,
  but the wise quietly holds it back.
¹² If a ruler listens to falsehood,
  all his officials will be wicked.
¹³ The poor and the oppressor have this in
    common:
  the LORD gives light to the eyes of both.
¹⁴ If a king judges the poor with equity,
  his throne will be established forever.
¹⁵ The rod and reproof give wisdom,
  but a mother is disgraced by a neglected child.
¹⁶ When the wicked are in authority,
    transgression increases,
  but the righteous will look upon their
    downfall.
¹⁷ Discipline your children, and they will give you
    rest;
  they will give delight to your heart.
¹⁸ Where there is no prophecy, the people cast
    off restraint,
  but happy are those who keep the law.
¹⁹ By mere words servants are not disciplined,
  for though they understand, they will not
    give heed.
²⁰ Do you see someone who is hasty in speech?
  There is more hope for a fool than for
    anyone like that.
²¹ A slave pampered from childhood
  will come to a bad end.[a]
²² One given to anger stirs up strife,
  and the hothead causes much transgression.
²³ A person's pride will bring humiliation,
  but one who is lowly in spirit will obtain
    honor.
²⁴ To be a partner of a thief is to hate one's own
    life;
  one hears the victim's curse, but discloses
    nothing.[b]
²⁵ The fear of others[c] lays a snare,

a Vg: Meaning of Heb uncertain   b Meaning of Heb uncertain
c Or human fear

NIV	NRSV
but whoever trusts in the LORD is kept safe. 26 Many seek an audience with a ruler, but it is from the LORD that man gets justice. 27 The righteous detest the dishonest; the wicked detest the upright.	but one who trusts in the LORD is secure. 26 Many seek the favor of a ruler, but it is from the LORD that one gets justice. 27 The unjust are an abomination to the righteous, but the upright are an abomination to the wicked.

COMMENTARY

29:1. The opening saying is reminiscent of Lady Wisdom's warnings in 1:25, 30 about the calamity that comes to those who stubbornly refuse to listen to (her) wise counsel and rebuke (also 13:18; 15:10; cf. 28:23). Verse 1*b* replicates 6:15*b*, where the villain of 6:12 receives his fate. To be "stiff-necked" is a common idiom for stubborn rebellion towards one who deserves obedience. Thus when Israel rebels against Yahweh, their new covenant Lord, they are stiff-necked (Exod 32:9-10; cf. Jer 7:25-26; 17:23). This saying illustrates the patience of the reprover and the persistence of the rebel, for the rebukes are multiple. As Delitzsch notes, "The door of penitence, to which earnest, well-meant admonition calls a man, does not always remain open."[307] Individuals can finally be broken beyond healing, but so can nations (Jer 19:10-11).

29:2. Here is another thematic verse on the weal or woe of the body politic in relation to righteous and wicked rulers (see Commentary on 28:12-28; 29:16). Here the emphasis is respectively on the joy people feel when right has the upper hand and the acute suffering of ordinary people when wrong reigns. Our century has illustrated both sides of this proverb, though one wonders if the second line does not predominate (see Commentary on 11:10-11 and Reflections on Proverbs 11:1-31).

29:3. The saying applies to all people (10:1; 28:7), but in the context of vv. 2 and 4, it may apply especially to the royal son (see 31:3). The contrast between "loves wisdom" and the illicit love of prostitutes (6:26) evokes the pervasive symbolism of chaps. 1–9, which associates the love of wisdom or folly with love of wife or the "strange woman" (see Overview on 1:1–9:18).

29:4. This verse is a specific illustration of v. 2. "Justice" (משפט *mišpāṭ*) is a word whose range of meaning includes "customary [and thus normative] practice," "law," and the giving of justice within and outside of the law court (see 29:14).[308] Lit., the king's justice "makes the land stand (firm)." "Country" (ארץ *'ereṣ*) or, rather, "land" also means "earth," and the cosmic overtones of the word should not be ruled out here. Social injustice leads to cosmic catastrophe (see Commentary on 30:21-23), but justice leads to blessing and a fruitful earth (see Psalms 65; 72).[309] The alternative translations, "who makes heavy exactions" (NRSV) or "who is greedy for bribes" (NIV), each interpret a unique Hebrew phrase, lit., "a man of gifts." The difficulty is that gift (תרומה *tĕrûmâ*) is a term that elsewhere consistently refers to sacral contributions. NIV understands a ruler or judge who takes bribes; NRSV suggests a ruler whose taxes are extreme. In either case, the issue is the government's misuse of income (perhaps intended for the sanctuary?) in a way that compromises its responsibility to do justice. For "tears it down," see the same verb in 11:11; 14:1.

29:5. The NIV better captures the ambiguity of the masculine gender Hebrew: Is the flatterer spreading a net for his own feet or for his neighbor's? The next verse suggests that, while the net is intended for the neighbor, it actually snares the flatterer (see 1:17-19; Pss 9:15-16; 57:6). For "flatterer," see Commentary on 26:28.

---

307. Ibid., 240.

308. See Moshe Weinfeld, *Social Justice in Ancient Israel and in the Ancient Near East* (Minneapolis: Fortress, 1995) for these terms.

309. H. H. Schmid, *Gerechtigkeit als Weltordnung*, BHT 40 (Tübingen: Mohr Siebeck, 1968).

29:6. Verse 6*a* ("snare") picks up on the previous verse; the thought is similar to 12:13. Verse 6*b* conveys the joy of those who escape from trouble (cf. Ps 67:5; Jer 31:7; Zech 2:10). Because the connection of the two lines is not entirely obvious, some scholars emend "sing" (ירון *yārûn*) to "run" (ירוץ *yārûs*; i.e., free of trouble) and are glad (cf. 4:12; 18:10).

29:7. "Know" here refers to active, caring concern, as is clear from 12:10 and 27:23. The just have compassion even for their cattle; how much more for their fellow humans, who are sometimes treated worse than beasts.[310] "Rights" (a term laden with modern, Enlightenment connotations) does not quite capture the sense of the Hebrew, which is closer to "cause" in a legal dispute (see Commentary on 23:10-11). The "knowing" of the righteous entails that they defend and rescue the poor from the powerful who have wronged them (see Commentary on 24:10-12). This happens especially in juridical but also in other ways.[311] Verse 7*b* is not entirely clear; lit., "a wicked person does not understand knowledge." Our translations convey the general sense.

29:8. The writer provides here another political observation. The Hebrew phrase underlying scoffers appears also in Isa 28:14, where it refers to rulers who have filled Jerusalem with lies—until that time when God will make justice and righteousness the standard (Isa 28:17; cf. Prov 29:12). Wrongdoers set the city on fire with conflict (see 26:18-21; Sir 28:8-12). It takes the wise to restore order and peace (see Commentary on 15:1-2).

29:9. This verse presents one of a number of reasons for the advice in 26:4: "Do not answer a fool according to his folly" (NIV). The general point is to avoid conflict, especially with fools, if possible (see also 13:20; 14:7; 26:17-19). NIV supplies "fool" as subject in the second line (probably rightly, see 29:11); NRSV renders the verbs impersonally. Because v. 9*b* lacks an explicit subject, some translations identify the subject as the "wise" person: "he [the wise man] may rage or laugh but can have no peace" (NAB).

29:10. Verse 10*b* is difficult and uncertain. At first glance, it means "and the upright [pl.] seek his life" (i.e., to kill him), which makes no sense.

This has led to a number of emendations. NRSV and NIV have the advantage of not modifying the text.[312] The issue is the murderous rancor that the wicked have toward the good. For descriptions of the "bloodthirsty" (lit., "men of blood") see Pss 26:9-10; 139:19-20.

29:11. The reading of NRSV is closer to the Hebrew than is the NIV, for the object of "holds it back" is "anger" (lit., "spirit," cf. Eccl 10:4), not the person. The restraining of rampant emotion is a frequent theme in Proverbs; it separates the wise from the foolish (12:16; 14:17; 15:1-2, 18; 16:32 18:2; cf. Sir 20:7; 21:26).

29:12. Citizens, like children, will generally do what they are permitted to do. Here the abdication of the ruler's responsibility leads to the corruption of his officials, with the consequent ruination of the land (29:4; see Commentary on 17:4). Psalm 101, as a "mirror for princes" demonstrates the care with which a righteous king chooses his servants. A king must search out the truth of things and judge accordingly (14:35; 25:2). Sirach 10:1-4 provides a generalized form of this saying with commentary.

29:13. This verse is a variant of 22:2, but the juxtaposition of "poor" and "oppressor" adds sharpness to the theology of this saying. The point is that God judges those who wrong the poor (see Commentary on 14:31). "Gives light to the eyes" is the same as giving life and the joy of life, because "to see light" means to live (see Job 3:16; Pss 13:4; 38:10; 49:19; cf. Prov 15:30).

29:14. This verse outlines one of the basic duties of government: the protection and defense of the poor from those stronger than they (Ps 72:4; Isa 11:4; Jer 22:16). This protection lies at the heart of royal "justice and righteousness"[313] and gives stability to the king's throne or government and to the land (see Commentary on 16:12; 25:5; cf. 28:2, 15-16; 29:2, 4).

29:15-21. Delitzsch notes that vv. 15-18 alternate the topics of household and people.[314] In the ancient world, relations in marriage and family, between masters and servants, and in the body politic were generally conceived as parallel hier-

---

310. See Delitzsch, "Proverbs," 245.
311. Weinfeld, *Social Justice in Ancient Israel,* 44-49

312. For the grammar implicit in the (somewhat paraphrastic) NIV and NRSV translations, see Bruce K. Waltke and M. O'Connor, *An Introduction to Biblical Hebrew Syntax* (Winona Lake: Eisenbrauns, 1990) ¶4.7, 76-77, ¶16.4.b, 303.
313. Weinfeld, *Social Justice in Ancient Israel,* 45-74.
314. Delitzsch, "Proverbs," 250.

archical structures, a fact still evident in the so-called domestic codes of the NT (Rom 13:1-7; Titus 2:1-3, 8; 1 Pet 3:13-22; see Commentary on 30:21-23).[315] The pattern seen by Delitzsch may be extended as far as v. 21, for v. 15 is linked, leap-frog fashion, with 29:17, 19, 21, all of which concern the discipline of sons or servants. Verses 19 and 20 reflect on two of the many functions of words.

29:15. For the context of this verse, both cultural and literary, see Commentary on 13:1; 23:13. The ancient oriental mode of corporal punishment is presupposed (see Commentary on 13:24). The proverb warns of "permissive" child rearing, for it assumes that children need to be trained because what is right and wise does not always come to them "naturally" (22:15). Sirach expands this saying and renders it more severe (Sir 22:3-6; 30:1-13).

29:16-17. Verse 16 is similar to 10:19, though the cause of transgression is different in each case. This verse is part of the thematic repetition noted in the Overview (see Commentary on 28:12; 29:2). It promises that tyrants will fall. The belief that God's justice will ultimately prevail is implicit. Psalms 11 and 12 may be seen as meditations on this point. For v. 17, see the Commentary on 10:1; 19:18; 29:15.

29:18. This verse is the only place in Proverbs where prophetic "vision" (חָזוֹן *ḥāzôn*) is mentioned. "Vision" can refer to various types of prophetic revelation (Ps 89:19; Dan 1:17; 8:1), and usually occurs as a dream (Isa 29:7; Mic 3:6). A sage can claim such a revelatory vision (Job 4:13 uses a cognate term). A vision can be written down (Hab 2:2), thus the term appears in the titles of prophetic books (Isa 1:1; Obad 1:1; Nah 1:1; cf. 2 Chr 32:32; Amos 1:1; Mic 1:1; only Hab 1:1 uses the verb).

There is diversity of opinion on 29:18. Many feel that its vocabulary should be understood in terms of typical wisdom concerns, so that "vision" and "law" refer to political guidance and wise instruction respectively (cf. 11:14). Others note that "vision" appears here in parallel with *tôrâ* (law or instruction)—a key word in this subsection of Proverbs (see Overview to chaps. 28–29).

Thus, taken together, these terms represent the "law and prophets" as twin, written sources of guidance for the people of God.[316]

If this is correct, 29:18 may represent editorial, "innerbiblical" reflection on the first two sections of the Hebrew canon: the law (of Moses) and the Prophets. The third section, Writings, includes Proverbs itself (see Commentary on 30:1-9 for intra-biblical references in Proverbs). The overall concern in this subsection of Proverbs for rulers, politics, and justice, brings to mind the deuteronomic dependence of the king on the Mosaic law (Deut 17:18-19; cf. 1 Kgs 2:2-4), and of king and people on prophecy (Deut 18:15-22; cf. 2 Sam 24:11). A comprehensive study of language common to Proverbs and the Pentateuch, Proverbs and the Prophets, and Proverbs and the other Writings remains to be written. It should be noted, however, that toward the end of canon formation, wisdom becomes an increasingly literary and learned scribal phenomenon, as is evident also from Ben Sira, Qumran, and the NT.[317] Judaism and Christianity in their formative periods were already "religions of the book."

Another view is that with the Babylonian exile active prophecy ceases, as does priestly teaching of the Mosaic law. At that time, Jerusalem's "king and princes are among the nations; the law is no more, and her prophets obtain no vision from the Lord" (Lam 2:9; cf. Ps 74:9; Jer 18:18; Ezek 7:26; 12:22). In such a situation, the individual (the Hebrew is singular) "who keeps the law" will still be blessed (see Commentary on 28:4, which uses the plural; see also Ps 1:1). McKane emends v. 18*b* to read, "but a guardian of the Law keeps it [the people] on a straight course."[318] The emendation is unnecessary (cf. 28:4, 7).

29:19. In the matter of discipline, the ancients believed that "actions speak louder than words." The servant (sg., masc.), like many people, follows the line of least resistance: he gets away with what he can (29:12; cf. 17:2). Without sanctions

---

315. See David L. Balch, *Let Women Be Submissive: The Domestic Code in 1 Peter,* SBLMS 26 (Chico, Calif.: Scholars Press, 1981) 28, 33-34, quoting Aristotle *Politics* 1.1253*b*.1-14.

316. W. O. E. Oesterley, *The Book of Proverbs* (London: Methuen, 1929) 263.

317. See, comprehensively, M. J. Mulder, ed., *Mikra: Text, Translation, Reading and Interpretation of the Hebrew Bible in Ancient Judaism and Early Christianity,* CRINT 2.1 (Philadelphia: Fortress, 1988); cf. R. C. Van Leeuwen, "Scribal Wisdom and Theodicy in the Book of the Twelve," in Leo G. Perdue, et al., eds., *In Search of Wisdom: Essays in Memory of John G. Gammie* (Louisville: Westminster/John Knox, 1993) 31-49.

318. See William McKane, *Proverbs: A New Approach,* OTL (Philadelphia: Westminster, 1970) 640-41.

---

authority has no power to command obedience. Sirach 33:24-33 treats the handling of servants ambiguously, advising not only harsh discipline, but also kindness (see Commentary on 29:15, 17, 21).

29:20. This verse is a near duplicate of 26:12 (cf. 22:29); it substitutes "who speaks in haste" for "wise in his own eyes." Haste in speech is an eminent form of folly (10:19; Eccl 5:1; Jas 1:19; see 19:2 for haste in general). It is better to be silent than to speak an ill word that cannot be called back (17:27-28).

29:21. This saying is the end of the leapfrog series on discipline and training of sons and servants. The final word in Hebrew is otherwise unknown and, despite many conjectures, uncertain. Thus, "bring grief" and "come to a bad end" are guesses. A possible solution is that מנון (*mānôn*), was an error for מדון (*mādôn*), "strife" (see 29:22). The general sense of the saying, against permissive indulgence, is clear.

29:22. Verse 22a is nearly identical to 15:18a. Verse 22b expands the thought, using vocabulary similar to 29:16, a key verse in this subsection.

29:23. The reversal of high and low, proud and humble is a topic encountered before (see Commentary on 15:33; 16:18-19; 18:12).

29:24. (see Commentary on 13:20; 14:7). The saying is not entirely clear. The partner of a thief, lit., "who shares [the spoils]," hates his own life, that is, puts his life at risk as in 1:18 (cf. 8:36). An Israelite's obligation is to help restore goods to their rightful owner(s), to break with wrongdoers, and to give testimony against them in court. Not to fulfill these obligations is a sin of omission that renders one subject to a curse (Lev 5:1; Judg 17:1-3). The accomplice of a thief pre-fers ill-gotten gain to the well-being of the community and disdains the curse that falls on wrongdoers. It is not clear that such a person has actually been put under oath.

29:25. The "fear of man" in v. 25a may be taken in one of two senses. In the first, the genitive "of" is objective, contrasting fear of other humans to trust in God (see Commentary on 28:25-26). This topic is familiar from the Psalms, "In God I trust; I will not be afraid./ What can man do to me?" (Ps 56:11 NIV; cf. Psalm 27). In the second, the genitive is subjective, as in the NRSV margin. Here the reference is to human terrors of any sort, with the implication that those who trust in God do not need to fear, for they are secure in him. The imagery is of a fortress or tower, literally "high" and thus safe (see Commentary on 18:10-11). The meaning in both cases is similar, though the second applies to any frightful human situation. This verse and the next contrast humans with Yahweh.

29:26. This saying contrasts the ruler—as that powerful human who is entrusted with the responsibility of giving "justice" to the many—and God as the ultimate source of justice. This is so, even when human rulers are the agents of God's justice on earth (20:22; 21:1-3; Psalm 72:1-2; Rom 13:1-7). The contrast between God and humans (see 29:25) is a foundation of OT thought and is expressed in a myriad of ways (Job 38; Psalms 8; 62; Eccl 5:2; Isa 55:8-9).

29:27. The final verse contrasts the mutual abhorrence of righteous and wicked humans, rather than God's abhorrence of the latter. For "abhorrent" ("abomination"; see Commentary on 11:1; cf. 11:20).

REFLECTIONS

1. Proverbs 28–29 casts a penetrating gaze at the interaction of government, money, justice, and poverty. These chapters call Christians to social and governmental reflection and reform. To reflection because uninformed reform does damage. To reform because much in the land is wrong and crooked. The sages were not prophets, but their standards for government and civic life have a prophetic ring. Their concern extends far beyond the red flag moral issues that exercise many religious folk in America today: (other people's sexual) immorality, abortion, and drugs. These issues are important, and in a pluralist society their resolution is complex. Unfortunately, passion about them is no substitute for a biblically informed, wise view of the government's task. Here Christians are desperately divided.[319]

319. See James W. Skillen, *The Scattered Voice: Christians at Odds in the Public Square* (Grand Rapids: Zondervan, 1990).

Curiously, evangelical Christians, who rightly proclaim the authority of Scripture, often restrict its message to the realm of private, personal conversion and the family-related moral issues noted above. But mainline Christians, who rightly proclaim the social, public relevance of the gospel, often struggle with biblical authority. And both camps struggle with ignorance of Scripture in a television culture. In both camps Scripture does not function as a reality guide for public and private life. In this regard, Abraham Lincoln's monumental second inaugural address shows that this need not be so. It provides a prophetic example of biblical wisdom illuminating the life of the nation in time of crisis.

The OT insists that the basic task of rulers is to do justice internationally by preserving the nation's boundaries and integrity, and domestically by protecting the boundaries of widows and orphans (see Commentary on 15:25) and righting wrongs. Royal justice, like Yahweh himself, is especially dedicated to the cause of the weak and defenseless (28:27; 29:7, 14; Psalm 72).[320]

To move to one example in our American context, the perennial debate about the size of government requires a clear understanding of its task. Christians cannot say that government is too big or too small without serious, biblically informed analysis of that part of creation that is government and politics (see Commentary on 8:15-16).[321] Government should be big enough to do its job and small enough to do it without inappropriate trespass into other spheres of life (28:2, 15-16; 29:2; 1 Sam 8:10-18). Indeed its delicate, necessary task includes the adjudicating of relationships among various persons and spheres of life and the prevention of one sphere from dominating others (e.g., does industry exploit workers; are products safe for consumers; are drivers competent to drive a car; may minors buy tobacco and alcohol?).[322] To do its task, government must often intrude into other spheres "for the sake of justice and righteousness" (e.g., when parents neglect or abuse their children; when a large company unfairly restricts trade; when Christian schools fail to meet public educational standards; when another country invades its borders). These issues and the tasks of justice are complex and crucial. Too often today Christian minds and hands neglect them.

Not only do Christians need clarity as to government's nature and task, they also need a sense of its right practice. For example, the Scriptures, including Proverbs, consistently warn that money diverts the government from heeding the truth and doing justice (see Commentary on 15:27b; 17:23; 28:16, 21; 29:4, 12). Thus Christians ought not to be silent when Congress perpetually fails to enact campaign finance reform, so allowing special interest lobbies to distort legislation. Again, Christians ought not to be silent when civil and criminal justice is affordable only to wealthy individuals and corporations who can afford expensive lawyers and professional "expert" witnesses.

Biblical wisdom and biblically informed common sense concerning government will grow, not by proof-texting this or that specific issue, but when God's people learn to read the Bible as a book of justice and to see their world in its light. For Proverbs 28–29 the "law" is both the "Torah" of Moses and the "teaching" of the wise (see Overview of 28:1–29:27). These chapters imply that knowledge of the Scriptures and wisdom concerning practical politics and good government cannot be separated (cf. Josh 1:6-9; 1 Kgs 2:1-4). We need to saturate our minds and imaginations in the Scriptures and then open our eyes to the reality around us. We need to act, not rashly, but wisely and decisively, not out of partisan interest, but with a humble passion for "justice and liberty for all."

2. Proverbs 28:5 and 29:27 portray the mutual intolerance of the righteous and the wicked.

---

320. See Keith W. Whitelam, "King and Kingship," *Anchor Bible Dictionary,* 6 vols. (New York: Doubleday, 1990) 4:40-48.

321. See Paul Marshall, *Thine Is the Kingdom: A Biblical Perspective on the Nature of Government and Politics Today* (Grand Rapids: Eerdmans, 1984); Oliver O'Donovan, *The Desire of the Nations: Rediscovering the Roots of Political Theology* (Cambridge: Cambridge University Press, 1996).

322. See Michael Walzer, *Spheres of Justice* (New York: Basic, 1983) 3-30; Peter L. Berger, "In Praise of Particularity: The Concept of Mediating Structures," in *Facing Up to Modernity* (New York: Basic, 1977) 130-41.

The assumption is that righteous folk understand and align themselves with the divine perspective on good and evil (28:5; 29:7). Wicked folk and wickedness are abhorrent to God (6:16-19; 8:7; 21:27), and in this the righteous imitate God. God's enemies are their enemies, because God's enemies do evil. This thought comes to strong expression in Ps 139:19-22 (from the divine side, cf. Gen 12:3; Num 24:9). Such sayings portray a world apparently without a middle ground, a world with a fundamental conflict between good and evil. In our tolerant, pluralistic society, such thinking seems troublesome, especially when we see the violence done by groups seeking to impose their understanding of good and evil on others. Should we not rather "live and let live"?

Yet Jesus also spoke in terms of conflict. "Whoever is not with me is against me, and whoever does not gather with me scatters" (Matt 12:30). How are we to understand such biblical language today?

Two extreme currents compete in contemporary culture, and yet they seem to feed on one another in a strange symbiosis. On the one hand there is a strong insistence—itself often dogmatic—on tolerance and avoiding dogmatic truth claims.[323] No one person or group may presume to have the truth because such claims are actually covert bids for power and self-aggrandizement.[324] A moral corollary, especially in the media, seems to be that "anything goes." On the other hand there is a fanaticism in which one's position or the position of one's group is absolutely right; nothing is ambiguous, and divergent views should be destroyed. To the extent that such thinking is theologically aware, human thought is identified with God's thought, ignoring that even divine revelation must be interpreted by fallible humans. In such thinking "the end justifies the means," including violence. All balance is lost; public discourse is destroyed.

Proverbs 29:27 offers a reproof to the first current rather than the second. And yet, unless this proverb is taken seriously, the second, fanatic current will be given free play. Proverbs reminds us that we may not elevate moral ambiguity and religious mystery to the point of relativism, where the lines between right and wrong, good and evil, true and false, are erased (see Isa 5:18-23). At that point tolerance is no longer a virtue, but moral indifference in the face of evil. It is an abandonment of the social responsibility to which the God of the Bible continually calls us. Christians cannot, for example, remain silent and inactive in the face of oppression or racial hate—whether in Nazi Europe or in America with its burning of black churches. Tolerance is not an adequate response to evil.[325]

The Scriptures insist that in and through creation God has shown *all* humans enough of God's own self and of good and evil that we are "without excuse" (Rom 1:18-20; 2:14-15). No one may say, "we did not know" (24:12; see Reflections on Proverbs 8:1-36). God has shown humans what is good, and what God requires is especially open to those who have the Scriptures (Mic 6:8; see Commentary on 29:18).

---

323. See Lesslie Newbigin, *The Gospel in a Pluralist Society* (Grand Rapids: Eerdmans, 1989), for an invaluable discussion of these issues.
324. On these themes, see Anthony C. Thiselton, *Interpreting God and the Postmodern Self: On Meaning, Manipulation, and Promise* (Grand Rapids: Eerdmans, 1995).
325. Bonhoeffer's *Ethics* is a crucial resource. See D. Bonhoeffer, *Ethics* (New York: Macmillan, 1965). In a public television interview, Philip Hallie, author of *Lest Innocent Blood Be Shed* (New York: Harper & Row, 1979), revealed that he no longer believed that the heroic pacifism described in his book was an adequate response to the Holocaust. It did not stop Hitler. See Bill Moyers, "Facing Evil: Light at the Core of Darkness," Videotape (KERA Dallas: Public Affairs Television, Inc., 1988).

THE WORDS OF AGUR, CURSES, AND NUMERICAL SAYINGS

NIV

30 The sayings of Agur son of Jakeh—an oracle[a]:

This man declared to Ithiel,
   to Ithiel and to Ucal:[b]

2 "I am the most ignorant of men;
   I do not have a man's understanding.
3 I have not learned wisdom,
   nor have I knowledge of the Holy One.
4 Who has gone up to heaven and come down?
   Who has gathered up the wind in the hollow
      of his hands?
Who has wrapped up the waters in his cloak?
   Who has established all the ends of the earth?
What is his name, and the name of his son?
   Tell me if you know!

5 "Every word of God is flawless;
   he is a shield to those who take refuge in
      him.
6 Do not add to his words,
   or he will rebuke you and prove you a liar.

7 "Two things I ask of you, O LORD;
   do not refuse me before I die:
8 Keep falsehood and lies far from me;
   give me neither poverty nor riches,
   but give me only my daily bread.
9 Otherwise, I may have too much and disown
      you
   and say, 'Who is the LORD?'
Or I may become poor and steal,
   and so dishonor the name of my God.

10 "Do not slander a servant to his master,
   or he will curse you, and you will pay for it.

11 "There are those who curse their fathers
   and do not bless their mothers;
12 those who are pure in their own eyes

a1 Or *Jakeh of Massa*   b1 Masoretic Text; with a different word division of the Hebrew *declared, "I am weary, O God; / I am weary, O God, and faint.*

NRSV

30 The words of Agur son of Jakeh.
      An oracle.

Thus says the man: I am weary, O God,
   I am weary, O God. How can I prevail?[a]

2 Surely I am too stupid to be human;
   I do not have human understanding.
3 I have not learned wisdom,
   nor have I knowledge of the holy ones.[b]
4 Who has ascended to heaven and come down?
   Who has gathered the wind in the hollow
      of the hand?
Who has wrapped up the waters in a garment?
   Who has established all the ends of the
      earth?
What is the person's name?
   And what is the name of the person's child?
   Surely you know!

5 Every word of God proves true;
   he is a shield to those who take refuge in
      him.
6 Do not add to his words,
   or else he will rebuke you, and you will be
      found a liar.

7 Two things I ask of you;
   do not deny them to me before I die:
8 Remove far from me falsehood and lying;
   give me neither poverty nor riches;
   feed me with the food that I need,
9 or I shall be full, and deny you,
   and say, "Who is the LORD?"
or I shall be poor, and steal,
   and profane the name of my God.

10 Do not slander a servant to a master,
   or the servant will curse you, and you will
      be held guilty.

a Or *I am spent.* Meaning of Heb uncertain   b Or *Holy One*

NIV

and yet are not cleansed of their filth;
¹³those whose eyes are ever so haughty,
  whose glances are so disdainful;
¹⁴those whose teeth are swords
  and whose jaws are set with knives
to devour the poor from the earth,
  the needy from among mankind.

¹⁵"The leech has two daughters.
  'Give! Give!' they cry.

"There are three things that are never satisfied,
  four that never say, 'Enough!':
¹⁶the grave,ᵃ the barren womb,
  land, which is never satisfied with water,
  and fire, which never says, 'Enough!'

¹⁷"The eye that mocks a father,
  that scorns obedience to a mother,
will be pecked out by the ravens of the valley,
  will be eaten by the vultures.

¹⁸"There are three things that are too amazing for
    me,
  four that I do not understand:
¹⁹the way of an eagle in the sky,
  the way of a snake on a rock,
the way of a ship on the high seas,
  and the way of a man with a maiden.

²⁰"This is the way of an adulteress:
  She eats and wipes her mouth
  and says, 'I've done nothing wrong.'

²¹"Under three things the earth trembles,
  under four it cannot bear up:
²²a servant who becomes king,
  a fool who is full of food,
²³an unloved woman who is married,
  and a maidservant who displaces her mistress.

²⁴"Four things on earth are small,
  yet they are extremely wise:
²⁵Ants are creatures of little strength,
  yet they store up their food in the summer;
²⁶coneysᵇ are creatures of little power,
  yet they make their home in the crags;
²⁷locusts have no king,
  yet they advance together in ranks;
²⁸a lizard can be caught with the hand,
  yet it is found in kings' palaces.

a16 Hebrew *Sheol*   b26 That is, the hyrax or rock badge

NRSV

¹¹ There are those who curse their fathers
  and do not bless their mothers.
¹² There are those who are pure in their own
    eyes
  yet are not cleansed of their filthiness.
¹³ There are those—how lofty are their eyes,
  how high their eyelids lift!
¹⁴ There are those whose teeth are swords,
  whose teeth are knives,
to devour the poor from off the earth,
  the needy from among mortals.

¹⁵ The leechᵃ has two daughters;
  "Give, give," they cry.
Three things are never satisfied;
  four never say, "Enough":
¹⁶ Sheol, the barren womb,
  the earth ever thirsty for water,
  and the fire that never says, "Enough."ᵃ

¹⁷ The eye that mocks a father
  and scorns to obey a mother
will be pecked out by the ravens of the valley
  and eaten by the vultures.

¹⁸ Three things are too wonderful for me;
  four I do not understand:
¹⁹ the way of an eagle in the sky,
  the way of a snake on a rock,
the way of a ship on the high seas,
  and the way of a man with a girl.

²⁰ This is the way of an adulteress:
  she eats, and wipes her mouth,
  and says, "I have done no wrong."

²¹ Under three things the earth trembles;
  under four it cannot bear up:
²² a slave when he becomes king,
  and a fool when glutted with food;
²³ an unloved woman when she gets a husband,
  and a maid when she succeeds her mistress.

²⁴ Four things on earth are small,
  yet they are exceedingly wise:
²⁵ the ants are a people without strength,
  yet they provide their food in the summer;
²⁶ the badgers are a people without power,

a Meaning of Heb uncertain

NIV

²⁹"There are three things that are stately in their
stride,
four that move with stately bearing:
³⁰a lion, mighty among beasts,
who retreats before nothing;
³¹a strutting rooster, a he-goat,
and a king with his army around him.ᵃ

³²"If you have played the fool and exalted yourself,
or if you have planned evil,
clap your hand over your mouth!
³³For as churning the milk produces butter,
and as twisting the nose produces blood,
so stirring up anger produces strife."

a31 Or *king secure against revolt*

NRSV

yet they make their homes in the rocks;
²⁷ the locusts have no king,
yet all of them march in rank;
²⁸ the lizardᵃ can be grasped in the hand,
yet it is found in kings' palaces.

²⁹ Three things are stately in their stride;
four are stately in their gait:
³⁰ the lion, which is mightiest among wild
animals
and does not turn back before any;
³¹ the strutting rooster,ᵇ the he-goat,
and a king striding beforeᶜ his people.

³² If you have been foolish, exalting yourself,
or if you have been devising evil,
put your hand on your mouth.
³³ For as pressing milk produces curds,
and pressing the nose produces blood,
so pressing anger produces strife.

a Or *spider*   b Gk Syr Tg Compare Vg: Meaning of Heb uncertain
c Meaning of Heb uncertain

COMMENTARY

30:1-9. The "Words of Agur" is one of the most difficult and controverted sections in Proverbs. Not only does it present serious textual and exegetical problems (especially in v. 1), but also its very meaning and purpose have received radically contrary interpretations.[326]

Some find here the words of a skeptic (vv. 1-4) who is either agnostic (denying human knowledge of God) or atheistic (denying God's existence). The next verses would be the words of a pious Jew who answers the skeptic in an orthodox way (vv. 5-6), praying to be spared similar impiety or sin (vv. 7-9).[327] A contrary reading—the view taken here—believes that the entire section needs to be taken as a whole and reflects a humble piety (cf. Job 42:1-6), recognizing the immense gap between God and humans (vv. 2-4). The arena in which this gap is revealed is creation itself, much

as in Job 38–39 and Isaiah 40–55. And like Isa 55:8-11, vv. 5-6 assert that the answer to the cosmic gulf between God and humans is a form of God's Word, prophetic and canonical Scripture respectively.

The main sections of the passage are linked by hymnic rhetorical questions based on the name of God (see Commentary on 30:4, 9). Moreover, in the light of God's provision for life, the sage prays that God give neither luxury nor poverty, lest faith be tempted to violence against the Giver's holy name.[328] Finally, there is an implicit contrast between the faithful Word of God (v. 5) and what faithless humans may say (v. 9—the Hebrew uses the same root [אמר *'āmar*]; cf. Rom 3:4).

Even the boundaries of the passage are disputed. The LXX version of Proverbs places vv.

326. James L. Crenshaw, "Clanging Cymbals," in Douglas A. Knight and Peter J. Paris, eds., *Justice and the Holy: Essays in Honor of Walter Harrelson* (Atlanta: Scholars Press, 1989) 51-64.

327. R. B. Y. Scott, *Proverbs–Ecclesiastes*, AB 18 (Garden City, N.Y.: Doubleday, 1965) 175-76.

328. See P. Franklyn, "The Sayings of Agur in Proverbs 30: Piety or Scepticism?" *ZAW* 95 (1983) 237-52; A. Gunneweg, "Weisheit, Prophetie und Kanonformel: Erwägungen zu Proverbia 30, 1-9," in *Alttestamentlicher Glaube und biblische Theologie: Festschrift für Horst Dietrich Preuss zum 65 Geburtstag*, Jutta Hausmann et al., eds. (Stuttgart: W. Kohlhammer, 1992) 253-60.

1-14 before 24:23 and places vv. 15-33 (plus 31:1-9) after 24:34 (using the Hebrew chapter and verse numbers). It is clear that vv. 1-14 comprise several subunits. Are they merely juxtaposed, or is there an implicit editorial logic that links them into a larger whole? Crucial here is the question of genre or genres in the passage.

Verses 1-3, 4, 5-6, 7-9 should be read together as an editorial, "anthological" poem. Reference to other passages of Scripture is an essential feature of this passage, and these allusions and quotations have a deliberate theological and canonical function. In this composite literary whole, the central issues arise from the questions concerning God's name and the believer's need to be free of sin regarding that name, lest one say contemptuously, "Who is the Lord?" (i.e., "Yahweh," which is the proper name of Israel's God; see Exod 3:14-15; 34:6-7). Conspicuously, the passage does not use the name until its last verse. As numerous commentators have noted, in contrast to the rest of Proverbs, which almost always uses "Yahweh"/"LORD," this passage avoids that name by using alternative terms for "God."

The passage begins with the limits of human knowledge, which nearly drive the writer to despair (vv. 1-4); yet it ends with a fervent prayer of faith (vv. 7-9), made possible by confidence in the written revelation of God (vv. 5-6; see also 29:18).

Verses 1-9 comprise several parts, but they are linked by rhetorical questions and their implicit answer, by thematic catch words, and by an overarching, implicit logic. Skehan argued that v. 4 was a riddle pointing to the Creator and that "his son" must be taken seriously. For Skehan, the riddle is resolved by seeing in "the Holy One" a reference to Yahweh, and in "Agur son of YQH" a reference to Jacob/Israel as Yahweh's "son" (What is his name and his son's name, if you know?), since Israel is God's "son" (Exod 4:22; Deut 32:19; Hos 11:1; cf. Matt 2:15). YQH is then an abbreviation for יהוה (YHWH, Qadôsh Hû, "Yahweh, Holy is He"), a precursor of the familiar later phrase, "The Holy One, blessed be He."[329]

Against Skehan's position, it may be noted that

these questions are not true riddles concerning Yahweh's name, which every Israelite knew. Rather, they concern the greatness of the Creator and the smallness of the creature. As questions about Yahweh's name, their counterpart is the triumphant hymnic declaration often found in creation contexts: "Yahweh (God of hosts) is his name!" (e.g., Isa 47:4; 48:2; 51:15; 54:5; Jer 31:35; Amos 4:13; 8:7-9; 9:6). As questions about divine activity in creation, they correspond to the rhetorical hymnic questions in Isaiah 40–55 (e.g., Isa 40:12, 26; 45:21). Agur's questions, like their counterparts in Job 38, are designed to exalt God and to humble human pretensions to knowledge (Job 38:4-11).

30:1. This opening verse abounds with difficulties. "Agur son of Jakeh" is unknown. "Agur" itself is not a usual Hebrew name. Again, "Jakeh" (properly, יקה yāqeh) is unknown. Agur's sayings are called not "an" but "the" oracle (המשא hammaśśāʾ); this term reappears, without the article, in 31:1. Many commentators prefer to make a minor emendation so that the word (in one or both cases) refers not to a prophetic utterance but to a north Arabic tribe to which Agur and Lemuel, both apparently non-Israelites, belonged (see Gen 25:14; 1 Chr 1:30). The most vexing part of the verse, however, is "to Ithiel, to Ithiel and to Ucal" (NIV) or "I am weary, O God, I am weary, O God. How can I prevail?" (NRSV). The only other occurrence of the Hebrew name "Ithiel" ("God is with me"; cf. "Immanuel") is in Neh 11:7. The NRSV makes one of many attempts to divide the consonants differently and repoint its vowels to give some coherent meaning that fits the context. Another, less plausible, attempt reads the text as Aramaic (see Dan 3:29): "There is no God, there is no God, and I can [not know anything]" (see Ps 14:1; Dan 2:10).[330] The phrase "thus says the man" (lit., "an oracle of the man") is a prophetic formula found only in Num 24:4, 15 and 2 Sam 23:1. The allusion to Numbers is nicely ironic. There Balaam, a prophet for hire, uses wisdom modes of speech. He "takes up his saying"—the same word found in the title of Proverbs (משל māšāl; not "oracle")—and gives a conventional invitation to hear, used frequently in Proverbs 1–9 (Num 23:18). Balaam claims to be

329. P. W. Skehan, "Wisdom's House," in *Studies in Israelite Poetry and Wisdom,* CBQM 1 (Washington, D.C.: Catholic Biblical Association of America, 1971) 42-43; Roland E. Murphy, *Wisdom Literature: Job, Proverbs, Ruth, Canticles, Ecclesiastes, Esther,* FOTL 13 (Grand Rapids: Eerdmans, 1981) 80.

330. R. B. Y. Scott, *Proverbs–Ecclesiastes,* AB 18 (Garden City, N.Y.: Doubleday, 1965) 175-76.

one who sees clearly, who "hears the words of God" (Num 24:4, 16; cf. Prov 30:5). He claims to have visionary "knowledge of the Most High" (Num 24:16; cf. Prov 30:3). Yet, Balaam is "son of Beor," a name that punningly may be read as "son of Stupid," the same root as in v. 2.

30:2-3. The writer does not mean to say that Agur considers himself subhuman. Rather, it is a hyperbolic and ironic confession of the limits of human existence and understanding, like the psalmist's "I am a worm and not a man" (Ps 22:6 NIV; cf. Ps 49:10, 12, 20). The same metaphorical denial of human understanding of God appears in the psalms.

> How great are your works, O Lord,
>   how profound your thoughts!
> The senseless man does not know
>   [בער לא ידע *ba'ar lō' yēdā'*],
> fools do not understand.
> (Ps 92:5-6 NIV)

Again, when the faith of the pious poet of Psalm 73 was tried, he failed to understand God's justice:

> I was senseless and ignorant [בער ולא אדע
>   *ba'ar welō' 'ēdā'*; cf. Jer 10:14];
>   I was a brute beast before you [see Prov 26:3].
> Yet I am always with you. (Ps 73:22-23a NIV)

There are people like Eliphaz and Balaam who think they know divine mysteries by personal revelation (Job 4:12-17). However, in the light of vv. 5-6, the specific focus of Agur's ignorance appears to be his failure to learn the wisdom that Moses taught to Israel (Deut 4:1, 6) and for which one does not need to ascend to heaven (Deut 30:11-14).

30:4. The four questions in this verse all presuppose the obvious answer: No one, except God or heavenly agents. These cosmic questions are traditional and rhetorical; they reveal the gap between God (or gods in the ancient Near East) and human beings. To ascend to and come down from heaven is impossible for humans (Gen 11:4-5, 7; 28:12-13; Deut 30:12; Judg 13:20; Bar 3:29-32; 2 Esdr 4:8; John 3:12-13), and this question was a standard proverb in the ancient

Near East.[331] It is mere presumption for humans to contemplate ascending to heaven (Gen 11:1-9; Job 11:7-9; Isa 14:13-15). In the Hellenistic period, however, apocalyptic claims to have seen hidden things, which had been revealed uniquely to them, arose in the name of heroes like Enoch (Gen 5:21-24):

> I know everything; for either from the lips of the Lord, or else my eyes have seen from the beginning even to the end . . . I know everything, and everything I have written down in books, the heavens and their boundaries and their contents. . . . What human being can see their cycles and their phases [i.e., of the heavenly bodies]? . . . I measured all the earth . . . and everything that exists. I wrote down the height from the earth to the seventh heaven, and the depth to the lowermost hell. . . . And I ascended to the east, into the paradise of Edem [i.e., into heaven; italics added].[332]

Perhaps an important function of vv. 1-9 is to reject such claims to know hidden things by directing readers to trust in God's scriptural word (v. 5) and to humble acceptance of the limits of the human condition (vv. 8-9).

The whole span of creation is covered in the four questions. The sequence of elements from "heaven" to "earth" spans reality from top to bottom and sets the four ancient elements in order (fire = heaven, air = wind, earth, water; cf. Eccl 1:4-11). Like the divine speeches in Job 38–41, these questions contrast the almighty Creator with puny humans (cf. Job 26:8; 28:26; Isa 40:12).

30:5. This saying is a quotation from 2 Sam 22:31 (= Ps 18:30; cf. Pss 2:12; 18:2), but uses an infrequent term for "God" in place of the original "Yahweh" (cf. Ps 18:31). This psalm in effect supplies the answer for Agur's questions, for immediately after the verse quoted here, David asks, "Who is God but Yahweh?" (2 Sam 22:32 = Ps 18:31). Significantly, the psalm portrays Yahweh as descending from the heavens (2 Sam 22:10, 17; for an ascent, see Judg 13:20; see Commentary on Prov 30:4).

30:6. The writer here alludes to the canonical

---

331. F. Greenspahn, "A Mesopotamian Proverb and Its Biblical Reverberations," *JAOS* (1994) 33-38; W. Lambert, *Babylonian Wisdom Literature* (Oxford: Clarendon, 1960) 41, 149, and esp. 327. See also *ANET* 79 (Gilgamesh), 101-2 (Adapa), 103, 508 (Nergal and Ereshkigal), 601 (Dialogue of Pessimism), 597 (I will Praise the Lord of Wisdom).

332. 2 Enoch 40, 41 [J], in J. H. Charlesworth, ed., *The Old Testament Pseudepigrapha,* 2 vols. (Garden City, N.Y.: Doubleday, 1983) 1:164, 168. See M. Stone's important study, "Lists of Revealed Things in the Apocalyptic Literature," in F. M. Cross, W. Lemke, P. D. Miller, eds., *Magnalia Dei* (New York: Doubleday, 1976) 414-54.

formulas in Deut 4:2; 5:22; 12:32. The purpose, in line with the questions asked in v. 4 and the confession about God's Word in v. 5, appears to be to exclude apocalyptic speculation and additions to the Scriptures held as authoritative by the editors of Proverbs (see Commentary on Prov 30:4).

30:7-9. This is the only prayer in Proverbs. It asks God for two seemingly unrelated things: first, to be kept from falsehood; second, to be given neither wealth nor poverty. Expressed in positive form, it is a request for one's daily bread. The petition from the Lord's prayer has its background here (Matt 6:11), as the NIV translation suggests. But the Hebrew term קֹח (ḥōq) here means a portion that is fitting (see Commentary on 26:1-12) or appropriate to one's needs and situation as a servant (31:15)—in this case, a servant of God.

Verse 9 provides the motive clauses that explain the reasons for the prayer's unusual requests. The one who prays knows that being poor is better than being a rich liar (19:22), who, like Pharaoh, thinks that Yahweh is an impotent nobody: "Who is the LORD?" (Exod 5:2 NRSV; cf. 3:13-15, "What is his name?" leading to the revelation of the name "Yahweh"). But the one who prays also knows that grinding poverty can break a person and lead to theft, which does violence to God's name. The verb here (and "deny" you) is linked elsewhere to "stealing" as something disloyal or unfaithful to God (Josh 7:11; Hos 4:1-2). But it can refer also to greedy, idolatrous reliance on wealth (Job 31:24-28; cf. Col 3:5). Joshua 24:27 uses the same verb to signal denying God by failing to keep all the "words of the LORD" (cf. v. 5; Job 6:10). In Hos 4:1-2, "stealing" and "lying" ("denying") are among the actions that demonstrate that Israel does not know God. Significantly, v. 9 provides the first explicit instance of God's revealed name, "Yahweh," in this passage. Its question, "Who is the Lord?" echoes the rhetorical questions of v. 4.

30:10-33. 30:10. This verse is loosely linked to vv. 11-14 by the theme of blessing and cursing (see Exod 21:17), while vv. 11-14 form a subunit, each beginning with "There are those. . . ." The remainder of the chapter, separated in the LXX, contains a variety of numerical sayings.

There are curses that are deserved (see Commentary on 26:2). Servants are in a vulnerable position with respect to their masters; the servants' only recourse may be the curse as an appeal to God for justice. Ecclesiastes 7:21 and Deut 23:15-16 appear to take note of the power imbalance between master and servant, so as to protect the servant. The saying in this verse assures the weak that God will give them justice when they are wrongly accused (cf. 22:22-23). The story of Joseph and Potiphar's wife provides a good illustration (Gen 39:6-23).

30:11-14. These verses form a catalogue of vice, reminiscent of the numerical saying in 6:16-19. "There are those who" is literally, "A generation of those who" or perhaps, "A circle of. . . . " Although this unit is in the third-person indicative, there is here a note of prophetic urgency and indignation. The focus is on the collective character of sin; wrongdoing is done in "packs" inspired by a common spirit of wickedness (cf. Jer 2:31; 7:29; Matt 3:7; 12:34). The cursing of parents is forbidden in the Torah (Exod 20:12; 21:17; see Commentary on 10:1; 20:20; 30:17). The deception of self-appraisal is a frequent theme in wisdom literature, signaled by the phrase "[pure] in their own eyes" (see Commentary on 16:2; 20:9; 26:12). "Lofty" eyes are a symbol of pride (see Commentary on 6:17; see also Ps 131:1). For the image of teeth as swords, see Ps 57:4. The rapacity of the powerful against the weak is a frequent OT theme (see 14:31; Ps 14:4; Mic 3:1-3).

30:15-16. Here begins the first of a series of explicitly numerical sayings, though one should note the number in v. 7 and the implicit numerical catalogue in vv. 11-14. Numerical sayings, especially those that use the pattern x, x + 1, are common in the ancient world, including the Homeric poems of Greece (see 6:16-19; Amos 1–2). Verse 15a appears to have been added to the three-plus-four saying in vv. 15b-16. Common to both is the insatiability of things, whether human or cosmic. Instead of the four elements—fire, earth, water, and air (see Commentary on v. 4)—here we have the addition of Sheol, the grave, which is never filled with the dead (see 27:20; Isa 5:14). For a related metaphorical use of "fire," see 26:20-21. The juxtaposition of Sheol and the "barren womb" is poignant, since it cannot replace what the grave devours. Rachel, Hannah, and Elizabeth each expresses the depth of an Israelite woman's longing for children (Gen 30:1-2; 1 Samuel 1–2; cf. Luke 1:5-25).

30:17. This verse corresponds to v. 11. The reference to eyes graphically portrays the law of retribution, in which the punishment fits the crime. When a corpse is abandoned, it is eaten by beasts or by the birds of the air (cf. 1 Sam 17:44, 46; 1 Kgs 14:11; 21:23-24), and the brutal harshness of this act means to convey the utter wrongness of cursing parents.

30:18-20. These verses portray simple wonder at marvelous phenomena in God's creation, culminating with the mystery of sexual love. If vv. 2-3 expressed the limits of human knowledge with regard to God above, then these verses declare that even the marvels of creation are beyond human comprehension. Verse 20 is linked to the preceding verses by the catch word "way" (דרך *derek*) and by a poignant awareness that the same activity can excite wonder and dismay. For a discussion of "way," see the Reflections on Proverbs 4:1-27.

The typical pattern of three and four is used here with reference to created phenomena. They are beyond understanding, not so much in a scientific sense, but in the sense of joyful, aesthetic awe at what God has made indescribably beautiful. Some scholars have thought that the four ways are linked by the disappearance of what has passed, as suggested by Wis 5:7-13. Here, however, each way somehow excites the poet's amazement and joy. And each image subtly suggests the most wonderful thing of all: "the way of a man with a girl." "Eagle" is the same word translated "vultures" (lit., "sons of the vulture"— i.e., birds of the vulture class) in v. 17*b*. Birds, which fly and soar through the air, have a way that, in its freedom and artlessness, seems to be no way at all. The snake moves mysteriously without feet; it is, not coincidentally, a universal phallic symbol. The ship makes its way, literally, "in the heart of the sea" (23:34; Exod 15:8), an image that suggests rhythmic movement as the ship plunges through wave after wave of waters with unfathomable, hidden depths.

The ways move from three realms of creation (again earth, air, water; see Commentary on 30:4, 16) to culminate in the human realm. Of all the creatures made by God, God's image, male and female, is the crown. The translations obscure

some of the parallelism of the images. Both the three natural images and the image of human love share the same pattern, and (except for the snake on a rock) use the same Hebrew preposition, ב (*b*). This preposition can mean both "in" and "with," and the translators choose the latter in the last line only: a vulture "in the sky, a ship on . . . the sea," but a man "with" a girl. The term "girl" is that used in the well-known passage Isa 7:14, where it refers to a young woman without specifying virginity or lack thereof. Using delicate imagery for love, this small poem sings implicit praise to God for the glories of creation, especially for sexual love (see Commentary on 5:15-20; Song of Songs).

Like 5:15-20, the present passage moves from delight and wonder at sexuality as a created good to a disturbing picture of good gone wrong. Adultery is not the way the Creator intended. Sex is compared to eating (a common trope, see Reflections on Proverbs 4:1-27; 5:1-23; Sir 26:12), and the casually wiped mouth may be literal or figurative. Perhaps more horrifying than the deed itself is the lack of guilt or remorse, as if the deed might be wiped away and leave neither physical nor moral tracks, like a ship on the seas.

30:21-23. These verses form another three plus four saying. Though some have seen this passage as merely humorous, it is an instance of the world upside down, a pattern of inversion or chaos that is found throughout the world from ancient times to the present.[333] Such pictures of inversion have a variety of functions ranging from the comic to the serious and sometimes combine both. Many a true word is spoken in jest. The ancients linked the natural world to the human world of culture and society (see Reflections on Proverbs 8:1-36). Chaos or harmony in one was correlate to chaos or harmony in the other. When God's messiah (anointed one) comes, people of low status are elevated and the high and mighty are brought low (see 1 Sam 2:4-8, 10*b*; Luke 1:51-53). But whether social inversion is good or bad depends upon the situation (see Isa 3:4-5). "The Bible delights in fruitful reversals of fortune . . . but has no use for upstarts."[334] If the wicked

333. R. C. Van Leeuwen, "Proverbs 30:21-23 and the Biblical World Upside Down," *JBL* 105 (1986) 599-610.

334. Derek Kidner, *Proverbs,* TOTC (Downers Grove, Ill.: InterVarsity, 1964) 181.

are in power, inversion is good, but if the good are brought low, the world upside down is bad. Moreover, the various spheres of life were seen as linked. Thus the political world of king and royal servant is parallel to the domestic world of husband, wife, and domestic servants (cf. Esth 1:16-22; see Commentary on 29:15-27).

The earth is meant not to tremble, but to be stable and carry its load (Amos 1:1; 7:10; 8:8; 9:5-6). The elevation of a royal servant to the position of king represents social anarchy (14:35; 19:10; Eccl 10:5-7), something that especially plagued the Northern Kingdom of Israel (but see Commentary on 17:2 for a contrary saying). A fool is here someone who behaves contrary to right custom and social norms (17:7), as does Nabal in 1 Samuel 25. In a subsistence farming society fools do not work appropriately and so lose the right to scarce resources (10:4-5; 19:10; 28:19; cf. 2 Thess 3:10).

The case of the unloved woman (lit., "disliked") may refer not to one gaining a husband, nor to one being divorced, but rather to a second wife in a polygamous household (see Deut 21:15-17) who comes to "lord it over" the household, as Peninnah did to Hannah (1 Samuel 1). The last instance of a topsy-turvy world is the case of a female servant displacing her mistress as mother of an heir. This pattern appears in the conflict of Hagar and Sarah (Genesis 16; 21) and often in the competition of royal wives or concubines to set their son on the throne (see 1 Kings 1). Here the domestic and the political combine.

30:24-28. Only the number four is mentioned in this passage, and the subject turns to the world of nature as a source of wisdom (see vv. 15-19; Job 12:7-10; Psalm 19). The sayings exploit the paradox that the small, weak, and insignificant can be wise and accomplish great things. The description of ants and (rock) badgers (Ps 104:18) as a people suggests that part of their wisdom and success lies in their grassroots social organization and cohesion, a point that is explicit in the case of the locusts, who have no king (contrast Judg 17:6 and Jotham's parable, Judg 9:7-15). The

devastating, quasi-military order of a myriad of locusts in the Near East is well known (Joel 1:4-7; 2:2, 4-9, 11). Their strength lies in their unity. The ant has already had a parable devoted to it (6:6-11). At key, perhaps editorial, points in the book, the advance preparation of food (lit., "bread;" 6:8; 12:11; 20:13; 27:27; 31:14, 27) and especially the building or care of a house have a powerful resonance as instances of fundamental wisdom (9:1; 14:1; 24:3, 27; 27:27; 31:15, 21, 27). Again, a lizard is small, insignificant, yet has free run of the king's palace. Though one can take it in one's hand, one does not harm it, for it serves the king by controlling noisome insects.

30:29-31. This unit is another three and four animal saying, which, if correctly translated, affords comparisons for the king in his majestic dignity. There are a number of linguistic uncertainties, however, and the last line is obscure. Verse 30 is quite clear. Even in English the lion is "king of beasts," known for its fearlessness (see Gen 49:9-10). "Strutting rooster" follows the ancient versions but is uncertain, (lit., "loins girded?"). The LXX amplifies, "the rooster marching boldly among his hens." If this reading is correct, it signals (perhaps with humor) the king's proud bearing: the rooster knows it rules the roost. In Dan 8:5-8, another word for "he-goat" is used as a metaphor for a leader, and this appears to be the point here, although the word used here appears only four times in the Bible.

30:32-33. These verses present a humorous sketch with a serious point. There is danger in elevating oneself (see Commentary on 25:6-7). If you've made that mistake, silence yourself by putting "hand to mouth," a symbol of dismay and humiliation (Job 21:5; 29:9). The pressing of the hand to one's mouth leads to a humorous chain of parallels in v. 33, nicely captured by NRSV's repeated "pressing . . . produces." There are here some delightful puns. The word for "curds" plays on a word for wrath. And in the last line, "pressing anger," which makes no real sense in English, puns in Hebrew because the word for "anger" is the dual form of the word for "nose"!

REFLECTIONS

1. To some readers, the Words of Agur (vv. 1-9) seem to offer biblical warrant for skepticism. Such a position appeals partly to uncertain readings of the very difficult first verse. But the thought of skepticism in the Bible is somehow appealing in our culturally uncertain times. We are often uncomfortable with those who possess more certainty than seems humanly appropriate. In my understanding, vv. 1-9 give no warrant for skepticism, but it does humble many of our proud certainties. As Ecclesiastes notes, God is in heaven and we are on earth (Eccl 5:2). The writer (or editor, if fragments have been combined) refuses even to claim the knowledge of divine things that other religious specialists of his day claim to know (vv. 2-3). But with the rhetorical questions of v. 4, he exposes their claims to superhuman, perhaps apocalyptic, knowledge as bogus: No human has made the journey to heaven and back.

The writer/editor's response to the limits of human knowledge is threefold. First, he points to the reliable, now written or canonical word of God (vv. 5a, 6). This is not something up in heaven and out of reach, but near at hand. Humans can know it and do it (Deut 30:11-14). However vast human ignorance of God and cosmic mysteries may be, this they can and must know. The writer quotes a canonical formula that warns against adding to (or subtracting from) the written word of God (v. 6). The scriptures provide the norm, the limit, the circle of truth within which human thought may operate, "lest you be found a liar." The writer is profoundly aware of the human tendency to (self) deception and denial of reality. Denial and deception were not discovered by Freud.[335]

Second, our source of security is not found in the perfection of our knowledge, but by taking refuge in the God who is made known in Scripture (v. 5, quoting Ps 18:30 = 2 Sam 22:31). This does not diminish the importance of human wisdom and knowledge (the focus of Proverbs), but puts it in an ultimate perspective.

Third, the writer prays for daily, ordinary bread—not too much and not too little (vv. 8-9)—for he knows how deeply we humans are embedded in this created world and how easily our earthly circumstances sway our devotion to God and distort our perception of the truth (cf. Luke 8:14). Thus the rich are tempted to rely on their wealth and to ignore God and deny God's radical requirements (vv. 8-9; cf. Deut 8:17-18; Luke 18:18-29). Conversely, the poor are tempted to mistrust God's goodness and promises. So they may offend the integrity of God's name (cf. Exod 6:9; 34:6-7) because hunger drives them to break the requirements of God's law (v. 9; cf. 6:30-31).

2. To ask a person's name and that of his or her son is not a Hebrew way of asking for someone's full identity (v. 4). That would require a person's name and hir or her father's name (and a mother's name, if royalty). One's child does not establish identity; even King David is "the son of Jesse" (1 Sam 20:30; 2 Sam 23:1). Some scholars conclude that the point is ironic; there is no such (human) person. But if the answer to the rhetorical questions is Yahweh, then a plausible candidate for "his son" must be found. In Israel there were two possibilities: Israel itself (Exod 4:22-23; Hos 11:1) or David and his royal heirs, sons of God by covenant (2 Sam 7:14; Pss 2:7; 89:26-27). In the New Testament, the identity of Israel is encompassed in Jesus Christ (Matt 2:15). There Jesus is known both as "son of David" (Matt 22:41-45) and as the "son of God" who ascended into heaven (John 3:12-13; Heb 4:14). In his Pentecost sermon, Peter is at pains to point out that "David did not ascend to heaven," but Christ did (Acts 2:33-34; cf. Eph 4:7-10; Heb 4:14; see Commentary on v. 5 and note the messianic ending in 2 Sam 22:51).

---

335. See the exposition of the classic Reformation creed, The Belgic Confession (1561), Article 7 ("The Sufficiency of Scripture") on this point. Concerning human opinions it declares, "All human beings are liars by nature and more vain than vanity itself."

THE WORDS OF LEMUEL AND A HYMN TO THE VALIANT WOMAN

OVERVIEW

The final chapter of the book begins with the words of a king, taught him by the queen mother (vv. 1-9). These verses are separated from vv. 10-31 in the LXX by chaps. 25–29, perhaps indicating they were once independent. Yet these passages are related in various ways. Through echoes and allusions, both passages, but especially the second, create an envelope around the book, with Proverbs 1–9.[336] More immediately, the royal focus in vv. 1-9 has been anticipated by the numerical sayings of the previous chapter, with their frequent reference to kings (30:21-31; cf. chaps. 28–29). The genre in vv. 1-9 is the royal instruction, a subcategory of the instruction form pervasive in chaps. 1–9.[337] The royal instruction also appears in Egypt and Mesopotamia, but the attribution to the queen mother (a position of no little importance) is exceptional.[338]

The last section of the book is formally an acrostic (alphabetic) hymn in praise of a "capable wife." It begins with an introduction of the woman (vv. 10-12), is followed by a catalogue of her heroic deeds (vv. 13-27), and concludes with an invitation to join the poet in praise of his subject (vv. 28-31).[339] One may compare the extended "praise" (הלל *hālal*, vv. 30-31; Sir 44:1) of distinguished men in Sirach 44–50. (When Sirach speaks of the good wife, however, his focus is relentlessly on her benefits to her husband, and the praise is commingled with fear of the bad wife; Sir 26:1-27.) The twenty-two letters of the Hebrew alphabet sum up wisdom, as it were, from A to Z, just as the extended acrostic in Psalm 119 sums up Torah piety. Wisdom is here embodied in a noble woman. And so the symbolism of wife as wisdom, which runs through Proverbs, is brought full circle (see Introduction).

---

336. See Claudia V. Camp, *Wisdom and the Feminine in the Book of Proverbs* (Sheffield: Almond, 1985) 186-208.

337. See James L. Crenshaw, "A Mother's Instruction to Her Son (Proverbs 31:1-9)," in *Urgent Advice and Probing Questions: Collected Writings on Old Testament Wisdom* (Macon, Ga.: Mercer University Press, 1995) 383-95.

338. N. A. Andreasen, "The Queen Mother in Israelite Society," *CBQ* 45 (1983) 179-94. Cf. Carole R. Fontaine, "Queenly Proverb Perfomance: The Prayer of Puduhepa," in *The Listening Heart*, ed. K. G. Hoglund et al. (Sheffield: JSOT, 1987) 95-126.

339. Al Wolters, "Proverbs XXXI 10-31 as Heroic Hymn: A Form-Critical Analysis," *VT* 38 (1988) 448-57.

PROVERBS 31:1-9, THE WORDS OF LEMUEL

NIV	NRSV
31 The sayings of King Lemuel—an oracle[a] his mother taught him:	**31** The words of King Lemuel. An oracle that his mother taught him:
[2]"O my son, O son of my womb, O son of my vows,[b]	[2] No, my son! No, son of my womb! No, son of my vows!
[a]1 Or *of Lemuel king of Massa, which* [b]2 Or */ the answer to my prayers*	[3] Do not give your strength to women,

NIV

³do not spend your strength on women,
  your vigor on those who ruin kings.

⁴"It is not for kings, O Lemuel—
  not for kings to drink wine,
  not for rulers to crave beer,
⁵lest they drink and forget what the law decrees,
  and deprive all the oppressed of their rights.
⁶Give beer to those who are perishing,
  wine to those who are in anguish;
⁷let them drink and forget their poverty
  and remember their misery no more.
⁸"Speak up for those who cannot speak for
    themselves,
  for the rights of all who are destitute.
⁹Speak up and judge fairly;
  defend the rights of the poor and needy."

NRSV

your ways to those who destroy kings.
⁴ It is not for kings, O Lemuel,
  it is not for kings to drink wine,
  or for rulers to desire*a* strong drink;
⁵ or else they will drink and forget what has
    been decreed,
  and will pervert the rights of all the afflicted.
⁶ Give strong drink to one who is perishing,
  and wine to those in bitter distress;
⁷ let them drink and forget their poverty,
  and remember their misery no more.
⁸ Speak out for those who cannot speak,
  for the rights of all the destitute.*b*
⁹ Speak out, judge righteously,
  defend the rights of the poor and needy.

*a*Cn: Heb *where*   *b*Heb *all children of passing away*

COMMENTARY

This instruction, like those in Proverbs 1–9, addresses "my son." Besides formal affinities, the passage has thematic connections with chaps. 1–9. The queen mother instructs her royal son not only concerning his duty to do justice (see Commentary on 8:14-16; Reflections on 28:1-18; 29:1-27), but reverts to the preoccupation with women found in chaps. 1–9.

31:1-2. Lemuel is otherwise unknown; for the alternatives, "an oracle" or "king of Massa" (NIV margin), see Commentary on 30:1. The foreign character of Lemuel is perhaps suggested by the Aramaic forms in this passage (which alternate with the corresponding Hebrew forms) and by the Aramaic word for "son" (בר *bar*). Similar literary mixing or alternating of Hebrew and Aramaic appears in Job and Daniel, for example. "No" or "O" is literally, "what?" and this form has not been adequately explained. An appeal to an Arabic expression, "Take heed," is far-fetched. Like Hannah (1 Samuel 1–2), this mother has dedicated her son to God.

31:3. "Your ways" seems an odd parallel to "your strength," and alternative explanations have been offered. But "ways" may simply allude to chaps. 1–9, where ways is a basic metaphor for

the conduct of life, especially in relation to women.

31:4-5. This passage warns the king against the subversive effect of alcohol on memory and judgment (cf. Lev 11:10). To "pervert the rights" is literally to "change the judgment," a judicial idiom known also in Mesopotamia.³⁴⁰ On things decreed, see Commentary on 8:15, which employs the royal terms used here. The concern is that the government protect those who cannot protect themselves and "speak for those who cannot speak" (see vv. 8-9, 20; 16:12; 28:3, 15; 29:4, 7, 14; Ps 72:1-4, 12-14; Jer 22:16).

31:6-7. In classic wisdom fashion (see Commentary on 26:4-5), these verses follow the warning against misuse of alcohol with an opposite, positive use. Wisdom is too perceptive to offer simplistic solutions to problems like alcohol abuse. To make an absolute prohibition of alcohol or other drugs would be to remove their proper use. The picture here is of a less chemically sophisticated society, where alcohol has an anesthetic function: Those in bitter anguish may drink to

340. See "The Code of Hammurabi," Law 5, in *Ancient Near Eastern Texts Relating to the Old Testament,* ed. James B. Pritchard, 3rd ed. (Princeton, N.J.: Princeton University Press, 1969) 166.

forget their sorrow, in contrast to kings who should not (v. 5; cf. Lev 10:11:10; Jer 16:7-8).

31:8-9. The mother's instruction to the young king concludes with a positive admonition not to be passive, but to be active and zealous in seeking the well-being of the poor and helpless. It has strong verbal and thematic connections with v. 20, precisely at the center of the next passage.

PROVERBS 31:10-31, HYMN TO THE VALIANT WOMAN

NIV

^{10a}A wife of noble character who can find?
    She is worth far more than rubies.
^{11}Her husband has full confidence in her
    and lacks nothing of value.
^{12}She brings him good, not harm,
    all the days of her life.
^{13}She selects wool and flax
    and works with eager hands.
^{14}She is like the merchant ships,
    bringing her food from afar.
^{15}She gets up while it is still dark;
    she provides food for her family
    and portions for her servant girls.
^{16}She considers a field and buys it;
    out of her earnings she plants a vineyard.
^{17}She sets about her work vigorously;
    her arms are strong for her tasks.
^{18}She sees that her trading is profitable,
    and her lamp does not go out at night.
^{19}In her hand she holds the distaff
    and grasps the spindle with her fingers.
^{20}She opens her arms to the poor
    and extends her hands to the needy.
^{21}When it snows, she has no fear for her household;
    for all of them are clothed in scarlet.
^{22}She makes coverings for her bed;
    she is clothed in fine linen and purple.
^{23}Her husband is respected at the city gate,
    where he takes his seat among the elders of the land.
^{24}She makes linen garments and sells them,
    and supplies the merchants with sashes.
^{25}She is clothed with strength and dignity;
    she can laugh at the days to come.
^{26}She speaks with wisdom,

a10 Verses 10-31 are an acrostic, each verse beginning with a successive letter of the Hebrew alphabet.

NRSV

^{10} A capable wife who can find?
    She is far more precious than jewels.
^{11} The heart of her husband trusts in her,
    and he will have no lack of gain.
^{12} She does him good, and not harm,
    all the days of her life.
^{13} She seeks wool and flax,
    and works with willing hands.
^{14} She is like the ships of the merchant,
    she brings her food from far away.
^{15} She rises while it is still night
    and provides food for her household
    and tasks for her servant-girls.
^{16} She considers a field and buys it;
    with the fruit of her hands she plants a vineyard.
^{17} She girds herself with strength,
    and makes her arms strong.
^{18} She perceives that her merchandise is profitable.
    Her lamp does not go out at night.
^{19} She puts her hands to the distaff,
    and her hands hold the spindle.
^{20} She opens her hand to the poor,
    and reaches out her hands to the needy.
^{21} She is not afraid for her household when it snows,
    for all her household are clothed in crimson.
^{22} She makes herself coverings;
    her clothing is fine linen and purple.
^{23} Her husband is known in the city gates,
    taking his seat among the elders of the land.
^{24} She makes linen garments and sells them;
    she supplies the merchant with sashes.
^{25} Strength and dignity are her clothing,
    and she laughs at the time to come.
^{26} She opens her mouth with wisdom,

NIV

and faithful instruction is on her tongue.
²⁷She watches over the affairs of her household
and does not eat the bread of idleness.
²⁸Her children arise and call her blessed;
her husband also, and he praises her:
²⁹"Many women do noble things,
but you surpass them all."
³⁰Charm is deceptive, and beauty is fleeting;
but a woman who fears the LORD is to be
praised.
³¹Give her the reward she has earned,
and let her works bring her praise at the city
gate.

NRSV

and the teaching of kindness is on her
tongue.
²⁷ She looks well to the ways of her household,
and does not eat the bread of idleness.
²⁸ Her children rise up and call her happy;
her husband too, and he praises her:
²⁹ "Many women have done excellently,
but you surpass them all."
³⁰ Charm is deceitful, and beauty is vain,
but a woman who fears the LORD is to be
praised.
³¹ Give her a share in the fruit of her hands,
and let her works praise her in the city
gates.

COMMENTARY

This section comprises a great wisdom hymn in praise of the "capable woman/wife." This phrase, which is variously translated, is the female counterpart to "capable men," persons who evidence a wise competence and vigor in a variety of tasks (Gen 47:6; Exod 18:21, 25 [with fear of God, see 31:30]; 1 Chr 26:8, 12-14) including warfare (2 Sam 11:16; Jer 48:14; cf. Isa 5:22, which is ironic: "heroes" at drinking). The acrostic Psalm 112 (see also its acrostic twin, Psalm 111) is somewhat parallel to vv. 10-31 and describes a man who fears the Lord.

Throughout vv. 10-31 the focus is on the woman's wise and energetic activity. The poem is rich in words of action. The common Hebrew root for doing and making, working and acting (עשׂה 'śh), appears five times (vv. 13, 22, 24, 29, 31), culminating in the declaration that her very works praise her (v. 31). The adjective "capable" is the same Hebrew word (חיל ḥayil) translated "strength" in v. 3 and "noble things" in v. 29. This repetition creates a thematic envelope linking the two sections of chap. 31, as well as an envelope marking the beginning and ending of the acrostic poem. The two poems in chap. 31 are also linked by the care for the poor and needy that king and capable woman exhibit, each in ways appropriate to them (vv. 9, 20). The expression "capable woman" appears only three times

in the Bible (v. 10; 12:4; Ruth 3:11). Significantly, Ruth follows Proverbs in Hebrew Bibles.[341]

31:10. This verse picks up the love language of finding wife and wisdom that has been pervasive in chaps. 1–9 (cf. 8:35; 18:22). The point of the rhetorical question, which expects the hyperbolic answer "no one," is not that such women do not exist, but that they are, as it were, a rare find and priceless, like Lady Wisdom herself. Pious Jewish husbands still recite this poem every Sabbath eve in praise of their own wives. "The sense is: Whoever has married such a woman knows from his experience how priceless is her worth."[342] The same rhetorical question appears with a male object in 20:6b (cf. Gen 41:38). A similar rhetorical idiom seems to inform Eccl 7:28, a passage often read as misogynist (cf. the numerical hyperbole in 1 Sam 18:7). The comparison to jewels/rubies links the woman to Wisdom (3:13-15; 8:11; cf. 20:15; Job 28:18).

31:11-12. These verses lay out the good the wife does for her husband (see vv. 23, 28; 12:4), because the book as a whole is addressed primarily to young men on the verge of marriage and adulthood (see Overview on chaps. 1–9). As the wise trust in God, so also a wise husband, on a human level, trusts in his wife, because she

341. Thomas P. McCreesh, "Wisdom as Wife: Proverbs 31:10-31," *RB* 92 (1985) 25-46.
342. Cohen, *Proverbs,* 211.

"brings him good, not harm" (for the phrase see 1 Sam 24:18; cf. 16:20; 28:25-26). "Gain" ("booty") contrasts with the ill-gotten gain of brigands in 1:13 (cf. 16:19). This term—unusual in this context—suggests the woman is like a warrior bringing home booty from her victories.

31:13-20. This section (to the end of the first half of the alphabet) details the woman's great industry and wise competence in a dialectic of acquisition and provision. The wife seeks/selects the raw materials that her hands will work into cloth; the verb used here connotes careful inquiry and investigation (see Ps 111:2; Eccl 1:13). The woman understands the nature of things; she knows the quality and use of the materials she acquires (see v. 16). The ending of this section (vv. 13-20) forms an envelope with its beginning, for her hands make yarn from the materials she sought (see Commentary on vv. 19-20). Throughout the poem, cloth, clothing, and cloth goods are symbols of industry, intelligence, and, when worn, of the glory (see Reflections on 26:1) appropriate to the woman and her house—also a key word (vv. 5, 21 [twice], 27). As Wisdom builds and supplies her house, so also the capable wife builds and fills her house with good (see Commentary on 9:1; 14:1; 24:3-4).

31:14. The woman's scope of action encompasses the entire creation: Both land and sea provide resources for her house as she brings goods from near and far (v. 14). She is like a trader's ship faring over the awesome sea (see Pss 104:24-26; 107:23-32). Israel was not a seafaring nation, but it made use of the Phoenician traders of Tyre, Sidon, and Byblos (see Commentary on v. 24; 1 Kgs 5:9). The Phoenician ships plied the coast, bringing grain from Egypt to the Levant. The woman, who appears to live in the rocky Judean hills (see Commentary on v. 21), probably brought grain for her household from the Jezreel Valley in the north, Israel's bread-basket. Her activity also spans night (vv. 15, 18) and day (vv. 12, 25). Verse 14*b*, however, turns from acquisition to provision.

31:15. This verse continues the turn to provision for the house and anticipates the nocturnal activity of v. 18. More important, this verse (of which the last phrase may be an editorial expansion) contains important links with other passages in Proverbs. "Portions" rather than tasks (for her

servant-girls) better translates חֹק *ḥōq*, for the point is provision of house(hold) members, each according to their appropriate measure (see Commentary on 30:7-9; cf. Job 24:5*b*). The phrase is parallel to 27:27, and the reference to servant girls (only three times in Proverbs) links it also to Lady Wisdom's house (9:3). Abigail, a wise, energetic, and godly woman had such servant girls ("maids," 1 Sam 25:42).

31:16. The woman astutely surveys and evaluates a field to see what it is good for and how it may be developed. The text probably does not describe the acquisition of the field, for Israelite women did not own land (cf. 27:26). Rather, she is like a general who conquers territory and subdues it (she takes it; this verb refers only rarely to buying; for conquest see Gen 48:22; Deut 3:14). To transform a Judean highland plot (as large as 10 acres) into a vineyard is a difficult, massive undertaking (Eccl 2:4; Isa 5:1-5, 10). It is done on rocky, hilly ground, not good for much else (Mic 1:6). The woman takes part in humanity's task to "master the earth" (Gen 1:28-29).[343] From the "fruit of her (working) hands," probably her textiles, the woman gains yet more (see 18:20-22) by financing and planting a vineyard to produce literal fruit. Commerce and creation join to produce prosperity.

31:17. "She girds her loins with strength" is an act that prepares one for heroic or difficult action, often for warfare (1 Kgs 18:46; 2 Kgs 4:29; Jer 1:17). It is a masculine image (see Reflections and 8:14; 24:5; 31:25; Job 38:3; 40:7).

31:18. This verse describes the wife with language attributed to Lady Wisdom; "that her merchandise is good" is identical in Hebrew to "for she is more profitable" in 3:14. The verb in v. 18*a* is literally, "She tastes" (see Gen 1:4; Ps 34:8). The beautiful woman in 11:22, however, lacks taste, that is, good sense. That the capable woman's light does not go out refers partly to rising early, while it is still dark (v. 15), but mainly to the adequate provision of oil, which keeps a lamp burning through the night, as in the temple. One may compare the foolish and wise virgins in Jesus' parable (Matt 25:1-13).

31:19-20. These two verses are a carefully

---

343. See Jeremy Cohen, *"Be Fertile and Increase, Fill the Earth and Master It": The Ancient and Medieval Career of a Biblical Text* (Ithaca, N.Y.: Cornell University Press, 1989).

constructed chiastic couplet that forms the heart of the poem. In Hebrew, the woman uses her hands/palms/palm(s)/hands both to produce and to provide for the needy. There is no evidence for the use of the distaff, however, in the ancient Near East. Also, a distaff is not grasped with both hands. The Hebrew term probably refers to a "doubling spindle."[344] "She puts her hands to" is an idiom that has military connotations of mastery, thus reinforcing the heroic character of the woman's activities. Moreover, her provision for the poor and needy links her activity to King Lemuel's (v. 9). The hands that grasp to produce open wide to provide.

31:21-31. The second half of the acrostic forms an envelope, beginning with "no fear" and ending with "a woman who fears the Lord" (v. 30).

31:21-25. Here the focus is on the woman's provision for her house (v. 21 twice, see v. 27), especially of the splendid clothing she makes, sells, and—with her household—wears (contrast 23:21). Snow was for Israelites an infrequent (except in the mountains of Lebanon) and awesome phenomenon (Ps 147:16-17). Its presence places the woman in the Judean hill country (2 Sam 23:20; 1 Macc 13:22). Because of her clothing, the woman has no fear; so she "laughs at the days to come" (v. 25; see Job 5:21-22; 39:22).

"Coverings" (מרבדים *marbaddîm*, v. 22) is an exotic word appearing only twice in the OT. It forms another link between the capable woman and the women of Proverbs 1–9, and a contrast with the wealthy adulteress (7:16). Purple, a foreign word, is another luxurious cloth, made with the famous Phoenician dye derived from shellfish.

At first glance, the appearance of the husband (v. 23; lit., "lord" [בעל *ba'al*], vv. 11, 28) seems unmotivated. Its explanation is probably to be found in v. 21*b* (see 2 Chr 18:9). The household, including the husband, are bedecked in clothing worthy of their status and glory (see Commentary on v. 13; Exod 28:2, 40; Ps 45:13-14; Dan 5:7, 16). From Exodus it is clear that to make garments that bespeak glory requires a "wise heart" (= "skill") and a "spirit of wisdom" (Exod 28:3; Jer 10:9), just as does building a tabernacle (see Commentary on Prov 9:1-18). For the signifi-

cance of the city gate, see Commentary on 8:1-3 and 24:7 (see also Lam 5:14). For "elders of the land," see 1 Kgs 20:7 and Jer 26:17.

"Linen garments" (v. 24) is another foreign term of uncertain meaning; it occurs in contexts that convey splendor (Judg 14:12-13; Isa 3:23;). She sells her goods to merchants (lit., "Canaanites," a term that came to mean "trader," from the renown of the Phoenician merchants; see v. 14; Job 41:6; Zech 14:21). "Sash" is a noun of the same root as "girds" in v. 17.

Verse 25 returns to the woman's own clothing (vv. 17, 21-22), but in a metaphorical sense. "Strength and dignity" (though not in combination) are clothing worn by the king (Pss 8:5; 21:5) and even by Yahweh (Pss 29:1; 93:1; 104:1). "She laughs" is an envelope parallel to "she has no fear" (see Commentary on vv. 21-25).

31:26. This forms the center of the second half of the poem. The woman's wisdom is not simply evident in her actions (though that is the hymn's main focus). The phrase, "opens her mouth" with wisdom (see v. 23*a*; 24:7) again links the capable woman to King Lemuel (vv. 8-9; see Commentary on vv. 19-20). It also suggests that she partakes of Wisdom's splendid words (see Commentary on 8:1, 6-10). The "teaching of kindness" or "faithful instruction" (cf. Mal 2:6) is a phrase that in the Bible only occurs here. If the former meaning is correct, one may think of Lemuel's mother, who teaches her son compassion for the destitute and afflicted (vv. 5-9; see also 1:8; 6:20). The woman herself practices what she preaches (v. 20).

31:27. A clever bilingual pun appears here. In v. 27*a*, the first Hebrew word forms a transliteration of the Greek word "sophia," or wisdom; the Hebrew word for wisdom appears in the previous verse. The line may then be translated, "The ways of her house are wisdom."[345] Similarly, v. 27*b* may be read, "and idleness [in the concrete sense of "idlers"] will not eat bread" (cf. 30:22). Along with clothing, food and eating are a recurrent theme in the poem (vv. 14, 15; vv. 16, 18, 31 use metaphors of food and eating). The provision of food is a sign of wise diligence and not idleness (see 6:6-11; "sluggard" translates the same Hebrew root).

---

344. Al Wolters, "The Meaning of Kîšôr (Proverbs 31:19)," *HUCA* 65 (1994) 91-104.

345. Al Wolters, "Ṣôpiyyâ (Prov 31:27) as Hymnic Participle and Play on *Sophia*," *JBL* 1054 (1985) 577-87.

31:28-31. The final verses turn to those who praise the woman and conclude with a hymnic invitation to praise. Her children (lit., "sons," the audience of vv. 1-9 and chaps. 1–9) "call her blessed" (see Ps 112:1) because she, like Wisdom, is a source of blessing (see 3:13-18). Perhaps "children" is another double entendre, meaning also that her works praise her (see v. 31*b*; Matt 11:19; parallel Luke 7:35). Her husband praises her (the Hebrew verb (הלל *hālal*) is familiar in English as "Hallelujah" or "Alleluia," "Praise the Lord") in the words of v. 28.

Verse 29 quotes the husband's words of praise, which express the wife's incomparability; similar idioms are often used in hymns praising Yahweh. "Women" is literally "daughters" (בנות *bānôt*), which echoes the "sons" of the previous verse. "Do noble things" captures the envelope structure of the poem (noble = capable, חיל *ḥayil*; see Commentary on v. 10), especially in combination with woman/wife in v. 30. This expression can refer to gaining wealth (Deut 8:17-18; Ezek 28:4), and to heroic military exploits, (Num 24:18; 1 Sam 14:48). Significantly, the "elders at the gate" encourage Ruth to "do noble things/valiantly" in the context of building a house (Ruth 4:11; the verbal parallel is obscured in the translations). "You surpass them all" uses an idiom (עלה על *ʿālâ ʿal*) that often refers to military activity.

The standards according to which the capable woman is to be praised are summarized in v. 30. Verse 30*a* may be seen as an implicit attack on the ancient (and modern) valuations of women only according to their external beauty and sex appeal (see Commentary on 11:16, 22). The ancient literature in praise of women is consistently erotic in focus, and the hymn in praise of the capable woman is a profound corrective to this. That she does her husband good "all the days of her life" is a reminder that a wife is also a treasure in old age. Finally, this woman fears the Lord. This is the ultimate source of her energetic and joyous wisdom. This it is that gives coherence, wholeness, and meaning to the activities of her life. Moreover, this phrase creates in Proverbs a grand envelope structure, not only with regard to women (chaps. 1–9 and 31), but with regard to its theological key: the fear of the Lord (see Commentary on 1:7; 9:10).

Verse 31 contains yet another rich word play. Since this is a heroic hymn, the primary sense of v. 31*a* is "extol her for the fruit of her hands ("extol" = root תנה *tnh*, see Judg 5:10[11]; 11:40). This reading provides the appropriate parallel to "praise" in v. 31*b*. The NIV and the NRSV, as well as the ancient versions, record the secondary sense of the line, probably because the verb for "extol" is rare (see Isa 3:10 for the thought). Finally, the woman's works—no doubt suffused with piety (see 16:3)—praise her in the center of life, at the city gates (see Commentary on 8:1-3; 31:28). This is a human parallel to the cosmic praise that Yahweh's works accord to him (Ps 145:10).

REFLECTIONS

1. If in the earlier chapters the strange woman could subvert ordinary males, here it is the king, cornerstone of ancient society, whose person and duty may be damaged by wine and women (vv. 1-9). This admonition speaks only indirectly to or about women. Rather, it is a warning to powerful men who are tempted to indulge themselves sexually. It is easy for the powerful to think that divine standards for conduct do not apply to them and that what is possible is permitted. The royal stories of David and Bathsheba, Amnon and Tamar, Solomon and his harem show that the problem was not imaginary (2 Samuel 11; 13; 1 Kings 11). It is no less a problem in our society, as well as in the church, where the vitality of Christ's body and the credibility of the gospel is damaged by sexual misconduct (see 1 Cor 5:1-12; 6:9-20).

One respected commentator has said that "the elite mother, if this passage is indeed by a woman, has internalized the male fear of women so prevalent throughout the book (31:3a)."[346] To this male author it seems that interpretation misreads the book's warnings about sex and

346. Carole Fontaine, "Proverbs," in Carol A. Newsom and Sharon H. Ringe, eds., *The Women's Bible Commentary* (Louisville: Westminster, 1992) 151.

does a disservice to the queen mother and her wisdom. If men are afraid of women, their fear is misplaced and dysfunctional. What people should fear is, rather, their "disordered passions" (Augustine), by which they inordinately desire created goods (wealth, wine, property, attractive sexual partners, etc.) that are not proper to them. To say that men fear attractive women is a little like saying the male robbers of 1:10-19 fear jewels and money. A reformed robber, I suppose, would say he fears and fights his greed for what is not his. To blame the beautiful jewels is a projection of his problem onto the object. No doubt men often engage in such rationalization and projection, especially with regard to wine and women. It makes no sense, however, for an alcoholic to say, "the glass of wine led me astray" (cf. 20:1) In the perspective of Proverbs, the male line, "she was asking for it," is no excuse for sexual misconduct, even in those cases where a woman offers a sexual invitation (see 7:10-21).

Testosterone-flooded men do have a problem, but it is not women. It is themselves. Proverbs challenges them to take responsibility for their sexual selves and to love and enjoy their wives with thanks to God.

2. Some commentators have been puzzled by the appearance of the phrase "fears the LORD" in the poem on the capable woman (v. 30), since it has been totally occupied with praising the woman's mundane activities. The woman's wisdom and fear of the Lord, however, come to expression precisely in her worldly activities.[347] For Proverbs there is no sacred-secular split. All of human life and action is to manifest reverence and obedience to God and show harmony with his cosmic order. This biblical perspective that ordinary life is to reflect and serve the Creator's glory and wisdom was especially prized in the early modern period by English and Dutch Calvinists. John Milton put this ideal succinctly:

> To know
> That which before us lies in daily life
> Is the prime wisdom.[348]

This view, with its biblical roots and elaboration in various Christian traditions, had a powerful shaping role in forming the modern mind.[349] And yet, when such an affirmation of ordinary life is severed from a wise love and service of the Creator and creation, it eventually descends into that confused worship and degradation of the creation that Paul described in Romans 1.

3. Like Wisdom in 9:1-6 and Abigail in 1 Samuel 25, this woman is a great lady, a wealthy member of the aristocracy. Her counterpart may be found in other cultures, among the noble ladies of archaic Greece, for example.[350] She has a great deal of authority and power. In all her dazzling activity, she manifests a vital joy in doing good. And yet, the ideal that she embodies should not be restricted to the upper classes. Such ideals of energy and wisdom can and should pervade all strata of society.[351] An ordinary person can model himself or herself after a great man or woman, and grow thereby (cf. Phil 3:17; Heb 11:1-12:13).

4. The use of masculine images in praise of a woman (vv. 17, 25) must be considered in the light of the poem's masculine audience. If ancient Israel admired the man of war (even Yahweh in Exod 15:1-3) who defended God's people from their enemies, and if Israelite males, like men throughout history, were sinfully prone to demean women as "the weaker sex," the praise of woman here is designed to alter errant male perceptions of women. The heroic terms of strength usually applied to men are here given to a woman so her splendor and wisdom may be seen by all.

---

347. Al Wolters, "Nature and Grace in the Interpretation of Proverbs 31:10-31," *Calvin Theological Journal* 19 (1984) 153-66.
348. John Milton *Paradise Lost* VIII.192-94.
349. See Charles Taylor, "The Affirmation of Ordinary Life," in *Sources of the Self: The Making of the Modern Identity* (Cambridge, Mass.: Harvard University Press, 1989) 211-302; Lee Hardy, *The Fabric of This World: Inquiries into Calling, Career Choice, and the Design of Human Work* (Grand Rapids: Eerdmans, 1990).
350. See Werner Jaeger, *Paideia: The Ideals of Greek Culture* (Oxford: Basil Blackwell, 1965) 1:22-24.
351. On this point, see the cogent argument of Simon Schama, *The Embarrassment of Riches: An Interpretation of Dutch Culture in the Golden Age* (Berkeley: University of California Press, 1988) 4-6.

THE BOOK OF ECCLESIASTES

INTRODUCTION, COMMENTARY, AND REFLECTIONS
BY
W. SIBLEY TOWNER

THE BOOK OF
ECCLESIASTES

INTRODUCTION

E cclesiastes has always had its fans among the original thinkers of the Jewish and Christian communities: skeptics, people with a dark vision of reality, recovering alcoholics. The rest of us know and love some of its individual epigrams and its more lyrical passages. On the whole, however, believers have found it at least baffling and at most wrongheaded. From the beginning serious efforts were made to exclude it from the list of sacred books, and even now in liturgical practice it enjoys only a very small place. The *Revised Common Lectionary* would have us read Eccl 3:1-13 every New Year's Day—not a day for much pious observance, except when it falls on Sunday—and offers Eccl 1:2, 12-14; 2:18-23 as the Old Testament alternative to Hos 11:1-11 on Proper 13 in cycle C. That's it! Theoretically, its place in Jewish liturgical practice is greater because it is one of the five "scrolls" (*megillot*) that are read during festivals. The book of Ecclesiastes is to be read in its entirety during the Feast of Sukkot (Tabernacles), but the number of worshipers who will sit still to hear all twelve chapters through or even, in modern synagogues, will have the opportunity to do so is surely small. Frequently this book excites talk about its partial grasp of the truth, its need for fulfillment, and its function as the dark background against which the light of the gospel shines forth.

All dismissive talk about the book of Ecclesiastes is banned from the following pages. This commentary has been written in the conviction that we need to hear the author of Ecclesiastes out. Time and time again one is driven to admit the truth of what Ecclesiastes has to say, even though one might not want to hear it. Here is the most real of the realists of the sacred writers. Here is the Hebrew writer least comfortable with conventional wisdom, and the most willing to challenge unexamined assumptions. No faith can survive long that is founded on the slippery slope of conceptually muddled piety, and in Qohelet, God has given us a tonic for our biblical faith.

Following this minimal, stage-setting introduction, each unit of the scriptural text will be discussed in a Commentary section designed to remove as many barriers to understanding as possible so that the communication of that unit can be set forth clearly. Technical discussions of philology, redactional history, ancient Near Eastern background, and the like are kept at a minimum, not because they are unimportant for understanding, but because they are available elsewhere. This interpretation has another task: to allow the clarifications of each commentary to flow directly into a Reflections section. The most original contributions of this commentary to the literature on Ecclesiastes are to be found in these Reflections. That must inevitably be the case, for these paragraphs move across more than two millennia from what the Teacher taught to what the Teacher's teachings can teach us.

THE NAMES OF THE BOOK: QOHELET AND ECCLESIASTES

We know the writer of the book of Ecclesiastes not by name but by the title קהלת (*qōhelet*). In two of its seven occurrences in the book, that title even appears in Hebrew with the definite article (7:27 [as amended]; 12:8). Traditionally this title has come over into English as "the Preacher." The real identity of the author is masked by this title, however. True, the word *qōhelet* offers slight warrant for claiming that the author was a woman, because it has the form of a feminine singular participle of the Hebrew verbal root קהל (*qhl*, "assemble"). Arrayed against this suggestion, however, are two weightier considerations: (1) Other titles, presumably of male persons, can be found in the Hebrew Bible in exactly the same grammatical form (e.g., Hassophereth ["the leatherworker"]; Pochereth-hazzebaim ["the gazelle-tender"] in Ezra 2:55, 57). This leads to the conclusion that the "feminine" form of the participle is merely an alternative form of the masculine. (2) A clearly male appellation, "the son of David," is appended to the title in Eccl 1:1, and the verbs accompanying the title here and in two of its other appearances (Eccl 12:8-9) are masculine. For better or for worse, then, in this commentary the speaker in the book of Ecclesiastes will be referred to as "him."

Now, one of the functions of the Hebrew participle is to serve as the noun that names the one who does the action of the verb. So a *qōhelet* is the agent of "assembly," the "assembler." If what he assembles is a קהל (*qāhāl*, "congregation"), one can translate *qōhelet* as "leader of the assembly" (see NIV note) or even, to use the title most frequently given by us to such a functionary, "preacher" (see NRSV note). Already in antiquity, the Greek translators of the Hebrew Bible accepted this sense of the term *qōhelet*. Their Septuagint translates it as Ἐκκλησιαστής (*Ekklēsiastēs*), "one who leads a congregation [ἐκκλησία *ekklēsia*]," and it is from them that the name reached the English language.

Working from the basic root meaning of "assemble" for the verb קהל (*qāhal*), some argue that a *qōhelet* is one who assembles sentences or proverbs or wisdom.[1] The translation "Teacher," favored by both the NIV and the NRSV, attempts to capture some of both of these senses of the term. A teacher not only assembles information to convey to students but also carries out this function in an assembly, perhaps even in a place of congregational worship. There are other perfectly good and far more common Hebrew words for "teacher," of course, and whether *qōhelet* would have been understood as a synonym for them is difficult to judge because this title occurs only in the book of Ecclesiastes. If this writer is essentially a teacher, then by the standards of the wisdom literature of the Hebrew Bible he is a highly original thinker, capable of uncommonly sustained argument.

A title always implies a social setting. No one is called "judge" except in a place in which decisions are handed down. People receive the title "pilot" by virtue of their vocation in the maritime or aeronautical industries. If we could be sure which way to construe it, we could provide Qohelet with at least a sketchy sociological setting from his title alone. If it is taken to mean "Preacher," the name Qohelet conjures up a social setting of a congregation of believers—e.g., an early synagogue. Taken to mean "Teacher," it suggests a place of instruction for one or more pupils—e.g., a tutor's chamber in a royal or high priestly household or another early school. Unfortunately, we know next to nothing about either places of worship (other than the Second Temple) or schools in third-century BCE Judea. So whichever way we go with the title, we gain only a hint about the work of the man.

It makes sense that the author of the book of Ecclesiastes should be referred to by his title, "the Teacher," only four times in the book: in the superscription (1:1) and in its reprise (12:8), once in the main body (7:27), and once in the epilogue (12:9). After all, he is presented as having written the book, and having done so mostly in the first person! In these four instances, some narrator or editor of the teacher's work butts in to say something about the man. Although the definite article appears in the Hebrew only in 7:27 (as amended) and 12:8, the NRSV and the NIV make all four occurrences definite: He is always "the Teacher."

LANGUAGE AND GENRE

The Hebrew language in which Qohelet wrote is distinctive. Either it is a late dialect peculiar to his place and time or, because his task was to offer a philosophical discussion of issues, he had to shape a new language for the purpose. Ancient Hebrew was not a literature given to abstract philosophy; however, if there was a philosopher in ancient Hebrew, Qohelet was the one, and to him fell the task of making the language of his people work for the purpose of sustained reflection.

Like other post-exilic writings in the Hebrew Bible, Qohelet's Hebrew betrays significant

---

1. James L. Crenshaw, *Ecclesiastes,* OTL (Philadelphia: Westminster, 1987) 33-34.

influence of the Aramaic language. Because Aramaic, like Hebrew, is a member of the family of northwest Semitic languages, the two always drew on a common vocabulary base. Periodically, however, new words or grammatical constructions would flood into Hebrew from Aramaic, leaving behind enriched linguistic soil. This happened during the period of the divided monarchy, especially in the northern kingdom of Israel, which had much intercourse with the Aramean kingdoms of Damascus and Hamath. It happened again after the exile. From the seventh century BCE down into Hellenistic times as late as 200 BCE, Official or Imperial Aramaic was the lingua franca of the Near East. The royal epistles and decrees preserved in the book of Ezra are written in this language. The Hebrew spoken and written in Judea during these years in this Aramaic milieu is distinctive enough to have been given its own name, Late Biblical Hebrew. Probable Aramaisms that occur only in Ecclesiastes in the Hebrew text of the Bible (though they often become common in Mishnaic and even modern Hebrew) include עִנְיָן (*inyan*, "business"; 1:13 and seven other times as a noun); כְּבָר (*kĕbār*, "already"; 1:10 and eight other times); חֶשְׁבּוֹן (*ḥešbôn*, "sum"; 7:25, 27; 9:10); פֵּשֶׁר (*pēšer*, "interpretation"; 8:1); and גוּמָּץ (*gûmmāṣ*, "pit"; 10:8). Many other Aramaic loan words and grammatical forms occur as well, including the synonymous terms רַעְיוֹן (*ra'yôn*) and רְעוּת (*rĕ'ût*), "chasing [after wind]," alternatively translated "feeding [on wind]" in the NRSV note (1:14 and seven other times). In all, 3.1 percent of Qohelet's vocabulary consists of Aramaisms.[2]

Quite apart from linguistic evidences of origin in late post-exilic culture, Qohelet simply forged his own distinctive literary style out of a repertoire both of standard clichés and of unique words or inflections of words. Five of his favorite terms are discussed below (see the section "The Vocabulary of Qohelet's Thought," 278-82), and others are pointed out along the way.

The very genre of the book of Ecclesiastes is a matter of debate. The editors of the NIV consider 60 percent of the text to be poetry, while the NRSV thinks it is 75 percent prose. The translators of the Good News Bible and the Revised English Bible think the only poetic passage in the entire book is 3:2-8. The criteria for identifying poetry in biblical Hebrew are subtle, and with Ecclesiastes they function hardly at all. As to the literary form of the book as a whole, von Rad's proposal that it follows the Egyptian genre of "royal testament" is now generally rejected because the pretense of kingly authorship is dropped after chap. 2. The Hellenistic genre "diatribe," too, has failed to convince critics, largely because of the absence of any explicit dialogue. Numerous sub-genres can be recognized (e.g., autobiographical narrative, rhetorical questions, parable, curses and blessings, proverbs), but for the book as a whole the very general rubrics "instruction" and "reflection" seem to be most satisfactory.[3]

2. Ibid., 31.
3. Roland E. Murphy, *Ecclesiastes,* WBC 23A (Waco, Tex.: Word, 1992) xxxi-xxxii.

AUTHORSHIP, DATE, AND HISTORICAL SETTING

The language of Ecclesiastes demands that it be placed among the later books of the Hebrew canon. Its language is not as late as that of Daniel, however. Almost half of Daniel is written in the so-called Middle Aramaic dialect that slowly displaced Official Aramaic in written texts after Greek became the more widely used official language in the Hellenistic period (after 200 BCE). Embedded in that Aramaic and in the Hebrew half of Daniel as well are loan words from Greek; furthermore, that book is rich with veiled historical allusions to the Ptolemaic and Seleucid successors of Alexander in Egypt and Antioch respectively. Indeed, because of those allusions, we can date Daniel in its canonical form quite confidently to 164 BCE. The language of Ecclesiastes shows no discernible influence from Hellenistic Greek, nor is it particularly reminiscent of the Hebrew of Daniel. It should, therefore, be dated earlier than 164 BCE. This *terminus ante quem* (the date before which it must have been written) is supported by the presence of fragmentary Ecclesiastes texts among the Dead Sea Scrolls of Cave 4, dated mid-second century BCE.

The book exhibits the "philosophical" spirit of the Hellenistic period to a degree more pronounced than any other book of the Hebrew canon, even though none of the Teacher's ideas can be directly linked to Greek originals. All things considered, it seems sensible to date the book to the period between 332 BCE, when Alexander the Great put an end to Persian political dominance in the Middle East and cemented the hold of Greek cultural influence in the area, and 200 BCE. Had Qohelet known of the wrenching political crises associated with the change from Ptolemaic to Seleucid suzerainty in Palestine around that time, he might have alluded to them. Without attempting a definitive statement on the matter, this exposition will assume that Ecclesiastes was written in the middle of the third century BCE, perhaps around 250.

Other books, such as Daniel, offer historical evidences that corroborate linguistic judgments about their dates. The narrator of the final form of the book of Ecclesiastes also offers a historical setting to the reader, though without reference to the Egyptian Ptolemies of his own day or to their rivals, the Seleucid monarchs of Antioch in Syria. Instead he reaches over centuries to the era of monarchy in Jerusalem. It is no surprise that the superscription (Eccl 1:1) attributes the book to a king. That a king would concern himself with wisdom might surprise people today, but it certainly would not have done so in antiquity. The importance of circles of scribes, seers, and teachers at the courts of Babylon, Persia, and Egypt can hardly be overestimated. In ancient Israel the court—whether royal, gubernatorial, or high priestly—was paired with the Temple as the center of learning, the patron of scribes and teachers, the arbiter of etiquette. Joseph and Daniel in their respective times act the parts of wise and learned courtiers. The wisdom writer, Jesus ben Sira, who may even have been a late contemporary of the author of Ecclesiastes, instructed the patrician youth of his age in the things that make for successful living, boldly claiming, "Hear but a little of my instruction,/ and through me you will acquire silver and gold" (Sir 51:28 NRSV).

It comes as no surprise either that "the Teacher" is not only a king but is, in the literary presentation given to his work, no other than "the son of David," King Solomon. After all, it was Solomon who, having asked God for the gift of wisdom, received it so abundantly that it "surpassed the wisdom of all the people of the east, and all the wisdom of Egypt." It was he who "composed three thousand proverbs, and his songs numbered a thousand and five." It was to hear his wisdom that "people came from all the nations . . . [and] from all the kings of the earth who had heard of his wisdom" (1 Kgs 4:29-34 NRSV). Pre-eminent among these visitors was the Queen of Sheba, who exclaimed to him, "Your wisdom and prosperity far surpass the report that I had heard" (1 Kgs 10:7). His father, David, might have been both warrior and lyricist, but to Solomon were attributed, among the canonical books, whole sections of the book of Proverbs, Ecclesiastes, and the great lyric of erotic love, the Song of Solomon (NRSV), or Song of Songs (NIV). Apocryphal works attributed to the wise king include a long sapiental book, the book of Wisdom, the *Psalms of Solomon, Odes of Solomon,* and a pseudepigraphical *Testament of Solomon,* which touts his greatness as a magician.

However, when all is said and done, one person who almost certainly was not the author of the book of Ecclesiastes was Solomon. First of all, the author drops any pretense of being a king after the fictional narrative of the royal experiment (Eccl 2:1-11). In the middle of the book, he offers advice to courtiers who come into the presence of the king as if he were standing beside them and whispering words of etiquette into their ears (Eccl 8:2-6; 10:4). He expresses views of monarchy very unlikely to have emanated from any actual royal throne (Eccl 4:13-16; 5:8-9). Finally, he is identified in the epilogue as a wise man or sage, who worked among the people (Eccl 12:9). Apart from these bits of internal evidence that the writer of Ecclesiastes, or the Teacher himself (if they are not one and the same person), was not a king of any kind is the linguistic evidence already alluded to, which places the book well after the time of any monarchy in Israel.

Who, then, was the author of Qohelet? For the purposes of this commentary, let us assume that the author of the bulk of the book is also the one who speaks in the first person. Only the epilogists and the author of the first verse of the book stand apart from the man who teaches through the rest of the text, and their identities are too pallid to obscure the thought and personality of the Teacher in any significant way.

He is a "sage" (Eccl 12:9). It is generally agreed that sages played important roles in the royal courts of the ancient Near East. This does not necessarily mean, however, that Qohelet was either a member or a servant of the elite, or that he shared their "upper-crust" attitudes. Some commentators find the bent of a patrician in passages like 7:21 and 11:1-2, but others dismiss as routine the references to a personal servant and investment of capital. The assertion that he worked among the common people (Eccl 12:9) might suggest a link with the traditional wisdom circles of the rural folk of Palestine. Nevertheless, a man who could read and write and who could draw even indirectly upon resources of the ancient Near Eastern sapiental tradition seems unlikely to have been a common peasant. At the same time, too little is known about the sages as a class (if, indeed, they constituted anything as definable as a class in ancient Israel) to make generalizations about their place in the social order.[4]

As for the provenance of the book of Ecclesiastes, efforts to show settings as diverse as Egypt and Phoenicia have not gained much support. While nothing in the book requires that its author had worked in Judea or Jerusalem, neither is there any compelling reason not to make that assumption.

THE CANONICITY OF QOHELET

Although not much is known about the process by which Qohelet came to be regarded as sacred scripture, controversy evidently surrounded its candidacy for the first few centuries. Fragments of Ecclesiastes from about 150 BCE appear at Qumran, but a book did not have to be regarded as Scripture in order to be included in the library of the Dead Sea community. The Mishnah reports challenges in rabbinic circles to the sacredness of Qohelet down to the time of Rabbi Akiba (died c. 135 CE). After setting forth the general principle that "All the holy writings render the hands [ritually] unclean," *M. Yad* 3:5 states, "The Song of Songs and Ecclesiastes render the hands unclean." The rabbis argued about the matter, however. Rabbi Akiba gave a ringing endorsement of the canonicity of the Song of Songs with these words: "God forbid!—no man in Israel ever disputed about the Song of Songs [that he should say] that it does not render the hands unclean . . . for all the Writings are holy, but the Song of Songs is the Holy of Holies." Then, as if to suggest that the argument about Qohelet continued on, the passage concludes, "And if aught was in dispute the dispute was about Ecclesiastes alone."[5] Ecclesiastes is mentioned in the very earliest Christian lists of canonical writings as well, such as that of Melito of Sardis (died c. 190 CE).

QOHELET'S RELATIONSHIP WITH ANCIENT WISDOM

The book of Ecclesiastes belongs to that third part of the canon of the Hebrew Scriptures known as the Ketubim ("Writings"). Into this section of the Bible the scribes of ancient Israel gathered all sacred texts that were neither Torah nor prophets: Ezra, Nehemiah, and the books of Chronicles (late historical writings); the book of Psalms (hymns of the Second Temple, though certain ones, such as Psalms 1; 37; 49; 73; 112; and 128, are recognized as "wisdom" psalms); Lamentations (a collection of laments or dirges over the loss of Judah that are traditionally treated as an appendix to Jeremiah); Daniel (placed among the prophets in the order of the Christian canon); Ruth and Esther (short stories); and the Song of Songs (nuptial poetry). Only the remaining three "Writings"—Proverbs, Job, and Ecclesiastes—remain in the true "wisdom" canon of the Hebrew Bible.

4. Ibid., xxi.
5. Herbert Danby, trans. and ed., *The Mishnah* (Oxford: Oxford University Press, 1933) 782.

That Ecclesiastes belongs in the company of Job and Proverbs cannot be doubted. The genres of writing, the strongly secular perspective, the sophisticated quarrel with conventional piety and theology—all belong to the effort of wisdom writers to make sense of life based on observation and practical experience. Like all of wisdom literature, both courtly and popular, the focus is on human nature, and the goal is to guide human beings into the path of successful living. Rules of proper behavior (i.e., etiquette), observations of natural phenomena, and even some sustained theological reflections (such as those on Dame Wisdom in Proverbs 1–9 and on theodicy in the book of Job) are the stuff of the classical sapiental writings of Israel.

The world of wisdom, however, stretched far beyond the narrow borders of Israel. Any reflection on the wisdom bed in which Ecclesiastes nestles, therefore, has to take account of this larger environment. The relationship was richer and more complex than a few sentences can indicate; the examples given here are merely illustrative. Mesopotamian wisdom traditions must have been known to writers and thinkers in Israel for nearly the first millennium of its existence as a people, since Assyria, Babylon, and finally Persia dominated the Levant during most of that time. The Babylonian exile may have given the displaced intellectuals of Jerusalem fresh purchase on the actual sapiental texts of their conquerors—the image of Daniel and his friends successfully gobbling up learning while picking delicately at their victuals in the Babylonian Academy of Wisdom (Dan 1:3-7, 18-21) might not be far off the mark. Among several witnesses to Babylonian theological pessimism about fair treatment for the righteous at the hands of the gods is *A Dialogue About Human Misery,* or "The Babylonian Ecclesiastes."[6] Ecclesiastes 3:11 resonates in a particularly striking way with v. 24 of this text, which says: "The mind of the god, like the center of the heavens, is remote; His knowledge is difficult, men cannot understand it."

Even a document as different in genre from Qohelet as the Mesopotamian epic of the primeval hero Gilgamesh provides evidence of the ubiquity of sage advice. The alewife, Siduri, tries to deflect the hero's quest for immortality with words of realism that have often been compared to the wisdom of the Teacher in Eccl 9:7-10:

Gilgamesh, whither rovest thou?
The life thou pursuest thou shalt not find.
When the gods created mankind,
Death for mankind they set aside,
Life in their own hand retaining.
Thou, Gilgamesh, let full be thy belly,
Make thou merry by day and by night.
Of each day make thou a feast of rejoicing,

---

6. *Ancient Near Eastern Texts Relating to the Old Testament,* ed. James B. Pritchard, 3rd ed. (Princeton, N.J.: Princeton University Press, 1969) 438-40.

Day and night dance thou and play!
Let thy garments be sparkling fresh,
Thy head be washed; bathe thou in water.
Pay heed to the little one that holds on to thy hand,
Let thy spouse delight in thy bosom!
For this is the task of [humankind]![7]

How the sapiental tradition of Egypt was mediated to the late post-exilic intellectual community in Judah is not entirely clear, although we know that a great deal of intellectual and cultural exchange between the two cultures took place right alongside commercial enterprise and the usual military incursions. That the sages of Egypt served in the ancient and universal role as counselors to nobility is demonstrated conclusively in wall paintings, tomb furnishings, and in such written works as *The Instruction of Amenemope*.[8] It is a role with which Qohelet was evidently familiar as well (e.g., Eccl 8:2-6). Other commonalities, if not direct influences, can be demonstrated in such works as *The Song of the Harper*,[9] which sounds the theme of *carpe diem* ("seize the day!") with words like these: "Fulfill thy needs upon earth, after the command of thy heart, until there come for thee that day of mourning" (cf. Eccl 7:14). *The Instruction of Ani*[10] offers admonitions about the proper approach to God, similar to those found in Eccl 5:1-7.

As far as relationship with Greek tradition, the consensus of scholars is that the parallels of ideas are frequent and broad enough to justify the contention that Qohelet was very much influenced by the Hellenistic culture that had spread throughout the domain of the Ptolemies, including Judea, in the third century BCE. Attempts to identify specific Greek influences in the terminology of the book or to discern overt borrowing by Qohelet from Greek philosophers or literature have all failed. It is clear, however, that he shared the quest of Greek philosophy in general, which was to help a human being live happily in a world that is not very friendly to human happiness.[11]

It remains to say something of the relation of Ecclesiastes to the two great deuterocanonical Jewish sapiental works of the last centuries before the turn of the era, Ecclesiasticus (the Wisdom of Ben Sira) and the book of Wisdom (also known as the Wisdom of Solomon). Many efforts have been made to link Qohelet's work with that of Ben Sira, whose book is dated about 180 BCE. Certainly, the two authors held one pedagogical objective in common: Both wished to imbue their students with ideas and etiquette sufficient to move successfully in the highest levels of society. Ben Sira differs markedly from Qohelet on the major wisdom theme of retribution by generally following the conventional expectation of his age that the system will requite fools and knaves for their deeds. Qohelet, of course, will have none of that. The two do agree that justice, if there is any, has to be achieved

---

7. Ibid., 90.
8. Ibid., 421-25.
9. Ibid., 467.
10. Ibid., 420-21.
11. M. V. Fox, *Qoheleth and His Contradictions*, BLS 18 (Sheffield: Almond, 1989) 16.

here and now because there is no life after death and in Sheol there is neither hope nor praise.

As far as the relationships with the first-century CE book of Wisdom, much effort has been made to show that it is in part an intentional refutation of Ecclesiastes. This polemic is centered particularly in Wisdom 2, which seems to target such passages in Ecclesiastes as 3:16-22 and 9:5-6 that speak of non-existence after death. One major innovation by the Wisdom of Solomon over against Ecclesiastes (and the rest of the canonical Hebrew wisdom writings, as well as Sirach) is the doctrine of blessed immortality. That doctrine, of course, takes care of a number of the laments raised by Ecclesiastes, including the obscure but poignant agnostic statement about the wise and the righteous in the hands of God: "whether it is love or hate, one does not know" (Eccl 9:1). The writer of Wisdom knows. He believes that in the life beyond death a loving God makes good with those who trust that God.

Nevertheless, rather than argue that the writer of the book of Wisdom is specifically attacking Ecclesiastes on this point, it seems preferable to take the later work as simply a fresh meditation for another generation on the great themes of justice and death, which were perennially raised by the Israelite wisdom tradition and were addressed powerfully in his own time by Qohelet.

THE PLOT OF THE BOOK

Every piece of literature, down to and including one's laundry list, has a plot. That is to say, it moves according to some logic. It aims at some end and follows some structure in order to reach that end. Certain essays and books display their plots prominently, while others conceal them in elaborate ways. People tend to enjoy reading the former more than the latter. The same is true of biblical texts. They all have internal emphases, main points, punch lines, and the like. Some, such as Jonah or the Joseph narrative, are novellas with rising action, climactic moment, and falling action—just like *Tom Jones* or *A Farewell to Arms.* Others, such as the epistles of Paul, follow a more tortuous route toward their main emphases.

Either the book of Ecclesiastes has one of the most tortuous plots of any book of the Hebrew Bible, or else it has an extremely minimal one. The latter seems to be more likely. There is no story line. Unlike any one of the prophetic books, the seams between individual units in Ecclesiastes are often invisible. In fact, it is more difficult to identify most of the individual pericopes of Ecclesiastes than in any other book of the Hebrew Bible, except perhaps the book of Proverbs. This much, however, is agreed upon by all: There is a narrator of all the material between Eccl 1:2 and Eccl 12:8. All of this material presents itself as being the thought of Qohelet, whose book it is. Ecclesiastes 1:1 is always conceded to be a superscription or title for the book, probably by some other hand, and nearly all commentators agree that the last two units of the book (12:9-11, 12-14) are by one or two other persons who have added some words at the end of the work of Qohelet to integrate that work somehow into the stream of canonical literature. Beyond this, there is no universally agreed-upon analysis of the structure of the book.

Efforts to provide such an analysis range from claims that the book is a systematic philosophical treatise with a discernible architecture,[12] through proposals that it is a series of intentionally created antitheses or "polar structures" by which the Teacher set his thought off against conventional wisdom,[13] to proposals that the book is given unity by one concept or another (e.g., ephemerality, goodness, divine freedom), to denials that any overarching structure is demonstrable.[14] Crenshaw simply lists twenty-five units, comparing their sequence to the apparently random but sometimes illuminating configurations of a kaleidoscope.[15] Murphy, on the other hand, adopts and adapts the structural analysis of Addison G. Wright.[16] This approach, based initially on repetition of key phrases, was elaborated by Wright's discovery of a numerological pattern that places the conceptual midpoint of the book exactly where the Masoretes, who were only counting verses, placed it—namely, after 6:9 (the 111th of the 222 verses in the book).

More recent commentators seem less eager than those of a generation ago to invoke a slew of editors and glossators (as Barton, e.g., did)[17] or extensive cryptic quotations from other sources (as Gordis did)[18] to account for the numerous and often-remarked upon contradictions within the book. Now its tensions strike people more as the natural inevitabilities of experience than as a dialectic between various voices. From one angle or another, everything that is said is true. Indeed, one might ask whether the failure of experience and observation to convince the writer of the truth either of traditional reward-and-punishment ideology or of an untraditional outlook of total moral randomness may have led him to despair of ever arriving at a working philosophy of life. Perhaps it led the writer to what is now called, in psychological jargon, "the doubting syndrome," in which he found reason to question everything simply because its opposite could also be found.

The outline of the book used in this commentary is merely descriptive of the contents and discerns no major organizing structure in the work. Certain structural features do stand out, however. (1) Specialized vocabulary, clichés, and refrains often signal the presence of major teachings. (2) Several important units can easily be demarcated: the thematic statement (Eccl 1:2; 12:8), the poem on times and seasons (Eccl 3:1-8), the sad but beautiful evocation of the ravages of old age (Eccl 12:1-7), and many individual epigrams and proverbs. (3) Elsewhere, it seems to be the case that the practice of gathering thematically related materials together in little collections is operative. (4) Beyond that, it

---

12. Norbert Lohfink, *Kohelet, Die neue Echter Bibel* (Würzberg: Echter Verlag, 1980).

13. J. A. Loader, *Ecclesiastes,* Text and Interpretation (Grand Rapids: Eerdmans, 1986).

14. R. N. Whybray, *Ecclesiastes,* NCB (Grand Rapids: Eerdmans, 1989).

15. James L. Crenshaw, *Ecclesiastes,* OTL (Philadelphia: Westminster, 1987) 47-49.

16. Roland E. Murphy, *Ecclesiastes,* WBC 23A (Waco, Tex.: Word, 1992) xxxviii-xli.

17. George A. Barton, *A Critical and Exegetical Commentary on the Book of Ecclesiastes,* ICC (New York: Scribner's, 1908).

18. Robert Gordis, *Koheleth: The Man and His World,* 1st ed. (New York: Schocken, 1951; 3rd ed., 1968).

is noteworthy that some sentences are stated in the first-person singular as if they were "reflections" by the author, and others, which can be called "instruction," are directed to the student in the second-person singular or even with the use of the imperative mood of the verb. These "reflections" and "instructions" interface throughout the book in a way that is almost as seamless as the tongue-and-groove joining of a good oak floor.

Perhaps Ecclesiastes is best viewed as a notebook of ideas by a philosopher/theologian about the downside and upside of life. In this notebook he reports much of his own inner life and then turns to his students or his public with instructions that flow from that inner life. All of this reflection and instruction is framed by the famous slogan of the book, "Vanity of vanities! All is vanity" (1:2; 12:8 NRSV). Perhaps that slogan itself, together with a few other key terms, provides the most solid principle of organization that we can grasp. As G. von Rad puts it, "There is . . . an inner unity which can find expression otherwise than through a linear development of thought or through a logical progression in the thought process, namely through the unity of style and topic and theme. . . . A specific, unifying function is fulfilled by a small number of leading concepts to which Koheleth returns again and again, concepts such as 'vanity,' 'striving after wind,' 'toil,' 'lot,' etc."[19]

THE VOCABULARY OF QOHELET'S THOUGHT

"All" (כל *kōl*). In the opening thematic statement of the book (Eccl 1:2), Qohelet uses the word "all," and he never lets up after that. The word occurs in 41 percent of the 222 verses of the book. The text of Ecclesiastes constitutes about 1.2 percent of the volume of the Hebrew Bible, and yet 2.1 percent of the verses in which "all" is used are in this book, almost double the expected rate. This frequency of the use of "all" in Ecclesiastes far outdistances any competitor in the Hebrew Bible. Other wisdom texts do not stress it. In Proverbs it occurs in 8.3 percent of the verses, and in Job 6.2 percent. This statistical study suggests that the universal perspective conveyed by the word "all" belongs in a very special way to Qohelet, the philosopher and theologian. It is useful to him because of his determination to reflect on the meaning of all of life—not just Israelite life, not even just human life, but all of life. Alone within the canon of the Hebrew Bible, Qohelet makes this kind of meditation a central concern; more than any other book of the Old Testament, this one attempts to arrive at understandings that will work everywhere and in every time.

"Vanity" (הבל *hebel*). The noun *hebel* occurs some sixty-nine times in the entire Hebrew Bible, five of which can be subtracted because they are the name of Abel, Cain's unfortunate younger sibling. Of the sixty-four remaining occurrences, thirty-eight, or almost 60 percent, occur in the book of Ecclesiastes alone, beginning in the opening thematic statement (Eccl 1:2). As if the great partiality of the Preacher for this term were not enough to drive home the centrality of the concept to his thought, the locations of

19. Gerhard von Rad, *Wisdom in Israel* (Nashville: Abingdon, 1972) 227.

most of its occurrences further underscore its importance. Usually it appears at the end of a discussion in the position of a punch line or a coda; furthermore, it is often used in longer formulas with one or both of two other stock expressions, "a chasing after the wind" and "under the sun."

In the light of this high visibility, one would suppose that the meaning of the Hebrew term *hebel* would be clear to all translators and interpreters. But such is not the case. This can quickly be illustrated by looking at the words used by various English versions simply to translate the first clause of Eccl 1:2: "Vanity of vanities" (KJV, RSV, NRSV, JB); "utterly vain, utterly vain" (Moffatt); "emptiness, emptiness" (NEB); "futility, utter futility" (REB); "it is useless, useless" (GNB); "utter futility!" (TNK); "nothing is worthwhile" (TLB); "utterly absurd" (Fox); "a vapor of vapors!" (Scott); "meaningless! meaningless!" (NIV).

These English renditions of the Hebrew word *hebel* do not all mean the same thing. They are not even all the same part of speech. Although most translators take the word to be a noun, the NIV treats it as an adjective. To say that something is a "vapor" captures a sense of ephemerality, but ephemerality and "utter futility" are not really the same thing. Something can be extremely substantial and not at all vaporous but still be utterly futile. Similarly, something can be meaningless without necessarily being worthless or vain. Perhaps the least satisfactory translation of the term *hebel,* because of the broadness of its meaning in English, is the traditional "vanity of vanities." What does that mean? That things are proud and stuck up? That things are a waste of time? That they are ineffectual?

Here, then, is the most important term in the book of Ecclesiastes, and its English equivalent is not agreed upon. No wonder. Even in Hebrew its sense is ambiguous. One way, of course, to make precise the meaning of the term in Ecclesiastes would be to go to the other 40 percent of its occurrences elsewhere in the Hebrew Bible to see what kind of sense can be made of it there. The standard biblical Hebrew dictionary gives the root meaning of the word as "vapor" or "breath"; that sense of the term in fact fits best with its use in Isa 57:13, where, in a polemic against idols, it is used in parallel with wind: "The wind will carry them off,/ a breath [*hebel*] will take them away" (NRSV). This sense of the term can also be found in post-biblical Hebrew texts. Other occurrences translated by the NRSV as "breath" (Job 7:16; Pss 39:5-6, 11; 62:9; 78:33; 94:11; 144:4; Prov 21:6) do not demand this rendition alone. The parallel with "shadow" in Pss 39:5-6 and 144:4 and the comparison with weightlessness in Ps 62:9 suggest "ephemerality." Qohelet, too, uses the term in this sense at least once (Eccl 11:10). Other texts imply a meaning of emptiness or worthlessness, as in Jer 10:15: "They are worthless, a work of delusion" (NRSV; see also Job 35:16; Jer 51:18). Elsewhere *hebel* means "falsehood" (e.g., 2 Kgs 17:15; Job 21:34; Zech 10:2).

From these comparisons it is evident that the term *hebel* describes something that is without merit, an unreliable, probably useless thing. Perhaps, in the manner of creative thinkers everywhere, the Teacher has welded new meaning onto this already extant term so that it can better serve his special purposes. Michael Fox thinks so, arguing that the most appropriate English rendition of *hebel* as Qohelet uses it is "absurd," "absurdity." In order to define "absurd," he appeals to the contention of Albert Camus that absurdity arises when two ideas that ought to be joined by links of causality and harmony are in fact divorced from each other. Something that is absurd just makes no sense. "To call something 'absurd' is to claim a certain understanding of its nature: It is contrary to reason."[20] That, says Fox, is what *hebel* is in Ecclesiastes. (Murphy agrees with the sense of "absurd, absurdity" for Qohelet's *hebel*, but thinks that "irrational" goes one nuance too far for the meaning of "absurd." "Incomprehensible" is plenty for him.)[21]

Fox follows the many uses of the term *hebel* in Qohelet as it is applied to human behavior, living beings, and divine behavior and finds that this sense of "absurdity" for the notion of *hebel* best comprehends them all. Human labor produces goods and achievement, and yet all avails for nothing in the face of chance and death. It is possible to find pleasure, wisdom, and the like, and yet they do not guarantee happiness or long life. Even the behavior that, according to the normal piety of ancient Israel and of many people today, ought to be rewarded by God appears instead to be punished: The system of reward and punishment is out of order. In all of these things a disparity exists between what people expect and what actually happens to them. By his widespread application of *hebel*, "there is not, Qohelet avows, a single unspoiled value in this life."[22]

"Toil" (עמל **ʿamal).** This Hebrew noun occurs some fifty-five times in the Bible. It has nothing to do with the honest, goal-oriented labor of what we know as the "work ethic," but almost always conveys such negative ideas as trouble (Job 3:10; 5:6), weariness (Ps 73:16), sorrow (Jer 20:18), mischief (Job 4:8; Ps 140:9), and even oppression (Deut 26:7). In Ecclesiastes alone the term appears twenty-two times as a noun (40 percent of its usage), which means that, as in the case of *hebel*, it supplies a major motif to the message of this book. The accents of suffering and pain remain even though the Teacher uses the term in a more focused way to refer to hard labor of the sort best conveyed in English by the word *toil* (see also Ps 107:12). For Qohelet, toil and life are practically identical.[23] Like the writer of the story of the fall in Genesis 3, he places human beings in a world from which both the presence and the friendship of God are withdrawn and people are left to fend for themselves on an accursed ground in lives of toil that end only in death.

"Wisdom" (חכמה ḥ*okmâ).* This noun occurs some twenty-six times in Ecclesiastes, beginning with 1:13. The related noun/adjective חכם (ḥ*ākām*, "sage," wise") also occurs nearly as frequently (22 times), and the verb occurs four times, twice in its usual stative sense, "to be wise" (2:15; 7:23), once in the unique preterit sense of "to act wisely" (2:19), and once in a reflexive form (7:16). These terms are part of the distinctive semantic repertoire of the Teacher, though their occurrence is not uniform throughout the book but clusters in those pericopes in which he reflects on the value of "wisdom" as such (1:12-18; 2; 7:10-13, 15-25; 9:10-18). Qohelet does not employ the entire semantic range

---

20. Michael V. Fox, "The Meaning of Hebel," *JBL* 105 (1986) 413.
21. Murphy, *Ecclesiastes,* lix.
22. Ibid., lix.
23. Fox, *Qoheleth and His Contradictions,* 54.

that the word *ḥokmâ* enjoys elsewhere in the Hebrew Bible. For example, he does not use it to mean the inspired skill of a craftsman (cf. Exod 35:35; 36:2, 8; 1 Kgs 7:13-14); nor does he personify it as Dame Wisdom, God's first creation and co-worker in the making of the world (cf. Prov 8:22-31; Sir 24:1-12; Wis 7:22–8:18).

Unlike the other "wisdom" books of the Hebrew Bible, Ecclesiastes never explicitly identifies wisdom as "the fear of the LORD" (cf. Job 28:28; Ps 111:10; Prov 15:33; Sir 1:14), though he often recommends fearing God (e.g., Eccl 5:7; 7:18; 8:12); nor does he use it as a synonym for Torah, God's revealed will (cf. Sir 24:23; Bar 4:10). By *ḥokmâ* Qohelet never means the rich tradition of mantic wisdom—the interpretation of dreams, the solution of riddles, and other occult arts at which, for example, the Jewish sage Daniel excelled (Dan 5:11) and with which Solomon was credited by later generations (Wis 7:15-22).

For all that, however, the Teacher does mean a variety of things by the term "wisdom." It is an intellectual skill to be used in the discovery of truth (e.g., 2:3; 7:23), or at least the discovery that truth is undiscoverable (1:12-14). It is the mental endowment of "wise" people (e.g., 2:9), from whose instruction one gains great profit (7:5; 9:17). It can be construed as a moral value, the opposite of folly (e.g., 10:1). Perhaps most frequently, it is a rich body of lore (1:16) that, because it provides the only possible avenue to the understanding of all of life (8:16), is a most precious asset (2:9; 7:11), even though the training necessary to acquire it can only be called vexing (1:18). The first epilogist sums up the work of the "wise" Teacher under the headings of teaching knowledge, studying, and "arranging" (i.e., writing down) proverbs (12:9).

Not only the intense preoccupation with "wisdom" as demonstrated by the frequency of the term but also the literary style and subject matter of the book won Ecclesiastes its place alongside Job and Proverbs in ancient Israel's canon of sapiental literature. As Israel practiced it in these books, and in the deuterocanonical books of Sirach and Wisdom, wisdom aimed at "practical knowledge of the laws of life and of the world, based upon experience."[24] Many of the values that are prominent in the earlier sections of the Hebrew Bible—Torah and Former and Latter Prophets—are largely absent in this wisdom canon: covenant, election of Israel, sacrificial cultus, God's action in history. The outlook of these books is anthropocentric rather than theocentric and universal rather than particular. God is not mentioned very often, but stands in the background as the providential upholder of a world of such orders as the connection of deed to consequence and the certainty of death. These orders work themselves out dependably and inexorably, without any need for direct divine intervention.

As is quite evident, Qohelet shares these same understandings. However, he radicalizes them in that he rejects the commonly held conviction of his age that the linkage of cause and effect can be resolved in the moral sphere into a scheme of distributive justice by which good is rewarded and evil punished. For him, bad things happen to good people, too. The only transcendent truths are God's sovereignty over all things and the universality

24. Gerhard von Rad, *Old Testament Theology* (New York: Harper & Row, 1962) 1:418.

of death. All other supposed moral orders are absurd. No wonder orthodox theologians have found this book objectionable!

In short, the "wisdom" this book seeks and offers bears the distinctive accents of the Teacher. Although challenging to standard thinking, this wisdom was, nevertheless, recognized by Israel as a gift from God. It won and maintained its place in the sacred canon in spite of attempts to purge it.

"Fate" (מקרה *miqreh*). At the end of 2:14, the Teacher mentions for the first time the word *miqreh,* "fate," "chance," "destiny." Seven of the ten biblical occurrences of the word are in Ecclesiastes. The other three occurrences of the word are in more or less mundane contexts: (1) When David, suspecting a plot against his life, fails for two days to turn up at Saul's table, Saul says to himself, "Something has befallen him; he is not clean, surely he is not clean" (1 Sam 20:26 NRSV). (2) Ruth happened to glean in the part of the field that belonged to Boaz (Ruth 2:3). Of course, neither of these was really a random and mysterious event, for which our word "fate" would be the appropriate translation. The protagonist and the reader can easily see that these occurrences have been engineered very consciously. (3) Readers know that the great harm the Philistines suffered after they captured the ark of God was not mere "chance"; however, the Philistines themselves could be sure of that fact only by putting the ark on an ox cart and letting it go (1 Sam 6:9).

In Ecclesiastes, the outcome of life's struggles is described with the same word (2:14-15; three times in 3:19; 9:2-3). Here, too, the "fate" that awaits human beings is far from mere chance or a random event, though from our point of view it may seem purely contingent since it overtakes us without apparent connection either to our behavior or to our wishes. For the Teacher, "fate" is fact. It is decreed by God, even though one can learn nothing about this decree; it is death.

THE IDEOLOGY OF THE BOOK OF ECCLESIASTES

The thought of any book flows out of its vocabulary. The five components of the vocabulary of Qohelet discussed in the preceding section are pillars upon which its view of the world rests. "All" of human experience is "absurd"—i.e., incomprehensible, even senseless. Life is "toil." With the help of "wisdom" a person may find happiness amid the toil, but only if that person is utterly realistic about the inevitable "fate" of death.

Murphy sagely remarks that "the message of Ecclesiastes has suffered from excessive summarizing."[25] The epilogist, perhaps even the Teacher himself, started doing it right within the book itself ("All is absurd" [1:2]; "The end of the matter. . . . Fear God, and keep his commandments" [12:13]), and the practice has continued to this present day. Yet, what are we interpreters to do? We need handles on this book of Scripture. We need pedagogical and homiletical strategies that flow straight out of the book's own current of thought and ultimately make confluence with our own.

25. Murphy, *Ecclesiastes,* lviii.

Ecclesiastes is not a book about God; it is a book about ideas. That is why one speaks of its ideology in preference to its theology. Its ideas are about human survival in a world in which work is pain, overwork is foolish, pleasure soon pales in the face of death, and wisdom is unable to comprehend even the simplest sequences that would make possible real understanding of the world. Such a world is absurd. Yet life in the face of the absurd did not create a Qohelet who, with desperate shouts of *carpe diem* ("seize the day!"), merely snatches at a few shreds of superficial happiness or lives a few fitful moments of bright joy against a relentlessly dark background. No, he comes forward as the Teacher, with sober and yet caring countenance, ready to help his pupils deal with such a world. He holds God in profound respect but will never claim to know too much about God. Above all he will not commit God to the program of distributive justice that Job's friends advocated. Is his God just, then? Is his God even good? Qohelet does not tell us, perhaps cannot tell us. His is not a book about God.

In his magisterial commentary on Qohelet, Robert Gordis identifies four themes that are basic to the thought of Qohelet: (1) Human achievement is weak and impermanent; (2) the fate of human beings is uncertain; (3) human beings find it impossible to attain to true knowledge and insight into the world; (4) the goal of human endeavors needs to be joy, which is the divine imperative.[26] Clearly, the fourth theme is the only one that boldly affirms life. The other three only point to the limitations and impossibilities within which human beings live. For Gordis, too, the book has no proper "theology" or doctrine of God other than that God exists in limitless sovereignty; its ideology is "anthropology." Deep within human nature is "an ineradicable desire for happiness," planted there by God.[27] To live a moral life by doing the will of God, then, is to pursue happiness.

Other commentators introduce at least a theological dimension into their summations of the meaning of the book of Ecclesiastes. Gerhard von Rad, for example, finds that the book continually circles around three basic ideas: "1. A thorough, rational examination of life is unable to find any satisfactory meaning; everything is 'vanity.' 2. God determines every event. 3. Man is unable to discern these decrees, the 'works of God' in the world."[28]

The notion that "God determines every event," based in large part on the famous passage in Eccl 3:1-8 (see Commentary), leads Murphy to write an entire section on who is the God of Qohelet.[29] He agrees that Qohelet teaches that whatever God is doing in the world is unintelligible to human beings and that little personal relationship with God can, therefore, exist apart from human attitudes of fear and awe. God is not revealed in any way in history. However, Murphy is convinced that Qohelet's God is not simply a god of origins who sets into motion inexorable natural laws and then walks away. Such a god is not the God of Israel, and Qohelet—though he never calls God "Yahweh," the name revealed to Moses at Sinai and uses only the generic name אלהים (*ĕlōhîm*)—is an Israelite

26. Gordis, *Koheleth,* 252.
27. Ibid., 113.
28. Von Rad, *Wisdom in Israel,* 227-28.
29. Murphy, *Ecclesiastes,* lxviii-lxix.

writer who stands squarely within the give and take of Israel's tradition of theological reflection. Qohelet believes that "everything happens because of the Lord's action. . . . God is portrayed as intimately involved in all that occurs."[30] Murphy quotes with favor L. Gorssen's remark that "God is utterly present and at the same time utterly absent. God is 'present' in each event and yet no event is a 'place of encounter' with God. . . . Events do not speak any longer the language of a saving God. They are there, simply."[31]

Here is the ideological crux of the book. Von Rad and Murphy are by and large correct in saying that for Qohelet events are both impenetrable and preordained by God. There can be no question of mastery of events, because they are out of human hands. The position is deterministic, but not fatalistic, as Murphy understands it, because human beings are still perfectly free and responsible to act. At the same time, it seems unnecessary to insist that this assertion about the predetermination of times by God is the central idea of the book. True, God "has made everything suitable for its time . . . yet they cannot find out what God has done from the beginning to the end" (Eccl 3:11 NRSV). Nevertheless, charges that God is arbitrary and capricious or even just plain absent pale beside the positive assertion that, by taking charge of what they can in their lives, human beings can find joy and happiness (Eccl 2:24-26; 3:12-13; 5:18-20; 8:15; 9:7-10; 11:7-10). This advice culminates in the remarkable sentence, "Follow the inclination of your heart and the desire of your eyes, but know that for all these things God will bring you into judgment" (Eccl 11:9 NRSV), in which the latter clause should be taken to mean that God holds every person responsible for following the heart and the eyes to find happiness (see Commentary on 11:7-10). Even in the middle of a maddeningly absurd world in which the fatal shadow of death hangs equally over the wise and the foolish (Eccl 2:10), human being and beast (Eccl 3:19), this passionate possibility exists for those who, with prudence and respect for the unknown and all-determining God, can seize it!

By the simple device of shifting the emphasis from the admitted determinism of an order in which God has already ordained everything to the human responsibility or freedom that Qohelet also admittedly affirms, the weight comes down not on a tragic fatalism—human beings in the hands of a distant, all-powerful, and arbitrary God who causes good and evil alike—but on the opportunity for human happiness in a world in which God is utterly sovereign and people are truly free.

Can we have it both ways—divine sovereignty over all things *and* human freedom? Let us hope so! Every book of the Bible mixes these ingredients of theological truth in different proportions. In the Hebrew Bible, the books of Samuel and Kings, Esther, and Ruth concern themselves largely with the free actions of human beings in the world, while the book of Daniel hints at a plan for the ages set down before ever a king or a saint began to act. Ecclesiastes pours heavy doses of sovereignty and predestination into the theological mixture, but it too reckons with the responsive human heart and the obedient human

30. Ibid., lxvi.

31. L. Gorssen, "La cohérence de la conception de Dieu dans l'Ecclésiaste," *ETL* 46 (1970) 314-15; quoted in Murphy, *Ecclesiastes,* lxviii-lxix.

will. Even though God remains cloaked in obscurity, God's predetermination sometimes seems more like prevenient grace; sometimes the ordained times and seasons seem more like the blessed and secure orders of nature. It is good that divine sovereignty and human freedom find a blend in this book, too, because faith assents to both ideas and finds each vital. If Qohelet spoke only for predetermined necessity, synagogue and church alike might have to put it aside, for most of us find such a doctrine both theologically obnoxious and intellectually impossible. But he does not; in the end, he seeks to lead his pupils to their own decision to walk humbly, sensitively, harmoniously with their God.

THE TEACHER FOR THE PREACHER

No attempt at an introduction to the Reflection sections of the book will be made here. To do so would be abstract; the move from Scripture to contemporary thought and preaching is best made in the presence of specific texts that raise burning questions one by one.

This section will serve, therefore, simply as a brief index of theological topics discussed in the Reflections that follow. Readers are invited to turn directly to them.

Topic	See Reflections on:
Absurdity of life	1:1
Advantage of the wise and rich	6:1-12
Death	3:16–4:8; 7:1-14; 9:1-12; 11:7–12:8
Envy	3:16–4:8
Fame	1:3-11
Feelings	7:1-14
Folly	9:13–10:7
Freedom to act	10:8–11:6
Happiness	1:1; 2:1-11, 24-26; 9:1-12; 11:7–12:8
Hatred of life	2:12-23; 3:16–4:8
Hopelessness	9:1-12
Moral perfectionism	7:15–8:1
Newness	1:3-11
Orders	3:1-15
Predetermination by God	3:1-15; 5:8-20; 6:1-12; 7:1-14
Resurrection, immortality, sheol	3:16–4:8; 9:1-12
Solidarity with the animals	3:16–4:8
Talk	4:9–5:7
Universal fate	2:12-23
Vocation	3:16–4:8; 8:10-17
Wisdom	1:12-18; 7:15–8:1; 12:9-14
Work	1:3-11

BIBLIOGRAPHY

Barton, George A. *A Critical and Exegetical Commentary on the Book of Ecclesiastes.* ICC. New York: Scribner's, 1908. Long a standard, still useful especially in philological matters.

Crenshaw, James L. *Ecclesiastes.* OTL. Philadelphia: Westminster, 1987. Careful exegesis, thorough documentation; stresses discussion of literary features.

Farmer, Kathleen A. *Who Knows What Is Good? A Commentary on the Books of Proverbs and Ecclesiastes.* ITC. Grand Rapids: Eerdmans, 1991. A more conservative viewpoint, aimed at preachers and teachers in the church.

Fox, M. V. *Qoheleth and His Contradictions.* BLS 18. Sheffield: Almond, 1989.

Gordis, Robert. *Koheleth: The Man and His World.* 1st ed. New York: Schocken, 1951; 3rd ed., 1968. Rich in command of the literature, Gordis offers fresh insights that have achieved wide acceptance. (Page references in this commentary are to the first edition.)

Murphy, Roland E. *Ecclesiastes.* WBC 23A. Waco, Tex.: Word, 1992. The most recent commentary, richly documented. Considerable theological reflection as well.

Rankin, O. S., and G. G. Atkins. "The Book of Ecclesiastes." In *The Interpreter's Bible.* Vol. 5. Edited by George A. Buttrick et al. Nashville: Abingdon, 1956.

Scott, R. B. Y. *Proverbs, Ecclesiastes.* AB 18. Garden City, N.Y.: Doubleday, 1965. Concise general introductions to the wisdom canon and to Ecclesiastes; commentary skimpy.

Whitley, C. F. *Koheleth: His Language and Thought.* BZAW 148. Berlin: de Gruyter, 1979. Intense work with philology.

Whybray, R. N. *Ecclesiastes.* NCB. Grand Rapids: Eerdmans, 1989. Nontechnical, compact, and readable. Intended for use in lay teaching.

OUTLINE OF ECCLESIASTES

THE SUPERSCRIPTION

NIV	NRSV
1 The words of the Teacher,[a] son of David, king in Jerusalem:	1 The words of the Teacher,[a] the son of David, king in Jerusalem.
[a]1 Or *leader of the assembly*; also in verses 2 and 12	[a] Heb *Qoheleth*, traditionally rendered *Preacher*

COMMENTARY

The superscription, or headline, of Ecclesiastes (1:1) appears to give us its social and historical settings. The appearance is deceptive, however. The lateness of the Hebrew language of the book puts its composition well after the time of Solomon or, for that matter, any later royal "son of David" (see Introduction). Nor does the title "Qohelet" reveal much about the author or the social setting of the book. (For more on this title, see Introduction.) In fact, the book was written by an unknown author, not the one to whom it is attributed in the superscription. This author created a main character, Qohelet, who impersonates the wise and pleasure-loving king Solomon from 1:1 through 2:11. Because of the sustained exploration of ideas he offers to the readers of his book, he is best known as "Teacher," the translation of his title used by both of the modern English versions before us.

ECCLESIASTES 1:2–12:8

THE WISDOM OF THE TEACHER

ECCLESIASTES 1:2, THEME

<table>
<tr><td>NIV</td><td>NRSV</td></tr>
<tr>
<td>

2"Meaningless! Meaningless!"
  says the Teacher.
"Utterly meaningless!
  Everything is meaningless."

</td>
<td>

2 Vanity of vanities, says the Teacher,[a]
  vanity of vanities! All is vanity.

[a]Heb *Qoheleth*, traditionally rendered *Preacher*

</td>
</tr>
</table>

COMMENTARY

The major theme of the entire book is set forth in 1:2. We can be certain of the importance of this verse because it introduces the term הבל (*hebel*; NRSV, "vanity"; NIV, "meaningless"), which becomes a veritable refrain throughout the book. Furthermore, if we set aside 1:1 as a headline and 12:9-14 as epilogue by other hands, then the notion of *hebel* forms a literary bracket (1:2 + 12:8) around the body of the Teacher's work.

Of the many proposals advanced by scholars about the precise meaning in Ecclesiastes of the key word *hebel* (see Introduction), the translation "absurdity"[32] best conveys the Teacher's meaning across the millennia into contemporary English. Under the impact of existentialist philosophy, an "absurdity" has become for our age more than simply a silly, foolish thing; it is a thing that cannot be made intelligible through any of the rubrics that people usually invoke to explain the meaning of their experience. An absurdity is not necessarily ephemeral ("a vapor"). It may in fact go on and on. But it makes no more sense at the end than it did at the beginning.

That is the very conviction with which Qohelet approaches his reflections on meaning in life. Everything is *hebel*. Nothing can be counted on to work out the way it ought to; nothing makes any ultimate sense. Certain things can be done; certain achievements can be made. Happiness is possible. However, over all experience stands the Teacher's general rule: "All is absurd." This judgment is "not cosmic, but designates the worldly realities with which humans must deal."[33] (For the signficance of the lowly word "all" for the universalism of Qohelet, see Introduction.) The traditional system by which life could be understood does not work, and randomness, pain, loss, failure, and death may break out unexpectedly and inexplicably.

The doubling of the word *hebel* into the form "vanity of vanities" creates a superlative; it heightens the absurdity to its ultimate possible degree. Similar constructions can be seen in Exod 26:33, "holy of holies"; Cant 1:1, "song of songs"; and Ezek 26:7, "king of kings."

---

32. M. V. Fox, *Qoheleth and His Contradictions,* BLS 18 (Sheffield: Almond, 1989).

33. Roland E. Murphy, *Ecclesiastes,* WBC 23A (Waco, Tex.: Word, 1992) 4.

REFLECTIONS

It is ironic that the best-known single verse in the book of Ecclesiastes is also the most maligned and despised. Sometimes the artistic and literary images that are the most mocked and parodied are those that are the most painfully true. Take, for example, Grant Wood's painting of the elderly Iowa farm couple, *American Gothic*. We hate it, we laugh at it, and some of us know in our hearts that we are in that picture, too. The case is similar with the slogan in the book of Ecclesiastes: "Vanity of vanities, says the Teacher,/ vanity of vanities! All is vanity." Since time immemorial the possibility that life really is absurd, that no sense can be made of it, has haunted human consciousness. In the heart of Herman Melville's novel *Moby Dick*, which is the story of a chase after evil that, because it is so futile and destructive, becomes evil and absurd in itself, Melville reveals his partiality for the book of Ecclesiastes. He rightly recognizes that the slogan of the book stands as a perpetual warning against superficiality and foolish, giggling hilarity.

> That mortal man who hath more joy than sorrow in him, that mortal man cannot be true—not true, or undeveloped. With books, the same. The truest of all men was the Man of Sorrows, and the truest of all books is Solomon's and Ecclesiastes is the fine hammered steel of woe. "ALL is vanity." ALL. This wilful world hath not got hold of un-christian Solomon's wisdom yet. But he who dodges hospitals and jails, and walks fast crossing grave-yards, and would rather talk of operas than hell . . . not that man is fitted to sit down on tomb-stones, and break the green damp mould with unfathomably wondrous Solomon.[34]

Twentieth-century literature, too, reflects the malaise of a Western culture in which boredom and meaninglessness squeeze the joy out of life. The despair and hollowness of Willy Loman in Arthur Miller's *Death of a Salesman*, the blurring of falsehood and truth in George Orwell's *1984*, the plight of T. S. Eliot's "Hollow Men"—all testify to the very real consciousness in our time that life might just be absurd. Interpreters do well not to play down the slogan in the book of Ecclesiastes.

At the same time, we do well to acknowledge that this truth is only a partial one. Life is absurd until, and unless, meaning is thrust upon it in acts of courage and faith. Even the author of this slogan, the Teacher, will cautiously propose responses to the challenge of absurdity in his own teachings. One of the salient themes of his book is that God wills that we enjoy our lives (see Introduction), and in that teaching lies at least an existential, if only temporary, respite from absurdity. Other biblical writers are not so cautious. The teller of the story of Esther (who worked at a time not far distant from that of the Teacher himself) relates how a Jewish woman and her uncle parlayed her potentially absurd position as a member of the king's harem into a powerful victory for justice against tyranny. The stories of Daniel 1–6 show how obedience and trust in the power of God can transmute scenes of pitiful persecution into scenes in which the very oppressor praises God. The man born blind (John 9) finds that his blindness is an occasion wherein the glory of God might be manifested. By his steadfastness in suffering for others, the man on the cross turned an instrument of torture and tragedy into a symbol of hope.

Our modern writers, too, sometimes believe that meaning and purpose can be forged out of the raw material of absurd pain and tyranny, not by the giggling words of Pollyanna, but by the faithful love of those who are determined here and now in their own lives of obedience to give foretastes of what life is like in the kingdom of heaven. One example of this juxtaposition of absurdity and meaning is P. D. James's novel *The Children of Men*, in which, against the background of the end of human reproduction and the slow demise of the human race, a flawed but brave couple bring forth a savior in a manger.[35]

---

34. Herman Melville, *Moby Dick*, chap. 96.
35. P. D. James, *The Children of Men* (New York: Alfred A. Knopf, 1993).

ECCLESIASTES 1:3–2:26, ILLUSTRATIONS OF THE THEME OF ABSURDITY

Ecclesiastes 1:3-11, The Tedious Cycle of Nonachievement

NIV	NRSV

3What does man gain from all his labor
    at which he toils under the sun?
4Generations come and generations go,
    but the earth remains forever.
5The sun rises and the sun sets,
    and hurries back to where it rises.
6The wind blows to the south
    and turns to the north;
round and round it goes,
    ever returning on its course.
7All streams flow into the sea,
    yet the sea is never full.
To the place the streams come from,
    there they return again.
8All things are wearisome,
    more than one can say.
The eye never has enough of seeing,
    nor the ear its fill of hearing.
9What has been will be again,
    what has been done will be done again;
    there is nothing new under the sun.
10Is there anything of which one can say,
    "Look! This is something new"?
It was here already, long ago;
    it was here before our time.
11There is no remembrance of men of old,
    and even those who are yet to come
will not be remembered
    by those who follow.
	3 What do people gain from all the toil
	    at which they toil under the sun?
	4 A generation goes, and a generation comes,
	    but the earth remains forever.
	5 The sun rises and the sun goes down,
	    and hurries to the place where it rises.
	6 The wind blows to the south,
	    and goes around to the north;
	round and round goes the wind,
	    and on its circuits the wind returns.
	7 All streams run to the sea,
	    but the sea is not full;
	to the place where the streams flow,
	    there they continue to flow.
	8 All things*a* are wearisome;
	    more than one can express;
	the eye is not satisfied with seeing,
	    or the ear filled with hearing.
	9 What has been is what will be,
	    and what has been done is what will be done;
	    there is nothing new under the sun.
	10 Is there a thing of which it is said,
	    "See, this is new"?
	It has already been,
	    in the ages before us.
	11 The people of long ago are not remembered,
	    nor will there be any remembrance
	of people yet to come
	    by those who come after them.
	
	aOr words

COMMENTARY

Having established a general but unconventional rule by which all life can be interpreted, the Teacher moves on to reflect on the first of a number of specific instances in which experience proves conventional wisdom to be absurd. In a haunting and melancholy poem (1:3-11), he poses a rhetorical question: "What do people gain from all the toil/ at which they toil under the sun?" The expected answer is, of course, "Nothing." In nature's endless round there is neither innovation, variation, nor remainder. For all their claims of unique creativity, human beings cannot escape this universal futility.

Clearly he had hoped that the עָמָל ('āmāl, "toil"; see Introduction) of a humble, righteous struggler would enjoy a payoff somewhere. After all, the psalmist had construed Israel's own history as such a reversal of fortune: "He gave them the lands of the nations,/ and they took possession of the wealth [עָמָל 'āmāl] of the peoples" (Ps 105:44 NRSV). Qohelet's observation that toil gains nothing confounds all notions of distributive justice.

The rhetorical question of v. 3 concludes with another formula, "under the sun." Used twenty-nine times in Ecclesiastes and nowhere else in the Hebrew Bible, this cliché, too (together with the variant "under heaven" found in 1:13; 2:3; and 3:1; see also Gen 6:17; Exod 17:14; Deut 7:24; 9:14), is part of the distinct repertoire of the Teacher. Like the "all" of 1:2 and 12:8, the expression points to all that human beings ever have to face and deal with. It is a gloomy assessment of the light of day.

Having established that nowhere on the face of the earth does hard labor produce the expected effect, the Teacher proceeds through a number of details illustrative of the point. In vv. 4-11, one of the most lyrical passages of the book, the Teacher draws upon the four elements of ancient cosmology—earth (v. 4), fire or sun (v. 5), wind or air (v. 6), and water (v. 7)—to describe repeating cycles of inevitability that touch upon all things except the earth itself. Just like the ever-repeating cycles of nature, human generations go and come. The sun also rises eastward and sets westward, then "hurries" to start over again.[36] The wind blows south, then north (unusual wind directions for Palestine), and the streams flow tiresomely and uselessly to the sea (v. 7). Just as endless and just as ineffectual as the endless cycles of nature are the futile efforts by human beings to observe and express these things (v. 8). In despair, the Teacher can only deny the possibility of any novelty or any randomness. All is predictable, for "there is nothing new under the sun" (v. 9). When some unseen adversary objects and says, "See, this is new" (v. 10), Qohelet once again affirms that whatever today seems innovative and fresh is only the latest manifestation of something that has always been around. By this point in the poem, readers are exhausted with the monotony of it all.

The passage 1:3-11 concludes with the devastating assertion that the "remembrance" of people past, present, and future will fail as well (v. 11). Considering that for Qohelet and all Israel before him this was the only form of immortality for which a person could hope, and was in fact a kind of reinstatement or recapitulation of the thing remembered, this is truly a hard saying. It calls into question the one means available for transcending death.

36. Gordis contrasts the sun's weariness here with the joy with which it runs the course ordained for it by God in Ps 19:4-6. See Robert Gordis, *Koheleth: The Man and His World,* 1st ed. (New York: Schocken, 1951; 3rd ed., 1968) 196.

REFLECTIONS

At least three major challenges to conventional piety lurk in the poem of Eccl 1:3-11. Contemporary faith will be enriched to the degree that these challenges can be faced squarely in theology and preaching.

1. *The Folly of the Work Ethic.* The implied answer "nothing" to the rhetorical question of v. 3 confounds more than simply the Protestant work ethic and other such propensities of modern readers. It confounded the ethic of the sages of ancient Israel as well. Their usual line was, "In all toil there is profit" (Prov 14:23). Teachers and parents have echoed that idea ever since. In contrast, Qohelet teaches that hard work is only an absurd waste of effort. He would have blessed the appealing heroine of Larry McMurtry's novel *Leaving Cheyenne,* Molly Taylor White, who always believed in living fully while she was alive (see Eccl 2:24); and he would have chastised the hard-working, driven hero, Gideon Fry, who never learned how to quit and enjoy.[37]

37. Larry McMurtry, *Leaving Cheyenne* (New York: Simon & Schuster, 1979).

2. *Nothing New Under the Sun.* The notion of the wearisome cycle of all things and the claim that "what has been is what will be" (vv. 8-9), capture an experience of *ennui* with which we are familiar. In another sense, however, they are dead wrong. To say that what has been is what will be is not the same as saying *Que será será*, "Whatever will be, will be." The latter is not only empirically justified, but it is also affirmed in biblical thought, even by Yahweh, who says, "I am what I will be" or "I am what I am becoming" (Exod 3:14). But to say that what has been is what will be is to speak of an eternal round of natural and moral orders that admits of no variation or innovation. Such a world truly would be absurd, for there would be no room for individualism, creativity, or contingencies of any kind. But the world is not really like that; although Qohelet may have captured a well-known feeling, he did not capture a physical reality. As far as the death of all living organisms goes, yes, that is an order that has been and will be true. Jerome caught the irony of v. 4 when he wrote, "What is more vain than this vanity: that the earth, which was made for humans, stays—but humans themselves, the lords of the earth, suddenly dissolve into dust?"[38] We now know, however, that the orders of creation do not move in cycles, but more nearly in spirals, never returning to the beginning point. The new science of chaos studies begins with evidence that even in physics there is a place for new things under the sun, for random, chance events and genuine innovations. What casts a pall of absurdity over our experience is neither the endless round that Qohelet imagines nor the relentless, invariable operation of natural laws that Newtonian physics has bequeathed us; rather, it is the knowledge that we are hurtling toward the end of the cosmos—the very thing the Teacher said does not happen (Eccl 1:4*b*)! Our faith ought to challenge us to face up to this ultimate absurdity. If the great monuments we construct and the great literature and art we pass on are all destined ultimately for the cosmic scrap heap, it becomes more urgent than ever for us to impose meaning upon existence through acts of courage, loving-kindness, and compassion. Although the memory of such acts will not survive, the acts themselves transcend the perishing nature of the world because they participate in the eternal reality of the love of God, which is revealed in the courage and compassion of Jesus Christ.

3. *No Abiding Fame.* The quest for fame, too, is brought under scrutiny by this passage. That people struggled since time immemorial to achieve for themselves a lasting name as a hedge against oblivion is acknowledged in the story of the Tower of Babel: "Come, let us build ourselves a city, and a tower . . . and let us make a name for ourselves" (Gen 11:4 NRSV). The ensuing story of the call of Abram counters Babel by teaching that a lasting name is a gift of God: "I will . . . make your name great" (Gen 12:2 NRSV). The Teacher, however, trusts neither the efforts of human beings to attain immortality through their works nor the promise of God to grant that "remembrance" that is a lasting heritage.

38. Cited by James L. Crenshaw, *Ecclesiastes*, OTL (Philadelphia: Westminster, 1987) 63.

Ecclesiastes 1:12-18, A King Gains Nothing from Wisdom

NIV

[12]I, the Teacher, was king over Israel in Jerusalem. [13]I devoted myself to study and to explore by wisdom all that is done under heaven. What a heavy burden God has laid on men! [14]I have seen all the things that are done under the sun;

NRSV

[12]I, the Teacher,[a] when king over Israel in Jerusalem, [13]applied my mind to seek and to search out by wisdom all that is done under heaven; it is an unhappy business that God has

[a] Heb *Qoheleth*, traditionally rendered *Preacher*

NIV

all of them are meaningless, a chasing after the wind.

¹⁵What is twisted cannot be straightened;
    what is lacking cannot be counted.

¹⁶I thought to myself, "Look, I have grown and increased in wisdom more than anyone who has ruled over Jerusalem before me; I have experienced much of wisdom and knowledge." ¹⁷Then I applied myself to the understanding of wisdom, and also of madness and folly, but I learned that this, too, is a chasing after the wind.

¹⁸For with much wisdom comes much sorrow;
    the more knowledge, the more grief.

NRSV

given to human beings to be busy with. ¹⁴I saw all the deeds that are done under the sun; and see, all is vanity and a chasing after wind.[a]

¹⁵ What is crooked cannot be made straight,
    and what is lacking cannot be counted.

16I said to myself, "I have acquired great wisdom, surpassing all who were over Jerusalem before me; and my mind has had great experience of wisdom and knowledge." ¹⁷And I applied my mind to know wisdom and to know madness and folly. I perceived that this also is but a chasing after wind.[a]

¹⁸ For in much wisdom is much vexation,
    and those who increase knowledge increase sorrow.

[a]Or *a feeding on wind.* See Hos 12.1

COMMENTARY

The Teacher who was also the "king" now addresses himself to the worth of wisdom. The structure of the passage (vv. 12-18) falls into two parts: A report by the Teacher culminating in the formula "all is vanity and a chasing after wind" is followed by a proverb quoted with approval, perhaps from a traditional source.[39] The same pattern is then repeated in vv. 16-18. The phrase "a chasing after wind,"[40] which occurs nine times in Ecclesiastes with slight variations in the Hebrew, conveys a sense of extreme intellectual futility and frustration.

1:12-15. Following a formula of royal declaration, "I, Qohelet" (v. 12; cf. Dan 4:4, 37), the Teacher-king "applies his mind" (v. 13 NRSV) or "devotes himself" (NIV) to see what wisdom will gain for him. His search is far-reaching. He will "study" and "explore" (TNK, "probe") experience, verbs that in Hebrew suggest that the effort has both breadth and depth.[41] In fact, he sets for himself a goal both universal and impossible in scope: Using wisdom as his instrument, he will examine "all that is done under heaven."

Now for the first time in the book, the Teacher-king mentions God (v. 13). He discovers that God has "laid upon" human beings "an unhappy business" (NRSV) or "a heavy burden" (NIV). What are we to make of this judgment? In one sense, the proverb of v. 15 helps to answer this question. We live in a world in which providence reigns supreme. The rules by which existence is structured are firm and reliable; however, they also dictate that some of the things against which we rail and struggle, such as crookedness and deficiency, remain.

1:16-18. In these verses, a similar point is made. Although the Teacher-king says, no doubt in all candor, that his wisdom exceeds that of anyone before him, he has learned that all wisdom leads to sorrow and knowledge to grief. The puzzling v. 17 may suggest the universality of the Teacher's quest for knowledge, which carries him into both the light and the shadow side of human experience. A better construal of the four Hebrew nouns in the verse—"wisdom" (חכמה *ḥokmâ*), "knowledge" (דעת *da'at*), "madness" (הוללות *hôlēlôt*), and "folly" (סכלות *siklût*)—would be to take them as doubly compound objects of the

---

39. Gordis has argued that Qohelet quotes extensively from otherwise unknown Israelite wisdom sentences, using them sometimes as evidence and sometimes as foils for his own argumentation. See Robert Gordis, *Koheleth: The Man and His World,* 1st ed. (New York: Schocken, 1951; 3rd ed., 1968) 95-108. Whybray, too, thinks Qohelet cites other sages, but he can positively identify only eight examples. He believes Qohelet used each of these sayings because he agreed with it. See R. N. Whybray, *Ecclesiastes,* NCB (Grand Rapids: Eerdmans, 1989) 35-40.

40. Scott translates "clutching at the wind." See R. B. Y. Scott, *Proverbs, Ecclesiastes,* AB 18 (Garden City, N.Y.: Doubleday, 1965) 216.

41. James L. Crenshaw, *Ecclesiastes,* OTL (Philadelphia: Westminster, 1987) 72.

infinitive "to know" (לדעת *lāda'at*)—that is, "to know that wisdom and knowledge [are] madness and folly."[42]

In any case, the entire effort comes to naught. Perhaps the closing proverb of the passage, "the more knowledge, the more grief" (NIV) was origi-

nally meant to be taken quite literally. If the cane was used liberally in school, the educational process might truly have been painful.[43] Qohelet radicalizes the teaching, however: The wiser one becomes, the more troubled and unhappy one is. Nevertheless, he pushes on.

42. Gordis, *Koheleth,* 203.

43. Crenshaw, *Ecclesiastes,* 76.

REFLECTIONS

It is true that what is by nature crooked cannot be made straight (v. 15*a*). Who would want to live in a world that was any different than that? To say that something that is absent can nevertheless be counted present (v. 15*b*) would be to say that the world is unreliable and crazy. However, things that should not be crooked or absent are, and people want to know why. The intellectual restlessness God placed in human beings that causes them to search for answers to such "Why?" questions is not a happy dimension of life.

Why not quit school, then, and just remain innocent? After all, "the more knowledge, the more grief" (v. 18). The notion has had echoes in traditional thinking ever since:

> . . . where ignorance is bliss,
> 'Tis folly to be wise.[44]

and:

> From ignorance our comfort flows,
> The only wretched are the wise.[45]

Yet the heart resists such a conclusion. A modern writer answered these counsels of despair with the aphorism, "Ignorance is not bliss—it is oblivion."[46] Even though the quest of the Teacher-king led him close to embracing ignorance, in the end he too cannot reject wisdom (Eccl 9:13-18).

44. Thomas Gray, "On a Distant Prospect of Eton College" (1742).
45. Matthew Prior, "To the Hon. Charles Montague" (1692).
46. Philip Wylie, *Generation of Vipers* (New York: Farrar & Rinehart, 1942).

Ecclesiastes 2:1-11, Pleasure Is an Absurdity

NIV	NRSV
2 I thought in my heart, "Come now, I will test you with pleasure to find out what is good." But that also proved to be meaningless. [2]"Laughter," I said, "is foolish. And what does pleasure accomplish?" [3]I tried cheering myself with wine, and embracing folly—my mind still guiding me with wisdom. I wanted to see what was worthwhile for men to do under heaven during the few days of their lives. [4]I undertook great projects: I built houses for myself and planted vineyards. [5]I made gardens and	2 I said to myself, "Come now, I will make a test of pleasure; enjoy yourself." But again, this also was vanity. [2]I said of laughter, "It is mad," and of pleasure, "What use is it?" [3]I searched with my mind how to cheer my body with wine—my mind still guiding me with wisdom—and how to lay hold on folly, until I might see what was good for mortals to do under heaven during the few days of their life. [4]I made great works; I built houses and planted vineyards for myself; [5]I made myself gardens and parks, and

NIV

parks and planted all kinds of fruit trees in them. [6]I made reservoirs to water groves of flourishing trees. [7]I bought male and female slaves and had other slaves who were born in my house. I also owned more herds and flocks than anyone in Jerusalem before me. [8]I amassed silver and gold for myself, and the treasure of kings and provinces. I acquired men and women singers, and a harem[a] as well—the delights of the heart of man. [9]I became greater by far than anyone in Jerusalem before me. In all this my wisdom stayed with me. [10]I denied myself nothing my eyes desired;

I refused my heart no pleasure.

My heart took delight in all my work,

and this was the reward for all my labor.

[11]Yet when I surveyed all that my hands had done

and what I had toiled to achieve,

everything was meaningless, a chasing after the wind;

nothing was gained under the sun.

[a]8 The meaning of the Hebrew for this phrase is uncertain.

NRSV

planted in them all kinds of fruit trees. [6]I made myself pools from which to water the forest of growing trees. [7]I bought male and female slaves, and had slaves who were born in my house; I also had great possessions of herds and flocks, more than any who had been before me in Jerusalem. [8]I also gathered for myself silver and gold and the treasure of kings and of the provinces; I got singers, both men and women, and delights of the flesh, and many concubines.[a]

9So I became great and surpassed all who were before me in Jerusalem; also my wisdom remained with me. [10]Whatever my eyes desired I did not keep from them; I kept my heart from no pleasure, for my heart found pleasure in all my toil, and this was my reward for all my toil. [11]Then I considered all that my hands had done and the toil I had spent in doing it, and again, all was vanity and a chasing after wind,[b] and there was nothing to be gained under the sun.

[a]Meaning of Heb uncertain   [b]Or a feeding on wind. See Hos 12.1

COMMENTARY

Having reasoned from experience that the acquisition of wisdom is an absurdity (which is to say it does not result in the happy outcome that its proponents had touted for it), Qohelet determines to "make a test of pleasure" (2:1). As before (1:13) he gives the result (vv. 1b-2) before he describes the experiment: Pleasure is vanity and of no use. The reward of uninhibited hedonism is unbounded disillusionment; it is all absurd and futile (v. 11).

According to 1 Kgs 10:1, the Queen of Sheba came to Jerusalem to "test" Solomon with riddles. True to form, the "Solomon" of Ecclesiastes readily subjects himself to tests in order to find the answer to the great riddle, Is anything in life not absurd? In vv. 3-8 the Teacher-king becomes a whirlwind of energy in carrying out his experiments. After fortifying himself with wine (v. 3) and putting folly under the control of wisdom for the time, he acts in grand style, filling his days by acquiring houses, vine-

yards, gardens,[47] parks, pools, slaves and cattle, silver and gold, servants of all kinds, and concubines[48] (vv. 4-8). He does not do all this in order to wallow in sensuality, but because "he is taking the measure of a life of pleasure."[49]

The royal perquisites are writ large here. The model is the fictional Solomon of the Song of Songs, whose "gardens" were veritable paradises (see Cant 4:12-15; 5:1; 6:2) and whose appetites were renowned. But the profile is also consistent with the report of Solomon's largeness and largess

47. The Hebrew word used here, פרדס (pardēs), is probably a corruption of a Persian word meaning "[forest] enclosure." A similar word meaning "park" also occurs in Akkadian. The Greeks borrowed the word as well (παράδεισος paradeisos), from whence we got our word "paradise." If its presence here betrays Persian influence, as seems likely, we have additional evidence that Qohelet's Hebrew is post-exilic, from the period when Persia was dominant in the Middle East.

48. The Hebrew word שדה (šiddâ) has been variously rendered "cup bearers" (LXX), "goblets" (Vg), and even "music" (Luther; see KJV). Its relation to "sad," "breast," and other considerations have led recent translators toward the women of the royal household. The NIV's "harem" captures the sense of abundance that the double use of the Hebrew term conveys.

49. Murphy, Ecclesiastes, 18.

in 1 Kgs 4:20-34 (see also 2 Chr 9:13-28). We are not told there that he planted forests and made reservoirs to provide irrigation for them (cf. 2:6), but such works were the king's to command. The mention in 2 Kgs 20:20 that King Hezekiah built a pool and a conduit in the Jerusalem water system (confirmed archaeologically by the eighth-century BCE Siloam inscription found on the wall of the conduit) and the mention of the king's pool in Neh 2:14 are evidence of royal interest in that precious commodity, water, in ancient Israel. It is no surprise, then, to read that "I became great and surpassed all who were before me in Jerusalem" (v. 9). We readers take hope when we hear that "my heart found pleasure in all my toil, and this was my reward for all my toil" (v. 10). Experience does not deny the possibility of pleasure and the possibility of reward. Yet the very word חֵלֶק (ḥēleq, "reward," "portion," "lot") provides a transition from the good news that pleasure is real to the bad news that follows. Qohelet uses the term eight times, usually in a positive sense. But what did his "reward" really amount to? The result of the Teacher-king's effort to escape from absurdity through pleasure replicates the outcome of his quest for meaning through wisdom; it is "vanity and a chasing after wind, and . . . nothing to be gained under the sun" (v. 11).

REFLECTIONS

Teachers of creative writing say that one should not give away the point of a story before the conclusion lest readers be deprived of an opportunity to imagine. Qohelet pays no attention to that rule, and tells us right away that the "test of pleasure" the king undertakes will prove that pleasure ultimately is meaningless (2:1-2). Had he not done so, we might have held our breath until the dénouement in v. 11. Many of us see a familiar sight as the Teacher-king sets out determinedly to do all the things that pleasure-loving people, hedonists, even affluent upper-middle-class Americans have always done. He tries to find meaning and happiness in property, produce, wealth, and sex. Furthermore, he craftily brings the whole effort under the rubric of a work ethic. Because he can say, "I made . . . I bought . . . I gathered . . . I got," he rightly gets to enjoy the fruits of his labor (v. 10). What is wrong with that?

Even though we readers knew the enterprise was doomed from v. 2 onward, we may have hoped for the best and found ourselves unprepared for the total rejection of the entire search for pleasure as absurdity or vanity, chasing after wind, and more of the same old thing (v. 11). That message will not play well in Peoria; in fact, it may not even be entirely true. Human beings all over the world, from the poorest peasants of Sudan to the teeming masses on the Ganges to the affluent residents of penthouses in New York, all agree that food, drink, comfort, and intimacy are goals to be pursued and are likely to produce a measure of human happiness. The notion is not foreign to our religious tradition either. The Song of Songs is a canticle to bounty and sensual pleasure. Jesus did not scruple to enjoy himself thoroughly at the wedding in Cana, and he added further pleasure to the occasion by improving the water (John 2:1-11).

Underlying the pessimistic assessment by the Teacher in this passage is the view later to be articulated (2:24-26) that the capacity to enjoy life is a gift of God alone. Unless God has made that gift, he believes, the most relentless struggle for wealth and the satisfaction of sensual appetites will fail. That view raises the difficult question of the predetermination of all things (see Introduction; Reflections at 2:24-26); but it also enables us to put something of a positive spin on the passage before us. It requires not that we deny the love of human beings for pleasure, but that we place human pleasure in its proper context. Qohelet is not too far from the faith of Torah or Gospel when he teaches that happiness is not a product of our own concupiscence, but of the prevenient grace of God.

Ecclesiastes 2:12-23, Wisdom Is an Absurdity

NIV

¹²Then I turned my thoughts to consider wisdom,
and also madness and folly.
What more can the king's successor do
than what has already been done?
¹³I saw that wisdom is better than folly,
just as light is better than darkness.
¹⁴The wise man has eyes in his head,
while the fool walks in the darkness;
but I came to realize
that the same fate overtakes them both.

¹⁵Then I thought in my heart,

"The fate of the fool will overtake me also.
What then do I gain by being wise?"
I said in my heart,
"This too is meaningless."
¹⁶For the wise man, like the fool, will not be long
remembered;
in days to come both will be forgotten.
Like the fool, the wise man too must die!

¹⁷So I hated life, because the work that is done under the sun was grievous to me. All of it is meaningless, a chasing after the wind. ¹⁸I hated all the things I had toiled for under the sun, because I must leave them to the one who comes after me. ¹⁹And who knows whether he will be a wise man or a fool? Yet he will have control over all the work into which I have poured my effort and skill under the sun. This too is meaningless. ²⁰So my heart began to despair over all my toilsome labor under the sun. ²¹For a man may do his work with wisdom, knowledge and skill, and then he must leave all he owns to someone who has not worked for it. This too is meaningless and a great misfortune. ²²What does a man get for all the toil and anxious striving with which he labors under the sun? ²³All his days his work is pain and grief; even at night his mind does not rest. This too is meaningless.

NRSV

12So I turned to consider wisdom and madness and folly; for what can the one do who comes after the king? Only what has already been done. ¹³Then I saw that wisdom excels folly as light excels darkness.

¹⁴ The wise have eyes in their head,
but fools walk in darkness.

Yet I perceived that the same fate befalls all of them. ¹⁵Then I said to myself, "What happens to the fool will happen to me also; why then have I been so very wise?" And I said to myself that this also is vanity. ¹⁶For there is no enduring remembrance of the wise or of fools, seeing that in the days to come all will have been long forgotten. How can the wise die just like fools? ¹⁷So I hated life, because what is done under the sun was grievous to me; for all is vanity and a chasing after wind.ᵃ

18I hated all my toil in which I had toiled under the sun, seeing that I must leave it to those who come after me ¹⁹—and who knows whether they will be wise or foolish? Yet they will be master of all for which I toiled and used my wisdom under the sun. This also is vanity. ²⁰So I turned and gave my heart up to despair concerning all the toil of my labors under the sun, ²¹because sometimes one who has toiled with wisdom and knowledge and skill must leave all to be enjoyed by another who did not toil for it. This also is vanity and a great evil. ²²What do mortals get from all the toil and strain with which they toil under the sun? ²³For all their days are full of pain, and their work is a vexation; even at night their minds do not rest. This also is vanity.

ᵃOr *a feeding on wind.* See Hos 12.1

COMMENTARY

Running through this section, and marked by numerous uses of the slogans with which Qohelet structures his meditations on meaning and absur-dity, is the underlying theme of the common fatal destiny of all things. That common destiny, hate-ful death, keeps the rich entrepreneur awake at night, seething in anger at the prospect that some unknown knave may live to enjoy the windfall of his inheritance. Although wisdom must be valued (vv. 13-14), it does not bring peace and happiness to one who contemplates this fate. In fact, it is not even attainable (7:23-24).

2:12-13. The exact meaning of v. 12*b* is difficult to ascertain. The NIV specifically identifies the speaker as the successor to the Teacher-king, who finds that he cannot improve on what his predecessor has done. Gordis, who translates the passage, "Of what value is a man coming after the king, who can only repeat what he has already done?" is surely correct in saying, "Koheleth, in his assumed role of Solomon, wishes to assure the reader that he has experienced the ultimate in both wisdom and pleasure and that there is no need for anyone else to repeat the experiment."[50]

2:14-17. In v. 14, the Teacher swings to the other side again, affirming the enterprise of wisdom, saying it is superior to folly, and even offering a proverb that, by use of antithetical parallelism, gives the edge to the wise who "have eyes in their head." Fools are as good as blind, because they walk in darkness. This is, of course, conventional wisdom, and it is consistent with the general drift of the metaphors for "light" (wisdom, goodness, Torah) and "darkness" (folly, evil) in the sapiental literature. But with his dialectical "Yet . . ." (v. 14*b*), the Teacher swings back to negate the values of wisdom that he has just briefly affirmed.

At v. 14*b* the Teacher uses for the first time another of his favorite words, "fate" (see the section "The Vocabulary of Qohelet's Thought," 278-82, in the Introduction). Powerful, predetermined "fate" is perhaps the major component of his sense of absurdity. Once again the Teacher's meditations drive him to the encompassing "all." Death, the great leveler of all distinctions between wise people and fools, workers and drones, "befalls all of them."

2:18. Who is the one that will come after the Teacher? The Hebrew text of this verse reads literally, "I must leave it to the individual who will be after me." (Here is a case in which the NRSV, in its effort to eliminate generic pronouns, obscures the meaning. The verse is improperly

understood when one reads it as "I must leave it to those who come after me," because the Masoretic text speaks only of האדם (*hā ʾādām*), "the [individual] human being," but not of a whole class. The NIV gets it right.) If this verse intends to continue the literary fiction that Ecclesiastes is the work of "the son of David who is a king in Jerusalem," this could be an oblique reference to Rehoboam, the unfortunate successor of Solomon, who inherited only half of his father's kingdom. However, one of the manuscripts from the Cairo Geniza[51] eliminates the article, thereby making the rule a general one: "I must leave it to whoever comes after me." This scribe was probably correct in understanding that Qohelet intended to teach a universal truth—even a truism—here. What finally happens to one's worldly goods after one dies lies beyond the reach of the "dead hand" of the grave.

2:19. The question, "Who knows?" is rhetorical in Ecclesiastes (which uses the expression four of the ten times it occurs in the Bible). The expected answer is "No one!" No one can say whether the beneficiary of a bequest will prove to be wise or foolish. But it really does not matter. Qualified or not, the successor will "be master" (NRSV) or "have control" (NIV; the cognate verb in Arabic gives rise to the noun "sultan") over all of one's hard-earned wealth. That is why toil is absurd.

2:20-23. The absurdity of inheriting the property and wealth of another person without working for it is underscored in v. 21. Crenshaw remarks, "The sages' egocentric perspective stands out here, for there is no indication that the donor derives genuine pleasure from bestowing happiness on someone else."[52] Perhaps Qohelet is selfish, but realism is on his side. The illusion that the goods and properties for which one has labored so mightily are inalienable is stripped away by the realization of death. When that occurs, it is possible to despair, even if one fantasizes that one's legacy gives happiness to the heir and contributes to the common good. Literally translated,

---

50. Gordis, *Koheleth,* 211.

51. During the second half of the nineteenth century, a trove of Hebrew manuscripts, some as early as the eighth century CE, was extracted from a forgotten storeroom (*geniza*) in the ancient Karaite synagogue of Old Cairo. Variant readings in the biblical texts from Cairo are now incorporated in the critical apparatus of the standard *Biblia Hebraica Stuttgartensia.*

52. Crenshaw, *Ecclesiastes,* 88.

the Hebrew of v. 23 reads, "Even at night his heart will not lie down." Because the biblical writers have no interest in the brain and make no reference to it, the seat of all the emotions is always the heart. Such a heart is the mind of a person, and, as we all know, the mind can be restless and worried. Like the proverbial rich person who tosses and turns at night in anxiety over all there is to lose (see 5:12), Qohelet makes sleeplessness the rule for anyone contemplating the disposition of a life's accumulation.

REFLECTIONS

This section is so rich with theological and homiletical possibilities that any discussion of it must necessarily be selective. Only two issues are explored here: (1) Qohelet's universalism and the fool's paradise and (2) the painful cry of the truth seeker.

1. *An Unhappy Universalism.* In that he recognizes no exceptions to the fate of human beings, Qohelet is a genuine universalist. In 2:14b-17, he looks with clear vision and great pain on the fact that the attainment of wisdom offers no guarantee of an enduring name. Two centuries before Qohelet flourished, the Greek philosophers undertook a threefold quest for knowledge, virtue, and happiness. Often knowledge held pride of place. Socrates, for example, held the highest good to be knowledge of the self; from that knowledge flowed all the rest. For Qohelet, in contrast, knowledge brings the tragically clear vision of universal obliteration. These verses elaborate the theme that in later times Paul will use as a foil to christology: "For as all die in Adam, so all will be made alive in Christ" (1 Cor 15:22 NRSV). Even though the Teacher has access to only the gloomy first half of that antithesis, he is not willing to deny the truth that his wisdom has brought him to see. Neither virtue nor happiness flows from this truth, but he intends to face it squarely and unhesitatingly. Herman Melville, whose poem "A Spirit Appeared to Me" takes its cue from these verses, was more prepared to pretend:

A spirit appeared to me, and said
"Where now would you choose to dwell?
In the Paradise of the Fool,
Or in wise Solomon's hell?"
   Never he asked me twice:
   "Give me the Fool's Paradise."

2. *A Painful Cry: "I Hate Life."* For Qohelet, who had no notion of a meaningful afterlife, death leveled the distinction between the wise and the foolish. Are you wise? So what! Why bother? It will not make any difference at all in the end; death relativizes, even trivializes wisdom. Until resurrection makes its first appearances late in the Old Testament period (see Isa 26:19; Dan 12:1-3), the hope of ancient Israelites for any transcendence of death lay only in "enduring remembrance" (v. 16). The individual life would be extinguished at death, but the memory of good deeds and wise words would linger on. Now, however, the utter realist—no detached observer here, but an anguished victim—arises to say what everyone knew anyway: that memory is short and the monuments raised by wise people and fools alike do not long endure. Fate is not kind to some and hard on others; it is hard on everyone. Was he wrong? Here the realism of the Teacher emerges to clear away any self-delusion about our common destiny of death. Modern Jews and Christians usually deny his premise of no afterlife, but as far as what we leave behind here, the man was absolutely correct. All of us have to say, "I must leave it to those who will come after me—and who knows whether they will be wise or foolish?" (See vv. 18-19.)

So bitter is this pill of absurdity that the Teacher claims that he hates life altogether (v. 17). The cry is the most extreme in the entire book, yet it is not a choice of death over life (Deut

39:19). In fact, the claim is hard to accept at all, for this central character of the book has a mind so lively and zeal so apt to challenge every orthodoxy that mere contact with him quickens the spirit of his readers. Even in his extremity, Qohelet continues to prefer light over darkness (v. 13), which means "life lived without self-deception, without despair, life lived in full questioning awareness."[53]

53. Kenneth R. R. Gros Louis, "Ecclesiastes," in *Literary Interpretations of Biblical Narratives,* ed. K. R. R. Gros Louis et al. (Nashville: Abingdon, 1974) 280.

Ecclesiastes 2:24-26, Living Happily Pleases God

NIV

[24]A man can do nothing better than to eat and drink and find satisfaction in his work. This too, I see, is from the hand of God, [25]for without him, who can eat or find enjoyment? [26]To the man who pleases him, God gives wisdom, knowledge and happiness, but to the sinner he gives the task of gathering and storing up wealth to hand it over to the one who pleases God. This too is meaningless, a chasing after the wind.

NRSV

24There is nothing better for mortals than to eat and drink, and find enjoyment in their toil. This also, I saw, is from the hand of God; [25]for apart from him[a] who can eat or who can have enjoyment? [26]For to the one who pleases him God gives wisdom and knowledge and joy; but to the sinner he gives the work of gathering and heaping, only to give to one who pleases God. This also is vanity and a chasing after wind.[b]

[a]Gk Syr: Heb *apart from me*   [b]Or *a feeding on wind.* See Hos 12.1

COMMENTARY

In the desert of absurdity baking everywhere around him under the sun, Qohelet now discovers a small but important oasis. Verse 24 introduces one of the principal themes of Qohelet (see Introduction): the commendation of eating, drinking, and pleasure in life (reiterated in 3:13; 5:18; 8:15; 9:7). The conventional wisdom scheme of distributive justice that Qohelet may have taught his students and in which he seems also to have wished to place his trust animates v. 26: God rewards those who please God with "wisdom and knowledge and joy," and even with the fruits of the labors of sinners who end up turning their gains over to the righteous. The familiar refrain "This too is meaningless, a chasing after the wind" (NIV) with which the paragraph closes (v. 26b) may sum up the self-serving effort of the "sinner." The word is probably without moral connotation; the Hebrew word that the NIV and the NRSV translate as "sinner" (חוטא *ḥôṭe'*) can also mean "fool," "bungler"—i.e., someone antithetical to

wisdom (see 9:18). It might even mean simply an "unlucky" person. A fool misses the mark by denying God's will that human beings should enjoy life. An unlucky person discovers that in God's utter freedom, the fruits of that person's toil just may end up in the hands of a "lucky" person.[54] For the Teacher, one's moral purity never guarantees that one gets the goods.

Nevertheless, the possibility of enjoying life remains open. True, that enjoyment is subject to the limitations of discretion (cf. 7:26); furthermore, it is evanescent. In the end all roads lead to the grave. However, in this passage we encounter the counterpoint to the Teacher's great theme of absurdity. There is a small space in life that, though not large enough to accommodate an abiding monument of any kind, is nevertheless tolerable. One can enjoy simple things such as

54. H. L. Ginsberg, "The Structure and Contents of the Book of Koheleth," in *Wisdom in Israel and the Ancient Near East,* ed. Martin Noth and D. W. Thomas, VTSup 3 (Leiden: Brill, 1955) 139.

food, drink, and life itself. If, in fact, these pleasures are "from the hand of God" (v. 24) and cannot be enjoyed apart from God (v. 25, as amended on the basis of the ancient Greek and Syriac versions), then surely it is the duty of human beings to receive them gratefully and to enjoy them. Putting the best spin on vv. 24b-26 leads the interpreter to say that, according to Ecclesiastes, it is the will of God that we should enjoy our life, pitching our tents in an oasis of peace and happiness in the middle of a desert of absurdity. While pleasure may fall short of an absolute goal for human life, "it remains the only practical program for human existence."[55]

55. Gordis, *Koheleth,* 216.

REFLECTIONS

This unit opens with advice that sounds like an echo of the words of Qohelet's contemporary Greek philosopher Epicurus (341–270 BCE). However, it was not he who first taught "Eat, drink and be merry for tomorrow we die," but the Hebrew Bible itself. Perhaps Isaiah was quoting the ironic words of an already well-known drinking song when he pictured the endangered inhabitants of Jerusalem partying on the eve of the Day of the Lord, saying, "Let us eat and drink, for tomorrow we die" (Isa 22:13 NRSV). Wherever he may have gotten the slogan, he put the stamp of prophetic disapproval upon it. Paul did not think much of this attitude, either, when he quoted Isa 22:13 in order to dismiss the hopelessness of those who denied the resurrection of the dead (1 Cor 15:32). Jesus, too, criticized this attitude in his parable of the rich fool, who was a fool precisely because he did not take the last clause of the saying seriously and died that very night (Luke 12:19).

Qohelet provides a needed canonical counterpoint to this criticism of existential despair. As contemporary theologians, we can be gratified that he identifies food, drink, and enjoyment as gifts of God and anodynes for upcoming death. The problem for us may be the muted, but implicit, notion (made explicit in 5:19; 6:2) that one can enjoy one's present moment only if God elects one into the happy company of those who can do so. If not only the values of "wisdom and knowledge and joy" (v. 26) are gifts of God, but also the very ability to enjoy these gifts, then an atmosphere of utter determinism and predestination lingers around even this one hopeful motif of the book. If one cannot even choose to enjoy what is given, but is given that capacity, too, as a gift, then Gordis is perhaps overly optimistic in thinking that Qohelet wants a person to reach out and take the glass of wine and the loaf of bread from the festive table as a religious duty, a *mitzvah,* that one eagerly and happily embraces. How could one answer for a willingness to enjoy life if that very capacity of enjoyment is bestowed on only a few by God? In the larger canonical context, particularly in the wisdom literature, the capacity to enjoy the good things of life is mated with more individual moral responsibility in decision making. To take pleasure in life is a choice that lies within the reach of every individual (e.g., Ps 1:1-3; Prov 12:20; 21:15; Matt 5:3-12; see also Sir 1:12, a variant of which reopens the "gift of God" theme).

As is true of so many beloved slogans, this one has enjoyed a life of repetition and paraphrase. The third of the three terms in Qohelet's version of the saying is "enjoyment." That third term is the one that has been most volatile in the replays through literature. In Isa 22:13 and 1 Cor 15:32, the third term is "death": "Let us eat and drink, for tomorrow we die" (NRSV). In *Don Juan,* Byron turned it into "love": " 'Eat, drink, and love, what can the rest avail us?'/ So said the royal sage, Sardanapalus" (2.207).

Arthur Hugh Clough, in his poem "Easter Day," turns the third term into "play":

"Eat, drink, and play, and think that this is bliss.
There is no heaven but this;

> There is no hell
> Save earth, which serves the purpose doubly well."

The list goes on and on. The theme of imposing meaning on fading life through eating, drinking, and merriment is reiterated in our modern literature in many ways. Irving Berlin's popular song "Let's Face the Music and Dance" captures the sentiment as well as any:

> Before the fiddlers have fled,
> Before they ask us to pay the bill,
> And while we still have a chance,
> Let's face the music and dance!

If inexorable, divine predetermination is the notion guiding the mind of the Teacher, the strange conclusion of the passage makes more sense. A sinner is simply one whom God has chosen to regard as a sinner, and the appropriate spirit of the onlooker is bafflement! (For another angle on the issue raised by 2:24-26, see the Reflections at 9:7-10.)

ECCLESIASTES 3:1-15, REFLECTIONS ON THE MEANING OF TIME

NIV

3 There is a time for everything,
and a season for every activity under
heaven:

² a time to be born and a time to die,
a time to plant and a time to uproot,
³ a time to kill and a time to heal,
a time to tear down and a time to build,
⁴ a time to weep and a time to laugh,
a time to mourn and a time to dance,
⁵ a time to scatter stones and a time to gather
them,
a time to embrace and a time to refrain,
⁶ a time to search and a time to give up,
a time to keep and a time to throw away,
⁷ a time to tear and a time to mend,
a time to be silent and a time to speak,
⁸ a time to love and a time to hate,
a time for war and a time for peace.

⁹What does the worker gain from his toil? ¹⁰I have seen the burden God has laid on men. ¹¹He has made everything beautiful in its time. He has also set eternity in the hearts of men; yet they cannot fathom what God has done from beginning to end. ¹²I know that there is nothing better for men than to be happy and do good while they live. ¹³That everyone may eat and drink, and find satisfaction in all his toil—this is the gift of God.

NRSV

3 For everything there is a season, and a time
for every matter under heaven:

² a time to be born, and a time to die;
a time to plant, and a time to pluck up what
is planted;
³ a time to kill, and a time to heal;
a time to break down, and a time to build up;
⁴ a time to weep, and a time to laugh;
a time to mourn, and a time to dance;
⁵ a time to throw away stones, and a time to
gather stones together;
a time to embrace, and a time to refrain from
embracing;
⁶ a time to seek, and a time to lose;
a time to keep, and a time to throw away;
⁷ a time to tear, and a time to sew;
a time to keep silence, and a time to speak;
⁸ a time to love, and a time to hate;
a time for war, and a time for peace.

⁹What gain have the workers from their toil? ¹⁰I have seen the business that God has given to everyone to be busy with. ¹¹He has made everything suitable for its time; moreover he has put a sense of past and future into their minds, yet they cannot find out what God has done from the beginning to the end. ¹²I know that there is nothing better for them than to be happy and

[14]I know that everything God does will endure forever; nothing can be added to it and nothing taken from it. God does it so that men will revere him.

[15]Whatever is has already been,
    and what will be has been before;
    and God will call the past to account.[a]

[a]15 Or *God calls back the past*

enjoy themselves as long as they live; [13]moreover, it is God's gift that all should eat and drink and take pleasure in all their toil. [14]I know that whatever God does endures forever; nothing can be added to it, nor anything taken from it; God has done this, so that all should stand in awe before him. [15]That which is, already has been; that which is to be, already is; and God seeks out what has gone by.[a]

[a]Heb *what is pursued*

COMMENTARY

3:1-8. This is perhaps the best-known passage in Ecclesiastes, the beloved list of things for which there is a proper time. The topic of time was a favorite one with wisdom writers. In Sir 39:16-34, as also elsewhere in Qohelet (e.g., Eccl 3:14-15; 6:10), time marches strictly to God's command. But not here. In these verses, God plays no explicit role in setting the "seasons" and "times." In this passage, Qohelet does not say why things occur at their appropriate times. They just do. Only as he reflects further in the enigmatic ensuing prose passage (vv. 9-15) does the Teacher invoke God's role in the matter of time.

The distinctive style of the passage may indicate that Qohelet drew it from another source. The seven verses 2-8 contain fourteen antitheses,[56] encompassing twenty-eight experiences known to all human beings, all organized under the twofold synonymous heading, "For everything [phenomenon] there is a season, and a time for every matter under heaven" (v. 1). Like 1:3-11, this pericope is simply a list of empirical observations. Except for the bracketing words "be born . . . peace," the list offers no order of importance or any other evaluation at all other than the principle stated in the heading. None of these times and seasons is a pregnant, potential-filled καιρός *kairos*. The "times" are moments of human-scale appropriateness intricately interwoven with implicit cosmic orders. The first item on the list, "a time to be born, and a time to die" (v. 2), is clearly out of human

hands, but the rest involve human choices. The wise person's task evidently is to know when the right time has come and to move visibly with whatever invisible program there may be.

In v. 3, the reference to "a time to kill and a time to heal" seems to give society two ways to respond to individual transgression. The first is capital punishment; the second is the work of physicians and other kinds of helpers to improve the life of an ailing person. Since sickness was regarded as a punishment from God, some may have thought nothing should be done for the sinner/invalid. Qohelet, however, seems to affirm the right of physicians to intervene in the sequence of cause-and-effect and to heal when it is time to do so.

The medieval midrash *Qohelet Rabbah* interprets the reference to scattering and gathering stones (v. 5*a*) as a strict parallel to embracing (v. 5*b*)—i.e., both are metaphors for sexual relations. Given the fact that stichs *a* and *b* of each verse in the series are closely related to stichs *c* and *d* of each verse, this seems preferable to taking v. 5*a* as a reference to the preparation of a field of rocky Palestine for farming (see Isa 5:2).

Surely the teaching that there is "a time to keep, and a time to throw away" (v. 6*b*) intends to do more than simply warn "pack rats" to get serious about cleaning out the attic. In a broader sense, this antithesis suggests that both prudence and providence—that boundless outpouring of help to other people—are genuine human virtues. If v. 7*a* refers to the ancient Israelite mourning custom of rending garments (see Gen 37:29; 2

56. Cf. Sir 33:15, "Look at all the works of the Most High;/ they come in pairs, one the opposite of the other" (NRSV).

Sam 13:31), then v. 7*b* would authorize the family to sew the rips back up again when the mourning was over. Mourning customs could also explain the coupling of v. 7*ab* with v. 7*cd,* "a time to keep silence and a time to speak," for as Job 2:13 suggests, silence was appropriate in the presence of bereavement. If, on the other hand, the picture is of a sewing bee, even in that context silence might, from time to time, be golden. When Ben Sira thought about this subject, he too tied talk to time: "The wise remain silent until the right moment" (Sir 20:7 NRSV).

The culminating v. 8, which raises the human experiences of love and hate, war and peace, reverses the order in the final clause, putting peace in the position of a "punch line." Thus do peace and birth (v. 2*a*) bracket the entire list. By this simple device, their antitheses, death and war, are demoted to realities that, though both profound and universal, have neither the first nor the last word.

3:9-15. In the prose section, which follows the poem of vv. 1-8, the notions of the rhythm and rightness of time are pursued further. "What gain have the workers from their toil?" the Teacher asks in v. 9. His answer takes the form of religious truth claims about human endeavor. In 1:13, the "business" that God gave human beings to do is "unhappy" or even "evil." Not so in v. 10, because now Qohelet has supplied an important context for human striving: It all takes place within "suitable" (יפה *yāpeh*) time. God "has made everything suitable for [NIV, beautiful in] its time" (v. 11 NRSV) and has given human beings a sense of having a place in the stately unrolling of the universal ("everything"), predetermined providential plan of God. The good news is that the (presumably) good God has provided direction, even finality, to the course of history (vv. 14-15). The bad news is that people "cannot find out what God has done from the beginning to the end" (v. 11). Withholding this knowledge is within the sovereign authority of God. By refusing to show the trump cards of the future, God keeps humanity—who want to know good and evil (Gen 3:22), who want to have an unassailable name (Gen 11:4), who want to compete with God—in awe and submission. It goes without saying that what cannot be known by human beings also cannot be changed by them. Verse 11

is the very epitome of one of Qohelet's principal themes: the impossibility of knowing what is truly going on in the world (see the section "The Ideology of the Book of Ecclesiastes," 282-85, in the Introduction; see also Eccl 6:10-12; 7:14, 27-28).

Both the NRSV and the NIV take the much debated word העלם (*hā 'ōlām*) in v. 11 to refer to time (NRSV, "sense of past and future"; NIV, "eternity"; cf. Eccl 3:14). Taken this way, the picture is of human creatures endowed by God with a keen consciousness of the passage of time, yet not endowed with the capacity to make any sense of it. In Murphy's words, v. 11*b* "is a fantastic statement of divine sabotage."[57]

The other meaning of the word *hā 'ōlām,* "world," has been advocated in modern times by such scholars as Ewald, Voltz, H. L. Ginsberg, and Gordis. Although the latter meaning of the word is largely a development in post-biblical Hebrew (see Sir 3:18; *M. 'Abot* 4:17), Ecclesiastes uses a number of other words of which the same could be said. For Gordis, this meaning yields a teaching that reinforces his proposal that enjoyment of life is at the heart of the message of the book: "He has also placed the love of the world in men's hearts, except that they may not discover the work God has done from beginning to end."[58] Scott relates the term back to the root sense of "that which is obscure, hidden," and translates, "Yet he has put in their minds an enigma."[59] Whitley suggests "ignorance."[60]

In favor of viewing *hā 'ōlām* as "eternity" (NIV) are the facts that this is the usual meaning of the noun in the Hebrew Bible and that the context establishes "time" (v. 11*a*) as the subject under discussion. The problem is to arrive at the exact nuance of time in this sentence. "Eternity" can be misleading, too, if a reader thinks of immortality or the spiritual contemplation of divine timelessness rather than history in its most inclusive sense. The paraphrase of the NRSV suggests frustration with the One who fixed the times of all things and gave humankind a sense of that reality,

57. Roland E. Murphy, *Ecclesiastes,* WBC 23A (Waco, Tex.: Word, 1992) 39.

58. Robert Gordis, *Koheleth: The Man and His World,* 1st ed. (New York: Schocken, 1951; 3rd ed., 1968) 146.

59. R. B. Y. Scott, *Proverbs, Ecclesiastes,* AB 18 (Garden City, N.Y.: Doubleday, 1965) 220.

60. C. F. Whitley, *Koheleth: His Language and Thought,* BZAW 148 (Berlin: de Gruyter, 1979) 31-33.

yet who withheld the timetable from those who might otherwise have understood it. Faced with this problem, Rankin argues for a revocalization of *hā ʿōlām* to העלם (*hā ʿelem*), "forgetfulness." The sense, then, would be that although God made everything excellent in its time, God also burdened people with "the inability to remember and record all the generations of human history," thereby depriving them of the means of making history comprehensible.[61]

Within the awful incomprehensibility of the big

picture (v. 14), however, God has made a "gift" of the possibility of human happiness. It is a gift made to "all" (כל *kōl*, v. 13)—a teaching that omits the deterministic reservation voiced in 5:19 and 6:12 that God "enables" only some to enjoy life. As Gordis has pointed out, Qohelet teaches that "joy is God's great commandment for man."[62] Verses 2-13, therefore, are ethical teachings. When the Teacher says, "Be happy and enjoy . . . eat and drink and take pleasure in . . . toil" (vv. 12-13; see 2:24), he means that to accept God's gift of life is to be obedient to the will of God.

61. O. S. Rankin and G. G. Atkins, "The Book of Ecclesiastes," in *The Interpreter's Bible,* 12 vols., ed. George A. Buttrick et al. (Nashville: Abingdon, 1956) 5:48-49.

62. Gordis, *Koheleth,* 118.

REFLECTIONS

In 3:1-8, the Teacher does not describe the inexorable cycling of times as another absurdity, nor does he frame it with despair. On the contrary, he endorses it. Time is not out of joint: "For everything there is a season." Here at last he finds solidity and dependability. It is good that there is order in life. It is good that there is a time to die that stands over and against the time of birth, for to have it any other way would be to admit that there is no order at all but only arbitrary and erratic events. In 3:1-8, the Teacher is able to affirm that the polarities within which life must be lived are both discernible and secure.

One can wax enthusiastic about the moral possibilities of some of the items on Qohelet's list of things for which there is a proper time. For example, that there is "a time to keep, and a time to throw away" (v. 16) invokes the two virtues of prudence and providence. It is good to know that the cosmic orders provide a place for saving against a future rainy day (even ants do it! see Prov 30:25). Qohelet seems to open the door to prudential moral behavior.

There is also a time to throw away. Now, the virtue we call generosity is about throwing away, about the unstinting pouring out of good things on those around about. We call God's generosity "providence"; the Bible also knows that human behavior can be providential. The idea reaches a keen point in Jesus' difficult teaching "Be perfect, therefore, as your heavenly Father is perfect" (Matt 5:48 NRSV). Taken by itself, that verse has served some people as a disastrous invitation to excessive scrupling and perfectionism. But taken in context, it is clear that the God-like perfection (i.e., "reaching the mark") that Jesus advocates is in human giving, "throwing away." The context of the saying in the Sermon on the Mount reads, "[God] makes his sun rise on the evil and on the good, and sends rain on the righteous and on the unrighteous. For if you love those who love you, what reward do you have? Do not even the tax collectors do the same?" (Matt 5:45-46 NRSV). For the Gospel writer, perfection consists in being like God in pouring out providential generosity onto others. In teaching that there is a time for divestiture, Qohelet, too, opens the door to providential moral behavior.

Similar discussions can be advanced about the other antitheses of the poem, as if they invited the individual to be sensitive to appropriate times for action and then to act, morally, perhaps decisively, to kill, to heal, to keep silence, to speak, to love, to hate, to make war, and to make peace. However, if we read this list through the lens of predetermination, as vv. 9-15 suggest we do, a number of things change radically. First of all, there can be no quarrel with any members of the list, such as hate and war. If everything occurs on the God-given schedule, then this list cannot be weeded. Second, there is little real possibility of moral action. If a time to make love is not a matter of a conscious human choice to act appropriately, but merely a matter of a timetable set forth in advance by God for organisms or even for human individuals, then there can be no question of moral agency in the lovemaking, but simply answering responses to the call of the hormones. All of the earlier remarks about perfection in giving (v. 6*b*) become simply nonsense. There simply comes a time to throw stuff away, no doubt because of the approach of death.

Commentators and preachers alike have generally not wanted to consign the beautiful poem of 3:1-8 into the grim jaws of necessity, and they have warrant. The uniqueness of its style and its logical coherence invite attention to this pericope in its own terms. Even if only for heuristic reasons, much can be gained by reading it independently of context—at least of vv. 9-15—and thereby seeing it in a different light from that given it through the (tinted) lens of predetermination. If one reads the poem with the understanding that the fixed orders provide structure rather than calendar, then individual human moral decision making is possible. One can then hear in this poem a challenge to be wise, to be ethical, to discern when one's actions are in keeping with God's time and then to act decisively.

Reading vv. 1-8 through a positive lens focuses on the grace inherent in the periodic structure of life. What would the gift of life be, for example, without the concomitant gift of death (v. 2)? Without the knowledge of death, life would lose its urgency and savor. Without death no poetry would be written, no music composed, no monuments raised, no children begotten. This is not to say that people actually welcome death, except those in the most dire states of emotional and physical distress. Nevertheless, a healthy acknowledgment that "there is a time to die" leads people "to improve each shining hour." In that sense, even if taken as a list of grim necessities, Qohelet's hymn serves as a gift of truth. And truth is grace!

A predestinarian rereading of the poem of 3:1-8 does seem to occur in the prose context in which the poem is now placed within the book of Ecclesiastes. For example, v. 15 situates life squarely in the middle of an endlessly repetitive and rigid scheme that cancels any intention by vv. 1-8 to make place for human free will: "That which is, already has been; that which is to be, already is." No innovation or creativity seems to be possible under those rules! Yet, the Teacher maintains a slight ambivalence even in this passage. The key to this chink in the armor of predisposition is the declaration "it is God's gift that *all* should eat and drink and take pleasure in all their toil" (v. 13, italics added). Not only is this option available to *all,* as opposed to only those who have been specially enabled for the task of enjoyment (contra 5:19; 6:2), but also it seems to be phrased in terms of a choice. If there is a choice, there is also the possibility of moral behavior. If there is a choice, then the Teacher's student can be as happy and as wise as the Teacher, if the student chooses gratefully to accept the small daily pleasures of life as gifts of God.

The tension between a radical predisposition of all things into an inexorable sequence of times and seasons, on the one hand, and, on the other hand, a small but secure place for human choice has troubled adherents of Islam—that most predestinarian of the Western religions. The tension is exemplified in the seventy-third stanza of the *Rubáiyát of Omar Khayyám:*

> With Earth's first Clay
> They did the Last Man knead,
> And there of the Last Harvest sow'd the Seed:
> And the first Morning of Creation wrote
> What the Last Dawn of Reckoning shall read.

In this view, nothing happens that was not already determined on the day of creation. That cannot easily be squared with any human initiative in happiness. What a way to make a world!

Omar's sad yearning to reorganize the world along very different lines, expressed in his 99th stanza, might have struck a chord of response in Qohelet, too:

Ah Love! could you and I with Him conspire
To grasp this sorry Scheme of Things entire,
Would not we shatter it to bits—and then
Re-mould it nearer to the Heart's Desire!

ECCLESIASTES 3:16–4:8, REFLECTIONS ON JUSTICE AND DEATH

NIV

[16]And I saw something else under the sun:

In the place of judgment—wickedness was
    there,
  in the place of justice—wickedness was there.

[17]I thought in my heart,

"God will bring to judgment
  both the righteous and the wicked,
for there will be a time for every activity,
  a time for every deed."

[18]I also thought, "As for men, God tests them so that they may see that they are like the animals. [19]Man's fate is like that of the animals; the same fate awaits them both: As one dies, so dies the other. All have the same breath[a]; man has no advantage over the animal. Everything is meaningless. [20]All go to the same place; all come from dust, and to dust all return. [21]Who knows if the spirit of man rises upward and if the spirit of the animal[b] goes down into the earth?"

[22]So I saw that there is nothing better for a man than to enjoy his work, because that is his lot. For who can bring him to see what will happen after him?

4 Again I looked and saw all the oppression that was taking place under the sun:
I saw the tears of the oppressed—
  and they have no comforter;
power was on the side of their oppressors—
  and they have no comforter.
[2]And I declared that the dead,
  who had already died,

a19 Or spirit b21 Or Who knows the spirit of man, which rises upward, or the spirit of the animal, which

NRSV

[16]Moreover I saw under the sun that in the place of justice, wickedness was there, and in the place of righteousness, wickedness was there as well. [17]I said in my heart, God will judge the righteous and the wicked, for he has appointed a time for every matter, and for every work. [18]I said in my heart with regard to human beings that God is testing them to show that they are but animals. [19]For the fate of humans and the fate of animals is the same; as one dies, so dies the other. They all have the same breath, and humans have no advantage over the animals; for all is vanity. [20]All go to one place; all are from the dust, and all turn to dust again. [21]Who knows whether the human spirit goes upward and the spirit of animals goes downward to the earth? [22]So I saw that there is nothing better than that all should enjoy their work, for that is their lot; who can bring them to see what will be after them?

4 Again I saw all the oppressions that are practiced under the sun. Look, the tears of the oppressed—with no one to comfort them! On the side of their oppressors there was power— with no one to comfort them. [2]And I thought the dead, who have already died, more fortunate than the living, who are still alive; [3]but better than both is the one who has not yet been, and has not seen the evil deeds that are done under the sun.

[4]Then I saw that all toil and all skill in work come from one person's envy of another. This also is vanity and a chasing after wind.[a]

[5] Fools fold their hands
  and consume their own flesh.

aOr a feeding on wind. See Hos 12.1

NIV

are happier than the living,
who are still alive.
³But better than both
is he who has not yet been,
who has not seen the evil
that is done under the sun.

⁴And I saw that all labor and all achievement spring from man's envy of his neighbor. This too is meaningless, a chasing after the wind.

⁵The fool folds his hands
and ruins himself.
⁶Better one handful with tranquillity
than two handfuls with toil
and chasing after the wind.

⁷Again I saw something meaningless under the sun:

⁸There was a man all alone;
he had neither son nor brother.
There was no end to his toil,
yet his eyes were not content with his wealth.
"For whom am I toiling," he asked,
"and why am I depriving myself of
enjoyment?"
This too is meaningless—
a miserable business!

NRSV

⁶ Better is a handful with quiet
than two handfuls with toil,
and a chasing after wind.ᵃ
7Again, I saw vanity under the sun: ⁸the case of solitary individuals, without sons or brothers; yet there is no end to all their toil, and their eyes are never satisfied with riches. "For whom am I toiling," they ask, "and depriving myself of pleasure?" This also is vanity and an unhappy business.

ᵃOr *a feeding on wind.* See Hos 12.1

COMMENTARY

The Teacher has new shocks in store in 3:16–4:8. He has come to see that the conventional law of retribution, *jus talionis,* in which his contemporaries believed and perhaps he taught his students, is not operative. How could it be, if everything is predetermined? On the other hand, he seems unwilling to charge God with being tolerant of evil.

3:16-22. Qohelet ferrets out the answer to the absurdity stated in v. 16 through the device of a dialogue with himself, punctuated by the formula "I said in my heart" (NRSV) or simply "I thought" (NIV). Prior even to these clichés is the formula "I saw," which unifies the entire pericope (see also 3:22; 4:1, 4, 7). At first he relates the issue back to the theme of appropriate times (v. 17*a*; cf. 3:1), with this nuance: At the time God appointed for it, God will judge the righteous and the wicked. This will not

occur, of course, in an afterlife of bliss or torment, but here in this world. Nevertheless, it may not happen right away. In fact, on a day-to-day basis, neither justice nor righteousness, but wickedness prevails. So much for the standard theodicy!

The insight of vv. 18-19 may not be very original, but it is profound, perhaps in more ways than Qohelet himself understood. The mysterious origins of life's experiences lie in God, who uses them to "test" humankind. The sense moves from testing as "proving" (as in "proving ground") to testing as "proving to"—driving people to the conclusion that they belong to the realm of beasts. Death, the common fate that animals and human beings share, is the final proof of this: "as one dies, so dies the other." In Qohelet's view, this lack of advantage of human beings is "absurd"

310

(הבל *hebel*). We who stand near the place of angels (Ps 8:5) and who have been invited into the council of heaven (1 Kgs 22:19-23) must all "turn to dust again" (see Gen 3:19; Job 10:9; Ps 104:29; Sir 40:11). In vv. 20-21, echoes of the Yahwistic creation story in Genesis are present. Qohelet assumes that the רוח (*rûaḥ*, "wind," "breath," "spirit") that God breathed into the original terracotta humanoid (Gen 2:7) is the animating principle of all living creatures and can be withdrawn by God from one species just as well as another (see Ps 104:27-30).

Upon the lowly but omnipresent word "all" (כל *kōl*, vv. 19-20; see Introduction) rides Qohelet's universal vision. There are no exceptions to this rule of death. In v. 21 the Teacher pleads ignorance on the question of the ultimate destiny of the human spirit. The discussion is introduced by a second use of the formula "Who knows?" (see 2:19; 6:12; 8:1). The question is not exactly rhetorical; that is, it does not seem to anticipate a particular answer. In fact, the formula is often invoked in the Hebrew Bible precisely when the question is to be left totally open-ended (see 2 Sam 12:22; Joel 2:14; Jonah 3:9). When the pupil asks, "Is there life beyond death?" the Teacher answers, "Who knows?"

The ancients believed that at death everything returns to its source. Consistent with that model, in 12:7 Qohelet distinguishes between the dust that descends to the ground from whence it came and the "breath" that arises to God, from whom it came (see Gen 2:7). However, the question of the continued existence of the creature that can live only because it is a *combination* of dust and life-breath is left totally unanswered. The logic of the Teacher's argument is to forge a solidarity in death between animals and human beings. There is no discernible reason why the "breath" of the former should behave differently at death than would that of the latter. The Hebrew underworld, Sheol, is not the source of the animal spirit, and there is no reason why it should descend thither after death in antithesis to the upward, "heavenly" movement alleged for the human spirit (v. 21).[63] Chances are good that the same fate awaits us all.

Contemplation of ultimate destiny or fate is of no comfort to Ecclesiastes, so he reverts to the comfort already set forth in 3:9-15: Happiness in their doings is the lot of human beings. That is not bad; it is a gift of God (v. 13). However, it is possible only when human beings accept the premise that they cannot know what lies ahead (v. 22*b*). The question, "Who can bring them to see what will be after them?" is, of course, a rhetorical one. The answer is, No one! For Qohelet the high probability exists that there is nothing after death. However, he refuses to speculate beyond that and instead carves out for human effort a little island of happiness in the midst of a sea of unknowability and, finally, nonexistence.

4:1-8. Qohelet continues his dialogue with himself by further meditations (vv. 1-3) on the intertwined themes of death and justice, introduced by the unifying formula "I saw." Oppressed people find no comfort from any quarter. Job, too, longed for an advocate, and even dared hope for a divine one (Job 9:33; cf. Job 16:18-22; 19:25-27). Qohelet holds out no such hope. In vv. 2-3, the Teacher returns to the theme of death. He divides all people into three categories according to an ascending order of happiness: those who are now living, those who have died, and those who were never born. The latter are happiest of all because they never have to see the horrors that occur in human history (see 7:1; Job 3:11-19; Jer 20:14-18). Therefore, nonexistence is preferable to existence, though the Teacher does not advocate suicide.

The Teacher's high estimation of the power of "envy" (קנאה *qin'â*, v. 4) to drive the engines of competition ought to gladden the hearts of capitalists everywhere. It does not gladden his heart, however, for in his judgment this is an absurd way to make a living. The NRSV's literal translation of the traditional saying of v. 5 leads one to contemplate self-cannibalism (the language is a figure of oppression in Isa 49:26; Mic 3:2-3), though no doubt it describes the fool who will not work, therefore cannot eat, and so destroys himself (see Prov 6:10-11; 19:15). This teaching seems to contradict the doubts about economic

---

63. Rankin points out that this is the first reference in the Hebrew Bible or any other Jewish source to "immortality"—i.e., the direct ascent of the human "breath" to God without resurrection or at least an interim state in Sheol. See O. S. Rankin and G. G. Atkins, "The Book of Ecclesiastes," in *The Interpreter's Bible,* 12 vols., ed. George A. Buttrick et al. (Nashville: Abingdon, 1956) 5:52. The notion was present in Mesopotamian astral

religion as well as in Greek thought, and it may have reached Israel from the east. In any case, Qohelet reports the view only to reject it. The reference in 12:7, too, does not suggest a life after death for the individual, but only the reclamation by God of the "life-breath" that had belonged to God in the first place.

drive in v. 4, insofar as the person who takes it easy is judged to be a fool. It connects better with the proverb in v. 6, which advocates modesty in consumption (see Prov 15:16-17; 16:8; 17:1). With whom is the Teacher more sympathetic, then, the workaholic or the skinny fool? Or is v. 6 his mediating position? Gordis discerns here another unattributed quotation that serves as an opponent to be refuted. He thinks that v. 5 should be introduced with "Some say" and v. 6 with "But I say."[64] Murphy, in contrast, thinks both sayings may be traditional and, in Qohelet's opinion, valueless.[65]

The case of the lonely person whose lust for riches is never satisfied and who never simply enjoys life (v. 8) leads to the plaintive question, "For whom am I toiling?" (On "toil" see Introduction.) Reflecting on a similar situation, Ben Sira remarks, "If one is mean to himself, to whom will he be generous?" (Sir 14:5 NRSV). Crenshaw, who accused the sage of selfishness in his account of the royal experiment (2:1-11), remarks that here "sapiental . . . egocentrism weakens appreciably."[66]

64. Gordis, *Koheleth,* 231.
65. Roland E. Murphy, *Ecclesiastes,* WBC 23A (Waco, Tex.: Word, 1992) 39.

66. James L. Crenshaw, *Ecclesiastes,* OTL (Philadelphia: Westminster, 1987) 51.

REFLECTIONS

This interesting passage provokes reflection on four of the Teacher's themes that continue to resonate in our lives: (1) the hatefulness of life; (2) our solidarity with the animals in death; (3) the ethics of envy; (4) the human need for a cause.

1. *The Hatefulness of Life.* How the mournful tenor of this pericope is supposed to square with Qohelet's recommendation to "eat and drink and take pleasure in all their toil" (e.g., 3:13) can only be guessed at. Perhaps he would simply have had his angst-ridden readers laugh in the face of onrushing doom. True, the attitude squares with the hatred of life the Teacher voiced in 2:17—a hatred that arose from the absurd fact that the righteous suffer oppression and justice seems blind. The orthodox faith he has abandoned would not have had it so. But it is so, and it is hateful. At the same time, this writer takes care, even delight, in exploring from all sides the meaning of life, and he does so with sustained energy. He does not behave as one who feels, like Macduff in Macbeth, that he should have been "from his mother's womb/ Untimely ripp'd"; he is more like his own model figures who "take pleasure in all their toil" (3:13). Besides, as he will later observe, "a living dog is better than a dead lion" (9:4 NRSV). For anyone today who seeks theological guidance from the Teacher, it is fortunate that the latter observation may be as close to his last word on the subject as this one is. After all, the view that it would have been better to never have been born is antithetical to most other biblical teaching. Modern theology, too, which often makes existence or being itself its central value, would cry out against a preference never to have been born. From Tillich's point of view, for example, because being is rooted in God the very Ground of Being, it stands in ontological opposition to the most profound antivalue, which is nonbeing.

2. *Our Solidarity with the Animals in Death.* Qohelet's expansion on his hatred of life is doubly interesting because it is articulated by a declaration of solidarity in death with all living things (3:19). He was right in making this identification, of course. He simply did not go far enough in talking about the commonalities that we share with the animal kingdom. We know now that we are made of the same stardust—carbon, oxygen, nitrogen—that makes up the cells of all living things and that our genetic makeup differs very little from that of the great apes. But even in the third century BCE, Qohelet knew that the gulf that continues to separate humankind from God is a great one in spite of human efforts to bridge it (Genesis 3). He knew that that gulf is far greater than the one that separates humankind from baboons and shrews. Qohelet's remark that all are driven by the brutal fact of death means that the world does not take moral sides, and we can no more manipulate our fate with virtue or with wickedness than can the animals.

In short, modern Jews and Christians have much to agree with in Qohelet's exclamation in 3:19 that the fate of all animals is the same. Our dispute with him comes more in relation to the following v. 20, in which he says, "All go to one place; all are from the dust, and all turn to dust again." Physically, of course, he is correct, but he means also to deny the possibility of any existence beyond physical death. In his own time, the dawn of the alternative doctrine of resurrection was at hand (Isa 26:19 probably predates him slightly, and Dan 12:2 follows not long after). The alien doctrine of blessed immortality had also begun to find acceptance in Judaism. At about 100 BCE, the writer of the book of Wisdom quoted a remarkably Qohelet-like opponent as saying:

> For our allotted time is the passing of a shadow,
> and there is no return from our death,
> because it is sealed up and no one turns back.
> Come, therefore, let us enjoy the good things that exist. (Wis 2:5-6 NRSV)

His answer to this opponent is clear: "God created us for incorruption, and made us in the image of his own eternity" (v. 23 NRSV). For Christians, the resurrection of Jesus of Nazareth tips the scale definitively away from blessed immortality and toward resurrection faith in the renewal of all things at the day of God's victory over death and evil (1 Cor 15:20-28).

Do we have an argument with 3:21-22? Does the human spirit go upward and the spirits of animals go downward at death or at a general resurrection? That is a fascinating question that remains surprisingly open in twentieth-century theology. A Tillichian approach, for example, assumes that anything that has being is finally reunited with the source of all being and that God wastes nothing. That would include animals, too, though the details remain sketchy.

3. *The Ethics of Envy.* Perhaps the Teacher intended to be cynical in attributing all effort and accomplishment to envy (4:4). Then again, perhaps he had grabbed human nature by the same lapel that Adam Smith and other capitalists seized it by in later times—competition (= envy) drives the engines of commerce. One wonders, however, how this insight fits with the conviction expressed in 3:11 that everything is predetermined. If time and chance are absolutely neutral, if the world is driven on by destiny, and if meaningful moral choice, therefore, is impossible, then a decision to push ahead of others in moneymaking because the time is right would be based on illusion. To compete out of envy is an ethical choice. It may be a perverse ethic, but it is a choice. It is a choice that is consistent with the kinds of energy that, released by the knowledge that death is inevitable, give rise to such human activities as empire building and childbearing, which seem to offer a way of transcending the inevitability of death (see Reflections at 3:1-8).

In short, Qohelet is inconsistent in his remarks about work that imply choices—even bad ones. Readers sometimes fault Qohelet for being inconsistent; some even postulate an editor who inserted occasional glosses to correct some of the Teacher's more egregious unorthodoxies. Perhaps the most we can say about the dissonant teachings of the book is to suggest that, as an assembler of proverbs (12:9), Qohelet was aware that the folk had spoken about the same subject in quite different ways on separate occasions. Perhaps he was ambivalent himself and could see both sides of such an issue as competition versus cooperation.

Actually, it is remarkable that so many contradictory thoughts about the same subject can have the ring of truth. On the one hand, it strikes the reader as true that we live in a web of fixed orders (3:1-8) and that, at the same time, we can make choices that are good and bad. It strikes one as true that people are urged on to toil and skill because they fear death and because they envy their neighbors. By nature, truth is multifaceted.

Modern literature explores this fact frequently, perhaps nowhere more successfully than in Akira Kurosawa's 1951 film *Rashomon.* In that film a murder in a forest is viewed from the perspectives of the victim, the murderer, and others. In the end, the viewer, who witnessed the original crime, is no longer sure what really happened because the same set of facts takes on different contours depending on who tells the story. Most of the things that Qohelet is saying about life are true, and a preacher ought not to ignore the fact, even though the same realities viewed from a post-resurrection perspective can be described in other ways.

4. *The Human Need for a Cause.* The delightful story in 4:7-8 tells about the lonely childless person who, like Ebenezer Scrooge after Marley's ghost had finished with him, asks, "Why am I joylessly struggling to acquire goods and property that I have nowhere to put in the end?" (His case is almost worse than that of the person who has to leave it all to some fool [2:19]!) None of us can prove that the deferred gratification that we practice now will have some payoff in the years ahead or in the world to come.

To be set alongside Qohelet's insight, however, is the equally important biblical realization that human beings require a cause, something bigger than themselves, in order to live happily and effectively. Both creation accounts in Genesis establish this as an ontological reality. In the J account (Gen 2:4*b*-25), there can be no plant of the field, no agriculture, no husbandry, until there is a human being. God plants the garden of Eden only after God creates Adam to be its farmer and keeper. Human beings are created with a vocation, and that vocation is essential to the larger cause of earth-keeping. The Priestly writer, too, recognized that human beings have a vocation from the very moment of their creation. Probably the best translation of Gen 1:26 is "Then God said, 'Let us make humankind in our image, according to our likeness, so that they may have dominion over the fish of the sea' " (NRSV). In other words, God's image in humankind is to be expressed in God-like, loving rule in the earth on God's behalf. This is our human vocation.

This biblically acknowledged need for a cause that is bigger than the self is confirmed by modern social science. Psychiatrist Robert Jay Lifton, for example, identifies a capacity toward resiliency and self-transformation present in all of us that enables us to survive personal and cultural traumas and to connect ourselves with the rest of humankind.[67] By effecting change in our self-preoccupation, we can join in community in working to end warfare, to enhance ecological safety, in short, to ensure human survival. This is our human vocation.

Put the insight of Genesis alongside that of the Teacher, and you have valid and useful doctrine. To put everything off to some future time while spending the present enslaved to moneymaking is foolish. Just say no to that! On the other hand, it is also true that we want to feel that our lives contribute to a larger good. Perhaps within the Teacher's doctrine of times and seasons there is a place for this truth, too, especially if moral choice survives within his scheme (3:6):

> There is a time to seek [one's self-interest] and a time to lose [one's life in the vigorous pursuit of a cause].

---

67. Robert Jay Lifton, *The Protean Self: Human Resilience in an Age of Fragmentation* (New York: Basic Books, 1993).

ECCLESIASTES 4:9–6:12, APHORISMS

Ecclesiastes 4:9–5:7, On Competition, Cooperation, and Vows

NIV

9Two are better than one,
  because they have a good return for their
    work:
10If one falls down,
  his friend can help him up.
But pity the man who falls
  and has no one to help him up!
11Also, if two lie down together, they will keep
    warm.
But how can one keep warm alone?
12Though one may be overpowered,
  two can defend themselves.
A cord of three strands is not quickly broken.

13Better a poor but wise youth than an old but foolish king who no longer knows how to take warning. 14The youth may have come from prison to the kingship, or he may have been born in poverty within his kingdom. 15I saw that all who lived and walked under the sun followed the youth, the king's successor. 16There was no end to all the people who were before them. But those who came later were not pleased with the successor. This too is meaningless, a chasing after the wind.

5 Guard your steps when you go to the house of God. Go near to listen rather than to offer the sacrifice of fools, who do not know that they do wrong.

2Do not be quick with your mouth,
  do not be hasty in your heart
  to utter anything before God.
God is in heaven
  and you are on earth,
  so let your words be few.
3As a dream comes when there are many cares,
  so the speech of a fool when there are many
    words.

4When you make a vow to God, do not delay in fulfilling it. He has no pleasure in fools; fulfill your vow. 5It is better not to vow than to make a vow and not fulfill it. 6Do not let your mouth lead you into sin. And do not protest to the

NRSV

9Two are better than one, because they have a good reward for their toil. 10For if they fall, one will lift up the other; but woe to one who is alone and falls and does not have another to help. 11Again, if two lie together, they keep warm; but how can one keep warm alone? 12And though one might prevail against another, two will withstand one. A threefold cord is not quickly broken.

13Better is a poor but wise youth than an old but foolish king, who will no longer take advice. 14One can indeed come out of prison to reign, even though born poor in the kingdom. 15I saw all the living who, moving about under the sun, follow that[a] youth who replaced the king;[b] 16there was no end to all those people whom he led. Yet those who come later will not rejoice in him. Surely this also is vanity and a chasing after wind.[c]

5[d] Guard your steps when you go to the house of God; to draw near to listen is better than the sacrifice offered by fools; for they do not know how to keep from doing evil.[e] 2[f]Never be rash with your mouth, nor let your heart be quick to utter a word before God, for God is in heaven, and you upon earth; therefore let your words be few.

3For dreams come with many cares, and a fool's voice with many words.

4When you make a vow to God, do not delay fulfilling it; for he has no pleasure in fools. Fulfill what you vow. 5It is better that you should not vow than that you should vow and not fulfill it. 6Do not let your mouth lead you into sin, and do not say before the messenger that it was a mistake; why should God be angry at your words, and destroy the work of your hands?

7With many dreams come vanities and a multitude of words;[g] but fear God.

aHeb the second bHeb him cOr a feeding on wind. See Hos 12.1 dCh 4.17 in Heb eCn: Heb they do not know how to do evil fCh 5.1 in Heb gMeaning of Heb uncertain

NIV

⌊temple⌋ messenger, "My vow was a mistake." Why should God be angry at what you say and destroy the work of your hands? 7Much dreaming and many words are meaningless. Therefore stand in awe of God.

COMMENTARY

4:9-16. This passage opens with pairs of people. Here are explored the virtues of companionship—perhaps even marriage—and teamwork. The imagery of vv. 10-12 suggests travel, though the "falling" of v. 10 may be metaphorical for "failing." The shift from ordinary narrative description to the metaphor of the three-stranded cord suggests that at least v. 12*b* is another popular proverb. If by cooperating two persons can ensure their mutual safety, three would offer even greater security. (If the bed in v. 11 in which the two snuggle to keep warm is a marriage bed, perhaps the third strand in v. 12 is a child.) Altogether, these three verses offer a positive alternative to the envy-driven rivalry declared absurd in 4:4.

Verses 13-16 also focus on two persons: a wise youth juxtaposed to a foolish king. (As the NRSV notes indicate, the Hebrew text seems to include both a first and a second successor to the original king.) The Joseph-like jail-to-throne motif of these verses is enhanced in the NRSV by considerable emendation of the obscure Hebrew text. The result fits the context, however. The fame and power based on popular acclaim is evanescent. The "doubting syndrome" of the Teacher reasserts itself when he points out that even the success of the youth who replaced the king is of limited duration and that hopes for generations yet to come to continue to grant him enduring praise are merely "chasing after wind." So much for the enduring legacy of Joseph, wise vizier to the pharaoh!

5:1-7. The last verse of chap. 4 in the Hebrew text is 5:1 in the English translations. The latter division makes sense, however, because the subject of 5:1-7 is coherent—all the aphorisms have to do with the vanity of speech. A literal translation of the beginning of 5:1 could be, "Watch

your step when you go to the house of God" (lit., "the god"). In the presence of God (presumably in the Temple), sincere listening is more pleasing to God than the sacrificial gestures of "fools." (Note that the condemnation of fools in v. 1*b* results from an emendation of the Hebrew text, which literally reads, "They do not know how to do evil." Murphy offers a helpful alternative: "They have no knowledge of doing evil.")[68] We do not know to what kind of preaching or instruction the contemporaries of the author of Ecclesiastes had the opportunity to listen in their temple environment, but evidently discourse was available for those who had ears to hear. Perhaps chanting of psalms and recitation of weekly portions of the Torah were what Qohelet had in mind. Even though his book makes little reference to worship in the Temple or elsewhere, the central cultic institution would very likely have been part of his experience. Gordis, who consistently finds evidence of social elitism in the Teacher's work, finds it here as well: "Koheleth here reflects the proto-Sadducean upperclass viewpoint, which regards the Temple as essential to the established order, and therefore required."[69] However he may have experienced it personally, Qohelet knew that in the presence of God a person's heart, ears, and mouth are all under scrutiny. Each person needs to be chastened by the humility of being an earthling (v. 2), subject to a heavenly sovereign who cannot be manipulated by words: "He does whatever he pleases" (Ps 115:3 NRSV).

Prophets and sages alike had always warned that cultic worship without serious intention and obedience is foolish and dangerous (see 1 Sam

68. Roland E. Murphy, *Ecclesiastes,* WBC 23A (Waco, Tex.: Word, 1992) 46.
69. Robert Gordis, *Koheleth: The Man and His World,* 1st ed. (New York: Schocken, 1951; 3rd ed., 1968) 236.

15:22-23; Prov 15:8; 21:27; Jer 7:22-23; Hos 6:6; Mic 6:6-8). The cautionary note "let your words be few" (v. 2) may refer to prayer; if so, it anticipates Jesus' warning to his disciples not to "heap up empty phrases as the Gentiles do" (Matt 6:7 NRSV). The linkage of dreams with cares (v. 3*a*) is less germane to the context than is the voice of the fool (v. 3*b*). The point is that excess—whether of business or of words—means trouble. Meaningless verbiage is the mark of a fool (10:12-14) and is inappropriate public behavior (Sir 7:14).

Verse 6 suggests that to tell the messenger who arrives to collect on a vow that you did not mean it is not at all wise. (The word translated "mistake" [שׁגה *šāgâ*] is used elsewhere to designate unintended sin; e.g., Num 15:22.) To do so would only alert God to the need for punitive action. The law was clear: "If you make a vow to the Lord your God, do not postpone fulfilling it; for the Lord your God will surely require it of you" (Deut 23:21 NRSV). Even though Qohelet pleads ignorance about what God is doing all the time (3:11), evidently he still believed that God would judge and punish human actions. Ben Sira, too, saw the danger of reneging on a vow (Sir 18:22), and the sages advised careful thought before even making one (Prov 20:25). The seven verses that caution against empty vows and excessive verbiage conclude with a simple admonition that, when taken seriously, negates both pomposity and carelessness in speaking: "Fear God!" (v. 7).

REFLECTIONS

In 5:1-7, the organ at issue is the mouth. Qohelet warns his students against the hollow, outward observance of religion, and he cautions them to be particularly careful in taking vows. In issues of faith and philosophy alike, having a big mouth can get one into a lot of trouble: "Do not let your mouth lead you into sin" (v. 6*a*). Perhaps it was this warning that vacuous words are also culpable words that led G. K. Chesterton to compose his poem "Ecclesiastes":

> There is one sin: to call a green leaf gray,
>   Whereat the sun in heaven shuddereth.
> There is one blasphemy: for death to pray,
>   For God alone knoweth the praise of death.
>
> There is one creed: 'neath no world-terror's wing
>   Apples forget to grow on apple-trees.
> There is one thing is needful—everything—
>   The rest is vanity of vanities.

Ecclesiastes 5:8-20, On the Love of Money

NIV	NRSV
[8]If you see the poor oppressed in a district, and justice and rights denied, do not be surprised at such things; for one official is eyed by a higher one, and over them both are others higher still. [9]The increase from the land is taken by all; the king himself profits from the fields. [10]Whoever loves money never has money enough; whoever loves wealth is never satisfied with his income.	[8]If you see in a province the oppression of the poor and the violation of justice and right, do not be amazed at the matter; for the high official is watched by a higher, and there are yet higher ones over them. [9]But all things considered, this is an advantage for a land: a king for a plowed field.*a* 10The lover of money will not be satisfied with *a* Meaning of Heb uncertain

NIV

This too is meaningless.

[11]As goods increase,
  so do those who consume them.
And what benefit are they to the owner
  except to feast his eyes on them?

[12]The sleep of a laborer is sweet,
  whether he eats little or much,
but the abundance of a rich man
  permits him no sleep.

[13]I have seen a grievous evil under the sun:

wealth hoarded to the harm of its owner,
[14] or wealth lost through some misfortune,
so that when he has a son
  there is nothing left for him.
[15]Naked a man comes from his mother's womb,
  and as he comes, so he departs.
He takes nothing from his labor
  that he can carry in his hand.

[16]This too is a grievous evil:

As a man comes, so he departs,
  and what does he gain,
  since he toils for the wind?
[17]All his days he eats in darkness,
  with great frustration, affliction and anger.

[18]Then I realized that it is good and proper for a man to eat and drink, and to find satisfaction in his toilsome labor under the sun during the few days of life God has given him—for this is his lot. [19]Moreover, when God gives any man wealth and possessions, and enables him to enjoy them, to accept his lot and be happy in his work—this is a gift of God. [20]He seldom reflects on the days of his life, because God keeps him occupied with gladness of heart.

NRSV

money; nor the lover of wealth, with gain. This also is vanity.

[11]When goods increase, those who eat them increase; and what gain has their owner but to see them with his eyes?

[12]Sweet is the sleep of laborers, whether they eat little or much; but the surfeit of the rich will not let them sleep.

[13]There is a grievous ill that I have seen under the sun: riches were kept by their owners to their hurt, [14]and those riches were lost in a bad venture; though they are parents of children, they have nothing in their hands. [15]As they came from their mother's womb, so they shall go again, naked as they came; they shall take nothing for their toil, which they may carry away with their hands. [16]This also is a grievous ill: just as they came, so shall they go; and what gain do they have from toiling for the wind? [17]Besides, all their days they eat in darkness, in much vexation and sickness and resentment.

[18]This is what I have seen to be good: it is fitting to eat and drink and find enjoyment in all the toil with which one toils under the sun the few days of the life God gives us; for this is our lot. [19]Likewise all to whom God gives wealth and possessions and whom he enables to enjoy them, and to accept their lot and find enjoyment in their toil—this is the gift of God. [20]For they will scarcely brood over the days of their lives, because God keeps them occupied with the joy of their hearts.

COMMENTARY

The second section of aphorisms offers a number of reflections on profit and wealth, all of which throw an unfavorable light on the person who makes the gain of wealth a high priority.

5:8-9. In the light of the teachings that follow it, we may take v. 8 to be a commentary not on political oppression as much as it is on economics. Every official "watches" those lower on the chain

of authority in order to secure a percentage of the tax or bribe revenue. The enigmatic v. 9 leaves translators and exegetes with serious problems, as the comparison of the NIV with the NRSV will demonstrate. The NIV solution fits best with the sense of the section: The heavy hand of taxation extends to the king at the very top, who claims revenue for the crown from fields worked by even the lowliest peasants. The king is devoted to agriculture all right (which may be the notion at work in the NRSV), but that devotion is self-interested. There is no reason to see in this sentence any positive affirmation by the Teacher of the institution of kingship. If the king, who, according to the prophets, had to guarantee that the system worked justly for all, had his own hand in the till, then no one should anticipate any recourse from unfair treatment by officials.

5:10-17. The plight of the acquisitive person is explored further in these verses. In 3:8, Qohelet linked greedy eyes to riches; here he speaks of unfulfilled passion, "love," for wealth of all kinds. Furthermore, with increased productivity and profitability come increased demands by interested parties. Sometimes the owner merely gets to look at personal gains before they are consumed by others (v. 11). The Teacher is then moved to restate an idea that he first raised in 2:23: Those who have nothing to lose sleep sweetly even on half-empty stomachs, while those who have more than they need lose sleep worrying about protecting their assets—or perhaps because they have overeaten.

The theme of vv. 13-17 is an echo of 2:18-23. It describes the evil effects of riches, on both the hoarder and the disappointed heirs of an estate. In words reminiscent of Job 1:21, the Teacher laments that we exit from the world just as naked and vulnerable as we entered it and that we have nothing to show for all of our toil. We work only for wind (v. 15). The passage culminates in v. 17 with the textually difficult reference to the one who eats in darkness "with great frustration, affliction and anger." One pictures an ancient

Scrooge who, in his unpleasantness and obsessiveness having driven off all friends and family, sits down to his supper alone.

5:18-20. These next verses, in contrast, bring the passage to a close with a reprise (see 2:24-26) of the only consistently positive theme of the book: that the proper goal of all human endeavor is joy (see Introduction). A good life of enjoyment of the fruits of human labor is possible if people will simply look on food, drink, and money as gifts from God and accept their "lot" (חלק *ḥēleq*, v. 18; cf. 2:10, "reward"; 3:22). This term, not to be equated with "fate" (מקרה *miqreh*, 2:14), refers to the individual's share of personal history and of earthly goods. God "enables" some to enjoy these gifts (v. 19), even though the gifts are limited both in quantity and in duration. Because God makes this available, acceptance of one's lot as a gift of God to be enjoyed becomes a moral responsibility.

The meaning of v. 20 is elusive, partly because the Hebrew verb "remember" (זכר *zākar*) is susceptible of various interpretations. By translating it as "brood," the NRSV suggests that the "remembering" in view here is not quite healthy and that it is better for human beings not to examine seriously the situations in which they find themselves. God keeps them so "occupied" (ענה *'ānâ*; taking the verb in the sense unique to Ecclesiastes; cf. 1:13; 3:10) that they do not have time to brood and despair, and so their "days flit pleasantly past."[70]

---

70. O. S. Rankin and G. G. Atkins, "The Book of Ecclesiastes," in *The Interpreter's Bible*, 12 vols., ed. George A. Buttrick et al. (Nashville: Abingdon, 1956) 5:60.

REFLECTIONS

This collection of aphorisms on the theme of the acquisition of wealth (5:8-20) seems contemporary in many ways. Verse 8, which cynically says that there is no need for surprise at the oppression of the poor by the rich and the powerful, could well be a text for one of today's liberation theologians. Systemic violation of the have-nots by the haves is as crucial an issue in our time as it ever was. Similarly, v. 10, "The lover of money will not be satisfied with money," expresses the very sentiment on which consumerism is built. In giving one of the simplest reasons why the rich tend to get richer, Qohelet incidentally discloses one of the bedrocks that underlie Wall Street.

A matter of more philosophical interest grows out of Qohelet's remarks in vv. 18-20. The fact that good things come from God suggests that Qohelet thought of God as more than simply a distant power, an omnipotent but amoral fabricator of the universe. God also appears here as the author and source of all that is available to human beings to make life joyous. To accept God's gracious gift is, in fact, the only moral responsibility laid by Ecclesiastes upon the reader of the book. The disturbing aspect of this otherwise positive situation is, of course, that the decision by God as to who gets wealth and who is "enabled" to enjoy it seems totally arbitrary. Although such a radical claim squares with Qohelet's general preference for a closed predestinarian system, the choice of the verb *enables* rather undercuts the moral possibilities inherent in doing God's will by humbly and gratefully accepting God's gifts. If even the very ability to make that choice is a gift of God, those who do not receive it will never find happiness.

A more positive spin on the word *enables* might take it this way: People cannot earn their happiness through good works, as the authors of the Hebrew Bible had sometimes imagined they could do (e.g., "The reward for humility and fear of the LORD is riches and honor and life" [Prov 22:4 NRSV]; see also Pss 19:11; 62:12; Isa 3:10). Like Job, who found that all his good deeds did not save him from the dunghill (Job 29:11-20), Qohelet realizes that there is no sure and certain hope and that one must simply have faith that God will make happiness possible. Whether this election by God of some people requires the rejection by God of others, whether that rejection follows as a consequence of human behavior or is simply God's arbitrary choice—these are questions of which Qohelet makes nothing. The conundrum he raises remains alive and well. Who among us has not puzzled at why some people who "have it all" struggle with self-doubt, low self-esteem, and general misery while others do not? We may attribute the difference to family systems, jumbled genes on some chromosome, or simple brain chemistry, though the definitive answer remains beyond our reach. Here Qohelet attributes the difference simply to God's "enabling."

Ecclesiastes 6:1-12, On Lowering Expectations

NIV	NRSV
6 I have seen another evil under the sun, and it weighs heavily on men: ²God gives a man wealth, possessions and honor, so that he lacks nothing his heart desires, but God does not enable him to enjoy them, and a stranger enjoys them instead. This is meaningless, a grievous evil.	**6** There is an evil that I have seen under the sun, and it lies heavy upon humankind: ²those to whom God gives wealth, possessions, and honor, so that they lack nothing of all that they desire, yet God does not enable them to enjoy these things, but a stranger enjoys them. This is vanity; it is a grievous ill. ³A man may beget a hundred children, and live many years; but however many are the days of his years, if he does not enjoy life's good things, or has no burial, I say that a stillborn child is better off than he. ⁴For it comes into vanity and goes into darkness, and in darkness its name is covered; ⁵moreover it has not seen the sun or known anything; yet it finds rest rather than he. ⁶Even though he should live a thousand years twice over, yet enjoy no good—do not all go to one place?
³A man may have a hundred children and live many years; yet no matter how long he lives, if he cannot enjoy his prosperity and does not receive proper burial, I say that a stillborn child is better off than he. ⁴It comes without meaning, it departs in darkness, and in darkness its name is shrouded. ⁵Though it never saw the sun or knew anything, it has more rest than does that man— ⁶even if he lives a thousand years twice over but fails to enjoy his prosperity. Do not all go to the same place?	
⁷All man's efforts are for his mouth, yet his appetite is never satisfied. ⁸What advantage has a wise man	7All human toil is for the mouth, yet the appetite is not satisfied. ⁸For what advantage have the wise over fools? And what do the poor have

NIV

over a fool?
What does a poor man gain
  by knowing how to conduct himself before
    others?
⁹Better what the eye sees
  than the roving of the appetite.
This too is meaningless,
  a chasing after the wind.

¹⁰Whatever exists has already been named,
  and what man is has been known;
no man can contend
  with one who is stronger than he.
¹¹The more the words,
  the less the meaning,
  and how does that profit anyone?

¹²For who knows what is good for a man in life, during the few and meaningless days he passes through like a shadow? Who can tell him what will happen under the sun after he is gone?

NRSV

who know how to conduct themselves before the living? ⁹Better is the sight of the eyes than the wandering of desire; this also is vanity and a chasing after wind.ᵃ

10Whatever has come to be has already been named, and it is known what human beings are, and that they are not able to dispute with those who are stronger. ¹¹The more words, the more vanity, so how is one the better? ¹²For who knows what is good for mortals while they live the few days of their vain life, which they pass like a shadow? For who can tell them what will be after them under the sun?

ᵃOr *a feeding on wind.* See Hos 12.1

COMMENTARY

Chapter 6 picks up the note upon which chap. 5 concluded: that possessions are gifts of God and that the ability to enjoy them is also a gift of God. This chapter follows through four stages the plight of those who do not have that gift of enjoyment: (1) Verses 1-2 present us such persons as the counterimage of the happy rich person of 5:18-20; (2) vv. 3-6 tell the story of two characters, a thwarted rich man who does not have the gift and a lucky stillborn child; (3) vv. 7-9 use the anatomical images of mouth and eyes to bring forward the painful truth that advantage is no advantage; (4) vv. 10-12 picture the human community in the grip of inexorable predetermination, true knowledge about which is not available to humankind.

6:1-2. The formula with which the chapter opens, "There is an evil that I have seen under the sun," echoes the language of 5:13. The evil is the situation of the individual whom God has not "enabled" to enjoy "wealth, possessions and honor." God's refusal to "empower" the rich man means that a "stranger" ends up enjoying the estate. Gordis points out that this stranger need not be a foreigner or even an unknown person:

"For Koheleth, the individualist, each man is a stranger to his fellows, even to members of his own family. There is a distinctly modern implication here of the essential loneliness of the individual personality."[71]

6:3-6. At v. 3 the contrast is drawn between the man who ostensibly has the things that constitute blessing—many children (e.g., Gen 24:60; Deut 11:21; 28:4) and a long life (e.g., Exod 23:26; Deut 30:20; Ps 91:16; Isa 65:20)—with the stillborn infant. The latter is better off, says the Teacher, because it finds rest more quickly than does the rich man. Although the stillborn child's progress through the world is from vanity to darkness (v. 4), that journey is mercifully brief. The passage culminates in a rhetorical question: "Do not all go to one place?" The intended answer is yes. If the distance between now and then is only a course of suffering, then why not recognize that the shorter life is the better? Like its precursor in 4:3, this text brings to mind Job's wistful longing to have ended his life "like a

71. Gordis, *Koheleth,* 247.

stillborn child,/ like an infant that never sees the light" (Job 3:16 NRSV). It raises questions about whether long life is in fact always a blessing. Indeed, with a consistency rare to him, Qohelet repeatedly expresses doubt about it (see also Eccl 8:12; 11:8).

The NRSV and the NIV do not reveal the difficulty in the semi-final clause of v. 3, translated by NRSV "or has no burial." It is true that a decent burial is one of the marks of blessing and that to be deprived of it is a curse (see Isa 14:19; Jer 22:19). The importance attached to the moving of Joseph's bones from Egypt (Gen 50:25; Exod 13:19) and to the proper burial of Saul and Jonathan (1 Sam 31:11-13; 2 Sam 2:5-7) illustrates the point. The problem with v. 3 is both logical and philological. Is it logical to suppose that a rich man who had a miserable life but an elaborate funeral could therefore be said to have been a happy man? Surely not. Crenshaw construes the pronoun implied in "and [he/she/it] does not receive proper burial" as anticipatory of the stillborn child. His result, then, is "but he is not satisfied with good things, then even if it does not have a burial, I say that the still-born is better off than he."[72]

However the verse may be fine-tuned, the point of the story remains the same. The rich man who does not enjoy his riches, whether he was properly buried or not, is less well off than the stillborn fetus who may not be buried at all.

6:7-9. These verses seem to be an amalgam of a traditional saying (v. 7) that is approved and enlarged upon by Qohelet (cf. Prov 16:26, "The appetite of workers works for them; their hunger urges them on," NRSV). Human beings struggle to stuff their mouths full, and yet they cannot satisfy their cravings. Some interpreters suggest that because "mouth" (פֶּה *peh*) is modified by a possessive pronoun ("his" or "its") in Hebrew, the "mouth" must be that of Sheol, the place to which all go (6:6*b*). The notion that Sheol has a hungry, gaping maw that swallows up the dead is graphically acknowledged in the list in Prov 30:15-16 of three and four things that never say "Enough" (see also Isa 5:14; Hab 2:5). Certainly the gaping mouth of hell (pictured as Leviathan, as Jonah's whale, or just as a cavelike opening into which

the damned are flung) became a staple feature of medieval Christian art. However, the fact that "appetite" (נֶפֶשׁ *nepeš*) lacks the possessive pronoun rather tips the interpretive scale back to seeing the proverb as a generalization about the human condition: Satiety can never be achieved.

The response to the problem of nonsatiety seems to be 6:9, which commentators take essentially to mean "a bird in hand is worth two in the bush." The seat of desire in the Hebrew Bible is the נֶפֶשׁ (*nepeš*), the "soul" or "life force" (see Cant 5:6). So the reference to "pursuing *nepeš*" (v. 9*a*) is no doubt correctly translated "wandering of desire" (NRSV) or "roving of the appetite" (NIV).

Bracketed by verses 7 and 9 is the rather puzzling v. 8. Does v. 8*b* describe a poor man who knows how to conduct himself in the face of opposition, or is Scott right in amending the text to read, "How then is a wise man better off than a fool? [Only] in knowing how to conduct himself during his life"?[73] In either case, v. 8 seems intended to give yet another painful example of the truth that the advantaged person finally has no advantage. Even if wisdom and wealth are joined, as Qohelet urges they be (see 7:11; 9:15), nothing necessarily is gained; nor is the humble virtue of the poor person of lasting merit.

6:10-12. These verses appear to comprise a separate, transitional unit devoted entirely to one of the Teacher's major themes: the impossibility of knowing what is truly going on in the world (see Introduction). It opens with the enigmatic statement that "it is known what human beings are." Assuming that the one who is stronger than the human individual is God (v. 10*b*; the NRSV obscures this possibility), this verse joins Job in decrying the uselessness of words spoken against God even while longing to enter into "dispute" with God. (In such passages as Job 9:32-35 and 16:18-22, Job tries to get God into court for a full hearing and adjudication of their dispute.) The Teacher—a lover of words in spite of his declarations against rhetoric—puts it with beautiful alliteration: "the more words, the more vanity [דברים הרבה מרבים הבל *děbarîm harbēh marbîm hābel*]" (v. 11).

"Who knows" indeed what is good for mortals

72. James L. Crenshaw, *Ecclesiastes,* OTL (Philadelphia: Westminster, 1987) 120.

73. R. B. Y. Scott, *Proverbs, Ecclesiastes,* AB 18 (Garden City, N.Y.: Doubleday, 1965) 231.

in the present moment (v. 12*a*)? Long ago Zimmerli credited Qohelet with having stated the "central question" faced by the wisdom writers of the Hebrew Bible: "What do people gain from all the toil at which they toil under the sun?" (1:3). How can a wise person gain "practical mastery" over life?[74] By this point in his book it is clear that Qohelet will be unable to answer his own

74. Walther Zimmerli, "Concerning the Structure of Old Testament Wisdom," in *Studies in Ancient Israelite Wisdom,* ed. James L. Crenshaw (New York: KTAV, 1976) 175-207, esp. 176, 198.

question and will be forced to leave it as an unanswerable conundrum. Nor can anyone say what lies in the future for human beings (v. 12*b*). Yet they can no more leave alone the question of the future than they can the question of the proper task of the present moment. Because of his curiosity about the fate of his descendants, Job could not live in peace: "Their children come to honor, and they do not know it;/ they are brought low, and it goes unnoticed" (Job 14:21 NRSV).

REFLECTIONS

Like the ancient dialectical theologian that he was, the Teacher circles once again around the themes of the means of joy in life, the illusory advantage of power and wealth, and inescapable predetermination.

1. In 6:1-2, the fatalistic dilemma into which Qohelet's radical logic carries him is restated in negative terms. In 5:19 the problem was stated softly and positively: To have the gift of enjoying good things is a grace of God. Now it is put harshly: To have it and never enjoy it is "an evil" that "lies heavy upon humankind." Unlike the rich fool in Jesus' story whose free choice it was to build ever bigger barns before he ate, drank, and was merry (Luke 12:13-21), the rich and famous people of Qohelet's tale could not have escaped their discontent and despair in any way. One sympathizes with Scott's effort to weaken the dilemma by describing this as the "case of a man who has everything that heart can desire, but is prevented by circumstances, or by his own attitude, from enjoying life."[75] Elsewhere the Teacher allows freer play to human choice and responsibility (see, e.g., Commentary and Reflections at 3:1-15). In this passage, however, Qohelet's mood is deterministic. God and God alone decides who will be able to enjoy and be happy—and faithful obedience, moral rectitude, prayer, and fasting will not affect this outcome in any way.

2. As Qohelet sees it (6:3-6), the stillborn or aborted fetus enjoys the advantage in the game of life by never having played it. Yet he does not advocate resigning the game by committing suicide. "Tough it out!" is his recommendation.

Someone among his contemporaries must have been advocating an afterlife as a way of offering advantage upon those who were willing to play the game fair and square now. Why else would the Teacher keep raising that possibility, only to reject it with a rhetorical question (v. 6*b*)? Now, even though we Christians are on the side of Qohelet's adversary because we accept Easter as the first step toward the renewal of all things, we need not scoff at Qohelet's gloomy assessment of non-advantage to anyone who stands before death. Our hope of participation beyond this life in the life of the kingdom of heaven is not based on any reward we may feel we have earned or have been given. It is based solely on God's love of us and commitment to our lives. So Qohelet's gloom can serve us in good stead when the snake oil seller or our own longings promise us the advantage. The fact is that we all do die, and, but for God alone, we probably would all lie forever in the same narrow bed of extinction. The game of life is always a deuce game; ultimate advantage lodged in the assertion of ourselves really is an illusion.

3. At the end of chap. 6, Qohelet conveys the sense that human beings move almost as

75. Scott, *Proverbs, Ecclesiastes,* 232.

automatons within the inexorable orders of the One who is stronger than we are (v. 10). We cannot know the future, but we know that whatever it will hold has already been named. As so often elsewhere, echoes of Qohelet's ineluctable doctrine reverberate in the rhymes of the Islamic predestinarian Omar Khayyám.

> We are no other than a moving row
> Of Magic Shadow-shapes that come and go
> Round with the Sun-illumin'd Lantern held
> In Midnight by the Master of the Show;
> But helpless Pieces of the Game He plays
> Upon this Chequer-board of Night and Days;
> Hither and thither moves, and checks, and slays,
> And one by one back in the Closet lays.

The view is an obnoxious one to modern Jewish and Christian sensibilities. Only if we construe Qohelet's line on predetermination as not so much a hard one involving election and rejection, but something more commonsensical, perhaps involving a softening of the heart into an attitude of grateful acceptance of life's allotment, does it begin to have possibilities for us.

ECCLESIASTES 7:1–8:17, A FIRST MISCELLANY

Ecclesiastes 7:1-14, Things That Are Good for Human Beings

NIV	NRSV
7 A good name is better than fine perfume, and the day of death better than the day of birth.	**7** A good name is better than precious ointment, and the day of death, than the day of birth.
[2] It is better to go to a house of mourning than to go to a house of feasting, for death is the destiny of every man; the living should take this to heart.	[2] It is better to go to the house of mourning than to go to the house of feasting; for this is the end of everyone, and the living will lay it to heart.
[3] Sorrow is better than laughter, because a sad face is good for the heart.	[3] Sorrow is better than laughter, for by sadness of countenance the heart is made glad.
[4] The heart of the wise is in the house of mourning, but the heart of fools is in the house of pleasure.	[4] The heart of the wise is in the house of mourning; but the heart of fools is in the house of mirth.
[5] It is better to heed a wise man's rebuke than to listen to the song of fools.	[5] It is better to hear the rebuke of the wise than to hear the song of fools.
[6] Like the crackling of thorns under the pot, so is the laughter of fools. This too is meaningless.	[6] For like the crackling of thorns under a pot, so is the laughter of fools; this also is vanity.
[7] Extortion turns a wise man into a fool, and a bribe corrupts the heart.	[7] Surely oppression makes the wise foolish, and a bribe corrupts the heart.
[8] The end of a matter is better than its beginning, and patience is better than pride.	[8] Better is the end of a thing than its beginning; the patient in spirit are better than the proud in spirit.
[9] Do not be quickly provoked in your spirit, for anger resides in the lap of fools.	[9] Do not be quick to anger,

NIV

10Do not say, "Why were the old days better than these?"
For it is not wise to ask such questions.

11Wisdom, like an inheritance, is a good thing
and benefits those who see the sun.
12Wisdom is a shelter
as money is a shelter,
but the advantage of knowledge is this:
that wisdom preserves the life of its possessor.

13Consider what God has done:

Who can straighten
what he has made crooked?
14When times are good, be happy;
but when times are bad, consider:
God has made the one
as well as the other.
Therefore, a man cannot discover
anything about his future.

NRSV

for anger lodges in the bosom of fools.
10 Do not say, "Why were the former days better than these?"
For it is not from wisdom that you ask this.
11 Wisdom is as good as an inheritance,
an advantage to those who see the sun.
12 For the protection of wisdom is like the protection of money,
and the advantage of knowledge is that wisdom gives life to the one who possesses it.
13 Consider the work of God;
who can make straight what he has made crooked?
14In the day of prosperity be joyful, and in the day of adversity consider; God has made the one as well as the other, so that mortals may not find out anything that will come after them.

COMMENTARY

At the end of the preceding chapter (6:12), the Teacher abandoned the search for "what is good for mortals." Apparently the mention of the word "good" jingled his memory or that of his compiler, for, having just abandoned his search, he promptly offers in 7:1-14 a collection of seven sayings precisely dealing with what is "good" (or even "better") for human beings (concluding with v. 14a, "When times are good, be happy"). No absolute good is proposed, and no perfection is attainable, but now (in contrast to 6:10; 7:14) Qohelet imagines that within their limits human beings do have competency to make moral decisions and to act accordingly. The "goods" that are discerned are behavioral virtues, things that a wise person should cultivate. They do not differ from the standard teachings of the sages except that they offer no guarantees, no certain outcomes; even the good of wisdom itself is limited in its capacity to comprehend the outcome of life (vv. 11-14). Verse 14 offers the perspective from which the Teacher guides his students through this examination of what is good for mortals. That verse says, as it were, *"Carpe diem,"* "Seize the day." If a day is good, be good with it—be happy. You can know neither the etiology of this good thing

nor its outcome; all life is tangled in a web of divine orders that can neither be known nor altered. God made both the good and the bad days, and one can expect to experience both, whether one's morals and etiquette bear the marks of wisdom or not. The appropriate way to approach life, then, is with realism, sobriety, and a low profile.

7:1. The series of epigrams begins with this beautifully crafted verse, the alliterative first stich of which reads in Hebrew, טוב שם משמן טוב (*ṭôb šēm miššemen ṭôb*): "A good name is better than good ointment." The relationship of v. 1a to v. 1b becomes clear only when one recognizes that the "good name" and the "day of death" are given preference respectively over "precious ointment" and "day of birth" (the logic being A > B : A′ > B′). This means that A and A′ also explicate each other, as do B and B′. Perhaps one can never really attain a "good name" prior to the completion of one's life: "Call no one happy before his death; by how he ends, a person becomes known" (Sir 11:28 NRSV). The Hebrew Bible is full of stories of people's efforts to make for themselves a good name or its near equivalent, a great name. The builders of the Tower of Babel were led into sin by their zeal to "make a name for ourselves" (Gen 11:4 NRSV). In Gen 12:2, the Lord offers as a precious gift to Abram and his descendants the very thing the tower builders could not achieve: "I will . . . make your name great, so that you will be a blessing" (NRSV). The sages did not leave the good name strictly up to God, however. Human beings have responsibility and can attain the goal: "A good name is to be chosen rather than great riches" (Prov 22:1 NRSV). If "good name" and the "day of death" are thus related, then so are "precious ointment" and "day of birth." This pairing of terms may refer to the actual practice in ancient Greece and Egypt of anointing infants at birth with fragrant unguents. Although the Bible does not describe this act narratively (Ezek 16:4 speaks only of bathing an infant and rubbing it with salt), we know that adults anointed themselves with oil after bathing (Ruth 3:3; Ezek 16:9; Jdt 10:3; see Luke 7:38), and there is reason to suppose that infants were similarly anointed. Perhaps v. 1*a* was a traditional proverb and v. 1*b* is Qohelet's expansion of that proverb in an unconventional direction. The resulting combination is similar to Hillel's teaching, "Trust not in thyself until the day of thy death."[76] Although elsewhere Qohelet is prepared to say that it is better never to have been born at all than to suffer the frustrations of life (6:3), here the "good name" and the "day of death" are linked into a rounded-out life history that includes an element of satisfactory achievement. There is a place for human responsibility and action after all!

7:2. The second "good" saying extends this direction of thinking in recommending visitation at wakes during the seven-day period of mourning (Sir 22:12) in preference to attendance at "the house of feasting" ("drinking house" [בית משתה *bêt mišteh*]). The modal auxiliary verb "should" (NIV) accurately captures the idea: A wise person should approach all of experience with a keen sense of mortality, aware that death "is the end of everyone." The same idea, that all behavior should be colored by the reality of death, is expressed by the well-known line in Ps 90:12: "So teach us to count our days/ that we may gain a wise heart" (NRSV).

7:3-4. The third of the "good" sayings introduces the notion that "a sad face is good for the heart." If we allow Scripture to be its own interpreter, this apparently absurd teaching takes on life because of its relationship to the other six sayings in the series. The overriding theme of the series is that one should be busy at all times preparing for days of adversity, rather than trying to deny their inevitability or drown the awareness of them in foolish mirth. In 1:18, Qohelet already observed that the suffering that accompanies wisdom is so intense that wisdom hardly seems worth seeking. This is not the same message as that brought to Job by his friends—namely, that suffering has pedagogical value and should be welcomed as a moral benefit (Job 5:17). Qohelet speaks here in a simple declaratory manner: Given all that one comes to know in life, sadness is more appropriate than laughter.

7:5-6. These verses make up the fourth of the "good" sayings in this pericope. Now the metaphor involves sound and hearing. It is possible that the "song" (Vg, *adulatio*) of fools is simply the insincere praise that the Teacher's student will receive from others. (Other instances in which "song" is synonymous with "praise" include Ps 149:1; Isa 42:10.) This kind of "song" would be the perfect antithesis to the rebuke of the wise. In an expansion of this theme, Qohelet once again employs the literary device of alliteration. In v. 5 he spoke of the "song" (שיר *šîr*) of fools; in v. 6 he speaks of the "thorns" (סירים *sîrîm*) that crackle under the "pot" (סיר *sîr*).[77]

7:8-10. The fifth of the "good" sayings reverts to the claim of v. 1 that the best perspective one can hope to attain on a matter is the perspective of its outcome (v. 8*a*; see King Ahab's message to the king of Aram: "One who puts on armor should not brag like one who takes it off" [1 Kgs 20:11 NRSV]). To do so requires patience (v. 8*b*); in turn, this requires resistance to quick, hot flashes of anger (v. 9; see Prov 16:32). Finally, a perspective from the end of life precludes the need to hark back to the good old days (v. 10).

---

76. *M. 'Abot* 2:5.

77. Barton's translation of v. 6*a*, "As the crackling of nettles under kettles," wonderfully preserves alliteration but diverts the eye of the mind away from the spiny desert plants and cacti that surely were in Qohelet's mind to the nasty stinging weeds of Bryn Mawr, where Barton taught. In Hos 2:6, *sîr* seems to mean a cactus hedgerow, like those still in use on farms in the Middle East. See George A. Barton, *A Critical and Exegetical Commentary on the Book of Ecclesiastes*, ICC (New York: Scribner's, 1908) 140.

The maturity and realism of age do not long for the past, because, from the perspective of the end (v. 8), they are able to assess the meaning of all of life and not simply its fresh beginnings. From such a perspective, it is clear that there is no general progress in justice and righteousness, no ethical evolution, but only individual examples of wise persons who acted prudently.

7:11-12. The Hebrew of v. 11, the beginning of the sixth "good" saying, reads, "Wisdom is good with an inheritance, and profitable to those who see the sun." This literal translation seems to make the point that wisdom is good, but wisdom with cash is even better. The idea is paralleled in *M. 'Abot* 2:2: "Excellent is study of the Law together with worldly occupation, for toil in them both puts sin out of mind." In other words, even such positive values as wisdom and Torah can benefit from the parallel practical responsibility of making a living. The NIV takes the Hebrew preposition "with" (עם *'im*) to mean "like" in this instance and sees a simile here: "Wisdom, like an inheritance, is a good thing." This places wisdom and money on a par; therefore, the value of wisdom can be illuminated by comparing it to an inheritance. By creating a comparison using the formula "as good as," the NRSV plays down the value of money in comparison with wisdom and says, in effect, that even without any money at all, one could still have in wisdom a possession of great value. Verse 12 tips the scale toward the more literal understanding, especially if one follows Gordis (and Ibn Ezra) in translating v. 12*a*, "For there is the double protection of wisdom and money."[78]

7:13-14. For Gordis these verses present the epitome of Qohelet's thought.[79] Because God is all powerful and cannot be challenged, human beings have to take whatever comes in stride, knowing that both the good and the bad are from God. In reference to what God "has made crooked" (see also 1:15), Crenshaw remarks, "The universe has wrinkles."[80] Some things out there seem to us not to be the way we would want them to be, but we cannot alter what God has made.

This then leads to the last of the seven "good" sayings (v. 14), the somewhat tentative affirmation that it is possible to find things that are good for human life (a rejoinder to 6:12); however, one has to reckon that God, who structures life by opposites (see 3:1-8), sends evil times along with the good ones. No reason exists, therefore, to hope that life will go on to perfection.

---

78. Robert Gordis, *Koheleth: The Man and His World,* 1st ed. (New York: Schocken, 1951; 3rd ed., 1968) 264.

79. Ibid., 265.

80. James L. Crenshaw, *Ecclesiastes,* OTL (Philadelphia: Westminster, 1987) 139.

REFLECTIONS

The collection of aphorisms that makes up 7:1-14 is not as miscellaneous as it might seem at first. Whether original with Qohelet or borrowed by him, all of these sayings have to do with what is good for the human being. Reflections on three facets of that discussion now follow.

1. It is well and good to contemplate the end of life. The first three "good" sayings (7:1-4) stress the superiority of sober contemplation of death to any giggling, foolish hilarity about life. Underlying these verses that juxtapose wisdom and foolishness, sobriety and mirth, is yet a deeper juxtaposition: birth and death. Verse 1 makes that juxtaposition explicit: The happiest outcome of life is to arrive at one's destiny with a good name and a record of probity rather than by virtue of being born to plunge the whole household into rejoicing and feasting (v. 2). Underlying this juxtaposition are the sacramental acts of mourning the dead and anointing the newborn child. The contrast between these two major life events and their liturgical accompaniments remains alive in both the Jewish and the Christian communities and in their respective houses of worship.

One of the most dramatic moments in the life of any Christian congregation is the baptism and chrismation of a child. This is particularly the case in Eastern Orthodox congregations in the modern Middle East, when the priest sweeps the infant three times through a great copper basin filled with warm water—once in the name of each of the members of the blessed Trinity. Then, with the child wrapped in a cozy towel, the priest makes the sign of the cross on the forehead, lips, ears, eyes, and feet of the child with the chrism, the sacred oil of unction. After communing the infant from the altar, priest and family parade around the sanctuary with the infant raised on high for all to see, accompanied by that peculiar gobbling shriek of women, called ululation. All of this signals reception of a new human being into the bosom of church and community.

Evidently Qohelet saw whatever version of that process was practiced in Jewish antiquity and was not impressed. He soberly concluded that it is more important to participate in the solemn ritual acts that even to this day accompany the end of life in the Middle East, when the professional mourners go wailing through the streets to mourn the departure of a loved one—if one is to live life with the gravity and care that it deserves.

2. It is worth noting that Qohelet teaches his student here that there is a discrepancy between the outer and the inner reality: A glad heart hides behind a sad face. This contradicts the usual exact proportionality between physiognomy and passion in the Hebrew Bible. Physical manifestations of inner states begin at least as early as Cain's nose burning (he was very angry) and his countenance falling (depression?) in Gen 4:5. Positive or negative feelings welling up from that innermost of organs, the heart, are also reflected in the voice and face (e.g., Ps 45:1; Prov 15:13; Sir 13:26). Even God's emotions are written straightforwardly on the divine countenance (e.g., Num 6:25-26).[81] Here, however, the sage turns the link inside out and teaches his students that they can identify persons whose hearts are whole and secure by their long faces. Other sages had seen the same reality, of course. Something similar to Qohelet's reversal of the usual congruence of the heart and the face is evident in Prov 14:13: "Even in laughter the heart is sad,/ and the end of joy is grief" (NRSV).

In his poem "Do Not Go Gentle into That Good Night," that quintessential voice of modernity, Dylan Thomas, challenged a war-torn and weary world to value life and make the most of it.

> Do not go gentle into that good night,
> Old age should burn and rave at close of day;
> Rage, rage against the dying of the light.
> Grave men, near death, who see with blinding sight
> Blind eyes could blaze like meteors and be gay,
> Rage, rage against the dying of the light.[82]

Thomas's sensibility is utterly opposed to the counsel of the Teacher. When the latter gentleman heard anyone ask him not to pull a long face all the time but to plunge vigorously back into the struggle, his response was, "Sorrow is better than laughter,/ for by sadness of countenance the heart is made glad" (v. 3). In short, Qohelet's advice is: Go gentle!

3. Verses 13-14 contain an essentially obnoxious doctrine—everything is from God—which, as has been pointed out, has to be put into some kind of canonical context in order to be used (see Introduction; also Reflections at 3:1-15). Although the verses may epitomize Qohelet's theodicy, it remains hard to accept that God made the bad times as well as the good ones. Is it possible to agree with Qohelet that "nothing can challenge God's sovereign power or secure human existence,"[83] and still deny the premise underlying vv. 13-14 that God conjured up everything—the good and the bad alike?

Now, in the larger canonical context this problem has been examined many times, and a

81. See Meyer I. Gruber, *Aspects of Nonverbal Communication in the Ancient Near East,* 2 vols. (Rome: Biblical Institute, 1980).

82. Dylan Thomas, from *The Poems of Dylan Thomas.* Copyright © 1952 by Dylan Thomas. Reprinted by permission of New Directions Publishing Corp.

83. Crenshaw, *Ecclesiastes,* 139.

variety of solutions has been offered. One solution is that human beings create their own destiny by their deeds, which are theirs alone and not God's. The notion that the wicked die prematurely or suffer injury and that the righteous prosper underlies the great retributional scheme of the deuteronomistic history and is hymned as an article of faith in the "psalms of the two ways" (Pss 1; 37). Qohelet is in business to deny that scheme its simplistic appeal with the message that "we have no sure and certain hope." He has to be heard on this point. The Christian, too, standing on the far side of the incarnation and the cross, only sees through a "glass darkly" when it comes to making iron-clad assertions about who has earned salvation. We do not have God in a box, and we are not able to predict what God will do. No formula exists by which we can assure our lives after death or even victory and success here. It is necessary that Qohelet be heard, for his teaching is profoundly true: "Who can tell [mortals] what will be after them under the sun?" (Eccl 6:12 NRSV).

However, the corollary Qohelet offers in 7:13-14 is not a mandatory one. The corollary to the premise that we do not have God in a box and cannot force our own salvation is not that all the bad stuff is sent on us by God. Even the writer of Job shied away from saying that, because it makes God the author of evil. (Job came very close to saying it, of course, when he cried, "The arrows of the Almighty are in me;/ my spirit drinks their poison;/ the terrors of God are arrayed against me" [Job 6:4 NRSV].) Even if we grant God a shadow side, we cannot go against the profound conviction of our tradition that God and God alone is good (Matt 19:17; Mark 10:18; Luke 18:19) and that God is good (Pss 100:5; 135:3; 136:1), without admixture of evil (1 John 1:5).

Biblical faith is theologically monistic and ethically dualistic. That means that God is good and good alone; we human beings are capable of both moral good and moral evil. This reality about human nature means that we need help from God when we confront the choice of good or evil. The appropriate corollary to the premise that we cannot know what lies ahead for us is the faith that when we confront crises in our life and have to make profound ethical decisions, God will be alongside, ready to muddle on through with us. Even though we cannot know what will happen, in the full context of the canon of Scripture we are assured that we can walk the road into the future with a friend. That is the message of the story of the man born blind in John 9. Jesus rejects the premise that the blindness is punishment for anyone's sin. Instead, it is an occasion wherein "God's works might be revealed in him" (John 9:3 NRSV). That is a far different way of looking at the adversities that inevitably confront us than to say, "God has made the one as well as the other."

Ecclesiastes 7:15–8:1, Common Sense

NIV

15In this meaningless life of mine I have seen both of these:

a righteous man perishing in his righteousness,
and a wicked man living long in his
wickedness.
16Do not be overrighteous,
neither be overwise—
why destroy yourself?
17Do not be overwicked,
and do not be a fool—

NRSV

15In my vain life I have seen everything; there are righteous people who perish in their righteousness, and there are wicked people who prolong their life in their evildoing. 16Do not be too righteous, and do not act too wise; why should you destroy yourself? 17Do not be too wicked, and do not be a fool; why should you die before your time? 18It is good that you should take hold of the one, without letting go of the other; for the one who fears God shall succeed with both.

NIV

why die before your time?
[18]It is good to grasp the one
and not let go of the other.
The man who fears God will avoid all
⌊extremes⌋.[a]

[19]Wisdom makes one wise man more powerful
than ten rulers in a city.

[20]There is not a righteous man on earth
who does what is right and never sins.

[21]Do not pay attention to every word people say,
or you may hear your servant cursing you—
[22]for you know in your heart
that many times you yourself have cursed
others.

[23]All this I tested by wisdom and I said,

"I am determined to be wise"—
but this was beyond me.
[24]Whatever wisdom may be,
it is far off and most profound—
who can discover it?
[25]So I turned my mind to understand,
to investigate and to search out wisdom and
the scheme of things
and to understand the stupidity of wickedness
and the madness of folly.

[26]I find more bitter than death
the woman who is a snare,
whose heart is a trap
and whose hands are chains.
The man who pleases God will escape her,
but the sinner she will ensnare.

[27]"Look," says the Teacher,[b] "this is what I
have discovered:

"Adding one thing to another to discover the
scheme of things—
[28] while I was still searching
but not finding—
I found one ⌊upright⌋ man among a thousand,
but not one ⌊upright⌋ woman among them
all.
[29]This only have I found:
God made mankind upright,
but men have gone in search of many
schemes."

NRSV

[19]Wisdom gives strength to the wise more
than ten rulers that are in a city.

[20]Surely there is no one on earth so righteous
as to do good without ever sinning.

[21]Do not give heed to everything that people
say, or you may hear your servant cursing you;
[22]your heart knows that many times you have
yourself cursed others.

[23]All this I have tested by wisdom; I said, "I
will be wise," but it was far from me. [24]That
which is, is far off, and deep, very deep; who can
find it out? [25]I turned my mind to know and to
search out and to seek wisdom and the sum of
things, and to know that wickedness is folly and
that foolishness is madness. [26]I found more bitter
than death the woman who is a trap, whose heart
is snares and nets, whose hands are fetters; one
who pleases God escapes her, but the sinner is
taken by her. [27]See, this is what I found, says the
Teacher,[a] adding one thing to another to find the
sum, [28]which my mind has sought repeatedly, but
I have not found. One man among a thousand I
found, but a woman among all these I have not
found. [29]See, this alone I found, that God made
human beings straightforward, but they have devised many schemes.

8 Who is like the wise man?
And who knows the interpretation of a
thing?
Wisdom makes one's face shine,
and the hardness of one's countenance is
changed.

NIV

8 Who is like the wise man?
Who knows the explanation of things?
Wisdom brightens a man's face
and changes its hard appearance.

COMMENTARY

7:15-18. The expectation promoted by conventional wisdom (e.g., Pss 1; 37; Prov 10:28; 11:21) that righteousness and wickedness respectively reap their just rewards is refuted once again in v. 15 (cf. Eccl 3:16). The Teacher then advocates a kind of wise moderation (vv. 16-17). It is impossible to know whether he had firsthand knowledge of Solon or Aristotle, but concepts such as "the golden mean" were in the air of third-century BCE Palestine. He urges realism about both righteousness and wickedness, wisdom and foolishness. Why should one be fanatically righteous or try to go on to moral perfection? Such proto-Wesleyan piety might only cause one to be set upon by others!

This first section concludes with the enigmatic indefinite pronouns of v. 18*a,* "the one . . . the other. . . . " This sounds for all the world as though Qohelet were advocating a modest ownership of the shadow side of life, anticipating Jung by several millennia! In any case, v. 18 appears to be the point of the entire discussion—namely, that by reverencing God one can keep a grip on righteousness and wisdom even though one will certainly—even prudently—fall short of perfection. If fanatical scrupling and perfectionism give way to modesty in well-doing, moral excellence is possible.

7:19–8:1. A series of reflections that culminates at 8:1 begins at 7:19, and the first and last verses of this series bracket the pericope with lofty evaluations of wisdom. Embedded in this frame are two proverbs that offer acknowledgment of human shortcomings as a component of wise behavior (vv. 20-21) and sad truths about human nature, which wisdom discerns (vv. 22-29).

7:19-20. Verse 19 itself sets a tenfold premium on the power of wisdom to strengthen the sages (cf. Prov 21:22; 24:5-6). Verse 20 echoes a line from the intercessory portion of Solomon's great prayer of dedication of the Temple (1 Kgs

8:46: "There is no one who does not sin" [NRSV]). Commentators suggest that it is placed here as an answer to v. 19, lest some sage claim too much for the advantage conferred by wisdom; however, the theme of v. 20 is righteousness, not wisdom, and the two are not synonymous. Perhaps this teaching of realism is simply one facet of the empowering wisdom a sage possesses.

7:21-22. Another may be the discretion in the handling of slander that the Teacher advises: A genuinely wise person knows that even to listen to gossip is to borrow trouble (v. 21). Furthermore, because the wise person knows that his or her own record on cursing others is not spotless (v. 22), the recommended style is acceptance rather than criticism. Crenshaw points out that the reference here to the sage's servant (v. 21) allows us to extrapolate to an element of the social setting of Qohelet and his pupils: They must have belonged to an elite, propertied, slaveholding class. Furthermore, he notes that the reference to "what your heart knows" (v. 22) comes close to being a discussion of conscience, though that term itself occurs for the first time in Jewish literature only in the first-century BCE extracanonical book of Wisdom (Wis 17:11).[84]

7:23-25. Although vv. 23-24 issue a caveat suggesting that theoretical wisdom is beyond the grasp of human beings, the remainder of the subsection vv. 23-29 sets forth some specific advances in understanding made by the principal character of the book, Qohelet the sage. The latter are the kind of learnings that assist in getting on with the business of life; only God possesses the former. The same contrast of wisdoms animates the book of Job and comes to the fore in the meditation on wisdom in Job 28. Only God knows the way to the secrets of the cosmos, but God imparts knowledge sufficient for human needs

84. Ibid., 143n. 107.

with these words: "Truly, the fear of the LORD, that is wisdom; and to depart from evil is understanding" (Job 28:28 NRSV). The theme that ultimate wisdom is elusive to humankind is sounded frequently in the sapiental writings of the ancient Near East as well as elsewhere in Jewish wisdom (Prov 30:1-4; Sir 24:28-29; Bar 3:9–4:4).

7:26-28. Qohelet turns to relations between the sexes and immediately warns against that standard character of ancient Near Eastern wisdom literature, the ensnaring woman (see Prov 5:4; 6:26). There is no use pretending that Qohelet's attitude toward women measures up to the standards of equality and respect we now expect. It is true that in 9:9 he recommends love and marriage for life; here, however, his attitude is grouchy, to say the least. The two characters who confront the woman here are not necessarily a good man and a sinner; the Hebrew terms would also support the translation "a lucky one" and "an unlucky one" (also true in 2:26).

The problem of vv. 27-28 is to make sense of the phrase "adding one thing to another to find the sum." Is this a description of the work of a "collector" (קהלת *qōhelet*) of proverbs? Or does it refer to Solomon and his collection of 700 wives and 300 concubines? Commentators often suggest that the verse points forward to v. 28*b*, where the result of the Teacher's research is given—i.e., that among a thousand persons, only one man (0.1 percent) is found worthy. Although the Hebrew term used here is the generic "human being" (אדם *'ādām*), it has to be translated "man" in this case, because it is antithetical to אשה (*'iššâ*), "woman," not a single worthy one of whom (= 0 persons) was to be found. Does this mean that, in Qohelet's view, males are only infinitesimally better than females? Or does it mean that they are infinitely better? The same

statistics could be read either way. Males have nothing to crow about in any case, for the ratio of good ones to bad ones is extremely low!

7:29. The conclusion of the subsection puts the responsibility for human behavior squarely on human beings themselves. God made people "straightforward" (NRSV) or "upright" (NIV), but they have "schemed" or devised many questionable things. This news that human beings are responsible for their own perversity is not new in the Hebrew Bible (see Job 5:6-7; Lam 3:31-42), nor does it come as a shock to Jews and Christians of later eras. In spite of his avowal of the radical predetermination of all things by God (6:10; 7:14), even Qohelet makes theological allowance for human freedom and, therefore, for human error and malfeasance, for which human beings must be deemed responsible.

8:1. As understood here, this verse closes out the passage. The verse begins with two rhetorical questions and concludes with a twofold statement about the effect of wisdom on outward human appearance. The verse closes the bracket opened by 7:19 and thus helps to embrace the more restrained and gloomy evaluations of human performance in 7:20-29.

In v. 1*a* the term פשר (*pēšer,* "interpretation") is used only in this place in biblical Hebrew. It is relatively common in the Aramaic text of Daniel and becomes a major concept at the Qumran community, whose Teacher of Righteousness had the key to *pēšer* and whose *Pēšer Habakkuk* is the most perfectly preserved of the sectarian documents from the Dead Sea Scrolls.

The shining face of the wise person in v. 1*b* reflects God's shining face in the context of a right relationship of blessing (see "the priestly benediction," Num 6:25). The "impudent look" is something simply to be masked (see Sir 13:24).

REFLECTIONS

1. *Modesty in the Attainment of Virtue.* The delightful realism of 7:15-18 has struck a cord with people through the centuries. It has the ring of realism, even humanism, in its willingness to acknowledge human limitations. Qohelet already expressed great dissatisfaction with the idea that the reward of virtue and the vindication of wisdom were sure and certain outcomes (e.g., 2:15-21). For him, no one-to-one relationship between piety and payoff exists either here or in some world to come. All through their lives, human beings need to be pushed to see that they have no advantage even over the animals (3:18-19). The world itself is morally neutral, and human history produces no mechanism that will respond positively to superscrupulous sanctity and perfectionism. Qohelet counsels, therefore, that we take it easy, do the best we can, and not make ourselves miserable trying for moral superiority when there is no point in it. To make that effort might be to miss the most fundamental moral direction God gives us, that "all should eat and drink and take pleasure in all their toil" (3:13 NRSV).

2. *The Difficulty of Attaining to Wisdom.* When the writer of Deuteronomy contemplated the accessibility of the truth that saves human life from death and disaster, he said:

> Surely, this commandment that I am commanding you today is not too hard for you, nor is it too far away. It is not in heaven, that you should say, "Who will go up to heaven for us, and get it for us so that we may hear it and observe it?" . . . No, the word is very near to you; it is in your mouth and in your heart for you to observe. (Deut 30:11-14 NRSV)

Other writers of Scripture have not been as sanguine when they have contemplated ultimate and saving truth. Job 28:12-28, for example, teaches that the true meaning of things, "the reality below all changing phenomena,"[85] cannot be known (see also Sir 24:28-29; Bar 3:15-23; Rom 11:33). No one stated this pessimistic point of view more dramatically than did the Teacher, who, when undertaking to know the reality behind the realities, cried out, "That which is, is far off, and deep, very deep; who can find it out?" (7:24).

In our time we have discovered that reality lies even deeper than Qohelet imagined. Against the apocalyptists of his day, for example, he was quite willing to assert that he knew that the earth would endure forever (1:4) and that the great cycles of nature would perdure (1:5-11). Beginning with the seventeenth century, we have lived with Newtonian physics, which in a secular way made the same assertion—that immutable laws provide for stable cycles in the natural order and allow us to predict the long-term behavior of objects as large as our planet and even the universe as a whole. Now the truth about matter has become "deep, very deep; who can find it out?" From meteorology to paleontology to astrophysics, science gives us evidence of flux, of chance occurrences, of randomness and chaos. Science and Scripture converge now, not at Eccl 1:4 ("the earth remains forever" [NRSV]), but at Eccl 7:24 ("That which is, is far off, and deep, very deep" [NRSV]). Order there is in the natural world, but it is a malleable order, the complexity of which grows exponentially as we learn more about it.

85. George A. Barton, *A Critical and Exegetical Commentary on the Book of Ecclesiastes,* ICC (New York: Scribner's, 1908) 146.

Ecclesiastes 8:2-9, Instructions on Appearing Before the King

NIV

[2]Obey the king's command, I say, because you took an oath before God. [3]Do not be in a hurry to leave the king's presence. Do not stand up for a bad cause, for he will do whatever he pleases. [4]Since a king's word is supreme, who can say to him, "What are you doing?"

[5]Whoever obeys his command will come to no harm,
and the wise heart will know the proper time and procedure.
[6]For there is a proper time and procedure for every matter,

NRSV

[2]Keep[a] the king's command because of your sacred oath. [3]Do not be terrified; go from his presence, do not delay when the matter is unpleasant, for he does whatever he pleases. [4]For the word of the king is powerful, and who can say to him, "What are you doing?" [5]Whoever obeys a command will meet no harm, and the wise mind will know the time and way. [6]For every matter has its time and way, although the troubles of mortals lie heavy upon them. [7]Indeed, they do not know what is to be, for who can tell them how it will be? [8]No one has power over

[a] Heb *I keep*

NIV

though a man's misery weighs heavily upon him.

[7]Since no man knows the future,
who can tell him what is to come?
[8]No man has power over the wind to contain it[a];
so no one has power over the day of his death.
As no one is discharged in time of war,
so wickedness will not release those who practice it.

[9]All this I saw, as I applied my mind to everything done under the sun. There is a time when a man lords it over others to his own[b] hurt.

[a]8 Or *over his spirit to retain it*   [b]9 Or *to their*

NRSV

the wind[a] to restrain the wind,[a] or power over the day of death; there is no discharge from the battle, nor does wickedness deliver those who practice it. [9]All this I observed, applying my mind to all that is done under the sun, while one person exercises authority over another to the other's hurt.

[a]Or *breath*

COMMENTARY

In this short passage the Teacher instructs his pupil on court etiquette. The writer makes no effort to validate the king's authority; he merely notes that it is real, it is supreme, and a wise person will approach the king accordingly. This leads, of course, to the dangers of obsequiousness and opportunism, alongside the achievements of survival and success.

Surely the king in view here is neither Solomon nor a member of the Davidic dynasty. In fact, he is probably not a Jewish king at all. Assuming a third-century BCE date for the book of Ecclesiastes, it is quite likely that his contemporaries among the wealthy merchant or priestly Jewish families would be involved in intercourse with the suzerain of the Ptolemaic family of Egypt. The Zeno Papyri and Josephus[86] describe exactly such affairs between the rich tax farmers, the Tobiad family of Qasr al Abd (a few miles west of modern Amman, Jordan), and the Ptolemies. Other clues in the book suggest that Qohelet either belonged to that class himself or worked for them. His counsel about court etiquette thus fits with the times and with the needs of his clients; the king in question, then, might have been an Egyptian.

8:2-5. If we understand that the last phrase of v. 2, literally translated "on account of an oath

of God," refers not to an oath God made to legitimate the king but rather to an oath the client made or would make to the king in the name of God, then v. 2 is clear enough. Verse 3, however, is not. Gordis suggests that the sense of the whole verse is something like: Do not leave your post when events are unfavorable.[87] The NIV takes the two parts of the verse as separate instructions in prudential etiquette. In v. 3*a*, the Teacher may mean that to dash suddenly out of the king's presence is to arouse suspicion. In v. 3*b*, he counsels the pupil to avoid espousing causes in which the king has no interest or about which he holds a different opinion. If such counsel sounds like an invitation to become a sycophant, to seize every opportunity to please the foreign despot, so be it. Proverbs 16:14, too, advises appeasement of the king's anger. After all, the position before the throne of the conquered subject has always been precarious, to say the least. This picture of the prudent Jew in the presence of the king belongs to a diverse collection of biblical stories about courtiers who range from the ideal servant of the king, Joseph, to the impressive but resistive young sages Daniel and his friends in the Babylonian court, to Esther and Mordecai, who were not above using stratagems to get their way with

86. Josephus *Antiquities of the Jews* 11.4.

87. Robert Gordis, *Koheleth: The Man and His World,* 1st ed. (New York: Schocken, 1951; 3rd ed., 1968) 278.

the king, to Judith, who simply tricked the leader of the enemy to death. Up to a point, but not beyond, all of these would have accepted Qohelet's advice of v. 3: Go along to get along. After all, the king's word goes (v. 4)! Bearing in mind the spirit of 7:16-17, Qohelet's advice in 8:4-5 may amount to saying, "It is better to violate your own scruples than to disobey the king's command." Where would he draw the line?

8:6. The Teacher believes that timing is everything (v. 6*a*). As he demonstrated in the beautiful poem of 3:1-8, the notion of the proper time was as fundamental to the thinking of Qohelet as it was to that of earlier wisdom teachers. Ben Sira epitomizes the usual sapiental attitude toward time when he says, "Watch for the opportune time, and beware of evil" (Sir 4:20 NRSV). For Qohelet, however, there is no comfort in the concept of the proper time, for unlike other wisdom teachers, he believes that one can do little on one's own to discern the proper time. Things are not a random jumble because God has predetermined them. On the other hand, one cannot discern the hand of God anywhere because God does not reveal that hand (v. 7). The strange dilemma in which he is left is summed up by Gerhard von Rad: "To Koheleth, the world and events appear to be completely opaque and . . . on the other hand . . . they are completely within the scope of God's activity."[88]

It is no wonder that Qohelet couples with the

announcement that everything has its proper time (v. 6*a*) a further reference to the misery human beings experience (v. 6*b*). But what exactly does this half verse mean? Are the "troubles of mortals" referred to there from this implacable conundrum of divine predetermination and divine secrecy, or are they simply the things people generate for themselves? Perhaps the "troubles" referred to here are not moral failures as much as they are human defects and ailments, like Job's boils (Job 2:7). The sense of v. 6 might be, therefore: Bide your time and wait until someone messes up and gives you your opening. Even if the meaning is ethically evil, as it is in v. 11, the sense may still be the same: When someone else slips up, the wise courtier can move in at that "proper time" to win the king's favor.

8:7-9. These verses restate one of Qohelet's major themes (see Introduction; cf. 9:3, 11-12; 11:6). Whatever decisions people may make, be they pragmatic, prudential, or highly principled, they cannot know the outcome because they cannot know the future. This is a painful truth. The NIV understands the sequence of v. 8 as a set of two analogies. Just as people have no power over the "wind" (or "the spirit [of life]"), so they also have no say about when they die. Just as there is no exit when a battle is underway, even though the law (Deut 20:1-9) exempts certain people from war duty, so also wickedness does not exempt its perpetrators from its consequences (see 10:8-11).

88. Gerhard von Rad, *Wisdom in Israel* (Nashville: Abingdon, 1972) 229.

REFLECTIONS

The closing observation of this unit weaves the reflections on court etiquette back into the fabric of the book as a whole using the key phrase "under the sun." The reader is left not with the usual message of absurdity but with something worse. Whatever else may happen, the abuse of the marginals by the powerful will continue. Qohelet offers this as a universal and timeless rule that applies not only to the relationships of kings and subjects, but also even more generally to those between the powerful and the vulnerable. The NIV debates whether the Hebrew pronoun at issue in the last clause refers to the abuser or to the one being abused, while the NRSV is clear that the teaching is not a moral homily (the bad person will get it in the end) but simply a gloomy reality check (the bad person will continue hurting other people).

Ecclesiastes 8:10-17, Retribution Is an Absurdity

NIV

[10]Then too, I saw the wicked buried—those who used to come and go from the holy place and receive praise[a] in the city where they did this. This too is meaningless.

[11]When the sentence for a crime is not quickly carried out, the hearts of the people are filled with schemes to do wrong. [12]Although a wicked man commits a hundred crimes and still lives a long time, I know that it will go better with God-fearing men, who are reverent before God. [13]Yet because the wicked do not fear God, it will not go well with them, and their days will not lengthen like a shadow.

[14]There is something else meaningless that occurs on earth: righteous men who get what the wicked deserve, and wicked men who get what the righteous deserve. This too, I say, is meaningless. [15]So I commend the enjoyment of life, because nothing is better for a man under the sun than to eat and drink and be glad. Then joy will accompany him in his work all the days of the life God has given him under the sun.

[16]When I applied my mind to know wisdom and to observe man's labor on earth—his eyes not seeing sleep day or night— [17]then I saw all that God has done. No one can comprehend what goes on under the sun. Despite all his efforts to search it out, man cannot discover its meaning. Even if a wise man claims he knows, he cannot really comprehend it.

a10 Some Hebrew manuscripts and Septuagint (Aquila); most Hebrew manuscripts *and are forgotten*

NRSV

10Then I saw the wicked buried; they used to go in and out of the holy place, and were praised in the city where they had done such things.[a] This also is vanity. [11]Because sentence against an evil deed is not executed speedily, the human heart is fully set to do evil. [12]Though sinners do evil a hundred times and prolong their lives, yet I know that it will be well with those who fear God, because they stand in fear before him, [13]but it will not be well with the wicked, neither will they prolong their days like a shadow, because they do not stand in fear before God.

14There is a vanity that takes place on earth, that there are righteous people who are treated according to the conduct of the wicked, and there are wicked people who are treated according to the conduct of the righteous. I said that this also is vanity. [15]So I commend enjoyment, for there is nothing better for people under the sun than to eat, and drink, and enjoy themselves, for this will go with them in their toil through the days of life that God gives them under the sun.

16When I applied my mind to know wisdom, and to see the business that is done on earth, how one's eyes see sleep neither day nor night, [17]then I saw all the work of God, that no one can find out what is happening under the sun. However much they may toil in seeking, they will not find it out; even though those who are wise claim to know, they cannot find it out.

*a*Meaning of Heb uncertain

COMMENTARY

Even though Qohelet closed the preceding unit on the note that wickedness cannot be guaranteed to pay, he is not prepared to say that righteousness will do so either. The section that follows, vv. 10-17, includes a complex interplay between the accepted wisdom set forth in vv. 12b-13 and his own profound doubts that the mechanism for rewarding wickedness according to its just deserts is in place. Although all of the themes in this passage have been stated before, it brings them together in a combination that sets forth with considerable pathos the failure of retributional theology to operate dependably, the impossibility of discerning the reason why this should be, and the retreat into the by now familiar advice to eat, drink, and be merry (v. 15) that is Qohelet's only positive recommendation. Rankin sums up the thought of this section succinctly: "There is no moral purpose working itself out in human destiny."[89]

8:10. With help from the LXX, scholars conclude that this obscure opening verse intends to say something like this: "I have seen the wicked brought to their grave with pomp; and when people walk from the holy place, they are praised in the city where they acted thus." The sense, then, is that even though the community knew these people were wicked, it gave the villains a decent burial (a mark of a successful life, according to Eccl 6:3). Before they are even cold in their graves, in the very city in which they committed their evil deeds, their names are being honored (another mark of distinction, according to Eccl 7:1). In short, the wicked do not get what is coming to them; they get much more! This Qohelet finds to be absurd.

8:11-15. Although it is clear that Qohelet advocates sentencing sinners in order to deter sin, vv. 11-12*a* offer no assurances that they will certainly be caught and treated appropriately. In

spite of the optimism of the traditional teaching of vv. 12*b*-13, the Teacher recurs to his own line in v. 14. In this topsy-turvy world, the very opposite of what ought to happen may in fact happen. In the light of these grim injustices, Qohelet once again advocates his type of hedonism (v. 15), sounding the hitherto unheard note that the pleasures of food and drink will accompany individuals into the difficult struggles of their lives. Whether this accompaniment into toil is simply a matter of memory or whether it is a full stomach or even genuine happiness and peace of mind cannot be determined from the text; however, the Teacher does seem to allow the possibility that times of leisure and pleasure positively affect the rest of life.

8:16-17. The passage closes with Qohelet's familiar diatribe against the claims of sages to have penetrated to the heart of life and to the work God is doing in the world (see Job 12:2, where Job sardonically mocks his friends for claiming to know such things). It is a canon of the preacher's faith that God's actions in history cannot be discerned.

89. O. S. Rankin and G. G. Atkins, "The Book of Ecclesiastes," in *The Interpreter's Bible,* 12 vols., ed. George A. Buttrick et al. (Nashville: Abingdon, 1956) 5:71.

REFLECTIONS

Advocates of the summary execution of judgment can no doubt take heart from the sentiments expressed in vv. 11-12*a*. In these verses, the Teacher might be heard to say, in effect, that crime and wickedness are rampant because there is too much parole, that too many offenders are let off with light sentences or released early from jail, and that deterrents of crime cannot be operative in such a climate. Perhaps he did toy with such ideas. At the same time, in the context of God's predetermination of the times and refusal to share the plan, there seems to be relatively little space for vigorous legal and moral action. The wages of sin are not necessarily death, nor are the wages of righteousness life; things happen when they must happen. Even though the spectacle of the wicked person's going unpunished and even prospering is sickening, one tires of looking at it. Then one turns to the swimming pool and to the lunch spread on the grass and to the enjoyment of such small things as are available to people who live with total lack of knowledge of the future and total lack of ability to shape or structure it. There is no use trying to get out ahead of events, to anticipate the future, be it economic, political, or personal. *Que será, será:* Whatever will be will be.

Such a climate seems to inhibit the building up of much enthusiasm for ridding a community of evil and building a better world. It drives one to quietism in the search for a little piece of happiness with food, drink, and loved ones. Even though there is a time to kill (3:3), and that might include the speedy execution of justice against evildoers (8:11), on the whole there is not much point in taking too many people before the firing squad. Innumerable others will spring up. By getting involved one only loses time to "eat, and drink, and enjoy" (8:15), which is the one sphere of real human freedom and autonomy that the Teacher is able to discern.

ECCLESIASTES 9:1-12, TIME AND CHANCE BEFALL ALL

NIV

9 So I reflected on all this and concluded that the righteous and the wise and what they do are in God's hands, but no man knows whether love or hate awaits him. [2]All share a common destiny—the righteous and the wicked, the good and the bad,[a] the clean and the unclean, those who offer sacrifices and those who do not.

As it is with the good man,
    so with the sinner;
as it is with those who take oaths,
    so with those who are afraid to take them.

[3]This is the evil in everything that happens under the sun: The same destiny overtakes all. The hearts of men, moreover, are full of evil and there is madness in their hearts while they live, and afterward they join the dead. [4]Anyone who is among the living has hope[b]—even a live dog is better off than a dead lion!

[5]For the living know that they will die,
    but the dead know nothing;
they have no further reward,
    and even the memory of them is forgotten.
[6]Their love, their hate
    and their jealousy have long since vanished;
never again will they have a part
    in anything that happens under the sun.

[7]Go, eat your food with gladness, and drink your wine with a joyful heart, for it is now that God favors what you do. [8]Always be clothed in white, and always anoint your head with oil. [9]Enjoy life with your wife, whom you love, all the days of this meaningless life that God has given you under the sun— all your meaningless days. For this is your lot in life and in your toilsome labor under the sun. [10]Whatever your hand finds to do, do it with all your might, for in the grave,[c] where you are going, there is neither working nor planning nor knowledge nor wisdom.

[11]I have seen something else under the sun:

[a]2 Septuagint (Aquila), Vulgate and Syriac; Hebrew does not have *and the bad.* [b]4 Or *What then is to be chosen? With all who live, there is hope* [c]10 Hebrew *Sheol*

NRSV

9 All this I laid to heart, examining it all, how the righteous and the wise and their deeds are in the hand of God; whether it is love or hate one does not know. Everything that confronts them [2]is vanity,[a] since the same fate comes to all, to the righteous and the wicked, to the good and the evil,[b] to the clean and the unclean, to those who sacrifice and those who do not sacrifice. As are the good, so are the sinners; those who swear are like those who shun an oath. [3]This is an evil in all that happens under the sun, that the same fate comes to everyone. Moreover, the hearts of all are full of evil; madness is in their hearts while they live, and after that they go to the dead. [4]But whoever is joined with all the living has hope, for a living dog is better than a dead lion. [5]The living know that they will die, but the dead know nothing; they have no more reward, and even the memory of them is lost. [6]Their love and their hate and their envy have already perished; never again will they have any share in all that happens under the sun.

[7]Go, eat your bread with enjoyment, and drink your wine with a merry heart; for God has long ago approved what you do. [8]Let your garments always be white; do not let oil be lacking on your head. [9]Enjoy life with the wife whom you love, all the days of your vain life that are given you under the sun, because that is your portion in life and in your toil at which you toil under the sun. [10]Whatever your hand finds to do, do with your might; for there is no work or thought or knowledge or wisdom in Sheol, to which you are going.

[11]Again I saw that under the sun the race is not to the swift, nor the battle to the strong, nor bread to the wise, nor riches to the intelligent, nor favor to the skillful; but time and chance happen to them all. [12]For no one can anticipate the time of disaster. Like fish taken in a cruel net, and like birds caught in a snare, so mortals are snared at a time of calamity, when it suddenly falls upon them.

[a]Syr Compare Gk: Heb *Everything that confronts them* [2]*is everything* [b]Gk Syr Vg: Heb lacks *and the evil*

NIV

The race is not to the swift
  or the battle to the strong,
nor does food come to the wise
  or wealth to the brilliant
  or favor to the learned;
but time and chance happen to them all.

12Moreover, no man knows when his hour will come:

As fish are caught in a cruel net,
  or birds are taken in a snare,
so men are trapped by evil times
  that fall unexpectedly upon them.

COMMENTARY

This section is a happy amalgam of two of the major themes of the book: The same fate happens to everyone, and *carpe diem* ("seize the day") and enjoy life (see Introduction). The passage also weaves together traditional proverbs with fresh reflections by Qohelet; it combines prose and poetry; it punctuates the entire mix with two of the slogans of the book, "all is vanity" and "under the sun." The overarching theme upon which the writer expands in this section is that the ultimate destiny of the good person is no better than that of the evil person and that all the achievements of life do not guarantee escape from death or obliteration. In no way does good behavior guarantee good results. In short, it is a sadly realistic, almost despairing passage; yet, it is animated by the lovely sentiments of 9:7-10. The combination of familiar elements makes those verses sound almost like a programmatic statement for the entire book.

9:1-3. The love and hate that await an individual (v. 1) are the attitudes of God, though one cannot know the divine verdict in advance. The last clause of the verse, which literally reads, "Everything is before them," is combined by the NRSV with an amended version of the beginning of v. 2. The NIV rightly decides to avoid the emendation and keep the two verses separate, making clear that the task of v. 2 is to expand on the gloomy theme of the common destiny of all humanity.

The list of "righteous" people in v. 2 has a somewhat antiquarian flavor. Perhaps Qohelet reached out for examples from the ranks of the superreligious. By his time, for example, sacrifice had begun to yield to prayer as the most basic act of personal piety. As for the swearing of oaths, including the curious custom of placing the hand on the genitals of the other oathtaker (see Gen 24:2-9; 47:29), the practice was coming into increasing disfavor in the later period of the Hebrew Bible and in the intertestamental period. Qohelet did not personally recommend it (5:5). Josephus[90] says that the turn-of-the-era Essenes banned oath taking, except for the binding vow taken upon entry into the covenant community. Nor did Jesus look upon the practice with favor: "Let your word be 'Yes, Yes' or 'No, No'; anything more than this comes from the evil one" (Matt 5:37 NRSV). In the background of this development stands the ninth commandment, against false testimony (Exod 20:16; Deut 5:20), which was Israel's safeguard of the integrity of sworn witnesses in court. Qohelet's point may be that even people who have become so scrupulous about the truth that they fear to take an oath have destinies neither more nor less positive than the moral leper who has sworn an oath and then violated it. Against the standard but flawed reward-and-punishment mentality of his day—and

90. Josephus *The Jewish War* 2.8.6; confirmed by 1QS 5:8.

every day—he asserts that what one does has no bearing on what finally happens to one. "The same fate comes to everyone" (v. 3): Everyone dies.

9:4. After the extremely dark picture of human beings painted in v. 3*b*, a ray of hope shines out of this verse—if, that is, "hope" is the correct translation of בטחון (*biṭṭāḥôn*), which in its other occurrences in biblical Hebrew (2 Kgs 18:19 = Isa 36:4) means "trust" and in modern Hebrew means "security." Perhaps v. 4*a* simply means that whoever is alive can have confidence in life, at least for the present moment. This is followed in v. 4*b* by another popular proverb that stresses the superiority of any kind of life at all over death. The dog is not admired in the Hebrew Bible (1 Sam 24:14; 2 Sam 3:8; 16:9), whereas the lion is the very emblem of royalty (Gen 49:9) and a metaphor for God's power (e.g., Isa 38:13; Lam 3:10; Hos 5:14; 13:7-8). Yet the nod is given to life, for "consciousness on any terms is preferable to non-existence."[91]

9:5-7. Nevertheless, the advantage of the living human being quickly deteriorates into the pain of knowing what lies ahead. The dead vanish in memory as if they never were. This is the theme of Qohelet that sticks in the craw of his putative antagonist, the author of the Wisdom of Solomon. The latter includes this motif in his condemnation of those who reason cynically that we can eat, drink, be merry, rob, and extort because:

Our name will be forgotten in time,
and no one will remember our works;
our life will pass away like the traces of a cloud,
and be scattered like mist
that is chased by the rays of the sun
and overcome by its heat.
For our allotted time is the passing of a shadow.
(Wis 2:4-5 NRSV)

Against this view, so profoundly asserted by Qohelet, the writer of Wisdom advocates a doctrine of blessed immortality and a dependable connection between righteousness and salvation: "But the souls of the righteous are in the hand of God, and no torment will ever touch them" (Wis 3:1 NRSV).

In response to the gloomy future sketched in vv. 1-6, vv. 7-10 sound the affirmation of Eccle-

siastes that the goal of humankind is to seek joy in all endeavors. Because all passions are extinguished by death (v. 6), it is imperative to seize the hour for happiness now. Appended to the injunction to eat, drink, and be merry is the extraordinary remark that "God has long ago approved what you do."

At issue between the NRSV and the NIV is the meaning in this verse of the word כבר (*kĕbār*, "already"). Using the perfect or completed tense, the Teacher claims that God has accepted or approved the hearer's deeds. (The same Hebrew verb is used when God accepts an offering; e.g., Deut 33:10-11; Amos 5:22). The use of the perfect (completed) tense is not definitive inasmuch as Qohelet sometimes uses it to refer to present and uncompleted acts as well (e.g., "gives," 2:26; "exercises authority," 8:9), but the word "already" seems intended to underscore the completedness of the divine decision. Thus the verse appears to be giving the hearer a blank check to spend on a life of gaiety and pleasure. The NIV tries to avoid this implication, it seems, by discerning the nuance "now" in the word *kĕbār* and by using an imperfect or uncompleted sense of the verb "accepted," "approved": "for it is now that God favors what you do." The NRSV comes closer to the literal understanding: Long ago God declared it to be morally correct that human beings should enjoy bread, wine, and life itself. It is not that God foreordains or approves of everything that one might do, but that God created human life good from the beginning and wills that human beings take legitimate pleasure in being alive. This approach differs from that of Crenshaw, who dismisses the problem by saying, "Since one's capacity to enjoy life depends on a divine gift, anyone who can eat and drink must enjoy divine favor. . . . Divine approval preceded human enjoyment."[92] Crenshaw's interpretation is indebted to 5:16 and 6:2, where the word השליט (*hišlît*, "empowered") is used to describe God's role in human pleasure. But here God's role is described by the verb רצה (*rāṣâ*, "approved"). If approval equals empowerment, the Teacher would not need to offer this instruction.

9:8. The passage continues to describe the joyful person as being clothed in white, the festal

---

91. Gordis, *Koheleth,* 295.

92. James L. Crenshaw, *Ecclesiastes,* OTL (Philadelphia: Westminster, 1987) 162.

color throughout the ancient Near East. Mordechai wears "robes of blue and white" on the day of the liberation of the Jews (Esth 8:15). The togas of the worshipers on the walls of the third-century CE synagogue at Dura Europas are white. White is the color of the garments of the saints (2 Esdr 2:40) and of the clothing of the transfigured Jesus (Matt 17:2 and parallels). The garments of the angels at the tomb of Christ (Matt 28:3 and parallels) and in Rev 3:4-5 and 7:9 are all white. When this invitation to wear the clothing of the holy ones is combined with the injunction to use oil freely (see Ps 133:2), the effect is a call to exuberance.

9:9-10. Qohelet reaches the zenith of his very restrained praise of women in v. 9. Evidently addressing an all-male audience, he links happiness with "a woman you love" (TNK) to the other means of happiness that are given to humankind. In this fourth and final use of the term "love" (אהב 'āhab), the Teacher for once is unambiguous. Elsewhere love may be opposed by hate (3:8; 9:1) or may be described as fleeting (9:6). Here, however, the love of a man for a woman is a simple component of joy. Both the NRSV and the NIV make the indefinite Hebrew word "a woman," "wife," definite, "the wife," and "your wife," respectively—no ambiguity for them! One need not go so far in the opposite direction as does Gordis, who says, "Koheleth was almost surely a bachelor, and was certainly no apologist for the marriage institution."[93] Yet the Teacher's analysis of how joy and morality intersect might not have been the same as those of today's Jews and Christians. The point here is not the exact arrangement within which a man and a woman find happiness in each other, but rather the importance of the ability to love amid the fleeting absurdity of life. This is because the destiny that confronts all people is Sheol (v. 10).

Sheol, the abode of the dead, is not the Hellenistic hades or the hell of later Judaism and Christianity. It is not the antithesis of heaven (although the reluctance of the NIV to use the term suggests that it wishes to reserve the concept of an underworld for later juxtaposition with heaven). Contra the NIV, it is not simply "the grave." Instead, it is a place in which all dead

93. Gordis, *Koheleth,* 296.

persons have a shadowy existence, a place to which the Lord can send people and from which God can also bring them back (1 Sam 2:2), a place from which the Lord could hear the cries of Jonah (Jonah 2:2). Sheol is mentioned some sixty-five times in the Hebrew Bible, and some of the writers allow the "shades" to continue to possess some kind of memory and existence in Sheol (e.g., Num 16:30-33; 1 Sam 28:8-14; Ps 143:3; Isa 14:14-17). One psalmist even imagined that God could be present in it: "If I ascend to heaven, you are there;/ If I make my bed in Sheol, you are there" (Ps 139:8).

But in this his only use of the term, Qohelet maintains the traditional view of ancient Israel: Sheol is a place from which no one exits, from which no prayers arise, beyond which there is no further hope (see Job 14:11-14; Ps 6:5). It is a place of nonbeing, where all consciousness and all passions have ceased (see 9:5-6). As we have seen (3:21), the Teacher maintains this view in the face of some of his contemporaries who were apparently already beginning to suggest that the dead might be resurrected to either of two places, one up and one down (see Isa 26:19; Dan 12:2). Perhaps Qohelet's view is a manifestation of a conservative, upper-class outlook, analogous to that of the patrician Sadducees of later times who denied the resurrection of the dead (Mark 12:18; Luke 20:27). Perhaps Qohelet's critic of a later generation, the writer of the Wisdom of Solomon, more accurately represented the hope of the rank and file of Jews even of Qohelet's day when he wrote, "Righteousness is immortal" (Wis 1:15 NRSV).

9:11-12. The lyrical v. 11 systematically demolishes all of the assurances of success to which people cling. The object of a runner is to win the race; the object of a valiant soldier is to win the battle; the object of intelligence is to gain riches. According to the Teacher, however, there is no sure and certain hope that any of these objectives can be met, because over all loom time and "chance" (see Introduction). Through all of life one can only repeat, "Curses, foiled again!" In this stern judgment Qohelet runs against conventional wisdom, which saw a one-to-one correlation between good sense and success—e.g., "Good sense wins favor,/ but the way of the faithless is their ruin" (Prov 13:15 NRSV). Although righteousness is not listed as one of the virtues that is demolished by time and chance, presumably Qohelet would include it as well (see 7:16), thereby confounding even hopes as fond as those expressed by the psalms of the two ways: "In all that [the righteous] do, they prosper" (Ps 1:3 NRSV). Sudden entrapment, sudden calamity, sudden death are the fates of human beings just as they are those of innocent fish and birds (v. 12), and one cannot anticipate, prevent, or gainsay this reality.

REFLECTIONS

Qohelet's characteristic ambivalence about life permeates 9:1-12. "The same fate comes to everyone" (v. 3), he says, and yet "whoever is joined with all the living has hope, for a living dog is better than a dead lion" (v. 4). The latter sentence is not exactly a thumping affirmation of life, but it is a reluctant admission that a bird in the hand is better than two in the bush (to maintain the idiomatic flavor of the discussion). The notion that life even at an attenuated level is better than no life at all has been affirmed by theologians and poets alike (see Reflections at 3:16–4:8). Thoreau, for example, in the conclusion to *Walden,* criticizes those who say that "we Americans, and moderns generally, are intellectual dwarfs compared with the ancients, or even the Elizabethan men. But what is that to the purpose?" He continues: "A living dog is better than a dead lion. . . . Let every one mind his own business, and endeavor to be what he was made." Somerset Maugham evidently thought Americans had a propensity to go for the main chance and that Eccl 9:4 describes that propensity. In his *Cakes and Ale,* when two young American literati prefer to tour the home of the deceased writer Edward Driffield with his widow rather than in the company of a distinguished younger writer, Maugham has the latter remark to a friend, "You don't know America as well as I do. . . . They always prefer a live mouse to a dead lion. That's one of the reasons I like America."

The poet Louis Untermeyer gave a rather different spin to the passage in question. In his poem entitled "Koheleth," he relates the message of the entire book to 9:4. He takes the living dog to be a moral midget that survives the moral giant, who perishes. Although he does not say it explicitly, to him this is vanity.

> I waited and worked
> To win myself leisure,
> Till loneliness irked
> And I turned to raw pleasure.
> I drank and gamed,
> I feasted and wasted,
> Till, sick and ashamed,
> The food stood untasted.
> I searched in the Book
> For rooted convictions
> Till the badgered brain shook
> With its own contradictions.
> Then, done with the speech,
> Of the foolishly lettered,
> I started to teach
> Life cannot be bettered:
> That the warrior fails
> Whatever his weapon,
> And nothing avails
> While time and chance happen.
> That fools who assure men
> With lies are respected,
> While the vision of pure men

Is scorned and rejected.
That a wise man goes grieving
Even in Zion,
While any dog living
Outroars a dead lion.[94]

As noted in the exegetical discussion, the clause "for God has long ago approved what you do," the most original and unexpected comment in this passage, is woven into the familiar advice of Qohelet to eat, drink, and be merry (9:7-10). Because the meaning is elusive, the interpretive possibilities are many! If Qohelet's point is that God foreordains everything, then even what one does by way of play has already been written in the book of life before history ever began. If Qohelet's point is that God gave advance approval in general terms to the things that make for human happiness, then interpreters can enlarge on the possibility of having a good life, if it is lived within those preapproved parameters.

The most likely construal of v. 7*b* is this: In the midst of the uncertainties and even the absurdity in which people live and in the face of the personal extinction that most certainly lies ahead, the best thing they can do now is to "eat . . . bread with enjoyment and drink . . . wine with a merry heart." Then they will be obeying the will of God for their lives and can enjoy divine approval. The nuances of how one eats bread and drinks wine and enjoys life are many, of course, and we heirs to the puritanical tradition will no doubt busy ourselves developing criteria by which to grade the degree of approval that God gives to our various modes of doing these things. Even so, the previous approval of vigorous, happy, human living seems to be the singular plus in the message of Qohelet. God knows there are many long faces and much unhappiness out there, some of which derives from the malpractice of religion. Qohelet's plus, therefore, is a gift from which contemporary Jews and Christians can take heart.

When Qohelet reverts to his theme of the certainty of death for everyone in 9:11-12, he sees no escape from the sudden onset of calamity. Virtue, wisdom, skill, riches, and strength cannot alter that immutable decree, expressed to our minds as "time and chance." When D. H. Lawrence read these verses, his reaction was to advocate a modest acceptance of fate even while clinging to the fragile beauty of life. In other words, he read 9:11-12 in terms of the life affirmation of vv. 7-10:

The race is not to the swift
but to those that can sit still
and let the waves go over them.
  The battle is not to the strong
  but to the frail, who know best
  how to efface themselves
  to save the streaked pansy of the heart
    from being trampled to mud.[95]

Christians have a basis for optimism about the future, because we are convinced that it belongs to God. By our eschatological vision of the New Jerusalem, we are drawn as with a magnet into that future. Having had a foretaste of the new age of peace and justice in the life, ministry, death, and resurrection of Jesus Christ, we are eager to get on with our work of building a world that looks as much as we can make it look like the kingdom of heaven on earth. Even so, there is a place in our faith for the kind of realism that Qohelet offers us and that D. H. Lawrence captures: In the misery of warfare and persecution or in the doldrums

---

94. Louis Untermeyer, "Koheleth," *Burning Bush.* Copyright © 1928 by Harcourt Brace & Company and renewed 1956 by Louis Untermeyer. Reprinted by permission of the publisher.

95. "Race and Battle" by D. H. Lawrence from *The Complete Poems of D. H. Lawrence* by D. H. Lawrence, ed. V. de Sola Pinto and F. W. Roberts. Copyright © 1964, 1971 by Angelo Ravagli and C. M. Weekley, Executors of the Estate of Frieda Lawrence Ravagli. Used by permission of Viking Penguin, a division of Penguin Books USA Inc.

of secularization and consumerism, sometimes the best we can do is to acknowledge the limits of our human capacity to achieve great ends and "save the streaked pansy of the heart."

ECCLESIASTES 9:13–11:6, A SECOND MISCELLANY

Ecclesiastes 9:13–10:7, Wisdom, Folly, Kings, and Fools

NIV	NRSV
[13]I also saw under the sun this example of wisdom that greatly impressed me: [14]There was once a small city with only a few people in it. And a powerful king came against it, surrounded it and built huge siegeworks against it. [15]Now there lived in that city a man poor but wise, and he saved the city by his wisdom. But nobody remembered that poor man. [16]So I said, "Wisdom is better than strength." But the poor man's wisdom is despised, and his words are no longer heeded.	[13]I have also seen this example of wisdom under the sun, and it seemed great to me. [14]There was a little city with few people in it. A great king came against it and besieged it, building great siegeworks against it. [15]Now there was found in it a poor wise man, and he by his wisdom delivered the city. Yet no one remembered that poor man. [16]So I said, "Wisdom is better than might; yet the poor man's wisdom is despised, and his words are not heeded."

[17]The quiet words of the wise are more to be heeded
    than the shouts of a ruler of fools.
[18]Wisdom is better than weapons of war,
    but one sinner destroys much good.
	[17] The quiet words of the wise are more to be heeded
	    than the shouting of a ruler among fools.
	[18] Wisdom is better than weapons of war,
	    but one bungler destroys much good.

10 As dead flies give perfume a bad smell,
    so a little folly outweighs wisdom and honor.
[2]The heart of the wise inclines to the right,
    but the heart of the fool to the left.
[3]Even as he walks along the road,
    the fool lacks sense
    and shows everyone how stupid he is.
[4]If a ruler's anger rises against you,
    do not leave your post;
    calmness can lay great errors to rest.
	10 Dead flies make the perfumer's ointment give off a foul odor;
	    so a little folly outweighs wisdom and honor.
	[2] The heart of the wise inclines to the right,
	    but the heart of a fool to the left.
	[3] Even when fools walk on the road, they lack sense,
	    and show to everyone that they are fools.
	[4] If the anger of the ruler rises against you, do not leave your post,
	    for calmness will undo great offenses.

[5]There is an evil I have seen under the sun,
    the sort of error that arises from a ruler:
[6]Fools are put in many high positions,
    while the rich occupy the low ones.
[7]I have seen slaves on horseback,
    while princes go on foot like slaves.
	[5]There is an evil that I have seen under the sun, as great an error as if it proceeded from the ruler: [6]folly is set in many high places, and the rich sit in a low place. [7]I have seen slaves on horseback, and princes walking on foot like slaves.

COMMENTARY

There is no need to regard this section as an intentional unity. It seems highly likely that a number of verses are quotations from popular wisdom (e.g., 9:18; 10:1), while others have been grouped together because of thematic commonalities. However, running through this section are the contrasts of wisdom and foolishness and of kings and commoners. As the NRSV understands it, the passage is bracketed on either end by little prose passages that can almost be called parables (9:13-16; 10:5-7).

9:13-16. These verses tell the story of a poor wise man who saved an entire city during a powerful siege by an enemy king, and yet in the end the poor man was overlooked. This passage almost has the quality of an apophthegm, a story developed to provide a narrative context for an already extant teaching or proverb. In this case, it enlarges on the difficulty a poor person has in being listened to with respect (cf. Sir 13:23). The punch line is the Teacher's gloomy dialectical reflection in v. 16. As elsewhere (e.g., 4:5-6; 9:18), he is able to make two contradictory points simultaneously. Perhaps he achieves this by quoting a traditional saying and then answering it; in any case, he seems to agree with both positions: "Wisdom is better than might," and, at the same time, "wisdom is despised." If Qohelet is speaking as a teacher of the children of the rich and powerful, he is warning them not to be too sanguine, not to expect that the rewards of wisdom will be acknowledgment and esteem. He will go on to urge realism. Even with such good attainments as wisdom, wealth, and power there is no sure and certain hope in this life, and absolutely no hope in any other life.

9:17–10:1. The sage Qohelet comments further on the values of wisdom and its limitations. After affirming the efficacy of wisdom, he offers another contradiction: "One bungler [חוטא *ḥôṭe*ʾ] destroys much good" (v. 18*b*). The NIV translates the term *ḥôṭe*ʾ as "sinner." The rendition is possible, but it substantially changes the meaning of the proverb. The contrast in this section is not sinner/saint but fool/wise person. That a *ḥôṭe*ʾ can be one who "misses the mark" and is therefore a fool and a bungler is demonstrated by Prov 19:2.

This little series of teachings about the supe-

riority of wisdom over folly combined with the infernal capacity of folly to win the day concludes with the much-quoted proverb of 10:1. The problems of the Hebrew text of this passage have led interpreters both ancient and modern to propose many emendations. However, all agree on the main point of the proverb: Just as worthless insects can ruin valuable ointment, so also little specks of folly can pollute an entire mass of "wisdom and honor."

10:2-3. These verses continue the wise/foolish antithesis, followed by vv. 4-7, which are dominated by the image of the ruler. Verse 2 puts an unfortunate onus on the leftward direction. Hebrew literature was not alone in this tendency. In many languages "left" is ominous and awkward (*sinister,* Latin; *gauche,* French), whereas "right" also means "balanced," "correct," "just" (*droit,* French; *recht,* German). Even God seems to be right-handed, for salvation is wrought by God's powerful right hand (Exod 15:6), which is "filled with victory" (Ps 48:10). When the Christ is raised to glory it is to sit at the right hand of God (Acts 2:33-34; Heb 1:3). From his throne of judgment, the Son of Man separates the saved sheep from the damned goats onto his right and left hands respectively (Matt 25:31-36). The judgment here, however, is not a moral but a practical one, for everyone can see the stupidity of the fool who drifts off in the wrong direction (v. 3). Although Qohelet was often unconventional, he was still a teacher of wisdom and often accepted standard ideas such as this one.

10:4. Gordis believes that in passages such as vv. 4-7 the conservative upper-class mentality of Qohelet the professional sage appears. Here, for example, he warns his prominent pupils that "an unstable society may give importance to upstarts and fools, while the rich and well-born (the contrast is instructive) may lose their positions."[96] The advice of this verse, aimed directly at the pupil in the second person, is in the mode of 8:1-9. It says, in effect, If you offend the ruler, do not run off, but face the music with composure. After all, "a soft answer turneth away wrath" (Prov 15:1, 4), and so on—conventional stuff.

---

96. Robert Gordis, *Koheleth: The Man and His World,* 1st ed. (New York: Schocken, 1951; 3rd ed., 1968) 306.

10:5-7. These verses deal in reversals. Qohelet cautions his pupils that the world can easily be turned upside down and that the unpredictability of life may result in debasement of those whose wealth and social standing would normally have given them preferential seating at banquets and on steeds. The ruler himself may even sanction such reversals. Verse 6 juxtaposes an abstract noun, "folly" (הסכל *hassekel*), with a concrete noun, "the rich" (עשירים *ʿăšîrîm*). In a similar juxtaposition in 9:18, abstract wisdom could be undone by the confusion of one specific bungler; here abstract folly dethrones the power of many leading citizens.

Crenshaw points out that, because of their use in warfare, horses had prestige that mules and donkeys lacked, even though royalty, too, rode mules in earlier times (2 Sam 18:9) and perhaps even later in ritual processions (Zech 9:9).[97] For members of the Jerusalem establishment, Jesus' Palm Sunday entry into the city—mounted on a donkey, not a horse—must have represented a reversal like that anticipated in this verse. See Matt 21:1-11 and parallels.

97. James L. Crenshaw, *Ecclesiastes*, OTL (Philadelphia: Westminster, 1987) 172.

REFLECTIONS

History provides numerous examples of the validity of 9:17. In our own lifetimes many of us have seen the contrast between the German contemporaries Dietrich Bonhoeffer and Adolf Hitler. The quiet words of the jailed theologian have proved to be of enduring worth. But who can quote a single phrase of the endless rantings of the dictator? The antithetical parallelism of v. 18 makes for useful reflection. A wooden translation of the Hebrew, "More good is wisdom than implements of warfare; but one bungler destroys much good," reveals that the contrasting assertions are tied together by the word "good." The effect is to say that the great quantity of good that wisdom can amass can be wiped out by one lowly fool. To express the theme in our vernacular wisdom, "One rotten apple can spoil the whole bushel."

The saying of 10:1 expands on this theme and in the process gives us our English adage "a fly in the ointment." Rottenness is manifested in folly as much as it is in outright sin. The historian Barbara Tuchman defines wisdom as "the exercise of judgment acting on experience, common sense and available information"; folly, in contrast, "is the pursuit of policy contrary to the self-interest of the constituency . . . involved."[98] Folly manifests itself in wooden-headed-ness, which is the source of self-deception, that fatal wish not to be deflected by the facts from a chosen course of action. Tuchman applies these criteria to the activities of kings and nations and in her book *The March of Folly,* subtitled *From Troy to Vietnam,* cites parade examples of public folly on a horrific scale. Qohelet's rule of 10:1 can be applied equally well to both the private and the public spheres, but it disagrees in no way with the insights of the modern historian. Wooden-headedness and self-deception can indeed overcome wisdom and honor! Nor need the folly be continuous and current; it can be a single act of long ago—a sexual contact with an HIV-infected person, a small unrepaid loan from a fund entrusted to one's keeping, a decision to invest in a fraudulent scheme. It all goes on the record, for every action has consequences sooner or later. The eighteenth-century English poet Matthew Prior addressed this in his poem "Pleasure: The Second Book of Solomon on the Vanity of the World," from which this stanza is excerpted:

> Oft have I said, the praise of doing well
> Is to the ear, as ointment to the smell.
> Now if some flies perchance, however small,
> Into the alabaster urn should fall;
> The odors of the sweets enclosed would die;

98. Barbara W. Tuchman, *The March of Folly: From Troy to Vietnam* (New York: Knopf, 1984) 4-5.

And stench corrupt (sad change!) their place supply.
So the least faults, if mixed with fairest deed,
Of future ill become the fatal seed:
Into the balm of purest virtue cast,
Annoy all life with one contagious blast.

Ecclesiastes 10:8–11:6, The Certainty of Cause and Effect

NIV

⁸Whoever digs a pit may fall into it;
  whoever breaks through a wall may be bitten
    by a snake.
⁹Whoever quarries stones may be injured by them;
  whoever splits logs may be endangered by
    them.
¹⁰If the ax is dull
  and its edge unsharpened,
more strength is needed
  but skill will bring success.

¹¹If a snake bites before it is charmed,
  there is no profit for the charmer.

¹²Words from a wise man's mouth are gracious,
  but a fool is consumed by his own lips.
¹³At the beginning his words are folly;
  at the end they are wicked madness—
¹⁴ and the fool multiplies words.

No one knows what is coming—
  who can tell him what will happen after him?

¹⁵A fool's work wearies him;
  he does not know the way to town.

¹⁶Woe to you, O land whose king was a servant[a]
  and whose princes feast in the morning.
¹⁷Blessed are you, O land whose king is of noble
    birth
  and whose princes eat at a proper time—
    for strength and not for drunkenness.

¹⁸If a man is lazy, the rafters sag;
  if his hands are idle, the house leaks.

¹⁹A feast is made for laughter,
  and wine makes life merry,
  but money is the answer for everything.

²⁰Do not revile the king even in your thoughts,
  or curse the rich in your bedroom,
  because a bird of the air may carry your words,

a16 Or *king is a child*

NRSV

⁸ Whoever digs a pit will fall into it;
  and whoever breaks through a wall will be
    bitten by a snake.
⁹ Whoever quarries stones will be hurt by them;
  and whoever splits logs will be endangered
    by them.
¹⁰ If the iron is blunt, and one does not whet the
    edge,
  then more strength must be exerted;
  but wisdom helps one to succeed.
¹¹ If the snake bites before it is charmed,
  there is no advantage in a charmer.

¹² Words spoken by the wise bring them favor,
  but the lips of fools consume them.
¹³ The words of their mouths begin in
    foolishness,
  and their talk ends in wicked madness;
¹⁴ yet fools talk on and on.
  No one knows what is to happen,
  and who can tell anyone what the future
    holds?
¹⁵ The toil of fools wears them out,
  for they do not even know the way to town.

¹⁶ Alas for you, O land, when your king is a
    servant,[a]
  and your princes feast in the morning!
¹⁷ Happy are you, O land, when your king is a
    nobleman,
  and your princes feast at the proper time—
    for strength, and not for drunkenness!
¹⁸ Through sloth the roof sinks in,
  and through indolence the house leaks.
¹⁹ Feasts are made for laughter;
  wine gladdens life,
  and money meets every need.
²⁰ Do not curse the king, even in your thoughts,

aOr *a child*

NIV

and a bird on the wing may report what you
say.

11 Cast your bread upon the waters,
for after many days you will find it again.
²Give portions to seven, yes to eight,
for you do not know what disaster may come
upon the land.

³If clouds are full of water,
they pour rain upon the earth.
Whether a tree falls to the south or to the north,
in the place where it falls, there will it lie.
⁴Whoever watches the wind will not plant;
whoever looks at the clouds will not reap.

⁵As you do not know the path of the wind,
or how the body is formed*ᵃ in a mother's
womb,
so you cannot understand the work of God,
the Maker of all things.

⁶Sow your seed in the morning,
and at evening let not your hands be idle,
for you do not know which will succeed,
whether this or that,
or whether both will do equally well.

ᵃ5 Or know how life (or the spirit) / enters the body being formed

NRSV

or curse the rich, even in your bedroom;
for a bird of the air may carry your voice,
or some winged creature tell the matter.

11 Send out your bread upon the waters,
for after many days you will get it back.
² Divide your means seven ways, or even eight,
for you do not know what disaster may
happen on earth.
³ When clouds are full,
they empty rain on the earth;
whether a tree falls to the south or to the
north,
in the place where the tree falls, there it
will lie.
⁴ Whoever observes the wind will not sow;
and whoever regards the clouds will not
reap.
5Just as you do not know how the breath
comes to the bones in the mother's womb, so
you do not know the work of God, who makes
everything.
6In the morning sow your seed, and at evening
do not let your hands be idle; for you do not
know which will prosper, this or that, or whether
both alike will be good.

COMMENTARY

The collection of miscellaneous proverbs found
in 10:8–11:6 pivots around the theme of the
inexorable tie of cause to effect. However, that
theme is not explored in a theoretical, abstract
way. By offering a number of examples of wise
and foolish behavior and their results, the text
shows that actions guided by prudence will enjoy
success. Not once in this passage does the Teacher
brand the outcome of good judgment and wise
behavior an absurdity! Put another way, these
proverbs assure the Teacher's student or reader
that disaster assuredly will follow folly and that
caution and good judgment help one to avoid such
disaster.

10:8-11. The possibility that one might fall
into a trap that one had dug for another person
(v. 8) recurs rather frequently in the Israelite
wisdom tradition (Pss 7:15; 9:15; 35:7; Prov

26:27; 28:10; Sir 27:26). In this and the following
verses, the Teacher expands on the idea, saying,
in effect, Do not blame anyone else if you are
"hoist with [your] own petar." If the pit traps or
the snake bites or the stones crush or the logs
injure or the axe is dull, the fault lies in your own
lack of preparation or even intellectual laziness,
for "wisdom helps one to succeed" (v. 10*b*). This
series of teachings on prudence culminates in the
charming v. 11, which conjours up the humorous
picture of "the master of the tongue" (the Hebrew
idiom for "snake charmer"), a man with a wooden
flute (or recorder) and a basket. Even today snake
charmers entertain that way in Middle Eastern
village markets. Biblical writers thought of the
charmer as more than an entertainer, however,
as someone necessary to control those pests that
were susceptible to charming (apparently adders

were not; see Jer 8:17). A certain skepticism about the efficacy of charming seems evident here, however. Either Qohelet's charmer came too late with too little or, as seems more likely, his charms just did not work. Ben Sira is skeptical not about the method but about the intelligence of the charmer, who has chosen such a high-risk vocation: "Who pities a snake charmer when he is bitten,/ or all those who go near wild animals?" (Sir 12:13 NRSV). We are doubly doubtful now, especially when music is involved, because we have learned that snakes have no hearing apparatus. It may be that charmers wave their recorders from side to side so that the snake will strike the end of the flute and not the flutist!

10:12-15. The next little collection of sayings pivots around the theme of the talk of fools, which is self-destructive (v. 12), malicious (v. 13), and deceptive (v. 14; Qohelet repeatedly asserts that the future is unknowable; see 6:12; 7:14; 8:7; 11:6). The section culminates in the obscure teaching that fools "do not even know the way to town" (v. 15b). Commentators find parallels elsewhere in ancient literature, suggesting that in the category of fool is the barbarian or rube who does not "know the territory."

10:16-17. These verses contrast a happy land with an unhappy one, the respective states of mind of which are dependent on the status of their leaders. As the notes in both the NRSV and the NIV show, the Hebrew of v. 16a literally reads, "Your king is a lad" (or "child" [נער *nāʿar*]). Rather than attempt to find a boy-king in Qohelet's time to whom this might be a cryptic reference (the Egyptian ruler Ptolemy V Epiphanes, 203–181 BCE, is probably too late), it is better simply to say that Qohelet was interested in maintaining the social order. If he was a retainer of the upper class who looked down his nose at impropriety, he would, of course, have preferred a land in which the king was mature and dignified and the princes did not get drunk in the morning. As Gordis points out, ancient sources in and out of the Bible took morning drinking to be a sign of dissoluteness (e.g., Isa 5:11-13).[99]

10:18-20. The section culminates in these verses, which contain both bad news about laziness and good news about the gladness of feasts and the worth of money. We may suppose that the warning of v. 20 not to say curses out loud against the rich and not even to think curses against the king suggests the relative menace posed by each. The king's informants are so ubiquitous that even an unguarded comment stemming from an "attitude" toward the king might cause trouble. As for the rich, gossip may reach their ears. It seems unlikely that the Teacher really intended to warn against talking birds (v. 20b), as if a parrot or a crow might spread one's curses all over town.[100] The key to Qohelet's meaning is probably to be found in Ahiqar's metaphor: "A word is a bird; once released no man can re[capture it]."[101] As our idiom puts it, "a little bird told me." The little bird might really have the shape of a servant or a spouse.

11:1-4. The collection of prudential epigrams continues. Since ancient times the famous v. 1 has been taken to advocate liberality motivated by the promise of a good return on generosity—not sevenfold, perhaps, but at least at a break-even rate.[102] However, when vv. 1-2 are taken together, the teachings emerge as practical advice about how to invest money: Export of goods abroad can be profitable (v. 1), and (speaking almost in the mode of a modern-day mutual fund broker) investments should be diversified (v. 2). Verse 2 contains the literary device of the "graded numerical dictum." Qohelet does not offer an actual list of seven or eight investment opportunities, though such lists often follow a headline like this. This literary device can be found in the prophetic canon (e.g., Amos 1:3–2:8; the figures seven and eight occur together in Mic 5:5), but it is used most commonly in sapiental texts. (In

100. It is, of course, conceivable that Qohelet meant it literally. The conceit was not unknown in his era, of course. Aristophanes used talking birds in his drama *The Birds* (601:4950). A note on the apocalyptic 2 Esdr 5:6 ("And one shall reign whom those who inhabit the earth do not expect, and the birds shall fly away together" [NRSV]) remarks, "Birds, possibly as creatures which soar aloft, were regarded in antiquity as possessing supernatural knowledge. They usually foresee impending events." See R. H. Charles, *Apocrypha and Pseudepigrapha of the Old Testament,* vol. 2 (Oxford: Clarendon, 1913) 569.

101. *Ancient Near Eastern Texts Relating to the Old Testament,* ed. James B. Pritchard, 3rd ed. (Princeton: Princeton University Press, 1969) 428b.

102. Rankin's suggestion that the exhortation to "send out your bread upon the waters" is an allusion to the popular practice in the cult of Adonis of flinging baskets of grain seedlings into streams or the sea in order to assure the fertility of the land has found little support. See O. S. Rankin and G. G. Atkins, "The Book of Ecclesiastes," in *The Interpreter's Bible,* 12 vols., ed. George A. Buttrick et al. (Nashville: Abingdon, 1956) 5:81.

99. Gordis, *Koheleth,* 315.

Prov 30:15-31, five full lists of three and four are given; see also Job 33:14, 29; Prov 6:16-19; Sir 26:5; 50:25-26.)

Verses 3-4 should be taken together, for they form a chiasm:

A rain;
   B wind (manifested in fallen tree);
   B' wind;
A' rain (clouds).

Although one can do nothing about the natural phenomena of the seasons, it is not prudent to stand gaping at the rain clouds and wind, perhaps waiting for the ideal moment in which to act. One has to sow and reap in harmony with these natural forces. Again, the Teacher affirms that "wisdom" is necessary for success.

11:5-6. The section culminates in two different teachings that reiterate Qohelet's major theme of the unknowability of the future (see Introduction). If one cannot figure out the miracle of conception, even though it is something that has happened to every human being, one cannot expect to know the workings of the Almighty (v. 5). This does not lead one to refrain from sexual activity, however. The same is true of agriculture: Sow your seed (not the sexual sense here; see v. 4) early and late. Even though you cannot be assured of any specific outcome (v. 6), your chances of harvesting a crop are immeasurably improved if at least you plant one!

REFLECTIONS

Every preacher ought to deliver a sermon on Ecclesiastes 10:8-11! Although this passage is not in any lectionary reading, it ought to be because it sets forth in a wonderful way the principle of the "destiny-producing deed."[103] In his realism, the Teacher finds no need to invoke God either as the proximate or the remote cause of things like snake bite, quarry and logging accidents, and the stupid and embarrassing position of a person who has fallen into the trap prepared for an enemy. In this text, a deed brings on its own unhappy destiny just as dependably as night follows day. No doubt, as Qohelet himself says (3:9-15), God is in ultimate control of the world and of history. That remains the faith of Judaism and Christianity. Within that large scheme, however, there is a circle of human hegemony in which we make our own decisions, shape our own immediate destinies, and have to act either foolishly or responsibly. In short, Ecclesiastes gives us canonical authority to give a certain secular, nonsacral interpretation to experience. God may have the whole world in the divine hands, but there is a sphere within that sphere in which human beings are fully responsible. In that sphere, people reap what they sow. In spite of the Teacher's highly predeterministic outlook, he secures a place for human autonomy.[104]

Writers from Jerome through Tolkein have been fascinated with the image of the pit (Eccl 10:8), which they usually take to be a metaphor for the commission of evil and its consequences. One who falls into a trap of one's own making experiences the appropriate self-inflicted penalty of sin. Even Sherlock Holmes offers us a sample of this long-lasting tradition. In "The Adventure of the Speckled Band," Holmes discovers that the villain, Grimesby Roylott, has been killed by the serpent that he intended to use to kill his stepdaughter. A. Conan Doyle has his sleuth remark, "Violence does, in truth, recoil upon the violent, and the schemer falls into the pit which he digs for another."

When, in his poem "All Is Vanity, Saith the Preacher," Byron contemplated Eccl 10:11, he thought of a snake more intellectual and spiritual than a real one that had failed to be charmed:

---

103. For his seminal discussion of the "destiny-producing deed," see K. Koch, "Does the Old Testament Have a Doctrine of Retribution?" in J. L. Crenshaw, ed., *Theodicy in the Old Testament* (Philadelphia: Fortress, 1983) 57-87. See also W. S. Towner, "The Renewed Authority of Old Testament Wisdom for Contemporary Faith," in *Canon and Authority,* G. W. Coates and Burke O. Long, eds. (Philadelphia: Fortress, 1977) 132-47.

104. Cited in David Lyle Jeffrey, ed., *A Dictionary of Biblical Tradition in English Literature* (Grand Rapids: Eerdmans, 1992) 336.

The serpent of the field, by art
And spells, is won from harming;
But that which coils around the heart,
Oh! who hath power of charming?
It will not list to wisdom's lore
Nor music's voice can lure it;
But there it stings forevermore
The soul that must endure it.

The proverb "Send out your bread upon the waters,/ for after many days you will get it back" (Eccl 11:1 NRSV) has made its way into the proverbial repertoire of the English language. No doubt there are people out there who think Benjamin Franklin first said it, but they are wrong; the credit goes to the Teacher. Although writers and preachers generally recognize that it is a call to providential behavior or disinterested benevolence, often it is used in an ironic sense. In his story "The Man Higher Up," for example, O. Henry renders for us a delightful cardsharp who, prior to a big gambling evening, bought every deck of cards in a small town and marked every card in every deck before he returned them to the shops for half credit (and for subsequent purchase by other gamblers). That caper cost him $75, but then, as he says, "trade and commerce had their innings, and the bread I had cast upon the waters began to come back in the form of cottage pudding with wine sauce."[105] An even more dramatic use of the maxim "bread upon the waters" to describe corruption is employed by Somerset Maugham in his story "The Fall of Edward Barnard," wherein he speaks of "the philanthropist who, with altruistic motives builds model dwellings for the poor and finds he has made a lucrative investment. He cannot prevent the satisfaction he feels in the ten per cent which rewards the bread he has cast upon the waters, but he has an awkward feeling that he detracts somewhat from the savor of his virtue."[106] In our own time, when television evangelists appeal for funds saying that they can guarantee that every dollar contributed will come back to the donor double or even sevenfold, we see a modern-day exploitation of the notion that charity is profitable.

The fallen tree of 11:3b, which is taken here to illustrate the need to act even when conditions are not completely favorable, was applied by Samuel Johnson and Boswell to the spiritual estate of a person on the deathbed. In the entry for Thursday, May 29, 1783, this colloquy is recorded. Boswell asked:

"Suppose a man who has led a good life for seven years, commits an act of wickedness, and instantly dies; will his former good life have any effect in his favour? JOHNSON. 'Sir, if a man has led a good life for seven years, and then is hurried by passion to do what is wrong, and is suddenly carried off, depend upon it he will have the reward of his seven years' good life; GOD will not take a catch of him. Upon this principle Richard Baxter believes that a Suicide may be saved. "If, (says he) it should be objected that what I maintain may encourage suicide, I answer, I am not to tell a lie to prevent it." ' BOSWELL. 'But does not the text say, "As the tree falls, so it must lie?" ' [Eccl. 11:3]. JOHNSON. 'Yes, sir; as the tree falls: but,—(after a little pause)—that is meant as to the general state of the tree, not what is the effect of a sudden blast.' In short, he interpreted the expression as referring to condition, not to position. The common notion, therefore, seems to be erroneous; and Shenstone's witty remark on Divines trying to give the tree a jerk upon a death-bed, to make it lie favourably, is not well founded."[107]

105. O. Henry, "The Man Higher Up," in *The Complete Works of O. Henry* (Garden City, N.Y.: Doubleday, 1953) 323.
106. Cited in David Lyle Jeffrey, ed., *A Dictionary of Biblical Tradition in English Literature* (Grand Rapids: Eerdmans, 1992) 105.
107. G. B. Hill, ed., *Boswell's Life of Johnson*, rev. ed., vol. 4 (Oxford: Clarendon, 1934) 225-26.

ECCLESIASTES 11:7–12:8, INSTRUCTIONS FOR A YOUNG PERSON AND CONCLUSION

NIV

⁷Light is sweet,
and it pleases the eyes to see the sun.
⁸However many years a man may live,
let him enjoy them all.
But let him remember the days of darkness,
for they will be many.
Everything to come is meaningless.

⁹Be happy, young man, while you are young,
and let your heart give you joy in the days
of your youth.
Follow the ways of your heart
and whatever your eyes see,
but know that for all these things
God will bring you to judgment.
¹⁰So then, banish anxiety from your heart
and cast off the troubles of your body,
for youth and vigor are meaningless.

12 Remember your Creator
in the days of your youth,
before the days of trouble come
and the years approach when you will say,
"I find no pleasure in them"—
²before the sun and the light
and the moon and the stars grow dark,
and the clouds return after the rain;
³when the keepers of the house tremble,
and the strong men stoop,
when the grinders cease because they are few,
and those looking through the windows grow
dim;
⁴when the doors to the street are closed
and the sound of grinding fades;
when men rise up at the sound of birds,
but all their songs grow faint;
⁵when men are afraid of heights
and of dangers in the streets;
when the almond tree blossoms
and the grasshopper drags himself along
and desire no longer is stirred.
Then man goes to his eternal home
and mourners go about the streets.

⁶Remember him—before the silver cord is
severed,

NRSV

7Light is sweet, and it is pleasant for the eyes
to see the sun.
8Even those who live many years should rejoice
in them all; yet let them remember that the days
of darkness will be many. All that comes is vanity.
9Rejoice, young man, while you are young, and
let your heart cheer you in the days of your youth.
Follow the inclination of your heart and the desire
of your eyes, but know that for all these things
God will bring you into judgment.
10Banish anxiety from your mind, and put
away pain from your body; for youth and the
dawn of life are vanity.

12 Remember your creator in the days of your
youth, before the days of trouble come,
and the years draw near when you will say, "I
have no pleasure in them"; 2before the sun and
the light and the moon and the stars are darkened
and the clouds return with^a the rain; 3in the day
when the guards of the house tremble, and the
strong men are bent, and the women who grind
cease working because they are few, and those
who look through the windows see dimly; 4when
the doors on the street are shut, and the sound
of the grinding is low, and one rises up at the
sound of a bird, and all the daughters of song are
brought low; 5when one is afraid of heights, and
terrors are in the road; the almond tree blossoms,
the grasshopper drags itself along^b and desire fails;
because all must go to their eternal home, and
the mourners will go about the streets; 6before
the silver cord is snapped,^{c} and the golden bowl
is broken, and the pitcher is broken at the fountain, and the wheel broken at the cistern, 7and
the dust returns to the earth as it was, and the
breath^d returns to God who gave it. 8Vanity of
vanities, says the Teacher;^{e} all is vanity.

^{a}Or *after*; Heb *'ahar* ^{b}Or *is a burden* ^{c}Syr Vg Compare Gk:
Heb *is removed* ^{d}Or *the spirit* ^{e}*Qoheleth*, traditionally rendered *Preacher*

NIV

or the golden bowl is broken;
before the pitcher is shattered at the spring,
or the wheel broken at the well,
⁷and the dust returns to the ground it came from,
and the spirit returns to God who gave it.

⁸"Meaningless! Meaningless!" says the Teacher.ᵃ
"Everything is meaningless!"

ᵃ8 Or *the leader of the assembly;* also in verses 9 and 10

COMMENTARY

With the final panel from the hand of the Teacher, the book of Ecclesiastes reaches a lyrical climax. Although the NRSV prints 11:7–12:8 as prose, a strong case can be made to join the NIV in viewing it as poetry. With the exception of the concluding verse, the entire section is a lengthy exploration of Qohelet's most positive theme: To be happy in the present moment is the goal of human endeavor, and to be so is the will of God for human beings (see Introduction). Evidently these words are addressed to Qohelet's student ("young man," 11:9). Such a young person was also the student of the epilogist ("my child," 12:12, the traditional addressee of wisdom teachings; e.g., Prov 1:10; 2:1; Sir 2:1). Even though his listener is young, Qohelet offers him a realistic assessment of the losses and terrors of old age contrasted with the opportunities that are presented to youth.

11:7-10. Beginning with the images of "light" and "sun" (v. 7), frequently used in ancient literature when the subject is the praise of life, the Teacher proceeds to urge people really to live while they are alive (cf. 2:3, 24; 3:12, 22; 5:18; 8:15). "Rejoice" during a time of light, but "remember" that the darkness is coming. The announcement in v. 8 that "the days of darkness will be many" is not so much a threat as it is a justification for enjoying the "many years" that one might live. Beyond vital living comes the endless darkness, the oblivion of Sheol, which in its pitiful contrast to light and life is the ultimate absurdity (v. 8). Gordis makes perhaps his greatest contribution to the understanding of the ideology of Qohelet in the way he reads passages like vv.

9-10: "For Koheleth, the enjoyment of life becomes the highest dictate of life."[108] Unlike many more austere writers of the Bible (e.g., Num 15:39), Qohelet has no problem with desire and encourages his readers to "follow the inclination of your heart and the desire of your eyes." In fact, for Qohelet the enjoyment of life is an imperative, which requires the use of the imperative mood (e.g., four times in 11:9, twice in 11:10). For this urgency for the enjoyment of life he advances two reasons: Life is fleeting (vv. 8*b*, 10*b*; 12:1*b*), and it is God's will that we enjoy life (v. 9*c*). This approach to vv. 7-10 hinges considerably on the conjunction "but," which connects v. 9*c* to the rest of the verse in the NRSV and the NIV. "But," of course, is an adversative conjunction; however, the same Hebrew particle ו (*wĕ*) also means "and." Taken that way, v. 9*c* becomes a simple narrative sequence: "and know that for all this God will call you to account." In other words, instead of a pious warning against getting carried away, the text may well be an announcement that God holds you responsible to "follow the inclination of your heart and the desire of your eyes." Such advice might be unconventional, but not really radical. The spirit is rather like that of Sir 14:11, 14, 16: "My child, treat yourself well, according to your means,/ and present worthy offerings to the Lord. . . . Do not deprive yourself of a day's enjoyment;/ do not let your share of desired good pass by you. . . . Give, and take, and indulge yourself,/ because in Hades one cannot look for luxury" (NRSV).

108. Robert Gordis, *Koheleth: The Man and His World,* 1st ed. (New York: Schocken, 1951; 3rd ed., 1968) 325.

If this reading is correct, the "judgment" of God (v. 9) is an evaluation of a life lived fully and not an *a priori* condemnation of desire and the love of life. Such a treatment of v. 9 is consistent with v. 10, in which the NIV and the NRSV substitute the psychological term "anxiety" for the more traditional renderings of "vexation" (RSV) or "sorrow" (KJV). Thus is manifested the changing influence of modernity on our reading of the unchanging ancient text! Anxiety and physical pain detract from happiness and challenge survival itself. Survival, God knows, is brief enough (v. 10*b*). The theme word הבל (*hebel*, "vanity") should be translated here as "ephemeral" or even "fleeting breath," on analogy with Job 7:16; Ps 144:4 (see Introduction). That makes it clear that v. 10*b* is really a motivation for v. 10*a*. The writer is not saying that "youth and vigor are meaningless" (NIV) or even that they are "vanity" (NRSV), but that they are painfully brief.

12:1-8. Such a reading accords well with this magnificent "allegory of old age," which is addressed to youth. Over the years, commentators have attempted to discern a consistent extended metaphor underlying the imagery of this passage. Some have imagined that the body and its organs are being allegorically described here; others have supposed that the verses picture a storm; yet others see the prevailing metaphor as a house and estate in decline. There is, in fact, no pressing reason to insist that the allegory be entirely consistent. The most satisfactory understanding of the imagery may simply be to let each image remind the reader of what it will. Poets write that way, after all, not intending to exercise strict control over the range of impressions their images evoke.

12:1-3. In his opening address to the young person (v. 1), Qohelet unexpectedly adjures his student to "remember your Creator in the days of your youth." Murphy summarizes suggested alternatives to the Hebrew word for "your Creator[s]" (בוראיך *bôrĕ'eykā;* expressed in the plural form), including "your well" ("your wife"), "your pit" ("your grave"), "your vigor," or even "your health."[109] While it is true that "your Creator[s]" does not fit the context of vv. 1-7, the ancient

manuscripts and versions do not support an emendation of the text. The Teacher has no illusions about old age.[110] Those are the "days of trouble," the days of joylessness. Since "the sun and the light and the moon and the stars" are not really darkened but only appear to the human observer to be so, v. 2 most likely refers to the progressive loss of vision and slow descent into depression that afflict the aged (although proponents of the storm metaphor find in this verse a picture of an approaching cloudburst). Verse 3 offers quite a good picture of a decaying estate in which the servants have grown old and unable to work; however, the imagery works with the storm metaphor, too, when the house shakes, work ceases, and darkness settles in. Proponents of the human body allegory equate the "house" with the body, "the guards" with the legs, "the strong men" with the arms, "the women who grind" with the teeth, "those who look through the windows" with the eyes. Perhaps the writer deliberately left all of these possibilities in the rich imagery of the poem. In any case, whatever prevailing metaphor one imagines to be at work here, the text conveys a powerful impression of creeping collapse.

The use of the word "windows" in v. 3 might

---

109. Roland E. Murphy, *Ecclesiastes*, WBC 23A (Waco, Tex.: Word, 1992) 113.

110. Who would the Teacher have considered to be an "old" person? Put aside the idealized lifespans of the prediluvian matriarchs and patriarchs and even the immediate pre-flood reduction to 120 years (Gen 6:3). The psalmist comes closer to human reality: "The days of our life are seventy years,/ or perhaps eighty, if we are strong" (Ps 90:10 NRSV). King David acted "old" with Abishag (1 Kgs 1:1-4) when David was seventy years of age (a figure arrived at by adding his thirty years at coronation in Hebron [2 Sam 2:15] to the forty years of his reign [1 Kgs 2:11]). The few physically superior persons who survived into their eighties would certainly fit the description of the losses of aging enumerated in Eccl 12:1-7. However, without the benefit of modern medicine the decline of eyesight, hearing, potency, and general vitality no doubt occurred earlier for most people. An average life expectancy for ancient Israel, were a reliable one available, would not help us to calculate when "old age" would have been recognized in individuals because the average would be seriously skewed downward by the high infant mortality rate. Recent studies of tombs in Jerusalem and Jericho from the first century BCE to the first century CE have shown that about 65 percent of the people interred therein had died before the age of thirty, and nearly half of those had died in infancy and early childhood. (The sources are cited by Rachel Z. Dulin, *A Crown of Glory: A Biblical View of Aging* [Mahwah, N.J.: Paulist, 1988] 23.) Persons who survived into their twenties had a much better chance of attaining something like "old age," although even most of them would not have outlasted their forties. Even though kings suffered from the occupational hazards of warfare and assassination, presumably they also enjoyed the nutritional and medical benefits of the elite. The fact that the average age at death of the seventeen kings of Judah whose ages are given in the books of Kings is forty-four (ibid., 21-23) suggests a life expectancy of around forty for adult commoners who did not enjoy the same advantages.

For the purposes of the discussion of Eccl 12:1-7, let us assume that people became "old" when their capacities began to fail in their late fifties and sixties, but that people in the category of "old" were a very small percentage of the population.

mislead readers into imagining panes of glass in a frame. Glass is mentioned only once in the Hebrew Bible, and then it is listed next to gold in value (Job 28:17). It is doubtful whether any ancient Israelite houses had glass windows. The word translated "windows" (ארבות 'ǎrubbôt) really means "lattices," no doubt similar to the decorative wooden *mushrabiya* still to be seen covering windows on old houses in Arab cities. These lattices enable women to look out on the scene in the street without being seen themselves.

12:4-5. The beautiful imagery continues in v. 4, allowing the body allegorists to find references to deafness ("the doors on the street"), to the digestive tract ("the sound of the grinding"), to inability to sleep in the morning ("rises up at the sound of a bird"), and to deafness again ("all the daughters of song [birds, not dancing girls] are brought low"). The same images can be applied to either the storm metaphor, taking them to refer to the cessation of activity and the shutting of doors, or the metaphor of the decay of a working household. The deterioration of the body seems to be the favored metaphor lying behind v. 5, for it culminates in death. The first clause is straightforward; the reference to the blossoming almond tree in the second perhaps refers to the white hair of old age, for almond blossoms turn quickly from pink to white. Much of the discussion of v. 5 has centered on the meaning of the clause "the grasshopper drags itself along." Some of the versions take the verb סבל (sābal) to mean "to grow fat"; the Talmud thinks "grasshopper" is a euphemism for "the rump."[111] If the clause is an allusion to the decline of sexual vitality, with the grasshopper's being a euphemism for male genitals, then the next clause of the verse, "and desire fails," follows logically. The problem with the latter clause is that the key word translated by the NRSV as "desire" (אביונה 'ǎbiyyônâ) occurs in this sense nowhere else. An alternative meaning, supported by the ancient versions and the late–second-century CE compilation of Pharisaic lore, the Mishnah,[112] is "caperberry," a plant believed to stimulate sexual appetite. With this culminating and

tragic picture of an old person whose body has failed in many respects, the picture turns at the end of v. 5 to the funeral itself. The "eternal home" must be the grave (see Tob 3:6). The "mourners" (see 3:4) are those professional wailers who could be hired to provide a suitable lamentation for the dead. Perhaps irony is intended: The man or woman who had enjoyed esteem and wealth in youth is honored at the end by hired hands!

12:6-7. Here the Teacher employs a different metaphor. The silver cord, golden bowl, pitcher, fountain, wheel, and cistern all appear to refer to the failure of a single well (although "silver cord" and "golden bowl" are excessive for a well rope and bucket and would better describe an elegant ceiling oil lamp). As elsewhere in 12:1-8, these verses contain rare or unique words and difficult textual problems. However, the sense remains clear: Live now, young person, before the precious water of life becomes unobtainable and (in a clear allusion to Gen 3:19) "the dust returns to the earth . . . and the breath returns to God who gave it" (v. 7). This does not contradict 3:21, for there the Teacher merely expressed skepticism that the respective life forces of human beings and animals had different destinies at death. As Gordis points out, "This verse affirms what Koheleth does not deny that life comes from God."[113] This is not, however, a teaching of immortality. The "breath" is not one's soul or one's identity, but simply the life force that came from God in the first place (Gen 2:7; see also Job 34:14-15; Ps 104:29).

12:8. This lyrical section concludes with nearly an exact repetition of the opening thematic statement of the book (1:2), which now serves as a conclusion to the message of Ecclesiastes. If v. 7b led anyone to think that the Teacher hoped for blessed immortality, this section dispels the idea. The two verses are not identical, however. The phrase "vanity of vanities" is not repeated here as it is in 1:2, and in the Hebrew of v. 8, the word "Qohelet" bears the article as if it were a title, "the Qohelet" (see Introduction).

---

111. *B.T. Shabb* 152a.
112. *M. Ma'aś* 4:6.

113. Gordis, *Koheleth,* 339.

REFLECTIONS

Except for the marvelously uninhibited affirmation of life and light in 11:7, the remaining verses of chapter 11 (vv. 8-10) moderate their affirmative cries of joy about life and youth with cautionary remarks. Nevertheless, these four verses have an almost defiantly existential quality. Rejoice, rejoice, follow the inclination of the heart and the desire of the eyes, banish anxiety and pain—these are the positive recommendations of the Teacher. They are motivated not only by the grim realizations that the darkness of death lasts a long time (v. 8) and that youth and vigor are ephemeral (v. 10), but also by the joyous conviction that God wills that we live life up to the limit. Qohelet's ideal religionists would never be the pale and hollow people that Nietzsche described; far from moping around in despair, he would have us really live while we are alive.

The true counterpoint to the joyous affirmations of vv. 11:7-10 is the lyric of 12:1-7. If the NRSV punctuation accurately reflects the Masoretic system of conjunctive and disjunctive accents (which, by reflecting the way in which the text of the Hebrew Bible was recited, provided it with most of the very minimal punctuation that it had), then this entire passage of seven verses is all one sentence. Because Hebrew literature is, on the whole, given to short and pithy utterances, such a stylistic variation has to be taken as a serious clue to the intended understanding of the passage. Lectors, cantors, preachers, and those who read Scripture out loud need to practice this passage over and over to capture the richness of oral interpretation that it provides.

Oral interpretation is that kind of rendition of a text that recapitulates its content in the way it is read. It "performs" the sentiment of the text. Verses 1-7 should be "performed" in the mode of a clock running down. The pitch should lower, and the speed should drop as the reader moves from the memory of the Creator and the days of youth through the dawning clouds of trouble; the covering of the sun with darkness; the shaking of the household; the loss of desire; the arrival of the mourners; then the loss of the bowl, the cord, the pitcher, and the wheel at the cistern; dryness; and finally death. The poem is a great inclined plane dropping to the lowest range of the voice and the lowest decibel of sound and culminating in extinction! The voice of the Teacher has died, the voice of the reader has died, and only dark silence remains.

If the text of 12:1-7 is "performed" in this way, the new sentence of v. 8 rings like a tocsin bell. With rich sonority, the opening slogan of the book is repeated in the firm, clear voice of the narrator of the book of Ecclesiastes: "Vanity of vanities, says the Teacher; all is vanity." That this is meant to be the final assessment of the Teacher's thought is evident from the fact that it mates with the initial thematic statement in 1:2 to form a perfect bracket around the body of the work.

More can be said about these verses than simply the literary role they play in the dénouement of the book of Ecclesiastes as a whole. First of all, the power of the imagery of 12:1-7 is revealed in the response it has awakened in readers throughout the years. In the survey of literary uses of the image of the broken golden bowl in Jeffrey's work, no less than eight modern writers, mostly North Americans, are shown to have alluded to this passage.[114] Not only Herman Melville, who, as we have seen, drew heavily on Ecclesiastes, but also Washington Irving, Oliver Wendell Holmes, Henry James, and Lytton Strachey used the image quite straightforwardly as a metaphor for the end of life. One of the more notable allusions is found in the first lines of Edgar Allan Poe's "Lenore":

Ah, broken is the golden bowl! the spirit flown for ever!
Let the bell toll!—a saintly soul floats on the Stygian river.

114. See David Lyle Jeffrey, ed., *A Dictionary of Biblical Tradition in English Literature* (Grand Rapids: Eerdmans, 1992) 313.

The picture of desolation and ruin that the passage invokes for body, household, and world itself, culminating in the loss of access to water, which is tantamount to the loss of life itself, is reminiscent of some of the more desolate landscapes by Salvador Dali. The apocalypses of modern literature, too, spring to mind. In Russell Hoban's novel *Riddley Walker,* the descendants of the survivors of a holocaust wander around in a world in which dogs and people fight for food, in which language is degraded and memory unreliable. Memory is imparted by a wandering bard who recalls the time when the "one big one" caused the beauty and the glory of civilization to wind down toward extinction.[115] In Walker Percy's book *Love in the Ruins,* the little world of the protagonist is choked with kudzu-like vines that are a metaphor for the approaching end.[116]

These literary images of our own time tend to be political and cultural. They reflect the fears of a generation that has seen the demons that its own hands have unleashed. As far as the decline of individual life into those days of which one says, "I have no pleasure in them" (12:1), the images and expectations are radically altered. We have difficulty even imagining a world in which the average life expectancy was only forty-some years, as it was in Qohelet's day. Many more people survive now into really old age, and not all lose the abilities to walk erectly, to see clearly, to chew painlessly, to enjoy sexuality—the losses alluded to in this poem. At the same time, many experience to the full the sequence of decay described in 12:1-7. For us, too, then, Qohelet's appeal in 11:7-10 remains vital: Do it while you can! Live while you are alive!

It is perfectly sound Christian doctrine to say that God wills that we love life. It was to the end that we might live abundantly and that we might renew with vigor and enjoyment our vocation of earth keeping, peace making, and loving that Jesus came into our midst. When Qohelet says, "Banish anxiety from your mind, and put away pain from your body" (11:10 NRSV), his motivation is the brevity and transience of life. When Jesus says the same thing, he offers an entirely different motivation. Jesus says, "And can any of you by worrying add a single hour to your span of life? And why do you worry about clothing? Consider the lilies of the field, how they grow; they neither toil nor spin, yet I tell you, even Solomon in all his glory was not clothed like one of these" (Matt 6:27-29 NRSV). This is an invitation to a life of trust, gratitude, and courage, driven not by a melancholy sense of the fleetingness of it all, but by the nearness and greatness of the kingdom of God and God's righteousness (Matt 6:33).

Of course, with Qohelet-like realism, Jesus also acknowledges that "today's trouble is enough for today" (Matt 6:34 NRSV). That cautionary note aside, however, he urges his followers to get on with the business of being merciful, making peace, comforting those who mourn, and living life abundantly. The fact that we can expect to do these things more than thirty years longer on average than the original readers of the Old Testament could have done is truly a cause for rejoicing. Yes, it is a foretaste of the kingdom of God in which we participate already.

The time in life described by 12:1-7 is now called dotage. Its hallmarks are the decline in quality of life and, sometimes in the end, post-personal existence. The knowledge that frail old age is a possibility for us may serve as a useful goad, just as Qohelet meant it to do. Teaching us that one day the light will fade, the "daughters of song" will no longer be audible, the life force will fail, and death will come is surely his way of enabling us to enjoy the light of the moon and the stars now, to appreciate the sound of the birds and the taste of food now, and to savor intimacy and love now. Not only to quiet enjoyment does the Teacher goad us, but to action as well. While we have time, we have work to do—the work of conceiving and raising children, the work of building monuments, of writing poems and sermons, of performing music and creating needlepoint, and cooking delicious dishes—now—before "the golden bowl is broken, and the pitcher is broken at the fountain, and the wheel broken at the cistern" (12:6 NRSV).

115. Russell Hoban, *Riddley Walker: A Novel* (New York: Summit Books, 1980).
116. Walker Percy, *Love in the Ruins* (New York: Avon, 1971).

THE EPILOGUES

NIV

⁹Not only was the Teacher wise, but also he imparted knowledge to the people. He pondered and searched out and set in order many proverbs. ¹⁰The Teacher searched to find just the right words, and what he wrote was upright and true.

¹¹The words of the wise are like goads, their collected sayings like firmly embedded nails—given by one Shepherd. ¹²Be warned, my son, of anything in addition to them.

Of making many books there is no end, and much study wearies the body.

¹³Now all has been heard;
here is the conclusion of the matter:
Fear God and keep his commandments,
for this is the whole ⌊duty⌋ of man.
¹⁴For God will bring every deed into judgment,
including every hidden thing,
whether it is good or evil.

NRSV

⁹Besides being wise, the Teacher*ᵃ* also taught the people knowledge, weighing and studying and arranging many proverbs. ¹⁰The Teacher*ᵃ* sought to find pleasing words, and he wrote words of truth plainly.

¹¹The sayings of the wise are like goads, and like nails firmly fixed are the collected sayings that are given by one shepherd.*ᵇ* ¹²Of anything beyond these, my child, beware. Of making many books there is no end, and much study is a weariness of the flesh.

¹³The end of the matter; all has been heard. Fear God, and keep his commandments; for that is the whole duty of everyone. ¹⁴For God will bring every deed into judgment, including*ᶜ* every secret thing, whether good or evil.

ᵃ Qoheleth, traditionally rendered *Preacher*   *ᵇ* Meaning of Heb uncertain   *ᶜ* Or *into the judgment on*

COMMENTARY

The book of Ecclesiastes closes with two epilogues that are widely agreed to be the work of hands other than those of the Teacher. The most obvious reason for this idea is that in this section Qohelet is referred to in the third person, whereas elsewhere (except in 1:1 and in the clause "says Qohelet" at 1:2; 7:27; 12:8) the writer speaks in the first person. The phrase "my child" or "my son" appears only in this section (12:12), even though it is used very commonly elsewhere in the wisdom literature to address the client of a sage. Perhaps the epilogists added these concluding verses sometime between the time of the composition of the book in the third century BCE and the time of Ben Sira (c. 190 BCE), who, many commentators believe, regarded Ecclesiastes as sacred Scripture. By the time a book came to be regarded as Scripture, the opportunity to amend it was over; therefore, the supplements

may have been attached during the years 250–200 BCE.

The writers of these last two short panels (vv. 9-11 and 12-14) use a form of Hebrew similar to that of Qohelet, thus they must have been reasonably close to the Teacher in time and place. It has often been asserted that the mission of the first epilogist was to bring the book closer to the mainstream of Hebrew thought, thereby to ensure its place in the library of sacred writings. He is not opposed to the ideas and temperament of the Teacher and gives valuable information about him in vv. 9-10. The second epilogist undertakes to correct certain key ideas of the book.

12:9-11. The first epilogist highlights the claim that Qohelet was a member of the royal family and calls him a "wise" man—i.e., a professional sage. More surprising, he claims that Qohelet "also taught the people" (v. 9). Evidently the

Teacher reached out to an audience larger than the narrow circle of the court and the aristocracy. Perhaps he weighed and studied and arranged sapiental texts for this mass audience, improving them stylistically and gathering them into collections (v. 9); the book of Ecclesiastes itself, however, seems too sophisticated to have been part of Qohelet's popularizing work. Verse 10a may contain a slight criticism of Qohelet, since "pleasing words" can also be vacuous or manipulative ones. Nevertheless, there is no reason to join Ehrlich in translating v. 10b as if it were intended to contradict v. 10a—i.e., "but what should be written are words of truth."[117] Verse 11 has caused no end of trouble (see NRSV note), largely because several of its words are unique in the Hebrew Bible. Particularly difficult is the phrase "the collected sayings"; the KJV's "masters of learned assemblies" only demonstrates how obscure the Hebrew really is. Assuming that the "one shepherd" refers to God, the epilogist appears not only to have valued highly the "sayings of the wise," even those that were unconventional and controversial, but he appears also to believe sapiental works like Ecclesiastes should and did have the status of inspired Scripture.

12:12-14. The assumption that the phrase "anything beyond these" (v. 12) introduces a second epilogue lends more sense to the strange warning against too much study (v. 12). Efforts to understand which writings he was speaking of when he said, "Of making many books there is no end," have not achieved consensus. It may be that this writer intended to offer a more cautious and orthodox perspective on Qohelet. Some have suggested that vv. 11-12 are intended to contrast canonical writings (the "sayings of the wise") with apocryphal or even non-Jewish ones, to the disparagement of the latter. Murphy takes the warning against writing more books to be a way of praising Qohelet's work: "There is no need of more wisdom writings! In this view one should not postulate a second redactor responsible for vv. 12-14."[118]

The book concludes with a standard formula for escaping the kinds of theological and moral dilemmas in which Qohelet has wallowed: "Fear God and keep his commandments" (cf. Ben Sira's summary of his thinking, Sir 43:27). This is followed by a ringing affirmation of the reliability of divine retribution, an affirmation that Qohelet himself was never able to make at all convincingly, though he allowed for the inevitable cause-and-effect sequence of the "destiny producing deed" (10:8-11). At this late date it is not possible either to affirm or to deny that the otherwise heterodox book made it into the canon because of the caveats contained in these verses. Certainly these last words would have been more familiar than other parts of the book to many of the readers of sacred Hebrew literature two centuries before the turn of the era. However, not only do they lack the nuance and probing energy of the rest of the book, but also they contradict two of its most important claims—namely, that human beings can know neither the future nor the activity of God (see 3:11; 7:14).

117. Cited by Robert Gordis, *Koheleth: The Man and His World,* 1st ed. (New York: Schocken, 1951; 3rd ed., 1968) 342.

118. Roland E. Murphy, *Ecclesiastes,* WBC 23A (Waco, Tex.: Word, 1992) 126.

REFLECTIONS

The epilogists who added the last six verses to the book of Ecclesiastes achieved their apparent end of making the book more conventional and palatable. The traditionally pious confidence of vv. 13-14 that God will bring all deeds into judgment and will reward those who fear God feels more comfortable to many people even today than does anything else in the book of Ecclesiastes. It is ironic that much of the preaching and thinking about this fascinating book is based on the words of someone other than its real author.

The epilogists also coined what for many people, particularly students, is one of the best-known slogans in the book: "Of making many books there is no end, and much study is a weariness of the flesh" (12:12b). In the days before the printing press, people took the first remark to mean that the awesomely wearisome business of copying and binding books had to go on endlessly in order to support human culture. The sight of medieval books chained to their reading desks, which can still be found in old libraries in Europe, gives some legitimacy to this reading of the verse. The Puritans, however, took the second of the two clauses of v. 12*b* to be the guide to the proper understanding of the first. They tended to see this verse as cautioning readers against relying on teachings other than those of sacred Scripture. As Matthew Henry put it, "Let men write ever so many books for the conduct of human life, write till they have tired themselves with much study, they cannot give better instructions than those we have from the Word of God."[119] John Milton, on the other hand, though a Puritan, was also a liberally educated Cambridge rationalist who, in his *Areopagitica,* observed that the choice among books is one that God has placed within the sphere of our responsibility: "Solomon informs us, that much reading is a weariness of the flesh; but neither he, nor other inspired author, tells us that such or such reading is unlawful; yet, certainly had God thought good to limit us herein, it had been much more expedient to have told us what was unlawful, than what was wearisome."[120]

In our age of the explosion of knowledge and the difficulty of information retrieval, the words of Hugh of St. Victor ring as true as any: "The number of books is infinite; do not pursue infinity! When no end is in sight, there can be no rest. Where there is no rest, there is no peace. Where there is no peace, God cannot dwell."[121] Perhaps he had in mind the writing of commentaries on books like Ecclesiastes, which, if they are to prove their worth, have to shed at least as much light as does the original itself. Experience teaches that this is an accomplishment not easily attained!

119. Matthew Henry, *Commentary on the Whole Bible,* 4.1051.
120. Cited in David Lyle Jeffrey, ed., *A Dictionary of Biblical Tradition in English Literature* (Grand Rapids: Eerdmans, 1992) 562.
121. Hugh of St. Victor *Didascalicon* 5.7.

THE SONG OF SONGS

INTRODUCTION, COMMENTARY, AND REFLECTIONS
BY
RENITA J. WEEMS

THE
SONG OF SONGS

INTRODUCTION

The content of Song of Songs, sometimes referred to as the Song of Solomon, represents a remarkable departure from that of other books in the Bible. To open the pages of this brief volume of poetry is to leave the world of exceptional heroism, tribal conflict, political disputes, royal intrigue, religious reforms, and divine judgment and to enter the world of domestic relations, private sentiments, and interpersonal discourse. Filled with language of sensuality, longing, intimacy, playfulness, and human affection, Song of Songs introduces the reader to the non-public world of ancient Israel. The relationships are private (i.e., a man and a woman), the conversation is between intimates (e.g., "darling," "beloved," "friend"), and the language hints of kinship bonds (e.g., mother, sister, brother, daughter). At last, readers of Scripture have the opportunity to focus not so much on the external politics that organized and dominated the lives of Hebrew people (e.g., palace intrigue, temple politics, prophetic conflict, international doom, natural disasters) but on the internal systems and attitudes that also shaped the lives of the people of Israel.

Song of Songs stands out in sharp contrast to the rest of the biblical books in two other ways. First, nowhere in its eight chapters is God mentioned. The book of Esther is the only work that shares this distinction. Although the religious significance of the latter is frequently debated as well, its religious significance is a little more self-evident, referring as it does to the rituals of fasting and prayer (Esth 4:16) and to the celebration of the Feast of Purim (Esth 9:20-32). A decidedly secular tone permeates Song of Songs; not only is God's name not mentioned in the book, but also no allusions are made to any of Israel's sacred religious traditions, be they covenant traditions (the Davidic or Sinai covenants) or

God's saving acts in Israel's history (e.g., deliverance at the sea). One possible allusion to a religious theme may indicate that the book had "religious" origins: The lovers exchange their love poems against the backdrop of a pastoral, utopian garden setting where images of animals, hillsides, and exotic flowers predominate. Such allusions suggest intimations of the Garden of Eden story (Genesis 2), with its focus on the first human couple and their portentous dealings with each other. (More will be said about this topic below.)

Second, Song of Songs is the only biblical book in which a female voice predominates. In fact, the protagonist's voice in Song of Songs is the only unmediated female voice in all of Scripture. Elsewhere, women's perspectives are rehearsed through the voice of narrators, presumably male (e.g., Esther and Ruth), and their contributions are overshadowed by male heroism and assorted male-identified dramas. But in Song of Songs, where more than fifty-six verses are ascribed to a female speaker (compared to the man's thirty-six), the experiences, thoughts, imagination, emotions, and words of this anonymous black-skinned woman are central to the book's unfolding. Moreover, the protagonist is not merely verbal; unlike many of the women in the Bible, she is assertive, uninhibited, and unabashed about her sexual desires.

The book's pronounced and unrelenting female point of view is reinforced further by its strong female imagery. The several interjections of the Jerusalem daughters into the lovers' discourse (5:9; 6:1, 13a) and the repeated mention of the "mother's house" (אֵם בֵּית *bêt 'ēm*, 3:4; 8:2) as opposed to the customary "father's house" (בֵּית אָב *bêt 'āb*), the patriarchal household, contribute to the book's impression of giving readers insights into the decidedly private, unexplored world of Hebrew women's special viewpoints and private sentiments. The presence of such important female imagery allows Song of Songs to be seen as a collection of meditations from a woman's heart. Casting the book as the private, journal-like reflections of a female may provide us just the insight needed to unlock the mystery behind the decision to include such patently erotic and secular musings within the canon. As meditations of a woman's heart, Song of Songs might have been viewed as the feminine counterpart to a book like, say, Ecclesiastes. In the latter, an unnamed speaker, who is most likely male, reflects on the chasm between traditional wisdom teachings and actual human experience. He does not hesitate to express profound disdain for traditional wisdom, arguing that even the best of life is plagued with transience, unpredictability, absurdity, vanity, and ultimately ends in death. And he is openly cynical about the contradictions he has observed in life, one being that good deeds do not always lead to good consequences. In the light of the patent limitation of human wisdom, and in the face of death and vanity, the Preacher repeatedly urges his audience to indulge themselves in life's few genuine pleasures—food, drink, love, work, and play—as gifts of God.

One might argue that the protagonist in Song of Songs accepts the author of Ecclesiastes' invitation and revels in the joys of nature, work, and play when one is in love. In its own way, Song of Songs meditates, among other things, on traditional thinking about (female) sexuality and a certain protagonist's life experiences as a woman in love. Speaking in the first person, as does the protagonist in Ecclesiastes, the woman allows herself a few outbursts of impatience and effrontery (1:6; 6:13 *b*; 8:1, 10), making it very clear that she is well aware that her own words and actions violate traditional teachings pertaining to womanhood and modesty. In the end, she is as impatient with traditional wisdom as her male counterpart in Ecclesiastes is scornful. But instead of expressing openly her contempt for and cynicism toward traditional wisdom, the speaker in Song of Songs takes the subtle approach and extols the erotic happiness she has found—despite all of its complications and limitations. One can see from both the striking amount of female speech and the decidedly female angle of vision of the book how easy it is to imagine that a female sage is responsible for the stirring meditations contained in Song of Songs.

AUTHOR AND TITLE

On the surface, the allusion to King Solomon in the superscription to the book (1:1) rules out a female as the author of Song of Songs. But the attribution to the last king of the united monarchy should not be taken as decisive. Because he was rumored to have married hundreds of wives (1 Kgs 11:3), many traditions inspired by Solomon's presumed vast knowledge about romance and matters of the heart no doubt emerged over the centuries. Song of Songs was likely one such composition. Attributing the love poems to Solomon probably represents an attempt by the scribes to associate the work with the wisest and most notorious king in Israel's history. Appending his name to the book would place it foremost within an intellectual stream of respected and authoritative theological reflection, the wisdom tradition. The king's reputation as a sage with more than several thousand wise sayings to his credit and a composer of more than one thousand lyrics (1 Kgs 4:32) lent to Song of Songs, especially in the light of the wisdom homily attached near the end of the book (Cant 8:6-7), the kind of sublimity and inspiration befitting royal compositions. This might explain one rendering of the book's title, "The Most Sublime of Songs."

There is no way to determine the gender of the person actually responsible for having written this collection of love poetry (although the preponderance of female speakers and experiences in the book has led me to refer to the lyricist throughout as female). But the book's class origins are conspicuous. Its author was acquainted with the accoutrements of the privileged class (e.g., the reference to the woman's vineyard in 1:6; the lavish royal wedding procession in 3:6-11; the scattered references to fine spices, fruits, and perfumes; the mention of Tirzah, once the capital city of the northern kingdom [6:4]). It is not farfetched to imagine that the lyrics were inspired by someone (a woman) from an elite class who, at least modestly educated, was familiar with the Hebrew lyrical heritage and aware of prevailing assumptions about the role of women and the prohibitions against marriages crossing class and ethnic lines.

The title of the book (שיר השירים *šîr haššîrîm*) cleverly hints at the work's contents.

Although its flat translation is better known among English-speaking audiences as the Song of Songs (NIV) and the Song of Solomon (NRSV), the title actually bears rich connotations ranging from the Song Comprised of Songs to the Most Excellent of Songs. (See Commentary on Cant 1:1). The book is a collection of love lyrics filled with candid longing and tender expressions of desire and desperation by both the lover and her beloved.

Although it is difficult to discern any straightforward rationale or logic to the book's structure, the poems' lyrical quality is unmistakable. These brief, evocative, unpredictable units of material, which were brought together on the basis of alliteration, intonation, and possibly rhythm surely made for memorable musical performances. In the second century CE, the lyrics to Song of Songs became a favorite in bawdy quarters, prompting Rabbi Aqiba (c. 135 CE) reportedly to protest that "he who trills his voice in chanting the Song of Songs in the banquet house and treats it as a sort of song has no part in the world to come."[1] We are not sure how successful the rabbi was in quelling secular enthusiasm for the lyrics. Nevertheless, for those who appreciate its subliminal nature, the content and character of Song of Songs continue to stir the religious imagination. Even today in some Jewish traditions, the text of Song of Songs is chanted at the end of the eight-day celebration of Passover. In other Jewish traditions, it is sung weekly in services prior to the sabbath. Even in many Protestant Christian traditions, some of the book's important themes continue to find their way into the church's most stirring compositions about human longing, divine compassion, and the beauty of creation.

LOVE LYRICS AND THEIR CONTENT

Lyrical poems cast as passionate dialogues, erotic soliloquies, and private dreams function in Song of Songs as the discourse of interior life and the rhetoric of heartfelt emotions. Hardly anything written in classical secular romance literature can match the exquisitely provocative exchanges between the anonymous female protagonist and her shepherd suitor in Song of Songs. To see Song of Songs merely as a collection of love poems that reclaims human sexuality and celebrates female sexuality, however, poems embodying gender balance and mutuality, is to fail to appreciate the deep and complicated emotions expressed in the book. Love lyrics are powerful forms of persuasion; they provide a modest way for communicating immodest sentiments, and they allow one to talk disingenuously about experiences and identities that defy official moral codes and fall outside the official cultural ideology. That being the case, the poetry of Song of Songs is the poetry of personal sentiment.[2] Its vocabulary and expressions are obscure because they are the private language of intimates. Identifying the speakers is complicated so as to protect the privacy of the partners. The descriptions of human longing, vulnerability, dependence, and

---

1. Tosefta, *Sanhedrin* XII 10.
2. For an illuminating discussion of the way poetry and songs are used to express personal, often unconventional sentiments in Arab bedouin communities, see Lila Abu-Lughod, *Veiled Sentiments: Honor and Poetry in a Bedouin Society* (Berkeley: University of California Press, 1986).

yearning are intended to capture the imagination and sympathy of the audience, forcing them to identify with the universal plight of lovers who want to be loved by the man or woman of their own choosing. Love poetry permits the speakers to comment on subjects from perspectives the audience might otherwise never consider. The woman argues for her right to pursue love, and her lover argues that in his eyes his maiden is beautiful.

When we compare the lyrics in Song of Songs with some of the psalms, we see that all lyrics are not the same. They differ according to their content, emotional tone, and social context. In our culture, gospel music, Scottish hymns, anthems, rap music, country music, hard rock, rock and roll, reggae, and jazz, to name a few, are all examples of oral literature that, while formulaic, ultimately originated out of very particular social contexts and represent unique forms of social commentary. The closest American musical parallel to the kind of material we find in Song of Songs may be the American blues tradition because of its comparable poignant interest in personal, individual struggles, the joys and sorrows of love, and the confounding chasm that exists between domestic reality and domestic fantasy. In both musical traditions, the speaker speaks in the first-person singular voice and the subject matter is deeply personal and gripping in intensity.

Many of the specific themes covered in Song of Songs also appear in classical women's romantic literature (e.g., personal relationships, thwarted love, sexual passion, the female body). In the classics, male self-identity develops and grows through a series of adventures that inevitably takes him away from his country and home, especially away from his intimate connections with women (e.g., mother, wife, sister). However, the female self in classic literature develops invariably through the woman's experiences with the impediments and frustrations of romantic love. In other words, women's education traditionally is "in or on the periphery of marriage."[3] Similarly, the lyrics of Song of Songs record the personal predicament of a certain black-skinned maiden—her struggles to love and be loved by a man for whom she has been deemed, for reasons not exactly clear to modern readers, an unsuitable mate. Readers are asked to understand the innocence of their love, to recognize the purity of their longing, and to empathize with the absurdity of the obstacles and frustrations, both internal and external, they are forced to endure. We watch the protagonist's selfhood unfold before our eyes as we observe her (1) as the innocent romantic who is propelled by her passion and her dreams of being loved and caressed by the man of her dreams (e.g., 1:2-4); (2) as defiant and impatient (1:5-6; 6:13b); (3) as a mature, intelligent, knowledgeable woman who passes on what she has learned in her experience of frustrated love to her impressionable female audience (2:7; 3:5; 8:4); and (4) as self-assured but pragmatic about the way the world operates and resolved to find happiness, despite the limitations imposed on her (8:10, 13-14).

The book's charm is its ability to elaborate on the erotic while at the same time critiquing prevailing cultural norms. In fact, the poet cunningly uses the former subtly to denounce

3. Elaine Hoffman Baruch, "The Feminine *Bildungsroman:* Education Through Marriage," in *Women, Love, and Power: Literary and Psychoanalytic Perspectives* (New York: New York University Press, 1991) 122-44.

the latter. So forward, so uncompromising, so urgent is the maiden's desire for and attachment to her lover that her comments border on the contentious in some places. Her insistence on three occasions that her beloved suitor belongs to her (2:16; 6:3; 7:10) is not mere assertion. Rather, seen in the context of her defense of her complexion (1:4), her bodily integrity (1:5; 6:13*b*), her small breasts (8:10), her continual adjuration (2:7; 3:5; 8:4), and in view of the Jerusalem daughters' continual skepticism (5:9; 6:13*a*), the protagonist's words have a polemical tone. For one thing, her black skin color, she suspects, immediately places her at odds with those around her (1:5-6).

The woman's daring love talk and explicit sexual longing invariably raise questions about the place of this book within the Bible. This is especially the case when one considers that the lovestruck female is as straightforward and aggressive about satisfying her libidinous urges as is her male suitor, or any other male character in Scripture. How, then, do we explain the radically different portraits of female sexuality in the Bible when we compare the sexually vivacious protagonist in Song of Songs with the sexually constrained women in so many other portions of Scripture? The former speaks openly and immodestly about her erotic desires, while the latter are portrayed as the archetypal other whose sexuality must be regulated and guarded against. These are not questions easily answered by cursory readings of the book. In fact, it has been difficult for scholars to arrive at answers to such important questions. Perhaps we are not supposed to come up with satisfying answers. Perhaps the fact that the book has been included in the canon is evidence enough of the rich, complex, and often ambivalent thinking about women, sex, and matters of the heart that existed in Israel throughout the centuries.

INTERTEXTUAL ALLUSIONS

Lyrical compositions, like all discursive forms, rely on a great store of intertextual comparisons for their affect and effect on their audiences. We have already seen how associating the book with King Solomon gave it an air of authority and legitimacy. When Song of Songs is viewed within its ancient Near Eastern setting, the influence of broader, extra-canonical texts lends the book a cosmopolitan note and situates it within the larger stream of internationally acclaimed compositions. For example, Song of Songs shares striking parallels with Egyptian love poetry. Both favor openness, tenderness, and frankness in their romantic speeches; the female lover in both traditions is referred to as "sister" (Cant 4:9, 10, 12) and is frequently addressed in superlative terms ("the most beautiful of women," Cant 5:9; 6:1).

Song of Songs also resonates with intertextual allusions to the story of the first human couple (Genesis 2–3).[4] Repeated mention of "garden" and garden-like settings in Song of Songs, whether used as a metaphor for the woman's sexuality (e.g., 4:12, 16; 5:1) or as

---

4. Phyllis Trible argues that Song of Songs was written as a counterpoint or response to the Genesis story and points to a number of remarkable resonances between the two in her work *God and the Rhetoric of Sexuality* (Philadelphia: Fortress, 1978) chap. 5.

a special location for the couple's lovemaking (6:11-12), may suggest that the book is a response to the "love story that goes awry"[5] back in the garden in Genesis 2–3. As a result of what happened in Eden, there is rupture in creation, disharmony between the first human couple, resulting in the subjugation of the woman and, by implication, the demise of mutual sexual fulfillment. In the garden of Song of Songs, by contrast, mutuality is reestablished and intimacy is renewed. Audiences encountering the content of Song of Songs for the first time would have had a repertoire of cultural information upon which to draw as they listened to the poems and placed them within the framework of what they understood love, relationships, and sex were or should entail.

A less commented upon, but equally suggestive parallel may be drawn between Song of Songs and Hosea 2.[6] Both use the trope of aggressive female sexuality to comment ambivalently on the relationship between love and power, on the one hand, and the erotic and the divine, on the other. In both texts, male figures threaten to imprison the women if they prove unchaste (cf. Cant 8:9 and Hos 2:6-7), and the women are beaten for pursuing the men they love (cf. Cant 5:2-8 and Hos 2:6-13). The woman in Song of Songs tells the woman's side of the drama; she is not depraved and incorrigible, as in Hosea. Instead, she is a woman in love and in trouble.

Whether Song of Songs was indeed written in response to these canonical examples of female/human sexuality is debatable. What is certain, however, is that like all poets, the author of Song of Songs appealed to what at that time was a store of cultural "texts" familiar to an ideal audience—some written and fixed, some oral and evolving, some ancient and tried, some contemporary and trendy, some expressly religious, and others, though secular, nevertheless inspired. Some of those texts are recoverable, such as the Garden of Eden story in Genesis and Egyptian love poems; but many of those intertextual allusions remain unrecoverable for the outsider. Regardless, they represent the kinds of material all readers bring to the reading process, consciously or unconsciously, that act as a sieve through which new information is assessed and organized, appropriated or resisted.

THE "BODY" IN SONG OF SONGS

With abandon, the lovers in Song of Songs delight in the physical pleasures of love. They revel in each other's body: taste (2:3; 4:11; 5:1), touch (7:6-9), smell (1:12-14; 4:16), and the sound (2:8, 14; 5:16) of each other's voice. The female body poses no ethical problems in Song of Songs, although in other parts of Scripture it is problematic. It bleeds (cf. Leviticus 12; 15:19-30); it breeds (Leviticus 12); it confounds male wisdom (Numbers 5); and it has enormous power over the male imagination (Lev 21:7; cf. 2 Samuel 11), or so it seems. So mysteriously powerful is a woman's body that it can compete with a man's religious obligations (Exod 19:15). Only in Song of Songs is the female body extolled and

5. This is the title of Trible's chapter on Genesis 2–3 in *God and the Rhetoric of Sexuality*, 72-143.

6. A frequently overlooked study of the parallels between Song of Songs and Hosea 2 that deserves more attention is Fokkelien van Dijk-Hemmes, "The Imagination of Power and the Power of Imagination," *JSOT* 44 (1989) 75-88.

praised for its difference and its beauty. With daring abandon the shepherd describes the maiden's eyes, neck, hair, feet, thighs, and navel using extravagant metaphors and sexually suggestive imagery. In fact, both lovers, using the genre of the *wasf,* or poetic passages describing with a series of images the various parts of the body, celebrate the integrity and uniqueness of the other's body. Four *wasfs* (Arabic for "description") can be found in Song of Songs (4:1-7; 5:10-16; 6:4-10; 7:1-9).[7] Three of the four *wasfs* praise the woman's form and flawless appearance, suggesting that the poet assumed that her audience might otherwise find some aspect of her physical makeup (perhaps her complexion?) objectionable (4:1-7; 5:10-16; 7:1-9). While only one *wasf* praises the man's body (6:4-10), nevertheless it stands out in both Song of Songs and in Scripture because it is the only description of masculinity and male beauty from the female point of view. No doubt drawn from the conventional stock of imagery and language poets and lyricists used during that period to describe the human body, *wasfs* do not attempt to be precise and concrete in their descriptions. They are deliberately imprecise and playful, where the intention is upon evoking the imagination and stirring the senses.[8] The focus on the human body allows both the poet and the audience to reflect simultaneously on at least three complex and highly symbolic themes that body imagery invokes in a culture: race, sex, and power.

The protagonist is unapologetic about the way she looks and relaxes in her beloved's desire for her. On one occasion she insists that her beloved's desire is for her only, presumably despite what others think (7:10). This is the talk of a woman under pressure both to conform and to relinquish her rights to be loved by the man of her choice. A possible context for the poem's origin was the post-exilic period, when the inhabitants of the tiny province of Judah were struggling to reestablish their identity. There are indications that canons of legal prescriptions were codified during this period to legitimate women's subjugation and that aggressive measures were taken to restrict social intermingling and to monitor marriage affiliations (Ezra 9:1–10:44; Neh 13:23-29; cf. Leviticus 12; 15; Numbers 5).

INTERPRETATION

Various proposals have been made for interpreting the book's secular and erotic contents. The major interpretations have viewed Song of Songs as (1) a dramatization of an ancient fertility rite in which the deity and humans were ceremonially united in sacred marriage;[9] (2) a single love poem structured around repetitive words, phrases, and motifs;[10] (3) a cycle of marriage songs;[11] and (4) an allegory idealizing, from the Jewish point of view, God's love for Israel, and from the Christian perspective, Christ's love for the church or

---

7. Richard N. Soulen, "The *Wasf* in the Song of Songs and Hermeneutic," *JBL* 86 (1967) 183-90.

8. See Marcia Falk's keen insights on *wasfs* in *The Song of Songs: A New Translation and Interpretation* (San Francisco: HarperCollins, 1990) 125-36.

9. T. J. Meek, "Canticles and the Tammuz Cult," *AJSL* 39 (1922-23) 1-14.

10. J. Cheryl Exum, "A Literary and Structural Analysis of the Song of Songs," *ZAW* 85 (1973) 47-79.

11. Michael D. Goulder, *The Song of Fourteen Songs,* JSOTSup 36 (Sheffield: JSOT, 1986).

for the individual's soul.[12] As for the latter, it is surprising to note that while Protestants have for the most part rejected the allegorical and tropological modes of interpretation that were characteristic of medieval biblical interpretation, when it comes to Song of Songs they are willing to rely on medieval and mystical allegorical interpretations to guide their thinking about the book's contents.

Readers tend to see the book as an allegory in part because the vocabulary of love poetry is obscure, the images are condensed, and the referents are ambiguous. The view that the lovers' pulsating passion and titillating sexual fantasies do not represent or point to any higher theological reality, that the book's significance is revealed in its literal meaning, and that the poet and editors who shaped the final poetry were not interested in elaborating on the nature of God and mediating sound religious doctrine has proved too incredible for those who remain bent on reading Song of Songs allegorically.

Today more and more interpreters are willing to read the book as a collection or anthology of love lyrics that capture the joys and sufferings of intimate relationships and of sensual love. The book chronicles one woman's journey to find fulfilling love with a man who, for reasons unknown to us, comes across as both enamored of her and forever elusive to her. Although the matter is never put so boldly in the poems, everyone who listens to the couple's plaintive outbursts empathizes with their dilemma, "to love or not to love." And although the drama appears to center around the heterosexual, erotic exchange between a woman and a man, Song of Songs is not in the end *about* heterosexual sex. Instead, it teaches us about the power and politics of human love. The lovers' humanity, not their genders, intends to captivate the audience. Audiences are supposed to recognize their own flawed demonstration and practice of love in these two characters, not because they recognize themselves in the characters' genders, but because they recognize themselves in their humanity. Audiences are first lured into contemplating the universal need by all to be loved, and then forced to confront their ambivalences about sexuality.

The black-skinned protagonist remains in many ways a product of her culture in her ambitions and her fantasies. Her continuous struggle to fulfill her desire to be loved and to retain her dignity as a woman invites audiences to ignore for the moment their inbred ethnic prejudices (against a Shulammite?), their class assumptions (about women who labor in the sun?), and their religious judgments about female sexuality, modesty, and impurity. The hope is that readers, whether male or female, will recognize themselves in this woman's very human need and desire simply to be loved.

STRUCTURE AND COMPOSITION

While the archaic grammatical and linguistic forms found in the book suggest that some version of the book dates back to the early period in Israel's history, lyrical compositions

---

12. This line of interpretation began, of course, with the Targum, but one European Catholic scholar in modern times was very influential in arguing the claim. See Paul Joüon, *Le Cantique des Cantiques: commentaire philologique et exégétique* (Paris: Gabriel Beauchesne, 1909).

are notoriously difficult to date with any accuracy. In fact, much of their appeal is the result of their seemingly timeless, universal application to the human situation. The themes of Song of Songs are those that belong to the commonplaces of human courtship and human sexual attraction: yearning for the lover's presence, the joys of physical intimacy, coded speech, and elusive behavior, intoxication with the charms and beauty of one's lover, overcoming social obstacles and impediments to be together. Such themes are typical of love lyrics both ancient and modern. In fact, scholars have long noted the similarities between the mood and lyrics in Song of Songs and those of ancient Egyptian love poetry dating from the period of the New Kingdom (c. 1567–1085 BCE).[13] Observing particular stylized features of Egyptian love songs associated with the Ramesside texts, Michael Fox posits that these ancient songs may have been composed for entertainment and were performed by professional singers at private banquets and public festivals.[14] This music, performed over centuries and for generations, was created to charm audiences through its use of erotic allusions, veiled speeches, and extravagant imagery. Indeed, in the Song of Songs, audiences are at least implicitly invited to assume the identities of the lovers, to identify with their plight, to sympathize with their dilemma, to share their resolve, to relish their tenacity, to enjoy their clever disguises, to mourn their losses and flaws, to celebrate their joys and strength, and to endure with them unto the end.[15] The mood and tone of the book change, sometimes within a few verses, as speakers move in and out of the drama, wooing, pleading, teasing, doubting, and interrupting each other. Audiences (and readers) are expected to be able to perceive within the poem's "progression" all the ambiguities, uncertainties, tensions, shortcomings, and suspense of love itself. In other words, drama and contents come together in the Song of Songs to create a poem intent upon gripping its audience.

Readers trained within the Western literary tradition invariably find a book like Song of Songs difficult to follow. Western readers expect literature to proceed in an orderly fashion and are frequently dismayed when a book like Song of Songs defies expectations of linearity, uniformity, transparency, and plot development. Whereas the presence of speakers, dialogue, and audiences gives the book an unmistakably dramatic quality, modern readers are struck by the way speakers, imagery, moods, and perspectives shift back and forth, seemingly without logic, sometimes within a span of one, two, or three verses. These otherwise oral speeches, which originally had their own performance quality, have been committed to a written form that has caused some tensions in its narrative development. Finding a uniform structure and consistent pattern to the book's content is not always possible. Those who perceive any literary unity to the poetry usually argue on the basis of their own aesthetic insights and not on the basis of any straightforward criteria. Commen-

13. See Adolf Erman, *The Literature of the Ancient Egyptians,* trans. Aylward M. Blackman (London: Methuen, 1927); John Bradley White, *A Study of the Language of Love in the Song of Songs and Ancient Egyptian Poetry,* SBLDS 38 (Missoula, Mont.: Scholars Press, 1978).

14. Michael Fox, *The Song of Songs and the Ancient Egyptian Love Songs* (Madison: University of Wisconsin Press, 1985) 244-47.

15. Roland Murphy, *The Song of Songs,* Hermeneia (Minneapolis: Fortress, 1990) 47.

tators who divide the work into poems see it as a composition of fourteen, eighteen, twenty-eight, or thirty-one (to name just a few examples) units of poetry.

The position taken in this commentary to divide the poem into eleven lyrical units is not based on unassailable perceptions into its unfolding direction. Although the poem seems to be framed by an inclusio (the book opens [1:2-6] and closes [8:8-14] on similar themes; e.g., vineyard, the protagonist's brothers, her bodily integrity), the major indications of the book's "organization" are shifts in speakers and moods. The thirteen blocks of material commented upon in this commentary reflect what seem to be thirteen shifts in speakers, in some instances, and moods of speeches (in other instances). Of course, in the numerous instances where it is difficult to determine exactly who speaks and who is the referent (e.g., 2:1; 6:11-12; 8:11-12), guesses are hazarded.

Although we see changing sides of the protagonist (romantic, defender, sage, and pragmatist), she switches back and forth between these different shades of herself, depending on the obscure attitudes challenging her right to love and to be loved by whomever she chooses. By the poem's end, the protagonist is leaning in her lover's arms in a satisfying embrace (8:5). But her fulfillment is short-lived. The curtain closes on the lovers' thwarted passion; the maiden hurries her lover's pleasure for fear of retaliation. As a woman in the Hebrew culture, she is aggressive and audacious, but as a sage and observer of human nature she is also profoundly realistic. The homily on wisdom in 8:6-7 may be correct that love is a powerful force, one that in the end conquers everything that opposes it. But love's victory does not come without a price.

Finally, Western readers expect compositions to exhibit some interest in progression or development of character(s) and plot. This cultural expectation is only casually satisfied in the Song of Songs. In the first five chapters the lovers yearn for each other, delight in each other's charms, and sing each other's praises. In the last three chapters of the book, having defended their relationship against forces from without and from within, they eventually embrace, consummate their love, and pledge that their love, though costly, is more powerful than the forces opposing it. Under no circumstances can one argue that the book closes on a note of resolution or conclusion. At the end the maiden is forced to shoo her lover away, leaving the audience to wonder whether the two are ever allowed to relax and revel in their relationship. What could be the meaning of such an unresolved ending? Is love worth it? Perhaps that is precisely the question the song wants the audience to ponder.

BIBLIOGRAPHY

Commentaries:

Falk, Marcia. *The Song of Songs: A New Translation and Interpretation.* San Francisco: HarperCollins, 1990. Although not a commentary per se, this translation of the Hebrew text by a Jewish scholar represents one of the most sensitive, contemporary, and daring attempts to capture the nuances of Hebrew love poetry in English.

Murphy, Roland. *The Song of Songs.* Hermeneia. Minneapolis: Fortress, 1990. This commentary by a Catholic Carmelite adds helpful insight into neglected literary and theological themes in Song of Songs.

Pope, Marvin. *Song of Songs.* AB 7C. New York: Doubleday, 1977. This most celebrated commentary on Song of Songs represents a meticulously detailed exposition on virtually every conceivable Near Eastern mythological intimation in the little Hebrew book.

Other Suggestive Studies:

Abu-Lughod, Lila. *Veiled Sentiments: Honor and Poetry in a Bedouin Society.* Berkeley: University of California Press, 1986. An exceptionally illuminating discussion of the structure, form, content, and social context of bedouin poems and songs reflecting the private sentiments of bedouin women in particular.

Baruch, Elaine Hoffman. *Women, Love, and Power: Literary and Psychoanalytic Perspectives.* New York: New York University Press, 1991. A social critique of prominent themes that recur in literature about women and romantic love from the Middle Ages to the present.

Biale, David. *Eros and the Jews: From Biblical Israel to Contemporary America.* New York: Basic, 1992.

Brenner, Athalya, ed. *A Feminist Companion to the Song of Songs.* Sheffield: JSOT, 1993. A collection of classic articles written on Song of Songs.

Merkin, Daphne. "The Woman on the Balcony: On Reading the Song of Songs," *Tikkun* 9, 3 (May–June 1994) 59-64.

Meyers, Carol. *Discovering Eve: Ancient Israelite Women in Context.* New York: Oxford University Press, 1988. An interdisciplinary look at the everyday lives of women in ancient Israel living in the Palestinian highlands during the Iron Age (1200–300 BCE).

Miles, Margaret R. *Carnal Knowing: Female Nakedness and Religious Meaning in the Christian West.* Boston: Beacon, 1989.

Nelson, James, and Sandra P. Longfellow, eds. *Sexuality and the Sacred: Sources for Theological Reflection.* Louisville: Westminster John Knox, 1994. A rich collection of writings reflecting a range of contemporary Christian thinking on sexuality.

Trible, Phyllis. *God and the Rhetoric of Sexuality.* Philadelphia: Fortress, 1978.

OUTLINE OF SONG OF SONGS

SUPERSCRIPTION

NIV	NRSV
1 Solomon's Song of Songs.	1 The Song of Songs, which is Solomon's.

COMMENTARY

The Hebrew title שיר השירים (*šîr haššîrîm*), usually translated flatly, though literally, as "the Song of Songs" (NIV) identifies the work before us as an exemplary literary creation. The Hebrew is a typical way of expressing the superlative and might be more accurately translated as "the Most Excellent of Songs" or perhaps "the Most Sublime of Songs" (cf. "the God of gods and the Lord of Lords," Deut 10:17 NIV; "vanity of vanities," Eccl 1:2; 12:8 NRSV).

The book's further association with King Solomon (שר השירים אשר לשלמה *šîr haššîrîm 'ăšer lišlōmōh*) situates it in the tradition of the wisest and most prolific king in Israel's history; hence the title in some translations, "the Song of Solomon" (NRSV). Less poetic, but equally defensible translations might be "the Song Composed of Songs" or "the Song of Many Songs." Each translation in its own way calls attention to the contents of the book as a special collection of songs or poems.

According to tradition, King Solomon uttered some three thousand "proverbs" (משל *māšāl*) and a thousand and five songs in his lifetime (1 Kgs 4:32[5:12]). It is unlikely that Solomon actually composed the Song of Songs, however, given many of the late linguistic forms scattered throughout the book. It is possible that the reputation of the infamous king as sage, composer, and husband to hundreds of wives inspired more than one composer through the centuries to draft provocative love lyrics in his memory. Rather than being viewed as an attempt to give a precise date and specific author, then, the superscription in 1:1 is best understood as a scribal effort to associate the book with a prominent figure in Israel's history and to place its contents within an established tradition of reflection—namely, the wisdom tradition.

Solomon's reputation as husband to seven hundred wives and three hundred concubines, both foreign and local women (1 Kgs 11:1-8; cf. Deut 17:17) must have made him a popular subject of folk tales and folk music. The six references to the king in the book may reflect some of the varied folk traditions that inevitably sprang up over the centuries about the king and came to be incorporated into a book under his name (1:1, 5; 3:7, 9, 11; 8:11). The many speculations about the king's love life, the banter about his powers of seduction and numerous marriages, and admiration of his godly insight into affairs of the heart made his name an ideal *nom de plume* to attach to the highly controversial, but profoundly human, contents of Song of Songs. Associating poetry luxuriating in human passion with such a renowned king accomplished three things: (1) It lent the work a semblance of authority, thus assuring its preservation and transmission; (2) it connected the book with a privileged school of thinking that was associated with Solomon—the wisdom tradition; and (3) it brought together for sacred reflection three topics (sex, power, and wisdom) that, combined, could evoke deeply felt emotions and tap into widely held social beliefs.

Biblical superscriptions, though rarely as precise about dating as modern interpreters would like, insist by their very placement at the opening of a work that the following material did not originate in abstraction. Its contents have been shaped by specific contexts, its conversations framed by shared histories and worldviews. "Let the reader beware," then, is the subtle warning behind every superscription; although the subject matter may appear oblique and quixotic in some places, downright obscure and baffling in others, and although its origin and apparent significance may seem puzzling, the following text has been judged sublime and urgent by past generations who were perfectly willing to wrestle with its message and whose patience is worthy of emulation.

REFLECTIONS

Throughout the ages in Jewish and Christian liturgy, the Song of Songs has played an important part of worship, being sung at Passover celebrations in the Jewish tradition and serving as sermon text to illustrate Jesus' love for the church in the Christian tradition. The melodramatic and highly passionate tone of the lyrics lends the book's contents to singing and reenactment in festive, celebrative gatherings where love and devotion are thematic.

Judging by the bits of songs and poetry scattered throughout the Old Testament, especially the 150 lyrical compositions assembled in the book known as Psalms, music and poetry were ideal media in biblical antiquity for chronicling profoundly sacred and profoundly human experiences. We find repeated examples of the people's attempt to articulate in song their greatest joys (e.g., "Sing to the LORD, for he has triumphed gloriously" [Exod 15:21a NRSV]), their deepest sorrows (e.g., "How shall we sing the LORD's song in a strange land?" [Ps 137:4 KJV]), and their most profound hopes ("Sing, O barren one who did not bear; burst into song and shout, you who have not been in labor! For the children of the desolate woman will be more than the children of her that is married, says the LORD" [Isa 54:1 NRSV]). According to tradition, King David, himself a musician, was so convinced of the powers of music to evoke the sublime that he made sure that music was a professional, institutionalized part of Israel's worship.

It is difficult to imagine worship without music. Certainly for those raised in traditions characterized by lively music, expressive chants, and dramatized sermons music and worship are virtually synonymous. Music, as musicians are wont to insist, is the language of the soul. And a book like Song of Songs is ideal reading in ceremonies where men and women gather to celebrate the perfecting of human love here on earth as it is in heaven.

Because lyrics use the sparsest amount of language to appeal to the deepest of emotions, capturing our joys and fears, recording our creeds and contradictions, rehearsing our ambitions and failures with meter and measure that lull and grip the imagination, music and poetry reflect upon a society's images of itself that it can hear, appreciate, digest, react to, and correct. Perhaps that is why artists are the first to be silenced in totalitarian governments. Theirs is a potential to unmask falsities bit by bit, in portions manageable to the masses and in unforgettable language.

Some of the most memorable hymns, anthems, and praise songs make imaginable and comprehensible to our congregations ideas and notions that continue to elude our best exegetical sermons: God's amazing grace, Jesus' redemptive love at the cross of Calvary, the faith of our beloved ancestors, a people's prayers for their children's children. Epiphanies like these tend to break the back of mundane speech. Often, music and poetry are needed to bridge the gap between heaven and earth, the world of strangers and enemies, the world of women and men. Love lyrics, like those in Song of Songs, invite their audience into the private world of intimates.

LET HIM KISS ME

NIV

²Let him kiss me with the kisses of his mouth—
    for your love is more delightful than wine.
³Pleasing is the fragrance of your perfumes;
    your name is like perfume poured out.
    No wonder the maidens love you!
⁴Take me away with you—let us hurry!
    Let the king bring me into his chambers.
We rejoice and delight in you*;
    we will praise your love more than wine.
How right they are to adore you!

a4 The Hebrew is masculine singular.

NRSV

² Let him kiss me with the kisses of his mouth!
    For your love is better than wine,
³   your anointing oils are fragrant,
    your name is perfume poured out;
    therefore the maidens love you.
⁴ Draw me after you, let us make haste.
    The king has brought me into his chambers.
We will exult and rejoice in you;
    we will extol your love more than wine;
    rightly do they love you.

COMMENTARY

Turning to the initial full unit (1:2-6), readers are gripped by the first-person narration that opens the book: "Let him kiss me with the kisses of his mouth!" One experiences the uneasy, but exhilarating, feeling that attends a public performance where actresses and actors invite audiences into the deeply personal world of private secrets and pent-up emotions. The audience is invited to share in each actor's pathos. To do that, however, one must be able to distinguish the players from one another and to follow the direction of the performance.

The opening verses of Song of Songs plunge the reader directly and without delay into one of the features of the book that makes it difficult to organize and frustrating to follow. Pronouns shift back and forth, as do verb forms, making it hard to identify speakers and subject matter from verse to verse. For example, the pronouns shift from the third person ("him") in v. 2 to the second person ("you") in v. 3, signaling a change from the narrative voice to direct address; and in v. 4 the verb forms change the speech from second-person narration to first-person singular ("Draw me after you") and first-person plural address ("We will exult and rejoice in you"). Readers are left to wonder how many speakers are involved

in this drama and exactly who is being spoken to and about. This kind of suspense was evidently used by composers of ancient lyrics to entice the audience to strain forward and listen intently.

1:2. The first speech opens on a note of yearning. The speaker is female. She introduces herself to the reader, not by giving her name, but by announcing her wish to be kissed by her lover: "Let him kiss me with the kisses of his mouth!" In a culture where casual touch between the opposite sexes was rare, a kiss was fantasized as the climax of sexual pleasure. After addressing no one in particular, but everyone in earshot, the woman turns to address her lover directly, beckoning him by speaking adoringly of his love, his scent, and his name (vv. 2*b*-3). She cherishes his "love" over wine (v. 2*b*)—no trivial matter when one considers that the black-skinned woman lives in a part of the world where vineyards were greatly prized and specially handled (cf. Exod 22:5; 23:11; Deut 20:6; 23:24). Comparing love to wine was common to male and female exchanges of love (cf. 4:10), much like the modern expression, "your love is sweeter than honey."

Because the Hebrew words for "breast" and "love" share a similar consonantal spelling (דוד

dwd), some ancient manuscripts, changing the vocalization of the noun, read "your breasts" (דדיך *daddayik*) over "your love" (דדיך *dōdeykā*), thereby rendering the verse as "your breasts are better than wine." But "breasts" is an unlikely translation. It assumes the speaker is male, and nothing in the remainder of the verse points indisputably to a male speaker. There *is* reason to believe that the woman remains the speaker. For one thing, the Hebrew word for "love" is a derivative of the same term she uses repeatedly in the poetry to refer to her suitor, דודי (*dôdî*), "beloved" (see 1:13, 14, 16).

1:3. The maiden insists that no one can escape her lover's powers: "No wonder the maidens love you!" (NIV). But she carefully refrains from divulging his name, simply comparing it to the perfumed oils of Mediterranean cultures. Such oils, regarded by the populace as powerful aphrodisiacs, were produced by combining perfumes with olive oil. Like spilled perfume, whose aroma fills the air, her lover's name is pleasant to the senses. Demonstrating in this verse her powers as a poet, the protagonist relies more on inference and imagination than on candor and the mundane to describe her love. She invites her audience to experience her suitor as she does, with the nose (e.g., perfume) and the tastebuds (e.g., kisses and wine).

1:4. In this verse, the protagonist's voice becomes insistent, and her request is cast in the imperative: "Draw me after you." She speaks assertively, insisting that her suitor take her quickly to his chambers (lit., "Draw me after you—let us hurry [until] the king has brought me into his chambers"). Her reference to the king is probably an expression of endearment and esteem, although some commentators have thought

that Solomon is being spoken of here. Whether "king" refers to an actual monarch or is a term of endearment for a special love, the sense of the verse is probably best captured by the NIV: "Let the king bring me into his chambers."

The narrative change from first-person singular to first-person plural in the next line ("We will rejoice and exult . . . extol your love") has prompted several translations and interpretations: Is this the speech of the maidens, presumably the daughters of Jerusalem (v. 5) who from time to time interrupt the speeches of the protagonist and suitor to challenge their views (5:9; 6:13)? Or is the protagonist speaking here, looking forward to the time when she and her suitor can frolic and luxuriate in royal or lavish settings, celebrating their love for each other and savoring each other's taste ("we will extol your love more than wine")? Listening in on the private world of human passion, we can only guess that the latter is the case.

Modern readers might marvel at such a bold portrait of a woman in biblical antiquity. Such immodest desires on a woman's lips run counter to the passive, reserved, submissive image of Hebrew women one finds in many other portions of the Old Testament. Hebrew women do not initiate sex, one might suppose, except in the cases of women like Tamar (Genesis 38) and Ruth (Ruth 3), who wanted to become pregnant. Yet there is no hint in these verses, or elsewhere in the poem, that the female protagonist has procreation on her mind as she yearns for her suitor. Indeed, the protagonist presents a portrait of Hebrew women different from the one cast throughout much of the Old Testament—indeed, the entire Bible. She boldly longs for intimacy with a special lover and does not hesitate to pursue him.

REFLECTIONS

Perhaps our ancestors were not so squeamish about using the erotic to contemplate transcendence as we have supposed. In Song of Songs all of the created order is invited to join in this paean to human eroticism, where two souls pine for each other in a lyrical drama of suspense, intrigue, and desperation. Audiences are invited to identify with a female protagonist who longs to be kissed and swept away by her lover. Does the woman's voice in Song of Songs, which is unparalleled in the rest of Scripture, make us recoil or surrender? How, if at all, might we react differently had her suitor opened the book with the same words and his was the dominant perspective? If the male voice were predominant, would the work's religious import be more apparent or plausible?

We should not dismiss the importance of our initial shock at the woman's voice and longing in the first few verses of a canonical book. The composer of the poem undoubtedly was hoping to pique her audience's attention. After all, nothing seizes an audience like the topic of sex. A sensual sermon illustration is sure to make the person dozing in the third pew take notice of the remainder of a sermon. Hearing a woman talk explicitly about her sexual fantasies can arrest an audience's wandering thoughts.

The composer probably did not expect her poetry to fall into the hands of audiences for whom combining the topics of sex and religion was unthinkable. But she was likely quite aware that poetry detailing a woman's intimate fantasies was not the stuff of normal public discourse. And like any good composer of a literary work, she incorporated the song's probable effects upon her audience—discomfort, embarrassment, curiosity—into the meaning and significance of her poetry. Notice that the composer does not postpone the ribald topic of sexual longing until after she has won her audience's sympathies for the lovers; nor does she prepare her audience for the steamy erotic exchanges of the lovers by explicating in detail the nature of the difficulties obstructing their love (cf. Psalm 137, where the poet delays introducing a cruel outcry to slaughter the babies of his enemy [Ps 137:8-9] until after he has first lured the audience into empathizing with the social distress of the speaker [Ps 137:1-6]). The poet counts on the tensions experienced by audiences wanting to believe in both love and social propriety to create an arresting drama. Sex forces audiences to confront head-on their deepest convictions, their unspoken preconceptions, and their own complicated desires. When sex is combined with religion, boundaries are transgressed and lines are blurred, because sex is rarely about just sex. It is about needs, longings, fears, fantasies—in a word, human passion. And passion never quite conforms to the neat and tidy categories and labels of religion.

The opening verses of Song of Songs force the reader to face his or her deepest convictions about marriage, love, and female sexuality. The Bible is full of stories in which male sexual aggression is taken for granted and assimilated into some of the most notable moments in redemptive history. In Genesis 6:1-4, intercourse between women and the "sons of God" (referring either to mythic angels or to ancient warriors of renown) represents one final act of corruption leading to God's decision to blot out humankind with a flood (Gen 6:9–9:17). In the prophecies of Hosea, Jeremiah, and Ezekiel in particular, male fantasies of whoring wives, female lasciviousness, and rape are the backdrop for divine judgment and prophetic predictions of destruction.[16] And in Exod 19:15 the men of Israel, before receiving divine law, are ordered to observe rituals of purification, which included refraining from sexual intercourse with women (the inference being that sexual contact with women obstructs divine revelation). Female sexuality poses problems for men and, according to our male narrators, for God. Unrestricted contact with women threatens boundaries and portends turmoil. Repeatedly fathers warn sons against falling into the sexual snares of loose women (cf. Prov 2:16-19; 5:3-14, 20-21; 6:24-35; 7:1-27; 9:13-18); and in both canonical and non-canonical literature one finds male narrators openly declaring their contempt for women (Eccl 7:26; Sir 25:24; 42:14).

Song of Songs represents a remarkable departure from much religious literature because the book's opening verses hurl the unsuspecting reader straight into the clutches of a *woman's* sexual fantasies. It forces the reader to see herself or himself, the world, and God (for those who read the book as an allegory of God and Israel's relationship) in an unfamiliar way—namely, through a woman's libidinous cravings. Whatever ambivalences one may have about hearing from God or discovering the sacred through the messy mysteries of the female body are forced to the surface. By beckoning the reader into the private world of female imagination and longing, the poet gambles on her audience's curiosity about sex and romance and fascination with tales of obstructed love winning out over whatever squeamishness the readers may have about associating women's bodies with divine revelations. Hence, the meaning of the opening verses of Song of Songs lies not only in what they tell us about God, but also in what they tell us about ourselves.

---

16. Renita J. Weems, *Battered Love: Marriage, Sex, and Violence in the Hebrew Prophets* (Minneapolis: Fortress, 1995).

I Am Black and Beautiful

NIV

NIV

⁵Dark am I, yet lovely,
  O daughters of Jerusalem,
  dark like the tents of Kedar,
  like the tent curtains of Solomon.ᵃ
⁶Do not stare at me because I am dark,
  because I am darkened by the sun.
My mother's sons were angry with me
  and made me take care of the vineyards;
  my own vineyard I have neglected.

ᵃ5 Or *Salma*

NRSV

⁵ I am black and beautiful,
  O daughters of Jerusalem,
  like the tents of Kedar,
  like the curtains of Solomon.
⁶ Do not gaze at me because I am dark,
  because the sun has gazed on me.
My mother's sons were angry with me;
  they made me keeper of the vineyards,
  but my own vineyard I have not kept!

Commentary

A good example of how the poetry of this book provokes the cultural imagination appears in 1:5-6. It is one of those Bible passages whose interpretation has engendered a lively amount of speculation and discussion, even though the Hebrew text is relatively uncomplicated.

After romancing her lover with flattery in 1:2-4, the protagonist speaks with pride, self-confidence, and, contrary to what some have argued, without apology as she describes herself (v. 5). She is, in her own words, "black and beautiful" (NRSV). The Hebrew word she uses to describe her complexion (שחורה *šĕḥôrâ*) is unambiguous, despite the numerous efforts by translators to render it more euphemistically and palatably as "dark," "very dark," "swarthy," "blackish," and so on. Derivative adjectival forms of the word appear elsewhere in the Old Testament where the color "black" is the indisputable meaning. In Lev 13:31, 37, "black" hair as a sign of health and cleanness is clearly being contrasted to yellowish diseased hair. In Zech 6:2, 6 the adjective distinguishes the "black" horses of the second chariot from the red, white, and dappled horses driving the other chariots. And elsewhere in Song of Songs the adjective describes the color of her beloved's wavy hair, "black as a raven" (Cant 5:11). In its only occur-

rence as a verb, שחר (*šāḥar*) describes Job's blackened, parched skin, the result of a protracted fever (Job 30:30). If "black" is the uncontested meaning of *šāḥar* elsewhere in the Old Testament, then there is no basis for debate about its meaning in Cant 1:5. If there is any dispute, and there has been considerable, it centers on whether the protagonist describes herself as "black and beautiful" or "black, but beautiful."

In the Septuagint (LXX), the Greek translators of the Old Testament had no misgivings about the matter. The Greek translation reads, "Black am I and beautiful." Some commentators, construing the protagonist's comment in v. 5 as apologetic point to v. 10 and Lam 4:7 to defend the view that the white and ruddy complexion was the prevailing standard of beauty at the time. That being the case, they argue, the accurate translation is, "I am black, but beautiful." Other evidence must be considered, however: (1) The word "black" appears five times in the emphatic position suggesting that the woman's tone is confident and her posture assertive—not apologetic. (2) Throughout the poem the woman's physical beauty is both praised and celebrated, not only by her lover but also by the maidens of the city, which means that others regard her as indisputably attractive. (3) Although the Song of Songs and Lamentations (and other portions of Scripture) suggest that a ruddy complexion was prized in men, the same does not automatically apply to women, since women were commonly judged by a different standard of beauty.

No other woman in the Bible describes herself in the way the black-skinned woman in Song of Songs does. Unlike Leah and Rachel, she is not seen through her male narrator's eyes (Gen 29:17). Unlike Tamar, she does not disguise who she really is to avoid rejection (Gen 38:15). And unlike Ruth, she does not apologize for being noticed, conspicuous, or different (Ruth 2:10). She is the only woman in Scripture who describes herself in her own words.

She is careful to explain how she became the color she is. Her brothers, she insists, forced her to work outdoors in their vineyards. She is not a freak, she insists, but a casualty of the sun (v. 6). Although there is no mistaking the defensive tone in her words, there is no reason to believe that the protagonist is apologetic about her color. That she is not embarrassed by her complexion can be seen in the fact that she compares her color to the stark sable fabric characteristic of the imposing tents of the Syro-Arabian nomadic tribe known as Kedar (whose root connotes darkness; cf. Jer 8:21; 14:2; Mic 3:6), and to the striking curtains in Solomon's palace. The inference is that hers is a color of distinction and nobility (at least in her own mind), hence her insistence that she is beautiful (נאוה *nā'wâ*).

Despite the brief references to her color, the protagonist remains nameless and virtually clanless throughout the whole poem (notwithstanding the one oblique reference to "Shulammite" in 6:13). Likewise, no mention is made of her patronymic or matronymic, which could shed light on her ancestral lineage. We are left to take heart in her bold act of self-assertion and description:

She speaks up for herself; she is the object of her own gaze: she is, by her own estimation, black *and* beautiful.

There remains the matter of her enigmatic statement in v. 6, "My brothers were angry with me and made me take care of the vineyards." Is this a reference to actual kindred? Familial terms are used casually throughout the book as literary devices and as part of cultural memory; the male lover refers to the protagonist repeatedly as his "sister" (4:9, 12; 5:1); she refers to "mother(s)" on several occasions (3:4, 11; 8:1, 5); and in 1:6 and 8:1 she alludes to the privileges a "brother" can take with his sister. But exactly why were her brothers angry with her, and, more important, what politely veiled cultural comment might she be making by claiming that her brothers forced her to tend "the vineyards"?

The protagonist's complaint that she was forced to labor in vineyards, a term with erotic overtones throughout Song of Songs (2:15; 7:12; 8:12), has led some commentators to draw sexual inferences from the verse. Marvin Pope, who has written an important commentary on the book, says, "The well-attested sexual symbolism of vineyard and field strongly suggests that the import of her statement is that she has not preserved her own virginity."[17] Specifically, Pope (and others) sees the protagonist as referring here to her body and sexual parts.[18] Taken this way, then, the woman admits here that she has not been able to safeguard her own virginity—as she ought or would have liked. Such an interpretation is consonant with the overall image throughout the book of a woman who persists in the face of incredible odds in pursuing an elusive relationship.

17. Marvin Pope, *Song of Songs,* AB 7C (New York: Doubleday, 1977) 329.
18. Ibid., 330.

REFLECTIONS

Curiously, God's name is never mentioned in Song of Songs. Neither is there any explicit comment on traditional religious themes. Readers are left to draw on their experiences of love, longing, mutuality, sensuality, and human connectedness to contemplate the book's meaning for conventional religious doctrines of faith, covenant, law, justice, hope, revelation, and reconciliation. We are invited to find God in ourselves, to perceive the parallels between human passion and religious pathos, to weigh our noblest ideas against our most senseless prejudices, and to let our deepest yearnings direct us to what is eternal. What better way of prompting audiences to probe the depths of their thinking about God, to examine their unexamined prejudices, and to dive below the surface of their narrow notions than to invite them to contemplate simultaneously love and bigotry? Indeed, to read the poetry of Song of Songs is to be caught up in unrelenting and enormous swings in emotions. The reader must be willing to switch from one emotion to another, sometimes in a span of one, two, or three verses, surrendering to passion and then playfulness, longing and then reserve, vanity and then defensiveness, awe and then anguish. It is also to be torn between one's deep cultural prejudices and one's noblest cultural ideals. We have already seen in vv. 5-6 that the reader follows the lovesick woman through at least two extremes of the human heart: confidence and defensiveness.

What is it about the color of a person's skin that can evoke the most banal impulses of the human heart? Why has color prejudice been such a pervasive and virtually universal mode of discrimination throughout the ages and around the world? Why in patriarchal cultures do foreign women whose physical characteristics deviate from the norm invariably become the subject of intense debate and condemnation? Addressing these questions would, perhaps, take us too far afield of our present study. But they are questions worth pondering as we reflect on the significance of Song of Songs for our cultural context. Time and again religious people have been at the forefront of campaigns to outlaw and subjugate people who think and look differently, and they have turned their heads when others were tortured, gassed, or hanged. The black-skinned woman in Song of Songs remains forever a meaningful trope for talking about the quest for authentic relationship and community.

Of course, this is not the first time in the Bible when a foreign woman becomes a reminder of how diverse is God's vision of covenant people (e.g., Ruth and Rahab). Nor is the protagonist in Song of Songs the first woman who functions as a mirror for self-scrutiny (e.g., Moses' Ethiopian wife, the Samaritan woman at the well). The stories of these deviant women, foreigners, harlots, and widows who part from cultural norms, not so much by their actions (although they frequently engage in heroic or gallant feats on behalf of their community), but by nature of their physical and cultural differences, become important rhetorical lessons on the ecumenicity of God's vision of the kingdom.

Forced to get into the skin of this black woman, the reader is made to see her as neither Amazon nor demon, the two extreme fears of the bigot. Her quest for love, her desire to be loved genuinely, and her willingness to give herself unselfishly to love are so familiar that even the bigot can identify with the protagonist. All of us are reminded that love has its own logic. It refuses to succumb to the human will. It is rarely predictable, and it delights in the unexpected. It forces us to do things we never anticipated, to say things we never heard ourselves say before, to submit to feelings we never felt before, and to pair ourselves with people we never imagined for ourselves. Love helps us risk stretching beyond our comfort zones. Indeed, nothing exposes us for who we really are—and who we are not—nothing divulges our secrets and unmasks our preconceptions like love. Song of Songs, with its hint at color prejudice, taps into our deepest cultural prejudices by making us confront the way they keep us from seeing certain people as individuals with needs, desires, ambitions for love, and intimacy just like ourselves.

Finally, the lovelorn female in the Song of Songs calls out our noblest yearnings. She does this first by forcing us to face our prejudices about the other, making us confront a base impulse: the propensity to differentiate ourselves from those who deviate from our expectations and fall outside the norm. She challenges the dominant aesthetics. She pooh-poohs the hegemonic standards of beauty. She leaves us conflicted. Do we endorse her quest to find satisfying love, irrespective of where such a search might take her? Or do we, along with her gawking audience, allow our prejudices against black, aggressive, forward women, to censure her, impose limits on her, and force her into vineyards not of her choosing?

SONG OF SONGS 1:7–2:7

I COMPARE YOU, MY LOVE

OVERVIEW

Turning to 1:7–2:7, we cannot help feeling that we are eavesdropping on an intimate tête-à-tête between lovers. It seems as though we are intruding upon a conversation intended for only the special ears involved. This is profoundly private talk between two people who share special intimacies and who have special intentions toward each other. Theirs is love talk, lusty and mischievous. Such talk is ablaze with mutual admiration and longing, while at the same time shrouded in cryptic references and secret allusions. What

keeps it from careening toward the vulgar, besides the fact that it is consensual, is that love talk is not blunt speech. Lovers bristling with passion and yearning rarely talk about their desires forthrightly. Instead, they talk around them. They talk in codes, relying on analogies, hiding behind innuendoes and figurative speech to convey what they are too shy, too embarrassed, too nervous, too straitlaced, or perhaps too modest to say outright. As for the subject of their whispers, why, it is sex, of course.

SONG OF SONGS 1:7-8, A SIMPLE QUESTION

NIV

⁷Tell me, you whom I love, where you graze
    your flock
  and where you rest your sheep at midday.
Why should I be like a veiled woman
  beside the flocks of your friends?
⁸If you do not know, most beautiful of women,
  follow the tracks of the sheep
and graze your young goats
  by the tents of the shepherds.

NRSV

⁷ Tell me, you whom my soul loves,
    where you pasture your flock,
    where you make it lie down at noon;
  for why should I be like one who is veiled
    beside the flocks of your companions?

⁸ If you do not know,
    O fairest among women,
  follow the tracks of the flock,
    and pasture your kids
    beside the shepherds' tents.

COMMENTARY

1:7. One detects a petulant tone in the protagonist's voice as she inquires as to her lover's whereabouts, a query repeated in one way or another throughout the book. To soften her impatience and boldness in asking, however, the black-skinned woman addresses her lover with a term of endearment that melts

away any possible taking of offense. The NRSV captures poetically her seduction: "you whom my soul loves." She inquires as to where he pastures his flock (which suggests that he is a shepherd), particularly where he leads his flock, as shepherds do, at the noon hour to rest. The implication is that midday might be the ideal time when she and her mate could steal away for some adventure.

Almost pouting, but maintaining a tone of seductiveness, the protagonist lets her lover know that she resents being in the dark as to his whereabouts, having to stumble about blindly, as if she wore a veil over her face, groping for him: "Why should I be like one who is veiled beside the flocks of your friends?" (v. 7*b*). She is not comparing herself to a prostitute whose face is cloaked in order to hide her identity, as one might think. Some scholars point to the ruse Tamar was forced to resort to in her efforts to woo her father-in-law, Judah (Gen 38:15; cf. Hos 2:2). The protagonist's meaning, then, would be something like, "Why should I have to resort to duplicity (like the ancestress Tamar) in order to get your attention?"

But the poetry makes clear throughout that it is not the woman who is evasive, but her lover. She is continually looking for him, groping for him, inquiring about him (2:8; 3:1-2; 5:6; 6:1-2). He is elusive, but she is persistent. The veil that she speaks of is the figurative one she feels she wears, which keeps her always uncertain about him.

1:8. To her question about his whereabouts, he answers with a tease: "If you do not know, most beautiful of women, follow the tracks of the sheep and graze your young goats by the tents of the shepherds." Like other maidens in antiquity who resided in rural, bedouin-like, semi-pastoral cultures, the protagonist was responsible for her share of the chores in the household, which among other things included tending the fields, dressing vines, and leading the family goats to grazing ground during the day. Seen in the light of her duties, her lover's comment in this verse should be taken to mean: "I am right under your nose." One might be tempted to ascribe this verse to the chorus of Jerusalem maidens who from time to time interject their opinion into the poetry (5:1*b*; 6:1, 10, 13; 8:5). But her question is not directed at the maidens. It addresses her lover.

Such a forthright answer on the shepherd's part contradicts his reputation throughout the book as inaccessible and elusive. More likely, his comment represents the kind of cryptic retort that skittish, evasive lovers are wont to make when pressed for more accountability: "You know where to find me." But that remains to be seen. So far we have a typical scene in love poetry: One party is frantic with desire, and the other party feigns disinterest by remaining elusive, not to be mean, but to heighten the romance and to prolong the foreplay. (See Reflections at 2:1-7.)

SONG OF SONGS 1:9-11, PRECIOUS METAPHORS

NIV

⁹I liken you, my darling, to a mare
   harnessed to one of the chariots of Pharaoh.
¹⁰Your cheeks are beautiful with earrings,
   your neck with strings of jewels.
¹¹We will make you earrings of gold,
   studded with silver.

NRSV

⁹ I compare you, my love,
   to a mare among Pharaoh's chariots.
¹⁰ Your cheeks are comely with ornaments,
   your neck with strings of jewels.
¹¹ We will make you ornaments of gold,
   studded with silver.

COMMENTARY

Like the protagonist, the shepherd in Song of Songs relies on metaphors in these verses to describe his admiration: "I compare you, my darling, to a mare harnessed to one of the chariots of Pharaoh" (1:9). The numerical incongruity between the Hebrew word for "mare" (סוסה *sûsâ*, sing.) and the Hebrew word for "chariotry" (רכבי *rikbê*, plural construct) is not a problem to be solved by grammarians when one considers the Egyptian custom of sending a mare out among the stallion-driven chariots of the enemy to distract and waylay the enemy. The implication is that the beloved female in Song of Songs is as tempting and alluring as a mare. Her earring-adorned cheeks and bejeweled neck heighten her allure (v. 10).

While comparing a woman to a mare may elicit a blank stare from a modern, urban audience—we are, after all, totally ignorant of mares' unique contribution to chariotry tactics—we can assume that at the time of its composition such a comment would have been easily understood by someone familiar with horses and their role in Egyptian tactical formations. A savvy audience knows a compliment when they hear one and knows when

to swoon with appreciation. Now, whether the average maiden in antiquity was familiar with the roles mares played in military affairs is another thing altogether. More likely, this is one of those instances, so common in courtship rituals, in which a man compliments a woman with imagery borne of androcentric activities (e.g., sports, warfare) and based on androcentric values (e.g., power, domination), which are foreign to the woman's domain of activities and to her values. We can only guess the maiden's knowledge of mares' role in warfare maneuvers. The shepherd redeems himself, however, by going on to compare his maiden to precious stones (v. 10). (See Reflections at 2:1-7.)

SONG OF SONGS 1:12-17, FRAGRANT METAPHORS

NIV

[12]While the king was at his table,
  my perfume spread its fragrance.
[13]My lover is to me a sachet of myrrh
  resting between my breasts.
[14]My lover is to me a cluster of henna blossoms
  from the vineyards of En Gedi.
[15]How beautiful you are, my darling!
  Oh, how beautiful!
  Your eyes are doves.
[16]How handsome you are, my lover!
  Oh, how charming!
  And our bed is verdant.
[17]The beams of our house are cedars;
  our rafters are firs.

NRSV

[12] While the king was on his couch,
  my nard gave forth its fragrance.
[13] My beloved is to me a bag of myrrh
  that lies between my breasts.
[14] My beloved is to me a cluster of henna
    blossoms
  in the vineyards of En-gedi.

[15] Ah, you are beautiful, my love;
  ah, you are beautiful;
  your eyes are doves.
[16] Ah, you are beautiful, my beloved,
  truly lovely.
  Our couch is green;
[17]   the beams of our house are cedar,
  our rafters[a] are pine.

[a] Meaning of Heb uncertain

COMMENTARY

It is the maiden's turn to return the compliment. Again, she affectionately refers to the shepherd as "king." But what exactly are we to make of "While the king was on his couch, my nard

gave forth its fragrance" (v. 12)? Is she fantasizing about a future moment, recalling a past event, or describing a present happening? She leaves those eavesdropping to wonder. On the one hand, v.

12 is simply too tantalizing not to be taken literally. On the other hand, it is one of those cryptic allusions to private intimacies only the lovers are able to decode. As for its meaning, is it "an allusion to the sexual smell" the woman emits when aroused in anticipation? To her lover's exclamation of her beauty (vv. 9-10), does she comment explicitly on his power to excite her (v. 12)? The scene is irresistible: As he reposes under a tree on a makeshift "couch" of leaves, nestled between her breasts, presumably whispering his flirtations in his sweetheart's ear, she admits that he stirs her in ways that make her emit aromas (vv. 12-14).

In v. 13, the protagonist refers to her lover as "beloved" (דודי *dôdî*), a term she will use more than twelve times. She compares him to choice fragrances, myrrh and henna (vv. 13-14), which by and large were not native to Canaan and had to be imported. Myrrh was used, among other things, as a cosmetic treatment on young girls preparing for sexual relations with their husbands-to-be (Esth 2:12). Because the springs of En-gedi made it a fertile oasis, such a site would have been an ideal lush garden for myrrh to grow.

The Hebrew in vv. 15-17 leaves open the possibility that two voices are heard here. Their words are precisely the kind of sweet talk lovers whisper to each other as they relax together. He admires her beauty (v. 15); she compliments him on being handsome (v. 16). With large broad trees towering above them, and with their leafy, green couch (or nuptial bed) spread beneath them, they are presumably ready for love. (See Reflections at 2:1-7.)

SONG OF SONGS 2:1-7, I ADJURE YOU

NIV

2 I am a rose[a] of Sharon,
　a lily of the valleys.
[2]Like a lily among thorns
　is my darling among the maidens.
[3]Like an apple tree among the trees of the forest
　is my lover among the young men.
I delight to sit in his shade,
　and his fruit is sweet to my taste.
[4]He has taken me to the banquet hall,
　and his banner over me is love.
[5]Strengthen me with raisins,
　refresh me with apples,
　for I am faint with love.
[6]His left arm is under my head,
　and his right arm embraces me.
[7]Daughters of Jerusalem, I charge you
　by the gazelles and by the does of the field:
Do not arouse or awaken love
　until it so desires.

[a]*1 Possibly a member of the crocus family*

NRSV

2 I am a rose[a] of Sharon,
　a lily of the valleys.

[2] As a lily among brambles,
　so is my love among maidens.

[3] As an apple tree among the trees of the wood,
　so is my beloved among young men.
With great delight I sat in his shadow,
　and his fruit was sweet to my taste.
[4] He brought me to the banqueting house,
　and his intention toward me was love.
[5] Sustain me with raisins,
　refresh me with apples;
　for I am faint with love.
[6] O that his left hand were under my head,
　and that his right hand embraced me!
[7] I adjure you, O daughters of Jerusalem,
　by the gazelles or the wild does:
do not stir up or awaken love
　until it is ready!

[a]*Heb crocus*

COMMENTARY

2:1-4. The popularity of v. 1 in Christian traditions as a metaphorical epithet for Jesus makes it disappointing to have to admit that we do not actually know much about the plants mentioned in v. 1. The KJV translates them "rose of Sharon" and "lily of the valley," and modern translators tend to follow suit. Ancient versions have not been helpful in determining the precise plant life cited. The problem is that the rose is actually a late transplant to the region, and there is no evidence that lilies ever really flourished in the area in any abundance.

Nevertheless, it seems certain that the protagonist is feigning modesty when she compares herself to *a* flower among many—namely, to one of a number of flowers that grow in Sharon and in valleys. Her lover counters that, in fact, she is more unique than she gives herself credit; indeed, she stands out among her peers (v. 2). She returns the compliment in v. 3*a* by reminiscing or fantasizing about rendezvous that turned into love feasts (the Hebrew is literally "wine house"). On those occasions, she exclaims, his "intentions," as seen in his eyes or "glance," are unmistakable (v. 4).

Marvin Pope argues that strong funerary echoes are evident throughout Song of Songs, prompting him to interpret the book as a text associated with funerary feasts common to the ancient Near East. Such love feasts, held to invoke fertility of the land, were celebrated with wine, women, and song.[19] Song of Songs celebrates the power of love over death (8:6), and, as seen in vv. 3-13, echoes language found in Ugaritic mythological and ritual texts in which sacrificial banquets, full of revelry and excesses, take on a funereal character as the gods become drunk almost to death. While Pope's interpretation of the book remains daring and debatable, there is no doubt that revelry, fantasy, and lightheartedness permeate much of the poetry.

Again, the protagonist delights in tantalizing the eavesdropper. This time she uses what appears to be a *double entendre,* which allows her to praise her lover while leaving those listening in to figure out her meaning (v. 3*b*): "With great delight I sat in his shadow, and his fruit was sweet to my taste." Exactly what was sweet to the protagonist's taste? An apple from the apple tree, or was it some part of her beloved's body? It is obviously something for the two of them to know—and the rest of us to find out.

2:5-7. The mere recall of their escapades and the very thought of his touch leaves her faint, flushed, and wistful (vv. 5-6). But greater still, we learn in v. 7, is the knowledge that love brings: "Daughters of Jerusalem, I charge you by the gazelles and by the does of the field: Do not arouse or awaken love until it so desires." In classic romance literature, of which Song of Songs can be viewed as something of a precursor, love is explored as the agent of a woman's self-development. Whereas men obtained their education, developed their identity, and matured in their consciousness through danger and a series of adventures, women turned to romance to achieve knowledge and the development of a higher level of consciousness. Similarly, in Song of Songs, the love-struck woman who earlier in the poem was lightheaded with passion becomes by 2:7 the worldly woman and savvy teacher. She passes her knowledge on to her impressionable female admirers. Love has taught her a few things about herself, about the opposite sex, about stolen intimacy, about love itself. She has learned that love must be allowed to run its course, neither interfered with nor prematurely provoked.

Scholars have offered various proposals for interpreting v. 7: "I adjure you, O daughters of Jerusalem, by the gazelles or the wild does: do not stir up or awaken love until it is ready!" The phrase appears in two other places in the poem (3:5; 8:4). It has been translated variously as an admonition (a) not to arouse love prematurely (NRSV, NIV), (b) not to awaken the male love until "he" determines (KJV), (c) not to awaken or rouse the female protagonist until she pleases (NEB), (d) not to disturb their lovemaking until it is satiated.[20] Each translation represents an effort to see in this recurring phrase the *crux interpretum* to unlocking the otherwise elusive message

---

19. Pope, *Song of Songs,* 210-29.

20. Marcia Falk, *The Song of Songs: A New Translation and Interpretation* (San Francisco: HarperCollins, 1990) 164-76.

of the entire book. Whatever its message, it is clear that there is a searching, unfulfilled, desperately longing mood to the entire book. The maiden's adjuration was probably formulaic and common to those who dwelled in desert settings: e.g., "I charge you by the gazelles and by the does of the field." In other words, we might say, "I beg you with everything within me." Of course, some of the imagery in the admonition appears in other contexts throughout the poetry: The male lover is associated with the swiftness and agility of gazelles in vv. 9, 17; the woman's breasts are compared to young fawns who browse (meaning probably "bounce" or "leap") among lilies.

In the end, the woman's experiences are supposed to serve as a lesson to her Jerusalem female friends. The admonition in v. 7 by the black-skinned woman not to interfere with love should be understood as a typical feature of women's romance literature, which offers a portrait of the love-worn but savvy female whose moral example becomes a prophylaxis, a warning and guide to the path of love for her sister neophytes (the Jerusalem daughters). The admonition represents the wisdom of a woman who has learned a lot about life and about herself through her experiences with "impeded" love. What exactly about love has she learned? For one thing, there is a time for love—a time to love and a time to wait for love. Perhaps it is her attempt, as a sage, to round out the litany of Qohelet (Eccl 3:1-8).

REFLECTIONS

Song of Songs can be a frustrating text to read for those who take seriously the responsibility to study and scrutinize God's Word. Zealous to be scrupulous exegetes and faithful interpreters, conscientious students of the Bible turn to commentaries for sober guidance into these sacred texts; but their zeal is met with equivocation and conjecture. A battery of questions is applied to each passage, and every word is weighed and studied; nonetheless, the book and its content refuse to submit easily to the arsenal of learned procedures we put them through. Song of Songs insists that we approach it on its own terms. Proving above all that language is rarely precise and emotions are hardly translatable, the love lyrics in the Song of Songs force serious, humorless religious types to get back in touch with the playfulness of the human spirit and the intensity of religious longing. As we listen in on lovers flirting with and teasing each other, whispering their deliciously oblique fantasies in each other's ear, and as we witness them playing hide and seek in each other's dreams, we are reminded of how resilient and trusting, and hence inscrutable, is the human heart.

We are warned against obstructing love. This is not the same as disturbing love. The consequences of the former can be more dire. Those who disturb love can be forgiven because what they do is frequently unintentional. But those who obstruct love, impede love, interfere with love—because of their own prejudices and fears—should beware. They do so at the risk of crushing lovers' enthusiasm, destroying lovers' faith in life, and bruising their sense of esteem. In this case the cliché that deserves repeating is: Human beings are born to love and to receive love. We are our happiest, our strongest, our most creative and most forgiving when we are in love. We are also our most confident and secure about ourselves as individuals when we know that we are loved unconditionally. In fact, our ability to love makes us capable of transcending our finitude, our humanity, our creatureliness. Our ability to love is also what makes us most like God. Part of what it means to be created "in the image of God" is to be capable of transcending oneself and loving another person unconditionally. Small wonder that at the center of both the OT and the NT is the repeated reminder that being a covenant people means loving God with all that is possible.

We have no transcripts of what were surely the many lively discussions about the propriety of including the ribald poetry of Song of Songs in the biblical canon. We are left only to wonder how it made its way into Scripture. Based on what criteria did those responsible decide it qualified as sacred, holy writ suffused with divine truth? It is unlikely that Solomonic authorship alone warranted its inclusion in the canon. The astute reader perceives something more. Its tale of love, courtship, compassion, intimacy, longing, and mutual delight resounds with many of the elements that characterize, according to the larger biblical drama, God's dealings with God's people. Bawdy, titillating, cryptic, and bordering sometimes on the lewd as the book may appear, the lovers' unpredictable love affair, which the poet tries desperately to capture—characterized by halts, jerks, lurches, twitches, and inconstancy—shows remarkable parallels with the history of the relationship between human and divine love. Powerful lessons await its readers. Seeing our relationship with God through the eyes of frustrated, but desperate, lovers, however baffling their behavior, forces us to ponder the powerful emotions underlying the divine-human bond: what it means to be demanding, yet fickle, desperate, but timid; what it means to wound those we love and to be wounded by love; what it means to disappoint those we love and to be disappointed by love; and what it means to be hopelessly attached to each other and trying to hear what the other is saying.

The Song of Songs provides its audience glimpses into two human beings' efforts at perfecting human love and building intimacy and the lessons they learn about themselves and each other along the way.

MY BELOVED IS MINE, AND I AM HIS

NIV

[8]Listen! My lover!
  Look! Here he comes,
leaping across the mountains,
  bounding over the hills.
[9]My lover is like a gazelle or a young stag.
  Look! There he stands behind our wall,
gazing through the windows,
  peering through the lattice.
[10]My lover spoke and said to me,
  "Arise, my darling,
  my beautiful one, and come with me.
[11]See! The winter is past;
  the rains are over and gone.
[12]Flowers appear on the earth;
  the season of singing has come,
the cooing of doves
  is heard in our land.
[13]The fig tree forms its early fruit;
  the blossoming vines spread their fragrance.
Arise, come, my darling;
  my beautiful one, come with me."
[14]My dove in the clefts of the rock,
  in the hiding places on the mountainside,
show me your face,
  let me hear your voice;
for your voice is sweet,
  and your face is lovely.
[15]Catch for us the foxes,
  the little foxes
that ruin the vineyards,
  our vineyards that are in bloom.
[16]My lover is mine and I am his;
  he browses among the lilies.
[17]Until the day breaks
  and the shadows flee,
turn, my lover,
  and be like a gazelle
or like a young stag
  on the rugged hills.[a]

[a]17 Or the hills of Bether

NRSV

[8] The voice of my beloved!
  Look, he comes,
leaping upon the mountains,
  bounding over the hills.
[9] My beloved is like a gazelle
  or a young stag.
Look, there he stands
  behind our wall,
gazing in at the windows,
  looking through the lattice.
[10] My beloved speaks and says to me:
  "Arise, my love, my fair one,
  and come away;
[11] for now the winter is past,
  the rain is over and gone.
[12] The flowers appear on the earth;
  the time of singing has come,
and the voice of the turtledove
  is heard in our land.
[13] The fig tree puts forth its figs,
  and the vines are in blossom;
  they give forth fragrance.
Arise, my love, my fair one,
  and come away.
[14] O my dove, in the clefts of the rock,
  in the covert of the cliff,
let me see your face,
  let me hear your voice;
for your voice is sweet,
  and your face is lovely.
[15] Catch us the foxes,
  the little foxes,
that ruin the vineyards—
  for our vineyards are in blossom."

[16] My beloved is mine and I am his;
  he pastures his flock among the lilies.
[17] Until the day breathes
  and the shadows flee,
turn, my beloved, be like a gazelle
  or a young stag on the cleft mountains.[a]

[a]Or on the mountains of Bether: meaning of Heb uncertain

COMMENTARY

Lovers are notoriously possessive. They demand to know each other's whereabouts, they insist upon commitment, they expect accountability, and they take advantage of every opportunity to remind each other, and those in earshot, of their special claims upon each other. Nowhere is their possessiveness more apparent than in the choice of pet names they use to describe each other. The protagonist consistently refers to her anonymous male lover throughout the book, beginning in 2:1-3, as "my lover" (NIV) or "my beloved" (NRSV). Elsewhere she refers affectionately to him as "my friend" (5:16) and "he whom my soul loves" (1:7; 3:1-4).

The suitor's store of pet names for his love is more inventive and diverse. He relies on a plethora of epithets to address the woman: "fairest among women" (1:8; 5:9; 6:1); "my darling" or "my love" (1:9, 15; 2:10, 13; 4:1, 7; 5:2; 6:4); "my fair one" or "my beautiful one" (2:10, 13); "my dove" (2:14; 5:2; 6:9); "my perfect one" or "my flawless one" (5:2; 6:9), and so on. His epithets for her, and those she applies to him, all have one very important thing in common: They are preceded by the first-person singular possessive pronoun "my." Nine occurrences of the pronoun "my" within a span of nine verses (vv. 8-17) is not a trivial matter, even in Song of Songs. This is not simply an example of the romantic drivel typical of new lovers. Something more is at stake here and throughout the poem. In fact, the more than fifty occurrences of "my" throughout this brief poem strongly suggests that they are not just asserting their mutual devotion: The lovers are *insisting* on it. To her, he is "my lover" (vv. 8, 9, 10, 16, 17 NIV). But to him, she is "my darling" (vv. 10, 13), "my beautiful one" (v. 10), "my dove" (v. 14). Perhaps they expect their audience to disapprove of their union. Perhaps they are aware that some might question the propriety of their relationship. Was theirs a forbidden union? Were they, because of class, ethnic, or economic differences, an unlikely pair? What did they have to prove? The poetry to this point is elusive, but tantalizing, about the matter. We will have to wait for answers. In the meantime, again and again the two lovers declare their ex-

clusive affection for each other, a declaration that climaxes in the beautiful "formula of mutual belonging" that we find in v. 16 and in altered form elsewhere in the poem: "My lover is mine and I am his" (דודי לי ואני לו *dôdî lî waʾănî lô*; cf. 6:3; 7:10). Here the Hebrew is both elliptic and unequivocal: "My lover to me and I to him."

Taken as a whole, the unit rhapsodizes the feeling of love that spring brings. The gifts of spring rain are everywhere. The sight of sprinting animals (vv. 8-9), the smell of figs and vines (v. 13), the sound of birds singing (v. 12), the feel of fresh flowers and new buds (v. 12) are enough to arouse love in the most cynical of persons. With springtime comes belief in new adventures, new possibilities, and, most of all, a new outlook on life. Even forbidden love looks different when viewed against the backdrop of spring rain, sprinting animals, budding flowers and vines, and the sound of chirping birds.

Drawing on the intoxicating feelings that nature and spring arouse, the shepherd refers to this time as "the season of singing" (v. 12), when the sound of the turtledoves can be heard throughout the land. No one wants to be unloved at this time of year, when all of nature is aroused to newness. He beckons her to come away with him (v. 13). But as usual, he is vague and does not specify exactly where he wants to take her. He changes the subject by asking to hear her voice (v. 14).

In fact, this unit is filled with the sound of the lovers' voices. Each luxuriates in the sound of the other's voice. She hears his "voice" (lit., "sound" [קול *qôl*]) before she actually sees him approaching from just over the mountains (v. 8). His words are what the ears of every lovestruck maiden yearns to hear: "Arise and come" (v. 10). We cannot be sure whether this is an actual quotation or simply what she imagines him saying on the day he arrives. From v. 10 to v. 15 the maiden replays the words of her beloved. Twice he encourages her to depart with him ("Arise, my love, my fair one, and come away," vv. 10, 13). With her safely in his arms, he imagines in v. 14 that he can luxuriate in the sound of her voice and in the loveliness of what both the NRSV and the NIV have translated as "face," but is more accurately "appearance" (מראה *mar'eh*; cf. 5:15). One might expect the shepherd to comment directly on the maiden's face or complexion in the light of her own defensive remarks in 1:5. But he does not. (For more discussion of his silence, see Commentary on 4:1–5:1.)

To keep the audience at bay, the lovers speak to each other in riddles: "Catch for us the foxes, the little foxes, that ruin the vineyards, our vineyards that are in bloom" (v. 15). One commentator has referred to this statement as "a saucy reply to the lover."[21] It may be saucy, but just how saucy, we may never know. The riddle's meaning is obscure. Some interpreters have understood it as a quotation of a well-known ditty that cryptically observes the manner in which foxes (young men) notoriously despoil the blooming vineyards (ripening female sexuality).[22] Others see in this verse a more ominous meaning, one in which the foxes are not prowling young men, but threatening city guards who take advantage of defenseless women on the streets (3:3).[23] The overall mood of this unit seems not to support Falk's ominous reading of the riddle, however. From beginning (v. 8) to end (vv. 16-17), the protagonist is not emphasizing danger, but seduction. Throughout she tries to woo the shepherd with promises of her anticipation. Both delight in sustaining the suspense between them by talking in riddles and romantic cryptograms. The reference to "foxes" and "vineyards" is probably an allusion to their

cunning stratagems to find opportunities to consummate their blossoming love while attempting simultaneously to avoid detection by others. They belong together; they belong to each other (v. 16). Her suitor rightfully "pastures," says the maiden, among the most delicate flower of all, the lily, the black-skinned maiden herself (cf. "lily of the valley" in 2:1).

Finally, the black-skinned maiden is not shy about trying to pin her elusive lover down on a time for them to meet. By the passage's end, she proposes the allure and romance of an evening rendezvous (v. 17) instead of a daytime tryst (1:7): "Until the day breaks and the shadows flee" (NIV). Her words from the beginning of the passage to its end echo one another. In both the opening (v. 8) and closing (v. 17) lines, she compares her lover to a gazelle and a stag who bound over hillsides. (The same imagery reappears in the final verse of the book, 8:14.) His swift, agile movements are of the sort that make young maidens imagine prowess and attribute strength to their lovers. The unit is dominated by her yearning, her imaginings of his presence, her fantasies of his seduction, her response to his diffidence, her imploring him to tread carefully. She commences her remarks by announcing his arrival (v. 8); she closes her remarks by shooing him away (v. 17). She urges him to hold off their consummation until a more opportune time, late evening. Her hesitation is unclear to us. But her passion is constant. As often as she beckons him to her, for reasons unknown she shoos him away until a later time.

21. Roland Murphy, *The Song of Songs*, Hermeneia (Minneapolis: Fortress, 1990) 141.

22. Ibid., 141; Marvin Pope, *Song of Songs*, AB 7C (New York: Doubleday, 1977) 402-5.

23. See Falk, *The Song of Songs*, 178.

REFLECTIONS

The love lyrics in Song of Songs are ideal for examining the pull and tug of romantic and spiritual commitment. The story of the beguiling young maiden and her skittish shepherd lover can be used as a thoughtful text for probing the dread of living in committed, covenant union. The book reminds us that intimacy can be as frightening as it is fulfilling. It is fraught with dangers, unknowns, demands, and unforeseeable consequences. Not simply a commentary on the fragility of human intimacy, the work captures the dilemma of the divine-human drama.

The Bible is full of stories of people who play hide and seek with God's calling. Their faith falters, their obedience is short-lived, their worship wanes, and their commitment must be tested and reestablished again and again. The stories of Elijah withdrawing to a lonely cave, Jeremiah refusing to preach, Jonah sailing away to Tarshish, and Paul prowling the Damascus road are stories of men who went to extraordinary lengths to resist God's claim upon them.

But before we see Song of Songs solely as an indictment of the inconstancy of commitment to and love for God, we would do well to pause and consider its honesty. These brief nine verses remind us that human-human relationships, like human-divine relations, must be cultivated, nurtured, safeguarded, and cherished. Special moments do not just happen; they are cultivated. Intimacy with God and with each other costs; it costs us our time and our energies. A willingness to be present, to remain, to be accountable, to see things through, to come out from hiding are necessary to nurture relationships.

Lovers cannot take their love for granted, no more than humans can take their relationship with God for granted. We must take care to spend time with those we love and to find time to talk with each other. Like lovers in search of the perfect time and place to mate, care should be given to creating an atmosphere in which conversation and intimacy can thrive. "Mindfulness," "attentiveness," and "dailiness" are popular terms within our culture to remind us that beauty, love, joy, abundance, the sacred, and the possibility for happiness surround us in the ordinary routines of human living if we would only take the time to notice and nurture them. The sound of children's laughter, the thoughtful gesture of a lover, the sound of church bells in the distance, the gentle breeze across the face after a day at the office, an unexpected call from a childhood friend, a helping hand from a stranger, a "thank you" from an admirer, the smell of fresh-baked bread, and the sight of fresh flowers on the nightstand are just a few of the gifts "angels" strew daily along our path. Straining as we do, like the lovers in Cant 2:14, to behold beauty and to hear the sacred in our routines, we must take care to lean closer and see God's face and to hear God's voice in our lives.

In preaching and teaching on this and other portions of the Song of Songs, modern interpreters should not be put off or intimidated by the titillating direction of the poetry. Readers should relax and enjoy the poet's playful use of language and exploration of human emotions. Allow the lovers' playful jostle back and forth and curious speech to inspire thinking about the way figurative and coded speech creates special memories for intimates. It might be a worthwhile exercise for preachers and teachers to listen to the way they try to tell their audiences about God's love for humankind. What imagery is repeatedly used? What language stirs an audience's emotions? From whence does language receive its power to make an impact on an audience? When do you know that the language has connected with your audience? Perhaps we should try rewriting the love story between God and human creation in our own modern jargon and imagery, comparing our images of God and ourselves, our symbols for love and passion with those of our biblical ancestors. What do human connectedness and intimacy look like to us? What do they feel like? To what do we compare them? What does this tell us about ourselves?

Song of Songs is an ideal text for comparing the changing history and context of romantic talk. The poet uses the language and imagery of a rustic, semi-pastoral culture to evoke passion and desire. Comparisons to goats, gazelles, and apple trees sound strange to those of us who reside in parts of the country where neighborhoods are treeless, apartment complexes have no lawns, and we ride underground in the earth's belly to get to our windowless downtown offices. We do not recognize seduction of the Song of Songs sort when we hear it. Our lives are too hurried and harried to bother with cryptograms from another time and another culture. And while it may be true that much of the speech in this little book is hopelessly lost on our modern ears because it does not speak to our experience, we must admit that our own language for intimacy is equally lost on those unfamiliar with our culture. How does a generation flatter and woo one another when they are raised on microwave ovens, computers, fax machines, voice mail, the Internet, camcorders, electronic games, space fantasies, and overnight express mail? How do they talk about love? "You've pushed the right button," perhaps. Or "My hormones are in warp speed for you"? The maiden and her suitor of Song of Songs would stagger down the slopes of En-gedi in amazement and laughter at the sound of twenty-first-century erotic speech.

I LOOKED FOR HIM BUT DID NOT FIND HIM

NIV

3 All night long on my bed
   I looked for the one my heart loves;
 I looked for him but did not find him.
²I will get up now and go about the city,
   through its streets and squares;
 I will search for the one my heart loves.
   So I looked for him but did not find him.
³The watchmen found me
   as they made their rounds in the city.
   "Have you seen the one my heart loves?"
⁴Scarcely had I passed them
   when I found the one my heart loves.
 I held him and would not let him go
   till I had brought him to my mother's house,
   to the room of the one who conceived me.
⁵Daughters of Jerusalem, I charge you
   by the gazelles and by the does of the field:
 Do not arouse or awaken love
   until it so desires.

NRSV

3 Upon my bed at night
   I sought him whom my soul loves;
 I sought him, but found him not;
   I called him, but he gave no answer.*ᵃ*
² "I will rise now and go about the city,
   in the streets and in the squares;
 I will seek him whom my soul loves."
   I sought him, but found him not.
³ The sentinels found me,
   as they went about in the city.
 "Have you seen him whom my soul loves?"
⁴ Scarcely had I passed them,
   when I found him whom my soul loves.
 I held him, and would not let him go
   until I brought him into my mother's house,
   and into the chamber of her that conceived
      me.
⁵ I adjure you, O daughters of Jerusalem,
   by the gazelles or the wild does:
 do not stir up or awaken love
   until it is ready!

ᵃ Gk: Heb lacks this line

COMMENTARY

When evening comes and the shepherd has not arrived, the maiden takes to the streets to search for her lover. Desperation, supplication, and longing fill this unit, and the audience is invited to ponder the experience of the distraught woman.

Scores of questions race through the maiden's mind as she scours the streets and squares of Jerusalem searching for her lover. Has she shooed her lover away this time, only to lose him forever? Where is he? Is he lost? Is he hiding? Why can he not be found? Will he return? She wonders now about the wisdom of putting him off until evening, a time she thought more auspicious for lovemaking (2:17). "Have you seen him whom my soul loves?" she anxiously inquires of the sentinels who guard the city at night (v. 3; the Hebrew actually reads more poetically and archaically: "Him whom my soul loves, have you seen?"). Her desperation touches her audience. Our emotions go out to her. We are as frustrated as she. "Where in God's creation is he?" we wonder aloud. How long will they continue to put each other off?

At last, it seems, the black-skinned woman finds her lover (v. 4*a*). We sigh with her. She holds him close, promising never again to let him go, determined to bring him into the house of her mother, into the very chambers where she herself was conceived (v. 4*b*). This expression "to my mother's house" (אל-בית אמי *el-bêt 'immî,* v. 4; 8:2) is odd, given the enormous emphasis throughout the Old Testament on the "father's house" (בית אב *bêt 'āb*), the patriarchal family compound.[24] With the emphasis in Song of Songs on family and with imagery drawn from the private domain, one would expect some reference to *bêt 'āb*, the place where a daughter's chastity was protected and controlled by the father or male head of household. But the Song of Songs is the poetry of domesticity and not the poetry of domination (cf. Gen 24:28; Ruth 1:8). It focuses on the private world of women's interior emotions and experiences. The references to the "mother's house" symbolize the private, enclosed world of women's secrets and sexuality. Where the maiden intends to lure her lover is no place for fathers, brothers, uncles, or other male guardians. The "chambers of her who conceived me" are where women's secret rituals, fantasies, speech, and private dramas (e.g., bathing, having babies) take place.

Once the maiden finds her lover, we hold our breath. We wonder if in her "mother's house" the two lovers will finally be able to consummate their love. She holds him, but can she keep him? She has him now, but will he stay? Is this a dream, or is it real? What is the point of the cat-and-mouse game the two lovers seem bent upon playing? How are contemporary audiences, accustomed to tales of speedy romance and uninhibited passion, supposed to read this story of frustrated love?

In a culture where casual sexual relations were virtually unheard of, where it was difficult for lovers to find opportunities to satisfy their lust, where social contact between the sexes was strictly limited, where lovers exchanged glances more than they did kisses, love songs about thwarted love affairs took on mythological propor-

tions. (The kind of myths mentioned above tend also to reinforce the culture's attitudes about courtship and romance.) Delayed gratification was the rule in antiquity, not the exception. Unmarried couples were not free to indulge their appetites for each other when and however they wanted, nor could married couples, for that matter (see Lev 18:19). Ancient audiences, thus, were enthralled by poetry like Song of Songs because it captured the longing, heightened the tension, gave drama to the pursuit, and reinforced the promise of awaiting ecstasy. In antiquity, love lyrics were not expected to describe the consummation of love, but the anticipation of its consummation. Some things were better left to the audience's imagination. Whereas modern audiences cannot figure out why the two lovers do things that forestall their getting together—he comes, and she puts him off; she inquires about his whereabouts, and he does not say; he invites her to come with him, but he does not say where—ancient audiences would have been patient with their failed attempts at love and amused by their blunders. Impediments and obstacles were typical devices of ancient love lyricists, designed to sustain the audience's interest in the subject and heighten the tension of the drama.

Parallel accounts of searching and finding, or not finding, for example, appear in romantic lore of neighboring cultures in antiquity. In Mesopotamian hymns and myths, Ishtar, the goddess of love and sexuality, supposedly travels to the netherworld in search of her lover, Dumuzi. On the way she contends with inimical forces and eventually meets up with him. Their meeting ends in a sacred marriage that was ritualized in the mating of the king with a sacred prostitute as a way of regenerating the fertile forces of nature. A similar motif appears in the Ugaritic myth of Anat's search for the body of her consort, Baal, who has been killed by Mot ("Death"). Upon finding Baal, Anat buries him and mourns him by inflicting wounds upon her own body. When the irate Anat avenges her lover's death and destroys Mot, Baal is revived and restored to power. In each of these texts, the female protagonist is the fierce, aggressive, and zealous one who sets out on a dangerous journey to find her missing comrade, rescuing him from opposing forces, restoring him to his rightful place of power, or, as in the case of Song of Songs,

24. For a helpful discussion of the presence of "mother's house" over the customary "father's house" in Song of Songs, see Carol Meyers, *Discovering Eve: Ancient Israelite Women in Context* (New York: Oxford University Press, 1988) 177-81.

receiving him into her arms as her consummate lover.

Finally, when the maiden exhorts her audience again to be patient with love, not to interfere prematurely with love, not to launch into love unadvisedly (v. 5), she is cautioning an audience already accustomed to postponing sexual pleasure. She is reminding them of what they know only too well: Love is a powerful force that should not be rushed into or provoked.

REFLECTIONS

Modern readers may tire of this roller-coaster love affair—now you see him, now you don't; now she has him, now she doesn't. We are not accustomed to delaying our passion. We are impatient with indecisive lovers and bored by repeatedly frustrated love scenes. In our sexually liberated culture, we do not understand unconsummated love affairs. "What is the problem with these two people?" we ask ourselves. Now that the protagonist has finally seized her lover and suggestively beckoned him and her audience toward the room where her own mother conceived her, do we dare allow ourselves to anticipate their passion?

The challenge for preachers and teachers alike is to use the Song of Songs as a way of reclaiming some of the virtue of patience, the wisdom of delayed gratification, and the joy of exploring each other's hearts long before we explore each other's bodies. This text is ideal for exploring new ways of discovering and building human intimacy, because it begins by celebrating and delighting in the human body. We are not asked, as in so much banal religious literature, to deny our need for physical contact and communion. Song of Songs takes the body seriously. But it also takes seriously that we are more than a body. Relationships cannot survive when they are based solely on physical attraction. Song of Songs, with its constant use of dialogue and conversation, riddles and allusions, reminds us of the importance of learning how to talk and how to listen to each other. Those who turn to this poetry for profound theological insight into the nature of God, the character of the divine, the lessons of the Christian faith (e.g., grace, mercy, free will, sovereign love) should not dismiss its teachings about what it means to live and to love as human beings. We can learn from the ancient audiences. One thing we can learn is to listen for the unspoken gestures of human communication.

One cannot help admiring the aggressive measures the protagonist takes to find her missing lover. She risks her life and reputation to find him (3:1-3). She is not daunted by the fact that she is female and that certain aggressions in women are unacceptable in her culture. She knows what she wants, and she goes after him. Better yet, she knows what belongs to her, and she searches for him. Love forces us to stretch beyond our boundaries, beyond our narrow self-interests, beyond our comfort zones. Love encourages us to take risks, to embrace other ways of thinking, other ways of being, and other ways of doing.

Again, our ability to love is the very quality that makes us most like God. We learn what it means to go to extraordinary lengths to reclaim our lovers. The search for a lover reminds those of us who read this poem with theological eyes how very precious love is. When you find it, do everything in your power to keep it. God, who is love, has created us to be able to give and to receive love.

Song of Songs reminds us that nothing in our upbringing prepares us for love's rocky journey. It is a journey filled with valleys and peaks, requiring of the lovers enormous patience with and commitment to each other. Love is something that must be worked at, sought after, and fought for. When it eludes the lovers, disappearing from their bedroom, escaping their embrace, it must be pursued, hunted down, recaptured, and brought back into their domain. Not only with lovers, but also in humans' relationship with God, closeness and intimacy must be nurtured. It cannot be taken for granted, nor is it a given. Human beings must be as vigilant about their relationship with God as they presumably are about their relationships with each other.

Who Is This Coming Up
from the Desert?

NIV

⁶Who is this coming up from the desert
  like a column of smoke,
perfumed with myrrh and incense
  made from all the spices of the merchant?
⁷Look! It is Solomon's carriage,
  escorted by sixty warriors,
  the noblest of Israel,
⁸all of them wearing the sword,
  all experienced in battle,
each with his sword at his side,
  prepared for the terrors of the night.
⁹King Solomon made for himself the carriage;
  he made it of wood from Lebanon.
¹⁰Its posts he made of silver,
  its base of gold.
Its seat was upholstered with purple,
  its interior lovingly inlaid
by*ᵃ* the daughters of Jerusalem.
¹¹Come out, you daughters of Zion,
  and look at King Solomon wearing the crown,
  the crown with which his mother crowned
    him
on the day of his wedding,
  the day his heart rejoiced.

ᵃ10 Or its inlaid interior a gift of love / from

NRSV

⁶ What is that coming up from the wilderness,
  like a column of smoke,
perfumed with myrrh and frankincense,
  with all the fragrant powders of the
    merchant?
⁷ Look, it is the litter of Solomon!
  Around it are sixty mighty men
  of the mighty men of Israel,
⁸ all equipped with swords
  and expert in war,
each with his sword at his thigh
  because of alarms by night.
⁹ King Solomon made himself a palanquin
  from the wood of Lebanon.
¹⁰ He made its posts of silver,
  its back of gold, its seat of purple;
its interior was inlaid with love.*ᵃ*
  Daughters of Jerusalem,
¹¹   come out.
Look, O daughters of Zion,
  at King Solomon,
at the crown with which his mother crowned
    him
  on the day of his wedding,
  on the day of the gladness of his heart.

ᵃ Meaning of Heb uncertain

COMMENTARY

Scholars have frequently observed that this section interrupts the poetry with its description of an ornate wedding ceremony. In the preceding unit, the woman describes her desperate search for her lover (3:1-5). In the unit that follows (4:1–5:1), the man describes the physical charms of the woman. At first glance, the lofty procession recounted in vv. 6-11 seems premature, if not out of place. Seeing the unit, however, as the protagonist's fantasy about her wedding day, when she will finally be given license to do precisely what she can only wish to do in v. 4—that is, to steer her lover into her secret chambers—we can forgive the unit its abruptness. Fantasies are by nature unpredictable.

The scenery described in these verses is her

daydream, a wedding scene reminiscent of the days of Solomon, when, in the light of the king's marriages to hundreds of women, lavish wedding processions with imposing military formations were a common sight on the streets of Jerusalem. Although we have no information from the OT about how ancient wedding ceremonies were actually conducted, we can see here in Song of Songs, especially in the description of the ornate carriage with its silver, gold, and purple upholstery and its cedar (v. 10), just how lavish and imposing a sight royal weddings were. (The pomp and circumstance associated with royal weddings are hinted at in Psalm 45.) Undoubtedly, special lyrics were composed for the occasion, parts of which have been incorporated into the book of Song of Songs.

Exactly who or what is being hailed by the speaker in v. 6? Solomon? The female protagonist? The "litter" (bed) of Solomon? The NIV translates the interrogative literally as "who." But one does not find in v. 7 a specific person stepping forward and identifying himself or herself, as one does in Isa 63:1, where a similar phrase appears. Instead, a procession is described ("Look!"), one associated with Solomon, which has led some translators to render the interrogative, following an Akkadian precedent, more accurately as, "What is this coming up from the wilderness?"

The question in v. 6 is the kind posed by sentries to persons, parties, or caravans as they drew near the city gates, or by inhabitants as strangers drew near their quarters. In this context, the question may have been ceremonially posed to an approaching wedding caravan, hailing the arrival of an awe-inspiring wedding procession as it drew near the awaiting guests. The military procession described in vv. 7-8 suggests that the bridegroom's party is arriving. Exactly why the procession is described as originating in the "desert" (NIV) or the "wilderness" (NRSV) remains uncertain. (If v. 6 represents the manner in which the bridegroom would have been hailed upon arrival at the ceremony, the parallel greeting for the approaching bride and her bridal procession may be found in 6:10: "Who is this that looks forth like the dawn?"; see note there.)

Although one is tempted to see the bridegroom and his party as the subject of vv. 6-11, the mention of an approaching "litter," or bed, naturally suggests a woman's being hoisted upon a canopy and carried ceremonially and suggestively into the wedding service. It seems, however, that the bridegroom is being hoisted onto the bed and carried to his awaiting bride. Such imagery would certainly be in keeping with the protagonist's earlier wish (3:4) that her lover be brought into her intimate chambers.

Furthermore, the mention of Solomon's name in v. 7 should not be taken literally, but as part of the lyrics of the song. It is yet another oblique term of endearment that a bride might use to compliment her lover for his dashing, romantic, regal side. A modern parallel might be to call a man "Romeo."

By now, the royal bridegroom is decked in attire befitting a king and warrior who is confident in his power. Surrounded by a swarm of virginal attendants, the bride, herself of royal heritage according to her daydream, is brought before the king adorned in embroidered garments and gold ornaments. So resplendent is the whole occasion that the Jerusalem daughters are urged to come out (vv. 10-11) and behold the bridegroom ("Solomon") and the entire wedding party, which by now presumably includes the bride.

"The crown with which his mother crowned him" (v. 11) does not apply exclusively to royal wedding ceremonies, but, as Robert Gordis has pointed out, to the standard headpiece worn during marriage ceremonies by both bride and groom in antiquity.[25] As for the reference to Solomon's mother (v. 11), mothers figure prominently in the protagonist's development of her female and sexual identities in Song of Songs. On the one hand, her own mother serves as the role model for her sexual identity, providing her with the charms and chambers for seduction (v. 4). On the other hand, the mother who gave birth to the bridegroom "crowned" him with life and conjugal possibilities. In a patriarchal culture, a mother's approval of her son's marriage was not necessary, since arranging marriages was largely in the hands of the male head of the house. However, it was signally important to have the mother-in-law's blessing, since brides upon marriage moved to their husband's locality, frequently in the compound where his father and mother lived.

25. Robert Gordis, *The Song of Songs: A Study, Modern Translation, and Commentary,* TextsS 20 (New York: Jewish Theological Seminary of America, 1954) 56.

Wedding ceremonies in ancient Israel were meant to be lavish occasions where each class attempted to approximate as much as it could afford the most ideal of all ceremonies, the royal wedding. In every culture and in every generation, women (and men) imagine their wedding day, when in the pageantry and splendor befitting their love, they are united with their sweethearts in everlasting bonds. We see here in the sketchy details of 3:1-5 how very much the black-skinned woman, in her fantasy of her wedding day, was a product of her culture.

REFLECTIONS

For those who are married, Song of Songs is a reminder of how naive and idealistic we were on our wedding day. We look back on our wedding photos at the slim, dashing young man with a full head of hair and the svelte, glowing young woman, and we say to ourselves, "Gosh, were we naive!" By luring those of us who are married into reliving our wedding day, and by enticing those not married to imagine that day, Song of Songs reminds us of what it means to pledge to live one's life with only one other individual. A man and a woman pledge to submit to each other and to expose his or her wounded self to each other for scrutiny and healing. We promise to allow our two lives to be melded into one brand-new life together. The man and woman in Song of Songs remind us of how much passion, enthusiasm, and utter idealism it takes to believe such things are even possible.

Throughout the Bible, marriage is viewed as the most sublime metaphor for the relationship between God and human beings. Old Testament prophets—Hosea, Jeremiah, Ezekiel—and others used marriage to symbolize the intimacy, love, and devotion characteristic of the covenant union between Yahweh and Israel. The author of the book of Ephesians relied on marriage imagery to describe the union between Christ and the church (Eph 5:25-33), noting that the union between man and woman, like the one between Christ and the church, is a mystery. Jesus himself told a parable in which a wedding feast became the symbolic setting for the coming of the kingdom (Matthew 22). Marriage is an apt metaphor for capturing the divine-human relationship because it captures best all the vicissitudes of trying to live faithfully and spontaneously with the Other. It is the closest bond possible for two human beings, one that teaches both partners lessons about grace, forgiveness, constancy, submission, and love. The love poetry in Song of Songs reminds us of how crazy, how innocent, how ardent is the passion that brings human beings together. But this one glimpse into the protagonist's fantasy also reminds us of how preposterous, how unthinkable, how supernatural is the actual union that takes place, often years after the ceremony is over, when passion fades and true love has a chance to emerge.

In marriage, each partner is given the opportunity to see one person as he or she has never seen another person before. Living as a child in a parent's home does not quite prepare a person for marriage. Neither does living with someone outside the bonds of marriage ensure that once married, one has a jump on marriage. Marriage, as a union of articulated vows and commitments, allows an individual the context in which to glimpse into the heart and soul of another, to behold another's nakedness and vulnerabilities, to handle and to nurse another's wounds and bruises. A covenant vow is needed to embark on this kind of undertaking, for it acknowledges that it takes an act of will *and* a power greater than two frail parties to prevent either or both from abandoning the tedious work that lies ahead. Physical attraction may draw the two together, but it will take a supernatural attraction to keep them together—in love. And while it is true that living in covenant union with another human being may prove the most unglamorous, exacting, and excruciating work a person will ever undertake, it is also the most extraordinary effort one can engage in. Behold, it is a mystery!

SONG OF SONGS 4:1–5:1

How Beautiful You Are, My Love

Overview

If there is any connection between the wedding scene that the protagonist fantasizes about and the lover's celebration of the beloved's body in 4:1–5:1, it is this: The flattery and praise he lavishes upon her in this unit are the stuff of wedding-night seductions. The shepherd extols the woman's beauty (4:1*a*), he admires her eyes (4:1*b*), he praises her hair (4:1*c*), he compliments her teeth (4:2), he relishes her lips and mouth (4:3*a*), he delights in her cheeks (4:3*b*), he loves her neck (4:4), and he fawns over her breasts (4:5). Hers is the kind of beauty, he says in 4:6-8, that draws him to her. As a shepherd, he uses the native gifts of the desert to describe his lover's beauty (e.g., fauna, pomegranate, the landscapes of Gilead). His lavish bodily compliments, known as *wasfs*, based on parallels with Syrian nuptial songs that poetically describe and celebrate a beloved's body, are unheard of elsewhere in Scripture. Of the four *wasfs* in Song of Songs (4:1-7; 5:10-16; 6:4-10; 7:1-9), three focus on the beauty of the woman's body (4:1-7; 6:4-10; 7:1-9). This one, belonging as it does to a larger paean to her beauty, is striking in both what it says and what it does not say.

SONG OF SONGS 4:1-8, A WOMAN'S BEAUTY

NIV

4 How beautiful you are, my darling!
  Oh, how beautiful!
 Your eyes behind your veil are doves.
Your hair is like a flock of goats
  descending from Mount Gilead.
²Your teeth are like a flock of sheep just shorn,
  coming up from the washing.
Each has its twin;
  not one of them is alone.
³Your lips are like a scarlet ribbon;
  your mouth is lovely.
Your temples behind your veil
  are like the halves of a pomegranate.
⁴Your neck is like the tower of David,
  built with elegance^a;
on it hang a thousand shields,
  all of them shields of warriors.
⁵Your two breasts are like two fawns,
  like twin fawns of a gazelle

^a4 The meaning of the Hebrew for this word is uncertain.

NRSV

4 How beautiful you are, my love,
  how very beautiful!
 Your eyes are doves
  behind your veil.
Your hair is like a flock of goats,
  moving down the slopes of Gilead.
² Your teeth are like a flock of shorn ewes
  that have come up from the washing,
all of which bear twins,
  and not one among them is bereaved.
³ Your lips are like a crimson thread,
  and your mouth is lovely.
Your cheeks are like halves of a pomegranate
  behind your veil.
⁴ Your neck is like the tower of David,
  built in courses;
on it hang a thousand bucklers,
  all of them shields of warriors.
⁵ Your two breasts are like two fawns,
  twins of a gazelle,

NIV

that browse among the lilies.
⁶Until the day breaks
and the shadows flee,
I will go to the mountain of myrrh
and to the hill of incense.
⁷All beautiful you are, my darling;
there is no flaw in you.

⁸Come with me from Lebanon, my bride,
come with me from Lebanon.
Descend from the crest of Amana,
from the top of Senir, the summit of Hermon,
from the lions' dens
and the mountain haunts of the leopards.

NRSV

that feed among the lilies.
⁶ Until the day breathes
and the shadows flee,
I will hasten to the mountain of myrrh
and the hill of frankincense.
⁷ You are altogether beautiful, my love;
there is no flaw in you.

⁸ Come with me from Lebanon, my bride;
come with me from Lebanon.
Depart[a] from the peak of Amana,
from the peak of Senir and Hermon,
from the dens of lions,
from the mountains of leopards.

aOr Look

COMMENTARY

After luxuriating in her beauty, the beloved hastens to the woman's scented bosom (v. 6, "mountain of myrrh and hill of frankincense"). The Hebrew word for "frankincense" (לבונה *lĕbônâ*), which appears also in 3:6, plays on the mountain name "Lebanon" and reappears in vv. 8 and 15. Overcome, the beloved beckons his "bride" to depart with him from known mountain sites to unspecified parts.

In his eyes, the maiden is perfect. But judging by the kind of imagery he uses to describe her, one thing is certain: Beauty is in the eyes of the beholder. Even more, seduction and erotica are culturally specific. For example, comparing beauty to the slopes of Gilead, halves of pomegranate, flocks of goats and ewes coming up from the washing, and a thousand bucklers on the tower of David is alien to the modern (Western) reader. Not only are seduction and erotica contextually determined, but also love talk can be especially frustrating to decode. While it is obvious that Lebanon, Amana, the peak of Senir, and Hermon are mountainous regions, exactly why these are peculiarly ominous places for his beloved to be wandering is all but lost on us. Presumably, predatory animals roam the peaks of these mountains, making them dangerous for both lover and beloved.

Even so, might these place names be his way of talking metaphorically about what he sees as her own inaccessibility? Typical twelfth-century courtly love poems, for example, focused on the theme of *amor de lonh,* love from far away, where love between a knight and his lady was unattainable and endlessly frustrated. Lovers in these lays are perpetually confronted externally and internally by obstacles, dangers, and impediments.[26] This theme continues to influence even modern androcentric literature, in which "men idealize women as the beautiful but unattainable *object."*[27] Nevertheless, his lover's inaccessibility and unattainability only add to the feverish desire of her beloved: "You have ravished my heart, my sister, my bride, you have ravished my heart" (v. 9).

Idiosyncratic as his descriptions of her body are, we have every reason to believe that comparisons to goats and slopes, to crimson thread and buckler shields, and to dangerous mountainsides were enough of an aphrodisiac to woo the heart of a young maiden and melt any resistance on her part. They were probably also stirring enough to convince any detractors of the shepherd's sincerity.

26. Elaine Hoffman Baruch, *Women, Love, and Power: Literary and Psychoanalytic Perspectives* (New York: New York University Press, 1991) 49.

27. See Elaine Hoffman Baruch and Lucienne J. Serrano, *Women Analyze Women: In France, England, and the United States* (New York: New York University Press, 1988) 327; see also Elaine Hoffman Baruch's chapter, "He Speaks/She Speaks: Language in Some Medieval Love Literature," in *Women, Love, and Power,* 31-51.

Oddly enough, the lover's compliments of his maiden stand in sharp contrast to her own defensive comments. In 1:6 she demanded that her onlookers not stare at her. While she did not apologize for her complexion, she did defend her black skin tone. So lavish is the shepherd's praise of the maiden's body, however, that one cannot help wondering who he is trying to convince. His beloved? Himself? Outsiders? Probably the latter. After all, lyrical poetry is frequently written to sway audiences as much as to entertain them.

One clue that something more is at stake in his poetry is the lover's claim that his darling is not only "altogether beautiful" in his eyes, but also "flawless" (v. 7). That is strong language, spoken perhaps to counter strong reservations on the part of his audience. He is quick to elaborate on his opinion of his lover's physical virtues (vv. 9-15).

Notice, however, that while the black-skinned woman defends her complexion in 1:5, the shepherd extols every part of her body except her complexion. While the woman's race or complexion is not the chief focus of the book, it would be inaccurate to assume that color played no role in standards of beauty, health, and social acceptability (cf. Miriam and Moses' Ethiopian wife in Numbers 12). Ancient lyricists were indeed aware of color differences and preferences. But the emphasis of Song of Songs is not on color so much as it is on the pain and power of love. Although the book opens with the maiden's somewhat defensive comments about her skin color (1:5-6), it seems odd that her suitor never addresses directly the matter of her color. With so much care given in this praise song to elaborating on the details of her body, one would expect to find in 4:1-15 some flattering comment about her complexion. One cannot deny the significance of his silence. Perhaps he did not think the matter worth commenting on; or perhaps dwelling on other aspects of her beauty and charm (i.e., eyes, hair, teeth, lips, cheeks, neck, scent) was the shepherd's way of rebuffing his critics and making it clear what attributes had for him the greater allure. In his eyes, she is "flawless" (v. 7). (See Reflections at 4:16–5:1.)

SONG OF SONGS 4:9-15, A LOCKED GARDEN

NIV

9You have stolen my heart, my sister, my bride;
  you have stolen my heart
with one glance of your eyes,
  with one jewel of your necklace.
10How delightful is your love, my sister, my bride!
  How much more pleasing is your love than wine,
  and the fragrance of your perfume than any spice!
11Your lips drop sweetness as the honeycomb, my bride;
  milk and honey are under your tongue.
  The fragrance of your garments is like that of Lebanon.
12You are a garden locked up, my sister, my bride;
  you are a spring enclosed, a sealed fountain.
13Your plants are an orchard of pomegranates
  with choice fruits,
  with henna and nard,
14 nard and saffron,

NRSV

9 You have ravished my heart, my sister, my bride,
  you have ravished my heart with a glance of your eyes,
  with one jewel of your necklace.
10 How sweet is your love, my sister, my bride!
  how much better is your love than wine,
  and the fragrance of your oils than any spice!
11 Your lips distill nectar, my bride;
  honey and milk are under your tongue;
  the scent of your garments is like the scent of Lebanon.
12 A garden locked is my sister, my bride,
  a garden locked, a fountain sealed.
13 Your channel[a] is an orchard of pomegranates
  with all choicest fruits,
  henna with nard,
14 nard and saffron, calamus and cinnamon,
  with all trees of frankincense,

aMeaning of Heb uncertain

NIV

calamus and cinnamon,
with every kind of incense tree,
with myrrh and aloes
and all the finest spices.
[15]You are[a] a garden fountain,
a well of flowing water
streaming down from Lebanon.

[a]15 Or *I am* (spoken by the *Beloved*)

NRSV

myrrh and aloes,
with all chief spices—
[15] a garden fountain, a well of living water,
and flowing streams from Lebanon.

COMMENTARY

The Hebrew verb (לבב *lbb*) used in v. 9 to describe the maiden's effect upon the shepherd can be interpreted in two ways: "to hearten" or "to dishearten." In this case, "hearten" makes the most sense, and both the NRSV ("you have ravished my heart") and the NIV ("you have stolen my heart") make gallant efforts to capture the meaning here. Put differently, his "sister" and "bride" has turned him on. "Sister" is a popular term of endearment in Egyptian love poetry. It no more suggests that the two lovers are siblings than does the word "baby," shared by modern lovers, suggest an incestuous relationship between the two.

"Bride" picks up on the wedding imagery introduced in chapter 3. Interestingly, of the ten times in the OT in which the word "bride" appears, six are in Song of Songs. All six occurrences appear in 4:8–5:1. Both "sister" and "bride" are terms not only of endearment, but also of intimacy.

In vv. 9-15, the lover abandons fauna metaphors and takes up flora metaphors. Not only is he a skillful lover, but also he is a versatile poet. Because the fruits and spices to which he compares his beloved are more familiar to us, we modern readers are better able to appreciate the scents and taste of romance evoked here: wine and spice (v. 10), nectar (v. 11*a*), honey and milk (v. 11*b*), cedar wood (v. 11*c*, "scent of Lebanon"), pomegranates and henna (v. 13), myrrh and aloes (v. 14). These are the fragrances and spices one expects to find in a "garden."

The repeated mention of "garden" in Song of Songs has prompted more than one feminist scholar to interpret the latter as an echo of and a redeeming counterpoint to the "love story that

goes awry" in the garden in Genesis 2–3.[28] Indeed, this entire poetic unit in Song of Songs has been categorized by more than one scholar as something of a "garden poem" in which the garden metaphor extends throughout as the ideal symbol of love. Lush with erotic imagery (e.g., flowers, spices, and delectable fruits), the garden is both the ideal place for sexual consummation and a metaphor for the woman's fertility. As for the physical garden described in Song of Songs, the unlikelihood that such a lush, variegated growth of plants and trees could have grown or been sustained in this region should pose no problem for the imagination. But that is the whole point of poetry: It specializes in the exaggerated, the extreme, the evocative—not in statistics, formalism, and the concrete. Rightly called a "utopian, fantasy-garden,"[29] the emphasis here is not on the known entity, but on an unknown, mysterious, unique place for love. The garden, therefore, is both the place to which they escape together and the place mentioned as a "well of living water" (v. 15), perhaps hinting at the flood of human body fluids that accompany arousal.

More interesting information could be cited on the garden image in the Song of Songs. Repeatedly, the woman, or some part of her anatomy, is referred to as a "garden" (4:12, 15-16; 5:1; 6:2, 11). In one instance, she is a "garden locked, a fountain sealed" (NRSV), a subtle allusion to the black-skinned woman's mystery and chastity. (The Targum, Midrash Rabbah, and Christian interpreters

28. See, e.g., Phyllis Trible, *God and the Rhetoric of Sexuality* (Philadelphia: Fortress, 1978) 144-65.
29. Roland Murphy, *The Song of Songs,* Hermeneia (Minneapolis: Fortress, 1990) 161.

have interpreted "locked" and "sealed" as emphasizing the woman's virginity.) The NIV follows other ancient manuscripts (e.g., the Septuagint, the Vulgate, and Syriac) in changing the parallel word from "garden" (גן *gan*) to "spring" or "fountain" (גל *gal*). Of course, seeing it as the latter picks up the connotation in Proverbs, where in a series of warnings against adultery "fountain" can be understood as referring to sexual intimacy:

Should your springs be scattered abroad,
   streams of water in the streets?
Let them be for yourself alone,
   and not for sharing with strangers.
Let your fountain be blessed,
   and rejoice in the wife of your youth,
   a lovely deer, a graceful doe. (Prov 5:16-19 NRSV)

(See Reflections at 4:16–5:1.)

SONG OF SONGS 4:16–5:1, THE SCENT OF A WOMAN

NIV

[16]Awake, north wind,
   and come, south wind!
Blow on my garden,
   that its fragrance may spread abroad.
Let my lover come into his garden
   and taste its choice fruits.

5   I have come into my garden, my sister, my bride;
   I have gathered my myrrh with my spice.
I have eaten my honeycomb and my honey;
   I have drunk my wine and my milk.
Eat, O friends, and drink;
   drink your fill, O lovers.

NRSV

[16] Awake, O north wind,
   and come, O south wind!
Blow upon my garden
   that its fragrance may be wafted abroad.
Let my beloved come to his garden,
   and eat its choicest fruits.

5   I come to my garden, my sister, my bride;
   I gather my myrrh with my spice,
I eat my honeycomb with my honey,
I drink my wine with my milk.

Eat, friends, drink,
   and be drunk with love.

COMMENTARY

Whether the black-skinned woman is mysterious or virginal (or both), the shepherd-lover will not be deterred. With the fragrance of her body stirring in the breeze (4:16), he gladly comes and immerses himself in the maiden's taste and smells (5:1). For the reader who appreciates subtlety and modesty, the man's language invites the mind to volley between the literal and the figurative. What in his "garden" might he be eating and drinking that tastes of myrrh and spice, honeycomb and honey, wine and milk? We can only guess and blush.

Finally, an anonymous but welcome voice encourages "friends" to eat and drink until they are satiated. Taste your fill of love, the anonymous voice admonishes. Is it the voice of the daughters of Jerusalem (5:1*b*)? We do not know.

REFLECTIONS

It is curious to note that a book that on the surface seems to celebrate human sexuality and luxuriate in the female body would come to be interpreted over the centuries by some parts of Christendom as a tract for renouncing fleshly passions. For example, for many years ascetics have seen in 4:1–5:1 a call to renounce the prevailing sociopolitical hegemonic structures of their day and to withdraw into the austere, disciplined life of monasticism. For these "dissidents," Song of Songs has epitomized the pleasures one experiences when bodily passions are subjugated for the blessed reward of achieving mystical union with God. Song of Songs 4:6-8 is particularly important because of its alleged call to a life of chastity and austerity. It progresses "from the many to the one, for the more we draw near to God in fleeing the world, that much more are we gathered into the one."[30]

Even Protestant preachers and teachers, who are otherwise ardent champions of setting biblical passages within their concrete historical settings in establishing the parameters of their interpretations, have rarely resisted the temptation to rehearse the allegorical and tropological interpretations of their ascetic counterparts. The blatantly sexual tone of the book has embarrassed the Protestant and the Catholic churches alike. Thus the shining peak of Lebanon, in the tradition of both, has become the hope and heart of the spiritual life, the embodied peak of the union between the Bridegroom (God) and the Bride (the human soul). The journey, therefore, is away from the carnality of the lion's den and the leopard's cave—that is, away from the temptations of the female body and female impurities—toward the spiritual peaks of Mount Seir and Mount Hermon.

In fact, in a great deal of Catholic and Protestant theological thinking nothing in the world is as tempting as the female body. She is as one feminist representation theorist has argued, "both desirable body and fascinating subjectivity. She is difference and *diffe'rance,* mysterious, and unknown. She localizes, focuses, reduces all temptation to the time and space occupied by her body. She is the litmus test of his ascetic practice, the 'trial of seduction' that proves his accomplishment."[31] All of the sexual pleasure and charm associated with the female body in Song of Songs are transferred onto a spirit relationship with God in androcentric interpretation, where union with God is a garden delightful and inviolable (4:12), and the process of union is one of perpetual wooing (4:1, 9), surrender (4:16), and luxuriating (5:1). This shows, perhaps, the extent to which both Protestant and Catholic male interpreters have tended to agree with one particular maxim that was popular during the medieval period, "A woman's body is fire."[32]

We see, then, that the lone book in the Bible that celebrates human sexuality and praises the female body has become in some hands the guiding tract for denying human desires and for mortifying human flesh. Why are we still inclined to read it so? The reasons are many and complex, but the first and easiest answer would be to say that the human body continues to embarrass us by its insistence upon bleeding and decaying. It disobeys us with disease and lust. It disappoints us by refusing to shape up to certain ideals. Even God, according to the purity laws in Leviticus 12–26, cannot countenance the discharges and messiness of the human body. The female body, being the messiest of all, poses the greatest problem when it comes to control (cf. Lev 12:1-8; 15:19-30; 18:1-20).

Song of Songs can be, if we allow it, an ideal book for guiding the Christian interpreter into reflecting on bodily integrity and religious meaning. It gives us permission to accept our bodies as gardens for exploring the human and divine parts of our nature. In Song of Songs,

---

30. A quotation from medieval Christian literature, found in Ann Matter's study of the medieval perspectives on Song of Songs, *The Voice of My Beloved: The Song of Songs in Western Medieval Christianity* (Philadelphia: University of Pennsylvania Press, 1990) 136.
31. Margaret R. Miles, *Carnal Knowing: Female Nakedness and Religious Meaning in the Christian West* (Boston: Beacon, 1989) 136.
32. Matter, *The Voice of My Beloved,* 33.

the female body poses no threat to the created order. It is a blank form on which many of the gifts of nature (flora and fauna) are inscribed. Reading Song of Songs in this way forces us to an entirely new bodily theology, one that acknowledges and celebrates the bodily self as an integral part of what it means to be human.

A second reason why modern readers continue to read Song of Songs in ways that shift the focus from sexual intimacy toward spiritual intimacy between God and human beings is the book's lack of moral precepts and divine law. It remains the one book in the Bible (hence, in our lectionaries) that continues to be elaborated on a level beyond its apparent meaning even though reading the Bible allegorically is no longer as popular as it was from the fourth century to the early Middle Ages. There is no mention of God by name or allusions to any of Israel's sacred historical traditions. Readers desperate to understand the book's religious significance are left to wonder whether beneath the sexual surface there might be hidden meanings and deeper revelations in the Song of Songs. Perhaps there are. Yet if the book was written to valorize the integrity of the human body and the mutual blessedness of human sexuality as gifts from God, why should not that be sufficient?

Because sex and power are virtually synonymous in our culture, we are in continuous need of material that helps us to model and celebrate intimacy that does not abuse power. In a society in which virtually every public debate about sexuality becomes a debate about power (e.g., rape, sexual abuse, pornography, incest, abortion marches, teenage pregnancy), it is refreshing to read an account of love in which lovers love without domination. The love songs of the beloved speak, among other things, of mutual love as the context for empowering the human spirit and for sharing bodily humanity. The shepherd in 4:1–5:1 praises the body of the black-skinned maiden without any attempt to dominate or subdue her. He just appreciates his beloved's beauty. That alone should be enough to give modern readers pause.

Finally, Song of Songs does not anticipate all of our questions and equivocations about human sexuality. The book celebrates the love of a man and a woman—in this case a man and a woman of, presumably, different skin colors. It does not argue against same-sex love, nor for that matter does it argue against sex between lovers of the same hue. The human body is relished and praised throughout the book, despite the fact that in much of Scripture, particularly the New Testament, the body poses a problem for those who desire to approach God. In the Song of Songs, a woman's sexuality is the delight of God's creation, despite overwhelming efforts elsewhere in the Bible to manage, regulate, and subjugate the chaos that female sexuality poses for the cult (Numbers 11; cf. Leviticus 12). A black-skinned woman is elevated as beautiful and desirable, although "black" and "dark" are associated elsewhere with things negative, sinister, and evil. Song of Songs does what it does well: It inspires modern audiences to find ways to bridge the chasm that divides lovers and to perfect human intimacy. Plain and simple.

IF YOU FIND MY BELOVED

OVERVIEW

As the longest poetic unit in the book, 5:2–6:13 (MT 7:1) has the trappings of a real drama. One gets the feeling of some progression of thought, action, movement, and speech. The lovers have an encounter; there is misunderstanding. The shepherd departs, and the maiden searches after him; in her pursuit she is attacked by city guards. She enlists help from the daughters of Jerusalem. They hesitate at first, but, upon hearing her song of adoration for the shepherd, the daughters of the city relent. The young man reappears, if only through his words (his whereabouts remain uncertain), and once more he speaks in strong seductive tones about his lover's beauty. The two lovers exchange endless adulations and confessions of their undiminished desire for each other. Although the language remains highly evocative and refuses to yield easy answers, the poem's sense of suspense, frustration, uncertainty, and tragedy was intended to keep the audience invested in the lovers' fate. With the words, "I slept, but my heart was awake," the writer conveys to the audience the feeling that at last the two lovers will meet. They will defy the odds and consummate their love.

The entire meaning of the unit seems to hinge upon how one interprets the opening scene in 5:2-8. Is this a "dream scene" as many have supposed,[33] or an account of an actual set of events[34] that helps to give the entire passage a note of dramatic unity? Is the black-skinned maiden asleep or awake, fantasizing or describing real events? The poet is ambiguous; she leaves open the possibility that the maiden is both asleep

and half-awake, fantasizing about what almost took place and also trying to discover what went wrong. Her opening line, "I slept, but my heart was awake," is not meant to draw an audience into a discussion of whether these are actual events (although there is no reason to reject out of hand the possibility that what she describes did take place). Rather, her comment is meant to admit that not all the impediments facing the lovers stem from their environment and their culture. Just as the shepherd, though effusive in his seductive remarks, remains strangely elusive, even slippery, is always running and hiding and must always be searched out, the maiden must carry her share of responsibility for the state of their romance. Whether a real or imaginary event, the description of her failure to rouse herself fully from her sleep in order to respond to her lover's knock at the door may be her own encrypted way of admitting her inability to separate fantasy from reality; when given the opportunity to face the love for which she has wished, she tends to prolong the coquetry and is reluctant to answer the call.

The poem is a complex structure of voices, changing scenery, shifting moods, drama, and dénouement. The shepherd comes for his beloved. Yet each, for his or her own reasons, recoils. The nighttime, when this all presumably takes place ("I slept"), is a fitting backdrop for their hapless disappointments. If what we have in some earlier passages are accounts of the protagonist's dreams and fantasies about her beloved (e.g., their wedding, his wedding-night seduction, the consummation of their love), then what we have here in 5:2-6:13 (MT 7:1) is what invariably follows upon fantasy—namely, the rude awakening of reality. It is the most bitter lesson of all young love: Reality hardly matches fantasy. Whether the events the long unit describes actually took place

---

33. Falk refers to it as the only self-proclaimed dream poem in the entire collection. See Marcia Falk, *The Song of Songs: A New Translation and Interpretation* (San Francisco: HarperCollins, 1990) 121.

34. Some have proposed seeing it as the actual events on the night after the wedding (4:1-7), or shortly afterward, when the bride is only half-awake and too sluggish to open the door when the bridegroom taps. See Michael D. Goulder, *The Song of Fourteen Songs,* JSOTSup 36 (Sheffield: JSOT, 1986) 40-43.

is beside the point. What matters is the torrent of emotions the lyrics invite the audience to relive. Here, the two extremes of the human heart are the focus: the joy of hope and the bitterness of disappointment.

SONG OF SONGS 5:2-8, I SLEPT, BUT MY HEART WAS AWAKE

NIV

²I slept but my heart was awake.
    Listen! My lover is knocking:
"Open to me, my sister, my darling,
    my dove, my flawless one.
My head is drenched with dew,
    my hair with the dampness of the night."
³I have taken off my robe—
    must I put it on again?
I have washed my feet—
    must I soil them again?
⁴My lover thrust his hand through the
        latch-opening;
    my heart began to pound for him.
⁵I arose to open for my lover,
    and my hands dripped with myrrh,
my fingers with flowing myrrh,
    on the handles of the lock.
⁶I opened for my lover,
    but my lover had left; he was gone.
    My heart sank at his departure.[a]
I looked for him but did not find him.
    I called him but he did not answer.
⁷The watchmen found me
    as they made their rounds in the city.
They beat me, they bruised me;
    they took away my cloak,
    those watchmen of the walls!
⁸O daughters of Jerusalem, I charge you—
    if you find my lover,
what will you tell him?
    Tell him I am faint with love.

[a]6 Or *heart had gone out to him when he spoke*

NRSV

² I slept, but my heart was awake.
    Listen! my beloved is knocking.
"Open to me, my sister, my love,
    my dove, my perfect one;
for my head is wet with dew,
    my locks with the drops of the night."
³ I had put off my garment;
    how could I put it on again?
I had bathed my feet;
    how could I soil them?
⁴ My beloved thrust his hand into the opening,
    and my inmost being yearned for him.
⁵ I arose to open to my beloved,
    and my hands dripped with myrrh,
my fingers with liquid myrrh,
    upon the handles of the bolt.
⁶ I opened to my beloved,
    but my beloved had turned and was gone.
My soul failed me when he spoke.
I sought him, but did not find him;
    I called him, but he gave no answer.
⁷ Making their rounds in the city
    the sentinels found me;
they beat me, they wounded me,
    they took away my mantle,
    those sentinels of the walls.
⁸ I adjure you, O daughters of Jerusalem,
    if you find my beloved,
tell him this:
    I am faint with love.

COMMENTARY

5:2-5. The sound of his knock at her door rouses the maiden from her sleep (v. 2). The Hebrew word קוֹל (*qôl*) is translated in both the NIV and the NRSV as the exclamation "Listen!" although the actual meaning is something like "noise" or "sound." The same word appears in 2:8 and in Isa 40:3, where the meaning has more to do with a human noise, specifically an "outcry" or "yell" that portends someone's approach. From the look of things, the Palestinian dew, which is characteristically heavy and frigid (see Judg 6:38; Hos 13:3), has left her suitor's head drenched. The protagonist hesitates and protests, even though the suitor prefaces his request with a string of pet names: "my sister," "my darling," "my dove," "my flawless one" (v. 2). "Will she open, or will she not?" the audience wonders as the song unfolds.

But before satisfying her audience's curiosity about the outcome of the lovers' encounter, the poet cleverly raises in her audience's minds other equally engaging questions. Is the maiden dreaming about her lover's visit, or is this an actual encounter between the two? Is she fantasizing about finding his hand thrust through the opening to her door, or speaking seductively about an intimate sexual touch?[35] Is the shepherd trying to get into the portal to the woman's home or into the portal to her womb? How do we explain her reluctance to open the door? After all, her response, "I have taken off my robe—must I put it on again? I have washed my feet—must I soil them again?" (v. 3) does not sound like the response of the lovesick woman elsewhere in the book (see 5:8). Whether their encounter is real or imagined, and whether their remarks are literal or figurative, neither shepherd's nor maiden's wishes are granted. She delays, and he goes away dejected—leaving the audience disappointed and perplexed. But, then, love and lovemaking rarely are as convenient, tidy, or graceful as they are in our dreams.

Proposals for translating the second half of v. 4 prove fascinating: "my heart began to pound for him" (NIV); "my inwards seethed for him";[36] "my

heart leaps for him";[37] "my innermost being yearned for him" (NRSV); "I trembled to the core of my being" (JB). The noun is literally "inward parts" (מעה *mēʿeh*), as in the belly, but the more poetic translations (NIV and JB, e.g.) have tried to capture the emotional timbre of the poetry. Proving again that the literal translation is not necessarily the most accurate, the KJV translation borders on the comical: "My bowels were moved for him." In this case, the meaning of the verse is completely lost. The verse can be taken to mean (a) upon hearing her lover fumbling with the door lock, the maiden confesses that his efforts stir her to her senses; or (b) the feel of his hands fumbling to unlock her sealed sexual parts is part of the steamy adventure of foreplay, which leaves her body trembling at and surrendering to his touch. In either case, it is not the maiden's bowels, but her genitals that respond.

5:6. Further, the maiden's disappointment in v. 6c is as heartrending as her description of ecstasy in v. 4 was titillating: "my heart sank at his departure" (NIV); "my soul failed me when he spoke" (NRSV); "I swooned when he left";[38] "my soul failed at his flight" (JB). The Hebrew reads literally, "my life went out," as in Gen 35:18, where Rachel dies while giving birth to Benjamin. The protagonist in Song of Songs does not die, but feels as though she had when she discovers that her beloved shepherd has left without her.[39] A better way of capturing her meaning might be "something inside me died when he left" (perhaps it was the same something that had earlier yearned for him). Once again, she sets out to search for her beloved (cf. 3:1-4). She searches, but cannot find him; she calls, but there is no answer. This time, love is not just elusive; it is all but gone forever. At least, that is what the audience is led to think.

True to its form, love poetry delights in the provocatively ambiguous. The composer of Song of Songs relishes words that leave her audience wondering. Ancient audiences would have known that wooden keys were needed to unlatch doors

---

35. "Hand" (יד *yād*) appears in one other place in the OT as a euphemism for the male sexual organ. See Isa 57:8-10.
36. Marvin Pope, *Song of Songs,* AB 7C (New York: Doubleday, 1977) 517-21.

37. Falk, *The Song of Songs,* 184.
38. Murphy, *The Song of Songs,* 164.
39. Falk omits the line altogether. See Falk, *The Song of Songs,* 184.

from the outside (Judg 3:25; Isa 22:22). But the composer of this work, like composers of love lyrics everywhere, exploited her audience's fascination with love and lighthearted attitude toward love lyrics. By using polyvalent language and oblique descriptions, she invites her audience to probe every statement, weigh every option, and imagine every possibility. The lyricist uses a variety of devices to invite the audience to ponder possibly different layers of the poem.

In the end, the maiden's excuses cost her her fantasies. Her suitor leaves dejected. She learns something about herself, perhaps: She is not the woman of her dreams.

She learns something also about the man of her dreams. He is not the dogged lover she has imagined him to be. At the slightest rejection he withdraws and walks away. While it is true that he attempts to open the lock and fails, still the

man in the rest of her dreams is much too gallant, too persistent, and too smitten with her to give up so easily.

5:7-8. This time the sentinels of the city are less forgiving at the sight of a woman roaming the city streets at night alone. Before they apparently did not interfere (3:3), but this time, as with the woman in Prov 7:11-12, whom the sentinels mistake for a prostitute, they attack the protagonist, beating and wounding her (v. 7). Not only does her heart suffer, but her body suffers as well. The mention of her torn cloak may be a veiled reference to the sentinels' having raped her. If gang rape is her payment for reluctance to open the door to her lover, then her adjuration to her Jerusalem girlfriends in v. 8 is understandably different from those elsewhere in Song of Songs (2:7; 3:5). She is not merely faint with love; love has made her sick (v. 8).

REFLECTIONS

Stories of women in love and in trouble abound in the Bible. Indeed, themes and imagery introduced in stories about women echo back and forth across chapters and books in the Bible as a way of binding books and women together. In Song of Songs we hear echoes of the first lovers in the garden in Eden, of the battered prostitute in Proverbs 7, and of the ever faint whisper of the bludgeoned concubine in Judges 19. Like the protagonist in Song of Songs, the latter is high spirited and independent thinking. The fates of both eventually hinge on the other side of closed doors, however. In a disgusting scene of extravagant violence against a woman, the concubine returns to the door from which her Levite husband had thrown her out, raped and brutalized by the perverse men of the town. She is left to die on the doorstep with her hands clasped to the threshold. Obviously, the mere recounting of this story can leave an audience reeling with outrage and sorrow. The informed listeners recognized the terrorizing echoes of Judges 19: both high-spirited women, both left to fend for themselves, both raped and abused, both left "dying" at the door, and both searching in vain for their lovers.

There is one difference between the concubine in Judges 19 and the black-skinned maiden in Song of Songs. The concubine in Judges is never given the chance to speak for herself. The maiden in Song of Songs speaks throughout the work. Interpreters should resist the urge to regard the story of the protagonist in Song of Songs as redeeming that of the concubine in Judges 19. The black-skinned maiden in Song of Songs has no more power over her relationship with her lover than did her counterpart in Judges. Although her speech extends beyond the mention of her rape, she is nevertheless raped by the sentinels in the city. Besides, she, too, never quite finds what she's looking for on the other side of the door.

What are we to do, then, with these stories of extravagant terror against women?[40] The fact that some are probably pure artistic creations with female characters who embody literary types—stories that do not recount the lives of real women in antiquity—does not get us off the hook. That the violence against women like Hagar, Jephthah's daughter, the Levite's

---

40. See Phyllis Trible, *Texts of Terror: Literary-Feminist Readings of Biblical Narratives* (Philadelphia: Fortress, 1984).

concubine, Gomer, and the black-skinned protagonist was *thinkable* is strangling enough to the senses. The question these stories ought to raise concerns the pervasive portrait of violated women in the Bible.

In a story like the Song of Songs, where the mood is largely playful and seductive and the social conflict behind the book is well disguised, what and how does the protagonist's beating contribute to the book's general meaning? Its mention is so oblique that it can go unnoticed. Why do repeated accounts of women's castigation and victimization appear in the biblical narratives? What is it about the lives and bodies of women that lend them to the mutilating purposes of writers? What is the cultural fascination with a woman's ravaged body? For one thing, it lends enormous emotional power to the plot of a book. Because of the attitudes attached to the female body, violence against it evokes great passion in audiences. One can manipulate a number of intense and contradictory emotions when trying to retain an audience's attention. Moved by feelings as contradictory as compassion, desire, rage, and disgust, audiences are gripped by these tales. Feelings reinforce themes, and themes reinforce feelings. Here, the maiden's regret at hesitating to open the door, her longing to be embraced by her beloved, her insistence upon searching for love become even more palpable in the light of the extent to which she goes for love. She is willing to lose her virtue to be with her beloved.

Texts that describe plundering and rape are not for the fainthearted reader. They are to be read, shared, and explored in settings in which the reader is unafraid to tap into the volcano of emotions lying just beneath faith. We should not overlook these tales for the more palatable stories that reinforce the religiously inspired fiction that bad things happen only to bad people. Bad, ugly, crushing things happen to good people also, sometimes for no apparent reason.

A cryptic, barely noticed line in Song of Songs like 5:7 does not have to be made to carry the weight of violence against women everywhere. In its own context, this passage is clear: With love comes suffering and disappointment. To love someone is to open oneself to the risk of being hurt and disappointed by that person. Indeed, it entails giving someone access to hurt you and discloses knowledge about you that only comes with intimacy—that is, the knowledge of what hurts you most. Song of Songs reminds us that the journey to satisfying love may bring us face to face with our greatest torment and disappointment.

SONG OF SONGS 5:9, WE DON'T GET IT

NIV

⁹How is your beloved better than others,
    most beautiful of women?
How is your beloved better than others,
    that you charge us so?

NRSV

⁹ What is your beloved more than another
    beloved,
    O fairest among women?
What is your beloved more than another
    beloved,
    that you thus adjure us?

COMMENTARY

The Jerusalem daughters act as interlocutors; they goad the speakers and action along with questions and instigations. "What is so special about your beloved?" they ask. "Why should we get involved?" they want to know. Even more, "If we are to help you find him (v. 8), how are we to recognize him?" After five chapters of listening in on the lovers' longing, the Jerusalem daughters remain unconvinced. "How is your beloved better than others?" they ask in this verse. They are made to ask the unspoken sentiments and reservations of the audience. The Jerusalem daughters verbalize the audience's doubts about the propriety and implication of the lovers' affair. The Jerusalem daughters' query functions as a welcome interjection into this protracted drama about the bewitching nature of love. "Explain to us, what is so special about your love?" Or better yet, "What makes your love so different from others?" The audience obviously does not get it.

SONG OF SONGS 5:10-16, DO YOU SEE WHAT I SEE?

NIV

¹⁰My lover is radiant and ruddy,
    outstanding among ten thousand.
¹¹His head is purest gold;
    his hair is wavy
    and black as a raven.
¹²His eyes are like doves
    by the water streams,
washed in milk,
    mounted like jewels.
¹³His cheeks are like beds of spice
    yielding perfume.
His lips are like lilies
    dripping with myrrh.
¹⁴His arms are rods of gold
    set with chrysolite.
His body is like polished ivory
    decorated with sapphires.ᵃ
¹⁵His legs are pillars of marble
    set on bases of pure gold.
His appearance is like Lebanon,
    choice as its cedars.
¹⁶His mouth is sweetness itself;
    he is altogether lovely.
This is my lover, this my friend,
    O daughters of Jerusalem.

ᵃ14 Or *lapis lazuli*

NRSV

¹⁰ My beloved is all radiant and ruddy,
    distinguished among ten thousand.
¹¹ His head is the finest gold;
    his locks are wavy,
    black as a raven.
¹² His eyes are like doves
    beside springs of water,
bathed in milk,
    fitly set.ᵃ
¹³ His cheeks are like beds of spices,
    yielding fragrance.
His lips are lilies,
    distilling liquid myrrh.
¹⁴ His arms are rounded gold,
    set with jewels.
His body is ivory work,ᵃ
    encrusted with sapphires.ᵇ
¹⁵ His legs are alabaster columns,
    set upon bases of gold.
His appearance is like Lebanon,
    choice as the cedars.
¹⁶ His speech is most sweet,
    and he is altogether desirable.
This is my beloved and this is my friend,
    O daughters of Jerusalem.

ᵃMeaning of Heb uncertain   ᵇHeb *lapis lazuli*

COMMENTARY

The protagonist patiently takes the time to describe her lover's charms in these verses. Of the four *wasfs,* or poetic descriptions of the body in Song of Songs, this one alone focuses on the man's body (cf. 4:1-7; 6:4-10; 7:1-9). The maiden begins her description with the upper part of his body (his hair and face) and proceeds from there to the lower part of his body (his legs and feet).

It is not an actual description of her lover, of course, but a portrait of ideal masculinity and male desirability according to ancient standards of physical beauty. The aim of her poetry is to persuade her audience to see what she sees in the shepherd.

This paean to male beauty is the only one of its kind in the Bible. It represents our only look at the male body through the eyes of a woman. It is a woman's subjective construction of male beauty: healthy complexion (v. 10); luxuriant black hair (v. 11); translucent eyes (v. 12); sweet-smelling cheeks (v. 13); brawny physique, with strong legs (vv. 14-15); tall, like the cedars in Lebanon (v. 15); and charming (v. 16). Strong white teeth should probably be added in view of v. 12*b* ("bathed in milk, fitly set"); we know from the shepherd's description of the maiden in 4:2 that healthy teeth were important to good looks. She describes him as she experiences him, using imagery her audience is sure to understand because it is inspired by the sights, sounds, and smells of their rural, pastoral, bedouin culture.

No one part of her description stands out, except perhaps her descriptions of his "body" in v. 14 (מעה *mē'eh*). The word usually refers to the internal organs, but in this context it obviously refers to the external region of the man's body. Some translators have translated it more precisely as "belly"[41] or more erotically as "loins."[42] The parallel clause "decorated/encrusted with sapphires" intensifies the description of the external region between the man's thighs and chest. In all likelihood the maiden is discreetly referring to the man's genitalia, hinting that his loins are a work of consummate firmness, rare and precious as gems.

When applied to the shepherd in v. 15, both the NRSV and the NIV translate *mar'eh* as "appearance." The maiden compares his appearance to choice timber. But the same word, in feminine form, when applied in 2:14 to the maiden is translated "face." The translators probably chose "your face is lovely" because it is paired with "your voice is sweet." But the shepherd is requesting to see more than her lovely face; he desires to behold her full "form" or "body." Male com-

mentators have tended to see the poetic imagination at work in this *wasf* as "less sensuous and imaginative" than the other three *wasfs,* which all describe the female body (4:1-7; 6:4-10; 7:1-9).[43] Whether the description of the man's physique and loins is "less sensuous and imaginative" than the descriptions of the woman's breasts and long hair may just be a matter of opinion.

To the maiden, the shepherd's most enduring and distinguishing quality is not his genital area, however, but his speech (v. 16). Twice in this unit, once indirectly (v. 13) and once explicitly (v. 16), the protagonist basks in the taste of and sounds from her beloved's mouth. Earlier in the book the shepherd pined for his soulmate's sweet-sounding voice (2:14) and admired her lips, which drip honey (4:11). Here in chap. 5, the maiden imagines the smell of spices on the shepherd's cheeks (v. 13*a*) and the taste of lips that drip honey (v. 13*b*). (A fragranced beard was perhaps common among Hebrew men, as noted in Ps 133:2, which describes the precious ointment the Aaronide priests wore on their beards.) In v. 16 she moves from her lover's smells and tastes to the sound of his speech in v. 16 (cf. "His conversation is sweetness itself" in the JB).

According to some biblical narrators, men in love speak in a certain tender way to the women they love and wish to woo (see Gen 34:3; Hos 2:14). Throughout Song of Songs the voice and sounds of the shepherd inspire the protagonist to act and react. His sound captures her attention in 2:8, and his beckoning in 2:10 arouses her. His silence sends the maiden searching the Jerusalem streets for him (3:1-2). Again in this chapter his words rouse her from her sleepy stupor and once more prompt her to take to the streets in search of him. This attention to speech and voice coheres within the very structure of the book. In a poem sculpted along the lines of soliloquies and dialogue, it is not surprising that compliments abound between the two lovers about their sweet-talking ways.

Although it would be futile to read the *wasfs* in Song of Songs literally, as precise descriptions of the lovers, we should not overlook what may be a very important allusion in v. 10. The maiden begins her one and only poetic sketch of her

41. Roland Murphy, *The Song of Songs,* Hermeneia (Minneapolis: Fortress, 1990) 164.

42. Pope, *Song of Songs,* 411.

43. Richard N. Soulen, "The *Wasf* of the Song of Songs and Hermeneutic," *JBL* 86 (1967) 183-90.

lover's body with a remark about his complexion. His complexion is the same as that of the shepherd boy turned king, David. Both are described as "ruddy," which refers to the color red (1 Sam 16:12; 17:42). A ruddy complexion was probably associated with the healthy tan of shepherds, whose work kept them under the sun's rays. But what are we to make of the different descriptions of the lovers' complexions? Hers, the result of laboring in the vineyard under the sun (1:5-6), is "black" and evidently odd; but his handsome, ruddy complexion, common to shepherds who labor in pastoral settings under the sun, is charming and handsome. Is this a hint of different standards for male and female beauty, different interpretations of the same physical characteristic?

Finally, after summing up the shepherd's charms, the protagonist closes contentedly and smugly, "This is my beloved and this is my friend, O daughters of Jerusalem" (v. 16*b*). In other words, "Now do you see what I mean?"

REFLECTIONS

In recent years feminist writing on the spiritual meaning of female body experiences has been rich and voluminous. Feminists have sought to create new frameworks for understanding women's embodiedness, showing how women's experiences of their body selves, from their anatomical parts (e.g., breasts, uterus, clitoris) to their biological potentials (e.g., menstruation, orgasm, pregnancy, labor and childbirth, infertility, and menopause) can be a resource for understanding and relating to God and to the larger world. What remains virtually uncommented upon in this new movement to reclaim embodied knowledge is the spiritual meaning of the male body, especially the moral significance of male genitalia.

It is, indeed, a great loss to those of us who want to affirm body experiences as good that, whereas the female character in Song of Songs claims her body as positive, good, and important—contrary to those who attempt to make her feel inferior because of her dark complexion (1:5-6) and small breasts (8:8-10)—the male character never comments upon his own body. Our only description of his body is from the woman's perspective. His thoughts about his appearance, his sexuality, his embodiedness remain unknown to us. What does it feel like, women may wish to know, to live inside a male body? What does it feel like to have a penis? More important, how do men experience and commune with God in the day-to-day bodily experiences of their maleness?

For example, if the experience of pregnancy puts many women in touch with the creative powers of God, and menstruation reinforces for others the atoning and purifying power of Christ's blood, then what analogous bodily experiences of spiritual revelation can men point to? In Song of Songs we perceive the male body from the female point of view. Her description is telling. We discover that standards of beauty and handsomeness and definitions of masculinity and femininity vary according to context. Not only is it true that "beauty is in the eyes of the beholder," but also what you see depends upon where you are standing. Human beings, depending upon what they have been taught, tend to ascribe different values to different shades of skin complexion. Likewise, we are taught to ascribe different values to different body shapes and builds, and we are taught to associate certain physical and emotional characteristics with women and others with men. The lovers in Song of Songs do not necessarily teach us new ways of thinking about beauty. Indeed, we discover from the poetry just how long prejudice against "black" complexions has existed in the world. But this book of poetry does allow us to come face to face with one couple's efforts to challenge color prejudice and cultural biases and stereotypes about what makes someone a suitable partner. In our own culture, men are expected to marry women who are shorter, younger, physically weaker, less educated, and who earn less money. Says who?

The lovers' odes to each other reinforce the notion that the singular most important thing about love is their experience and perceptions of each other. Although those experiences and perceptions may sometimes be influenced by the culture, they are not hopelessly determined by it. Love by its very nature arouses lovers to see and hear each other in ways no other ever has. We should recognize in the maiden's description of the shepherd her effort to describe what she sees as special about her lover. Yes, her imagery is conventional. Of course, her description is generic. But her experience of otherwise conventional beauty is unique: "This is my lover, this is my friend" (v. 16b). We should not dismiss their descriptions of one another because they focus on physical characteristics, with hardly any mention of the things we value in potential mates: character, social ambitions, family background. After all, theirs was a culture where physical contact, though not impossible, was rare and kissing was the stuff of sexual fantasy. Sex was a fantasy, and kissing was a pleasure that demanded one's most ingenious talents for hiding, sneaking, and talking abstrusely. If we tire of their endless elaborations, it is perhaps because we cannot understand their delay. Song of Songs reacquaints the modern reader with the art and pleasure of old-fashioned courtship.

SONG OF SONGS 6:1-3, BUT WHERE IS HE?

NIV	NRSV

6 Where has your lover gone,
   most beautiful of women?
Which way did your lover turn,
   that we may look for him with you?
²My lover has gone down to his garden,
   to the beds of spices,
to browse in the gardens
   and to gather lilies.
³I am my lover's and my lover is mine;
   he browses among the lilies.
	6 Where has your beloved gone,
	   O fairest among women?
	Which way has your beloved turned,
	   that we may seek him with you?
	
	² My beloved has gone down to his garden,
	   to the beds of spices,
	to pasture his flock in the gardens,
	   and to gather lilies.
	³ I am my beloved's and my beloved is mine;
	   he pastures his flock among the lilies.

COMMENTARY

The Jerusalem daughters' interest is piqued: "Where has your beloved gone, O fairest among women? Which way has your beloved turned, that we may seek him with you?" (6:1). They want a glance at him for themselves. But the protagonist is oblique about his whereabouts, alluding once more to the image of the garden, their private and sensuous utopia, insisting that the two of them belong to each other and to no one else (6:3).

SONG OF SONGS 6:4-10, ONE-OF-A-KIND BEAUTY

NIV

⁴You are beautiful, my darling, as Tirzah,
    lovely as Jerusalem,
    majestic as troops with banners.
⁵Turn your eyes from me;
    they overwhelm me.
Your hair is like a flock of goats
    descending from Gilead.
⁶Your teeth are like a flock of sheep
    coming up from the washing.
Each has its twin,
    not one of them is alone.
⁷Your temples behind your veil
    are like the halves of a pomegranate.
⁸Sixty queens there may be,
    and eighty concubines,
    and virgins beyond number;
⁹but my dove, my perfect one, is unique,
    the only daughter of her mother,
    the favorite of the one who bore her.
The maidens saw her and called her blessed;
    the queens and concubines praised her.
¹⁰Who is this that appears like the dawn,
    fair as the moon, bright as the sun,
    majestic as the stars in procession?

NRSV

⁴ You are beautiful as Tirzah, my love,
    comely as Jerusalem,
    terrible as an army with banners.
⁵ Turn away your eyes from me,
    for they overwhelm me!
Your hair is like a flock of goats,
    moving down the slopes of Gilead.
⁶ Your teeth are like a flock of ewes,
    that have come up from the washing;
all of them bear twins,
    and not one among them is bereaved.
⁷ Your cheeks are like halves of a pomegranate
    behind your veil.
⁸ There are sixty queens and eighty concubines,
    and maidens without number.
⁹ My dove, my perfect one, is the only one,
    the darling of her mother,
    flawless to her that bore her.
The maidens saw her and called her happy;
    the queens and concubines also, and they
    praised her.
¹⁰ "Who is this that looks forth like the dawn,
    fair as the moon, bright as the sun,
    terrible as an army with banners?"

COMMENTARY

In these verses the shepherd extols his black-skinned lover's beauty. Here he repeats and expands upon much of the imagery he used to describe her in 4:1-3. He admires the maiden's flowing hair (like "a flock of goats moving down the slopes of Gilead"), her perfect teeth (like "a flock of ewes . . . all of them bear twins and not one of them is bereaved"), and her blushing cheeks ("like halves of a pomegranate"). In his eyes, the maiden is beautiful. Indeed, if there is one thing the Jerusalem daughters and the shepherd agree on, it is that she is physically striking. Both use various Hebrew word forms to describe the maiden as "beautiful" (יפה *yāpâ*; Jerusalem daughters: 1:8; 5:9; 6:1; the lover: 1:15; 2:13;

4:1; 6:4). In this *waṣf* praising the woman's beauty, the shepherd reinforces the idea that the maiden is unique, one of a kind.

As lovers tend to do, the shepherd gushes with hyperbole and rattles on indecipherably when he talks about his love. For example, it is unclear exactly what similarities he has in mind when he compares the black-skinned maiden to "an army with banners" (v. 4c) or "bannered troops." In Hab 1:7 a different form of the same Hebrew word for "banner" (אים *'āyōm*) appears, referring to the formidable invading Chaldean troops (translated variously as "terrible," NRSV; "majestic," NIV; "formidable," JB). Whatever its exact translation, the sense in Song of Songs is that the woman's beauty is captivating and arresting. The idiosyncratic manner in which he compliments her should probably be viewed as the typical blather of the lovestruck.

Contrasted with the protagonist's defensive comments in 1:6 ("Do not gaze at me because I am black"), the descriptions of her beauty by her observers are noteworthy. Is there a conflict in perspectives here? Does the black-skinned woman see herself in a way (e.g., stigmatized, object of scorn and ridicule) that is different from the way her lover and friends see her (e.g., beautiful, striking, unrivaled)? Why do the others repeatedly make reference to the protagonist's beauty? Must the black-skinned woman be convinced of something she sometimes doubts herself? Why does one of the only two comments she makes about her own body (the other in 8:4 comments obliquely on her breasts) pertain to her complexion? Why does her lover remark again and again about her beauty, insisting in 6:9 that hers is a bodily self that is unique, perfect, and flawless? Should we see this simply as the conventional formulaic romantic gush of a lovestruck paramour? Or might this be a clue that theirs was a romance that violated the boundaries and norms of acceptable coupling, transgressing class, ethnic, or tribal barriers, which forever necessitated defense and special pleading before a disapproving audience?

The comparison of the protagonist's beauty to two capital cities, Tirzah and Jerusalem, though less remarkable, has left a number of commentators baffled. It should not, however, since one finds capital cities symbolized as female throughout the OT (see Ezekiel 16; 23). Influenced by ancient Near Eastern mythology, which understood the capital city as the patron city of the deity, the prophets, for example, characterized Jerusalem, and frequently Samaria as well, variously as a bride, a widow, a pubescent girl, a promiscuous wife, a woman raped, a whore, and a mother writhing with labor pains. Whether in the first three chapters of the book of Hosea or in chapters 16 and 23 of Ezekiel, or in scattered texts throughout Jeremiah, the capital cities Jerusalem and Samaria are repeatedly depicted as women, loose, wanton, brazen, and shocking in their indifference to the social norms regulating female sexuality. Song of Songs 6:4 stands out because it is the only occurrence where, in the language of linguists, the tenor (the subject) and the vehicle (the figurative language) are reversed. Usually in the OT the capital city (tenor) is compared to a woman (vehicle). Here in v. 4, however, a woman (tenor) is compared to a capital city (vehicle).

The mention of Tirzah (v. 4) instead of Samaria, which one would expect in parallel with Jerusalem, has prompted different interpretations. First, one can point to v. 4 as strong evidence for dating the book to the period of Solomon's reign. Tirzah was the capital city of the northern kingdom from the time of Jeroboam, just after the division of the united kingdom to the time of Omri, when the latter built Samaria as the new capital (see, e.g., 1 Kgs 14:17; 15:21, 33; 16:6). A second approach to this verse follows the lead of the LXX and other ancient manuscripts in translating the Hebrew as a nominal form of רצה (rāṣâ), meaning "pleasing." A third approach regards Tirzah as a gloss inserted in place of Samaria, either because of the circumstances surrounding its destruction or because the long-standing aversion to the Samaritans made Samaria unmentionable in polite settings. Although each is a likely explanation for the verse, none can be proven correct.

Lovers everywhere boast that their beloved is somehow different from others. If the beloved is male, his courage and stature are unlike other men's. If the beloved is female, her beauty, poise, and modesty are unparalleled. The reference to "sixty queens and eighty concubines" (v. 8) is a way of talking about the countless number of women among whom the black-skinned woman stands out as unique. Not only is the maiden praised by countless royal and peasant women alike, but also she is the apple of her mother's eye ("the darling of her mother," NRSV), says the shepherd lover.

In v. 10, the shepherd quotes what likely was a conventional way of hailing a beautiful or exceptional person when the latter entered a room: "Who is this that looks forth like the dawn, fair as the moon, bright as the sun, majestic as the stars in procession?" In fact, this greeting is probably the parallel to 3:6, which hailed the bridegroom's arrival. In 3:6, the "sixty mighty men" and other skilled swordsmen in Solomon's litter are mentioned as surrounding the bridegroom. Here sixty maidens and eighty concubines (vv. 8-9) surround and praise the black-skinned maiden. (See Reflections at 6:13.)

SONG OF SONGS 6:11-12, THE GARDEN OF LOVE

NIV

[11]I went down to the grove of nut trees
  to look at the new growth in the valley,
to see if the vines had budded
  or the pomegranates were in bloom.
[12]Before I realized it,
  my desire set me among the royal chariots of
    my people.[a]

[a]12 Or *among the chariots of Amminadab;* or *among the chariots of the people of the prince*

NRSV

[11] I went down to the nut orchard,
  to look at the blossoms of the valley,
to see whether the vines had budded,
  whether the pomegranates were in bloom.
[12] Before I was aware, my fancy set me
  in a chariot beside my prince.[a]

[a]Cn: Meaning of Heb uncertain

COMMENTARY

Verses 11-12 are easily the most difficult in the entire book. They stand apart from the preceding unit and do not fit with what follows. The greatest difficulty with these verses has to do with identifying the speaker. A case can be made that the shepherd continues to speak, albeit obliquely, about his love affair with the maiden. A case can be made also that the black-skinned woman is the speaker. Of course, the allusion to the garden in v. 11 is reminiscent of repeated references throughout the book to the woman as a garden (cf. 4:12, 16; 5:1), and of her own fantasies of endless hours of lovemaking amid the fertile fields and villages. She fantasizes in 7:12 of just such lovemaking, using language and imagery similar to what we find in 6:11. The LXX editors obviously understood the woman as speaker in 6:11; on the basis of 7:13, they added to 6:11 the additional line, "There I will give my love to you."

Even if one can reasonably ascribe v. 11 to a female speaker and determine that the inference of the verse is about lovemaking in the springtime, there remains the matter of v. 12. The latter invariably brings even the most intuitive interpreter to her or his exegetical knees.

Various emendations have been offered to restore the meaning of v. 12, but none has achieved a consensus among interpreters. With the NRSV and the NIV, these are among the speculations:

"Before I knew my desire had hurled me onto the chariots of Amminadib." (JB)

"Before I knew it, my heart made me (the blessed one) of the prince's people."[44]

"Unawares I was set in the chariot with the prince."[45]

"Or ever I was aware, my soul made me like the chariots of Ammi-nadib." (KJV)

Falk admits defeat and simply refuses to hazard a guess about the translation or the meaning of the verse. In a bold move, she omits the line from her translation.[46] But we should allow the verse to stand as an eloquent reminder (1) of the cultural distance between our world and the ancient world of biblical love poetry; (2) of how formidable love poetry can be to the rigid, unimaginative exegete; and (3) of how imprecise language often is.

44. Roland Murphy, following a NAB rendering. See Murphy, *The Song of Songs*, 176.
45. Marvin Pope, *Song of Songs*, AB 7C (New York: Doubleday, 1977) 584-91.
46. Marcia Falk, *The Song of Songs: A New Translation and Interpretation* (San Francisco: HarperCollins, 1990) 187.

SONG OF SONGS 6:13, THE DAUGHTERS' REQUEST

NIV

NIV

¹³Come back, come back, O Shulammite;
  come back, come back, that we may gaze on
  you!
Why would you gaze on the Shulammite
  as on the dance of Mahanaim?

NRSV

¹³ᵃ Return, return, O Shulammite!
  Return, return, that we may look upon you.

Why should you look upon the Shulammite,
  as upon a dance before two armies?ᵇ

ᵃCh 7.1 in Heb   ᵇOr *dance of Mahanaim*

COMMENTARY

Translators differ as to whether this verse (MT 7:1) belongs with the preceding unit or with the *wasf* that follows in chapter 7. Where do the words of the Jerusalem daughters belong? Indeed, theirs are the words of the interlocutors who play each partner off the other. In 5:9 they questioned the protagonist about what she saw in the shepherd lover. This time they wish to know what the shepherd sees in the maiden. Their request to examine the maiden for themselves comes between the shepherd's two praise songs (*wasfs*) and acts to heighten the tension in the drama. Because they are not quite convinced of his reasons, the shepherd must once again defend what he sees in the Shulammite.

But first the woman is forced to (re)turn (from the nut orchard? v. 11) and face her doubters: "Come back, come back, O Shulammite; come back, come back, that we may gaze on you!" (NIV). This is the first time an epithet is applied to the protagonist that does not necessarily signify her as a sexual object (e.g., "my darling," "my bride") or refer to her by her physical looks (e.g., "fairest one," "perfect one"). Unfortunately, the word does not show up anywhere else in the Old Testament, so its meaning is difficult to determine. One way to view the epithet is to see it as a feminine form of the name of the monarch with whom the book is associated, King Solomon.[47] Another possibility is to view it as a title of nobility, reinforced by the parallel appellation בת-נדיב (*bat-nādîb*),

which is translated as "queenly maiden."[48] Regardless of how one understands her new epithet, the inference of the daughters' request is unmistakable: "Let us find out for ourselves what is so special and unique about this Shulammite!"

Before the shepherd can resume his defense, the protagonist speaks up in v. 13*b*. She is prepared to challenge anyone who tries to undermine her sense of self (see 1:5; 8:10). Her rebuff in modern idiom might be something like, "Why are you looking at me as though I were a freak or something?" The dance she mentions, "the dance of two armies," while unknown to us, was probably outstanding for its unusual, spectacular, exotic choreography. Regardless, the black-skinned Shulammite refuses here, as in 1:6, to be an object of people's stares and speculations.

In summary, a look at the unit as a whole, from its opening (v. 4) to its closing (v. 13) lines, shows that the emphasis is on asserting in sundry ways the protagonist's inherently unique beauty and worth. The shepherd finds different ways to defend his lover's attractiveness: He first asserts that she is beautiful (v. 4) and then enumerates the many physical attributes that prove it (vv. 5-7); even when compared to other women, say, those of royal or privileged circumstances, she stands out as unique (v. 8). Not only is she uniquely favored in her own mother's eyes (v. 9), but also she captures the attention of onlookers whenever she enters the room (v. 10). In the end, we

---

47. H. H. Rowley, "The Meaning of 'the Shulammite,'" *AJSL* 56 (1939) 84-91.

48. For a helpful history of interpretations given to this term, see Marvin Pope, *Song of Songs,* 596-600.

discover that she does not need the shepherd to plead her case and defend her self-worth. The black-skinned maiden is quite able to defend herself. He can speak about her, but he cannot speak for her. To those who remain skeptical about what he sees in her, the black-skinned woman steps forward and speaks for herself (v. 13). She is not something to be gawked at and pointed to as though she were a freak show. The implication is that she is a person with value and an identity apart from her appearance.

REFLECTIONS

1. Song of Songs 6:4-10 portrays a man who defends the depth of his love and sentiments for a certain unknown young maiden who, for reasons unclear to us, has been deemed an unsuitable mate. We hear his defense of this maiden as unique and his defense of their love as special. This is a rare glimpse at male love. Accounts of men driven by anger, jealousy, hatred, and cynicism, all in the name of God, abound in the Bible. But by comparison only a few stories exist in the Bible about men falling in love: Adam rejoices at Eve's creation (Gen 2:23); Jacob falls for Rachel (Gen 29:9-11); Shechem is smitten by Dinah (Gen 34:3); David lusts after Bathsheba (2 Sam 11:2). But outside the poetry of Song of Songs there are no descriptions of what it feels like to be a man in love. This is the case despite the fact that the biblical story of salvation is often inspired by, and sometimes thwarted because of, the romantic entanglements of many of the male protagonists. Indeed, the sage of Proverbs all but warns of the mysterious effects that love has on the male psyche:

Three things are too wonderful for me;
    four I do not understand:
the way of an eagle in the sky,
    the way of a snake on a rock,
the way of a ship on the high seas,
    and the way of a man with a girl. (Prov 30:18-19 NRSV)

That the shepherd uses much of the same imagery he employs elsewhere to describe his true love should not be surprising. How many ways are there to describe one's love? This explains why love poetry repeats time-worn expressions. It draws from a repertoire of stock themes, phrases, and imagery to talk about topics otherwise risqué and immodest. Borrowing this traditional language makes erotic talk both legitimate and honorable. His descriptions of his beloved's spellbinding gaze, her flowing hair, perfect teeth, and blushing cheeks were the stuff of the Mediterranean man's dreams. And we should take heart in knowing that the shepherd is as eager to defend his love for the maiden as she is to defend her love for him.

2. As for the maiden herself, it is interesting to note that her harshest words in the entire poem (6:13) are directed at her female peers, the Jerusalem daughters. Their views represent the cultural prejudices against which the lovers must defend themselves. And while the maiden is not a radical feminist, we do witness some remarkable things about her character. Here, for example, she defends her integrity as a person; she is not an object to be stared at and inspected. Interpreters should resist the temptation to portray the black-skinned protagonist in Song of Songs as something of a feminist and independent thinker in her day. She is sassy and aggressive, to be sure. But she is not asserting the universal right of women to be judged according to their character, rather than their physical looks and bodily functions. For what it is worth, she is insisting on her right to love the man of her dreams.

Still her portrait provides us a glimpse of a rare female self. The maiden belongs both to herself and to her lover (2:16; 6:3). The woman, or man for that matter, who is able to experience sensuous autonomy and selfhood and at the same be present to another person is not plagued by the kind of dualistic tension so characteristic of Christian patriarchal thinking. This kind of thinking leaves us feeling as though we must continually choose between autonomy and dependence, between the self and the other to be whole. Patriarchy so frequently leaves us "split at the roots," forcing us to choose between domination and submission, power and powerlessness, sex and intimacy, friendship and eroticism, spirituality and materiality. The black-skinned Shulammite woman in Song of Songs insists upon the integrity of her physical, bodily self as the source and resource for her understanding of herself and her relationship with others.

3. Finally, the guiding premise throughout this commentary is that Song of Songs is about more than just sex. To the extent that it is *about* anything, it is especially about male and female expressions of love and intimacy, the communion of self with the other, and the riddled journey toward mutuality. If this little book of love poetry can teach the church anything about sex, it is that sex is more than what we do with our genitals. Thus the church's sometimes hysterical outbursts against sexuality (e.g., adult unmarried sex, homosexuality, teenage sex) frequently completely miss the point. Sex is a physical reenactment of our emotional, physical, cognitive, and spiritual need to experience intimate communion with other(s). Making love involves partners exploring and searching for *their* own expressions of love for each other without the detractions of naysayers, without the diminishment of oneself in order to enhance the other, and without being forced to live up to or according to certain predetermined roles. Those who are rightly distressed by many of the abusive and extreme expressions of human sexuality we regularly witness in our culture (e.g., rape, pornography, pregnant teenagers) must face the fact that we have lost touch with the true meaning of love. Inasmuch as the perfecting of human love has always been a recognized goal of religion, Song of Songs—with its spotlight on the trials of impeded love and the pleasures of "making love" beyond the impediments—is an appropriate text for modern readers to consider again and again.

WHO IS THIS LEANING ON HER BELOVED?

OVERVIEW

This block of material, which contains speeches by the protagonist (7:10-13; 8:1-4, 5b, 6-7), the shepherd (7:1-9), and the maidens (8:5a), propels the entire book toward yet another climactic possibility: The lovers at last experience the passion they have longed for throughout the book. This section consists, then, of four subunits (7:1-9, 10-13; 8:1-5, 6-7), which are organized around the shifts in speeches. After an unusually explicit seduction speech by the shepherd (7:1-9), there follows an intimation of the maiden's surrender (7:10-13) and her subsequent fantasy of the ideal circumstances for their affair and the reply of the Jerusalem daughters (8:1-5). The section ends with a wisdom homily (8:6-7) extolling the power of love.

SONG OF SONGS 7:1-9, THE SHEPHERD'S SEDUCTION

NIV

7 How beautiful your sandaled feet,
O prince's daughter!
Your graceful legs are like jewels,
the work of a craftsman's hands.
²Your navel is a rounded goblet
that never lacks blended wine.
Your waist is a mound of wheat
encircled by lilies.
³Your breasts are like two fawns,
twins of a gazelle.
⁴Your neck is like an ivory tower.
Your eyes are the pools of Heshbon
by the gate of Bath Rabbim.
Your nose is like the tower of Lebanon
looking toward Damascus.
⁵Your head crowns you like Mount Carmel.
Your hair is like royal tapestry;
the king is held captive by its tresses.
⁶How beautiful you are and how pleasing,
O love, with your delights!
⁷Your stature is like that of the palm,

NRSV

7 How graceful are your feet in sandals,
O queenly maiden!
Your rounded thighs are like jewels,
the work of a master hand.
² Your navel is a rounded bowl
that never lacks mixed wine.
Your belly is a heap of wheat,
encircled with lilies.
³ Your two breasts are like two fawns,
twins of a gazelle.
⁴ Your neck is like an ivory tower.
Your eyes are pools in Heshbon,
by the gate of Bath-rabbim.
Your nose is like a tower of Lebanon,
overlooking Damascus.
⁵ Your head crowns you like Carmel,
and your flowing locks are like purple;
a king is held captive in the tresses.[a]

⁶ How fair and pleasant you are,

[a] Meaning of Heb uncertain

NIV

and your breasts like clusters of fruit.
[8]I said, "I will climb the palm tree;
     I will take hold of its fruit."
May your breasts be like the clusters of the vine,
     the fragrance of your breath like apples,
[9] and your mouth like the best wine.
May the wine go straight to my lover,
     flowing gently over lips and teeth.[a]

[a]9 Septuagint, Aquila, Vulgate and Syriac; Hebrew *lips of sleepers*

NRSV

O loved one, delectable maiden![a]
[7] You are stately[b] as a palm tree,
     and your breasts are like its clusters.
[8] I say I will climb the palm tree
     and lay hold of its branches.
O may your breasts be like clusters of the vine,
     and the scent of your breath like apples,
[9] and your kisses[c] like the best wine
     that goes down[d] smoothly,
     gliding over lips and teeth.[e]

[a]Syr: Heb *in delights*   [b]Heb *This your stature is*   [c]Heb *palate*
[d]Heb *down for my lover*   [e]Gk Syr Vg: Heb *lips of sleepers*

COMMENTARY

In the final seduction scene, the shepherd yearns for his lover, praises her bodily charms once more, and teeters close to violating the codes of decency and public performance by talking explicitly about his fantasies of his lover's breasts. He begins this *wasf* by praising her feet (v. 1). This is the first time in the book that the man compliments a body part below the woman's waistline. And what he has to say about her thighs, navel, and belly is much too personal to take lightly. In fact, his luxurious comments do not sound like the talk of a man who is keeping the required distance between himself and a veiled, or even diaphanous veiled, virgin. The body parts he describes in this *wasf* are of a more intimate nature than those described elsewhere. By poeticizing her feet, thighs, and navel, the shepherd's sweet talk has moved from blather to daring. If his daring details of her intimate places were without feeling, commitment, and genuine adoration for the maiden, his description would be pornographic. But he is not a voyeur, peeping vulgarly at a naked woman; he is a man smitten by a woman others overlook.

The setting of these verses has been seen as a reference to the dance before the two armies (מחנים *maḥănayim*) alluded to in 6:13. Drawing on parallels with modern Near Eastern sword dance ceremonies, the bride, who supposedly wields a sword on her wedding day, presumably wears an outfit that exposes significant portions of her body, especially her mid-section. This might explain the shepherd's racy remarks about her feet, thighs, navel, and belly. Another context

might be the palace dance, which was common during festival seasons, when the king showed off the beauty of the women in his harem by asking them to dance. (King Ahasuerus's summons of Queen Vashti to display herself before his guests may reflect just such a ceremony [Esth 1:10-13].) Although commentators are inclined to see hints of just such dance rituals, the parallels are in the end unconvincing. Indeed, in 6:13*b* the protagonist seems to reject any efforts to associate her with exotic exhibitionism. Her sentiment on the matter throughout is unmistakable (see 1:6): While she is perfectly willing to revel in her lover's exploratory glances, she refuses to be an object of other people's fantasies. What we have here then is not the raucous shouts of male revelry at the sight of a woman's gyrations. It is a man who is gingerly, carefully, discreetly fantasizing about the contours of his lover's frame. He explores her body with poetic relish.

Beginning his remarks in v. 1 with yet another pet name for his lover ("O prince's daughter," NIV; "O queenly maiden," NRSV), the shepherd describes a body that has form and definition, flesh and sinew, shape and cultural meaning. In the other three *wasfs,* the direction of description was from top to bottom (e.g., 4:1-7; 5:10-16; 6:4-10). Here the shepherd begins his compliments from the bottom up, beginning with the woman's feet. (In a rustic, pastoral, bedouin environment people's feet surely take an incredible beating, since women and men stand on their feet for long periods of the day on rocky, uneven surfaces and in brutal weather.) His description of her thighs ("legs," NIV), her navel, and her belly suggests that hers is the body of a round, full-figured, fertile woman. Her breasts, like "two fawns," are firm and supple (v. 3). Ivory ornaments adorn her long graceful neck (v. 4). This woman stands in sharp contrast to the image of the ideal Western woman in contemporary times, who is gaunt, curveless, and boyish in form. As disquieting as it may be to read such erotic descriptions of a woman's body parts in the Bible, it is important that we savor the descriptions. Such careful delineation of her body reinforces the notion that the woman in Song of Songs is a real flesh-and-blood woman with emotions, desires, ambitions, and bodily integrity. She is not a convenient blank form, like the concubine in Judg 19:27-30. She is more than the sum total of her body parts, to be sure, but at the same time she will not be dismissed because of her body.

To describe the maiden's face, the imagery moves from the mundane to the ethereal. Before the shepherd was content to compare the maiden's beauty generally to the glory and splendor of capital cities (6:4). In vv. 4-5, however, he elaborates upon each part of her face by drawing comparisons with ancient place names, each no doubt renowned for its own wondrous features. Unfortunately, those unique features are all but lost on most modern Western readers: Heshbon (v. 4b), Bath-rabbim (v. 4c), Lebanon (v. 4d), Damascus (v. 4e), Carmel (v. 5a).

In the end, the maiden's elegant pose is like that of a palm tree (v. 6).[49] The maiden had compared the shepherd to the trees in Lebanon, erect and tall (5:15b). Here he uses the same tree to describe her as graceful and smooth. Each lover has a gender-biased way of understanding trees: For him their forms sway gracefully with the wind; for her their upright, unbowed nature is striking.

Accentuating the woman's body are her breasts (vv. 7-8). The shepherd dreams out loud of mounting the black-skinned woman's body and clutching her breasts (v. 8)—which surely must have been a shockingly explicit statement for a Mediterranean man, governed by modesty and honor, to have uttered. He longs in v. 8 to taste her mouth and smell her breath, imagining both to bring to his mind the fragrance of apples and the taste of a smooth wine (v. 9). (See Reflections at 8:6-7.)

49. Three women in the Old Testament share the name "Tamar," which in Hebrew means "palm tree" and symbolizes poised beauty. See Gen 38:6; 2 Sam 13:1; 14:27.

SONG OF SONGS 7:10-13, THE SHULAMMITE'S SURRENDER

NIV	NRSV
[10]I belong to my lover, and his desire is for me. [11]Come, my lover, let us go to the countryside, let us spend the night in the villages.[a] [12]Let us go early to the vineyards to see if the vines have budded, if their blossoms have opened, and if the pomegranates are in bloom— there I will give you my love. [13]The mandrakes send out their fragrance, and at our door is every delicacy, both new and old, that I have stored up for you, my lover.	[10] I am my beloved's, and his desire is for me. [11] Come, my beloved, let us go forth into the fields, and lodge in the villages; [12] let us go out early to the vineyards, and see whether the vines have budded, whether the grape blossoms have opened and the pomegranates are in bloom. There I will give you my love. [13] The mandrakes give forth fragrance, and over our doors are all choice fruits, new as well as old, which I have laid up for you, O my beloved.
a11 Or henna bushes	

COMMENTARY

The woman interrupts the man's speech in v. 10. She stakes her possessive claim upon him ("I am my beloved's, and his desire is for me") as she did using similar language in 2:16 and 6:3. If part of God's curse upon the woman in Gen 3:16 was that she be ruled by her "desire" (תשוקה *tĕšûqâ*) for her husband, then certainly the woman in Song of Songs comes to restore mutuality to life outside Eden, where the man's desire for a woman is equally determinative. She repeats his invitation to join in a pastoral tryst (2:10), but this time she has a tryst of her own in mind and beckons him into the fields and villages (lit.,

"henna flowers") to survey the plants that bloom there (e.g., vines, grapes, pomegranates, mandrakes), each of which was associated with sensuality and fertility. In v. 11 she openly beckons him to the fields and leaves no doubt in the audience's mind as to her intentions: "There I will give you my love" (v. 12d). In a book filled with coded, figurative speech between lovers, this is perhaps the protagonist's boldest, most open declaration. She recalls the image of the mandrake as a recognized aphrodisiac in Israel's national fiction (see Gen 30:14-16). (See Reflections at 8:6-7.)

SONG OF SONGS 8:1-5, IN MY MOTHER'S HOUSE

NIV

8 If only you were to me like a brother,
who was nursed at my mother's breasts!
Then, if I found you outside,
I would kiss you,
and no one would despise me.
²I would lead you
and bring you to my mother's house—
she who has taught me.
I would give you spiced wine to drink,
the nectar of my pomegranates.
³His left arm is under my head
and his right arm embraces me.
⁴Daughters of Jerusalem, I charge you:
Do not arouse or awaken love
until it so desires.
⁵Who is this coming up from the desert
leaning on her lover?
Under the apple tree I roused you;
there your mother conceived you,
there she who was in labor gave you birth.

NRSV

8 O that you were like a brother to me,
who nursed at my mother's breast!
If I met you outside, I would kiss you,
and no one would despise me.
² I would lead you and bring you
into the house of my mother,
and into the chamber of the one who bore
me.ª
I would give you spiced wine to drink,
the juice of my pomegranates.
³ O that his left hand were under my head,
and that his right hand embraced me!
⁴ I adjure you, O daughters of Jerusalem,
do not stir up or awaken love
until it is ready!

⁵ Who is that coming up from the wilderness,
leaning upon her beloved?

Under the apple tree I awakened you.
There your mother was in labor with you;
there she who bore you was in labor.

ª Gk Syr: Heb *my mother; she* (or *you*) *will teach me*

COMMENTARY

8:1-2. The shepherd does not seem to be aware of or fazed by any restraints on his fantasy of kissing his lover (7:8-9). The protagonist, however, hints that the circumstances are not quite right for engaging in their fantasies. In Mediterranean cultures, where consanguinity usually provides the only culturally approved basis for forming close social relationships and where the cultural ideal for many tribal societies is the marriage of patrilateral parallel cousins (preferably the children of brothers), it is likely that we have in v. 1 the first hint that the tension in the shepherd and black-skinned woman's romance has to do with the possibility that it violates the norms governing marriage affiliations. The maiden wishes that her lover were her "brother," by which in all likelihood she means a close relative. That would be the ideal circumstance for their union in that culture.

The protagonist's complaint in v. 1 that had the shepherd nursed at her mother's breasts their intimacy would have been permissible brings several possibilities to mind. Perhaps we have here an indication that matrilineal unions were allowable during the time of the composition of the Song of Songs. Of course, such a supposition flies in the face of overwhelming evidence in the OT that Israelite tribal societies were based on patrilineal lineage. Indeed, in most Middle Eastern societies, kinship is usually reckoned patrilineally (through the male line) and kinship-based family units are structured patrilocally around what in Hebrew is called the בית אב (*bêt ʾāb*), the "father's house." The wife leaves her *bêt ʾāb* to reside within the *bêt ʾāb* of her husband.[50]

But there is evidence that matrilineal unions were not unknown in biblical Israel. In Genesis 28–29, the story of the marriage of Jacob and Rachel (and Leah), we see an instance in which a matrilineal kinship-based relationship was arranged and encouraged, in this case between a son and his mother's brother's daughter. Some commentators have taken the protagonist's references to her mother in vv. 1-2, particularly the expression "mother's house" (בית אם *bêt ʾēm*), as an indication of the possibility of just such a union.

The other kinship possibility that the protagonist may be alluding to brings under the control of one *bêt ʾāb* a variety of women (e.g., co-wives, sisters-in-law, nieces, aunts, wives of dependent hired workers) who share collectively in the domestic affairs of the household and in the care and upbringing of children. In this household arrangement, common in Mediterranean cultures, marriage among some children of the same "household" is permissible. The emphasis here is on the close bond that exists between families raised in the same compound/household. Because they are bound by shared blood and common interests, and typically have been raised in the same household (since close genealogical kin ideally live near each other), cousins in Eastern cultures are considered ideal marriage partners. They frequently know each other and have had sufficient contact with each other to be virtual sisters and brothers. (The marriage of Abraham and Sarah was probably a marriage of cousins, since more than once Abraham refers to Sarah as his "sister" [Gen 12:10-20; 20:2-18; cf. Gen 26:7-11].)

On a more poetic level, of course, the protagonist's reference to her "mother's house" (*bêt ʾēm*) may be a veiled reference to a private, secret chamber in her imagination, if not actually in her house, where female passion could be explored and luxuriated in (see Commentary on 3:4).

The protagonist is brazen in her courtship, but when the time comes for actual consummation of the relationship, she remains a product of her culture. She would like to be able to embrace her beloved freely and without public hassle. If they were kin, she imagines, she could invite him into her mother's house and there be instructed by him in the ways of lovemaking (v. 2). It is not clear in the MT whether she means, "I would lead you and bring you to my mother's house—she who has taught me" (NIV), or "I would lead you and bring you into the house of my mother, and into the chamber of the one who bore me"

---

50. For a helpful discussion of this topic, see Carol Meyers, *Discovering Eve: Ancient Israelite Women in Context* (New York: Oxford University Press, 1988) chaps. 5 and 7; Naomi Steinberg, *Kinship and Marriage in Genesis: A Household Economics Perspective* (Minneapolis: Fortress, 1993).

(NRSV), or "I would lead you, I would take you into my mother's house, and you would teach me!" (JB). Following the example of similar statements in 3:4 and 8:5, one would have to emend the Hebrew to read "she who bore me." The more conservative position, however, would be to leave the Hebrew as is and to follow the unusual statement, "she who [has] taught me."

8:3. Despite her apprehension, the black-skinned Shulammite still yearns for her beloved's embrace, his left hand under her head, his right hand clasping her. In a book of poetry filled with passionate verses, this is one of the few explicit references to the lovers actually touching each other. There are plenty of steamy descriptions of their bodies and several veiled references to tastes and smells, but hardly any direct talk about embracing, kissing, or stroking. Allusions abound, of course (cf. 2:4; 5:1, 4; 7:8), but they are just that—allusions. The only other explicit reference to body contact is in 1:2, where the maiden opens the poetry by expressing her desire that her lover kiss her. Only intimates dared touch each other openly (Isaac and Rebecca, Gen 26:8; Jacob and Rachel, Gen 29:11).

8:4. The protagonist repeats her earlier adjuration (2:7; 3:5). Her accumulated wisdom about love, her lover, and lovemaking result from her experience of obstructed, but now consummated love. She is a wiser, more experienced woman by chap. 8 than she was in chap. 1. Her message to her peers, however, is constant: For everything there is a time and a place. There is a time and a place for love(making). And it is best not to hurry or interfere with the natural course of love.

8:5. We can only imagine that by now the Shulammite has consummated her dreams. She emerges from her chambers of blossom and budding refreshed, energized, inspired, and a little fatigued, possessed of new knowledge about herself and fascinating knowledge about him. The maiden arrives embraced by her shepherd lover, and the look on their faces captures the attention of the Jerusalem daughters. The city women hail the lovers' arrival with a conventional question: "Who is this coming up from the wilderness, leaning upon her beloved?" (see 3:6; 6:10). It is a moment of joy, to be sure; but it is also, after journeying in the wilderness, the look of post-coital relaxation. (See Reflections at 8:6-7.)

SONG OF SONGS 8:6-7, THE POWER OF LOVE

NIV	NRSV
[6]Place me like a seal over your heart, / like a seal on your arm; / for love is as strong as death, / its jealousy[a] unyielding as the grave.[b] / It burns like blazing fire, / like a mighty flame.[c] / [7]Many waters cannot quench love; / rivers cannot wash it away. / If one were to give / all the wealth of his house for love, / it[d] would be utterly scorned.	[6] Set me as a seal upon your heart, / as a seal upon your arm; / for love is strong as death, / passion fierce as the grave. / Its flashes are flashes of fire, / a raging flame. / [7] Many waters cannot quench love, / neither can floods drown it. / If one offered for love / all the wealth of one's house, / it would be utterly scorned.

[a]6 Or *ardor* [b]6 Hebrew *Sheol*
[c]6 Or / *like the very flame of the* LORD [d]7 Or *he*

COMMENTARY

The contemplative mood of this passage is a curious change from the flirtatious tone that dominates most of the other portions of the book. Cast as a homily on the power of love, this piece of worldly lyrics is reminiscent of the aphoristic material one finds in the wisdom texts of Proverbs and Ecclesiastes. This unit alone lends to the entire poem a kind of wisdom-like quality, where the object of the lyrics' message, like that of Proverbs and Ecclesiastes, is to transmit a very important lesson about life. In this case, vv. 6-7 impart one of the most important lessons of love: Love is possibly the most powerful force on earth. Even chaotic forces (i.e., fire and flood) cannot subdue it. Whereas the sages who stand behind books like Proverbs and Ecclesiastes use aphorisms and irony to impart such hard-earned wisdom, the sage behind the Song of Songs uses love lyrics to ponder the lessons of human experience.

The "seal" the maiden wishes to be placed upon her lover's heart (v. 6) signals her desire to be inseparably united with the shepherd by a sacred oath. The "seal ring" was a symbol of the kind of oath new lovers tend to make with each other when, after lovemaking, they awaken to the reality of the immense risk they have taken in exposing such intimate knowledge of themselves. (Tamar asked for just such an object from Judah before having sex with him [Gen 38:18]). Lovers pledge themselves in love, the only force on earth believed capable of circumventing the inexorable power of death and the grave. In other words, say the lovers, may our love outlive death and destruction.

Death and the grave (v. 6) are paired elsewhere in the Bible, notably in the other book renowned for its ambivalent message about love and passion: the book of Hosea. In Hos 13:14, death is personified in language reminiscent of Canaanite mythology, in which Mot, god of death, engages in battle with Baal and loses. Also in that verse, however, Israel's God boldly proclaims victory over the forces of death and the grave:

Shall I ransom them from the power of Sheol?
  Shall I redeem them from Death?
O Death, where are your plagues?

O Sheol, where is your destruction?
(Hos 13:14 NRSV)

Sheol, the Hebrew word for "grave" (שאול *šĕʾôl*) in both Song of Songs and Hosea, is the underworld where the departed go according to Hebrew cosmology, and it should not be confused with the modern notion of hell. The idea of hell—namely, a place of endless punishment, especially by fire—derives from Greek mythology, whose influence we see in both intertestamental literature (*1 Enoch* 18:11-16; 108:3-7, 15; 2 Esdr 7:36-38) and Christian writings (Rev 19:20; 20:14-15; 21:8). In Song of Songs, and elsewhere in the Old Testament, it is a force that is powerful and devouring. Like divine love, human love, according to v. 6, is capable of overcoming the negative natural forces (i.e., death/grave, fire, water) that threaten human existence.

But the seal upon the shepherd's heart is not merely a pledge; it also carries a warning. Beware, for "human passion" (קנאה *qinʾâ*) sometimes manifests itself in a number of intense and indistinguishable shades. "Jealousy" (NIV), which is frequently the translation of the Hebrew word (*qinʾâ*), is the dark, dangerous side of love, as unrelenting as the grave itself and as vehement and intense as a blazing fire. The last part of v. 6 is perhaps deliberately multivalent. Human passion is compared to "a mighty/raging flame" or "a flame of fire from Yahweh/God." Human love can be as intense as divine love, but divine jealousy can be as intense as human jealousy. This kind of intense love cannot be put out by another force of nature, the "floods" (מים רבים *mayim rabbîm,* v. 7). Nor can this love be bought with a price.

Verses 6-7 address the wise, contemplative souls who are prepared to reckon with the impediments and frustrations to love, the social norms and cultural opinions that legislate love, and the changing mutations and irrational sides of love. This is not knowledge that one acquires through hearsay. This kind of knowledge, acquired through experience and careful observation of life's rhythms, is savored by the wise.

REFLECTIONS

For all of its titillating descriptions of the male and female anatomy, for all of its lush intimations about erotica and lovemaking, Song of Songs does not mislead its readers about the dark, dangerous, and complicated sides of human passion. Couples who clamor to include sections of the poetry in their wedding vows and to reproduce portions in their wedding announcements, without reflecting on its ominous undertones, have missed a valuable look into the future that awaits them. Unwed, casual lovers who glibly take the book as divine permission for their unbridled sexual appetites patently profane its purposes. Song of Songs is about neither romance nor sex, not entirely anyway. It is about love struggling against the odds. In this unit, where the shepherd speaks for what perhaps is the last time (7:1-9) and the maiden in the boldest of fashion (7:10-13), theirs is a love that has been beset by powers and forces that have threatened to overwhelm them (8:6-7).

EPILOGUE

<table>
<tr><td>

NIV

⁸We have a young sister,
  and her breasts are not yet grown.
 What shall we do for our sister
  for the day she is spoken for?
⁹If she is a wall,
  we will build towers of silver on her.
 If she is a door,
  we will enclose her with panels of cedar.
¹⁰I am a wall,
  and my breasts are like towers.
 Thus I have become in his eyes
  like one bringing contentment.
¹¹Solomon had a vineyard in Baal Hamon;
  he let out his vineyard to tenants.
 Each was to bring for its fruit
  a thousand shekels*a* of silver.
¹²But my own vineyard is mine to give;
  the thousand shekels are for you, O Solomon,
  and two hundred*b* are for those who tend its
   fruit.
¹³You who dwell in the gardens
  with friends in attendance,
  let me hear your voice!
¹⁴Come away, my lover,
  and be like a gazelle
 or like a young stag
  on the spice-laden mountains.

a11 That is, about 25 pounds (about 11.5 kilograms); also in verse 12
b12 That is, about 5 pounds (about 2.3 kilograms)

</td><td>

NRSV

⁸ We have a little sister,
  and she has no breasts.
 What shall we do for our sister,
  on the day when she is spoken for?
⁹ If she is a wall,
  we will build upon her a battlement of
   silver;
 but if she is a door,
  we will enclose her with boards of cedar.
¹⁰ I was a wall,
  and my breasts were like towers;
 then I was in his eyes
  as one who brings*a* peace.
¹¹ Solomon had a vineyard at Baal-hamon;
  he entrusted the vineyard to keepers;
  each one was to bring for its fruit a thousand
   pieces of silver.
¹² My vineyard, my very own, is for myself;
  you, O Solomon, may have the thousand,
  and the keepers of the fruit two hundred!

¹³ O you who dwell in the gardens,
  my companions are listening for your voice;
  let me hear it.

¹⁴ Make haste, my beloved,
  and be like a gazelle
 or a young stag
  upon the mountains of spices!

aOr finds

</td></tr>
</table>

COMMENTARY

This unit consists of disparate pieces of material that seem to lack any obvious coherence to one another and that fail to show any obvious dramatic connection to the unit that precedes it. Three distinct subunits make up this final section: vv. 8-10, vv. 11-12, and vv. 13-14. Intriguing as each element is, the unit itself comes off as anticlimactic after the wisdom homily in 8:6-7, which summarizes what seems to be the conspicuous contents of the book. The material in this unit repeats or elaborates upon themes presented elsewhere in the book (vineyard, breasts, Solomon), yet it does not seem to bring any further closure to the poetry, as one would expect. A possible exception may be vv. 8-9. If the protagonist's brothers are the speakers of this first segment ("We have a little sister, and she has no breasts"), then their words act as an inclusio, or repetition of closure, echoing the reference to the brothers in 1:6. Their words bring the poem full circle.

Aside from the obscure remarks about the maiden's breasts, there is the matter of the meaning of v. 9. As her male guardians who safeguard or avenge their "sister's" chastity (see Dinah's brothers in Gen 34:25-31; and Absalom, Tamar's brother, in 2 Sam 13:20-22), the speakers, presumably the maiden's brothers, promise to reward their sister with silver adornments on her wedding day ("the day when she is spoken for") if she has remained chaste ("if she is a wall"). If, however, she fails to be chaste ("if she is a door"), they threaten to hem her in with cedar to prevent her from chasing after her lovers. A similar warning appears in Hos 2:6, where the prophet threatens to build a wall of thorns so that his wife cannot get to her lovers.

The brothers' taunt and threat are in all likelihood quoted here by the maiden, who replies impudently in v. 10 that she has been chaste ("I am a wall"); and as for her breasts, they are ample enough, thank you. The only person whose opinion matters is her lover, and in his eyes she is "whole" (שׁלום *šālôm*). Here again the black-skinned maiden is sassy and headstrong. She resists the efforts of those around her, including her male guardians, her brothers, to define her, to censure her, or to meddle in the affairs of her heart. Her protest here is in keeping with repeated admonitions in the book not to interfere with the course of love.

It is impossible to say with certainty who is speaking in vv. 11-12. This boastful song, if it is comparing the speaker's vineyard, or sexual property, to King Solomon's vineyard, is the kind one might expect from a male lover. Despite Solomon's larger holdings, the speaker presumably has the choicest woman. The unknown site "Baal-hamon" (בעל המון *ba'al hāmôn*) means literally "possessor of abundance" and may be a *double entendre* referring to what was then a well-known private vineyard owned by King Solomon. Again, cryptic references to vineyards and royal sexual encounters echo material already introduced in the book.

In the final moment of this dramatic poem (vv. 13-14) the protagonist warns her beloved of impending danger. She shoos him away from "the gardens"—that is, his intimate exploration of her body (see Commentary on 4:1–5:1). Conventionally these verses are interpreted as the protagonist's effort to shoo her beloved away for fear they will be caught together. Unidentified persons around her watch for his arrival ("my companions are listening for your voice"). She is concerned for the shepherd's safety. This conservative, straightforward way of interpreting these final verses has a lot to commend it, for it follows the literal wording of the verse. Yet such an interpretation leaves the audience dangling and mystified about what all this means, even though it coincides with the larger theme of coming and going, hasty departure, and fleeting encounters, which marks much of the poetry.

Another admittedly daring way to interpret these final verses considers the cryptic edge of the overall poem and sheds light on the entire epilogue: the maiden's and the shepherd's words as exchanged in the context of their lovemaking. In these final verses, the maiden is hurrying her lover's sexual climax. Her defiant exclamation in vv. 8-10 and his boastful outburst in vv. 11-12 are the stuff of lovers' intimate exchanges in a moment of special privacy. Referring to herself as a "garden" (v. 13), she awaits the sound of his culminating pleasure in v. 14. She encourages him to hurry like a swift and graceful young antelope (gazelle) and stag (male deer) "upon a mountain of spices" who must come and go quickly and gracefully to avoid becoming prey for dangerous animals. Her brothers, or other male relatives, lurk in the background determined to catch not only the shepherd's dishonorable advances toward their sister, but also their socially unacceptable attempt to unite. Seen in this way, the epilogue concludes the book with a description of the consummation of their love as the protagonist's continual defiance of the social norms. Or, on a more realistic note, the ancient audience is left to contemplate the final episode in their thwarted passion. That is, rebellion against cultural norms—no matter how moving, inspiring, and legitimate—is in the end *very* costly.

REFLECTIONS

The composer who brought together this little book of love poems known as the Song of Songs was not an idealist. She was quite aware of the cost lovers must pay for defying social customs. Despite the homily on the power of love in 8:6-7, she is not saying simply that love conquers all. Love may conquer all, but not without a price. It will have to survive the forces of cultural ideology, family beliefs, outside opinions, and the lovers' own individual quirks and limitations. The poet is apparently sympathetic to the lovers' desire to plead for their right to love whom they choose, irrespective of norms and prejudices, and to their desire to explore their love. But the composer also respects the power that the combined weight of custom, tradition, and attitudes has to distort even the most laudable attempts at reform. No matter how noble their cause, because of the power and influence of culture, nonconformists must always look over their shoulders.

Song of Songs is for the contemplative and the realist. It does not lend itself easily to some of the "God said it, and I believe it, and that settles it" preaching that bellows from so many pulpits every Sunday morning. Its lessons are not that banal. It demands introspection and honesty on the part of its audience. It invites them to explore the complicated world of emotions and feelings that clash with inherited values and cherished traditions. Nothing is as simple as it seems, not even falling in love.

Finally, Song of Songs can teach modern audiences a lot about the power and politics of love. It invites its audience to weigh the risks of love and asks us indirectly whether love is worth it. Those of us who think that it is worth it must decide so wisely. The recurring narrative plot of the Bible is that of the power of divine love to subvert the external systems that oppress human existence. The poetry of Song of Songs gives us a glimpse into the battle of human love to subvert the internal systems that thwart human relations.

THE BOOK OF WISDOM

INTRODUCTION, COMMENTARY, AND REFLECTIONS
BY
MICHAEL KOLARCIK, S.J.

THE BOOK OF
WISDOM

INTRODUCTION

T his book has been referred to over the centuries and still today as the book of Wisdom (from the Vulgate) or the Wisdom of Solomon (from the Septuagint). The latter title derives from the middle section of the book where the unnamed speaker is immediately recognized as Solomon—the king who preferred the wisdom of God to fame and riches. In Jewish tradition, Solomon became a model for the "true sage" in whom the best of human wisdom and the most ardent faithfulness to the ways of God were joined. Standing under the authority of this figure of Solomon, the unknown author of this work presents us with a dramatic exhortation to seek justice. It is the gift of wisdom that makes it possible to live justly and to receive friendship with God. The extraordinary deliverance of the Israelites from Egypt and the subsequent guidance through the desert testify to the strength of justice and to the wisdom of God. These three concerns—the exhortation to justice, the gift of wisdom, and the deliverance from Egypt—make up the rich tapestry of the three main sections of the Wisdom of Solomon.

The style of writing is clearly poetic with a strong emphasis on paradoxical and forceful images rather than on logical arguments. Yet the images are arranged and orchestrated in such a way as to sustain an argument for justice and faithfulness. In the first part of the book, the Hebrew poetic device of parallelism between lines is used to great effect—so much so that earlier scholars presumed the text had been written first in Hebrew and subsequently translated into Greek, as in the case of Sirach. But the use of such Greek words as those representing "immortality" (ἀθανασία *athanasia*) and "incorruptibility" (ἀφθαρσία *aphtharsia*) makes it difficult to imagine a Hebrew original. In any event, we have no references to a Hebrew text of Wisdom, and the most ancient manuscripts that relate the book of Wisdom are in Greek. Furthermore, the latter part of the book makes use of a freer prosaic style of writing that reveals the author's familiarity and ease with Greek prose.

AUTHOR, DATE, AND PLACE OF COMPOSITION

The first unambiguous reference to the book of Wisdom stems from the second century CE in the writings of Irenaeus (c. 140–202 CE). Two references are made to Wis 2:24 and 12:10: "Everyone follows the desires of his depraved heart, nurturing a wicked jealousy through which death entered the world";[1] "from generation to generation the Lord gives an opportunity to repent to all those who desire to return."[2] References become multiple in the writings of Clement of Alexandria (c. 175–230 CE), who continuously refers to the book of Wisdom and treats it as a canonical book. The book of Wisdom is cited among the list of books held to be canonical by the church in the Muratorian Canon (c. 180–190 CE). Interestingly, in the Muratorian Canon, the book of Wisdom is located among the canonical books of the New Testament.

Although Origen (c. 185–255 CE) cites the book of Wisdom among his writings and commentaries on Scripture, he shares the uncertainty of its canonical status with others. Jerome follows Origen's hesitancy and accepts as canonical the twenty-two books of the Hebrew canon (according to a certain combination of books), the number of which corresponds to the twenty-two letters of the Hebrew alphabet. The greatest impetus for the formal inclusion of the book of Wisdom in the canon of Scripture came from Augustine (354–430 CE). For Augustine, the long and venerable reading of the book of Wisdom in the liturgy by all Christians revealed its veritable canonical status.[3]

However, it was very clear to early Christian writers like Origen and Augustine that the Solomonic authorship of the book was practically impossible. Although many candidates had been proposed (from the nephew of Ben Sira to Philo of Alexandria), there was no consensus regarding the authorship of this fascinating work.

The great affinity between many phrases in the book of Wisdom and in the writings of Philo (c. 20 BCE–50 CE) has brought attention to their relationship. Although they share a common set of concerns and many phraseological affinities, there are no clear citations between them. It would be tempting to see in the book of Wisdom the result of Philo's personal attempt to write a more religious and poetic work over and above the philosophical and allegorical works for which he is famous. The greatest stumbling block to identifying Philo as the author of the book of Wisdom is his penchant for allegorical interpretation and its absence in Wisdom. Similarly, although Wisdom's personification of wisdom bears similarities to the Logos theology of Philo, the former does not employ platonic philosophical

---

1. Irenaeus *Against Heresies* 3:4.
2. Ibid., 7:5.
3. Augustine *Patrologia latina* 44.979-980.

categories as Philo does. Still, the affinities between the two testify to the distinct likelihood that they shared a common cultural background and could not have been far apart in time.

The relationship of the book of Wisdom to Philo suggests the Roman period of Alexandria to be the likely time frame for the book's composition (30 BCE–40 CE). There are many factors to support this time frame and the location of Alexandria in Egypt for the book's composition. The particular nuances of numerous Greek words and phrases, for example, in the book of Wisdom belong to the first century CE.[4]

The tension between the Jewish community and the Greeks in Alexandria under Roman rule explains the many concerns for justice that abound in the book of Wisdom. Moreover, the author's familiarity with Greek poetry and philosophy as well as the author's presupposition that the reader is conversant with Hellenism would suggest a cultural center with strong Jewish participation. Alexandria provides precisely such a cultural context. Under Ptolemy I (323–285), Alexandria became the capital of Egypt. With its museum and library, Alexandria soon became the leading center of Hellenistic philosophy and art. It is not surprising, then, that Alexandria became the focus for the translation of the Hebrew Bible into Greek.[5]

According to Philo, the Jewish population in Egypt reached one million,[6] and much of it lived in Alexandria. Although that number may be an exaggeration, there is no doubt that the Jewish community was a major force in the economic and cultural fabric of the city. The Jews formed their own *politeuma,* an organization with economic and educational rights. Such Jewish literary figures as Aristobulos (180–145 BCE) and Philo show how far the Jewish community had integrated many aspects of Hellenism into its own tradition. Whether they gained access to the gymnasium or established their own educational centers parallel to those of the Greeks is difficult to establish. What is certain is that their leading figures were thoroughly conversant with Hellenism.

The tension that the author of the book of Wisdom highlights between justice and injustice, between the Egyptians and the righteous, also mirrors the tension between the Jewish community and other inhabitants of Alexandria. Although Alexandrian Jews had been granted certain rights by Emperor Augustus in continuity with the policies of the Ptolemies, the poll tax that was introduced in 24 BCE threw the status of the Jewish community into question. The criteria for applying the tax made a distinction among Greek citizens who were exempt, Hellenes who paid a lower tax, and the Egyptian natives who paid the tax in full. The Jews of Alexandria sought to establish Greek citizenship, and the Greeks vehemently barred them from doing so.

The tension reached tragic proportions in 38 CE when the Jews were attacked in a pogrom-like manner. Synagogues were destroyed or desecrated with portraits of Caligula

---

4. For a discussion on the time frame for many words and phrases employed in the Wisdom of Solomon see David Winston, *The Wisdom of Solomon,* AB 43 (New York: Doubleday, 1979) 20-25. Winston places the date for the composition of Wisdom around the reign of Caligula (37–41 CE), though it could very well have been written over a longer period of time.

5. See *The Letter of Aristeas* c. 150–100 BCE.

6. Philo *Flaccus* 43.

bearing divine titles. The following year, Philo himself led the Jewish delegation to Emperor Caligula to argue for the rights that had originally been granted them by Augustus. But no positive results were forthcoming. With the assassination of Caligula in 41 CE, the Jews revolted in Alexandria. This led the new Emperor Claudius to settle the dispute once and for all with his forceful letter to the Alexandrians in 41 CE. The letter of Claudius essentially maintained the status quo. Greeks were reprimanded for their hostility toward the Jewish community, but the Jews were told to be satisfied with their position and not to strive for Greek citizenship. In effect, even though the letter brought a certain peace to Alexandria, it was a bitter blow to the Jewish community. Without access to the gymnasium, the Jews had no access to Alexandrian citizenship. This restriction paved the way for future strife and rebellion, which would eventually see the annihilation of the Jewish community in Alexandria during Trajan's suppression of the Jewish revolt in 115–117 CE.[7]

This combination of a thorough familiarity with and respect for the best in Hellenism that the Jewish community manifested, as well as the tension between the Greeks and the Jewish community, makes Alexandria the likely site for the composition of the book of Wisdom. The argument that Wisdom could not have been written in Alexandria if Philo does not mention it or quote it is quite weak if, in fact, Philo and the writer of Wisdom were contemporaries.

The question as to whether the New Testament writers were familiar with the book of Wisdom is difficult to resolve. There are, however, special affinities between Paul and John and the book of Wisdom. But the common phraseology and ideas are general enough to suggest that they arise from common concerns and values rather than from literary dependency.

INFLUENCES

The two major influences on the author's thought and arguments in the book of Wisdom are Hellenism and the Hebrew Bible itself. Throughout the argumentation and imaginative language employed in the work, the author essentially retains a Hebrew mentality while conversing in language familiar to various strains within Hellenism. The author has not gone as far as Philo did in applying philosophical categories from Middle Platonism to the interpretation of the biblical stories. Yet, as in the case of Philo, Middle Platonism provided distinctions and concepts that the Wisdom author employed.

Hellenism is, of course, a wide cultural umbrella that covers diverse philosophical systems and cultural values. With Platonism we can see points of contact all through the author's argumentation: the respect for beauty, the advantage of virtue, the superiority of the soul, the relationship between body and soul, the ethical perspective on justice and injustice. A certain contact may exist between Epicureanism and the author's presentation

7. For a thorough treatment of the ambiguous status of the Jews in Alexandria during the Roman period, see Martin Hengel, *Judaism and Hellenism,* trans. J. Bowden (Philadelphia: Fortress, 1974).

of the wicked person's project in life (Wisdom 2). In this case, the author was making reference to a popular ethical stance of pleasure that the disciples of Epicurus postulated. The author seems to have borrowed a number of terms and phrases from Stoic philosophers without using them in the precise manner of the Stoics. The Stoic concern to convey a coherent presentation of reality that is permanent and in flux is reflected in the interpretation of the plagues. The Neo-Pythagoreans especially flourished in Alexandria in the Roman period and, with their insistence on heavenly immortality, offered a counterbalance to the Stoics. Other motifs that are close to the Pythagoreans find an echo in the imagery of the book of Wisdom: the order of numbers (Wis 11:20*b*), the metaphor of music for order and harmony in the universe (Wis 19:18), the seriousness of perjury (Wis 14:28-31).

However, the prime source for the author of Wisdom is Scripture itself. Throughout every section of the book of Wisdom, the author makes reference to authoritative images, concepts, and stories from the Torah, the Prophets, and the Writings.

In the first section, Wis 1:1–6:21, the images from the creation and fall episodes form a veritable backdrop for the author's arguments on justice, death, and immortality (Genesis 1–3). Moreover, there is a particular concentration on successive images from Isaiah 52–58 that highlights the author's arguments against injustice and in favor of justice (the suffering servant, the sterile woman, the eunuch, the just, divine judgment).

In the second section, Wis 6:22–11:1, the author builds on the personification of wisdom exemplified in Proverbs 8 and Sirach 24. The prayer for wisdom that the figure of Solomon articulates in Wisdom 9 is formulated through the author's adaptation of Solomon's night vision in 1 Kings 3 and 2 Chronicles 1. Finally, Wisdom 10 is a eulogy of salvation history that recounts wisdom's role in saving and guiding humanity from the time of creation right up to the events of the exodus from Egypt.

The third and largest section, Wis 11:2–19:22, has been termed a "midrash" on the events of the exodus from Egypt and the journeying in the desert. The books of Exodus and Numbers provide the backdrop for the author's extended treatment of the liberation of the Israelites from Egypt. There are two large digressions on God's power and mercy and on the critique of false worship. In the course of these digressions, the author makes continuous reference to the prophets. Although the image of the covenant itself does not command a central focus in the book, such related features to the covenant as election, God's faithfulness, and the responsibility of humans to decide and act constantly emerge throughout all sections of the book.

UNITY

One feature that may be striking, at first, from a surface reading of the book of Wisdom is the great divergence of imagery and style among its three large sections. The first section displays a dramatic struggle between injustice and virtue, against which the images of life and death constantly emerge. It is a forceful exhortation to justice as if the issue of justice is a matter of life and death for the author and the reader alike. The second section moves almost indiscernibly to a contemplative tranquility. Here the author offers eloquent praise to the wisdom that comes from God and that guides humans effortlessly in their journeys. In the third section, the positive role of wisdom appears to recede into the background, and it is God who intervenes directly in the affairs of the wicked and the righteous during the exodus events. The conflict between the wicked and the just, which we found already in the first part of the book, is exemplified again in the exodus narrative.

All of these differences between the major sections of the book of Wisdom have led scholars to postulate divergent authors for the respective sections. However, studies on the unity of the language have essentially dispelled the theories of diverse authorship, even though different styles of writing were employed. At most, the author may have written these sections over a longer period of time. The surface dissimilarities among the three sections are matched by their deep unity of imagery and purpose.

One particular image that is used throughout all three sections of the book is the positive role of the cosmos. In the first section, the positive function of the forces of creation is set in relief against the backdrop of the struggle between justice and injustice. It is the cosmos itself that God arms to wage a battle against injustice. In the second section, wisdom's role to save humanity is assured through wisdom's presence at the creation of the world and humanity. Wisdom and the cosmos are intertwined in order to bring life and prosperity to the just and the wise. In the third section, the author emphasizes the role of the forces of creation in bringing justice to the wicked and sustenance to the righteous.

In terms of the unity of purpose, each section focuses on a particular concern within the author's overarching argument. The author is attempting to bolster the faith of the Jewish community under attack by powerful forces (such as those present in the Alexandrian community during Roman rule). The first section is an exhortation to justice that attempts to strip away the facade of the power of injustice and unfaithfulness. It would have been attractive to many Jews to give up their tradition in favor of Greek citizenship. The author counters such deprecation of the Jewish tradition by unmasking the powerlessness of injustice in the face of virtuous justice. Essentially, it is a dissuasion from injustice and death. The second section is more of a persuasion to the faith through the beauty and power of wisdom and virtue. Finally, the last part of the second section (chap. 10) and the midrashic treatment of the exodus events (chaps. 11–19) give historical support to the author's message. The wisdom of God has continuously accompanied humanity to bring the righteous to prosperity and well-being even through trials and tribulation (chap. 10). God has intervened with the forces of the cosmos itself to bring the wicked to justice and to sustain the righteous (chaps. 11–19).

GENRE

The book of Wisdom in its entirety does not fit into any particular genre. The work is the result of a creative and imaginative writer who has produced a rather unique piece of literature. Two forms of discourse that stem from Aristotelian rhetoric have been proposed: *Protreptic* discourse, which is governed by exhortation and persuasion, and the *Epideictic* discourse of the *Encomium,* which praises a figure and entertains throughout a sustained argument.[8] Both genres, however, include exhortation and praise. The question is, Which is at the service of the other? Since we are lacking extant sources and examples of these forms of literature from the time of the book of Wisdom, it is not an issue that can be easily decided. David Winston has summarized well the situation regarding the genre: "It is thus extremely difficult to determine whether Wisdom is an epideictic composition with an admixture of protreptic, or essentially a protreptic with a considerable element of epideictic."[9]

The author makes use of several forms of writing throughout the work. There is the *diatribe,* especially noticeable in the first part, where the author sets up speakers in order to critique their arguments. There are *literary diptychs,* which make use of the comparing and contrasting features of *synkrisis.* These are especially noticeable in the first part of the book, where the lives of the just are contrasted with the lives of the wicked, and in the later part of the book, where the Egyptians are contrasted with the Israelites. The second part of the work makes use of the *eulogy* in order to sustain the contemplation of the beauty and attractiveness of wisdom. Finally, though it is difficult to call the style of writing known as a *midrash* a genre because of its loose structure, it is clear that the author makes use of this general style of interpretation when treating biblical texts. In the first part of the book, the author employs a series of images from Isaiah in a manner that has been called midrashic or homiletic.[10] In commenting on the events of the exodus in the last part of the book, the author is clearly following the events as recounted in Exodus and Numbers and attempting to give them a specific interpretation from a unique point of view. This is typical of midrashic writing. All of these styles of writing have been combined by a skilled writer who was able to make use of devices and forms according to the movement of the argument.

STRUCTURE

The book of Wisdom is a highly structured literary work. It is helpful for the interpretation of specific passages to keep in mind the overall structure of the book and the structure of individual sections. The structures that give shape to the author's argument and arrangement of images are often dense. They help to bring images in relation to each other, both for comparison and for contrast.

8. Aristotle *The Art of Rhetoric* III.xiv.10-xv.9.
9. D. Winston, book review, *CBQ* 48 (1986) 527.
10. J. Suggs, "Book of Wisdom II,10-V: A Homily Based on the Fourth Servant Song," *JBL* 76 (1957) 26-33.

There are two literary structures that the author particularly favors: the concentric structure and the parallel structure of literary diptychs. A concentric structure derives its name from the geometric image of circles sharing a common center (ABCDD'C'B'A'). By paralleling phrases, images, or types of speech at the beginning of a unit to the end, the author skillfully draws the reader's attention to comparisons, to contrasts, and to development. Often the center of such a unit contains a focus of concentration. Parallel structures draw together images or ideas in parallel fashion (ABCDA'B'C'D'). The term *literary diptych* is derived from iconography, where two images are set side by side for the purpose of complementarity or contrast. The parallel structure of literary diptychs is particularly suited for developing and emphasizing contrasts.

The opening section of the book is formulated in a rather elegant concentric structure:

A		1:1-15	exhortation to justice
			warning against death
	B	1:16–2:24	speech of the wicked
			their defense of injustice through power and might
	C	3:1–4:20	three diptychs contrast the just with the wicked
			the defense of injustice by the wicked is dismantled
	B'	5:1-23	speech of the wicked
			their confession of error
A'		6:1-21	exhortation to wisdom
			warning against injustice

Even within this concentric structure, the parallel diptych system is used in the central unit, where the situation of the just is contrasted with that of the wicked:

3:1-13*a*	—	the just are in the hand of God
	—	the wicked will be punished
3:13*b*–4:6	—	the just who appear fruitless will bear much fruit
	—	the wicked who appear fruitful will not benefit from their wickedness
4:7-20	—	the virtuous youth who dies is with God
	—	the aged wicked will be condemned by the youth

The second section of the book of Wisdom contains two concentric structures—7:1–8:21, Solomon's desire for wisdom, and 9:1-18, Solomon's prayer for wisdom—and a parallel structure of diptychs—10:1-21, where God's wisdom is shown to have intervened in the life of humanity in order to save the just.

A						7:1-6	Solomon is mortal and limited
	B					7:7-12	Wisdom is superior to all goods
		C				7:13-22*a*	God is the guide of wisdom God gives knowledge and wealth
			D			7:22*b*–8:1	eulogy of wisdom twenty-one attributes of wisdom
		C'				8:2-9	Solomon desires to have wisdom as a bride Wisdom knows all things and is a source of wealth
	B'					8:10-16	Wisdom grants success and fame
A'						8:17-21	as a child, Solomon was gifted but still needs God's wisdom

The concentric structure of chapter 9:

A						9:1-3	God has formed humanity through wisdom
	B					9:4	Solomon asks for the wisdom that sits beside God's throne
		C				9:5-6	Solomon is weak and limited
			D			9:7-8	yet called to be king and judge over God's people
				E		9:9	Wisdom knows what is pleasing to God
					F	9:10*ab*	prayer for God to send wisdom
				E'		9:10*c*-11	so that Solomon may learn what is pleasing to God
			D'			9:12	Solomon will judge God's people justly
		C'				9:13-17*a*	for human beings are weak and burdened
	B'					9:17*b*	unless God's wisdom and Spirit come from on high
A'						9:18	and through wisdom humanity is saved

Chapter 10 consists of seven brief diptychs that show how wisdom accompanied various persons from the Torah and helped them against adversaries: (1) 10:1-3, Adam/Cain; (2) 10:4, Noah/those who perished in the flood; (3) 10:5, Abraham/the nations of Babel; (4) 10:6-8, Lot/those who perished in the cities of the plain and his wife; (5) 10:6-12, Jacob/Esau and his personal enemies; (6) 10:13-14, Joseph/his brothers and Potiphar's wife; (7) 10:15-21, the Israelites and Moses/their oppressors.

The final section of the book is a rather developed series of five diptychs that relate the punishment of the plagues to a particular sin of the Egyptians. The contrast in each diptych focuses on the means of punishment against the oppressors and the means of salvation in favor of the righteous. In addition, two major digressions occur within the second diptych. The digression on false worship (chaps. 13–15) is formulated in three parts that progress from the least blameworthy to the most blameworthy: (1) 13:1-9, philosophers incur slight blame; (2) 13:10–15:13, idol worship is condemned; (3) 15:14-19, the idol and animal worship of Egypt is severely condemned.

Figure 1: The Five Diptychs and the Seven Antitheses in the Book of Wisdom

Causal relationship	Antithetical relationship
11:16	11:5, 13

Sins	Plagues	Blessings
1. 11:6-14 killing of infants	1. 11:6-14 undrinkable water	water in the desert
2. 11:15–16:14 animals adored	2. 16:1-4 animals suppress the appetite	delicious animals (quails)

1st digression 11:17–12:27 — God's power and mercy to save and to punish
2nd digression 13–15 — the origins of false worship
minor digression 16:5-14 — the brazen serpent; God has power over life and death

	3. 16:5-14 animals that kill	the saving brazen serpent
3. 16:15-29 refusal to recognize the true God	4. 16:15-29 rain, hail; creation destroys by fire; lack of food	creation saves; the manna resists burning by fire
4. 17:1–18:4 enslaving the Hebrews	5. 17:1–18:4 captivity by darkness	pillar of fire in the darkness Aaron stops the destroyer
5. 18:5–19:21 killing of infants in river	6. 18:5-25 death of the firstborn	Israel passes through the Red Sea
	7. 19:1-9 drowning in the sea	

minor digression 18:20-25—
minor digression 19:6-12—Creation

The central section of the critique that treats idol worship specifically is organized concentrically:

A		13:10-19	gold, silver, stone, wooden idols—carpenter
	B	14:1-10	reflection on God's providential care
		C 14:11-31	invention and result of idolatry punishment of idolatry
	B'	15:1-6	reflection on God's mercy and power
A'		15:7-13	clay idols—potter

MAJOR CONTRIBUTIONS

Death, Immortality, Justice. The author advances significantly the formal treatment of the status of an individual human being after death. Although the problem of God's faithfulness to the just who suffer arose in such works as Job and Ecclesiastes, the unambiguous declaration of the survival of the individual is a late phenomenon (Dan 12:2-3; 2 Macc 7:9). The background for the author's unambiguous declaration of human immortality is the covenantal faithfulness of God to the just. God is faithful to the just, and no torment will destroy them; God's grace and mercy remain with the elect (3:1-9).

Although the language the author employs to convey the belief in an afterlife is Greek, a uniquely Hebraic ethical understanding is given to that language. The author sustains the idea of the survival of the just after death with such words as "immortal" (Wis 1:15; 3:4; 4:1; 8:17; 15:3) and "incorruptible" (2:23; 6:18-19). But an ethical perspective is brought in to condition this notion of immortality. The author is not positing an inherent immortality that all humans possess. Rather, immortality depends on the inner life of virtue. Immortality is the divine life toward which all human beings have been destined from the dawn of creation (Wis 2:23). But the decisions and actions of human beings that affect others determine the quality of final life.

A life of justice and virtue leads to immortality (Wis 3:4; 6:17-20). A life of injustice and wickedness leads to death (Wis 1:16; 2:24; 5:17-23). Death here is understood not simply as the experience of mortality, which the just experience as well, but as divine judgment. Similarly, the immortal life of the just is not presented as an inherent quality, but as the result of a positive divine judgment over one's decisions and actions (Wis 5:15-16). Although the author's presentation of the immortality of the just could be reconciled with the notion of a bodily resurrection, nowhere is a bodily resurrection formally posited in the book of Wisdom.

Even the notion of justice, which figures so dominantly throughout the book, retains its Hebraic nuances rather than the Greek qualities of balance and equality that are associated with justice. The two perspectives are not incompatible, but for the author of the book of Wisdom justice involves the support and respect for the weak. Solomon asks for wisdom to be able to judge God's people justly (Wis 9:12). Injustice is identified as oppressing and exploiting the weak and defenseless. The wicked employ their power to oppress the widow, the aged, the poor, and the just (Wis 2:12-20).

Personification of Wisdom. In focusing on the wisdom of God through personification, the author picks up the sapiential traditions from Proverbs 8 and Sirach 24. However, what is unique to the author of the book of Wisdom is the emphasis on the specific role of wisdom both in creation and in human affairs. The wisdom that comes from God is able to help humans because it was present at creation. As a result of this, wisdom is a bridge between humans and God. Wisdom knows God's works, knows what is pleasing to God, and brings friendship with God.

The author integrates the current Greek views of wisdom with the Hebrew sapiential tradition of the personification of wisdom. For the Greeks, wisdom is essentially a means of gaining knowledge, both cosmic and divine. For the Wisdom author, wisdom lives with God and is revealed and given to humans by God. The wisdom that comes from God is a gift that brings to completion the wisdom through which humans were formed at creation. According to the author's anthropology, human beings have been shaped and formed by the wisdom of God in such a way that they yearn to be completed by the wisdom of God, which comes only as a gift. Solomon provided the ideal figure through which the author presents this anthropology. He is presented as naturally gifted, yet as realizing the limitations of his being and yearning for the wisdom that comes from God.

It is not surprising, then, to see how the author attaches the wisdom of God to the just. Injustice is inimical both to the structures of the cosmos and to the human heart. Wisdom flees from the unjust and the wicked, but waits for the just and actively seeks them out.

The author has gone as far as possible in the personification of God's wisdom without creating a separate entity as an intermediate being between human beings and God. Wisdom is the manner in which God has created the world and fashioned the human heart. Wisdom is the manner in which God continuously intervenes in history both to save the just and to thwart the designs of injustice.

CANONICAL STATUS

The canonical status of the book of Wisdom differs among the Christian communities. Discussion regarding the book's status hinged essentially on the acceptance or rejection of the wider canon of the LXX, the Greek version of the Old Testament. The doubt regarding its acceptance can be traced to the strong voice of Jerome (345–419 CE), who preferred the smaller canon of the Hebrew Scriptures. The authoritative voice of Augustine provided the greatest impetus for acceptance. In the ambit of the Latin Church, the Council of Carthage (397 CE) and the letter of Innocent I to the Bishop of Toulouse (405 CE) follow the list of canonical books presented by Augustine.[11]

The acceptance of the wider canon was settled definitively in the Roman Church at the Council of Trent (1546 CE). The Orthodox Church accepted the Roman canons of Scripture at the Council of Jerusalem in 1672. But since the eighteenth century a renewed discussion has emerged among the Orthodox communities regarding the inspiration of the deutero-canonical books. The Protestant and Reformed traditions follow the lead of Martin Luther, who was inspired by Jerome's preference for the smaller canon. However, even Martin Luther accepted the deuterocanonical/apocryphal books as inspirational reading while withholding their canonical status. So it is not surprising to note that one of Wisdom's best modern commentaries stems from the pen of a Protestant scholar.[12] Since there is little doubt as to the Jewish origin of the work, Jewish scholars also study Wisdom as a source for understanding the currents of Jewish thought during the Hellenistic period.[13]

11. Augustine, *De Doctrina Christiana* 2,8; *PL* 34,40.
12. C. L. W. Grimm, *Das Buch der Weisheit* (Leipzig: Hirzel, 1837).
13. Y. Amir, "The Figure of Death in 'The Book of Wisdom,'" *JJS* 30 (1979) 154-78.

BIBLIOGRAPHY:

Kolarcik, Michael. *The Ambiguity of Death in the Book of Wisdom (1–6)*. AnBib 127. Rome: Pontifical Biblical Institute, 1991. Explores the various levels of meaning that the image of death presents to the reader in the first part of the book of Wisdom.

Larcher, C. *Le Livre de la Sagesse ou La Sagesse de Salomon.* Vols. 1-3. Études Biblique, nouvelle série. 1, 3, 5. Paris: Gabalda, 1983–85. The most extensive treatment by a single author on the book of Wisdom stems from a French exegete. The three-volume commentary was preceded by a collection of studies by the author on the cultural backdrop for the book of Wisdom (*Études sur le Livre de la Sagesse.* Études Bibliques. Paris: Gabalda, 1969).

Nickelsburg, George W. E. *Resurrection, Immortality and Eternal Life in Intertestamental Judaism.* HTS 26. Cambridge, Mass.: Harvard University Press, 1972. This work sets the context for the Wisdom author's views of immortality in the larger picture of Judaism. Of particular interest for the book of Wisdom is chapter 2, "Religious Persecution: The Story of the Persecution and Exaltation of the Righteous Man," 48-92.

Reese, James M. *Hellenistic Influence on the Book of Wisdom and Its Consequences.* AnBib 41. Rome: Pontifical Biblical Institute, 1970. The precise influence of Hellenism on the author of Wisdom is difficult to determine. Reese explains that though the Wisdom author employs language and images from Hellenistic culture, the mentality of the author remains Hebraic.

Taylor, Richard J. "The Eschatological Meaning of Life and Death in the Book of Wisdom I-V," *ETL* 42 (1966) 72-137. Examines the notion of the afterlife that can be discerned in the first five chapters of the book of Wisdom.

Vílchez, Jose. *Sabiduría.* Sapienciales V. Nueva Biblia Española. Estella: Editorial Verbo Divino, 1990. Complete commentary on the book of Wisdom that combines textual analysis with an examination of sources and with theological interpretation. The extensive introduction and appendixes treat the cultural milieu of Judaism in the diaspora. Vílchez's work has been of great help in the writing of this commentary.

Winston, David. *The Wisdom of Solomon.* AB 43. New York: Doubleday, 1979. Provides an excellent introduction with an overview of the main themes in Wisdom; includes a thorough treatment of the difficulties of translating obscure words and phrases. One of its greatest uses lies in the many references to other parts of Scripture, to Hellenistic philosophy and literature, and to rabbinic sources.

Wright, Addison G. "Wisdom." *NJBC.* Englewood Cliffs, N.J.: Prentice Hall, 1990. Synthesizes various insights into the structure of the book of Wisdom that Wright has presented in other articles.

OUTLINE OF WISDOM

WISDOM 1:1–6:21

EXHORTATION TO JUSTICE

OVERVIEW

The opening chapters of the book of Wisdom appeal to the mind and the heart. We are presented with a spectacle of human life filled with tragedy and great hope. The author, speaking like a sage, invites the reader to look behind the scenes and below the surface of appearances to appreciate fundamental truths. The agonizing mystery we confront in the dramatic presentation of a condensed slice of human life is the struggle between justice and injustice. How do we interpret the reality of injustice in life? Why should we value integrity and authenticity in the face of the apparent power of injustice? The author offers us a dramatic scene to lend us eyes that perceive beyond the surface and behind appearances. By weaving a concise nexus between the practice of injustice and the consequence of death, the argumentation exhorts the reader to reject injustice and embrace virtue. What is at stake is nothing less than life and death. Arguments of thought unfold to engage the heart to choose justice and life. The section opens with an exhortation to love justice (1:1), and it closes with a parallel exhortation to learn wisdom (6:9-11). But what transpires throughout the body of the exhortation is a dynamic argument that attempts to uncover the insidious source of injustice as well as the transforming power of virtue.

Although the exhortation at the outset points to a positive value—namely, that of loving justice—it quickly turns to a warning against bringing on death (1:12). Death is presented as a fundamental obstacle to the practice of justice. This death implies a nihilistic judgment on human dignity viewed from the side of mortality, human weakness, and suffering that reduces ethical perspectives to those of evasive pleasure, arrogant power, and brutal violence (2:6-20). By uncovering the false reasoning implied in the nihilistic judgment on human dignity, the argument attempts to liberate the reader from the fear of death to the love of justice and wisdom.

A major innovation in the argument of this work is the unambiguous declaration of a life after death (3:1; 4:10, 16). Although the declaration is unambiguous, the precise when, where, and how are left open and undefined. This eternal life is not simply a state of being but a relationship with the divine. It is the result of God's faithfulness to those who have been faithful (3:9). Humans were created for incorruption (2:23). The practice of injustice destroys a person's relationship with God and even with the cosmos. The practice of virtue, despite appearances to the contrary, issues in an indissoluble relationship with God and with the cosmos.[14] Immortality is the positive motive for dissuading the reader from a life of injustice.

Death is the prime negative motive for loving justice and seeking God. In these opening chapters, the image of death retains the contours of its threatening ambiguity in life. Death may signify an end, but it may also signify a new beginning. There is the death of mortality in general, which for the wicked renders life meaningless (2:1-5); for the righteous, mortality is a stepping stone to divine life (3:2-6). There is the death that is experienced as the consequence of unjust actions (5:9-14). Finally, there is a death that is ultimate, a final judgment of God and the cosmos against injustice (5:20-23).

Both eternal life and ultimate death are viewed from the perspective of ethical decisions. The author is not so much concerned with states of being inherent in nature as much as with decisions that lead to just or unjust actions toward others, toward oneself, and toward God. In this

---

14. See Richard J. Taylor, "The Eschatological Meaning of Life and Death in the Book of Wisdom I–V," *ETL* 42 (1966) 72-137; J. J. Collins, "The Root of Immortality: Death in the Context of Jewish Wisdom (Sir WisSol)," *HTR* 71 (1978) 177-92.

regard, the book of Wisdom continues the great Israelite heritage of stressing the value of ethical conduct.

The first section of the book of Wisdom actually takes the shape of the procedures of a trial. First there is an accusation against the unjust, expressed through a statement: Lawlessness leads to death (1:1-11). Second, the wicked, who represent lawlessness, put forth a defense for their lives of pleasure, power, and violence (2:1-20). The conclusion of their defense issues in a counteraccusation of the incoherence of the lives of the just. Third, the author dismantles both the wicked's defense and their counteraccusation through a deliberation and examination of the evidence. In four series of comparisons and contrasts, the author sifts through the evidence of appearances and reality (3:1–4:20). Fourth, the wicked confess to their error and guilt (5:2-14). Fifth, the verdict and sentencing are conveyed through an apocalyptic judgment in which the just receive a royal award and the unjust are hurled to oblivion (5:15-23). Finally, the concluding exhortation to rulers calls the readers to apply the judgment rendered during the metaphorical trial to their own lives (6:1-21).[15]

The stylistic device that gives formal shape to the opening section of Wisdom is that of a concentric structure (see the diagram on p. 446). This is a favorite device used throughout the book of Wisdom. A concentric, or chiastic, structure has the effect of intensifying the images used during the argumentation by rendering them parallel in the reader's imagination. In this way, we more readily notice the repetitions and transformations in the flow of the statements.

15. Michael Kolarcik, *The Ambiguity of Death in the Book of Wisdom 1–6,* AnBib 127 (Rome: 1991) 111-12.

WISDOM 1:1-15, LOVE RIGHTEOUSNESS

NAB

1 Love justice, you who judge
  the earth;
 think of the LORD in goodness,
 and seek him in integrity of heart;
2 Because he is found by those who test him
  not,
 and he manifests himself to those who do
  not disbelieve him.
3 For perverse counsels separate a man from
  God,
 and his power, put to the proof, rebukes
  the foolhardy;
4 Because into a soul that plots evil wisdom
  enters not,
 nor dwells she in a body under debt of sin.
5 For the holy spirit of discipline flees deceit
 and withdraws from senseless counsels;
 and when injustice occurs it is rebuked.
6 For wisdom is a kindly spirit,

The original language of the Book of Wisdom is Greek. The basic text used here is the Greek text as found in H. B. Swete, *The Old Testament in Greek,* 3 ed, Vol. II, Cambridge, 1907.

NRSV

1 Love righteousness, you rulers of
  the earth,
 think of the Lord in goodness
 and seek him with sincerity of heart;
2 because he is found by those who do not put
  him to the test,
 and manifests himself to those who do not
  distrust him.
3 For perverse thoughts separate people from
  God,
 and when his power is tested, it exposes the
  foolish;
4 because wisdom will not enter a deceitful soul,
 or dwell in a body enslaved to sin.
5 For a holy and disciplined spirit will flee from
  deceit,
 and will leave foolish thoughts behind,
 and will be ashamed at the approach of
  unrighteousness.

6 For wisdom is a kindly spirit,
 but will not free blasphemers from the guilt of
  their words;

NAB

yet she acquits not the blasphemer of his
    guilty lips;
Because God is the witness of his inmost self
    and the sure observer of his heart
    and the listener to his tongue.
7 For the spirit of the LORD fills the world,
    is all-embracing, and knows what man says.
8 Therefore no one who utters wicked things
    can go unnoticed,
  nor will chastising condemnation pass him by.
9 For the devices of the wicked man shall be
    scrutinized,
    and the sound of his words shall reach the
    LORD,
  for the chastisement of his transgressions;
10 Because a jealous ear hearkens to everything,
    and discordant grumblings are no secret.
11 Therefore guard against profitless grumbling,
    and from calumny withhold your tongues;
  For a stealthy utterance does not go
    unpunished,
    and a lying mouth slays the soul.
12 Court not death by your erring way of life,
    nor draw to yourselves destruction by the
    works of your hands.
13 Because God did not make death,
    nor does he rejoice in the destruction of
    the living.
14 For he fashioned all things that they might
    have being;
    and the creatures of the world are wholesome,
  And there is not a destructive drug among
    them
    nor any domain of the nether world on
    earth,
15 For justice is undying.

NRSV

because God is witness of their inmost feelings,
    and a true observer of their hearts, and a
    hearer of their tongues.
7 Because the spirit of the Lord has filled the
    world,
    and that which holds all things together knows
    what is said,
8 therefore those who utter unrighteous things
    will not escape notice,
    and justice, when it punishes, will not pass
    them by.
9 For inquiry will be made into the counsels of
    the ungodly,
    and a report of their words will come to the
    Lord,
    to convict them of their lawless deeds;
10 because a jealous ear hears all things,
    and the sound of grumbling does not go unheard.
11 Beware then of useless grumbling,
    and keep your tongue from slander;
    because no secret word is without result,[a]
    and a lying mouth destroys the soul.

12 Do not invite death by the error of your life,
    or bring on destruction by the works of your
    hands;
13 because God did not make death,
    and he does not delight in the death of the living.
14 For he created all things so that they might
    exist;
    the generative forces[b] of the world are
    wholesome,
    and there is no destructive poison in them,
    and the dominion[c] of Hades is not on earth.
15 For righteousness is immortal.

a Or will go unpunished   b Or the creatures   c Or palace

COMMENTARY

This opening exhortation places before the imagination of the reader the lofty value of righteousness. The conclusion to the exhortation buttresses the importance for humans of embracing this value through the bold assertion that righteousness is immortal (v. 15).[16] "Righteousness"

(δικαιοσύνη dikaiosynē) is a word that aptly describes an aspect of Israelite heritage that highly values ethical conduct. In the Torah and the Prophets, righteousness engulfed an ethical perspective regarding all facets of life: relationships to God, to oneself, and to others. The nuances of this word are colored by the subject, whether God or Israel, and by the specific relationship to which

16. The Vg added a contrasting colon to 1:15: Righteousness is immortal; injustice is the acquisition of death.

it refers.[17] It is a value that demands or presumes a conscious choice and a course of action. When God is righteous, human beings are saved through the deliberate actions of God. When humans are said to be righteous, they have made decisions for justice (Abram, Gen 15:6) or carried out righteous conduct as in response to the law (Deut 16:19-20). More than a mere concept, righteousness denotes an entire program of conduct in life that demands commitment and clarity of vision.

The idea of immortality that is introduced at the conclusion of this exhortation is a key concept for the Wisdom author. This is the only occurrence of the adjective "immortal" (ἀθάνατος *athanatos*) in the entire book. The noun "immortality" (ἀθανασία *athanasia*) is employed on several occasions (3:4 in relation to hope; 4:1 in relation to the memory of virtue; 8:13 in relation to remembrance; 8:17 in relation to wisdom; 15:3 in relation to righteousness). It does not refer to an independent quality of being as much as to an aspect of the enduring relationship between the just and the realm of the divine achieved through virtue. This idea of immortality achieved in relation to God through virtue will constitute the author's main argument for dismantling the reasoning of the unjust.[18]

The exhortation itself is reminiscent of the call of personified wisdom in Proverbs who goes about the streets exhorting people to learn (Proverbs 8). All the words of her mouth are said to be righteous; they will help humans find life. In Proverbs the exhortation is directed to all who are willing to hear. With a similar universalistic aim, the Wisdom exhortation is directed to the rulers of the earth.

Opening exhortations on the value of ethical conduct are typical of sapiential writings. A Hebrew wisdom writing from the Cairo Geniza (probably written during the Middle Ages) begins its proverbial type of teaching with an exhortation similar to the Wisdom text: "Seek wisdom and the right path so that you will be great in the eyes of God and people. All those who remove foolishness and haughtiness from their lives will become wise and strong."[19]

The addressees are referred to as "the rulers of the earth." This title is parallel to that in the closing exhortation, where the addressees are called "kings" and "judges of the ends of the earth," those who "rule over multitudes and boast of many nations" (6:1-2 NRSV). Although it is possible to see in these titles an allusion to Roman or at least to foreign powers, we should not overlook the function of the royal image to denote humanity. Humans are human precisely in their ability to reign over their thoughts and actions. This royal image is not lacking in the Genesis account of creation, in which God generously gives to humanity the command to fill the earth and the task to have dominion and care over the animals (Gen 1:26, 28). The royal image will extend to the reward of the just when they receive the royal gifts of a "glorious crown" and a "beautiful diadem" (5:16 NRSV). In the second major section of the book of Wisdom, we will soon identify the unnamed speaker as the wise Solomon, pre-eminent in judgment. The reader is being addressed as one who reigns over thoughts and actions, words and deeds. The reader, then, is ultimately one who bears kingly responsibility for both just and unjust actions.

Although the exhortation begins and ends on the positive note of the value of righteousness, sets of opposites dominate the body of the exhortation. There is resistance to righteousness. On one side are righteousness, the Lord, God, wisdom, a holy and disciplined spirit, a kindly spirit, the Spirit of the Lord (vv. 1-7). On the other side are perverse thoughts, a deceitful soul, foolish thoughts, unrighteousness, blasphemers, and death (vv. 3-13). These sets of opposites raise the stakes in the exhortation. They are antagonistic to one another. To love righteousness and to seek the Lord with sincerity imply the burden of overcoming resistance to justice.

In setting up these series of opposites, the Wisdom author is delving into the cherished sapiential doctrine of the two ways (Psalm 1). The way of wisdom and virtue leads to life; the way of foolishness and injustice leads to death. And

17. For an excellent treatment of the various senses of "righteousness" in the OT, see J. J. Scullion, "Righteousness, Old Testament," *Anchor Bible Dictionary*, 6 vols. (New York: Doubleday, 1992) 5:724-36.

18. For a review of the development of the belief in immortality in the intertestamental period, see G. W. E. Nickelsburg, *Resurrection, Immortality and Eternal Life in Intertestamental Judaism*, HTS 26 (Cambridge, Mass.: Harvard University Press, 1972). Nickelsburg treats Wisdom 2 and 5 specifically among other apocalyptic works.

19. *The Wisdom Writing from the Cairo Geniza* 1:1, in Klaus Berger, *Die Weisheitsschrift aus der Kairoer Geniza* (Tübingen: Francke Verlag, 1989).

there is opposition between the two ways. The sets of opposites exclude each other. Both correct and wrong thinking have serious repercussions on one's social life. People with perverse thoughts are separated from God. Wisdom will not enter a deceitful soul. A disciplined spirit flees from deceit and is ashamed at the very approach of unrighteousness (1:2-5). The opposition that is being described between these two ways of justice and injustice sets the scene for a more dramatic confrontation.

Other sapiential biblical works, such as Job and Ecclesiastes, highlight the incongruity between the doctrine of the two ways and life experiences in which the wicked thrive and the just perish. This was an observation as disturbing in ancient times as it remains today. The book of Wisdom confronts this particular incongruity through the lenses of appearance and reality. What appears to be the case in fact is not. What appears not to be the case in fact is. The focus of the author's argument is to look beyond appearances to the heart of the matter.

The anticipation of a confrontation between justice and injustice is heightened as the arena for the sets of opposites subtly shifts to that of a trial. Opposition is now expressed in images borrowed from juridical terminology (1:6-11). The kindly spirit will not free blasphemers from the guilt of their words (v. 6). God is a witness, a true observer. Justice will punish. An inquiry or report will be made. The unjust will be convicted of their lawless deeds. Much of the emphasis in these allusions to forensic procedures focuses on the eventual revelation of what is done in secret. Because God pervades the cosmos as a witness and an observer, nothing will remain hidden (cf. Mark 4:22; Luke 8:17: "For there is nothing hidden, except to be disclosed; nor is anything secret, except to come to light" [NRSV]). This metaphor of the trial is strengthened through images relating to the power of speech: "words," "jealous ear," "sound of grumbling," "tongue," "slander," "lying mouth."

Speech is considered a powerful force. Therefore, to speak untruth is understood to have serious consequences for the speaker. There is a consistency between thought and action that is taken for granted and presumed. Bad thinking leads to destructive actions. The ominous warning against "useless grumbling" and against a "lying mouth which destroys the soul" (v. 11) prepares the reader to view critically the speech of the wicked, which will follow the opening exhortation.

What is at stake in loving justice is nothing short of avoiding death (vv. 12-15). What had begun as a positive exhortation is now being transformed into a warning against bringing on death. To find life through justice demands the explicit rejection of all that leads to death. From now on death and its parallel side, injustice, are seen as prime obstacles to the practice of justice and to the life that ensues.

A rather daring statement is made that radically separates God from death: "God did not make death" (v. 13). On the one hand, the fact that God is said not to "delight in the death of the living" (v. 13) is consistent with the parallel phrases in Ezekiel, "I have no pleasure in the death of the wicked, but that the wicked turn from their ways and live" (Ezek 33:11 NRSV; cf. Ezek 18:23). On the other hand, traditionally, God is understood to be the author of both life and death, the one who makes alive and kills (Deut 32:39; Sir 11:14). The question then arises as to which death is radically opposed to God. Is it mortality in general that God did not make? Is it death as punishment for injustice? Is it the ultimate death that signifies an ultimate separation?

In the opening of the next unit, a direct parallel is made between death and the wicked (v. 16). The ungodly are said to summon death, "they consider him a friend," they "made a covenant with him," "they are fit to belong to his company." This parallel would suggest that the death God did not make is not the death of mortality, which applies to the righteous and to all the living; rather, it is the death of an ultimate judgment that signifies a broken relationship with both God and the cosmos.

Creation itself is being drawn into close parallel with God. God is said to have created all things for good. This close parallel between God and the cosmos prepares the reader for the positive role the cosmos will play in helping the cause of the just in the rest of the book. At the same time, the realm of death is being separated from the realm of creation and the cosmos. All that exists is described as wholesome. There is no destructive poison in creation, and the power of Hades does not reside on earth (v. 14). The death that the author dissuades the reader from bringing on through injustice is not some destructive power that resides somewhat magically in the forces of the cosmos. Rather, the power to bring on such a death resides in the free decision of human beings.

The author may very well be criticizing some contemporary positions among the Hellenists or the native Egyptians that viewed the world in a dualism of forces of good and evil. Such a critique is pointedly aimed at placing the responsibility of injustice squarely on people who make decisions and not on some controlling or deterministic, cosmic power.

The contrast to this death brought about through injustice is the immortality of righteousness (vv. 12-15). Individuals who are free to choose and to reject bear the responsibility for receiving the gift of immortality or for bringing on death. This personal responsibility makes the exhortation to justice so urgent and the need to uncover the masks of injustice so compelling. The effect of the sets of oppositions that have been created in the exhortation is to build up an expectation of resolution.

REFLECTIONS

1. A word in our own contemporary setting that conveys perhaps some of the evocative force that *righteousness* has for biblical faith is *integrity.* A person of integrity is one who adheres to given values even in the face of opposition. In one sense, integrity is tested and known only through opposition. We know whether we adhere to the values of honesty, justice, and respect for others and our world by facing the test of resistance to such values.

The opposition that the Wisdom text envisages between justice and injustice is one that permeates life. It is a part of the human situation and predicament that choices be made for the sake of justice and integrity. Failing to make such choices, human beings collapse into the structures of silence, passivity, and injustice, which ultimately lead to death. Not to speak out against injustice is to succumb to its lure. Much of the drama of human greatness and tragedy devolves on the choices human beings make.

2. It is tempting to shirk responsibility in the face of overwhelming social, environmental, and structural problems. What can one person do in the face of massive injustice? What can one person do in the face of years of environmental abuse? But the voice of one person does matter. The Wisdom text refuses to displace the responsibility for injustice onto foreign cosmic powers or onto an inherent determinism. By the "error of our lives" and by the "works of our hands" we invite death into our world (1:12). Responsibility for greatness and for tragedy ultimately resides in the concrete choices of human beings. We do need to take sides in the polarity of justice and injustice.

3. The author presents a profound basis for optimism in the human struggle against injustice. A rather unique emphasis in the book of Wisdom is placed on the "wholesomeness" of the cosmos (1:14). We have here in the forces of nature an ally in the struggle for authenticity and for maintaining integrity.

This positive view of the cosmos is evidently the author's interpretation of the Priestly account of creation, "God saw everything that he had made, and indeed, it was very good" (Gen 1:31 NRSV). The idea that the cosmos is an ally to the cause of justice is introduced in the opening exhortation, and it will recur with added force throughout the entire book. The basis for this positive outlook lies in God, the creator. Since God is the creator of all things, the existence of all things ultimately is wholesome. Injustice, though it pervades human existence, essentially remains foreign to human life. As an intruder, it dismantles what is essentially wholesome and good.

WISDOM 1:16–2:24, THE REASONING OF THE UNJUST

NAB

16 It was the wicked who with hands and words invited death,
    considered it a friend, and pined for it,
    and made a covenant with it,
    Because they deserve to be in its possession,

2   they who said among themselves, thinking not aright:
    "Brief and troublous is our lifetime;
    neither is there any remedy for man's dying,
    nor is anyone known to have come back from the nether world.
2 For haphazard were we born,
    and hereafter we shall be as though we had not been;
    Because the breath in our nostrils is a smoke
    and reason is a spark at the beating of our hearts,
3 And when this is quenched, our body will be ashes
    and our spirit will be poured abroad like unresisting air,
4 Even our name will be forgotten in time,
    and no one will recall our deeds.
    So our life will pass away like the traces of a cloud,
    and will be dispersed like a mist
    pursued by the sun's rays
    and overpowered by its heat.
5 For our lifetime is the passing of a shadow;
    and our dying cannot be deferred
    because it is fixed with a seal; and no one returns.
6 Come, therefore, let us enjoy the good things that are real,
    and use the freshness of creation avidly.
7 Let us have our fill of costly wine and perfumes,
    and let no springtime blossom pass us by;
8 let us crown ourselves with rosebuds ere they wither.

2, 5: (ho) kairos (hēmōn): so LXX^MSS.
2, 7: earos: so LXX^A.

NRSV

16 But the ungodly by their words and deeds summoned death;[a]
    considering him a friend, they pined away
    and made a covenant with him,
    because they are fit to belong to his company.

2   For they reasoned unsoundly, saying to themselves,
    "Short and sorrowful is our life,
    and there is no remedy when a life comes to its end,
    and no one has been known to return from Hades.
2 For we were born by mere chance,
    and hereafter we shall be as though we had never been,
    for the breath in our nostrils is smoke,
    and reason is a spark kindled by the beating of our hearts;
3 when it is extinguished, the body will turn to ashes,
    and the spirit will dissolve like empty air.
4 Our name will be forgotten in time,
    and no one will remember our works;
    our life will pass away like the traces of a cloud,
    and be scattered like mist
    that is chased by the rays of the sun
    and overcome by its heat.
5 For our allotted time is the passing of a shadow,
    and there is no return from our death,
    because it is sealed up and no one turns back.

6 "Come, therefore, let us enjoy the good things that exist,
    and make use of the creation to the full as in youth.
7 Let us take our fill of costly wine and perfumes,
    and let no flower of spring pass us by.
8 Let us crown ourselves with rosebuds before they wither.
9 Let none of us fail to share in our revelry;

a Gk him

NAB

9 Let no meadow be free from our
   wantonness;
      everywhere let us leave tokens of our
      rejoicing,
      for this our portion is, and this our lot.
10 Let us oppress the needy just man;
      let us neither spare the widow
      nor revere the old man for his hair grown
      white with time.
11 But let our strength be our norm of justice;
      for weakness proves itself useless.
12 Let us beset the just one, because he is
      obnoxious to us;
      he sets himself against our doings,
      Reproaches us for transgressions of the law
      and charges us with violations of our training.
13 He professes to have knowledge of God
      and styles himself a child of the Lord.
14 To us he is the censure of our thoughts;
      merely to see him is a hardship for us,
15 Because his life is not like other men's,
      and different are his ways.
16 He judges us debased;
      he holds aloof from our paths as from
      things impure.
   He calls blest the destiny of the just
      and boasts that God is his Father.
17 Let us see whether his words be true;
      let us find out what will happen to him.
18 For if the just one be the son of God, he will
      defend him
      and deliver him from the hand of his foes.
19 With revilement and torture let us put him
      to the test
      that we may have proof of his gentleness
      and try his patience.
20 Let us condemn him to a shameful death;
      for according to his own words, God will
      take care of him."
21 These were their thoughts, but they erred;
      for their wickedness blinded them,
22 And they knew not the hidden counsels of God;
      neither did they count on a recompense of
      holiness
      nor discern the innocent souls' reward.

2, 9: (*mēdeis*) *leimōn*: cf V *pratum.*
2, 12: Omit *de*: so LXX[MSS].
2, 19: *dokimasōmen*: so LXX[MSS].
2, 22: (*mystēria*) *theou*: so LXX[MSS].

NRSV

   everywhere let us leave signs of enjoyment,
   because this is our portion, and this our lot.
10 Let us oppress the righteous poor man;
   let us not spare the widow
   or regard the gray hairs of the aged.
11 But let our might be our law of right,
   for what is weak proves itself to be useless.

12 "Let us lie in wait for the righteous man,
   because he is inconvenient to us and opposes
      our actions;
   he reproaches us for sins against the law,
   and accuses us of sins against our training.
13 He professes to have knowledge of God,
   and calls himself a child[a] of the Lord.
14 He became to us a reproof of our thoughts;
15 the very sight of him is a burden to us,
   because his manner of life is unlike that of
      others,
   and his ways are strange.
16 We are considered by him as something base,
   and he avoids our ways as unclean;
   he calls the last end of the righteous happy,
   and boasts that God is his father.
17 Let us see if his words are true,
   and let us test what will happen at the end of
      his life;
18 for if the righteous man is God's child, he will
      help him,
   and will deliver him from the hand of his
      adversaries.
19 Let us test him with insult and torture,
   so that we may find out how gentle he is,
   and make trial of his forbearance.
20 Let us condemn him to a shameful death,
   for, according to what he says, he will be
      protected."

21 Thus they reasoned, but they were led astray,
   for their wickedness blinded them,
22 and they did not know the secret purposes of
      God,
   nor hoped for the wages of holiness,
   nor discerned the prize for blameless souls;
23 for God created us for incorruption,
   and made us in the image of his own eternity,[b]

[a] Or *servant*   [b] Other ancient authorities read *nature*

NAB	NRSV
23 For God formed man to be imperishable; 　　the image of his own nature he made him. 24 But by the envy of the devil, death entered 　　the world, 　　and they who are in his possession 　　experience it.	[24] but through the devil's envy death entered the 　　world, 　　and those who belong to his company 　　experience it.

COMMENTARY

1:16, Introduction to the Speech of the Wicked. The author introduces the speech of the wicked with an explanation as to the way they bring ultimate death upon themselves. Through their words and deeds, which flow from unsound reasoning, the wicked beckon the stark, negative reality of death. Personalistic language is employed to highlight the personal responsibility they bear for inviting death. They summon death through their words and actions; they consider death a friend; they pine away in longing for death; they even make a covenant with death, for they belong to death's company. This last image encloses the entire unit of 1:16–2:24. In both the opening and the closing of the unit, the wicked are said to belong to the company of death (1:16*d*; 2:24).

The idea of making a covenant with death highlights the deliberate and responsible choice implied in achieving an alliance. This death has not sought out the wicked; rather, through their thoughts and actions they have sought out death. The phrase is reminiscent of that in Isa 28:15: "We have made a covenant with death, and with Sheol we have an agreement" (NRSV). Here Isaiah is criticizing the ruling classes during Hezekiah's reign (716–686 BCE) for placing their trust in an alliance with Egypt, famous for its respect for the dead.

The inner reflection of the wicked constitutes their defense for a project in a life of injustice. The author has the wicked speak for themselves, and this they do with an elegance and poetic flare that belie the nihilism and violence that seethe underneath.

The defense has four major parts: (1) the wicked's reflection on the ephemeral value of life

that portrays their nihilistic judgment (2:1-5), (2) a despairing exhortation to pleasure (2:6-9), (3) an exhortation to power (2:10-11), and (4) an exhortation to oppose the righteous one (2:12-20).

2:1-5, The Ephemeral Value of Life. This reflection on the fleeting value of human life is portrayed in uncommonly rich, poetic imagery. It will be matched in the wicked's confession of guilt with a parallel reflection using similar imagery to depict their lack of moral virtue (5:9-14). Much of the imagery echoes the depiction of human sorrow and limitations that can be found in other sapiential works, such as Job and Ecclesiastes. The books of Psalms and Prophets also provide parallels for the imagery used in this reflection. Still, a number of images and concepts throughout this section depicting the reasoning of the wicked can be seen to have been borrowed from Hellenistic thought.[20]

The very first line states the wicked person's negative judgment on life. It is short and sorrowful. Job, in his laments, utters similar phrases that touch upon the fragility and evanescence of life: "Are not the days of my life few?" (Job 10:20 NRSV); "A mortal, born of woman, few of days and full of trouble, comes up like a flower and withers" (Job 14:1-2 NRSV).

All the images used in this unit illustrate the irrevocability of death without the word "death" ever passing through the lips of the wicked. Instead of the usual word for "death," they use metaphors to portray what they judge to be the destroyer of human value ("end," vv. 1, 5; "Ha-

---

20. There are several excellent works that study the sources used for the speech of the wicked. See David Winston, *The Wisdom of Solomon,* AB 43 (New York: Doubleday, 1979) 113-23; M. Kolarcik, *The Ambiguity of Death in the Book of Wisdom (1–6),* AnBib 127 (Rome: Pontifical Biblical Institute, 1991) 114-23.

des," v. 1; "we shall be as though we had never been," v. 2; "extinguish," "dissolve," v. 3; "pass away," "scattered," v. 4). It is as if the unspeakable reality of death cannot be named.[21]

The wicked insist upon the irreversibility of death. There is no remedy for it. No one has been known to free us from Hades. There is no return from our fate; it is sealed, and no one turns back. Just as our fate and end are judged to be insignificant and pointless, so too is our beginning. We have come into being by mere chance. In order to portray as vividly as possible the evanescence of life, the wicked compare aspects and elements of the body—such as breath, the heartbeat, reason, the soul—to smoke, mist, a spark, and air. All of these are described as vanishing or dissolving without a trace.

Again, these statements echo similar biblical descriptions of the fragility of life. Qohelet's speeches abound with such ruminations: "No one has . . . power over the day of death" (Eccl 8:8 NRSV); "in the days to come all will have been long forgotten" (Eccl 2:16 NRSV); "For who knows what is good for mortals while they live the few days of their vain life, which they pass like a shadow?" (Eccl 6:12 NRSV). The psalms, especially the laments, also share similar sentiments: "For my days pass away like smoke, and my bones burn like a furnace" (Ps 102:3 NRSV); "For the ransom of life is costly, and can never suffice that one should live on forever and never see the grave" (Ps 49:8-9 NRSV).

Several images in this unit have no biblical parallels but can be related to contemporary currents in Greek philosophical thought and literature. The Wisdom author has the wicked use these images to depict their denial of an afterlife, which abrogates the context for ethical conduct. The idea of coming into being by mere chance (v. 2) was a common explanation for the origin of the cosmos and all life in late Epicurean thought and was found as well in preceding authors, such as Leucippus and Democritus.

The idea that human thought is but a spark in the beating of our heart (v. 2d) is a unique formulation of the Wisdom author. In the ancient

world, both Greek and Hebrew, it was common to locate the reasoning processes with the heart ("there were great searchings of heart" [Judg 5:15 NRSV]). In Epicurean and Stoic thought, the association of the soul with fire was meant to express the superiority of reasoning to matter. But the Wisdom author uses the image of reason's being but a spark in the heart to show its transitoriness and perhaps even its insignificance. When the spark is extinguished, every function ceases. The body turns to ashes, and the soul dissolves like empty air.

Since much of the imagery employed in this unit has concrete parallels to other biblical sources, we can legitimately ask, Where is the difficulty or fallacy in reasoning? The author has alerted the reader at the outset that the wicked reason unsoundly. The difficulty in their logic does not rest in the assertion of the inevitability of mortality, but in the negative judgment of purposelessness that they ascribe to it.

Here is the crux of the erroneous reasoning of the wicked. They claim that we have come into the world by mere chance and afterward we will be as though we had never been. The wicked espouse a purely mechanistic concept of life. They deny any form of life beyond mortality and any form of divine intervention at death. Just as no divine being gives purpose to life at the beginning, so also there is no divine reality that awaits humans at the end. Perhaps it is for this denial of divine relevance that the wicked are introduced as the "ungodly" (ἀσεβής asebēs, 1:16); this designation for the wicked will continue throughout the author's rebuttal (3:10; 4:3, 16). Essentially what the wicked's rumination on life expresses, couched as it is in poetic imagery, is that human life in the face of death is void of meaning. The wicked's preoccupation with physical death issues in a judgment that portrays despair and hopelessness.

The author chooses to have the wicked speak in eloquent language for a reason. By presenting the wicked's judgment on life in expressive and poignant imagery, the author is holding up for careful scrutiny what could be construed as a tenable and convincing philosophy of life. Of course, since the wicked speak in their own defense, we would expect their positions on life to be presented in as positive a light as possible.

---

21. In v. 2:5b, "there is no return from our death," the NRSV is translating the Greek word for "end" (τελευτή teleutē) as "death." The word teleutē actually functions as the image that encloses this entire unit of 2:1-5. It stands parallel to the statement "there is no remedy when a life comes to its end" (2:1).

The background image of the trial warns the reader to look below the surface, to sift through appearances to understand the heart of the matter. If the wicked's judgment on life is described in poetic language that only masks their negative judgment, in the end it will be revealed for what it is: unrelenting despair.

2:6-9, A Despairing Exhortation to Pleasure. The negative judgment on life provides the wicked with a philosophical basis for their project in life. They exhort each other to enjoy life's apparently innocent pleasures. The series of subjunctives through which they exhort one another serves as a counterpoint to the author's imperatives that inaugurate the opening exhortation to love righteousness and to seek the Lord. Poetic imagery carries over from the previous unit.

Although the exhortation of the wicked appears positive enough, it soon takes on frenetic proportions that belie the appearance of healthy pleasure. The wicked call for the enjoyment of the good things that exist, and they encourage each other to make use of creation as they did in youth. Luxurious items are the order of the day: costly wines, perfumes, and rosebuds (vv. 7-8). A crown of rosebuds is to be worn before they fade and wither. The memory of the evanescence of life in reference to the fading rosebuds carries over from the negative judgment of life. An exaggerated call to revelry betrays signs of strain and despair, almost as if the wicked need to suffocate the cries of despair with frenzied activity. Everyone should take part in revelry and leave signs of diversion everywhere (v. 9). What began as a call to innocent pleasures appears to be heading toward a sinister end.

The conclusion of the wicked's exhortation to pleasure boasts in such revelry to be their due "portion and lot in life" (v. 9c). The phrase parallels the author's critique of the speech of the wicked both at the beginning ("they belong to his *company,*" 1:16d) and at the end ("those who belong to his *company,*" 2:24b). In both cases, when the wicked are said to belong to death, the same Greek word for "portion" or "company" (μερίς *meris*) is employed. By making evasive pleasure that leads to a grasping for power through violence their project in life, the wicked unwittingly bring upon themselves the very realities they so despise: weakness and death.

Two main proponents have been proposed as the target of the Wisdom author's criticism in this section: Qohelet and the Epicureans. On the one hand, the exhortation to enjoy life does have certain parallels to that of Qohelet (Ecclesiastes), but they are quite minimal. Qohelet on numerous occasions calls for the enjoyment of life: "There is nothing better for mortals than to eat and drink, and find enjoyment in their toil. This also, I saw, is from the hand of God" (Eccl 2:24 NRSV; cf. Eccl 3:13; 5:18; 8:15; 9:7-9; 11:9). In each case where Qohelet exhorts the reader to enjoy life, God's presence is assured. Either pleasure is seen as God's gift or God is understood as one who sets a limit and calls excess into judgment (Eccl 11:9). Since the very presence or relevance of God is denied rather forcibly by the wicked in Wisdom, only with a strained effort could one construe the Wisdom speech as a critique of the preacher in Ecclesiastes.

On the other hand, the call to enjoy life is so diffused in the literature of the ancient world that it is difficult to pinpoint a single source for the Wisdom author. It was a favorite motto for funerary inscriptions. On a tomb inscription from the XIth Dynasty in Egypt we read, "Follow your heart as long as you live. Sprinkle perfumes on your head; clothe yourself in fine linen, anoint yourself with the most marvelous of essences" (author's trans.).

The exhortation to pleasure became closely identified with Epicurus, who gave enjoyment noble stature as the end to be sought in life. But when Epicurus postulates pleasure as the goal to strive for, he does not identify pleasure with a dissipated life, but understands pleasure to be the result of sober reasoning. Even the garden gatherings associated with followers of Epicurus were renowned for their simplicity and frugality.[22]

Other disciples of Epicurus promoted the famous "discussion-dinner party," whose attendees perhaps on occasion fell into excesses of drinking special wines and eating lavish foods. Marc Anthony and Cleopatra adopted the customs of the symposium in Alexandria. It became customary on such occasions to spice the best of wines with fragrances and for attendees to adorn themselves in flowers. Lucian criticizes the waste associated

---

22. Diogenes Laertius 10-11.

with such gatherings. His description contains resemblances to the Wisdom author's portrayal of the wicked people's exhortation to pleasure. "It is they," said he, "who buy expensive dainties and let wine flow freely at dinners in an atmosphere of saffron and perfumes, who glut themselves with roses in midwinter, loving their rarity and unseasonableness and despising what is seasonable and natural because of its cheapness, it is they who drink myrrh."[23]

It would appear that the author is culling ideas from various representatives of hedonism of his day to portray the dynamic of false reasoning. Although some of the Epicurean ideas, such as the finality of death, the denial of divine presence, and the legitimacy of pleasure, have been used to portray the hedonism of the wicked, it is not possible to single out a specific group as the target of the Wisdom author's criticism.[24] It is the reasoning process of the wicked that is being criticized rather than a philosophical group or political faction contemporaneous to the author.

2:10-11, An Exhortation to Power. A sudden and menacing turn of events has the wicked extolling the oppression of the poor, widows, and the elderly. The call for oppression finally betrays the appearance of innocent pleasures that followed from the judgment on the ephemeral value of life. The sinister reality of despair that was masked in poetic imagery is raising its head. The call to oppress the weak in society stands in clear contradiction to the law, which protects the weaker members of Israelite society.

This combination of the poor, the widow, and the elderly to designate the weak and the helpless in society is unique in the OT. To be sure, all three groups, along with the sojourner and the orphan, were especially protected under Israelite law (for sojourners, orphans, and widows, see Deut 14:29; for the poor, see Exod 23:6; for the respect of the elderly, see Lev 19:32).

The combination of the poor and the widow occurs more often with the orphan or the sojourner to designate the weak person who stands under special protection (Job 24:3-4; 29:12-13; 31:16-18; Isa 10:2; Jer 7:6; Zech 7:10). The triad

of the poor, the widow, and the orphan has the closest parallel to the Wisdom designation of the poor, the widow, and the elderly. Why the Wisdom author has replaced the more usual designation of the orphan with the aged will become clear in the ensuing argumentation. But the wicked persons' adulation of youthful strength (v. 6) anticipates this derogatory view of old age. In other biblical references, the aged are represented as being vulnerable and in need of protection in various associations with orphans, widows, and the needy (2 Chr 36:17; Jer 6:11; 2 Macc 8:30).

The wicked justify the arbitrary oppression of the weak with a double-sided principle: Power makes right; weakness is useless (v. 11). This idea of power and strength making right is as old as the stars and has found justification in many circles throughout history. The nihilistic judgment of the wicked that the value of life is ephemeral lends its support to the principle that might makes right. On the one hand, if there is no divine reality that gives purpose to human origins or human destination, then the basis for ethical conduct devolves on arbitrary power. On the other hand, if life's value is radically depressed by the limitations of space and time, then any manifestation of mortality in weakness, sickness, and death should be curtailed and held in derision. What surfaces unmistakably is that the victorious tone of the wicked only serves to mask an abysmal despair in the value of human life.

2:12-20, An Exhortation to Oppose the Righteous One. The reasoning of the wicked takes on a life of its own and focuses with a frightening consistency on the righteous, who oppose their way of life. If might makes right and what is weak is useless, then whoever opposes the wicked will be subject to the weapons of their wrath. What had begun as an exhortation to seemingly innocent pleasure (vv. 6-9) ends in calling for an unambiguous act of injustice, the brutal death of the just (vv. 17-20).

For the first time, the image of the just one comes onto the scene. In tension with the wicked and the godless, the just will occupy center stage for the rest of the first section of Wisdom. The idea of the wicked "ambushing" the just or "lying in wait" (ἐνεδρεύω *enedreuō*) for the righteous is a familiar description of the wicked in the

---

23. Lucian *Nigrinus* 31.
24. D. Winston summarizes well the various arguments for not postulating a single group as the target of the Wisdom author's criticism. See Winston, *The Wisdom of Solomon,* 114.

psalms, particularly the psalms of lament. In Ps 10:8-11 the wicked are presented as a lion lying in wait for the helpless and to seize the poor (cf. Pss 17:8-12; 37:12; 59:3-4; 64:2-6).[25] The wicked are always many. The just stand alone.

The opening motive for the wicked's oppression of the just one is the opposition directed against them (v. 12). It is the just who are inconvenient in that they oppose the actions of the wicked; they reproach them for sins against the law and accuse them of sins against their training. This motif of antagonism between the just and the wicked echoes the radical separation between God and justice in the opening exhortation. It confirms the standard of the "two ways" in that the just are encouraged to separate themselves from the ways of the wicked (see Pss 1:1; 6:4-5; 38:20; 139:21-22).

The second series of motives for oppressing the just focuses on the claims of the just, which contradict the wicked's judgment on life and death (2:13-16). The just claim to have knowledge of God. They are children of God; their end will be happy; and they boast that God is their father. These claims are interpreted by the wicked with disdain as opposing their way of life. Hence, the just one is considered to be reproof of their thoughts, a burden for them simply to behold.

Two of the claims of the just that fundamentally contradict the nihilistic judgment of the wicked are the fatherhood of God (v. 16) and the sonship of the just (vv. 13, 18). Moreover, the particular aspect of this filial and paternal relationship that the wicked question in their counteraccusation is the just's *trust* in God.

All three themes of God's fatherhood, the sonship of the just, and their trust in God have their root in the psalms of lament. The fundamental stance of the one who laments is to trust in God despite all odds: "But I trusted in your steadfast love; my heart shall rejoice in your salvation" (Ps 13:5 NRSV); "I believe I shall see the goodness of the LORD in the land of the living" (Ps 27:13 NRSV).

Just as the wicked in Wisdom accuse the just of unfounded trust in God (vv. 17-20), so also the wicked in the psalms of lament deride the just for their trust in God. "Many are saying to me, / 'There is no help for you in God' " (Ps 3:2 NRSV). "Commit your cause to the LORD; let him deliver—let him rescue the one in whom he delights!" (Ps 22:8 NRSV). "They say, 'Pursue and seize that person whom God has forsaken, for there is no one to deliver' " (Ps 71:11 NRSV).

The fatherhood of God is an image that has its sources in the devout and religious prayer of the psalms and in the messianic texts in which the king/messiah is the adopted son of God. To describe God's loving care for the weak, the psalms speak of God as a caring father: "Father of orphans and protector of widows is God in his holy habitation" (Ps 68:5 NRSV). "As a father has compassion for his children, so the LORD has compassion for those who fear him" (Ps 103:13 NRSV; cf. Deut 1:30-31; 8:5; 32:6; Isa 63:16; 64:8; Jer 3:19; Mal 1:6).

The theme of adoption that marked Israel's relationship to God in monarchic theology stresses the fatherhood of God. "He said to me, 'You are my son; / today I have begotten you' " (Ps 2:7 NRSV). "He shall cry to me, 'You are my Father, my God, and the Rock of my salvation' " (Ps 89:26 NRSV; cf. 2 Sam 7:14).

Various formulations for the phrase "son of God" (v. 18) are attested throughout Scripture with differing nuances (a holy people, Deut 14:1-2; restoration of Israel, Hos 2:10-11; vocation, Hos 11:1). Still, one particular prophetic source can be identified in the author's formulation of the opposition between the wicked and the just: the suffering servant of Isaiah, especially the fourth servant song (Isa 52:13–53:12).[26] In Wis 2:13, the wicked recall the just's claim to be children of God. The Greek word for "child" (παῖς *pais*) can also mean "servant"; in fact, the LXX translates the Hebrew word for "servant" (עבד *'ebed*) in Isaiah alternately as "child" (*pais*) and as "servant" (δοῦλος *doulos*). The term is meant to express a special relationship between the Lord and the servant. It is precisely this special relationship of the just to God that the wicked hold

---

25. Wis 2:12a is almost identical to a sentence added in the LXX version of Isa 3:10, "Let us kill the righteous man because he is inconvenient to us." But it is more likely that the Wisdom text influenced the Greek writing of Isaiah, rather than Isaiah's being the source for Wisdom in this instance.

26. The Wisdom author's use of texts from Isaiah is virtually certain. In fact, an entire series of images from Isaiah 42–56 are borrowed for the author's arguments in Wisdom 2–5. See Patrick W. Skehan, "Isaiah and the Teaching of the Book of Wisdom," *CBQ* 2 (1940) 289-99; M. J. Suggs, "Wisdom of Solomon II, 10-V: A Homily Based on the Fourth Servant Song," *JBL* 76 (1957) 26-33.

in derision. Just as the servant suffers a shameful death and is despised by others (Isa 53:3, 7), so also the wicked propose to inflict a shameful death on the just. A major difference between the persecution of the just in Wisdom and the servant in Isaiah is the vicarious suffering of the servant. For the obvious reason of the developed antagonism between the just and the wicked in Wisdom, the theme of the vicarious suffering of the servant in Isaiah was dropped.

The final part of the wicked's speech constitutes their counteraccusation against the just (vv. 17-20). They decide to put the just one through the trial of an ignoble death to test whether his claims are true. Of course, the test is a rhetorical one. The wicked inflict on the just the experience of mortality, which they have judged to be the destroyer of human value. Since the just stand for a way of life with ethical parameters that contradicts their project in life, the wicked inflict on others the very conditions of mortality that led them to their nihilistic judgment on life.

Taken as a whole, the speech of the wicked contains a logic that involves a progressive dynamic of evil. The negative judgment on mortality, expressed through poetic imagery, provides a basis for an amoral perspective on life. The commitment to transient, youthful pleasure simply masks the underlying despair that is dimmed or softened through the clamor of busy activity. The other side of the adulation of youthful pleasure is the despising of human weakness and the reliance on power. The sinister side of the nihilistic judgment on life emerges with frightening clarity, until the blatant and brutal project to kill the just reaches the climax. What had begun as a poetic rumination on mortality ends with a frightful project to inflict a shameful death on the just. The wicked's speech progresses from a nihilistic judgment on life to a project in life that embraces sensuality, that in its turn despises weakness and relies on power, and that finally, when challenged, unmasks itself as an unbridled license to brutal violence.

Since the speech of the wicked provides an explanation and defense of their way of life, it also constitutes the author's attack against a project of injustice, which brings death. The wicked are being accused of a false judgment on human life, of a pointless sensuality, of a ruthless reliance

on power, and of a blatant and brutal act of violence. Their principal line of defense rests in the claim that death renders life meaningless. Therefore, the author will have to explain the shameful death of the just in order to prove effectively that the reasoning process of the wicked is false. The wicked's call for the death of the just as proof of the validity of their life of despair is the climax of their speech. In the context of the trial scene, it raises an expectation of resolution for the reader.

2:21-24, Conclusion to the Speech of the Wicked. The author reiterates the falseness of the wicked's reasoning (cf. 2:1). In both the introduction and the conclusion, the author stresses that through their injustice the wicked bring death upon themselves. The author introduces an etiology for both immortality and death to prepare for the dismantling of the false reasoning of the wicked.

However, a new basis for their false thinking is added. Their evil ways have blinded them (v. 21). Their blindness has caused the wicked to overlook three essential realities: the secret purposes of God, the wages of holiness, and the prize for blameless souls. In other words, their wickedness has brought about a blindness to a fundamental truth. This metaphor of blindness prepares the reader for the author's rebuttal, which will depend heavily on sifting through appearances and reality.

The fundamental reality the wicked overlook is the destiny for which God created human beings: incorruption (v. 23). This declaration contradicts the wicked's claim that human beings have come to exist arbitrarily and that after death it will be as though they had never been. To sustain the bold claim for immortality, the author appeals to the powerful "image of God" in the Genesis narrative (Gen 1:26-27; 5:1). God has created human beings for immortality because we are made in the image of God's identity or eternity (v. 23b).[27]

If the origin of human immortality is based on

---

27. With a change of a single letter, different versions offer a word that means either God's "identity" (ἰδιότης *idiotēs*) or God's "eternity" (ἀιδιότης *aidiotēs*). The idea of eternity draws out more explicitly the author's claim that life does not end with physical death. For an excellent review of the import of the image of God in the history of interpretation, see Gunnlaugur A. Jonsson, *The Image of God: Gen 1:26-28 in a Century of Old Testament Research*, ConBOT 26 (Stockholm: Almqvist & Wiksell International, 1988).

the image of God, then where does death origi-nate? The author has already declared that God did not make death (1:13). Human beings bring on death through their own words and actions. Since the human destiny of immortality is rooted in creation itself, the author appeals to the Genesis narrative to give an etiology for death as well. Through the envy of the adversary, death has entered the cosmos (2:24).[28] The adversary,[29] like the serpent in Genesis 3 or the satan in Job, is opposed to the liberal act of God's generosity to human beings. It is the adversary who occasions the human option for wickedness, and those who belong to the adversary experience death (2:24b).

The author presents a nuanced idea of immor-tality. Human beings are not created immortal; they are created *for* immortality. In other words, human beings, who are created in the image of God, form or shape the original image into God's identity of immortality through their ethical con-duct. With a life of injustice, the initial figure of God can be deformed into death, which God did not create. The death that is presumed here signifies a total separation from God and the cosmos, not the experience of mortality that all human beings, even the virtuous, experience.

Sirach relates the image of God to human mortality in a similar fashion to that of Wisdom. It does not, however, draw out the ethical impli-cations for life and death: "The Lord created human beings out of earth, and makes them return to it again . . . He endowed them with strength like his own, and made them in his own image" (Sir 17:1-3 NRSV).

In terms of the trial image that has been subtly working in the background, the speech of the wicked constitutes the defense of their purpose in life, which in its turn ends in the counteraccusa-tion of the incoherence of the just's purpose in life. For the wicked, the rhetorical test of death is proof enough of the validity of their entire reasoning process. To disprove the false reasoning of the wicked, the author must resolve the issue of the tragic death of the righteous.

If the death of the just is resolved, then the entire reasoning process of the wicked, beginning with the end, falls apart. If the death of the just is not a tragic manifestation of meaninglessness, then the limitations of human mortality do not render human life worthless and empty. If human life is not worthless, then the experience of youth-ful pleasures is not merely an evasion of underly-ing despair. If the experience of youthful pleasure is not meant to smother despair, then power over the weak, who remind us of mortality, does not make any right. The original nihilistic judgment on the vacuity of human mortality, which is the basis for the wicked's project of injustice, will be proved false.

---

28. Several legends that recount the creation and fall narratives in haggadic fashion actually ascribe envy to the devil (*Enoch, Apocalypse of Moses, Life of Adam and Eve*): "And the devil sighed and said, 'O Adam, all my enmity and envy and sorrow concern you, since because of you I am expelled and deprived of my glory which I had in the heavens in the midst of angels, and because of you I was cast out onto the earth' " (*Life of Adam and Eve*, 12:1). It is probable that the Wisdom author was familiar with one or more of these stories. Paul used a similar phrase in which death is replaced by sin: "Therefore, just as sin came into the world through one man, and death came through sin, and so death spread to all because all have sinned" (Rom 5:12 NRSV).

29. The original meaning of the Greek word διάβολος (*diabolos*), from which the English word "devil" derives, is "accuser" or "slanderer." This is the usual manner in which the LXX translates the Hebrew word for "the satan," "the adversary" (הַשָּׂטָן *haśśāṭān*; Job 1:6; 2:1).

REFLECTIONS

1. In the speech of the wicked, the author provides us with a rather profound understanding of the psychology involved in the dynamic of injustice. Self-justification for blatant violence does not rest on mere rationalization but has its source in a fundamental judgment on the value we place on life. The nihilistic stance of the wicked flows from despair. Like a chain reaction, their despair elicits a form of escapism from the manifestations of human limitations. At first, in this form of escapism they turn to evasive sensuality. In the case of the wicked, the adulation of youthful pleasure serves only to mask and to deny the underlying despair. The victorious tone in their voice is more like a clamoring noise that tries to fill a deafening silence. It is as if their ensuing project in life is simply to blunt and mask the reality of human limitations and suffering.

Another form of escapism opposes manifestations of mortality. The call of the wicked to exercise power over others, especially over the weak, who remind them of the "uselessness" of a life stamped with mortality, is only a brief and tenuous denial of the "weakness" that awaits everyone in the face of mortality.

Finally the blatant expression of injustice over one who opposes them reveals the full consequence of the wicked's original judgment on mortality. In their call to kill the just, the wicked only affirm their nihilistic despair and inflict it on others.

There are serious consequences in our lives that flow from the fundamental value we attribute to life. The dynamic of injustice in the wicked's project shows how difficult it is to isolate one decision from another.

A concrete example of a similar dynamic of injustice can be gleaned from the story of David and Bathsheba (2 Samuel 11–12). One decision on the part of David leads to another. What appears relatively trivial at the beginning is revealed to be quite hideous at the end. The conclusion of the dynamic is a blatant and unjust killing of an innocent person. But whereas the Wisdom author stresses the initial nihilistic judgment as the source for the spiral of violence, the story of David and Bathsheba concentrates on the final outcome of the dynamic of evil.

2. The author chooses to portray the wicked's nihilistic judgment on life through poetic imagery. There is a tremendous difference between the reflection on the ephemeral value of life by the wicked in Wisdom and the reflections on human limitations and suffering in the books of Job and Ecclesiastes. The reflection of the wicked issues in despair; that of Job and Qohelet issues in hope. What is constant in both is that the experience of human limitations and suffering elicits an important and fundamental human response. On the one hand, the experience of sickness, failure, loss, and death can elicit a destructive despair as it does in the case of the wicked; on the other hand, it can elicit a response of sustaining hope, as it does in the case of the just. Suffering is not neutral. In the end, our response, whether it be the silence of despair or the serenity of respect, will be revealed in our actions.

3. Human dignity resides in our relationship to the divine. The author of Wisdom sustains the value of human dignity in the face of the wicked's deadening ruminations on mortality. This value is maintained by the affirmation of a relationship with a transcendent being. The ungodly deny a divine presence both in our origins and in our finality. From that denial issues the wicked's despair and judgment on life, which in turn elicits the final turn to violence.

Both prior to the speech of the wicked (1:12-15) and afterward (2:22-23) the author affirms the dignity of the universe itself and the dignity of human beings in their relationship to the divine creative act. All the generative forces of the world are wholesome. Human beings were created for incorruption and were made in the image of God.

The denial of divine relevance opens the problematic and enduring issue of power constituting right. If there is no God, why do power and might not constitute the only right? We have not substantially advanced the arguments presented in Wisdom over the years. In the face of arbitrary and relative laws based on power, the dignity of human beings becomes arbitrary and relative.

I recall the arguments of Alexander Solzhenitsyn and Vadim Borisov in their analyses of the regime of power in the Soviet Union. If the concept of the human personality is deprived of divine authority, then the personality can be defined conditionally and inevitably arbitrarily. If the personality is not absolute but conditional, then respect for humans is something one can disregard or claim at whim.[30] Of course, various agnostic or humanistic philosophies still try to maintain an ethic that does not reduce the human being to arbitrary power. But to do so they still appeal to a larger framework, such as society, the community of humanity, or the universe, for the basis of their ethic.

---

30. See Vadim Borisov, "Personality and National Awareness," in *From Under the Rubble,* ed. Alexander Solzhenitsyn (Toronto: Little, Brown, 1975) 200.

WISDOM 3:1–4:20, IN DEFENSE OF VIRTUE AND JUSTICE

OVERVIEW

In the conclusion of the wicked's defense, the righteous one is accused of incoherence. The wicked's proof for such incoherence is the projected death of the righteous. This tragic death is meant to belie the claim of the just that their end is full of hope. In this way, the entire reasoning process of the wicked and their life project of exploiting creation, oppressing the weak, and doing violence against the just depends on the interpretation of the tragic death of the just. The author must disprove this interpretation for the entire argument of the wicked to collapse. The author examines the evidence by sifting through the appearance of tragedy in the lives of the just and the appearance of strength in the case of the wicked.

In three diptychs, the author examines the way of virtue in the case of the just, who suffer, and the way of the wicked, who appear to thrive over the just. Each diptych begins with a picture of the just, who appear to have suffered, and then turns to the other side to examine the picture of the wicked, who appear to have thrived. The examination constitutes the author's defense of the virtuous life and an attack against a project of life that consists of injustice.

Each diptych picks up the themes within the speech of the wicked in exactly the reverse order in which they appear. The shameful and tragic death of the just is picked up in the very first diptych (3:1-12), which declares the life of the virtuous to be in the hand of God. The call to oppress the poor man and the widow and the aged is treated in the second diptych (3:13–4:6), which deals with the barren woman, the eunuch, and the virtuous who are childless. This second diptych actually contains two sets of comparisons and contrasts on each side. The one side deals with the barren woman and the eunuch (3:13-

19), and the second deals with virtuous people who are childless (4:1-6). What unites them into a single diptych with four parts is the image of the fruit of virtue and wickedness (3:13; 4:5). Finally, the wicked's call to exploit creation as "in youth" is confounded in the third diptych (4:7-20), which elaborates the blessing of the virtuous youth who has had an early death.

The argumentation of the author cannot be considered purely philosophical or logical. More than not, the critique is based on declarative statements that show the strength of the wicked to be false in the light of the blessedness of the just. The key technique in the criticism is the examination of appearances and reality. This perspective is particularly suitable to the background image of the trial, which examines appearances, reality, and intentionality. What really happened? Why did it happen? And what are the consequences? Such are the questions the author explores within the declarative statements regarding the just and the wicked. The author defends the virtuous life of the just and attacks the unjust lives of the wicked.

The unraveling of the argumentation of the wicked reveals their entire reasoning process as flawed. The death of the just is not the dreaded tragedy the wicked claim it to be. The oppression of the old, the widow, and the poor does not in the end confine the virtuous, who had "little strength to show" during their life. The call to exploit life "as in youth" is shown to be groundless in the face of a youth who has died an early death, yet is blessed in the presence of God. In its turn, the wicked's nihilistic judgment on the mortality of human beings is shown to be the true cause of a death that goes far beyond the contours of mortality, which they despise.

Wisdom 3:1-13a, The Just Are in the Hand of God

NAB

3 But the souls of the just are in the hand of God,
and no torment shall touch them.

2 They seemed, in the view of the foolish, to be dead;
and their passing away was thought an affliction

3 and their going forth from us, utter destruction.
But they are in peace.

4 For if before men, indeed, they be punished,
yet is their hope full of immortality;

5 Chastised a little, they shall be greatly blessed,
because God tried them
and found them worthy of himself.

6 As gold in the furnace, he proved them,
and as sacrificial offerings he took them to himself.

7 In the time of their visitation they shall shine,
and shall dart about as sparks through stubble;

8 They shall judge nations and rule over peoples,
and the LORD shall be their King forever.

9 Those who trust in him shall understand truth,
and the faithful shall abide with him in love:
Because grace and mercy are with his holy ones,
and his care is with his elect.

10 But the wicked shall receive a punishment to match their thoughts,
since they neglected justice and forsook the LORD.

11 For he who despises wisdom and instruction is doomed.
Vain is their hope, fruitless are their labors,
and worthless are their works.

12 Their wives are foolish and their children wicked;
accursed is their brood.

NRSV

3 But the souls of the righteous are in the hand of God,
and no torment will ever touch them.

2 In the eyes of the foolish they seemed to have died,
and their departure was thought to be a disaster,

3 and their going from us to be their destruction;
but they are at peace.

4 For though in the sight of others they were punished,
their hope is full of immortality.

5 Having been disciplined a little, they will receive great good,
because God tested them and found them worthy of himself;

6 like gold in the furnace he tried them,
and like a sacrificial burnt offering he accepted them.

7 In the time of their visitation they will shine forth,
and will run like sparks through the stubble.

8 They will govern nations and rule over peoples,
and the Lord will reign over them forever.

9 Those who trust in him will understand truth,
and the faithful will abide with him in love,
because grace and mercy are upon his holy ones,
and he watches over his elect.[a]

10 But the ungodly will be punished as their reasoning deserves,
those who disregarded the righteous[b]
and rebelled against the Lord;

11 for those who despise wisdom and instruction are miserable.
Their hope is vain, their labors are unprofitable,
and their works are useless.

12 Their wives are foolish, and their children evil;

13 their offspring are accursed.

3, 9: (*eleos*) *en tois hosiois autou kai episkopē en tois eklektois autou:* so with LXX[S].

---

[a] Text of this line uncertain; omitted by some ancient authorities. Compare 4.15   [b] Or *what is right*

COMMENTARY

3:1-9, The Reward of the Just. 3:1-4. As opposed to the shameful death the wicked projected for the just one, the author declares the just to be in the hand of God. Three images are used to create a sharp contrast between the blessedness of the just and the anticipated tragedy and shame projected by the wicked. The just are in the hand of God (v. 1); they are in peace (v. 3); and their hope is the fullness of immortality (v. 4). The hand of God traditionally signifies divine power and protection (Ps 95:4). To be in peace intimates the fullness of rest and well-being (Pss 4:8; 29:11). The hope of immortality refers to the author's declaration that justice is immortal (1:15). This noun "justice" (δικαιοσύνη *dikaiosynē*), along with its adjective, "immortal" (ἀθάνατος *athanatos*), is late and quite rare in the LXX (cf. Wis 3:4; 4:1; 8:13, 17; 15:3; 4 Macc 14:5; 16:13). It is a concept borrowed from the Greek that expresses Israel's hope in God's faithfulness to the promises of the covenant.[31]

The author concedes the appearance of tragedy and shame, but contends that the reality of the just is one of blessedness (vv. 2-4). Only from the perspective of the foolish do the just seem to have died, and their death seems to have been disaster, destruction, and even punishment.

3:5. By creating this disjunction between appearances and reality, the author is inviting the reader to look behind appearances for enduring values. The author introduces the idea of God's "testing" the just and offers two traditional metaphors of transformation and applies them to the case of the just who have died.

The idea of God's testing the people is often associated with the wanderings in the desert after the exodus from Egypt. In the theology of Deuteronomy, the desert experience of Israel is presented as a time of testing and an opportunity for inculcating discipline and knowledge (Deut 4:36;

8:2-5). This theme will be picked up in the later part of the book, when the specific history of the exodus will be treated. The sapiential tradition developed the notion of "testing in order to teach" as a means of passing on the insights of wisdom (Prov 3:11-12; Sir 2:1-5; 4:17-18).

3:6. The two metaphors that facilitate the notion of the transformation of the just in the context of God's testing are borrowed from metallurgy and the temple cult. Both metaphors share the image of fire as the element that causes transformation. The transformation of the just is compared to gold's being tested or purified in fire (v. 6; cf. Ps 66:10; Prov 17:3; Zech 13:9; Mal 3:2-3; Sir 2:5). The testing of gold in fire has the double function of verification and purification. The second metaphor, the burnt offering, accentuates the union between the just and God. The just are literally compared to a burnt offering that, though consumed by fire, is accepted by God as a pleasant fragrance (see Gen 8:21). If the metaphor of gold's being tested in fire stresses transformation and purification, the second metaphor stresses God's acceptance and union with the just.

3:7-8. The transformation of the just includes also a heightening of their activity at the time of judgment (vv. 7-8). Until now, the just have been passive, both during the wicked's speech and during the author's declaration of their blessedness. They are at peace in the hand of God. But at the time of judgment they will "shine forth"; they will run like "sparks through the stubble"; they will "govern nations." This idea of the righteous shining with brilliance is often associated with the vindication of the just at the time of judgment in apocalyptic writings. In Dan 12:3, for instance, the wise and the righteous are described as shining forth like the brightness of the sky and the stars (cf. Matt 13:43).

Several descriptions in the wicked's speech are reversed in the author's presentation of the just. The just were in the hands of the wicked, but now they are in the hands of God (2:18–3:1). The wicked were to put the just to torment, but now no torment will touch them (2:19–3:1). The wicked planned to test what would happen to the just, but it was really God who had tested the

---

31. Although the book of Wisdom presents an unambiguous belief in an afterlife, it does not affirm a clear belief in the resurrection (though other sources already affirm such a belief; cf. 2 Macc 7:9). Richard J. Taylor argues concisely that the Wisdom author's belief in an afterlife follows more from the theology of Israel's covenant than it does from Greek philosophical positions. The presence of specifically covenantal terms such as "grace," "mercy," and "the elect" (ἐκλεκτός *eklektos*, Wis 3:9) would indicate the value the author attributes to covenantal realities. See Richard J. Taylor, "The Eschatological Meaning of Life and Death in the Book of Wisdom I-V," *ETL* 42 (1966) 72-137.

just and found them worthy (2:17–3:5). The wicked were to try the forbearance of the just, but God is the one who has tried them like gold in the furnace (2:19–3:6).

3:9. The final brief comments on the just reiterate the faithfulness of God in covenantal terms. The just abide with God in love. Grace and mercy rest on the holy ones, and God's providence watches over the elect. The author's belief in an afterlife is rooted more deeply in covenantal theology than in Greek philosophical ideas concerning the immortality of the soul.[32]

3:10-13a, The Punishment of the Wicked. 3:10-11. In contrast to the active blessedness of the just, the author declares the hope and strength of the wicked to be empty and useless (v. 11). As a result of their injustice, the wicked will be punished according to their reasoning (v. 10). The wicked will not be punished simply because they have sinned. Rather, in the very manner of their wickedness, they will experience the punishment of their own reasoning.

The author draws a close connection between the false reasoning of the wicked and the experience of punishment. This is a unique perspective in the work that once again reveals the author's profound psychological understanding of the relationship among thought, praxis, and consequences. The entire reasoning process of the wicked contains the seeds of their own destruction. The nihilistic judgment on life, the invitation to evasive pleasure, the beckoning to oppress the weak, and the call to kill the just—all of these principles informing their view are understood by the author to turn against the wicked.

It is not as if the punishment is an external penalization that has no bearing on the manner of the injustice perpetrated. The author envisages an internal coherence between one's actions and their consequences. This will be particularly emphasized in the latter half of the book, where the author treats the issues of idol worship (11:16; 12:23-27; 14:30-31) and the punishment of the

enemies of the righteous ones in the plague episodes (15:18–16:1; 18:4-5). An explicit relationship will be drawn between their sin and the punishment for it.

This idea of a relationship between sin and punishment is implicit in several psalms of lament in which the psalmist calls on God for liberation and for the wicked's punishment according to their very means of wickedness: "Their mischief returns upon their own heads, and on their own heads their violence descends" (Ps 7:16 NRSV; cf. Pss 5:10; 9:15; 35:8; 37:14-15; 109:29; 141:10).

Although the punishment of the wicked for their false reasoning and injustice is envisaged as taking place in the future (they "will be punished as their reasoning deserves," v. 10), the seeds of destruction are already operative in their lives. Their lives really are miserable, their hope is vain, their labors are unprofitable, and their works are useless. These images are the very antitheses of the experience of the just, who are in peace, whose hope is the fullness of immortality, and whose future is to govern nations and rule over peoples.

3:12-13a. The concluding declaration of the first diptych focuses on the fruit of the wicked, the topic for the next diptych. The wives of the wicked are foolish, their children are evil, and their offspring are cursed. The author's judgment of punishment for the wicked here is rather harsh and comprehensive, without distinctions and exceptions. Even the children and the wives of the wicked will experience destruction.

The author takes pains to attribute the cause of ultimate death to the words and actions of the wicked. Why does the curse of the wicked extend to wives and children who may not have any guilt? Of course, the author is continuing in a longstanding tradition that claimed that blessings and curses continue to the fourth generation (cf. Exod 20:5; 34:7; Num 14:18; Deut 5:9; Sir 41:5-10). Actions do have consequences on other people, for better or for worse. If the wicked hope to accumulate advantages and wealth through injustice, they will be sorely dismayed. This irony introduces the contrast in the next diptych between the hopeless fruitfulness of the wicked and the hopeful sterility of the just.

---

32. Scholars once thought that the Wisdom author was deeply entrenched in Greek philosophy and anthropology. The fact that the work was written in Greek, including unique words with no Hebrew counterparts, lent substance to such a view. However, with careful analysis it is evident that the author is thoroughly established in Hebrew anthropology with a great deal of sympathy for Greek philosophy and literature. See J. M. Reese, *Hellenistic Influence on the Book of Wisdom and Its Consequences,* AnBib 41 (Rome: Pontifical Biblical Institute, 1970).

REFLECTIONS

1. This passage, which declares the hope of the just who have died (3:1-9), is one of the many biblical texts offered for selection at funerals. The author encourages the embracing of pain and loss, but offers hope as well. The declarations and images in the text have the unique capability of offering hope without bypassing or diminishing the pain of loss. Recognition is given to the suffering and death of others in the image of gold's being tested and purified in fire and in the image of the burnt offering. To lament and mourn the loss of family and friends is an important element in human relations, and it is not wise to pass over mourning lightly.

Yet, at the same time, pain and loss may be transformed into hope. The purification of gold leads to brilliance; the burnt offering signifies union. This is the unique perspective the author wishes to bring to the tragedies of life. In contrast to the perspective of the wicked, who see in human tragedy a destroyer of human value, the author focuses on the relationship between the just and God that emerges from their experience of tragedy. Far from being destructive tragedies, experiences of pain and loss can become moments of purification, resolution, and even deeper union with others.

2. The interpretation of tragedy in our own lives and in the lives of others remains ambivalent. Perhaps it is almost an instinctive reaction to interpret tragedy as punishment and a consequence of guilt. Instead of seeing tragedy, loss, sickness, and even death as a call to care and to be concerned for union, we judge either other people or ourselves as being accursed. Perhaps we simply try to avoid the realities of those who suffer altogether.

"Though in the sight of others they were punished,/ their hope is full of immortality" (3:4 NRSV). The Wisdom text offers a different perspective on the reality of tragedy and limitations in human life. Tragedy, loss, and death are not the destroyers of ultimate human value. The book of Job is the great precursor to the Wisdom text for modulating the perception and interpretation of tragedy in life. The tragedy of Job's life and family was not the result of his guilt, no matter how much the tradition and the three friends tried to impose such an interpretation on his experience. Christ, likewise, modulated the interpretation of tragedy in the case of the man who was blind from birth. The disciples presumed guilt to have been the cause of his blindness, "Rabbi, who sinned, this man or his parents, that he was born blind?" (John 9:2 NRSV). Jesus's response transformed the perspective on tragedy. He denied sin to be the cause for that tragedy and instead stated that the response to the man's blindness will be the manifestation of God's works (John 9:1-3).

3. In the author's critique of the lives of the wicked, a parallel is drawn between their sin and their punishment. Implicit in this parallel lies the age-old belief that injustice will finally catch up with the perpetrators. The reward of justice and the punishment of injustice too easily may be understood as extrinsic to moral conduct. For the Wisdom author, the fruit of a moral life is already implicit in the concrete decisions and actions of individuals. Even if the explicit or public revelation of justice and injustice resides in the future, the personal consequences of moral acts, like planted seeds, are active from the start.

Wisdom 3:13*b*–4:6, The Moral Strength of the Virtuous

13 Yes, blessed is she who, childless and
    undefiled,
    knew not transgression of the marriage
        bed;
    she shall bear fruit at the visitation of souls.
14 So also the eunuch whose hand wrought
    no misdeed,
    who held no wicked thoughts against the
        LORD—
    For he shall be given fidelity's choice reward
    and a more gratifying heritage in the LORD's
        temple.
15 For the fruit of noble struggles is a glorious
    one;
    and unfailing is the root of understanding.
16 But the children of adulterers will remain
    without issue,
    and the progeny of an unlawful bed will
        disappear.
17 For should they attain long life, they will
    be held in no esteem,
    and dishonored will their old age be at last;
18 While should they die abruptly, they have
    no hope
    nor scomfort in the day of scrutiny;
19 for dire is the end of the wicked
    generation.

4   Better is childlessness
    with virtue;
    for immortal is its memory:
    because both by God is it acknowledged,
    and by men.
2 When it is present men imitate it,
    and they long for it when it is gone;
    And forever it marches crowned in triumph,
    victorious in unsullied deeds of valor.
3 But the numerous progeny of the wicked
    shall be of no avail;
    their spurious offshoots shall not strike
        deep root
    nor take firm hold.
4 For even though their branches flourish for
    a time,
    they are unsteady and shall be rocked by
        the wind

    For blessed is the barren woman who is
        undefiled,
    who has not entered into a sinful union;
    she will have fruit when God examines souls.
14 Blessed also is the eunuch whose hands have
        done no lawless deed,
    and who has not devised wicked things against
        the Lord;
    for special favor will be shown him for his
        faithfulness,
    and a place of great delight in the temple of
        the Lord.
15 For the fruit of good labors is renowned,
    and the root of understanding does not fail.
16 But children of adulterers will not come to
        maturity,
    and the offspring of an unlawful union will
        perish.
17 Even if they live long they will be held of no
        account,
    and finally their old age will be without honor.
18 If they die young, they will have no hope
    and no consolation on the day of judgment.
19 For the end of an unrighteous generation is
        grievous.

4   Better than this is childlessness
    with virtue,
    for in the memory of virtue[a] is immortality,
    because it is known both by God and by
        mortals.
2 When it is present, people imitate[b] it,
    and they long for it when it has gone;
    throughout all time it marches, crowned in
        triumph,
    victor in the contest for prizes that are
        undefiled.
3 But the prolific brood of the ungodly will be
        of no use,
    and none of their illegitimate seedlings will
        strike a deep root
    or take a firm hold.
4 For even if they put forth boughs for a while,
    standing insecurely they will be shaken by the
        wind,

[a] Gk *it*   [b] Other ancient authorities read *honor*

NAB

and, by the violence of the winds,
uprooted;
5 Their twigs shall be broken off untimely,
and their fruit be useless, unripe for eating,
and fit for nothing.
6 For children born of lawless unions
give evidence of the wickedness of their
parents, when they are examined.

NRSV

and by the violence of the winds they will be
uprooted.
5 The branches will be broken off before they
come to maturity,
and their fruit will be useless,
not ripe enough to eat, and good for nothing.
6 For children born of unlawful unions
are witnesses of evil against their parents when
God examines them.[a]

[a] Gk *at their examination*

COMMENTARY

3:13b-15, The Moral Fruit of Virtue. 3:13b-14. This central diptych is aimed at dismantling the wicked's despising of everything that is weak and useless (2:10-11). Again, the issues of appearance and reality in the case of the just and the wicked are paraded before the reader for critical examination. This is done in two sets of comparisons and contrasts of the childless, who are righteous, and the wicked, who thrive. The particular image that unites the elements of this double comparison and contrast is "fruit" (καρπός karpos). The sterile woman will have "fruit" in the day of accounting (v. 13*b*), whereas the "fruit" of the wicked will be useless (4:5). Where there appears to be fruitlessness in the virtuous, there will be fruit. Where there appears to be fruit in injustice, there is no lasting fruit.

In order to recast the reader's perspective on human tragedy, the author chooses two traditional images of the accursed and raises them to a status of "blessedness." Because of the virtue of the barren woman and the eunuch, what appears to be human weakness and tragedy turns out to be a stage or a passage toward blessedness.

The barren woman and the eunuch are traditional images of curse and misfortune. The corollary image of blessing is that of fruitfulness. The abundance of children was considered a major sign of God's blessing. The initial divine blessing and command at creation, "Be fruitful and multiply . . . " (Gen 1:28), constitutes procreation as one of the intrinsic blessings of humanity (cf. Psalm 128). The gift of children was a sign of blessing associated with the Abrahamic covenant

(Gen 12:2; 15:3-5; 17:15-21) and also in a particular manner with the deuteronomic covenant (Deut 30:16). Sterility for both women and men was considered a grave misfortune (Gen 30:23; 1 Sam 1:4-8). The eunuch was barred from the priesthood and the assembly of the Lord (Lev 21:20; Deut 23:2). As such, the images of the barren woman and the eunuch are extreme examples of human limitation and weakness.

In a turnabout of events, the author declares both the barren woman and the eunuch to be blessed because of their moral integrity. The barren woman who is undefiled will bear fruit during the final judgment (v. 13*b*); the eunuch who has done no lawless deed will have a place of great delight in the temple of the Lord (v. 14). In this way the reader is being challenged to evaluate what constitutes true blessedness. The author has not flinched from choosing traditional images of curse as possible examples of blessedness.

Although there is no other biblical passage in which these two traditional images of curse are transformed precisely into declarations of blessedness, it is evident that the Wisdom author is borrowing themes from Isaiah.[33] In Isaiah 54, the prophet exhorts the barren woman, who represents Jerusalem, to rejoice, for she will have many children (Isa 54:1-3). In Isaiah, the city of Jerusalem is referred to as a barren woman (Isa 54:1)

---

33. Two works draw the parallels that can be found between Isaiah and the Wisdom of Solomon: M. J. Suggs, "Wisdom of Solomon II,10-V: A Homily Based on the Fourth Servant Song," *JBL* 76 (1957) 26-33; J. Schaberg, "Major Midrashic Traditions in Wisdom 1,1-6,25," *JSJ* 13 (1982) 75-101.

and a widow (Isa 54:4); Jerusalem is like a wife abandoned by her husband (Isa 54:6-7); the city is afflicted (Isa 54:11) and oppressed (Isa 54:14). In each case, the image of affliction is transformed into an image of restoration. Jerusalem will have many children; God is declared to be her husband; the covenant of peace shall not be taken away; the city will be rebuilt with magnificent stones; the city will become a safe haven. The author of Wisdom has condensed and focused on the image of the barren woman from the Isaiah passage. But the added perspective is that of her virtue. Because of her virtue, which is stated in negative terms ("undefiled," "not entered into a sinful union"), the barren woman will have fruit.

Similarly, the idea of righteous eunuchs' receiving a place in the Temple is borrowed from Isaiah. In Isaiah 56, the covenant of the Lord is extended to all who maintain justice and who keep the sabbath. Specifically this includes the foreigner who loves the name of the Lord, eunuchs who hold fast to the covenant, and the outcasts of Israel.

3:15. The temporal fruitlessness of the virtuous barren woman and the virtuous eunuch is reduced to mere appearance when compared to the fruitfulness they will have in their virtue. The author continues the attack on the reasoning of the wicked by transforming the perspectives on ordinary human limitations and weaknesses. Just as the death of the just appeared to be a final tragic event only in the eyes of the foolish, so too is the fruitlessness of virtuous individuals who hold to their integrity only apparent. In fact, the virtuous, who bear little or no temporal fruit, have the root of understanding, which ultimately does not fail. Perhaps no other biblical author has pushed the concept of blessedness so far as to exclude from it material goods and to include within it the experience of suffering.

3:16-19, The Apparent Fruit of the Wicked. In direct contrast to the moral fruitfulness of the just, the author declares the temporal fruit of the wicked to be of no account. On the day of judgment there will be no consolation for the unrighteous generation. Whatever temporal fruit they have acquired through unrighteous means will not come to the hoped-for maturity. The final outcome of the unrighteous generation is grievous.

If we understand the expression "children of adulterers" literally as the children of the unrighteous, then the author's reasoning would appear to be entering a rather awkward position. Innocent children would appear to be punished for the sins of their parents. As in the case of vv. 12-13, the author's argument has more nuances than the literal sense would suggest. In prophetic literature, terms relating to adultery signify Israel's faithlessness to God, idolatry, and abandonment of the law (cf. Isa 57:3-13; Jer 5:7-9; 7:8-10; Ezekiel 16; Hos 2:2-13; 3:1-5; 4:2-19). Adultery referred to the whole complexity of Israel's faithlessness to God.[34] Children from such an "adulterous" relationship signified the advantages and privileges gained from alliances and cultic practices. Instead of relying on the covenantal promises, Israel adopted cultic practices and entered political intrigues through which Israel hoped to secure advantages and privileges; thus the children of adultery represent these advantages. Even within prophetic teaching, the judgment of God is presented as demolishing the children of adultery—that is, the advantages that Israel hoped to secure through idolatry, foreign alliances, and cultic practices (cf. Jer 5:8-9; Hos 9:12).

The particular nuance that the Wisdom author is deriving from the image of the hopelessness of the children of adultery is that the wicked's hoped-for consolation will turn to nothing. Children represent hope and strength. They provide a guarantee for the future. However, for those who practice injustice, all the apparent advantages that have been thus gained will fail, like children of an adulterous relationship. The fruit of wickedness, contrary to its appearance of blessedness, will become a curse.

The wicked had declared might to be their right, and they judged weakness to be useless (2:11). The author is focusing on the image of fruitfulness as an external sign of might and strength and fruitlessness as an external sign of weakness and helplessness. The apparent fruit of unjust actions will not bring the hoped-for consolation. The apparent fruitlessness of the righteous will in fact bring forth the fruit of virtue.

4:1-2, The Advantage of Virtue. Unlike the

---

34. For a concise treatment of the nuances of adultery in prophetic literature, see Elaine A. Goodfriend, "Adultery," *Anchor Bible Dictionary,* 6 vols. (New York: Doubleday, 1992) 1:82-86.

opening and closing diptychs, the central diptych contrasts the hope of the virtuous who are childless with that of the wicked in a double set of comparisons. In this second half of the diptych, the author declares the particular advantage of virtue to be immortality. Parents live on in their children. But how do the childless continue? Through their virtue and honor, the just will live on in relation to God and to others. In virtue there is immortality. Therefore, it is better to be childless and virtuous than to have the abundance of the wicked (cf. Ps 37:16, "Better is a little that the righteous person has than the abundance of many wicked" [NRSV]).

What was stated negatively for the barren woman and the eunuch is stated positively in the case of virtuous people who are childless. The righteousness of the barren consisted of their refraining from unlawful conduct, whereas the righteousness of the childless consists of being rooted in virtue.

The author has adapted familiar Greek ideas on the value of virtue to the case of the just who are childless. For Plato, the life of the soul was far more important than the life of the body. In the examination of justice from the point of view of who is happier, the just or the unjust, Plato champions the enduring value of virtue, which lives on.[35]

Virtue is personified as a victorious athlete who marches with the crown of victory after having won spotless prizes (v. 2). In 1:8, justice was personified as one who punishes. In the following section of the book, wisdom will be personified as the object of the unnamed Solomon's admiration.

4:3-6, The Disadvantage of the Wicked. In contrast to the advantage of virtue, the prolific brood of the wicked is declared to be of no use. Whereas virtue was compared to a victorious athlete, the results of wickedness are compared to a doomed tree and a rootless plant.

Vegetation is used often in Scripture as a metaphor for the flourishing of moral life. The righteous are compared to trees that are planted by streams of water and that yield their fruit in due time (Ps 1:3; Jer 17:7-8). Perhaps even more frequently, especially in the prophetic writings, we find the image of vegetation, and particularly the vine, as a metaphor for judgment against the unfaithful (Isa 5:1-7; 27:1-6; Jer 2:21; 5:10-11; 8:13; 12:10-13; Ezekiel 15; Amos 4:9). The destruction of the vine, which is ordinarily a symbol of life and abundance, is a striking image that portrays the precariousness of an immoral and unfaithful life.

The author of Wisdom adapts the vegetation metaphor for the life of the wicked to include the progressive stages of growth: seedlings, roots, boughs, branches, fruit. By following the progressive growth of the plant from the illegitimate seedling to its useless fruit, the author stresses the thoroughness of the plant's ineffectiveness. Even if the seedlings take root, those roots will not be deep; even if they put forth boughs, they will be shaken by the wind; even if they sprout branches, they will be broken off; and even if they should provide a semblance of fruit, it will be useless (vv. 4-5).

The metaphor for the children of adultery veers away from vegetation and returns to that of a trial. Even more useless than fruit, the children of the wicked become witnesses against their parents when God examines them (v. 6). This is the pivotal issue in the author's argument on the apparent fruit of the wicked. The author is unmasking the illusion of strength and power that the wicked gain through injustice. Not only are the advantages and privileges of the wicked said to be useless, like unripe fruit that cannot be digested, but also this fruit actually testifies against them for their injustice.

Since the wicked had regarded weakness as useless and power as making right, then the fruit of their injustice would appear to be a vindication for their stance in life. The author counters this erroneous reasoning by declaring the fruit of the wicked to be both useless and accusatory. The wicked will fail not because they will not achieve success from their injustice, but because their supposed success will not bring them the hoped-for security; instead, it will be a source for their own condemnation at the time of accounting.

To elucidate the change in perspective from appearance to reality, the author provides several reversals of fortune in the case of the just and the wicked. The barren woman and the eunuch who are virtuous have the "root" of understanding

35. Plato *Republic* 2:362.

(3:15), whereas the wicked do not plant deep "roots" (4:3). The wicked lamented that there would be no "memory" (μνημονεύω *mnēmoneuō*) of them after their death (2:4), whereas in the "memory" of virtue there is immortality (4:1). In their frenetic boasting, the wicked called for wearing "crowns" of roses before they fade (2:8), whereas it is virtue that marches victoriously carrying the "crown" (στέφανος *stephanos*, 4:2). The wicked claimed evasive pleasure to be their lot in life (2:9), whereas it is the righteous eunuch who will have a "lot" (κλῆρος *klēros*) in the Temple (3:14). The wicked had planned to inflict a shameful death on the just one to see what the end of his life would be (2:17), whereas the "end" (τέλος *telos*) of the unrighteous generation is said to be grievous (3:19). The wicked had judged weakness to be useless (2:11), whereas the apparent success of the wicked is shown ultimately to be "useless" (ἄχρηστος *achrēstos*, 4:5).

The reversal of fortune regarding the apparent fruitlessness of the just and the supposed fruitfulness of the wicked is aimed at countering the wicked's despising of what is weak and extolling the virtue of sheer might and success. The author's counterattack relies heavily on the distinction between appearance and reality. What appears to be a weakness of the righteous in the end turns out to be the strength of their virtue. What appears to be a strength of the ungodly—namely, all the benefits and privileges accrued from injustice—in the end turns against them and reveals their moral weakness and depravity.

REFLECTIONS

The author's treatment of the theme of childlessness points to a more general and universal problem: How do we interpret the many forms of human weakness and limitations that we encounter in ourselves and in our world? If the first diptych aimed at facing the issue of the human tragedy of a violent and unjust death, the second diptych focuses on the less obvious tragedies that the unfulfillment of human possibilities presents.

In ancient Israel, children were considered one of the great gifts and rewards in life. They were a sign of God's blessing. Childlessness was considered to be a lack and even a curse. The image of the "fruit" of the wicked and the righteous relies on the presence of children, but goes beyond the metaphor of procreation to include all the consequences of injustice. The fruit of one's actions includes all the strengths, achievements, and failures of one's labor of righteousness or of injustice. The Wisdom author explores the apparent lack of the "fruit" of the righteous and the apparent strength of the "fruit" of the wicked to face the issue of the meaning of human weakness and the propensity for false hope.

1. The strength of injustice is only apparent and illusory. The seeming strength of injustice is one of the great problems that emerges with growing intensity among the sapiential circles of Israel. The wicked appear to thrive while the just appear to founder. The apparent thriving of injustice runs head on against the covenantal promises. Obedience and faithfulness to the law bring life; injustice and faithlessness bring death (Deut 30:11-20).

A number of eloquent voices in Scripture speak to this perennial problem. Psalm 73 is dedicated entirely to the theme of the apparent success of injustice. The psalmist confesses to having been sorely tempted to envy the arrogant for their prosperity. What saves the psalmist from succumbing to this temptation is the realization of the ultimate end of the wicked at the time of judgment. Job, in confronting the accusation of his three friends, contemplates the bitter paradox of the just who perish and the wicked who thrive (Job 21). Qohelet continuously raises the issue of the apparent strength of folly or injustice to jolt the reader from reducing reward and punishment to an automatic consequence of one's actions (Eccl 2:12-17; 4:1-3; 7:15; 8:10-17).

The particular nuance that the Wisdom author brings to the paradox is the dichotomy between appearance and reality. The author concedes the appearance of strength to the practice of injustice but denies its strength to be effective in the long run. Moreover, the effect of the author's reversal of images between the just and the wicked is to raise the importance of being critical of appearances. For our culture, which relies so heavily on appearances and first impressions, this exhortation to reflect on the essentials and arrive at the heart of the matter can be a significant voice for integrity. It calls for a critical examination of the fruit of one's action and its effect in the long run: "Thus you will know them by their fruits" (Matt 7:20 NRSV). Although the fruit of injustice may appear strong in the short term, in the long run it reveals its origins in nihilism. Success, strength, and achievements brought about unjustly are false sources of hope. In the end, these very strengths will reveal their function of simply masking the abysmal despair that breeds injustice.

2. The weakness of integrity is only apparent. In antithesis to the paradox of the seeming strength of injustice is the apparent weakness of integrity. What benefit is there to following a way of life of justice and integrity? Weakness, limitations, and surface failure put integrity and justice as a way of life to a sore test.

But the author challenges the reader to set his or her gaze beyond the immediate, beyond appearances, to view the result of justice in the long run. Virtue is respected by God and by people (4:1). A life of virtue places one in relationship to God and in a relationship of integrity with others. Again, it is in the long run that the true strength of justice is grasped with all its clarity. What cannot be destroyed in a life of integrity is the enduring relationship with God and others.

Ultimately, the author is affirming the covenantal promises. Faithfulness to God's way of justice does bring life; the way of injustice does bring death. But this defense is not sustained in a naive or superficial manner. The defense of justice and the critique of injustice are sustained by an examination of the ultimate fruit that is derived from ethical conduct. For a critical assessment of the strength and weakness of justice, one has to go all the way. What is the ultimate result of having achieved success, security, and temporary glory through a life of injustice? What is the ultimate result of clinging to a life of integrity and justice while enduring failure, threat, and a seeming anonymity? In the long run, a life of injustice leads to the alienation it presumes, whereas a life of justice places one into relationship with others.

Wisdom 4:7-20, The Death of a Virtuous Youth

NAB	NRSV
7 But the just man, though he die early, shall be at rest.	7 But the righteous, though they die early, will be at rest.
8 For the age that is honorable comes not with the passing of time, nor can it be measured in terms of years.	8 For old age is not honored for length of time, or measured by number of years;
9 Rather, understanding is the hoary crown for men, and an unsullied life, the attainment of old age.	9 but understanding is gray hair for anyone, and a blameless life is ripe old age.
10 He who pleased God was loved; he who lived among sinners was transported—	10 There were some who pleased God and were loved by him, and while living among sinners were taken up.
11 Snatched away, lest wickedness pervert his mind or deceit beguile his soul;	11 They were caught up so that evil might not change their understanding or guile deceive their souls.
	12 For the fascination of wickedness obscures what is good,

NAB

12 For the witchery of paltry things obscures
        what is right
    and the whirl of desire transforms the
        innocent mind.
13 Having become perfect in a short while, he
        reached the fullness of a long career;
14   for his soul was pleasing to the LORD,
        therefore he sped him out of the midst of
            wickedness.
    But the people saw and did not understand,
        nor did they take this into account.
16 Yes, the just man dead condemns the sinful
        who live,
    and youth swiftly completed
        condemns the many years of the wicked
            man grown old.
17 For they see the death of the wise man
        and do not understand what the LORD
            intended for him,
        or why he made him secure.
18 They see, and hold him in contempt;
    but the LORD laughs them to scorn.
19 And they shall afterward become
        dishonored corpses
    and an unceasing mockery among the
        dead.
    For he shall strike them down speechless
        and prostrate
        and rock them to their foundations;
    They shall be utterly laid waste
        and shall be in grief
        and their memory shall perish.
20 Fearful shall they come, at the counting up
        of their sins,
    and their lawless deeds shall convict them
        to their face.

4, 12: *metalloioi*: cf 16, 25 and V.
4, 15: Omit: conj; cf 3, 9.

NRSV

    and roving desire perverts the innocent mind.
13 Being perfected in a short time, they fulfilled
        long years;
14 for their souls were pleasing to the Lord,
    therefore he took them quickly from the midst
        of wickedness.
15 Yet the peoples saw and did not understand,
    or take such a thing to heart,
    that God's grace and mercy are with his elect,
    and that he watches over his holy ones.

16 The righteous who have died will condemn
        the ungodly who are living,
    and youth that is quickly perfected*a* will
        condemn the prolonged old age of the
            unrighteous.
17 For they will see the end of the wise,
    and will not understand what the Lord
        purposed for them,
    and for what he kept them safe.
18 The unrighteous*b* will see, and will have
        contempt for them,
    but the Lord will laugh them to scorn.
    After this they will become dishonored corpses,
    and an outrage among the dead forever;
19 because he will dash them speechless to the
        ground,
    and shake them from the foundations;
    they will be left utterly dry and barren,
    and they will suffer anguish,
    and the memory of them will perish.

20 They will come with dread when their sins are
        reckoned up,
    and their lawless deeds will convict them to
        their face.

a Or ended   *b* Gk *They*

COMMENTARY

4:7-15, The Righteous Are Pleasing to God. The final diptych contrasts the death of a virtuous youth with the prolonged life of the wicked. Just as children in ancient Israel were a sign of great blessing, so too was a ripe old age

considered to be a blessing (Gen 15:15; 25:8; 35:29; Exod 20:12; Deut 4:40; Judg 8:32). Old age was presented as a sign of wisdom and as a reward for right conduct in the sapiential traditions as well (Job 42:17; Prov 3:1-2; 10:27; 16:31;

Sir 1:12). Again, as with the case of the barren, the author has not shrunk away from choosing an image that ordinarily evokes tragedy and misfortune to propel the reader to seek out the deeper source of human dignity. What is truly disastrous is not a brief life lived out with integrity, but a long life filled with the perpetration of injustice.

An early death was considered a great calamity; it was a curse one wished only on enemies (Ps 109:8). But viewed from the perspective of virtue, an early death may even signify a blessing. The author is advocating the same change in perspective as in the case of the violent death of the just and the fruitless lives of the righteous. From the point of view of justice and integrity, what appears tragic is only a stage in further growth.

The author argues that an honorable old age is not something that can be established by external signs of age, such as gray hair. Neither can it be measured by number of years. Rather, an honorable age is achieved in a life of innocence, understanding, and inner maturity (vv. 8-9). The idea of progressive internal growth is portrayed through the images of "a life become pleasing to God" (v. 10) and "coming to perfection in a short time" (v. 13).

Pushing away even further the interpretation of an early death as necessarily tragic, the author goes so far as to consider the early death of a virtuous youth to be an expression of divine favor (vv. 10-15). This certainly is a novel position within the biblical writings. More than likely, the idea was facilitated by the popular axiom in Greek and Roman literature, "He whom the gods love dies young."[36] It is parallel to our own popular expression, "The good die young." The Wisdom author is adapting this idea in the light of the Enoch stories in Genesis and Sirach. Two links to the Genesis account of Enoch (LXX) exist in the Wisdom text: The idea of Enoch's pleasing God and the idea of transference: "Enoch was pleasing to God, then he was found no more, for God transferred him" (Gen 5:24). Notice that in the Hebrew Bible the opening phrase reads, "Enoch walked with God . . . " unlike the Greek text, which Wisdom employs. Sirach makes a similar reference to the Enoch account of the Greek version of Genesis in the hymn that honors the

ancestors: "Enoch pleased the Lord and was taken up, an example of repentance to all generations" (Sir 44:16 NRSV; cf. Heb 11:5).

The particular nuance attributed to God's pleasure in the case of the virtuous youth's being removed from the world is that of saving the youth from evil and calamity. God has taken up the virtuous youth, who has achieved maturity early, lest the future corrupt him (vv. 11-12). This idea was also present in Greek, Roman, and rabbinic literature: "For who knows but that God, having a fatherly care for the human race, and foreseeing future events, early removes some persons from life untimely."[37]

The Wisdom author stresses God's motivation of care and love in the early death of the virtuous youth. As with the case of the tragic and violent death of the just in the first diptych, people misinterpret the untimely death as tragic and void of divine care (v. 15). But from a perspective of justice and virtue, even events of seeming tragedy are interpreted in the light of God's grace, mercy, and providence.

4:16-20, The Righteous Youth and the Aged Wicked. The conviction of the wicked frames the second half of the diptych. At the outset, the righteous ones and the just youth are said to condemn the ungodly and the prolonged age of the unrighteous (v. 16). In the conclusion, the lawless deeds of the wicked will convict them to their face (v. 20). The author stresses the quality of judgment in the righteous youth. It is the youth, ordinarily not renowned for judgment, who will condemn the aged, who are commonly associated with wisdom, for their wickedness.

There are biblical precedents for the image of a wise youth who criticizes the wicked or foolish people who have the respect that belongs to elders. In the book of Job, Elihu defends his right to speak out because the source of wisdom resides in the breath of God and not in length of years. As a younger man, inspired by the Spirit of God, Elihu is critical of his elders for not responding effectively to the laments of their friend Job (Job 32:6-9). Qohelet speaks of the advantages of a

---

36. Menander 425; cf. Plautus *Bacchides* IV.816.

37. Plutarch *Consolatio ad Apollonium* 117D. David Winston provides several sources in rabbinic, Roman, and Greek literature that give expression to this idea, developed by the Wisdom author, whereby God "removes" those who are at the prime of their virtuous life, lest they change their minds. See David Winston, *The Wisdom of Solomon,* AB 43 (New York: Doubleday, 1979) 140-41.

poor and wise youth over an old and foolish king (Eccl 4:13). God is said to have aroused Daniel, a youth with a holy spirit, in order to confound the wicked elders and liberate Susanna from false judgment (Sus 45).

The author's judgment against the wicked is expressed in apocalyptic language. This language anticipates the similar expression of the formal judgment that occurs after the wicked's confession (5:17-23). In part, the language of destruction may have been inspired by Isaiah's judgment on the downfall of the king of Babylon (Isa 14:3-21). The Lord "will laugh" the wicked to scorn; they will become "dishonored corpses"; they will be "dashed, shaken," and "left utterly dry" (vv. 18-19). At the time of reckoning, the lawless deeds of the wicked will convict them.

The issue of appearance versus reality is applied to the case of the virtuous youth who dies an early death. Although it appears to be a tragedy, such a death need not be interpreted as a calamity or disaster. On the contrary, from the perspective of virtue and maturity, such a death may be a sign of God's special favor. People may see such events and not understand their true meaning or take such ideas into consideration (v. 15).

A number of images are taken up by the author from the original speech of the wicked and the previous diptychs in order to dismantle the reasoning of the wicked and counter their false accusation of the just. The wicked wanted to see whether the claims of the just were true, and so test him to the end (2:17); now the wicked will see the end of the wise and still not understand (v. 17). Just as the righteous were to become active and govern nations and peoples in the first diptych (3:7-8), so too the just and the righteous youth condemn the wicked in the third diptych (v. 16). Just as the children of the wicked become witnesses against them at the time of accounting in the second diptych (v. 6), so too the lawless deeds of the unrighteous convict them at the day of reckoning in the third diptych (v. 20).

By taking up another image of disaster and tragedy—namely, that of the early death of a virtuous youth—the author is countering the wicked persons' adulation of youthful pleasures (2:6-9) and their negative judgment on the transience of human life (2:1-5). In this way, all three diptychs counter the judgment and exhortation to injustice that reflect the wicked's approach to life. And this they do in reverse order as they appear in the wicked's speech.

During the sifting of appearances and reality, the author systematically uncovers the true meaning of the violent death of the just, the final fruitfulness of the barren woman and the eunuch, the special divine favor shown to the virtuous youth. The first diptych refutes the challenge of the wicked, who project the shameful death of the just one to be a confirmation of the validity of their stance toward life. The second diptych counters the wicked's decision to make might their right and to oppress those who are weak, the poor, the widow, and the elderly. The third diptych on the wise youth refutes the negative view of the wicked's judgment on physical death, which had led to their initial exhortation to evasive youthful pleasures. The interpretation of physical death plays a critical role in the author's refutation of a style of life that justifies injustice. The entire reasoning process of the wicked falls apart and prepares the reader for the day of judgment, when they will confess the error of their ways and their sin.

REFLECTIONS

1. The author's declaration of the blessedness of the wise youth who has died is not meant to be an answer to someone who is grieving the loss of a child or young friend. The death of a young person increases the poignancy of the loss of life, the waste of human possibilities, and the transience of life. Precisely for this reason, the author chose this common enough experience of human affliction to heighten the appreciation of a life of virtue and justice. Far from being an ultimate tragedy, even a short life can be considered a full life if it is measured by integrity and not by the ordinary standards of human strength. By looking behind the appearance of loss, in the case of a youth who has died, the author celebrates the power of virtue, justice, and inner maturity.

2. Wisdom and virtue can be found in the most unlikely places. The author holds up the example of a virtuous and wise youth in contrast to the wicked elderly in a manner that challenges our ordinary perspectives on wisdom and virtue. Wisdom and virtue traditionally are associated with the tried, the experienced, and the aged. But it is more important to assess the acts and judgments of human beings in the light of wisdom and virtue than it is to assess their appearances and places in society. Christ would proclaim a similar change in perspective in even more drastic terms: "Truly I tell you, the tax collectors and the prostitutes are going into the kingdom of God ahead of you" (Matt 21:31 NRSV; cf. Luke 18:9-14).

3. In the context of the author's refutation of the wicked's argument, the image of the death of a youth calls into question an absolutely negative judgment of the loss of youthful energies. The wicked regard the experience of the loss of life so negatively that this judgment justifies their escape to youthful pleasures. If youthful pleasures are pursued simply to evade the limitations and afflictions of life, they will never completely satisfy the desire for communion. Communion and integrity can be achieved even when youthful energies are diminished to the point of death.

4. The negative interpretation of an early death is mitigated by two realizations. The first is communion with God. God's faithfulness to the promises of the covenant has elicited the faith in an afterlife (4:15). The communion that is envisaged between the youth that has died an early death and God depends not so much on the immortality of the human being as much as on the enduring covenantal relationship. This communion is realized through the virtuous life of a youth that has been found pleasing to God.

The second is the idea of the inner maturity of virtue, whereby the essence of life reaches its completion. What is critical for the author of Wisdom is the inner life of virtue. The failings and shortcomings of life in their physical contours—even including early death—pale in comparison to the dignity of a life lived out with integrity.

5. The appearance of wisdom and achievement of the aged is not to be confused with virtue. As with the earlier cases of the tragic death of a virtuous person and the apparent fruitlessness of a barren person, the author calls for an examination of the true nature of human strength and wisdom. What appears to be a tragic loss of life in the case of the wise youth indeed is not. Presumably the author could have chosen other figures to signify human strength, such as people of wealth or those with educational and political might. Instead he uses three extreme examples of human misfortune to highlight with clarity the significant values of virtue and justice for determining the dignity of human beings. The true failures, tragedies, and disasters in life are not what the wicked think they are. Moral vacuity expressed through a life of evasive pleasure, exploiting the weak, and perpetrating violence brings on a death and destruction that is far more devastating than the experience of mortality, which all human beings encounter.

WISDOM 5:1-23, THE FINAL JUDGMENT

NAB

5 Then shall the just one with great
    assurance confront
    his oppressors who set at nought his labors.
2 Seeing this, they shall be shaken with
    dreadful fear,
    and amazed at the unlooked-for salvation.
3 They shall say among themselves, rueful
    and groaning through anguish of spirit:
    "This is he whom once we held as a
    laughingstock
    and as a type for mockery, 4 fools that
    we were!
    His life we accounted madness,
    and his death dishonored.
5 See how he is accounted among the sons of
    God;
    how his lot is with the saints!
6 We, then, have strayed from the way of
    truth,
    and the light of justice did not shine for
    us,
    and the sun did not rise for us.
7 We had our fill of the ways of mischief and
    of ruin;
    we journeyed through impassable deserts,
    but the way of the LORD we knew not.
8 What did our pride avail us?
    What have wealth and its boastfulness
    afforded us?
9 All of them passed like a shadow
    and like a fleeting rumor;
10 Like a ship traversing the heaving water,
    of which, when it has passed, no trace can
    be found,
    no path of its keel in the waves.
11 Or like a bird flying through the air;
    no evidence of its course is to be found—
    But the fluid air, lashed by the beat of
    pinions,
    and cleft by the rushing force
    Of speeding wings, is traversed:
    and afterward no mark of passage can be
    found in it.

5, 11: *diaptantos*: so LXX^MSS; trsp *tarsōn mastizomenon*: so LXX^MSS.

NRSV

5 Then the righteous will stand with
    great confidence
    in the presence of those who have oppressed
    them
    and those who make light of their labors.
2 When the unrighteous^a see them, they will be
    shaken with dreadful fear,
    and they will be amazed at the unexpected
    salvation of the righteous.
3 They will speak to one another in repentance,
    and in anguish of spirit they will groan, and
    say,
4 "These are persons whom we once held in
    derision
    and made a byword of reproach—fools that
    we were!
    We thought that their lives were madness
    and that their end was without honor.
5 Why have they been numbered among the
    children of God?
    And why is their lot among the saints?
6 So it was we who strayed from the way of
    truth,
    and the light of righteousness did not shine on
    us,
    and the sun did not rise upon us.
7 We took our fill of the paths of lawlessness
    and destruction,
    and we journeyed through trackless deserts,
    but the way of the Lord we have not known.
8 What has our arrogance profited us?
    And what good has our boasted wealth
    brought us?

9 "All those things have vanished like a shadow,
    and like a rumor that passes by;
10 like a ship that sails through the billowy water,
    and when it has passed no trace can be found,
    no track of its keel in the waves;
11 or as, when a bird flies through the air,
    no evidence of its passage is found;
    the light air, lashed by the beat of its pinions
    and pierced by the force of its rushing flight,
    is traversed by the movement of its wings,

^a Gk *they*

NAB

12 Or as, when an arrow has been shot at a mark,

the parted air straightway flows together again

so that none discerns the way it went through—

13 Even so we, once born, abruptly came to nought

and held no sign of virtue to display,

but were consumed in our wickedness."

14 Yes, the hope of the wicked is like thistledown borne on the wind,

and like fine, tempest-driven foam;

Like smoke scattered by the wind,

and like the passing memory of the nomad camping for a single day.

15 But the just live forever,

and in the LORD is their recompense,

and the thought of them is with the Most High.

16 Therefore shall they receive the splendid crown,

the beauteous diadem, from the hand of the LORD—

For he shall shelter them with his right hand,

and protect them with his arm.

17 He shall take his zeal for armor

and he shall arm creation to requite the enemy;

18 He shall don justice for a breastplate

and shall wear sure judgment for a helmet;

19 He shall take invincible rectitude as a shield

20 and whet his sudden anger for a sword,

And the universe shall war with him gainst the foolhardy.

21 Well-aimed shafts of lightnings shall go forth

and from the clouds as from a well-drawn bow shall leap to the mark;

22 and as from his sling, wrathful hailstones shall be hurled.

The water of the sea shall be enraged against them

and the streams shall abruptly overflow;

23 A mighty wind shall confront them

and a tempest winnow them out;

NRSV

and afterward no sign of its coming is found there;

12 or as, when an arrow is shot at a target,

the air, thus divided, comes together at once,

so that no one knows its pathway.

13 So we also, as soon as we were born, ceased to be,

and we had no sign of virtue to show,

but were consumed in our wickedness."

14 Because the hope of the ungodly is like thistledown[a] carried by the wind,

and like a light frost[b] driven away by a storm;

it is dispersed like smoke before the wind,

and it passes like the remembrance of a guest who stays but a day.

15 But the righteous live forever,

and their reward is with the Lord;

the Most High takes care of them.

16 Therefore they will receive a glorious crown

and a beautiful diadem from the hand of the Lord,

because with his right hand he will cover them,

and with his arm he will shield them.

17 The Lord[c] will take his zeal as his whole armor,

and will arm all creation to repel[d] his enemies;

18 he will put on righteousness as a breastplate,

and wear impartial justice as a helmet;

19 he will take holiness as an invincible shield,

20 and sharpen stern wrath for a sword,

and creation will join with him to fight against his frenzied foes.

21 Shafts of lightning will fly with true aim,

and will leap from the clouds to the target, as from a well-drawn bow,

22 and hailstones full of wrath will be hurled as from a catapult;

the water of the sea will rage against them,

and rivers will relentlessly overwhelm them;

23 a mighty wind will rise against them,

and like a tempest it will winnow them away.

Lawlessness will lay waste the whole earth,

and evildoing will overturn the thrones of rulers.

5, 14: *achnē*: so LXX[MSS], V, P.
5, 23: *pasan*: so LXX[MSS].

[a] Other ancient authorities read *dust*   [b] Other ancient authorities read *spider's web*   [c] Gk *He*   [d] Or *punish*

NAB

> Thus lawlessness shall lay the whole earth
>> waste
> and evildoing overturn the thrones of
>> potentates.

COMMENTARY

5:1-3, Introduction to the Scene of Judgment. The author has refuted the entire reasoning process of the wicked in a series of diptychs that uphold the integrity of the just and condemn the ways of the unjust. Despite appearances to the contrary, the blessedness of the just is assured by virtue of their relationship with God, whereas the downfall of the wicked is guaranteed by the vacuity of their moral life. The lynch pin in the wicked's argument was their final project to condemn the just one to a shameful death (2:20). In their minds, a shameful death would disprove the just's pretensions to an enduring divine relationship and would confirm their own negative judgment on the transiency of life. In turn, the negative interpretation of life justified their flight to evasive pleasure, their grasping of power, and their exercising of violence. By having the just one stand with confidence before the oppressors in a final judgment, the author strips away any vestiges of the wicked's claim to truth. The author brings the reader to the lofty heights of a divine perspective whereby the blessedness of the just shines clearly against the moral tragedy of the wicked. The power of injustice and the impotence of virtue are reversed. The just one will stand before the oppressors.

The theme of a final judgment has continuously been brought to the fore by the author. In a sense, a final judgment functions as a "trump card" for eliciting in the present a reflection on the eventual outcome of one's judgments and actions. The terms of this judgment are general and descriptive. It is called an "inquiry" and a "report" that will be brought to God (1:9). The author's favored term ἐπισκοπή (*episkopē*) refers to God's day of visitation or accounting, in which God cares for the just and punishes the wicked (2:20; 3:7, 9, 13; 4:15; cf. Isa 10:3; 23:17; 29:6). But this day

of judgment is also described as a time when God will examine or judge human beings (3:18; 4:6).

The mere presence of the just one who stands before the oppressors constitutes irrefutable evidence against the wicked. The very act of standing up has juridical overtones. A judge stands in order to inquire and to pronounce judgment (Job 31:14; Ps 82:1). A witness stands to accuse or to defend (Deut 19:15-16; Job 33:5). A person who cannot stand has nothing further to add for his or her defense (Ps 1:5). Therefore, the very presence of the just one constitutes a condemnation. Not a word need be spoken, yet the wicked are accused and condemned. The wicked had wanted "to see" whether the words of the just were true (2:17); now in divine judgment they "see" the end of the just and are overtaken with fear (v. 2).

The wicked confess their guilt. Just as the author provided the reader with the privileged position of following the wicked persons' perspective on life, so too is the reader allowed to listen in on the wicked's confession of guilt. A confession can have one of two purposes. In the context of a relationship, confessing one's sins or wrongdoing can have the function of expressing conversion or a change of heart that seeks reconciliation. We confess our sins in order to elicit the forgiveness of God (Ps 32:5). In the context of a trial, the confession confirms the validity of the accusation and justifies the condemnation (see the story of Achan, who confesses his sin of taking booty and is promptly executed after the misdeed is verified, Josh 7:10-26).

The confession of the wicked in the book of Wisdom takes place only among themselves. It does not take place in the presence of God and not even in the presence of the just one. The wicked are not seeking reconciliation through their confession. They simply are admitting to their error among themselves. Even though they are said to speak with remorse and in anguish, the purpose of the confession is not to indicate a change of heart but to provide incontrovertible evidence that their reasoning has been false. After the three diptychs that defend the just and accuse the wicked, even the unrighteous admit they are wrong.

5:4-14, Confession of the Wicked. Just as the author's defense of the just in three diptychs unraveled the wicked's argumentation in the reverse order of their project in life, so too does the wicked's confession disclaim their project in reverse order. The death of the just is not their final and tragic end (vv. 4-5); the wicked's paths of lawlessness and exploitation brought only destruction (vv. 6-7). Their arrogance and wealth have not provided profit (v. 8). As a result, their lives have become the meaningless and hopeless reality that they feared mortality had decreed for all human beings (vv. 9-14).

The wicked's confession of error covers their entire reasoning process, not just their miscalculation of the final end of the just one. A shadow is cast right back onto their original ruminations on the transience of life, and it covers their evasive pleasures, exploitation of the weak, and violence.

There are several touches of irony in the wicked's confession in phrases referring to images employed in their project of life. The wicked had derided the just one for claiming to be a "child of God" (2:13); now they acknowledge that the just one is counted among "the children of God" (υἱοὶ θεοῦ *huioi theou*, v. 5). The wicked had described revelry as their proper "lot" (κλῆρος *klēros*, 2:9) in life, but now they acknowledge that the just have their "lot" among the saints (v. 5). The wicked acknowledge that they have "taken their fill" (ἐμπίμπλημι *empimplēmi*) of lawlessness and destruction (v. 7), whereas they had exhorted one another "to take their fill" of costly wines and perfumes (2:7).

The recognition of their error and guilt leads the wicked to a lengthy reflection on the vacuity of their moral lives (vv. 9-14). This reflection stands in parallel fashion to the opening reflection on the transience of life (2:1-5). Both sections are marked by poetic images. Just as the wicked had judged their lives to be stamped fatally by the sign of mortality, so now they recognize that their

moral conduct is stamped by hopelessness as well. Whereas in the first reflection the wicked ruminated on the transience of their physical existence, now they lament the transience of their moral existence. Their hopelessness and rootlessness in the moral sphere are parallel to their judgment of meaninglessness in the physical sphere. They are being punished according to their very own reasoning (3:10).

Two brief images open the disclosure of the illusory nature of their project in life. All the appearances of their wealth have vanished like a shadow and like a rumor (v. 9). These images are followed by the elaboration of several metaphors depicting the transience of their project. First comes the metaphor of the boat with its oars, which after its passing leaves no sign of its presence (v. 10). Next comes the metaphor of the bird that pushes itself through the air and leaves no sign of its coming (v. 11; cf. Job 9:26). Finally there is the metaphor of the arrow shot through the air toward a target whose trajectory cannot even be recognized (v. 12). All of these metaphors emphasize the common feature that no trace is left of an object's passing.

The wicked profess what they had denied in their opening reflection: There is an enduring value in the transience of life—virtue. But as a result of their unjust actions they have nothing of it. Four poetic images conclude the wicked's confession whereby the rootlessness of their hope is emphasized. Without virtue, their hope is like chaff in the wind, frost in a storm, smoke in the wind, and the passing memory of an occasional guest (v. 14). It is possible that this last image of an occasional guest is formulated in the light of the Near Eastern custom of traveling in the evening and spending the day in hostels so as to avoid the heat of the day. Such guests would come and go and not be noticed.

The confession of the wicked continues to follow the pattern in Isaiah. Just as the author borrowed themes of the suffering servant, the barren woman, the eunuch, and the wise one from Isaiah, so too do we find a confession from Israel that precedes a scene of God's judgment. In Isa 59:9-13, the people confess their sin with at least one image similar to that employed by the wicked in Wisdom: They recognize how they walk in darkness and how they grope like the blind because of injustice (Isa 59:9-10; cf. Wis 5:6-7). Similarly, various parts of the wicked's confession allude to sections of the suffering servant of Isaiah ("hold in derision," Wis 5:3-4 = Isa 53:3; "we have strayed," Wis 5:6 = Isa 53:6).

The author has chosen to express the confession of the wicked in eloquent language similar to the wicked's ways of injustice. On the surface, the reasoning of the wicked remains polished, erudite, and even sophisticated. For the sake of the reader, the author does not wish to strip away from the wicked the attractive facade of their erroneous positions. The effect of the eloquent language of the confession is to underscore the importance of judging not on the surface appearance, but according to the results of judgments and actions. Although the wicked can speak with eloquence and even though they have the appearance of strength, their injustice is heading them toward a death that is far more devastating than the physical death they lament in their opening ruminations.

5:15-23, The Apocalyptic Scene of Judgment. The confession of the wicked confirms the author's argument in the three diptychs. It prepares the way for judgment to be established with respect to both the just and the wicked. The image of a royal reward is used to depict the victory of the just (vv. 15-16), whereas the image of a final and cosmic conflagration is employed to depict the punishment of the wicked (vv. 17-23).

In sharp contrast to the transience of the wicked's hope, the righteous are said to live forever (v. 15). The author here confirms the destiny that God has determined for human beings (1:15; 2:23). Faith in an enduring relationship with God is the hallmark of the just (3:1; 4:7; 5:1). The transcendent image of God as "the most high" is joined to the image of God's immanent "care," which reflects the concern of a parent watching over his or her child (v. 15b).

Two royal images are used to convey the dignity of the just person's future and eschatological reward: the crown and the diadem (v. 16). The author's use of these two images may have been inspired by Isa 62:3, where the downcast of Zion are assured that they will become a "crown of beauty" and a "royal diadem" in the hand of the Lord. The royal reward is consistent with the opening address, in which kings and rulers are exhorted to justice (1:1), and it anticipates the final address, in which kings are encouraged to listen and judge correctly (6:1).

God protects the just like a warrior whose hand covers them and whose arm shields them. The image of the divine warrior who prepares for battle is an adaptation of the metaphor that occurs in Isa 59:17-19. The analogy is expanded somewhat from Isaiah's use of breastplate, helmet, garments, and mantle to the use of the full armor of a *hoplite* in Wisdom. Each weapon of a hoplite is compared to a divine attribute: zeal = armor, justice = breastplate, impartial judgment = helmet, holiness = shield, wrath = sword.

Particularly innovative in the metaphor of the divine warrior in Wisdom is the role of the cosmos.[38] The Lord is arming creation as well (vv. 17, 20), and creation will join God in battle against the enemy (vv. 20-23). This positive role of creation on the side of justice is consistent with the author's declaration of the positive forces of the cosmos (1:14). The forces of creation are on the side of the righteous against injustice.

The ultimate conflagration is depicted in a limited apocalyptic fashion in which meteorological phenomena bring about the destruction of wickedness.[39] The forces of the cosmos—lightning, hail, water, rivers, winds, storms—will ravish the earth as a result of lawlessness (cf. Pss 18:7-15; 97:1-5; Isa 29:6).

Little can be deduced regarding the specific eschatological beliefs of the author from this restrained apocalyptic account. Such beliefs as the resurrection of the body, a definitive annihilation of the physical cosmos, and the location of blessedness cannot be presumed. In this respect, the apocalyptic judgment in Wisdom differs from other presentations of the ultimate conflagration in its brevity and in its restrained descriptions. The author is not so much interested in focusing on the end times as in portraying the importance of living a life based on justice and virtue in the

---

38. In all three parts of the book of Wisdom, the author displays consistency in portraying the positive role of the cosmos: in relation to God's judgment in the first, in relation to wisdom in the second, and in relation to the exodus in the third. See John J. Collins, "Cosmos and Salvation: Jewish Wisdom and Apocalyptic in the Hellenistic Age," *HR* 17 (1977) 121-42.

39. For a thorough review of the genre and language of apocalyptic sources, see John J. Collins, *The Apocalyptic Imagination* (New York: Crossroad, 1989). The judgment and destruction of the wicked is one of the dominant and consistent features of apocalypses (ibid., 6).

present. The final conflagration simply affirms the royal reward of the just and the destruction of wickedness. It functions as the cosmic sentencing in the context of the trial that has been working in the background of the author's debate (cf. Job 34:21-30).

This somber but noble account of God's judgment brings to a close the tension that was raised in the opening exhortation between justice and injustice. It is this ultimate death portrayed in apocalyptic fashion that became the negative motive for the author's exhortation to love justice

and to seek God. This death is the result of the deliberate judgments and actions of the wicked, which they have brought upon themselves through their words and deeds. This is the undesirable destiny of alienation from God and the cosmos that the author dissuades the readers from bringing upon themselves. Through a false reasoning on mortality that leads to a life of evasive pleasure, exploitation of the weak, and reliance on violence, a death far worse than mortality is experienced.

REFLECTIONS

1. Considering the final day of judgment is relevant for the present. It may appear that the consolation for the just and the punishment of the wicked reside in a future so distant that the day of judgment is irrelevant for the present moment. This could become a difficulty if the issue of time becomes the overriding factor. But for the author of Wisdom, the consideration of the ultimate judgment is meant to focus the reader on the present situation. Judgments and actions of virtue or of injustice already initiate the dynamics of immortality and of moral death. By bringing the reader to the lofty heights of a divine perspective at an ultimate judgment, the author is focusing the lens on the true outcome of a life of virtue and a life of injustice.

2. The fruit of injustice has no enduring significance. This hard truth is one that the author argues in the three diptychs and is confirmed in the wicked's confession. The contrast between appearances and reality is heightened from the perspective of the ultimate judgment. When we examine the final outcome, what remains of our actions and relationships in the long term says a great deal about the quality of life in the present. In the case of the wicked, the strength and benefits of injustice disappear, and their status is shown to be transient.

The wicked are said to perceive this dissonance from the perspective of the enduring relationship between the just and God. What the wicked had embraced as signs of pleasure, strength, and power turn out to be hollow and transient benefits from the perspective of justice. The illusion of strength that accrues from unjust actions is built on a false hope that eventually is revealed for what it is. False hope leaves them rootless and hopeless.

3. The forces of the cosmos have both a positive and a negative function. They are positive toward justice and negative toward injustice. The unique viewpoint of the author of Wisdom interprets the forces of creation as having a concrete function for the human world. This is an extension, or perhaps an adaptation, of the creation story in Genesis. God saw everything that had been created and declared it good. For the author of Wisdom, then, the source of evil resides in the human heart and not in the forces of the world. In fact, even the forces of creation aid human beings in the pursuit of justice and hinder the practice of injustice. The exodus event will be interpreted in the latter half of the work as an instance in history of the forces of the cosmos coming to the aid of the just and hindering those who pursue injustice.

4. A good example in our own time of the principle that justice is an inherent aspect of the cosmos is our concern for the conservation of the environment. Perhaps at no other time in history have human beings been more acutely aware of the consequences of exploiting the resources of nature. Nature does have its way of reconstituting a balance with powerful and even cataclysmic events. Actions in the present, along with all of the negligence of the past, do have serious consequences for the future. We can either align ourselves with the forces that balance nature or set ourselves over and against the environment. In either case the environment will work for us or against us.

WISDOM 6:1-21, EXHORTATION TO WISDOM

NAB

6 Hear, therefore, kings,
and understand;
learn, you magistrates of the earth's
expanse!

2 Hearken, you who are in power over the
multitude
and lord it over throngs of peoples!

2 Because authority was given you by the LORD
and sovereignty by the Most High,
who shall probe your works and scrutinize
your counsels!

4 Because, though you were ministers of his
kingdom, you judged not rightly,
and did not keep the law,
nor walk according to the will of God,

5 Terribly and swiftly shall he come against
you,
because judgment is stern for the exalted—

6 For the lowly may be pardoned out of
mercy
but the mighty shall be mightily put to the
test.

7 For the Lord of all shows no partiality,
nor does he fear greatness,
Because he himself made the great as well as
the small,
and he provides for all alike;

8 but for those in power a rigorous scrutiny
impends.

9 To you, therefore, O princes, are my words
addressed
that you may learn wisdom and that you
may not sin.

10 For those who keep the holy precepts
hallowed shall be found holy,
and those learned in them will have ready
a response.

11 Desire therefore my words;

NRSV

6 Listen therefore, O kings,
and understand;
learn, O judges of the ends of the earth.

2 Give ear, you that rule over multitudes,
and boast of many nations.

3 For your dominion was given you from the
Lord,
and your sovereignty from the Most High;
he will search out your works and inquire into
your plans.

4 Because as servants of his kingdom you did
not rule rightly,
or keep the law,
or walk according to the purpose of God,

5 he will come upon you terribly and swiftly,
because severe judgment falls on those in high
places.

6 For the lowliest may be pardoned in mercy,
but the mighty will be mightily tested.

7 For the Lord of all will not stand in awe of
anyone,
or show deference to greatness;
because he himself made both small and great,
and he takes thought for all alike.

8 But a strict inquiry is in store for the mighty.

9 To you then, O monarchs, my words are
directed,
so that you may learn wisdom and not
transgress.

10 For they will be made holy who observe holy
things in holiness,
and those who have been taught them will
find a defense.

11 Therefore set your desire on my words;
long for them, and you will be instructed.

12 Wisdom is radiant and unfading,
and she is easily discerned by those who love
her,

NAB

long for them and you shall be instructed.

12 Resplendent and unfading is Wisdom,
and she is readily perceived by those who
love her,
and found by those who seek her.
13 She hastens to make herself known in
anticipation of men's desire;
14 he who watches for her at dawn shall
not be disappointed,
for he shall find her sitting by his gate.
15 For taking thought of her is the perfection
of prudence,
and he who for her sake keeps vigil shall
quickly be free from care;
16 Because she makes her own rounds, seeking
those worthy of her,
and graciously appears to them in the ways,
and meets them with all solicitude.
17 For the first step toward discipline is a very
earnest desire for her;
then, care for discipline is love of her;
18 love means the keeping of her laws;
To observe her laws is the basis for
incorruptibility;
19 and incorruptibility makes one close to
God;
20 thus the desire for Wisdom leads up to
a kingdom.
21 If, then, you find pleasure in throne and
scepter, you princes of the peoples,
honor Wisdom, that you may reign as
kings forever.

6, 12: Add *kai heurisketai hypo tōn zētountōn autēn* at end: so LXX[MSS].

NRSV

and is found by those who seek her.
13 She hastens to make herself known to those
who desire her.
14 One who rises early to seek her will have no
difficulty,
for she will be found sitting at the gate.
15 To fix one's thought on her is perfect
understanding,
and one who is vigilant on her account will
soon be free from care,
16 because she goes about seeking those worthy
of her,
and she graciously appears to them in their
paths,
and meets them in every thought.

17 The beginning of wisdom[a] is the most sincere
desire for instruction,
and concern for instruction is love of her,
18 and love of her is the keeping of her laws,
and giving heed to her laws is assurance of
immortality,
19 and immortality brings one near to God;
20 so the desire for wisdom leads to a kingdom.

21 Therefore if you delight in thrones and
scepters, O monarchs over the
peoples,
honor wisdom, so that you may reign forever.

[a] Gk *Her beginning*

COMMENTARY

In returning to words of exhortation similar to those of the opening, the author is bringing to a conclusion the first part of the work. Almost immediately, the opening exhortation to love justice and to seek God turned into a warning against a way of life that would hinder those values. The main negative image behind the warning is death: "Do not invite death by the error of your life" (1:12 NRSV).

The defense of the wicked for an unjust way

of life was motivated by the negative judgment on mortality and human weakness. Their counter-accusation envisaged a shameful death for the just one. This would disprove the claims of the just and conclusively prove the validity of their own position. Through the metaphor of a trial, the author has paraded before the imagination of the reader the various scenes of the just in the hand of God—the barren woman, the eunuch, and the virtuous youth. In the examination of these scenes, the author has cut through the appearance of tragedy and injustice. These scenes function, therefore, as witnesses for justice against injustice. Finally, the scene of a final judgment elicits the confession of the wicked. They retract their entire reasoning process, which exemplified the defense of the way of injustice. The wicked are sentenced to annihilation, and the just are vindicated.

But the exhortation does not conclude with the sentencing. In suitable sapiential fashion, the author invites the reader to learn and to appropriate the lessons of the trial scene. These lessons are a matter of vital importance—the dissuasion from death, the persuasion to life. By appropriating the lessons of a warning against death, the reader can then pursue the love of justice and wisdom. With an uncluttered mind that is not mesmerized by the appearance of the power of injustice and the impotency of virtue, the attractiveness of wisdom will be readily accessible.

6:1-11, Exhortation to Kings. 6:1-2. The addressees of the exhortation are formally referred to as "kings" (βασιλεῖς *basileis*) and "judges" (δικασταί *dikastai*) who rule over multitudes (vv. 1-2; cf. "monarchs" [τύραννοι *tyrannoi*] in vv. 9, 21). These terms pick up the opening scene where the addressees are called "rulers of the earth" (1:1). As is the case in the opening address, the exhortation "to listen," "to learn," and "to give ear" is reminiscent of personified wisdom, who goes about the streets to convince listeners of the importance of her message (Proverbs 8). Sages would introduce their wisdom with similar exhortations (Job 13:6; 21:2; Prov 4:1; Eccl 3:1). There is a sense of urgency in the plea that has been accruing since the author introduced the stark image of death (1:12).

On the one hand, there is no need to look to specific contemporary rulers, kings, or emperors as if they are the direct addressees of the book of Wisdom. The "king" is a metaphor for human beings who are human insofar as they judge, act, and rule (Gen 1:26-27). Especially in sapiential circles, the royal image becomes the metaphor of the sage who understands and knows how to judge and to act. This royal metaphor, which begins explicitly in the closing exhortation, will become concrete in the unnamed king and sage, Solomon, for the second part of the book.

On the other hand, this does not mean that the author is not intending a critique of political power. The function of the ruler is important to understand from the point of view of faith for subjects as well as for rulers. The declaration "you that rule over multitudes and boast of many nations" (v. 2), could very well have been inspired by the extension of Roman authority during the diaspora. This does not, however, make the Roman emperor the addressee of the entire work. The Jewish community in the diaspora also had to come to terms with the meaning of such power in their cities and the role of Roman authority in their own self-understanding.

6:3-4. The author introduces a key element of the faith of Israel regarding the true source of kingship and sovereignty. The Lord is the one who confers dominion; the Most High is the source of sovereignty (cf. Judg 8:22-23; 1 Chr 29:10-13; Prov 8:15-17; Dan 2:20-23). As such, the Lord remains the unrelenting defender of justice before those who administer power in the world. God is the guarantor of justice, the one who inquires into the dealings of human beings (cf. v. 8). Therefore, the same judgment against the wicked that the author has presented in the trial scene awaits anyone who does not rule rightly and who transgresses the law and the purposes of God.

6:5-8. A corresponding theme that the author develops in the exhortation is the heightened responsibility of those in power (cf. Luke 12:48). The greater the power, the greater the accountability. To heighten the effect of this axiom, the author appeals to the longstanding tradition of God's not deferring to the powerful and the mighty. This is especially consistent with the author's penchant of looking behind appearances to the heart of judgment and action. Judgment is not partial to appearances. Since God is the source of all, everyone is accountable to God (cf. Deut 1:17; Job 34:19; Ps 104:27-30; Prov 22:2). God holds all accountable, especially those with greater responsibility. The lowly may find some leniency, but the mighty will be judged with severity (v. 6; cf. Luke 12:47-48).

6:9-11. The final purpose of the exhortation is to learn wisdom in order not to transgress. The reader is challenged to appropriate the insights and the understanding that emerge from the entire sequence of the trial scene in the earlier chapters. If we do not appropriate the importance of loving justice, then the death from which the author has dissuaded the reader will come with its full force as God's justice.

This short counsel within the larger exhortation (vv. 1-21) marks the switch from the author's warning against bringing on death to the persuasion to love wisdom as a means of practicing justice. The first part has concentrated on what one must not do to avoid the judgment of God. The second part concentrates on what must one do (learn wisdom, observe holy things, set one's desire on the words of the sage). If the reader has appropriated the insights and understanding that follow from the results of the wicked's ruminations on life, then all the more important will it be to learn wisdom. To avoid death, one must pursue wisdom so as to learn justice.

6:12-21, The Qualities of Wisdom. Wisdom is presented as a person who seeks out the sage. The author is freely adapting the personification of wisdom from the book of Proverbs (Prov 8:1-17). The literary device of personification is frequently employed by the sages (cf. Proverbs 8; Sir 6:18-31). Very briefly the author had employed the personification of justice in the opening exhortation (1:8). With this introduction to wisdom, the author is anticipating the second part of the work, which focuses on the sage Solomon, who seeks out wisdom as a bride.

The double movement of the encounter between wisdom and the sage characterizes this opening presentation of wisdom. An encounter may take place with one person moving to another, or by two people moving toward each other. The author uses the double movement of both the sage and wisdom for the meeting. The sage is instructed at first to seek wisdom, to rise up early to meet her, to fix his thought on her, to be vigilant. But wisdom is not passive. She does not simply wait for the sage. She "hastens to make herself known"; "she sits at the gate"; "she goes about seeking those who are worthy of her"; "she appears to them in their paths"; "she meets them in every thought." Since wisdom is intimately connected to God, it is not difficult to recognize the author's understanding of divine grace and intervention operating in the figure of wisdom.

Two adjectives characterize the quality of wisdom. She is "radiant" (λαμπρά *lampra*) and "un-fading" (ἀμάραντος *amarantos*, v. 12). Both adjectives serve to describe the encounter between wisdom and the sage. Wisdom as radiant light is easily discernible to the one who seeks her. Wisdom as unfading light shows her constancy and permanence, her immortality. One has time to meditate and concentrate on her with one's whole mind and heart. Both images reflect the double movement of the encounter between wisdom and the sage. Wisdom actively seeks out human beings, and she lets herself be discovered by those who seek her.

A chain syllogism (*sorites*) encapsulates the surprising conclusion that the love of wisdom leads to a kingdom (vv. 17-20). Chain syllogisms were a popular literary device used to condense insights and propositions with a playful effect. The classical sorites was a six-part chain syllogism in which each proposition led to another and finally concluded with a surprise declaration.[40] But there were many variations of it. The end of each proposition would become the opening for the next. The playfulness in these syllogisms was meant to lead the reader along with several propositions that one could easily give assent to and then surprise the reader with a more difficult proposition. In our case, the surprise ending consists of the proposition that the desire for wisdom leads to a kingdom. The kingdom is an appropriate goal for the addressees, who are described as kings, judges, and monarchs.

With the offering of a kingdom through wisdom, the exhortation of the first part reaches its conclusion. The reader has been encouraged to divest a way of life of injustice, which leads to death. The argumentation of the diptychs is subtle. By sifting through appearances and reality, the author has enhanced a change in perspective according to the light of virtue and justice. The dissuasion from death has now been transformed into a persuasion toward life. Wisdom is an illuminating source for justice that brings one into proximity to God and to immortality. For the second part of the book, wisdom becomes the central concern. The focus will concentrate on the wisdom that comes from God and how it accompanies human beings throughout their struggles for a just life.

40. See Linda Claire Burns, *Vagueness: An Investigation into Natural Languages and the Sorites Paradox* (Boston: Kluwer Academic, 1991); H. A. Fischel, "The Uses of Sorites in the Tannaitic Period," *HUCA* 44 (1973) 119-51.

REFLECTIONS

1. God is the source of power. The exhortation by the author for kings and judges to learn and understand puts matters of authority into perspective. Throughout the diptychs and in the trial scenes, the author has stripped away the appearance of the strength of injustice as well as the apparent weakness of virtue. In the final exhortation, even the act of ruling and judging is declared to be rooted in the sovereignty of God. The mere fact that one has authority over others is no reason to attribute such power to oneself. Such a misconception opens the way for the abuse of power. The forms of injustice that follow are subject to the same judgment of God and creation. The author cautions everyone who acts with authority not to be mesmerized by the appearance of strength as if it were rooted in oneself.

The tendency to attribute strength and authority to oneself is recognized within the Torah, and so too is the need to be reminded of the ultimate source of governance in God. The homilies of Moses in the book of Deuteronomy offer a point of comparison with Wisdom's exhortation. The Israelites are poignantly reminded of their relative insignificance before crossing the Jordan River. It was not their strength in numbers or even their moral conduct that prompted God to elect them and to bring them success and blessings in the land. It was out of God's love that Israel was chosen. Only by remaining rooted in God will Israel be blessed in the land (Deut 8:1–9:7).

2. Responsibility brings accountability. This reflection concretely places the function of authority into greater perspective. For whatever reason one is given authority, one will be held accountable for the exercising of that authority. The theme of judgment permeates the exhortation. In fact, it is the perspective of the ultimate judgment that allows the author to critique the ways of injustice in the present. Similarly, in the case of authority, the more authority a person has, the more justice will be expected from that person. The Wisdom author foreshadows Christ's parable of the unfaithful slave: "From everyone to whom much has been given, much will be required; and from the one to whom much has been entrusted, even more will be demanded" (Luke 12:48 NRSV; cf. Matt 25:14-30; Luke 19:11-27).

3. There is a paradox in the experience of seeking God and discovering in the encounter that it is the seeker who has been sought and found by God. The Wisdom author recognizes the double movement in the human relationship to God. The background metaphor of encounter is used to portray the movements of the sage who seeks wisdom. The sage and personified wisdom strive to meet each other. They each set out to encounter the other. The sage "seeks" wisdom, "desires" her, "gets up early" to find her, and "fixes the mind" on her. But wisdom also "hastens to make herself known," "she goes about seeking those worthy of her," "she graciously appears . . . and meets them in every thought" (6:12-16 NRSV). No matter how hard we strive to find God in our lives and in our world, the moment of encounter often reveals how, in fact, it is God who has been seeking us out, speaking to us through others with many words and in different languages of silence and action.

4. Wisdom makes one intimate with God. A life of injustice brings death, but a life of justice brings one into union with God. The way to a life of justice is through wisdom. Wisdom is a value to be sought even as God seeks out human beings to give them wisdom. The way is clear for the author to advance a way of understanding the human condition in a manner other than that of the wicked. The second part of the book becomes a eulogy of wisdom that began in the conclusion of the exhortation. Wisdom is on intimate terms with God, and it is through wisdom that human beings come close to God.

If anything, the complexity of human life and the challenge of discerning between justice and injustice should bring about a humble desire for wisdom to guide us through life.

WISDOM 6:22–10:21

IN PRAISE OF WISDOM

OVERVIEW

On the surface, the tone of these chapters is quite different from the first part of the book. Speech in the first person signals the main shift in perspective and in emphasis. The various scenes of the trial that mediated an argument against injustice had been presented through a narrator speaking in the third person. Now, the author speaks personally, "I will tell you what wisdom is and how she came to be" (6:22), as if to heighten the understanding of the author's personal knowledge of wisdom.

If the first part of the book can be understood as the tense drama between justice and injustice, represented in the conflict between the righteous and the wicked, the second part can be understood as the creative drama between wisdom and the righteous, represented in Solomon's love of and desire for wisdom. The first section of Wisdom presented an argument against a life of injustice and death. The second part presents a persuasion to the wisdom that comes from God. Understood in this light, the sections complement each other.

The main shift in perspective focuses on the unnamed speaker: Solomon. By attributing the eulogy and praise of wisdom to Solomon, the author is garnishing authority for the values of wisdom. The Hebrew tradition idealized Solomon as the wise sage who was able to govern through wisdom. The well-known story of Solomon's first act of judgment, which uncovered the true mother of a child, formed a basis for the process of idealization (1 Kgs 3:16-28).

In keeping with the policy of not naming names throughout the book, the author uses descriptions that lead the reader to identify the speaker as Solomon. This feature is well known in certain genres of Greek writing that belong to protreptic discourse and to the encomium.[41] It is a stylistic feature that is meant to engage the reader's mind playfully to make judgments of identification.

The significance of Solomon, who praises wisdom, is that he offers a counterpart to the wicked in the first part of the book. Like the wicked, Solomon offers a perspective on mortality that issues in a concrete project in life. Unlike the wicked, Solomon's ruminations on mortality lead to a profound desire for wisdom so as to govern justly.

The main shift in emphasis from the first part focuses on personified wisdom. These chapters are permeated with Solomon's desire for, praise of, and love of wisdom. The personification of wisdom is perhaps the unique contribution of the sapiential tradition to Israel's theological heritage. In the book of Wisdom, wisdom is presented through the imagery of romantic courtship.[42] Solomon desires to win wisdom over as a suitor who woos his lover. In the other sapiential sources for the personification of wisdom (Proverbs 1–9; Sirach 24), wisdom speaks on her own behalf. But all three sources share the common feature of relating wisdom to the act of God's creation.

The author highlights two functions of wisdom in the process of personification: (1) the creative role of wisdom for humans (7:12, 22; 8:5-6; 9:2, 10-11, 18; 10) and (2) the cosmic function of wisdom in the universe (7:24; 8:1). These emphases contrast with the Hellenistic concept, whereby wisdom is primarily understood as

41. For examples of the technique of "riddling speech" in Hellenistic writings, see David Winston, *The Wisdom of Solomon*, AB 43 (New York: Doubleday, 1979) 141-42.

42. For an excellent treatment of the personification of wisdom in the Wisdom of Solomon, see John S. Kloppenborg, "Isis and Sophia in the Book of Wisdom," *HTR* 75 (1982) 57-84. This work compares the Hellenistic version of the Isis cult (as opposed to the Egyptian version, which celebrates the healing power of the goddess Isis over the poisonous forces in the world) to the qualities of wisdom as presented in the book of Wisdom.

a means of attaining knowledge and of contemplating God. For the Wisdom author, wisdom is a gift and a revelation of God that works with humans and in creation.

As in the first part of the book, the technique of concentric structuring abounds in this central section of Wisdom. Chapters 7–8 are concentrically structured with the description of the nature of wisdom standing at the center:

A 7:1-6
  B 7:7-12
    C 7:13-22*a*
      D 7:22*b*–8:1
    C′ 8:2-9
  B′ 8:10-16
A′ 8:17-21

The extreme sections describe what prompts Solomon to pray for wisdom. In the two mid-sections, Solomon extols wisdom by comparing her favorably to other commonly recognized goods.

Chapter 9 presents the climax of Solomon's eulogy of wisdom. Here he adamantly prays for the wisdom that is a gift of God. The prayer begins with his recalling how the world and human beings were created through wisdom, and it ends declaring wisdom to be the one who has saved humans continuously throughout history. In the center stands the request for God to send forth wisdom from the holy heavens and from the throne of God's glory.

A 9:1-3
  B 9:4
    C 9:5-6
      D 9:7-8
        E 9:9
          F 9:10*a*
        E′ 9:10*b*-11
      D′ 9:12
    C′ 9:13-17*a*
  B′ 9:17*b*
A′ 9:18

In addition, the unit C′, 9:13-17*a*, is also arranged concentrically within itself.

The conclusion of Solomon's prayer provides the theme for the rest of the work. Wisdom is the one who saves the righteous in their difficult conditions of life. Chapter 10 specifically describes how wisdom accompanies righteous persons throughout history to prompt them through the crises and difficulties of life. Beginning with Adam and ending with Moses, the author tersely charts wisdom's saving role in history. As in the case of Enoch (Wis 4:10) and Solomon (Wisdom 7–9), the biblical characters remain unnamed, but their descriptions allow for relatively easy identification.

Chapter 10 provides the link between the eulogy of wisdom (chaps. 6–9) and the midrashic treatment of the exodus and the desert experience in the concluding part of the work (chaps. 11–19). The concluding part picks up the thread of the argument from wisdom's role in raising up Moses to save the troubled people and compares the Israelites in the desert to the plague-ridden Egyptians. The subject of the last part of Wisdom is not personified wisdom, but God. Wisdom recedes into the background, having completed her function of drawing the righteous into an immediate relationship with God.

WISDOM 6:22–8:21, SOLOMON'S DESIRE FOR WISDOM

Wisdom 6:22–7:12, The Sage Seeks Wisdom

NAB

22 Now what Wisdom is, and how she came
        to be, I shall relate;
    and I shall hide no secrets from you,
    But from the very beginning I shall search
        out
        and bring to light knowledge of her,
        nor shall I diverge from the truth.
23 Neither shall I admit consuming jealousy to
        my company,
        because that can have no fellowship with
        Wisdom.
24 A great number of wise men is the safety
        of the world,
        and a prudent king, the stability of his
        people;
25   so take instruction from my words, to
        your profit.

7   I too am a mortal man, the same
        as all the rest,
    and a descendant of the first man formed
        of earth.
    And in my mother's womb I was molded
        into flesh
2   in a ten-months' period—body and blood,
        from the seed of man, and the pleasure
        that accompanies marriage.
3 And I too, when born, inhaled the common
        air,
        and fell upon the kindred earth;
        wailing, I uttered that first sound common
        to all.
4 In swaddling clothes and with constant care
        I was nurtured.
5 For no king has any different origin or birth,
6   but one is the entry into life for all; and
        in one same way they leave it.
7 Therefore I prayed, and prudence was given
        me;
    I pleaded, and the spirit of Wisdom came
        to me.
8 I preferred her to scepter and throne,

NRSV

22 I will tell you what wisdom is and how she
        came to be,
    and I will hide no secrets from you,
    but I will trace her course from the beginning
        of creation,
    and make knowledge of her clear,
    and I will not pass by the truth;
23 nor will I travel in the company of sickly envy,
    for envy[a] does not associate with wisdom.
24 The multitude of the wise is the salvation of
        the world,
    and a sensible king is the stability of any
        people.
25 Therefore be instructed by my words, and you
        will profit.

7   I also am mortal, like
        everyone else,
    a descendant of the first-formed child of earth;
    and in the womb of a mother I was molded
        into flesh,
2 within the period of ten months, compacted
        with blood,
    from the seed of a man and the pleasure of
        marriage.
3 And when I was born, I began to breathe the
        common air,
    and fell upon the kindred earth;
    my first sound was a cry, as is true of all.
4 I was nursed with care in swaddling cloths.
5 For no king has had a different beginning of
        existence;
6 there is for all one entrance into life, and one
        way out.
7 Therefore I prayed, and understanding was
        given me;
    I called on God, and the spirit of wisdom came
        to me.
8 I preferred her to scepters and thrones,

a Gk this

NAB

And deemed riches nothing in comparison
with her,

9 nor did I liken any priceless gem to her;
Because all gold, in view of her, is a little sand,
and before her, silver is to be accounted
mire.

10 Beyond health and comeliness I loved her,
And I chose to have her rather than the light,
because the splendor of her never yields
to sleep.

11 Yet all good things together came to me in
her company,
and countless riches at her hands;

12 And I rejoiced in them all, because Wisdom
is their leader,
though I had not known that she is the
mother of these.

7, 12: *genetin*: so LXX^A, etc.

NRSV

and I accounted wealth as nothing in
comparison with her.

9 Neither did I liken to her any priceless gem,
because all gold is but a little sand in her sight,
and silver will be accounted as clay before her.

10 I loved her more than health and beauty,
and I chose to have her rather than light,
because her radiance never ceases.

11 All good things came to me along with her,
and in her hands uncounted wealth.

12 I rejoiced in them all, because wisdom leads
them;
but I did not know that she was their mother.

COMMENTARY

6:22-25, Introduction to Solomon's Discourse. This passage displays the author's literary penchant for linking major units with transitional sections. As such, it has striking parallels of phrases to the first part of Wisdom and to the eulogy of wisdom in the second. Royal imagery from vv. 9 and 21 is continued in the reference to a sensible king's being the stability of the people (v. 24). The exhortation to "honor wisdom" recalls the enclosing exhortations of the first part to rulers, judges, and kings (vv. 21, 25; cf. "my words," vv. 11, 25). Solomon will not hide any "secrets" (μυστήρια *mystēria*, v. 22; cf. 2:22, "they did not know the secret purposes of God" [NRSV]). Envy is dissociated from wisdom (v. 23; cf. 2:24, through the devil's envy death entered the world). Of course, the unit has even stronger links to the eulogy of wisdom of the second part. The origins and qualities of wisdom, which Solomon promises to reveal in the introductory speech, become the focus and the subject for the ensuing chapters.

The unique theological perspective in this short introduction to Solomon's eulogy on wisdom rests with the author's emphasis on the universality and openness of the revelation of wisdom. Solomon will tell of wisdom's origins and her function in history. No secrets will be hidden, and the truth will not be sidestepped. This openness to the gifts of personified wisdom is consistent with the figure of wisdom in Proverbs and Sirach, in which wisdom proclaims openly her values and gifts.

Solomon's insistence on revealing wisdom's origins freely without reservation is the author's counterpoint to the secretive initiation procedures of the mystery cults. In such cults, such as those developed in Egypt around the veneration of Isis and Osiris, there would be a combination of public expressions of celebration (processions, rituals of purification and sacrifice) and secretive rites of initiation of which very little is known.[43] In contrast to the value of secrecy in the mystery cults, the Wisdom author champions the openness of wisdom's revelation. Wisdom has a universal appeal that is readily available for all who have the disposition of virtue.

A proverbial saying that highlights the value of

43. For a concise treatment of the mystery religions that flourished during the Greco-Roman period, see Marvin W. Meyer, "Mystery Religions," *Anchor Bible Dictionary,* 6 vols. (New York: Doubleday, 1992) 4:941-45.

wisdom ends the introduction. Many wise people and a sensible king are said to be the salvation of the world and the stability of the people (v. 24). This proverbial statement echoes Prov 29:4, where justice replaces wisdom as the virtue that brings stability, "By justice a king gives stability to the land" (NRSV; cf. Eccl 10:16-17; Sir 10:1-50).

Since the first part of the work identified the just with the wise, especially in the diptych on the virtuous youth (cf. 4:16-18), the multitude of the wise and the sensible king represent those who have learned justice through wisdom. They are the source of salvation. Wisdom's positive role in the salvation of humanity throughout history in general and in the case of Israel specifically (9:18; 10:1-21) is consistent with the author's positive stance toward the world (1:14).

7:1-6, Solomon Is Mortal and Limited. Solomon's resolve to pursue the wisdom that comes from God is preceded by a brief, yet touching, reflection on his mortal condition. This reflection serves as a direct counterpart to the ruminations of the wicked on the transience of life (2:1-5).

Solomon recognizes his common lot with humanity. The reflection is not evasive. Solomon declares his mortality (v. 1). But what accompanies the recognition of the mortal condition is the solidarity of Solomon with the rest of humanity. Solomon is mortal, equal to and like everyone else. Since he is a son of Adam, he belongs to humanity. His origin is described not like that of the wicked, by mere chance, but out of the desire of his mother and father, "from the pleasure of marriage" (v. 2).

The author's description of the formation of the embryo is informed especially by Greek science. The idea of the embryo's being molded into flesh in the mother's womb through the compacting, or "curdling," of the semen in the blood was common in Greek writings.[44] In Ps 139:13-16 and in Job 10:10 we have references to the formation of the embryo in which God is said to be the author of life or the creator who knows intimately the workings of human beings.

Solomon's formation in the womb for a period of ten months is like that of all other people. The Hebrew tradition understood the time of human gestation to be nine solar months ("I carried you nine months in my womb" [2 Macc 7:27 NRSV]; but see 4 Macc 16:7, where pregnancy translates the Greek word δεκαμηνιαῖος [*dekamēniaios*] to mean "a ten-month period"). The Greeks and the Romans often referred to a ten-month period for pregnancy; Roman law understood ten lunar months to comprise the period of gestation. Aristotle noted that for human beings the period of gestation differs from seven to eleven months, with the ninth month being the most common for birth.[45]

Solomon recalls how at his birth he breathed the "common" air and fell upon the "kindred" earth. The world is not presented as a hostile, transient environment. Rather, the earth constitutes a home that is "common" and compassionate. Even though his first sound was a cry, like that of all healthy newborns, he was cared for and nursed in swaddling clothes. Solomon recognizes that his first cry of need was met by the care of another human being.

The conclusion of the reflection stresses Solomon's equality with everyone else. For everyone there is one entrance into life and one exit from it (7:6). Solomon's egalitarian status could very well be an implicit critique of the divine status attributed to Egyptian pharaohs and to the kings of the Hellenistic period. But the author's purpose of stressing Solomon's commonality with humans has a more immediate aim. Solomon does not have a status separate from other humans that guarantees special wisdom. The wisdom that Solomon will seek and attain is open to everyone.

Instead of issuing in despair, as is the case with the wicked, Solomon's ruminations on mortality bring him into solidarity with humanity. The world is not perceived as a hostile environment in which might makes right. Rather, the experience of human limitations, like the first cry of a newborn, elicits care and concern for others. Recognizing the common limitations of all human beings, Solomon is led to yearn for the transcendent reality of God.

7:7-12, Solomon Prays, and Wisdom Is Given. Whereas the wicked's negative judgment on the value of human life led to a project of

---

44. See, e.g., Aristotle *Generation of Animals* 739b21.

45. Ibid., VII 4, 584ab.

evasive pleasure, power, and violence, Solomon's recognition of the solidarity among humans in their limitations leads to an openness to God.

The reference to prayer and wisdom in v. 7 unmistakably employs the dream episode of 1 Kings (cf. 2 Chr 1:6-12), where Solomon came to Gibeon to offer sacrifices, and God appears in a dream to offer him a choice (1 Kgs 3:1-15). In the dream, Solomon recognizes the great task of being king and his own need to be guided in government and in judgment. Therefore, he requests an understanding mind and the ability to discern between good and evil. God responds by giving Solomon a wise and discerning mind, and God also grants him what he did not request: riches and honor.

Similarly, in the Wisdom text, Solomon recalls how he prayed and called out. The reflection on his smallness, fragility, and commonality with humanity leads him to search for a source to guide him. Understanding and a spirit of wisdom are given to him so that he will prefer wisdom to all else. Yet, all good things come to him as well through wisdom.

The author relates the gift of wisdom to the human goods that became associated with the life of Solomon (1 Kgs 4:20-34; 7:1-51). First, wisdom is declared to be superior to all that is most esteemed among humans: power and wealth (v. 8); precious stones and wealth (v. 9); health, beauty, and light (v. 10). This technique of comparing wisdom to riches, gems, and honor for exalting the benefits of wisdom was common in the sapiential tradition (Job 28:12-19; Prov 3:13-18; 8:10-11, 19).

At the same time, through wisdom, all good things have come to Solomon, and he rejoices in them. Solomon's delight in the natural qualities of health, riches, and beauty serves as a counterpoint to the wicked's evasive adulation of sensual pleasure (2:6-9). The author is adding nuances to the notion of blessedness, offered in the first part of the work. Earlier, in the diptychs, the author had argued that blessedness rooted in virtue endures even in the face of suffering and in the lack of natural human goods. The author is not pessimistic or strictly ascetic toward the pleasures of human life. Pleasure is not meant to be evaded; it is a gift of wisdom. The Preacher's exhortation in Ecclesiastes to enjoy life as God's gift finds an echo in the Wisdom text (see Eccl 2:24; 3:13; 5:18; 8:15; 9:7-9; 11:9).

The relationship between physical goods and virtue was much discussed in Greek philosophy. The Stoics held a position whereby virtue is considered the only quality necessary for human happiness. Aristotle offered a notion of happiness that integrates the good functioning of the three fundamental aspects of human life: the outside world, the body, and the soul.[46] Philo offered positions on human happiness that resemble those of Wisdom: A person attains happiness and bliss, "when there is welfare outside us, welfare in the body, welfare in the soul, the first bringing ease of circumstance and good repute, the second health and strength, the third delight in virtue."[47]

The conclusion of the passage adds a nuance to the relationship between wisdom and human goods that supersedes the source in 1 Kings. In 1 Kgs 3:10-13, the gifts of "riches and honor" are given in addition to the gift of a wise and discerning heart. The Wisdom author refers to wisdom as the engenderer of human goods (the rarely used Greek word γενέτις [*genetis*, v. 12*b*] is the feminine form of γενέτης [*genetēs*], which means "the begetter" or "father"). The image of the mother is a rare metaphor for wisdom. Ordinarily, wisdom is presented as a lover. In Sir 15:2, wisdom is compared to a mother in parallel fashion to the young bride, "She will come to meet him like a mother, and like a young bride she will welcome him" (NRSV). In Proverbs, personified wisdom is not called a mother; yet she exhorts others as a mother would her children (cf. Prov 7:24; 8:32). Philo describes wisdom as a mother and nurse.[48] As is the case with the author's view on the internal consistency between sin and punishment, the author postulates an intimate and intrinsic connection between wisdom and human goods. Wisdom is not passive in the world; rather, like a mother, wisdom actively engenders the human possibilities for happiness.

The fact that Solomon comments on not having known that wisdom was the mother of all goods singles out his pristine love for wisdom. He did

---

46. Aristotle *Nicomachean Ethics* 1098b.
47. Philo *Who Is the Heir* 285-86. For other Greek and Latin references to the various definitions of human happiness, see David Winston, *The Wisdom of Solomon*, AB 43 (New York: Doubleday, 1979) 168.
48. Philo *On Drunkenness* 31.

not pursue wisdom in order to have these goods. Rather, in discovering and receiving wisdom he has unearthed a value that goes far beyond his desires and expectations.

REFLECTIONS

1. Gratitude leads to generosity. The eulogy for wisdom is introduced with Solomon's desire to impart knowledge of her freely and without restriction (6:22-25). This unfettered placement of knowledge at the disposition of others corresponds to the universal accessibility of the wisdom that comes from God. The figure of wisdom in the sapiential writings who proclaims the ways of God from the rooftops and in the marketplace is consistent with the figure of Solomon, who imparts wisdom freely (Prov 1:20-21; 8:1-4; Sir 16:24-25). Another strain in the sapiential tradition will insist on the limits of human wisdom and will stress its inaccessibility (Job 28:1-28; Eccl 7:23-25; 8:16-17).

In the case of the Wisdom author, what has been freely given to Solomon is likewise given freely in return. This attitude of generosity is explicitly and concisely formulated in the preaching of Jesus, "You received without payment, give without payment" (Matt 10:8 NRSV). Jesus' exhortation to the disciples not to hold their light under a bushel basket but to put it on a stand for all to see likewise is concretely exemplified in Solomon's disposition to impart freely the knowledge of wisdom (cf. Matt 5:15; Mark 4:21; Luke 11:33).

2. Solomon's appreciation of human weakness elicits a sense of solidarity with humanity. It is interesting to notice how both the wicked (2:1-5) and Solomon (7:1-6) provide short reflections on the human condition of mortality prior to elucidating their projects in life. What for the wicked leads to despair for Solomon leads to solidarity with humanity.

Solomon's reflection on his own mortality and smallness constitutes his commonness with humanity. Recalling his frailty as a crying infant is not something that belittles him. Instead, his memory serves to remind him of the care and solicitude shown to him in his fragile state: "I was nursed with care in swaddling cloths (7:4 NRSV). A reflection on the limitations of human life in space and time need not lead to despair if the experience of suffering and weakness draws human beings together. On the one hand, suffering and weakness can remind us of our commonness with humanity. On the other hand, perceiving another person's need may draw out of us the care and solicitude that issues in unbreakable bonds.

3. Human weakness may open a person to transcendence. A parallel result of Solomon's reflection on mortality is his openness to transcendence. The realization of his "smallness" not only solidifies Solomon's commonness with the rest of humanity, but it also leads him to search, to desire, and to reach out. Again, in Solomon's outreach is the counterpoint to the inner despair of the wicked. Their negative judgment on life leads them to collapse in on themselves to mask the abyss with evasive pleasure and violence. Solomon's acceptance of his limitations leads him to pray and to call out.

4. A spirituality for suffering can be found in Solomon's two responses to his reflection on mortality: solidarity and desire. These responses provide the author's counterpoint to the response of the wicked. Suffering will always remain a mystery that cannot be resolved by conceptual formulations. But the author's treatment of the wicked's and Solomon's responses to human mortality provides clues for approaching the mystery of suffering both in ourselves and in others. Human suffering elicits solicitude and care. The anguish of human limitations reminds us of our solidarity with all of humanity. In facing the suffering of others, we sense the need to speak a word of solidarity and to reach out with solicitude. Finally, suffering in its many forms, from the normal experience of human finitude to the horrendous displays of despair and violence, invites or even shocks a person to reach out for answers. Suffering leaves us restless. Instead of collapsing in on himself in despair, like the wicked, however, Solomon accepts his "commonness" with all of humanity. He remembers the solicitude and care shown to him in his fragility. He looks beyond the self through prayer to find a response to the enigma of his situation in life.

5. Wisdom abounds with gifts. The description of wisdom's many attributes exemplifies the principle of abundance. Solomon recognizes that in wisdom all of life is ordered to bring forth the best of human goods. Solomon's response to receiving wisdom is the fullness of gratitude that rejoices in all of wisdom's gifts. Gratitude issues in his generosity to impart knowledge of wisdom without restriction. The figure of the wise Solomon epitomizes the principle of abundance. The more he has, the more he receives and the more he gives. When Solomon pursues wisdom first, all other gifts are showered on him with wisdom. A similar perspective on abundance is found in the teaching of Christ. The figure of wisdom is replaced with the kingdom of God and righteousness: "But strive first for the kingdom of God and his righteousness, and all these things will be given to you as well" (Matt 6:33 NRSV; cf. Luke 12:31).

Wisdom 7:13–8:1, The Nature and Qualities of Wisdom

NAB	NRSV
13 Simply I learned about her, and ungrudgingly do I share— her riches I do not hide away;	13 I learned without guile and I impart without grudging; I do not hide her wealth,
14 For to men she is an unfailing treasure; those who gain this treasure win the friendship of God, to whom the gifts they have from discipline commend them.	14 for it is an unfailing treasure for mortals; those who get it obtain friendship with God, commended for the gifts that come from instruction.
15 Now God grant I speak suitably and value these endowments at their worth: For he is the guide of Wisdom and the director of the wise.	15 May God grant me to speak with judgment, and to have thoughts worthy of what I have received; for he is the guide even of wisdom and the corrector of the wise.
16 For both we and our words are in his hand, as well as all prudence and knowledge of crafts.	16 For both we and our words are in his hand, as are all understanding and skill in crafts.
17 For he gave me sound knowledge of existing things, that I might know the organization of the universe and the force of its elements,	17 For it is he who gave me unerring knowledge of what exists, to know the structure of the world and the activity of the elements;
18 The beginning and the end and the midpoint of times, the changes in the sun's course and the variations of the seasons.	18 the beginning and end and middle of times, the alternations of the solstices and the changes of the seasons,
19 Cycles of years, positions of the stars,	19 the cycles of the year and the constellations of the stars,
20 natures of animals, tempers of beasts, Powers of the winds and thoughts of men,	20 the natures of animals and the tempers of wild animals, the powers of spirits[a] and the thoughts of human beings,

7, 19: *astrōn*: so LXX[S].

[a] Or *winds*

NAB

uses of plants and virtues of roots—
21 Such things as are hidden I learned, and
such as are plain;
22 for Wisdom, the artificer of all, taught
me.
For in her is a spirit
intelligent, holy, unique,
Manifold, subtle, agile,
clear, unstained, certain,
Not baneful, loving the good, keen,
unhampered, beneficent, 23 kindly,
Firm, secure, tranquil,
all-powerful, all-seeing,
And pervading all spirits,
though they be intelligent, pure and very
subtle.
24 For Wisdom is mobile beyond all motion,
and she penetrates and pervades all things
by reason of her purity.
25 For she is an aura of the might of God
and a pure effusion of the glory of the
Almighty;
therefore nought that is sullied enters into
her.
26 For she is the refulgence of eternal light,
the spotless mirror of the power of God,
the image of his goodness.
27 And she, who is one, can do all things,
and renews everything while herself
perduring;
And passing into holy souls from age to age,
she produces friends of God and prophets.
28 For there is nought God loves, be it not one
who dwells with Wisdom.
29 For she is fairer than the sun
and surpasses every constellation of the
stars.
Compared to light, she takes precedence;
30 for that, indeed, night supplants,
but wickedness prevails not over Wisdom.
8 Indeed, she reaches from end to end
mightily
and governs all things well.

NRSV

the varieties of plants and the virtues of roots;
21 I learned both what is secret and what is
manifest,
22 for wisdom, the fashioner of all things, taught
me.

There is in her a spirit that is intelligent, holy,
unique, manifold, subtle,
mobile, clear, unpolluted,
distinct, invulnerable, loving the good, keen,
irresistible, 23 beneficent, humane,
steadfast, sure, free from anxiety,
all-powerful, overseeing all,
and penetrating through all spirits
that are intelligent, pure, and altogether subtle.
24 For wisdom is more mobile than any motion;
because of her pureness she pervades and
penetrates all things.
25 For she is a breath of the power of God,
and a pure emanation of the glory of the
Almighty;
therefore nothing defiled gains entrance into
her.
26 For she is a reflection of eternal light,
a spotless mirror of the working of God,
and an image of his goodness.
27 Although she is but one, she can do all things,
and while remaining in herself, she renews all
things;
in every generation she passes into holy souls
and makes them friends of God, and prophets;
28 for God loves nothing so much as the person
who lives with wisdom.
29 She is more beautiful than the sun,
and excels every constellation of the stars.
Compared with the light she is found to be
superior,
30 for it is succeeded by the night,
but against wisdom evil does not prevail.
8 She reaches mightily from one end of the
earth to the other,
and she orders all things well.

COMMENTARY

7:13-22a, God Is the Guide of Wisdom.
7:13. The author had affirmed the relationship among wisdom, justice, and God in the opening exhortation (1:1-4). Now that the speaker is to divulge ungrudgingly and without guile what has been learned (v. 13), the relationship between wisdom and God comes to the fore with striking emphasis. The repetition of the idea of not holding back or hiding the wealth of wisdom reiterates the author's critique of the secretive methods of induction into the mystery cults (cf. 6:22-23; Sir 20:30-31).

7:14. Through the gift of wisdom comes friendship with God (v. 14; cf. vv. 27-28). Friendship was highly valued in the wisdom tradition, and it became an ideal for fostering a faithful and personal relationship with God (Job 29:4; Ps 25:14; Prov 7:14; 18:24; 27:10; Sir 6:5-17). Friendship with God was one of the highest epithets that could be given to a person. Abraham received the appellation of God's friend, and Moses spoke to God as a friend (Abraham, 2 Chr 20:7; Isa 41:8; Jas 10:23; Moses, Exod 33:11; cf. Christ and the disciples, John 15:13-15).

7:15-16. In the preceding passage, the author had just finished highlighting the superiority of wisdom to all human goods. Wisdom is described as the author or mother of good things. Now the intimate relationship between wisdom and God is laid bare. God is declared to be the source and guide of wisdom, the corrector of the wise (v. 15). Although wisdom has been personified according to the tradition of Proverbs and Sirach, the image of wisdom does not have a separate status apart from God. This intimate relationship between wisdom and God will allow the author to drop references to wisdom in the third part of the work as the subject who acts and to replace the subject with God, who acts on behalf of Israel. God is the giver of wisdom, and wisdom brings one into unity with God.

To impart the wisdom that comes from God, the sage asks for God's help and inspiration (v. 15). To be able to speak well and to express oneself with convincing artistry was a particular value of the sapiential tradition, as its literary activity testifies (Eccl 12:9-12). Yet the sage calls

upon God and recognizes that even this acquired talent is a gift to be sought from God. Wisdom was described as the source of all human goods; yet, wisdom itself has its source in God. Therefore, all the gifts that belong to wisdom, "our words," "all understanding," and "skill in crafts," are in God's hand.

7:17-20. The knowledge that the sage attests contains several references to Hellenistic philosophy and science of the day. The range in knowledge covers chronology and astronomy (vv. 18-19), zoology, demonology, the human psyche, botany, and pharmacology (v. 20). The author is appealing to the traditional motif of extraordinary wisdom and knowledge that became associated with Solomon, considered pre-eminent among sages (1 Kgs 4:29-34).

On the one hand, such phrases as "structure of the world," "activity of the elements," "the beginning and end and middle of times," "alternations of the solstices," and "cycles of the year" (v. 19) belong to technical and popular Hellenistic ideas on the universe. Alexandrian astronomy was famous for calculating the corrections needed for the public calendar to match the solar calendar. It was under Ptolemy III Euergetes (246–221 BCE) that an extra day was added to the calendar every four years so that the seasons would fall into regular cycles. In 45 BCE, Julius Caesar employed the Alexandrian astronomer Sosigenes to oversee the implementation of the Julian calendar.

On the other hand, such phrases as "the natures of animals," "the varieties of plants," and "the virtues of roots" (v. 20), point to the traditional knowledge attributed to Solomon. In the eulogy of Solomon's wisdom, both botany and zoology are included in his vast knowledge: "He would speak of trees, from the cedar that is in the Lebanon to the hyssop that grows in the wall; he would speak of animals, and birds, and reptiles, and fish" (1 Kgs 4:33 NRSV). Ordinarily, God is presented as the one who understands the thoughts of human beings (Ps 94:11; Jer 17:9-10). Yet this knowledge is attributed to Solomon, based perhaps on the "discerning mind" he received in the dream sequence (1 Kgs 3:12). The phrase "powers of spirits" (or "of winds") can be understood either as meteorological or magical knowledge. Magical knowledge would appear to be somewhat out of place in a list of specialties that reflect Hellenistic concerns, but later Jewish tradition attributed to Solomon knowledge of magical arts. Josephus, for example, describes Solomon's magical knowledge and how it was used against demonic spirits for the purpose of healing the sick.[49]

7:21-22a. The concluding sentence forms an inclusion to the opening part of the passage with the idea of learning (vv. 13, 21). Solomon learned and taught because wisdom, the fashioner of all things, taught him. The book of Wisdom is the only book in Scripture in which wisdom is presented as the fashioner of the cosmos (cf. 8:6, where she is the fashioner of what exists). But this idea is in continuity with the presentation of wisdom in Proverbs. There wisdom is the first act of God's creation, present to God and to the cosmos as it is being created and formed (Prov 8:22-36; cf. Wis 9:9). Wisdom is personified as a master worker or a darling child taking delight in the creation of the cosmos.[50] By attributing a stronger nuance of creation to personified wisdom, the author is once again bridging the distance between the transcendent God, creator of all, and the palpable experience of the cosmos.

7:22b–8:1, Wisdom Is Praised. Through the figure of Solomon, the author had promised to reveal the origins of wisdom and to trace her activities from the dawn of creation (6:22). This is precisely what takes place in the very center of the second part of the book of Wisdom. Wisdom is praised both for who she is and for what she does. This eulogistic passage forms the central unit of the concentric structure of 7:1–8:21. The author eulogizes wisdom through a description of her innate, natural qualities (7:22b-23), through an explanation of her origins in God (7:24-26), and through a presentation of her activities in the world and in history (7:27–8:1).

7:22b-23. The description of wisdom's innate and natural qualities takes the form of a list of attributes. There are numerous examples of this device for eulogies or for praise in both Hellenistic and rabbinic writings. The goddess Isis, for example, has so many names attributed to her that one epithet for her is "countlessnames."[51] In similar fashion, Philo attributes the epithet "manynames" to wisdom, referring to the several names given to wisdom by Moses.[52]

In this passage, the number of qualities attributed to wisdom, twenty-one (vv. 22-23), is not arbitrary. Three sets of the perfect number seven signify complete perfection. For the most part, the adjectives or qualities are borrowed from Greek thought, especially that of the Stoics. Of themselves the terms do not offer precise connotations. Rather, they are approximations and nuances that point to the subtlety, authenticity, and permeation of wisdom in the cosmos.

Intelligent, holy, unique, manifold, subtle, mobile, clear; unpolluted, distinct, invulnerable, loving the good, keen, irresistible, beneficent; humane, steadfast, sure, free from anxiety, all-powerful, overseeing, penetrating—it is not easy to discern a clear-cut pattern in the list of attributes, but three general concentrations of qualities can be recognized in the three sets of seven attributes. The qualities of the first set point to the mobility and transparency of wisdom. Appropriately, this series begins with the image of intelligence. Wisdom will be described as "an initiate in the knowledge of God" (8:4 NRSV), who "knows and understands all things" (9:11 NRSV). The second set points to the moral good associated with wisdom. Wisdom is dissociated from the opposite of the good, as in the opening exhortation (1:4). She is unpolluted and loves the good. The third set begins to point to wisdom's indomitable relationship to humanity. Wisdom is humane, pervading and permeating all that exists. Wisdom's pervasiveness in the cosmos makes her immediate and immanent to human beings.

7:24-26. Of the twenty-one attributes, the mobility and the pervasiveness of wisdom in the cosmos are singled out for special attention (v. 24). The idea that thought is faster than any physical motion was a common reflection in Greek philosophy. Philo likewise made use of the idea of swiftness in praising the speed of the

---

49. Josephus *Antiquities of the Jews* 8.2.5.
50. For a discussion on the images behind the personification of wisdom in Proverbs, see Mitchell Dahood, "Proverbs 8,22-31," *CBQ* 30 (1968) 512-21; Gale A. Yee, "The Theology of Creation in Proverbs 8:22-31," in *Creation in the Biblical Traditions,* ed. Richard J. Clifford and John J. Collins, CBQMS 24 (1992) 85-96.

51. *The Oxyrhynchus Papyri* XI 1380.
52. Philo *Allegorical Interpretation* 1.43.

Logos[53] and commented on the speed of the mind: "For the mind moves at the same moment to many things material and immaterial with indescribable rapidity."[54] The idea of the pervasiveness of knowledge that penetrates all things was a typically Stoic idea. Even the use of the double verbs "pervade" (διήκω *diēkō*) and "permeate" (χωρέω *chōreō*) points to its Stoic source, which makes use of these verbs to describe the presence of the spirit.[55] Because of its mobility and pervasiveness, wisdom is readily accessible to human beings as a source of right conduct.

Five metaphors are used in the central part of the unit to indicate the relationship of wisdom to God (vv. 25-26). Each metaphor attempts to relate wisdom to an aspect of God. Wisdom is the breath of God's "power" (δύναμις *dynamis*), an emanation of the "glory" (δόξα *doxa*) of the Almighty, a reflection of the eternal "light" (φῶς *phōs*) of God, a mirror of the "working" (ἐνέργεια *energeia*) of God, and an image of the "goodness" (ἀγαθότης *agathotēs*) of God. All of these varied metaphors attempt to root wisdom in God through images that point to wisdom's flowing, emanating, or originating from an aspect of God.

The metaphors themselves are quite an innovation for the Wisdom author, in comparison to the descriptions of the origins of wisdom in Proverbs 8 and Sirach 24. The author is combining various terms and metaphors that refer to divine or spiritual activity from Greek and Hellenistic sources.[56] Yet, the author is evidently applying such metaphors to the traditional Jewish concept of wisdom.[57]

The use of "breath," which in general denotes exhalation, signifies the close connection between wisdom and the power of God. The Greek word for "breath" (ἀτμίς *atmis*) comes closer to signifying the effect of the mist on our nostrils than it does to the breath of God in the Genesis creation accounts. As such, it often refers to the fragrance of incense (Lev 16:13; Sir 24:15). Wisdom, then, is like the fragrance of the power of God. The metaphor of the pure emanation (NRSV) or effusion (NAB) of God's glory brings us into the semantic range of water, although light can be said to flow as well (Ezek 1:13, lightning issues from the fire). Wisdom is being compared to the flowing of water from the source, which is God's glory. With the qualification of wisdom as being a pure flowing, the author is intensifying the authenticity of wisdom's relationship to God. Just as pure water flows freely from a good source, so too nothing defiled or impure contaminates wisdom, whose source is God (cf. 1:4; 6:23).

The comparison of God to various forms of light is a frequent and effective image in the OT, especially as light relates to the theophanies of God (Exod 24:17; Isa 60:1-3; Ezek 1:27-28; Hab 3:4). The psalms often speak of God's light and the light of God's countenance brightening up the life and path of humans (Pss 4:6; 27:1; 36:8; 43:3; 44:3; 89:15; 104:2). The author has already applied images of light to wisdom. Wisdom is radiant and unfading (6:12). Wisdom is said to surpass the brightness of light and the sun (7:10, 29). But here, wisdom is presented as the reflection of the eternal light. The same idea is continued in the following metaphor, which employs the image of a spotless mirror reflecting the activity of God (v. 26*b*). Philo also uses the metaphor of the mirror to describe how the activity of order and management in the cosmos mirrors the powers of God.[58] Wisdom, essentially, is busy with the activity of God (7:22; 8:6).

The metaphor of the image of God's goodness confirms the attribute of goodness and friendship that has continuously been applied to wisdom. Wisdom has been called a "kindly spirit" (1:6), the mother of all good things (7:11-12) who provides "friendship with God" (7:14; cf. 7:27) and who "loves the good" (7:22). The metaphor of "image" is biblical, used to convey the relationship between humans and God (2:23; cf. Gen 1:27; 5:1; 9:6). But with the specific nuance of explaining the relationship of God's goodness to wisdom, the metaphor in Wisdom is particularly at home with the platonic metaphor of a copy,

53. Philo *On the Cherubim* 28.

54. Philo *On the Change of Names* 179.

55. *Stoicorum Veterum Fragmenta*, ed J. von Arnim, 4 vols. (Leipzig, 1903–24; reprint Stuttgart, 1966; New York, 1986) 2.416: "the spirit pervades all things"; 2.1021: "the spirit permeates the whole."

56. For a source of multiple references to Philo's metaphors for the relationship of the Logos to God and for those of the Isis cult, see Winston, *The Wisdom of Solomon,* 184-87.

57. For an excellent presentation on the Wisdom author's sympathy for Greek thought and for attempting to express traditional Israelite faith through Hellenistic forms, see Alexander A. Di Lella, "Conservative and Progressive Theology: Sirach and Wisdom," *CBQ* 28 (1966) 139-54, also in *Studies in Ancient Israelite Wisdom,* ed. James L. Crenshaw (New York: KTAV, 1976) 401-16.

58. Philo *Questions and Answers on Genesis* 1.57.

"It is wholly necessary that this Cosmos should be a copy of something,"[59] and with Philo's application of the metaphor to relate the Logos to God, "The Divine Logos is himself the Image of God."[60]

The novelty for the author of Wisdom in identifying the proximity of wisdom to God lies in the density of the images, not in creating a new personality for wisdom. No other biblical source provides the variety of metaphors for relating personified wisdom to God. Yet all of these metaphors of fragrance, flowing, reflection, mirroring, and image relate only aspects of God (God's power, glory, light, activity, and goodness) to wisdom. The Wisdom author is expanding the traditional images of God's Word and God's deed—which relate the transcendent God to the life of Israel—to include images that portray causality and relation in God's dealings with humanity.

7:27–8:1. This unit explains the activity of wisdom in the life of the cosmos and humanity. Here the author highlights wisdom's effective influence on humanity. Cognizant of wisdom's effective role in the cosmos and in the lives of the just, Solomon will proceed to desire her above all else and to discover how to obtain wisdom (8:2-21).

The paradox of wisdom's being one, yet able to do all things, perhaps is inspired by the Greek paradox of the one and the many, or the problem of change and permanence, as put forward by Parmenides (504–456 BCE). It was a paradox applied to the many faces of Isis, who is described as being one, yet able to do everything.[61] However the same general idea is not absent in Scripture, "You [God] change them like clothing, and they pass away; but you are the same" (Ps 102:26-27 NRSV). The simplicity of wisdom is comparable to the unicity of God (Deut 6:4). Similarly, the parallel idea in the same verse has its roots in Greek philosophy. While remaining in herself, wisdom renews all things. In Greek philosophy, God is described as the "unmoved mover," who "remains in the same place," "not moving at all."[62] However, the idea that wisdom renews all things has particular biblical overtones. Making

things new is the activity of God's Spirit: "When you send forth your spirit, they are created; / and you renew the face of the ground" (Ps 104:30 NRSV). The author is drawing close parallels between wisdom and the activity of God in creation. Wisdom is God's activity in the cosmos and in humanity that renews the earth and restores human beings.

The turn to the specific focus on wisdom's relationship to humanity (7:27c) is consistent with the image of wisdom in Prov 8:31, where wisdom is said to rejoice in the inhabited world and to take delight in the human race. Wisdom enters into holy ones to make them friends and prophets of God. Both ideas have already been asserted by the author. Divine providence especially cares for the just (3:9), and those who have wisdom obtain God's friendship (7:14). What had been stated negatively in 1:3-6—namely, that wisdom flees from deceit—is now stated positively. Wisdom collaborates with the holy ones. Both friend and prophet refer to relationships of personal friendship and affiliation (Isa 6:1-9; Jer 1:4-10; Ezek 2:1-3:11).

The notion of God's loving the person who lives with wisdom anticipates the following unit, in which Solomon seeks to obtain wisdom as his spouse. The image of "living with wisdom" conjures up the parallel that the relationship between the just and wisdom is comparable to that of husband and wife (cf. Isa 62:5). They are completely faithful to each other, and their mutual love reaches a completion that goes beyond themselves.

To complete the eulogy, the author returns to the superiority of wisdom over light and ends with wisdom's pervasiveness over the earth, which effectively orders all things well. What is particularly striking and new in the comparison (from that of 7:8-10 and 7:24) is the introduction of a moral perspective. Wisdom is superior to light not because of brightness, since night follows day, but because evil does not prevail over wisdom. The tension between injustice and wisdom that dominated the first part of the work resurfaces, but with the emphatic superiority of wisdom assured.

The concluding remark also contains echoes of the Stoic belief in God's providence. The author has prepared for the conclusion that wisdom reaches from one end of the earth to the other

---

59. Plato *Timaeus* 29B.
60. Philo *On Flight and Finding* 101.
61. *Isis Aretalogy* Cyrene 6, 15.
62. See Plato *Timaeus* 42E; Aristotle *Physica* 256b25.

and orders everything well in the description of wisdom and in the metaphors relating wisdom to aspects of God. Wisdom is mobile and actively present in the world and in humans. However, the image of wisdom stretching through the universe is similar to the Stoic belief of the *pneuma* stretching from one end of the universe to the other. Similarly, the idea of wisdom's ordering all things well is parallel to the Platonic and Stoic ideas that God orders the universe continuously.

REFLECTIONS

1. Knowledge of the cosmos is consistent with the wisdom of God. The author of Wisdom presents, essentially, a positive view of the cosmos, of human beings, and of human knowledge. The role of God and God's wisdom in creation confers upon the cosmos and human beings a primary dignity that endures even during the conflicts between justice and injustice. The author, therefore, welcomes the insights of Greek and Hellenistic philosophy and integrates them into Israel's faith. Within the controversy of faith and science, the book of Wisdom comes down on the side of the integration of faith and knowledge. Since God has created the cosmos through wisdom, then knowledge of the cosmos leads to God.

In praising the origin of knowledge in God, the author's list of insights into the cosmos, into nature, and into the thoughts of human beings seems like a litany of praise for God and wisdom. It is as if the wonder and amazement of the intricate functioning of the cosmos lead to the awe and the astonishment of the source, who is God (7:17) and God's wisdom (7:22). The list of insights embraces the major fields of Greek knowledge: the activity of the elements, the calculation of time through astronomy, the variety of animal species, vegetation, human psychology, and medicine. At the beginning of the list of various forms of knowledge, God is praised as the originator of knowledge. At the end of the list, wisdom, the fashioner of all, is praised as the teacher. In the reflection on the origin of false worship, the author will reiterate the consistency between knowledge of the cosmos and divine origin (13:1-9) with greater philosophical precision.

The constant growth and expansion of our knowledge of science, of human psychology, of medicine, and of technology can appear rather daunting in terms of faith in a personal creator. Other voices in Scripture warn humans of the folly of holding one's own knowledge up with arrogance, thereby considering humans the center of the universe. The story of the tower Babel in Genesis signals the danger of truncating knowledge of the universe from the purposes of the creator. At the same time, the belief in the creation of the world by a personal God reminds us that the cosmos is imprinted with signs that point to a divine origin. The voice we hear in the book of Wisdom reminds us that the wonder we experience in understanding the universe can lead to the contemplation of the source of God's wisdom.

2. The eulogy of wisdom shows signs of attempting to bridge the distance between God's transcendence and God's immanence. The distance yet proximity of God is a paradox at the heart of Israel's faith. God, at once, is understood as reigning high in the heavens, beyond human understanding, yet intervening in human history to call Israel and to save the just (see Psalms 33; 113; 136). God's face cannot be seen; yet God is the one who cares for Israel as a parent. Traditional images that bridged the distance between God Almighty and God, compassionate love, rested on God's Word and deed. Through Word and deed, God would reach into human history to save the just and destroy resistance.

Personified wisdom is the later sapiential contribution to theology that bridges the gap between God's distance and God's proximity. The author understands God's proximity to human beings as being realized in the signs of intelligence in creation itself. The twenty-one attributes of wisdom attempt to describe wisdom's pervasiveness in and through the universe and the solicitude for human beings in calling them to the moral good. Wisdom is not personified to the point of becoming a separate entity. Rather, through five metaphors, wisdom is presented as God's intervention in history: a breath of God's power, a flowing of God's glory, a reflection of eternal light, a mirror of God's activity, and an image of God's goodness. The whole point of wisdom's activity is to bring human beings into proximity to God. It is wisdom who makes humans friends of God.

3. Although it remains unclear whether the NT writers were familiar with the book of Wisdom, some of the christological formulations in the letters associated with Paul have strikingly close parallels to the metaphors for wisdom's relationship to God in 7:25-26. Paul employs the image of a mirror reflecting the glory of the Lord to portray the manner in which God's glory transforms human beings in Christ:

> And all of us, with unveiled faces, seeing the glory of the Lord as though reflected in a mirror, are being transformed into the same image from one degree of glory to another. (2 Cor 3:18 NRSV)

Just as wisdom is called the image of God's goodness (7:26c), so too does Paul refer to Christ as "the image of God" (2 Cor 4:4 NRSV). Similarly, in Col 1:15, Christ is referred to as "the image of the invisible God" (NRSV) through whom all things were created. The author of Hebrews employs the rare Greek word for "reflection" to explain how Christ "is the *reflection* of God's glory and the exact imprint of God's very being" (Heb 1:3 NRSV, italics added; cf. Wisdom 7). Since the personification of wisdom became a literary device for presenting the immanence of God in human history, it was natural enough for the NT writers to employ similar language in presenting Christ as the image of God.

Wisdom 8:2-21, Solomon's Love for Wisdom

NAB	NRSV
2 Her I loved and sought after from my youth; I sought to take her for my bride and was enamored of her beauty.	2 I loved her and sought her from my youth; I desired to take her for my bride, and became enamored of her beauty.
3 She adds to nobility the splendor of companionship with God; even the LORD of all loved her.	3 She glorifies her noble birth by living with God, and the Lord of all loves her.
4 For she is instructress in the understanding of God, the selector of his works.	4 For she is an initiate in the knowledge of God, and an associate in his works.
5 And if riches be a desirable possession in life, what is more rich than Wisdom, who produces all things?	5 If riches are a desirable possession in life, what is richer than wisdom, the active cause of all things?
6 And if prudence renders service, who in the world is a better craftsman than she?	6 And if understanding is effective, who more than she is fashioner of what exists?
7 Or if one loves justice, the fruits of her works are virtues; For she teaches moderation and prudence, justice and fortitude, and nothing in life is more useful for men than these.	7 And if anyone loves righteousness, her labors are virtues; for she teaches self-control and prudence, justice and courage; nothing in life is more profitable for mortals than these.
	8 And if anyone longs for wide experience,

NAB

8 Or again, if one yearns for copious learning,
    she knows the things of old, and infers
        those yet to come.
    She understands the turns of phrases and the
        solutions of riddles;
        signs and wonders she knows in advance
        and the outcome of times and ages.
9 So I determined to take her to live with me,
    knowing that she would be my counselor
        while all was well,
    and my comfort in care and grief.
10 For her sake I should have glory among the
        masses,
    and esteem from the elders, though I be
        but a youth.
11 I should become keen in judgment,
    and should be a marvel before rulers.
12 They would abide my silence and attend my
        utterance;
    and as I spoke on further,
    they would place their hands upon their
        mouths.
13 For her sake I should have immortality
    and leave to those after me an everlasting
        memory.
14 I should govern peoples, and nations would
        be my subjects—
15   terrible princes, hearing of me, would be
        afraid;
    in the assembly I should appear noble, and
        in war courageous.
16 Within my dwelling, I should take my
        repose beside her;
    For association with her involves no
        bitterness
    and living with her no grief,
    but rather joy and gladness.
17 Thinking thus within myself,
    and reflecting in my heart
    That there is immortality in kinship with
        Wisdom,
18   and good pleasure in her friendship,
    and unfailing riches in the works of her
        hands,
    And that in frequenting her society there is
        prudence,
    and fair renown in sharing her discourses,

8, 8: *eikazei*: so LXX^MSS.

NRSV

she knows the things of old, and infers the
    things to come;
she understands turns of speech and the
    solutions of riddles;
she has foreknowledge of signs and wonders
and of the outcome of seasons and times.
9 Therefore I determined to take her to live with
        me,
    knowing that she would give me good counsel
    and encouragement in cares and grief.
10 Because of her I shall have glory among the
        multitudes
    and honor in the presence of the elders,
        though I am young.
11 I shall be found keen in judgment,
    and in the sight of rulers I shall be admired.
12 When I am silent they will wait for me,
    and when I speak they will give heed;
    if I speak at greater length,
    they will put their hands on their mouths.
13 Because of her I shall have immortality,
    and leave an everlasting remembrance to those
        who come after me.
14 I shall govern peoples,
    and nations will be subject to me;
15 dread monarchs will be afraid of me when they
        hear of me;
    among the people I shall show myself capable,
        and courageous in war.
16 When I enter my house, I shall find rest with
        her;
    for companionship with her has no bitterness,
    and life with her has no pain, but gladness and
        joy.
17 When I considered these things inwardly,
    and pondered in my heart
    that in kinship with wisdom there is
        immortality,
18 and in friendship with her, pure delight,
    and in the labors of her hands, unfailing
        wealth,
    and in the experience of her company,
        understanding,
    and renown in sharing her words,
    I went about seeking how to get her for myself.
19 As a child I was naturally gifted,
    and a good soul fell to my lot;

NAB	NRSV
I went about seeking to take her for my own.	20 or rather, being good, I entered an undefiled body.
19 Now, I was a well-favored child, and I came by a noble nature;	21 But I perceived that I would not possess wisdom unless God gave her to me—
20 or rather, being noble, I attained an unsullied body.	and it was a mark of insight to know whose gift she was—
21 And knowing that I could not otherwise possess her except God gave it— and this, too, was prudence, to know whose is the gift—	so I appealed to the Lord and implored him, and with my whole heart I said:
I went to the LORD and besought him, and said with all my heart:	

COMMENTARY

8:2-9, Solomon Desires Wisdom. This passage corresponds to the unit 7:13-22 within the concentric structure through a parallel of several themes and images (i.e., wealth, riches, understanding, wisdom as fashioner of what exists, as knower of the seasons). After praising wisdom's nature, her origin in God, and her effect on humanity, the figure of Solomon turns to a more personal note. It is for these reasons that Solomon is personally caught up in the pursuit of wisdom. There is a return to speech in the first person. The language changes to that of love, courtship, and marriage. The same issues of wisdom's nature, relationship to God, and benefits for humanity are pursued, but now from Solomon's personal point of view. It is as if the speaker is contemplating the precious moments of falling in love with a value of extreme importance.

8:2. The underlying metaphor of courtship is unmistakable. Solomon recounts how he had sought wisdom from his youth, desired to take her as a bride, and became enamored of her beauty. The literary device of treating wisdom or other abstract values as a lover and wife who is to be sought and cherished was common in both the Israelite and the Greek traditions.[63] Both Proverbs and Sirach provide excellent examples in the sapiential tradition of offering advice on the importance of choosing a good wife (Proverbs 31;

Sirach 25–26). In Proverbs, wisdom is personified as a woman calling attention to her values in the streets (Prov 1:20-33; 8:1-21), as the woman of a household who prepares a feast for those who are willing to hear insight (Prov 9:1-6), as a sister and an intimate friend (Prov 7:4). Sirach uses several metaphors for the pursuit of wisdom: a hunter (Sir 14:22), a suitor (Sir 14:23-25), a youth in quest (Sir 51:13-22). In a very brief metaphor, wisdom is presented as a bride and a steadfast wife (Sir 15:2-6).

The Wisdom author extends the treatment of the personification of wisdom as a lover and a bride. The figure of Solomon, whom tradition held to have cherished wisdom (1 Kgs 3:9), lends itself to the metaphor of courting wisdom as a lover. The metaphor of human sexual love to connote the passionate pursuit of values or faithfulness to God has its precursors in the Song of Songs and in the extensive metaphor of Israel's being the bride of God (Isa 62:4-5; Hos 2:14-23). Here the metaphor is held up to the reader's imagination to contemplate the values associated with wisdom.

8:3-4. The metaphor is applied not only to Solomon and wisdom, but also to God and wisdom. Wisdom's divine origin is dignified through a symbiosis of God and wisdom. Wisdom lives with God. The Lord loves her. The term used to characterize wisdom's relationship to God as an "initiate" ($\mu\acute{u}\sigma\tau\iota\varsigma$ *mystis*) in knowledge is a technical term used in the mystery cults to designate

---

63. For several examples of the wife metaphor for virtue or wisdom in Greek literature, see David Winston, *The Wisdom of Solomon,* AB 43 (New York: Doubleday, 1979) 192-93.

the highest level of illumination for their members.[64]

8:5-8. Four conditional sentences introduce wisdom's effective role for humanity in creation. If riches are a value to be pursued, then even more so is wisdom the source of wealth. If understanding is a value, then even more so is wisdom, the fashioner of whatever exists. The author appeals to wisdom's enduring role in creation to highlight her benefits (cf. 7:11, 22).

If righteousness is a value to be loved, then so much more so is wisdom, the origin of the four virtues: self-control, which moderates the use of pleasure; prudence, which discerns the means for ends; justice, which determines what belongs to each; and courage, which gives strength to surmount difficulties and trials. This is the first clear reference in Scripture to the famous debate of the four virtues in Greek literature. Plato classified virtue into four categories as expressing the harmony or health of the soul.[65] Although the Epicureans rejected the platonic division, they discussed all four virtues in the pursuit of pleasure.[66] The Stoics and Philo continued to speak of the four virtues, and Philo attributed the origin of the virtues to the divine Logos very much as our author attributes them to wisdom.[67] The author may very well have been inspired to integrate the Greek philosophical debate on the virtues with the traditional understanding of wisdom. In Proverbs 2, for example, wisdom is presented as the origin and bestower of several virtues (cf. 4 Macc 1:18).

Finally, if wide experience is a value, then so much more so is wisdom, who knows the past and the future, who understands speech and riddles, and who has foreknowledge of signs and wonders. The underlying allusion here is to Solomon's ability to solve riddles and enigmas (1 Kgs 5:9-14; 10:1-9). Among the sages, the ability to communicate with effective speech was highly regarded. The disciples of Qohelet valued this particular ability in their master (Eccl 12:9-13).

The common word pair "signs and wonders" (σημεῖα καὶ τέρατα *sēmeia kai terata*, 8:8) is ordinarily associated with the great events surrounding the exodus (Exod 7:3; Deut 4:34; 6:22; 7:19; Ps 135:9). In reverse order, it appears in 10:16 referring precisely to the great events of liberation that wisdom inspired through Moses. These signs and wonders associated with the exodus will become the focus in the last part of the book. The phraseology here anticipates the wisdom of God to be the one who saves the people and guides them through the desert with signs and wonders.

8:9. To conclude the series of conditional sentences, Solomon expresses his decision to have wisdom live with him. This decision continues the metaphor of courting wisdom as a lover in the opening sentence of the unit (v. 2). For the author, to accept wisdom into one's life is like engaging oneself in marriage. The commitment to live with wisdom will assure Solomon good counsel and encouragement in the trials of life.

8:10-16, Wisdom Grants Success. This unit corresponds to the declaration of wisdom's superiority over all goods within the concentric structure (7:8-12). The image that is treated throughout the unit is Solomon's fame, both during his life and after his death. Two phrases introduce the alleged fame Solomon will have through wisdom. The first addresses the fame he will have during his rule (v. 10), and the second introduces the fame of immortality that will belong to him (v. 13). The time frame focuses on the future, and the form of discussion is a personal and interior reflection of the unnamed speaker, Solomon.

The allusion to Solomon's fame is based on two features in the historical accounts of Solomon's rise to power. The first is to the youthfulness of Solomon, who recognizes his need for experience and wise counsel. In the dream sequence, Solomon confesses that he is but a child and does not know how to govern. Therefore, he asks for an understanding mind so that he can govern wisely and continue in the footsteps of his father, David (1 Kgs 3:7-9). In his reflection on Wisdom, Solomon realizes how he will have glory and respect before the multitudes and his elders, even though he is young. The idea of youths having understanding beyond their years was already addressed in the third diptych (4:7-20). Other examples in

---

64. The initiate (*mystis*) is one who has experienced the mysteries of the cult and is bound by a vow of silence not to divulge its secrets. See Marvin W. Meyer, "Mystery Religions," *ABD*, 4:941-42. Wisdom, however, is one who has the complete experience of the mysteries of God, but divulges the secrets to the just.
65. Plato *Republic* 443D-E, 444D.
66. Cicero *De Finibus Bonorum* 1.42-54.
67. Philo *Allegorical Interpretation* 1.63-65.

Scripture would be those of Joseph, who could interpret dreams (Gen 41:33-45); Elihu, who confronts the elders (Job 32:6-14); and Daniel, whose wisdom saved Susanna (Sus 44-46, 64). Solomon confesses that the reputation he has acquired is based on his commitment to wisdom.

The second feature in the historical accounts to which the author makes an allusion is the reputation Solomon will earn as a wise statesman both in Israel and beyond. His keen judgment is represented in the astute action he took to determine the true mother of a child (1 Kgs 3:16-28). His fame is alleged to have spread throughout all the neighboring lands (1 Kgs 4:29-34), and his rule extended far and wide (1 Kgs 4:20-21). Even the Queen of Sheba came to Solomon to verify his fame as the wisest of kings (1 Kgs 10:1-13). For the author of Wisdom, Solomon's reputation as a wise and powerful statesman was made possible because of the gift of wisdom that he received from God.

The claim that wisdom will confer immortality on Solomon is consistent with the previous association of wisdom with immortality (6:17-20). Wisdom brings one close to God and confers immortality. In the Isis cult, the goddess Isis was considered to have been the conferer of immortality, which she confered on her husband, Osiris, and on her son Horus. The immortality Solomon will enjoy is the honored reputation that will last even after his death. This reputation of immortality stands in sharp contrast to the reflection of the wicked, who were denied any lasting memory after death (2:2-5).

Finally, the metaphor of loving wisdom as a wife concludes this part of Solomon's inner reflection on the advantages of living according to wisdom. Wisdom is the one who brings complete rest and joy. All of Solomon's activity in planning and ruling finds its culmination in rest and peace through wisdom (v. 16). Both Solomon's public life and his private life will become well ordered so that he may enjoy in peace the fruit of his labor.

8:17-21, Wisdom Is a Gift of God. This unit corresponds to the opening unit of the concentric structure (7:1-6). The opening of Solomon's reflection on his human limitations and mortality led to the realization of his solidarity with all humanity and his openness to the tran-

scendence of God. Here at the conclusion of Solomon's reflection and eulogy for wisdom, we return to the concrete awareness of his need to ask from God the wisdom that is graciously bestowed as a gift.

8:17-18. The speaker recaps the essential features of the lengthy reflection on wisdom (vv. 17-18). In kinship with wisdom, there is immortality (cf. v. 13); in friendship with her, pure delight (cf. v. 16); in laboring with her, unfailing wealth (cf. 7:11); and in the experience of her companionship, understanding and knowledge (cf. 7:21-22). The conclusion of the summary leads to Solomon's awareness that he must actively seek the gift of wisdom.

8:19-20. The theme of Solomon's birth and childhood binds the unit to the opening reflection on his first cry as an infant (7:3). What is critical to the author of Wisdom is Solomon's awareness that even his good corporeal and spiritual nature needs to be completed by the wisdom that comes from God. The author is balancing the positive dynamic of the human structure against the incompleteness of human nature. It is as if the wisdom of God has fashioned human beings in such a way that they are complemented by the wisdom that is bestowed as a gift. The very structure of human beings is oriented to being completed by the transcendence of God (cf. 9:5-6, 13-17).

The controversial theory of the pre-existence of the soul has played a part in the formulation of the author's positive view of Solomon's nature.[68] A good soul fell to Solomon's lot—or, rather, being good, Solomon entered an undefiled body (vv. 19-20). The author's qualification of the priority of the soul over the body was probably influenced by nuances of Greek ideas treating the pre-existence of the soul. The notion of pre-existence had already worked its way into Jewish thought as exemplified in Philo and Josephus. But,

68. The pre-existence of the soul received its authoritative expression in Plato's complex doctrine (see *Phaedo, Republic*). The Wisdom author is clearly referring to the primacy of the soul with a notion of its pre-existence without reference to the more complex and negative aspects of Plato's doctrine—the transmigration of souls and the "fall" of the soul into matter. The negative interpretation of matter and the "fall" of the soul into a material body is quite foreign to the author of Wisdom. But, as David Winston points out, a few Middle Platonists already offered the perspective of a positive view of the joining of souls to bodies. For a thorough discussion of the various views of the pre-existence of the soul in Platonism, in Stoicism, and in rabbinic and apocalyptic writings, see Winston, *The Wisdom of Solomon*, 25-32.

in both formulations of vv. 19-20, the author is asserting the natural harmony that exists between Solomon's soul and body. What the qualification stresses is not so much the pre-existence of the soul as the moral perspective of the relationship between body and soul. By the virtue of "being good" Solomon entered an undefiled body. This is consistent with the author's ethical stance toward immortality.

8:21. Even though Solomon's natural disposition is as good as anyone could expect, he realizes that he will achieve the goal of his desires only through the gift of the wisdom that comes from God. Solomon's naturally good disposition gives him the insight that there is a gift from God that completes his desires.

At the beginning of the reflection, Solomon ponders the aspects of wisdom in his heart (v. 17), and at the end he prays to God with all his heart (v. 21). The idea of praying to God with all one's heart and soul and might was firmly ensconced in Hebrew piety. The author may very well be alluding to the shema in describing the ardor in which Solomon prays to God for wisdom, "You shall love the LORD your God with all your heart, and with all your soul, and with all your might" (Deut 6:5 NRSV).

REFLECTIONS

1. The effect of Solomon's reflection on the beauty of wisdom provides an insight into the self-appropriation of values. Solomon's pursuit of wisdom does not issue from a blind obedience or from outside pressure. Rather, by contemplating the reality of the wisdom that comes from God, the author engages the intellectual and the affective capacities of the mind and the heart. The author provides the reader with the inner dispositions of the unnamed Solomon that lead him to embrace the value of wisdom: the appreciation of beauty, wealth, intelligence, the virtues, and the desire for wisdom's intimacy with God, and even the knowledge of human experience. The pursuit of wisdom leads to the balance and harmony of a full human life.

The appropriation of the value of wisdom with all of its associated virtues in the figure of Solomon provides a contrast to what the wicked do with their lives (2:1-20). Despair motivates their judgments and actions in life. Love motivates Solomon's decision to embrace wisdom.

2. The mystical marriage between Solomon and wisdom continues a long-standing tradition of highlighting the personal engagement involved in choosing and appropriating values through the metaphor of human love. Just as courtship and marriage fully engage the entire spectrum of our intellectual and affective concerns, so too does the pursuit of God's wisdom demand the engagement of the entire person. The relationship between Israel and God is portrayed often enough through the image of a marriage. Hosea made extensive use of courtship and marriage to portray the painful consequences of unfaithfulness as well as the freshness, intimacy, and beauty of God's "first love" for Israel (Hos 2:1-23), and Paul used the metaphor to depict the relationship between Christ and the church (Eph 5:22-33). This marriage metaphor, then, both heightens the beauty of the exchange of love in the covenant and sharpens the pain of loss due to unfaithfulness.

In Christian mysticism, the use of language of human love to express divine love was inspired by these metaphors from the scriptures. John of the Cross rewrote the Canticle of Canticles based on a contemplative discussion between God as the bridegroom and the soul as the bride:

> Bridegroom
> She has entered in, the bride,
> To the long desired and pleasant garden,
> And at her ease she lies,
> Her neck reclined
> To rest upon the Loved One's gentle arms.[69]

69. John of the Cross *The Spiritual Canticle* 28.

Teresa of Avila spoke of the final stage in one's relationship with God in terms of a spiritual marriage. In the *Interior Castle,* she sets out to explain the progression of the soul in its spiritual journey as being led by God through a series of mansions. The seventh mansion represents the complete fusion of the soul with God through the image of a spiritual marriage.[70] Human friendship, love, and commitment provide images through which we can grasp both the challenge of wisdom and its gifts of rest, completion, and intimacy.

3. A spirituality from abundance emerges through Solomon's eulogy of wisdom. Solomon's awareness of his natural gifts does not lead to arrogance or complacency, but to the contemplation of the origin of his being. The awareness of having been given abundant gifts brings him to recognize the source of those gifts. In his final reflection on wisdom's many benefits (8:17-21), Solomon offers the counterpoint to his opening reflection on mortality and limitations (7:1-6), which offers a spirituality of privation and suffering. The final reflection offers a spirituality of abundance. Human limitation can be the birth of desire and longing. Solomon's realization of his mortality led him to yearn for completion in God. The experience of life in abundance also can lead to a yearning for union with the source of all gifts.

The eulogy of wisdom suggests that there is also a proper way to live with abundance. In the wicked, despair brought forth a plan in which abundance and power simply masked a nihilistic stance in life. They used the natural gifts of life to cover the abyss of weakness and mortality. Solomon's many gifts, which he received from his natural environment, however, lead him to reflect on the source of his blessedness. Instead of collapsing in on himself, Solomon reaches out to the source of blessedness.

What do we have that we have not received as a gift? Even the most personal achievements of insight or works of art never occur in a vacuum. Someone gave us encouragement or provided the right conditions for us to receive insight or inspiration. It may be easy to forget the giver in the experience of abundance (see Deut 8:1-20), but to reflect on the source of prosperity brings the purpose of abundance to its completion: union between the lover and the beloved.

70. Teresa of Avila *The Interior Castle,* Seventh Mansion II.

WISDOM 9:1-18, SOLOMON'S PRAYER FOR WISDOM

NAB

9   God of my fathers,
       LORD of mercy,
     you who have made all things by your word
2 And in your wisdom have established man
     to rule the creatures produced by you,
3 To govern the world in holiness and justice,
     and to render judgment in integrity of
       heart:
4 Give me Wisdom, the attendant at your
       throne,

9, 1: (*eleous*): omit *sou:* so LXX[MSS], Vrs.
9, 2: *kataskeuasas:* so LXX[MSS].

NRSV

9   "O God of my ancestors and
       Lord of mercy,
     who have made all things by your word,
2 and by your wisdom have formed humankind
     to have dominion over the creatures you have
       made,
3 and rule the world in holiness and
       righteousness,
     and pronounce judgment in uprightness of
       soul,
4 give me the wisdom that sits by your throne,

NAB

and reject me not from among your
children;

5 For I am your servant, the son of your
handmaid,
a man weak and short-lived
and lacking in comprehension of judgment
and of laws.

6 Indeed, though one be perfect among the
sons of men,
if Wisdom, who comes from you, be not
with him,
he shall be held in no esteem.

7 You have chosen me king over your people
and magistrate for your sons and
daughters.

8 You have bid me build a temple on your
holy mountain
and an altar in the city that is your
dwelling place,
a copy of the holy tabernacle which you
had established from of old.

9 Now with you is Wisdom, who knows
your works
and was present when you made the world;
Who understands what is pleasing in your eyes
and what is conformable with your
commands.

10 Send her forth from your holy heavens
and from your glorious throne dispatch her
That she may be with me and work with me,
that I may know what is your pleasure,

11 For she knows and understands all things,
and will guide me discreetly in my affairs
and safeguard me by her glory;

12 Thus my deeds will be acceptable,
and I shall judge your people justly
and be worthy of my father's throne.

13 For what man knows God's counsel,
or who can conceive what the LORD intends?

14 For the deliberations of mortals are timid,
and unsure are our plans.

15 For the corruptible body burdens the soul
and the earthen shelter weighs down the
mind that has many concerns.

16 And scarce do we guess the things on earth,
and what is within our grasp we find with
difficulty;

9, 10: (hagiōn) sou (ouranōn): so 1 LXX^MS, V, Arm, Copt.

NRSV

and do not reject me from among your
servants.

5 For I am your servant[a] the son of your serving
girl,
a man who is weak and short-lived,
with little understanding of judgment and laws;

6 for even one who is perfect among human
beings
will be regarded as nothing without the
wisdom that comes from you.

7 You have chosen me to be king of your people
and to be judge over your sons and daughters.

8 You have given command to build a temple
on your holy mountain,
and an altar in the city of your habitation,
a copy of the holy tent that you prepared from
the beginning.

9 With you is wisdom, she who knows your
works
and was present when you made the world;
she understands what is pleasing in your sight
and what is right according to your
commandments.

10 Send her forth from the holy heavens,
and from the throne of your glory send her,
that she may labor at my side,
and that I may learn what is pleasing to you.

11 For she knows and understands all things,
and she will guide me wisely in my actions
and guard me with her glory.

12 Then my works will be acceptable,
and I shall judge your people justly,
and shall be worthy of the throne[b] of my
father.

13 For who can learn the counsel of God?
Or who can discern what the Lord wills?

14 For the reasoning of mortals is worthless,
and our designs are likely to fail;

15 for a perishable body weighs down the soul,
and this earthy tent burdens the thoughtful[c]
mind.

16 We can hardly guess at what is on earth,
and what is at hand we find with labor;
but who has traced out what is in the heavens?

17 Who has learned your counsel,
unless you have given wisdom
and sent your holy spirit from on high?

a Gk slave   b Gk thrones   c Or anxious

NAB

but when things are in heaven, who can
search them out?
17 Or who ever knew your counsel, except
you had given Wisdom
and sent your holy spirit from on high?
18 And thus were the paths of those on earth
made straight,
and men learned what was your pleasure,
and were saved by Wisdom.

NRSV

18 And thus the paths of those on earth were set
right,
and people were taught what pleases you,
and were saved by wisdom."

COMMENTARY

This eloquent prayer for wisdom has been recognized by many commentators as the climax of the book of Wisdom. The eulogy of wisdom, which began at the end of chapter 6, flows into a dramatic appeal to God by the unnamed Solomon for the gift of wisdom. Throughout the chapters that dissuaded the reader from bringing on the reality of death by living a life of injustice (chaps. 1–6), the need for guidance in the turbulent sea of life has been coming to the fore. The wisdom of God offers the context of a positive vision for creation and humanity. With the wisdom that comes from God, humans find completion for their energies. And so Solomon pleads with God for the gift of wisdom.

The prayer is located near the central position of the book, especially when considered from the point of view of lines in the manuscripts.[71] It is modeled on the dream sequence in 1 Kgs 3:1-15 and the nocturnal appearance of the Lord in 2 Chronicles 1. Both stories relate how God appeared to Solomon in a dream or in a vision to grant him any request. Instead of choosing riches, fame, or a long life, the standard values, Solomon asks for a discerning mind and wisdom. The significant difference between Wisdom and those accounts is that the original context of a dream or a vision has been changed into a prayer initiated by Solomon.[72]

The prayer is crafted exquisitely from a literary perspective. It is as if the density of insight and feeling enclosed in the prayer needs an appropriate form to express and contain what otherwise would be dissipated. A curious fact is that the most moving passages of Scripture, upon a little probing, turn out to have been crafted with great artistic care.[73] It would appear that insight and profundity favor an aesthetic expression.

The three sections of the concentric structure of 9:1-18 may be outlined as follows:

```
A   9:1-3                        A′  18
   B   4                           B′  17b
      C   5-6                        C′13-17a
   ─────────────────────────────────────
      D   7-8            D′  12
       E   9         E′   10b-11
              F   10a
```

Through this structure, the author balances ideas and images within the prayer. The first section within the structure (vv. 1-6) speaks of

---

71. For a discussion on the central position of Solomon's prayer for wisdom in the book of Wisdom, see A. G. Wright, "The Structure of the Book of Wisdom," *Bib* 48 (1967) 165-84. Chapter 9 concludes the first half of the book, with chapter 10 added as link to balance the two halves of the book: chaps. 1–9; 10; 11–19.

72. Maurice Gilbert uncovered the concentric structure of Solomon's prayer and pointed out the author's creative transformation of the sources from 1 Kings and 2 Chronicles. See Maurice Gilbert, "La structure de la prière de Salomon (Sg 9)," *Bib* 51 (1970) 301-31. For a treatment of this work in English, see Michael Kolarcik, *The Ambiguity of Death in the Book of Wisdom (1–6)*, AnBib 127 (Rome: Pontifical Biblical Institute, 1991) 17-18.

73. The concentric structure, which relates images and expressions through a mirror-like reflection from top to bottom, is only one literary device employed frequently throughout Scripture. Several key passages in both the OT and the NT contain elements of concentric structuring: e.g., the Priestly creation account, Gen 1:1–2:3; the Priestly Abrahamic covenant, Gen 17:1-27; the sacrifice of Isaac, Gen 22:1-19; the disciples on the road to Emmaus, Luke 24:1-33.

wisdom's role in creation for all humanity. This section stands parallel to the last section (vv. 13-18) in which the tasks of life in general again are addressed. In the beginning, it is wisdom's role in creation that assures wisdom's intimacy with God (v. 1). At the end, it is wisdom's role in salvation history that assures humanity its intimacy with God (v. 18). The middle section (vv. 7-12) concentrates specifically on the task of kingship placed on the shoulders of Solomon. In itself, it is balanced by two halves that treat Solomon's call to govern, and in its center rests the formal request that God send to him the wisdom that is with God (v. 10). The prayer synthesizes the broad perspectives of the author's view of the human relationship to God and to the cosmos. It balances the reflection on human limitations and potential with the essential function of wisdom in creation and in salvation.

9:1-6, Wisdom Fashioned Humanity. Key themes are touched upon in the opening address of the prayer: the God of the ancestors, the God of creation, the creation of humanity through wisdom, the call of humanity to rule over the world in justice, the limitations of humanity for this great task, the need for human knowledge to be completed by the wisdom of God.

God is addressed in traditional Hebrew fashion as the God of the ancestors and the God of mercy (v. 1). The image of the God of the ancestors recapitulates the providence and care shown to Israel through the history of the patriarchs Abraham, Isaac, and Jacob (cf. Gen 26:24; 28:13; 32:10; Exod 3:13-16; 4:5; Deut 1:11, 21; 4:1; 12:1). During the divine intervention into the life of Moses in the desert, God's name is revealed precisely through the image of the God of the ancestors (Exod 3:13-16). But immediately the image of the God who saves is juxtaposed to the image of the God who creates the world (v. 1) and humanity (v. 2).[74] God is the savior and creator.

The reference to the Priestly account of creation is unmistakable. God creates by the spoken

word (Gen 1:3-29; cf. Ps 33:6). Humanity is given dominion over God's creatures and the task to rule the world (Gen 1:26-28). This task represents the ideal of God's plan for humanity: to rule as God rules, through justice and mercy. The author adds a clarification of wisdom's role in creation. Humanity has been formed by God's wisdom (cf. Ps 104:24; Prov 3:19; Jer 10:12, the same verb for "to form" is used in Wis 13:4). The relation of God's wisdom to creation and to humanity has already been addressed by the author on several occasions (Wis 1:6; 6:12-20; 7:14, 22, 27; 8:6, 13). It is a key idea that guarantees the efficacy of wisdom in bringing humanity continuously into union with God.

In the light of the great task that belongs to humanity, Solomon recalls the limitations and weaknesses that humanity equally shares. Humans are weak and short-lived, with little understanding in comparison to the complexities of the world (vv. 4-6). As in the earlier instances of this reflection on human weakness (7:1-6; 8:19-21), the awareness of limitations is no cause for despair. Rather, the reflection propels Solomon outside himself to seek wisdom in someone greater. The reflection is double-sided. Humans are limited, yet these limitations are subsumed by the wisdom of God (9:4-6). Humans also have many strengths. But if the wisdom of God is lacking, then even these gifts and strengths will lack their full power (v. 6). From the point of view both of human weakness and of human strength, Solomon realizes the efficacy of the wisdom that comes from God.

9:7-12, Solomon Needs God's Wisdom. 9:7-8. The prayer turns to the great tasks that have been placed on the shoulders of Solomon. First there is the call for him to be king over Israel (see 1 Kgs 1:28-40; 3:7), and, second, there is the call to build the Temple on the holy mountain (see 2 Sam 7:12-14; 1 Chr 28:11-19). The various terms employed for the construction of the Temple combine the image of the tabernacle in the desert with that of the Temple in Jerusalem ("a temple on your holy mountain," v. 8a; "an altar in the city of your habitation," v. 8b; "a copy of the holy tent," v. 8c).

The instruction to Solomon to build the Temple is parallel to the instruction to Moses to build the tabernacle (tent of meeting) so that God may

---

74. Ordinarily, Scripture seems to give precedence to the saving interventions of God as the fundamental bedrock of Israelite faith. Creation theology takes second place as a development from salvation theology. In an interesting article, Walter Vogels points out that the author of Wisdom appears to reverse this perspective. See Walter Vogels, "The God Who Creates Is the God Who Saves: The Book of Wisdom's Reversal of the Biblical Pattern," *Église et Théologie* 22 (1991) 315-35.

dwell among the people (Exod 25:8-22). The tabernacle housed the ark and the incense altar as well as a table, a candelabrum, an eternal flame, Aaron's staff, the priestly vessels, and a book written by Moses. The Temple in Jerusalem was meant to function as the tabernacle had done throughout Israel's early history. It became God's dwelling place (Psalm 84). When Solomon dedicated the Temple after its completion, the ark and the tent of meeting were placed in it (1 Kgs 8:4; 2 Chr 5:5). The relationship between the tent of meeting and the Temple was already implicit in David's plan to build a temple to house the ark (2 Samuel 7).

It would appear that a platonic concept enters the author's formulation when the Temple is described as a "copy of the holy tent" prepared by God from the beginning (v. 8c). The chronicler speaks of a "plan" for the Temple that David gave to Solomon, which likewise was given to David by the Lord (1 Chr 28:11-19). Sirach also may contain an allusion to a heavenly tent where personified wisdom is said to minister to God and that, therefore, was established in Jerusalem (Sir 24:10).

Although the precise formulation may very well be under platonic influence, the idea of an earthly temple reflecting a heavenly one is old, indeed. Gudea, the governor of Lagash in the second millennium BCE, spoke of the ground plan of a temple to be built, given to him in a dream.[75] Sennacherib (704–681 BCE) likewise spoke of the founding of the city of Nineveh as having been planned long ago in heaven. Philo made use of the platonic theory of forms to explain how the tabernacle envisaged by Moses was modeled on a prototype produced by immaterial and invisible forms.[76]

9:9. The abrupt switch to the theme of wisdom in the prayer has been prepared in the opening reference to wisdom. Because Solomon has been given such a great task and is so limited, he needs the wisdom that has fashioned human beings and, therefore, understands what is right. The author contends once again that wisdom is with God (cf. 7:21; 8:3, 21). But the particular

nuance that adds force to the affirmation is wisdom's presence at creation. Wisdom knows God's works, was present at creation, and, therefore, understands what is pleasing to God. The author is continuing in the sapiential tradition of Proverbs and Sirach regarding wisdom's presence in creation (Prov 3:19-20; 8:22-31; Sir 1:1-10; 24:1-7).

9:10. At the very center of the prayer stands the formal request that God send forth wisdom to Solomon from heaven. The phrase is formulated chiastically:

A send her forth
  B from the holy heavens
  B′ from the throne of your glory
A′ send her

The purpose of receiving the gift of wisdom is that wisdom "labor" at the side of Solomon, thereby enabling him to be united to God in his life and in his work. Wisdom is the one who makes friends with God (cf. 7:27), because she is intimately in union with God and a collaborator with human beings (cf. 6:12-16; 8:16-18; 9:2). The emphasis on learning what is pleasing to God (vv. 9, 10d, 18) may well be an echo of the central statement in the dream narrative of 1 Kgs 3:1-15, where Solomon's request for a discerning mind is described as "pleasing" the Lord (1 Kgs 3:10).

9:11-12. Wisdom's presence at creation (v. 9) guarantees efficacy in her collaboration with Solomon. Since wisdom knows all things, she will guide and protect Solomon in his decisions and actions. The idea of the glory of wisdom guiding and protecting Solomon may be an allusion to the pillar of cloud and fire that guided the Israelites in their flight from Egypt (Exod 13:17-22; 14:19-20). The theme of Solomon's task to rule and to judge is picked up positively in the second half of the prayer. With wisdom, his works will be acceptable; he will be able to judge justly; he will be a king worthy to follow in the footsteps of his father, David.

9:13-18, Wisdom Saves Humanity. Completing the concentric structure of the opening section of the prayer, the author addresses the phenomenon of human limitation with the concluding summary of wisdom's role in salvation. Just as the opening dealt with both wisdom's role in creation

---

75. *Inscription of Gudea, CAH* 1, part 2, 103.
76. Philo *Moses* 2.74-76. For other references in Greek and rabbinic literature to the idea of the Temple's being a copy of a heavenly prototype, see David Winston, *The Wisdom of Solomon,* AB 43 (New York: Doubleday, 1979) 202-5.

and a reflection on human weakness, so too does the conclusion show how human weakness is taken up and compensated for by the teaching and saving wisdom of God.

On first reading, it would appear that the author's formulation of human weakness in this section combines Greek and sapiential ideas on the limits of human knowledge. Greek philosophy holds the idea of the body burdening down or hindering the mind's activity.[77] However, for the Wisdom author it is not matter that separates humans from God but injustice (5:1-23). The idea of the soul's being imprisoned in matter would be quite foreign to the author of the book of Wisdom (see 1:14; 8:19-20).[78] The Hebraic notion of the "flesh" symbolizing human weakness and fragility comes much closer to the author's understanding of human limitations than do the precise nuances of the Platonic distinction between the body and the soul (see the use of the term "flesh" throughout the flood narrative in Genesis 6–9).

From the sapiential tradition, the author makes reference to the limits of human knowledge with respect to the wisdom of God. The poem to wisdom in Job 28 emphasizes the human incapability of finding wisdom (Job 28:12-15). The preacher in Ecclesiastes likewise emphasizes the limits of human wisdom: "That which is, is far off, and deep, very deep; who can find it out" (Eccl 7:24 NRSV). Whereas the sages caution against arrogance and hubris in their emphasis on the limits of wisdom, however, the Wisdom author stresses that human knowledge *is* completed by the wisdom that comes from God. The reflection on human weakness is formulated through a series of apparently rhetorical questions: Who can learn? Who can discern? Who has traced out what is in the heavens? Who has learned God's counsel? The surprising answer is affirmative when God grants wisdom. The conclusion to the reflection is that with the wisdom that is given by God all of these endeavors are possible (v. 17). This is consistent with the author's view of the function of human weakness, treated earlier. Human limitation and suffering need not be interpreted as signs of human despair and meaninglessness, as the wicked interpret them (2:1-11). Rather, like Solomon, the experience of fragility and weakness can propel one to seek the wisdom that comes from God (7:1-7; 9:4-6).

The conclusion to the prayer draws a direct parallel between creation and salvation.[79] It is through wisdom that human paths are set right, and people are saved by wisdom. Just as wisdom was present at creation (vv. 1-2), then, so too is wisdom continuously present to save human beings (vv. 18). Salvation is the theme that will dominate the remaining part of the book (10:4; 14:4-5; 16:7, 11; 18:5). Chapter 10 will follow wisdom's role in saving the just ones in their trials from the time of Adam right up to Moses. Then in the last section of the book, the focus will be on the exodus events, the foundational saving event for Israel.

---

77. The most notable reference would be in Plato *The Phaedo* 81C, where the soul is described as being burdened by the body.

78. Richard J. Taylor examines in detail the links and differences of the Wisdom author's anthropology to that of Platonic and Neo-Platonic philosophies. The conclusion is that although many terms are borrowed from Greek philosophy, the characteristic underpinning of the author's philosophy is essentially Hebraic. See Richard J. Taylor, "The Eschatological Meaning of Life and Death in the Book of Wisdom I-V," *ETL* 42 (1966) 92-95.

79. The author has broadened the perspective of salvation throughout the entire book of Wisdom to include creation, exodus, and ultimate judgment. For the author of Wisdom, salvation is understood as God's effort to bring humanity to the point of realizing the original intentions of creation. See Michael Kolarcik, "Creation and Salvation in the Book of Wisdom," in *Creation in the Biblical Traditions,* ed. Richard J. Clifford and John J. Collins, CBQMS 24 (1992) 97-107.

REFLECTIONS

1. Wisdom is not the same as knowledge. Solomon's recognition of his need for wisdom is a paradigm for humanity, particularly for our own time, when our technical knowledge has grown exponentially. There is a fundamental distinction in Solomon's prayer between knowledge and wisdom. Solomon is acutely aware of both the limits and the strength of his knowledge. Knowledge represents the human familiarity with the world that enables people to move and act within it. It bestows the power to act. But how will Solomon act? How will he act out of both the limits and the strengths of his knowledge? How will he assess and judge rightly the tasks before him? How will he choose the good from the myriad possibilities open to him?

It is through the divine wisdom given as a gift and welcomed as a friend that Solomon hopes to use wisely the power entrusted to him. This wisdom is elusive, and the author has attempted to describe its many facets throughout the eulogy of wisdom. It is close to the human mind and heart. It is divine. Because humans have been "fashioned" by wisdom, it enables people to judge well and act for the good.

Our contemporary situation is not essentially different from that of Solomon, described in the prayer. Our knowledge in the areas of technology, medicine, and psychology is more extensive than at any time in history. At the same time, it has become evident that without the will to act wisely we leave behind a wake of turmoil in the environment and in the social fabric of life. Both our knowledge and our awareness of our limitations should propel us like the unnamed Solomon to seek with humility and with passion the wisdom that judges wisely and acts with respect for the world.

2. Divine wisdom is not set over and against human knowledge. It is not as if Solomon must deny his knowledge to embrace the wisdom that comes from God. The prayer affirms with a particular nuance the essential relationship between humans and God presented in the account of creation (see Gen 1:27). Humans were fashioned according to God's wisdom (Wis 9:2). It is as if human energy is directed to being completed by the wisdom that comes from God. This means that without this wisdom, human knowledge becomes truncated from its divine source and will fail (Wis 9:6). But with the gift of wisdom that comes from God, human knowledge reaches its full potential (Wis 9:13-17).

3. Both human weakness and human strength lead to God. In the prayer, Solomon's view of his own weakness and his strength supplements what was already treated in 7:1-7; 8:19-21. Together these passages form a contrast with the view of weakness and strength offered by the author through the perspective of the wicked (2:1-20). For the wicked, human weakness in all of its forms is a cause for despair, and human strength is an occasion for hubris and exploitation. The portrait of Solomon painted by the author offers the very antithesis to such an interpretation. Solomon viewed his limitations and weakness (9:5) from the perspective of his tasks in life and his relationship to God. Instead of collapsing in on himself, Solomon confesses his limitations and seeks wisdom to overcome his limitations. Similarly, Solomon recognizes the strengths of his standing before others and in his selection to be king and judge. This is no occasion for hubris. He recognizes that without right judgment and action these strengths will come to nothing (9:6). The interpretation we give to weakness and strength is a perennial gauge of our moral perspective.

4. The prayer's enclosure of themes that relate creation and salvation reveals a synthetic theological panorama. God is the creator who has fashioned humans according to wisdom. And it is through the wisdom of God that humanity is continuously being saved. In some circles it has become customary to view creation theology and salvation theology as somewhat in opposition. Salvation theology emphasizes the unique interventions of God in history to liberate and redeem humanity from oppression and sin. Creation theology emphasizes the immanence of God's presence through the structure of the universe and humanity as continuously calling humanity to its original dignity and harmony with God and the world.

In older biblical scholarship, it was thought that creation theology was a very late addition to Israelite faith.[80] In more recent theological scholarship, it has been suggested that the salvation

---

80. Gerhard von Rad, *Old Testament Theology,* 2 vols., trans. D. M. G. Stalker (London: SCM, 1975). Von Rad's basic approach to understanding Israel's faith is to explore the creedal statements within the biblical narrative. Since these statements are expressed in the form of praising God for salvation, it is only natural that the salvational perspective of Israel's faith would be highlighted. In a later book, Von Rad explores the theme of creation within the wisdom tradition. See Gerhard von Rad, *Wisdom in Israel,* trans. J. D. Martin (London: SCM, 1978).

theology of the Bible has so dominated the last centuries of Christiandom that we need to recover the creational perspective.[81] The two perspectives of creation and salvation are not in opposition in the Bible. Certainly, the author of Wisdom envisions a harmony between the God who has created the world and humanity through wisdom and the God who continuously saves humanity through wisdom. Precisely because God is the creator and fashioner of the human heart, this same God intervenes to bring humanity to freedom and liberation. In the last part of the book, which deals with the saving event of the exodus, for example, the author presents the exodus as a new creation (19:6, 18).

81. Thomas Berry captures the importance of a holistic approach to creation through a renewed understanding of the context of growth—the earth. The creational perspective is present in the symbolic representations of our understanding of the earth in the Bible, but it can be overshadowed by the salvational perspective. See Thomas Berry, *The Dream of the Earth* (San Francisco: Sierra Club, 1988); Thomas Berry and Thomas Clarke, *Befriending the Earth: A Theology of Reconciliation Between Humans and the Earth* (Mystic, Conn: Twenty-Third, 1991).

WISDOM 10:1-21, WISDOM ACCOMPANIES THE RIGHTEOUS

NAB	NRSV
10 She preserved the first-formed father of the world when he alone had been created; And she raised him up from his fall,	**10** Wisdom[a] protected the first-formed father of the world, when he alone had been created; she delivered him from his transgression,
2 and gave him power to rule all things.	2 and gave him strength to rule all things.
3 But when the unjust man withdrew from her in his anger, he perished through his fratricidal wrath.	3 But when an unrighteous man departed from her in his anger, he perished because in rage he killed his brother.
4 When on his account the earth was flooded, Wisdom again saved it, piloting the just man on frailest wood.	4 When the earth was flooded because of him, wisdom again saved it, steering the righteous man by a paltry piece of wood.
5 She, when the nations were sunk in universal wickedness, knew the just man, kept him blameless before God, and preserved him resolute against pity for his child.	5 Wisdom[a] also, when the nations in wicked agreement had been put to confusion, recognized the righteous man and preserved him blameless before God, and kept him strong in the face of his compassion for his child.
6 She delivered the just man from among the wicked who were being destroyed, when he fled as fire descended upon Pentapolis—	6 Wisdom[a] rescued a righteous man when the ungodly were perishing; he escaped the fire that descended on the Five Cities.[b]
7 Where as a testimony to its wickedness, there yet remain a smoking desert, Plants bearing fruit that never ripens, and the tomb of a disbelieving soul, a standing pillar of salt.	7 Evidence of their wickedness still remains: a continually smoking wasteland, plants bearing fruit that does not ripen,
8 For those who forsook Wisdom	

10, 5: *egnō (ton dikaion)*: so LXX[MSS].
10, 6: *ex apollymenōn*: so with V, Arm, Copt.

[a] Gk *She*   [b] Or *on Pentapolis*

NAB

first were bereft of knowledge of the right,
And then they left mankind a memorial of
their folly—
so that they could not even be hidden in
their fall.

9 But Wisdom delivered from tribulations
those who served her.

10 She, when the just man fled from his
brother's anger,
guided him in direct ways,
Showed him the kingdom of God
and gave him knowledge of holy things;
She prospered him in his labors
and made abundant the fruit of his works,

11 Stood by him against the greed of his
defrauders,
and enriched him;

12 She preserved him from foes,
and secured him against ambush,
And she gave him the prize for his stern
struggle
that he might know that devotion to God
is mightier than all else.

13 She did not abandon the just man when he
was sold,
but delivered him from sin.

14 She went down with him into the dungeon,
and did not desert him in his bonds,
Until she brought him the scepter of royalty
and authority over his oppressors,
Showed those who had defamed him false,
and gave him eternal glory.

15 The holy people and blameless race—it was
she
who delivered them from the nation that
oppressed them.

16 She entered the soul of the LORD's servant,
and withstood fearsome kings with signs
and portents;

17 she gave the holy ones the recompense
of their labors,
Conducted them by a wondrous road,
and became a shelter for them by day
and a starry flame by night.

18 She took them across the Red Sea
and brought them through the deep
waters—

10, 9: *therapeuontas:* so LXX^MSS.

NRSV

and a pillar of salt standing as a monument to
an unbelieving soul.

8 For because they passed wisdom by,
they not only were hindered from recognizing
the good,
but also left for humankind a reminder of their
folly,
so that their failures could never go unnoticed.

9 Wisdom rescued from troubles those who
served her.

10 When a righteous man fled from his brother's
wrath,
she guided him on straight paths;
she showed him the kingdom of God,
and gave him knowledge of holy things;
she prospered him in his labors,
and increased the fruit of his toil.

11 When his oppressors were covetous,
she stood by him and made him rich.

12 She protected him from his enemies,
and kept him safe from those who lay in wait
for him;
in his arduous contest she gave him the
victory,
so that he might learn that godliness is more
powerful than anything else.

13 When a righteous man was sold, wisdom[a] did
not desert him,
but delivered him from sin.
She descended with him into the dungeon,

14 and when he was in prison she did not leave
him,
until she brought him the scepter of a kingdom
and authority over his masters.
Those who accused him she showed to be
false,
and she gave him everlasting honor.

15 A holy people and blameless race
wisdom delivered from a nation of oppressors.

16 She entered the soul of a servant of the Lord,
and withstood dread kings with wonders and
signs.

17 She gave to holy people the reward of their
labors;
she guided them along a marvelous way,

a Gk *she*

NAB	NRSV
19 But their enemies she overwhelmed, and cast them up from the bottom of the depths. 20 Therefore the just despoiled the wicked; and they sang, O LORD, your holy name and praised in unison your conquering hand— 21 Because Wisdom opened the mouths of the dumb, and gave ready speech to infants.	and became a shelter to them by day, and a starry flame through the night. 18 She brought them over the Red Sea, and led them through deep waters; 19 but she drowned their enemies, and cast them up from the depth of the sea. 20 Therefore the righteous plundered the ungodly; they sang hymns, O Lord, to your holy name, and praised with one accord your defending hand; 21 for wisdom opened the mouths of those who were mute, and made the tongues of infants speak clearly.

COMMENTARY

Most commentators understand the function of chap. 10 as a link that joins the eulogy of wisdom in chaps. 6–9 to the midrashic treatment of the exodus events in chaps. 11–12. This it does admirably well by continuing the praise of wisdom through examples of her accompanying the righteous of humanity from Adam to Moses and by introducing the final theme of the book: the exodus. Specifically, the concluding reference in the prayer to people's being saved by wisdom is concretely exemplified through biblical support. Of the author's three approaches to personified wisdom (7:22b–8:1; 8:2-8)—namely, to expound on her beauty, on her rootedness in God, and on her beneficial qualities for humanity—the latter is highlighted to conclude the eulogy on wisdom.

Seven loose sets of contrasts from personages in the Torah are brought forward to emphasize the positive function of wisdom in the lives of the just: (1) Adam/Cain (vv. 1-3); (2) Noah/the flooded earth (v. 4); (3) Abraham/the nations put to confusion (v. 5); (4) Lot/the five cities and Lot's wife (vv. 6-8); (5) Jacob/Esau and Laban (vv. 9-12); (6) Joseph/Potiphar's wife (vv. 13-14); (7) Israel-Moses/Pharaoh-enemies (vv. 15-21). In each case, wisdom is understood to have accompanied the righteous in their trials in order to protect them and bring them success. The contrasts are grouped into six sections (vv. 1, 5-6, 13, 15-16), each beginning with the pronoun "she" (αὕτη *hautē*). All the noble personages in the contrasts are described as "righteous," except for the first—Adam. The reason why the author does not describe him as righteous is likely that it was precisely from his transgression that wisdom had delivered him. The contrast between the righteous and their enemies or oppressors continues the contrast from the first section of the book, where the apparent fate of the righteous was contrasted with the fate of the wicked. At times, the contrast emphasizes the debilitating result of evading wisdom, as is the case with Cain, the enemies of Lot, and the Egyptians. Other contrasts focus on the positive guiding force of wisdom, as in the case of Jacob and Joseph especially.

The passage looks upon God's interventions in history in typical sapiential fashion. In wisdom literature, God is seen to act in history from within creation, so to speak. Through wisdom, God works within historical events and within the cosmos to bring the plan of creation to completion. There is a difference of emphasis in the prophetic perspective, which tends to look upon God's interventions as extraordinary acts of power that break into human history.[82] In the prophetic

---

82. For a discussion on the unique function of wisdom in relation to history, see John J. Collins, "Cosmos and Salvation: Jewish Wisdom and Apocalyptic in the Hellenistic Age," *HR* 17 (1977) 121-42.

view, we see God reaching out into the cosmos and into human history. In the sapiential view, we see the cosmos and humanity reaching out toward God with the aid of divine wisdom. Covenantal theology forms the backdrop for prophetic literature, whereas creation theology forms the backdrop for wisdom literature.

The form of writing in this chapter (and for a good part of the remainder of the book) is midrashic. Because of its loose style, it is difficult to call midrash a literary genre (it is a rabbinic term meaning "investigation"). In its broadest definition, a midrash is a type of literature that contains explicit allusions to the fixed canonical text.[83] The author is presuming knowledge of the accepted text and interprets the events of the Torah in a manner that attributes them to the wisdom of God. (For other examples of midrashic praises of illustrious persons in the Bible, see Sirach 44–50; 1 Macc 2:49-64; Heb 11:4-40.)

10:1-3, Adam/Cain. Three details from the Genesis accounts of Adam are singled out to show wisdom's protective role for all humanity: (1) he had been created alone, (2) he transgressed, (3) he received the strength to rule over all things. Adam's "aloneness" alludes to the second creation account, in which the creation of humanity is described through a double process: First, Adam is created and then Eve, and together they constitute the beginning of humanity (Gen 2:4-24). The transgression alludes to Adam's eating of the fruit in disobedience to the divine command (Gen 3:6). The third point reaches back to the first creation account, in which humanity is given the task of ruling over the living creatures (Gen 1:26, 28). Wisdom's protective role encompasses both the weaknesses and the strengths of humanity.

Adam is called the father of the world (v. 1). Although an abundance of literature surrounding the figure of Adam had arisen in the mystery cults and in gnostic writings, it is unlikely that the Wisdom author is alluding to some "ideal man" or demiurge through whom the creation of the world took place.[84] Adam is immediately described as the "first-formed" father of the world who was created alone. The term "world"

(κόσμος kosmos) most likely refers to the world of humanity. As the father of Cain and Abel, Adam is called the father of humanity.

In contrast to Adam, Cain is described as having departed from wisdom in anger, and as a result he is said to have perished. When his sacrifice of the fruit of the ground was not accepted by God, Cain became exceedingly angry and plotted to kill his brother Abel (Gen 4:3-8). For the author, Cain is a figure of unrighteousness; consequently the tradition of God's protective mark on Cain and his family is ignored (Gen 4:15-17).[85]

10:4, Noah/the Flooded Earth. The author mentions Cain's sin as the cause of wickedness that occasions the flood. Actually, in the Genesis narrative, Cain's murder of Abel is treated only as the first expression of violence among humans, which eventually leads to the wickedness that occasions divine wrath in the form of a flood. The earth is described as being saved by wisdom, who steers Noah, a righteous man, on "a paltry piece of wood." The author singles out the fragility of "a piece of wood," referring to the ark, to highlight the directive quality of wisdom's action for humanity (cf. Gen 7:17-24).

10:5, Abraham/the Nations. Three events from Abraham's life are depicted as being directed by wisdom: the tower of Babel (Gen 11:1-9), Abraham's righteousness (Gen 15:6), and the sacrifice of Isaac (Gen 22:1-19). The description of the nations that are put to confusion because of their wicked agreement refers to the episode at the tower of Babel (11:1-9). Although in the Genesis narrative there is no mention of Abraham's being involved in those events, the genealogy that follows the episode leads up to Terah, the father of "Abram." The Rabbinic tradition, moreover, made Abraham contemporaneous to those events: "Abraham said to the men of the generation of the Tower of Babel: What do you seek from God? Has He said to you, "Come and provide for me?" He created and He provides; He made and He sustains."[86]

83. See Gary G. Porton, "Midrash," *Anchor Bible Dictionary,* 6 vols. (New York: Doubleday, 1992) 4:818-22.

84. See Plato *Timaeus* 28C, where the demiurge is described as the "father of this world." See also *Life of Adam and Eve, Apocalypse of Adam, Apocalypse of Moses.*

85. Conspicuously absent from the list of righteous persons is Enoch, who had become one of the biblical characters who personified the sage and the beloved of God. Perhaps his absence is due to the fact that the author had already alluded to Enoch in the diptych regarding the untimely death of a just youth (Wis 4:10-15).

86. *Tanhuma,* Wayera, 50a.

Wisdom is said to have recognized Abraham's righteousness and to have maintained his integrity before God. This is a reference to the covenant episode between God and Abram (Genesis 15), where Abram expresses hope in God's promises and this action is reckoned to him as righteousness. With respect to the testing of Abraham (Genesis 22), the author explains how it was the wisdom of God that strengthened Abraham to follow God's command in the face of sacrificing his own son Isaac. The author had described wisdom as a friend of humans who seeks out those who are just in order to guide them and to make them friends of God. The references to famous persons of the Torah are meant to be concrete examples of what the author has argued in general terms.

10:6-9, Lot/the Five Cities. Although Lot is not presented in exemplary fashion in the Genesis narrative, the Wisdom author attributes the divine intervention of the two angels who save him to the working of wisdom (cf. Gen 19:1-29). Two features from the Genesis story of Sodom and Gomorrah are put into relief: the destruction of the cities by fire and the fateful glance backward of Lot's wife, who turns into a pillar of salt. The Genesis narrative mentions only three cities of the plain by name, Sodom, Gomorrah, and Zoar (the city that was spared for Lot). In the previous battle between the two groups of five kings against four, all five cities are mentioned (Gen 14:1-2). Although the accepted tradition understands only four of the cities to have been destroyed (see Deut 29:23), other traditions generalize the destruction as affecting the five cities of the plain (cf. Gen 19:24-25).[87]

The story of the destruction of Sodom and Gomorrah had become a proverbial epithet to characterize the ensuing devastation of wickedness (Deut 29:33; Isa 13:19; Jer 50:40; Amos 4:11; Matt 10:15; 2 Pet 2:6; Rev 11:8). It gives occasion for the author to elaborate the connection between devastation and wickedness. The desolate land around the southwestern part of the Dead Sea had given rise to many legends regarding its rocky, inhospitable terrain. The wisdom author refers to two of these legends: the destruction by fire, which renders the land hostile to

cultivation, and the pillar of salt. The mention of the plant whose fruit does not ripen echoes the author's earlier critique of the "brood of the ungodly" (4:3-5 NRSV). The pillar of salt refers to the legend of Lot's wife, who was punished for her unbelieving gesture of turning back (Gen 19:26). This legend playfully explained the erosion in the salty rock around the Dead Sea that created all sorts of eerie forms, one of which resembles a human being and is called "the wife of Lot." The author uses these images to drive home the importance of collaborating with wisdom. Because these people passed wisdom by, they could not recognize the good (cf. 2:21-22). In contrast to the folly of the wicked, the passage concludes on a positive note, highlighting the manner in which those who serve wisdom are rescued from their troubles. This theme of wisdom's protecting the righteous in their trials will be picked up in the examples of Jacob and Joseph.

10:10-12, Jacob/Esau and Laban. A series of events from the life of Jacob are picked up in order to illustrate the positive working of divine wisdom: Jacob's flight from his brother, Esau (Gen 27:41-45); Jacob's vision of the ladder at Bethel (Gen 28:10-17); Jacob's growing prosperity despite Laban's restrictions (Gen 30:25–31:54); Jacob's wrestling with the divine at Peniel (Gen 32:22-32). In each instance, wisdom is shown to be working in the background to bring about success for Jacob against those who would have harmed him. Wisdom guides him; shows him the kingdom of God; helps him to prosper at the expense of Laban, who had been oppressing him; and even gives him the victory in his arduous contest with the "angel." Jacob's vision at Bethel had been expanded in pseudepigraphal works to include explanations of divine plans.[88] The emphasis in the Jacob/Esau contrast is not on the negative source of wickedness, as with Lot, but on the positive accompaniment of wisdom that brings success out of trying circumstances.

10:13-14, Joseph/Potiphar's Wife. One might have expected Isaac to have been listed among the illustrious personages whom wisdom has aided. The author selected Joseph, perhaps, because the trials he faced in life were more amenable to showing wisdom's creative power to

---

87. See also Josephus *The Jewish War* 4.8.4; *Antiquities of the Jews* 1.11.4.

88. See, e.g., *Testament of Levi* 9:3.

transform situations of distress into occasions of divine blessing. Joseph was known for his sagacity in his interpretation of dreams and in his rising to great heights within the ranks of the Egyptian government. However, the author passes over the sapiential themes already present in the Genesis narrative (Genesis 37–50) and concentrates instead on two episodes: the attempted seduction of Joseph by Potiphar's wife, which eventually caused his imprisonment, and his rising out of prison to the heights of power in Egypt.

Wisdom did not abandon Joseph in his solitary position. Wisdom accompanied him to protect his righteousness and to be with him in the pit and in the dungeon. His resistance to the seduction of Potiphar's wife is attributed to wisdom. Wisdom is described as staying with him right to the point of reversing his misfortune. He ends up having authority over his previous masters (his brothers), and his accusers (Potiphar and his wife) are shown to be false. As a result of wisdom's accompanying presence, Joseph receives "everlasting honor." Wisdom was described by the unnamed speaker Solomon as one who leads people to a kingdom (6:20) and who confers an everlasting remembrance (8:13). Not only is this the case for Solomon, but also, according to the author, history itself has already exemplified wisdom's creative role.

10:15-21, Israel-Moses/Pharaoh-Enemies. The final contrast is more complex than the previous one in that the righteous consist of the entire people Israel and their singular leader, Moses. By contrast, the enemies are the Egyptian oppressors and their leader, the pharaoh. The protagonist throughout the contrast is wisdom. Wisdom delivers Israel by entering into Moses to guide the people and bring them over the Red Sea. Likewise, wisdom is the protagonist in thwarting the resistance to Israel's liberation. It is wisdom who drowned the enemies and cast them up. Wisdom is the one who inspires praise for God's marvelous liberation from the mouths of mutes and infants.

10:15. The Israelites are called "holy and blameless" and later in the passage "righteous" (v. 20). This is not to say that the author is unaware of the memory of Israel's own resistance to liberation, which is entrenched in the tradition. The

book of Exodus insists on a triple source of resistance to God's intervention: Moses (Exod 4:1-17), the people themselves (Exod 6:9; 14:11-12), and, of course, the pharaoh (Exod 14:5-9). Later in the book of Wisdom, the author alludes to Israel's resistance in the desert and to the punishment inflicted on the people as a result of Korah's rebellion (18:20-25; cf. Num 16:25-35; 17:1-15). But for the purpose of an effective contrast here, the author singles out Israel's righteousness under Egyptian oppression.

10:16. Moses is designated the Lord's servant, which is a much-used title for Moses in the Torah (Exod 4:10; 14:31; Num 11:11; 12:7-8; Deut 3:24; 34:5). The ancestors as well as Israel as a whole are referred to as God's servants (Exod 32:13; Deut 9:27; Lev 25:42, 55). In Isa 63:11, God is described as the protagonist of liberation who put his Spirit into the people and raised up Moses. Similarly, the author of Wisdom attributes the power of the Spirit that enters into Moses to the workings of God's wisdom.

10:17-19. Various events from the exodus narrative are attributed to the guiding and inspiring activity of wisdom: Moses and Aaron bargaining with Pharaoh using signs and wonders (Exodus 7–11); the acquisition/reception of goods from the Egyptians (Exod 11:2-3; 12:33-36); the remarkable journey from under Pharaoh's power guided by the cloud by day and by fire at night (Exod 13:17-22); the crossing of the Red Sea (Exod 14:13-25); the destruction of the army in the waters (Exod 14:26-31; 15:19); the song of praise by Moses, the people, and Miriam (Exod 15:1-21).

10:20-21. Two details in the Wisdom account are based on later interpretations of the events surrounding the exodus: the plundering of the Egyptian army (v. 20) and the singing of praises to God by mutes and infants (v. 21). The first detail, the plundering of the Egyptian army, was developed to explain how the Israelites acquired arms to thwart Amalek's attack at Rephidim (Exod 17:8-13). Josephus gives an account of this interpretation:

On the morrow, the arms of the Egyptians having been carried up to the Hebrews' camp by the tide and the force of the wind setting in that direction, Moses, surmising that this too was due to the providence of God, to ensure that even in weapons they should not be wanting, collected them and, having accoutred the Hebrews therein led them forward to Mount Sinai.[89]

The reference to wisdom's opening the mouths of the mute may be the author's clever reference to the song of Moses, which praises God's liberation (Exod 15:1-18). When God called Moses forth to lead the Hebrews out of Egypt, Moses resisted by claiming he did not know how to speak (Exod 4:10-16). The author thus attributes to wisdom God's concrete intervention to give Moses the power of speech and the ability to sing spontaneous praise.

Even the infants are singled out as singing God's praise under wisdom's inspiration (v. 21). Inspired, perhaps, by Ps 8:2, "Out of the mouths of babes and infants you have founded a bulwark because of your foes, to silence the enemy and the avenger" (NRSV), a very early rabbinic tradition attributes the singing of God's praises to infants: "When the babe lying on its mother's lap and the suckling at his mother's breast saw the divine presence, the former raised his neck, and the latter let go of his mother's breasts, and they all responded with a song of praise, saying, 'This is my God, and I will glorify him.' "[90]

89. Josephus *Antiquities of the Jews* 2.16.6.

90. *Tosefta Sotah* 6.4.

REFLECTIONS

1. Through wisdom God provides providential care for humanity. The sweeping survey of biblical figures from Adam to Moses is meant to expound on the saving role of wisdom. This saving role formulated the concluding remark of Solomon's prayer: Through wisdom God has fashioned the human heart, and through wisdom God saves humanity continuously (cf. 9:1, 18). The author has chosen familiar biblical characters to illustrate how the difficult circumstances of their lives fell under the providential gaze of God. In each case the saving activity of God is attributed to God's wisdom.

The providential care of God rests on the immanent workings of wisdom in creation. Providential care is at work in the forces of the cosmos, in the human heart, and in the history of human events. Where the standard biblical texts envisage God as intervening in the affairs of the ancestors, often dramatically and against the course of events, the sages understand God's interventions to be implicit in the ordinary activities of human decisions for justice or for injustice.

The Wisdom author's commentary on the ark that is guided by wisdom is a good case in point. The Genesis narrative highlights God's majestic command for Noah to build the ark to save humanity and the various animal species (Gen 6:11-22). The Wisdom author emphasizes the implicit guiding hand of wisdom that "steers" the fragile piece of wood to safety. God's providence need not be seen simply in the extraordinary events that bring liberation, but in the everyday circumstances that allow for injustice to be redressed as well.

2. Through wisdom, God reverses the misfortune of the just. The saving activity of wisdom not only intervenes on behalf of the righteous but also thwarts the plans of the unjust. The contrasts of righteous biblical figures and their wicked counterparts mirror the author's treatment of the just and the wicked in the first part of the book (3:1–4:20). In each case, the author recalls the trying situations of the righteous to show how, in fact, through wisdom the lingering threat is transformed into fortune. Only in the first case, Adam, is the trying situation brought about by one's own transgression. In this way, all of humanity, which originates from Adam, can be understood to be under the guiding providence of God's wisdom.

Wisdom had already been associated with righteousness in the opening part of the book. So it comes as no surprise that the author argues for wisdom's being God's means of saving the just and hindering the wicked. Cain is described as having "departed from" wisdom (v. 3); the populations of the destroyed cities "passed wisdom by" (v. 8); wisdom had shown

Joseph's accusers to be false (v. 14), and to wisdom is ascribed the role of having drowned the enemies of the Hebrews at the Red Sea (v. 20).

3. History is a forum for discovering God's action toward humanity. In the first part of the book, the author had argued out of principles. The reversal of fortune in the case of the righteous and the wicked was established through a series of declarations. The fortune of the wicked and the misfortune of the just were stripped of their appearances. In large part, the redress of injustice took place by the author's postulation of an ultimate judgment. It is the ultimate judgment that reveals the true nature of the reward of the righteous and the moral vacuity of the wicked. But what is the author's basis for postulating an ultimate judgment? In chap. 10s and throughout the rest of the book, history provides the data to argue for the merits of justice and the peril of injustice.

The series of incidents from the ancestral stories is presented to our imaginations with a particular intent. We see concrete examples of the righteous, who are rewarded by wisdom for justice during their own lifetime. These references to past incidents that are open to reflective scrutiny form the basis for contemplating the relationships between justice and wisdom and between wisdom and life. Contemplating the stories with the connections the author draws leads to an appreciation of wisdom and to a respect for justice. Since these connections are palpable in the illustrious persons of the tradition, there is hope that they are valid for the future.

The technique of recasting faith history to establish fundamental truths lies at the heart of the biblical narrative.[91] The particular examples of recasting ancestral history, besides the Wisdom text, are few: Sirach 44–50; 1 Macc 2:49-64; Heb 11:4-40. Sirach, the most extensive of the ancestral eulogies, begins with Enoch and ends with Simon son of Onias. In 1 Maccabees, Mattathias recounts stories of ancestral heroes from Abraham to Daniel to show how they were rewarded or saved for their virtue. The eulogy of the ancestors in Hebrews is the closest parallel to Wisdom. Faith replaces personified wisdom as the architect of salvation. Hebrews begins with the sacrifice of Abel and concludes by mentioning Samuel and the prophets to show how they had all been protected and saved by faith.

---

91. For an interesting discussion of the function of history in the articulation of Israel's faith, see Claus Westermann, *Praise and Lament in the Psalms,* trans. K. R. Crim and R. N. Soulen (Edinburgh: T. & T. Clark, 1981) esp. "The 'Re-presentation' of History in the Psalms," 214-49.

WISDOM 11:1–19:22

THE JUSTICE OF GOD REVEALED
IN THE EXODUS

OVERVIEW

The praise of wisdom's role in the history of the ancestors leads to the reflection of the foundational saving event for Israel: the exodus. The events of the exodus, ranging from the plagues of Egypt to God's providence for the Israelites in the desert, are presented as signs of God's wisdom and commitment to justice. As different as this final section of the book appears on the surface from the first two parts, the inner cohesion is nonetheless striking as well. This is the most "Israelite" section of the book, focusing as it does on the foundational event of Israel's consciousness. In it the author integrates God's commitment to justice, from the first section of the book, and the wisdom of God working through creation to bring union between humans and God, from the second part of the book. In the first two parts, the dramatic personae are individuals: the just one who suffers unjustly and Solomon, the seeker of wisdom. This initial focus on individuals allows the author to generalize and to philosophize on the nature of justice, life, death, wisdom, and God. In the third part, the forum for the conflict between justice and injustice is the collective unity of Israel. In God's action on behalf of the righteous in the exodus, the author draws out the confirmation of the principle of justice from the first part of the book and the sagacity of God's interventions from the second part of the book.

Given the author's tendency to organize literary units in dense forms, it is not surprising to see the further use of intricate concentric structures (chaps. 13–15). However, the major organizing device of the entire section is comparison and contrast, which is similar to the diptychs of the first part of the book. The various means of punishment of people who resist Israel's liberation are set in relief to the ways God intervenes on behalf of the just. The similarity to the diptychs that compare the just and the wicked in the first part of the book is noticeable.

This form of writing shows remarkable similarities to the literary genre *syncrisis,* which involves a comparison and contrast of antitheses.[92] In the classical forms of *syncrisis,* there are only two elements that are both compared and contrasted. The Wisdom author has adapted this Greek literary device to include a third party—namely, God, who intervenes in the case of the Egyptians and on behalf of the Israelites.

Since the basis for the author's comparisons and contrast is the story of the exodus as presented in the Torah, the form of writing is midrashic.[93] A midrash is an interpretation of a text that follows the contents and events of the narrative or poetic text explicitly or implicitly. In the book of Wisdom, the author follows carefully, though at times loosely, the events as related in the text of Exodus and interprets them as signs of God's justice. The author has made use of the older Scripture in both previous parts of the book (part one relies on Isaiah 42–60; part 2, 1 Kings 3). However, these biblical references in the first half functioned more as allusions to authoritative figures than as the organizing basis for interpretation. Here, in the third part, the references to selected events of the exodus are sustained throughout the entire section.

Exegetes have noticed two organizing features for the author's interpretation of the plagues associated with the exodus (see Fig. 1, 446).

92. See James M. Reese, "Plan and Structure in the Book of Wisdom," *CBQ* 27 (1965) 391-99.
93. See R. T. Siebeneck, "The Midrash of Wisdom 10–19," *CBQ* 22 (1960) 176-82.

One is a system of antitheses that compare and contrast the Egyptian punishments with Israel's blessings.[94] This system follows a moral principle enunciated in 11:5, 13: The very means that

94. J. M. Reese, "Plan and Structure in the Book of Wisdom," *CBQ* 27 (1965) 391-99.

God uses to punish the Egyptians are used to save the Israelites. Thus seven plagues are chosen for these diptychs; notice how these plagues compare loosely with the ten plagues and the final destruction of the army in Exodus.

Wisdom		Exodus
1. water turned to blood	—	1. water turned to blood (Exod 7:14-25)
2. animals suppress the appetite	—	2. frogs (Exod 8:1-15)
3. animals that kill	—	3. gnats (Exod 8:16-19)
	—	4. flies (Exod 8:20-32)
	—	5. livestock diseased (Exod 9:1-7)
	—	6. boils (Exod 9:8-12)
4. rain, hail, and fire	—	7. thunder and hail (Exod 9:13-35)
	—	8. locusts (Exod 10:1-20)
5. darkness	—	9. darkness (Exod 10:21-29)
6. death of the firstborn	—	10. the firstborn die (Exod 12:29-32)
7. drowning in the Red Sea	—	Pharaoh's army drowns (Exod 14:26-29)

The other system consists of five diptychs that draw a parallel between Egypt's sins and the ensuing punishments of the plagues.[95] This system follows the moral principle enunciated in 11:16: God punishes the Egyptians according to the very manner in which they sin. This principle is consistent with that of the first part of the book, where the author declares that the wicked are punished according to their false reasoning (3:10-13).

The contrasts within the first four diptychs are introduced by the adverb "instead" (ἀντί *anti*; 11:6; 16:2; 16:20; 18:3). The last diptych is more complex. Instead of there being a single punishment for one sin, there is a sin with two punishments. The sin of killing the Israelite infants elicits both the death of the Egyptian firstborn and the drowning in the sea of the Egyptian army. Both the first and the last diptychs concentrate on the identical sin of the Egyptians, the killing of the Israelite newborn.

The comparison and contrast within the diptychs afford the author the opportunity to reflect on and interpret the significance of the enemy's sins, the blessings for Israel, and God's actions.

95. See A. G. Wright, "The Structure of Wisdom 11-19," *CBQ* 27 (1965) 28-34.

These reflections have been coined "digressions" whenever they are sustained for a longer period. Two major digressions occur within the second diptych, which treats the worship of animals. The first major digression deals with God's grace and moderation (11:17–12:27). The second concentrates on the origins of false worship (chaps. 13–15). From within the five-diptych system, three other minor digressions can be noted: the digression on God's power over life and death, derived from the episode of the brazen serpent (16:5-14); a digression on the death experienced also by the righteous, which Aaron stops (18:20-25); and a concluding digression on creation (19:6-21).

One of the reasons why a number of exegetes earlier had posited different authors for the three sections of the book is the absence of personified wisdom in the midrash on the exodus. Indeed, on the surface this absence appears rather striking. Wisdom is the protagonist in the sweeping review of the history of illustrious figures from the book of Genesis until Moses (10:1–11:1). Afterward (11:2–19:22), God alone is the protagonist who acts in favor of the righteous and in opposition to the enemies of the righteous. Moses and Aaron function as mediators, but it is always God who is presented as the actor who inspires even the mediators to act. Wisdom is mentioned only twice in the third part of the book in the reflection on the origin of idolatry (14:2, 5).

There remains the convenient explanation that the Wisdom author may very well have written the various sections of the book at different intervals. This distance in time, then, might account for the different focus in images and themes within a style of writing that bears striking consistency of vocabulary. However, there is a theological consistency in the relative silence on wisdom in the third part that should not be overlooked. For the author, personified wisdom is not a separate entity from the divine sphere. Wisdom is the particular outreach of God to humans in the cosmos. The purpose of wisdom for humans is to guide them to God. Wisdom is described as making people friends of God (7:27). Therefore, for the author to focus on God as the protagonist in the events of the exodus shows the transparency of personified wisdom. Wisdom recedes into the background, but it permeates the exodus events because of wisdom's subdued role in the first two sections of the book. Philo likewise would alternate between speaking of personified wisdom or the Divine Mind as the outreach of God in the world and the personal God who acts immediately in the affairs of human history.[96]

One of the unifying features throughout the diptychs on the plagues that relates the third part to the first is God's justice and judgment. The author's interpretation of the exodus event applies the principle of justice from the first part of the book to the foundational experience of Israel. God intervenes in Israel's history to restore justice. Justice implies the restoration of life to the Israelites and the thwarting of the resistance to liberation in the case of the Egyptians. The Israelites are constantly named the righteous, whereas the Egyptians are often called the enemies. The polarity between the righteous and the enemies in the exodus interpretation parallels the polarity between the wicked/godless and the righteous in the first part.

In fact, there is a deliberate correlation between God's ultimate judgment in the first part of Wisdom and the judgment of God against the enemies of the righteous and in behalf of Israel in the third part. In both cases, the cosmos acts in unison with God's activity of justice. God makes use of the cosmos to bless and to punish. The author had posited an ultimate judgment that would reveal the true nature of the blessedness of the just and the empty hope of the wicked. The basis for positing such an ultimate judgment lies in Israel's own history. Since God has acted to restore life and to thwart resistance to life in Israel's history, then there is hope that this is the guiding principle of God's justice in the present time and in the future.

Another theological consistency in the author's unique interpretation of the exodus event and in the first two parts of Wisdom centers on the role of the cosmos in sustaining the creative activity of God. Salvation and creation become fused into a continuum of God's activity. The unique saving event of Israel, the liberation of the Israelites from Egypt, is portrayed as a new creation (19:9-22). God used the cosmos to thwart the resistance of the lawless in the apocalyptic judgment of the first part of the book. In the second part of the book, it is because of wisdom's work in and through the cosmos at the time of creation that allows wisdom to save the righteous throughout history. Through wisdom, God is able to direct the positive force of creation to establish justice continuously. The author derives proof for such divine activity in the reflection on the episodes of the exodus drawn from the Torah.

---

96. David Winston notes Philo's tendency to move almost unconsciously from speech about wisdom to speech about God. See Philo *On the Sacrifices of Abel and Cain* 98 and *On the Migration of Abraham* 128. See also *The Wisdom of Solomon,* AB 43 (New York: Doubleday, 1979) 226.

WISDOM 11:1-5, THE WILDERNESS

NAB

11 She made their affairs prosper through the holy prophet.
2 They journeyed through the uninhabited desert,
    and in solitudes they pitched their tents;
3   they withstood enemies and took vengeance on their foes.
4 When they thirsted, they called upon you,
    and water was given them from the sheer rock,
    assuagement for their thirst from the hard stone.
5 For by the things through which their foes were punished
    they in their need were benefited.

NRSV

11 Wisdom[a] prospered their works by the hand of a holy prophet.
2 They journeyed through an uninhabited wilderness,
    and pitched their tents in untrodden places.
3 They withstood their enemies and fought off their foes.
4 When they were thirsty, they called upon you,
    and water was given them out of flinty rock,
    and from hard stone a remedy for their thirst.
5 For through the very things by which their enemies were punished,
    they themselves received benefit in their need.

a Gk *She*

COMMENTARY

11:1. The exposition on the role of personified wisdom in the lives of the righteous leads the author to the contemplation of the activity of God in the events of the exodus. Wisdom is said to be the one who prospers the activities of the righteous through the prophet Moses (v. 1). This verse brings to a conclusion the exposition of wisdom's role in the lives of the righteous and introduces specifically the events of the exodus from Egypt and the wandering in the desert. The figure of Moses towers over the events of the exodus. The wisdom author, however, attributes the guiding hand of God for the entire people and for their mediators to personified wisdom.

11:2-4. Interestingly, the introduction to the exodus events focuses on the image of the wilderness, which actually follows those events as narrated in Exodus. After the extraordinary deliverance at the Red Sea, the Israelites face the antagonism of the desert. The wilderness refers to a space that is hostile to life and to a time that is volatile and unsure. It is described as being uninhabited and untrodden (v. 2). There is a threat to life not only from the natural circumstances of drought in the wilderness, but also from the deliberate hostility of enemies (v. 3). The

combination of drought and enemies that the author employs to characterize Israel's existence in the desert is more than likely a reference to Exodus 17, where the two episodes of thirsting in the desert and of waging war with Amalek are narrated side by side. However, the entire period of Israel's life in the desert was characterized by thirst and hunger (Exod 15:22-27; 16:1-26; 17:1-7; Num 11:1-14; 11:31-35; 20:1-13) and by threat from enemies (Exod 17:8-16; 21:1-33; Deut 2:1–3:22). The threat to life in the wilderness actually highlights the extraordinary intervention of God for the benefit of the righteous. They call upon God because they are thirsty, and water is given through the flinty rock (v. 4).

11:5. The reflection on the source of water in the wilderness brings the author to one of the two key principles through which the exodus events will be interpreted. The very means of punishment against the Egyptians are the means of salvation for the Israelites. In this case, water was used to punish the enemies of the Israelites both when the Nile was turned to blood and when the Egyptian army drowned in the Red Sea. But for the righteous, the gift of water in the wilderness brings the quenching of thirst and survival.

The use of identical means of blessing and punishment is rare in biblical literature. In Sirach we find a similar idea, although it is formulated differently. In a comparison between the gifts given to the righteous and the punishments given to sinners, the author notes: "All these are good for the godly, but for sinners they turn into evils" (Sir 39:27 NRSV). In a rabbinic source, the same idea is formulated much in the way the Wisdom author understands it: "The Holy One blessed be He heals by the same means whereby He smites."[97]

The principle implies that God is the Lord of both creation and history. The elements of creation are ambivalent. God can use them to bless and to punish. Creation itself, as noted in the first half of the book, is on the side of justice and the righteous. The events of the exodus, viewed from this perspective, become the author's clinching proof for the judgment that justice and wisdom bring life.

97. *Wayyikra Rabba* 18.5.

REFLECTIONS

1. The backdrop of the wilderness experience highlights the gift of life. No matter how much the Israelites may have struggled for survival against the harshness of the environment and against the threat of enemies, their memory records their survival as a gift and as an extraordinary deliverance. The Wisdom author introduces the exodus events by setting them in the context of this wilderness experience. Where the threat to life is extreme, so much more does the awareness of life and its gift become acute. The purpose of the comparisons between the acts of deliverance of the righteous and the acts of punishment of the enemies is to heighten the appreciation of the gift of life.

In the book of Deuteronomy we see how a tradition within Israel had idealized the wilderness experience as Israel's privileged moment of faith and trust in God (see Deut 8:1-20). Exodus and Numbers record the "grumbling in the desert" and the acts of "faithlessness" even in the leadership of Moses, Aaron, and Miriam. The authors of Deuteronomy interpret the wilderness experience after the great acts of rebellion as the in-between time of learning trust and faith in God (Deuteronomy 1–3). The Wisdom author shares this perspective on the wilderness experience. To reflect on the difficulties and tragedies in life is not a morbid or depressing exercise. What is extracted from the memories of the threat to existence is the energy and the gift of life.

2. The principle enunciated by the author reinforces the positive function of the energies of the cosmos. Through the very elements in which the Egyptians experienced punishment, the righteous experienced benefit in their need. There is an inherent parallel between the apocalyptic judgment presented in the first part of the book and the continuous judgment exercised throughout the midrash on the exodus and wilderness episodes. Just as all of creation was understood to be armed by God to wage battle against lawlessness (Wis 5:15-23), so too are the elements of the cosmos used to bring punishment to the enemies and life to the righteous.

The ambiguity of the elements of the cosmos, as symbolized by water and fire, elicits a healthy respect for the environment. The forces of the cosmos cannot be possessed through knowledge or manipulation without regard to justice. Because creation is guided continuously by the wisdom of God, the relationship between justice and the forces of the cosmos remains dynamic. In the case of the exodus episodes, the captivity and enslavement of the Hebrews in Egypt elicit even from the forces of the cosmos the redressing of injustice.

WISDOM 11:6-14, THE NILE DEFILED WITH BLOOD—ABUNDANT WATERS

NAB

6 Instead of a spring, when the perennial river
   was troubled with impure blood
7 as a rebuke to the decree for the slaying
   of infants,
   You gave them abundant water in an
   unhoped-for way,
8 once you had shown by the thirst they then
   had
   how you punished their adversaries.
9 For when they had been tried, though only
   mildly chastised,
   they recognized how the wicked, condemned
   in anger, were being tormented.
10 the latter you tested, admonishing them
   as a father;
   the former as a stern king you probed and
   condemned.
11 Both those afar off and those close by were
   afflicted:
12 For a twofold grief took hold of them
   and a groaning at the remembrance of the
   ones who had departed.
13 For when they heard that the cause of their
   own torments
   was a benefit to these others, they
   recognized the LORD.
14 Him who of old had been cast out in
   exposure they indeed mockingly
   rejected;
   but in the end of events, they marveled at him,
   since their thirst proved unlike that of the just.

11, 6: *tarachthentos:* so LXX[MSS].
11, 10f: Trsp 11, 11 before 11, 10: conj.
11, 12: *mnēmōn (tōn) parelthontōn:* so LXX[MSS].
11, 14: *hon (gar):* so LXX[A], etc.

NRSV

6 Instead of the fountain of an ever-flowing river,
   stirred up and defiled with blood
7 in rebuke for the decree to kill the infants,
   you gave them abundant water unexpectedly,
8 showing by their thirst at that time
   how you punished their enemies.
9 For when they were tried, though they were
   being disciplined in mercy,
   they learned how the ungodly were tormented
   when judged in wrath.
10 For you tested them as a parent[a] does in
   warning,
   but you examined the ungodly[b] as a stern king
   does in condemnation.
11 Whether absent or present, they were equally
   distressed,
12 for a twofold grief possessed them,
   and a groaning at the memory of what had
   occurred.
13 For when they heard that through their own
   punishments
   the righteous[c] had received benefit, they
   perceived it was the Lord's doing.
14 For though they had mockingly rejected him
   who long before had been cast out and
   exposed,
   at the end of the events they marveled at him,
   when they felt thirst in a different way from
   the righteous.

[a] Gk *a father*   [b] Gk *those*   [c] Gk *they*

COMMENTARY

The first diptych contrasts the thirst of the Egyptians due to the defilement of the Nile (Exod 7:14-24) with the abundant waters the righteous received in the wilderness (Exod 15:22-27; 17:1-7). The brief introduction to the diptychs prepares for the elaboration on the first plague with the reference to the Israelites' calling out to God from their thirst (Wis 11:4).

11:6-7. An explanation is given for the specific punishment the Egyptians experience by means of the Nile's defilement (v. 7). The Nile is defiled in rebuke to Pharaoh's decree that the newborn males be drowned in the Nile (Exod 1:22). This explanation for the first plague inaugurates the author's technique of relating the specific plague experienced by Egypt to a correlating sin. For the author, there is an inherent relationship between sin and punishment. This principle will be formally announced in the second diptych: "so that they might learn that one is punished by the very things by which one sins" (v. 16 NRSV). This correlation between sin and punishment was also present in the author's argumentation in the first part of the book. The wicked, who had reasoned falsely, were said to have experienced punishment according to their reasoning (3:10). Since they judged mortality to be meaningless and decided to subject the righteous to a shameful death, the wicked finally will experience an ultimate death as punishment.

11:8-10. One difficulty the author faces throughout the contrast between the righteous and their enemies is the experience of suffering on Israel's part as well as that of Egypt. Whereas in the diptychs of the first part of the book the suffering of the righteous was not the result of their sin, the suffering of the Israelites in the wilderness at times was caused by their own rebellion. In the case of the first plague, the author notes how Israel also experienced thirst. But even here the author contrasts the thirst of the Israelites with that of the Egyptians. Israel's thirst is meant to be disciplinary. The thirst of the enemies is punitive. The deuteronomic interpretation of Israel's suffering in the wilderness is harnessed to appreciate the Israelites' desert trials (Deuteronomy 8). Israel's suffering is a time for learning God's faithfulness and power. God tests the righteous as a parent does in warning, but the Lord tests the ungodly as a stern king in judgment (11:10; cf. Deut 8:5). This positive function of God's testing the righteous is parallel to the author's explanation of the suffering of the just in

the first part (3:4-6). There, too, the righteous were tested by God as gold would be tested in fire. They were found to be worthy and acceptable as an offering to God.

11:11-13. The thirsting of the righteous gives them an appreciation of God's judgment against Egypt. The anguish of the Egyptians' punishment by thirst is twofold. In addition to the plague ruining the water supply while the Israelites were present in Egypt, the Egyptians suffer further from the realization that the Israelites receive abundant water in the desert. The author is telescoping the events of the exodus and the wilderness and imagining what the Egyptians would experience by realizing that blessings are bestowed on the righteous. The first principle is elaborated (vv. 5, 13). When the ungodly realize that the righteous are blessed through the very means by which the wicked are punished, their anguish doubly increases.

The turn to direct speech toward God (vv. 7-10) signals the quality of laudatory prayer. The entire midrash on the exodus is enclosed by the author's direct praise of God (vv. 7-10; 19:22). Throughout the midrash, the author turns to God in praise of the marvelous interventions in Israel's history.

11:14. The conclusion to the diptych focuses on Moses, on both his tenuous clinging to life at birth and his power as an adult. Moses had narrowly escaped the death sentence decreed by the pharaoh. Now, at the end, the Egyptians are forced to marvel at the events wrought by Moses both in Egypt and in the desert. The formulation of this scene is reminiscent of the scene of judgment in the first part of the book. In the final scene of judgment, the ungodly are amazed at the salvation of the righteous. With anguish they recognize that those whom they had held in derision are numbered among the children of God (5:1-5). Similarly with Moses, the Egyptians marvel at the one they had cast out and exposed to death.

REFLECTIONS

1. The principle whereby one is punished by the very means by which one has sinned presumes an inner coherency between sin and punishment. This idea was introduced in the first part of the book when the author declared that the wicked are punished according to their reasoning (3:10). The author constantly applies this principle throughout the diptychs that deal with the plagues preceding the exodus. The Wisdom author is advocating a psychological truth. Often enough, both blessing and punishment are conceived of as being extraneous to the activities that are being rewarded or penalized. On many levels, this is an adequate representation. But in the case of both faithfulness and sinfulness, there is an internal consistency between acts of faithfulness and acts of sinfulness and their corresponding consequences. The author is stressing this consistency between the sin of injustice and the suffering that the Egyptians experience as a result of their sin. There is an internal reward for faithfulness that, in the long run, even against all appearances, reveals itself through abundance and joy. There is an internal destruction of the source of injustice that, in the long run, despite appearances to the contrary, reveals itself in despair and anguish. The very earth lets the blood of Abel cry out to God for a murder done in secret (Gen 4:10-11). The arguments the author labored to maintain in the first part of the book regarding the blessedness of the righteous and the wretchedness of the unjust are sustained through a reflection on Israel's salvation history. An act of injustice, as small as it may appear, eventually finds a way of raising its head toward destruction. Even a small act of kindness, as unnoticeable as it may be, carries with it the expression of love.

2. God tests the righteous in order to bring discipline and knowledge to them (11:6-10). The author explains the suffering of the righteous, both deserved and undeserved, as a process of purification and learning. The model is that of a parent who disciplines children for their benefit, a procedure enshrined in the Torah (Deut 8:5). It is always difficult to attribute human suffering to God without making God appear to be a tyrant or a merciless taskmaster. The writer of the book of Job rebels against a rigid application of the laws of retribution to all forms of human suffering. But, at the same time, the God who speaks from the whirlwind does not shy away from praising Behemoth and Leviathan, the symbols of enduring chaos (Job 40:6–41:34). Perhaps the very function of chaos and human limitations within creation is that they constitute a condition for freedom and decision.

For the author of the book of Wisdom, human limitations are not the destroyer of value. Suffering and tragedy do not destroy the soul, but injustice does. On the contrary, the awareness of his limitations propels Solomon to seek God and wisdom. According to the book of Wisdom, the God who tries and tests the righteous is the God who out of love attempts to stir them to knowledge and discipline. The end result is that Solomon's relationship to God is assured through wisdom—wisdom makes humans friends of God.

WISDOM 11:15–16:14, ANIMALS PUNISH EGYPT, AND QUAILS ARE FED TO THE RIGHTEOUS

OVERVIEW

The second diptych contrasts the plaguing of Egypt with various animals to the special foods provided the Israelites in the wilderness. Although in itself the contrast is quite brief, the entire diptych is rather lengthy. The image of animals in the plagues elicits the two major digressions or theological reflections of the last part of the book (the reflection on the moderation of God, 11:17–12:27; the reflection on false worship, chaps. 13–15), as well as a minor digression that treats God's power over creation in the episode of the brazen serpent (16:5-14). The two major digressions are well composed and theologically dense. Therefore, an understanding of their structure will facilitate their interpretation.

The first reflection on the moderation of God toward both the enemies of Israel as well as Israel itself is elicited by the awareness of the progressive infliction of the plagues. God sent various plagues against Egypt. The author reasons that since God could have destroyed Egypt in a single show of might (11:17-21), then God's reluctance to use the full force of power expresses the moderation and mercy of God (11:26–12:2). Through moderation and mercy, God provides room for human conversion.

The treatment of the moderation and mercy of God is composed in three parts: (1) God's moderation in dealing with the Egyptians, 11:15–12:2; (2) God's moderation in dealing with the Canaanites, 12:3-18; and (3) a double lesson for Israel, 12:19-27.

The first two sections, on the moderation of God with the Egyptians and the Canaanites, are parallel in theme and in structure.

| 11:15-20 | the Egyptians—the Canaanites | 12:3-11 |
| 11:21–12:2 | God is sovereign and merciful | 12:12-18 |

By noticing how God treats the weak and the haughty from the examples of the exodus, the wilderness, and the conquest, the righteous are to learn and to appropriate the same compassion and mercy of God.

The second reflection or digression is more directly motivated by the central image of the second diptych. The main contrast of the diptych fluctuates between the animal worship of Egypt and the animals that become a source of food for Israel. Egypt's sin of animal worship occasions a thoughtful critique of false worship in general. The entire critique progresses in three parts from the least blameworthy form of false worship to the most blameworthy: (1) philosophers incur slight blame, 13:1-9; (2) idol worship is condemned, 13:10–15:13; (3) both the idol worship and the animal worship of Egypt are severely condemned, 15:14-19.

The first critique centers on the various forms of nature worship, from worship of the elements of nature to worship of the heavenly bodies. Only slight blame, but blame nonetheless, is attributed to such persons who come to identify the divine with natural phenomena.

The most extensive part of the critique concentrates on the central section, which deals with idol worship. Here the critique attempts to explain the origins of the worship of idols and the dreadful moral consequences of such worship in life. The critique (13:10–15:13) is arranged concentrically:

A	13:10-19	gold, silver, stone, wooden idols—carpenter
B	14:1-7	reflection on God's providential care
C	14:8-31	punishment of idols / invention and result of idolatry / punishment of idolatry
B′	15:1-6	reflection on God's mercy and power
A′	15:7-13	clay idols—potter

In addition to the progressive blame attributed to forms of false worship within the overall structure of the critique (chaps. 13–15), we can notice a progression in the matter of the idols (13:10–15:13). The overall progression moves from the least blameworthy to the most blameworthy. The internal progression moves from precious metals, like gold and silver, to the common, lower-value substance clay.

In the third and final critique of animal worship, the author is at a loss to find a conceivable explanation or source of such worship. Therefore, the most severe condemnation is attributed to animal worship. This return to the image of animals, which occasioned the two reflections on God's moderation and on false worship, continues the thread of the argument in the second diptych. Animals torment the enemies of Israel, yet animals provide sustenance to the righteous.

Wisdom 11:15–12:27, The Moderation of God

NAB

15 And in return for their senseless, wicked
    thoughts,
        which misled them into worshiping dumb
        serpents and worthless insects,
    You sent upon them swarms of dumb
    creatures for vengeance;
16   that they might recognize that a man is
        punished by the very things through
        which he sins.
17 For not without means was your almighty
    hand,
        that had fashioned the universe from
        formless matter,
        to send upon them a drove of bears or
        fierce lions,
18 Or new-created, wrathful, unknown beasts
        to breathe forth fiery breath,
    Or pour out roaring smoke,
        or flash terrible sparks from their eyes.
19 Not only could these attack and completely
    destroy them;
        even their frightful appearance itself could
        slay.
20 Even without these, they could have been
    killed at a single blast,
        pursued by retribution
        and winnowed out by your mighty spirit;
    But you have disposed all things by measure
    and number and weight.
21 For with you great strength abides always;
        who can resist the might of your arm?
22 Indeed, before you the whole universe is as
    a grain from a balance,
        or a drop of morning dew come down
        upon the earth.
23 But you have mercy on all, because you can
    do all things;
        and you overlook the sins of men that they
        may repent.
24 For you love all things that are
        and loathe nothing that you have made;
        for what you hated, you would not have
        fashioned.

11, 18: *bromon:* so LXX^MSS.

NRSV

15 In return for their foolish and wicked thoughts,
        which led them astray to worship irrational
        serpents and worthless animals,
    you sent upon them a multitude of irrational
        creatures to punish them,
16 so that they might learn that one is punished
        by the very things by which one sins.
17 For your all-powerful hand,
        which created the world out of formless
        matter,
        did not lack the means to send upon them a
        multitude of bears, or bold lions,
18 or newly-created unknown beasts full of rage,
    or such as breathe out fiery breath,
    or belch forth a thick pall of smoke,
    or flash terrible sparks from their eyes;
19 not only could the harm they did destroy
        people,[a]
    but the mere sight of them could kill by fright.
20 Even apart from these, people[b] could fall at a
        single breath
    when pursued by justice
    and scattered by the breath of your power.
    But you have arranged all things by measure
        and number and weight.

21 For it is always in your power to show great
        strength,
        and who can withstand the might of your arm?
22 Because the whole world before you is like a
        speck that tips the scales,
        and like a drop of morning dew that falls on
        the ground.
23 But you are merciful to all, for you can do all
        things,
        and you overlook people's sins, so that they
        may repent.
24 For you love all things that exist,
        and detest none of the things that you have
        made,
        for you would not have made anything if you
        had hated it.
25 How would anything have endured if you had
        not willed it?

[a] Gk *them*   [b] Gk *they*

NAB

25 And how could a thing remain, unless you
willed it;

or be preserved, had it not been called
forth by you?

26 But you spare all things, because they
are yours, O LORD and lover of souls,

12 for your imperishable spirit is
in all things!

2 Therefore you rebuke offenders little by
little,

warn them, and remind them of the sins
they are committing,

that they may abandon their wickedness
and believe in you, O LORD!

3 For, truly, the ancient inhabitants of your
holy land,

4 whom you hated for deeds most
odious—

Works of witchcraft and impious sacrifices;

5 a cannibal feast of human flesh
and of blood, from the midst of . . .—

These merciless murderers of children,

6 and parents who took with their own
hands defenseless lives,

You willed to destroy by the hands of our
fathers,

7 that the land that is dearest of all to you
might receive a worthy colony of God's
children.

8 But even these, as they were men, you
spared,

and sent wasps as forerunners of your army
that they might exterminate them by
degrees.

9 Not that you were without power to have the
wicked vanquished in battle by the just,

or wiped out at once by terrible beasts or
by one decisive word;

10 But condemning them bit by bit, you gave
them space for repentance.

You were not unaware that their race was
wicked

and their malice ingrained,

And that their dispositions would never
change;

NRSV

Or how would anything not called forth by
you have been preserved?

26 You spare all things, for they are yours,
O Lord, you who love the living.

12 For your immortal spirit is in
all things.

2 Therefore you correct little by little those who
trespass,

and you remind and warn them of the things
through which they sin,

so that they may be freed from wickedness and
put their trust in you, O Lord.

3 Those who lived long ago in your holy land

4 you hated for their detestable practices,
their works of sorcery and unholy rites,

5 their merciless slaughter[a] of children,
and their sacrificial feasting on human flesh
and blood.

These initiates from the midst of a heathen
cult,[b]

6 these parents who murder helpless lives,
you willed to destroy by the hands of our
ancestors,

7 so that the land most precious of all to you
might receive a worthy colony of the servants[c]
of God.

8 But even these you spared, since they were
but mortals,

and sent wasps[d] as forerunners of your army
to destroy them little by little,

9 though you were not unable to give the
ungodly into the hands of the
righteous in battle,

or to destroy them at one blow by dread wild
animals or your stern word.

10 But judging them little by little you gave them
an opportunity to repent,

though you were not unaware that their origin[e]
was evil

and their wickedness inborn,

and that their way of thinking would never
change.

11 For they were an accursed race from the
beginning,

and it was not through fear of anyone that you
left them unpunished for their sins.

12, 5: *teknōn te phoneas aneleēmonas* trsp before *kai authentas.*
12, 6: conj. (parallelism); (*ek mesou*) *thysiastēriou:* conj: not translated;
mystathetasou: so LXX^MSS; unintelligible.

---

[a] Gk *slaughterers*   [b] Meaning of Gk uncertain   [c] Or *children*
[d] Or *hornets*   [e] Or *nature*

NAB

11   for they were a race accursed from the beginning.
   Neither out of fear for anyone
   did you grant amnesty for their sins.

12 For who can say to you, "What have you done?"
   or who can oppose your decree?
   Or when peoples perish, who can challenge you, their maker;
   or who can come into your presence as vindicator of unjust men?

13 For neither is there any god besides you who have the care of all,
   that you need show you have not unjustly condemned;

14 Nor can any king or prince confront you on behalf of those you have punished.

15 But as you are just, you govern all things justly;
   you regard it as unworthy of your power to punish one who has incurred no blame.

16 For your might is the source of justice;
   your mastery over all things makes you lenient to all.

17 For you show your might when the perfection of your power is disbelieved;
   and in those who know you, you rebuke temerity.

18 But though you are master of might, you judge with clemency,
   and with much lenience you govern us;
   for power, whenever you will, attends you.

19 And you taught your people, by these deeds, that those who are just must be kind;
   And you gave your sons good ground for hope that you would permit repentance for their sins.

20 For these were enemies of your servants, doomed to death;
   yet, while you punished them with such solicitude and pleading,
   granting time and opportunity to abandon wickedness,

21 With what exactitude you judged your sons, to whose fathers you gave the sworn covenants of goodly promises!

12, 16: (*pheidesthai*) se (*poiei*): so LXX[MSS].

NRSV

12 For who will say, "What have you done?"
   or will resist your judgment?
   Who will accuse you for the destruction of nations that you made?
   Or who will come before you to plead as an advocate for the unrighteous?

13 For neither is there any god besides you, whose care is for all people,[a]
   to whom you should prove that you have not judged unjustly;

14 nor can any king or monarch confront you about those whom you have punished.

15 You are righteous and you rule all things righteously,
   deeming it alien to your power
   to condemn anyone who does not deserve to be punished.

16 For your strength is the source of righteousness,
   and your sovereignty over all causes you to spare all.

17 For you show your strength when people doubt the completeness of your power,
   and you rebuke any insolence among those who know it.[b]

18 Although you are sovereign in strength, you judge with mildness,
   and with great forbearance you govern us;
   for you have power to act whenever you choose.

19 Through such works you have taught your people
   that the righteous must be kind,
   and you have filled your children with good hope,
   because you give repentance for sins.

20 For if you punished with such great care and indulgence[c]
   the enemies of your servants[d] and those deserving of death,
   granting them time and opportunity to give up their wickedness,

21 with what strictness you have judged your children,

a Or *all things*   b Meaning of Gk uncertain   c Other ancient authorities lack *and indulgence*; others read *and entreaty*   d Or *children*

NAB

22 Us, therefore, you chastise, and our enemies
	with a thousand blows you punish,
	that we may think earnestly of your
		goodness when we judge,
	and, when being judged, may look for
		mercy.
23 Hence those unjust also, who lived a life of
		folly,
	you tormented through their own
		abominations.
24 For they went far astray in the paths of
		error,
	taking for gods the worthless and
		disgusting among beasts,
	deceived like senseless infants.
25 Therefore as though upon unreasoning
		children,
	you sent your judgment on them as a
		mockery;
26 But they who took no heed of punishment
		which was but child's play
	were to experience a condemnation
		worthy of God.
27 For in the things through which they
		suffered distress,
	since they were tortured by the very things
		they deemed gods,
	They saw and recognized the true God
	whom before they had refused to know;
	with this, their final condemnation came
		upon them.

NRSV

	to whose ancestors you gave oaths and
		covenants full of good promises!
22 So while chastening us you scourge our
		enemies ten thousand times more,
	so that, when we judge, we may meditate
		upon your goodness,
	and when we are judged, we may expect
		mercy.

23 Therefore those who lived unrighteously, in a
		life of folly,
	you tormented through their own
		abominations.
24 For they went far astray on the paths of error,
	accepting as gods those animals that even their
		enemies[a] despised;
	they were deceived like foolish infants.
25 Therefore, as though to children who cannot
		reason,
	you sent your judgment to mock them.
26 But those who have not heeded the warning
		of mild rebukes
	will experience the deserved judgment of God.
27 For when in their suffering they became
		incensed
	at those creatures that they had thought to be
		gods, being punished by means of
		them,
	they saw and recognized as the true God the
		one whom they had before refused to
		know.
	Therefore the utmost condemnation came
		upon them.

[a] Gk *they*

COMMENTARY

11:15-16. The second diptych contrasts the animals that were sent to punish Egypt with the quails that were sent to feed Israel in the desert (Wis 11:15-16; 16:1-4). Direct speech to God signals the quality of prayer that the reflection is taking for the author (11:15-17). The diptych continues to emphasize the relation between sin and its inherent punishment. In the case of the Egyptians, the worship of animals is perceived to be the cause of plagues of various animals. The

author is conflating into a single diptych the several plagues of animals and insects from Exodus (frogs, gnats, flies, pestilence in livestock, locusts).

The author's explanation that irrational animals were sent to plague Egypt for their sin of animal worship reinforces the inherent relationship between sin and punishment. Again, the author is exerting great effort to explain that punishment is not extrinsic to thought and action, but is implicit in the very structure of sin. Since for the author the worship of animals is irrational, then irrationality seizes the minds of the Egyptians as irrational animals plague the land.

This principle is both similar to and distinct from the longstanding principle of taliation (*lex talionis,* "an eye for an eye, a tooth for a tooth"). In the law of talion, the damage to or injury of the claimant is equated with the punishment of the culprit (see Exod 21:23-25; Deut 19:18-21).[98] For the author of Wisdom, the principle of retaliation equates the means of punishment to the sin. The idea of the similarity of the means of punishment to the means of the injury emphasizes the inherent relationship between sin and its consequences. As a clearly enunciated principle, it is an idea that is seen infrequently in ancient texts. Perhaps the closest parallel to the author's principle can be found in the *Testament of the Twelve Patriarchs*: "For by whatever capacity anyone transgresses, by that also is he chastised."[99]

11:17–12:2, Moderation Toward the Egyptians. This brief introduction to the second diptych elicits a reflection on God's treatment of the Egyptians in the plague episodes. The author focuses on God's moderation. The progressive harshness of the plagues reveals God's attempt to teach the Egyptians through the experience of lack and suffering that their injustice brings. To highlight God's moderation, the author notes that the enemies of Israel could have been destroyed by a single show of force (11:20) and by horrendous and unimaginable animals. Instead, they are tormented by rather insignificant pests.

11:17-20. God's reign over the universe through creation is one of moderation and balance. The author employs a platonic term to paraphrase God's creation of the heavens and the earth in Genesis. The image of "formless matter" (11:17) corresponds to the "formless void" of Gen 1:2. This image, which opens the reflection, is parallel to another platonic idea that closes the unit before the contemplation of God's mercy. As if to summarize the moderation of God's reign, the author in 11:20 harnesses the popular platonic

triad of "measure, number and weight."[100] These references to elements of physics were employed by many classical writers to denote the harmony and balance of the universe. In Scripture, similar terms were used to indicate the harmony and balance of God's creation (weight, measure, decree, way, Job 28:25-26; measured, weighed, Isa 40:12).

11:21–12:2. The contemplation of God's moderation combines the two poles of God's power and mercy. God is powerful yet merciful. The two poetic images that contrast the smallness of the world with the majesty of God are reminiscent of Solomon's description of his own transience (7:1-6). Just as Solomon's reflection on his insignificant stature propelled him to seek God and wisdom, so too the author's reflection on the smallness of the universe elicits the contemplation of God's mercy and compassion. The world is compared to a speck that tips the scales and to a drop of morning dew. Both images point out the smallness and insignificance of the universe in comparison to the majesty of God. Similar images are used in Isaiah to illustrate the smallness of the nations ("a drop from a bucket, dust on the scales" [Isa 40:15 NRSV]).

The power and majesty of God highlight the Lord's compassion and mercy (11:23). The purpose of the moderation of God is to give space for conversion and repentance. The author recalls the relationship between God and the universe, enunciated in the beginning of the book. God loves all that exists and does not detest anything that has been created (11:24-26; cf. 1:14). The earlier reflection on the irrationality of animals has probably elicited this reaffirmation of the positive qualities of creation. It is not the animals that are detested by the author, even if their appearance may be repulsive (15:18-19); rather, the author abhors the falsity of animal worship.

The passage 11:21–12:2 is stamped through and through with the value of universalism, which characterizes sapiential literature in general. God is merciful to all, loves all things that exist, and spares all things. The universal goodness of God is affirmed within the polemic against Israel's

---

98. *Laws of Hammurabi,* 196, 200; For the varieties of the principle of retaliation found in Ancient Law Codes and in the Bible, see the brief treatment by H.B. Huffmon in "Lex Talionis," *ABD,* 4:321-22.

99. The *Testament of the Twelve Patriarchs, Gad, the ninth son,* 5:10.

100. Plato *Philebus* 55E, measurement and weights are essential for art; *Republic* 602D, measuring, counting and weighing are correctives to illusory art; *Laws* 757B, the equality determined by measure, weight, and number is meant to ensure good politics.

opponents. The power and mercy of God extend to all of creation. This is quite remarkable for a work that clearly is marked with polemics against the injustice suffered by the Jewish community in the diaspora.

God's mercy is expressed in moderation. As harsh as the polemic appears in the midrashic treatment of the narrative of the plagues in Exodus, the author of Wisdom interprets the punishments within the context of God's compassion and moderation. The unit closes with the purpose of God's moderation in the administration of punishment. Punishments are meant to elicit conversion. Those who sin are reminded of their sin precisely in order that they may be freed from sin (12:2).

12:3-18, Moderation Toward the Canaanites. The same principle of moderation is applied to God's treatment of the Canaanites. Here the author is interpreting the events of the conquest and the infiltration of the promised land as predicted in Exodus and Deuteronomy. The idea of God's punishing the Canaanites for their sins gradually and in stages, sending "wasps" as forerunners, is an interpretation of Exod 23:20-33. The description of the various forms of the sins of the Canaanites that result in their losing the land in favor of the Israelites is an interpretation of Deut 18:9-14 (cf. Deut 9:5). Their sins include child sacrifice, divination, and sorcery (cf. Wis 12:3-6). Although the author is evidently making reference to human sacrifices in the cult of Moloch, as described in the biblical texts (Lev 18:21; Deut 12:31; Jer 32:35), it is also true that human sacrifice extended well into the Roman period, at least among some groups, even in Egypt.[101]

The author's purpose in recalling the destruction of the pre-Israelite dwellers of the land is to highlight the moderation and mercy of God. As with the Egyptians, God could have destroyed them in one blow (v. 9). Instead, they were judged little by little, precisely to give them an opportunity to repent (v. 10). The author appeals to the very same image of wasps or hornets being sent out before the invading Israelites to weaken the enemies of Israel as related in Exod 23:28 (cf.

Deut 7:20; Josh 24:12). The Hebrew word for "hornets" or "wasps" is unclear, and it could very well refer to disease or pestilence, as the root meaning would suggest. The LXX translates the Hebrew by the Greek word σφήξ (*sphēx*), which means "wasps" or "hornets." Interestingly, a difference in the comparison between the Egyptians and the Canaanites is that the suppression of the means of punishment is equal to the means of their sin. The author is content to stress that the reason for the Canaanites' loss of the land is their sin. Perhaps the author could not think of an immediate correlation between the forms of sin and the punishment of the loss of land.

The reflection on the plight of the first dwellers of the land serves to underscore the sovereignty of God (vv. 12-18). God cannot be accused of acting unjustly, since no one is condemned without recognition of his or her sin (v. 15). But precisely because God is sovereign over creation and history, God acts with care, mildness, and forbearance. God's motive for such moderation is love for all people. The universal aspect of God's love for what exists (11:24-26) is reiterated in the reflection on the treatment of the Canaanites (vv. 15-18).

Just as the reflection on the destruction of Egypt elicited the author's praise of God's power and mercy, so too the reflection on the destruction of the Canaanites elicits the praise of God's sovereignty and compassion (vv. 12-18). The two sections stand parallel, 11:21–12:2 = 12:12-18. In both cases, the reflection on God's treatment of Israel's enemies leads to the perception of God's universal love and moderation.

12:19-27, A Double Lesson for Israel. 12:19-22. What the righteous are to learn from the meditation on the plight of the unrighteous is summarized succinctly in v. 22. They are to learn to be compassionate and moderate, and they are to trust in the mercy of God. The double lesson touches upon their relationship to God and their relationship to enemies. The points in the argument the author has constructed regarding the treatment of the unrighteous are now applied to the righteous as well. The main issue the author holds up for consideration is the moderation of God (vv. 19-21). God provides repentance for sinners and gives time and space for the unrighteous to turn from their injustice.

---

101. For references to the debate on cannibalism and the practice of human sacrifice, see David Winston, *The Wisdom of Solomon,* AB 43 (New York: Doubleday, 1979) 239-40.

12:23-27. The concluding section of the first reflection on the moderation of God returns to the punishment of the Egyptians. In its context, this unit returns to the theme of the opening section of the digression and prepares for the second digression on false worship. In itself, it continues the theme of the second diptych—namely, the animals that torment Egypt are understood as a punishment in accord with the sin of animal worship. This section could very well have been a part of the second diptych before the two major theological reflections were inserted into the text (11:15-16; 12:23-27; 16:1-14).

The language applied to the Egyptians is reminiscent of the language applied to the wicked in the scene of judgment in the first part of Wisdom.

Just as the wicked recognized that they had strayed from the way of truth and had taken their fill of the paths of lawlessness (5:6-7), so too are the Egyptians described as straying onto the paths of error (12:24). Just as the wicked reproached themselves for their folly (5:4), so too are the Egyptians accused of living unjustly in a life of folly (v. 23). Just as the wicked recognized the blessed end of the just (5:5), so too do the Egyptians finally recognize the true God, whom they hitherto refused to acknowledge (v. 27). The final verse, which introduces the idea of recognizing the true God, allows the argument of the author to pass smoothly onto the next major digression on false worship.

REFLECTIONS

1. There is an ethical difficulty in reflecting on the fall of one's enemy. How does one reflect on the demise of anyone, even one's enemies or opponents, without gloating over their fall in such a manner as to take on their very attributes and values? The oppressed only too easily become the oppressor, the victim the victimizer. How does one face injustice without falling into the pitfalls of destructive anger and revenge? The difficulties inherent in this reflection are similar to those found in the psalms of complaint, in which the just lament over the power of the enemies and plead with God for salvation and vindication (e.g. Psalms 5; 10; 17; 35; 58; 59). Only a fine line, indeed, separates the righteous anger of the oppressed from destructive thoughts and desires for revenge. Throughout the latter part of Wisdom, the author reflects on the demise of Israel's enemies. But instead of this reflection building up a sense of arrogance and self-righteousness over their demise, it leads to an appreciation of God's sovereignty and mercy. The reflection on the power and tolerance of God provides a necessary context for pondering the power and folly of the unjust.

It should be borne in mind that the polemical character of the latter part of Wisdom reflects the situation of a Jewish community under siege in the diaspora. Although at times Jewish communities achieved great autonomy and flourished in the fields of philosophy, art, and commerce, especially in Alexandria, they often fell prey to the jealousy of local centers of power. The careful reflection the author is offering over the demise of the unjust powerful is not meant to foster gloating over the fall of one's enemies. Rather, the examples of an unjust and unfair use of power from Israel's history are brought to the fore in order to bolster commitment to and trust in justice. The example of the exodus is set forth by the author as historical proof for the vindication of justice over the appearance of the power and might of injustice. What had been argued in the first part of Wisdom regarding the folly of injustice and the strength of virtue is now bolstered by examples from Israel's history. Injustice *does* lead to death. Justice *does* lead to life. The exodus is the author's supreme example that constitutes Israel's hope in virtue and justice for the present and the future.

2. Ironically, perhaps, the examples of the demise of Egyptian and Canaanite power are used to foster compassion and mercy. The focus is not so much on the fall of Egypt and Canaan as it is on God's treatment of the just and the unjust. Using the example of the punishment of the wicked, the author continuously asserts the inner dynamic of the self-destruction of injustice. The unjust are punished by the very means by which they sin. From the example of God's treatment of those who wield power unjustly, the author derives the tolerance and mercy of God. Like Ezekiel, the author interprets the activity of God toward sinners as a call to conversion: "Have I any pleasure in the death of the wicked, says the Lord GOD, and not rather that they should turn from their ways and live?" (Ezek 18:23 NRSV; cf. 33:11-16).

3. The moderation of God toward Egypt and Canaan teaches the Israelites to be tolerant. Israel is to be compassionate and kind because that is God's approach, even to Israel's enemies. The author's reflection on the universal love of God instills an ethical imperative toward one's opponents. The author may very well have had in mind the extraordinary extension of God's blessing to Israel's traditional enemies, Egypt and Assyria, as narrated in Isa 19:18-25, "Blessed be Egypt my people, and Assyria the work of my hands, and Israel my heritage" (NRSV). This openness to opponents, or at least to the stranger in one's midst, is also consistent with the deuteronomic call to be kind to the sojourner in the midst of Israel because the Israelites were sojourners in the land of Egypt (Deut 10:18-19; 23:7; 24:21).

The way one treats one's opponents in life reveals a great deal about one's appropriation of the virtue of justice. The tolerance and moderation proposed by God's treatment of Egypt and Canaan is similar to the tolerance proclaimed by Christ. Tolerance is not a sign of weakness, but of strength and compassion. In the parable of weeds among the wheat, there is the concern of uprooting the wheat along with the weeds, the good along with the bad (Matt 13:24-30). Although the parable is more directly concerned with the final judgment, which separates the weeds from the wheat, it also gives space to the coexistence of good and evil. In this in-between time, the wicked subsist along with the good and are not to be eliminated but tolerated. The Wisdom author's explanation for God's tolerance is the desire for conversion, as is the case with Ezekiel (Ezek 18:23). The parable's explanation for tolerance is the protection of the good. Both, of course, recognize the final judgment as a time of reckoning.

The theme that true power is sublimely expressed through love or mercy has been cast into the cinematic form. In *Schindler's List,*[102] the ruthless commanding officer at Plaszow boasts to Oscar Schindler that power is control. Schindler, the business tycoon who feels compelled to save the Jews who had worked for him, responds with a story. He relates how a common thief who was unmistakably guilty was given the death sentence. But the emperor, who had every right and all the power to confirm the sentence, for no apparent gain acquitted the thief out of mercy toward him. "Now that is power," ruminates Schindler to the officer.

102. Steven Spielberg, director and producer, *Schindler's List,* Universal City Studios and Amblin Entertainment, 1993.

Wisdom 13:1–15:19, Critique of Pagan Cults

OVERVIEW

The principle of the means of punishment being equal to the form of sin generates a second major theological reflection in the second diptych: a critique of pagan cults. Egypt is punished by animals for the sin of worshiping animals. The theme of Egypt's animal cult elicits the critique of pagan cults in general. The critique is carefully balanced into three parts, the largest of which deals with idolatry in the very center. There is a qualitative progression from the least blameworthy (the foolish, who cannot recognize God, 13:1), to the more blameworthy (the miserable, who put their hope in dead idols, 13:10), finally to the most blameworthy (the most foolish, who go further and, in addition to dead idols, worship the most hateful animals, 15:14). The *Letter of Aristeas* (134-141) from the second century BCE (c. 150–100) also contrasts two forms of worship—namely, idol worship, attributed to the Greeks, and animal worship, attributed to the Egyptians.

The division of various forms of cultic worship into two or three types is also well-known within Hellenistic/Jewish writings contemporaneous to the book of Wisdom. Philo makes a distinction between the worship of natural elements or celestial bodies and the worship of idols or animals.[103] The Stoics made a threefold distinction in forms of worship: the mythical type, the philosophical type, and the legislative type.

103. See Philo *On the Decalogue* 52; *On the Special Laws* 1.13.

Wisdom 13:1-9, Nature Worship

NAB	NRSV
13 For all men were by nature foolish who were in ignorance of God,	**13** For all people who were ignorant of God were foolish by nature;
and who from the good things seen did not succeed in knowing him who is, and from studying the works did not discern the artisan;	and they were unable from the good things that are seen to know the one who exists, nor did they recognize the artisan while paying heed to his works;
2 But either fire, or wind, or the swift air, or the circuit of the stars, or the mighty water, or the luminaries of heaven, the governors of the world, they considered gods.	2 but they supposed that either fire or wind or swift air, or the circle of the stars, or turbulent water, or the luminaries of heaven were the gods that rule the world.
3 Now if out of joy in their beauty they thought them gods, let them know how far more excellent is the Lord than these; for the original source of beauty fashioned them.	3 If through delight in the beauty of these things people assumed them to be gods, let them know how much better than these is their Lord, for the author of beauty created them.
4 Or if they were struck by their might and energy, let them from these things realize how much more powerful is he who made them.	4 And if people[a] were amazed at their power and working, let them perceive from them how much more powerful is the one who formed them.
5 For from the greatness and the beauty of created things their original author, by analogy, is seen.	5 For from the greatness and beauty of created things comes a corresponding perception of their Creator.
6 But yet, for these the blame is less; For they indeed have gone astray perhaps, though they seek God and wish to find him.	6 Yet these people are little to be blamed, for perhaps they go astray while seeking God and desiring to find him.
7 For they search busily among his works, but are distracted by what they see, because the things seen are fair.	7 For while they live among his works, they keep searching, and they trust in what they see, because the things that are seen are beautiful.
8 But again, not even these are pardonable.	8 Yet again, not even they are to be excused;
9 For if they so far succeeded in knowledge	

13, 5: *kai kallonēs* : so LXX[MSS].

a Gk *they*

NAB	NRSV
that they could speculate about the world, how did they not more quickly find its LORD?	[9] for if they had the power to know so much that they could investigate the world, how did they fail to find sooner the Lord of these things?

COMMENTARY

The author's main argument against nature worship rests on the failure to recognize God, the creator, in the beauty of creation. The prime metaphor used throughout the argument is the image of the artist and the artifact. One may recognize the artist in the quality of the work of art (vv. 1, 5). This critique is done with a great deal of sympathy for the natural desire to search for God in the forces of creation (vv. 6-7). Since creation itself is the work of God, the author acknowledges the naturalness of recognizing the beauty of creation inherent in the various forms of nature worship. The fault in nature worship is the failure to recognize the creator behind the works of creation. In contrast to this failure, the believer moves easily from the contemplation of the beauty of nature to the personal God who is the creator (v. 9; cf. Psalm 8).

The relationship between the artist and the artifact was a frequent metaphor in Greek philosophical circles: "Assuredly from the very structure of all made objects we are accustomed to prove that the work is certainly the product of some artificer and has not been constructed at random."[104] Similarly, as a work of art, the universe was the workplace of the divine artist for Stoic philosophers.[105]

God is explicitly called the artisan (τεχνίτης technitēs, v. 1), the same term the author had used earlier for personified wisdom (7:22; 8:6). Wisdom will be called the artisan who builds the vessels in which people put their trust on the raging waters of the sea (14:2). The term used for God as artisan in the first half of the unit is parallel to "Creator" (v. 5), "God" (v. 6), and "the Lord" (v. 9) in the second half. Otherwise, God is never referred to as artisan in Scripture. Apply-

ing the term "artisan" to God is another sign of the author's deliberate joining together of the role of wisdom in human affairs to that of God in the exodus in the final part of the book of Wisdom.

The two general forms of nature worship that are singled out are those of the natural forces (fire, wind, air, water) and that of celestial bodies (circle of the stars and luminaries of heaven, v. 2). The author is combining the traditional biblical critique of luminary cults (cf. Deut 17:3; Job 31:26-28; Jer 8:2; 19:13; Ezek 8:16) to the particular critique of the deification of natural forces, associated loosely with Stoic tenets. In particular, the author of Wisdom pays attention to the polyvalent understanding of the *pneuma* in Stoic writings. In Stoic philosophy, the *pneuma* is the unifying principle of the universe. For the Stoic philosopher Chrysippus, *pneuma* consists of fire and air, which on occasion appear to be deified.[106] All three elements that focus on the concept of *pneuma* in Stoic philosophy—fire, wind, and air—are represented in v. 2.

The fundamental argument of the author is that if people are swayed by the beauty of the created universe, so much more should they come to appreciate the creator who stands behind it (vv. 3-9). The search for the divine reality in the universe among peoples who worship natural phenomena, therefore, receives the author's sympathy and approbation (vv. 6-7). Philo likewise apportions less blame to those who magnify the subject above the ruler in nature worship than to those who worship dead idols.[107] What is lacking in the many forms of nature worship is the further step of recognizing the personal creator God behind the beauty of the universe (13:8-9).

104. Epictetus 1.6.7.
105. Cicero *De Natura Deorum* 1.20.53.
106. Chrysippus *Stoicorum Veterum Fragmenta* 2.310.442.786.
107. Philo *On the Decalogue* 66.

REFLECTIONS

1. The reason for the author's reticent and limited critique against adherents of nature cults resides in their implicit desire to seek God in creation. Behind this reticence we can recognize the author's admiration for some of the noble features of Greek philosophy and religious tenets: the relentless search for truth, the desire to understand human society and the universe, and the respect for principles and laws in nature. While the author does not exculpate them for their failure to take the final step and recognize the creator of the universe, there is strong recognition of the inherent goodness and appropriateness of groups who genuinely seek God and meaning in life (13:7).

The author recognizes a certain affinity to biblical faith in the search for God manifested among the Greeks. This restrained attitude on the part of the author, even within criticism, can serve as a good reminder of the fact that faith in an ultimate being is based on a search for meaning and desire. Faith involves a journey, a search, and a willingness to find God. The author lauds the desire to search for God in creation, but criticizes the failure of adherents of nature cults for being satisfied with the gifts of the giver and not reaching the beauty of the creator.

2. The author's metaphor of the artisan, in which the artist is recognized in an admired artifact, is a powerful analogy for the process of recognizing the creator behind the beauty of the universe. God is understood inherently as the artist who has fashioned a great work of art in the universe. Aesthetics and faith have been allies for a long time. Take the covenant with Abram. To assure Abram that the promise of progeny would be fulfilled, God called Abram to contemplate the heavens and the stars, "Look toward heaven and count the stars, if you are able to count them" (Gen 15:5 NRSV). Even more to the point is the contemplation of God's love for humanity through a reflection on the beauty of the heavens: "When I look at your heavens, the work of your fingers, the moon and the stars that you have established; what are human beings that you are mindful of them, mortals that you care for them?" (Ps 8:3-4 NRSV). Even in the NT, which is more prone to advancing the "cross of Christ" as the privileged moment of encounter between humans and God, the contemplation of the beauty of nature elicits wonder in God's care for humanity:

> "Consider the lilies of the field, how they grow; they neither toil nor spin, yet I tell you, even Solomon in all his glory was not clothed like one of these. But if God so clothes the grass of the field, which is alive today and tomorrow is thrown into the oven, will he not much more clothe you—you of little faith." (Matt 6:28-29 NRSV)

It was quite fashionable until recently, perhaps, for many scientists and artists to declare their agnosticism (if not direct hostility) with respect to belief in an ultimate being guiding the universe. Yet, many scientists who face the beauty and intricacy of the universe every day in their routine experimentation, from analyzing the constellations of the stars to the mapping of the genetic code, are led to a mystery behind the universe that cannot be denied. The sheer majesty of the universe continues to evoke questions of faith and ultimate meaning.

3. Perhaps the closest parallel in our own time to the author's ambivalent critique of nature cults is the Christian response to secular humanism. Although many of the values promoted by secular humanism are based on Judeo-Christian values—such as the dignity of the person, the right to education and health, and social justice—there remains a fundamental antagonism between the two approaches on the issue of belief and commitment to a personal divine being. Extremists on both sides have argued that the respective approaches of each side belittle humanity. On the one hand, for some secular humanists, positing a divine being unnecessarily reduces human beings to the category of servants or slaves. On the other hand, Christian critics have argued that if the authority of a divine being is not acknowledged, human beings are easily discounted and subjected to the whims of the majority and the powerful.

The author of Wisdom is not willing to compromise the values that the nature cults and Israelite faith have in common—namely, respect and admiration for the universe. At the same time, the critique is a challenge to anyone who may be tempted to remain within the sphere of the natural and, in the author's words, "fail to find sooner the Lord of these things" (13:9). Similarly, in the debate between secular humanism and the Judeo-Christian tradition, the antagonisms should not blind us to the values shared in common. The mysterious and beautiful voice of creation should be allowed to speak of the artist behind the great works.

Wisdom 13:10–15:13, Origin and Consequences of Idolatry

WISDOM 13:10-19, THE CARPENTER AND IDOLS

NAB	NRSV
10 But doomed are they, and in dead things are their hopes, who termed gods things made by human hands: Gold and silver, the product of art, and likenesses of beasts, or useless stone, the work of an ancient hand.	10 But miserable, with their hopes set on dead things, are those who give the name "gods" to the works of human hands, gold and silver fashioned with skill, and likenesses of animals, or a useless stone, the work of an ancient hand.
11 A carpenter may saw out a suitable tree and skillfully scrape off all its bark, And deftly plying his art, produce something fit for daily use, 12 and use up the refuse from his handiwork in preparing his food, and have his fill; 13 Then the good-for-nothing refuse from these remnants, crooked wood grown full of knots, he takes and carves to occupy his spare time. This wood he models with listless skill, and patterns it on the image of a man 14 or makes it resemble some worthless beast. When he has daubed it with red and crimsoned its surface with red stain, and daubed over every blemish in it, 15 He makes a fitting shrine for it and puts it on the wall, fastening it with a nail. 16 Thus lest it fall down he provides for it,	11 A skilled woodcutter may saw down a tree easy to handle and skillfully strip off all its bark, and then with pleasing workmanship make a useful vessel that serves life's needs, 12 and burn the cast-off pieces of his work to prepare his food, and eat his fill. 13 But a cast-off piece from among them, useful for nothing, a stick crooked and full of knots, he takes and carves with care in his leisure, and shapes it with skill gained in idleness;[a] he forms it in the likeness of a human being, 14 or makes it like some worthless animal, giving it a coat of red paint and coloring its surface red and covering every blemish in it with paint; 15 then he makes a suitable niche for it, and sets it in the wall, and fastens it there with iron. 16 He takes thought for it, so that it may not fall,

[a] Other ancient authorities read *with intelligent skill*

NAB

knowing that it cannot help itself;
    for, truly, it is an image and needs help.
17 But when he prays about his goods or
        marriage or children,
    he is not ashamed to address the thing
        without a soul.
    And for vigor he invokes the powerless;
18   and for life he entreats the dead;
    And for aid he beseeches the wholly
        incompetent,
    and about travel, something that cannot
        even walk.
19 And for profit in business and success with
        his hands
    he asks facility of a thing with hands
        completely inert.

NRSV

because he knows that it cannot help itself,
    for it is only an image and has need of help.
17 When he prays about possessions and his
        marriage and children,
    he is not ashamed to address a lifeless thing.
18 For health he appeals to a thing that is weak;
    for life he prays to a thing that is dead;
    for aid he entreats a thing that is utterly
        inexperienced;
    for a prosperous journey, a thing that cannot
        take a step;
19 for money-making and work and success with
        his hands
    he asks strength of a thing whose hands have
        no strength.

COMMENTARY

The more serious nature of idol worship is signaled at the outset of the critique. Miserable are those who worship "dead things" (v. 10). This critique against idol worship continues a long tradition in the biblical writings. The making of idols counters the supreme prohibition against creating a graven image of God (Deut 5:8, "You shall not make for yourself an idol, whether in the form of anything that is in heaven above, or that is on the earth beneath, or that is in the water under the earth" [NRSV]; cf. Lev 26:1). The author's ridicule of the making and worshiping of idols is formulated in a manner similar to that found in several other scriptural passages (e.g., Pss 97:7; 115:3-8; 135:15-18; Isa 2:8-20; 40:18-20; 44:9-20; 45:16-20; 46:5-7; Jer 10:1-16; Hab 2:18; Bar 6:8-73).

What is emphasized throughout the author's sustained critique is the origin behind the practice of making and worshiping idols. Just as the author attempted to portray the process whereby humans came to deify the elements of the universe, so too is there an attempt to understand the process whereby idol worship came into practice.

The language applied to the creators of idols is reminiscent of the language applied to the wicked in the first part of Wisdom. The points of contact focus on the origin of idol worship, the moral depravity associated with idol worship, the deserved punishment for idol worshipers, and the judgment against both idol makers and the idols.

The author is deliberately drawing parallels between the perpetrators of injustice in the first part and the idol makers and worshipers in the second part. For instance, death was said to have entered the world through the adversary's envy (2:24). Here it is said that idols have entered the world through human vanity (14:14). The wicked's project in life was described through images of moral corruption and injustice (2:6-20). Even more so are the consequences of idol worship presented through images of moral depravity and licentiousness (14:22-29). The wicked were described as being fit to belong to the company of death (1:16). The idol worshipers are said to be fit for the dead objects they worship (15:6). The day of reckoning for the wicked was presented vividly, where the righteous were rewarded with royal dignity, whereas wickedness was utterly demolished through a cosmic upheaval (4:18–5:14). Similarly in the critique against idolatry, a day of divine reckoning is assured for both idol makers and their idols (14:8-11).

The pejorative language used to speak of the cult of idols is highlighted at the outset with the emphasis on the lifeless quality of idols. At least in nature worship the human mind is taken up with the beauty of God's creation. In idol worship, the human mind is mesmerized by the lifeless works of human hands, works of gold, silver, stone, and wood (vv. 10-11). The progression from quality metals to less valuable materials used in fashioning idols accentuates the author's criticism. Idol worship represents for the author a movement of degradation. To worship idols made of precious metals like gold and silver or made of valuable stone is deplorable, but to worship items made of useless bits of wood and of odd pieces of clay reveals the moral vacuity of such worship.

The focus of the critique rests on the carpenter who from the less valuable commodity of wood makes all sorts of useful utensils with artistry. The ridicule is based on the distance between the useful tools made from wood for daily needs and the "cast-off" pieces of wood chosen for idols. Not being useful for anything practical, such crooked and knotted blocks of wood are then carefully shaped into human or animal form, their blemishes are covered with paint, and they are set in a niche in the wall.

The author highlights the helplessness and lifelessness of the idol, which sets up the irony of praying for human values and needs to a lifeless thing. The idol cannot walk or stand by itself and must be fastened in the niche. To such a helpless image the idol worshiper entrusts things of great value: marriage and children, health, life, a safe journey, a prosperous business transaction (vv. 16-19). The final statement clinches the essential argument: Idol worshipers ask for strength from something whose hands have no strength at all.

The author is adapting at least two biblical arguments against idols into a unified argument: the process of making the idol and the lifeless qualities of the idol. In Isa 44:9-20 is a critique of ironsmiths and carpenters who make practical objects from the same substance from which they make idols. The prophet concentrates on the same process used in the book of Wisdom whereby a carpenter fashions both practical utensils and lifeless idols from the same block of wood (see also Isa 40:18-20; Jer 10:3-5). Psalm 115:3-8 is a poetic analysis of the lifelessness of idols made of silver and gold. They have a mouth that cannot speak, eyes that cannot see, ears that cannot hear, a nose that cannot smell, hands that cannot grasp, and feet that cannot walk (see also Deut 4:27-28;

Ps 135:15-18; Bar 6:8-16, 53-59). These idols need to be fixed into a niche and fastened so that they will not topple over (vv. 15-16; cf. Isa 40:18-20).

The author of Wisdom highlights, in a similar manner, the lifeless qualities of the statue. At this point, however, instead of using the metaphor of the bodily senses (as will be done in 15:15), the author juxtaposes the prayers for human needs against the lack of human vitality in idols. The prayer for possessions, marriage, and children is juxtaposed to the lifelessness of an idol; praying for health is juxtaposed to the weakness of an idol; praying for life to the "deadness" of an idol; praying for help in life to the utter inexperience of idols; praying for a prosperous journey to an idol that cannot move; praying for success in business and work to an image whose hands have no strength (vv. 17-19).

It should be pointed out that in Greek and Hellenistic circles there was both a critique of the naiveté of idol worship and a defense for a more sophisticated view of an idol's function in prayer. The author's critique presumed a parody of idol worship. The lifeless quality of images and statues of worship was a subject of scorn for Heraclitus and Timaeus of Tauromenium.[108] But Plato defended the use of idols to remind humans of the living gods. The idol is to the living god what the shadow is to the object in Plato's allegory of the shadows in the cave: "The ancient laws of all men concerning the gods are two-fold: some of the gods whom we honor we see clearly, but of others we set up statues as images, and we believe that when we worship these, lifeless though they be, the living gods beyond feel great good-will towards us and gratitude."[109]

In terms of the author's overall argument, it should be noted that the image of wood continues to be used in the next part of the critique (14:1-10), when the fearful sailor prays to a wooden idol for protection aboard the wooden vessel. The theme of the carpenter who fashions idols is matched at the outer level of the concentric structure with the theme of the potter who gives shape to statues from clay (15:7-13).

---

108. See David Winston, *The Wisdom of Solomon*, AB 43 (New York: Doubleday, 1979) 259-61, for references to the practice of idol worship in Egypt and in Greek writings.
109. Plato *Laws* 931A.

REFLECTIONS

The author gives a name to a disorder that stifles human growth: idolatry. This disorder, which can be described in so many different ways, essentially seeks life where in fact there is no life. Appropriately, at the beginning of the critique the idol is described as "dead" (13:10). At the end of the critique what is highlighted is the discrepancy between the worshiper's attempt to secure values of life through idols and the "lifeless" quality of the idols themselves (13:17-19). Idolatry rests on a false hope, much as the wicked's reckless purposes and projects in life in the earlier chapters of the work rest on their false understanding of power and might (2:1-24).

With respect to the idol worshiper, the idol is described as the work of "human hands" (13:10). Herein lies the author's essential criticism of idolatry. It involves a lifeless absorption with the "self." Those who worship an idol made of human hands are locked into a preoccupation with the self that stifles transcendence. In the author's argument, there is in nature worship at least the minimal amount of transcendence involved because of its appreciation of the beautiful works of creation. But in the worship of idols made by human hands, the focus of the worshiper is drawn more and more toward the self.

Although it would be rather difficult to find idol worshipers in the strict sense in our contemporary societies and cultures, the essential function of idol worship still abounds. The idols of our own time may not be ones fashioned into images of gold, silver, or wood. There are the idols of consumerism with their many faces through which an entire generation has been trained to focus on the self. The resulting alienation and purposelessness that arise from not living out one's life for another are as lifeless as the helpless idols the author of Wisdom holds up for ridicule.

WISDOM 14:1-10, THE NAVIGATOR AND IDOLS

NAB	NRSV
14 Again, one preparing for a voyage and about to traverse the wild waves cries out to wood more unsound than the boat that bears him.	**14** Again, one preparing to sail and about to voyage over raging waves calls upon a piece of wood more fragile than the ship that carries him.
2 For the urge for profits devised this latter, and Wisdom the artificer produced it.	2 For it was desire for gain that planned that vessel, and wisdom was the artisan who built it;
3 But your providence, O Father! guides it, for you have furnished even in the sea a road, and through the waves a steady path,	3 but it is your providence, O Father, that steers its course, because you have given it a path in the sea, and a safe way through the waves,
4 Showing that you can save from any danger, so that even one without skill may embark.	4 showing that you can save from every danger, so that even a person who lacks skill may put to sea.
5 But you will that the products of your Wisdom be not idle; therefore men trust their lives even to frailest wood, and have been safe crossing the surge on a raft.	5 It is your will that works of your wisdom should not be without effect; therefore people trust their lives even to the smallest piece of wood, and passing through the billows on a raft they come safely to land.
6 For of old, when the proud giants were being destroyed,	

NAB

the hope of the universe, who took refuge
on a raft,
left to the world a future for his race, under
the guidance of your hand.
7 For blest is the wood through which justice
comes about;
8 but the handmade idol is accursed, and
its maker as well:
he for having produced it, and it, because
though corruptible, it was termed a
god.
9 Equally odious to God are the evildoer and
his evil deed;
10 and the thing made shall be punished
with its contriver.

NRSV

6 For even in the beginning, when arrogant
giants were perishing,
the hope of the world took refuge on a raft,
and guided by your hand left to the world the
seed of a new generation.
7 For blessed is the wood by which
righteousness comes.

8 But the idol made with hands is accursed, and
so is the one who made it—
he for having made it, and the perishable thing
because it was named a god.
9 For equally hateful to God are the ungodly and
their ungodliness;
10 for what was done will be punished together
with the one who did it.

COMMENTARY

The critique of worshiping a wooden idol focuses on the contrast between entrusting one's
survival on the sea to a piece of wood and calling
upon an idol made of wood that is more fragile
than the ship itself. Entrusting one's life to the
forces of creation and to one's knowledge of them
is rooted in the goodness of creation. The artistry
involved in the fashioning of the ship is praised
as the work of wisdom, the artisan (v. 2). It is
God's providence that steers the the ship through
the laws governing the winds and the currents.

As an example of genuine human trust in the
forces of creation, the author presents the ark of
Noah, which provided a saving benefit to all
humanity (vv. 3-7). Trust in this piece of wood
was rooted in God's providence. God supplements
the natural disposition of human intelligence with
a providence that brings to completion the desired
goal of safety (v. 5). By highlighting the wood in
the ark as a means of rescue, the author is
drawing a distinction between the goodness of the
materials of creation and the corruption of misus-
ing those materials to make idols. God is being
praised for the gift of wood that sustains human
beings in precarious moments on the sea. The
reflection takes on the quality of thankful praise
to God for the wonders of creation and for God's
providential care in and through creation.

The praise to God ends in a statement of
beatitude reminiscent of the declaration of blessedness for the virtuous sterile woman and the
eunuch (3:13-14, different Greek words for "blessedness" are used in each passage). The very wood
by which the righteousness of Noah brought salvation to humanity is proclaimed blessed.

It is quite understandable how the early church,
which on occasion favored an allegorical interpretation of Scripture as exemplified in Origen of
Alexandria, recognized in this statement a reference to the blessedness of the cross of Christ.
Ambrose comments on Wis 14:7-8 by juxtaposing
the matter that is considered blessed with matter
that is considered accursed. He explains the reference to wood as representing the cross of Christ
and the reference to the work of human hands
as representing wooden idols.[110]

The NT employed the same Greek word to
designate "cross" that can be translated as "wood"
in general or even "tree" (ξύλον *xylon;* Acts 5:30;
10:39; 13:29; Gal 3:13; 1 Pet 2:24). The tree of
life and the tree of the knowledge of good and
evil are represented by the same Greek word in
the creation text (Gen 2:9). The book of Revelation also employs the same word for references

110. Ambrose *Sermon* 8,23; *Patrologia latina* 15, 130A.

to the tree of life (Rev 2:7; 22:2; 22:14, 19). The Wisdom author had already employed the same word in an evident reference to the ark of Noah ("wisdom again saved it, steering the righteous man by a paltry piece of wood" [Wis 10:4 NRSV]). Since there was an evident interpolation to the cross in Ps 96:10 LXX, "The Lord reigns from the wood," which the oldest Greek MSS (B, S, and A) had already expunged, it was thought that perhaps the text of Wis 14:7 was also a Christian insert. The Muratori Canon (c. 180–190 CE) includes the Wisdom of Solomon in its list of NT writings, and this could very well have been the verse that caused the compiler to include it on the oldest list of NT writings that we have. However, as reflecting a reference to the ark of Noah, the verse fits well into the argument of the author, which lauds the matter through which human beings come to salvation and to justice. The author's firm assertion of the health and beauty of creation perhaps elicited this emphasis on the integrity of matter itself to distinguish the matter of wood from the idols made of wood that are accursed (vv. 8-11).

The turn to direct speech (vv. 3-7), which is found throughout the midrashic treatment of the exodus, points to the contemplative nature of the reflection. God is invoked directly as Father (v. 3). Although the image of father is used for God throughout Scripture, the address to God as Father in direct prayer is very late.[111] God is described through various images as a father (as father of orphans, Ps 68:5; as a father who has compassion or provides discipline, Ps 103:13; Prov 3:12; cf. Deut 8:5). At times God wishes that Israel would call upon the Lord as a father (Jer 3:4; 3:19; 31:9; Mal 1:6; 2:10).

There are occurrences of God's being addressed directly as a father in the texts representing the Davidic covenant (Ps 89:26), whereby the king is understood to be the adopted son of God (2 Sam 7:14). The closest parallels to the Wisdom text to God's being called father in direct speech is in Isa 63:16: "For you are our father . . . you O LORD are our father; our Redeemer from of old is your name" (NRSV; cf. Isa 64:8), and in Sir 23:1, "O Lord, Father and Master of my life" (NRSV; cf. Sir 23:4). It was common in rabbinical stories for God to be addressed as a father, "Hanin ha-Nehba was the son of the daughter of Honi the Circle-drawer. When the world needed rain, the Rabbis would send schoolchildren to him, who would pull him by the corners of his garments, and say to him: 'Father, Father! Give us rain!' Said Hanin: 'Master of the world! Do it for the sake of these who do not distinguish between the Father who gives rain and a father who does not give rain.' And the rain came."[112]

Philo and Josephus employ the metaphor of father for God in a universal manner, as does the author of Wisdom. The ambiance, therefore, was already very fertile indeed for Jesus of Nazareth to address God through the personal designation of God as "Abba, father" (Matt 5:16; 6:1-32; Mark 19:36).

In contrast to the blessedness of the wood that saves, the author declares the idols made by human hands to be accursed (vv. 8-10). Both the makers of idols and the idols themselves fall under the disapproval of God. Since the author had declared that all creatures stand under God's providential care (1:14; 11:24-26), a distinction is made between the material of the idol and its function of "snaring" human souls and "trapping" the feet of the gullible (v. 11). Human beings, through their deliberate choices, have transformed a material that is part of God's creation into something that is not. Just as the responsibility for bringing on death lies squarely on the shoulders of human beings, according to the first part of the book, so too does the responsibility for transforming something blessed into a thing accursed rest on the idol makers.

---

111. On the fatherhood of God in direct prayer, see Eileen M. Schuller, "The Psalm of 4Q372 1 Within the Context of Second Temple Prayer," *CBQ* 54 (1992) 67-79.

112. *Babylonian Talmud, Ta'an*, 23b.

REFLECTIONS

1. The author's critique of sailors who beseech for safety a wooden idol more fragile than the ship that carries them elicits the author's contrasting admiration of God's providence. This admiration is occasioned by the juxtaposition of the groundless trust in a wooden idol and the marvelous trust exemplified by Noah, who entrusted the future of the living also to a "piece of wood" (14:5). The piece of wood is one of God's "many works of wisdom" through which human beings can develop their potential for life. The author recognizes the providential care of God within the works of creation that are placed at the service of human beings. Creation itself is there for human beings to find sustenance and security. The author's positive view of the forces of creation that stand under God's providence surfaces again and again throughout the work. The reflection ends in a declaration of praise of the very material of creation, "Blessed is the wood by which righteousness comes" (14:7 NRSV).

2. But the positive forces of creation are open to abuse from human manipulation. The idol symbolizes the human abuse of the created material of the universe. Instead of using wood for its many positive functions, the idol makers transform it into objects that misguide and ensnare human beings so that they do not perceive the originator of the universe. The particular nuance of this critique against idol makers highlights the importance of reflecting on our use of material goods, of the environment, and of the earth itself.

WISDOM 14:11-31, ORIGINS AND EVILS OF IDOLATRY

NAB	NRSV
11 Therefore upon even the idols of the nations shall a visitation come, since they have become abominable amid God's works, Snares for the souls of men and a trap for the feet of the senseless.	11 Therefore there will be a visitation also upon the heathen idols, because, though part of what God created, they became an abomination, snares for human souls and a trap for the feet of the foolish.
12 For the source of wantonness is the devising of idols; and their invention was a corruption of life.	12 For the idea of making idols was the beginning of fornication, and the invention of them was the corruption of life;
13 For in the beginning they were not, nor shall they continue forever;	13 for they did not exist from the beginning, nor will they last forever.
14 for by the vanity of men they came into the world, and therefore a sudden end is devised for them.	14 For through human vanity they entered the world, and therefore their speedy end has been planned.
15 For a father, afflicted with untimely mourning, made an image of the child so quickly taken from him, And now honored as a god what was formerly a dead man and handed down to his subjects mysteries and sacrifices.	15 For a father, consumed with grief at an untimely bereavement, made an image of his child, who had been suddenly taken from him; he now honored as a god what was once a dead human being, and handed on to his dependents secret rites and initiations.
16 Then, in time, the impious practice gained strength and was observed as law, and graven things were worshiped by princely decrees.	16 Then the ungodly custom, grown strong with time, was kept as a law,

14, 12: *heuresis*: so LXX [S, V.]

NAB

17 Men who lived so far away that they could
      not honor him in his presence
    copied the appearance of the distant king
    And made a public image of him they wished
      to honor,
      out of zeal to flatter him when absent, as
        though present.
18 And to promote this observance among
      those to whom it was strange,
    the artisan's ambition provided a stimulus.
19 For he, mayhap in his determination to
      please the ruler,
      labored over the likeness to the best of his
        skill;
20 And the masses, drawn by the charm of the
      workmanship,
      soon thought he should be worshiped who
        shortly before was honored as a man.
21 And this became a snare for mankind,
      that men enslaved to either grief or tyranny
    conferred the incommunicable Name on
      stocks and stones.
22 Then it was not enough for them to err in
      their knowledge of God;
      but even though they live in a great war
        of ignorance,
    they call such evils peace.
23 For while they celebrate either child-slaying
      sacrifices or clandestine mysteries,
    or frenzied carousals in unheard-of rites,
24 They no longer safeguard either lives or
      pure wedlock;
      but each either waylays and kills his
        neighbor, or aggrieves him by adultery.
25 And all is confusion—blood and murder,
      theft and guile,
      corruption, faithlessness, turmoil, perjury,
26 Disturbance of good men, neglect of
      gratitude,
      besmirching of souls, unnatural lust,
      disorder in marriage, adultery and
        shamelessness.
27 For the worship of infamous idols
      is the reason and source and extremity of
        all evil.
28 For they either go mad with enjoyment, or
      prophesy lies,

14, 26: *amnēstia*: so LXX^MSS.

NRSV

and at the command of monarchs carved
  images were worshiped.
17 When people could not honor monarchs[a] in
      their presence, since they lived at a
        distance,
    they imagined their appearance far away,
    and made a visible image of the king whom
      they honored,
    so that by their zeal they might flatter the
      absent one as though present.

18 Then the ambition of the artisan impelled
    even those who did not know the king to
      intensify their worship.
19 For he, perhaps wishing to please his ruler,
    skillfully forced the likeness to take more
      beautiful form,
20 and the multitude, attracted by the charm of
      his work,
    now regarded as an object of worship the one
      whom shortly before they had honored
        as a human being.
21 And this became a hidden trap for humankind,
    because people, in bondage to misfortune or
      to royal authority,
    bestowed on objects of stone or wood the
      name that ought not to be shared.

22 Then it was not enough for them to err about
      the knowledge of God,
    but though living in great strife due to
      ignorance,
    they call such great evils peace.
23 For whether they kill children in their
      initiations, or celebrate secret
        mysteries,
    or hold frenzied revels with strange customs,
24 they no longer keep either their lives or their
      marriages pure,
    but they either treacherously kill one another,
      or grieve one another by adultery,
25 and all is a raging riot of blood and murder,
      theft and deceit, corruption,
      faithlessness, tumult, perjury,
26 confusion over what is good, forgetfulness of
      favors,
    defiling of souls, sexual perversion,

a Gk *them*

NAB

or live lawlessly or lightly forswear
themselves.

29 For as their trust is in soulless idols,
they expect no harm when they have
sworn falsely.

30 But on both counts shall justice overtake
them:
because they thought ill of God and
devoted themselves to idols,
and because they deliberately swore false
oaths, despising piety.

31 For not the might of those that are sworn
by
but the retribution of sinners
ever follows upon the transgression of the
wicked.

NRSV

disorder in marriages, adultery, and
debauchery.

27 For the worship of idols not to be named
is the beginning and cause and end of every
evil.

28 For their worshipers[a] either rave in exultation,
or prophesy lies, or live unrighteously, or
readily commit perjury;

29 for because they trust in lifeless idols
they swear wicked oaths and expect to suffer
no harm.

30 But just penalties will overtake them on two
counts:
because they thought wrongly about God in
devoting themselves to idols,
and because in deceit they swore unrighteously
through contempt for holiness.

31 For it is not the power of the things by which
people swear,[b]
but the just penalty for those who sin,
that always pursues the transgression of the
unrighteous.

a Gk *they*   *b* Or *of the oaths people swear*

COMMENTARY

14:11-14. The idols fashioned by human hands
fall under the same judgment as their makers and
worshipers. This argument, which relies on a distinction between the function of the idol and the
material of the idol itself, is similar to that found in
the first part of the book. Human beings have been
made for immortality. Their rightful destiny is to be
in union with God. But they can choose a life of
justice that brings immortality or a life of injustice
that brings death. The case with idols is similar.
From their very material they are part of what God
had created. Yet through human choice they have
become an abomination because they have led people astray. The final judgment includes God's visitation not only on the makers and worshipers of idols,
but also on the idols themselves.

Nonetheless, the argument appears somewhat
forced and awkward. It would appear that the
author is including the idols under the judgment
of God in continuity with the prohibition against
idols that arose during the prophetic period. One

of the arguments for the validity of the idol is that
it endures in time and space. Judgment against
the false worship of idolatry includes the revelation of the idol's worthlessness or ineffectiveness.
The story of the statue of Dagon that stood beside
the ark in captivity is a case in point. Twice it
had fallen before the ark as a judgment against its
worshipers (1 Sam 5:1-5).

An interesting reflection on the problem of the
endurance of idols occurs in the Mishnah, where
some Romans questioned the rabbis about idols:
"The elders in Rome were asked, 'If your God
has no pleasure in the worship of idols, why does
he not destroy them?' They replied, 'If men had
worshiped the things which the world does not
need, He would have destroyed them. But, they
worship sun, moon, stars and planets; is He to
destroy His world because of the fools?' "[113] God

113. Quoting this, the Gemara adds, "The world maintains its course,
but the fools who have corrupted their ways, will be judged hereafter."
Aboda Zara 4.7.

spares the wicked, providing a time for conversion (Wis 11:26–12:1-2, 10). The idols belong to their worshipers and fall under the cloud of the final judgment along with them.

The explanation for the origin of idolatry (vv. 12-21) continues the author's tendency to probe under the surface to arrive at the causes of injustice and death. In the first part of the book, the author provided an explanation for the origin of sin and death. Human beings bring on death through living unjustly (1:12-15). Through the envy of the adversary, death had entered the cosmos (2:24). In the critique of nature worship, the author probed the origins of identifying the forces of creation with divine reality (13:1-9). The critique of the carpenter ridiculed the idol-making process, but it did not offer an explanation for idolatry. In the very center of the concentric structure, the author attempts to enter into the mind-set of those who have come to worship an idol made by human hands.

The language that introduces the explanation for idol worship reflects the author's previous concerns and explanations: the essential goodness of all that exists and the entrance of idol worship into the world. Since God loves all that exists, the author reiterates how idols did not exist at the beginning. God is not their creator. They entered the cosmos through human vanity (v. 14); therefore, their end is assured (cf. Isa 45:16; Jer 16:19-21).

The relationship between idol worship and fornication (v. 12) is one that the author adapts primarily from prophetic teaching. The Greek word representing "fornication" (πορνεία porneia) refers to various forms of sexual disorders. The corresponding Hebrew term is often used to designate more precisely the worship of false gods, as is the case with the Wisdom author. The image of marital infidelity is implied in the prophetic use of the metaphor of fornication with idols (Jer 3:6-8; Ezek 16:15-43; Hosea 1–2; 4:11-19; cf. Exod 34:15-17; Judg 2:16-23). Infidelity to the faithful God of the covenant is understood as a breach of the covenant agreement. The author is adapting the uniquely Israelite understanding of fidelity to the One God for its application to all humanity in the explanation of the origin of idol worship.

14:15-21. Two brief examples of the origin

of idol worship are presented in the story of a father who is bereft over the sudden death of a child (vv. 15-16) and the monarch who commands the worship of carved images (vv. 16-17). The latter example is further developed with the illustration of the artisan who, perhaps not even having known the monarch, embellishes the likeness with a charm that attracts a multitude (vv. 18-21). Neither example is attested in Scripture as an explanation for the cult of idols, but each relates to general practice in the Greco-Roman age of setting up images of either one's beloved or monarchs.

Many of the clear examples of the Greco-Roman practice of idol worship are posterior to the book of Wisdom. For example, there is the cult of Antinoos, which the Emperor Hadrian set up in memory of his young friend who drowned tragically in Egypt (c. 130 CE). There is a story from the fourth century CE that explains how a statue became an idol that is very similar to the case envisaged in Wisdom. In that story, an Egyptian named Syropahnes sets up a statue of his dead son in his house in order to ease the family's grief at their loss. The family members decorate the statue to please the father, and eventually the household slaves begin to flee to it for protection. In this way, a statue honoring the memory of a son was understood to have become eventually the object of cultic worship.[114]

The author adds to the critique of the origin of such idol worship the falsity of the artist's embellishment of the idol. Plato had expressed a certain ambivalence toward art that was motivated primarily by the tendency of artists to embellish their subjects. For Plato such a tendency led to a falsification of the true form and represented an aberration from true art itself.[115] Philo added the same argument found in Wisdom, which ridicules the artist's embellishment of the subject, in his critique of idol worship, "Further, too, they have brought in sculpture and painting to cooperate in the deception, in order that with the colors and shapes and artistic qualities wrought by their fine workmanship they may enthrall the spectators and so beguile the two leading senses, sight and hear-

114. For several examples of the custom of honoring the dead and monarchs in the Greco-Roman world, see the references in David Winston, *The Wisdom of Solomon*, AB 43 (New York: Doubleday, 1979) 270-78.
115. Plato *Republic* 604D.

ing."[116] The attraction to works of art is viewed as a snare that entraps humans to worship idols made of stone or wood (v. 21).

14:22-26. What follows is a list of vices that arise from not having knowledge of God. The passage is reminiscent of the speech of the wicked, in the first part of the book, who perpetrated injustice against the just one (chap. 2). The wicked have no knowledge of God, and this lack of knowledge blinds them to the gifts of justice and wisdom. Whereas the author's presentation of the wicked's aberration to injustice was subtle, with a progressive and sinister momentum, the author's invectives are unrestrained with respect to idol worshipers.

The list of vices follows a much-used literary device in which disorders and aberrations are accumulated to highlight the perversions that stem from a single cause. In the Greek *Apocalypse of Baruch* is a series of disorders attributed to the fall and to drunkenness, "Brother does not have mercy on brother, nor father on son, nor children on parents, but by means of the Fall through wine come forth all (these): murder, adultery, fornication, perjury, theft, and similar things.[117]

The combination of blood, murder, theft, and deceit in v. 25 is a reference to Hos 4:1-2, where the list of vices follows the similar declaration of a lack of knowledge of God: "There is no faithfulness or loyalty, and no knowledge of God in the land. Swearing, lying, and murder, and stealing and adultery break out; bloodshed follows bloodshed" (NRSV). The list of vices, in the Greek translation of Hosea especially, appears to be structured according to a section of the decalogue in Exod 20:13-16 (LXX): "You shall not murder. You shall not commit adultery, You shall not steal, You shall not bear false witness against your neighbor" (cf. Matt 15:19; Mark 7:21-22). Paul made frequent use of a list of vices in his letters (Rom 1:24-32; 1 Cor 5:9-11; 2 Cor 12:20-21; Gal 5:19-21; Col 3:5-9; 1 Tim 1:9-10), at times juxtaposing them to a list of virtues (Gal 5:22-23; Col 3:11-17).

At the outset of the list of vices, the author highlights one particular feature that had surfaced earlier in the book: The lack of virtue confuses the perspective on the good (vv. 22*b*, 26). In the concluding summary, regarding the reasoning of the wicked (2:21-24), the author explained how the injustice of the wicked blinded them to the purposes of God, the wages of holiness, and the prize for blameless souls. When the figure of Solomon speaks in the second part of Wisdom, emphasis is placed on the openness of wisdom and on the revelatory character of Solomon's teaching (6:22-23). All good things came to Solomon through wisdom, who makes people friends with God (7:11, 27). In the criticism of idol worship, the author postulates that the lack of knowledge of the true God confuses the perception of the good and devolves into secrecy and disorder.

The theme of mistaking war for peace was immortalized in the famous epithet of Tacitus (c. 55–117 CE): "To plunder, butcher, steal, these things they misname empire; they make a desolation and they call it peace."[118] Tacitus was criticizing the *Pax Romana,* which was often achieved through a brutal exercising of power through violence. For the victors, the outcome is called peace, but for the victims it is sheer desolation. Just as injustice blinds the wicked from perceiving the plan of God, so also the lack of knowledge of God in idol worship confuses the perception of the good (v. 26). Idol worshipers consider the internal and external disorders that throw them into great strife as peace (v. 22).

The critique of idolatry includes an attack on the secret mystery cults (v. 23). In the second part of the book, the author implied a critique of the mystery cults by deliberately presenting personified wisdom as transparent and open (7:22–8:1). Likewise, Solomon was presented as having transmitted his knowledge acquired through friendship with wisdom openly, ungrudgingly, and without restriction (6:22-23; 7:13-14). This open style of pedagogy on the part of personified wisdom and exemplified in the persona of Solomon stands in stark contrast to the secretive initiation rites common to mystery cults in the Greco-Roman world.

14:27-31. The concluding section on the origin and evils of idolatry focuses on the cause of disorders and the accompanying judgment against

---

116. Philo *On the Special Laws* 1.29.
117. 3 Bar 4:17; see also Philo *On the Decalogue* 168 and *Who Is the Heir* 173.

118. Tacitus *Agricola* 30.

idolatry. In this way, we are brought back to the themes in the beginning of the unit by the repetition of the image of the origin of evils (v. 12 = v. 27), and the image of judgment and punishment for idol worshipers (v. 11 = vv. 30-31). The unit begins with the declaration of the punishment of the idols themselves and the connection between the origin of evil and the making of idols. The unit concludes with the declaration of the origin of every evil residing in idolatry and the punishment of idol worshipers.

One of the criticisms of idol worship in this unit focuses on the Israelite prohibition of the naming of idols and swearing oaths by them (cf. Exod 23:13; Josh 23:7; Ps 16:4). But the particular nuance that the Wisdom author emphasizes in this critique is the loss of moral direction that results from the worshiping of false gods made by human hands.

In effect, the worship of idols brings about a life of injustice (v. 28). Without moral direction, the idolater's life is easily caught in false "exultation," "prophesying lies," "living unrighteously,"

"committing perjury," "swearing unjust oaths" without realizing the destructive consequences of such actions (vv. 28-29). The tension between justice and injustice is brought to the fore with six words in the Greek text: "unrighteously" (ἀδίκως *adikōs*, v. 28), "wicked oaths" (κακῶς ὀμόσαντες *kakōs omosantes*, v. 29), "just penalties" (δίκαια *dikaia*, v. 30), "unrighteously" (ἀδίκως *adikōs*, v. 30), "just penalty" (δίκη *dikē*, v. 31), and "unrighteous" (ἄδικοι *adikoi*, v. 31).

The generalization whereby the origin of every evil is said to reside in idolatry (v. 27) parallels the generalization in the first part of the book whereby injustice is described as being the cause of death (1:12-16). More immediately, the phrase parallels the opening volley against the making of idols in v. 12, "For the idea of making idols was the beginning of fornication, and the invention of them was the corruption of life." The generalizations are not meant to exclude each other. Rather, they intensify the level of disorder that the author judges injustice and idolatry to cause.

REFLECTIONS

1. The declaration of divine judgment against idols and their worshipers (14:11) recalls the author's assertion of divine judgment against the wicked in the first part of the book. The wicked had placed their hope in the apparent "fruit" of their injustice. But on the day of judgment the very fruit of the wicked accuses them and, therefore, does not bring its hoped-for strength (3:13–4:9). The idols that entrap and snare human beings fall under the same divine judgment (14:11). Whatever prevents human beings from realizing their relationship with God and with one another is to be destroyed.

The severity of the judgment the author extends to the idols is based on their continuous entrapping function. Idols are like structures of injustice. They have become somewhat independent from their originators, the hands that crafted them; yet they continue to be a snare and a trap that hinder people from achieving a more just and equitable balance in society.

2. The aberration of idol worship produces a confusion over what is good: "They call such great evils peace" (14:22 NRSV); "and all is . . . confusion over what is good" (14:25-26 NRSV). The author offers insight into the moral confusion that results from the sin of idolatry. Sin brings about a confusion over what is good and what is evil. This same misdirection was evident in the author's critique of the reasoning of the wicked in the first part of the book. The wicked's judgment, that mortality renders life arbitrary, caused them to value power and might and to despise weakness and frailty (2:11). As a result, they perceived death in weakness when in fact the weakness of the virtuous is transformed into life; they perceived life in their exercise of unjust power when, in fact, the power of the wicked is revealed as being groundless and empty of virtue.

A similar understanding of the confusion over good and evil, and life and death, that results from unfaithfulness to God is presented in the book of Deuteronomy. When the spies had returned from reconnoitering the promised land, they announced that the land God was giving them was a good land (Deut 1:25). But instead of perceiving life in the new land as good, the people thought only of death: "It is because the LORD hates us that he has brought us out of the land of Egypt, to hand us over to the Amorites to destroy us" (Deut 1:27 NRSV). The nonsequitur that stands between the spies' positive assessment of the land and the people's interpretation of the divine motive can be explained only by the blindness and confusion caused by their sin of faithlessness.

The same lack of trust prompted the people to announce their preference for life as slaves in Egypt to the tenuous existence in the wilderness, where they perceived death. At the imminent moment of deliverance the people accused Moses of bringing them to the desert to die (Exod 14:10-14). The author of Wisdom attributes the same confusion over the good to the idolatry that focuses on the self, symbolized in the idol, "the work of human hands." Those caught in idolatry perceive the turmoil of misdirection as peace. Sin carries with it the consequence of a moral blindness that induces a misinterpretation of what is good and brings life in the long term and of what is evil and brings death in the long run. Only the shock of a tragedy or an amazing expression of love and respect can jolt the one who is blind into reexamining the moral consequences of his or her actions.

3. A just punishment pursues those who devote themselves to idolatry (14:30). This idea affirms the author's particular understanding that punishment arises from seeds of destruction inherent in the paths of injustice or untruth. It is not as if the punishment comes from the outside and somehow could be avoided if the perpetrators of injustice or followers of untruth go unseen or are not caught by the legal authorities. The seeds of turmoil are inherent in a path of life that focuses on the self (on the works of human hands). Such a life excludes the transcendence (going beyond oneself) that brings human beings into communion with one another. As in the case of an addiction, whatever semblance of human fulfillment may appear to be in the beginning, eventually the relentlessness of the addiction brings about the evident signs of destruction.

WISDOM 15:1-6, REFLECTION ON GOD'S MERCY AND POWER

NAB	NRSV

15 But you, our God,
   are good and true,
 slow to anger, and governing all with mercy.
 2 For even if we sin, we are yours, and know your might;
   but we will not sin, knowing that we belong to you.
 3 For to know you well is complete justice,
   and to know your might is the root of immortality.
 4 For neither did the evil creation of men's fancy deceive us,
   nor the fruitless labor of painters,
	15 But you, our God,
	   are kind and true,
	 patient, and ruling all things*a* in mercy.
	 2 For even if we sin we are yours, knowing your power;
	   but we will not sin, because we know that you acknowledge us as yours.
	 3 For to know you is complete righteousness,
	   and to know your power is the root of immortality.
	 4 For neither has the evil intent of human art misled us,
	   nor the fruitless toil of painters,
	   a figure stained with varied colors,
	 5 whose appearance arouses yearning in fools,

15, 2: (*ouch hamartēsometha*) *de:* so LXX^MSS.

a Or *ruling the universe*

NAB

A form smeared with varied colors,

5   the sight of which arouses yearning in the
         senseless man,
     till he longs for the inanimate form of a
         dead image.

6 Lovers of evil things, and worthy of such hopes
     are they who make them and long for
         them and worship them.

15, 5: *aphroni eis orexin:* so LXX[MSS].

NRSV

so that they desire[a] the lifeless form of a dead
         image.

⁶ Lovers of evil things and fit for such objects of
         hope[b]
     are those who either make or desire or worship
         them.

[a] Gk *and he desires*   [b] Gk *such hopes*

COMMENTARY

Within the concentric structure of the critique of idolatry, the author turns briefly to praise God for the mercy and power shown to the righteous. The unit stands parallel to the prayerful reflection on God's providential care in the treatment of the sailor who prays to a wooden idol (14:1-10). The difference in tone is noted immediately by the use of direct speech. God is addressed directly in the second person and is praised for the merciful sovereignty exercised over creation.

15:1-3. One notable difference in the language of this reflection from that on God's providence is the author's explicit identification with the people of God. This sense of identification with the community under divine protection is inaugurated in v. 1 with the image of *"our* God," and it continues with the persistent use of the first-person plural in v. 2: "even if *we* sin, *we* are yours . . . but *we* will not sin, because *we* know that you acknowledge *us* as yours" (italics added). The vocabulary depicting this personal bond between the righteous and God is reminiscent of the terms describing the bond between Israel and God in covenantal language:

They shall know that I, the LORD their God, am with them, and that they, the house of Israel, are my people, says the Lord GOD. You are my sheep, the sheep of my pasture and I am your God, says the Lord GOD. (Ezek 34:30-31 NRSV; cf. Ezek 11:20; 14:11; 37:27; 39:7)

The bond between the righteous and God is highlighted and intensified by the contrast to the relationship between idolaters and their lifeless idols (vv. 4-6). The God of the righteous is full of power and mercy (v. 1); the many gods of the idolatrous are powerless (13:17-19).

The opening phrase of the unit, "But you, our God," contrasts the personal God of the righteous to the previously described lifeless idols of the unrighteous. A series of four descriptive words and phrases characterizes the mercy and power God exercises over creation and the righteous. God is depicted as kind, true, patient, and ruling all things in mercy. Verse 1 evidently was inspired by the poetic vocabulary of God's declaration to Moses in the giving of the second set of tablets. As God passed before Moses,

"The LORD, the LORD,
a God merciful and gracious,
slow to anger,
and abounding in steadfast love
     and faithfulness,
keeping steadfast love for the
     thousandth generation."
(Exod 34:6-7 NRSV)

Three of the four descriptive expressions in the Wisdom text are found in the Greek text of the Exodus source: "true" = "faithfulness" (Exod 34:6) "patient" = "slow to anger" (Exod 34:6), "ruling all things in mercy" = "merciful" (Exod 34:6). The first adjective, "kind" (χρηστός *chrēstos*) is not found in Exod 34:6, but it is frequently used in the psalms as a translation of the Hebrew word for "good" (טוב *ṭôb*; Pss 25:8; 34:9; 86:5; 100:5; 106:1). Moreover, the same root in the adverbial form was used by the Wisdom author to describe the manner in which wisdom guides the cosmos, wisdom "guides" all things *well* (8:1).

The phrase "ruling all things" (v. 1), had already been employed by the author in 8:1, where personified wisdom was described as "guiding all things well." The Greek phrase was particularly in common use among the Stoics. The Wisdom author is applying the coined phrase to the gracious manner in which God guides the cosmos without the pantheistic and materialistic overtones of Stoic philosophy. The covenantal language of the verse maintains the tension between God's transcendence and God's care for all things.

This tension was maintained by the author in several previous passages in which God's mercy and power are held together to portray the marvelous manner in which God guides the cosmos. In 8:1, personified wisdom is described as "reaching mightily from one end of the earth to the other" as well as "ordering all things well." In 11:21-24, both God's power and God's mercy are praised as giving expression to God's love for all things that exist. In 12:15-18, the description of God's justice concentrates on the consistency between God's righteousness and God's power: "You rule all things righteously, deeming it alien to your power to condemn anyone who does not deserve to be punished" (12:15 NRSV). The sovereignty of God is described as combining strength and mildness, power and forbearance.

The bond between God and the righteous is said to be stronger than sin itself (v. 2). Even if the righteous sin, they still belong to God. This awareness of the indissoluble covenantal bond prompts the author's declaration that the righteous will not sin. It is rare in the book of Wisdom for the author to treat the sin of the righteous. Of course, the biblical traditions from which the author heavily draws support, particularly Isaiah and Deuteronomy, are filled with an explicit awareness of the sin of Israel. In the diptychs of the first part of Wisdom, which contrasted the righteous and the wicked, the author employed Isaiah's image of the suffering servant. Yet the feature of the vicarious suffering of the servant in Isaiah was suppressed by the Wisdom author. The reason for this suppression is evident when one considers that the author is contrasting the righ-

teous one who suffers unjustly with the powerful wicked who oppress. In Isaiah the servant suffers for the sake of Israel. The themes of conversion and reconciliation associated with the suffering servant are replaced with themes of judgment against the wicked and the integrity of the righteous by the Wisdom author. The issue of the righteous person's also experiencing punishment for infidelity will surface again later in the diptychs. The author will have to face the possible objections or protests that naturally arise in the contrast between the enemies of Israel and the righteous. Not only the enemies of the Israelites but also the righteous themselves experience the tragic consequences of injustice (16:5-6; 18:20-25).

The reference to the sin of the righteous was more than likely prompted by the same source (Exod 34:6-7) that was used for the image of God's mercy and compassion in v. 1. The merciful and gracious God of Moses is also a forgiving God who pardons iniquity, transgression, and sin (Exod 34:7). Israel had committed the sin of idolatry by worhiping the golden calf immediately after the giving of the law to Moses at Sinai. Yet, this sin did not eradicate their belonging to God. Because of God's mercy and faithfulness, Israel remained God's special people before whom great wonders would be done (Exod 34:8-10).

Since the author of Wisdom is criticizing the worship of false gods in the broader context of the argument, the particular sin being alluded to is probably idolatry. The supreme demand of the covenantal bond for Israel is to worship the Lord alone and not bow down to false gods (Exod 20:2; 34:11-17; Deut 5:6-11). The prophetic voice that continually reprimands Israel for apostasy and idolatry testifies to the tenacious rootedness that idolatry had in ancient Israel.

The author's confidence that the righteous will not fall into the sin of idolatry stems from the general belief in the eradication of idolatry among the Jews at the time of the author's writing. This belief was voiced in the book of Judith: "For never in our generation, nor in these present days, has there been any tribe or family or people or town of ours that worships gods made with hands, as was done in days gone by" (Jdt 8:18 NRSV). Even Tacitus (55–117 CE) acknowledges that the Jewish cult showed no signs whatsoever of tolerating idolatry as an expression of faith: "The Jews conceive of one god only, and that with the mind alone: they regard as impious those who make from perishable materials representations of god in man's image; that supreme and eternal being is to them incapable of representation and without end."[119] The tone of confidence is not one of arrogance arising from merit on the side of Israel, but is one of humility arising from the realization of God's continuous expression of mercy and forgiveness.

The effective result of the covenantal bond between the righteous and their merciful God is perfect justice and possession of the root of immortality. The verse expresses its thought through complete parallelism. To know God is righteousness; to know God's sovereignty is the root of immortality. As in the first part of Wisdom, justice and immortality meet once again (3:1-4; 4:1; 6:17-20).

The nuance that the verb "to know" ($\epsilon\check{\imath}\delta\omega$ *eidō*) carries in the verse is twofold, "to be intimate with" and "to acknowledge." In v. 2*b* the force of the verb "to know" in the phrase "knowing your power" is that of acknowledging or recognizing the power and sovereignty of God. Even if they sin, the righteous still will acknowledge and recognize the dominion of God. This acknowledgment of God's sovereignty follows from knowing that God claims them.

The author has made frequent use of the verb "to know" in the triple relationship among Solomon, wisdom, and God in the second part of Wisdom. Personified wisdom is described as an initiate in the ways of God (8:2-8). Solomon prays to God for the gift of wisdom, who knows the works of God and, therefore, can guide him wisely in his actions (9:9-12). In effect, one sees in the prayerful reflection on God's mercy and power the results of Solomon's prayer for the wisdom that comes from God. Wisdom brings a knowledge of God that makes one an intimate friend of God and enables one to acknowledge God's dominion.

Acknowledging the sovereignty of God is the root of immortality. The gift of immortality is as inchoate as a tree with its root growing in the

soil. Eventually the tree will come to full maturity. Whereas in the first part of the book immortality was presented more as a gift in response to the fidelity of the righteous, here the inchoate presence of immortality is more explicitly seen to exist as a root that will come to a complete fullness of union with God. In the case of the barren woman and the faithful eunuch, a similar image was employed to show the eventual fruitfulness of virtue: "The root of understanding does not fail" (3:15 NRSV). It is not simply the sovereignty of God that assures immortality; rather, the acknowledgment of God's dominion is the root of immortality.

A different line of interpretation of the expression "to know your power is the root of immortality" would understand the force of meaning to be that God is the one who has power over death.[120] In this case, God's power over death is the source of immortality. God's power, of course, is open to signifying either a concrete expression of God's sovereignty or the general dominion of God. Interpreting the verb "to know" as "to acknowledge" would suggest that God's power refers to the general dominion of God over all creation. It is not simply God's power that is the root of immortality. Rather, God's dominion is the context, the soil for the root of immortality. Those who acknowledge God's sovereignty and who have come to experience the fidelity of God even in the face of their own resistance have the root of immortality.

15:4-6. The concluding part of the unit contrasts the root of immortality, which the righteous have in recognizing the true God, with the hopeless situation of idolaters. The righteous have not been led into idolatry by the misguided attempts of artistry that embellishes the lifelessness of the idols (v. 4).

The author has already criticized the duplicity of artists who embellish the surface of idols (13:13-15; 14:18-21). The author's own critique in this regard parallels the criticism of such prac-

---

119. Tacitus *Histories* 5.5.

120. R. E. Murphy, "To Know Your Might Is the Root of Immortality (Wisd 15,3)," *CBQ* 25 (1963) 88-93. Murphy understands God's power specifically as God's power over death. This interpretation explains the reference to immortality and ties the argument to the first part of the book, where death is seen as the obstacle to justice and virtue. Even this interpretation can be broadened to include the general dominion of God over life and death, indeed, over all creation.

tices by Plato and the Stoics.[121] At this point the author focuses briefly on the sexual aberrations associated with idolatry. The embellishment of the idols goes so far as to bring about an aberrant yearning for the lifeless idol. Stories and legends were in circulation at the author's time regarding such behavior. One such story, that of Pygmalion, was known in several versions. This legendary king of Cyprus had a statue of a woman made from ivory whose form was so real and beautiful that he fell in love with it.[122]

The author stresses the lifeless and dead qualities of the idol that become the source of affection

in the idolater: "they desire the lifeless form of a dead image" (v. 5). The idolater is called a "lover of evil things" who is worthy of the object that is loved. The parallel to the wicked in the opening part of the book is unmistakable. There the wicked were described as the friends of death who pined away and made a covenant with death (1:16). In turn, this passage contrasts the "lovers of evil things" (v. 6) and Solomon's love for wisdom (8:2; cf. Prov 8:36, "all who hate me love death" [NRSV]). Just as the wicked are said to be worthy of death, so too are idolaters worthy of the lifeless idols in which they base their hopes (v. 6).

---

121. Plato *Republic* 602D-603B; Seneca *Letters* 88:18.

122. Ovid *Metamorphoses* 10.243-297.

REFLECTIONS

1. Four descriptive terms for "God" initiate the author's praise of God for the mercy and kindness shown to the righteous. God is kind, true, and patient, ruling all things in mercy (15:1). God's transcendent power and immanent compassion are held together in these descriptive images. The power of God is balanced by compassion and mercy. The compassion of God is expressed through God's ruling all things in mercy. What a contrast to the idols, which have no power! They cannot even stand up on their own, but have to be fastened to a niche in the wall (13:15-16). Neither do they afford mercy and kindness, because they are lifeless, weak, inexperienced, and dead (13:17-18).

2. The praise of the powerful and merciful God of the righteous conveys a sense of communal pride. God's power and mercy created a people and sustains them even in their rising and falling fortunes. The turn to the first-person plural in the verbal forms points to the author's being caught up in the praise of God's mercy and compassion shown to the righteous. This is one of the few occurrences in the entire book in which the author formally identifies with the righteous through the first-person plural form of "we" and "us." In the first part of the book, the author as narrator has an objective viewpoint. In the second part of the book, the subjective viewpoint takes over as the author identifies with the figure of Solomon and speaks in the first person. In the third part of the book, the author speaks through both the objective viewpoint of a narrator and the subjective viewpoint in the first-person singular. Only rarely, as in this brief unit, does the author's identification with the righteous surface explicitly (cf. 12:18-22; 18:8).

The communal sense of pride in the God of power and mercy that the author expresses in this passage has parallels in the book of Deuteronomy. The reflection on the history that brought the people to the land of Moab elicits from the figure of Moses the praise of God for the gift of the Torah and for the extraordinary interventions of mercy and power: "For what other great nation has a god so near to it as the LORD our God is whenever we call to him? And what other great nation has statutes and ordinances as just as this entire law that I am setting before you today?" (Deut 4:7-8 NRSV; cf. Deut 4:32-40). If we are correct in locating the time of composition of this passage from Deuteronomy during the exile, then the similarity of the function of praise here is like that in the book of Wisdom. A community under siege, feeling weak and threatened, becomes cognizant of the great strength of its tradition. A reflection on the living tradition becomes a source of strength and pride. Although the author of Wisdom is sympathetic to the best of Hellenistic contributions to literature and culture, and incorporates terminology and philosophical arguments from them, the author is attempting here to strengthen the Jewish community in the diaspora. It is a community under siege and weakened both from without and from within, not unlike the community in exile. The sense of pride the author expresses in belonging to a special people is based on a reflection of history and the quality of faith. Thus the author offers this reflection to strengthen the community's faith. The values that accrue from being faithful to the true God overshadow the dismal facade of trust in idols.

3. We receive what we love. In contrast to the sure hope of immortality for the righteous, the idolaters receive what they love in idolatry: lifeless hope. Again, the author's understanding of punishment comes to the foreground. The form of punishment is intimately connected to the false hope in which the idolater trusts. On one side, we have Solomon, who loves wisdom; wisdom makes one a friend of God and brings the assurance of immortality (6:18-19; 7:27; 8:2). On the other side, we have idolaters, who desire "the lifeless form of a dead image" (15:5). Such lovers of evil things are fit for the lifelessness that idols represent. The author uses the similar phrase that was employed for the wicked in the first part of the book, describing them as being fit for death, with which they make a covenant, pining away for it as for a friend (1:16).

The idea that one receives what one loves is taken up in several forms in the teaching of Christ. In the teaching concerning treasures, Jesus contrasts the treasures of earth, which can be stolen or consumed by moths or rust, to the treasures of heaven. Wherever people place their treasure, they will find that their heart is there as well (Matt 6:19-21; Luke 12:33-34). They receive what, in fact, they love. In one case they receive something perishable; in the other, they receive something enduring.

The parables regarding the talents to be invested (Matt 25:14-30; Luke 19:11-27) and stories about the measure that is given out (Matt 7:1-5; Mark 4:21-25; Luke 6:37-38) make a direct correlation between what one gives and what one receives. Here as well there is a continuity between what one actually receives and what one has given or invested. The reward or punishment does not come from the outside, but is a direct consequence of the fruit of one's own decisions and actions. Giving and investing are the themes that replace "loving." But in all three cases, a direct correlation is made between the fruit of one's actions and the intention behind the decision to love, to give, or to invest.

For the author of Wisdom, it is important to pay attention to what one seeks and loves. If one seeks and loves, like Solomon, the wisdom that makes one close to God, then the gift of immortality is assured. If one seeks and loves the lifeless security of idolatry, then one's own hope becomes as lifeless and dead as idols.

WISDOM 15:7-13, THE POTTER AND CLAY IDOLS

NAB	NRSV
7 For truly the potter, laboriously working the soft earth, molds for our service each several article: Both the vessels that serve for clean purposes	[7] A potter kneads the soft earth and laboriously molds each vessel for our service, fashioning out of the same clay both the vessels that serve clean uses and those for contrary uses, making all alike; but which shall be the use of each of them

15, 7: *hen* (*hekaston*): so LXX[MSS]; omit *all' ek tou autou pēlou aneplasato*: dittog; cf 15, 8; (*toutōn de*) *hekaterōn*: so 1 LXX[MS].

NAB

and their opposites, all alike;
As to what shall be the use of each vessel of
either class
the worker in clay is the judge.
8 And with misspent toil he molds a
meaningless god from the selfsame
clay;
though he himself shortly before was made
from the earth
And after a little, is to go whence he was
taken,
when the life that was lent him is
demanded back.
9 But his concern is not that he is to die
nor that his span of life is brief;
Rather, he vies with goldsmiths and
silversmiths
and emulates molders of bronze,
and takes pride in modeling counterfeits.
10 Ashes his heart is! more worthless than
earth is his hope,
and more ignoble than clay his life;
11 Because he knew not the one who
fashioned him,
and breathed into him a quickening soul,
and infused a vital spirit.
12 Instead, he esteemed our life a plaything,
and our span of life a holiday for gain;
"For one must," says he, "make profit
every way, be it even out of evil."
13 For this man more than any knows that he
is sinning,
when out of earthen stuff he creates fragile
vessels and idols alike.

NRSV

the worker in clay decides.
8 With misspent toil, these workers form a futile
god from the same clay—
these mortals who were made of earth a short
time before
and after a little while go to the earth from
which all mortals are taken,
when the time comes to return the souls that
were borrowed.
9 But the workers are not concerned that mortals
are destined to die
or that their life is brief,
but they compete with workers in gold and
silver,
and imitate workers in copper;
and they count it a glorious thing to mold
counterfeit gods.
10 Their heart is ashes, their hope is cheaper than
dirt,
and their lives are of less worth than clay,
11 because they failed to know the one who
formed them
and inspired them with active souls
and breathed a living spirit into them.
12 But they considered our existence an idle
game,
and life a festival held for profit,
for they say one must get money however one
can, even by base means.
13 For these persons, more than all others, know
that they sin
when they make from earthy matter fragile
vessels and carved images.

COMMENTARY

Within the concentric structure of the author's treatment of idolatry, the judgment of the potter stands parallel to the critique of the carpenter (13:10-19). Both the carpenter and the potter form a natural substance into many shapes, including ones that eventually become objects of worship. The author moves from gold, silver, stone, and wood in the critique of the carpenter to the less valuable clay in the critique of the potter. As a result of this progression of blame-

worthiness, the critique of the clay idols and the potter is more severe than that of the carpenter. The author offered no motives for the carpenter's slipping into the fabrication of idols. But in the case of the potters, they are described as forging counterfeits, motivated by greed and profit (v. 12).

The unit is enclosed by images that capture the theme of the critique: "earth," "earthy" (vv. 7, 13); "vessels," "vessel" (vv. 7, 13). The very substance of these idols as "earthy vessels" is the same matter from which humans were formed and to which they return (v. 8). Several of the themes from the critique of idolatry and even the critique of the wicked from the first part of the book are condensed in this judgment of the potter: the motive of profit, the idols as counterfeit, the distinction between useful vessels and useless idols, the contrast between the lifeless clay idol and the dignity of the human being who is made of clay. A contrast is developed between the duplicitous creativity of the potter and the creativity of God, who has molded human beings out of the earth. There is a clear emphasis on the personal responsibility of the makers of clay idols. Because of their full knowledge of the process of deception, these idol makers know what they are doing in setting up works of clay as idols.

The opening description of the technique of molding clay is as innocuous as the opening description of the technique of carpentry (13:11-12 = 15:7). Of itself, the description betrays no signs of criticism at first. Only when the ordinary labor of fashioning utensils is applied to idols does the discrepancy between useful tools and deified objects leap into view. Elsewhere in Scripture, the technique of the potter is used positively to describe God's care for Israel or to highlight Israel's unfaithfulness to such care (e.g., Jer 18:1-11; cf. Gen 2:7; Isa 64:8; Job 10:9; Sir 33:13). The carpenter and the potter alike give shape to useful vessels for noble and necessary needs. However, both become misguided when they use their skill to form idols.

In the case of clay idols, the author draws attention to the existence of the same earthly substance in the clay idol and in the human being who fashions it. In fashioning clay idols, the potter is falsely imitating the work of the Creator. Potters make idols from earth, the very substance from which they have been made and to which they will return upon death.

The moment of death is described through an image that appears in only late canonical texts. The soul is described as being on lease and as returning to the Creator at death (v. 8*b*; cf. v. 16). In the famous passage on death in Ecclesiastes, the moment of death is depicted through the double movement of the body's returning to the earth and the spirit's returning to God, who had originally given it (Eccl 12:6-7; cf. 3:20-21).

The Wisdom text describes death as the body returning to the earth (from which it was taken) when the time comes for the soul that was borrowed to be returned. The obvious source for such imagery is the Yahwist version of the creation of Adam. Adam was formed from the earth, and the breath of life was breathed into his nostrils so that he became a living being (Gen 2:7). But in the account of the punishment for his and Eve's disobedience, the Genesis text speaks only of the return of Adam to the earth. Nothing is said of the living breath returning to God. In the Gospel of Luke, such an image sways in the background when the rich fool is reprimanded: "This very night your life is being demanded of you" (Luke 12:20 NRSV). Only in v. 8 do we have the explicit comparison of death to the return on a lease.

The idea that life is borrowed and that death constitutes the return of life to the proprietor was known in both Greek and Roman literature as well. "Life is granted to no one as formal possession, but to all on lease."[123] Philo employs the same idea on several occasions: "Now, the creator of life has given you on loan life, speech and sensation."[124] Josephus appeals to the same idea when he explains to his fellow Jews why he did not commit suicide and, as a result, was captured by the Romans: "Those who die at the time when the Creator demands it by following the natural law and give back to God the loan they had received, they will obtain immortal glory."[125]

The author criticizes the clay-idol makers for not recognizing the limits of the span of human life (v. 9*a*). The clay should be a reminder to the potter that human beings are made of clay, to which they return at death. From the very substance that defines human mortality, the idol makers conceive idols that are but pale imitations of those made of gold, silver, and copper (v. 9*b*). The counterfeit is doublefold; not only are the clay idols false in themselves, but also they are doubly so as imitations of idols made of precious metals.

The author juxtaposes three images of clay to three images of the interior life in order to highlight the lack of life in the clay idol makers: Their hearts are ashes, their hope is dirt, their lives are

---

123. Lucretius 3.971.
124. Philo *Who Is the Heir* 104-108.
125. Josephus *The Jewish War* 3.374.

clay. By choosing the very image through which the idol makers sin to characterize their moral bankruptcy, the author continues to draw a link between sin and the lifelessness that ensues from it.

The guilt of the idol makers is highlighted by their failure to recognize in their work and skill the Creator (cf. 13:9), who like a potter fashioned human beings from clay and breathed a living spirit into them. Instead, they consider human existence to be an "idle game" in which one must gain profit through whatever means possible. The imagery contains allusions to the wicked in the first part of the book. Since they had declared that human beings come into the world by mere chance (2:2), their project in life took on the form of a festival (2:6-9), which in turn led to the conclusion that their might makes them right (2:11).

The motive of might is transformed in the case of the clay-idol makers into the motive of gain and money. The author is attributing to the clay idol makers the motive of gain and profit regardless of the source (v. 12*b*). The theme regarding dishonorable gain appears quite frequently in Greek and Roman literature. Creon declares that it is "not well to love gain from every source."[126] Horace argues for the merit of virtue over the gain of those who say, "Make money, money by fair means if you can, if not, by any means money."[127]

The author attributes greater responsibility for sin to the clay idol makers (v. 13). Since they know very well that the objects they fashion are made from clay and perishable materials, they bear greater responsibility for the counterfeit than do those who worship the lifeless objects.

126. Sophocles *Antigone* 312.
127. Horace *Letters* 1.1.65.

REFLECTIONS

1. Most of the author's arguments regarding idol creation and idol worship have already been covered in the treatment of the carpenter (13:10–14:10) and in the explorations of the origin of idolatry (14:11-31). Essentially, the arguments revolve around the inexplicable tendency of those who practice idolatry to deify a lifeless object that is less valuable than the human being, who has received the gift of life. The author continually highlights the discrepancy between the lifeless object and its worshiper, who is alive. In the case of the carpenter, the idol was described through the very antitheses to the prayers of the idolater—prayers for family, health, life, help, a prosperous journey, success, and strength. The misguided sailor puts trust in a wooden idol more fragile than the marvelous piece of wood crafted by wisdom that keeps the sailor afloat. The clay idol makers fashion images from the earth, the very substance God had used to fashion Adam. But God has breathed into humans the gift of life, something the potter cannot do for the idol.

2. The critique of the potters marks an intensification of responsibility through the potter's obvious motive of gain and profit. It is out of personal gain that the potter fashions counterfeit images. With respect to the carpenter and to the explanations of the origin of idolatry, ordinary human needs and tragedies formed the basis of the misguided deification of images and statues. But in the case of those who make clay idols, the author draws attention to the willful and deliberate fashioning of counterfeit objects for personal profit and gain. Greater responsibility rests on those who deliberately misguide people into placing their hope on unfounded principles. Consequently, greater guilt resides with them as well. Their own hope is less than the very substance they use to fashion the counterfeit image. They are not unlike the ungodly in the first part of the book whose hope is compared to dust carried by the wind or to frost driven away by a storm (5:14).

Wisdom 15:14-19, Idolatry and Animal Worship in Egypt

NAB

14 But all quite senseless, and worse than
    childish in mind,
      are the enemies of your people who
      enslaved them.
15 For they esteemed all the idols of the
    nations, gods,
      which have no use of the eyes for vision,
      nor nostrils to snuff the air,
    Nor ears to hear,
      nor fingers on their hands for feeling;
      even their feet are useless to walk with.
16 For a man made them;
      one whose spirit has been lent him
      fashioned them.
    For no man succeeds in fashioning a god like
      himself;
17   being mortal, he makes a dead thing with
      his lawless hands.
    For he is better than the things he worships;
      he at least lives, but never they.
18 And besides, they worship the most
      loathsome beasts—
    for compared as to folly, these are worse
      than the rest,
19 Nor for their looks are they good or
      desirable beasts,
    but they have escaped both the approval
      of God and his blessing.

NRSV

14 But most foolish, and more miserable than an
    infant,
      are all the enemies who oppressed your people.
15 For they thought that all their heathen idols
    were gods,
      though these have neither the use of their eyes
      to see with,
    nor nostrils with which to draw breath,
    nor ears with which to hear,
    nor fingers to feel with,
    and their feet are of no use for walking.
16 For a human being made them,
    and one whose spirit is borrowed formed
      them;
    for none can form gods that are like
      themselves.
17 People are mortal, and what they make with
      lawless hands is dead;
    for they are better than the objects they
      worship,
    since*a* they have life, but the idols*b* never had.

18 Moreover, they worship even the most hateful
    animals,
      which are worse than all others when judged
      by their lack of intelligence;
19 and even as animals they are not so beautiful
      in appearance that one would desire
      them,
    but they have escaped both the praise of God
      and his blessing.

a Other ancient authorities read *of which*   *b* Gk *but they*

COMMENTARY

In all its brevity, this passage brings to a close the author's critique of idolatry. The particular idolaters under discussion are identified as the enemies of God's people (v. 14). This is the typical designation for the Egyptians throughout the midrashic treatment of the exodus from Egypt (e.g., 11:5; 12:20; 16:8; 18:1). Other designations for the Egyptians link the oppressors of Israel to the wicked in the first part of the book ("wicked,"

12:10-11; "ungodly," 16:16; "unjust," 12:23; "foolish," 15:14; 19:3).

The quality of the false worship exhibited by the enemies of God's people elicits the most severe reprimand from the author of Wisdom. Within the concentric structure of the passage on idolatry (chaps. 13–15), the worship of the Egyptian gods and goddesses is contrasted with the worship of the elements of nature and the heavenly bodies (13:1-9). This contrast intensifies the reprehensible form of zoolatry. Those who deify the elements of creation are at least making divine the great works of God. But those who deify the visually abhorrent species have lost touch even with the aesthetics of creation. The intensification of the reprimand is noticeable also in the progression throughout the entire critique: the worship of nature and heavenly bodies made by God, counterfeit images of God's creation made by humans (gold, silver, copper, clay), and finally the inexplicable deification of animals.

The return to the image of animal worship brings the author's argument right back to the punishment of the Egyptians through animals, which occasioned the two major digressions on God's power (11:17–12:27) and false worship (chaps. 13–15). This return at the end of the critique against false worship also allows for the continuation of the second diptych, which deals with the animals that punish the Egyptians and the animals that help sustain the righteous (16:1-14).

The critique against the Egyptians' false worship focuses on two forms: syncretistic idolatry (15:14-17) and zoolatry (15:18-19). The acceptance of all the idols of the nations, and not merely one's own, condenses the author's critique of idolatry. Various arguments already alluded to in the earlier treatment of idolatry provide proof for the most severe judgment reserved to the Egyptians (13:10-19; 14:4-5; 15:7-8). This tendency to attribute divine status to the various idols was particularly acute in Hellenism. It was especially predominant in Ptolemaic Egypt. The lifelessness of all such idols is again recounted in traditional fashion. Although the idols may appear in bodily form, they have no organs of sight, smell, hearing, or touch. They are not able even to walk (cf. Pss 115:3-8; 135:15-18; Isa 44:18).

More important, the author concentrates on the discrepancy between the life of the human being who makes an idol and the lifelessness of the idol (v. 16). The idol maker has a spirit that is borrowed (cf. v. 8), but he or she cannot give the gift of life to the idol. The author's perplexity revolves around the obvious irony that is present in idolatry. The idol makers are human beings—that is, they are alive and have been given the gift of life and thus are more valuable than the lifeless objects they create. Philo is perplexed by the same inconsistency in idolatry, "In their general ignorance they have failed to perceive even that most obvious truth which even 'a witless infant knows,' that the craftsman is superior to the product of his craft both in time, since he is older than what he makes and in a sense its father, and in value, since the efficient element is held in higher esteem than the passive effect."[128]

The final two verses of the critique focus on a particular form of idolatry—namely, animal worship (vv. 18-19). As mentioned at the outset, the theme of animal worship occasioned the major digressions within the second diptych. These two verses refer to 11:15, where the enemies are described as being led astray to worship irrational serpents and worthless animals, and to 12:27, where it is recalled how the Egyptians were punished by the very animals they thought to be gods.

The idea that these animals worshiped as deity are so abhorrent that they have escaped divine blessing (v. 19b) appears to go against much of what the author has previously stated on the essential dignity of all creation (1:14; 11:24). In Zoroastrianism, which presumes a radical dualism between good and evil, certain animals, such as reptiles and dangerous insects, along with poisonous plants were considered evil creatures. To destroy such creatures was the equivalent of destroying evil and wickedness.[129] Although the author does not adhere to such a dualism of good and evil as that of Zoroastrianism, it is possible that some of the formulations of its ideas have influenced the author's argument.

For an explanation of this judgment against the deified reptiles, it is helpful to recognize the parallel the author is drawing between idols and deified animals. In the critique against the carpenter and the sailor who worships a wooden idol, the author concluded with the divine judgment against idols. Although they are a part of God's creation, they have become an abomination through their deliberate fabrication by human beings (14:8-11). The author's purpose in highlighting the lack of intelligence of the animals

128. Philo *On the Decalogue* 69.
129. For a presentation of Zoroastrian thought, see Robert Charles Zaehner, *The Dawn and Twilight of Zoroastrianism* (London: Weidenfeld and Nicolson, 1961).

worshiped in Egypt's zoolatry is to put into relief the misguided nature of false worship. Like the idols, the sacred animals stand under God's judgment. But instead of turning to the judgment against such animals, the author focuses on the inexplicable choice of human beings to deify the lesser animals of God's creation.

REFLECTIONS

1. The author's rather lengthy digression, which offers a severe critique of false worship, concludes with the utter foolishness of idolatry. The brevity of this final passage within the entire concentric structure (chaps. 13–15) reveals the author to be at a loss to explain the aberration of syncretistic idolatry and zoolatry. The progression from the least blameworthy form of false worship of natural phenomena to the most blameworthy—namely, zoolatry—reflects a similar progression as that found in the wicked's reflection on their project in life (2:1-20). What had begun in the wicked as a rather innocuous reflection on human mortality ended in the blatant and sinister plot to humiliate and destroy the just one. In a similar manner, the author presents the tendency of false worship to move from the beautiful works of God's creation to the inexplicable adoration of the strangest and most dangerous animals.

2. The opposite side of the critique highlights the importance of being rooted in the worship of the true God. Just as the practice of justice through the gift of wisdom in the first part of the book brings the assurance of immortality, so also the worship of the true God brings protection in danger and immortality to the righteous (14:2-7; 15:1-4). The author's critique of the seduction of injustice and of false worship is meant to present before the imagination of the reader the compelling attraction of justice and the true God. The incoherence of idolatry and the aesthetic repugnance of zoolatry render the worshiping of the true God much more plausible.

Wisdom 16:1-14, The Plague of Animals and Delicacies for the Righteous

NAB	NRSV
16 Therefore they were fittingly punished by similar creatures, and were tormented by a swarm of insects. 2 Instead of this punishment, you benefited your people with a novel dish, the delight they craved, by providing quail for their food; 3 That those others, when they desired food, since the creatures sent to plague them were so loathsome, should be turned from even the craving of necessities, While these, after a brief period of privation, partook of a novel dish.	**16** Therefore those people[a] were deservedly punished through such creatures, and were tormented by a multitude of animals. 2 Instead of this punishment you showed kindness to your people, and you prepared quails to eat, a delicacy to satisfy the desire of appetite; 3 in order that those people, when they desired food, might lose the least remnant of appetite[b] because of the odious creatures sent to them, while your people,[a] after suffering want a short time, might partake of delicacies. 4 For it was necessary that upon those oppressors inescapable want should come,
16, 3: *eidechtheian:* so LXX[C], etc; *houtoi* (*de ep᾽ oligon*): so LXX[MSS].	a Gk *they* b Gk *loathed the necessary appetite*

NAB

4 For upon those oppressors, inexorable want
     had to come;
   but these needed only be shown how their
     enemies were being tormented.
5 For when the dire venom of beasts came
     upon them
   and they were dying from the bite of
     crooked serpents,
   your anger endured not to the end.
6 But as a warning, for a short time they were
     terrorized,
   though they had a sign of salvation, to
     remind them of the precept of your
     law.
7 For he who turned toward it was saved,
   not by what he saw,
   but by you, the savior of all.
8 And by this also you convinced our foes
   that you are he who delivers from all evil.
9 For the bites of locusts and of flies slew
     them,
   and no remedy was found to save their
     lives
   because they deserved to be punished by
     such means;
10 But not even the fangs of poisonous reptiles
     overcame your sons,
   for your mercy brought the antidote to heal
     them.
11 For as a reminder of your injunctions, they
     were stung,
   and swiftly they were saved,
   Lest they should fall into deep forgetfulness
   and become unresponsive to your
     beneficence.
12 For indeed, neither herb nor application
     cured them,
   but your all-healing word, O Lord!
13 For you have dominion over life and death;
   you lead down to the gates of the nether
     world, and lead back.
14 Man, however, slays in his malice,
   but when the spirit has come away, it does
     not return,
   nor can he bring back the soul once it is
     confined.

NRSV

   while to these others it was merely shown how
     their enemies were being tormented.

5 For when the terrible rage of wild animals
     came upon your people[a]
   and they were being destroyed by the bites of
     writhing serpents,
   your wrath did not continue to the end;
6 they were troubled for a little while as a
     warning,
   and received a symbol of deliverance to remind
     them of your law's command.

7 For the one who turned toward it was saved,
     not by the thing that was beheld,
   but by you, the Savior of all.
8 And by this also you convinced our enemies
   that it is you who deliver from every evil.
9 For they were killed by the bites of locusts and
     flies,
   and no healing was found for them,
   because they deserved to be punished by such
     things.
10 But your children were not conquered even
     by the fangs of venomous serpents,
   for your mercy came to their help and healed
     them.
11 To remind them of your oracles they were
     bitten,
   and then were quickly delivered,
   so that they would not fall into deep
     forgetfulness
   and become unresponsive[b] to your kindness.
12 For neither herb nor poultice cured them,
   but it was your word, O Lord, that heals all
     people.
13 For you have power over life and death;
   you lead mortals down to the gates of Hades
     and back again.
14 A person in wickedness kills another,
   but cannot bring back the departed spirit,
   or set free the imprisoned soul.

a Gk *them*   b Meaning of Gk uncertain

16, 4: (*ekeinois*) *men* . . . (*toutois de*): so LXX^MSS.

COMMENTARY

16:1-4. The final critique of zoolatry brings the argument back to the second diptych, which had begun in 11:15. The diptych contrasts the plagues of the various animals upon Egypt with the marvelous gift of quails for the righteous in the desert. The argument of the diptych picks up exactly where it left off regarding the principle of punishment through the very means of one's sin (11:5, 16). Since the enemies of the righteous reached the extreme form of idolatry and worshiped animals, it is only to be expected that through animals they will experience the consequences of their sin. The short unit that focuses the diptych on the hunger of the Egyptians is enclosed by the image of torment: They "were tormented by a multitude of animals" (v. 1); "their enemies were being tormented" (v. 4).

The turn in the diptych contrasts the torment of the enemies by animals with the marvelous gift of quails provided to the righteous in the desert (v. 2). The author is condensing the several plague episodes of the exodus that deal with animals into a single diptych (v. 2, frogs; v. 3, gnats; v. 4, flies; v. 5, diseased livestock; v. 8, locusts). In order to provide a contrast with the gift of quails in the desert, the author adds one particular element to the Exodus narrative—namely, that of the Egyptians' hunger. Although in the plague narratives Egypt's sources of water, food, and livestock had been destroyed by the plagues, nowhere does the book of Exodus mention that the Egyptians actually hungered. However, this is a reasonable assumption the Wisdom author is making in condensing the stories of the plagues in Exodus 8:1–9:7.

In response to the Israelites' hunger, God provides them with quails. The author is following episodes from the narrative of the Israelites in the desert from Exod 16:1-13 and from Num 11:4-35. In both sources, the meager signs of food and water in the desert contrast sharply with the abundance of food in Egypt (Exod 16:3; Num 11:5). The people complain. They demand food, and they are given the extraordinary gift of manna and quails.

The motif of the people's grumbling and complaining in the desert is suppressed in the author's contrast of the Egyptians' hunger with that of the righteous. The suppression of the theme of Israel's sin and need for repentance regarding the desert wandering is consistent with the author's suppression of the theme of the vicarious suffering of God's servant in the wicked's plan to kill the just one (2:12-25). But the theme of Israel's resistance to God's law will emerge in a subtle manner through the experience of punishment and death that the author feels compelled to address later in the diptychs (16:5-6; 18:20-25). The righteous will hunger for a short while to enable them to appreciate the depth of hunger their enemies will experience.

16:5-14. This reflection on the hunger of the righteous moves the author to another digression within the diptych on animals. The author is reminded of the threat to life that the Israelites experienced in the desert, as recounted in Num 21:6-9. The reflection of Israel's salvation from the venomous serpents occasions the author's praise of God's power over life and death. Some exegetes understand the unit to be another comparison or antithesis that contrasts the killing of the Egyptians through the bites of locusts and flies with the saving symbol of the brazen serpent for the righteous.[130] But the author does not use the word "instead" (ἀντί *anti*), which introduces the contrast. A type of antithesis is introduced in a negative form in v. 10, "But your children were not conquered even by the fangs of venomous serpents." Instead of considering the passage a full diptych, A. G. Wright perceives the unit's digressional form of reflection and praise within the second diptych.[131]

In the book of Numbers, the episode of the poisonous serpents in the desert is narrated as God's response to the people's continuous complaints: "Why have you brought us up out of Egypt to die in the wilderness? For there is no food and no water, and we detest this miserable food" (Num 21:5 NRSV). After many Israelites had died from the bites of venomous snakes, the people confessed their sin and pleaded with Moses

---

130. J. M. Reese, "Plan and Structure in the Book of Wisdom," *CBQ* 27 (1965) 391-99.
131. A. G. Wright, "The Structure of the Book of Wisdom," *Bib* 48 (1967) 165-84.

to beseech God for healing. In response to God's command, Moses formed a bronze serpent, put it on a pole, and whoever looked upon it was healed. We come across the bronze serpent again far later in the historical books, where Hezekiah is noted to have broken in pieces the bronze serpent Moses had made (2 Kgs 18:4).[132]

The author of Wisdom is interpreting this event within the second diptych from two points of view: The people's suffering in the desert is a warning that is meant to prevent them from being unresponsive to God's kindness, and the extraordinary healing of the people is a sign of the power of God's healing word.

The author does not focus directly on the sin of the righteous that evoked the punishment by the serpents in the desert. To focus on Israel's sin in a work that contrasts the righteous and the wicked on the one hand, and Israel and Egypt, on the other, would be out of place within the style of the diptychs. But the author alludes to the wrath of God and interprets its beneficial results for the righteous (v. 5). Instead of continuing to the end, God's wrath provides punishment, which serves as a warning (v. 6). The bronze serpent is interpreted as a symbol of deliverance that is meant to remind the Israelites of the command of the law. Similarly, the punishment is meant to remind them of God's commands and word (v. 11; cf. 12:2).

Since the image of the bronze serpent comes very close to that of the idols the author has just criticized, an explanation for the serpent is provided. The author draws attention to the power of God's Word. The people were not healed by the image they had beheld but by God, the savior

of all (v. 7; cf. 9:18, where wisdom is the one who saves). It was God's mercy that came to help them and heal them. The bronze serpent does not contain in itself a cure for sickness. Medicine was not applied to the bite wounds (neither herb nor poultice cured them, v. 12). Rather, God cured them through the Word, "It was your word, O Lord, that heals all people" (v. 12; cf. Exod 15:26).

Both Philo and the Mishnah interpret the healing of the Israelites as recounted in Num 21:6-9 in a spiritual manner, like that of the author of Wisdom: "He, then, who has looked with fixed gaze on the form of patient endurance, even though he should perchance have been previously bitten by the wiles of pleasure, cannot but live; for, whereas pleasure menaces the soul with inevitable death, self-control holds out to it health and safety for life."[133] "But could the serpent kill or could the serpent keep alive? But rather, whenever Israel looked on high and subjected their heart to their Father in heaven were they healed, but if not, they perished."[134] *Targums Pseudo-Jonathan* and *Neophyti I* on Num 21:8 also add to the canonical text the idea that all those who looked upon the bronze serpent also lifted their hearts to God in heaven and lived. The entire reflection focuses finally on the merciful power of God. God alone has power over life and death, to bring people to Hades and back again (v. 13). The author is alluding to a traditional formulation regarding God's power over life and death (cf. Deut 32:39; 1 Sam 2:6; Ps 49:15; Hos 6:1-2; Tob 13:2). The power of God is contrasted with the human powerlessness to bring people to life. Although human beings can kill others, they cannot bring them back to life (v. 14).

132. For a brief outline on the serpent as a religious symbol in the ancient Near East, see Lowell K. Handy, "Serpent (Religious Symbol)," *Anchor Bible Dictionary*, 6 vols. (New York: Doubleday, 1992) 5:1113-1116.

133. Philo *On Husbandry* 98.
134. Mishnah *Rosh Hashanah* 3.8.

REFLECTIONS

1. The author's reflection on the plague narratives focuses on discernment between good and evil. The source of evil is concentrated in the enemies of the righteous. The source of good is concentrated in the hand of God, who intervenes constantly to direct events in favor of the righteous. By holding up before the imagination of the reader the conflict between good and evil in the plague episodes, the author is laying bare the ultimate tragedy of injustice and the eventual success of integrity. Oppression leads to the loss of one's own source of life, as in the case of the oppressing Egyptians. Integrity leads to unexpected sources of life, as in the case of the faithful righteous. The author uses the episodes from Israel's distant history, as recorded in the Torah, as the basis for learning the consequences of injustice and the success of integrity. What was argued from a more philosophical position in the first part of the book is confirmed in the reflection of Israel's foundational history.

2. The righteous are called to learn from their suffering. Although the author does not touch directly upon the sin of the righteous, the suffering that results from the wrath of God in response to their sin is addressed (16:5-6). The righteous also experienced hunger, and they were ravaged by venomous serpents. What the author asks the reader to conclude from this experience is the purpose of God's punishment to bring back and to heal ("they were troubled for a little while as a warning" [16:6 NRSV]; "To remind them of your oracles they were bitten, and then were quickly delivered" [16:11 NRSV]; cf. 11:21-24; 12:2; 12:10).

Human suffering is paradoxical and ambiguous at best. Much of the pain and injustice people endure results from others' disregard for life or unscrupulous desire for gain. It is not easy to differentiate the suffering that comes from outside from the suffering that results from one's own injustice or failure. Still, so much pain is associated with the mere fact of living, of growing, and of dying. Yet, the suffering that the righteous are said to experience is meant to be a source of learning. They are asked to learn from the consequences of their resistance to God's ways with the assurance of God's mercy and power.

The author's perspective on the suffering of the righteous is consistent with that of the writers of Deuteronomy. The curses of the covenant are meant to be a source of conversion:

> When all these things have happened to you, the blessings and the curses that I have set before you, if you call them to mind among all the nations where the LORD your God has driven you, and return to the LORD your God, and you and your children obey him with all your heart and with all your soul, just as I am commanding you today, then the LORD your God will restore your fortunes and have compassion on you. (Deut 30:1-3 NRSV)

Similarly, from the perspective of Deuteronomy, the period of wandering in the desert is the privileged moment of learning God's ways. Where resources for life are so feeble, the perception of life is intensified (Deuteronomy 8).

For the author of Wisdom, the reflection on the suffering of the righteous, which is due to their own resistance, leads to a reminder of the purpose of God's interventions. God is powerful and merciful. Even in the midst of trying situations, such as those of the Israelites in the desert, the unexpected can occur to bring healing and sustenance.

WISDOM 16:15-29, THE PLAGUE OF STORMS AND MANNA FROM HEAVEN

NAB	NRSV
15 But your hand none can escape.	15 To escape from your hand is impossible;

16 For the wicked who refused to know you
    were punished by the might of your arm,
    Pursued by unwonted rains and hailstorms
        and unremitting downpours,
    and consumed by fire.
	16 for the ungodly, refusing to know you,
	    were flogged by the strength of your arm,
	    pursued by unusual rains and hail and
	        relentless storms,
	    and utterly consumed by fire.

NAB

17 For against all expectation, in water which
      quenches anything,
   the fire grew more active;
   For the universe fights on behalf of the just.
18 For now the flame was tempered
      so that the beasts might not be burnt up
      that were sent upon the wicked,
      but that these might see and know they
         were struck by the judgment of God;
19 And again, even in the water, fire blazed
         beyond its strength
      so as to consume the produce of the
         wicked land.
20 Instead of this, you nourished your people
         with food of angels
      and furnished them bread from heaven,
         ready to hand, untoiled-for,
      endowed with all delights and conforming
         to every taste.
21 For this substance of yours revealed your
         sweetness toward your children,
      and serving the desire of him who received it,
      was blended to whatever flavor each one
         wished.
22 Yet snow and ice withstood fire and were
         not melted,
      that they might know that their enemies'
         fruits
   Were consumed by a fire that blazed in the
      hail
      and flashed lightning in the rain.
23 But this fire, again, that the just might be
         nourished,
      forgot even its proper strength;
24 For your creation, serving you, its maker,
         grows tense for punishment against the
         wicked,
      but is relaxed in benefit for those who trust
         in you.
25 Therefore at that very time, transformed in
         all sorts of ways,
      it was serving your all-nourishing bounty
      according to what they needed and
         desired;
26 That your sons whom you loved might
         learn, O Lord,

16, 20: *arton ap' ouranou paresches autois akopiatōs*: so LXX[MSS], V.
16, 25: *metalloiōmenē*: cf 4, 12 and V.

NRSV

17 For—most incredible of all—in water, which
      quenches all things,
   the fire had still greater effect,
   for the universe defends the righteous.
18 At one time the flame was restrained,
      so that it might not consume the creatures sent
         against the ungodly,
      but that seeing this they might know
      that they were being pursued by the judgment
         of God;
19 and at another time even in the midst of water
         it burned more intensely than fire,
      to destroy the crops of the unrighteous land.

20 Instead of these things you gave your people
         food of angels,
      and without their toil you supplied them from
         heaven with bread ready to eat,
      providing every pleasure and suited to every
         taste.
21 For your sustenance manifested your sweetness
         toward your children;
      and the bread, ministering[a] to the desire of the
         one who took it,
      was changed to suit everyone's liking.
22 Snow and ice withstood fire without melting,
      so that they might know that the crops of their
         enemies
      were being destroyed by the fire that blazed
         in the hail
      and flashed in the showers of rain;
23 whereas the fire,[b] in order that the righteous
         might be fed,
      even forgot its native power.

24 For creation, serving you who made it,
      exerts itself to punish the unrighteous,
      and in kindness relaxes on behalf of those who
         trust in you.
25 Therefore at that time also, changed into all
         forms,
      it served your all-nourishing bounty,
      according to the desire of those who had
         need,[c]
26 so that your children, whom you loved,
         O Lord, might learn

[a] Gk *and it, ministering*   [b] Gk *this*   [c] Or *who made supplication*

NAB

that it is not the various kinds of fruits that
  nourish man, but it is your word that
  preserves those who believe you!
27 For what was not destroyed by fire,
  when merely warmed by a momentary
    sunbeam, melted;
28 So that men might know that one must give
  you thanks before the sunrise,
  and turn to you at daybreak.
29 For the hope of the ingrate melts like a
    wintry frost
  and runs off like useless water.

16, 28: *gnōstonę:* so LXX[MSS].

NRSV

that it is not the production of crops that feeds
  humankind
but that your word sustains those who trust
  in you.
27 For what was not destroyed by fire
  was melted when simply warmed by a fleeting
    ray of the sun,
28 to make it known that one must rise before
    the sun to give you thanks,
  and must pray to you at the dawning of the
    light;
29 for the hope of an ungrateful person will melt
    like wintry frost,
  and flow away like waste water.

COMMENTARY

This third diptych is located centrally within the diptych system of the midrashic commentary. Its theological import matches its centrality. The author's positive view of the forces of the universe, which had been touched upon earlier (1:14; 5:17-23; 7:15-22; 9:1-3, 9), reaches its sharpest focus. The forces of the cosmos reside under the sway of divine providence in order to save the just and to thwart the wicked. Essentially, the author contrasts the plague of storms against the Egyptians with the extraordinary rain of manna for the Israelites in the desert. The sources for this contrast are the seventh plague of thunder and hail from Exod 9:13-35 and the episode of the manna's being provided to the people from Exod 16:1-36 and Num 11:4-9.

16:15-23. All three principles that the author employs throughout the interpretation of the plague narratives coalesce into a unified argument in the third diptych: (1) the source of one's sin becomes the source of one's punishment; (2) the very means by which the ungodly are punished are the means of salvation for the just; (3) the cosmos exerts itself on behalf of the righteous and against the ungodly. The main principle being applied in the contrast is that of 11:5; the very source of punishment for the Egyptians becomes the source of blessing for the Israelites. The density of the theological perspective is achieved in the joining of this principle to that of the positive

view of creation and the cosmos. Creation itself labors to bring life to the just and justice to the wicked. Finally, the justice of God, which wreaks havoc from the heavens upon the ungodly, is a response to their refusal to recognize God (v. 16).

The particular elements of the cosmos that the author adapts for the plague and manna episodes are those of fire and water. The author interprets these episodes to show how the forces of creation become transformed in order to bring about salvation for the Israelites. Against the ungodly, fire is transformed so that in one case water cannot extinguish it (v. 17); yet in another story water actually intensifies the fire's heat and destructive power (v. 19). In favor of God's people, water (snow and ice) withstands the fire (v. 22), and fire itself, even as it is destroying the crops of the ungodly, forgets its natural destructive power regarding the food sent from heaven (v. 23). Some of the Stoic theories contemporary to the author of Wisdom regarding the transforming qualities of the elements are joined to the traditional theme of God's overriding providence in creation and history.

The opening phrase of the diptych actually links the unit to the preceding reflection of the power of God (v. 15). The idea that it is impossible to escape from God's hand alludes to Deut 32:39, "no one can deliver from my hand" (NRSV), and to Tob 13:2, "there is nothing that can escape his hand" (NRSV).

In response to their sin of refusing to recognize God, the ungodly are pursued by the strength of God's power from the heavens in the form of rain and fire. The author extracts two primal elements of the cosmos, water and fire, from the natural phenomenon of the storm with its rain and lightning in the seventh plague of Exodus. The unusual characteristic of these opposing forces is that they unite in destruction (v. 17). On the one hand, fire had an even greater effect within water, its very opposite. On the other hand, not even water could quench the fire so that it might not destroy the other creatures sent against Egypt. The author is supposing the punishments of animals and storms to be taking place contemporaneously, whereas in Exodus they occur sequentially.

The idea that the universe defends the righteous in the symbols of fire and water (v. 17*b*) is consistent with the positive view of the cosmos the author expounded in the first part of the work. The corollary statement that the universe punishes the unrighteous is made in the second half of the diptych (v. 24). In this way a careful balance is achieved: The ungodly are punished through the cosmos, for the universe defends the righteous (vv. 15-19); the ungodly know this is the judgment of God (v. 18). The righteous are sustained by the cosmos, for creation exerts itself to punish the unrighteous (vv. 20-24). The people of God know that the same destruction relaxed on their behalf that they might be fed (v. 23).

The turn in the diptych (v. 20) contrasts the ravaging storms sent against Egypt with the special food provided to God's people in the desert. The author employs images of ease, abundance, and rest in association with the bread that came from heaven. They did not toil for it; it provided every pleasure suited to every taste; it was expressive of God's kindness to them (cf. Deut 6:10-11; 8:3-10).

The contrast of the manna from heaven with the storms from the heavens continues with the images of water and fire. The manna is compared to snow and ice that would not melt in the face of burning fire. The author is exploiting the metaphor of frost, which is employed for the manna in Exod 16:14, "When the layer of dew lifted, there on the surface of the wilderness was a fine flaky substance, as fine as frost on the ground" (NRSV). The comparison of manna to snow based on the metaphor of frost in Exodus is made by Philo and Josephus as well.[135] The miraculous endurance of the manna in the threat of fire allows the righteous to know that the fire has relaxed (forgotten its own power) in order that they might survive (vv. 22-23). Just as the ungodly came to know that they were being pursued by the judgment of God (v. 18), so also the righteous came to know that fire was transformed so that they might live.

16:24-29. The final part of the diptych is a theological reflection on the transforming qualities of creation in the light of the gift of manna in the desert. The notion of creation's exerting itself to punish the wicked is in direct continuity with the ultimate judgment recounted in the first part of Wisdom (5:17-23). There the image of an apocalyptic storm was the author's vehicle for declaring the eventual demise of lawlessness and injustice. This image of the storm unites the plague diptych of storms and manna to the storm of destruction in the apocalyptic judgment.

A new feature that is articulated clearly in the function of the cosmos is that it actively labors on behalf of those who trust in God (v. 24). Although the idea is expressed in a new formation within the book, it is consistent with the author's positive view of the universe. Moreover, the direct relationship that was drawn between personified wisdom and creation in the second part of the book (9:1-2, 9-11, 18) prepares for the transference of the positive function of wisdom from human beings to the cosmos. It was through wisdom that human beings were made; wisdom was present at the creation of the world. As a result of its relationship to creation, wisdom knows God's works and can guide humans to set their paths straight so they may be saved. The wisdom of God and the forces of creation are intimately connected for the wisdom author. Creation is the work of God through wisdom, so that the forces of the cosmos stand on the side of the just and against the wicked (cf. 14:2-7).

The author's background metaphor for the adaptation of creation to justice and injustice employs two verbs, "exert" (ἐπιτείνω *epiteinō*)

---

135. Philo *Moses* 1.200; Josephus *Antiquities of the Jews* 3.1.6.

and "release" (ἀνίημι *aniēmi*). Creation exerts or tenses itself against the unrighteous, but relaxes or releases itself on behalf of the just. These verbs connote the tension and release of a cord, whether for a bow or for a musical instrument. Tonal assonance and dissonance were used frequently in Greek philosophical circles. It was a favorite metaphor employed by the Stoics to describe the harmony or disharmony of the constitution of the *pneuma*.[136] The right tension constituted health; the wrong tension involved sickness. The wisdom author will return to the metaphor of musical tones to describe the transforming qualities of creation that make a many-faceted harmony (19:18-21).

The author finally draws forth from the argument of the transformation of creation its intent and purpose, which the just will learn from their experience. The focus on the intent "to know" was already made within the diptych, both with respect to the unjust and to the righteous (vv. 18, 22). The just are to learn and take to heart the fact that the source of sustenance and life for human beings is the Word of God (v. 26).

The author's turn of phrase is a more rigorous adaptation of the declaration in Deut 8:3 that human beings do not live on bread alone but by every word that comes from the mouth of God (cf. Matt 4:4). Although the manna that is referred to in Deuteronomy did not come directly from the mouth of God, God's Word commanded its presence. What is stated as a gradation in Deuteronomy is articulated through antithesis in Wisdom. It is not the production of crops that feeds humans, but the Word of God that sustains those who trust in God. Philo adapted the phrase in

Deut 8:3 into a similar antithetical formulation, making a formal distinction between the body and the soul, which the Wisdom author presumes: "You see that the soul is fed not with things of earth that decay, but with such words as God shall have poured like rain out of that lofty and pure region of life to which the prophet has given the title 'heaven.' "[137]

The author draws one final moral conclusion from observing the adapting qualities of the manna to fire and to the rays of the sun. It is important to be grateful to God for the marvelous interventions in one's life. The manna could not be destroyed by fire, yet a single ray of sunlight would melt it at the appropriate time (v. 27). The mention of the rays of the sun melting the manna is an allusion to Exod 16:21. Moses commanded that the manna be collected by the Israelites in the morning, according to the need of each person, for when the sun grew hot the manna would melt. From this observation the author draws forth an exhortation to observe the pious practice expressed in the psalms: The faithful rise before the sun to express their prayer of thanksgiving or lament to God (Pss 5:3; 55:17; 57:8-9; 88:13).

The concluding remark in which the hopelessness of an ungrateful heart is compared to melting frost (v. 29) is occasioned by the previous image of the melting manna (v. 27). It recalls the language and imagery associated with the wicked in the first part of the book. The wicked had compared the evanescence of their lives to mist that is chased away by the rays of the sun (2:4). After their confession of guilt, the hope of the ungodly is compared to thistledown carried by the wind and to a frost driven away by a storm (5:14).

---

136. *Stoicorum Veterum Fragmenta,* ed. J. von Arnim, 4 vols. (Leipzig, 1903–24; reprint Stuttgart, 1966; New York, 1986) 3.92,525,259,471.

137. Philo *Allegorical Interpretations* 3.162-163.

REFLECTIONS

1. The particular virtue that the author expounds from the diptych on the plague of storms and the gift of manna is gratitude. Although gratitude has not been a particular focus throughout the arguments and presentations of the author, the author's disposition of praising God throughout the midrashic treatment of the exodus is certainly marked by a pervading attitude of thanksgiving. It is out of thanksgiving that the author turns to God directly throughout the final part of Wisdom in order to express praise and wonder (10:20-21; 11:21-26; 12:15-16; 14:3-7; 15:1-3; 16:12-13; 19:9, 22). Reflection on Israel's blessed history brings knowledge of the extraordinary interventions of God and the workings of creation on behalf of the faithful.

2. The forces of creation are on the side of justice. Even though this principle marks the entire book of Wisdom, nowhere is the author's theological perspective on creation enunciated with greater clarity. Creation rests in service of God, who formed it by battling injustice and coming to the aid of the righteous (16:24). Assertions on the positive function of creation dominate all three parts of the book. It is one of the unifying themes of the three divergent sections (chaps. 1–6; 7–10; 11–19) that form the author's argument into a coherent whole. The forces of creation are declared to be wholesome (1:14). Creation itself is armed by God to redress injustice (5:17-23). Personified wisdom is able to direct human beings on their paths because it was present at the creation of the universe and knows all of God's works (9:9). Throughout the author's presentation of the exodus events, the principle of the goodness of creation becomes the interpretative key for explaining the plight of the oppressors and the sustenance of the faithful.

3. Are natural phenomena an expression of moral integrity or dissolution? The third diptych presents the principle of the goodness of creation in terms of the punishment of the ungodly and the sustenance of the faithful through the natural phenomena of atmospheric storms and food. Does the author imply that all natural disasters are creation's response to human moral bankruptcy? Conversely, are all forms of deliverance and sustenance creation's response to human moral virtue? The answer must be an unequivocal no.

In the first part of Wisdom, the author argued vehemently against the apparent success of injustice and the apparent fruitlessness and failure of virtue. There the author argued that, in the long run, the moral vacuity of unjust people would be laid bare. In the long run, the moral fruitfulness of the virtuous would bring immortality. But tragedies, failures, and death itself befall all human beings. The experience of death for the just was tragic, like a holocaust and like gold tested in fire. Even Solomon recognizes the fragility of his life through the image of his cry at birth, which was like that of all human beings.

The emphasis on the author's application of the principle of the goodness of creation is consistent with the argument in the first part of the book. Eventually, moral vacuity is laid bare for what it is. There are consequences to a life of injustice. Injustice bears within it the seeds of its own destruction. Similarly, there are consequences to a life of justice. Although appearances may be to the contrary, a life of justice contains within it the seeds that eventually will blossom into union with God. The author employs the exodus events as a sign of divine judgment from Israel's foundational history. The interpretation of the plagues against the oppressors of Israel and the extraordinary interventions of God on behalf of the faithful are meant to assure the reader of the eventual consequences of injustice and justice.

WISDOM 17:1–18:4, PLAGUE OF DARKNESS AND A PILLAR OF FIRE

NAB	NRSV
17 For great are your judgments, and hardly to be described; therefore the unruly souls were wrong. 2 For when the lawless thought to enslave the holy nation, shackled with darkness, fettered by the long night,	**17** Great are your judgments and hard to describe; therefore uninstructed souls have gone astray. 2 For when lawless people supposed that they held the holy nation in their power, they themselves lay as captives of darkness and prisoners of long night,

NAB

they lay confined beneath their own roofs
as exiles from the eternal providence.

3 For they who supposed their secret sins were hid
under the dark veil of oblivion
Were scattered in fearful trembling,
terrified by apparitions.

4 For not even their inner chambers kept them
fearless,
for crashing sounds on all sides terrified
them,
and mute phantoms with somber looks
appeared.

5 No force, even of fire, was able to give light,
nor did the flaming brilliance of the stars
succeed in lighting up that gloomy night.

6 But only intermittent, fearful fires
flashed through upon them;
And in their terror they thought beholding
these was worse
than the times when that sight was no
longer to be seen.

7 And mockeries of the magic art were in
readiness,
and a jeering reproof of their vaunted
shrewdness.

8 For they who undertook to banish fears and
terrors from the sick soul
themselves sickened with a ridiculous fear.

9 For even though no monstrous thing
frightened them,
they shook at the passing of insects and
the hissing of reptiles,

10 And perished trembling,
reluctant to face even the air that they
could nowhere escape.

11 For wickedness, of its nature cowardly,
testifies in its own condemnation,
and because of a distressed conscience,
always magnifies misfortunes.

12 For fear is nought but the surrender of the
helps that come from reason;

13 and the more one's expectation is of itself
uncertain,
the more one makes of not knowing the
cause that brings on torment.

17, 9: *teratōdes*: so 2 LXX^MSS, V, P, Arm.

NRSV

shut in under their roofs, exiles from eternal
providence.

3 For thinking that in their secret sins they were
unobserved
behind a dark curtain of forgetfulness,
they were scattered, terribly[a] alarmed,
and appalled by specters.

4 For not even the inner chamber that held them
protected them from fear,
but terrifying sounds rang out around them,
and dismal phantoms with gloomy faces
appeared.

5 And no power of fire was able to give light,
nor did the brilliant flames of the stars
avail to illumine that hateful night.

6 Nothing was shining through to them
except a dreadful, self-kindled fire,
and in terror they deemed the things that they
saw
to be worse than that unseen appearance.

7 The delusions of their magic art lay humbled,
and their boasted wisdom was scornfully
rebuked.

8 For those who promised to drive off the fears
and disorders of a sick soul
were sick themselves with ridiculous fear.

9 For even if nothing disturbing frightened them,
yet, scared by the passing of wild animals and
the hissing of snakes

10 they perished in trembling fear,
refusing to look even at the air, though it
nowhere could be avoided.

11 For wickedness is a cowardly thing,
condemned by its own testimony;[b]
distressed by conscience, it has always
exaggerated[c] the difficulties.

12 For fear is nothing but a giving up of the helps
that come from reason;

13 and hope, defeated by this inward weakness,
prefers ignorance of what causes the torment.

14 But throughout the night, which was really
powerless
and which came upon them from the recesses
of powerless Hades,
they all slept the same sleep,

15 and now were driven by monstrous specters,

a Other ancient authorities read *unobserved, they were darkened behind a dark curtain of forgetfulness, terribly*   *b* Meaning of Gk uncertain   *c* Other ancient authorities read *anticipated*

NAB

14 So they, during that night, powerless though
it was,
that had come upon them from the
recesses of a powerless nether world,
while all sleeping the same sleep,
15 Were partly smitten by fearsome apparitions
and partly stricken by their soul's surrender;
for fear came upon them, sudden and
unexpected.
16 Thus, then, whoever was there fell
into that unbarred prison and was kept
confined.
17 For whether one was a farmer, or a
shepherd, or a worker at tasks in the
wasteland,
Taken unawares, he served out the
inescapable sentence;
18 for all were bound by the one bond of
darkness.
And were it only the whistling wind,
or the melodious song of birds in the
spreading branches,
Or the steady sound of rushing water,
19 or the rude crash of overthrown rocks,
Or the unseen gallop of bounding animals,
or the roaring cry of the fiercest beasts,
Or an echo resounding from the hollow of
the hills,
these sounds, inspiring terror, paralyzed them.
20 For the whole world shone with brilliant
light
and continued its works without interruption;
21 Over them alone was spread oppressive night,
an image of the darkness that next should
come upon them;
yet they were to themselves more
burdensome than the darkness.

18 But your holy ones had very
great light;
And those others, who heard their voices but
did not see their forms,
since now they themselves had suffered,
called them blest;
2 And because they who formerly had been
wronged did not harm them, they
thanked them,

17, 21: *epetetato*: conj.
18, 1: (*phōnēn*) *men . . . (morphēn de*): so LXXMSS.
18, 2: *eucharistoun*: so LXXMSS.

NRSV

and now were paralyzed by their souls'
surrender;
for sudden and unexpected fear overwhelmed
them.
16 And whoever was there fell down,
and thus was kept shut up in a prison not
made of iron;
17 for whether they were farmers or shepherds
or workers who toiled in the wilderness,
they were seized, and endured the inescapable
fate;
for with one chain of darkness they all were
bound.
18 Whether there came a whistling wind,
or a melodious sound of birds in
wide-spreading branches,
or the rhythm of violently rushing water,
19 or the harsh crash of rocks hurled down,
or the unseen running of leaping animals,
or the sound of the most savage roaring beasts,
or an echo thrown back from a hollow of the
mountains,
it paralyzed them with terror.
20 For the whole world was illumined with
brilliant light,
and went about its work unhindered,
21 while over those people alone heavy night was
spread,
an image of the darkness that was destined to
receive them;
but still heavier than darkness were they to
themselves.

18 But for your holy ones there was very
great light.
Their enemies[a] heard their voices but did not
see their forms,
and counted them happy for not having
suffered,
2 and were thankful that your holy ones,[b] though
previously wronged, were doing them
no injury;
and they begged their pardon for having been
at variance with them.[b]
3 Therefore you provided a flaming pillar of fire
as a guide for your people's[c] unknown journey,
and a harmless sun for their glorious
wandering.

a Gk *They*   *b* Meaning of Gk uncertain   *c* Gk *their*

NAB	NRSV

and pleaded with them, for the sake of the difference between them.
3 Instead of this, you furnished the flaming pillar
  which was a guide on the unknown way,
  and the mild sun for an honorable migration.
4 For those deserved to be deprived of light
  and imprisoned by darkness,
  who had kept your sons confined
  through whom the imperishable light of
  the law was to be given to the world.
	4 For their enemies^a deserved to be deprived of light and imprisoned in darkness,
	  those who had kept your children imprisoned,
	  through whom the imperishable light of the
	  law was to be given to the world.
	
	^a Gk *those persons*

COMMENTARY

The fourth diptych contrasts the plague of darkness that engulfed the Egyptians during the ninth plague with the light that accompanied the Israelites in the desert. This diptych shows the author's imaginative, interpretative, and poetic skills at their highest level. The source from Exodus regarding the ninth plague is brief, indeed (Exod 10:21-23). Yet, the fourth diptych, which is inspired by it, is of considerable length. The passage contains a varied vocabulary with more than fifty words occurring only in this unit within the entire book. Some words are familiar, but others are rare and carefully selected.

The author combines several literary and stylistic features that betray a complex style of Alexandrian writing. Often, it is difficult to recognize or appreciate these features in translation. Hebrew does not make extensive use of adjectives, but the author employs the Greek technique of using adjectival phrases throughout the diptych ("a dark curtain," 17:3; "the powerless night," 17:14; "the inescapable fate," 17:17; "a whistling wind," 17:18). Nouns are employed as qualities ("curtain of forgetfulness," 17:3; "power of fire," 17:5; "the rush of water," 17:18). Metaphors abound throughout the passage ("self-kindled fire," 17:6; "one chain of darkness," 17:17; "the heavy night," 17:21). Antitheses are used with dramatic effect ("lawless people"/"holy nation," 17:2; "brilliant flames"/"hateful night," 17:5). Use is made of a seven-part linked series of images of terror in 17:18-19, which is reminiscent of the six-part

chain syllogism of the sorites employed in 6:17-20.

In addition, the relative brevity of the description of the ninth plague in Exodus invites the author to explore the symbolism and the psychological drama of the terror of darkness. This entrance into the symbolism and drama of the fear caused by the heavy darkness parallels the author's entrance into the reasoning process and confession of the wicked in the first part of the book (5:2-14). The two passages are made parallel by the concentration of the dramatic result of terror and fear: "they will be shaken with dreadful fear" (5:2 NRSV); "they perished in trembling fear" (17:10). The author may very well have been familiar with the literary genre known as "descents into Hades," which at one point attempted to portray the terror and fear of those who are burdened with guilt.[138]

Although this is the only diptych in which God or the Lord is not explicitly mentioned, the direct speech both at the beginning (17:1) and at the end of the unit (18:15) retains the quality of praise directed to God.

17:2-6. The sin of the oppressors, which elicits the punishment of the imprisoning night, is described through two images: the imprisonment of the holy nation and the hiding of their sin behind the dark curtain of forgetfulness (vv. 2-3). Again the author attempts to show how the particular punishment of the ninth plague corresponds to the manner in which the oppressors sinned

138. See, e.g., Virgil *Aeneid* 6.

against the righteous. Since the righteous have been imprisoned, the oppressors experience an imprisonment of paralyzing fear arising from darkness.

A considerable amount of effort is spent to dramatize the elusive form of terror that has stricken the Egyptians. The author makes up for the relative brevity of the ninth plague with a vivid imagination of the terrors of the night. But all of the images of fear and terror are interpreted by the author finally as metaphorical language. The terror of the night represents the burden of guilt the oppressors are to themselves (v. 21). The author displays a great deal of psychological dexterity in exploring the debilitating effects of fear and hopelessness caused by a guilty conscience.

The idea of the Egyptians' hiding or concealing their oppression (v. 3) recalls Adam and Eve hiding in the garden after their disobedience (Gen 3:8; cf. Cain's disclaimer of knowing the whereabouts of his brother, Gen 4:9). The terrible darkness that engulfs them cannot be illumined either by fire or by the shining stars (vv. 3-6). In this way the author continues the theme that the elements change their normal qualities and functions for the purpose of redressing injustice, from the third diptych. Their inner fear is described by the author as a "self-kindled fire" (v. 6), which emphasizes their personal responsibility for their punishment.

17:7-10. The idea that the magic art and wisdom of the Egyptians was humbled with their failure to dispel the darkness depends on a contrast between the first few plagues and the later ones. The Egyptian magicians were able to match the signs and wonders of the first two plagues of blood and frogs (Exod 7:22; 8:7; cf. Exod 7:11). But during the third plague, that of gnats, the magicians failed to reproduce the signs of Moses and Aaron and admitted that the finger of God was present (Exod 8:18-19). The magicians themselves would become helplessly covered with boils in the sixth plague (Exod 9:11).

17:11-15. The author enters into a quasi-philosophical presentation of the fear that pursued the oppressors in the darkness (vv. 11-13). The punishing fear is brought into moral perspective. It is the result of wickedness, which is condemned by its own testimony of cowardice. It is compared to the burden of conscience that exaggerates the

difficulties at hand. Fear is defined as the abrogation of reason, which prefers the stupor of not knowing the cause of punishment.

Where exactly the author derives such reflections is unclear. The idea of the conscience is more at home in the Greek philosophical schools than in Hebrew thought. However, the reflection is consistent with the views the author has enunciated throughout the work regarding the responsibility of wickedness and the positive function of reason. The idea that wickedness is condemned by its own testimony parallels the author's declaration regarding the fruit of the wicked, which will bear witness against the parents at the time of accounting (4:4-6). The idea that wickedness gives up on reason and prefers ignorance contrasts well with the positive function of wisdom, which is the source of understanding and virtue (7:7-14; 8:2-8).

The philosophical currents of Hellenism, particularly of the moralists, such as the Epicureans and the Stoics, gave considerable space to the anguish that a guilty conscience could exercise.[139] The author of the book of Wisdom appears to be arguing that the resulting fear and cowardice of the oppressing conscience prefers ignorance, which actually compounds the torment of the one plagued by guilt. Plutarch relates a similar idea, "But fear alone, lacking no less in boldness than in power to reason, keeps its irrationality impotent, helpless and hopeless."[140]

17:16-17. The author continues with a series of images that are meant to describe and even mimic the perplexing and debilitating fear that resulted from the punishing darkness. Fear is described as an imprisoning power ("a prison not made of iron," v. 16), which contrasts with the power Egypt exercised over the holy nation (v. 2). It is all inclusive. The Exodus narrative insists on the general application of the plagues on humans, animals, and the land itself. Here the author chooses three specific walks of life to characterize the all-encompassing darkness. Darkness strikes farmers, shepherds, and laborers (v. 17). The qualification of the laborer who toils in the wilderness has led to several conjectures. What would a worker be doing in the wilderness? The Greek noun that signifies "wilderness" (ἐρημία

139. Lucretius 3.1011; Seneca *Epistulae* 41, 97.15.
140. Plutarch *Moralia* 165D.

erēmia) also refers to solitude. Thus it could very well refer to a qualitative aspect of laboring in solitude rather than to one of location, laboring in the desert. David Winston offers another possibility that could have arisen from the social conditions of Egypt in the first century CE. Due to heavy taxes levied on the inhabitants during the Ptolemaic period, but especially in the Roman period, workers escaped to the desert as a form of protest.[141] In any event, the import of the author's argument is that the chain of darkness bound all who were part of the oppression against the holy nation.

17:18-19. The seven-part linked series of images of terror describes through poetic imagery the paralysis of terror. Images from the animal world and from the elements of creation describe poetically a cause of terror that goes beyond all expectations: whistling wind, the sound of birds, rushing water, crash of rocks, leaping animals, roaring beasts, and the echo from mountains. This concentration of poetic imagery to convey the punishment of the wicked is reminiscent of the poetic imagery used by the wicked in the first part of the book. There the author employed poetic imagery from nature to describe the transience and the hopelessness of the wicked (2:1-5; 5:9-14).

17:20-21. The final reflection on the all-encompassing darkness contrasts the darkness that fell on the Egyptians with the light of the whole world. Everyone else goes about his or her work unhindered, whereas the Egyptians are plagued with the heaviness of darkness. As if to single out the personal responsibility of those who have oppressed the holy nation, the author emphasizes that on them alone the heavy night had spread. This is consistent with the events as described briefly in the ninth plague in Exod 10:21-23. Even heavier than this all-encompassing darkness are the guilty to themselves. This perception of personal guilt parallels the confession of the wicked in the first part of the book. After seeing the deliverance of the righteous, the wicked are tormented by a dreadful fear (5:2).

18:1-2. While the dreadful darkness plagued Egypt, the righteous experienced a very great light (v. 1). The reference to this light for Israel is the

same as that mentioned in 17:20. While the Egyptians were experiencing darkness, the holy ones experienced a great light. The positive response of the Egyptians to the Israelites' escape from the darkness (vv. 1-2) is an interpretation of Exod 11:2-3 and 12:33-36. After the tenth plague, the Egyptians themselves urged the Israelites to flee. They even gave the Israelites the silver and gold they asked for. The author interprets this external gesture as a brief sign of repentance before the foolish decision to pursue them once again is made (19:3).

18:3. The theme of light leads the author to reflect on the pillar of fire that accompanied Israel in the desert during the night and on the harmless sun during the day. The pillar of fire constitutes the prime antithesis to the plague of darkness. In this way, the righteous experience a blessing through the light in darkness just as the oppressors experience a punishment through the all-encompassing darkness. The source for the image of the pillar of fire is Exod 13:21-22. Only in this passage from Exodus in addition to the Wisdom text is the source of fire described as a "pillar." Elsewhere the source of light is described as a "cloud" or as a "fiery light" (Exod 40:38; Num 9:15-16; Ps 78:14, the fiery light is parallel to the cloud by day; cf. Ps 105:39).

The author makes no reference to the pillar of cloud by day (Exod 13:21), perhaps in order to sustain the theme of light. The sun was the source of light during the day, and it had no scorching or burning effect (cf. Isa 49:10).

18:4. The conclusion to the diptych reaffirms the connection between the oppressors' sin of imprisoning the righteous and the ensuing punishment of imprisoning darkness. It illustrates one of the main principles the author has been expounding throughout the diptychs: One is punished in accordance with one's sins. The very seed of punishment is contained in the sin. In this way, the diptych is enclosed by the inclusion of the theme of imprisoning darkness (17:2; 18:4).

The theme of light is reintroduced through the image of the universality of the law. The imprisoned people were the ones through whom the light of the law was to be given to the world. The author interprets the gift of the law as a light not only for Israel but also for the world. This understanding of the universality of the law fol-

141. David Winston, *The Wisdom of Solomon,* AB 43 (New York: Doubleday, 1979) 309-10.

lows that of Isaiah and Micah: "All nations shall stream to the holy mountain, for out of Zion shall go forth instruction" (Isa 2:2-3; Mic 4:1-4, author's trans.). Philo likewise stressed the universal purpose of the law by describing it as "a law for the world."[142] Earlier the author of Wis-dom described the wicked as not walking in the light of justice (5:6). The light of the law will illuminate the paths of truth. The responsibility of the righteous, then, is to transmit the law of justice to the world.

142. Philo *Questions and Answers on Exodus* 2.42.

REFLECTIONS

1. The fourth diptych explores primarily the psychologically damaging effect of injustice as it is conveyed through fear and hopelessness. The antithesis regarding the pillar of light is treated briefly in comparison to the imprisoning darkness that engulfs the enemies. One of the interesting features the author picks up from the exodus narrative to emphasize the unguided nature of injustice is the absence of reason. Through fear the unjust give up the help of reason. The author is interpreting the resistance of Pharaoh from the exodus narrative as the absence of reason. Despite all the evidence accumulated from the plagues, and despite the advice of his own wise counselors, Pharaoh persists in a policy of injustice that leads to destruction. Whereas Exodus attributes this folly to the hardening of Pharaoh's heart, the Wisdom author attributes this action on the part of the oppressors as resulting from the absence of reason (17:12-13). By refusing to read the signs of the times and interpret them with humility, the oppressors prefer ignorance. This ignorance begins to weigh heavily on them in the form of fear and guilt. In the Gospels, Christ also is said to interpret the refusal to read the signs of the times as a consequence of wickedness or moral blindness (Matt 16:1-4; Mark 8:11-13; Luke 12:54-56).

2. The theme of the first half of the diptych revolves around irony. The oppressors who imprison the righteous become imprisoned by terror and darkness themselves. This irony is reflective of the situation of the wicked in the first part of the book. There the wicked had formulated a plot whereby they would test the claims of the just by subjecting them to a "shameful death" (2:20). Yet in the end, at the time of accounting, the wicked experience terror and fear over their lack of virtue when they face the blessing of the righteous. They describe their state of anguish through images of death (5:9-14). They planned to subject the just one to a shameful death, yet they become subjected to the shame of their virtueless lives. Similarly, with the oppressors of the "holy nation," those who imprison the righteous are themselves in a prison of darkness. The master becomes enslaved in the process of enslaving others. The very form of one's injustice determines one's punishment.

3. Another side to this irony is the distance between the bravado and apparent strength of the oppressors and their cowardly behavior before seemingly innocent natural phenomena and harmless animals. This state also parallels the wicked in the first part of the book, whose apparent bravado with respect to the pleasures of life only masked the underlying despair and terror they finally revealed.

4. The extraordinary deliverance of the just through light parallels the deliverance of the just in the first part of the book. The author postulates firm hope in the promises of life for the just because of the great memories of deliverance of the righteous from the past. What takes place in history is seen to form a basis for imagining the unseen future. Although the author did not explain the where, when, and how of the deliverance of the just in the first part of the book, the firm belief in such a deliverance is postulated through a reflection on Israel's foundational history.

WISDOM 18:5–19:12, DEATH OF THE ENEMIES AND ISRAEL'S DELIVERANCE

NAB

5 When they determined to put to death the
   infants of the holy ones,
   and when a single boy had been cast forth
   but saved,
   As a reproof you carried off their multitude
   of sons
   and made them perish all at once in the
   mighty water.
6 That night was known beforehand to our
   fathers,
   that, with sure knowledge of the oaths in
   which they put their faith, they might
   have courage.
7 Your people awaited
   the salvation of the just and the destruction
   of their foes.
8 For when you punished our adversaries,
   in this you glorified us whom you had
   summoned.
9 For in secret the holy children of the good
   were offering sacrifice
   and putting into effect with one accord the
   divine institution,
   That your holy ones should share alike the
   same good things and dangers,
   having previously sung the praises of the
   fathers.
10 But the discordant cry of their enemies
   responded,
   and the piteous wail of mourning for
   children was borne to them.
11 And the slave was smitten with the same
   retribution as his master;
   even the plebeian suffered the same as the king.
12 And all alike by a single death
   had countless dead;
   For the living were not even sufficient for the
   burial,
   since at a single instant their nobler
   offspring were destroyed.
13 For though they disbelieved at every turn
   on account of sorceries,

18, 9: *proanamelpontes*: so LXX^{MSS}.
18, 10: (*diephereto*) *phōnē*: so LXX^{MSS}.

NRSV

5 When they had resolved to kill the infants of
   your holy ones,
   and one child had been abandoned and
   rescued,
   you in punishment took away a multitude of
   their children;
   and you destroyed them all together by a
   mighty flood.
6 That night was made known beforehand to our
   ancestors,
   so that they might rejoice in sure knowledge
   of the oaths in which they trusted.
7 The deliverance of the righteous and the
   destruction of their enemies
   were expected by your people.
8 For by the same means by which you punished
   our enemies
   you called us to yourself and glorified us.
9 For in secret the holy children of good people
   offered sacrifices,
   and with one accord agreed to the divine law,
   so that the saints would share alike the same
   things,
   both blessings and dangers;
   and already they were singing the praises of
   the ancestors.^a
10 But the discordant cry of their enemies echoed
   back,
   and their piteous lament for their children was
   spread abroad.
11 The slave was punished with the same penalty
   as the master,
   and the commoner suffered the same loss as
   the king;
12 and they all together, by the one form^b of death,
   had corpses too many to count.
   For the living were not sufficient even to bury
   them,
   since in one instant their most valued children
   had been destroyed.
13 For though they had disbelieved everything
   because of their magic arts,

^a Other ancient authorities read *dangers, the ancestors already lead-
ing the songs of praise*   ^b Gk *name*

at the destruction of the first-born they
acknowledged that the people was
God's son.

14 For when peaceful stillness compassed
everything

and the night in its swift course was half
spent,

15 Your all-powerful word from heaven's royal
throne

bounded, a fierce warrior, into the doomed
land,

16 bearing the sharp sword of your
inexorable decree.

And as he alighted, he filled every place with
death;

he still reached to heaven, while he stood
upon the earth.

17 Then, forthwith, visions in horrible dreams
perturbed them

and unexpected fears assailed them;

18 And cast half-dead, one here, another there,
each was revealing the reason for his
dying.

19 For the dreams that disturbed them had
proclaimed this beforehand,

lest they perish unaware of why they
suffered ill.

20 But the trial of death touched at one time
even the just,

and in the desert a plague struck the
multitude;

Yet not for long did the anger last.

21 For the blameless man hastened to be their
champion,

bearing the weapon of his special office,

prayer and the propitiation of incense;

He withstood the wrath and put a stop to the
calamity,

showing that he was your servant.

22 And he overcame the bitterness

not by bodily strength, not by force of
arms;

But by word he overcame the smiter,

18, 14: Omit *ta panta* at end: dittog from (*pariechousēs ta panta*)
preceding.
18, 17: (*oneirōn*) *deinōn*: so LXXMSS.
18, 20: (*dikaiōn*) *pote*: so 4 LXXMSS.
18, 22: (*enikēsen*) *de*: so LXXMSS; *ton cholon*: conj; cf *thymō* 18,
21 and *orgēn*, 18, 23.

yet, when their firstborn were destroyed, they
acknowledged your people to be God's
child.

14 For while gentle silence enveloped all things,

and night in its swift course was now half
gone,

15 your all-powerful word leaped from heaven,
from the royal throne,

into the midst of the land that was doomed,
a stern warrior

16 carrying the sharp sword of your authentic
command,

and stood and filled all things with death,

and touched heaven while standing on the
earth.

17 Then at once apparitions in dreadful dreams
greatly troubled them,

and unexpected fears assailed them;

18 and one here and another there, hurled down
half dead,

made known why they were dying;

19 for the dreams that disturbed them forewarned
them of this,

so that they might not perish without knowing
why they suffered.

20 The experience of death touched also the
righteous,

and a plague came upon the multitude in the
desert,

but the wrath did not long continue.

21 For a blameless man was quick to act as their
champion;

he brought forward the shield of his ministry,

prayer and propitiation by incense;

he withstood the anger and put an end to the
disaster,

showing that he was your servant.

22 He conquered the wrath[a] not by strength of
body,

not by force of arms,

but by his word he subdued the avenger,

appealing to the oaths and covenants given to
our ancestors.

23 For when the dead had already fallen on one
another in heaps,

he intervened and held back the wrath,

[a] Cn: Gk *multitude*

NAB

recalling the sworn covenants with their
fathers.

23 For when corpses had already fallen one on
another in heaps,
he stood in the midst and checked the
anger,
and cut off the way to the living.

24 For on his full-length robe was the whole
world,
and the glories of the fathers were carved
in four rows upon the stones,
and your grandeur was on the crown upon
his head.

25 To these names the destroyer yielded, and
these he feared;
for the mere trial of anger was enough.

19 But the wicked, merciless wrath assailed
until the end.
For he knew beforehand what they were
yet to do:

2 That though they themselves had agreed to
the departure
and had anxiously sent them on their way,
they would regret it and pursue them.

3 For while they were still engaged in funeral
rites
and were mourning at the burials of the dead,
They adopted another senseless plan;
and those whom they had sent away with
entreaty,
they pursued as fugitives.

4 For a compulsion suited to this ending drew
them on,
and made them forgetful of what had
befallen them,
That they might fill out the torments of their
punishment,

5 and your people might experience a
glorious journey
while those others met an extraordinary
death.

6 For all creation, in its several kinds, was
being made over anew,
serving its natural laws,
that your children might be preserved
unharmed.

18, 24: *lithōn* : so LXX^{MSS}.
18, 25: *ephobēthē*: so LXX^{MSS}.

NRSV

and cut off its way to the living.

24 For on his long robe the whole world was
depicted,
and the glories of the ancestors were engraved
on the four rows of stones,
and your majesty was on the diadem upon his
head.

25 To these the destroyer yielded, these he[a]
feared;
for merely to test the wrath was enough.

19 But the ungodly were assailed to the end
by pitiless anger,
for God[b] knew in advance even their future
actions:

2 how, though they themselves had permitted[c]
your people to depart
and hastily sent them out,
they would change their minds and pursue
them.

3 For while they were still engaged in mourning,
and were lamenting at the graves of their dead,
they reached another foolish decision,
and pursued as fugitives those whom they had
begged and compelled to leave.

4 For the fate they deserved drew them on to
this end,
and made them forget what had happened,
in order that they might fill up the punishment
that their torments still lacked,

5 and that your people might experience[d] an
incredible journey,
but they themselves might meet a strange
death.

6 For the whole creation in its nature was
fashioned anew,
complying with your commands,
so that your children[e] might be kept unharmed.

7 The cloud was seen overshadowing the camp,
and dry land emerging where water had stood
before,
an unhindered way out of the Red Sea,
and a grassy plain out of the raging waves,

8 where those protected by your hand passed
through as one nation,

a Other ancient authorities read *they*   *b* Gk *he*   *c* Other ancient
authorities read *had changed their minds to permit*
d Other ancient authorities read *accomplish*   *e* Or *servants*

NAB

7 The cloud overshadowed their camp;
   and out of what had before been water,
      dry land was seen emerging:
   Out of the Red Sea an unimpeded road,
      and a grassy plain out of the mighty flood.
8 Over this crossed the whole nation sheltered
      by your hand,
   after they beheld stupendous wonders.
9 For they ranged about like horses,
   and bounded about like lambs,
      praising you, O Lord! their deliverer.
10 For they were still mindful of what had
      happened in their sojourn:
   how instead of the young of animals the
      land brought forth gnats,
   and instead of fishes the river swarmed
      with countless frogs.
11 And later they saw also a new kind of bird
   when, prompted by desire, they asked for
      pleasant foods;
12 For to appease them quail came to them
      from the sea.

NRSV

after gazing on marvelous wonders.
9 For they ranged like horses,
   and leaped like lambs,
      praising you, O Lord, who delivered them.
10 For they still recalled the events of their
      sojourn,
   how instead of producing animals the earth
      brought forth gnats,
   and instead of fish the river spewed out vast
      numbers of frogs.
11 Afterward they saw also a new kind[a] of birds,
   when desire led them to ask for luxurious food;
12 for, to give them relief, quails came up from
      the sea.

a Or production

COMMENTARY

The fifth and final diptych contrasts the death of the Egyptians with the extraordinary deliverance of the Israelites. The antithesis is presented in two stages: (1) The death of the firstborn in Egypt contrasts with the deliverance of the Israelites at the hands of Aaron's intercession in the desert (18:5-25); (2) the death of the ungodly in the sea contrasts with the extraordinary deliverance of the Israelites through the sea (19:1-12).[143] The sin of the oppressors, which the author cites as the root for the double-pronged punishment, is the killing of the Hebrew children by drowning them in the Nile (18:5). The oppressors experience a punishment according to the manner in which they mete out injustice. For the killing of the children, they will lose their own children. For killing the children by drowning, they will

experience punishment by drowning in the sea. The book of *Jubilees* draws the same connection between the killing of the Hebrew infants and the punishment by drowning in the sea:

And all of the people whom he brought out to pursue after Israel the LORD our God threw into the middle of the sea into the depths of the abyss beneath the children of Israel. Just as the men of Egypt cast their sons into the river he avenged one million. And one thousand strong and ardent men perished on account of one infant whom they threw into the midst of the river from the sons of your people. (*Jub.* 48:14)

Note the parallelism drawn between the first and the final diptych. Both diptychs deal with the same sin of the oppressors against the righteous. The sin the author cites as eliciting the punishment of water turning to blood is the decree that the infants be killed in the Nile (11:6-7). In this way, the entire series of diptychs (chaps. 11–19) is enclosed by the theme of water. The Nile itself became a source of punishment at the beginning of the cycle of plagues, and the sea turns into a

143. A. G. Wright argues for a single, double-pronged diptych stating that the author of Wisdom explores one event with two results. The tenth plague of death and the destruction of Pharaoh's army at sea are joined together as a response to the decree to kill the infants in the Nile (18:5). See A. G. Wright, "The Structure of Wisdom 11–19," *CBQ* 27 (1965) 28-34.

source of punishment at the very end. Just as the righteous experienced a blessing through the gift of water in the desert, so too did they experience their foundational deliverance by a safe passage through the sea. Moreover, the theme of water returns the reader to the conclusion of the history of wisdom's interventions on behalf of the just in chap. 10. It was the theme of the extraordinary deliverance at the Red Sea that occasioned the lengthy midrashic treatment of the exodus events (10:15-21).

18:5-19, Death of the Firstborn. At the very beginning of the diptych, the author brings together the double response of God's punishment to Pharaoh's decree regarding the Hebrew infants (v. 5). The first response refers to the tenth plague, the death of the firstborn among the Egyptians. The second response refers to the destruction of Pharaoh's army at the Red Sea. The brief reference to the abandonment and rescue of the infant Moses provides a familiar link to Pharaoh's decree (Exod 1:22; 2:1-10). The threat and deliverance of the infant Moses prefigure the threat and extraordinary deliverance of the entire people.

The theme of the ancestors' foreknowledge of both the destruction of Egyptian oppression and their own deliverance underscores the continuous providence of God. In addition to the ancestors at the time of Moses, the author is alluding to the ancestors of the patriarchs. The ancestors' foreknowledge (v. 6) alludes to the covenant with Abram during the terrifying darkness that descended upon him. The message given to Abram after the "fire pot" descends and passes between the animal parts offered for sacrifice includes the history of Israel's four-hundred-year oppression. That period of oppression will be followed by judgment against the Egyptians and by the Israelites' extraordinary deliverance (Gen 15:12-16).

The author contrasts the situations of the righteous and the oppressors just before the administration of the tenth plague. The reference to the offering of sacrifices by the holy children in accordance with the divine law alludes to the institution of the passover feast (Exod 12:1-28). The paschal meal is understood as an expression of the praise of God in anticipation of the blessings and dangers that all would share and witness (v.

9). The image of "holy children of good people" is a new formulation for designating the righteous.

In contrast to this sacrifice of praise on the part of the holy ones, the oppressors' lament at the loss of their children passes throughout the land, from the greatest to the least. The universality of the tragedy is presented through word pairs, slave and master, commoner and king (vv. 10-12). The image of the tragedy's being so massive that the oppressors can hardly bury their dead (v. 12) is not present in Exodus. It may very well have been inspired by Num 33:3-4: "the Israelites went out boldly in the sight of all the Egyptians, while the Egyptians were burying all their firstborn, whom the LORD had struck down among them" (NRSV).

The particular wording the author employs to describe the release of God's people after the experience of the tenth plague is reminiscent of the speech of the wicked. The oppressors acknowledged the just to be "God's child" (v. 13). The author attributes the Egyptians' reluctance to release the Hebrews to their magic arts. Only the death of their firstborn forced the Egyptians to recognize their slaves as "God's children." In the first part of the book, the wicked had derided the just one for claiming God's paternity (2:16). Moreover, they planned to subject the just one to a shameful death because of this claim (2:18-20). Just as the wicked had to acknowledge that the just are counted among the "children of God" (5:5), so too do the oppressors of God's people acknowledge those whom they had oppressed to be "God's child." The author's use of this image in the tenth plague is facilitated by the reason given in Exodus for the release of the Hebrews: "Thus says the LORD: Israel is my firstborn son. I said to you, 'Let my son go that he may worship me'" (Exod 4:22-23 NRSV).

The parallel between the judgment of death in the fifth diptych and the judgment against the wicked in the first part of the book continues with the description of the "destroyer" from Exod 12:23 (5:17-23; 18:15-16). The destroyer is described as God's "all-powerful word" and as "a stern warrior" stretching from heaven to earth (v. 15), who wields a sharp sword filling all things with death (v. 16; cf. 5:20). Wickedness undergoes a judgment of cosmic proportions in the first part of the book, just as the oppressors of the holy ones meet their judgment of death in the final part.

Finally, the author alludes to the previous plague of darkness in the fourth diptych. The purpose of this is to highlight the effect of judgment to reveal the purpose of the punishment. The same apparitions, dreadful dreams, and unexpected fears as in the plague of darkness came upon them to remind them of their function of forewarning. In this way they understood why death had touched them and why they suffered (vv. 18-19).

18:20-25, Aaron's Intercession. The contrast to the destruction of the oppressors' firstborn is markedly different from the previous contrasts of the four diptychs. The contrast ordinarily presents the principle that the very means used to punish the Egyptians are used in some manner to deliver the just. In this case, the punishment that befalls the destroyer will occur to the just for their rebellion in the desert. The contrast consists of the saving intervention on the part of Aaron.

It would appear that the author is addressing a possible objection that might arise in the mind of the reader. It is true that Israel experienced extraordinary acts of deliverance in the desert. However, the Israelites also experienced death and destruction in response to their stubbornness and rebellious spirits. The author addresses their punishment without dwelling on the spirit of rebellion. The situation of the righteous differs from that of the oppressors in that the punishment of the righteous was not total. Because of the intercession of Aaron, the hand of the destroyer was stayed.

The episode being addressed is the punishment of the plague, which the Israelites experienced in the desert (Num 16:1-50). In response to the punishment meted out for the levitical rebellion of Korah, Dathan, and Abiram, the people assembled against Moses and Aaron. The plague destroyed 14,700 people before Aaron stopped it by making atonement for the people.

This episode picked up by the author in the fifth diptych is similar to the episode of the venomous serpents, treated as a digression in the second diptych. In both cases, the punishment of the just, which is only temporary, is a response to their rebellion. It was stopped by the intercession of Moses (through the brazen serpent) and

Aaron. Similarly, in both cases, the punishment is addressed without stressing the sinfulness of the people that had given rise to the experience of death. The reason for this is probably that the author judged it unfitting to be overtly critical of the righteous while contrasting their plight to that of their oppressors. Nonetheless, the recognition of the punishment in the episode of the venomous serpents and the plague in the desert reaffirms the author's judgment from the first part of the book: Punishment and ultimate death are brought upon people through their unjust decisions and actions.

The author employs a number of images for the plague that struck the righteous to make it parallel to the tenth plague against the Egyptians. The plague is referred to as "the experience of death" (v. 20; cf. 2:24). In both cases, the end result of the plague was numerous dead ("corpses too many to count," v. 12; "when the dead had already fallen on one another in heaps," v. 23).

The contrast between the punishment of the oppressors and the punishment of the righteous also is related through similar imagery. Whereas God's word against the oppressors was described as a "stern warrior" who carried a "sharp sword" (vv. 15-16), Aaron's intercession is described as a "shield" that subdued "the avenger" through his "word" (vv. 21-22).

To supplement the brief description of Aaron's atonement with the censer of atonement from Num 16:47, the author describes Aaron's intervention as an appeal to God's oaths and promises. In Numbers, Aaron does not intercede for the people. Rather, in response to Moses' command, he conducts a ritual of atonement with the censer for the people. The idea of intercession is borrowed from the intercessory interventions of Moses to save the people from God's wrath. In order to stave off the wrath of God against the people, Moses appeals to the promises of God sworn to the ancestors (Exod 32:11-14; cf. Num 14:13-24).

Finally, the author alludes to the priestly robe of Aaron, with its ephod, and the diadem before which the destroyer yielded (vv. 24-25). The ephod, which was placed on Aaron's priestly robe, was to contain two onyx stones on which "all the names of the sons of Israel" were to be engraved (Exod 28:6-14). The idea that the robe contained a depiction of the world (v. 24) expresses the author's universalistic perception of God's rule. The cosmos is on the side of God, for God is its creator. Philo makes a similar point with allegorical overtones that the Wisdom author is less prone to make. The robe of the high priest is described as a likeness and copy of the entire universe. Its dark blue color symbolizes the air, its full length symbolizing the recesses of the earth; its breastplate symbolizes heaven; the twelve precious stones arranged in four rows symbolize the twelve signs of the zodiac.[144]

19:1-5, The Strange Death. In contrast to the temporary anger of God against the righteous, the oppressors experienced the pitiless anger of God to the end (v. 1). The author alludes to Pharaoh's foolish decision to change his mind despite the release granted to the Israelites. The underlying dynamic here is that the oppressors' injustice is to reach completion in their punishment (v. 4). This idea is consistent with the author's emphasis throughout the work that injustice bears the seeds of its own destruction. Very little is said regarding the final judgment against the oppressors. It is summarized in the concise image of "a strange death." In contrast to the strange death of the oppressors, the righteous experience an incredible journey.

19:6-12, Creation Is Fashioned Anew. The contrast with the strange death of the oppressors is dramatized through the extraordinary moment of deliverance at the Red Sea. The author harnesses the positive function of the cosmos to highlight the final moment of salvation for God's people. Creation itself was transformed in order to redress injustice (cf. 16:24). It is as if the crossing of the sea unhindered on "a grassy plain" summarizes succinctly both the punishments of the oppressors and all the acts of deliverance recounted in the diptychs. Just as the sea was the means of the ultimate judgment against the oppressors (18:5), so too is the sea the means of the ultimate deliverance of the righteous (v. 7).

The praise of God expressed through images of ranging horses and leaping lambs (v. 9) recalls the joy expressed for deliverance in the Song of Moses (Exod 15:1-18) and in the Song of Miriam (Exod 15:20-21). Psalm 114 employs the image of skipping rams and lambs (Ps 114:4-6) to express the joy of creation at the deliverance of Israel. The comparison of the joyful righteous to ranging horses may be a contrast to the traditional image of the destruction of the "horse and rider" (Exod 15:1, 21 NRSV). Isaiah speaks of Israel's passing through the depths like "a horse in a desert" (Isa 63:13 NRSV).

In experiencing the extraordinary deliverance through the sea, the righteous remember the manner in which creation had come continuously to their aid against the unjust (v. 10). Against the unrighteous, the earth produced gnats and the river spewed forth frogs instead of fish, recalling the third (Exod 8:16) and second plagues (Exod 8:1-6). In favor of the righteous, a new kind of bird came up from the sea to give them relief when they desire food (v. 12; cf. Num 11:31). The creation of animals, as recounted in Gen 1:20-25, undergoes a metamorphosis in the exodus event in favor of the righteous.

144. Philo *Moses* 2.1117-1135; *On the Cherubim* 100; *Questions and Answers on Exodus* 2.73, 76, 91.

REFLECTIONS

1. The author has been drawing a parallel between the wicked in the first part of the book and the Egyptian oppressors in the latter half of the book. That parallel is all the more evident in the final diptych with the judgment of the final plague and the strange death at the Red Sea. Just as the judgment against wickedness is exercised through the arming of creation, so too is the final judgment against the oppressors of God's people exercised through the transformation of creation itself. The images that highlight the parallelism in the two sections are the following: creation's being armed to repel the enemies (5:17); "stern wrath for a sword" (5:20 NRSV); "the water of the sea" (5:22 NRSV); "the whole creation in its nature was fashioned anew" (19:6 NRSV); "a stern warrior carrying the sharp sword" (18:15-16 NRSV); "you destroyed them all together by a mighty flood" (18:5 NRSV).

Note the pedagogical function of the author's interpretation of the final plague. In the first part of the book, the author labored to defend a life of virtue and justice in the face of apparent failure and weakness. The virtue and justice of the righteous appeared to be weak and fruitless compared with the apparent strength of the unjust. Death, in its many expressions of mortality, punishment, and ultimate judgment, was uncovered as being an obstacle to the exercise of justice. The wicked feared and despised a life stamped by mortality and weakness. By postulating an ultimate judgment, the author strips away the apparent weakness of the just as well as the facade of the wicked's power. The entire midrashic treatment of the exodus interprets the foundational experience of Israel's liberation as the basis for postulating the final judgment. Just as creation labors on the side of the just to bring salvation and judgment to the righteous and to the wicked, as seen throughout the exodus narrative, so also then will there be an ultimate judgment that reveals the ultimate power and fruitfulness of a virtuous and just life.

2. A further parallelism is drawn between the Word of God in the final diptych and personified wisdom in the center of the book. Wisdom was described as residing beside the throne of God (9:10), as being all powerful (7:22). In the final diptych, God's all-powerful word leaps from heaven, from the royal throne (18:15). Although wisdom by name does not play a crucial role in the final part of the book, the saving activity of wisdom continues to be present. The activity of wisdom is to guide, to protect, and to rescue human beings on their paths in life (7:27; 8:2-8; 9:18; 10:1-21). In the final diptych, the activity of wisdom is fulfilled through God's Word and in the forces of creation, which were made through wisdom. The forces of the cosmos fulfill the function of wisdom, and wisdom becomes transparent in the struggle for justice between the righteous and their oppressors.

3. The experience of death touches the righteous as well as the wicked (18:20). The author does not develop to a great extent the theme of conversion. Perhaps the literary technique of comparing and contrasting the wicked and the righteous did not lend itself to developing the theme of conversion. In the digression on God's power and mercy, the issue of conversion was addressed at least in part. The experiences of punishment are interpreted as providing an opportunity for a change of heart and for conversion in one's life (11:23; 12:2, 10, 20). However, the recognition that the righteous experience punishment underscores the life-and-death consequences of decisions and actions. Even the righteous, treated collectively, rebelled against God and experienced the consequences of their actions. But it was a punishment that did not lead to an ultimate, tragic judgment. Aaron's intercession is a sign of the people's conversion. Just to test the wrath of God was enough (18:25).

4. The theme of creation's being fashioned anew highlights the author's positive view of the forces of creation. This reflection has accompanied the reader throughout the midrashic treatment of the exodus narrative. It is one of the unitive themes that weave a thread throughout the three diverse parts of the book. The elements of creation that served to thwart the resistance of the oppressors are transformed continuously to guide and protect the righteous in their struggle for life. The locus for evil and tragedy is not to be found in the forces of creation. Rather, tragedy resides in the decisions and actions of human beings. Creation itself is a creature of God whose energies are ultimately directed to bringing life to completion. The function of wisdom to guide, to protect, and to save is exercised by creation, which was made according to God's wisdom.

WISDOM 19:13-22, FINAL REFLECTIONS

NAB

13 And the punishments came upon the sinners
> only after forewarnings from the violence of the thunderbolts.
> For they justly suffered for their own misdeeds,
> since indeed they treated their guests with the more grievous hatred.
14 For those others did not receive unfamiliar visitors,
> but these were enslaving beneficent guests.
15 And not that only; but what punishment was to be theirs
> since they received strangers unwillingly!
16 Yet these, after welcoming them with festivities,
> oppressed with awful toils those who now shared with them the same rights.
17 And they were struck with blindness,
> as those others had been at the portals of the just—
> When, surrounded by yawning darkness,
> each sought the entrance of his own gate.
18 For the elements, in variable harmony among themselves,
> like strings of the harp, produce new melody,
> while the flow of music steadily persists.
> And this can be perceived exactly from a review of what took place.
19 For land creatures were changed into water creatures,
> and those that swam went over on to the land.
20 Fire in water maintained its own strength,
> and water forgot its quenching nature;
21 Flames, by contrast, neither consumed the flesh
> of the perishable animals that went about in them,

19, 13: *progegonotōn* : so LXX[MSS].
19, 17: *hautou* or *heautou* : so LXX[MSS] V, P.
19, 20: (*sbestikēs*) *physeōs* : so LXX[MSS].
19, 21: *oud¹ etēkon krystalloeides eutēkton* (*genos*); for *etēkon*, cf V, Arm, Syr[Hex]; for trsp of *krystalloeides* cf LXX[MSS].

NRSV

13 The punishments did not come upon the sinners
> without prior signs in the violence of thunder,
> for they justly suffered because of their wicked acts;
> for they practiced a more bitter hatred of strangers.
14 Others had refused to receive strangers when they came to them,
> but these made slaves of guests who were their benefactors.
15 And not only so—but, while punishment of some sort will come upon the former for having received strangers with hostility,
16 the latter, having first received them with festal celebrations,
> afterward afflicted with terrible sufferings those who had already shared the same rights.
17 They were stricken also with loss of sight—
> just as were those at the door of the righteous man—
> when, surrounded by yawning darkness,
> all of them tried to find the way through their own doors.

18 For the elements changed[a] places with one another,
> as on a harp the notes vary the nature of the rhythm,
> while each note remains the same.[b]
> This may be clearly inferred from the sight of what took place.
19 For land animals were transformed into water creatures,
> and creatures that swim moved over to the land.
20 Fire even in water retained its normal power,
> and water forgot its fire-quenching nature.
21 Flames, on the contrary, failed to consume the flesh of perishable creatures that walked among them,
> nor did they melt[c] the crystalline, quick-melting kind of heavenly food.

[a] Gk *changing*   [b] Meaning of Gk uncertain   [c] Cn: Gk *nor could be melted*

NAB

nor melted the icelike, quick-melting kind
of ambrosial food.
22 For every way, O LORD! you magnified and
glorified your people;
unfailing, you stood by them in every time
and circumstance.

NRSV

22 For in everything, O Lord, you have exalted
and glorified your people,
and you have not neglected to help them at
all times and in all places.

COMMENTARY

The final reflections of the author can be divided into three brief sections: (1) vv. 13-17, the punishment of the Egyptians; (2) vv. 18-21, the transformation of creation; and (3) v. 22, a concluding summary of praise to God. The author is distilling the essential features from the reflections of the extraordinary deliverance of the Israelites from Egypt. The oppressors suffered justly because of their wickedness toward the righteous (v. 13). The elements of the cosmos underwent a transformation in order to maintain harmony (v. 18). God's faithfulness has exalted and glorified the righteous (v. 22). Although the author is bringing the reflection on the exodus to a close, new themes are introduced to emphasize the extraordinary salvation of the just.

The statement that declares the punishment of the oppressors to be just corresponds to the ethical perspective the author has been pursuing throughout the book. There were signs that warned the wicked of the sinister results of their actions (v. 13; cf. 12:1-2, 10; 14:30-31). The successive plagues in the exodus narrative were meant to warn the oppressors of the inherent tragedy of their injustice.

19:13-17. A new argument for the just punishment of the oppressors is introduced with the theme of hospitality to guests and strangers (vv. 13d-14). The author interprets the Israelites' sojourn in Egypt as their being strangers and guests who originally were welcome benefactors, yet became enslaved. The background detail for the author's observation on hospitality is the story of Joseph and his brothers, who were welcomed in Egypt as strangers. The children of these strangers became the benefactors of the Egyptians in the governorship of Joseph. They became enslaved, however, by the very people who had benefited from his services (Genesis 41–42; 46–47; Exodus

1). The reference covers a large span of history. The book of Exodus recounts how after Jacob's family had multiplied and grown strong in Egypt, a pharaoh arose who did not know Joseph. This pharaoh set a policy in motion that treated the Hebrews as slaves.

The guilt of the Egyptian oppressors is highlighted by the comparison between those who did not welcome guests in the first place and those who welcome them only to enslave them. The author is alluding to the inhabitants of Sodom who wanted to abuse the guests of Lot (Gen 19:1-11). The punishment of the inhabitants of Sodom became a paradigmatic motif of sin and punishment in Scripture (cf. Deut 29:23; 32:32; Isa 1:9; 3:9; 13:19; Jer 23:14; 50:40; Lam 4:6; Ezek 16:48-56; Matt 10:15; 11:23; Luke 17:29; 2 Pet 2:6; Jude 7). Often the comparison of a contemporary sin to that of Sodom is made in order to highlight the greater culpability of the contemporary generation (cf. Lam 4:6; Matt 10:15). This greater seriousness and culpability of the sin of Egypt is exactly what the Wisdom author wishes to emphasize by comparing Egypt to Sodom. If it is a great sin not to receive a stranger with hospitality, as in the case of the inhabitants of Sodom, so much greater is the sin of receiving strangers only to enslave them, as in the case of Egypt.

Corresponding to the sins of both Sodom and Egypt is the punishment of darkness. The author draws a comparison between the form of punishment for the sins of inhospitality and slavery. The Egyptians were stricken with the loss of sight in the ninth plague (Exod 10:21-23; cf. Wis 17:1-21). The aggressors against Lot were struck by blindness so that they could not find the entrance to the door (Gen 19:11).

Two details in the author's treatment of the

hostility of Sodom and Egypt toward strangers possibly relate to the contemporary situation of the author. These details consist of the theme of hospitality to strangers (vv. 13-14) and the notice of someone's being enslaved who had shared the same rights as those who enslave him (v. 16).

Reference to the inhospitality of Egypt to the ancestors may be the author's reversal of the polemic levied against Jews by contemporary pagans. The Jews were often accused of secluding themselves from people of other nationalities and fostering a hatred of aliens.[145] Philo vehemently attacked such false accusations and interpreted the slavery of the Hebrews in Egypt in the same manner as did the Wisdom author:

"So, then, these strangers, who had left their own country and came to Egypt hoping to live there in safety as in a second fatherland, were made slaves by the ruler of the country. . . . And in thus making serfs of men who were not only free but guests, suppliants, and settlers, he showed no shame or fear of the God of liberty and hospitality and of justice to guests and suppliants."[146]

The reference to the Hebrews' being reduced to slavery after having shared equal rights (v. 16) possibly alludes to the polemic for equal rights and citizenship that Alexandrian Jews waged under Roman rule. Originally, the Jews welcomed Roman authority, to the consternation of the Egyptian natives and Greeks alike. According to Philo, Augustus confirmed the right for the Jewish community in Alexandria to maintain its autonomous status.[147]

Between the death of Augustus in 14 CE and the letter of Claudius (41–54 CE) to the Alexandrians, confirming the status quo, the Jewish community was in serious conflict with the Greek population in Alexandria. Not only was a special tax imposed on all non-Greek citizens by the Romans in 24 BCE, but also Emperor Caligula (37–41 CE) demanded divine status for himself. Both burdens were rejected by the faithful within the Jewish community. This put them into conflict with the Greeks, who successfully barred those who were demanding access to the gymnasia from

attaining Greek citizenship. Philo headed the delegation sent to Caligula to reestablish equal rights, but without success. Caligula's successor, Claudius, finally intervened to stop the arguments and mutual recrimination in Alexandria by imposing the status quo.

It is possible that the Wisdom author is not limiting the reference of "sharing the same rights" to the equal status enjoyed by the Hebrews under Joseph in ancient Egypt. The reference could equally apply to the autonomous status of the Jews in Ptolemaic Egypt who then subsequently became the object of attack by an aggressive Hellenism.

19:18-21. The second reflection in the concluding remarks picks up the theme of the metamorphosis of the elements. Creation is transformed for the benefit of the righteous. The metaphor the author uses to convey the quasi-mystical harmony of the exodus event is the symphony of sound. The elements of nature are compared to the varying notes played on a harp. Although the sound of a musical instrument is a new metaphor in the work, there was a fleeting reference to the same idea of creation's adjusting itself for different effects. In the third diptych, the author appealed to the transforming elements of creation to explain the paradoxical food of manna from heaven. Creation was described as tensing and relaxing itself to punish the unjust and to help those who trust in God (16:24). The author wishes to account for the transformation of the permanent elements of creation using the metaphor of a symphonic melody. Just as the notes of a melody may vary or stay the same to give shape to a harmonious tune, so too does creation exert itself to bring about a harmony of creation and salvation.

The various schools of Greek philosophy habitually spoke of four elements of nature: water, earth, fire, and air. The author's subsequent explanation of the transforming elements in the exodus deals with only three of these: land, water, and fire (vv. 19-21). Although the author may appear to be using technical language from physics and music to forge harmony, the argument is essentially a poetic one lacking the precision of both physics and musical science.

In order to present an account of permanence and variation for the "miracle stories" of the exodus, the author appeals to an ancient Greek

145. For references to allegations and polemics against Jewish views of aliens by pagan authors, see David Winston, *The Wisdom of Solomon,* AB 43 (New York: Doubleday, 1979) 327-28.
146. Philo *Moses* 1.36.
147. Ibid.

tradition. Under the influence of the Pythagoreans, various Greek philosophical schools would use the analogy of musical harmony to explain or to present the order of the universe.[148] Although the author may lack detail and precision in presenting the metaphor, the choice of the concept of a musical harmony is a felicitous one. The author makes use of the analogy of music to explain the creativity of divine action. Through the metaphor of music, God is imagined as an instrumentalist (or even a composer) who plays the various components and multiple variations of human history into a unity and a harmony. The entire midrashic treatment of the exodus is transformed before our eyes into a perspective on a new creation. Harmony is achieved through the transformation of notes in melodies and tones. Injustice is redressed through the salvation of the righteous, which is presented through the lens of a new creation.

The various images the author holds up briefly as a sign of the transforming qualities of creation are taken from the previous diptychs. They are all paradoxical images that deal with land, water, and fire to express punishment of the oppressors and salvation of the righteous. The image of land animals who are transformed into water creatures is a clever description of the passage of the Israelites through the sea (v. 19*a*). The swimming creatures that moved over to land refer to the plague of frogs that invaded all the land of Egypt (v. 19*b*).

The following two verses contain images that highlight the transformed functions of fire and water (vv. 20-21). These images are all taken from the third diptych, which contrasted the plague of rains, storm, and hail to the gift of manna in the desert (16:18-27). Fire burned more strongly in the hail, which rained down upon the crops of the oppressors (16:22); the function of water to quench fire was transformed so that the fire would burn even more strongly (16:17). On the contrary, in favor of the righteous, flames did not consume the flesh of the animals that were sent to plague the oppressors (16:18), nor did the rays of the sun melt the special gift of manna (16:23).

Note that the author concludes the images of the metamorphosis of creation with that of the

gift of "heavenly food" (lit., "food of ambrosia"). The author used two different metaphors for the gift of manna in 16:20, "food of angels" and "bread from heaven" (NAB). In this final image, the "ambrosia" is employed (the food of the gods that brings immortality). The sixth day of creation came to completion with the gift of food to humans and to animals alike: "See, I have given you every plant yielding seed that is upon the face of all the earth, and every tree with seed in its fruit; you shall have them for food" (Gen 1:29 NRSV). In Wisdom, the gift of manna as "heavenly food" occurs also after the transformation of creation through water, land, and animals. This situation of the gift of food parallels the situation in Genesis where God's generous gift of vegetation to humanity for food takes place at the end of creation, on the sixth day, after the separation of light and darkness, earth and waters, and the creation of the animals. By mentioning the gift of the manna as the culmination of the reflection on the exodus, the author places the exodus into the context of a new creation. Just as a life of justice achieved through the gift of wisdom brings immortality, so also divine intervention on behalf of the righteous brings the gift of immortality.

19:22. The author's final word is directed personally to God as a final hymn of praise. The doxology is formulated through a double, antithetical statement. The first half states the praise of God positively, "you have exalted and glorified your people." The second half states the praise of God negatively, "and you have not neglected to help them at all times and in all places." This final doxology forms a great inclusion to the doxology that was begun at the outset of the re-reading of the exodus narrative (10:20-21). It is an apt ending that focuses on the fidelity of God to a people who have experienced trials and hardship. The doxology is a confirmation of the validity of the opening exhortation of the entire work: "Love righteousness, you rulers of the earth . . . and seek the Lord with uprightness of heart" (1:1, author's trans.). The author's praise of God at the end of the book does not refer only to the divine interventions throughout the exodus (chaps. 11–19). Since the midrashic treatment of the exodus is meant to be a concrete example of the author's argument supporting God's fidelity to the just and of the author's praise of divine wisdom, the dox-

---

148. Aristotle *Metaphysica* I 5,986a3; *De mundo* 5,396b,7; Plato *Republic* VII 12,530d.

ology refers to God's fidelity, expressed in all three parts of the book. It includes the praise of God's fidelity to the just who suffer unjustly throughout history (chaps. 1–6). And it includes the praise of God's wisdom, which continuously accompanies humanity (chaps. 6–10). The midrashic treatment of the exodus confirms God's fidelity to the just and reveals the wisdom of God that forges a harmony of creation and salvation. What begins as an exhortation to seek God and love justice ends with a personal dialogue of praise to God.

REFLECTIONS

1. The author describes the extraordinary deliverance of the Israelites in the exodus through the imagery of a new creation. The very elements and creatures of the universe undergo transformation to effect a harmony of justice. Although this is not necessarily an innovation on the part of the author (cf. God as creator and redeemer, Isaiah 48; a new creation, Isa 65:17-25; the valley of dry bones, Ezek 37:1-14), this idea has followed the author's reflection throughout the work. There is a continuity in the mind of the author between the positive forces of God's creation and the extraordinary interventions of salvation.

This continuity, perhaps, has not been so boldly depicted in any other biblical work. Moments of salvation and deliverance are understood as being rooted in the positive forces of creation itself. Creation wages a battle against injustice and strives to support the efforts of the just. The explanation for the positive role of the universe is provided in the first two parts of the book. The universe is God's creature, and there is no "destructive poison" in its forces (1:14). It has been fashioned according to God's Word and divine wisdom (9:1-2). The author's tangible example of the world's positive forces is the foundational experience of the exodus. From a reflection on God's fidelity to the righteous in history, the author formulates a paradigm of creation and salvation for the present and the future.

One concrete effect that this continuity of creation and salvation offers is a set of criteria for assessing perspectives of theology. It is relatively easy to truncate creation from salvation, and vice versa, in our visions and theologies of life. A theological perspective that is one-sided in favor of salvation and redemption may offer a pessimistic and derogatory view of the natural forces of creation, and even of the human spirit. Creation and humanity become crushed at the expense of maintaining the extraordinary signs of God's redemption. On the contrary, a theological perspective that is one-sided in favor of creation and the harmonious force of the human spirit may neglect to assess the horrors of injustice. The book of Wisdom has an extraordinary coherence that allows the reader to view the horrors of injustice in the context of a world that is marked through and through with the beauty and wisdom of God.

2. The image of the symphonic harmony at the end of the book is an invitation to contemplate the extraordinary fidelity of God. Where the author has earlier provided somewhat philosophical arguments for the defense of virtue and the critique of injustice, the author now moves to the level of quasi-mystical language. Music has that capacity of suppressing one level of thought in order to heighten another level. The image of the symphonic harmony that God achieves in orchestrating the universe is an image that raises us to the level of contemplating God's fidelity tangibly in our lives. God's fidelity engulfs the paradoxes involved in life and death, in virtue and injustice, in apparent strength and weakness.

3. The final doxology bolsters the hope of those who suffer unjustly. The entire series of reflections in the book is brought to a conclusion that focuses on the enduring relationship between God and the righteous. God is the faithful one. God has not abandoned the just who suffered an ignoble death at the hands of the wicked. God has not abandoned the righteous in the course of their tenuous journey through the wilderness. Through the wisdom of God, which directs the forces of creation (7:7–8:21) and illumines the paths of humans (9:9-18), people are taught to trust in the path of justice. Despite weakness, despite the apparent power of injustice, people who follow the path of justice are not abandoned to the despair of death. Instead of ultimate death, the just will find themselves giving thanks to God in the community of the faithful.

THE BOOK OF SIRACH

INTRODUCTION, COMMENTARY, AND REFLECTIONS
BY
JAMES L. CRENSHAW

THE BOOK OF
SIRACH

INTRODUCTION

I n English Bibles the titles for the book under consideration lack consistency. The NRSV calls it "Ecclesiasticus, or the Wisdom of Jesus Son of Sirach." The TNK, or new Jewish translation, opts for "Ecclesiasticus," a title derived from many Latin Vulgate manuscripts. The GNB uses "Sirach: the Wisdom of Jesus, Son of Sirach (Ecclesiasticus)," and the REB has "Ecclesiasticus or the Wisdom of Jesus son of Sirach." This commentary refers to the book as Sirach and designates its author as Ben Sira.

WISDOM LITERATURE IN THE BIBLE

The books of Proverbs, Job, and Ecclesiastes differ markedly from the rest of the Old Testament, in both style and content. Their closest parallels occur outside the Bible, particularly in ancient Egyptian and Mesopotamian literature associated with educational contexts, either in the training of courtiers or the instruction of temple personnel. On the basis of sustained interest in wisdom within these biblical texts, scholars have labeled them "wisdom literature."[1] Specialists in Egyptian and Mesopotamian literature have adopted

---

1. One can obtain entry into this realm of discourse from several introductions, most notably James L. Crenshaw, *Old Testament Wisdom* (Atlanta: John Knox, 1981); Gerhard von Rad, *Wisdom in Israel* (Nashville: Abingdon, 1972); and Roland E. Murphy, *The Tree of Life* (New York: Doubleday, 1990). Several volumes of collected essays cover the entire spectrum of ancient wisdom, particularly *The Sage in Israel and the Ancient Near East,* eds. John G. Gammie and Leo G. Perdue (Winona Lake: Eisenbrauns, 1990); *In Search of Wisdom,* eds. Leo G. Perdue, Bernard Brandon Scott, and William Johnson Wiseman (Louisville: Westminster/John Knox, 1993); James L. Crenshaw, *Urgent Advice and Probing Questions* (Macon, Ga.: Mercer University Press, 1995); and *Wisdom in Ancient Israel,* eds. John Day, Robert P. Gordon, and H. G. M. Williamson (Cambridge: Cambridge University Press, 1995).

this nomenclature,[2] although it brings together texts with quite different settings and purposes.

Egyptian literature in this genre arose in the third millennium BCE in connection with the instruction of rulers, at first given by pharaohs and later by counselors who taught potential rulers. Several texts have survived the ravages of time, including *The Instruction of Ptah-hotep, The Instruction of Amenemope, The Instruction of Ani, The Instruction of Ankhsheshanky,* and Papyrus Insinger. In addition, several scribal texts illuminate the educational enterprise, attesting to lazy students and vigorous disciplinary measures by teachers. A text called *A Satire of the Trades* or *The Teaching for Duauf* makes fun of several occupations and praises the profession of the scribe above all others.[3]

Scribal texts from Sumerian times in ancient Mesopotamia describe conditions at the school house (*edubba*) and indicate that similar conditions existed there as in Egypt. A Sumerian instruction attributed to Šuruppak advises his son about the duties of kingship. An early prototype of the book of Job and a collection of Sumerian proverbs round out this early literature from Sumer.[4] Babylonian texts of this kind include *Counsels to a Prince,* various collections of proverbs, and parallels to the books of Job (*I Will Praise the Lord of Wisdom, The Babylonian Theodicy*) and Ecclesiastes (*The Dialogue of a Master and His Slave*).[5] *The Sayings of Ahiqar,* an Aramaic document, purports to have come from an adviser to an Assyrian king, Sennacherib (704–681 BCE). This text of early "Jewish" wisdom was enormously popular, being translated into several languages.[6] Although very little evidence of Canaanite wisdom has been preserved, many interpreters think that these peoples must also have had such texts.[7]

Resemblances between biblical wisdom and these extra-biblical texts from Egypt and Mesopotamia sometimes are so striking that a relationship of some kind appears likely. Most noteworthy is the case of *The Instruction of Amenemope* and a collection within the book of Proverbs, specifically Prov 22:17–23:33, where eleven sayings overlap.[8] The

---

2. W. G. Lambert, *Babylonian Wisdom Literature* (Oxford: Clarendon, 1960); and Miriam Lichtheim, *Late Egyptian Wisdom Literature in the International Context: A Study of Demotic Instructions,* OBO 52 (Fribourg: Fribourg University Press, 1983).

3. Miriam Lichtheim, *Ancient Egyptian Literature,* 3 vols. (Berkeley: University of California Press, 1973, 1976, 1980), includes wisdom literature among other genres, offering fresh translations of all the texts referred to above.

4. In addition to Lambert's translation of these texts, see Bendt Alster, *The Instructions of Šuruppak: A Sumerian Proverb Collection,* Mesopotamia 2 (Copenhagen: Akademisk Forlag, 1974); *Studies in Sumerian Proverbs,* Mesopotamia 3 (Copenhagen: Akademisk Forlag, 1975); and *Proverbs of Ancient Sumer: The World's Earliest Proverb Collection* (Bethesda, Md.: CDL, 1996).

5. Translations can be found in *Ancient Near Eastern Texts Relating to the Old Testament,* ed. James B. Pritchard, 3rd ed. (Princeton, N.J.: Princeton University Press, 1969).

6. James M. Lindenberger, *The Aramaic Proverbs of Ahiqar* (Baltimore: Johns Hopkins University Press, 1983).

7. No satisfactory study exists, as one can readily see from Loren R. Mack-Fisher's two entries in Gammie and Perdue, *The Sage in Israel and the Ancient Near East.* The first, "A Survey and Reading Guide to the Didactic Literature of Ugarit: Prolegomenon to a Study on the Sage" (67-80) suffers badly from an ill-defined grasp of wisdom literature, and the second, "The Scribe (and Sage) in the Royal Court at Ugarit" (109-15) fares no better.

8. See Harold C. Washington, *Wealth and Poverty in the Instruction of Amenemope and the Hebrew Proverbs,* SBLDS 142 (Atlanta: Scholars Press, 1994); Glendon E. Bryce, *A Legacy of Wisdom: The Egyptian Contribution to the Wisdom of Israel* (Lewisburg: Bucknell University Press, 1979). Both assess the relationship between these two texts from different countries. Nili Shupak, *Where Can Wisdom Be Found? The Sage's Language in the Bible and in Ancient Egyptian Literature,* OBO 130 (Fribourg & Göttingen: University Press & Vandenhoeck & Ruprecht, 1993), offers a valuable analysis of linguistic affinities between Israelite and Egyptian sages.

---

similarities between the book of Job and earlier prototypes from Mesopotamia are only slightly less remarkable, as is the affinity of Ecclesiastes with the ideas put forward in *The Dialogue of a Master and His Slave* and the *Epic of Gilgamesh,* a story about a hero who goes in search of eternal life and retrieves a branch from the tree of life, thanks to advice from the survivor of the flood, Utnapishtim, only to lose it to a serpent.[9]

These close similarities in teachings from three distinct environments in the ancient Near East illustrate a characteristic of wisdom literature: its tendency to present ideas in a universalistic context, one grounded in creation.[10] To the sages, truth was not bound by national ties. Nothing specifically Israelite appears in the books of Proverbs, Job, and Ecclesiastes. Scholars have often noted an absence in these texts of anything about the patriarchs Abraham, Isaac, and Jacob; nothing about early leaders like Moses, Joshua, Samuel; no mention of the judges; no celebration of Israelite kings—except to attribute wisdom literature to Solomon—and no mention of the prophets or a covenant between the Lord and Israel, a special people. In short, the entire history of salvation is missing from these texts. For this reason, wisdom literature has been largely ignored until recently in efforts to describe the theology of the Bible.[11]

Besides being applicable to all people, wisdom literature addresses the fundamental question, "What promotes well-being?" It offers advice on coping with difficult circumstances, in a sense giving parental counsel to growing children, but also offering popular advice to people of all ages. One type of wisdom literature explores existential questions, chiefly the matter of innocent suffering and what this implies about divine justice. Naturally, this questioning attitude does not stop short of asking about death and its consequences.[12]

Another characteristic of this literature is its preoccupation with the search for wisdom, which appears as a feminine personification associated with God in the creative process. She also actively woos young men to deeper intellectual and moral pursuits; in this endeavor she has a rival, folly, also personified as a woman. Often called a foreign woman, or strange, she seduces young men with the aid of powerful rhetoric (cf. Prov 9:17).[13]

The extent of biblical wisdom has elicited considerable debate, some interpreters wishing

9. Alexander Heidel, *The Gilgamesh Epic and Old Testament Parallels* (Chicago: University of Chicago Press, 1946); Jeffrey Tigay, *The Evolution of the Gilgamesh Epic* (Philadelphia: Fortress, 1982); Jeffrey Tigay, *Empirical Models for Biblical Criticism* (Philadelphia: Fortress, 1985); Jack M. Sasson, "Gilgamesh Epic," *ABD* 2:1024-1027; William L. Moran, "The Gilgamesh Epic: A Masterpiece from Ancient Mesopotamia," in *Civilizations of the Ancient Near East,* ed. Jack M. Sasson (New York: Scribner's, 1995) 4:2327-2336.

10. Leo G. Perdue, *Wisdom and Creation: The Theology of Wisdom Literature* (Nashville: Abingdon, 1994).

11. In addition to the last-cited work, see Ronald E. Clements, *Wisdom in Theology* (Grand Rapids: Eerdmans, 1992). William P. Brown, *Character in Crisis: A Fresh Approach to the Wisdom Literature of the Old Testament* (Grand Rapids: Eerdmans, 1996), emphasizes the development of moral character in the sapiential literature; Joseph Blenkinsopp, *Wisdom and Law in the Old Testament* (Oxford: Oxford University Press, 1995), draws attention to the ordering of society in ancient Israel, one dubiously located in the school by E. W. Heaton, *The School Tradition of the Old Testament* (Oxford: Clarendon, 1994). Lennart Boström, *The God of the Sages: The Portrayal of God in the Book of Proverbs,* CBOTS 29 (Lund: Almqvist & Wiksell, 1990); James L. Crenshaw, "The Concept of God in Old Testament Wisdom," in Perdue et al., *In Search of Wisdom,* 1-18 (reprinted in Crenshaw, *Urgent Advice and Probing Questions,* 191-205), and James L. Crenshaw, "The Contemplative Life," in Sasson, *Civilizations of the Ancient Near East,* 4:2445-2457.

12. James L. Crenshaw, "The Shadow of Death in Qoheleth," in *Israelite Wisdom* (Philadelphia: Fortress, 1979) 205-16; reprinted in Crenshaw, *Urgent Advice and Probing Questions,* 573-85.

13. J. N. Aletti, "Seduction et parole en Proverbs 1–9," *VT* 27 (1977) 129-44.

to broaden the category to include much of the Bible (e.g., Genesis 1–11; Deuteronomy; the story of David's rise to power and the succession, 2 Samuel 9–20; 1 Kings 1–2; Esther; Jonah).[14] These attempts merely demonstrate the fact that sages did not own a distinct vocabulary but used the ordinary language of their time. Their influence does seem to manifest itself in the book of Psalms, especially in 37; 49; and 73.

Sirach definitely belongs to biblical wisdom, although its teachings represent a transition from a nonspecific national audience to Jewish hearers whose intellectual heritage faces obliteration by Hellenism. Its author, Ben Sira, unites the unique legacy of Israel's saving history to the wisdom tradition. Although the language echoes that within the book of Proverbs, the content weaves together an account of the merciful guidance of Israel's Lord with advice on coping with life's eventualities. Like the book of Proverbs, Sirach also praises personified wisdom, further elaborating a myth of her activity at creation and identifying her with the accessible Mosaic law. Ben Sira describes the various professions, like *The Satire of the Trades,* and evidences a strong personal piety resembling that in *The Instruction of Ani.*[15]

A new dimension in Sirach, the praise of Israel's "saints" (men of piety), relates Israelite spiritual leadership to the guidance of wisdom. The other wisdom text, also from the Apocrypha, that develops this approach to Israel's history is the book of Wisdom. Its author praises personified wisdom, now a hypostasis (or manifestation) of God's essential character, and describes the period of the exodus from Egypt as one during which wisdom guided God's people into freedom. Prayer and praise unite in this thoroughly Hellenistic text, one composed in Greek and making extensive use of Greek rhetoric.[16]

THE ORIGINAL TITLE OF THE BOOK AND ITS CONTENTS

The title of this book in most Greek manuscripts identifies its genre and author: Σοφία Ἰησοῦ υἱοῦ Σιραχ (*Sophia Iēsou huiou S(e)irach*, "the Wisdom of Jesus the son of Sirach"). A shorter form occurs in the Syriac text: the Wisdom of Bar Sira (the Wisdom of the Son of Sira). And an altogether different title appears in the Latin tradition, where one finds such descriptive categories as the church book (Ecclesiasticus) in the Vulgate and *Parabolae* ("Wise Sayings") in a Hebrew copy, according to Jerome. On two occasions later Jewish writers preface a citation from Sirach with the words המשל אמר (*hammōšēl 'āmar,* "the one who spoke in Proverbs"). The tenth-century Jewish scholar Saadia refers to Sirach as ספר מוסר (*sēper mûsār,* "the book of Discipline/Instruction"), and Rabbi Joseph calls it משלי בן סרא (*mišlê ben sirā',* "The Proverbs of the Son of Sira").

14. Donn F. Morgan, *Wisdom in the Old Testament Traditions* (Atlanta: John Knox, 1981). James L. Crenshaw, "Method in Determining Wisdom Influence upon 'Historical' Literature," *JBL* 88 (1969) 129-42 (= Crenshaw, *Urgent Advice and Probing Questions,* 312-25) evaluates such attempts to find wisdom in various parts of the OT.

15. A shift from confident self-reliance, characteristic of early Egyptian wisdom, seems to occur in the new kingdom with Ani and Amenemope and to grow stronger with the passing of time, as evidenced by demotic instructions (Papyrus Insinger and the *Instruction of Ankhsheshanky*).

16. See James L. Crenshaw, "The Restraint of Reason, the Humility of Prayer," in Crenshaw, *Urgent Advice and Probing Questions,* 206-21.

Although the opening chapter of Sirach has not survived in the Hebrew manuscripts, a remark in Sir 50:27 attributes the book to Simeon ben Eleazar ben Sira, and Sir 51:30 adds: "Thus far the words of Simeon, the son of Jeshua, who is called Ben Sira. The Wisdom of Simeon, the son of Jeshua, the son of Eleazar, the son of Sira." The name "Simeon" (Σίμων Simōn) seems to have come from Sir 50:1, 24a; the probable name of the author is Jeshua ben Eleazar ben Sira. Most Greek and Latin manuscripts partially confirm the identity of the author, reading "the Wisdom of Jesus son of Sira" and "the book of Jesus son of Sirach" respectively. The *ch* ending on Sirach in Greek manuscripts represents either a Greek χ (*chi*), indicating an indeclinable word, or the Hebrew א ('*aleph*).

The prologue to the book, written by Ben Sira's grandson, confirms the tradition that identifies the author's name with Jeshua (Jesus). Ben Sira's patronymic includes the name of his father (Eleazar) and his grandfather (Sira). Within the book several self-references occur, identifying Ben Sira as a professional wise man, describing his disciplined life-style, and inviting young boys to study in his academy.[17]

The first of several authorial self-references, 24:30-34 (cf. 34:12-13; 39:12-15, 32-35; 41:16; 43:32; 50:25-29; 51:1-30) implies that Ben Sira understood his teachings as inspired utterances that began small but grew unexpectedly, like a canal expanding into a huge stream. His own learning, directed initially toward personal enjoyment ("I will water my garden/ and drench my flower-beds" [24:31 NRSV]), soon lost its selfish character and became available to everyone ("Observe that I have not labored for myself alone,/ but for all who seek wisdom" [24:34 NRSV]). In 33:16-18, Ben Sira repeats the latter remark; in doing so he compares himself to gleaners following grape pickers. This image suggests an awareness that the period of divine inspiration is rapidly coming to an end ("Now I was the last to keep vigil," 33:16). Later rabbinic teaching limited the era of divine inspiration to that begun by Moses and ended by Ezra. In the context of discussing the wide experience of educated persons, he mentions extensive travel and the danger associated with journeys in the ancient world (34:9-13).

Within an elaborate treatment of various professions in his day, Ben Sira demonstrates the advantages of being a scholar (38:24–39:11). The similarities to a popular Egyptian text, *The Instruction for Duauf,* often called *A Satire of the Trades,* has long been known and commented on, although the texts differ in tone and subject matter. (Ben Sira does not satirize, and his list of vocations is much shorter.) Having given his strong endorsement of the scribe's profession, yet without disparaging the works of one's hands, Ben Sira states that he has more to say, being full like the full moon, and invites students to blossom comparably, joining knowledge and worship (39:12-15). He proceeds to sing praise to the Creator:

17. Wolfgang Roth, "Sirach: The First Graded Curriculum," *The Bible Today* 29 (1991) 298-302, thinks the book was used as a textbook. The curious silence about circumcision and the sabbath, noted by J. Marböck, *Weisheit im Wandel: Untersuchungen zur Weisheitstheologie bei Ben Sira,* BBB 37 (Bonn: Peter Hanstein, 1971) 93, shows that, whatever its use, a certain haphazardness exists. The same principle was operative in law codes in the Bible, where significant gaps occur, and in ethical texts, such as Proverbs, that omit many important areas of life.

So from the beginning I have
  been convinced of all this
  and have thought it out and
    left it in writing:
All the works of the Lord are good,
  and he will supply every need in its time.
(39:32-33 NRSV)

Expressing a teacher's desire for respect, Ben Sira urges students to observe his instruction (41:16). In the Greek text of 43:32 (but not in the Hebrew, which has the plural "we," Ben Sira acknowledges the inevitable mystery that humans encounter when reflecting on transcendence: "Many things greater than these lie hidden,/ for I have seen but few of his works" (NRSV). An epilogue, 50:25-29, expresses Ben Sira's extreme animosity toward Samaritans, Idumeans, and Philistines (Hellenists), along with some comments reflecting an entirely novel idea in Hebraic thought: pride of authorship.

Instruction in understanding and knowledge
  I have written in this book,
Jesus son of Eleazar son of
    Sirach of Jerusalem,
  whose mind poured forth wisdom.
Happy are those who concern
    themselves with these things,
  and those who lay them to
    heart will become wise.
For if they put them into practice,
    they will be equal to anything,
  for the fear of the Lord is their path.
(50:27-29 NRSV)

The final chapter, consisting of a prayer, an autobiographical poem on wisdom, and an appeal to readers (51:1-30), is rich with personal references, although employing literary conventions. This practice of using traditional language of self-reference already appears in the book of Proverbs (cf. Prov 4:1-9) and Ecclesiastes (Eccl 1:12–2:2 and throughout the book).[18] For this reason, some of the self-references in Sirach may reveal nothing about the author's personal experiences (e.g., adventures during traveling).

The information that Ben Sira enjoyed the leisurely status of a professional teacher suggests that one can find in Sirach the sort of teachings he conveyed to his students. The book stands in the tradition of Proverbs and Ecclesiastes, especially the former. It consists, therefore, of brief aphorisms, maxims, and clever statements in poetic form having to do

---

18. For different views about the frequency of first-person language in Ecclesiastes and its function, see James L. Crenshaw, *Ecclesiastes,* OTL (Philadelphia: Westminster, 1987); and Michael V. Fox, *Qoheleth and His Contradictions,* JSOTSup 71 (Sheffield: Almond, 1989).

with practical daily existence.[19] Like the initial collection in Proverbs (Proverbs 1–9), the sayings in Sirach frequently make up brief paragraphs on a particular topic. The subjects range widely, extending from inner feelings, like a sense of shame,[20] to external behavior, such as slander, from deeply religious acts of charity to self-serving conduct at banquets, from proper attitudes toward money to the disgrace of being reduced to begging, from various kinds of friends to the trouble occasioned by bad daughters, and much more.

The teachings also take up existential issues, such as sickness and death,[21] wrestling with the ethical question of whether one should consult a physician, who in popular imagination was seen to interfere with divine punishment for sin. Ben Sira takes no refuge in belief in a future life, and that refusal to do so allows the matter of divine justice—or more correctly its absence—to press heavily on him, as it did on the author of the book of Job.[22] This vexing problem surfaces frequently in argumentative contexts, suggesting that Ben Sira encountered a vocal group who denied God's just governance of the world. Ben Sira subscribed to traditional religious teachings and expressed his own faith quite tangibly, either in prayer or in hymnic praise. Moreover, he identified the divine revelation in the Torah with the figure of wisdom, who descended from heaven to dwell in Jerusalem. True knowledge, as he saw it, consisted of worship, its origin and destination.

Ben Sira's teachings have no discernible order, except for the lengthy section praising faithful men (אנשי חסד *anšê ḥesed*; 44:1–50:24), and even there some confusion occurs as to actual sequence.[23] Occasional vocatives ("my son") give the book an appearance of

19. Research in the area of OT wisdom has made significant progress, yet without actually clarifying the precise sociological context within which ancient sages worked. For an understanding of the complex issues, see Gerhard von Rad, *Wisdom in Israel* (London: SCM, 1972); James L. Crenshaw, *Old Testament Wisdom* (Atlanta: John Knox, 1981); Roland E. Murphy, *The Tree of Life* (New York: Doubleday, 1990); R. N. Whybray, *The Intellectual Tradition in the Old Testament* (Berlin: Walter de Gruyter, 1974); Claus Westermann, *The Roots of Wisdom* (Louisville: Westminster/John Knox, 1995); Claus Westermann, *Forschungsgeschichte zur Weisheitsliteratur 1950–1990,* AzT 71 (Stuttgart: Calwer, 1991); Stuart Weeks, *Israelite Wisdom,* OTM (Oxford: Clarendon, 1994).

20. Jack T. Sanders, "Ben Sira's Ethics of Caution," *HUCA* 50 (1979) 73-106.

21. Friedrich Vinzenz Reiterer, "Deutung und Wertung des Todes durch Ben Sira," *Die Alttestamentliche Botschaft als Wegweisung: Festschrift für Heinz Reinelt,* ed. Josef Zmijemski (Stuttgart: Katholisches Bibelwerk, 1990) 203-36; the focus of attention in this article falls on Sir 41:1-4. L. J. Prockter, " 'His Yesterday and Yours Today' (Sir 38:22): Reflections on Ben Sira's View of Death," *J Sem* 2 (1990) 44-56, claims that Ben Sira combines Jewish piety with the best of popular Hellenistic philosophy, accepting life and death as part of God's providential order, like a good Stoic.

22. On theodicy as perceived by biblical authors, see James L. Crenshaw, ed., *Theodicy in the Old Testament* (Philadelphia: Fortress, 1983), particularly the opening essay, "Introduction: The Shift from Theodicy to Anthropodicy," 1-16. See also Crenshaw, *Urgent Advice and Probing Questions,* 141-54.

23. Interpreters usually emphasize the random character of the teachings in Sirach, viewing the book as a compendium of the accumulated lectures of a lifetime of work, with no fundamental structure. Rejecting a theory of accidental juxtaposition of wholly unrelated teachings, Wolfgang Roth, "On the Gnomic-Discursive Wisdom of Jesus Ben Sirach," *Semeia,* 17 (1980) 59-79, thinks Ben Sira wrote an original book consisting of 1:1–23:27 and 51:1-30, later supplementing this first edition with three additional units (24:1–32:13; 32:14–38:23; 38:24–50:24, 29). A prologue introduces each new section (24:1-29; 32:14–33:15; 38:24–39:11), and an autobiographical note intervenes between the prologue and the body of the unit (in contrast to the original edition, where prologues occur [1:1–2:18; 4:11-19; 6:18-37; 14:20–15:10], but no autobiographical note). Roth sees 39:2-3 as programmatic for Ben Sira's "hermeneutic-pedagogic theory: from understanding to explanation, from assimilation to exposition, from learning to teaching, from apprenticeship to mastery" (ibid., 63). In Ben Sira's oral instructions (e.g., 6:35; 17:10; 25:9; 42:15–43:33; 44–50), he sees a forerunner to *haggadah* (homiletic discourse); in other teachings (18:30–19:30; 20:27-31; 31:12–32:13) he recognizes early *halakah* (legal instruction). Roth thinks Ben Sira's warning against exceeding the scope of assignments (3:21-22) means exactly that: Stick to the day's lesson (ibid., 64). Roth also believes that Ben Sira organized the original four sections alphabetically: אב (*'āb,* "father") in 3:1-16; בשת (*bōšet,* "shame") in 4:20-28; גאות (*gā'ôt,* "arrogance") in 7:17 and 10:5-18; דעת (*da'at,* "knowledge") in 16:25b–23:27, following the order of the first four letters in the Hebrew alphabet (ibid., 74). The first two sections comprise, in Roth's view, elementary instruction; the third section "is more hortative-ethical and society oriented in character," while the fourth is more explorative-theological and individualistic (ibid., 74-75).

actual classroom use, although this form of address is standard in wisdom literature, occurring in ancient Sumerian and Egyptian instructions and in Proverbs. The expressions "father" and "son" eventually came to be used for "teacher" and "student." The advice in the book of Sirach certainly accords with the supposition that a professional teacher is busily at work in Jerusalem preparing his Jewish students to cope with reality in a Hellenistic environment (50:27).

Viewing the book as a text for the academy, Wolfgang Roth understands the book in terms of "seven teaching units set off from each other through brief passages that reassure and encourage the struggling student."[24] In his view, the book moves from simple matters to more complex ones on the assumption that students learn by stages. Moreover, Ben Sira uses himself as an example, describing his own progress from early discipline to later success. Marking the stages of a student's progress, an exhortation to prepare for testing (2:1-18) leads to instruction about filial devotion and duty to associates (2:7–4:10). A call to cling to wisdom (4:11-19) then introduces section two, an instruction on sincerity and justice, on humility, consistency, and friendship (4:20–6:17). An exhortation to accept wisdom's fetters follows introducing section three, teaching about social issues (7:1–14:19). The fourth section (15:11–23:27) praises students for staying in Wisdom's shelter, debates the matter of free will, and closes with a discourse by Wisdom (24:1-27). The fifth section (25:1–33:15) deals with social relationships in general, giving a "mini-sociology of early Judaism." The sixth section (33:19–39:11), introduced by a report on Ben Sira's progress (33:16-18), deals with such intimate issues as dreams and the inner springs of piety (providence, prayer, temperance, and illness), "a sort of mini-psychology." The seventh section (39:16–50:24) begins with a reflection on divine presence in human thinking and experience (39:16–42:14) and treats God's presence in the universe (42:15–43:35), reaching its climax in the praise of faithful Israelites (44:1–50:24), "a theological survey."[25]

THE HISTORICAL SETTING

A prologue introduces the Greek translation of Sirach. Ben Sira's grandson, who rendered the Hebrew text into Greek for the Jewish community in Egypt, gives the precise date of his arrival in Egypt as the thirty-eighth year of Euergetes. That epithet was applied to only two Lagid rulers, Ptolemy III Euergetes I (246–221 BCE) and Ptolemy VII Physkon Euergetes II (170–164, and 146–117 BCE). Only the latter king held office long enough to meet the translator's specified thirty-eight years; the date 132 BCE, therefore, marks his entry into Egypt. The translation was completed after the death of Euergetes II in 117 BCE (note the participle συγχρονίσας [sygchronisas], which ordinarily implies simultaneity, hence, "I was there as long as Euergetes reigned").[26]

24. Ibid., 302.
25. Ibid., 298-302.
26. Rudolf Smend, *Die Weisheit des Jesus Sirach erklärt* (Berlin: Reimer, 1906) 3-4.

Ben Sira lavishly praises a high priest named Simeon, son of Jochanan (called Onias in some Greek MSS). From 219 to 196 BCE, Simeon II was high priest in Jerusalem, which accords well with the information provided by Ben Sira's grandson. The grandfather lived during Simeon's rule over the religious life of the Jews, and Ben Sira vividly describes an occasion in which the high priest presided over the ritual at the Temple on a special holy day, perhaps the Day of Atonement, or possibly the daily whole offering.[27] The tone of Ben Sira's remarks about Simeon suggests that he had already died.

Assuming that Ben Sira lived during Simeon's tenure as high priest, when did he die? One thing is certain: He does not mention the social chaos that erupted during the Maccabean revolt against Syrian oppression in 167 BCE, although that seethed for some time prior to open resistance. In 175 BCE the Seleucid ruler Antiochus IV Epiphanes came to power, intensifying the policy of Hellenization already in force. Jason, the son of the high priest Simeon, joined in this effort, having replaced his own brother, Onias III, in that office, a prize secured through a bribe of 360 silver talents, plus the promise to hasten Hellenization through the construction of a gymnasium in Jerusalem. According to 2 Macc 4:23-26, the prize of the office of high priest later went to Menelaus, who offered an even higher sum to Antiochus.

In 167 BCE, this Seleucid king went so far as to proscribe Judaism, forbidding the celebration of festivals and sacrifices, the practice of circumcision and observance of dietary laws, and setting up a statue of Zeus over the altar in the Temple at Jerusalem. The horrified author of Dan 8:13; 9:27; 11:31; and 12:11 designates this statue "the abomination of desolation." Ben Sira has nothing to say about these disturbing events, and one can plausibly assume that he died before they took place. On the basis of a somewhat nostalgic depiction of Simeon, seemingly directed at his successor, Onias, and urging him to imitate his father's good deeds, scholars generally date Sirach in the period between 195 and 180 BCE. A date c. 185 BCE seems likely.[28]

27. F. O'Fearghail, "Sir 50, 5-21: Yom Kippur or The Daily Whole Offering," *Bib* 59 (1978) 301-16, argues that Ben Sira describes the daily whole offering rather than the Day of Atonement. Alexander Di Lella accepts this view; see Patrick W. Skehan and Alexander A. Di Lella, *The Wisdom of Ben Sira*, AB 39 (New York: Doubleday, 1987) 550-51.

28. James D. Martin, "Ben Sira—A Child of His Time," in *A Word in Season: Essays in Honour of William McKane*, eds. James D. Martin and Philip R. Davies, JSOTSup 42 (Sheffield: JSOT, 1986) 141-61, examines Ben Sira's teachings in the light of emerging apocalypticism in the Jewish world. The changing circumstances associated with the Babylonian defeat of Jerusalem and dislocation of a large segment of the Judean populace contributed to an attitude quite different from earlier optimism. Portions of the books of Ezekiel (chaps. 38–39), Isaiah (chaps. 26–29), and Zechariah (chaps. 9–14) reflect an early apocalypticism (sometimes called proto-apocalypticism). Full-blown developments occur in the books of Daniel and Revelation. Apocalyptic thought includes, among other things, a belief in a transcendent God (momentarily inactive in Israel's history), the temporary victory of evil, and imminent judgment on all peoples. This message assumes the form of revelation attributed to ancient worthies but kept hidden for years, strange imagery involving animals and beasts, coded language, heavenly journeys, visions, and martial conflicts. Sometimes a work asks difficult questions and ponders the existence of wickedness in a world supposedly ruled by a benevolent deity (cf. 2 Esdras, a masterpiece that asks why God's people are subjected to such harsh treatment from persons less devout than they). The idea of a final battle between the forces of good and the forces of evil finds expression in *The Wars of the Sons of Light Against the Sons of Darkness*, a text from Qumran; earlier expressions of this conflict occur in Ezekiel 38–39 and Joel 3–4 (Eng. 2:28-32; 3:1-21). The closest kinship with Ben Sira's panegyric of the fathers exists, in Martin's view, in Wisdom and 1 Maccabees (ibid., 145); such cult-centered historiography may thus be the origin of apocalyptic's historical expression (ibid., 147), although Ben Sira opposes idle speculation and apocalyptic excesses (ibid., 154). For Ben Sira in the Hellenistic context, see Martin Hengel, *Judaism and Hellenism*, I-II (Philadelphia: Fortress, 1974) 131-53.

Seleucid kings had not always looked on Jews as enemies. Antiochus III the Great (223–187 BCE) waged aggressive campaigns from Asia Minor to India, then turned his attention to Egypt. He was defeated at Raphia in 217 by Ptolemy IV Philopator, but succeeded in crushing the Egyptian army at Panium in 198 during the reign of Ptolemy V Epiphanes (203–181 BCE). The Jewish historian Josephus claims that the Jews assisted Antiochus in these early years, providing supplies and elephants and fighting to remove the garrison of Egyptian soldiers in the citadel at Jerusalem.

In gratitude, Antiochus made a number of concessions: (1) to help defray the cost of daily sacrifices; (2) to exempt from taxation the materials for building the Temple; (3) to obligate the people to live according to the Torah; (4) to exempt from taxation the senate, priests, scribes, and sacred singers; (5) to exempt Jerusalem citizens from taxation for three years; and (6) to let the remaining citizens reduce their taxes by a third and to emancipate slaves.[29] When the Syrians were routed by Romans at Magnesia in 190 BCE, the situation changed noticeably, and, pressed for revenues, Antiochus rescinded the exemptions from taxes and reduced the privileges previously granted to Jews. In 187, Antiochus was assassinated at Elymais while attacking one of Bel's sacred places to make payment to Rome. His son, Seleucus IV Philopator (187–175 BCE), succeeded him. Seleucus's treatment of the Jews was somewhat ambiguous, at first restoring the privileges earlier granted them by his father, but later sending Heliodorus to confiscate the treasures in the Temple at Jerusalem (2 Macc 3:4-40). In 175, Seleucus IV Philopator was assassinated, and Antiochus IV Epiphanes (175–164 BCE) assumed the reins. Among Jews he earned the nickname "Epimanes" ("Madman"), from his cruel treatment of them.[30]

The internal situation reflected the political climate abroad. Opportunists chose sides, hoping to find themselves on the side of the eventual winners in the struggle for power. Competing families—Tobiads and Oniads—strove for popular support, and old rivalries—Jews versus Samaritans—extended the dissension beyond the streets of Jerusalem. Avarice and greed ran free, touching the highest office, turning the religious priesthood into a coveted prize up for grabs to the highest bidder. Jason's and Menelaus's willingness to compromise ancestral practices in favor of Greek ways demonstrates the degradation of the priesthood and explains Ben Sira's glowing praise of Simeon, who stood as a sharp contrast to the weak son, Onias III. Antiochus IV Epiphanes's removal of Onias showed how far a foreign ruler was willing to go in carrying out his policy of Hellenization.

A few allusions in Sirach may suggest the volatile situation. In 50:25-26, Ben Sira voices contempt for Idumeans, Philistines (Hellenizers), and Samaritans, and in 7:4-7; 40:25-26; and 50:1, 23-24 (Hebrew text) he may criticize contenders for the office of high priest. Finally, the prayer for renewed deeds of deliverance and signs of divine leadership (36:1-22)

---

29. Josephus *Antiquities of the Jews* 12.138-144.

30. Skehan and Di Lella, *The Wisdom of Ben Sira,* 8-16, sketches this history and locates Ben Sira within the general period 250–175 BCE, with Sirach being written when Ben Sira was an old man, probably about 180 BCE. This interpretation of the data has obtained the status of consensus, rare among biblical critics.

suggests that Ben Sira thought that belief in the ancient experience of divine watchcare could soon disappear from the collective memory.[31] Nevertheless, such remarks fall readily within the historical situation envisioned by an activity for Ben Sira between 200 and 180 BCE.

FORMS OF EXPRESSION

Ben Sira stands in a venerable tradition of wisdom teachers.[32] His speech forms resemble those in Proverbs, Job, and Ecclesiastes, which he studied thoroughly (along with the Torah and prophetic literature).[33] Truth statement and instruction, the base forms of the מָשָׁל (*māšāl*), loosely translated "proverb" but etymologically implying a likeness and an authoritative word, occur with great frequency.

Truth Statements. Often called sentences, truth statements capture fleeting insights and express them in poetic form so as to seize the imagination and linger in memory. They capture the experience of many and couch it in words that individualize the discovery, giving it a timeless quality. Such aphorisms and maxims have the force of legal injunction in some societies;[34] ancient Israelites employed them as incontrovertible evidence. They need only be spoken to command assent: "A new friend is like new wine;/ when it has aged, you can drink it with pleasure" (9:10*b* NRSV). Who can deny that "all living beings become old like a garment,/ for the decree from of old is, 'You must die!' " (14:17 NRSV)? These sentences pronounce judgment on human nature: "A rich person does wrong, and even adds insults;/ a poor person suffers wrong, and must add apologies" (13:3 NRSV); "Like music in time of mourning is ill-timed conversation,/ but a thrashing and discipline

31. J. Marböck, "Das Gebet um die Rettung Zions Sir 36,1-22 (Gr: 33.9-13a; 36,16b-22) im zusammenhang der Geschichtsschau ben Siras," in *Memoria Jerusalem,* ed. J. B. Bauer (Jerusalem and Graz: Akademische Druck-und Verlagsanstalt, 1977) 93-116. In examining this remarkable prayer, Marböck points out that Ben Sira's appeal for renewed action on behalf of an elect people accords with Sir 17:17, which refers to Israel as Yahweh's special portion.

32. Walter Baumgartner, "Die literarischen Gattungen in der Weisheit des Jesus Sirach," *ZAW* 34 (1914) 161-98; James L. Crenshaw, "Sirach," *Harper Bible Commentary* (San Francisco: Harper & Row, 1988) 836-54; James L. Crenshaw, "Wisdom," in *Old Testament Form Criticism,* ed. John H. Hayes, TUMS 2 (San Antonio: Trinity University Press, 1974) 225-64. See also James L. Crenshaw, *Urgent Advice and Probing Questions* (Macon, Ga.: Mercer University Press, 1995).

33. J. L. Koole, "Die Bibel des Ben-Sira," *OTS* 14 (1965) 374-96; Douglas E. Fox, "Ben Sira on OT Canon Again: The Date of Daniel," *WTJ* 49 (1987) 335-50; T. Middendorp, *Die Stellung Jesu Ben Siras zwischen Judentum und Hellenismus* (Leiden: Brill, 1973); Eckhard J. Schnabel, *Law and Wisdom from Ben Sira to Paul: A Tradition-Historical Enquiry into the Relation of Law, Wisdom, and Ethics* (Tübingen: J. C. B. Mohr, 1985). The last two authors calculate the extent of Ben Sira's allusions to scripture (70 allusions to the Torah, 46 to historical books, 51 to prophetic books, and over 160 to the writings, according to Middendorp's reckoning). A more exacting criterion for establishing an allusion would reduce the number appreciably.

34. The advisory nature of sentences, as opposed to mandatory instructions, can no longer be maintained. See James L. Crenshaw, *Prophetic Conflict,* BZAW 124 (Berlin and New York; Walter de Gruyter, 1971), excursus B, " *'eṣa* and *dabar:* The Problem of Authority/Certitude in Wisdom and Prophetic Literature," 116-23; James L. Crenshaw, "Wisdom and Authority: Sapiential Rhetoric and Its Warrants," *Congress Volume Vienna 1980,* SVTP 32 (Leiden: Brill, 1981) 10-29 (see also Crenshaw, *Urgent Advice and Probing Questions,* 326-43); Claus Westermann, "Weisheit im Sprichwort," *Schalom. Festschrift A. Jepsen* (Stuttgart: Calwer Verlag, 1971) 73-85; Claus Westermann, *The Roots of Wisdom* (Louisville: Westminster/John Knox, 1995); Friedemann W. Golka, *The Leopard's Spots* (Edinburgh: T. & T. Clark, 1993).

are at all times wisdom" (22:6 NRSV).[35] Long experience with poor learners rests behind this one: "Whoever teaches a fool is like one who glues potsherds together,/ or who rouses a sleeper from deep slumber" (22:9 NRSV). Fools in biblical wisdom were morally bankrupt, not devoid of intellect.

These ancient truth statements came in various forms: "Better are the God-fearing who lack understanding/ than the highly intelligent who transgress the law" (19:24 NRSV). Echoing a sentiment within Proverbs, this truth statement expresses the pathos of being dependent on others: "Better is the life of the poor under their own crude roof/ than sumptuous food in the house of others" (29:22 NRSV). Failing to speak at the right time evokes the following comment: "Better are those who hide their folly/ than those who hide their wisdom" (41:15 NRSV).

Numerical sayings enable teachers to combine similar things to achieve maximum effect when the last item finally appears:

> I take pleasure in three things,
>> and they are beautiful in the sight of God
>>> and of mortals:
> agreement among brothers and sisters,
>> friendship among neighbors,
> and a wife and a husband who
>> live in harmony. (25:1 NRSV)

Sometimes these sayings become somewhat wordy:

> Two kinds of individuals multiply sins,
>> and a third incurs wrath.
> Hot passion that blazes like a fire
>> will not be quenched until it
>>> burns itself out;
> one who commits fornication with
>> his near of kin
> will never cease until the fire
>> burns him up. (23:16 NRSV)

> At two things my heart is grieved,
>> and because of a third anger comes over me:
> a warrior in want through poverty,
>> intelligent men who are treated contemptuously,

---

35. John J. Pilch, " 'Beat His Ribs While He Is Young' (Sir 30:12): A Window on the Mediterranean World," *BTB* 23 (1993) 101-13, examines the ancient understanding of parenting, concluding that respect for parents was more important than actual deeds and that strict (harsh) discipline fit nicely into such a worldview. His use of modern Mediterranean concepts raises the question of how appropriate is the analogy. Modern educators question the universality of the statement about the value of corporal punishment.

---

and a man who turns back from
    righteousness to sin—
the Lord will prepare him for the sword! (26:28 NRSV)

Some truth statements are introduced by a particle of existence; e.g., שׁ (yēš, "there is").[36]

Some [yēš] people keep silent and are
    thought to be wise,
while others are detested for being talkative.
Some people keep silent because
    they have nothing to say,
while others keep silent because
    they know when to speak. (20:5-6 NRSV)

There are those who work and
    struggle and hurry,
but are so much the more in want.
There are others who are slow and need help,
  who lack strength and abound in poverty;
but the eyes of the Lord look
    kindly upon them;
  he lifts them out of their lowly condition
and raises up their heads
    to the amazement of the many.
(11:11-13 NRSV)

There is the gift that profits you nothing,
    and the gift to be paid back double. (20:10 NRSV)

Some truth statements take the form of benediction or malediction, blessing and curse: "Happy are those who do not blunder with their lips,/ and need not suffer remorse for sin./ Happy are those whose hearts do not condemn them,/ and who have not given up their hope" (14:1-2 NRSV). Ben Sira characterizes pursuit of wisdom in this manner:

Happy is the person who meditates on wisdom
    and reasons intelligently,
who reflects in his heart on her ways
    and ponders her secrets,[37]

36. On this type of proverbial saying, see Pancratius C. Beentjes, " 'Full Wisdom Is Fear of the Lord.' Ben Sira 19, 20-20, 31: Context, Composition and Concept," *EstBib* 47 (1989) 27-45, esp. 37-40. In the existing Hebrew manuscripts, שׁ (yēš) occurs 64 times, involving 46 different verse lines; in 20:5-6, 22-23 they appear in "absolute condensation" (ibid., 37).

37. Martin, "Ben Sira—A Child of His Time," 154, thinks of the warning against seeking hidden things as being aimed at apocalyptic speculation. Others think it refers to Hellenistic philosophy.

pursuing her like a hunter,
>and lying in wait on her paths;
who peers through her windows
>and listens at her doors;
who camps near her house
>and fastens his tent peg to her walls;
who pitches his tent near her,
>and so occupies an excellent lodging place;
who places his children under her shelter,
>and lodges under her boughs;
who is sheltered by her from the heat,
>and dwells in the midst of her glory.
(14:20-27 NRSV)

The benedictions contrast mightily with these maledictions: "Woe to timid hearts and to slack hands,/ and to the sinner who walks a double path!/ Woe to the fainthearted who have no trust!/ Therefore they have no shelter./ Woe to you who have lost your nerve!/ What will you do when the Lord's reckoning comes?" (2:12-14 NRSV). These two forms reflect the sapiential tendency to think in polarities, making clear distinctions between the wise and fools, good and evil.

The simple sentence, or *māšāl,* also occurs as a rhetorical question: "Whose offspring are worthy of honor?/ Human offspring./ Whose offspring are worthy of honor?/ Those who fear the Lord./ Whose offspring are unworthy of honor?/ Human offspring./ Whose offspring are unworthy of honor?/ Those who break the commandments" (10:19 NRSV). Apostrophe, direct rhetorical address, livens the speech about death in 41:1-2: "O death, how bitter is the thought of you/ to the one at peace among possessions,/ who has nothing to worry about and is prosperous in everything,/ and still is vigorous enough to enjoy food!/ O death, how welcome is your sentence/ to one who is needy and failing in strength,/ worn down by age and anxious about everything;/ to one who is contrary, and has lost all patience!" (NRSV).[38]

Instruction. The other base form, instruction, sets the tone for Ben Sira's teaching, for he speaks as an authoritative figure addressing students. The direct address varies from the usual בני (*běnî*), "my son," to "holy sons" (39:13), "children" (3:1), "my children" (23:7; 41:14), and "you who need instruction" (51:23). His prescriptive advice, often resembling brief paragraphs on specific topics, is reinforced with warnings and admonitions, the proverbial dangling carrot employed to motivate people. Frequently, refrains set this material apart from what precedes or follows.

Throughout the book positively expressed instructions alternate with negative ones: "Honor your father by word and deed,/ that his blessing may come upon you" (3:8 NRSV);

---

38. The rhetorical device apostrophe occurs in the final acrostic (alphabetic poem) to capture students' interest and to give the impression of intimacy.

"Do not glorify yourself by dishonoring your father,/ for your father's dishonor is no glory to you" (3:10 NRSV). Frequently these instructions lack motivation, e.g., "Do not be ashamed to confess your sins,/ and do not try to stop the current of a river" (4:26 NRSV). Sometimes a series of instructions is followed by a single motivating clause: "My child, do not cheat the poor of their living,/ and do not keep needy eyes waiting./ Do not grieve the hungry/ or anger one in need./ Do not add to the troubles of the desperate,/ or delay giving to the needy . . . for if in bitterness of soul some should curse you,/ their Creator will hear their prayer" (4:1-6 NRSV). The appeal to reward for good conduct balances threats aimed at misbehavior: "Give to the Most High as he has given to you,/ and as generously as you can afford./ For the Lord is the one who repays,/ and he will repay you sevenfold" (35:12-13 NRSV).

Ben Sira demonstrates a fondness for refrains and repetitive phrases, as if stopping the readers in midthought and suspending them there: "You who fear the Lord, wait for his mercy;/ do not stray, or else you may fall./ You who fear the Lord, trust in him,/ and your reward will not be lost./ You who fear the Lord, hope for good things,/ for lasting joy and mercy" (2:7-9 NRSV; cf. 2:15-17). Similarly:

> Question a friend; perhaps he did not do it;
>   or if he did, so that he may not do it again.
> Question a neighbor; perhaps he did not say it;
>   or if he said it, so that he may not repeat it.
> Question a friend, for often it is slander;
>   so do not believe everything you hear.
>
> .   .   .   .
>
> Question your neighbor before you threaten him;
>   and let the law of the Most High take its course.
> (19:13-15, 17 NRSV)

Other Literary Forms. Besides the two base forms, truth statement and instruction, several other forms of literary expression liven Ben Sira's teaching. He includes two prayers, a rare feature in earlier wisdom (cf. Prov 30:7-9 for a profound invocation of help, presumably from above).[39] In 22:27–23:6, Ben Sira asks for effective control over his speech and thoughts, as well as mastery of pride and illicit sensual desire. This moving expression of piety addresses God as "O Lord, Father and Master of my life" and as "O Lord, Father and God of my life" (23:1, 4 NRSV). Ben Sira welcomes divine chastisement as early warning against repeating one's sins, lest one also become subject to human mockers. The other prayer, 36:1-22, invokes the "God of All," Yahweh, the sacred name of the deity in Jewish literature, and the "God of the ages." Here Ben Sira gives vent to frustration over God's apparent inactivity, praying for renewed signs and defeat of enemies,

---

39. On prayer in wisdom literature, especially in Sirach, see James L. Crenshaw, "The Restraint of Reason, the Humility of Prayer," in Crenshaw, *Urgent Advice and Probing Questions,* 206-21. See also James L. Crenshaw, *Origins: Early Judaism and Christianity in Historical and Ecumenical Perspective,* Brown Judaic Studies, forthcoming.

hastening the day of reckoning.[40] He longs for the return of all exiled Jews, and he asks for pity on Zion. Remembering ancient recitations of Yahweh's mighty deeds on Israel's behalf, together with prophetic promises yet unfulfilled, Ben Sira begs the Lord to confirm the truth of both in his own time.

Several hymns also appear in Sirach, most notably 42:15–43:33 and 51:1-12 (the Hebrew text of MS B after 51:12 has another hymn of sixteen verses modeled on Psalm 136).[41] In these hymns, Ben Sira extols the wonders of the created world in the same way the author of Job did. The awesome power of the Creator and a humble awareness of mystery, still unseen, establish the mood for these hymns. Ben Sira knows that human eyes merely touch the surface, but his exquisite use of poetic imagery suggests that even this limited knowledge is something marvelous. He mentions the way pools put on ice like a breastplate, and he describes frost as pointed thorns. The rapid descent of snow reminds him of birds in the sky. Such poetic flourish does not detract from the impression of order and precision, the existence of complementary pairs, and the purposive attention to design and function where the heavenly bodies are concerned.[42]

Two didactic compositions resemble the hymns, but their mood places more distance between the singer and the Creator (16:24–17:14; 39:12-35). One has the feeling that these learned meditations grew out of rational reflection and studious instruction. Exploring the place of human beings in the universe, they affirm a legitimate role for everything, even those things that seem out of place in a harmonious universe. These didactic compositions function as a defense of divine justice, like the debate form,[43] which Ben Sira uses freely.

Also known from Egyptian wisdom literature, this device to stave off dissent first appears within the Bible in Ecclesiastes: "Do not say, 'Who can have power over me?'/ for the Lord will surely punish you./ Do not say, 'I sinned, yet what has happened to me?'/ for

---

40. Several scholars have addressed the issue of eschatology and messianism in Sirach, usually reaching a minimalist position that only hints of each appear. See James D. Martin, "Ben Sira's Hymn to the Fathers: A Messianic Perspective," in *Crises and Perspectives: Studies in Ancient Near Eastern Polytheism, Biblical Theology, Palestinian Archaeology and Intertestamental Literature: Papers Read at the Joint British-Dutch Old Testament Conference Held at Cambridge, U.K., 1985,* Oudtestamentische Studien, deel 24, ed. A. S. Van der Woude (Leiden: E. J. Brill, 1986) 107-23; Stanley Frost, "Who Were the Heroes? An Exercise in Bitestamentary Exegesis, with Christological Implications," in *The Glory of Christ in the New Testament,* eds. L. D. Hurst and N. T. Wright (Oxford: Clarendon, 1987) 65-172; Burton L. Mack, "Wisdom Makes a Difference: Alternatives to 'Messianic' Configuration," in *Judaisms and Their Messiahs at the Turn of the Christian Era,* eds. Jacob Neusner, William Scott Green, and Ernest S. Frerichs (Cambridge: Cambridge University Press, 1987) 15-48; Robert Hayward, "The New Jerusalem in the Wisdom of Jesus Ben Sira," *ScanJT* 6 (1992) 123-38. A. Caquot, "Ben Sira et le Messianisme, *Sem* 16 (1966) 43-68, finds no evidence for messianism in Sirach. Hayward contrasts the lackluster Greek translation of Sirach 36 with the vibrant Hebrew, arguing that the grandson thought too much emphasis had been put on Zion in the past, an era that was "dead and gone" (Hayward, "The New Jerusalem in the Wisdom of Jesus Ben Sira," 137).

41. C. Deutsch, "The Sirach 51 Acrostic: Confession and Exhortation," *ZAW* 94 (1982) 400-409, studies "the passage as the statement of the sage, the focus of the acrostic." Deutsch emphasizes the affective language and lessons from Ben Sira's own life. Pamela F. Foulkes, " 'To Expound Discipline': The Portrait of the Scribe in Ben Sira," *Pacifica* 7 (1994) 75-84, thinks of Ben Sira as a reflective scholar fit for judicial or ambassadorial posts.

42. Marböck calls it "very abstract, indeed almost philosophical." See J. Marböck, *Weisheit im Wandel: Untersuchungen zur Weisheitstheologie bei Ben Sira,* BBB 37 (Bonn: Peter Hanstein, 1971) 137.

43. On the debate form, see James L. Crenshaw, "The Problem of Theodicy in Sirach: On Human Bondage," *JBL* 94 (1975) 47-64. See also Crenshaw, *Urgent Advice and Probing Questions,* 155-74.

the Lord is slow to anger. . . . Do not say, 'His mercy is great,/ he will forgive the multitude of my sins,'/ for both mercy and wrath are with him,/ and his anger will rest on sinners" (Eccl 5:3-4, 6 NRSV). This debate form warns against presuming too much about God's patience, mercy, and sovereignty. It challenges those who think they can sin with impunity: "Do not say, 'I am hidden from the Lord,/ and who from on high has me in mind?/ Among so many people I am unknown,/ for what am I in a boundless creation?' " (16:17 NRSV).

In two places Ben Sira sings wisdom's praise (1:1-10; 24:1-23), moving beyond Job 28, where wisdom remains altogether inaccessible to human beings, and Prov 8:1-36, where she is present alongside Yahweh as the first act of creation. Ben Sira affirms this earlier tradition, attesting to her innate inaccessibility and declaring her the initial creative act. At the same time, he insists that the Lord dispensed wisdom on all God's works and on those who love God (1:1-10). According to Sirach 24, wisdom searched the whole world for a suitable resting place until the Creator chose Israel as her place of residence. In Zion she blossomed and produced fruit, inviting those who desired her to eat their fill. Ben Sira identifies wisdom with the Mosaic law, making it accessible to everyone in Israel. The universal motif of wisdom's covering the earth like mist gives way to a particularistic tradition. The erotic relationship between wisdom and students, present in Proverbs 8–9, achieves new expression in an acrostic poem that concludes Sirach (51:13-20, 30), an earlier form of which was discovered in cave 11 at Qumran.[44]

Ben Sira also heaps praise on a select group of ancestral heroes (Sir 44:1–50:24).[45] He walks through the gallery of biblical characters, and in doing so prepares the way for a eulogy on the high priest of his day, Simeon. These descriptions resemble Greek encomia in some respects,[46] but suitable antecedents from biblical literature exist.[47] The choice of heroes, highly selective, betrays a decided preference for priestly figures[48] and for others

44. James A. Sanders, *The Dead Sea Psalms Scroll* (Ithaca, N.Y.: Cornell University Press, 1967); James A. Sanders, *The Psalms Scroll of Qumran Cave 11 (11 Q Ps[a]*), DJD 4 (Oxford: Clarendon, 1965). Sanders interprets the psalm as highly erotic, but see T. Muraoka, "Sir 51:13-30. An Erotic Hymn to Wisdom?" *JSJ* 10 (1979) 166-78.

45. The panegyric on ancestral worthies has generated considerable discussion, the most thorough recent studies being those of Burton L. Mack, *Wisdom and the Hebrew Epic: Ben Sira's Hymn in Praise of the Fathers,* Chicago Studies in the History of Judaism (Chicago: University of Chicago Press, 1985); Thomas R. Lee, *Studies in the Form of Sirach 44–50,* SBLDS 75 (Atlanta: Scholars Press, 1986). Other important essays include Maurice Gilbert, "L'eloge de la Sagesse [Siracide 24]," *Revue Théologique* 5 (1974) 326-48; Edmond Jacob, "L'Histoire d'Israel vue par Ben Sira," in *Mélanges bibliques rédigés en l'honneur de André Robert* (Paris: Bloud and Gay, 1958) 288-94.

46. Lee understands the section lauding Israel's heroes as an encomium (a Greek device praising a notable figure; it consisted of a prooemium, a genealogy, a narration of the person's accomplishments, and an epilogue with its concluding exhortation). The object of praise, in this view, is Simeon, not Israel's ancestors. See Lee, *Studies in the Form of Sirach 44–50,* 81. The record of Simeon's predecessors is proof from example. Mack thinks in terms of a hymn with decidedly encomiastic features (*Wisdom and the Hebrew Epic*). Chris A. Rollston, "The Non-Encomiastic Features of Ben Sira 44–50" (M.A. thesis, Emmanuel School of Religion, Johnson City, Tennessee, 1992), challenges their interpretation.

47. The unknown authors of the book of Wisdom and 1 Maccabees imitate Ben Sira's recitation of ancient history with emphasis on human accomplishments. Biblical antecedents of Ben Sira glorify God even when referring to similar history (cf. Psalms 68; 77–78).

48. J. G. Snaith, "Ben Sira's Supposed Love of Liturgy," *VT* 25 (1975) 167-74, plays down the author's priestly interests in favor of prophetic social justice, but John F. A. Sawyer, "Was Jeshua Ben Sira a Priest?" *Proceedings of the Eighth World Congress of Jewish Studies,* Div. A. (Jerusalem: World Union of Jewish Studies, 1982) 65-71, and Saul M. Olyan, "Ben Sira's Relationship to the Priesthood," *HTR* 80 (1987) 261-86, argue persuasively for identifying Ben Sira as a priest/sage. H. Stadelmann, *Ben Sira als Schriftgelehrter,* WUNT 6 (Tübingen: Mohr-Siebeck, 1980), develops the thesis that Ben Sira was a priestly, learned scribe.

who contributed to Israel's cult in some material way. One looks in vain for a woman in the list, despite the presence of remarkable females in the sacred traditions (e.g., Deborah, Huldah, Hannah, Samson's mother, Ruth). Pride of position goes to Aaron and Phinehas, with Moses, David, Solomon, Hezekiah, Josiah, Zerubbabel, and Joshua being invoked for their part in reforming and strengthening the cult of the temple. Prophets who make the list do so on the basis of miraculous acts rather than oracular proclamations. The sequence of heroes follows the canonical divisions, first those characters whose lives are recorded in the Pentateuch; then prophets, including Job; and finally Nehemiah, from the writings. An afterthought leads Ben Sira to return to the beginning, Enoch, and work backward to Adam.

BEN SIRA'S USE OF BIBLICAL TRADITIONS

Although Ben Sira patterns his teaching after Israel's wisdom literature, the extensive praise of ancestral heroes moves outside that body of texts to embrace the whole Hebrew canon.[49] This appeal to special revelation and its confessional attestations marks a radical departure from the books of Proverbs, Job, and Ecclesiastes. Sacred history thus becomes subject matter for consideration, and that shift compromises the fundamental character of wisdom as accessible to all people, regardless of nationality or geographical location.

To be sure, the author of Proverbs 1–9 introduces the notion of divine legislation (תורה *tôrâ*) and discipline (מוסר *mûsār*), together with the concept of reprehensible conduct (תועבה *tô'ebâ*), all of which come perilously close to providing a link with Deuteronomy. Their non-specific use with reference to the will of God and its punitive action against despicable behavior complicates matters and prevents firm resolution of the question of whether the author had Deuteronomy in mind when using these ideas. With Ben Sira, the issue is no longer ambiguous.

The integration of sacred history and wisdom instruction pervades the entire book of Sirach, not just 44:1–50:24. Allusions to Israel's history as recorded in the canon of his day function as examples of praiseworthy conduct and as warnings against deeds that provoke divine anger. No longer content to study nature and human nature in search of instructive analogies, Ben Sira draws freely on the special relationship between an elect people and its deity. He actually quotes King David's response to divine anger occasioned by obedience to a command to number the people, a perplexing story of a vacillating deity that prompted the chronicler to introduce Satan as the instigator of David's action. According to 2 Sam 24:14, David opted to take his chances with an angry Yahweh in preference to three years of famine or three months of fleeing from enemies. Ben Sira

49. J. G. Snaith, "Quotations in Ecclesiasticus," *TThS* 18 (1967) 1-12, finds very little citation of Scripture in Sirach. Other interpreters think Ben Sira made use of an anthological style, using brief phrases with telling effect. On the larger problem of citations, see *It Is Written: Scripture Citing Scripture. Essays in Honour of Barnabas Lindars, SSF*, eds. D. A. Carson and H. G. M. Williamson (Cambridge: Cambridge University Press, 1986).

observes: "Let us fall into the hands of the Lord,/ but not into the hands of mortals;/ for equal to his majesty is his mercy,/ and equal to his name are his works" (2:18 NRSV).

From the book of Genesis, Ben Sira alludes to Adam (Sir 33:10; 40:1), to Eve (Sir 25:24),[50] to Lot (Sir 16:8), to Sodom and Gomorrah (Sir 39:23), to the fallen angels (Sir 16:7), to the flood (Sir 40:10), to the covenant with Noah (Sir 17:12), to the image of God (Sir 17:3), to the creation account (Sir 39:16, 21), and to Jacob's descendants (Sir 23:12). Given the dearth of biblical references to Adam and Eve outside Genesis, Ben Sira's clear mention of Adam in 40:1—only the Greek text has the proper name in 33:10—and his placing on Eve the sole responsibility for the origin of sin show that he was influenced by a growing trend to speculate about such biblical persons as Adam, Eve, and Enoch.

Allusions to incidents associated with the signal event of Israelite history, the exodus, also occur. Ben Sira mentions the six hundred thousand Israelites who perished in the wilderness because of their idolatrous conduct (Sir 16:9-10), as well as the tree that turned bitter water sweet (Sir 38:5). He refers to Yahweh as the "Holy One" (Sir 4:14) and mentions the Sinaitic legislation transmitted through Moses to the people (Sir 24:23).

Sometimes Ben Sira alludes to a cluster of ideas from specific biblical themes. In 24:1-12, he refers to the Yahwistic notion of creation by means of a heavenly mist; to the pillar of cloud that symbolized Yahweh's guiding presence with the Israelites under Moses' leadership; to the tabernacle, also a sign of Yahweh's coming to meet the chosen spokesman for the wandering people; to sacred names—Israel/Jacob, Jerusalem—and to an elect people. Similarly, 36:1-17 mentions divine signs and wonders, echoing those associated with the exodus from Egypt and its immediate aftermath; the regular cultic recitation of Yahweh's "mighty deeds" (צדקות *şĕdāqôt*); the tribes of Jacob and their inheritance, the land promised to Abraham; the people on whom the divine name Yahweh had been pronounced; Israel, the firstborn of God; Zion, the city of God's sanctuary; unfulfilled prophecies uttered in Yahweh's name; and Aaron's priestly blessing.

Such allusions to the major sacral traditions, creation and exodus, also appear within didactic psalms, becoming at times somewhat tedious. Ben Sira stops short of giving a

---

50. Jack Levison, "Is Eve to Blame? A Contextual Analysis of Sirach 25:24," *CBQ* 47 (1985) 617-23, makes an interesting case for understanding the reference in this verse (Sir 25:24) as being directed to wicked wives, no thanks to whom husbands die. Levison rightly observes that elsewhere Ben Sira implies that death belongs to the natural order of things. An allusion to Eve in the context of discussing evil wives seems entirely natural, however, and Levison must assume remarkable gaps in Ben Sira's expression, which are supplied by brackets in Levison's translation: "From the [evil] wife is the beginning of sin, / and because of her we [husbands] all die." Moreover, the evidence from the use of γυνή *gynē* (ἀπὸ γυναικός *apo gynaikos*) is inconclusive, for the word refers to "wife" and to "woman" generally. Levison's claim that women are depraved is then cancelled by a recognition that good wives benefit husbands. Finally, the text from Cave 4 at Qumran entitled "The Wiles of the Wicked Woman," to which Levison alludes, deals with a mythic reality, personified evil, just as Sir 25:24, on the traditional reading, refers to the primal myth. See R. Moore, "Personification of the Seduction of Evil: 'The Wiles of the Wicked Woman,' " *RevQ* 10 (1979–81) 505-19. Levison's attempt to reorient scholarly thinking about Sir 25:24 resembles Norbert Lohfink's reading of Eccl 7:23-29: "War Kohelet ein Frauenfeind?" in *La Sagesse de l'Ancien Testament,* ed. Maurice Gilbert (Leuven: University Press, 1979) 259-87.

detailed account of these historical events connected with the wilderness, thus avoiding the tedium of learned psalmography (cf. Psalms 78; 105; 106; 136). The surprising aspect of his selection from Israel's sacred story is what he does not choose. Given the illustrative force of Joseph's refusal to succumb to seduction, the powerful negative potential of Saul, the perennial temptation to idolatry afforded by the story about Balaam, and so forth, one marvels at Ben Sira's reticence. When warning against the dangers of uncontrolled passion, he does not appeal to the examples of David and Bathsheba or Amnon and Tamar (cf. 6:2-4). To combat the strong lure of Hellenism, especially for young men, Ben Sira does not use the episode about Balaam or even the incident involving Elijah and the prophets of Baal.[51]

Ben Sira may very well have alluded to far more biblical texts than suggested thus far, inasmuch as his language frequently echoes ideas from them. For example, the designation of the Lord as compassionate and merciful (2:11)[52] undoubtedly reflects an abbreviated version of Exod 34:6-7, the ancient proclamation to Moses of the divine attributes. This oft-cited creed—only the positive attributes—left an indelible print on subsequent characterizations of Yahweh. Ben Sira often offers advice that has its point of reference in ancient teachings, such as the command to honor one's parents (Sir 3:3), although he provides a different rationale for such filial allegiance than one finds in the Decalogue.

Comparison with a wisdom text later than Ben Sira is instructive, for the author of the book of Wisdom also weaves sacred story into his instructions, always without specific names of the persons being recalled (Wis 10:1–19:22). He traces the long account of Israel in Egypt and the escape into the wilderness without ever naming anyone. The clear implication is that the audience knew the story intimately and filled in the missing names. This author adheres to the story line from beginning to end. The resulting treatment approaches the type of interpretation known as midrash, a running commentary on a biblical text. Furthermore, this midrash-like interpretation heightens the psychological features of a divine drama between Israel's God and the Egyptians. Their offense, idolatry, provides focus for the entire analysis.

The characters behind the story in Wis 10:1–19:22 include Adam, Cain, Abel, Noah, Abraham, Isaac, Lot, Lot's wife, Jacob, Esau, Joseph, and Moses. The full narrative explores the familiar events in considerable detail, leaving little to the imagination. Nevertheless, the incidents lead up to and set the stage for a sharp attack on idolatry, including three explanations for its appeal to the popular imagination (the aesthetic, a parent's grief over a son, a desire to honor a distant emperor).

With a single exception, Ben Sira withholds the names of persons to whom he refers

---

51. Mary Douglas, *In the Wilderness: The Doctrine of Defilement in the Book of Numbers* (Sheffield: Academic Press Limited, 1995), interprets the Balaam story as satire directed at the harsh policies of Ezra and Nehemiah. A recently found text from Deir 'Alla attests the popularity of the prophetic legend in relatively late times.

52. See James L. Crenshaw, "Who Knows What YHWH Will Do? The Character of God in the Book of Joel," in *Fortunate the Eyes That See: Essays in Honor of David Noel Freedman in Celebration of His Seventieth Birthday,* eds. Astrid B. Beck et al. (Grand Rapids: Eerdmans, 1995) 185-96.

in 1:1–43:33. That one specific reference is Lot (Sir 16:8). Ben Sira does mention Jacob, but the reference seems always to be national, hence synonymous with Israel. In the section praising ancestral heroes (Sir 44:1–50:24), Ben Sira specifically names the individuals under discussion. The difference probably relates to the literary form being employed; one mentions the name of the deceased in a "eulogy."

The practice of rehearsing ancient history by means of allusions raises the question, "Who was the intended audience?" In the light of the expense of owning scrolls of the entire Bible, one may reasonably conclude that both Ben Sira and the author of the book of Wisdom directed their teachings to a small group of prospective scribes. These young men would have studied the Scriptures just as Ben Sira is said to have done. Still, one cannot rule out the possibility that communal worship, especially singing the didactic psalms, and parental teaching may have familiarized the people with certain biblical traditions, particularly the story of the beginnings.

In some ways, Sirach resembles the book of Tobit, Baruch, the *Testament of the Twelve Patriarchs,* and *Pirqe 'Abot,* devotional literature from the wider Jewish environment. The author of Tobit emphasizes acts of piety as an expression of loyalty to the Mosaic law and regularly lifts up a voice in prayer. In Tob 12:6-10 the angel Raphael assumes the venerable role of wisdom teacher, insisting that "a little with righteousness is better than wealth with wrongdoing" (Tob 12:8 NRSV) and promising reward for virtuous living. Tobit both prays for and experiences divine activity; like Job, his misfortune was eventually reversed. The poem on wisdom in Bar 3:9–4:4 does not integrate mythic themes concerning wisdom's function at creation with the notion that wisdom finds concrete expression in the law of Moses. Instead, it proceeds in the manner of Job 28, stressing the inaccessibility of wisdom to all but God, who passed it on to Israel in the Torah.[53] The *Testament of the Twelve Patriarchs* transcends the ritual features of worship in favor of ethical dimensions to an unprecedented degree; Ben Sira endeavors to combine the two.[54] Like *Pirqe 'Abot,* Ben Sira offers ethical advice to students steeped in torah piety.

---

53. Lewis J. Prockter, "Torah as a Fence Against Apocalyptic Speculation: Ben Sira 3:17-24," *Proceedings of the Tenth World Congress of Jewish Studies,* Div. A (Jerusalem: World Union of Jewish Studies, 1990) 245-52. Prockter writes: "To seek in heaven what is already on earth, namely Torah given once and for all to Moses, is not only foolish but perilous. To seek what is 'beyond you' is to display pride, and by so doing to wilfully cut yourself off from God, who reveals his will to the humble here below, not to those trying to ascend to the heavenly *hekhalot* (3:17-20)" (ibid., 251). On the limitations to knowledge generally, see James L. Crenshaw, "Wisdom and the Sage: On Knowing and Not Knowing," *Proceedings of the Eleventh World Congress of Jewish Studies,* Div. A (Jerusalem: World Union of Jewish Studies, 1994) 137-44.

54. J. G. Snaith, "Ben Sira's Supposed Love of Liturgy," *VT* 25 (1975), emphasizes the teachings about social justice in Sirach. Ben Sira maintains a healthy balance between observing the niceties of cultic ritual and deeds of kindness, and he provides theological underpinnings for both in divine commands and the nature of Yahweh as merciful. Otto Kaiser, "Die Begrundung der Sittlichkeit im Buche Jesus Sirach," *ZTK* 55 (1958) 51-63, examines the basis for ethical actions in Sirach.

BEN SIRA AND HELLENISM

Occasional similarities between Sirach and Greek authors raise the issue of Ben Sira's dependence on popular Hellenistic philosophers.[55] The comparison of death to falling leaves in 14:18 (and in the *Iliad* vi.146-149) belongs to folk wisdom. The image would naturally occur to anyone who gave much thought to the process of growth and decay in nature and among humans. Ben Sira proclaims at one point: "He is the All." This expression was common in Stoic philosophy, but Ben Sira could easily have arrived at such an understanding of God on the basis of his reading of Isa 45:5-7 and Deut 32:39. Unlike Stoic thinkers, Ben Sira did not equate God with the created universe. The Stoic ideal of world citizenship did not drive out Ben Sira's conviction that God had chosen Israel as a special heritage.[56]

Ben Sira's affirmation of physicians shows that he did not reject Greek ideas without careful consideration (Sir 38:1-15). He combines traditional Jewish belief about sin and disease with Hellenistic teachings, although the two seem mutually contradictory. In the end, piety prevailed, and because both Greeks and Jews prayed for healing, he could argue for combining the physician's treatment with fervent prayer. Greek customs and ideas filled the air Ben Sira breathed, expressing themselves in many ways: a eulogy of ancestors, the notion of a rational universe with perfectly balanced pairs, human freedom and divine providence, dining customs, pride of authorship, and much more.

The last two deserve further comment. Ben Sira refers to the Hellenistic practice of selecting a person to preside over a banquet, and he gives advice on fulfilling that honor in an acceptable manner (Sir 32:1-13). He even mentions the reward for good service, the customary wreath awarded for leadership. His advice on table etiquette in 31:12-24 presupposes dinners like Greek banquets followed by symposia. Such dinners included contests at drinking wine, musical entertainment, speeches demonstrating wit and wisdom, seating of guests according to rank, and a blessing to the gods at the end of the dinner.

Greek pride of authorship influenced Ben Sira so strongly that he departed from the

---

55. T. Middendorp, *Die Stellung Jesus ben Siras zwischen Judentum und Hellenismus* (Leiden: Brill, 1973), overstresses Ben Sira's dependence on Hellenistic thinkers. The fault lies in his method, for similarities in phrases and ideas between Sirach and various Greek philosophers indicate literary dependence only when (1) the language and concepts are otherwise unique to Hellenism and (2) similarities in biblical literature are lacking. Moreover, two other factors enter the picture: Only a limited sample of Jewish literature from the ancient world has survived, and intelligent people can arrive at similar ideas independently. Even the expression "He is the all" does not necessarily derive from Stoic thinkers, for biblical precedent exists (Deut 32:39; Isa 45:5-7). These caveats notwithstanding, Ben Sira does show Hellenistic influence in the way he understands the universe as an orderly arrangement of complementary pairs. His almost mathematical tone in describing the universe, his endorsement of physicians, his description of banquets and symposia, and his pride of authorship place him squarely within the Hellenistic world. On the broader issue, see Jonathan Goldstein, "Jewish Acceptance and Rejection of Hellenism," in *Jewish and Christian Self-Definition,* eds. E. P. Sanders et al. (Philadelphia: Fortress, 1981) 2:64-87.

56. Stoic influence on Ben Sira has also been exaggerated; for a sober assessment, see David Winston, "Theodicy in Ben Sira and Stoic Philosophy," in *Of Scholars, Savants, and Their Texts,* ed. Ruth Link-Salinger (New York: Peter Lang, 1989) 239-49. An earlier study, Raymond Paultrel, "Ben Sira et le Stoicisme," *RSR* 51 (1963) 535-49, challenges Smend's claim that Ben Sira declares war against Hellenism. Paultrel also remarks on the omissions within such a long work as Sirach, noting Ben Sira's silence about angels, the Messiah, and the prohibition against images (ibid., 547).

---

usual anonymity or pseudonymity of those who composed the books of Proverbs, Job, and Ecclesiastes. He saw no particular virtue in attributing his teachings to King Solomon; given the nature of the book, he could not have done so, for the praise of ancestral heroes required an author from a much later time than the Solomonic era. The author of the book of Wisdom avoided a historical resume that would place him in the second or first centuries.

Egyptian influence can probably be detected in the comparison of professions in 38:24–39:11, although this text differs fundamentally from the *Satire of the Trades.* Ben Sira offers no hint of satire in describing the work of the farmer, the artisan, the smith, and the potter. Instead, he merely points out that their work consumes both time and energy, leaving no opportunity for study. In no way does he disparage their contribution to society, which he thinks depends on what they do for survival. The Egyptian *Instruction for Duauf,* or the *Satire of the Trades,* ridicules considerably more occupations than the four Ben Sira mentions. Both Ben Sira and the Egyptian author contrast the scribe's profession with all other kinds of work; their intent was to attract students to intellectual pursuits.

The ethic of caution based on shame and regard for one's reputation as expressed in Sirach closely resembles that in Papyrus Insinger; similarities also exist between this late Egyptian instruction and Ecclesiastes.[57] If Ben Sira relies on this work, he varies it in significant ways (cf. Sir 6:13; 13:1–42:2; 32:23; 41:11-13). His allusion to the bee to illustrate the importance of tiny things hardly confirms dependence on Papyrus Insinger, for such an analogy seems like a natural conclusion to an observant reader.

Links with Aramaean wisdom through the *Sayings of Ahiqar,* although possible, may derive from folk tradition: the futility of opposing a turbulent stream (*Ahiqar* 3.83 and Sir 4:26) and the revelation of character through the clothes one wears (*Ahiqar* 2.39 and Sir 19:29-30).[58] Anyone could easily draw these conclusions without having heard or read either work.

This meager evidence of Greek influence on Ben Sira[59] indicates that he drew far more extensively from biblical literature than from extra-biblical, even when trying to persuade Jews that their legacy was just as universal as Greek philosophy. That was the point of identifying the Mosaic law with cosmic wisdom. Ben Sira's teachings demonstrate an awareness of the seductive power of Hellenism, especially to young people, and he wages battle for the next generation of Jews. This struggle introduces new types of discourse:

57. J. T. Sanders, "Ben Sira's Ethics of Caution," *HUCA* 50 (1979); *Ben Sira and Demotic Wisdom,* SBLMS 28 (Chico, Calif.: Scholars Press, 1983). On the influence of "Papyrus Insinger" on Qoheleth, see James L. Crenshaw, *Ecclesiastes,* OTL (Philadelphia: Westminster, 1987), and for a modern translation of the Egyptian text, see Elizabeth Lichtheim, *Ancient Egyptian Literature,* 3 vols. (Berkeley: University of California Press, 1973–80) 3:184-217.

58. These references come from Edmond Jacob, "Wisdom and Religion in Sirach," in *Israelite Wisdom: Theological and Literary Essays in Honor of Samuel Terrien,* eds. John G. Gammie et al. (Missoula: Scholars Press, 1978) 250. They do not appear in James M. Lindenberger, *The Aramaic Proverbs of Ahiqar* (Baltimore: Johns Hopkins University Press, 1983), but the popular sayings attributed to Ahiqar have survived in various translations, chiefly Syriac, Armenian, Arabic, and Slavonic. See Lindenberger, *The Aramaic Proverbs of Ahiqar,* 354. The saying about stopping a river occurs frequently in ancient literature.

59. Martin Hengel, *Judaism and Hellenism,* 2 vols. (Philadelphia: Fortress, 1974) 1:115-254, examines the extent of Hellenistic influence on Jewish literature of the last three centuries before the emergence of the church.

psychological and philosophical arguments in the service of theodicy, discussion of free will and determinism, reflection about two ways (Sir 2:12). In essence, he sought to provide rational backing for his ancestral heritage.[60] The assertion that wisdom comes from the Lord constitutes a declaration of war against Hellenism, where it was a product of human inquiry. Ben Sira dismisses all astrological speculation—and apocalyptic—as sheer arrogance or pride. "Be content with the knowledge God has bestowed on you" sums up his attitude toward striving to unlock hidden mysteries.[61]

Did Ben Sira venture forth into the Hellenistic world as an ambassador like John, the father of Eupolemus, who was sent to Rome to negotiate a treaty (cf. 2 Macc 4:11), or Philo, who represented the Jews of Alexandria before Caligula? Did Ben Sira occupy a position as judge or counselor in the *gerousia?* Did he work as a scribe in the Temple? Perhaps one could say more about his relationship with Hellenism if these questions could be answered.

RELIGIOUS TEACHINGS IN SIRACH

The two primary themes in the book, fear of the Lord[62] and wisdom,[63] are interwoven from first to last, making it difficult to determine the dominant one. The author of Proverbs 1–9 subjugated piety to knowledge, viewing the fear of the Lord as the main ingredient and first principle of learning. Wisdom thus consisted of something above and beyond obedience to God, although religion comprised its very core. For Ben Sira, fear of the Lord has no rival, not even the acquisition of wisdom: "How great is the one who finds wisdom!/ But none is superior to the one who fears the Lord./ Fear of the Lord surpasses everything;/ to whom can we compare the one who has it?" (25:10-11 NRSV). Like the word translated "wisdom" (חכם *ḥakam*), the expression "fear of the Lord" (יראי יהוה *yirʾê yhwh*) appears often in Sirach (over fifty times).

Such elevation of religion prompts Ben Sira to conclude that wisdom's garland and root exist in the fear of the Lord, making religious achievement the sole justification for pride (Sir 10:22). Human wisdom expresses itself in deeds of kindness, true obedience to the

60. Ryan thinks of Ben Sira's "holistic response to the divisions within Israel" as a "comprehensive act of identification." See Michael D. Ryan, "The Act of Religious Identification in Ben Sirach and Paul," *The Drew Gateway* 54 (1983) 4-16.

61. Ben Sira acknowledges that the intellect can only touch the surface of divine mystery; at the same time, he wishes to assert that God has revealed to Israel all that is necessary for living in obedience to Yahweh. Maintaining a balance so as to discourage idle speculation, whatever its nature, was no easy matter. This struggle to appreciate the revelation of Torah without discrediting a sense of the unknown and unknowable has persisted in Judaism. Michael Fishbane, *The Garments of Torah: Essays in Biblical Hermeneutics* (Bloomington: Indiana University Press, 1989), treats this problem with his usual freshness and passion.

62. Joseph Haspecker, *Gottesfurcht bei Jesus Sirach: Ihre religiöse Struktur und ihre literarische und doctainäre Bedeutung,* AnBib 30 (Rome: Pontifical Biblical Institute, 1967), argues forcefully that the fear of God, not wisdom, occupies the prominent position in Sirach.

63. Gerhard von Rad, *Wisdom in Israel* (Nashville: Abingdon, 1972) 242, insists that wisdom subordinates everything else to it. The summary statement in 50:27 that Ben Sira poured forth wisdom from his heart does not settle the issue, for 50:29 balances knowledge with action. For Ben Sira, wisdom expressed itself in religious devotion ("fear of the Lord").

law of Moses. Divine wisdom manifests itself in the Torah. Whereas the later wisdom has assumed the form of legal statute and passionate exhortation, men and women have no excuse for choosing folly. It has been said that wisdom manifests itself subjectively as fear of the Lord and objectively as the law of Moses.[64]

Ben Sira urges submission to the yoke of divine discipline (מוסר *mûsār*), noting that it withholds itself like its name. Acknowledging the difficulty encountered by most students when they first endeavor to become wise, he describes wisdom as a hard taskmaster until people have demonstrated their worth. In time, however, she shows herself as the ardent lover, making them consider her earlier afflictions as nothing. This erotic language for intellectual curiosity and obedience to the Lord links up with the passionate discourse about love for God in the book of Deuteronomy.

Another theme pervading Sirach concerns God's justice and mercy. Ben Sira subscribes to the traditional belief in God's justice, but he knows that skepticism has imprinted itself indelibly on the minds of his audience. He uses the standard arguments—that God waits patiently, giving sinners an opportunity to repent; that things can change in a moment; that the hour of death will settle the score; that suffering serves as a test of character or as discipline; that human knowledge is partial; that praise is the proper response—and seeks to improve on them from Greek arguments about the design of the universe and punishment by mental and psychological anxiety.[65] He refuses to endorse an answer that seems to have been emerging slowly in the Jewish community: the conviction that righteous individuals will receive eternal life (17:27-28).[66] The Greek and Syriac texts introduce this belief at crucial junctures (Sir 7:17*b;* 48:11*b;* Greek II, Sir 2:9*c;* 16:22*c;* 19:19; Syriac, Sir 1:12*b,* 20; 3:1*b*). In this respect, Ben Sira resembles later Sadducees rather than Pharisees, who believed in life after death. That conservative tendency on the part of Ben Sira explains why he places so much emphasis on preserving honor or reputation, the one thing that survives after a person dies (Sir 41:11-13).

The origin of sin in a perfect universe placed a special burden on defenders of divine justice, particularly when it was attributed to the Creator. The serpent's presence in the garden indirectly indicted the Lord. Later biblical texts compromise divine justice further, insisting that God overrides human freedom, forcing pharaohs and others to persist in obstinacy. Ben Sira stoutly resisted such ideas, for he believed that everyone acts with absolute freedom (Sir 15:11-20). Nevertheless, he realized that irresistible forces put extraordinary pressure on free will (Sir 33:11-13). That ambiguity characterizes much

---

64. "Subjectively, wisdom is the fear of God; objectively, the Mosaic lawbook (chapter 24)." ("Subjektiv ist die Weisheit daher die Gottesfurcht, objektiv ist sie das Gesetzbuch Moses, c 24.") This succinct statement appears in Rudolf Smend, *Die Weisheit des Jesus Sirach erklärt* (Berlin: Reimer, 1906) xxiii.

65. See these works by James L. Crenshaw: *Theodicy in the Old Testament* (Philadelphia: Fortress, 1983); "Theodicy," in *Anchor Bible Dictionary,* 6 vols. (New York: Doubleday, 1992) 6:444-47; and "The Problem of Theodicy in Sirach: On Human Bondage," *JBL* 94 (1975).

66. Vincenz Hamp, "Zukunft und Jenseits im Buche Sirach," *Alttestamentliche Studien, Festschrift Nötscher,* BBB 1 (Bonn: Hanstein, 1950) 86-97. Hamp finds no evidence that Ben Sira thought of retribution in the next life.

biblical thinking about sin, but Ben Sira brings the issue of free will into the arena of public discussion.

Ben Sira's frequent attribution of mercy to the deity stands out when one observes the rarity of this idea in earlier wisdom literature. If an individual can rely on reward for virtuous conduct, the presupposition of much earlier wisdom, then divine mercy really does not fit into the picture. That understanding probably explains why sages did not characterize God as merciful. The shift takes place in Sirach, perhaps because earlier optimism had faded under the barrage of questions in the books of Job and Ecclesiastes.[67] Historical circumstances no longer favored such optimistic reading of the human situation, if they ever did, and a greater consciousness of human frailty produces existential anxiety. The extent to which such alarm over sinful dominance and the sorry future of the human race, both in this life and in the next, can be grasped by studying 2 Esdras. In the light of the weighty burden hanging over humanity, Ben Sira takes some comfort in divine compassion. The source of his confidence in God's mercy lies outside the wisdom literature, most likely in the ancient creedal confession in Exod 34:6-7.

The God whom Ben Sira worshiped was the Creator, a concept at the very heart of wisdom thinking.[68] This majestic fashioner of an orderly universe saw whatever transpired and therefore ruled with exact justice. This sovereign demanded social justice (Sir 4:8-10), the demonstration of one's true worship through ritual *and* charitable deeds, as well as pure thoughts. Ben Sira honors God as father, shepherd, and judge (Sir 18:13, 40; 23:1, 4; 51:10; 16:12-14).

It was noted earlier that Ben Sira did not believe in life beyond the grave, and in this regard he could be labeled a proto-Sadducee. Rejecting a meaningful existence after death alone hardly suffices to place him in the camp with later Sadducees, for he shared this skepticism with virtually all OT authors (Psalm 73; Isa 26:19; and Dan 12:2 being the only exceptions). Like the Sadducees of the first century CE, Ben Sira had strong interests, if not actual membership, in the priesthood. Moreover, he belonged to the elite ranks of upper-class citizens, and with this status came ultraconservatism aimed at maintaining the status quo. In addition, the temple cult represented the center of religious life for him, despite a commendable concern for doing acts of kindness when the occasion presented itself. In a sense, he understood the fundamentals of hasidic piety, but he never let the emotions seize control.

Later Pharisaism lacked this elitism and the strong attachment to the temple cult; it also appealed to the masses much more readily than did Sadduceeism. The destruction of the

---

67. James L. Crenshaw, "The Concept of God in Old Testament Wisdom," in *In Search of Wisdom: Essays in Memory of John Gammie,* eds. Leo G. Perdue, Bernard B. Scott, and William J. Wiseman (Louisville: Westminster John Knox, 1993) 1-18, explores the function of the idea of mercy in Sirach. Earlier optimism has given way to a sense of utter dependence on God's compassion; obedience has become more difficult and temptations harder to resist, perhaps because of declining influence from the family. Moreover, confidence in divine sovereignty, as well as faith that God works wonders on Israel's behalf, has begun to fade.

68. See the recent analysis of creation theology in Leo G. Perdue, *Wisdom and Creation: The Theology of Wisdom Literature* (Nashville: Abingdon, 1994).

Temple in 70 CE brought the sacrificial cult to an end, as well as placing the priesthood in jeopardy. The Pharisees were able to continue their worship in synagogues, which offered a natural setting for prayer and religious training of the young. Ben Sira's influence may well have suffered along with the priests whose life centered in the Temple. The sectarians at Qumran also cared deeply about the temple cult, but Ben Sira did not share their strong attention to divine mystery. Nor did he subscribe to their apocalyptic fervor, midrashic exegesis, celibacy, and so much more.

BEN SIRA'S ATTITUDE TOWARD WOMEN

Much has been said about biblical patriarchalism,[69] a subjecting of women to their husbands' whims and placing them in the category of property to be disposed of at will. Daughters depended on their fathers to arrange marriages, husbands could negate solemn oaths taken by their wives, and women usually did not inherit property. Husbands could marry more than one wife, but women had no such freedom. Two standards operated in the area of sexual misconduct, and husbands punished wives for infidelity. In a sense, primary responsibility for sin's origin fell to a woman, and a prophet could even personify evil as a woman (Zech 5:5-11). In traditional lore, if not also in fact, a father could sacrifice his daughter if he so wished (Jephthah), but sons were equally vulnerable (Isaac).

We should not lose sight of the fact that the male authors of the biblical texts often portrayed women in a highly favorable light (cf. the depiction of Samson's mother over against that of Manoah,[70] Ruth, Deborah, and Susanna). They may have acknowledged the threat presented by the notorious foreign woman of Proverbs,[71] but they balanced this figure with wisdom, personified as a woman, and with the portrait of an ideal wife. To be sure, they also personified folly as a female and praised the wife in Prov 31:10-31, largely from the point of view of the husband whom she benefits. Numerous instances of mutual love between husband and wife in the Bible suggest that not all women considered themselves oppressed. Sages considered good wives gifts of God, and the unknown author of 1 Esdr 3:1–4:41 praises woman as the strongest thing on earth, exceeded only by truth and its Author.[72] The erotic passion expressed in Song of Songs testifies to a society that values the power stronger than death that draws men and women to each other.

Nevertheless, rare expressions of misogynism reveal the darker side of Israelite society, the result of centuries of double standards and jokes that have long since lost their humor. The author of Ecclesiastes expresses disdain over his, or someone else's, inability to discover

69. Phyllis Trible, *God and the Rhetoric of Sexuality* (Philadelphia: Fortress, 1978); Phyllis Trible, "Depatriarchalizing in Biblical Interpretation," *JAAR* 41 (1973) 30-48.

70. James L. Crenshaw, *Samson* (Atlanta: John Knox, 1978) 65-98.

71. Carol A. Newsom, "Woman and the Discourse of Patriarchal Wisdom: A Study of Proverbs 1–9," in *Gender and Difference in Ancient Israel,* ed. Peggy L. Day (Minneapolis: Fortress, 1989) 142-60; Joseph Blenkinsopp, "The Social Context of the 'Outsider Woman' in Proverbs 1–9," *Bib* 72 (1991) 457-73.

72. James L. Crenshaw, "The Contest of Darius' Guards in 1 Esdras 3:1-5:3," in *Images of Man and God: The Old Testament Short Story in Literary Focus,* ed. Burke O. Long (Sheffield: Almond, 1981) 74-88, 119-20. See also Crenshaw, *Urgent Advice and Probing Questions*, 222-34.

a single trustworthy woman, although he does proceed to indict men almost equally, giving them only one one-thousandth of an advantage over women (Eccl 7:23-29). The heroine Judith stands above all the men in the little town of Bethulia as courageous, virtuous, and pious (Jdt 8:1-34; 15:8-10). In the book of Tobit, both Anna and Sarah appear above reproach (Tob 2:11-14; 3:7-15), suggesting that misogynistic views may have been less dispersed than has often been claimed. Examination of the Greco-Roman environment and of rabbinic Judaism reveals rampant misogynism, making the attitude of the Bible toward women look tame by comparison.[73]

Ben Sira inherits the mixed biblical tradition with respect to women, but he may be subject to Hellenistic views as well. In any event, he adds a new dimension, the discussion of daughters as a separate category.[74] Moreover, he places the adjective "wicked" (רעה *rāʿâ*) before the noun "daughters" (בנות *bānôt*). His obscene characterization of them as opening their quiver for every arrow (Sir 26:12) represents the ultimate in disrespect, and his rancorous opinion that the birth of a daughter is a loss (Sir 22:3) can hardly be justified by anxiety over what that entails—finding a husband for her, securing her virginity until marriage and her faithfulness afterward, worrying about her ability to bear children. Worse still, he places the entire blame for sin and death on the first woman (Sir 25:24) and apparently makes the ridiculous statement that a man's wickedness is better than a woman's goodness.[75]

The positive evaluation of woman also finds expression in Sirach, demonstrating Ben Sira's awareness that life without women would be drab, indeed. He recognizes the value of a faithful wife, and he sees the pathos of impossible "love" (using the image of a eunuch who beholds a desirable young woman and groans). Ben Sira scolds foolish old men who stray from their nests like birds, and he mentions restless sighing brought on by loneliness. His erotic appreciation for a woman's physical beauty seems boundless, issuing in effusive language based on the holy artifacts in the Temple ("Like the shining lamp on the holy lampstand,/ so is a beautiful face on a stately figure./ Like golden pillars on silver bases;/ so are shapely legs and steadfast feet" [Sir 26:17-18 NRSV]).

THE PRAISE OF ANCESTRAL HEROES

Such lavish praise of women did not induce Ben Sira to include a woman in his praise of loyal people, which comprises the last major section of the book, 44:1–50:24. If his

73. Charles E. Carlston, "Proverbs, Maxims, and the Historical Jesus," *JBL* 99 (1980) 87-105, esp. 95-97, gives some examples of maxims in the Greco-Roman world that denigrate women. Patrick W. Skehan and Alexander A. Di Lella, *The Wisdom of Ben Sira,* AB 39 (New York: Doubleday, 1987) 91, also give some repugnant maxims about women culled from M. R. Lefkowitz and M. B. Fant, *Women's Life in Greece and Rome* (Baltimore: Johns Hopkins University Press, 1982). Di Lella wishes to judge Ben Sira in the light of attitudes prevalent in his own time, a valid procedure.

74. Karla G. Bohmbach, "With Her Hands on the Threshold: Daughters and Space in the Hebrew Bible" (Ph.D. diss., Duke University, 1996).

75. W. C. Trenchard, *Ben Sira's View of Women: A Literary Analysis,* BJS 38 (Chico, Calif.: Scholars Press, 1982), goes too far in condemning Ben Sira for hostility to women. The positive treatment of some women, like the negative attitude toward some others, requires proper nuancing. On this problem, see Maurice Gilbert, "Ben Sira et le femme," *RTL* 7 (1967) 426-42. Modern corrective to such thinking receives impetus from Brenner, ed. *A Feminist Companion to Wisdom Literature* (Sheffield: Sheffield Academic Press, 1995).

primary criterion for selection relates to their contribution to and active participation in the temple cult, then silence with regard to women is mandated. That particular perspective certainly applies to Moses, Aaron, Phinehas, David, Solomon, Hezekiah, Josiah, Zerubbabel, Jeshua, Nehemiah, and Simeon. A secondary criterion, the desire to achieve canonical coverage, may explain the inclusion of Joshua and Caleb, along with the unnamed Judges, and the prophetic figures Nathan, Elijah, Elisha, Isaiah, Ezekiel, Job(!), and the unnamed twelve. That leaves two royal reprobates, Rheoboam and Jeroboam, and three priestly villains (Korah, Dathan, and Abiram) who merely stand out because of their infamy. Perhaps the addition of pre-Israelite worthies—Enoch, Noah, Abraham, Isaac, Jacob at first, then Enoch, Joseph, Shem, Seth, Enosh, and Adam later—represents a feeble effort to universalize the list.

This unusual journey through the portrait gallery of notables has recently been described as a complete reading of epic history that served as a mythic etiology for Judaism in the period of the Second Temple.[76] The hypothesis runs like this: The hymn consists of a tripartite architectonic structure with transitional units: (1) the establishment of covenants with the conquest of the land as transition; (2) the history of the prophets and kings, with the story of the restoration as transition; and (3) the climax in Simeon the high priest. Themes unite the figures within each major unit, for example, the promise of a blessing joins together the individuals from Abraham to Jacob. The poem resembles an encomium with four parts: (1) a prooemium in 44:1-15, (2) a genealogy in 44:17–49:16, (3) the narration of the subject's achievements in 50:1-21, and (4) an epilogue in 50:22-24.

According to this theory, Sir 49:14-16 serves as a bridge linking past and present, juxtaposing Adam and Simeon in a manner that renders praise of the latter both appropriate and effective. This praise commemorates rather than entertains, although many rhetorical encomiastic devices occur, such as amplification by syncrisis (the juxtaposition of opposites for rhetorical effect), hyperbole, rhetorical questions, appeal to experience acquired through traveling, a reference to a person's character and reputation for good deeds, the claim that words cannot adequately describe an individual, and an assertion that a person's contribution to society lacks precedent. Thus far, the theory.

The hypothesis would be more persuasive if Ben Sira had used the four essential characteristics of encomia (prooemium, ancestry, deeds, epilogue) in proper proportion and in a manner so that they could easily be recognized.[77] Stated differently, if Ben Sira borrowed the form of an encomium, he changed it radically. Moreover, the chronicler

76. Burton L. Mack, *Wisdom and the Hebrew Epic: Ben Sira's Hymn in Praise of the Fathers,* Chicago Studies in the History of Judaism (Chicago: University of Chicago Press, 1985). R. A. F. MacKenzie, "Ben Sira as Historian," in *Trinification of the World: A Festschrift in Honor of F. E. Crowe,* eds. T. A. Dunne and J. M. Laport (Toronto: Regis College Press, 1978) 313-27. MacKenzie observes that Ben Sira does not mention the Babylonian exile in his account of Israel's heroes. Was there any compelling reason to do so? After all, he concentrates on the high points, illustrating them with the names of persons involved in those momentous events.

77. Rollston illustrates the difficulty of proving literary dependence when an author adapts material or exercises exceptional selectivity. The resulting product differs appreciably from the presumed source, casting doubt on the presumption itself. See Chris A. Rollston, "The Non-Encomiastic Features of Ben Sira 44–50" (M.A. thesis, Emmanuel School of Religion, Johnson City, Tennessee, 1992).

provides a number of parallels to Ben Sira's use of biblical material, remaining silent about embarrassing aspects of David's character and dropping people from the record. Everything in the list could easily have occurred to a Jewish sage with no knowledge of Greek encomia. Most of the rhetorical features above occur in the Samson narrative, as well as in numerous other stories in the Hebrew Bible.

Why does Ben Sira overlook Ezra?[78] Was the omission intentional? At least five competing explanations for this anomaly deserve consideration. First, the socioeconomic circumstances had changed radically between the late fourth and early second centuries BCE in Jerusalem, making mixed marriage a matter of indifference.[79] This view assumes that Ezra's strict legislation concerning marriage with foreigners failed because it did not take into account long-standing practice among the Jews. Ben Sira, on this view, remained quiet about Ezra out of embarrassment over his strict policy and the ensuing suffering it generated.

A second explanation focuses on the venerable profession of scribes, to which Ben Sira belonged. In Ezra's day scribes had become narrowly and exclusively oriented toward the Mosaic law, but Ben Sira understands the scribal profession much more broadly. For him, an interest in the law went hand in hand with research in the tradition of the wise. To some degree, Ben Sira transforms the office of priest-scribe into that of teacher, whose authority rests ultimately on scholarship, insights, and communicative ability.[80]

A third response to the silence about Ezra focuses on the state of the priestly office during the immediate period after Simeon's death. Although Simeon's son and successor, Onias III, was a pious leader, he lacked the qualities of bold leadership. Like Ezra, he was a political quietist. For this reason, Ben Sira did not want to laud Ezra as someone whom Onias could emulate. Instead, Ben Sira skips over Ezra and commends Onias's father, hoping to stimulate a desire on the son's part to pattern his actions after his father and predecessor in the office of high priest.[81]

A fourth explanation for Ben Sira's omission of Ezra in the list of ancestral heroes takes its cue from a feature common to several individuals—active participation in constructing

---

78. Peter Höffken, "Warum schwieg Jesus Sirach über Esra," *ZAW* 87 (1975) 184-201, argues that Ben Sira omitted Ezra from the list of ancestral worthies because of his championing of Levites. Ben Sira rejects the chronicler's plea for the levitical priesthood and returns to the earlier priestly emphasis on the Aaronide line. Höffken understands the choice of the priestly tradition as theological. Christopher Begg, "Ben Sirach's Non-Mention of Ezra," *BN* 42 (1988) 14-18, finds the key to Ben Sira's silence about Ezra in his absence from participation in building projects related to the Temple. Begg detects no anti-Levitical polemic in Sirach.

79. Changing socioeconomic circumstances may explain many emphases in Sirach, on which see Martin Hengel, *Judaism and Hellenism,* 2 vols. (Philadelphia: Fortress, 1974).

80. Ben Sira does not stand in the direct line of Ezra, whose responsibility for instructing the people in the law of their God was tantamount, and yet both men were teachers. Ben Sira links up much more closely with the unknown authors of Proverbs, but with decisive differences. He embraces the entire sacral tradition and integrates it into wisdom instruction.

81. With the assassination of the weak Onias III, Simeon's line came to an end. According to P. C. Beentjes, " 'The Countries Marveled at You.' King Solomon in Ben Sira 47:12-22," *BTfuT* 45 (1984) 13, Ben Sira's goal in writing the history of Israel was "the perpetuation of and the succession of the priestly dynasty of Simeon and his descendants," their rule signifying divine activity.

or repairing the Temple.[82] In this view, Ezra was omitted in favor of Nehemiah, whose vital role in repairing the wall of the city was essential to the successful operation of the cult.

A fifth attempt to explain Ben Sira's failure to mention Ezra focuses on the chronicler's championing of Levites, which did not accord with the elevation of the Aaronide priestly lineage in Ben Sira. For this reason, he did not wish to mention a scribe who championed the cause of a rival priestly group.[83]

Two other prominent omissions call for comment, Joseph and Saul. In the body of the poem, one expects a reference to Joseph after the mention of Jacob, but it does not occur. The name "Joseph" appears in a brief "afterthought," along with the pre-deluvians Shem, Seth, and Adam (Sir 49:14-16; Enoch occurs here for a second time but is missing in the Masada text and the Syriac). Perhaps Joseph's connection with the northern tribes of Ephraim and Manasseh and his blessing of these sons gave the appearance of approving the despised Samaritans, who now occupied the area originally granted to Ephraim and Manasseh. The active campaign waged by the Tobiads in Transjordan and the leaders of Samaria against the policies of Simeon II and the Tobiads in Jerusalem may have generated sufficient antipathy to cause Ben Sira to remain silent about Joseph. Alternatively, Ben Sira may have removed the name of Joseph to blot out any record of his role as adviser to the pharaoh. Again, in the light of Onias III's switch of allegiance from the Seleucids to the Ptolemaic ruler, Ben Sira may have avoided giving the impression that he approved this shift.

Naturally, these attempts to explain Ben Sira's silence about Joseph presuppose the secondary character of the name in Sir 49:15. Viewing his presence in the latter text as comparison rather than praise lacks persuasiveness; excising the entire unit 49:14-16 as secondary solely to restore a sequence of two persons, Nehemiah and Simeon II, who were responsible for engineering improvements in Jerusalem, seems problematic at best.[84]

One further notable omission is the first king, Saul. The biblical story ascribes enough negative features to his character to explain the lack of any reference to him. In addition, his rivalry with David and his connection with northern tribal groups made Saul an unlikely candidate for Ben Sira's list of worthy men.

SIRACH AND THE CANON

The preface to Sirach, written by Ben Sira's grandson, refers to the law, the prophets, and the other writings, suggesting that the first two divisions of the Hebrew Bible existed as distinct entities and that the third group may or may not have been relatively fixed in his day. Ben Sira's praise of ancestral heroes supports this evidence, pushing the date back

---

82. P. C. Beentjes, "Hezekiah and Isaiah: A Study on Ben Sira xlviii 15-25," *OTS* 25 (1989) 77-88, esp. 81-82, calls attention to differences between the biblical account of Hezekiah's fortifications and that by Ben Sira.

83. Peter Höffken, "Warum schwieg Jesus Sirach über Esra."

84. Christopher Begg, "Ben Sirach's Non-Mention of Ezra," *BN* 42 (1988).

to the early second century BCE for at least two closed units, the law and the prophets.[85] He knows the chief characters in Genesis through Deuteronomy, and he mentions Isaiah, Jeremiah, Ezekiel, and the Twelve, as well as prominent persons from the Former Prophets (Joshua, Judges, Samuel, and Kings). Unfortunately, he does not provide enough information to enable scholars to identify the exact books making up the third category. Among them he mentions Job and Nehemiah, but he probably knew Psalms and other books as well.[86]

Although Sirach was excluded from the Hebrew Bible, it was frequently cited in rabbinic circles until the tenth century CE, occasionally introduced by the formula "it is written," which indicates Scripture.[87] Akiba, the noted rabbi of the second century (d. c. 132 CE), thought it belonged among the חסנים (*ḥisônîm*, "outside") or extra-canonical books, those that did not, in the language of the day, "defile the hands." A severe penalty accompanied their reading, forfeiture of any participation in the next life.[88] The same assessment of Sirach appears in *Tosephta*,[89] which states that the book does not defile the hands. Nevertheless, Sirach is quoted eighty-two times in the Talmud and other rabbinical writings.

Recent evidence from Masada and Qumran confirms that the Jewish communities in the area of the Dead Sea viewed the book as sacred, for the copy from Masada and the two tiny fragments from Cave 2 at Qumran are written stichometrically, with parallel columns, the first half of each colon beginning on the right side and the second half appearing on the left side. Moreover, the inclusion of Sirach in the Septuagint and the Palestinian revisions of this Greek text and the Hebrew indicate its acceptance as sacred. The formulation of specific criteria for canonicity, resulting from the debates associated with the so-called council of Jamnia and related discussions, automatically excluded Sirach, if one limits inspiration to the period from Moses to Ezra. In addition, several aspects of the book are closer to Sadducaic teaching than to Pharisaic, and this may have influenced its checkered history.

The situation is equally ambiguous in Christian tradition. The presence of the book of Sirach in the Septuagint implied at least quasi-sacred character, but the translator of the Vulgate, Jerome, denied a place in the canon to the additional books, labeling them deuterocanonical.[90] These books include 1–2 Esdras, Tobit, Judith, the Additions to Esther, the book of Wisdom, Sirach, Baruch, the Letter of Jeremiah, the Song of the Three Jews, Susanna, Bel and the Dragon, the Prayer of Manasseh, and 1–2 Maccabees. Augustine

85. Harry M. Orlinsky, "Some Terms in the Prologue to Ben Sira and the Hebrew Canon," *JBL* 110 (1991) 483-90, insists that the first two divisions of the HB were already fixed in the time of Ben Sira's grandson, hence should be capitalized—Law and Prophets.

86. The inclusion of Job among the prophets accords with an ancient Jewish tradition, although the book usually appears, in varying sequence, among the Writings.

87. Israel Levi, "Sirach, the Wisdom of Jesus the Son of," *The Jewish Encyclopedia* 11 (New York and London: Funk and Wagnalls, 1905) 390-92, discusses the book's popularity among Jews and Christians.

88. *Sanhedrin* 28a.

89. *Yadayim* 2.13.

90. According to Gilbert, "The Book of Ben Sira: Implications for Jewish and Christian Traditions," in *Jewish Civilization in the Hellenistic-Roman Period,* ed. Shamaryahu Talmon (Sheffield: JSOT, 1991) 87, Jerome quotes Ben Sira eighty times in his works.

disagreed with Jerome's estimate, considering all the books in the Septuagint equally authoritative.

Following Jerome, Martin Luther rejected the sacred character of the additional books in the Septuagint, which he called apocrypha and placed in a separate group between the two Testaments in his German translation of 1534. John Calvin rejected these books altogether. Nevertheless, the Apocrypha appeared in the King James translation in English until the third decade of the nineteenth century, when they were removed for a combination of reasons, partly theological and partly economic. The Roman Catholic Church still considers these books sacred, but deuterocanonical, except for 1–2 Esdras and the Prayer of Manasseh.

The author of the Epistle of James was particularly fond of Sirach.[91] Other works of the early church used Sirach as a source of inspiration, including the *Didache,* the *Shepherd of Hermas,* and the *Epistle of Barnabas.* So did the church father Clement of Alexandria. The early Latin fathers included Sirach as one of the five books written by Solomon, and Cyprian accepted its sacred character. This position eventually prevailed at the Council of Trent.

THE TEXT

Slightly more than two-thirds of Sirach has survived in Hebrew manuscripts (approx. 68 percent).[92] Between 1896 and 1900, the Cairo Geniza, a place for discarded sacred texts in the old synagogue in Cairo, yielded four distinct manuscripts of Sirach (A, B, C, D), dating from the tenth to the twelfth centuries. Another leaf (E) was discovered in 1931, and additional fragments of B and C came to light in 1958 and 1960. Three years later a fragmentary and mutilated scroll, resembling B, was discovered at Masada. In 1982 a new leaf of Sirach from the Cairo Geniza was identified (F). These manuscripts contain the following texts from Sirach:[93]

A		3:6*b*–16:26 (six leaves)
	B	30:11–33:3; 35:11; 38:27*b*; 39:15*c*–51:30
		(nineteen leaves, written stichometrically)
	C	4:23, 30-31; 5:4-7, 9-13; 6:18*b*-19, 28, 35;
		7:1-2, 4, 6, 17, 20-21, 23-25; 18:31*b*–19:3*b*;
		20:5-7; 37:19, 22, 24, 26; 20:13; 25:8, 13, 17-24;
		26:1-2*a* (a florilegium)
	D	36:29–38:1*a* (one leaf)
	E	32:16–34:1 (one leaf, written stichometrically)
	F	31:24–32:7; 32:12–33:8 (one leaf, written stichometrically)

91. Luke Timothy Johnson, *The Letter of James,* AB 37A (New York: Doubleday, 1995) 33-34, calls attention to similarities and differences between wisdom literature generally and the Epistle of James. Hubert Frankemolle, "Zum Thema des Jakobusbriefe im Kontext der Rezeption von Sir 2:1-18 und 15:11-20," *BN* 48 (1989) 21-49, stresses the affinities, at least in one respect.

92. Patrick W. Skehan and Alexander A. Di Lella, *The Wisdom of Ben Sira,* AB 39 (New York: Doubleday, 1987) 53.

93. Ibid., 52.

A fragment from Cave 2 at Qumran has Sir 6:20-31 in stichometric arrangement (only the ends of the lines have survived).

The Greek text exists in two forms: (1) codices such as the four major uncials: Sinaiticus, Vaticanus, Alexandrinas, and Ephraemi; and (2) a longer form in the Lucianic rescension and Origen's recension of the Septuagint. The Old Latin and Vulgate used the Greek text of Sirach, which has also influenced the *Peshitta* to some degree.

Both the Greek and the Hebrew texts contain titles for individual sections (Greek, 20:27; 23:7; 24:1; 30:1, 16; 44:1; 51:1; Hebrew, 31:12 = Greek 34:12; 41:14; 44:1) and transitions (42:25 to 43:1; 43:33 to 44:1; 49:16 to 50:1). In the Hebrew text an extra psalm resembling Psalm 136 follows Sir 51:12 (cf. 11QPs[a]). The sequence from Sirach 31 to 36 differs in the Hebrew, the Vulgate, and the Syriac from the Greek, which offers a less likely order at this point.

SELECT BIBLIOGRAPHY

Commentaries, Concordances, Monographs:

Barthelemy, D., and O. Rickenbacher. *Konkordanz zum hebräischen Sirach.* Göttingen: Vandenhoeck & Ruprecht, 1973. A comprehensive survey of the vocabulary in the Hebrew text of Sirach.

Hengel, Martin. *Judaism and Hellenism.* 2 vols. Philadelphia: Fortress, 1974. Illuminates the interplay of cultures during the period in which Ben Sira lived.

Lee, T. R. *Studies in the Form of Sirach 44–50.* SBLDS 75. Atlanta: Scholars Press, 1986. Views the Greek encomium as the literary model for Ben Sira's praise of honorable men.

Mack, Burton L. *Wisdom and the Hebrew Epic: Ben Sira's Hymn in Praise of the Fathers.* Chicago Studies in the History of Judaism. Chicago: University of Chicago Press, 1985. Claims that Ben Sira fashions a national epic from the lives of past heroes.

Marböck, J. *Weisheit im Wandel: Untersuchungen zur Weisheitstheologie Bei Ben Sira.* BBB 37. Bonn: Peter Hanstein, 1971. Emphasizes the changes in wisdom represented by Sirach over against earlier texts, specifically Proverbs, Job, and Ecclesiastes.

Oesterley, W. O. E. *The Wisdom of Jesus the Son of Sirach or Ecclesiasticus.* Cambridge: Cambridge University Press, 1912. An excellent commentary on Sirach, particularly rich with respect to Jewish sources.

Sanders, J. T. *Ben Sira and Demotic Wisdom.* SBLMS 28. Chico, Calif.: Scholars Press, 1983. Finds traces of Egyptian influence on Ben Sira, especially Papyrus Insinger.

Schrader, Lutz. *Leiden und Gerechtigkeit. Studien zu Theologie und Textgeschichte des Sirachbuches.* BBET 27. Frankfurt am Main: Peter Lang, 1994. Examines the themes of suffering and justice in Sirach.

Skehan, Patrick, and Alexander A. Di Lella. *The Wisdom of Ben Sira.* AB 39. New York: Doubleday, 1987. The best commentary on Sirach, although better in treating stylistic matters than in theological analysis.

Snaith, John G. *Ecclesiasticus or The Wisdom of Jesus, Son of Sirach.* CBC, NEB. Cambridge: Cambridge University Press, 1974. Brief notes on Sirach.

Stadelmann, Helga. *Ben Sira als Schriftgelehrter: Eine Untersuchung zum Berufsbild des vor-Maccabäischen Sofer unter Berucksichtigung seines Verhältnisses zu Priester-, Propheten und Weisheitslehretum.* WUNT 2/6. Tübingen: Mohr, 1981. Stresses Ben Sira's occupation as a learned scribe.

Trenchard, W. C. *Ben Sira's View of Women: A Literary Analysis.* Brown Judaic Studies 38. Chico, Calif.: Scholars Press, 1982. Emphasizes Ben Sira's misogyny, although in need of more nuancing.

Wischmeyer, Oda. *Die Kultur des Buches Jesus Sirach.* BZNW 77. Berlin: Walter de Gruyter, 1994. Examines the cultural setting of Ben Sira.

Yadin, Yigael. *The Ben Sira Scroll from Masada.* Jerusalem: Israel Exploration Society, 1965. Textual notes on the portion of Sirach discovered at Masada.

Ziegler, J. *Sapientia Iesu Filii Sirach.* Septuaginta 12/2. Göttingen: Vandenhoeck & Ruprecht, 1965. The Greek text of Sirach.

For Further Reading:

Crenshaw, James L. *Old Testament Wisdom.* Atlanta: John Knox, 1981. Provides a general introduction to the wisdom literature in the Bible and in neighboring cultures, Egypt and Mesopotamia.

———. "Sirach." *Harper Bible Commentary.* San Francisco: Harper & Row, 1988.

———. *Urgent Advice and Probing Questions: Collected Writings on Old Testament Wisdom.* Macon, Ga.: Mercer University Press, 1995. Extensive articles on various aspects of biblical wisdom.

Day, John, Robert P. Gordon, and H. G. M. Williams, eds. *Wisdom in Ancient Israel.* Cambridge: Cambridge University Press, 1995. Treats a wide variety of topics related to ancient wisdom.

Duesberg, H. *Les Scribes Inspirés: Introduction aux livres sapientiaux de la Bible.* 2 vols. Paris: Maredsous, 1966. Attention to intra- and extra-biblical parallels to wisdom literature.

Gammie, John G., and Leo G. Perdue, eds. *The Sage in Israel and the Ancient Near East.* Winona Lake: Eisenbrauns, 1990. A comprehensive look at professional sages and their literature.

Levine, Amy-Jill, ed. *"Women Like This": New Perspectives on Jewish Women in the Greco-Roman World.* Atlanta: Scholars Press, 1991. Claudia Camp's article on Ben Sira's view of women (pp. 1-39) is particularly valuable.

Murphy, Roland E. *The Tree of Life: An Exploration of Biblical Wisdom Literature.* ABRL. New York: Doubleday, 1990. An introduction to wisdom literature.

Nickelsburg, G. W. E. *Jewish Literature Between the Bible and the Mishnah: A Historical and Literary Introduction.* Philadelphia: Fortress, 1981. A good introduction to the rich corpus of Jewish literature from the general period in which Ben Sira lived.

Perdue, Leo G., Bernard Brandon Scott, and Wiliam Johnston Wiseman, eds. *In Search of Wisdom: Essays in Memory of John Gammie.* Louisville: Westminster/John Knox, 1993. Articles on wisdom in both Testaments.

Rad, Gerhard von. *Wisdom in Israel.* Nashville: Abingdon, 1972. An introduction to wisdom literature, with special emphasis on the limits of knowledge.

Schnabel, E. J. *Law and Wisdom from Ben Sira to Paul: A Traditional Historical Inquiry into the Relation of Law, Wisdom, and Ethics.* WUNT 2/16. Tübingen: Mohr, 1985. A comprehensive examination of the relationship between law and wisdom.

OUTLINE OF SIRACH

THE PROLOGUE

NAB

THE PROLOGUE

Many important truths have been handed down to us through the law, the prophets, and the later authors; and for these the instruction and wisdom of Israel merit praise. Now, those who are familiar with these truths must not only understand them themselves but, as lovers of wisdom, be able, in speech and in writing, to help others less familiar. Such a one was my grandfather, Jesus, who, having devoted himself for a long time to the diligent study of the law, the prophets, and the rest of the books of our ancestors, and having developed a thorough familiarity with them, was moved to write something himself in the nature of instruction and wisdom, in order that those who love wisdom might, by acquainting themselves with what he too had written, make even greater progress in living in conformity with the divine law.

You therefore are now invited to read it in a spirit of attentive good will, with indulgence for any apparent failure on our part, despite earnest efforts, in the interpretation of particular passages. For words spoken originally in Hebrew are not as effective when they are translated into another language. That is true not only of this book but of the law itself, the prophets and the rest of the books, which differ no little when they are read in the original.

I arrived in Egypt in the thirty-eighth year of the reign of King Euergetes, and while there, I found a reproduction of our valuable teaching. I therefore considered myself in duty bound to devote some diligence and industry to the translation of this book. Many sleepless hours of close application have I devoted in the interval to

This translation of Sirach is based on the original Hebrew as far as it is preserved, and corrected from the ancient versions, but often interpreted in the light of the traditional Greek text, here called LXX although it is the work of the author's grandson. For easy reference H. L. Strack, *Die Sprüche Jesus, des Sohnes Sirachs*, is used for the Hebrew text; the texts from Masada (39, 27–44, 17) and Qumran (51, 13–19.30) have been drawn upon.

Prolog, 1.9: (*toutōn*) *enēchoi* (*genomenoi*): so LXX[Sca, A].

Prolog, 1.17: *eurōn* (*ou mikras*).

NRSV

THE PROLOGUE

Many great teachings have been given to us through the Law and the Prophets and the others[a] that followed them, and for these we should praise Israel for instruction and wisdom. Now, those who read the scriptures must not only themselves understand them, but must also as lovers of learning be able through the spoken and written word to help the outsiders. So my grandfather Jesus, who had devoted himself especially to the reading of the Law and the Prophets and the other books of our ancestors, and had acquired considerable proficiency in them, was himself also led to write something pertaining to instruction and wisdom, so that by becoming familiar also with his book[b] those who love learning might make even greater progress in living according to the law.

You are invited therefore to read it with goodwill and attention, and to be indulgent in cases where, despite our diligent labor in translating, we may seem to have rendered some phrases imperfectly. For what was originally expressed in Hebrew does not have exactly the same sense when translated into another language. Not only this book, but even the Law itself, the Prophecies, and the rest of the books differ not a little when read in the original.

When I came to Egypt in the thirty-eighth year of the reign of Euergetes and stayed for some time, I found opportunity for no little instruction.[c] It seemed highly necessary that I should myself devote some diligence and labor to the translation of this book. During that time I have applied my skill day and night to complete and publish the book for those living abroad who wished to gain learning and are disposed to live according to the law.

[a] Or *other books*

[b] Gk *with these things*

[c] Other ancient authorities read *I found a copy affording no little instruction*

NAB

finishing the book for publication, for the benefit of those living abroad who wish to acquire wisdom and are disposed to live their lives according to the standards of the law.

COMMENTARY

Like Greek historical expositions by Herodotus, Thucydides, and Polybius and treatises by Dioscorides Pedamus, Hippocrates, Aristeas, and Josephus, the book of Sirach begins with a brief prologue, to which may also be compared Luke 1:1-4. Written in three elegant sentences by Ben Sira's grandson, the prologue demonstrates the author's mastery of Greek rhetoric to an extent not found in the rest of the book, where he translates in a manner that reflects the style of the original Hebrew being rendered into Greek. The three sentences (1) explain Ben Sira's reasons for writing the book; (2) request readers to study it in its Greek form, making allowances for infelicities in translation; and (3) provide an autobiographical note about the actual date of the translation and extent of care involved in producing it.

The grandson, who does not give his own name, identifies the author of the book he is translating as "Jesus," which is the Greek form of the popular Hebrew name "Jeshua," and characterizes him as a learned teacher of sacred writings. The author views these texts as channels of divine instruction and for the first time in extant literature refers to Scripture in the tripartite division that came to characterize the Hebrew Bible—the law, the prophets, and the later writings. This initial sentence also mentions the law, the prophets, and the other books of the ancestors; the second sentence varies the expression further, mentioning the law, the prophets, and the rest of the books. Like this loose language, the third group remained open as late as the first century CE (cf. Luke 24:44; in Matt 22:40, Luke 16:16, and Acts 13:15 the expression stops with the mention of the law and the prophets). The Greek text contains a suggestion of discipleship in the reference to the other books that followed. Like Deut 4:6, the author of the prologue sounds a strong note of ethnic pride to encourage readers living in the Egyptian dispersion.

The reference to "those who read the scriptures" echoes the technical expression for professional scribes entrusted with the preservation and transmission of sacred texts. In 1 Esdras the expression takes several forms, always with reference to Ezra: "priest and reader of the law of the Lord" (1 Esdr 8:8-9 NRSV); "priest and reader of the law of Most High God" (1 Esdr 8:19 NRSV); "priest and reader" (1 Esdr 9:39 NRSV); "priest and reader of the law" (1 Esdr 9:42 NRSV); "chief priest and reader" (1 Esdr 9:49 NRSV; cf. Neh 8:8-12). Such "readers" explained the meaning of Scripture written in a language that had ceased to be the vernacular—for Ezra's compatriots, Hebrew texts and Aramaic as the spoken language; for the present readers, a Greek translation of a Hebrew text for outsiders. This reference to non-Jews implies an effort to foster among Egyptians an appreciation for the religious insights of the Jewish tradition. The author attributes inspiration to his learned grandfather, whose book continues the legacy of sacred texts, and views the finished product as progress, the wise teacher adding to the accumulated insights of the ancestors.

The second sentence in Greek voices the anxiety felt by most, if not all, conscientious translators. The early rabbis formulated the problem concisely, attributing the witticism to Eliezer: "Whoever translates literally is a liar, and whoever adds to the text is guilty of blasphemy." Modern translators phrase the issue similarly, juxtaposing two fundamentally different principles—formal correspondence or dynamic equivalence. In brief, should the grammar and syntax of the source language prevail in the target language, or should the idiom of the target language dominate? W. O. E. Oesterley observed that "the numerous instances in which the translator misunderstood the original . . . show that his misgivings were fully justified."[94] In his own defense, the grandson of Ben Sira charged the translators of the Septuagint with similar unintentional misrepresentation of the original sense of the Hebrew text. That translation, probably completed in the mid-second century BCE in Alexandria, was necessitated by the large Jewish population in Egypt.

Jewish presence was felt in Egypt as early as the sixth century BCE; according to the biblical account, the prophet Jeremiah ended his long career there (Jeremiah 43–45). A Jewish community at Elephantine near Aswan has yielded important papyri from the fifth century, one of which mentions a celebration of the Passover; the Zenon papyri provide much information about the economic life of Jews in the second century BCE. In 162 BCE the priest Onias was exiled to Egypt and proceeded to build a rival temple at Leontopolis. From the late third century, when one of Alexander the Great's generals, Ptolemy, assumed control in Egypt, Jewish citizens assisted in maintaining authority over the indigenous population. The first-century CE Jewish philosopher Philo claimed that the Jewish population in Egypt totaled nearly one million.[95] The city of Alexandria granted Jewish citizens full rights, although conflicts in various areas of the country occasionally erupted, such as the burning of the temple to Yahweh at Elephantine. Two quite opposite responses to living in dispersion are evident within Jewish literature of the period: (1) harsh polemic as found in the book of Wisdom and (2) apologetic as exemplified by Josephus's *Antiquities of the Jews* and *Against Apion,* as well as Philo's many writings.

The third sentence in the Greek prologue states that the translator arrived in Egypt during the reign of Euergetes II Ptolemy VIII Physkon, who ruled Egypt from 170 to 164 and 146 to 117 BCE. The Greek word συγχρονίσας (*sygchronisas,* "a synchronizing") indicates that the grandson lived in Egypt from 132 to 117 BCE, completing the translation after Euergetes' death. The translator states that he had access to a copy of the book, ἀφομοιόν (*aphomoion,* "like"), but some manuscripts read ἀφορμήν (*aphormēn,* "opportunity"), implying "access to" and thus opportunity (cf. the different translations in the NRSV text and note).

The three sentences in this prologue employ three thematic expressions: (1) the law, the prophets, and later books (or the variants on the third category, the other writings, the rest of the books); (2) discipline and wisdom; and (3) law. The first of these occurs three times, the other two only two times. Alexander A. Di Lella overlooks the symmetry of these three expressions, for he views the first and last reference to "law" as an inclusio, a statement, a phrase, or a word occurring at the beginning and end of a bracketed unit of thought.[96] Actually, the first sentence uses all three thematic expressions, the first two twice. The second sentence refers to the law, the prophets, and the rest of the books, whereas the third sentence mentions only the law. The phrase "instruction and wisdom" identifies the two major components of the book of Sirach, the teachings of the Mosaic law and proverbial instructions, here linked together for the first time.

94. W. O. E. Oesterley, *The Wisdom of Jesus the Son of Sirach or Ecclesiasticus* (Cambridge: Cambridge University Press, 1912) 3.

95. Philo *Flaccus* VI.43.

96. Patrick W. Skehan and Alexander A. Di Lella, *The Wisdom of Ben Sira,* AB 39 (New York: Doubleday, 1987) 135.

REFLECTIONS

For everyone except the original recipients, God's Word is always at least once removed. This introduces a human element into all Scripture. Those to whom God entrusted a message were required to pass that word along to others whose vocabulary, experience, and psyche differed to some extent. In transmitting the revelation, these human spokespersons for the deity reflected on what they heard and then clothed the message in appropriate rhetoric, along with motive clauses and warnings. In short, they did their best to communicate the essence of the message from God to those who themselves had no direct access to the deity.

Christians today may find it extraordinary that God actually communicated with human beings; most of us would undoubtedly lift an eyebrow if confronted with someone who claims receiving a direct message from God. We should remember that the ancients were not all that different, for not everyone who asserted that God had spoken in his or her life was automatically accepted as an authentic messenger of transcendence. The mere affirmation that the living God, the source of all life and mystery, broke the silence of eternity and entered into dialogue with humans, made in the divine likeness, must surely be as bold a thought as humans can imagine. Viewed in this way, the testimony to this divine-human encounter becomes precious beyond measure. At the same time, its present form cautions against an idolatry that honors the literary medium rather than the God to whom all words point.

By its very nature, every revelation necessitates translation into the language of ordinary discourse. That is no easy task, for a vast chasm separates the two realms, human and divine. We know far more about the former than the latter, and we endeavor to use our greater knowledge to understand the less well-known. The primary means of relating the two realms is analogy. On the basis of the better-known constitutive element, often called *the vehicle* by literary critics, we try to grasp the meaning of the unknown, which critics designate *the tenor*. For Ben Sira and for subsequent interpreters, the Mosaic legislation, particularly the Ten Commandments, functions as the vehicle. The contents of the law are well known, for the legislation touches on matters of everyday experience. The tenor, however, is a construct of the human imagination. It goes by the name of divine wisdom. We know far more about the specific statutes than we do about the broad concept of divine instruction. Nevertheless, together the law and divine wisdom enable us to understand something about God's solicitous concern in guiding humans along safe paths.

In the important task of translating the revealed Word to society at large, faithful transmitters of the tradition were required to preserve accuracy through the ages. The ancient guardians of sacred texts were governed by the spiritual needs of various communities rather than any rigid concern to repeat verbatim earlier versions of the communicative effort. As a result, the tradition grew and retained vitality; in essence, religious texts took on the character of the living Word, a divine communication always both old and new. At the same time, these sacred texts bore witness to the human response to them, often questioning and protesting but, in the end, yielding to divine mystery.

This interrogative mood punctuates prophetic literature and occasionally makes an unexpected appearance in the narrative material in the Torah. The third division of the Hebrew Bible, the writings, witnesses an eruption of protest against the heavens that reaches a crescendo with the books of Job and Ecclesiastes. Ben Sira's teachings belong to this third division; appropriately they combine features of both perspectives, affirming praise and doubt about divine justice. In this extensive collection of a teacher's advice to professional sages, one comes face to face with human wit and wisdom, as in the book of Proverbs, but Ben Sira places this exploration of reality from below within the larger context of divine disclosure.

The language of the prologue, which describes the necessary process of transmitting religious texts across generations and cultures, calls attention to professionals from the religious establishment and to people entirely outside the community of believers. Although regrettable, not all members of a religious group have the inclination or capacity to become proficient in its sacred texts. Consequently, professional interpreters, here called readers, immerse themselves thoroughly in the texts and devote their lives to explaining the hidden meanings of God's interactions with the community. According to the unknown author of the prologue to the book of Sirach, Ben Sira belonged to this elite class of readers. His task was to assist in worship by explaining the meaning of the sacred text in the language of ordinary speech. A danger inherent in this practice is obvious: Others in the religious community relax their natural curiosity and leave the matter of interpretation to specialists.

This tendency to leave the Scriptures to the experts is buttressed by the mysterious character of so many texts, linguistic difficulties, and cultural gaps. Nevertheless, some rabbis spun stories that gave voice to the desire of numerous ordinary people to sit down together and discuss Torah from dawn to dusk. One extraordinary vision of heavenly existence pictured those who love Torah spending eternity while the true meaning of God's gift in sacred words unfolded before their eyes.

In the real world, there will always be outsiders and insiders; perhaps religious people should take heart from the fact that this situation offers an occasion for proclaiming the good news of God at work in human lives. Although the missionary endeavor was not central to ancient Israel, rare insights do acknowledge the need to be a blessing or a light to all nations. By nature evangelistic, Christians feel compelled to declare the good news that is transforming their lives. Often the most effective witness comes through example, not words. The goal to bring outsiders into the fellowship entails faithfulness to the integrity of a religious community; otherwise dissension and ultimately a rift within the body will result.

Possibly the most instructive feature of this prologue to Sirach is the apology for mistakes in translating the original Hebrew text into Greek. Concern over authentic rendering of one language into another has not disappeared from the scene, despite a lapse of over two millennia. The difficulty involved in translation should temper heated contemporary controversies over the inerrancy of Scripture. Because a certain amount of interpretation takes place in every translation, we would do well to adopt a stance of humility with respect to all renderings of the Bible into a language other than the originals. Today we are particularly fortunate in having several excellent translations, among which three stand out as superb representatives of two different principles: the NRSV (cf. also the NIV) for formal correspondence, the TNK, and the REB for dynamic equivalance. Because languages change with time, the task of translation never ends.

The prologue implies that God's people invariably move about from one country to another, often placing them in an alien context, imposing special demands. Existence in exile presents unusual temptations at the same time it offers considerable potential for good, especially the dissemination of the good news. This proclamation takes place through voluntary or involuntary exile, for God's people declare the Word in altogether new settings and unfamiliar languages. That religious message always occurs in the midst of political realities, as the mention of Pharaoh Euergetes suggests. The sacred text emerged in quite particular cultural contexts, a fact we ought always to keep in mind. God's Word certainly includes universal and absolute claims, but these claims are clothed in temporal garb. Separating the timeless from the temporal is exceedingly difficult.

The last verse of the prologue poses an intriguing problem. It can be read in two entirely different ways, one of which has stronger theological resonance. Which of the two should one treat as original? One actually does not need to choose, inasmuch as both readings address God's people, although at different times and in different settings. In one context, the emphasis on God's maternal love spoke with particular force, as it does once more. Another setting took special comfort in connecting God's compassion with scriptural warrant, in this instance the praise of God in Exod 34:6-7. Whether maternal feelings or sacred texts, the allusion captures the poignancy of God's affection for those who lovingly assist victims of a cruel society.

SIRACH 1:1–4:10

PART I

OVERVIEW

Like the book of Proverbs and, to some extent, Ecclesiastes, Sirach has no clear logical progression. Scholars, therefore, have difficulty when trying to divide its contents into distinct units. A few ancient manuscripts have topical headings here and there, although they lack consistency. The divisions that follow represent but one of many possible readings of the material.

Part I consists of five smaller units: (1) 1:1-10, an opening hymn to wisdom; (2) 1:11-30, the meaning and value of the fear of the Lord; (3) 2:1-18, faithfulness during testing; (4) 3:1-16, filial duty; and (5) 3:17–4:10, humility and almsgiving. The hymn to wisdom anticipates a far more elaborate celebration of divine wisdom in chap. 24, and the remarks about the fear of the Lord function as a theological statement for the whole book. The next two sections elaborate on the implications of the first and fifth commandments. The last section deals with responsibilities toward God and fellow human beings, particularly the social mandate to provide aid and comfort for needy persons in the community.

SIRACH 1:1-10, A HYMN TO WISDOM

NAB	NRSV

1 All wisdom comes from the LORD
    and with him it remains forever.
	1 All wisdom is from the Lord,
	    and with him it remains forever.

2 The sand of the seashore, the drops of rain,
    the days of eternity: who can number these?
	² The sand of the sea, the drops of rain,
	    and the days of eternity—who can count them?

3 Heaven's height, earth's breadth,
    the depths of the abyss: who can explore these?
	³ The height of heaven, the breadth of the earth,
	    the abyss, and wisdom[a]—who can search them out?

4 Before all things else wisdom was created;
    and prudent understanding, from eternity.
	⁴ Wisdom was created before all other things,
	    and prudent understanding from eternity.[b]

5 To whom has wisdom's root been revealed?
    Who knows her subtleties?
	⁶ The root of wisdom—to whom has it been revealed?
	    Her subtleties—who knows them?[c]

6 There is but one, wise and truly
        awe-inspiring,
    seated upon his throne:
	⁸ There is but one who is wise, greatly to be feared,
	    seated upon his throne—the Lord.

7 It is the LORD; he created her, has seen her and taken note of her.	
8 He has poured her forth upon all his works,	

a Other ancient authorities read the depth of the abyss b Other ancient authorities add as verse 5, The source of wisdom is God's word in the highest heaven, and her ways are the eternal commandments. c Other ancient authorities add as verse 7, The knowledge of wisdom—to whom was it manifested? And her abundant experience—who has understood it?

1, 3: Omit kai sophian: so P, Lat*.

NAB

upon every living thing according to his
bounty;
he has lavished her upon his friends.

NRSV

[9] It is he who created her;
he saw her and took her measure;
he poured her out upon all his works,
[10] upon all the living according to his gift;
he lavished her upon those who love him.[a]

[a]Other ancient authorities add *Love of the Lord is glorious wisdom;
to those to whom he appears he apportions her, that they may see
him.*

COMMENTARY

Marböck concludes his analysis of the opening hymn to wisdom (vv. 1-10) with these words: "the hymnic introduction . . . contains the outline and most significant elements for a theology of wisdom in Ben Sira."[97] To be sure, Marböck's observations are directed at refuting the thesis of Josef Haspecker that the fear of Yahweh, not wisdom, lies at the heart of Sirach and that the hymn in vv. 1-10 introduces only 1:1–2:18, a treatise on the fear of God.[98] Both of these scholars have clearly observed the signal importance of the opening hymn to divine wisdom.

The language and mood of this hymn are charged with polemical overtones, probably resulting from Ben Sira's encounter with Hellenistic philosophy, especially the Stoic philosophers' emphasis on the antiquity of their wisdom. For Ben Sira, only one God could rightly be called wise, and that one was Yahweh, the personal God of the Jews. Ben Sira attributes all wisdom to this God and concedes that humans acquire knowledge solely as a divine gift. With one sweep of the pen, he rules out human experience as a valid means of discovering the hidden subtleties of God's wisdom. The only bridge from human to divine knowledge starts with God's initiative, in which wisdom serves as a medium of divine presence and a revelation to human beings. In the words of C. J. Kearns, wisdom is "the multifareous gift that He has made of Himself, personified so as to be rendered comprehensible."[99]

Ben Sira reaches back into prophetic tradition to describe Yahweh's generous dispersal of wisdom on all flesh, but particularly on the elect. The expectation of an outpouring of the divine spirit, first articulated by Moses (Num 11:29) and subsequently endorsed by Ezekiel (Ezek 39:29) and Joel (Joel 3:1-5[Eng. 2:28-32]), furnishes the language for God's gift of wisdom to all flesh ($\mu\epsilon\tau\grave{\alpha}$ $\pi\acute{\alpha}\sigma\eta\varsigma$ $\sigma\alpha\rho\kappa\grave{o}\varsigma$ *meta pasēs sarkos,* 1:10*a*). Just as Joel 3:1[2:28] restricts the outpouring of the divine vitality to Jews, so also Ben Sira places "those whom Yahweh loves" in a special category. Similarly, Ben Sira borrows traditional language from prophecy and wisdom to describe the inaccessibility of wisdom. The rhetorical questions in vv. 2-3 and 6 recall Job 38:4; Prov 30:4; Isa 40:12-14; and Bar 3:15. Even the expressions "the sand of the seashore" and "drops of rain" echo Gen 32:12; 1 Sam 13:5; Ps 78:27; and Job 36:27 respectively. The creation of wisdom recalls the hymn in Prov 8:22-30, while wisdom's hiddenness is remarked on in Job 28:28. Ben Sira's use of impossible questions (vv. 2-3) gives expression to a cosmology that seems strange to modern readers, one composed of spatially limited heavens, a flat earth floating on top of underground waters, the circuit of which can be traversed in a day by the sun god (Ps 19:4*b*-6). The form of the impossible questions resembles numerical proverbs.[100]

The rare Greek word in v. 6 for wisdom's sub-

97. J. Marböck, *Weisheit im Wandel: Untersuchungen zur Weisheitstheologie bei Ben Sira,* BBB 37 (Bonn: Peter Hanstein Verlag GMBH, 1971) 34.

98. Ibid., 93-104, and Josef Haspecker, *Gottesfurcht bei Jesus Sirach,* AnBib 30 (Rome: Pontifical Biblical Institute, 1967).

99. C. J. Kearns, "La vie intérieure à l'école de l'Ecclésiastique," *La Vie Spirituelle* 82 (1950) 146.

100. Cf. James L. Crenshaw, "Impossible Questions and Tasks in Israelite Wisdom," *Gnomic Wisdom,* Semeia 7 (1981) 19-34 (also in James L. Crenshaw, *Urgent Advice and Probing Questions* [Macon, Ga.: Mercer University Press, 1995] 265-78), and "Questions, Dictons et Épreuves Impossibles," in *La Sagesse de l'Ancien Testament,* ed. Maurice Gilbert, BETL 51 (Leuwen: Duculot, 1979) 96-111.

tleties (πανουργεύματα *panourgeumata*, "secrets") occurs elsewhere in Sirach only at 42:18; together with σοφία (*sophia*) and ἐπιστήμη (*epistēmē*, vv. 6*a*, 7*a*, "wisdom" and "understanding"), it occurs also in Jdt 11:8, the only other place these three words appear in close proximity.[101] Ben Sira uses "root" and "subtleties" to indicate the origin and essence of divine wisdom; the Hebrew word ראשׁית (*rē'šît*) in Prov 1:7 includes the ideas of "source," "essence," and "primacy." Like the unknown author of the prologue to the first collection of the book of Proverbs (Proverbs 1–9; or to the whole book), Ben Sira associates fear of the Lord with wisdom, but in reverse sequence if one takes *rē'šît* to be temporal, a moment of beginning.

The interpretative addition to v. 4, found in some manuscripts, anticipates Ben Sira's later discourse on his inspiration that began as a small stream and grew to unexpected size (24:23-33). It reads: "The source of wisdom is God's word in the highest heaven, and her ways are the eternal commandments" (v. 5 NRSV). The gloss after v. 6 is repetitive: "The knowledge of wisdom—to whom was it manifested? And her abundant experience—who has understood it?" (v. 7). The addition to v. 10*ab* elaborates on the notion of God's friends (lit., "those who love God"). Marböck rightly focuses on vv. 1 and 8-10, the former verse as a great superscription and the latter verses as its obvious development.[102] Certain features of the original hymn in vv. 1-4, 6, 8-10*b* (omitting the two interpretative glosses in vv. 5 and 7) anticipate ideas that Ben Sira will take up later, specifically in the rest of chap. 1 and in chap. 18. The hymn extols different forms of wisdom, creation, and the fear of God. The brief allusion in v.

9 to mercy provides a clue for the interpretation of the entire first chapter, and indeed for the whole book. Marböck recognizes the importance of divine mercy to Ben Sira, although without adequate discussion of the tension thus produced with older sapiential views, according to which individuals received exactly what they deserved.[103] The centrality of mercy in the brief hymn in 18:1-13 and similarities with the initial one under discussion here, especially the idea of divine largess to all, suggest that Ben Sira considered these themes crucial to his teaching. The hymn in vv. 1-4, 6, 8-10*b* also clearly relates to vv. 25-27, which unites the themes of wisdom and fear of the Lord. The latter concept occupies center stage in vv. 11-30.

This opening hymn to wisdom actually extols its Creator, who alone has complete access to its mysteries and thus deserves the epithet "Wise." By enumerating various secrets of the universe that continue to mystify humans, the author contrasts our limited knowledge with God's immediate control of such facts as those that defy human inquiry. As the first created one, wisdom was subsequently mediated to other creatures, particularly to those who love God. Here in this simple observation Ben Sira sums up the exquisite praise of wisdom in Prov 8:22-31 and Job 28, to which he will return (cf. Sirach 24), using considerably more lavish language. The present hymn strikes a note of awe, both in the references to the unknown and unknowable, and in the reminder that the Wise Sovereign must be revered.

---

101. Skehan and Di Lella, *The Wisdom of Ben Sira*, 138.
102. Marböck, *Weisheit im Wandel*, 23.

103. Ibid., 28-30; and James L. Crenshaw, "The Concept of God in Old Testament Wisdom," 1-18 in *In Search of Wisdom: Essays in Memory of John G. Gammie*, ed. Leo G. Perdue et al. (Louisville: Westminster John Knox, 1993) 1-18. See also Crenshaw, *Urgent Advice and Probing Questions*, 191-205.

REFLECTIONS

The hymn about wisdom's true source arises from recognition that mystery always remains in any intellectual quest. Critical inquiry can do no more than touch the hem of the garment of truth. Jewish mystics spoke about the world as the garments of Torah, an insight Christians would do well to acknowledge. Such an understanding of reality gives the world a sacred character, including the declaration that the universe consists of divine disclosure, an accommodation necessitated by human weakness and ignorance. Ben Sira intimates that the universe conceals sufficient mystery to satisfy the curiosity of average citizens as well as gifted overachievers in intellectual quests. Whereas God has access to all wisdom, that unique possession does not create in the deity a wish to keep it for selfish purposes. Instead, God freely offers bits and pieces of this knowledge to deserving human beings. Here, too, humility is in order, for individuals who acquire huge amounts of knowledge owe much of it to divine generosity. Seminal thinkers know this fact well.

SIRACH 1:11-30, THE MEANING AND VALUE OF THE FEAR OF THE LORD

NAB

9 Fear of the LORD is glory and splendor,
    gladness and a festive crown.

10 Fear of the LORD warms the heart,
    giving gladness and joy and length of days.

11 He who fears the LORD will have a happy end;
    even on the day of his death he will be blessed.

12 The beginning of wisdom is fear of the LORD,
    which is formed with the faithful in the womb.

13 With devoted men was she created from of old,
    and with their children her beneficence abides.

14 Fullness of wisdom is fear of the LORD;
    she inebriates men with her fruits.

15 Her entire house she fills with choice foods,
    her granaries with her harvest.

16 Wisdom's garland is fear of the LORD,
    with blossoms of peace and perfect health.

17 Knowledge and full understanding she showers down;
    she heightens the glory of those who possess her.

18 The root of wisdom is fear of the LORD;
    her branches are length of days.

19 One cannot justify unjust anger;
    anger plunges a man to his downfall.

20 A patient man need stand firm but for a time,

1, 11: (*teleutēs autou*) *eulogēthēsetai*: so LXX^MSS, Vrs.
1, 12, 22: *yir'at yhwh.*
1, 13: 'im 'anšê ḥesed mē 'ôlām qānāh, we 'im zar'ām nē'ēmān ḥasdāh: so with P; cf 44, 10f.
1, 17: Omit *kai eiden kai exērithmēsen autēn*: so LXX^MSS, P; dittog: cf v 7b.

NRSV

11 The fear of the Lord is glory and exultation,
    and gladness and a crown of rejoicing.

12 The fear of the Lord delights the heart,
    and gives gladness and joy and long life.[a]

13 Those who fear the Lord will have a happy end;
    on the day of their death they will be blessed.

14 To fear the Lord is the beginning of wisdom;
    she is created with the faithful in the womb.

15 She made[b] among human beings an eternal foundation,
    and among their descendants she will abide faithfully.

16 To fear the Lord is fullness of wisdom;
    she inebriates mortals with her fruits;

17 she fills their[c] whole house with desirable goods,
    and their[c] storehouses with her produce.

18 The fear of the Lord is the crown of wisdom,
    making peace and perfect health to flourish.[d]

19 She rained down knowledge and discerning comprehension,
    and she heightened the glory of those who held her fast.

20 To fear the Lord is the root of wisdom,
    and her branches are long life.[e]

22 Unjust anger cannot be justified,
    for anger tips the scale to one's ruin.

[a]Other ancient authorities add *The fear of the Lord is a gift from the Lord; also for love he makes firm paths.* [b]Gk *made as a nest* [c]Other ancient authorities read *her* [d]Other ancient authorities add *Both are gifts of God for peace; glory opens out for those who love him. He saw her and took her measure.* [e]Other ancient authorities add as verse 21, *The fear of the Lord drives away sins; and where it abides, it will turn away all anger.*

NAB

and then contentment comes back to him.
21 For a while he holds back his words,
    then the lips of many herald his wisdom.
22 Among wisdom's treasures is the paragon of
        prudence;
    but fear of the LORD is an abomination to
        the sinner.
23 If you desire wisdom, keep the
        commandments,
    and the LORD will bestow her upon you;
24 For fear of the LORD is wisdom and culture;
    loyal humility is his delight.
25 Be not faithless to the fear of the LORD,
    nor approach it with duplicity of heart.
26 Play not the hypocrite before men;
    over your lips keep watch.
27 Exalt not yourself lest you fall
    and bring upon you dishonor;
28 For then the LORD will reveal your secrets
    and publicly cast you down,
29 Because you approached the fear of the
        LORD
    with your heart full of guile.

1, 21: (*kai cheilē*) *pollōn*: so LXX^(S,A), V.
1, 26: *lipenê* or *le·ênê*: cf P, V; MS 253: *enōpion*; but LXX originally *en ommasin?*
1, 29: Omit *ou*: so P, V; or read *sy?*

NRSV

23 Those who are patient stay calm until the right
        moment,
    and then cheerfulness comes back to them.
24 They hold back their words until the right
        moment;
    then the lips of many tell of their good
        sense.

25 In the treasuries of wisdom are wise sayings,
    but godliness is an abomination to a sinner.
26 If you desire wisdom, keep the
        commandments,
    and the Lord will lavish her upon you.
27 For the fear of the Lord is wisdom and
        discipline,
    fidelity and humility are his delight.

28 Do not disobey the fear of the Lord;
    do not approach him with a divided mind.
29 Do not be a hypocrite before others,
    and keep watch over your lips.
30 Do not exalt yourself, or you may fall
    and bring dishonor upon yourself.
The Lord will reveal your secrets
    and overthrow you before the whole
        congregation,
because you did not come in the fear of the
        Lord,
    and your heart was full of deceit.

COMMENTARY

A poem of twenty-two bicola (a line of poetry with two half-lines as separate cola), the same number of letters in the Hebrew alphabet, serves as a programmatic statement for the entire book. It identifies wisdom with the fear of God—that is, religion—and enumerates the fruits of living according to wisdom's dictates. Ben Sira infuses his statements about the fear of the Lord with the warmth of personal piety. The expression "fear of the LORD" and its variant occur ten times in this poem (twelve times if one counts the addition to v. 12, together with v. 21) and function as an inclusio to delimit the unit (vv. 11, 30). The heart of the poem equates wisdom, fear of the Lord, discipline, and observing the Mosaic law (vv.

25-27). A thematic statement (v. 11) leads to a promise of a long and blessed life to those who fear the Lord (vv. 12-20, where "long life" in vv. 12, 20 forms an inclusio), which abruptly veers off into warnings against loss of self-control (vv. 22-24) before returning to stress the need for keeping the commandments (vv. 25-27) and avoiding duplicity (vv. 28-30).

For the most part, Ben Sira's teachings in this poem derive from the book of Proverbs, especially the introductory collection Proverbs 1–9, which gives prominence to personified wisdom, but also the final praise of woman in Prov 31:10-31. Some of these images of wisdom as a crown, a garland, a tree, health and life, happiness, produce, root and branches came to prominence in later wisdom texts also (e.g., Wis 6:17-21; 7:1–9:18). At least two expressions in Ben Sira's poem about the identification of wisdom as fear of the Lord echo the larger canon, Torah and the Prophets. The concept of abomination (v. 25) is a cultic expression in Deuteronomy, although the notion belongs to the wisdom tradition in Egypt and the book of Proverbs as well. The connection in v. 26 with the commandments points to the original deuteronomic context in which God's law is proclaimed (cf. Exod 20:2-17; Deut 5:1-21) in capsular form. Ben Sira may actually allude to the entire Mosaic legislation. In v. 14, Ben Sira expresses a concept that was regularly associated with the birth of a prophet or a special servant of Yahweh in Israel (Isa 44:24; Jer 1:5) and with royal births in Mesopotamia. In this view, God chooses special persons to carry out individual assignments, whether prophetic or royal.

The reference to a happy end to life (v. 13) does not imply anything beyond the grave, for in this respect Ben Sira sides with those who later formed the party of the Sadducees. He accepts the usual teaching about the end (אחרית 'aḥărît) in the OT—that a person dies and joins the ancestors in a ghost-like existence in Sheol, the body returning to dust whence it came, according to hallowed narrative. Ben Sira's reference to the dead being blessed lacks any indication of the one doing the blessing, whether God or the human survivors (cf. 11:25-28, however, where Ben Sira attributes the blessing to God). According to the wisdom teachers who composed the book of Proverbs, an intimate connection existed between morality and happiness, with rare exceptions. These exceptions became the rule for the authors of the books of Job and Ecclesiastes, and yet Ben Sira was hardly touched by their poignant attacks on traditional wisdom. Events soon after he wrote his book threw an even greater question mark on this optimism, for the frequency of martyrdom during the Maccabean revolt (167–164 BCE) made it difficult to describe the end of such faithful ones as blessed. The author of Dan 12:2 breaks sharply with Hebrew tradition in a desperate effort to salvage divine reputation for justice and to provide comfort for those who either faced a martyr's end or grieved for someone who had.

Many features of this poem manifest an exuberance equal to that of the final verse in the prologue, which speaks of God's lavishing gifts on friends. Drawing on the poem about personified wisdom's building her house and inviting guests to a feast (Prov 9:1-6), Ben Sira actually uses a word for "inebriation" (μεθύσκω methyskō, v. 16). The allusion in v. 15 to her building a nest (ἐνόσσευσεν enosseusen) anticipates 24:8-12, a section on wisdom's coming to dwell in Jerusalem that reaches a crescendo at the close of the first half of the book. At the same time, this allusion looks back on the similar poem about personified wisdom in Prov 8:22-31.

The resemblances between this figure of wisdom and the Egyptian goddess ma'at have been acknowledged for some time, especially the picture of her holding the ankh, a symbol of long life, in one hand and riches in the other. That idea certainly resembles Ben Sira's description of wisdom's gifts. In addition, Egyptian wisdom emphasizes silence so much that the word becomes a technical term for the person of character, one who controls anger and is, therefore, the opposite of the heated person. Egyptian instructions also describe the good person as one who is like a tree with well-watered roots (cf. v. 20 and more fully 24:13-14, 16-17), and they characterize wise behavior in terms of restraint, eloquence, timing, and integrity. The wise person, thus, practices self-discipline, speaks effectively at the appropriate moment, and declares the truth. In vv. 22-24, Ben Sira refers to self-control and the right time (καιρός kairos) for speaking. The image of wisdom as a garland and a crown has its exact counterpart in Egyptian wisdom literature.

The interplay between free will and divine gift finds expression in v. 26, where human initiative evokes divine largess. To the unspoken question, "How can one become wise?" Ben Sira answers, "Keep the commandments." The author of the Epistle of James offers yet another response to this query: "Ask God for wisdom" (Jas 1:5 NRSV). The closing section of Ben Sira's poem introduces a powerful element of social control in the ancient world: honor and shame, one that he returns to several times (3:2-11; 4:21; 7:7; 10:19–11:6; 41:17–42:8). In his first reference to the loss of honor (v. 30), Ben Sira probably reflects on a text in Proverbs in which a dying victim of the "strange woman" confesses his mistake:

Oh, how I hated discipline,
and my heart despised reproof!
I did not listen to the voice of my teachers
or incline my ear to my instructors.
Now I am at the point of utter ruin
in the public assembly. (Prov 5:12-14 NRSV)

Presumably, Ben Sira thinks of disgrace in the context of the synagogue, although the greater Jewish community functioned as a social arena dispensing honor or shame. The language of duplicity, a double heart, occurs in Ps 12:3 and Jas 1:8; 4:8, and the notion of watching over one's lips recalls Ps 141:3, a theme that recurs in Sir 23:2-3.

Ben Sira's deep piety comes to expression in vv. 25-27, where the Greek words σοφία (*sophia*, "wisdom"), παιδεία (*paideia,* "instruction"), πίστις (*pistis*, "faith"), and πραότης (*praotēs,* "humility") recall venerable Hebrew terms for "wisdom" (חכמה *ḥokmâ*), "instruction" (מוסר *mûsār*), "faithfulness" (אמונה *'ĕmûnâ*), and "humility" (ענוה *'ănāwâ*). The noun *'ĕmûnâ* consists of active fidelity and passive trustworthiness, senses conveyed by various renderings in the Septuagint (*pistis,* "faith"; πιστός *pistos* "faithful"; ἀλήθεια *alētheia*, "truth"; ἀληθινός *alēthinos*, "truthful"; ἀξιόπιστος *axiopistos*, "reliable"). It thus becomes clear that the word includes far more than the cognitive dimension; mere intellectual assent expresses itself by means of appropriate action, as the author of the Epistle of James recognized.

To reiterate, this elaboration of the primacy of religious devotion within intellectual inquiry leaves no doubt about Ben Sira's allegiance. He elevates piety above all else, but it is an informed piety. Wisdom determines one's speech and actions, as it were, watching over those who fear God and keep the divine commandments. Such wisdom embraces every dimension of human existence, in Ben Sira's opinion. It informs one's silence, bringing rich dividends both in material wealth and in prestige among one's peers. It shapes virtue and strenghtens one in the fight against vice. Wisdom also gives loyal followers integrity, enabling them to avoid hypocrisy. Under its instruction, the faithful learn to compose wise sayings and thus to transmit a valuable legacy to others. Ben Sira will spell out these insights, and more, in what follows.

REFLECTIONS

For Ben Sira, genuine religious faith is the clearest indication of wisdom. A person cannot, in his view, be wise without acknowledging the priority of God in one's life. Possibly the most daring suggestion of all concerns the personification of wisdom as a woman, given the frequent disparaging of women in ancient proverbial sayings. This bold move was undoubtedly dictated by two factors: the circumstances of instruction, where boys comprised the students; and the feminine form of abstractions, such as wisdom, truth, and righteousness in the Hebrew and Greek languages. Viewing wisdom as feminine definitely introduced an erotic component into learning precisely at a stage in the life of young boys when they could make optimal use of attraction to the opposite sex.

This practice, while potentially enervating, is also fraught with danger. The natural curiosity about the opposite sex among young people easily leads to conduct that threatens both their spiritual well-being and their physical safety. At the same time, this heightening of the erotic brings the whole realm of sex into the clear light of day, requiring youth to come to terms with powerful feelings while striving to discover God's will for their lives. This struggle, begun in tender years, lasts into later years as well, and the church will do well to harness erotic energy so as to channel it into productive endeavors. Sacred dance and drama can add a powerful dimension to worship, particularly when one sees the body as a place of residence for the divine.

SIRACH 2:1-18, FAITHFULNESS DURING TESTING

NAB

2 My son, when you come to serve the LORD,
  prepare yourself for trials.
2 Be sincere of heart and steadfast,
  undisturbed in time of adversity.
3 Cling to him, forsake him not;
  thus will your future be great.
4 Accept whatever befalls you,
  in crushing misfortune be patient;
5 For in fire gold is tested,
  and worthy men in the crucible of
  humiliation.
6 Trust God and he will help you;
  make straight your ways and hope in him.

7 You who fear the LORD, wait for his mercy,
  turn not away lest you fall.
8 You who fear the LORD, trust him,
  and your reward will not be lost.
9 You who fear the LORD, hope for good
  things,
  for lasting joy and mercy.
10 Study the generations long past and
  understand;
  has anyone hoped in the LORD and been
  disappointed?
  Has anyone persevered in his fear and been
  forsaken?
  has anyone called upon him and been
  rebuffed?
11 Compassionate and merciful is the LORD;
  he forgives sins, he saves in time of
  trouble.

12 Woe to craven hearts and drooping hands,
  to the sinner who treads a double path!
13 Woe to the faint of heart who trust not,
  who therefore will have no shelter!
14 Woe to you who have lost hope!
  what will you do at the visitation of the
  LORD?
15 Those who fear the LORD disobey not his
  words;

2, 1: Omit *theọ* : so LXX[S,A,C].
2, 9: (*aiōnos kaì*) *eleos*: so a few LXX[MSS]; cf V.

NRSV

2 My child, when you come to
  serve the Lord,
  prepare yourself for testing.[a]
2 Set your heart right and be steadfast,
  and do not be impetuous in time of
  calamity.
3 Cling to him and do not depart,
  so that your last days may be prosperous.
4 Accept whatever befalls you,
  and in times of humiliation be patient.
5 For gold is tested in the fire,
  and those found acceptable, in the furnace
  of humiliation.[b]
6 Trust in him, and he will help you;
  make your ways straight, and hope in him.

7 You who fear the Lord, wait for his mercy;
  do not stray, or else you may fall.
8 You who fear the Lord, trust in him,
  and your reward will not be lost.
9 You who fear the Lord, hope for good things,
  for lasting joy and mercy.[c]
10 Consider the generations of old and see:
  has anyone trusted in the Lord and been
  disappointed?
  Or has anyone persevered in the fear of the
  Lord[d] and been forsaken?
  Or has anyone called upon him and been
  neglected?
11 For the Lord is compassionate and merciful;
  he forgives sins and saves in time of distress.

12 Woe to timid hearts and to slack hands,
  and to the sinner who walks a double path!
13 Woe to the fainthearted who have no trust!
  Therefore they will have no shelter.
14 Woe to you who have lost your nerve!
  What will you do when the Lord's
  reckoning comes?

15 Those who fear the Lord do not disobey his
  words,

a Or *trials* *b* Other ancient authorities add *in sickness and poverty put your trust in him* *c* Other ancient authorities add *For his reward is an everlasting gift with joy.* *d* Gk *of him*

NAB	NRSV
those who love him keep his ways.	and those who love him keep his ways.
16 Those who fear the LORD seek to please him, / those who love him are filled with his law.	16 Those who fear the Lord seek to please him, / and those who love him are filled with his law.
17 Those who fear the LORD prepare their hearts / and humble themselves before him.	17 Those who fear the Lord prepare their hearts, / and humble themselves before him.
18 Let us fall into the hands of the LORD / and not into the hands of men, / For equal to his majesty / is the mercy that he shows.	18 Let us fall into the hands of the Lord, / but not into the hands of mortals; / for equal to his majesty is his mercy, / and equal to his name are his works.[a]

^aSyr: Gk lacks this line

COMMENTARY

This section consists of three stanzas and a concluding couplet (vv. 1-6, 7-11, 12-16 + 17-18). Its ornate rhetorical style—three verses beginning with "You who fear the Lord" (vv. 7-9), three rhetorical questions (v. 10), three verses with introductory "woe to" (vv. 12-14), and three verses with an initial phrase consisting of "Those who fear the Lord" (vv. 15-17)—suggests oral use in classrooms. These *repetits* (refrain-like phrases) aided the memory and enhanced the rhetorical style of the unit. The key to understanding the first stanza, v. 6 has the catchwords "trust" (πιστεύω *pisteuō*) and "hope" (ἐλπίς *elpis*), whereas "mercy" (ἔλεος *eleos*) in vv. 7-9 provides a cohesion for the second stanza, and the correspondence between vv. 11 and 18 links the last two stanzas.

2:1-6. The idea of testing, discipline attributed to a loving father in Prov 3:11-12, follows naturally from the previous poem, which ends by warning against hypocrisy. Adversity has the potential for unmasking such insincere religion. The literature on divine testing in the OT is set within such a context (e.g., the offering of Isaac, Gen 22:1-18; the trials of Joseph in Egypt, Genesis 37–50; and the afflictions of Job). Biblical texts frequently describe this testing in the language of separating impure dross from precious metal (cf. Prov 17:3; Wis 3:6; Jas 1:12). The biblical writers maintain firm confidence that genuinely virtuous people will emerge victoriously in the end, just as the worst-case scenario, Job, exemplifies. Only the author of Ecclesiastes resolutely refuses to view testing in positive terms (perhaps also the

author of Jeremiah's laments in Jer 11:18–12:6; 15:10-21; 17:14-18; 18:18-23; 20:7-18). The three young men who enter the furnace, according to the devotional legend in Daniel 3, confess their readiness to die even if God elects not to rescue them (Dan 3:16-18). In some instances, these experiences of testing forged a special bond between the worshiper and God, eliciting profound expressions of piety.[104]

An important manuscript, MS 248, sets this unit apart by means of a heading, "On Patience" (περι ὑπομονῆς *peri hypomonēs*). The initial vocative, "my son" (τέκνον *teknon*) appears frequently in the book (3:12, 17; 4:1; 6:32; 10:28; 11:10; 14:11; 31:22; in the plural, 3:1; 23:7; 39:13; 41:14). This direct address of a son is typical of wisdom instruction throughout the ancient Near East, beginning as early as the third-millennium Sumerian *Instructions of Šuruppak* and Egyptian royal instructions. In this same vein, Israelite teachers directed their words to sons ("my son," Prov 1:8, 10, 15; 2:1; often in Proverbs 1–9; occasionally in Prov 22:17–24:22; "sons," Prov 4:1; 5:7). From earliest times this language of "father" and "son" was used in educational settings to designate "teacher" and "student." Sumerian schools also had a monitor who went by the title of "big brother." At first this familial language referred to kinship, but over the years the terms "father" and "son" lost their original

---

104. Cf. Ps 73:23-28. On these texts, see James L. Crenshaw, *A Whirlpool of Torment* (Philadelphia: Fortress, 1984) 99-100, 106-9.

connotations entirely and came to designate "teachers" and "students" only. That is exactly how בני (*bĕnî*; τέκνον *teknon*) functions for Ben Sira.

One of the most difficult aspects of testing was the necessity of holding firm in one's expectation of promised gratification for faithful conduct. Hence the necessity for encouraging words like Ben Sira's, "Trust in him, and he will help you" (v. 6a). Hoping in God's eventual deliverance of the worshiper occupies central place in much of the Bible, although sounding a rare note in wisdom literature, which emphasized human achievement. Ben Sira unites the traditional piety of psalms, prophecy, and sacred narrative with the more down-to-earth teachings of the sages. In this respect, Ben Sira continues the views attributed to Job's three friends who urge him to place his hope in God.[105]

2:7-11. In v. 10, Ben Sira uses a traditional argument of the sages, the appeal to accumulated experience. His long rhetorical question:

Has anyone trusted in the Lord
and been disappointed?
Or has anyone persevered in the
fear of the Lord and been forsaken?
Or has anyone called upon him
and been neglected?

anticipates a negative response (cf. Ps 22:4-5). This answer scarcely follows if one actually examines Israel's recorded past, particularly the tragic disappointment ending King Josiah's faithful reliance on the promises articulated in the book of Deuteronomy. Religious belief seldom coincides, however, with brutal reality, and people always seem capable of interpreting even the most adverse circumstances as confirmation of dogmatic expectations (cf. Ps 37:25-26).

Like numerous worshipers who preceded him in Israel, Ben Sira bases his confidence on Yahweh's much-cited proclamation to Moses of the divine attributes:

"The LORD, the LORD,
a God merciful and gracious,
slow to anger,
and abounding in steadfast love and faithfulness,
keeping steadfast love for the thousandth generation,

forgiving iniquity and transgression and sin,
yet by no means clearing the guilty,
but visiting the iniquity of the parents
upon the children
and the children's children,
to the third and the fourth generation."
(Exod 34:6-7 NRSV; cf., e.g., Pss 86:5; 103:3-4; 145:8-9; Joel 2:13; Jonah 4:2; Neh 9:17)

Predictably, later citations of this text omit the threatening traits of the divine character and appeal to the Lord's compassionate nature (except for Nah 1:2-3, directed against Nineveh). Liturgical use of this text extends beyond the Bible to the contemporary Jewish Passover seder, in which children respond to their parents' question, "Who knows?" (מי ידע *mî yôdēaʿ*), in numerical gradations from one to thirteen, ultimately reaching a devotional crescendo with the recitation of the thirteen divine attributes. Modern interpreters have understandably mined this biblical text as a mother lode of theological insight.[106]

2:12-14. For Jewish compatriots who consider Hellenistic thought and culture superior to ancestral traditions of the Jews, Ben Sira reserves the strongest language. Three times in these verses he utters the language of curse ("woe to" [הוי *hôy*; οὐαι *ouai*]). Persons whose hands slacken in observing the Mosaic statutes and who neglect to lift them in prayer occasion the first of these harsh curses. The other two uses of the curse accentuate cowardice and loss of nerve. All three refer to the body: heart and hand, heart, and nerve, respectively. The Lord's reckoning to which Ben Sira refers is entirely this-worldly; it manifests itself in various forms of sickness and disaster. The image of walking a double path, almost comic, underlines the absurdity of all attempts to reconcile Jewish and Hellenistic worldviews, according to Ben Sira. He was prepared to make modest compromises to accommodate those who valued Hellenistic ways, but that principle did not extend to matters affecting the divine commandments concerning good deeds. He will-

---

105. For this theme in the HB, see Walther Zimmerli, *Hope in the Old Testament* (London: SCM, 1971).

106. See Michael Fishbane, *Biblical Interpretation in Ancient Israel* (Oxford: Clarendon, 1985) 335-50; Thomas B. Dozeman, "Inner-Biblical Interpretation of Yahweh's Gracious and Compassionate Character," *JBL* 108 (1989) 207-23; David Noel Freedman, "God Compassionate and Gracious," *Western Watch* 6 (1955) 6-24; and James L. Crenshaw, "Who Knows What YHWH Will Do? The Character of God in the Book of Joel," in *Fortunate the Eyes That See: Essays in Honor of David Noel Freedman in Celebration of His Seventieth Birthday,* ed. Andrew H. Bartelt et al. (Grand Rapids: Eerdmans, 1994) 185-96.

ingly adopted Greek views and practices without any real drawing of the line. Perhaps the political situation permitted him such freedom. That changed with the oppressive policies inaugurated by Antiochus IV.

2:15-17. The concluding stanza stresses the interior motive for serving God and enjoins humility. The author of the saying in the Jewish tractate *Pirqe 'Abot* ("The Sayings of the Fathers") that elevates the love of God over desire for reward ("Be not as slaves that minister to their master in order to receive reward; but be as slaves that minister to their master without a view of receiving reward," *Pirqe 'Abot* 1:3) follows the clear teaching of Ben Sira. According to v. 16, religious devotion arises out of desire to please God. The keeping of the law, suspect to those Jews who have fallen under Hellenism's seduction, issues from love for God. This theme will recur many times throughout the book. For now, however, Ben Sira endeavors to put the fear of God into his hearers—and readers.

2:18. The final couplet evokes an episode in King David's life when he became vulnerable to divine wrath by, of all things, obeying Yahweh's explicit order to take a census of the people. Ben Sira quotes, not entirely accurately, David's decision to take his chances with God's wrath rather than endure three years of famine or three months of fleeing before enemies (cf. 2 Sam 24:1-17, esp. vv. 13-14). Choosing a three-day pestilence, David entertains the hope that Yahweh's unpredictable anger will give way before the reliable divine compassion: "I am in great distress; let us fall into the hand of the LORD, for his mercy is great; but let me not fall into human hands" (2 Sam 24:14 NRSV). The appeal to this text, like so much application of Scripture to later situations, stretches it to the limits, for an innocent David awaits divine punishment, whereas Ben Sira appears to view dependence on Yahweh as a means of *escaping* wrath. In any event, he closes this unit with a pun on the Hebrew word from Exod 34:6 for divine compassion, רחום (*raḥûm*; cf. 50:19), which he equates with God's name.

To sum up, in this section Ben Sira acknowledges that all who strive to do good inevitably encounter obstacles along the way. They need not despair, however, for the author of such trials uses difficulty to build character. Facing tests of various kinds, one should faithfully rely on divine assistance, knowing that the outcome will be favorable. This confidence rests above all in the nature of God, whose compassion is well known and whose faithfulness is attested from of old. Nevertheless, one's trust should have a solid basis in piety, for God's mercy is exacting.

REFLECTIONS

Ben Sira was convinced that true wisdom accompanied the keeping of the law. In Christian terms, this means that we become wise as a direct result of obeying God's will. True knowledge depends on faithfulness to divine guidance. To be sure, some people only pretend to be religious, necessitating rigorous examination of the conduct of those who claim to be wise. True religion is evident in those who worship God alone; Ben Sira knew that such devotion was difficult, for moments of testing inevitably arise. To stave off such temptation, he urged people to become thoroughly familiar with religious history. In his view, the testimony of predecessors provided adequate support for believing in divine mercy. In Hasidic Judaism and in Christian worship of the recent past, at least among some fellowships, testimony to God's faithfulness became a significant part of communal life. We may not wish to revert to this practice liturgically, but we can surely benefit from conversations with elderly members of congregations in which they bear witness to God's faithfulness during their days in our midst. The active participation of the elderly in worship thus provides an inspiration and a model for younger people, for whom the older generation stands as a permanent witness to the truth of the gospel and its claims on their lives.

Ben Sira's brief reference to David's struggle to endure divine anger in the least destructive manner introduces readers to a valuable means of relating to Scripture. In this instance, readers are instructed to search the sacred texts for occasions when someone experienced something similar to the circumstances confronting them. The assumption underlying this anecdote is that God is faithful. If in David's case God's fury was clothed in mercy, God will most probably behave similarly now.

SIRACH 3:1-16, FILIAL DUTY

NAB

3 Children, pay heed to a father's right;
  do so that you may live.

2 For the Lord sets a father in honor over his children;
  a mother's authority he confirms over her sons.

3 He who honors his father atones for sins;

4 he stores up riches who reveres his mother.

5 He who honors his father is gladdened by children,
  and when he prays he is heard.

6 He who reveres his father will live a long life;
  he obeys the Lord who brings comfort to his mother.

7 He who fears the Lord honors his father,
  and serves his parents as rulers.

8 In word and deed honor your father
  that his blessing may come upon you;

9 For a father's blessing gives a family firm roots,
  but a mother's curse uproots the growing plant.

10 Glory not in your father's shame,
  for his shame is no glory to you!

11 His father's honor is a man's glory;
  disgrace for her children, a mother's shame.

12 My son, take care of your father when he is old;

NRSV

3 Listen to me your father, O children;
  act accordingly, that you may be kept in safety.

2 For the Lord honors a father above his children,
  and he confirms a mother's right over her children.

3 Those who honor their father atone for sins,

4 and those who respect their mother are like those who lay up treasure.

5 Those who honor their father will have joy in their own children,
  and when they pray they will be heard.

6 Those who respect their father will have long life,
  and those who honor[a] their mother obey the Lord;

7 they will serve their parents as their masters.[b]

8 Honor your father by word and deed,
  that his blessing may come upon you.

9 For a father's blessing strengthens the houses of the children,
  but a mother's curse uproots their foundations.

10 Do not glorify yourself by dishonoring your father,
  for your father's dishonor is no glory to you.

11 The glory of one's father is one's own glory,
  and it is a disgrace for children not to respect their mother.

12 My child, help your father in his old age,
  and do not grieve him as long as he lives;

13 even if his mind fails, be patient with him;

3, 1: *dîn ʾāb*: so P, V.
3, 5: Omit *kai hōs . . . mētera autou*: so LXX[S,A,C], P, V; dittog of v 4.
3, 7a: Insert *ho phoboumenos Kyrion timēsei patera*: so a few LXX[MSS]; cf V.s
3, 8: Omit *benî*: so LXX, V.
3, 11b: With LXX.
3, 12: (*benî*) *haḥăzēq beśêbat*(ʾ *ābîkā*), (*weʾal taʿaśebēhû*(*kol-yemê*) *ḥayyāyw*: so LXX; cf V.
3, 13: *syggnōmēn eche*(*tor ʾăzōb lô*: dittog from v 12b); (*bekol-yemê* *ḥêlekā*: so LXX, V; cf P v 12b.

[a] Heb: Other ancient authorities read *comfort*   [b] In other ancient authorities this line is preceded by *Those who fear the Lord honor their father,*

NAB

> grieve him not as long as he lives.
> 13 Even if his mind fail, be considerate with
> him;
> revile him not in the fullness of your
> strength.
> 14 For kindness to a father will not be
> forgotten,
> it will serve as a sin offering—it will take
> lasting root.
> 15 In time of tribulation it will be recalled to
> your advantage,
> like warmth upon frost it will melt away
> your sins.
> 16 A blasphemer is he who despises his father;
> accursed of his Creator, he who angers his
> mother.

3, 16b: *ûmᵉqullal bôrᵒô makˈîs ˈimmô*: so LXX, V; cf P.

NRSV

> because you have all your faculties do not
> despise him.
> ¹⁴ For kindness to a father will not be forgotten,
> and will be credited to you against your sins;
> ¹⁵ in the day of your distress it will be
> remembered in your favor;
> like frost in fair weather, your sins will melt
> away.
> ¹⁶ Whoever forsakes a father is like a blasphemer,
> and whoever angers a mother is cursed by
> the Lord.

COMMENTARY

Whereas the preceding poem takes up human obligation, expressed in the first commandment—honor the Lord—the present unit much more self-consciously provides a commentary on the fifth commandment—honor your parents (Exod 20:2-3, 12; Deut 5:6-7, 16). Many ideas in these three subunits (vv. 1-6, 7-11, 12-16) derive from the book of Proverbs, where duty toward parents is mentioned often.[107]

Ben Sira's sharp comments (cf. v. 16) may have been provoked by changing economic conditions that put enormous pressure on the stability of the large family. Carol A. Newsom has perceived the beginnings of this conflict in Proverbs 1–9, the latest collection within the book of Proverbs. There the younger generation is tempted to adopt extreme measures to obtain its heritage without the delay occasioned by the long life of parents.[108] New ideas about longevity also began to surface, perhaps in the wake of Hellenistic influence, in the late third and second centuries BCE, particularly elevating youth and questioning the value of long life. A telling instance of this attitude occurs in 2 Macc 4:40, which refers to a certain Auranus as "advanced in years and no less advanced in folly." Ben Sira endeavors to preserve the traditional Jewish value of a definite hierarchy in the family structure, where parents and children relate to one another, in regard to power, in the same way masters and slaves do (v. 7).

The fifth commandment is the first to introduce reinforcements, specifically the promise of prolonged existence on earth (Exod 20:12) and well-being (Deut 5:16). This emphasis in ancient Israel on showing honor for one's parents reflects a sociological context where adult sons continued to live in the family complex long after marrying. This situation naturally increased the occasions for conflict between grown sons and their aging parents. The fifth commandment, therefore, covers more than the obligations of young children to their parents. In vv. 12-13, Ben Sira reinforces this broader understanding of the obligation to parents, for he urges his readers to remain constant in their respect for parents even when de-

---

107. In the Vg text a verse precedes the entire poem: "The children of wisdom are the congregation of the just; obedience and love are what they beget." A Christian interpolation in the LXX of v. 1 extends the promise of long life to existence beyond the grave.

108. Carol A. Newsom, "Woman and the Discourse of Patriarchal Wisdom: A Study of Proverbs 1–9," in *Gender and Difference in Ancient Israel,* ed. Peggy L. Day (Minneapolis: Fortress, 1989) 142-60.

crepitude and senility place extraordinary strains on the relationship.

3:1-6. The first unit opens with the conventional appeal from a teacher to a student, in this instance, but originally the language of father and son was literal. The probable Hebrew verb (שמע *šāmaʿ*, "*Listen* to me your father, O children"), when followed by the preposition ב (*bĕ*), implies obedience; here Ben Sira explicitly urges action in accord with the advice. The Greek purpose clause "so that you may be saved" (ἵνα σωθῆτε *hina sōthēte*) should not be understood in its New Testament sense, for it probably translates the Hebrew expression for "faring well" (cf. Deut 5:16: יטב [*yāṭab*, "that you may be kept in safety"]). The second verse attributes the authority of parents over their children to a divine gift rather than to societal convention. Nothing in this section indicates that honor for mothers was secondary, which should give pause to interpreters inclined to decry ancient Israel as an unmitigated patriarchal society.

Something relatively new in Hebraic thought, the atoning power of good deeds and the amassing of credit in the heavenly record book, finds expression in vv. 3-4. The emphasis on the efficacy of charitable acts arose as a consequence of the increased esteem in which piety was held during the second and first centuries BCE. The book of Tobit frequently acknowledges the positive correlation between acts of kindness and divine approval (cf. Tob 14:10-11). The notion of laying up treasure in God's sight, familiar to students of the NT, has an analogue in rabbinic literature that refers to meritorious conduct, both inherited and personally acquired. According to the *The Sayings of the Fathers* (*Pirqe ʾAbot*), charitable works and repentance erect a shield against evil.[109] Presuming too much, earlier sages carried such promises of divine blessing for faithful service to the limit and refused to acknowledge huge cracks in this system of theological accounts. Such calculating morality, challenged by the books of Job and Ecclesiastes, continues unabated in Sirach. The Greek expression for laying up treasure occurs elsewhere only in 1 Tim 6:19, although the idea itself occurs also in Matt 6:9-20 and Luke 12:21.

Ben Sira moves beyond a meritocracy based entirely on almsgiving and charitable works, for he knows that all such human deeds count in God's sight only when accompanied by prayer. Therefore, Ben Sira promises those who honor their parents that their own children will bring joy and that God will hear the parents' prayer (v. 5). In v. 6, Ben Sira returns to the motivation for honoring parents in the fifth commandment, specifically the prolonging of life, but he places selfish interests in a broader context of religious devotion: Those who honor their parents obey the Lord.[110]

3:7-11. The second unit (if indeed a separate entity) begins with a break in the text at v. 7, which MS 248 fills with typical teaching from Sirach, now applied to the subject under consideration ("Whoever fears the Lord will honor his father"). The description of children's service to parents uses the Greek word for the work of slaves, although with a qualifying expression "just like": "he will follow his parents just like masters" (ὡς δεσπόταις δουλεύσει *hōs despotais douleusei*). The singular form of the word for "masters" (δεσπότης *despotēs*) designates "God" in the LXX of 23:1 and 34:29. The next two verses (vv. 8-9) echo an earlier concept of patriarchal blessing, one that provides an important ingredient of the plot in the stories about Isaac and his two sons, Jacob and Esau (Genesis 27; cf. Genesis 48). Ben Sira knows that children can dissimulate, like Jacob, saying one thing while behaving in a deceptive manner. True honor for parents, Ben Sira insists, unites practice with speech. The image of a deeply rooted plant in v. 8 conveys Ben Sira's idea of the beneficent paternal blessing, just as Psalm 1 conveys the Lord's blessing by means of the image of a tree planted beside abundant waters. The second half of v. 9 states that not even such well-fed roots can protect a plant from a maternal curse (cf. Prov 20:20 for the reverse idea that a son who curses his parents will lose his lamp, a metaphor for life).

The final two verses of this subunit (vv. 10-11) introduce the concept of rivalry between a father and a son. Ben Sira observes that sons gain nothing through exalting themselves at their fathers' expense but that they benefit from their

---

109. *Pirqe ʾAbot* 4:11.

110. The promise of rest for the mother (cf. Prov 29:17) marks the beginning of the Hebrew text in MS A. The Hebrew runs to Sir 16:25.

fathers' honor. He extends this notion to include respect for mothers as well. Alexander Di Lella quotes Sophocles' *Antigone* (703-4), for a similar idea: "For me, my father, no treasure is so precious as your welfare. What, indeed, is a nobler ornament for children than a prospering father's fair fame, or for father than son's?"[111] Sophocles' last observation goes considerably beyond Ben Sira's exclusive emphasis on deriving benefit from a *father's* honor, with no mention of a father's benefiting from a son's honor.

3:12-16. The third subunit takes up special circumstances in which aging parents become a source of acute exasperation, tempting sons to seize authority. What should one do when parents lose control of their faculties, whether physical, emotional, or intellectual? Returning to the form of address "my son," perhaps to regain a sense of intimacy, Ben Sira urges the son to assist his father and not to stoop to the level of a father who has lost his ability to reason anymore.[112]

The next two verses (vv. 14-15), describe the atoning power of respect for parents. From early times, ancient Egyptians pictured the heart being weighed on scales against a feather, which represented justice. Israelites believed that God kept a book in which were recorded the names of those persons reckoned for life (cf. Exod 32:32, Moses' bold request to have his name blotted out of that book if the Lord did not forgive the sinful people). Later rabbinic literature also alludes to "that which balances."[113] Presumably, the people thought God kept a careful record of people's actions, whether good or evil, to assure that divine judgment was completely impartial—like blind justice. Naturally, such an idea stood in tension with an equally widespread belief in God's mercy. Believing that deeds of kindness atoned for sin, the author of the saying in the rabbinic tractate *Sukka* 49*b* concludes that almsgiving is superior even to sacrifice. In the same vein, Ben Sira remarks that the accumulation of credit for honoring one's parents will pay off in time of calamity, sins melting like frost in warm weather. The Greek ἐλεημοσύνη (*eleēmosynē*) of v. 14 translates a similarly technical Hebrew word, צדקות (*ṣĕdāqôt*), signifying "deeds of kindness."

The final verse in this unit under discussion presupposes the harsh legal statute that condemns to death anyone who curses his or her parents (Exod 21:17; Lev 20:9). Ben Sira equates dishonoring one's parents with blasphemy; the way one behaves toward parents thus becomes an indicator of religious allegiance.[114]

---

111. See Patrick W. Skehan and Alexander A. Di Lella, *The Wisdom of Ben Sira*, AB 39 (New York: Doubleday, 1987) 156.

112. The Hebrew has "Do not abandon him all the days of your life," whereas the Greek has "his life."

113. *Qiddushin* 40*b*.

114. The two Hebrew MSS, C and A, have different verbs for the son's treatment of parents: "abandon" (זאב *z'b*) and "despise" (בזה *bāzâ*), respectively. The Hebrew of the second half of v. 16 reads: "and whoever curses his mother provokes his Creator."

REFLECTIONS

Looking back over these sixteen verses, one is struck by the way Ben Sira comments from several perspectives on a particular commandment: Honor your father and your mother. The tendency of members of an extended family to reside in close quarters must have put enormous strain on younger family members when parents became old and lacking in judgment. Kindness to such individuals yields rich dividends, according to Ben Sira, atoning for earlier offenses.

True religion moves beyond love of God; it includes love for one's fellows, too. The recipients of acts of love are personalized here—parents in their waning years when they may become difficult and excessively demanding. In this way need becomes highly visible, and one cannot escape responsibility by entering the realm of an idealized and vague love of humankind.

SIRACH 3:17–4:10,
HUMILITY AND ALMSGIVING

NAB

17 My son, conduct your affairs with humility,
  and you will be loved more than a giver
    of gifts.
18 Humble yourself the more, the greater you
    are,
  and you will find favor with God.
19 For great is the power of God;
  by the humble he is glorified.
20 What is too sublime for you, seek not,
  into things beyond your strength search
    not.
21 What is committed to you, attend to;
  for what is hidden is not your concern.
22 With what is too much for you meddle not,
  when shown things beyond human
    understanding.
23 Their own opinion has misled many,
  and false reasoning unbalanced their
    judgment.
24 Where the pupil of the eye is missing, there
    is no light,
  and where there is no knowledge, there is
    no wisdom.

25 A stubborn man will fare badly in the end,
  and he who loves danger will perish in it.
26 A stubborn man will be burdened with
    sorrow;
  a sinner will heap sin upon sin.
27 For the affliction of the proud man there is
    no cure;
  he is the offshoot of an evil plant.
28 The mind of a sage appreciates proverbs,
  and an attentive ear is the wise man's joy.

29 Water quenches a flaming fire,
  and alms atone for sins.

3, 17: (*benî*) *ba asāqèkā* (cf 11, 10): so LXX, V.
3, 18: (*ma ęt napš^ekā*) *bekol ğ dullāt ekā*; omit *ôlām*: so LXX, V.
3, 19: With LXX.
3, 23: With LXX.
3, 24ff: Order of vv as in LXX[70,248,253]; cf LXX[S,A,C].
3, 25b: With LXX[S,A,C].
3, 27: Omit *al tārûş ḟ rapp^e ôt* and *kî*: so LXX, P, V.
3, 28: (*yābîn*) *mešālîm*: so P; cf LXX.

NRSV

17 My child, perform your tasks with humility;[a]
  then you will be loved by those whom God
    accepts.
18 The greater you are, the more you must
    humble yourself;
  so you will find favor in the sight of the
    Lord.[b]
20 For great is the might of the Lord;
  but by the humble he is glorified.
21 Neither seek what is too difficult for you,
  nor investigate what is beyond your power.
22 Reflect upon what you have been commanded,
  for what is hidden is not your concern.
23 Do not meddle in matters that are beyond you,
  for more than you can understand has been
    shown you.
24 For their conceit has led many astray,
  and wrong opinion has impaired their
    judgment.

25 Without eyes there is no light;
  without knowledge there is no wisdom.[c]
26 A stubborn mind will fare badly at the end,
  and whoever loves danger will perish in it.
27 A stubborn mind will be burdened by troubles,
  and the sinner adds sin to sins.
28 When calamity befalls the proud, there is no
    healing,
  for an evil plant has taken root in him.
29 The mind of the intelligent appreciates
    proverbs,
  and an attentive ear is the desire of the wise.

30 As water extinguishes a blazing fire,
  so almsgiving atones for sin.
31 Those who repay favors give thought to the
    future;
  when they fall they will find support.

4 My child, do not cheat the poor of
    their living,
  and do not keep needy eyes waiting.

[a] Heb: Gk *meekness*   [b] Other ancient authorities add as verse 19,
*Many are lofty and renowned, but to the humble he reveals his se-
crets.*   [c] Heb: Other ancient authorities lack verse 25.

NAB

30 He who does a kindness is remembered
    afterward;
  when he falls, he finds a support.

4   My son, rob not the poor man of his
    livelihood:
  force not the eyes of the needy to turn
    away.

2 A hungry man grieve not,
  a needy man anger not;

3 Do not exasperate the downtrodden;
  delay not to give to the needy.

4 A beggar in distress do not reject;
  avert not your face from the poor.

5 From the needy turn not your eyes,
  give no man reason to curse you;

6 For if in the bitterness of his soul he curse
    you,
  his Creator will hear his prayer.

7 Endear yourself to the assembly;
  before a ruler bow your head.

8 Give a hearing to the poor man,
  and return his greeting with courtesy;

9 Deliver the oppressed from the hand of the
    oppressor;
  let not justice be repugnant to you.

10 To the fatherless be as a father,
  and help their mother as a husband would;
  Thus will you be like a son to the Most High,
  and he will be more tender to you than a
    mother.

4, 1-5: With LXX.
4, 10d: With LXX.

NRSV

2 Do not grieve the hungry,
  or anger one in need.

3 Do not add to the troubles of the desperate,
  or delay giving to the needy.

4 Do not reject a suppliant in distress,
  or turn your face away from the poor.

5 Do not avert your eye from the needy,
  and give no one reason to curse you;

6 for if in bitterness of soul some should curse
    you,
  their Creator will hear their prayer.

7 Endear yourself to the congregation;
  bow your head low to the great.

8 Give a hearing to the poor,
  and return their greeting politely.

9 Rescue the oppressed from the oppressor;
  and do not be hesitant in giving a verdict.

10 Be a father to orphans,
  and be like a husband to their mother;
  you will then be like a son of the Most High,
  and he will love you more than does your
    mother.

COMMENTARY

The present unit consists of two distinct subunits, 3:17-31 and 4:1-10, each of which begins with the traditional appeal, "my son." Verses 30-31 provide a transition from a discussion of humility and pride to consideration of almsgiving. Two sayings (vv. 25, 29) offer self-conscious reflection on wisdom, in this regard resembling Hos 14:9 and similar reflective comments ("Those who are wise understand these things;/ those who are discerning know them" [Hos 14:9 NRSV]). The best Greek MSS actually lack v. 25, although it appears in MS 248.

3:17-31. The section on humility begins with conventional teaching about the virtue of humility, specifically that it incurs favor with humans and God. Ben Sira observes that persons in authority ought to be especially humble, because the Lord is honored by the lowly. The argument from the greater to the lesser is not entirely consistent, inasmuch as the supremely powerful One does not offer an example of humility. Nevertheless, various traditionists in ancient Israel acknowledged the centrality of humility—from Mosaic legislation and the description of the meek Moses to prophetic summaries of essential piety, such as Mic 6:6-8. Similarly, wisdom sayings link humility and piety ("The reward for humility and fear of the LORD/ is riches and honor and life" [Prov 22:4 NRSV]).

Perhaps the greatest temptation confronting sages was intellectual pride, particularly in a Hellenistic environment that encouraged the pursuit of every imaginable mystery. Traditional Judaism combined revelatory knowledge with human achievement but gave precedence to the former. Jewish leaders acknowledged the significance of intellectual inquiry, although imposing certain restrictions as a result of dangerous speculations into the unknown and unknowable. For example, they prohibited liturgical reading or study of the creation narrative, the mystifying description of Ezekiel's vision recorded in Ezek 1:4-28, and the list of sexual transgressions in Lev 18:6-18.

On the basis of Deut 30:11-14 and similar texts, one may conclude that some Israelites assumed that nothing worthwhile came cheaply, for the speaker insists that God's gift of the law requires no human effort at all beyond willing acceptance. The presumption that the people were prepared to ascend mountains or cross perilous seas to attain such a valuable treasure makes the announcement of a free gift all the more noteworthy. The gracious instruction leading to life could be had for the asking, but such an arrangement seemed too simple for persons accustomed to rigorous intellectual pursuits with minimal results.

Ben Sira recognizes the appeal of the unknown to the young students whom he addresses, but he also understands the hidden dangers inherent in astrological calculations among the Greeks and some forms of wisdom speculation in Jewish circles (cf. Sir 18:4-7). Hence he cautions against probing into areas that resist analysis, for in his view God has made known everything that human beings need to know.

One finds here no inkling of dissatisfaction like that expressed by Qohelet over God's restriction of knowledge (Eccl 3:11). This poignant complaint in the midst of praise for an orderly universe and a vigorous intellectual curiosity (if that is the real meaning of the obscure Hebrew word העלם [hā ʿōlām]) contrasts mightily with Ben Sira's stern warning against investigating the secrets of the universe. In a sense, however, he merely serves as a guardian of sanity, inasmuch as some facts will forever remain locked in mystery, and as a reminder that sacred tradition already contains enough mystery to keep most students occupied for the remainder of their lives. As for anything else, a statement in Deut 29:29[28] suffices: "The secret things belong to the LORD our God, but the revealed things belong to us and to our children forever, to observe all the words of this law" (NRSV).

The psalmist recognizes the need for controlling intellectual pride and boasts about mastering that temptation (Psalm 131). This modest person pleads not guilty to preoccupation with things too great and marvelous. The dominant image in v. 2 is either that of an infant cuddling against its mother's breast, suggesting that the probing mind has finally achieved rest, or that of a weaned child who has begun to venture forth on his or her own, a fine image for intellectual progress toward independent thought. This attitude, too, differs greatly from that of Qohelet, who complains that knowledge lies beyond human perception (Eccl 7:24).

The language of these texts on the proper scope of intellectual inquiry includes a wide range of expression, but a few words stand out. Among them are the ordinary word for "seeking" (דרש *dāraš*), a verb expressing penetrating study (חקר *ḥāqar*), and four adjectives for the hidden (נסתרות *nistārôt*), the wonderful (פלאות *pělā ʾôt*; נפלאות *niplāʾôt*), the deep (עמק *ʿāmōq*), and the distant (רחוק *rāḥôq*). Ben Sira's use of this weighty vocabulary lends credence to the hypothesis that he has in mind Greek speculation of a cosmogonic and theosophical character. Cosmogonic speculation centered in the question of the governance of the universe, and theosophical ruminations explored the hidden or mystical nature of the deity. The psalmist who composed Psalm 139 marvels that, unlike human knowledge, God's knowledge of the worshiper has no limit; here one finds some of the same vocabulary listed above, specifically the verb for rigorous investigation (*ḥāqar*) and the adjectives for "distant" (מרחוק *mērāḥôq*), "wonderful" (פליאה *pělî ʾâ*; cf. v. 14), and "secret" (בסתר *bassēter*). One can easily concur in the exuberant conclusion that such divine knowledge is too wonderful, beyond human grasp (v. 6).

Verses 25-31 contrast obstinate individuals with persons who listen to sound advice, attributing salvific generosity to sages who experience the joy of helping needy persons.[115]

Ben Sira characterizes obdurate persons as sinners who lack enough good deeds to ward off inevitable calamity, whereas responsive individuals perform acts of kindness that prevent harm from striking them. The concept of reward and retribution underlies such thinking, and the language echoes the description of Pharaoh as hardhearted in Exod 7:14 and the sage par excellence, Solomon, who requested a hearing heart to equip him for the task of ruling the nation. The Hebrew for an obdurate mind or will ("a hard heart" [לב כבד *lēb kābēd*]) indicates a heavy weight of arrogance that increases with every obstinate act; and its opposite ("a wise heart" [לב חכם *lēb ḥākām*]) becomes even lighter when overcome by joy.

Ben Sira's notion of retribution has no reference to a future life; "at the end," therefore, indicates disaster in this present existence. The scorner (לץ *lēṣ*) frequently provoked scathing rebuke in the book of Proverbs, but to no avail. Ben Sira even associates such persons with madness and describes them as active lovers of evil, not merely acquiescing in loathsome conduct. From such scoundrels only evil can proceed, so deep-rooted have their misdeeds become.

According to 3:29, an obedient will understands the sayings of the wise, and an attentive ear brings joy to a sage. Both qualities apply to teachers and to students, the former needing obedient listeners and the latter becoming wise through obedience.

Like fire, obstinate conduct threatens the existence of sinners. Ben Sira lacks confidence in the judgment of sinners to take advantage of the available antidote to sin, although the wise provide examples of almsgiving that atones for wrongdoing. Belief in the efficacy of charitable deeds led to an expression, attributed to Rabbi Aqiba, that God placed the poor on earth to provide a means for the rich to attain salvation through almsgiving.[116]

4:1-10. The final section of Part I (1:1–4:10) takes up the matter of duties toward marginalized citizens of the community, specifically the poor, widows, orphans, and sojourners. Ben Sira grounds social ethics in God's conduct toward the needy and promises divine approval for acts of kindness. The teacher recognizes the facts of life, the temptation for rulers to curry favor among powerful citizens, but he offsets this reality with the reminder that God hears the cry of the oppressed when they curse those who spurn them.

The Hebrew text of v. 1 has "mock" (לעג *lāʿag*) instead of "defraud" (ἀποστερέω *apostereō*) in the Greek text, recalling Prov 17:5 ("Those who mock the poor insult their Maker" [NRSV]; cf. Prov 14:31, "Those who oppress the poor insult their Maker" [NRSV]). This verse also has a reference to embittered eyes, presumably made that way through harsh experience. Ben Sira urges his listeners to offer assistance without delay (cf. 29:8), thus conferring dignity on persons reduced to poverty. In v. 3, the Hebrew reads "boil" (חמר *ḥāmar*) and "bowels of the oppressed" (מעי דך *mʿy dk*), conveying the idea of seething emotions. Ancient Israelites thought of the intestines as the seat of turbulent feelings.

Verses 4-6 warn against incurring the wrath of needy persons through outright rejection of their petition or a furtive glance away so as to avoid eye contact with them. The operative words in v. 6, "cry out" (צעק *ṣāʿaq*) and "cry" (צעקה *ṣĕʿāqâ*), belong to liturgical tradition (cf. Exod 22:23[22], "If you do abuse them, when they cry out to me, I will surely heed their cry" [NRSV]; Ps 22:25).[117]

Verses 7-10 treat the relationships among the several social classes in the Jewish community. Ben Sira offers advice on how to ingratiate oneself to the entire "congregation" (עדה *ʿēdâ*). That includes proper respect for the ruling aristocracy as well as for those in need. Under the Ptolemaic rulers in Egypt, Jerusalem had a number of officials, a pattern that continued in the Sanhedrin. These aristocrats demanded respect, which was easy enough to give; as for the poor, one should acknowledge their salutation, which preceded a request for alms. Ben Sira's reference to rescuing the oppressed recalls similar advice from Lemuel's

---

115. The place of v. 25 varies in the MS tradition; it occurs after v. 27 in the Hebrew and Syriac texts.

116. *Baba Bathra* 10a.

117. The Hebrew of v. 6, צורו (*ṣûrô*, "his Rock") may be a mistake for יצרו (*yôṣērô*, "his Maker"), which the Greek MSS attest (ὁ ποιήσας αὐτόν *ho poiēsas auton*).

mother in Prov 31:8-9, for royal ideology demanded that kings rescue the needy. This ideal seldom found expression in actual practice; most kings occupied themselves with military ventures aimed at securing—or improving—their political situation. The allusion to courageous rendering of a verdict does not necessarily imply membership in the legal profession, for ordinary citizens were often called upon to render judicial decisions.

Ben Sira presses his point home by calling upon everyone to assume parental responsibility for those in need. The reward makes such behavior worth the effort, according to Ben Sira. He promises that God will call these surrogate parents "children." Such imagery of God as parent, although rare, occurs enough times to make it particularly poignant.[118] The section closes on a high note, the staggering assurance that "God will be gracious and deliver you from harm," or if one follows the Greek, "God will love you more than your mother does."

118. Cf. Job 29:16; 31:18; Ps 68:6; Isa 1:17; 49:15; 66:13. See M. J. Lagrange, "La Paternité de Dieu dans l'ancien Testament," *RB* 5 (1908) 481-99.

REFLECTIONS

In this section, Ben Sira addresses an issue that was dear to the pious in Israel: the role of humility in the presence of divine mystery and human need. Beginning with appreciation for the humble by their peers, the unit closes by asserting that God, too, looks with favor on the humble. Two areas in which humility finds expression are highlighted: (1) intellectual inquiry and (2) the attitude toward marginalized citizens. Ben Sira recognizes the enormous gulf between human and divine knowledge, indeed the utter reliance of people on God for insight, here understood as the gift of Torah; but the teacher also perceives the practical implications of humility. Anyone who truly understands the meaning of humility will perform acts of kindness in a way that allows recipients to retain their dignity.

PART II

OVERVIEW

This section consists of discrete proverbs concerning relationships, both private and public. A brief poem in praise of wisdom (4:11-19) introduces the sayings, with alternating third- and first-person narrative. (The Greek text lacks this particular feature, describing wisdom throughout in third person.)

SIRACH 4:11-19, IN PRAISE OF WISDOM

NAB	NRSV

11 Wisdom instructs her children
     and admonishes those who seek her.
	11 Wisdom teaches[a] her children
	     and gives help to those who seek her.

12 He who loves her loves life;
     those who seek her out win her favor.
	12 Whoever loves her loves life,
	     and those who seek her from early morning
	          are filled with joy.

13 He who holds her fast inherits glory;
     wherever he dwells, the LORD bestows
          blessings.
	13 Whoever holds her fast inherits glory,
	     and the Lord blesses the place she[b] enters.

14 Those who serve her serve the Holy One;
     those who love her the LORD loves.
	14 Those who serve her minister to the Holy One;
	     the Lord loves those who love her.

15 He who obeys her judges nations;
     he who hearkens to her dwells in her
          inmost chambers.
	15 Those who obey her will judge the nations,
	     and all who listen to her will live secure.

16 If one trusts her, he will possess her;
     his descendants too will inherit her.
	16 If they remain faithful, they will inherit her;
	     their descendants will also obtain her.

17 She walks with him as a stranger,
     and at first she puts him to the test;
     Fear and dread she brings upon him
     and tries him with her discipline;
     With her precepts she puts him to the proof,
     until his heart is fully with her.
	17 For at first she will walk with them on tortuous
	          paths;
	     she will bring fear and dread upon them,
	     and will torment them by her discipline
	     until she trusts them,[c]
	     and she will test them with her ordinances.

18 Then she comes back to bring him happiness
     and reveal her secrets to him.
	18 Then she will come straight back to them again
	          and gladden them,
	     and will reveal her secrets to them.

19 But if he fails her, she will abandon him
     and deliver him into the hands of despoilers.
	19 If they go astray she will forsake them,
	     and hand them over to their ruin.

4, 12b.13a: Omit *myy.*
4, 14b: With LXX.
4, 15-19: "wisdom" in third person, with LXX.
4, 16: (*ean*) *empisteusē, kataklēronomēsei.* so LXX[Bb,S,A,C].
4, 17, c-f: With LXX, but trsp e and f.
4, 19: Omit a.b as variant of c.d: so LXX, P, V.

[a] Heb Syr: Gk *exalts*   [b] Or *he*   [c] Or *until they remain faithful in their heart*

COMMENTARY

The Hebrew of this poem is patterned after Prov 1:22-33 and 8:4-36, where Wisdom extols her virtues. This mode of address returns in Sir 24:3-22. The first-person account in the Greek echoes the style of comparable poems praising Isis (aretologies). A remarkable link between serving wisdom and serving God occurs in v. 14. Moreover, wisdom possesses the power to turn over those who resist her instruction to their own destruction. Such a figure is no ordinary person, and the poem comes close to hymnic praise of deity.

Using the image of treacherous paths and rigorous testing, Ben Sira acknowledges the difficulty of acquiring wisdom, but he insists that persistence pays off eventually. Earlier religious thinkers attributed testing to Yahweh, assuming that genuine faithfulness could best be ascertained when believers faced adversity and triumphed. Only as loyal servants demonstrated integrity could one be sure that religious devotion would endure, regardless of the circumstances. Ben Sira closely associates loyalty to wisdom and divine service (v. 14).

4:11. The initial verse in the Greek text echoes Prov 4:8, which promises that wisdom will exalt those who value her. The Hebrew and Syriac texts in v. 11 have a different verb, "to teach" (למד lāmad), as if to emphasize the stage of learning rather than the end result of respect among peers. The spelling of "wisdom" as חכמות (ḥokmôt) rather than the more usual חכמה (ḥokmâ) resembles Prov 1:20 and 9:1, which state that wisdom cries out in the busy streets and that she has built a house containing seven pillars.[119] A pun on the two consonants, ב (b) and נ (n), occurs in the Hebrew words for "sons" and their activity ("her sons" [בניה bānêhâ]) and מבינים (mĕbînîm), a participle from the verb בין (bîn, "to understand"). The NRSV's "her children" captures the wider sense of the expression bānêhâ, although in the context of the classroom it had the more restricted meaning of "sons" and "students."[120]

4:12. In keeping with wisdom's hiddenness and her readiness to put individuals to a test, this verse assures those who actively search for wisdom that they will obtain favor. The Hebrew text identifies the Lord as the source of favor, agreeing with the statement in Prov 8:35 ("For whoever finds me finds life and obtains favor from the Lord"), where the first colon uses the verb מצא (māṣā') and a participle from the same root with the sense of "finding" instead of בקש (bāqaš), as here, "to seek." The Greek text does not indicate whether the favor derives from God, from wisdom, or from human beings. In the thinking of Israel's sages, conformity with wisdom's dictates entitles persons to rewards from all three sources. An epithet for Yahweh, "the living one," can be viewed in the context of Canaanite religion in which Baal dies and rises again in accord with seasonal patterns. The divine title "the living one" asserts that Israel's God does not die and consequently must be reckoned with at all times. The concept of a deity who transcends natural seasons reinforces notions of both justice and mercy in that Yahweh always observes human conduct and watches over the faithful.

4:13. This verse moves beyond the images of loving and seeking wisdom to holding her fast. Together, these three ideas refer to an individual's prizing the life of the intellect, expending enormous energy to acquire an education, and building moral character that embodies the learning. The persons who embrace woman wisdom, an idea implicit in loving her (v. 12), and hold on to her for dear life will discover honor. Here Ben Sira uses the verb māṣā', along with כבוד (kābôd, "glory," "honor"; δοξα doxa) as the direct object of the verb. In this instance, both the Hebrew and the Greek indicate that the Lord bestows blessing on faithful individuals. The concept of blessing (ברכות bĕrākôt, plural), included long life, a loving family, and prosperity. The benefits that accrue from successful pursuit of wisdom thus pertain to one's status in the community and to the privacy of a family. The Greek text states that the Lord blesses every place wisdom enters,

119. Patrick W. Skehan, "The Seven Columns of Wisdom's House in Proverbs 1–9," *CBQ* (1947) 190-98, and in revised form Skehan, *Studies in Israelite Poetry and Wisdom*, CBQMS 1 (Washington, D.C.: Catholic Biblical Association of America, 1971) 9-14.

120. B. Couroyer, "Un Égyptianisme dans Ben Sira IV,11," *RB* 82 (1975) 206-17.

whereas the Hebrew concentrates on wisdom's followers.

According to Prov 9:1-6, wisdom has constructed a grand house with seven columns and invites guests to a banquet. Naturally, her house is believed to be a dwelling in which blessing abounds. In a later poem (14:20-27), Ben Sira describes those who meditate on wisdom as being blessed and urges them to pursue her like hunters on a chase, daring to pitch their tents near her house.

Ancient peoples imagined blessing and curse as states of mind and body subject to outside control. Professional cursers like Balaam, whom Balak, king of Moab, hired to denounce Israel in the story preserved in Numbers 22–24, were thought to have possessed considerable power. This tradition about Balaam survived outside the Bible and has been confirmed by a stroke of good fortune that yielded a text, discovered at Deir 'Alla near the Dead Sea, that actually refers to a prophet named Balaam. Such professionals were naturally feared, although the biblical narrative portrays this prophet as being subject to a greater power, the will of Yahweh.

Blessings, too, carried immense weight.[121] They also inspired certain incidents in the Bible, notably the story about Jacob's deceit of his father and receipt of the paternal blessing, to Esau's great dismay. The contravening divine will entered the picture, too, when human wishes did not coincide with Yahweh's plans; the strange scene describing Jacob's last words in Gen 48:8-22 sets aged father against son and ignores once more the right of primogeniture, giving the blessing to Ephraim rather than to Manasseh, the firstborn. These stories suggest that neither the curse nor the blessing automatically achieved its goal, contrary to much that has been written over the years.

4:14. The image moves beyond "seeking," "loving," and "holding" to that of "serving." The language belongs to Israel's cultic life; a noun formed from the verb שרת (*šārat*) applies to priestly ministers of the altar (משרתי מזבח *mĕšārtê mizbēaḥ;* cf. Joel 1:13, also called "ministers of

Yahweh" [משרתי יהוה *mĕšārtê YHWH*] in Joel 1:9 and 2:17). Similarly, the verb בקש (*bāqaš,* "to seek") belongs alongside other terms like דרש (*dāraš*) in describing inquiry of the Lord at the cultic center. The verb for "loving" (אהב *'āhab*), also functions as liturgical vocabulary in addition to its use in the secular realm. These verbs from the experience of worship indicate how Ben Sira allowed his personal piety to shape his everyday language. In vv. 11-13, the religious dimension of these verbs remains obscure, whereas it comes to prominence in v. 14. Now Ben Sira equates divine service with intellectual pursuit. This idea differs appreciably from the earlier notion that religion both orients knowledge and makes it possible, or that spiritual insight crowns all true knowledge. The older formulation, "The fear of God is the beginning/first principle of knowledge," has yielded an even bolder claim: Devotion to a life of the mind is identical to that of religious leaders. Both scholars and priests minister to the Lord, each in his or her own way.

The epithet "the Holy One"[122] occurs often in the Isaianic corpus, especially in the longer form, "the holy one of Israel." One can read the Hebrew for "Holiness" (קדוש *qādôš*; or קדש *qōdeš*) as a reference to a person or to a place. This title for God became the favorite of rabbinic Judaism, where it is often followed by "Blessed be He." Like v. 12, where a participle form of the operative verb occurs (those who *love* her *love* life), this verse employs a verb and a noun from the same root (those who *serve* the Holy One *serve* her). This feature of Hebrew syntax occurs frequently, indicating no aversion to repeating an idea in close proximity. Unlike the second colon of v. 14 in Hebrew, the Greek is perfectly clear: "and the Lord loves those who love her."[123]

4:15. The next verse continues the general topic of the preceding four, although shifting in the Hebrew to first-person address. In the thought of ancient Israelites, as also in Egyptian wisdom,

---

121. The classic analysis of blessing and curse appears in Johannes Pedersen's monumental work, *Israel,* vols. 1-2 (London: Oxford University Press, 1926) 182-212, 411-52. In the context of Yahweh's covenant with Israel, blessings are promised to those who serve the Lord faithfully, and those who turn away are threatened with curses.

122. Rudolf Otto, *The Idea of the Holy* (New York: Oxford University Press, 1958; originally 1923), made the concept of the numinous a household word in theological discourse. His analysis of holiness, which he described as a *mysterium tremendum et fascinans,* an awesome yet alluring mystery, brings Isa 6:1-13 into the heart of the discussion of all religious experience.

123. By transposing two consonants, the Syriac rendering of this colon, "and God loves her dwellings," misreads the present Hebrew "and his God" as "her tent" (ואלהו ואהלו *w' lhw = w' hlw*).

the verb שמע (šāmaʿ, "to hear") indicates obedience. "Those who hear me" are persons who
conduct their lives in compliance with wisdom's
proclamation. Such persons, Ben Sira avers, will
judge accurately, with integrity; the Hebrew אמה
(ʾĕmet) suggests "truth" or "reliability." The idea
that the righteous will judge nations, which the
Greek declares, derives from an ingenious reading
of the Hebrew word for "truth," ʾĕmet. By repointing the consonants to אמת (ʾummōt), a rare
expression for nations results. In this way, the
translator introduces a concept that was more at
home in the Alexandrian context, specifically Israel's relationship to non-Jews. The same idea that
wise Jews will judge nations appears in Wis 3:8
(cf. the Prov 29:9a LXX). In popular Hellenistic
thought, the wise were entitled to rule over the
people (cf. the idea of philosopher kings associated
with Plato). The initial verb in the second colon
of v. 15 parallels the verb for "hearing" in the
first colon: "Those who listen to me" // "Those
who obey me." The sentence concludes with a
promise of secure dwelling in the inner recesses
of wisdom's house. The language has an erotic
undertone, implying that obedient ones will reside
in wisdom's bedroom. Such fantasy enjoyed free
rein in ancient speculation about wisdom.[124] Reading ישכן (yiškan) as "dwells," one can translate as
follows: "Whoever obeys me dwells in safety;
whoever listens to me resides in the inner chamber of my house."

4:16. This verse is lacking in the Hebrew. The
Greek text, which turned the idea of faithfulness
in v. 15 into an entirely different notion (ʾemet,
"truth" to אמה [ʾummōt, "nations"]), now introduces faithfulness. In doing so, it promises an
inheritance to those who remain loyal to wisdom,
extending the legacy to their descendants. That
inheritance consists of personified wisdom, who
freely bestows herself and all accompanying blessings on faithful lovers. Because the Hebrew of this
verse is not extant, we cannot tell whether the
language was intended to evoke ancient sentiment
connected with the divine promise that Israel
constituted Yahweh's private possession (see, e.g.,
Exod 19:5-6).

4:17-19. The last section in this unit issues a
somber warning that pursuit of wisdom's blessings
entails arduous effort and not a little danger. The
image of testing suggests that wisdom will intentionally lead people along false paths in order to
determine their worth, in the end returning to a
straight path and rewarding the faithful but abandoning others to thieves. The difficult experiences
in classrooms probably inspired this talk about
trials, for the life of students included numerous
unpleasantries ranging from harsh whippings to
painful thinking. The latter included tedious
memorization of texts, extensive practice of cal-
ligraphy, copious recitations, and rigorous thinking—all at the expense of frivolity and fun with
persons of the opposite sex.

The excessively long initial verse (v. 17) cannot
stand alone, although it introduces the situation
that vv. 18-19 resolve. It states that wisdom
disguises herself, accompanying her followers and
putting them to tests. Earlier sages often spoke of
discipline as an unpleasantry that must be endured
in the educational task. The Hebrew verb signifying "disguise" has the basic sense of forgiveness;
the word recalls the notorious נכריה (nokriyyâ,
"strange or foreign woman") in Proverbs 1–9,
which Joseph Blenkinsopp plausibly interprets in
the light of exclusivism during the time of Ezra
and Nehemiah.[125] Another term for this dangerous
foe in Proverbs 1–9 is אשה זרה (ʾiššâ zārâ), "the
foreign woman."

The exact nature of her alienness is unclear,
but possibilities include ethnicity, spirituality, and
moral character. In short, the foreign woman may
have been a non-Israelite whose strange ways and
relative freedom set her apart and enhanced her
seductive powers; she may have been a practi-
tioner of a rival cult to Yahwism, particularly one
associated with sexual license; she may have been
an Israelite with loose morals. Ben Sira's choice
of vocabulary brings all this speculation to bear
on the experience of acquiring knowledge.

The language of v. 17 emphasizes wisdom's
active involvement in testing her followers, first
by specifying that she walks alongside them and
then by indicating that she probes them directly
(lit., "to their face"). Furthermore, the noun for
"trials" (מסה massâ) contains the consonants of

---

124. By changing two consonants in the verb פת (pat), Rudolf Smend
arrives at two perfectly synonymous cola: "whoever obeys" // "whoever
listens." See Smend, *Die Weisheit des Jesus Sirach* (Berlin: Verlag von
Georg Reimer, 1906) 40.

125. Joseph Blenkinsopp, "The Social Context of the 'Outsider
Woman' in Proverbs 1–9," *Bib* 72 (1991) 457-73.

the verb "to test" (נסה *nāsâ*), which occurs in Gen 22:1 to describe God's action in testing Abraham by demanding that he sacrifice his son Isaac. The same verb appears in the story about King Ahaz, recorded in Isaiah 7, this time in the mouth of the outwardly pious Judean ruler. His smug, hypocritical remark, "I should not petition nor test Yahweh" (Isa 7:12, author's trans.) outraged the prophet Isaiah, who endeavored to persuade the king to rely on the Lord rather than on the might of Assyrian soldiers.[126]

The Hebrew text of vv. 17-18 completes the thought as follows: "when his mind concurs with mine, I will once more put him on a straight path and make known to him my secrets." The Greek expands the idea of trials, noting that wisdom will bring fear and dread (cf. Exod 15:16), testing followers with discipline (παιδεία *paideia*). Here the Greek verb βάσανισει (*basanisei*) suggests "rubbing on a touchstone" to determine an object's authenticity.[127]

The imagery in the Hebrew involves the heart's becoming full of wisdom and the person's then being led on an accurate ("straight") route, until full disclosure takes place. Occasional hints of esoteric lore surface in biblical literature, e.g., Job 11:6*a*, "that [God] would tell you the secrets of wisdom" (NRSV), and Dan 2:22, "He reveals deep and hidden things;/ he knows what is in the darkness,/ and light dwells with him" (NRSV). Similarly, Qohelet speaks about obscurity and deep mystery, first in Eccl 3:11 ("He has made

everything beautiful in its time; also he has put the unknown[128] in their mind, because of which no one can find out the work God has done from beginning to end") and later in Eccl 7:24 ("Distant—whatever is—and extraordinarily deep; who can find it?").

The Greek text adds what is surely implicit in the Hebrew of v. 18: "and she will gladden him." The last verse (v. 19) returns again to the threatening posture, wisdom's final words here. If he turns away from her, she warns, she will cast him off, abandoning him to destruction. The image of a simpleton attempting to negotiate life on his own and ending up like the ruins of a deserted village or in the hands of robbers (cf. Obad 5, "plunderers by night" [NRSV]) brings this unit to an effective conclusion. The doublet in Hebrew makes the warning even more poignant.

In sum, this poem praises wisdom by associating her with life and its divine source. It asserts that wisdom's loyal followers attain joy, exalted position, and honor. Ben Sira's language inclines toward the sacral when describing wisdom's devotees as ministers—i.e., priests at the altar. The picture is not completely rosy, for Ben Sira acknowledges the unpleasant fact that intellectual inquiry demands arduous toil, particularly in the early stages until the pursuit becomes natural. Ben Sira understands this initial hardship as wisdom's testing of individuals to determine whether they will remain resolute in their study. The dire consequences of turning away from wisdom contrast with an unveiling of secrets to the faithful.

---

126. For discussion of testing in the HB, see James L. Crenshaw, *A Whirlpool of Torment* (Philadelphia: Fortress, 1984) 1-7, indeed throughout the book.

127. Patrick W. Skehan and Alexander A. Di Lella, *The Wisdom of Ben Sira,* AB 39 (New York: Doubleday, 1987) 172.

128. A nominal form of the verb עלם (*'elem,* "to be dark, obscure") occurs in Job 11:6 and Eccl 3:11. This use of עלם (*'elem*) has also shown up in Ugaritic texts.

REFLECTIONS

A significant feature of this section is the place of the intellect in biblical religion. The modern tendency to disdain intellectual pursuits as the domain of nerds and eggheads has made a negative impact on the church at every level. Social pressure on bright young people often places demands on them to hide their intellectual achievements and aspirations rather than risk rejection by less motivated peers. Society's refusal to value education has forced potential teachers to enter more lucrative professions like medicine, law, business, and scientific research. School standards, therefore, continue to decline, threatening society at large. The lowering of the reading level in textbooks, known in the trade as "dumbing down," and the constant pressure from competing interest groups to highlight private readings worsen the situation. Addiction to television compounds the problem, contributing to vastly shortened attention spans and mental laziness.

In years past, pastors belonged to the intellectually elite members of society, having received formal education in the classics. The situation has changed dramatically today, and many intellectually gifted individuals choose more lucrative professions. Few pastors now excel in the life of the mind, partly because of disinterest, but also because of mounting pressure on every hand to attend to all kinds of professional responsibilities. Moreover, many highly successful televangelists fill the airwaves with messages that extol the life of the Spirit at the expense of the mind. Some of these preachers even consider intellectual pursuits alien to spirituality, partly because of residual fallout from the historical-critical study of the Bible and partly because of well-known extremists in some universities.

Ben Sira elevates the life of the mind, equating divine service with devotion to the pursuit of knowledge. This attitude suggests that religious people need to take another look at the way they spend leisure time, as well as their commitment to education. Perhaps one can serve the Creator by studying just as effectively as one can by doing good deeds. Using the brain to explore the unknown may please God just as much as any number of acts, and applying the intellect to devout meditation may be looked upon with even more favor than some deeds of kindness. Both intellectual rigor and moral rectitude belong in the arsenal of religious people.

Furthermore, childlike curiosity should be encouraged in intellectual research. Ben Sira's stress on active seeking furnishes a vivid contrast to contemporary passive education. The beauty of intellectual pursuit is its open-endedness, for no one actually ever achieves the goal. The treasure at rainbow's end simply sits there, always beckoning but ever receding in the distance. Most of the excitement comes from the search; those individuals who sit at home and wait for wisdom to drop down upon them miss everything. In a similar vein, Mary L. Caldwell proposes that much of the value in prayer comes in the act itself, not in the answer.[129]

129. Mary L. Caldwell, *Praying for Fishhooks* (Macon, Ga.: Smyth & Helwys, 1994). The title for this book on intercessory prayer is taken from an incident in Twain's *The Adventures of Huckleberry Finn,* in which Huck prays for fishhooks and gets fishing line instead.

SIRACH 4:20-31, SOCIAL STATUS, SHAME, AND SPEECH

NAB	NRSV
20 Use your time well; guard yourself from evil, and bring upon yourself no shame.	20 Watch for the opportune time, and beware of evil, and do not be ashamed to be yourself.
21 There is a sense of shame laden with guilt, and a shame that merits honor and respect.	21 For there is a shame that leads to sin, and there is a shame that is glory and favor.
22 Show no favoritism to your own discredit; let no one intimidate you to your own downfall.	22 Do not show partiality, to your own harm, or deference, to your downfall.
23 Refrain not from speaking at the proper time,	23 Do not refrain from speaking at the proper moment,[a] and do not hide your wisdom.[b]

4, 20: Omit *benî* and *hāmôn*: so LXX, P.
4, 22: (*ʾal tiśśā) pānîm . . . (weʿal) tikkālēm*: cf LXX, P.
4, 23: (*dābār) beʿittô*: so P.

[a] Heb: Gk *at a time of salvation*   [b] So some Gk Mss and Heb Syr Lat: Other Gk Mss lack *and do not hide your wisdom*

NAB

and hide not away your wisdom;
24 For it is through speech that wisdom
    becomes known,
    and knowledge through the tongue's
        rejoinder.
25 Never gainsay the truth,
    and struggle not against the rushing
        stream.
26 Be not ashamed to acknowledge your guilt,
    but of your ignorance rather be ashamed.
27 Do not abase yourself before an impious
        man,
    nor refuse to do so before rulers.
28 Even to the death fight for truth,
    and the LORD your God will battle for you.
29 Be not surly in your speech,
    nor lazy and slack in your deeds.
30 Be not a lion at home,
    nor sly and suspicious at work.
31 Let not your hand be open to receive
    and clenched when it is time to give.

4, 25f: With LXX, but order of vv: 25a.26b.26a.25b.
4, 27 Omit ʾal tišēb . . . ʾimmô: So LXX, P; gloss (cf 8, 14).
4, 30: (ʾal tĕhî) kelābî (or: kᵉʾaryēh with MS C): so LXX, P.

NRSV

24 For wisdom becomes known through speech,
    and education through the words of the
        tongue.
25 Never speak against the truth,
    but be ashamed of your ignorance.
26 Do not be ashamed to confess your sins,
    and do not try to stop the current of a river.
27 Do not subject yourself to a fool,
    or show partiality to a ruler.
28 Fight to the death for truth,
    and the Lord God will fight for you.

29 Do not be reckless in your speech,
    or sluggish and remiss in your deeds.
30 Do not be like a lion in your home,
    or suspicious of your servants.
31 Do not let your hand be stretched out to
        receive
    and closed when it is time to give.

COMMENTARY

This section contains practical advice, largely stated negatively, on speaking one's mind regardless of the social classes involved, and on generosity. Ben Sira distinguishes two kinds of shame, one desirable and the other undesirable. He will discuss shame more thoroughly in later chaps. (41:14–42:8; cf. 20:22-23).

4:20. The customary address by a teacher to a student, derived from that of parent to child, opens this unit in the Hebrew and the Latin. The first observation, "Guard the time and noise," reverses usual sentence order in Hebrew, perhaps to emphasize the objects, which usually come after verbs. On the basis of Eccl 3:1, where the nouns for "season" and "time" (עת ומן zĕmān wĕ ʿēt) occur, one may conjecture that המון (hāmôn, "noise") is a corruption of an original zĕmān. The verb שמר (šāmar), the imperative of which is translated "guard," also has the sense of "observe." Ben Sira urges students to watch over the

occasions that come along, alert to opportune moments (καιροί *kairoi*). The Greek term καιρός (*kairos*) distinguishes these quality times from uneventful ordinary times (χρόνος *chronos*). Wise students inspect the different situations that emerge over the course of a day and seize the opportune moment for action.

This simple admonition to watch for promising moments possibly relates to the venerable practice of observing the times in order to control events magically. Specialists who knew the times are mentioned in Daniel; such individuals who studied the stars and chronicled seasonal changes sought mastery of astrology for the purpose of controlling events for themselves and their clients. The practice thrived in Mesopotamia, where wisdom has been plausibly defined as magic,[130] and in Egypt, where the well-known *Book of the Dead*

130. See Wilfred L. Lambert, *Babylonian Wisdom Literature* (Oxford: Clarendon, 1960) 1.

was compiled. Priestly groups in Israel, particularly those belonging to the sect at Qumran, devoted much energy to calendrical matters. They believed that God had specified exact times for sacred observances.

Precisely what "the evil" had to do with the times remains unclear, unless it signifies a misfortune for which omens were sought. Ben Sira continues with "And fear the evil," without elaborating on the nature of this object of dread. Alexander Di Lella understands the potential threat as Hellenism, the tendency to glorify Greek customs and ideas at the expense of Jewish practices and thoughts.[131] Nothing in this context points in such a specific direction, however deplorable attempts to become more Greek than Jewish may have been reckoned in later literature. In contrast to the unknown author of 1 Macc 1:11-15, who expresses chagrin over the efforts of Jews in the time of Antiochus IV Epiphanes (175–164 BCE) to efface all evidence of circumcision so they could participate in athletic contests in gymnasia, Ben Sira remains silent about such activity. Similar contempt for priests who highly prized Greek honors while despising Jewish values issues from the pen of the writer of 2 Macc 4:13-15.

Ben Sira warns against conduct that prevents students from standing up for what they believe. Being ashamed of taking a stand covers any number of situations, although embarrassment over identification with people whose customs seem backward and uncultured certainly fits the context. So does reticence to espouse unpopular causes when persons of power and influence resist them. Ben Sira may have in mind the many different ways influential, but corrupt, people pressure the wise to keep silent for fear of unwelcome consequences, for their livelihood often depended on the goodwill of the affluent. He urges students to guard their integrity in the same way they watch over opportune moments.

4:21. This verse reminds the reader that not all shame is the same, some being an indication of honor while other instances signify disgrace. One ought to be ashamed of deplorable conduct, which entails sin ("iniquity" עֲוֹן *'āwôn*; ἁμαρτία *hamartia*), but a person should not be ashamed of actions worthy

131. Skehan and Di Lella, *The Wisdom of Ben Sira*, 175-76.

of honor and favor (כבוד וחן *kābôd wĕḥēn*; δόξα καὶ χάρις *doxa kai charis*). The literary form of this statement consists of a particle of existence, "there is" (שׁ *yēš*), followed by predicate nominatives. In this instance, the two cola use synonymous parallelism but specify opposite types of shame: "For there is a shame that leads to sin,/ and there is a shame that is glory and favor." The LXX adds this verse after Prov 26:11.

At some point during the transmission of the HB, the divine name "Baal" caused sufficient unease to prompt changes in some personal names using this appellation. The name "Ishbosheth" thus resulted (2 Sam 1:1), with the implausible meaning "man of shame" instead of "man of Baal." In at least one instance, the change did not take place in every occurrence of the name, for Saul's son Meribbaal (1 Chr 8:34) is also called Mephibosheth (2 Sam 4:4). Clearly, Ben Sira's sensitivity toward shame has ancient precedent in Jewish scribal circles and does not, therefore, necessarily reflect the influence of Mediterranean culture, with its strong emphasis on honor and shame.

4:22. "Show no favoritism to the detriment of your true self" seems to represent the sense of v. 22*a*, although the Hebrew may warn against partiality toward oneself—i.e., selfishness. The Hebrew phrase "to lift up your face" implies showing favor toward someone, often in warning against being unduly influenced by wealth (cf. 42:1*b* and 35:16*a* for additional uses in Sirach). The second colon in v. 22 may advise against a sense of shame that leads to one's downfall. The Hebrew "do not stumble at your stumblings" can be improved by adopting the verb from the Greek, "do not be ashamed" (μὴ ἐντραπῇς *mē entrapēs*). The verse then warns against a shame that leads to ruin, but it does not indicate what Ben Sira has in mind. This generality leaves the saying open to many applications.

4:23. This verse counsels against withholding comment when the occasion for speech presents itself, thereby concealing one's intelligence. The use of the weighty expression for time in v. 23 (עולם *'ôlām* instead of עת *'ēt*) might indicate that speculation about the world to come and this age has already begun. Ben Sira has no use for such optimistic hopes of existence after death, but he knows that some moments are filled with potential, and he does not want his students to let them pass unnoticed. On the basis of 8:9 in Greek, "to give answer in time of need" (ἐν καιρῷ χρείας δοῦναι ἀπόκρισιν *en kairō chreias dounai apokrisin*), Rudolf Smend reads χρεία (*chreia*) for σωτηρία (*sōtēria*, "need" for "safety").[132] The author of Eccl 3:7 also recognizes a time for speech—indeed a time for everything under the sun.

The second colon in v. 23 acknowledges that wisdom can go unnoticed if one lacks the courage to speak up or the ability to recognize an opportune moment. To be sure, the adage that "remaining quiet and being thought a fool is better than opening one's mouth and removing all doubt" possesses some truth. One aim of ancient education was to equip young people for effective speech, which entails a capacity to discern the right time to respond.

4:24. The adverb כִּי (*kî*; γάρ *gar*), signals an explanation of the sentiment expressed in v. 23: "Through speech intelligence is made known and understanding through the tongue's response." This artful literary inclusio ABB'A':

A "through speech"

  B intelligence (חכמה *ḥokmâ*)

  B' understanding (תבונה *tĕbûnâ*)

A' "tongue's response"

employs technical vocabulary of the sages and gives voice to traditional beliefs in their circles. Despite this extraordinary praise of eloquence (cf. Prov 15:23; 16:1), these intellectuals knew that successful rogues also possessed smooth tongues. This theme found expression in the frequent warnings within the book of Proverbs about a seductress with her smooth line.[133] Quick answers and glib answers often go hand in hand, indicating that one needs to analyze the content of what is said and not just its eloquence.

4:25. The Hebrew here has contrasting parallelism: "Do not contradict God [האל *hā'ēl*] but bow before God [אלהים *'ĕlōhîm*]." An Aramaic loan word, סרב (*sārab*) connotes verbal lying, a bold resistance to the truth. The Greek has "Do

not oppose the truth" (μὴ ἀντίλεγε τῇ ἀληθείᾳ *mē antilege tē alētheia*). In Jewish piety of the first century CE, "truth" (אמת *'ĕmet*) actually served as a divine appellation; the Gospel of John has Jesus identify himself as "the way, the truth, and the life." Similarly, the Babylonian Talmud Sanhedrin 1:18*a* mentions Truth as one of God's names.[134]

In contrast to the Hebrew of this verse, the Greek second colon introduces the concept of folly and returns to the earlier notion of shame. According to this version, one ought to be ashamed of foolishness.

4:26. Here Ben Sira advises against pride that prevents persons from confessing fault. In these circumstances, embarrassment facilitates remorse, enabling one to admit guilt. The verb שוב (*šûb*) signifies an about-face, a turning from iniquity to true confession and moral resolve confirmed by subsequent conduct. In rabbinic times a noun form, תשובה (*tĕšûbâ*) indicated the act of repentance. The second colon in v. 26 probably alludes to an ancient proverb pointing to the futility of trying to resist the inevitable—in this instance God. "Do not stand in front of a flood" calls attention to the impossibility of resisting God's will. The image of an overflowing river occurs in Isaiah 8 with reference to Assyria's might. An Eygptian proverb about the impossibility of concealing a river appears several times, attesting the popularity of such thinking. The Syriac translation of the Aramaic collection of aphorisms titled *The Sayings of Ahiqar* includes the following comment: "My son, struggle not against a man in his day, and oppose not the current of a river."

4:27-28. Ben Sira next advises against spineless surrender before fools, "spreading oneself out" to be walked on, and showing favoritism to rulers (v. 27). At this point the Hebrew has a variant of 8:14, which states the obvious fact that litigation against a judge stands little chance of succeeding. The remark about rulers leads naturally to v. 28, which admonishes sages to fight to the death for righteousness (Greek and Syriac, "for truth") and promises assistance from above. The Hebrew adds 5:14*a* at this point.

4:29-30. Speech and actions form the two subjects of v. 29. Ben Sira advises against hasty—

132. Rudolf Smend, *Die Weisheit des Jesus Sirach erklärt* (Berlin: Reimer, 1906) 44.
133. J. N. Aletti, "Seduction et Parole en Proverbes I–IX," *VT* 27 (1977) 129-44.
134. W. O. E. Oesterley, *The Wisdom of Jesus the Son of Sirach or Ecclesiasticus* (Cambridge: Cambridge University Press, 1912) 32.

or haughty—speech and slovenly actions. The next verse resists the display of power in the presence of subjects: "Do not rage like a lion [or a dog] in your house or be wily and suspicious among servants." The rare expression for "your servants" (עבדתך 'ăbuddātāk) appears elsewhere only in Job 1:3 and Gen 26:14. According to Eccl 7:21-22, suspicion about slaves' criticism of their masters was fully justified.

4:31. The final aphorism in this unit addresses the problem of stinginess and greed by ridiculing persons whose hands open wide to receive gifts but clamp shut when others beg for alms. A hypothetical situation in Deut 15:7-8 mentions the same concept of an open and a closed hand. The idea persists into the early second century CE,

for example in *Did.* 4:5 and the *Epistle of Barnabas* 19:9, where the expression is exactly the same in Greek: "Be not one who stretches out his hands to receive, but shuts them when it comes to giving."

To recapitulate, this brief section concentrates on speech, both its timing and its integrity. It warns against concealing one's intelligence, but also against exposing ignorance. Because life seldom unfolds in simple patterns, one needs to cultivate the ability to discriminate between a time for speech and a time for silence. The same discernment applies to shame, which can be both positive and negative. In all circumstances, courage plays a role, and the person who possesses power is advised to practice restraint.

REFLECTIONS

1. The issue of shame seldom surfaces today. There once was a time when honor and shame governed human conduct, particularly in the ancient Near East, as it still does in modern Asian communities. Pilch and Malina contend that this code survives in the Mediterranean world today.[135] He and others find this ancient viewpoint among obscure villagers. When asked which son in Jesus' story did the right thing, the one who said yes but did nothing or the one who said no and later obeyed his father, modern Arabs praise the first son because he honored his dad in public. They denounce the other son for dishonoring his father openly.[136]

We live in a society whose people have forgotten how to blush. Honor and shame have little value to countless individuals. The parading of private lives on television talk shows, the restoration to respectability of junk bond traders on Wall Street, and contributing to the fortunes of criminals by purchasing their stories—all these and more bear witness to a loss of the concept of honor. Christians have an obligation to recapture the virtue of honor and reinstitute the notion of shame. Any society that ignores or rewards reprehensible behavior has a terrible mark against it. Shameless individuals who disgrace public office and cavalierly run again bear witness to our moral bankruptcy. Christians who reward such candidates by helping to elect them seriously compromise the office and demonstrate shameful disregard for honor.

Ben Sira recognized different kinds of shame. Christians rightly feel shame when the nation embarks on activities that bring death and starvation to people elsewhere. A sense of outrage may, indeed, be the strongest reaction one can make to military aggression, sales of weapons, and unjust economic policies that supplement the income of a few rich citizens.

2. The most reliable indication of intellectual acumen is found in deeds, for wisdom manifests itself in moral character. In the view of ancient sages, anyone who truly listened and understood the teaching acted in accordance with its demands.

This emphasis on deeds as the evidence of wisdom provides a balance for the earlier elevation of the intellect. Ben Sira realized the necessity of complementary pairs, for some truth resides in each side. Both doing and knowing are vital components of wisdom. In religious matters, one easily slips into a type of thinking that offers simplistic answers, for consistency seems desirable at all costs. Unfortunately, most such thinking distorts the truth while lulling people

---

135. John J. Pilch and Bruce J. Malina, *Dictionary of New Testament Culture* (Peabody, Mass.: Hendrickson, 1993).
136. John J. Pilch, " 'Beat His Ribs While He Is Young,' (Sir 30:12): A Window on the Mediterranean World," *BTB* 23 (1993) 104.

to sleep. Rather than taking comfort in single-minded answers, religious people need to be reminded of faith's complexity and fragility. A false sense of ease, a pseudo-simplicity, thus characterizes many Christians' approach to crucial issues precisely when they should be forced to work out the intricacies of their faith with fear and trembling.

3. This section also makes a point that Jesus subsequently reiterated: Money can capture the heart and push God out (see also 5:1-8). The ultimate longing of the heart, whether God or mammon, determines the character of joy and the nature of security. Modern society measures a secure future in terms of a good job, adequate medical coverage, and access to a good education. Without promise of these things, people become anxious about what is denied them, bestowing unreasonable importance on the missing element.

Those who have a disproportionate share of the world's wealth have great difficulty imagining the way basic things like daily food and shelter occupy the attention of Third World peoples from dawn to dusk. We who can reasonably expect to have adequate food and a place to sleep are fortunate in that our minds are freed from the cares of subsistence. Christians have an opportunity to demonstrate gratitude by easing the burdens on those who have less.

Ben Sira knew that wealth influences those who lack it in unhealthy ways. Like so many ethicists of the ancient world, he tried to counter the temptation to curry the favor of influential citizens. The author of the Epistle of James also brought this matter to the attention of early Christians, many of whom displayed favoritism whenever rich visitors arrived in their midst. He reminded Christians that their worst enemies were wealthy citizens.

The modern church has considerable difficulty living up to the ideals of a people who do not show partiality toward those persons with money and prestige. One reason why, surely, is the need for money to fund an operating budget. Most churches need a certain number of reasonably affluent members whose generosity enables them to carry out a program. A potential problem arises, however, when persons who will undoubtedly be a drain on the budget apply for church membership. Many congregations find themselves torn between a desire for security and status, on the one hand, and a sincere wish to minister to the needy, on the other hand. Ben Sira was sufficiently observant to know that the scales naturally tilt in favor of the rich. Perhaps we should be thankful for the visible presence of those who represent real need, for they give those who have sufficient resources an occasion to be truly generous.

SIRACH 5:1-8, ON PRESUMING TOO MUCH

NAB

5 Rely not on your wealth;
   say not: "I have the power."
2 Rely not on your strength
   in following the desires of your heart.
3 Say not: "Who can prevail against me?"
   for the LORD will exact the punishment.
4 Say not: "I have sinned, yet what has befallen me?"
   for the LORD bides his time.

5, 2: Omit ' *al tēlēk . . . rā' â*: variant of preceding; cf LXX, P, V.
5, 3: (*mî yûkal*) *lî*: so LXX; v 3b: so with LXX; but omit *se* with LXX[S,A].
5, 4: Omit *m*[e]' *ûmâ*: so LXX.

NRSV

5 Do not rely on your wealth,
   or say, "I have enough."
2 Do not follow your inclination and strength
   in pursuing the desires of your heart.
3 Do not say, "Who can have power over me?"
   for the Lord will surely punish you.

4 Do not say, "I sinned, yet what has happened to me?"
   for the Lord is slow to anger.
5 Do not be so confident of forgiveness[a]

[a] Heb: Gk *atonement*

NAB

5 Of forgiveness be not overconfident,
   adding sin upon sin.
6 Say not: "Great is his mercy;
   my many sins he will forgive."
7 For mercy and anger alike are with him;
   upon the wicked alights his wrath.
8 Delay not your conversion to the LORD,
   put it not off from day to day;
9 For suddenly his wrath flames forth;
   at the time of vengeance, you will be
   destroyed.
10 Rely not upon deceitful wealth,
   for it will be no help on the day of wrath.

NRSV

   that you add sin to sin.
6 Do not say, "His mercy is great,
   he will forgive[a] the multitude of my sins,"
for both mercy and wrath are with him,
   and his anger will rest on sinners.
7 Do not delay to turn back to the Lord,
   and do not postpone it from day to day;
for suddenly the wrath of the Lord will come
   upon you,
   and at the time of punishment you will
   perish.
8 Do not depend on dishonest wealth,
   for it will not benefit you on the day of
   calamity.

[a] Heb: Gk *he* (or *it*) *will atone for*

COMMENTARY

The author of the profound prayer in Prov 30:7-9 knew that wealthy people face a special temptation to rely on their own resources rather than trusting in God. Ben Sira also recognizes this danger, but he links it to certain additional attitudes that deny divine sovereignty. These attitudes fall into the category of theodicy, for they assert that God does not really punish evil people. In this brief section on theodicy,[137] Ben Sira takes up at least three arguments that sinners often use in defense of their presumption with regard to God's mercy: (1) Acquired wealth proves divine favor; (2) expected retribution for sin has not fallen; and (3) God's readiness to forgive gives one ample time to repent. The mention of wealth in v. 8 provides an inclusio with the first verse in chap. 5 and brings the unit to a close.

The language of this entire section assumes a combative posture, an authoritative figure issuing negative commands or prohibitions. The operative command "Do not" occurs at least once in every verse, twice in vv. 1 and 7. Ben Sira adopts an ancient formula from debates, "Do not say," which is then followed by proscribed sentiments.[138] He appears to address distinct attitudes toward the relationship between sin and punishment.

5:1-3. The first of these commands relates to possessions. One who has amassed a fortune tends to lean on it rather than trust in God. The Hebrew word for "wealth" (חיל *ḥayil*) implies vigor, hence it fits nicely into a context of self-reliance. The pregnant expression is matched by an idiom for control over one's destiny, "There is power in my hand."[139] The second verse reiterates the thought, repeating the verb "to lean" (שען *šā'an*), but using a different word for "his strength" (כחו *kōḥô*) before the final phrase about pursuing one's desire (cf. Job 31:7*b*). Confident in his or her own might, the bold sinner is thought to boast, "Who can prevail over my strength?" Ben Sira reminds those who would speak in this way that Yahweh will seek out the persecuted, which must mean that the oppressors cannot escape punishment. The same expression occurs in Eccl 3:15.

5:4. A second attitude toward delayed punishment surfaces in this verse. Ben Sira warns against saying, "I sinned and what has happpened to me?" Here we come up against an age-old di-

---

137. On this "compendium" of theodicy, see G. L. Prato, *Il problema della teodicea in Ben Sira,* AnBib 65 (Rome: Pontifical Biblical Institute, 1975) 367-69; and James L. Crenshaw, "The Problem of Theodicy in Sirach: On Human Bondage," *JBL* 94 (1975) 47-64. See also James L. Crenshaw, *Urgent Advice and Probing Questions* (Macon, Ga.: Mercer University Press, 1995) 155-74.

138. Crenshaw, "The Problem of Theodicy in Sirach," 48-51.
139. W. G. E. Watson, "Reclustering לאליד *l'lyd*," *Bib* 58 (1977) 213-15, claims that לאה (*lā 'ā,* "to be strong") has yielded a noun, לא (*lā '*, "power"). He divides לאליד (*l'lyd*) as לאליד (*l'leyā d*) and translates "power in the hand of."

lemma: People do wrong and appear to suffer no ill consequences for their actions. As time elapses and nothing unpleasant comes their way, they conclude that God does not punish the wicked. To counter such skepticism, Ben Sira reaffirms traditional belief that God is longsuffering. The expression "God is longsuffering" (אל ארך אפים הוא *ʾēl ʾerek ʾappayim hûʾ*) echoes the liturgical confession in Exod 34:6-7, in this instance the divine patience. The image "long of nose" suggests that God's anger does not flare up quickly but requires considerable provocation. Here, again, comparison with Ecclesiastes is instructive: "Because sentence against an evil deed is not executed speedily, the human heart is fully set to do evil" (Eccl 8:11 NRSV).

5:5-6. A third presumptive attitude concerns God's readiness to forgive. According to this opinion, the scope of one's sins does not really matter so long as they are atoned for by sacrifice and good works. Thinking forgiveness a light matter, the sinner freely indulges, "multiplying iniquity." Ben Sira warns against this kind of overconfidence, which trusts in Yahweh's compassionate nature to forgive an abundance of sin. Here, too, the decisive language for divine compassion (רחום *raḥûm*) derives from Exod 34:6-7. The apostle Paul combats a similar view in Rom 6:1; it seems that some Christians argued that the greater the sin the more copiously God's forgiveness manifests itself. Such reasoning provides a dubious justification for continuing in a state of rebellion,

indeed, for excelling in evil. The Mishnah offers evidence of similar presumption, warning against thinking that one can sin and ask forgiveness only to repeat the offense.[140] The rabbi responsible for this saying believed that for such persons the Day of Atonement had no efficacy.

5:7. Another attitude that Ben Sira rejects outright consists of calculated delay in the act of repentance. Assuming that God's wrath comes rather slowly, people hope for enough warning to enable them to repent at the last moment. In this way, they do not miss out on any fun, having the best of both worlds. Ben Sira reminds such thinkers that God's vengeance strikes suddenly, without warning, for at the time of reckoning they will perish.

5:8. Returning to the previously mentioned reliance on wealth to protect one from danger, Ben Sira insists that such ill-gotten wealth will not secure anyone in the day of God's vengeance. Trusting in lies ("deceitful riches" נכסי שקר *nĕkāsê šeqer*), the sinners will be completely vulnerable when divine fury "passes over" them (cf. Prov 11:4).

Verses 1-8 bracket presumptuous thoughts within overreliance on wealth. Ben Sira warns against ill-placed confidence, one based on faulty reasoning about delayed punishment. Both mercy and wrath belong to God, he insists, and one should act accordingly.

140. *M. Yoma* 8:8-9.

REFLECTIONS

This text probes the human psyche, exploring the rationale for shifting the blame for people's conduct to an unjust God. The several defenses given for adopting a life of sin imply fuller knowledge of the universe than is accessible to anyone except God. Such attacks on divine justice, and ultimately on God's benevolence, grow out of an unwillingness to accept the inevitable status of creature. Being finite means living in a condition of limited potential, and that limitedness includes such important qualities as power and knowledge. The arrogance of Job and all others like him becomes ludicrous when faced with the real problem of evil, mythologically symbolized in the two creatures Behemoth and Leviathan.

No human being can obtain sufficient distance from the scene to observe everything that transpires in the universe and to pass judgment on its appropriateness. Our view always takes place from below, as it were, and suffers from severe myopia. Even if one could bring together all human perspectives into a single view of things, the result would still lack the one essential ingredient for understanding the whole picture—*telos,* "the end." Hidden from our eyes is the larger picture in which God's purpose plays itself out on the earthly stage.

In some ways our lives resemble a great patchwork quilt. The individual pieces of cloth that make up the final design vary considerably in aesthetic appeal, with some actually falling into the category of ugly. Once the quilt maker finishes the design, the total picture completely transforms former unattractive pieces. The viewer now sees each individual square of cloth as it contributes to the beauty of the whole quilt.[141] Perhaps God weaves together the separate strings of human existence, intricately mixing and matching the different colors and textures so that they ultimately form a beautiful garment.

Biblical imagery suggests a similar analogy. If our bodies constitute a temple in which God resides, perhaps the master builder takes the individual stones and constructs an edifice from the different sizes, shapes, and colors. Together these building blocks make up a splendid house, God's dwelling place. In the final design, every single stone contributes to the whole just as every piece of cloth adds something necessary to the patchwork quilt.

This argument implies that the ugly incidents of our lives, those events that cause us to question divine justice, may fit into the larger picture in a way that our limited perspective obscures. In any event, most arguments for rebelling against God are so self-serving that they scarcely convince those using them, much less anyone else. The ones that Ben Sira cites lack the grandeur and power of struggles by loyal servants to comprehend things so thoroughly incongruent with belief in a loving God.

141. See *A Quilter's Wisdom: Conversations with Aunt Jane* (San Francisco: Chronicle Books, 1994) based on a historical text by Eliza Calvert Hall.

SIRACH 5:9–6:1, ON DISSIMULATION THROUGH SPEECH

NAB	NRSV
11 Winnow not in every wind, and start not off in every direction.	9 Do not winnow in every wind, or follow every path.[a]
12 Be consistent in your thoughts; steadfast be your words.	10 Stand firm for what you know, and let your speech be consistent.
13 Be swift to hear, but slow to answer.	11 Be quick to hear, but deliberate in answering.
14 If you have the knowledge, answer your neighbor; if not, put your hand over your mouth.	12 If you know what to say, answer your neighbor; but if not, put your hand over your mouth.
15 Honor and dishonor through talking! A man's tongue can be his downfall.	13 Honor and dishonor come from speaking, and the tongue of mortals may be their downfall.
16 Be not called a detractor; use not your tongue for calumny;	14 Do not be called double-tongued[b] and do not lay traps with your tongue; for shame comes to the thief,
17 For shame has been created for the thief, and the reproach of his neighbor for the double-tongued.	and severe condemnation to the double-tongued.
6 Say nothing harmful, small or great; be not a foe instead of a friend;	15 In great and small matters cause no harm,[c]

5, 11: *w^e ' al tēlēk l^ekol šebîl*: so MS C, LXX; cf P.
5, 16: Omit *rēa'*: cf 4, 28d.
6, 1: (*w^eqālôn*) *tîraš*: cf P; omit *ḥerpâ*.

a Gk adds *so it is with the double-tongued sinner* (see 6.1)
b Heb: Gk *a slanderer*   c Heb Syr: Gk *be ignorant*

NAB	NRSV
A bad name and disgrace will you acquire: "That for the evil man with double tongue!"	**6** ¹and do not become an enemy instead of a friend; for a bad name incurs shame and reproach; so it is with the double-tongued sinner.

COMMENTARY

Two images from popular proverbs in 5:9 provide a fitting transition to a new theme that evokes a triple use of the idiom "master of two" with reference to duplicity in speech. The remarks about winnowing indiscriminately, regardless of the direction of the wind, and trying out various paths apply equally well to the preceding discussion of different attitudes to retribution as they do to what follows. Another widespread expression, "to put the hand to the mouth," indicates humility and respect in the presence of greatness, perhaps also the lack of an adequate response. This symbolic gesture is mentioned in Job 21:5; 29:9; 40:4 and elsewhere in the OT (Prov 30:32; Mic 7:16; cf. Wis 8:12). Like so much in wisdom literature, it also appears in Egyptian texts.[142]

Ben Sira recommends quickness in hearing but a considered response, one "long in spirit" (the same advice can be found in Jas 1:19). The

necessity of hearing rightly before responding captured popular imagination much earlier, for it finds expression in Prov 18:13. Years later Qohelet contrasts a patient person with an arrogant individual in Eccl 7:8.

The slanderer comes in for Ben Sira's strongest censure. The double-tongued person resembles a thief in robbing innocent people of their good reputation. Just as speech with integrity brings honor in its wake, so also deceitful remarks cause shame. The purpose of such duplicity is described in the language of hunting—lying in wait. Thus the double-tongued person lays a trap for the unwary. The significant terms in 5:14 comprise an ABB'A' pattern: double-tongued/shame/reproach/double-tongued. The next verse combines two opposites: minute and large, friend and enemy. A third occurrence of "double-tongued" for emphasis or completion, plus the combination of "shame" and "reproach," offers a suitable conclusion to the section.

142. See B. Couroyer, "Mettre la main sur la bouche en Égypte et dans la Bible," *RB* 67 (1960) 197-209.

SIRACH 6:2-4,
ON UNCONTROLLED PASSIONS

NAB	NRSV
2 Fall not into the grip of desire, lest, like fire, it consume your strength;	² Do not fall into the grip of passion,[a] or you may be torn apart as by a bull.[b]
6, 2b: *pen tᵉbāʾer ḥêlᵉkā kāʾēš*: cf Ex 22, 5 (LXX).	[a] Heb: Meaning of Gk uncertain [b] Meaning of Gk uncertain

NAB	NRSV
3 Your leaves it will eat, your fruits destroy, and you will be left a dry tree,	[3] Your leaves will be devoured and your fruit destroyed, and you will be left like a withered tree.
4 For contumacious desire destroys its owner and makes him the sport of his enemies.	[4] Evil passion destroys those who have it, and makes them the laughingstock of their enemies.

COMMENTARY

The subject of this short unit probably falls into the realm of sexual misconduct. The warning applies generally to powerful passions of all kinds, but the images for the consequences apply particularly well to sins of the flesh. Ben Sira likens illicit sex to a raging bull, all the more apt because of the association of bulls with fertility, and he warns that sexual misbehavior destroys a tree, causing its fruit and leaves to drop off. The description elsewhere of a eunuch as a dry tree (Isa 56:3) indicates the dire consequences of ungoverned lust. Like the mighty Samson, the person who loses control of his or her passions falls into the hands of the enemy (Judg 15:18), the same expression used here in v. 2.

Later on Ben Sira uses the popular image of leaves falling from a tree as a powerful reminder of death.[143] This graphic image contrasts with that of a healthy tree situated near an abundance of water (Ps 1:3). The closing reference in v. 4 to an insatiable desire (נפש עזה *nepeš ʿazzâ*) acknowedges the strength of sexual lust, an appetite similar to hunger for essential nourishment. Uncontrolled, this desire turns one into an object of ridicule. According to Anderson's interpretation of שמחה (*śimḥâ*) as a rabbinic cipher for legitimate sex within marriage,[144] Ben Sira's choice of this noun to indicate enemies' happiness ("rejoicing") is especially fortuitous. The subject of sexual lust will occupy Ben Sira's attention again (cf. 18:30–19:3).

143. Homer uses this same image in discussing death (*Iliad* 6.146ff.), but one need not draw the conclusion that Ben Sira knew the *Iliad*. The idea would naturally have occurred to anyone who reflected on nature's transformation each year.

144. Gary A. Anderson, *A Time to Mourn, a Time to Dance* (University Park: Pennsylvania State University Press, 1991) 27-45.

SIRACH 6:5-17, ON FRIENDSHIP

NAB	NRSV
5 A kind mouth multiplies friends, and gracious lips prompt friendly greetings.	[5] Pleasant speech multiplies friends, and a gracious tongue multiplies courtesies.
6 Let your acquaintances be many, but one in a thousand your confidant.	[6] Let those who are friendly with you be many, but let your advisers be one in a thousand.
7 When you gain a friend, first test him, and be not too ready to trust him.	[7] When you gain friends, gain them through testing, and do not trust them hastily.
8 For one sort of friend is a friend when it suits him, but he will not be with you in time of distress.	[8] For there are friends who are such when it suits them, but they will not stand by you in time of trouble.
9 Another is a friend who becomes an enemy,	[9] And there are friends who change into enemies,

6, 5: šᵉʾēlôt (šālôm): so P; cf LXX.
6, 8: wᵉlōʾ (yaʿămôd): so LXX, P, V.

NAB

and tells of the quarrel to your shame.

10 Another is a friend, a boon companion,
    who will not be with you when sorrow
      comes.

11 When things go well, he is your other self,
    and lords it over your servants;

12 But if you are brought low, he turns against
      you
    and avoids meeting you.

13 Keep away from your enemies;
    be on your guard with your friends.

14 A faithful friend is a sturdy shelter;
    he who finds one finds a treasure.

15 A faithful friend is beyond price,
    no sum can balance his worth.

16 A faithful friend is a life-saving remedy,
    such as he who fears God finds;

17 For he who fears God behaves accordingly,
    and his friend will be like himself.

6, 11b: With LXX.
6, 14: ʾ ôhel (teqôp): so LXX.
6, 16: ṣôrî (ḥayyîm): so LXX, P, V. yaśśîgô: so LXX, V.
6, 17a: With LXX, P; trsp Heb v 17a to 17b; omit v 17b.

NRSV

and tell of the quarrel to your disgrace.

10 And there are friends who sit at your table,
    but they will not stand by you in time of
      trouble.

11 When you are prosperous, they become your
      second self,
    and lord it over your servants;

12 but if you are brought low, they turn against
      you,
    and hide themselves from you.

13 Keep away from your enemies,
    and be on guard with your friends.

14 Faithful friends are a sturdy shelter:
    whoever finds one has found a treasure.

15 Faithful friends are beyond price;
    no amount can balance their worth.

16 Faithful friends are life-saving medicine;
    and those who fear the Lord will find them.

17 Those who fear the Lord direct their friendship
      aright,
    for as they are, so are their neighbors also.

COMMENTARY

This section on the value of faithful friends is the first of several in the book dealing with a subject that was widely discussed in Hellenistic literature of the time. Jack T. Sanders has examined the affinities between this advice from Ben Sira and similar counsel in Theognis's elegiac poems of Book 1 and Phibis, another name for Papyrus Insinger.[145] Sanders's analysis demonstrates extensive cross-fertilization of ideas throughout the Greek world. Popular philosophers wandered from town to town and taught anyone who would listen to their ideas, and merchants traveled from port to port and inland, exchanging both goods and concepts. Ben Sira's frequent use of "lover" (אוהב ʾôhēb) instead of the usual word for "friend" (רע rēaʿ) probably betrays an unconscious influence from the Greek world.

145. Jack T. Sanders, *Ben Sira and Demotic Wisdom* (Chico, Calif.: Scholars Press, 1983) 27-59, esp. 30 (for Theognis), 69-100 (for Phibis/Papyrus Insinger). The primary text of Theognis is *Elegy and Iambus with the Anacreontea I*, LCL (Cambridge, Mass.: Harvard University Press, 1968).

Nevertheless, two expressions clearly mark this advice as authentically Hebraic. The language of greeting, "to ask about one's well-being" (שאל שלום šāʾal šālôm) characterizes genuine friendship, according to v. 5. In v. 16, the image of the soul's residing in a protective vessel, "the bag of the living" (צרור חיים ṣĕrôr ḥayyîm), recalls ancient folklore from 1 Sam 25:29, Abigail's rhetorical flourish about divine protection for David. Although the expression "one in a thousand" occurs in Job 9:3 and Eccl 7:28, it also appears in Egyptian wisdom literature and thus cannot be considered exclusively Hebraic. Ben Sira connects this expression with an interesting collocation, "lord of your counsel" (בעל סודך baʿal sôdekā). He therefore advises his students to have many companions ("persons of your well-being") but to restrict their intimates to one in a thousand (v. 16). The same advice is found in *Sanhedrin* 100b: "Let the men of thy peace be many; reveal thy secret to one out of a thousand."

Just as wisdom withholds her secrets from her followers until she has submitted them to various trials, so also should Ben Sira's students do. He suggests that they not share confidences with friends hastily, waiting until circumstances have tested their reliability. The reason for such caution concerns the harsh reality that some friends stay around only during fair weather. In Ben Sira's language, they do not withstand calamity with you, but they hang around as long as things go well. Furthermore, some friends become enemies for whatever reason and proceed to tarnish one's reputation by divulging embarrassing intimate details to everyone eager to devour delicious morsels of slander. The fact that this former friend once shared food at table seems to mean nothing, despite the rich symbolism of eating together in ancient Israel. The former table companion cannot be found to assist one in an evil day (v. 10). In the light of questionable character in friends, Ben Sira urges caution in every instance pertaining to friends but extraordinary wariness in the presence of enemies.

Despite its pitfalls, Ben Sira certainly esteems friendship highly. He likens a friend to treasure (הון *hôn*, a word much loved by the sages), and he recognizes the high cost of obtaining (קנה *qānâ*, "to purchase," "to acquire") a true friend. The threefold use of "a faithful friend" (אוהב אמונה *'ôhēb 'ĕmûnâ*) in vv. 14-16 has almost a touch of fantasy, as if Ben Sira wished to describe a perfect state of things on earth. Only deeply religious people, he asserts, will experience such friendship. Naturally, he understands true friends as God's gift for faithful service in spiritual living.

In contrast to the unit about deceptive speech in 5:9–6:1, this one emphasizes the positive power of language to foster friendship. The section opens with a beautiful expression for courteous greeting, "gracious lips" (שפתי חן *šiptê ḥēn*), the

pleasant response to a sweet palate (הין ערב *hēk 'ārēb*). The adjective *'ārēb* is as rare in the Bible as the sweet palate itself, occurring only in Prov 20:17 and Cant 2:14. Other links to the unit on duplicitous language include the word "reproach" (חרפה *ḥerpâ*) and the thrice-repeated particle of existence, "there is" (יש *yēš*) in vv. 8-9.

The Greek text of v. 16 changes the image of "a bag of the living," which the translator probably did not understand (or he considered "bundle," "bag" [צרור *sĕrôr*] a mistake for צרי [*sŏrî*]), to an expression compatible with Hellenistic thought. The resulting statement, "a faithful friend is a medicine of life" (φίλος πιστὸς φάρμακον ζωῆς *philos pistos pharmakon zōēs*), illustrates the way changes occur whenever texts are translated into a language with entirely different concepts and images.

The realization that even intimate friends sometimes "change into" enemies (the Hebrew verb הפך [*hāpak*] has this meaning in v. 9) does not give Ben Sira a jaundiced view of friendship. The ease with which a wisdom teacher could move over into suspicion of all relationships can be seen in *The Instruction of Amenemhet:* "Trust not a brother, know not a friend, make no intimates, it is worthless."

The Jewish tractate *Pirqe 'Abot* sums up the value of friends as follows: "Let a man buy himself a friend who will eat and drink with him, who will study with him the written and the oral law, and to whom he will entrust all his secrets."[146] Ben Sira would surely concur in these sentiments, as his return to this topic again and again suggests (cf. 11:29–12:18; 22:19-26; 37:1-6).

146. *T. Pirqe 'Abot* 1:6. See W. O. E. Oesterley, *The Wisdom of Jesus the Son of Sirach or Ecclesiasticus* (Cambridge: Cambridge University Press, 1912) 41. Oesterley is quoting from Solomon Schechter, *Studies in Judaism* (Philadelphia: Jewish Publication Society of America, 1924) 93.

REFLECTIONS

The importance of true friendship can hardly be overemphasized. Modern patterns of work put enormous strain on friendships, for people constantly change locations, making it difficult to maintain long-term relationships. Awareness that one will likely move to a new location in a few years works against the formation of close friendships, as does the time factor itself. To quote Ben Sira, "True friends are like wine; when it [friendship] has aged, you will enjoy it." Genuine friendship grows with the passing of time as two people share experiences and confidences over the years.

Extending a hand in friendship always makes one vulnerable. Ben Sira certainly recognized this unwelcome aspect of friendship, as did Jesus, who addressed his betrayer with the stinging word "friend." Many victims of false friends walk around and pose a staggering problem for trusting Christians. How much should a person divulge of his or her own hurts and joys? How far should an individual go toward cultivating friendships with those who have a long history of wearing their feelings on their sleeves? If friendship implies vulnerability, then Christians willingly become vulnerable by being friends at tremendous cost.

SIRACH 6:18–14:19

PART III

OVERVIEW

The third major unit in Sirach begins, like the first two, with a reflection on wisdom (6:18-37). It concludes with a solemn reminder of death's universality and urges young men to make the most of life by applying the advantages derived from wisdom (14:11-19). The final observations return to the contrasting stages of life, youth and old age, that introduce the initial poem (6:18), and reiterate the notion of fruits from one's labor (6:19; 14:15). Between the opening and closing sections, Ben Sira offers random advice about appropriate behavior; various responsibilities; warnings about different types of people, particularly women; caution in selecting associates; and unreliable friends.

SIRACH 6:18-37, WISDOM'S RIGOROUS DISCIPLINE

NAB	NRSV

18 My son, from your youth embrace discipline;
     thus will you find wisdom with graying hair.
 19 As though plowing and sowing, draw close to her;
     then await her bountiful crops.
 20 For in cultivating her you will labor but little,
     and soon you will eat of her fruits.
 21 How irksome she is to the unruly!
     The fool cannot abide her.
 22 She will be like a burdensome stone to test him,
     and he will not delay in casting her aside.
 23 For discipline is like her name,
     she is not accessible to many.
 	
 24 Listen, my son, and heed my advice;
     refuse not my counsel.
	18 My child, from your youth choose discipline,
	     and when you have gray hair you will still find wisdom.
	 19 Come to her like one who plows and sows,
	     and wait for her good harvest.
	 For when you cultivate her you will toil but little,
	     and soon you will eat of her produce.
	 20 She seems very harsh to the undisciplined;
	     fools cannot remain with her.
	 21 She will be like a heavy stone to test them,
	     and they will not delay in casting her aside.
	 22 For wisdom is like her name;
	     she is not readily perceived by many.
	
	 23 Listen, my child, and accept my judgment;
	     do not reject my counsel.
	 24 Put your feet into her fetters,
	     and your neck into her collar.
	 25 Bend your shoulders and carry her,
	     and do not fret under her bonds.
	 26 Come to her with all your soul,
	     and keep her ways with all your might.

6, 18: With LXX, P, V.
6, 22: (ʾeben) massâ: so LXX; cf V.
6, 23: Omit kᵉlî . . . ʾeḥād: duplicate of 27,5f.
6, 24f.27: With LXX; cf P.

NAB

25 Put your feet into her fetters,
   and your neck under her yoke.
26 Stoop your shoulders and carry her
   and be not irked at her bonds.
27 With all your soul draw close to her;
   with all your strength keep her ways.
28 Search her out, discover her; seek her and
      you will find her.
   Then when you have her, do not let her
      go;
29 Thus will you afterward find rest in her,
   and she will become your joy.
30 Her fetters will be your throne of majesty;
   her bonds, your purple cord.
31 You will wear her as your robe of glory,
   bear her as your splendid crown.

32 My son, if you wish, you can be taught;
   if you apply yourself, you will be shrewd.
33 If you are willing to listen, you will learn;
   if you give heed, you will be wise.
34 Frequent the company of the elders;
   whoever is wise, stay close to him.
35 Be eager to hear every godly discourse;
   let no wise saying escape you.
36 If you see a man of prudence, seek him out;
   let your feet wear away his doorstep!
37 Reflect on the precepts of the LORD,
      let his commandments be your constant
         meditation;
   Then he will enlighten your mind,
      and the wisdom you desire he will grant.

6, 29: $w^e t\bar{e} h\bar{a} pek$: so MS C, LXX, V.
6, 30: $w^e h\bar{a}y^e t\hat{a}$ $l^e k\bar{a})$ $h\bar{a}b\bar{a}l\grave{e}h\bar{a}$ $(m^e k\hat{o}n$ 'ōz), ($w^e m\hat{o}s^e r\bar{o}t\grave{e}h\bar{a}$ $p^e t\hat{\imath}l$ $t^e k\bar{e}let$); omit the rest.
6, 32: ($b^e n\hat{\imath}$) $tiww\bar{a}s\bar{e}r$: so LXX; cf v 33b.
6, 33: ($li\check{s}^e m\bar{o}a$') $tilmad$: so P; w^e ' im $tatteh$ (' $ozn^e k\bar{a}$) $tithakk\bar{a}m$: so LXX; cf 32a.
6, 34: With LXX, P.
6, 36: (r^e ' $\bar{e}h$) $m\hat{\imath}$ ($y\bar{a}b\hat{\imath}n$) . . . $sipp\bar{a}yw$: so LXX, P.
6, 37: ($w^e hitb\bar{o}n\bar{a}nt\bar{a}$) $bet\hat{o}rat$ $yhwh$, $\hat{u}b^e$ $mis wôt\bar{a}yw$ $tehgeh$: so LXX; cf P.

NRSV

27 Search out and seek, and she will become
      known to you;
   and when you get hold of her, do not let
      her go.
28 For at last you will find the rest she gives,
   and she will be changed into joy for you.
29 Then her fetters will become for you a strong
      defense,
   and her collar a glorious robe.
30 Her yoke[a] is a golden ornament,
   and her bonds a purple cord.
31 You will wear her like a glorious robe,
   and put her on like a splendid crown.[b]

32 If you are willing, my child, you can be
      disciplined,
   and if you apply yourself you will become
      clever.
33 If you love to listen you will gain knowledge,
   and if you pay attention you will become
      wise.
34 Stand in the company of the elders.
      Who is wise? Attach yourself to such a one.
35 Be ready to listen to every godly discourse,
   and let no wise proverbs escape you.
36 If you see an intelligent person, rise early to
      visit him;
   let your foot wear out his doorstep.
37 Reflect on the statutes of the Lord,
      and meditate at all times on his
         commandments.
   It is he who will give insight to[c] your mind,
      and your desire for wisdom will be granted.

[a] Heb: Gk *Upon her*   [b] Heb: Gk *crown of gladness*
[c] Heb: Gk *will confirm*

COMMENTARY

Three distinct sections make up the larger unit of twenty-two bicola: 6:18-22, 23-31, 32-37 (for the entire section, the Vg supplies the title *De Doctrina Sapientia*, "On Wise Teaching"). An inclusio, built on the noun "wisdom" (חכמה *ḥokmâ*), links vv. 18 and 37. An introductory "my son" (בני *běnî*), sets each of the three sub-sections apart. A single theme unites the whole discussion: the necessity for and rewards of seeking wisdom regardless of the obstacles one may encounter. Images of farming and hunting consistently dominate the material in the first two subsections; the third, vv. 32-37, shifts to the picture of lively conversation and deep thought.

The Hebrew of v. 18 is lacking in MS A, and only the last two words appear in MS C. For vv. 23-24, the Hebrew has 27:5-6, and vv. 26 and 34 are completely missing. In v. 19, the twin images of plowing and sowing are broken up in the Hebrew, but not in the Greek; an unlikely sowing and *reaping* occur in Hebrew, the context calling only for the preparatory stage of planting. This brief unit demonstrates the difficulty of determining precisely what the original Hebrew text of Sirach actually included. Often, as here, insufficient clues exist to enable interpreters to decide which option comes closer to the autograph.

6:18-22. Ancient Israelites believed that wisdom accompanied old age, the result of long experience. Naturally, because young people lacked exposure to the tradition and to the realities of life, they also could make no legitimate claim on knowledge. The sole means of attaining this worthy goal was by submitting to discipline and by persevering through all difficulties. Young people, like Elihu in the book of Job, were expected to listen while their elders gave their view of things and were to speak only briefly, if at all.

The weight of this preference for the aged in intellectual matters fell heavily on the prophet Jeremiah, who unsuccessfully pleaded youthful innocence as a way of escaping the divine commission. In his case, the narrative reports, the one who summoned him to prophesy would grant eloquence and courage so that he could stand up to ridicule (Jer 1:5-10). Within wisdom circles, the elevation of a young man or woman to a position of authority and leadership was unlikely. Wisdom and its advantages came at the end of much hard work; gray hairs signaled to others that one had lived long enough to acquire some valuable insights. This claim becomes problematic in the book of Job, for Elihu rejects it outright, and Job insists that he knows as much as his older friends.

The Bible often uses agricultural imagery, primarily because Scripture arose in an agrarian society. Claus Westermann has emphasized this aspect of wisdom literature, especially the older sayings in the book of Proverbs.[147] In his plausible view, this instruction is the product of simple villagers whose central concern was the family and its survival. Their discourse revolved around the daily routine in the fields and vineyards, at the gates, and in the intimacy of tents and small dwellings.

Although Ben Sira appears to have lived in a city, probably Jerusalem, he continues to use agricultural images, partly because of his conservative nature and partly because even in his day many city dwellers owned small plots outside Jerusalem and worked them daily during the growing season. He issues an invitation to approach wisdom in the same way one begins the day in the fields. Just as workers go about various tasks, here symbolized by plowing and sowing, with eager expectation of a successful yield, so also young students can start their long journey with confidence that the harvest will, indeed, be a time of rejoicing.

For ancient peoples, the metaphor of plowing and sowing often functioned as a euphemism for sexual relations, and a woman was described as a fruitful field to be plowed by her husband. This widespread metaphor, familiar to readers of the Samson narrative, in which one of his riddle-like sayings accuses the Philistine companions of dallying with his wife ("plowing with his heifer"), links up with the rich and varied imagery of eroticism associated with personified wisdom.[148] In addition, such language of explicit sexual expectation was fully at home at harvesttime, as the beautiful story about Ruth and Boaz demonstrates.[149] The eating of wisdom's bountiful produce, like the enjoyment of sexual union, makes the work involved in all former cultivation seem inconsequential, almost trivial. In Prov 8:19, Wisdom boasts that her fruit surpasses gold and silver in value; a similar point is made in 1 Esdr 4:18-19 with reference to a man's delight in a woman.

147. Claus Westermann, *Roots of Wisdom: The Oldest Proverbs of Israel and Other Peoples* (Louisville: Westminster John Knox, 1995).
148. On the metaphor "plowing with my heifer," see James L. Crenshaw, *Samson* (Atlanta: John Knox, 1978) 118-20; and for personified wisdom, see Bernhard Lang, *Wisdom and the Book of Proverbs* (New York: Pilgrim, 1986); Samuel Terrien, *Till the Heart Sings* (Philadelphia: Fortress, 1985); Claudia Y. Camp, *Wisdom and the Feminine in the Book of Proverbs,* BLS (Sheffield: Almond, 1985).
149. A stimulating and unconventional interpretation has recently come from Danna Nolan Fewell and David Miller Gunn, *Compromising Redemption* (Louisville: Westminster/John Knox, 1990).

Dropping precious ore like refuse, he stares at a beautiful woman with mouth agape.[150]

Ben Sira urges young boys to draw near to wisdom, eagerly anticipating her produce (v. 19); the verb קוה (*qāwâ*) connotes lively hope, a confidence born out of experience and reinforced by hard work. Simpletons and uninformed individuals, indicated by traditional terms from the book of Proverbs ("foolish" אויל *'ĕwîl*] and "unintelligent" קצר לב *qāṣar lēb*]), encounter her like an uneven path, unless the idea of plowing continues in v. 20 and suggests rocky terrain. Stopping momentarily to pick up a heavy stone, they quickly throw it down rather than moving it to an area in the field where its bulk would be useful, probably in helping to form a terrace to slow erosion and to retain water for agricultural use.

Verse 22 offers an explanation for such short-sightedness in persons of insufficient intellect and consequently inadequate resolve, and in doing so it draws on views about wisdom's hiddenness. Although Ben Sira's play on words is not entirely clear to modern interpreters, it probably involves מוסר (*mûsār*), a synonym for "wisdom," and a participle form of the verb סור (*sûr*, "to turn away") with passive force, "withdrawn."[151] The same root returns in the verb תוסר (*tiwasser*) of v. 33, "you will become wise."

This puzzling observation that wisdom, like her name, is not manifest to the crowds sounds somewhat elitist, particularly in its Greek translation, "and is not manifest to the populace" (καὶ οὐ πολλοῖς ἐστιν φανερά *kai ou pollois estin phanera*). She does not appear to ordinary citizens, *hoi polloi*. The Hebrew text has "obvious" or "plain" (נכחה *nōkḥâ* or נכחה *nĕkōḥâ*), perhaps continuing the idea of a path or furrow. The form is laid out in an ABB'A' pattern: wisdom: she: she: not straight. Ancient peoples believed that a name encapsulated one's essence, hence should be carefully guarded. A deity who divulged his or her name risked being controlled by magical incantation,

which probably explains the story about Yahweh's reluctance to share the divine name with Moses (Exod 4:13-15). Other traditionists did not subscribe to this theory about the divine name and, therefore, used "Yahweh" freely.

6:23-31. Whereas the first section emphasizes the harsh discipline involved in acquiring an education, the second unit continues its emphasis but moves beyond the idea of toil in splendid fashion. What once appeared to be fetters and a yoke will be transformed into royal garments. Now at last those students who persisted realize that wisdom only *seemed* harsh but was actually acting in their best interests. Like the symmetry in the book of Joel, where the destructive results of invading locusts are replaced in every detail by their opposite,[152] each unpleasant feature connected with trials imposed by wisdom on young students will be changed into highly desirable attire (Joel 1:2–2:17 // 2:18-27). The language of putting on moral traits like clothing was common in Israel and Greece at this time.

The form of v. 23, an imperative followed by its opposite with a negation, recalled earlier teaching in the book of Proverbs ("listen, accept // do not reject"). The teacher asserts his authority by means of a threefold possessive pronoun, "my" (אתי *'ōtî*) in the Hebrew; the Greek translator drops one of these but makes up for the loss with an intensive verb, "do not refuse" (μὴ ἀπαναίνου *mē apanainou*).

The dominant image in v. 24 comes from plowing; imagining an ox submitting to a yoke and collar, Ben Sira uses this symbol for the process of getting an education. This idea caught on rapidly in the Jewish community, for it appears prominently both in rabbinic literature and in the New Testament. According to Matt 11:29, Jesus invited followers to take his yoke upon their necks and learn from him; he promised, however, that his yoke would be easy and his burden light.[153] A passage in *Pirqe 'Abot* reads as follows: "Every one who receives on himself the yoke of Torah, they remove from him the yoke of the kingdom and the yoke of worldly occupation. But every one who breaks off from him the yoke of Torah,

150. James L. Crenshaw, "The Contest of Darius' Guards in 1 Esdras 3:1–5:3," in *Images of Man and God: The Old Testament Short Story in Literary Focus*, ed. Burke O. Long (Sheffield: Almond, 1981) 74-88, 119-20. See also James L. Crenshaw, *Urgent Advice and Probing Questions* (Macon, Ga.: Mercer University Press, 1995) 222-34.

151. John G. Snaith, *Ecclesiasticus*, CBC (Cambridge: Cambridge University Press, 1974) 39. Snaith thinks the pun occurs between מוסר (*mûsār*) and מוסר (*môsēr*), "bond," "halter," and provides a link with "fetters" of v. 24.

152. Discussed in James L. Crenshaw, *Joel*, AB (New York: Doubleday, 1995) 83-163.

153. M. Jack Suggs, *Wisdom, Christology, and Law in Matthew's Gospel* (Cambridge, Mass.: Harvard University Press, 1970) 99-127.

they lay upon him the yoke of the kingdom and the yoke of worldly occupation."[154] According to *Erubin* 54*a* of the Babylonian Talmud, whoever brings the neck under the yoke of Torah will enjoy her protective care.[155]

The reference to bonds or fetters in v. 24 is difficult; the Hebrew text actually has a word for "net" in v. 28. Perhaps the language suggests the stocks that were used to punish uncooperative slaves or weights that athletes employed during practice to strengthen their ankles and increase their speed. The expression may even be a rather loose way of describing the cords that secured yokes around the necks of oxen. In any event, v. 25 continues the image of an ox willingly submitting to a yoke. The following verse recalls deuteronomic language of resolve ("with your whole mind [heart] and strength").

Three imperatives describing the quest for wisdom signal the importance Ben Sira placed on the hunt. Lying between two imperatives for searching, דרש (*dĕrāš*) and בקש (*baqqēš*), the imperative of חקר (*ḥāqar*) suggests tracing out a route. Together the three verbs indicate thorough research,[156] a probing into the realm of the unknown. Actually, a fourth imperative appears in the initial colon of the Hebrew text, but the Greek translator probably read a verb, "and you will discover" (ותמצא *wĕtimṣāʾ*). The language of the second colon in this verse (v. 27) derives from Prov 4:13; once you have taken hold of (חזק *ḥāzaq*) wisdom, do not relinquish her. This verse furnishes a contrast to the conduct of the uninformed who abruptly threw away the stone he had picked up, presumably because of its heavy weight (v. 21).

Completely transformed, wisdom will present herself as rest and exquisite delight. Two verbs stand out here, "to find" (מצא *māṣāʾ*) and "to overturn (הפך *hāpak*).[157] The former is governed

by an adverb of time, "at last," while the latter is qualified by the personal pronoun "for you." Finally, worthy students see wisdom as she truly is and as she has always been. Verses 29-31 describe the splendid clothing that, with the cooperation of her industrious students, she has woven for them. The collar has become a beautiful robe, the yoke a golden ornament, the bonds a purple cord. Royal imagery abounds in this fanciful description, and even the color purple signifies kingship. The expression "purple cord" comes from Num 15:38-39 and later played into rabbinic speculation about a determent from adultery, the cord becoming visible when clothes are removed and serving as a reminder that God observes everything one does.

6:32-37. The third subsection proclaims that "where there is a will there also exists a way," offers useful advice about seizing every opportunity to learn, and provides a religious interpretation of the intellectual journey. The conclusion to the Egyptian "Instruction of Anii" demonstrates that some students seriously doubted their ability to live up to their teacher's moral requirements. Here the son, Khonshotep, objects that he lacks his father's moral stamina, although approving the teachings. Anii responds that everyone can learn, and he reinforces this view with specific examples taken from nature and society in general. Ben Sira, too, has full confidence in his students' ability. Having settled the matter of motivation, he encourages them to look for learned sources of knowledge among older people and become willing followers. The idea of peripatetic teachers flourished in the Greek environment, and Jewish teachers of the first century CE established rival schools, those of Hillel and his rival, Shammai.

Two things stand out in this bit of advice. First, education takes place by listening to intelligent discourse rather than through reading texts, and second, it assumes the form of a witty saying (משל *māšāl*; proverb, aphorism, witticism, allegory, riddle). The Hebrew שיחה (*śîḥâ*, "meditation") occurs only three times in the OT, Job 15:4 and Ps 119:97, 99. It conveys a sense of wonder and gratitude in the presence of God's mystery and statutes (cf. Amos 4:13, where a related form occurs [שחו *śēḥô*, "his thoughts"]). Verse 36 almost urges students to make a nuisance of themselves, rising early and wearing out the stone at

---

154. *Pirqe 'Abot* 3:6.
155. Quoted in Oesterley, *The Wisdom of Jesus the Son of Sirach*, 44.
156. The term *midrash* comes from the verb דרש (*dāraš*) and refers to the act of searching for the meaning of a sacred text. In the Middle Ages, Jews and Christians employed a fourfold method of interpretation. In Jewish circles, an acronymn, PaRDeS, indicated פשט (*pešat*, the literal meaning), רמז (*remez*, the allegorical meaning), דרש (*deraš*, the tropological and moral meaning), and סוד (*sôd*, the mystical meaning).
157. Jack Sasson, *Jonah*, AB (New York: Doubleday, 1990) 234-35, illustrates the rich ambiguity of this word הפך (*hāpak*) in Jonah 3:4 (in the feminine form). When Jonah proclaimed that Nineveh would be overturned (*nehpak*) in forty days, the word conveyed two possibilities: "destroyed" and "converted." Jonah understood the former sense of the verb, and the Ninevites heard the latter sense.

the entrance of a wise man's house. The Hebrew imperative of v. 36 further stresses the active responsibility to observe (ראה *rĕʾēh*) intelligent behavior.

The final verse in this unit reveals Ben Sira's extensive theological bent. He urges students to ponder the fear of the Most High and to meditate on the statutes continually ("daily" [תמיד *tāmîd*]). The ABB'A' structure returns in the first bicolon of v. 37 ("reflect on/the fear of Elyon/his state/meditate on") and persists to the end ("and he/will give insight to your mind/what you desire/he will make you wise").

REFLECTIONS

1. Ben Sira's remarks about cultivating a sense of self-worth are hardly needed in modern American society, which seems almost obsessed with universal self-congratulation, regardless of ethical character. The growth of the human potential movement and the widespread popularity of self-help literature have encouraged people toward an uncritical self-esteem and self-acceptance. The important thing, feeling good about yourself, has virtually extinguished the concept of guilt and banished the notion of sin. This attitude has led to disastrous pedagogy, ruling out the idea of learning from one's mistakes and accepting mediocrity, laziness, and slovenly habits.

While in the moral sphere, as well as the educational, the contemporary message promotes accepting the status quo and even glorying in it; in the area of body building and diet precisely the opposite message goes forth: "No pain, no gain." Here nothing worthwhile comes without effort, and no one tries to conceal this reality. To lose weight and to tone the muscles, one must submit to a rigorous regimen of food and exercise. The judgment that we are not always and completely okay underlies the entire enterprise.

The latter understanding of things resembles the ancient worldview, one in which discipline played a central role. Without practice, no one becomes really good at anything, whether sports, music, dance, cooking, parenting, or anything else. The apostle Paul applied this principle to the spiritual life, acknowledging that one begins as an infant and then grows in faith and knowledge through diligent study and moral discipline. Ancient moralists adopted images from sports, the martial arts, and agriculture in the effort to encourage people to grow in character.

2. Jesus, like Paul, made strict demands on his disciples, warning against an enthusiastic initial surrender followed by a slackening of resolve (Luke 9:62). He expected followers to forsake everything they valued and to take his yoke on their shoulders. Nevertheless, he did promise that, in retrospect, they would recognize his burden as easy and his yoke as light (Matt 11:29-30). The sect at Qumran also emphasized the difficult discipline facing initiates, and to ease that process the religious teacher provided a manual of discipline by which to organize their daily lives.

Christians today can profit from plain directions about living, particularly because absolutes have fallen under attack from every quarter. We may no longer render a categorical no about this or that practice, but one thing surely remains as fixed as ever: Growth in Christian discipleship comes only as a result of constant effort. In this struggle to become mature in faith, only Christians who exercise self-discipline will make any ascertainable progress. Jesus' exclusive language made the price of following him absolutely clear; the symbolism of a narrow way, and straight, implied that discipleship was only for the select few. That exclusive language clashes with the legitimate need to be inclusive today, and many Christians merely bypass the rigorous demands. The result is a brand of Christian witness lacking moral commitment.

SIRACH 7:1-17,
THE CONSEQUENCES OF SIN

NAB

7 Do no evil, and evil will not overtake you;
2 avoid wickedness, and it will turn aside from you.

3 Sow not in the furrows of injustice,
lest you harvest it sevenfold.

4 Seek not from the LORD authority,
nor from the king a place of honor.

5 Parade not your justice before the LORD,
and before the king flaunt not your wisdom.

6 Seek not to become a judge
if you have not strength to root out crime,
Or you will show favor to the ruler
and mar your integrity.

7 Be guilty of no evil before the city's populace,
nor disgrace yourself before the assembly.

8 Do not plot to repeat a sin;
not even for one will you go unpunished.

9 Say not: "He will appreciate my many gifts;
the Most High will accept my offerings."

10 Be not impatient in prayers,
and neglect not the giving of alms.

11 Laugh not at an embittered man;
be mindful of him who exalts and humbles.

12 Plot no mischief against your brother,
nor against your friend and companion.

13 Delight not in telling lie after lie,
for it never results in good.

14 Thrust not yourself into the deliberations of princes,
and repeat not the words of your prayer.

15 Hate not laborious tasks,
nor farming, which was ordained by the Most High.

7, 1: (ʾal taʿś) raʿ wᵉlōʾ (yaśśigᵉkā) raʿ: so MS C, LXX, P.
7, 3: (ʾal) tizraʿ ʾal ḥărûšê ʾāwel: so LXX, P.
7, 5: (ʾal tiṣtaddeq lipᵉnê) yhwh, wᵉlipᵉnê (melek): so LXX, P.
7, 6d: wᵉnatattā pešaʿ bᵉtummātekā: so LXX; cf P.
7, 7: (baʿădat) šāʿar: so LX, P; dittog.
7, 9: With LXX, P.
7, 15: ʾal tāqôṣ bišᵉbāʾ mᵉlāʾ ka, waʾ ăbôdâ mēʿ ēl neḥĕlāqâ: so LXX, V.

NRSV

7 Do no evil, and evil will never overtake you.

2 Stay away from wrong, and it will turn away from you.

3 Do[a] not sow in the furrows of injustice,
and you will not reap a sevenfold crop.

4 Do not seek from the Lord high office,
or the seat of honor from the king.

5 Do not assert your righteousness before the Lord,
or display your wisdom before the king.

6 Do not seek to become a judge,
or you may be unable to root out injustice;
you may be partial to the powerful,
and so mar your integrity.

7 Commit no offense against the public,
and do not disgrace yourself among the people.

8 Do not commit a sin twice;
not even for one will you go unpunished.

9 Do not say, "He will consider the great number of my gifts,
and when I make an offering to the Most High God, he will accept it."

10 Do not grow weary when you pray;
do not neglect to give alms.

11 Do not ridicule a person who is embittered in spirit,
for there is One who humbles and exalts.

12 Do not devise[b] a lie against your brother,
or do the same to a friend.

13 Refuse to utter any lie,
for it is a habit that results in no good.

14 Do not babble in the assembly of the elders,
and do not repeat yourself when you pray.

15 Do not hate hard labor
or farm work, which was created by the Most High.

16 Do not enroll in the ranks of sinners;
remember that retribution does not delay.

a Gk *My child, do*   b Heb: Gk *plow*

NAB

16 Do not esteem yourself better than your
     fellows;
    remember, his wrath will not delay.
17 More and more, humble your pride;
    what awaits man is worms.

7, 16: ʾal taḥšōbᵉkā mimmᵉtê ʿām, zᵉkôr ʿibbarôn lōʾ yitʿabbar.
7, 17: Omit ʾal-tāʾ îs . . . darkô : so LXX, V.

NRSV

17 Humble yourself to the utmost,
    for the punishment of the ungodly is fire
     and worms.[a]

[a] Heb *for the expectation of mortals is worms*

COMMENTARY

This section opens with a thematic sentence about how to avoid trouble and closes with a graphic description of punishment for evil. In between these powerful motivators, Ben Sira gives some advice about aspiring to a position of power and responsibility, warns against presumption and loose speech, and recommends manual labor. The grammatical form, the negative particle אל (*ʾal*) plus a jussive, runs through the entire section, except for v. 17, actually extending through v. 20. The repeated negative command builds up to a crescendo, emphasizing the teacher's concern for students' welfare. Two features of vv. 1-17 require comment, first the personification of evil and, second, the difference between the Hebrew and Greek texts.

Like wisdom, evil is personified in vv. 1-2 and thus capable of chasing someone and overtaking a hapless victim or turning its back on persons who show no interest in it. Such a move had already occurred in Prov 9:13-18, which describes a personified folly as a seductress who invites young boys to a banquet, reminding them of the pleasure derived from eating forbidden fruit. Interpreters generally consider this personification of evil to have been modeled on wisdom, although the reverse sequence has been proposed.[158] This descriptive language of personification characterizes prophetic speech, too, the prophet Amos likening the fallen nation Israel to a raped virgin (Amos 5:2), and Jeremiah threatening destruction from pestilence, sword, famine, and captivity (Jer 15:2). Similarly, a psalmist referred to righteousness and truth as kissing each other (Ps 85:10).

158. Lennart Boström, *The God of the Sages*, CBOTS 29 (Lund: Almquist & Wiksell International, 1990) 56.

7:17. The most striking difference between the Hebrew and the Greek texts in this unit occurs in this verse. Whereas the Hebrew only mentions the natural decomposition of the body ("worms") as the destiny of evil people, the Greek translator wrote "fire and worms" (πῦρ καὶ σκώληξ *pur kai skōlēx*). Critics usually see the addition of "fire" as evidence that Hellenism strongly influenced Ben Sira's grandson in Egypt. The Greek concept of perdition has thus invaded the thinking of pious Jews in the late second century BCE, according to this view. One should probably not make so much of this textual difference, for the expectation of "fire and worms" as punishment for rebels against the Lord occurs already in Isa 66:24: "for their worm shall not die, their fire shall not be quenched, and they shall be an abhorrence to all flesh" (NRSV). Nevertheless, the shorter version of Sir 7:17 (without any reference to fire) probably represents Ben Sira's view and, therefore, will be followed here.

7:1-3. The thematic sentence "Do no evil, and evil [misfortune] will never overtake you" struck later Jewish religionists as worthy of wider dissemination, for it is quoted several times in midrashic literature. The optimistic worldview underlying the sentiment owes nothing to the questioning of divine justice pursued in the books of Job and Ecclesiastes, as well as in Psalm 73. Instead, Ben Sira here reaffirms the dominant view of earlier wisdom within the book of Proverbs—namely, that individuals can control their own fate by the way they conduct their lives (Prov 10:16; 12:14; 13:18; 22:4). The agricultural metaphor in v. 3 about sowing "in the furrows of injustice" and reaping "a sevenfold crop" sounds like a popular aphorism. An erotic nuance probably clung to the saying, given the customary use of the metaphor for sexual relationships and the personification of evil as a woman.

7:4-7. The attempt by Ben Sira to dissuade young boys from aspiring to high office comes as a total surprise, for elsewhere he praises the office of sage above all other professions and states that they will serve among rulers (39:4; cf. 8:8). Martin Hengel has viewed the negative counsel against the dark background of Seleucid politics,[159] which is characterized in the book of 2 Maccabees as thoroughly corrupt (2 Macc 4:1-20). Where high office goes to the highest bidder and foreign control over internal Jewish decisions existed, service as judge or in any one of a number of official positions would have seriously compromised an individual. The more positive advice in the latter part of the book could have arisen in an earlier period, perhaps during the Ptolemaic rule prior to 198 BCE or early in the Seleucid era before a hostile attitude developed toward the Jews.

Less probably, in vv. 4-7 Ben Sira simply enjoins humility: "Don't seek office, but be prepared to serve if it searches you out." The warning against boasting about goodness to God and calling the king's attention to your intelligence supports the latter alternative. Verse 6 points away from that reading, suggesting that the demands of the office would be so taxing that the individual would inevitably fail. Either he would lack authority to expel wickedness, or he would be vulnerable to bribery and to the subtle influence of persons in power.

This brief section concerns four distinct entities: God, king, judge, and people. The first two, God and king, are brought together as supreme (heavenly) and terrestrial authorities respectively. By Ben Sira's time, the older concept of judge as warrior had given way to a more modern understanding of one who pronounces verdicts in litigation. The fourth category, the public at large, lacks the power inherent to the king and the judge, but it controls people in a much subtler fashion, through withholding honor and imposing shame.

7:8-14. The third subdivision deals with presumption. Ben Sira describes arrogant people who

think they can treat everybody lightly, indeed contemptuously, with impunity. They even treat God in this manner. Ben Sira warns against doing the same sinful act twice, the sinner presumably gathering courage from the absence of immediate punishment (cf. v. 16). Verse 9, missing in Hebrew, offers another rationale for sin, specifically that generosity toward God atones for one's deeds. The notion that money can buy anything, even forgiveness, has often lurked in the nooks and crannies of the religious mind. In v. 8 the image suggesting conspiracy is that of "binding up," the opposite of binding the precepts of the law on the hands and forehead (cf. Deut 6:8; 11:18).

Ben Sira advises against taking prayer lightly and uttering the same thing over and over (cf. Eccl 5:2). Finding the right balance between liturgical petition through refrains and offering spontaneous adoration did not come easily in the ancient world, any more than today. Warnings against excessive use of epithets for God and adjectives for divine attributes occur in rabbinic literature, and Jesus is quoted as cautioning against empty repetitions in prayer (Matt 6:7). At the same time, he teaches a model prayer to his followers and is pictured as repeating himself three times at prayer during his final hours in the garden of Gethsemane (Matt 26:39-44). For Ben Sira, the proper combination seemed to have been energetic prayer followed by the dispensing of alms to the needy.

The power of the spoken word for good and ill seems to have occupied Ben Sira's mind here. The negative side of speech, both ridicule and outright falsehood, provoke his ire, as does loose talk generally. Because the assembly of elders conducts important business, one's talk ought to be to the point and circumspect.

7:15-16. In the Hebrew text, v. 15 replaces v. 9 and belongs to the present subsection. Unique in subject matter, the verse reflects a viewpoint that will be explored more thoroughly in 38:24–39:11. Ben Sira recognizes manual labor as divinely ordained and therefore honorable; he derives this positive assessment of work from the ancient story about Adam and Eve in the garden of Eden before their sin. The changed sociological environment in the early second century BCE, with the opening up of numerous professions besides

159. Martin Hengel, *Judaism and Hellenism* (Philadelphia: Fortress, 1974) 1:133-34.

farming and the commercial situation that rewarded venturesome investments, may have prompted Ben Sira to come to the defense of traditional values here. He knew that society could not survive without products from the farm, and he also understood the reluctance of young boys to work with animals when they could avoid such backbreaking toil.

Ben Sira's favorable attitude toward work was also shared by the rabbis, finding expression in *Pirqe 'Abot* 2:2, "Excellent is Torah study together with worldly business . . . all Torah without work [i.e., manual labor] must fail at length, and occasion iniquity," and in Qiddushin 99*a*, "Whoever does not teach his son work, teaches him to rob."

SIRACH 7:18-28, DOMESTIC ADVICE

NAB

18 Barter not a friend for money,
    nor a dear brother for the gold of Ophir.

19 Dismiss not a sensible wife;
    a gracious wife is more precious than corals.

20 Mistreat not a servant who faithfully serves,
    nor a laborer who devotes himself to his task.

21 Let a wise servant be dear to you as your own self;
    refuse him not his freedom.

22 If you have livestock, look after them;
    if they are dependable, keep them.

23 If you have sons, chastise them;
    bend their necks from childhood.

24 If you have daughters, keep them chaste,
    and be not indulgent to them.

25 Giving your daughter in marriage ends a great task;
    but give her to a worthy man.

26 If you have a wife, let her not seem odious to you;
    but where there is ill-feeling, trust her not.

27 With your whole heart honor your father;
    your mother's birthpangs forget not.

28 Remember, of these parents you were born;
    what can you give them for all they gave you?

7, 18: (*w*ᵉ ᵃ*ḥ*) *tālîm* (?): cf LXX, P, V.
7, 20: (ᵃ*al tāra*ᵃ) ᵉ*ebed* (ᵉ*ôbēd*): so MS C; LXX, P.
7, 23b: With LXX, V; cf 30, 12.
7, 27f: With LXX, P, V.

NRSV

18 Do not exchange a friend for money,
    or a real brother for the gold of O'phir.

19 Do not dismiss[a] a wise and good wife,
    for her charm is worth more than gold.

20 Do not abuse slaves who work faithfully,
    or hired laborers who devote themselves to their task.

21 Let your soul love intelligent slaves;[b]
    do not withhold from them their freedom.

22 Do you have cattle? Look after them;
    if they are profitable to you, keep them.

23 Do you have children? Discipline them,
    and make them obedient[c] from their youth.

24 Do you have daughters? Be concerned for their chastity,[d]
    and do not show yourself too indulgent with them.

25 Give a daughter in marriage, and you complete a great task;
    but give her to a sensible man.

26 Do you have a wife who pleases you?[e] Do not divorce her;
    but do not trust yourself to one whom you detest.

27 With all your heart honor your father,
    and do not forget the birth pangs of your mother.

[a] Heb: Gk *deprive yourself of self*   [b] Heb *Love a wise slave as yourself*   [c] Gk *bend their necks*   [d] Gk *body*   [e] Heb Syr lack *who pleases you*

NRSV

28 Remember that it was of your parents *a* you
were born;
how can you repay what they have given
to you?

a Gk *them*

COMMENTARY

7:18-21. With this section Ben Sira moves into the privacy of the home, mentioning brother, wife, slaves, children, and parents. The opening statement about the exceptional worth of a brother sets the tone for the entire discussion of the family circle. Ophir, the source of the gold that was most valued in biblical literature, was either in southern Arabia or in Egypt (1 Kgs 9:28; 10:11; 22:48; Job 22:24; 28:16; Ps 45:9). Ben Sira places an intelligent and good wife alongside a brother as worth more than gold. His remarks about slaves reflect both Hebraic and Greek ideas, Hebraic in the reaffirmation of the ancient legislation enjoining owners to release slaves after six years (Exod 21:2; Deut 15:12-15), and Greek in the comment about intelligent slaves. Often Hellenistic slaves were learned educators acquired through conquest.

7:22-26. The sequence in these verses is somewhat jarring, particularly the abrupt move from mentioning cattle to mentioning children, but one observes a similar, although reverse, movement in the prologue to the book of Job (Job 1:2-3). To some degree, children and wives were understood as a man's property, although this does not rule out deep affection on both sides.

Ben Sira uses a rhetorical question four times: "Do you have cattle . . . children . . . daughters . . . a wife?" After each question he offers some timely advice, always from the standpoint of self-interest. Take care of valuable cattle, discipline children, protect a daughter's virginity and choose a sensible husband for her, and keep a wife whom you love. Conceivably, fathers chose husbands for their daughters without soliciting their wishes, but one can naturally assume that many young girls made their desires known. Ben Sira will have much more to say about daughters, not all positive (42:9-14). The Hebrew text has strong language for disciplining sons: "bend their necks," but it adds "and acquire wives for them while they are young"—that is, before awakening lust gets them in trouble.

7:27-28. These verses do not appear in the Hebrew text; they were probably omitted through a scribal error—after the scribe wrote, "with the whole heart" in v. 27, his eye then may have fallen on the similar phrase in v. 29. The sentiment expressed in these verses moves from the greater to the lesser. Your parents gave life to you; how can you ever match that gift?

SIRACH 7:29-36, OBLIGATIONS TO PRIESTS AND TO THE POOR

NAB

29 With all your soul, fear God,
revere his priests.
30 With all your strength, love your Creator,
forsake not his ministers.

NRSV

29 With all your soul fear the Lord,
and revere his priests.
30 With all your might love your Maker,
and do not neglect his ministers.

NAB

31 Honor God and respect the priest;
  give him his portion as you have been
    commanded:
  First fruits and contributions,
    due sacrifices and holy offerings.
32 To the poor man also extend your hand,
  that your blessing may be complete;
33 Be generous to all the living,
  and withhold not your kindness from the
    dead.
34 Avoid not those who weep,
  but mourn with those who mourn;
35 Neglect not to visit the sick—
  for these things you will be loved.
36 In whatever you do, remember your last
    days,
  and you will never sin.

7, 31c: *rê šit ût rûmat yad.*
7, 35a: With LXX, P, V.

NRSV

³¹ Fear the Lord and honor the priest,
  and give him his portion, as you have been
    commanded:
  the first fruits, the guilt offering, the gift of the
    shoulders,
  the sacrifice of sanctification, and the first
    fruits of the holy things.

³² Stretch out your hand to the poor,
  so that your blessing may be complete.
³³ Give graciously to all the living;
  do not withhold kindness even from the
    dead.
³⁴ Do not avoid those who weep,
  but mourn with those who mourn.
³⁵ Do not hesitate to visit the sick,
  because for such deeds you will be loved.
³⁶ In all you do, remember the end of your life,
  and then you will never sin.

COMMENTARY

7:29-31. Ben Sira's fondness for the priestly office finds frequent expression in the book, particularly within the section praising biblical heroes and ending with a magnificent poem eulogizing the high priest, Simeon II. The social status of priests varied over the centuries; because of competing sacerdotal families, the rise to power of one group naturally marked the decline of another in rank and privilege (1 Sam 3:10-14). The Levites endured this kind of demotion at one time, prompting the author of the book of Chronicles to come to their defense. Similarly, the family of Abiathar had fallen from royal favor in earlier days (1 Kgs 2:26-27). It follows that one can hardly describe all priests as privileged, although their status had certainly risen considerably during Ben Sira's time.[160] He urges his readers to obey biblical legislation with respect to supporting priests (cf. Deut 14:28-29; Lev 6:14-18). The two verbs, פחד (*pāḥad*) and כבד (*kābēd*), imply awe and high regard respectively. An ancient epithet for Yahweh was "the Fear of Isaac" (Gen 31:42), although an

alternative translation of פחד יצחק (*paḥad yiṣḥāq*) is "kinsman of Isaac." Either rendering of the phrase emphasizes Yahweh's protection of Isaac in times of danger. The careful delineation of different types of sacrifice involving gifts to priests suggests that Ben Sira left little to chance where priests were concerned.

7:32-36. The addition of some remarks about responsibilities toward the needy shows that Ben Sira linked duties to God and to human beings. The positive evaluation of offerings to the dead is surprising, for the funerary cult fell into disfavor quite early in Israelite history. Nevertheless, ancient and venerable practices such as this one survived through the centuries because of strong feelings for departed loved ones. One explanation for idolatry points to a parent's grief over a lost child and the desire to have a reminder in tangible form (Wis 14:15). The cult, widely practiced among Greeks and Romans, persisted into Christian times, according to F. X. Murphy. Catacombs of St. Sebastian have yielded a banquet room with graffiti on the walls "signifying that pil-

160. M. Stern, "The Social and Governmental Structure of Judea Under the Ptolemies and Seleucids," in *A History of the Jewish People,* ed. H. H. Ben-Sasson (Cambridge, Mass.: Harvard University Press, 1976) 194.

grims had satisfied a vow by celebrating a memorial banquet in honor of Sts. Peter and Paul."[161]

161. F. X. Murphy, "Refrigerium," *New Catholic Encyclopedia*, ed. M. R. R. McGuire (1967) 12:197. See also Charles A. Kennedy, "Dead, Cult of the," *ABD*, 2:105-8; Theodore J. Lewis, *Cults of the Dead in Ancient Israel and Ugarit*, HSM 21 (Cambridge, Mass.: Harvard University Press, 1989); and Paola Xella, "Death and the Afterlife in Canaanite and Hebrew Thought," in *Civilizations of the Ancient Near East* (New York: Charles Scribner's Sons, 1995) 3:2059-2070.

The Greek text tones down the reference to a cult of the dead, turning the remark into an admonition to attend burial rites, so important to the pious Tobit (Tob 1:16-20; 2:3-9).

SIRACH 8:1-19, SOME THINGS TO AVOID

NAB	NRSV
8 Contend not with an influential man, lest you fall into his power.	**8** Do not contend with the powerful, or you may fall into their hands.
2 Quarrel not with a rich man, lest he pay out the price of your downfall; For gold has dazzled many, and perverts the character of princes.	2 Do not quarrel with the rich, in case their resources outweigh yours; for gold has ruined many, and has perverted the minds of kings.
3 Dispute not with a man of railing speech, heap no wood upon his fire.	3 Do not argue with the loud of mouth, and do not heap wood on their fire.
4 Be not too familiar with an unruly man, lest he speak ill of your forebears.	4 Do not make fun of one who is ill-bred, or your ancestors may be insulted.
5 Shame not a repentant sinner; remember, we all are guilty.	5 Do not reproach one who is turning away from sin; remember that we all deserve punishment.
6 Insult no man when he is old, for some of us, too, will grow old.	6 Do not disdain one who is old, for some of us are also growing old.
7 Rejoice not when a man dies; remember, we are all to die.	7 Do not rejoice over anyone's death; remember that we must all die.
8 Spurn not the discourse of the wise, but acquaint yourself with their proverbs; From them you will acquire the training to serve in the presence of princes.	8 Do not slight the discourse of the sages, but busy yourself with their maxims; because from them you will learn discipline and how to serve princes.
9 Reject not the tradition of old men which they have learned from their fathers; From it you will obtain the knowledge how to answer in time of need.	9 Do not ignore the discourse of the aged, for they themselves learned from their parents;[a] from them you learn how to understand and to give an answer when the need arises.
10 Kindle not the coals of a sinner, lest you be consumed in his flaming fire.	10 Do not kindle the coals of sinners, or you may be burned in their flaming fire.
11 Let not the impious man intimidate you; it will set him in ambush against you.	11 Do not let the insolent bring you to your feet, or they may lie in ambush against your words.
12 Lend not to one more powerful than yourself;	

8, 1: Omit *lāmmâ . . . mimmekkā* : so LXX, V; cf P.
8, 2: ʾ*al tārîb* ʿ*im* ʾ*îs lô hôr*: so LXX, V; cf Heb v lc.
8, 4: (*pen yābûz) môlîdèkā*: so LXX, V; dittog from v 2d.
8, 6: (*kî) mimmennû mazqînîm*: so LXX, V; cf P.
8, 8: (*kî) mēhem*: so LXX, P, V; dittog from v 9c.
8, 10: ʾ*al taṣṣît b*ᵉ*gaḥelet*: so LXX, V.

a Or *ancestors*

NAB

and whatever you lend, count it as lost.

13 Go not surety beyond your means;
   think any pledge a debt you must pay.

14 Contend not at law with a judge,
   for he will settle it according to his whim.

15 Travel not with a ruthless man,
   lest he weigh you down with calamity;
   For he will go his own way straight,
   and through his folly you will perish with
   him.

16 Provoke no quarrel with a quick-tempered
   man
   nor ride with him through the desert;
   For bloodshed is nothing to him;
   when there is no one to help you, he will
   destroy you.

17 Take no counsel with a fool,
   for he can keep nothing to himself.

18 Before a stranger do nothing that should be
   kept secret,
   for you know not what it will engender.

19 Open your heart to no man,
   and banish not your happiness.

8, 15: (*pen*) *yakbîd*: so LXX[MSS], P, V.
8, 16: (' *al*) *tinnāṣ* (cf v 3) *maṣṣâ* . . . (' *immô*) *bammidbār*: so LXX, P, V.

NRSV

12 Do not lend to one who is stronger than you;
   but if you do lend anything, count it as a
   loss.

13 Do not give surety beyond your means;
   but if you give surety, be prepared to pay.

14 Do not go to law against a judge,
   for the decision will favor him because of
   his standing.

15 Do not go traveling with the reckless,
   or they will be burdensome to you;
   for they will act as they please,
   and through their folly you will perish with
   them.

16 Do not pick a fight with the quick-tempered,
   and do not journey with them through
   lonely country,
   because bloodshed means nothing to them,
   and where no help is at hand, they will
   strike you down.

17 Do not consult with fools,
   for they cannot keep a secret.

18 In the presence of strangers do nothing that is
   to be kept secret,
   for you do not know what they will divulge.[a]

19 Do not reveal your thoughts to anyone,
   or you may drive away your happiness.[b]

[a] Or *it will bring forth*   [b] Heb: Gk *and let him not return a favor to you*

COMMENTARY

8:1-7. The central theme of this unit, competing against someone with vastly more resources than you have, reminds Ben Sira of some related dangers, such as associating with violent people and revealing one's intimate secrets to strangers. The Hebrew verb ריב (*rîb*) is primarily juridical, connoting litigation in the court, but it also implies competition in other ways. Ben Sira deals with aging and the prospect of death in a humorous vein, quite differently from Qohelet's treatment of these issues in Eccl 11:7–12:7.[162] The eternal

162. James L. Crenshaw, "The Shadow of Death in Qoheleth," in *Israelite Wisdom: Theological Essays in Honor of Samuel Terrien* (Missoula, Mont.: Scholars Press, 1979) 205-16. See also James L. Crenshaw, *Urgent Advice and Probing Questions* (Macon, Ga.: Mercer University Press, 1995) 573-85.

decree, "You must die," did not carry terror for Ben Sira, unless he managed to hide it successfully. For him, death meant "a gathering in" just as earlier narrators spoke of the patriarchs' being gathered to the ancestors (Gen 25:8, 17; 49:29).

8:8-9. The next subsection emphasizes the importance of tradition, a point that *Pirqe 'Abot* dramatizes by imagining a great chain of tradition spanning the generations. In this way, the link between past and present was assured, as was the accuracy of what was transmitted. Ben Sira uses technical terms for careful pondering (שׂיח *śîaḥ*), riddles (חידות *ḥîdôt*) and teaching (למד *lāmad*) in v. 8 and that for accepting the instruction (שׁמע

šāmaʿ) in v. 9. The primary source of wisdom is aged people; according to *Pirqe 'Abot* 4:26, "He who learns from the old, to what is he like? To one who eats ripe grapes and drinks old wine." Similarly, in *Pirqe 'Abot* 4:1 the question is asked, "Who is wise?" and answered, "He who learns from every man."

8:18-19. In v. 18, Ben Sira achieves a striking pun through reversing the consonants of the Hebrew word for "stranger" (זר *zār*, yielding רז *rāz*, "secret"). The latter word plays an important role

in the *War Scroll* from Qumran with its esoteric knowledge and strong emphasis on being initiated into divine knowledge of mysteries that was not available to ordinary citizens.[163] The word *rāz* also occurs in the book of Daniel (2:18-19, 27-30, 47; 4:6), where a mystery must be unveiled by God's special representative. For Ben Sira, the secrecy implied by *rāz* had nothing to do with celestial mysteries.

163. 1QM 3:9; 14:9; 16:11.

SIRACH 9:1-9, RELATIONSHIPS WITH WOMEN

NAB	NRSV
9 Be not jealous of the wife of your bosom, lest you teach her to do evil against you.	**9** Do not be jealous of the wife of your bosom, or you will teach her an evil lesson to your own hurt.
2 Give no woman power over you to trample upon your dignity.	2 Do not give yourself to a woman and let her trample down your strength.
3 Be not intimate with a strange woman, lest you fall into her snares.	3 Do not go near a loose woman, or you will fall into her snares.
4 With a singing girl be not familiar, lest you be caught in her wiles.	4 Do not dally with a singing girl, or you will be caught by her tricks.
5 Entertain no thoughts against a virgin, lest you be enmeshed in damages for her.	5 Do not look intently at a virgin, or you may stumble and incur penalties for her.
6 Give not yourself to harlots, lest you surrender your inheritance.	6 Do not give yourself to prostitutes, or you may lose your inheritance.
7 Gaze not about the lanes of the city and wander not through its squares;	7 Do not look around in the streets of a city, or wander about in its deserted sections.
8 Avert your eyes from a comely woman; gaze not upon the beauty of another's wife— Through woman's beauty many perish, for lust for it burns like fire.	8 Turn away your eyes from a shapely woman, and do not gaze at beauty belonging to another; many have been seduced by a woman's beauty, and by it passion is kindled like a fire.
9 With a married woman dine not, recline not at table to drink by her side, Lest your heart be drawn to her and you go down in blood to the grave.	9 Never dine with another man's wife, or revel with her at wine; or your heart may turn aside to her, and in blood[a] you may be plunged into destruction.

9, 2: (ʿal) tittēn: so LXX, P; dittog from v 1a.
9, 4: ʿim mᵉnaggènet ʾal tistayyēd, pen-tillākēd baḥālāqôtèha: so LXX, P; omit the rest of Heb vv 3f: variant.
9, 6: (pen) tāsēb (ʾet-naḥălātekā): so LXX, P.
9, 7: ʾal tabbēṭ bimᵉbôʿ ê hāʿîr, wᵉʾ al tᵉšôṭēṭ birᵉhôbôtèha: so V; cf LXX.
9, 8c: bᵉtōʾ ar (ʾiššâ): so LXX, P, V.
9, 9b: ʿimmāh: so LXX, P, V.

ᵃ Heb: Gk *by your spirit*

COMMENTARY

Such recognition of dangers inherent to inter-action between males and females characterizes wisdom literature from the very beginning, al-though the later Jewish concern for purity of lineage gave more bite to the warnings. Ben Sira cautions against jealous suspicions on the basis that they might become self-fulfilling prophecy, and he uses an ancient metaphor for dominance, treading on one's back (cf. the advice to her son Lemuel by the Queen Mother in Prov 31:3).[164] This entire section reflects the perspective of a male who views women as dangerous seduc-tresses. That was true of all women, in Ben Sira's view, but particularly was the case with dancing women, prostitutes, and partygoers. A gloss on v. 4 reads: "Do not sleep with singing women lest they burn you with their mouths."

The allusion to fire in the context of seduction

recalls the extended treatment of passion in Prov 6:20-35, where a probable pun occurs between "fire" (אש '*ēš*) and "woman" (אשה '*iššâ*). Here, too, the adulterer is threatened with ruin, for the cuckolded husband will have no mercy on the offender. In this text from Proverbs, two images are juxtaposed, that of a cozy lamp guiding one's eyes and that of a burning fire destroying one's very existence (cf. Job 31:9, 12). The former is parental teaching, the latter an adulteress. Ben Sira's discussion of this danger is more prosaic and comprehensive than Prov 6:20-35. He takes up this issue again in 25:13–26:27, where more emphasis is put on loyal wives than in 9:1-9.

The astonishing tendency to blame the woman even in cases not involving active seductresses places Ben Sira among a host of other male teachers of his day. If men could not control their lust when a beautiful woman came into view, it was not the woman's fault. Like the rabbi who advised against walking behind a woman, Ben Sira blamed the victim of passion.

164. James L. Crenshaw, "*wĕdōrēk' al bamôtê 'āreṣ*," *CBQ* 34 (1972) 39-53; and "A Mother's Instruction to Her Son (Prov 31:1-9)," in *Perspectives in the Hebrew Bible* (Macon, Ga.: Mercer University Press, 1988) 9-22. See also James L. Crenshaw, *Urgent Advice and Probing Questions* (Macon, Ga.: Mercer University Press, 1995) 383-95.

REFLECTIONS

In Ben Sira's teaching, a negative understanding of women in society outweighs his few positive comments. Modern sensibilities about sexual harassment have brought about an enormously complex situation. In such a context, the church can function as an agent of reconciliation, helping to maintain pressure on those who think the issue is trivial and to encourage women and men to learn how to relate in a manner that guarantees dignity to both sexes. In coming to terms with the relationship between males and females, one does well to remember that Jesus' attitude toward women contrasted sharply with that of most others in the first century, both in the Jewish and the Greco-Roman worlds. The modern elevation of women owes much to his openness to them regardless of their reputation, as Charles E. Carlston pointed out some years ago.[165]

165. Charles E. Carlston, "Proverbs, Maxims, and the Historical Jesus," *JBL* 99 (1980) 87-105.

SIRACH 9:10-16,
FRIENDS AND NEIGHBORS

NAB

10 Discard not an old friend,
  for the new one cannot equal him.
 A new friend is like new wine
  which you drink with pleasure only when
   it has aged.
11 Envy not a sinner's fame,
  for you know not what disaster awaits him.
12 Rejoice not at a proud man's success;
  remember he will not reach death
   unpunished.
13 Keep far from the man who has power to
   kill,
  and you will not be filled with the dread
   of death.
 But if you approach him, offend him not,
  lest he take away your life;
 Know that you are stepping among snares
  and walking over a net.
14 As best you can, take your neighbors'
   measure,
  and associate with the wise.
15 With the learned be intimate;
  let all your conversation be about the law
   of the LORD.
16 Have just men for your table companions;
  in the fear of God be your glory.

9, 10b: *lōʾ yidmeh lô*: so LXX, V.
9, 15: (*wᵉkol sôdᵉkā*) *bᵉtôrat yhwh*: so LXX; cf P.

NRSV

[10] Do not abandon old friends,
  for new ones cannot equal them.
 A new friend is like new wine;
  when it has aged, you can drink it with
   pleasure.

[11] Do not envy the success of sinners,
  for you do not know what their end will be
   like.
[12] Do not delight in what pleases the ungodly;
  remember that they will not be held
   guiltless all their lives.

[13] Keep far from those who have power to kill,
  and you will not be haunted by the fear of
   death.
 But if you approach them, make no misstep,
  or they may rob you of your life.
 Know that you are stepping among snares,
  and that you are walking on the city
   battlements.

[14] As much as you can, aim to know your
   neighbors,
  and consult with the wise.
[15] Let your conversation be with intelligent
   people,
  and let all your discussion be about the law
   of the Most High.
[16] Let the righteous be your dinner companions,
  and let your glory be in the fear of the Lord.

COMMENTARY

Returning to some topics already treated in 8:1-9, Ben Sira uses an arresting simile: Friendship resembles wine in that both need time before they can be fully enjoyed. This saying may be a proverb that he quotes for effect, but he may actually have coined the saying himself. The delay in retribution can be misleading, he insists, and one should be careful about associating with powerful people whose anger can spell one's end. Ben Sira never seemed to tire of using the language of snares and nets. Here he offers an antidote to sin: constant conversation about Torah and religion in the presence of wise and good people.

SIRACH 9:17–10:5, ON RULERS

NAB

17 Skilled artisans are esteemed for their deftness;
   but the ruler of his people is the skilled sage.
18 Feared in the city is the man of railing speech,
   and he who talks rashly is hated.

10 A wise magistrate lends stability to his people,
   and the government of a prudent man is well ordered.
2 As the people's judge, so are his ministers;
   as the head of a city, its inhabitants.
3 A wanton king destroys his people,
   but a city grows through the wisdom of its princes.
4 Sovereignty over the earth is in the hand of God,
   who raises up on it the man of the hour;
5 Sovereignty over every man is in the hand of God,
   who imparts his majesty to the ruler.

9, 17: *yēḥāšēb* (*yôšēr, ûmôšēl*) *b*ᵉ ʿ*ammô ḥakambînâ:* so LXX.
9, 18: Omit *bîtâ:* dittog of *bînâ* (v 17); (*nôrā*ʾ) *bā*ʿ*îr . . . ûnôšē* (?) . . . *yiśśānē*ʾ; so LXX; cf P.
10, 1: *šôpēṭ ṭa*ʿ*am* (*yôsēd* ʿ*ammô*): cf LXX, P.
10, 2f: Order of vv as in LXX, P, V. (*kēn*) *yôšᵉbèhā.* (*yašḥît*) ʿ*ammô:* cf LXX, P; dittog.
10, 4f: Order cf vv as in LXX, P, V.

NRSV

[17] A work is praised for the skill of the artisan;
   so a people's leader is proved wise by his words.
[18] The loud of mouth are feared in their city,
   and the one who is reckless in speech is hated.

10 A wise magistrate educates his people,
   and the rule of an intelligent person is well ordered.
[2] As the people's judge is, so are his officials;
   as the ruler of the city is, so are all its inhabitants.
[3] An undisciplined king ruins his people,
   but a city becomes fit to live in through the understanding of its rulers.
[4] The government of the earth is in the hand of the Lord,
   and over it he will raise up the right leader for the time.
[5] Human success is in the hand of the Lord,
   and it is he who confers honor upon the lawgiver.[a]

[a] Heb: Gk *scribe*

COMMENTARY

Two things stand out here, the positive correlation between eloquence and success in rulers and the optimistic view of providence in appointing wise individuals to govern. The Greek text focuses on the way clever speech reflects an artisan's craft, whereas the Hebrew emphasizes the manipulative power of language. The persistence of belief in universal providence regardless of the political situation is testimony to the force of tradition, and Ben Sira's readiness to compromise universalism with particularist views about special divine interest in scribes (in the Greek text, at least) shows how both understandings of providence often co-existed. One wonders whether Ben Sira would have affirmed God's hand in appointing Antiochus IV Epiphanes to the Seleucid throne. This ruler proceeded to wage a campaign to destroy Jewish identity, proscribing the observance of the law and legislating the practice of idolatry. Ben Sira could not have foreseen any of this. Perhaps one could view Ben Sira's remarks as applicable only to Judah, for ארץ (ʾ*ereṣ,* "land") can have this restricted meaning, but the sages usually cast their nets much more widely than this reading allows. He appears to have framed his statement with thought only of

the relative freedom enjoyed by Jerusalem under the Ptolemies.

SIRACH 10:6–11:1, PRIDE AND HONOR

NAB

6 No matter the wrong, do no violence to your
    neighbor,
    and do not walk the path of arrogance.
7 Odious to the LORD and to men is arrogance,
    and the sin of oppression they both hate.
8 Dominion is transferred from one people to
    another
    because of the violence of the arrogant.
9 Why are dust and ashes proud?
    even during life man's body decays;
10 A slight illness—the doctor jests,
    a king today—tomorrow he is dead.
11 When a man dies, he inherits corruption;
    worms and gnats and maggots.
12 The beginning of pride is man's
    stubbornness
    in withdrawing his heart from his Maker;
13 For pride is the reservoir of sin,
    a source which runs over with vice;
    Because of it God sends unheard-of afflictions
    and brings men to utter ruin.
14 The thrones of the arrogant God overturns
    and establishes the lowly in their stead.
15 The roots of the proud God plucks up,
    to plant the humble in their place:
16 He breaks down their stem to the level of the
    ground,
    then digs their roots from the earth.
17 The traces of the proud God sweeps away
    and effaces the memory of them from the
    earth.

10, 7: *ûmeśunnêhem* (= *ûmeśunnā ʾhem*).
10, 9: *yārôm* (*gᵉwiyyô*): cf LXX (*erripse*), P.
10, 10: *šemeş = mikron*: cf V *brevem*.
10, 12: (*yāsûṇ libbô*: so LXX, P.
10, 13: (*miqwēh*) *ḥēṭ ʾ zādôn*: so P; cf LXX; (ʾ*al-kēn*) *hipliʾ* (ʾ*elōhîm*):
so LXX, P.
10, 14: (*wayyōšeb*) ʾ*ănāwîm*: so LXX, P.
10, 15: Cf LXX, P.
10, 16: *šoršām ʾad ʾereş qiʾāqēaʾ, wayyissᵉhem mēʾere
wayyittᵉšēm*.
10, 17: ʾ*aqàbat gēʾîm ṭēʾtēʾ ʾelōhîm, wayyašbēt mēʾereş zikrām*.

NRSV

6 Do not get angry with your neighbor for every
    injury,
    and do not resort to acts of insolence.
7 Arrogance is hateful to the Lord and to mortals,
    and injustice is outrageous to both.
8 Sovereignty passes from nation to nation
    on account of injustice and insolence and
    wealth.[a]
9 How can dust and ashes be proud?
    Even in life the human body decays.[b]
10 A long illness baffles the physician;[c]
    the king of today will die tomorrow.
11 For when one is dead
    he inherits maggots and vermin[d] and worms.
12 The beginning of human pride is to forsake the
    Lord;
    the heart has withdrawn from its Maker.
13 For the beginning of pride is sin,
    and the one who clings to it pours out
    abominations.
    Therefore the Lord brings upon them
    unheard-of calamities,
    and destroys them completely.
14 The Lord overthrows the thrones of rulers,
    and enthrones the lowly in their place.
15 The Lord plucks up the roots of the nations,[e]
    and plants the humble in their place.
16 The Lord lays waste the lands of the nations,
    and destroys them to the foundations of the
    earth.
17 He removes some of them and destroys them,
    and erases the memory of them from the
    earth.
18 Pride was not created for human beings,
    or violent anger for those born of women.

19 Whose offspring are worthy of honor?

[a]Other ancient authorities add here or after verse 9a, *Nothing is
more wicked than one who loves money, for such a person puts
his own soul up for sale.*   [b]Heb: Meaning of Gk uncertain
[c]Heb Lat: Meaning of Gk uncertain   [d]Heb: Gk *wild animals*
[e]Other ancient authorities read *proud nations*

NAB

18 Insolence is not allotted to a man,
  nor stubborn anger to one born of woman.

19 Whose offspring can be in honor? Those of
    men.
  Which offspring are in honor? Those who
    fear God.
  Whose offspring can be in disgrace? Those of
    men.
  Which offspring are in disgrace? Those
    who transgress the commandments.

20 Among brethren their leader is in honor;
  he who fears God is in honor among his
    people.

21 Be it tenant or wayfarer, alien or pauper,
  his glory is the fear of the LORD.

22 It is not just to despise a man who is wise
    but poor,
  nor proper to honor any sinner.

23 The prince, the ruler, the judge are in
    honor;
  but none is greater than he who fears God.

24 When free men serve a prudent slave,
  the wise man does not complain.

25 Flaunt not your wisdom in managing your
    affairs,
  and boast not in your time of need.

26 Better the worker who has plenty of
    everything
  than the boaster who is without bread.

27 My son, with humility have self-esteem;
  prize yourself as you deserve.

28 Who will acquit him who condemns
    himself?
  who will honor him who discredits
    himself?

29 The poor man is honored for his wisdom
  as the rich man is honored for his wealth;

30 Honored in poverty, how much more so in
    wealth!
  Dishonored in wealth, in poverty how
    much the more!

10, 18: (lōʾ) neḥĕlaq (leʾĕnôš): so LXX, P.
10, 20: (wîrēʾ yhwh) beʾammô: (Smend).
10, 21: (gēr) weᶻār.
10, 24: (ʾebed maśkîl) ḥōrîm yaʾäbōdû, weʾîš nābôn (lō yitʾ
ônān): so LXX; cf P, V.
10, 26: waḥasar māzôn: so LXX, P.
10, 27: weten lāh ṭaʾam keʾerkāh: so LXX, P, V.
10, 29b: weyēš ʾāšîr (nikkād): so P; cf LXX, V.
10, 30: (nikbād) beʾonyô (beʾošrô ʾēkākâ, weniqleh)
beʾošrô beʾonyô (ʾēkākâ): so LXX, P. Omit hammitkabbēd . . . : gloss.

NRSV

  Human offspring.
  Whose offspring are worthy of honor?
    Those who fear the Lord.
  Whose offspring are unworthy of honor?
    Human offspring.
  Whose offspring are unworthy of honor?
    Those who break the commandments.

20 Among family members their leader is worthy
    of honor,
  but those who fear the Lord are worthy of
    honor in his eyes.[a]

22 The rich, and the eminent, and the poor—
  their glory is the fear of the Lord.

23 It is not right to despise one who is intelligent
    but poor,
  and it is not proper to honor one who is
    sinful.

24 The prince and the judge and the ruler are
    honored,
  but none of them is greater than the one
    who fears the Lord.

25 Free citizens will serve a wise servant,
  and an intelligent person will not complain.

26 Do not make a display of your wisdom when
    you do your work,
  and do not boast when you are in need.

27 Better is the worker who has goods in plenty
  than the boaster who lacks bread.

28 My child, honor yourself with humility,
  and give yourself the esteem you deserve.

29 Who will acquit those who condemn[b]
    themselves?
  And who will honor those who dishonor
    themselves?[c]

30 The poor are honored for their knowledge,
  while the rich are honored for their wealth.

31 One who is honored in poverty, how much
    more in wealth!
  And one dishonored in wealth, how much
    more in poverty!

11 The wisdom of the humble lifts their
    heads high,
  and seats them among the great.

[a] Other ancient authorities add as verse 21, *The fear of the Lord is
the beginning of acceptance; obduracy and pride are the beginning
of rejection.* [b] Heb: Gk *sin against* [c] Heb Lat: Gk *their own
life*

NAB

11 The poor man's wisdom lifts his head high
and sets him among princes.

COMMENTARY

10:6-18. The essential question posed for interpreters of this section, "Does the language have
a specific referent?" cannot be answered. To be
sure, certain events in the political world of the
day resemble Ben Sira's remarks rather closely.
They could refer to Antiochus III's victory over
Ptolemy Philopator at Panium in 198 BCE, as well
as to the story about the excruciating death of the
latter king. The comment in v. 14 makes one
think of Joseph, the "ruler" who rose from a lowly
state to a place of honor (Genesis 39–50), but the
resemblance is minor. Even if Ben Sira wished to
describe the situation involving political jockeying
for control of Judea, he would have veiled his
language to avoid arousing the rulers' ire. The
description is sufficiently general to apply in any
number of contexts, and it may never have been
intended as satire against the ruling Seleucids or
Ptolemies.

Similarly, the remark about someone who became ill and died promptly, either because the
physician did not recognize its seriousness (the
Greek text) or because he was helpless to stop its
progress (the Hebrew), does not necessarily relate
to a specific instance in Ben Sira's memory. Transference of power, helplessness in the face of
illness, and eventual decomposition represent general occurrences of which almost everyone would
be aware. Ben Sira uses these powerful illustrations to emphasize the universal and personal
nature of defeat. Every vestige of pride becomes
ludicrous in the light of human makeup ("dust
and ashes" עפר ואפר *ʿāpār wāʾēper*]; cf. 17:32;
40:3; Gen 18:27).

Having witnessed a transferral of power of great
magnitude, Ben Sira knew that even "pretend-
gods" succcumbed to death's grim horror. Today's
king is tomorrow's corpse. That realization, to-

gether with the anecdote about a worthless physician, prompted Ben Sira to write that, in the
face of boundless pride, God turns things upside-
down. Egyptian wisdom literature often deals with
a topsy-turvy world of societal unrest, but it lacks
Ben Sira's optimism. The price of pride, according
to Ben Sira, exceeds loss of life in a most humili-
ating manner; it also involves total extinction,
even with all recollection of an individual being
erased.

10:19-25. Verses 19-22 employ a rhetorical
device, catechetical instruction (v. 19), that became popular in later times, both in Jewish pedagogy and in the Christian church. The simple
question, "Whose offspring are worthy of honor?"
is matched by its opposite, and the first answer
fits both questions. Human beings deserve both
honor and dishonor. The device permits the
teacher to contrast the two types, rebels and
God-fearers. Social status actually means nothing
where honor is concerned. The comment about
despising a poor wise man echoes Eccl 9:15-16.
The Hebrew sociological categories in v. 22,
largely monosyllabic, imply meager existence ("sojourner," "stranger," "foreigner," "impoverished"
[גר *gēr*, זר *zār*, נכרי *nokrî*, רש *rāš*]). Ben Sira
acknowledges their worth on the basis of a religious standard, whether they fear God or not.

Lest this graphic description of the fate awaiting
all humans, proud or not, the concentration on
divine intervention to frustrate human efforts, and
the attention paid marginalized citizens lead to
self-contempt, Ben Sira moves ahead to salvage
personal esteem and to base self-worth on intelligence. He recognizes the necessity for a certain
measure of pride lest others treat one like a
doormat.

SIRACH 11:2-28,
DECEPTIVE APPEARANCES

NAB

2 Praise not a man for his looks;
   despise not a man for his appearance.
3 Least is the bee among winged things,
   but she reaps the choicest of all harvests.
4 Mock not the worn cloak
   and jibe at no man's bitter day:
   For strange are the works of the LORD,
   hidden from men his deeds.
5 The oppressed often rise to a throne,
   and some that none would consider wear
   a crown.
6 The exalted often fall into utter disgrace;
   the honored are given into enemy hands.

7 Before investigating, find no fault;
   examine first, then criticize.
8 Before hearing, answer not,
   and interrupt no one in the middle of his
   speech.
9 Dispute not about what is not your concern;
   in the strife of the arrogant take no part.
10 My son, why increase your cares,
   since he who is avid for wealth will not
   be blameless?
   Even if you run after it, you will never
   overtake it;
   however you seek it, you will not find it.
11 One may toil and struggle and drive,
   and fall short all the more.
12 Another goes his way a weakling and a
   failure,
   with little strength and great misery—
   Yet the eyes of the LORD look favorably upon
   him;
   he raises him free of the vile dust,
13 Lifts up his head and exalts him
   to the amazement of the many.

11, 2: Omit *m^eko'ar*: so LXX; gloss.
11, 5: *ubal 'alû* ('*al lēb*): so LXX, P.
11, 6: Omit *w^e hošpālû yahad*: cf LXX, P; gloss.
11, 8: Omit *b^enî*: so LXX, P; dittog.
11, 9a: '*al tithār*: so LXX, P.
11, 10c.d: Omit *b^enî*: so LXX, V; dittog. *w^e 'im tārûṣ . . .
w^e im t^e baqqēš*: cf V.
11, 11: (*yēs*) *rōšēl* (?) . . . (*ḥāsaḥ*) *kōaḥ* (*w^e yôtēr*) '*onî*.

NRSV

2 Do not praise individuals for their good looks,
   or loathe anyone because of appearance
   alone.
3 The bee is small among flying creatures,
   but what it produces is the best of sweet
   things.
4 Do not boast about wearing fine clothes,
   and do not exalt yourself when you are
   honored;
   for the works of the Lord are wonderful,
   and his works are concealed from
   humankind.
5 Many kings have had to sit on the ground,
   but one who was never thought of has worn
   a crown.
6 Many rulers have been utterly disgraced,
   and the honored have been handed over to
   others.

7 Do not find fault before you investigate;
   examine first, and then criticize.
8 Do not answer before you listen,
   and do not interrupt when another is
   speaking.
9 Do not argue about a matter that does not
   concern you,
   and do not sit with sinners when they judge
   a case.

10 My child, do not busy yourself with many
   matters;
   if you multiply activities, you will not be
   held blameless.
   If you pursue, you will not overtake,
   and by fleeing you will not escape.
11 There are those who work and struggle and
   hurry,
   but are so much the more in want.
12 There are others who are slow and need help,
   who lack strength and abound in poverty;
   but the eyes of the Lord look kindly upon
   them;
   he lifts them out of their lowly condition
13 and raises up their heads

NAB

14 Good and evil, life and death,
poverty and riches, are from the LORD.

15 Wisdom and understanding and knowledge
of affairs,
love and virtuous paths are from the LORD.

16 Error and darkness were formed with
sinners from their birth,
and evil grows old with evildoers.

17 The LORD's gift remains with the just;
his favor brings continued success.

18 A man may become rich through a miser's
life,
and this is his allotted reward:

19 When he says: "I have found rest,
now I will feast on my possessions,"
He does not know how long it will be
till he dies and leaves them to others.

20 My son, hold fast to your duty, busy
yourself with it,
grow old while doing your task.

21 Admire not how sinners live,
but trust in the LORD and wait for his light;
For it is easy with the LORD
suddenly, in an instant, to make a poor
man rich.

22 God's blessing is the lot of the just man,
and in due time his hopes bear fruit.

23 Say not: "What do I need?
What further pleasure can be mine?"

24 Say not: "I am independent.
What harm can come to me now?"

25 The day of prosperity makes one forget
adversity;
the day of adversity makes one forget
prosperity.

26 For it is easy with the LORD on the day of
death
to repay man according to his deeds.

27 A moment's affliction brings forgetfulness of
past delights;
when a man dies, his life is revealed.

NRSV

to the amazement of the many.

14 Good things and bad, life and death,
poverty and wealth, come from the Lord.[a]

17 The Lord's gift remains with the devout,
and his favor brings lasting success.

18 One becomes rich through diligence and
self-denial,
and the reward allotted to him is this:

19 when he says, "I have found rest,
and now I shall feast on my goods!"
he does not know how long it will be
until he leaves them to others and dies.

20 Stand by your agreement and attend to it,
and grow old in your work.

21 Do not wonder at the works of a sinner,
but trust in the Lord and keep at your job;
for it is easy in the sight of the Lord
to make the poor rich suddenly, in an
instant.

22 The blessing of the Lord is[b] the reward of the
pious,
and quickly God causes his blessing to
flourish.

23 Do not say, "What do I need,
and what further benefit can be mine?"

24 Do not say, "I have enough,
and what harm can come to me now?"

25 In the day of prosperity, adversity is forgotten,
and in the day of adversity, prosperity is not
remembered.

26 For it is easy for the Lord on the day of death
to reward individuals according to their
conduct.

27 An hour's misery makes one forget past
delights,
and at the close of one's life one's deeds are
revealed.

28 Call no one happy before his death;
by how he ends, a person becomes known.[c]

11, 15: *Omit first myhwh hû*: dittog. *ḥibbâ* (*ûderākîm*): so LXX[MSS], P, V.

11, 16b: (*'immām*) *tityaśśēn* (?): cf LXX[MSS], P, V.

11, 17a: With LXX, V; cf P.

11, 19c: (*mâ*) *yihyeh ḥuqqô* (?): cf LXX, P.

11, 20: (*beni*) *'āmōd*: so MS.

11, 23: (*'al tō'mar*) *mâ ḥepṣî*: so LXX, V.

11, 26: With LXX, V. Omit *we 'aḥarît . . . 'ālāyw*: variant of v 27b.

[a]Other ancient authorities add as verses 15 and 16, 15Wisdom, understanding, and knowledge of the law come from the Lord; affection and the ways of good works come from him. 16Error and darkness were created with sinners; evil grows old with those who take pride in malice. [b]Heb: Gk *is in* [c]Heb: Gk *and through his children a person becomes known*

NAB

28 Call no man happy before his death,
 for by how he ends, a man is known.

11, 28: Omit a.b: variant of c.d.

COMMENTARY

The international character of wisdom literature comes through nicely in this section. The Egyptian Papyrus Insinger uses the illustration about the bee's smallness and the wonderful delicacy it produces. The entire twentieth instruction warns against overlooking small things (e.g., a small ilness, a little fire, a tiny lie, a small snake) and mentions some advantageous small things such as bread, dew, wind, and good news. Similarly, the *Instruction of Ankhsheshanky* has this comment: "Do not disdain a small document, a small fire, a small soldier."[166]

Several Greek writers observe that one's life cannot be evaluated until death. Solon, for instance, wrote: "Until he is dead, do not yet call a man happy, but only lucky"; Aeschylus stated, "Only when man's life comes to its end in prosperity can one call that man happy"; and Sophocles declared:

Let every man in mankind's frailty
Consider his last day; and let none
Presume on his good fortune until he find
Life, at his death, a memory without pain.[167]

Ben Sira may well have heard a popular saying like one of these, but the ideas are sufficiently general to occur in any cultural context. His formulation of the matter speaks volumes in few words: "A man's end tells about him."

The similarity between the teaching in v. 2 and the biblical story about Yahweh's selection of David to rule over Israel instead of Saul (1 Sam 16:6-13) does not necessarily indicate that Ben

Sira had that incident in mind. Remarkably, the account of David's anointing takes pains to add, "Now he was ruddy, and had beautiful eyes, and was handsome" (1 Sam 16:12 NRSV), after having discounted external appearance on the basis of the Lord's penetrating sight (1 Sam 16:7). Perhaps the narrator merely acknowledged a natural preference among human beings for attractive features. Ben Sira tries to overcome this tendency.

The enigmatic remark about concealed divine works probably plays on an epithet for Yahweh, the "Worker of Wonders" (Exod 15:11; Ps 77:14; cf. Jdg 13:19). The reference may be to God's activity in human lives—the exalting of the lowly and the humbling of the proud—rather than the works of creation, which are for the most part gloriously manifest. Ben Sira gives several examples of God's hidden work, particularly in changing the lives of paupers, but also by mocking arrogance among the wealthy.

In the ancient world, the deity, or deities, were said to be responsible for everything, whether good or evil. Ben Sira accepts this belief without expressing the slightest reservation (v. 14). The fuller exposition in vv. 15-16, widely attested, suggests that a later editor thought Ben Sira's straightforward remark needed further elaboration in the direction of spiritual qualities. This practice attests to the vitality of the interpretive community and to the biblical text's character as a living tradition.

The idea that work does not necessarily pay dividends (v. 11) runs counter to the fundamental teaching of early wisdom in the book of Proverbs. Sometime later, Qohelet certainly doubted the lasting value of human toil. Ben Sira's point, that God's peculiar actions defy human standard, arises from a strong concept of divine freedom. The allusion to the eyes of the Lord does not reflect

---

166. *Instruction of Ankhsheshanky* 16.25. See Miriam Lichtheim, *Ancient Egyptian Literature,* 3 vols. (Berkeley: University of California Press, 1973–80) 3:172.

167. The quote from Solon is preserved by Herodotus *Histories* I.32, Aeschylus's remark occurs in his *Agamemnon* 1.928, and Sophocles' observation appears in *Oedipus Rex* l.1529. Each is cited in Patrick W. Skehan and Alexander A. Di Lella, *The Wisdom of Ben Sira,* AB 39 (New York: Doubleday, 1987) 241.

Persian influence in this instance, although the notion of personified eyes roving the empire seems to be found in the book of Zechariah, but expressed differently (Zech 1:8-17, horsemen patrolling the earth).

Once again, Ben Sira returns to the issue of theodicy (vv. 20-28) and mocks the rich, who rely on their wealth to protect them from adversity. Like the rich fool whom Jesus ridiculed for overlooking one small matter (Luke 12:13-21), the fact of death, these powerful individuals take their ease and wait for more good to come their way. The debate formula, "Do not say," occurs twice (vv. 23-24) and a variant as well, "Do not wonder" (v. 21). Ben Sira points out that appearances often deceive, for instantaneous changes can reverse present circumstances. The final declaration of a person's character, the balancing of virtuous deeds against wicked works (cf. Dan 5:27), was thought to take place at the hour of death. The reward for faithful service was an honorable name that survived in children (so the Greek translation of באחריתו [bĕ'aḥărîtô, "at the end of his life"]) and in grateful memories of the entire community. The word סוף (sôp, "end") as an indication of life's termination occurs in Eccl 7:2. The idea of an exact balancing of the account soon took on great importance among the Pharisees, who enthusiastically endorsed belief in life after death.

SIRACH 11:29–14:19, ON FRIENDSHIP AND WEALTH

NAB

29 Bring not every man into your house,
  for many are the snares of the crafty one;
30 Though he seem like a bird confined in a cage,
  yet like a spy he will pick out the weak spots.
31 The talebearer turns good into evil;
  with a spark he sets many coals afire.
32 The evil man lies in wait for blood,
  and plots against your choicest possessions.
33 Avoid a wicked man, for he breeds only evil,
  lest you incur a lasting stain.
34 Lodge a stranger with you, and he will subvert your course,
  and make a stranger of you to your own household.

12 If you do good, know for whom you are doing it,
  and your kindness will have its effect.
2 Do good to the just man and reward will be yours,

11, 29: (ûmâ rabbû) 'arbē nôkēl: so LXX, P, V.
11, 30: kᵉ'ôp 'āḥûz bikᵉlûb hû, wᵉkimᵉraggēl yir'eh 'erwâ. Omit rest of v: variants and dittog.
11, 31f: Trsp to read: 31a.32a.32b.31b.
11, 33: Omit lō' tidbaq with LXX: variant of v 34.
11, 34–12, 1: Follow order of LXX, V. haškēn zār wᵉyahăpōk dᵉrākèkā: cf LXX, V. 'im tēṭîb da': so LXX, V; cf P.

NRSV

29 Do not invite everyone into your home,
  for many are the tricks of the crafty.
30 Like a decoy partridge in a cage, so is the mind of the proud,
  and like spies they observe your weakness;[a]
31 for they lie in wait, turning good into evil,
  and to worthy actions they attach blame.
32 From a spark many coals are kindled,
  and a sinner lies in wait to shed blood.
33 Beware of scoundrels, for they devise evil,
  and they may ruin your reputation forever.
34 Receive strangers into your home and they will stir up trouble for you,
  and will make you a stranger to your own family.

12 If you do good, know to whom you do it,
  and you will be thanked for your good deeds.
2 Do good to the devout, and you will be repaid—
  if not by them, certainly by the Most High.
3 No good comes to one who persists in evil
  or to one who does not give alms.
4 Give to the devout, but do not help the sinner.

a Heb: Gk downfall

NAB

if not from him, from the LORD.

3 No good comes to him who gives comfort to
the wicked,
nor is it an act of mercy that he does.

4 Give to the good man, refuse the sinner;
refresh the downtrodden, give nothing to
the proud man.

5 No arms for combat should you give him,
lest he use them against yourself;

6 With twofold evil you will meet
for every good deed you do for him.

7 The Most High himself hates sinners,
and upon the wicked he takes vengeance.

8 In our prosperity we cannot know our
friends;
in adversity an enemy will not remain
concealed.

9 When a man is successful even his enemy is
friendly;
in adversity even his friend disappears.

10 Never trust your enemy,
for his wickedness is like corrosion in
bronze.

11 Even though he acts humbly and peaceably
toward you,
take care to be on your guard against him.
Rub him as one polishes a brazen mirror,
and you will find that there is still
corrosion.

12 Let him not stand near you,
lest he oust you and take your place.
Let him not sit at your right hand,
lest he then demand your seat,
And in the end you appreciate my advice,
when you groan with regret, as I warned
you.

13 Who pities a snake charmer when he is bitten,
or anyone who goes near a wild beast?

14 So is it with the companion of the proud
man,

12, 3: (ʾēn tôbâ) lammēniaḥ (rāšāʾ).
12, 4-7: Order of vv as in LXX; but omit dos tǭ agathǭ . . .
hamartalou of LXX (variant of v 4).
12, 6: Omit beʿēt ṣôrek: so LXX; gloss.
12, 11c.d: (hěyēh lô kimegalleh) reʿî, (wēdaʾ ʾaḥărît) helʾâ: cf
LXX. Omit welôʾ yimṣāʾ leḥaṣẖîtekā: so LXX; gloss.
12, 13: (mî) yāḥōn: so LXX, P, V.
12, 14: ʾîš (zādôn): so LXX, P, V. Omit lôʾ yaʿăbôr . . .
leḥaṣṣîlekā: so LXX, V; cf 23, 16.

NRSV

5 Do good to the humble, but do not give to
the ungodly;
hold back their bread, and do not give it to
them,
for by means of it they might subdue you;
then you will receive twice as much evil
for all the good you have done to them.

6 For the Most High also hates sinners
and will inflict punishment on the ungodly.[a]

7 Give to the one who is good, but do not help
the sinner.

8 A friend is not known[b] in prosperity,
nor is an enemy hidden in adversity.

9 One's enemies are friendly[c] when one
prospers,
but in adversity even one's friend
disappears.

10 Never trust your enemy,
for like corrosion in copper, so is his
wickedness.

11 Even if he humbles himself and walks bowed
down,
take care to be on your guard against him.
Be to him like one who polishes a mirror,
to be sure it does not become completely
tarnished.

12 Do not put him next to you,
or he may overthrow you and take your
place.
Do not let him sit at your right hand,
or else he may try to take your own seat,
and at last you will realize the truth of my
words,
and be stung by what I have said.

13 Who pities a snake charmer when he is bitten,
or all those who go near wild animals?

14 So no one pities a person who associates with
a sinner
and becomes involved in the other's sins.

15 He stands by you for a while,
but if you falter, he will not be there.

16 An enemy speaks sweetly with his lips,
but in his heart he plans to throw you into
a pit;
an enemy may have tears in his eyes,

[a] Other ancient authorities add and he is keeping them for the day
of their punishment   [b] Other ancient authorities read punished
[c] Heb: Gk grieved

NAB

who is involved in his sins:

15 While you stand firm, he makes no bold
move;
but if you slip, he cannot hold back.

16 With his lips an enemy speaks sweetly,
but in his heart he schemes to plunge you
into the abyss.
Though your enemy has tears in his eyes,
if given the chance, he will never have
enough of your blood.

17 If evil comes upon you, you will find him
at hand;
feigning to help, he will trip you up,

18 Then he will nod his head and clap his
hands
and hiss repeatedly, and show his true face.

13 He who touches pitch blackens his hand;
he who associates with an impious man
learns his ways.

2 Bear no burden too heavy for you;
go with no one greater or wealthier than
yourself.
How can the earthen pot go with the metal
cauldron?
When they knock together, the pot will be
smashed:

3 The rich man does wrong and boasts of it,
the poor man is wronged and begs
forgiveness.

4 As long as the rich man can use you he will
enslave you,
but when you are exhausted, he will
abandon you.

5 As long as you have anything he will speak
fair words to you,
and with smiles he will win your
confidence;

6 When he needs something from you he will
cajole you,
then without regret he will impoverish
you.

7 While it serves his purpose he will beguile
you,

NRSV

but if he finds an opportunity he will never
have enough of your blood.

17 If evil comes upon you, you will find him there
ahead of you;
pretending to help, he will trip you up.

18 Then he will shake his head, and clap his
hands,
and whisper much, and show his true face.

13 Whoever touches pitch gets dirty,
and whoever associates with a proud
person becomes like him.

2 Do not lift a weight too heavy for you,
or associate with one mightier and richer
than you.
How can the clay pot associate with the iron
kettle?
The pot will strike against it and be
smashed.

3 A rich person does wrong, and even adds
insults;
a poor person suffers wrong, and must add
apologies.

4 A rich person[a] will exploit you if you can be
of use to him,
but if you are in need he will abandon you.

5 If you own something, he will live with you;
he will drain your resources without a
qualm.

6 When he needs you he will deceive you,
and will smile at you and encourage you;
he will speak to you kindly and say, "What
do you need?"

7 He will embarrass you with his delicacies,
until he has drained you two or three times,
and finally he will laugh at you.
Should he see you afterwards, he will pass you by
and shake his head at you.

8 Take care not to be led astray
and humiliated when you are enjoying
yourself.[b]

9 When an influential person invites you, be
reserved,
and he will invite you more insistently.

10 Do not be forward, or you may be rebuffed;
do not stand aloof, or you will be forgotten.

NAB

then twice or three times he will terrify
  you;
  When later he sees you he will pass you by,
    and shake his head over you.
 8 Guard against being presumptuous;
    be not as those who lack sense.
 9 When invited by a man of influence, keep
      your distance;
    then he will urge you all the more.
10 Be not bold with him lest you be rebuffed,
    but keep not too far away lest you be
      forgotten.
11 Engage not freely in discussion with him,
    trust not his many words;
  For by prolonged talk he will test you,
    and though smiling he will probe you.
12 Mercilessly he will make of you a
      laughingstock,
    and will not refrain from injury or chains.
13 Be on your guard and take care
    never to accompany men of violence.

14 Every living thing loves its own kind,
    every man a man like himself.
15 Every being is drawn to its own kind;
    with his own kind every man
      associates.
16 Is a wolf ever allied with a lamb?
    So it is with the sinner and the just.
17 Can there be peace between the hyena
      and the dog?
  Or between the rich and the poor can there
      be peace?
18 Lion's prey are the wild asses of the desert;
    so too the poor are feeding grounds for the
      rich.
19 A proud man abhors lowliness;
    so does the rich man abhor the poor.
20 When a rich man stumbles he is supported
      by a friend;
    when a poor man trips he is pushed down
      by a friend.

13, 9: *Qārā᾽* (*nādíb*): so LXX, V.
13, 10b: (*pen*) *tinnāšeh:* so LXX, V.
13, 12: (᾽*akzārî*) *yittenkā l̲e̲māšāl,* (*we̲lō᾽ yaḥmōl᾽ al*) *ra᾽ ûk̲e̲šārîm:* cf LXX.
13, 16: Omit *we̲kēn . . . re᾽ēsāl:* so LXX, P, V; variant of 16b or 17b.
13, 17: *mâ* (*šālôm*) (*bis*): so LXX, P, V.
13, 20: (᾽*āšîr*) *nāmôt nismak:* so LXX, V. Omit ᾽*el rēa᾽:* so LXX, V.

NRSV

11 Do not try to treat him as an equal,
    or trust his lengthy conversations;
  for he will test you by prolonged talk,
    and while he smiles he will be examining
      you.
12 Cruel are those who do not keep your secrets;
    they will not spare you harm or
      imprisonment.
13 Be on your guard and very careful,
    for you are walking about with your own
      downfall.[a]

15 Every creature loves its like,
    and every person the neighbor.
16 All living beings associate with their own kind,
    and people stick close to those like
      themselves.
17 What does a wolf have in common with a
      lamb?
    No more has a sinner with the devout.
18 What peace is there between a hyena and a
      dog?
    And what peace between the rich and the
      poor?
19 Wild asses in the wilderness are the prey of
      lions;
    likewise the poor are feeding grounds for
      the rich.
20 Humility is an abomination to the proud;
    likewise the poor are an abomination to the
      rich.

21 When the rich person totters, he is supported
      by friends,
    but when the humble[b] falls, he is pushed
      away even by friends.
22 If the rich person slips, many come to the
      rescue;
    he speaks unseemly words, but they justify
      him.
  If the humble person slips, they even criticize
      him;
    he talks sense, but is not given a hearing.
23 The rich person speaks and all are silent;
    they extol to the clouds what he says.

[a]Other ancient authorities add as verse 14, *When you hear these
things in your sleep, wake up! During all your life love the Lord,
and call on him for your salvation.*   [b]Other ancient authorities
read *poor*

712

NAB

21 Many are the supporters for a rich man
    when he speaks;
      though what he says is odious, it wins
        approval.
      When a poor man speaks they make sport of
        him;
      he speaks wisely and no attention is paid
        him.

22 A rich man speaks and all are silent,
      his wisdom they extol to the clouds.
    A poor man speaks and they say: "Who is
        that?"
      If he slips they cast him down.

23 Wealth is good when there is no sin;
      but poverty is evil by the standards of the
        proud.

24 The heart of a man changes his countenance,
      either for good or for evil.

25 The sign of a good heart is a cheerful
        countenance;
      withdrawn and perplexed is the laborious schemer.

14 Happy the man whose mouth brings him
      no grief,
    who is not stung by remorse for sin.

2 Happy the man whose conscience does not
        reproach him,
      who has not lost hope.

3 Wealth ill becomes the mean man;
      and to the miser, of what use is gold?

4 What he denies himself he collects for others,
      and in his possessions a stranger will revel.

5 To whom will he be generous who is stingy
        with himself
      and does not enjoy what is his own?

6 None is more stingy than he who is stingy
        with himself;
      he punishes his own miserliness.

7 If ever he is generous, it is by mistake;
      and in the end he displays his greed.

8 In the miser's opinion his share is too small;

13, 21c: (dal) mᵉdabbēr (ga' ga') yiśśā' û: so P.
13, 25b: (wᵉśîg) wᵉśîaḥ.
14, 1b: With LXX, V; Heb: wᵉlō' 'ābal 'al dᵉwōn 'āwôn?
14, 2: (lō') ḥissᵉdattô (napšô): so LXX, P.
14, 3: (ûlᵉ'iš ra' 'ayin) lāmmâ (ḥārûṣ): so LXX, V.
14, 5b: (wᵉlō') yiqdeh (?): so P; cf LXX, V (yeḥdeh?).
14, 7: With LXX, P, V.
14, 8ff: bᵉ'en ra' 'ayin mᵉaṭ ḥelqô, miṭ'allēm mērē'ēhû
ûmᵉ'abbēd napšô; 'ên ra' 'ayin tā'iṭ 'al leḥem, wᵉyābēš śîm 'al
šulḥānô. Omit the rest: variants and dittog.

NRSV

  The poor person speaks and they say, "Who
      is this fellow?"
    And should he stumble, they even push him
        down.

24 Riches are good if they are free from sin;
      poverty is evil only in the opinion of the
        ungodly.

25 The heart changes the countenance,
      either for good or for evil.[a]

26 The sign of a happy heart is a cheerful face,
      but to devise proverbs requires painful
        thinking.

14 Happy are those who do not blunder
      with their lips,
    and need not suffer remorse for sin.

2 Happy are those whose hearts do not condemn
        them,
      and who have not given up their hope.

3 Riches are inappropriate for a small-minded
        person;
      and of what use is wealth to a miser?

4 What he denies himself he collects for others;
      and others will live in luxury on his goods.

5 If one is mean to himself, to whom will he be
        generous?
      He will not enjoy his own riches.

6 No one is worse than one who is grudging to
        himself;
      this is the punishment for his meanness.

7 If ever he does good, it is by mistake;
      and in the end he reveals his meanness.

8 The miser is an evil person;
      he turns away and disregards people.

9 The eye of the greedy person is not satisfied
        with his share;
      greedy injustice withers the soul.

10 A miser begrudges bread,
      and it is lacking at his table.

11 My child, treat yourself well, according to your
        means,
      and present worthy offerings to the Lord.

12 Remember that death does not tarry,
      and the decree[b] of Hades has not been
        shown to you.

[a]Other ancient authorities add *and a glad heart makes a cheerful
countenance* [b]Heb Syr: Gk *covenant*

NAB

9 he refuses his neighbor and brings ruin on
    himself.
10 The miser's eye is rapacious for bread,
    but on his own table he sets it stale.
11 My son, use freely whatever you have
    and enjoy it as best you can;
12 Remember that death does not tarry,
    nor have you been told the grave's
      appointed time.
13 Before you die, be good to your friend,
    and give him a share in what you possess.
14 Deprive not yourself of present good things,
    let no choice portion escape you.
15 Will you not leave your riches to others,
    and your earnings to be divided by lot?
16 Give, take, and treat yourself well,
    for in the nether world there are no joys
      to seek.
17 All flesh grows old, like a garment;
    the age-old law is: All must die.
18 As with the leaves that grow on a vigorous
    tree:
    one falls off and another sprouts—
    So with the generations of flesh and blood:
    one dies and another is born.
19 All man's works will perish in decay,
    and his handiwork will follow after him.

14, 11: Omit *ʾim yeš lᵉkā šārēt mapšᵉkā w*: so LXX, V; dittog of
16b.
14, 12: Omit *lōʾ bišeʾôl taʾănûg w*: so LXX, P; dittog of v 16b.
14, 14: *wᵉheleq ḥemed ʾal taʾābōr*, and omit v 14c (variant of c
14b): so LXX.

NRSV

13 Do good to friends before you die,
    and reach out and give to them as much as
      you can.
14 Do not deprive yourself of a day's enjoyment;
    do not let your share of desired good pass
      by you.
15 Will you not leave the fruit of your labors to
    another,
    and what you acquired by toil to be divided
      by lot?
16 Give, and take, and indulge yourself,
    because in Hades one cannot look for
      luxury.
17 All living beings become old like a garment,
    for the decree[a] from of old is, "You must
      die!"
18 Like abundant leaves on a spreading tree
    that sheds some and puts forth others,
    so are the generations of flesh and blood:
    one dies and another is born.
19 Every work decays and ceases to exist,
    and the one who made it will pass away
      with it.

[a] Heb: Gk *covenant*

COMMENTARY

This section vividly illustrates the difficulty of dividing the contents of Sirach into discrete units. A glance at the commentaries reveals little agreement on this and many other larger units, each interpreter viewing the material from a different perspective. Riches, the unifying theme of 11:29–14:19, provokes various thoughts from Ben Sira, chiefly cautionary advice about the dangers involved in trying to relate to wealthy people. He uses several arresting images to convey his insights.

11:29–12:9. The first picture comes from a hunter's practice of placing a bird in a cage to lure other birds into it (11:30). The cage has a special entrance that opens from below; once another bird has entered the enclosed place, it cannot spring the door from above and is thus trapped. Ben Sira likens the proud to a decoy bird attracting the attention of its victims, perhaps also to the hunter who watches from a hiding place until its prey has entered the cage. As if this image of vulnerability were not sufficient, Ben Sira observes that a single spark ignites coals (11:32). An ancient proverb warned against underestimating a little fire, a tiny rumor, a small soldier. Experience had taught society that some small things did enormous harm. A "worthless person" (אִישׁ בְּלִיַּעַל *'iš běliyya'al*) lurks in the shadows to shed blood (cf. Prov 1:11, "to lie in wait, to ambush" [אָרַב *'rb*]). This use of the expression *'iš běliyya'al* is unique in Sirach, but it occurs elsewhere in Job 38:18 and Prov 6:12; 16:27; 19:28. The application of these images to the problem at hand, inviting strangers into one's home, uses a wordplay for "stranger"/"estrange" (זָר/זָהִיר *zār/zāhîr*).

12:10-12. Another image in this unit compares enemies to a corrosive pot or to a "magic mirror" that was thought to divulge the identity of friend and foe when carefully polished and examined. Ben Sira advises caution, taking the form of constantly polishing the metal surface of a mirror to prevent its copper from becoming discolored (12:10-11). The reference to the right hand (12:12) implies the place of honor, which should be zealously protected from impostors.

12:13-18. The picture of a snake charmer, once bitten, pleading for sympathy from onlookers, or a thoughtless daredevil who tempts ferocious beasts and then asks for pity when they have mauled him, accurately describes the behavior of anyone who gets cozy with an enemy. Shedding insincere tears and whispering feigned affection (12:16), the enemy awaits an opportunity to throw a victim into a pit (cf. Joseph's brothers in Gen 37:12-24).

13:1-20. The principle that the person who touches tar becomes dirty (13:1) gave rise to a proverb long before Ben Sira's day, for the idea of being tainted through association with base fellows already appears in a text by Theognis.[168] Its popularity has persisted to the present, occurring in two of Shakespeare's works.[169] Similarly, the concept of "like associating with like" was enunciated frequently in various forms (cf. the Latin "like delights in like," *Similis simili gaudet*). In Isa 11:6, the prophet envisions a total reversal of the usual pattern of things, an era when a wolf will lie down with a lamb, a leopard with a goat, a calf with a lion, a cow with a bear, and when an infant will play over the hole of an asp, a weaned child will touch an adder's den. The real

world, one in which a clay vessel that collides with an iron kettle shatters (13:2), does not deal gently with opposites who try to forge close friendship. Ben Sira lays out some areas of vulnerability when people of ordinary material resources attempt to become close friends with persons who possess extraordinary wealth.

In the first place, he argues, "like loves like" (13:15). The argument from analogy with animals like wolves, hyenas, dogs, wild asses, and lions contains a fundamental flaw, for rich and poor belong to the same genus. Ben Sira selects predatory animals to make his point: hyenas, wolves, lions. Their prey—or natural enemy, in the case of dogs (cf. Job 30:1; Isa 56:10; Jer 12:9)—illustrates the precarious position of people who aspire to be friends with the rich. Once the poor have served their purpose, whether for amusement or for their meager resources, they are promptly cast off like refuse. Moreover, in the process of responding to the hospitality of the wealthy by the customary follow-up, people of modest means deplete their resources through an endless round of entertainment.

In the second place, Ben Sira observes, those who befriend the wealthy walk a difficult tightrope, trying to be noticed without being too conspicuous and inviting contempt. The situation has been compared to sitting at a fire; one needs to get close enough to feel the warmth of the flame, but must remain far enough away to avoid getting burned.[170]

A third point of vulnerability issues from the inevitable self-denial demanded by limited resources, now stretched to the limit by competing with people who have greater wealth. One has to adopt a miserly life-style, and that, says Ben Sira, makes absolutely no sense for any number of reasons. The third and second centuries BCE, with surging interest in amassing a fortune, also produced advocates of personal enjoyment, such as Qohelet, Ben Sira, and the rabbi who insisted that everyone must give an account of every good thing not enjoyed. One can infer from the heated

168. Theognis #35.
169. See William Shakespeare *Much Ado About Nothing* III.3.61 and *King Henry IV*, Part I II.4.460

170. Gracian notes the skepticism regarding the political life: "First make an obligation, of what you are paid for afterwards; it is a trick of the political giants, to yield favor before it is earned, for it betokens that the men concerned are men of honor. The favor thus advanced, has double merit, for in the readiness with which it was bestowed, it lays greater obligation upon him who receives it, and if later it is mere pay, given earlier, it constitutes a promissory note." See Baltasar Gracian, *The Art of Worldly Wisdom* (New York: Barnes and Noble, 1993) 236.

attack in Wis 1:16–2:24 on such indulgence that things quickly got out of hand, leading to lawless conduct by young robbers. Qohelet's sevenfold encouragement to enjoy life had found a receptive audience, one prepared to do so without any consideration for those harmed by this commitment to gathering rosebuds before they wither.

13:21–14:2. Yet another source of difficulty lay in society's natural disposition, a bias in favor of the rich. The plain fact must be faced, Ben Sira observes (13:23), that the crowds praise the wealthy even when the latter utter nonsense, and the masses condemn the lowly who may speak eloquently; the word for "ridiculing" in 13:22 (געגע *ga' ga'*) imitates the croaking of frogs; if one reads גגע (*gaga'*), it may refer to cackling. In other words, people who endeavor to cross that invisible line between poverty and riches only fool themselves. As Qohelet rightly perceived, the poor wise man received no one's gratitude (Eccl 9:16). Small wonder a clever individual wryly observed that "God loves the poor but helps the rich."

The judgment that riches in themselves are not evil (13:24) introduces a wholly unexpected sentiment. Just as Ben Sira's advice about charitable giving in 12:1-7 presents an insuperable challenge—ascertaining authentic goodness in others—his opinion of the wealthy requires a similar looking into the hearts of others. Happily, he believed that goodness was reflected in one's countenance (13:26; cf. Prov 15:13; Ps 104:15; Eccl 8:1; Matt 6:16-18).

14:3-19. Finally, Ben Sira points to the absurdity of being stingy, "small of heart" (לב קטן *lēb qāṭān*) and denying oneself life's pleasure when standing under a sentence of death. This allusion to the story about Adam and Eve and the divine decree, "You must die!" (14:17), is virtually without precedent. Ben Sira will take the

reflection one additional step, blaming the woman for all subsequent misfortune. For now, he restricts himself to drawing a comparison between leaves falling from a tree and people dying. The analogy, although appropriate in the case of individual people, becomes strained when applied to generations, for usually when leaves fall from a tree on their own, others do not take their place until the seasons have changed. Ben Sira's expression for humankind, "flesh and blood" (בשר ודם *bāśār wĕdām*) occurs often in rabbinic literature.

When leaves fall to the ground, they decompose, enriching the soil. Human beings also rot (the verb רקב [*rāqēb*] occurs here and in two other places, Prov 10:7 and Isa 40:20), but the Israelites thought of the deceased as somehow existing in Sheol. The reference to this shadowy domain in 14:12 is the first one in Sirach. It was originally thought to be outside Yahweh's realm, but the prophet Amos recognized no such limit to God's authority (Amos 9:2). The unknown author of Job believed that a certain leveling of social distinctions occurred there, resulting in rest for the weary (Job 3:13-19). In the opinion of at least one psalmist, the residents of Sheol do not chant Yahweh's praises (Ps 6:5). Those who entered Sheol, so it was thought, take up permanent residence.[171] This opinion was replaced in NT times by a conviction that Sheol was only a temporary resting place, at least for the righteous. A change also took place in the character of Sheol, perhaps under Persian influence, in common thinking. No longer a neutral domicile, Sheol came to be depicted as hell, a realm of punishment by fire.

171. Theodore J. Lewis, "Dead, Abode of the," *ABD* 2 (New York: Doubleday, 1972); and N. J. Tromp, *Primitive Conceptions of Death and the Nether World in the Old Testament,* BibOr 21 (Rome: Pontifical Biblical Institute, 1969).

REFLECTIONS

1. Still another area in which Ben Sira's views have suffered over time concerns wealth. For the most part, he looked on rich people as enemies; the author of the Epistle of James shared this suspicion (Jas 2:1-7). Given the social context producing the Scriptures, such an attitude is understandable. Ben Sira does qualify his criticism of wealth in the end, observing that riches not associated with wickedness cannot be totally bad. Perhaps that appreciation for wealth rightly used should become a mainstay of Christian teaching—particularly in the light of the enormous financial resources in the coffers of the church. One can scarcely imagine modern society apart from the contributions of philanthropists who have donated funds for private hospitals, colleges and universities, churches, foundations that bestow seed money on all kinds of worthy causes, and the like.

Furthermore, many persons who have prospered materially encounter a problem peculiar to the wealthy: the difficulty of distinguishing between genuine friends and others who seek to use them for personal gain. The church serves these people faithfully when it also recognizes this problem and welcomes the rich into its circle in the same way it does the poor—that is, as persons needing Christian love. In this way, churches can help wealthy people learn to use their resources for worthy causes just as they teach those with meager possessions to be stewards of their resources.

2. Ben Sira has a few observations about death's inevitability that ring true today just as they did long ago, although the church has introduced the *hope* of the resurrection that alters the situation emphatically. This hope, fundamental to Pauline theology and to the early Christians generally, rests in God's character and in the belief that God raised Jesus from the dead. Ultimately, the hope in the resurrection symbolizes an unwillingness to believe in the victory of evil over good. No one really knows what happens at death, and Christians need to face up to that fact, readily admitting that they live by faith. In the meantime, the church can bear faithful witness to the hope of the resurrection by helping those who stare death in the face more immediately than the average individual. By providing hospices, visiting the dying, helping people die with dignity, preparing members to face the inevitable reality, remembering the dead, and teaching Christian workers to deal comfortably with the terminally ill, churches can demonstrate to society at large that their members take death seriously but do not let it paralyze them into inaction.

PART IV

OVERVIEW

Reminiscent of Psalm 1, with its language of blessing and the imagery of a flourishing tree, the opening poem about wisdom lays the groundwork for serious reflection on free will and divine retribution for wickedness. This discussion leads naturally to thoughts about God as judge, a concept that arose often in the volatile ancient Near East. Confident that God rewards virtue and punishes sin, Ben Sira urges his hearers to exercise their free will wisely, attending to small matters like giving alms to the needy, exercising caution and self-discipline, gaining control over speech by avoiding harmful utterances and by skillful elocution when speech was preferable to silence. He recognizes the favorable circumstances afforded wickedness and distinguishes between the wise and fools, who take different paths to distinct destinies. Ben Sira stresses the importance of long-term friendships, the proper use of language, and entering exclusively into appropriate sexual relationships. A prayer focuses his compelling desire to utter only what issues in favor from both God and humans.

SIRACH 14:20–15:10, SEEKING WISDOM AND BEING WELCOMED BY HER

NAB	NRSV

20 Happy the man who meditates on wisdom,
    and reflects on knowledge;
	20 Happy is the person who meditates on[a] wisdom
	    and reasons intelligently,

21 Who ponders her ways in his heart,
    and understands her paths;
	21 who[b] reflects in his heart on her ways
	    and ponders her secrets,

22 Who pursues her like a scout,
    and lies in wait at her entry way;
	22 pursuing her like a hunter,
	    and lying in wait on her paths;

23 Who peeps through her windows,
    and listens at her doors;
	23 who peers through her windows
	    and listens at her doors;

24 Who encamps near her house,
    and fastens his tent pegs next to her walls;
	24 who camps near her house
	    and fastens his tent peg to her walls;

25 Who pitches his tent beside her,
    and lives as her welcome neighbor;
	25 who pitches his tent near her,
	    and so occupies an excellent lodging place;

26 Who builds his nest in her leafage,
    and lodges in her branches;
	26 who places his children under her shelter,
	    and lodges under her boughs;

27 Who takes shelter with her from the heat,
    and dwells in her home.
	27 who is sheltered by her from the heat,
	    and dwells in the midst of her glory.

14, 21: *ûbinᵉtîbōtèhā* (*yitbônān*): so P (LXX: *atrapois?;* cf Jb 24, 13).
14, 24: (*wᵉhēbî*) *yᵉtēdāyw*: cf LXX.

[a] Other ancient authorities read *dies in*   [b] The structure adopted in verses 21-27 follows the Heb

NAB

15 He who fears the LORD will do this;
he who is practiced in the law will come
to wisdom.

2 Motherlike she will meet him,
like a young bride she will embrace him,

3 Nourish him with the bread of
understanding,
and give him the water of learning to
drink.

4 He will lean upon her and not fall,
he will trust in her and not be put to
shame.

5 She will exalt him above his fellows;
in the assembly she will make him
eloquent.

6 Joy and gladness he will find,
an everlasting name inherit.

7 Worthless men will not attain to her,
haughty men will not behold her.

8 Far from the impious is she,
not to be spoken of by liars.

9 Unseemly is praise on a sinner's lips,
for it is not accorded to him by God.

10 But praise is offered by the wise man's
tongue;
its rightful steward will proclaim it.

NRSV

15 Whoever fears the Lord will do this,
and whoever holds to the law will obtain
wisdom.[a]

2 She will come to meet him like a mother,
and like a young bride she will welcome
him.

3 She will feed him with the bread of learning,
and give him the water of wisdom to drink.

4 He will lean on her and not fall,
and he will rely on her and not be put to
shame.

5 She will exalt him above his neighbors,
and will open his mouth in the midst of the
assembly.

6 He will find gladness and a crown of rejoicing,
and will inherit an everlasting name.

7 The foolish will not obtain her,
and sinners will not see her.

8 She is far from arrogance,
and liars will never think of her.

9 Praise is unseemly on the lips of a sinner,
for it has not been sent from the Lord.

10 For in wisdom must praise be uttered,
and the Lord will make it prosper.

a Gk *her*

COMMENTARY

This praise of wisdom consists of two parts, 14:20-27 and 15:1-10; 15:1 then provides a thematic verse uniting the description of those who pursue wisdom with that of her receiving them with open arms. The remarkable resemblance between this hymn and Psalm 1 is both linguistic and theological. Each begins with the formula of blessing, "Blessed are" (אשרי 'ašrê), then goes on to describe the behavior of the happy ones—their meditating on Torah and subsequent prosperity—while using the image of a flourishing tree. Each one also contrasts two groups, the favored ones and the unfortunate victims of their own wickedness and folly.

14:20-27. The opening section focuses on the lively pursuit of wisdom; it does so by concentrating at first on the images of spies (in the Hebrew)

or hunters (in the Greek), then shifting to that of a passionate lover, only in the end changing the metaphor for wisdom to that of a tree with birds building nests in its branches and finding refuge from the scorching sun. All of this comprises a single sentence in Hebrew with various linking devices in the explanatory appositional clauses. The Greek reading in v. 20, "will die" (τελευτήσει *teleutēsei*), may have arisen through reflection on 11:28, the insistence that only at death can one really consider anyone happy. The verb "to meditate" (הגה *hāgâ*) also occurs in 6:37 and 50:28. In v. 22, the Greek manuscripts have "ways" (ὁδοῖς *hodois*), with only Codex Vaticanus reading "in her entrances" (ἐν ταῖς εἰσοδοις αὐτῆς *en tais eisodois autēs*), which agrees with the Hebrew. The idea suggests that spies observe every single entrance to wisdom's dwelling. The dominant image in the Greek text, that of hunting, implies that wisdom's pursuers lie in wait at all her paths and demonstrate their skill at tracking wild animals.

The change to lover occurs in vv. 23-25, where his action demonstrates strong passion at the expense of proper decorum, at least to the modern way of thinking, where peering into a window of a beloved hardly accords with acceptable conduct. On the basis of Cant 2:9, which has the young woman rejoice that her beloved stands outside and peers into her window, one may assume that the practice did not offend some segments in ancient society. Wishing to be near the object of his ardor, the young man in v. 24 pitches his tent against the wall of her house. The word אהלו ('ŏhŏlô, "his tent") has both a literal and a figurative meaning here and in Job 8:22; 22:23; and 29:4, approximating the sense of one's physical and psychological existence.

In vv. 26-27, the earlier image of wisdom as a shade tree recurs, with the lover now being described as a bird. The Hebrew text has "its nest" (קנו qinnô) in v. 26, whereas the Greek has "his children" (τέκνα αὐτοῦ tekna autou). The idea of wisdom's providing shelter occupies the thought of Qohelet in Eccl 7:12, an extremely enigmatic verse. The divine object lesson in Jonah 4:6-11 dramatizes the deep feelings generated by adequate protection from the sun's sweltering rays in the ancient Near East.

15:1-10. Part two of this poem shifts the point of view to the object of hot pursuit. As this section illustrates, wisdom gladly lets herself be captured by worthy pursuers but holds herself at a distance from those lacking intelligence. The thematic verse equates fear of Yahweh—that is, "piety"—with keeping the law and then relates both to wisdom. The expression "the one who handles the law" (תופש תורה tôpēš tôrâ) refers to a scribe in 15:1, but in Jer 2:8 it indicates a priest (alongside rulers [shepherds] and prophets). The verb תפש (tāpaś) connotes catching and holding an object securely, hence skill at warfare (cf. Num 31:27) and expertise at interpreting the law, as here.

The tame imagery of wisdom as a mother in v. 2 quickly yields to the more customary picture of a passionate young bride ("a wife of youth"; cf. Prov 5:18). Both Deutero- and Trito-Isaiah

compare Yahweh to a mother who cannot forget her children and who offers comfort (Isa 49:14-15; 66:13). Verse 3 echoes the ancient tradition about wisdom's feast as proclaimed in Prov 9:1-6, but the language comes closer to that uttered by wisdom's rival, folly, in 9:13-18. Although wisdom is said to serve bread and wine, folly offers stolen water and bread consumed in secret (v. 17). Ben Sira carefully specifies the nature of the bread and water ("bread of astuteness" and "water of understanding"). The clandestine and erotic features of illicit sex in Prov 9:17 have given way here to intellectual categories. This symbolic use of bread and water for religious instruction and its rewards gained popularity in Jewish literature after Ben Sira.[172] The idea has a long history, beginning as early as the period of return from Babylonian exile. In Isa 55:1-2, Yahweh offers water, milk, and bread to the hungry.

The literary structure of vv. 1-4 merits closer attention. In vv. 1 and 4 an ABA'B' parallelism reigns: "one who fears Yahweh/will do this // one who handles torah/will obtain her" (v. 1); "whoever leans on her/will not totter // whoever trusts her/will not be shamed" (v. 4). The ruling pattern of vv. 2-3 differs greatly, an ABB'A' structure obtaining: "she will meet him/like a mother // like a woman of youth; she will receive him" (v. 2); "and she will feed him/bread of astuteness // and water of understanding/she will give him to drink" (v. 3). Besides essential spiritual nourishment, wisdom grants honor and eloquence (v. 5). The explosion of sibilants in v. 6 almost gives the impression that Ben Sira wished to demonstrate his own skill at persuasive and pleasant communication: ששון (śāśôn, "joy"), ושמחה (wěśimḥâ, "and rejoicing"), ימצה yimṣâ, "he will discover"), ושם עולם (wěšēm 'ôlām, "and an everlasting name"), תורישנו (tôrîšennû, "she will bequeath to him"). The teasing sound of the consonants is balanced by content that evokes a desirable mood.

The poem ends on a threatening note: Sinners will not even catch a glimpse of wisdom. The contrast between the fate of foolish people and the reward of persistent lovers could hardly be

---

172. W. O. E. Oesterley cites several references (in the Midrashim: an early Tannaitic reference, *Sifre* 84a, as well as sayings from the Amoraim, *Shir Rabba* i 2, *Bereshith Rabba* lxxi, and in the Babylonian Talmud: *Shabbath* 120a). See W. O. E. Oesterley, *The Wisdom of Jesus the Son of Sirach or Ecclesiasticus* (Cambridge: Cambridge University Press, 1912).

starker. On the one hand, the lover camps beside wisdom's house and "nests" in her branches, and wisdom receives him with open arms, treating him to a sumptuous meal. On the other hand, the fool stands in the remote distance, having failed to capture her. Such arrogant sinners are not worthy of singing her praise (v. 9), and only divinely sent praise enjoys God's blessing.

REFLECTIONS

One of the most useful symbols for human existence is that of pilgrimage. We are *homo viator,* people on the road. Ben Sira's use of imagery from Bedouin who dwell in tents reminds us all of the temporary nature of earthly existence. "This world is not my home, I'm just passing through"—the words of this spiritual touch a responsive chord, describing how we are embarking on a journey, with its final destination by no means certain.

Whether we subscribe to that hope grounded in Jesus' resurrection or limit our concerns to the present existence, we can undoubtedly profit from clear signs laid by the trailblazer from Nazareth, for the journey will take us along dangerous routes. Ancient Romans set up milestones along the way, some of which survive to this day. As Christians, we can begin to think of ways to erect markers that indicate progress in coming to terms with ourselves and with God—over and above the customary moments of birth and conversion. Careful chronicling of spiritual progress, together with an honest listing of the unfortunate byways we frequently take, will serve as useful road maps for us and, at times, for others. We are not alone after all, and we bear some responsibility for fellow travelers.

The symbol of a pitched tent also suggests that every illusion of permanency will be exposed. In God's world, we do not own the land but merely occupy it for a short time and then move on to another place. Moreover, those committed to pilgrimage travel light, even in a day when success is measured in terms of material wealth. A readiness to go where need arises and to take up our tent pegs in God's service comes much more easily when one views life as a journey and sees every dwelling as temporary. Then the plight of dispossessed persons throughout the world becomes one every person can comprehend.

SIRACH 15:11–16:23, ON FREE WILL AND DIVINE RECOMPENSE

NAB	NRSV
11 Say not: "It was God's doing that I fell away"; for what he hates he does not do.	11 Do not say, "It was the Lord's doing that I fell away"; for he does not do[a] what he hates.
12 Say not: "It was he who set me astray"; for he has no need of wicked man.	12 Do not say, "It was he who led me astray"; for he has no need of the sinful.
13 Abominable wickedness the LORD hates, he does not let it befall those who fear him.	13 The Lord hates all abominations; such things are not loved by those who fear him.
14 When God, in the beginning, created man, he made him subject to his own free choice.	14 It was he who created humankind in the beginning, and he left them in the power of their own free choice.

15, 14: Omit *wayᵉšîtēhû bᵉyad ḥôtᵉpô*; so LXX, P, V; gloss on following words.

[a] Heb: Gk *you ought not to do*

NAB

15 If you choose you can keep the
    commandments;
    it is loyalty to do his will.
16 There are set before you fire and water;
    to whichever you choose, stretch forth
        your hand.
17 Before man are life and death,
    whichever he chooses shall be given him.
18 Immense is the wisdom of the LORD;
    he is mighty in power, and all-seeing.
19 The eyes of God see all he has made;
    he understands man's every deed.
20 No man does he command to sin,
    to none does he give strength for lies.

16 Desire not a brood of worthless children,
    nor rejoice in wicked offspring.
2 Many though they be, exult not in them
    if they have not the fear of the LORD.
3 Count not on their length of life,
    have no hope in their future.
    For one can be better than a thousand;
    rather die childless than have godless
        children!
4 Through one wise man can a city be peopled;
    through a clan of rebels it becomes
        desolate.
5 Many such things has my eye seen,
    even more than these has my ear heard.
6 Against a sinful band fire is enkindled,
    upon a godless people wrath flames out.
7 He forgave not the leaders of old
    who rebelled long ago in their might;
8 He spared not the neighbors of Lot
    whom he detested for their pride;
9 Nor did he spare the doomed people
    who were uprooted because of their sin;
10 Nor the six hundred thousand foot soldiers
    who perished for the impiety of their
        hearts.

15, 15: we᾽ĕmûnâ (la᾽ăśôt reṣônô): so LXX. Omit ᾽im ta᾽ămîn . . .
tiḥyeh: so LXX; gloss (cf Hb 2, 4) on preceding.
15, 20: Omit we᾽lō᾽ merahēm . . . sôd: so LXX; gloss.
16, 1: (᾽al tit᾽ awweh) rōb: so LXX, P.
16, 3: Omit kî lō᾽) . . . tôbâ: so LXX, P, V; gloss. Omit ᾽ôśeh rāṣôn and
mimmî . . . lāh û: so LXX; gloss.
16, 4: (mē᾽ ĕḥād) mēbîn (tēšēb ᾽îr): so LXX, V.
16, 5: (wa᾽ ăṣūmôt) mē᾽ ēlleh: so LXX, P, V.
16, 7: Omit ᾽ăšer: so LXX, P. (hammôrîm) mē᾽ ôlām.
16, 8: hametō᾽ abîm (be᾽ga᾽ ăwātām): so LXX.

NRSV

15 If you choose, you can keep the
    commandments,
    and to act faithfully is a matter of your own
        choice.
16 He has placed before you fire and water;
    stretch out your hand for whichever you
        choose.
17 Before each person are life and death,
    and whichever one chooses will be given.
18 For great is the wisdom of the Lord;
    he is mighty in power and sees everything;
19 his eyes are on those who fear him,
    and he knows every human action.
20 He has not commanded anyone to be wicked,
    and he has not given anyone permission to
        sin.

16 Do not desire a multitude of
    worthless[a] children,
    and do not rejoice in ungodly offspring.
2 If they multiply, do not rejoice in them,
    unless the fear of the Lord is in them.
3 Do not trust in their survival,
    or rely on their numbers;[b]
    for one can be better than a thousand,
    and to die childless is better than to have
        ungodly children.
4 For through one intelligent person a city can
    be filled with people,
    but through a clan of outlaws it becomes
        desolate.

5 Many such things my eye has seen,
    and my ear has heard things more striking
        than these.
6 In an assembly of sinners a fire is kindled,
    and in a disobedient nation wrath blazes up.
7 He did not forgive the ancient giants
    who revolted in their might.
8 He did not spare the neighbors of Lot,
    whom he loathed on account of their
        arrogance.
9 He showed no pity on the doomed nation,
    on those dispossessed because of their
        sins;[c]

[a] Heb: Gk unprofitable   [b] Other ancient authorities add For you
will groan in untimely mourning, and will know of their sudden
end.   [c] Other ancient authorities add All these things he did to
the hard-hearted nations, and by the multitude of his holy ones he
was not appeased.

NAB

11 And had there been but one stiffnecked
 man,
  it were a wonder had he gone unpunished.
 For mercy and anger alike are with him
  who remits and forgives, though on the
   wicked alights his wrath.
12 Great as his mercy is his punishment;
  he judges men, each according to his
   deeds.
13 A criminal does not escape with his plunder;
  a just man's hope God does not leave
   unfulfilled.
14 Whoever does good has his reward,
  which each receives according to his
   deeds.
15 Say not: "I am hidden from God;
  in heaven who remembers me?
 Among so many people I cannot be known;
  what am I in the world of spirits?
16 Behold, the heavens, the heaven of heavens,
  the earth and the abyss tremble at his
   visitation;
17 The roots of the mountains, the earth's
   foundations,
  at his mere glance, quiver and quake.
18 Of me, therefore, he will take no thought;
  with my ways who will concern himself?
19 If I sin, no eye will see me;
  if all in secret I am disloyal, who is to
   know?
20 Who tells him of just deeds
  and what could I expect for doing my
   duty?"
21 Such are the thoughts of senseless men,
  which only the foolish knave will think.

16, 11d: *(wᵉ ʿal rᵉšāʿîm) yanniaḥ (rogzô)*: cf 5, 6.
 16, 13: *tiqwat (ṣāddîq)*: so LXX, P.
 16, 14: *(kᵉmaʿăśāyw) yimṣa*: so LXX, P. Omit *yhwh hiqšâ . . . ḥālaq
lāʾ ādām*: so LXX, V.
 16, 15: Omit *kol bᵉnê ʾ ādām*: so LXX, V.
 16, 16b: *tᵉhôm wāʾāreṣ môʿ ădîm bᵉpoqdô*: so LXX. Omit the rest:
glosses.
 16, 20: *(kî) ʾ eṣṣôr (ḥôq)*.

NRSV

¹⁰ or on the six hundred thousand foot soldiers
  who assembled in their stubbornness.ᵃ
¹¹ Even if there were only one stiff-necked
   person,
  it would be a wonder if he remained
   unpunished.
 For mercy and wrath are with the Lord;ᵇ
  he is mighty to forgive—but he also pours
   out wrath.
¹² Great as is his mercy, so also is his
   chastisement;
  he judges a person according to his or her
   deeds.
¹³ The sinner will not escape with plunder,
  and the patience of the godly will not be
   frustrated.
¹⁴ He makes room for every act of mercy;
  everyone receives in accordance with his or
   her deeds.ᶜ

¹⁷ Do not say, "I am hidden from the Lord,
  and who from on high has me in mind?
 Among so many people I am unknown,
  for what am I in a boundless creation?
¹⁸ Lo, heaven and the highest heaven,
  the abyss and the earth, tremble at his
   visitation!ᵈ
¹⁹ The very mountains and the foundations of the
   earth
  quiver and quake when he looks upon them.
²⁰ But no human mind can grasp this,
  and who can comprehend his ways?
²¹ Like a tempest that no one can see,
  so most of his works are concealed.ᵉ
²² Who is to announce his acts of justice?
  Or who can await them? For his decreeᶠ
   far off."ᵍ
²³ Such are the thoughts of one devoid of
   understanding;
  a senseless and misguided person thinks foolishly.

ᵃOther ancient authorities add *Chastising, showing mercy, striking,
healing, the Lord persisted in mercy and discipline.* ᵇGk *him*
ᶜOther ancient authorities add ¹⁵The Lord hardened Pharaoh so that
he did not recognize him, in order that his works might be known
under heaven. ¹⁶His mercy is manifest to the whole of creation, and
he divided his light and darkness with a plumb line. ᵈOther ancient authorities add *The whole world past and present is in his
will.* ᵉMeaning of Gk uncertain: Heb Syr *If I sin, no eye can
see me, and if I am disloyal all in secret, who is to know?*
ᶠHeb *the decree*: Gk *the covenant* ᵍOther ancient authorities
add *and a scrutiny for all comes at the end*

COMMENTARY

In a fictional debate, Ben Sira tries to answer some accusations against God and to counter justification for wicked conduct.[173] Several biblical texts come very close to blaming Yahweh for human rebellion, especially Exod 11:10, Yahweh's hardening of Pharaoh's heart; 2 Sam 24:1, Yahweh's prompting David to carry out a census of young men who were eligible for conscription into the army; Jer 6:21 and Ezek 3:20, Yahweh's imposing obstacles to life; and Isa 6:9-13, Yahweh's use of the prophet to hinder repentance on the part of the nation. Furthermore, the claim that both weal and woe come from the Lord in Deut 32:39 and Isa 45:7, when coupled with a firm denial of any rival deities, can easily lead to belief that both good and evil human beings derive from God.

The fundamental problem arose from widespread belief that Israel's God had created a world in which sin was a live possibility. The skeptic asked why such a universe was formed when a deity capable of creation could surely have made one that rendered transgression impossible. Three possibilities for the origin of evil naturally came to mind: (1) God created both good and evil; (2) Satan introduced sin into the world; and (3) human beings brought evil into a perfect world. At this point, Ben Sira strongly attaches blame to men and women, who willingly opt to rebel against their maker. In three verses, he uses the Hebrew word חפץ (*ḥāpēṣ*, "to desire," "to choose") as many times, emphasizing human choice (15:15-17). In his view, any attempt to shift blame from humans to God ignored one essential fact: God cannot do that which God despises.

Skepticism about divine recompense for sinful deeds seemed to support the claim that Yahweh either approved of evil or simply overlooked it. When a delay in divine visitation coincided with reverse expectation, such as numerous children being born to wicked people, traditional understandings of divine justice became suspect. That situation existed in early second-century BCE Jeru-

salem and demanded a thoughtful response from a teacher like Ben Sira. In offering a rebuttal to such skepticism, he put forth at least one bold statement at odds with tradition: Barrenness with virtue surpasses a large family of wicked children (16:1-4). To overcome doubt about divine punishment, he lets Scripture demonstrate the reality of God's wrath on sinners of all sorts. Ben Sira's answer to those who considered their little actions inconsequential in God's eyes amounts to a teacher's harsh rebuke for sloppy thinking.

15:11-20. The initial section echoes Moses' speech in Deut 30:15, 19, which offers the people of Israel a choice between good and evil, life and death. This unit also draws on Gen 1:1 and insists that *from the beginning* God has opposed sin absolutely. The formula of debate, "do not say" (אל תאמר *ʾal tōmar*) and a variant, "lest you say" (פן תאמר *pen tōmar*), appear in vv. 10-12 (*ʾal tōmar* in 16:17). The attribution of rebellion (פשע *peša'*) and violence (חמס *ḥāmās*) to God evokes in Ben Sira a twofold use of the word שנא (*śānēʾ*, "to hate"; cf. vv. 11, 13; in the latter instance, רעה [*rāʿâ*, "wicked"] in hendiadys with ותועבה [*wĕtôʿēbâ*, "abomination"] precedes the verb). The Epistle of James also refutes a claim that God incites sinners to do evil; it, too, stresses human desire as the origin of sin (Jas 1:13-15).

Verses 15-16 breathe the spirit of Hab 2:4, where human faithfulness is said to bring justification before God. The strong intellectual component in faith thus finds a worthy complement in actions demonstrating one's convictions. Fire and water (v. 16) serve as metaphors for life's destruction and generation; and the idea of two ways was familiar in the Hellenistic world, as well as in Judaism. The rabbis frequently refer to two inclinations, the יצר הרע (*yēṣer hārāʾ*) and the יצר הטוב (*yēṣer haṭṭôb*). The first, the evil disposition, antedates the second, the good tendency, by a dozen years, according to rabbinic speculation. Biblical grounds for two inclinations existed in Gen 6:5 and 8:21 (for the evil bias) and 1 Chr 29:28 and Isa 26:3 (for the good inclination). The rabbis even noticed two spellings of the crucial nouns for mental disposition, לב (*lēb*) and לבב

---

173. Readers can quickly recognize the complexity of the problem of theodicy and become familiar with various ways of dealing with it in James L. Crenshaw, ed., *Theodicy in the Old Testament*.

lēbāb, "heart") and יצר (*yēṣer*, "inclination") in the biblical text.

16:1-23. In the second unit, which the Vg titles *De filiis impiis* ("On Wicked Children"), Ben Sira draws the consequences of his belief in an all-seeing God: Sinners will pay dearly for their offenses. He first takes up the mistaken notion that numerous progeny demonstrate God's favor. That is true, Ben Sira says, only when the children fear God. Indeed, one good person is better than a thousand sinners (cf. Eccl 9:15), and a single worthy individual can generate enough children to fill a city. Here Ben Sira probably alludes to Gen 15:1-5, the promise to Abraham that he will be the father of countless descendants.

Verse 5 raises a provocative issue for interpreters of wisdom literature: When does the personal ego surface? Peter Höffken has discussed this problem as it pertains to Qohelet, where the authorial "I" occurs often.[174] Does Ben Sira appeal to his own private experience in alluding to what he has seen and heard, or does he merely transmit information by means of a literary convention? Interestingly, he stops short of recording these personal insights; instead he promptly enters into an allusive account of divine wrath in biblical narrative. He recalls the punishment of Korah, Dathan, and Abiram in Num 16:1-35, that of the rebellious giants in Gen 6:1-4, the destruction of Sodom and Gomorrah in Gen 19:1-28, and the erasure of a whole generation of Israelites in the wilderness (cf. Exod 12:37 for the number 600,000).

The avoidance of the Hebrew word for "giants" (נפלים *nĕpilîm*) may represent Ben Sira's aversion

to speculation about their role in the fall of humankind that characterized the Enochic literature and the book of *Jubilees*.[175] Ben Sira's choice of "giants of old" (נסיכי קדם *nĕsîkê qedem*) may also allude to the myths preserved in Isaiah 14 and Ezekiel 28.[176]

Several psalms take up the problem of doubters who emphasize the vastness of the universe and the inconsequentiality of human deeds, whether good or bad (cf. Pss 10:4, 11, 13; 14:1; 53:2). Ben Sira combines such skepticism with vocabulary taken from theophanic descriptions of earth's response to God's coming, the prayers attributed to Solomon at the dedication of the Temple and to Jonah in the belly of the fish (1 Kgs 8:27; Jonah 2:6), and acknowledgment of mystery where God's actions are concerned. The exact grammatical relationship from vv. 17-23 is unclear, although vv. 18-19 may be parenthetical. In the Hebrew text, v. 20 links up with v. 17, whereas the Greek has v. 20 as a continuation of v. 19. The glosses on this unit (vv. 15-16) and the many variants in other languages attest to the lively debate generated by such skepticism (cf. 17:15-20; 23:18; Wis 3:7; 14:11). For now, Ben Sira seems content to adopt the practice of diatribe, a vibrant form of persuasive discourse in which an imaginery audience is addressed directly, often going so far as to label his opponents "misguided, senseless, and foolish."

---

174. Peter Höffken, "Das Ego des Weisen," *Theologische Zeitschrift* 4 (1985) 121-35. Occasionally, an author of brief proverbial sayings in the book of Proverbs slips into an "autobiographical style" (cf. the imagined speech in Prov 5:12-14, but also 25:30-34; and 30:18-19; the instructions naturally use the first-person address of a teacher, as in Prov 22:19-21; 30:1-14; and 31:1-9).

175. James VanderKam, *Enoch: A Man for All Generations* (Columbia: University of South Carolina Press, 1995), has examined this growth of a corpus of literature about Enoch in great detail; in doing so, he has thrown considerable light on the context of second- and first-century BCE Judaism.

176. Mythical language abounds in Isaiah 14 (Day Star, Dawn, Mountain of the North, the Pit, the Most High), all of it reminiscent of Canaanite mythology. The unspecified object of ridicule—Nebuchadrezzar? Babylon? Persia?—is depicted as having fallen because of extreme pride. The king of Tyre, according to Ezekiel 28, also was brought low because of overweening pride. Here, too, mythological concepts from Ugaritic literature occur, but so do Israelite mythic ideas (the wise Dan'el, the Pit, Mount Saphon, the garden of Eden, cherubim).

REFLECTIONS

Generation after generation of religious people have struggled to understand the implications of divine knowledge and sovereignty. Does God know everything that happens even before it takes place, and does divine power leave any room for human freedom? Experience teaches us that we make free choices when confronted with alternatives, but we also know that those decisions are shaped to a great extent by genetics and culture. How free, then, are people? In the religious realm, a similar ambiguity reigns. We choose God or spurn the divine invitation to holiness, but how much real choice do we have in that decision?

The biblical manner of addressing this problem began with the result and argued backward to causal factors. When people turned their backs on God, that action must surely have been willed by God, whose intention cannot be frustrated, given the operative understanding of divine power. The real difficulty with this view came in incidents involving people who desired to change but whose will was subjected to a contrary divine power (e.g., Pharaoh) or in circumstances where it was believed that God blocked human inclinations to repent (e.g., Isa 6:9-10; Mark 4:10-12). Possibly these texts represent mistaken assessments of the situation, but how can the church hold in proper tension our potential for good or ill and God's sovereignty? That struggle has divided the church and continues to baffle theologians, who usually take their cue from the rabbinic affirmation of free will *and* divine authority. That mystery is not the only one in the religious life of modern Christians.

SIRACH 16:24–18:14, THE RELATIONSHIP BETWEEN THE CREATOR-JUDGE AND HUMANKIND

NAB	NRSV
22 Hearken to me, my son, take my advice, apply your mind to my words,	24 Listen to me, my child, and acquire knowledge, and pay close attention to my words.
23 While I propose measured wisdom, and impart accurate knowledge.	25 I will impart discipline precisely[a] and declare knowledge accurately.
24 When at the first God created his works and, as he made them, assigned their tasks,	26 When the Lord created[b] his works from the beginning, and, in making them, determined their boundaries,
25 He ordered for all time what they were to do and their domains from generation to generation. They were not to hunger, nor grow weary, nor ever cease from their tasks.	27 he arranged his works in an eternal order, and their dominion[c] for all generations. They neither hunger nor grow weary, and they do not abandon their tasks.
26 Not one should ever crowd its neighbor, nor should they ever disobey his word.	28 They do not crowd one another, and they never disobey his word.
27 Then the LORD looked upon the earth, and filled it with his blessings.	29 Then the Lord looked upon the earth, and filled it with his good things.
28 Its surface he covered with all manner of life which must return into it again.	30 With all kinds of living beings he covered its surface, and into it they must return.
17 The LORD from the earth created man, and in his own image he made him. 2 Limited days of life he gives him and makes him return to earth again.	17 The Lord created human beings out of earth, and makes them return to it again.

16, 22: *šeemaʿ beenî ʾēlay weqaḥ . . . śîm* so LXX, V.
17, 1-3: Trsp to order of 1a.3b.2a.1b.3a.2b: cf V.

[a] Gk *by weight*   [b] Heb: Gk *judged*   [c] Or *elements*

NAB

3 He endows man with a strength of his own,
 and with power over all things else on
 earth.

4 He puts the fear of him in all flesh,
 and gives him rule over beasts and birds.

5 He forms men's tongues and eyes and ears,
 and imparts to them an understanding
 heart.

6 With wisdom and knowledge he fills them;
 good and evil he shows them.

7 He looks with favor upon their hearts,
 and shows them his glorious works,

8 That they may describe the wonders of his
 deeds
 and praise his holy name.

9 He has set before them knowledge,
 a law of life as their inheritance;

10 An everlasting covenant he has made with
 them,
 his commandments he has revealed to
 them.

11 His majestic glory their eyes beheld,
 his glorious voice their ears heard.

12 He says to them, "Avoid all evil";
 each of them he gives precepts about his
 fellow men.

13 Their ways are ever known to him,
 they cannot be hidden from his eyes.

14 Over every nation he places a ruler,
 but the LORD's own portion is Israel.

15 All their actions are clear as the sun to him,
 his eyes are ever upon their ways.

16 Their wickedness cannot be hidden from
 him;
 all of their sins are before the LORD.

17 A man's goodness God cherishes like a
 signet ring,
 a man's virtue, like the apple of his eye.

18 Later he will rise up and repay them,
 and requite each one of them as they
 deserve.

19 But to the penitent he provides a way back,
 he encourages those who are losing hope!

17, 5a: *yāṣar lāšôn w ʿênayim wᵏᵇ ʾoznaim:* cf P.
17, 8: Order as in LXX^MSS, P. *wîsaprû miple ʿ ôywt:* cf LXX^MSS, V (v
8b).
17, 9: *proethēken:* so P.
17, 11: (*phōnēs*) *autou:* so LXX^MSS.

NRSV

2 He gave them a fixed number of days,
 but granted them authority over everything
 on the earth.ᵃ

3 He endowed them with strength like his own,ᵇ
 and made them in his own image.

4 He put the fear of themᶜ in all living beings,
 and gave them dominion over beasts and birds.ᵈ

6 Discretion and tongue and eyes,
 ears and a mind for thinking he gave them.

7 He filled them with knowledge and
 understanding,
 and showed them good and evil.

8 He put the fear of him intoᵉ their hearts
 to show them the majesty of his works.ᶠ

10 And they will praise his holy name,

9 to proclaim the grandeur of his works.

11 He bestowed knowledge upon them,
 and allotted to them the law of life.ᵍ

12 He established with them an eternal covenant,
 and revealed to them his decrees.

13 Their eyes saw his glorious majesty,
 and their ears heard the glory of his voice.

14 He said to them, "Beware of all evil."
 And he gave commandment to each of them
 concerning the neighbor.

15 Their ways are always known to him;
 they will not be hid from his eyes.ʰ

17 He appointed a ruler for every nation,
 but Israel is the Lord's own portion.ⁱ

19 All their works are as clear as the sun before
 him,
 and his eyes are ever upon their ways.

20 Their iniquities are not hidden from him,
 and all their sins are before the Lord.ʲ

22 One's almsgiving is like a signet ring with the
 Lord,ᵏ

ᵃLat: Gk *it*   ᵇLat: Gk *proper to them*   ᶜSyr: Gk *him*
ᵈOther ancient authorities add as verse 5, *They obtained the use of
the five faculties of the Lord; as sixth he distributed to them the
gift of mind, and as seventh, reason, the interpreter of one's faculties.*   ᵉOther ancient authorities read *He set his eye upon*
ᶠOther ancient authorities add *and he gave them to boast of his
marvels forever*   ᵍOther ancient authorities add *so that they may
know that they who are alive now are mortal*   ʰOther ancient
authorities add 16*Their ways from youth tend toward evil, and they
are unable to make for themselves hearts of flesh in place of their
stony hearts.* 17*For in the division of the nations of the whole
earth, he appointed*   ⁱOther ancient authorities add as verse 18,
*whom, being his firstborn, he brings up with discipline, and allot-
ting to him the light of his love, he does not neglect him.*
ʲOther ancient authorities add as verse 21, *But the Lord, who is gracious and knows how they are formed, has neither left them nor
abandoned them, but has spared them.*   ᵏGk *him*

NAB

20 Return to the LORD and give up sin,
   pray to him and make your offenses few.
21 Turn again to the Most High and away from
      sin,
   hate intensely what he loathes;
22 Who in the nether world can glorify the
      Most High
   in place of the living who offer their praise?
23 No more can the dead give praise than
      those who have never lived;
   they glorify the LORD who are alive and
      well.
24 How great the mercy of the LORD,
   his forgiveness of those who return to him!
25 The like cannot be found in men,
   for not immortal is any son of man.
26 Is anything brighter than the sun? Yet it can
      be eclipsed.
   How obscure then the thoughts of flesh and
      blood!
27 God watches over the hosts of highest
      heaven,
   while all men are dust and ashes.

18 The Eternal is the judge of all
      things without exception;
   the LORD alone is just.
2 Whom has he made equal to describing his
      works,
   and who can probe his mighty deeds?
3 Who can measure his majestic power,
   or exhaust the tale of his mercies?
4 One cannot lessen, nor increase,
   nor penetrate the wonders of the LORD.
5 When a man ends he is only beginning,
   and when he stops he is still bewildered.
6 What is man, of what worth is he?
   the good, the evil in him, what are these?
7 The sum of a man's days is great
   if it reaches a hundred years:
8 Like a drop of sea water, like a grain of sand,
   so are these few years among the days of
      eternity.
9 That is why the LORD is patient with men

17, 25a: *ki lō ̕ kā ̕ ēlleh bā ̕ ādām*: so P.
17, 26b: *ûmâ ra ̕ miyyēṣer* (?) *bāṣār wādām*: so LXX^{Sa}, V.
18, 1: (*ho zōn eis ton aiōna*) *ekrinen*: cf P.
18, 2: *tini* (*exepoiēsen*): so LXX^{MSS}, Vet Lat^{MSS}, P.
18, 3b: *yāsûp* for *yôsip* (= *prosthēsei*).
18, 7b: Cf P.
18, 8b: *en hēmerais* (*aiōnos*): so LXX^{MSS}.

NRSV

   and he will keep a person's kindness like
      the apple of his eye.[a]
23 Afterward he will rise up and repay them,
   and he will bring their recompense on their
      heads.
[24] Yet to those who repent he grants a return,
   and he encourages those who are losing
      hope.

[25] Turn back to the Lord and forsake your sins;
   pray in his presence and lessen your offense.
[26] Return to the Most High and turn away from
      iniquity,[b]
   and hate intensely what he abhors.
[27] Who will sing praises to the Most High in
      Hades
   in place of the living who give thanks?
[28] From the dead, as from one who does not
      exist, thanksgiving has ceased;
   those who are alive and well sing the Lord's
      praises.
[29] How great is the mercy of the Lord,
   and his forgiveness for those who return to
      him!
[30] For not everything is within human capability,
   since human beings are not immortal.
[31] What is brighter than the sun? Yet it can be
      eclipsed.
   So flesh and blood devise evil.
[32] He marshals the host of the height of heaven;
   but all human beings are dust and ashes.

18 He who lives forever created the
      whole universe;
[2]   the Lord alone is just.[c]
[4] To none has he given power to proclaim his
      works;
   and who can search out his mighty deeds?
[5] Who can measure his majestic power?
   And who can fully recount his mercies?
[6] It is not possible to diminish or increase them,
   nor is it possible to fathom the wonders of
      the Lord.

[a]Other ancient authorities add *apportioning repentance to his sons
and daughters*   [b]Other ancient authorities add *for he will lead
you out of darkness to the light of health.*   [c]Other ancient
authorities add *and there is no other beside him;* [3]*he steers the
world with the span of his hand, and all things obey his will; for
he is king of all things by his power, separating among them the
holy things from the profane.*

NAB

and showers upon them his mercy.
10 He sees and understands that their death is
    grievous,
    and so he forgives them all the more.
11 Man may be merciful to his fellow man,
    but the LORD's mercy reaches all flesh,
12 Reproving, admonishing, teaching,
    as a shepherd guides his flock;
13 Merciful to those who accept his guidance,
    who are diligent in his precepts.

NRSV

7 When human beings have finished, they are
    just beginning,
    and when they stop, they are still perplexed.
8 What are human beings, and of what use are
    they?
    What is good in them, and what is evil?
9 The number of days in their life is great if they
    reach one hundred years.[a]
10 Like a drop of water from the sea and a grain
    of sand,
    so are a few years among the days of
    eternity.
11 That is why the Lord is patient with them
    and pours out his mercy upon them.
12 He sees and recognizes that their end is
    miserable;
    therefore he grants them forgiveness all the
    more.
13 The compassion of human beings is for their
    neighbors,
    but the compassion of the Lord is for every
    living thing.
    He rebukes and trains and teaches them,
    and turns them back, as a shepherd his
    flock.
14 He has compassion on those who accept his
    discipline
    and who are eager for his precepts.

aOther ancient authorities add *but the death of each one is beyond
the calculation of all*

COMMENTARY

This section consists of four (or five) distinct poems: 16:24-30; 17:1-24 (or 17:1-14 and 17:15-24); 17:25-32; 18:1-14. It treats the dual themes of God's creative and judicial functions, especially divine retribution, extends an invitation to repent, and elaborates on God's compassion for frail human beings. The former resembles a midrash on Genesis 1, while much of the language recalls Psalms 8 and 104. The brief unit in 17:15-24 provides further response to the earlier skeptical attitude articulated in 16:17-22.

16:24-30. The initial poem praises the Creator for the orderliness of the universe, its appropriate-

ness in every detail. The detached language and mathematical precision emphasize the divine plan (κοσμέω *kosmeō*, "to order," "to arrange") in Greek, from which comes the noun "cosmos." The Greek text has a vocative in v. 24, "my son," lacking in both Hebrew and Syriac. Verses 24-25 serve as an introduction to this initial poem, perhaps also to the larger section. Ben Sira stresses the reliability of his teaching by such terms as "weighing" (שקל *šāqal*) and "preserving" (צנע *ṣnʿ*). He implies that he has carefully examined God's works and retained his findings for posterity. From Prov 1:23 he borrows the concept of pouring out God's Spirit (אביעה *ʾabbîʿâ*), although in 50:27 he uses the causative form of the verb (נבע *nāba'*).

The poem describing God's creative act that brought forth the universe (vv. 26-30) reflects on the narrative in Gen 1:1-25, but the Hebrew is fragmentary from the second bicolon of v. 26 to 30:11. The Greek κρίσει (*krisei,* "judged") is a mistake for κτίσει (*ktisei,* "created"), for which the Hebrew has an infinitive construct form of the verb ברא (*bārā'*, "to create"), a verb used only with God as subject in the Bible. Whereas Gen 1:1 has בראשית ברא אלהים (*běrē'šît bārā' 'elōhîm*),[177] Ben Sira used the syntactically correct בברא אל (*bibrā' 'ēl,* "when God created") plus מראש (*mērōš,* "from the beginning"). These works, in contrast to human beings, always obey God's commands; indeed, they deserve the divine affirmation of extraordinary goodness (cf. the refrain in Genesis 1, where God makes this judgment often). Still, these creatures must return to the earth whence they came (cf. 40:11).

17:1-24. In 17:1-14, Ben Sira turns to the account of God's creation of human beings, merging the two different descriptions in Genesis 1–2 with the separate tradition from Sinai about the giving of the commandments. Ben Sira understands the image of God to imply authority over the animals comparable to God's sovereignty in the heavens. The Greek concept of the five senses (sight, touch, smell, sound, and taste), together with two additional faculties from Stoic philosophy, knowledge and reason, have evoked a gloss in v. 5, perhaps prompted by the listing of gifts in v. 6. The abrupt shift to the Sinaitic theophany in v. 13 follows the notion of fearing God, an accompaniment of praise, and emphasizes responsibility toward neighbors. The reference is probably to the second tablet of the Decalogue.

Contrary to the opinions expressed by "foolish persons" in 16:17-22, Ben Sira is convinced that God does see every human being and rewards or punishes each according to his or her actions. That assurance comprises the next seven verses, which

conclude with a promise of forgiveness to the repentant.

Verse 17 refers to ancient speculation about Israel's special relationship to God. Whereas God appointed secular rulers for the other nations (or angelic mediators with Yahweh on their behalf), Ben Sira observes, as God's portion, Israel has direct access to God. In short, Israel exists as the private people of God. Ben Sira's high esteem for good works shows in the metaphors employed in v. 22, where both a "signet ring" and "the apple of the eye" describe almsgiving. The signet ring, or seal, worn on the finger or around the neck, when pressed in wax, left a person's insignia on important papers (cf. Gen 38:18; Cant 8:6; Jer 22:24). The other metaphor appears in Deut 32:10; Ps 17:8; Prov 7:2; and Zech 2:12, the first and last of these references with regard to Israel and Judah as God's special portion.

Jewish reflection on the relationship of other peoples to God acknowledged their place in the divine scheme of things. *Sifre* 40 states that "God does not provide for Israel alone, but for all people," and the Targum to Pseudo Jonathan at Gen 11:7-8 observes that every nation has its own guardian angel (cf. Deut 32:8-9 LXX). Ben Sira believed in the universal domain of Israel's God, but he also considered some nations inveterate foes. His harshest comments occur in 50:25-26 with reference to Idumeans, Philistines, and Samaritans.

The threat of retribution in v. 23 resembles that in Joel 4:4-7[3:4-7, Eng.], where the prophet stresses an exact recompense for offenses against the Judeans. Ben Sira implies that God may remain inactive for the time being, as the skeptics in 16:17-22 suspected, but that patient waiting will eventually give way to divine visitation. Nevertheless, Ben Sira offers hope to the despairing.

17:25-32. The Latin text sets the next section apart with the title *De Conversione* ("On Repentance"); these verses urge mortals to repent in order to sing Yahweh's praises. Extolling the Lord's glory represented for Sirach the highest form of life (cf. 15:9-10; 17:10; 18:4-7; 39:8, 15, 35; 43:28-30; 51:1, 22), one forbidden those in Sheol. Ben Sira uses an analogy in v. 31 that also occurs in 1 Esdr 4:33-41 and in a fragmentary Sumerian text, specifically that if even the sun is eclipsed, how much more the feeble light of

---

177. Because of the peculiar pointing of the first two words in the Bible, interpreters have had difficulty deciding whether to translate the initial construction as absolute or temporal, both being possible grammatically. Context often leads scholars to understand the words temporally, thus "When God began to create the heavens and the earth, the earth was already waste and void." This translation, adopted by the NRSV, although phrased differently, seems to have more to recommend it than the alternative, "In the beginning God created the heavens and the earth."

humankind. The contest of Darius's guards appropriately concludes with praise of the Lord of truth, just as this poem sings of divine mercy in the context of human dust and ashes.

18:1-14. The final unit characterizes Yahweh as a righteous and merciful judge whose majesty surpasses human imagination. This thought prompts Ben Sira to reflect momentarily on the lowliness of men and women when compared with God's grandeur. The frailty of humankind even moves the Lord to compassion, according to Ben Sira, and evokes in the deity a shepherding role. This image of the divine shepherd enjoyed wide coverage in the Bible (cf. Psalms 2; 23; 80; Isa 40:11; Ezek 34:11-16; John 10:11-18; Heb 13:20; 1 Pet 2:25; Rev 7:17).

The title in v. 1 for Yahweh, "the One who lives forever," occurs in Dan 4:31; 6:27; and

12:17. This epithet probably constitutes the author's reaction against predominant extra-Israelite views of gods who die and rise each year. It follows that none could possibly adequately grasp Yahweh's mystery; Ben Sira expresses this point beautifully: When one has finished, one is actually still at the very beginning, having progressed little in recounting God's glory (cf. 1:3, 6; 42:17; Job 9:10; Ps 145:3). The rhetorical question in v. 8 links this verse with Pss 8:5; 144:3; and Job 7:17. Papyrus Insinger also likens the human life span to a grain of sand (see v. 10), and Egyptian texts generally calculate one's existence on earth as a maximum of one hundred years (see v. 9; cf. Ps 90:10; Isa 65:20). Ben Sira concedes in v. 13 that human beings limit their compassion to immediate neighbors, while Yahweh extends a merciful hand to everyone.

REFLECTIONS

The religious life stands under the promise of divine blessing, which comes in the midst of a broken world and makes life tolerable. A significant number of texts in the Bible either invite God's people to rejoice or actually characterize them as wholly surrendering to joyful praise. The sound of benediction, the blessing, may have served as the concluding note of congregational gatherings, but that affirmation had its basis in the earlier happiness created by God's presence in the company of good people. The "positive thinking" preachers of modern Christianity have rightly seized this feature of religion, although often by overlooking the biblical realism that gives that joy a moral obligation to ease others' suffering.

The church has an unenviable record of suppressing happiness, although unwittingly. Emphasis on negatives in one's personal moral conduct arose from purely good intentions, a desire to avoid every appearance of evil. Applying the Johannine principle of residing in the world without being a party to its values has never been easy. Too often the church has chosen withdrawal from the world as the safer option, despite the clear rejection of this approach in the New Testament.

Good Friday and Easter Sunday serve in the liturgical calendar as perennial reminders that both sadness and joy belong to the very center of Christian experience. Reflecting on the prevalence of sin and suffering in society, as well as contemplating the cost in human lives and in the divine economy, brings streams of tears. Nevertheless, meditating on God's bountiful love and acceptance of transgressors who turn away from their self-centered ways, along with thinking about the beauty and goodness in God's creatures, elicits rapturous songs of joy. The challenge is to give equal rein to each feeling. The long face must not become permanently fixed, for happiness comes with the dawn. That hope springs eternal in the human breast, awakened by every pronouncement of blessing on the people of God.

SIRACH 18:15-18, ON GIVING ALMS

NAB	NRSV
14 My son, to your charity add no reproach, nor spoil any gift by harsh words.	[15] My child, do not mix reproach with your good deeds, or spoil your gift by harsh words.
15 Like dew that abates a burning wind, so does a word improve a gift.	[16] Does not the dew give relief from the scorching heat? So a word is better than a gift.
16 Sometimes the word means more than the gift; both are offered by a kindly man.	[17] Indeed, does not a word surpass a good gift? Both are to be found in a gracious person.
17 Only a fool upbraids before giving; a grudging gift wears out the expectant eyes.	[18] A fool is ungracious and abusive, and the gift of a grudging giver makes the eyes dim.
18 Be informed before speaking; before sickness prepare the cure.	

COMMENTARY

The elaborate praise of God for unlimited generosity in the preceding section leads to some observations about acts of kindness among humans. They are to model their giving on that of the Lord (cf. Jas 1:5). Ben Sira realizes that the prevalent view about God's blessing on good persons and the opposite on sinners implies that prosperous people deserve their wealth just as the poor suffer appropriately for laziness or wickedness. The temptation, therefore, was to look on the poor with contempt, even when giving them a handout. Ben Sira advises that words should match deeds, a charitable act being accompanied by gentle remarks.

The analogy from daily experience—relief from oppressive heat that dew brings to plants suffering distress—prompts an exuberant overstatement, which Ben Sira hastens to qualify. A (kind) word is better than a gift, *but* a truly gracious individual unites both word and action. Ignorant persons do just the opposite, they compound a niggardly gift by harsh language. The Babylonian Talmud makes the point effectively: "Whoever gives a farthing is blessed sixfold, but the one who adds words elevenfold."[178]

178. *Baba Bathra* 96.

SIRACH 18:19-29, ON CAUTION

NAB	NRSV
19 Before you are judged, seek merit for yourself, and at the time of visitation you will have a ransom.	[19] Before you speak, learn; and before you fall ill, take care of your health.
20 Before you have fallen, humble yourself; when you have sinned, show repentance.	[20] Before judgment comes, examine yourself; and at the time of scrutiny you will find forgiveness.
21 Delay not to forsake sins, neglect it not till you are in distress.	[21] Before falling ill, humble yourself; and when you have sinned, repent.
	[22] Let nothing hinder you from paying a vow promptly,

18, 19a: (*pro kriseōs*) *etoimason seauton kalliergein:* so 1 LXX[MS], V (19a).
18, 21: With P; accidentally omitted in LXX.

NAB

22 Let nothing prevent the prompt payment of
    your vows;
    wait not to fulfill them when you are
    dying.
23 Before making a vow have the means to
    fulfill it;
    be not one who tries the LORD.
24 Think of wrath and the day of death,
    the time of vengeance when he will hide
    his face.
25 Remember the time of hunger in the time
    of plenty,
    poverty and want in the day of wealth.
26 Between morning and evening the weather
    changes;
    before the LORD all things are fleeting.
27 A wise man is circumspect in all things;
    when sin is rife he keeps himself from
    wrongdoing.
28 Any learned man should make wisdom
    known,
    and he who attains to her should declare
    her praise;
29 Those trained in her words must show their
    wisdom,
    dispensing sound proverbs like life-giving
    waters.

18, 23a: *b*ᵉ*terem tiddôr hākēn nidrekā*: so Tanchuma LXX^MSS, P.
18, 28f: cf P̣.

NRSV

and do not wait until death to be released
    from it.
23 Before making a vow, prepare yourself;
    do not be like one who puts the Lord to
    the test.
24 Think of his wrath on the day of death,
    and of the moment of vengeance when he
    turns away his face.
25 In the time of plenty think of the time of
    hunger;
    in days of wealth think of poverty and need.
26 From morning to evening conditions change;
    all things move swiftly before the Lord.

27 One who is wise is cautious in everything;
    when sin is all around, one guards against
    wrongdoing.
28 Every intelligent person knows wisdom,
    and praises the one who finds her.
29 Those who are skilled in words become wise
    themselves,
    and pour forth apt proverbs.ᵃ

ᵃOther ancient authorities add *Better is confidence in the one Lord
than clinging with a dead heart to a dead one.*

COMMENTARY

This brief unit may also have been inspired
by the poem on divine mercy and forgiveness
in 18:1-14. Ben Sira encourages his readers to
plan for unpleasant intrusions, particularly sickness and death. The Syriac of v. 19 urges
readers to consult a physician; because illness
was thought to strike those who had offended
God, one could not get well until obtaining
forgiveness. Physicians did not fit into this understanding of sin and its consequences very
well, for they interfered with that process. Ben
Sira wrestles with this vexing problem in 38:1-
15, where he combines the traditional view of

sin's relationship to sickness with a more modern
concept of doctors and medicines.

Reflection on the day of God's visitation and
the prospect of rejection puts the fear of the
Lord in people, according to v. 24. One should
observe a similar caution in making vows (cf.
Eccl 5:3), for one's circumstances may change
quickly, rendering it impossible to fulfill a promise despite its accompanying solemn oath. Ben
Sira reverses the usual order in the phrase "from
morning to evening" (see similar usage in late
texts, such as 1 Chr 16:40; 2 Chr 2:4; but cf.
Gen 1:5; Ps 55:7; Dan 8:26), perhaps because
political decisions and commercial transactions,

the primary means of quick reversals, occurred during the daylight hours.[179]

In Judaism, various ways to obtain forgiveness were advocated. Sickness and its accompanying suffering atone for sin, according to a Tannaitic source,[180] if one also repents. In this regard, W. O. E. Oesterley refers to *Bereshith Rabba* (chap.

65), which states that Isaac prayed to be given suffering to turn away divine judgment in the next life.[181] Another means of forgiveness, according to *Yoma* 86b is repentance, and almsgiving was yet another (*Baba Bathra* 10a). Death, the supreme suffering, also brought reconciliation (*Sifre* 33a). These texts reveal an eagerness to find ways to make God's forgiveness as far reaching as possible.

179. Frank Crüsemann, "The Unchangeable World: Reflections on the 'Crisis of Wisdom' in Koheleth," in *The God of the Lowly,* eds. Willi Schottroff and Wolfgang Stegemann (Maryknoll, N.Y.: Orbis, 1984) 57-77, has emphasized the excessive concern to get rich during the time of Qohelet, although he overemphasizes the author's greed.
180. *Sifre* 73b.

181. W. O. E. Oesterley, *The Wisdom of Jesus the Son of Sirach or Ecclesiasticus* (Cambridge: Cambridge University Press, 1912) 125-26.

SIRACH 18:30–19:17, ON SELF-CONTROL

NAB

30 Go not after your lusts,
　　but keep your desires in check.
31 If you satisfy your lustful appetites
　　they will make you the sport of your enemies.
32 Have no joy in the pleasures of a moment
　　which bring on poverty redoubled;
33 Become not a glutton and a winebibber
　　with nothing in your purse.

19 He who does so grows no richer;
　　he who wastes the little he has will be
　　　stripped bare.
2 Wine and women make the mind giddy,
　　and the companion of harlots becomes
　　　reckless.
4 He who lightly trusts in them has no sense,
　　and he who strays after them sins against
　　　his own life.
3 Rottenness and worms will possess him,
　　for contumacious desire destroys its owner.

5 He who gloats over evil will meet with evil,
　　and he who repeats an evil report has no sense.
6 Never repeat gossip,
　　and you will not be reviled.
7 Tell nothing to friend or foe;
　　if you have a fault, reveal it not,

18, 32–19, 2: With Heb; but trsp 2b to 3b (so LXX).
19, 3f: Trsp v 3 and v 4.
19, 5: *šāmēaḥ bᵉrāʾ* (so P, V: trsp *kardia* and *kakia*) *yērôaʾ*, *wᵉ šônēh dābār ḥăsar lēb*: so P.
19, 6b: *wᵉʾ iš lōʾ yᵉḥassᵉdekā* : so P.
19, 7b: Omit *mē* before *estin*: so P, V; dittog.

NRSV

30 Do not follow your base desires,
　　but restrain your appetites.
31 If you allow your soul to take pleasure in base
　　　desire,
　　it will make you the laughingstock of your
　　　enemies.
32 Do not revel in great luxury,
　　or you may become impoverished by its
　　　expense.
33 Do not become a beggar by feasting with
　　　borrowed money,
　　when you have nothing in your purse.ᵃ

19 The one who does thisᵇ will not
　　become rich;
　　one who despises small things will fail little
　　　by little.
2 Wine and women lead intelligent men astray,
　　and the man who consorts with prostitutes
　　　is reckless.
3 Decay and worms will take possession of him,
　　and the reckless person will be snatched away.

4 One who trusts others too quickly has a
　　shallow mind,
　　and one who sins does wrong to himself.
5 One who rejoices in wickednessᶜ will be
　　condemned,ᵈ

ᵃOther ancient authorities add *for you will be plotting against your own life*　ᵇHeb: Gk *A worker who is a drunkard*　ᶜOther ancient authorities read *heart*　ᵈOther ancient authorities add *but one who withstands pleasures crowns his life.* 6*One who controls the tongue will live without strife,*

NAB

8 For he who hears it will hold it against you,
   and in time become your enemy.
9 Let anything you hear die within you;
   be assured it will not make you burst.
10 When a fool hears something, he is in labor,
   like a woman giving birth to a child.
11 Like an arrow lodged in a man's thigh
   is gossip in the breast of a fool.
12 Admonish your friend—he may not have
   done it;
   and if he did, that he may not do it again.
13 Admonish your neighbor—he may not have
   said it;
   and if he did, that he may not say it again.
14 Admonish your friend—often it may be
   slander;
   every story you must not believe.
15 Then, too, a man can slip and not mean it;
   who has not sinned with his tongue?
16 Admonish your neighbor before you break
   with him;
   thus will you fulfill the law of the Most
   High.

19, 13: (*elegxon ton*) *plē sion sou*: so LXX[MSS], P, V; dittog.

NRSV

6   but one who hates gossip has less evil.
7 Never repeat a conversation,
   and you will lose nothing at all.
8 With friend or foe do not report it,
   and unless it would be a sin for you, do not
   reveal it;
9 for someone may have heard you and watched
   you,
   and in time will hate you.
10 Have you heard something? Let it die with
   you.
   Be brave, it will not make you burst!
11 Having heard something, the fool suffers birth
   pangs
   like a woman in labor with a child.
12 Like an arrow stuck in a person's thigh,
   so is gossip inside a fool.

13 Question a friend; perhaps he did not do it;
   or if he did, so that he may not do it again.
14 Question a neighbor; perhaps he did not say
   it;
   or if he said it, so that he may not repeat
   it.
15 Question a friend, for often it is slander;
   so do not believe everything you hear.
16 A person may make a slip without intending
   it.
   Who has not sinned with his tongue?
17 Question your neighbor before you threaten
   him;
   and let the law of the Most High take its
   course.[a]

[a]Other ancient authorities add *and do not be angry.* 18 *The fear of
the Lord is the beginning of acceptance, and wisdom obtains his
love.* 19 *The knowledge of the Lord's commandments is life-giving
discipline; and those who do what is pleasing to him enjoy the
fruit of the tree of immortality.*

COMMENTARY

Before v. 30, the Greek has a title, "Self-control of the Disposition" (ἐγκράτεια ψυχῆς *egkrateia psychēs*), a title that appeared at v. 15 in Codex Sinaiticus. Such headings occur elsewhere at 19:29; 20:27; 24:1; 30:1, 16; 44:1; and 51:1. This section contains brief poems about sensual desire (18:30–19:3) and gossip (19:4-17). The

chapter division interrupts a unit of thought (v. 1), indicating the consequences of living beyond one's means.

18:30–19:3. The surrender to extravagant lust impoverishes a person and brings mockery and contempt. Ben Sira associates lavish parties with sexual license, here symbolized by an expression that has become proverbial, "wine and women." He knows the power of carnal lust, a desire so strong as to tempt men to squander savings and to borrow with abandon in order to satisfy their lust. He warns that such debased conduct often brings venereal disease in its wake, although the reference could be to an untimely death by other means. The Hebrew emphasizes the complete exposure of the one who indulges in such conduct: "He will become utterly naked," probably a metaphor for an impoverished condition.

19:4-17. The unit on gossip urges those who hear unpleasant tales about others to put an end to the vicious rumor and to report what has been said only to the person about whom the gossip has revolved. The purpose is to warn that individual to be more circumspect or to repent, if the gossip contained any truth. The one exception to remaining silent (v. 8) alludes to Lev 5:1, legisla-

tion concerning testimony when someone knows a fact that bears on another's guilt or innocence. The graphic illustrations (bursting from holding a word inside; writhing, as if feeling the pains of giving birth; suffering from an arrow that has penetrated one's thigh) mock the ludicrous behavior of avid gossipmongers.

The anaphrous style of vv. 13-15, referring to a previously mentioned person or object (e.g., "friend . . . he"), with the repeated imperative, "Question . . . perhaps . . . or if . . . so that" with a variant in the third and fourth instances, arrests the attention of those who hear the successive items. In this manner, Ben Sira achieves maximum effect for the rhetorical question, "Who has not sinned with his tongue?" and the admonition to give free rein to the law (cf. Lev 19:17-18). The generous attitude toward the subject of gossip alone can successfully counter a natural tendency to believe the worst in others.

SIRACH 19:20-30, WISDOM AND CLEVERNESS

NAB	NRSV

17 All wisdom is fear of the LORD;
    perfect wisdom is the fulfillment of the law.
	20 The whole of wisdom is fear of the Lord,
	    and in all wisdom there is the fulfillment of the law.[a]

18 The knowledge of wickedness is not wisdom,
    nor is there prudence in the counsel of sinners.
	22 The knowledge of wickedness is not wisdom,
	    nor is there prudence in the counsel of sinners.

19 There is a shrewdness that is detestable,
    while the simple man may be free from sin.
	23 There is a cleverness that is detestable,
	    and there is a fool who merely lacks wisdom.

20 There are those with little understanding who fear God,
    and those of great intelligence who violate the law.
	24 Better are the God-fearing who lack understanding
	    than the highly intelligent who transgress the law.

21 There is a shrewdness keen but dishonest,
    which by duplicity wins a judgment.
	25 There is a cleverness that is exact but unjust,
	    and there are people who abuse favors to gain a verdict.

22 There is the wicked man who is bowed in grief,
    but is full of guile within;
	26 There is the villain bowed down in mourning,
	    but inwardly he is full of deceit.

23 He bows his head and feigns not to hear,	27 He hides his face and pretends not to hear,

19, 19: (*estin) panourgia . . . (elattoumenos) hamartias.* so P.
19, 20: *yēš ḥasar maddā* wirē yhwh, *w*ʰ*yēš yôtēr maddā* w*ᵉ* *ôbēr miṣwā.* cf P.

[a] Other ancient authorities add *and the knowledge of his omnipotence.* 21 *When a slave says to his master, "I will not act as you wish," even if later he does it, he angers the one who supports him.*

NAB

but when not observed, he will take
    advantage of you:
24 Even though his lack of strength keeps him
    from sinning,
    when he finds the opportunity, he will do harm.
25 One can tell a man by his appearance;
    a wise man is known as such when first met.
26 A man's attire, his hearty laughter and his gait,
    proclaim him for what he is.

NRSV

but when no one notices, he will take
    advantage of you.
28 Even if lack of strength keeps him from
    sinning,
    he will nevertheless do evil when he finds
    the opportunity.
29 A person is known by his appearance,
    and a sensible person is known when first
    met, face to face.
30 A person's attire and hearty laughter,
    and the way he walks, show what he is.

COMMENTARY

The reference to the law links this short poem to the preceding one. Ben Sira observes that wisdom can be both positive and negative, hence one who fears God is better than a shrewd sinner. Such a statement in a Hellenistic context invited mockery, given the Greek emphasis on intelligence. Earlier Jewish tradition illustrates the evil potential of knowledge—e.g., the serpent's craftiness in Gen 3:1 and Jonadab's clever but unscrupulous use of intelligence to enable Amnon to seduce his sister (2 Sam 13:3). In this brief section, Ben Sira unites the two fundamental themes of the book: wisdom and the fear of the Lord.

The insights in vv. 26-28 reveal profound psychological awareness; the outward demeanor of an unscrupulous person masks an inner hostility awaiting a chance to express itself openly, and the juxtaposition of competing claims about judging someone by external appearance. Although Ben Sira realizes that appearances can deceive, he insists that one can know another person by examining three things: clothing, laughter, and gait. Whoever maintains this cautious realism refuses to give up on the necessary task of making judgments about the character of those with whom one comes into contact. Some books *can* be judged by their covers, as everyone knows all too well.

SIRACH 20:1-31, ON SPEECH AND SILENCE

NAB

20 An admonition can be inopportune,
    and a man may be wise to hold his peace.
2 It is much better to admonish than to lose
    one's temper,
    for one who admits his fault will be kept
    from disgrace.
3 Like a eunuch lusting for intimacy with a
    maiden
    is he who does right under compulsion.

20, 2b: *mē ḥesed* for *mē ḥôser* (=*apo elattoseōs*).
20, 3: Cf Heb 30, 20c.b.: *kᵉne ü ëmān* (*lān*).

NRSV

20 There is a rebuke that is untimely,
    and there is the person who is wise
    enough to keep silent.
2 How much better it is to rebuke than to fume!
3 And the one who admits his fault will be kept
    from failure.
4 Like a eunuch lusting to violate a girl
    is the person who does right under
    compulsion.
5 Some people keep silent and are thought to be
    wise,
    while others are detested for being talkative.

NAB

4 One man is silent and is thought wise,
   another is talkative and is disliked.

5 One man is silent because he has nothing to
   say;
   another is silent, biding his time.

6 A wise man is silent till the right time comes,
   but a boasting fool ignores the proper time.

7 He who talks too much is detested;
   he who pretends to authority is hated.

8 Some misfortunes bring success;
   some things gained are a man's loss.

9 Some gifts do one no good,
   and some must be paid back double.

10 Humiliation can follow fame,
   while from obscurity a man can lift up his
   head.

11 A man may buy much for little,
   but pay for it seven times over.

12 A wise man makes himself popular by a few
   words,
   but fools pour forth their blandishments in
   vain.

13 A gift from a rogue will do you no good,
   for in his eyes his one gift is equal to seven.

14 He gives little and criticizes often,
   and like a crier he shouts aloud.
   He lends today, he asks it back tomorrow;
   hateful indeed is such a man.

15 A fool has no friends,
   nor thanks for his generosity;

16 Those who eat his bread have an evil
   tongue.
   How many times they laugh him to scorn!

17 A fall to the ground is less sudden than a
   slip of the tongue;
   that is why the downfall of the wicked
   comes so quickly.

18 Insipid food is the untimely tale;
   the unruly are always ready to offer it.

19 A proverb when spoken by a fool is
   unwelcome,
   for he does not utter it at the proper time.

NRSV

6 Some people keep silent because they have
   nothing to say,
   while others keep silent because they know
   when to speak.

7 The wise remain silent until the right moment,
   but a boasting fool misses the right moment.

8 Whoever talks too much is detested,
   and whoever pretends to authority is hated.[a]

9 There may be good fortune for a person in
   adversity,
   and a windfall may result in a loss.

10 There is the gift that profits you nothing,
   and the gift to be paid back double.

11 There are losses for the sake of glory,
   and there are some who have raised their
   heads from humble circumstances.

12 Some buy much for little,
   but pay for it seven times over.

13 The wise make themselves beloved by only
   few words,[b]
   but the courtesies of fools are wasted.

14 A fool's gift will profit you nothing,[c]
   for he looks for recompense sevenfold.[d]

15 He gives little and upbraids much;
   he opens his mouth like a town crier.
   Today he lends and tomorrow he asks it back;
   such a one is hateful to God and humans.[e]

16 The fool says, "I have no friends,
   and I get no thanks for my good deeds.
   Those who eat my bread are evil-tongued."

17 How many will ridicule him, and how often![f]

18 A slip on the pavement is better than a slip of
   the tongue;
   the downfall of the wicked will occur just
   as speedily.

19 A coarse person is like an inappropriate story,
   continually on the lips of the ignorant.

20 A proverb from a fool's lips will be rejected,
   for he does not tell it at the proper time.

21 One may be prevented from sinning by poverty;

20, 4b: *w eyēš (nim' ās) b*e*rôb (sîaḥ)*: so LXX, P.
20, 12: *ḥākām bim*e*' aṭ (en oligois* for *en logǭ) napšó ya' aḥíb,
w*e*ṭôbot k*e*sîlîm yiššap*e*kû ḥinnām.*
20, 13b: *kî b*e*' ênāyw ' aḥat taḥat šeba'* (?): cf P, V.
20, 15-16a: With V; cf LXX^MSS.
20, 18a: *' alyâ b*e*lō' melaḥ millâ b*e*lō' ' ēt:* cf P.

*a*Other ancient authorities add *How good it is to show repentance
when you are reproved, for so you will escape deliberate sin!*
*b*Heb: Gk *by words*   *c*Other ancient authorities add *so it is with
the envious who give under compulsion*   *d*Syr: Gk *he has many
eyes instead of one*   *e*Other ancient authorities lack *to God and
humans*   *f*Other ancient authorities add *for he has not honestly
received what he has, and what he does not have is unimportant
to him*

NAB

20 A man through want may be unable to sin,
  yet in this tranquility he cannot rest.
21 One may lose his life through shame,
  and perish through a fool's intimidation.
22 A man makes a promise to a friend out of
  shame,
  and has him for his enemy needlessly.
23 A lie is a foul blot in a man,
  yet it is constantly on the lips of the unruly.
24 Better a thief than an inveterate liar,
  yet both will suffer disgrace;
25 A liar's way leads to dishonor,
  his shame remains ever with him.
26 A wise man advances himself by his words,
  a prudent man pleases the great.
27 He who works his land has abundant crops,
  he who pleases the great is pardoned his
  faults.
28 Favors and gifts blind the eyes;
  like a muzzle over the mouth they silence
  reproof.
29 Hidden wisdom and unseen treasure—
  of what value is either?
30 Better the man who hides his folly
  than the one who hides his wisdom.

20, 28a: Omit *sophōn*: so P.
20, 30f: In Heb (MS B) after 41, 13.

NRSV

so when he rests he feels no remorse.
22 One may lose his life through shame,
  or lose it because of human respect.*ᵃ*
23 Another out of shame makes promises to a
  friend,
  and so makes an enemy for nothing.

24 A lie is an ugly blot on a person;
  it is continually on the lips of the ignorant.
25 A thief is preferable to a habitual liar,
  but the lot of both is ruin.
26 A liar's way leads to disgrace,
  and his shame is ever with him.

27 The wise person advances himself by his
  words,
  and one who is sensible pleases the great.
28 Those who cultivate the soil heap up their
  harvest,
  and those who please the great atone for
  injustice.
29 Favors and gifts blind the eyes of the wise;
  like a muzzle on the mouth they stop
  reproofs.
30 Hidden wisdom and unseen treasure,
  of what value is either?
31 Better are those who hide their folly
  than those who hide their wisdom.*ᵇ*

*ᵍ*Other ancient authorities read *his foolish look*   *ʰ*Other ancient authorities add ³²*Unwearied endurance in seeking the Lord is better than a masterless charioteer of one's own life.*

COMMENTARY

Random sayings comprise this unit, often juxtaposing an idea and its "opposite" in the two bicola. The central issue, the right use of speech, stands over against appropriate and inappropriate, or misleading, silence, on the one hand, and lying, on the other hand. The paradoxical circumstances involving speaking and refraining from talk lead to a discussion of paradoxes in general. The Greek heading, "Proverbial Sayings," before v. 27 indicates that an ancient scribe divided this section differently from that suggested here.

20:1-8. The sages in Israel and Egypt spoke often about right speech and silence, the latter

idea serving to characterize a professional sage, among others, in Egypt as "the silent one." Egyptian instructions develop a concept of rhetoric to serve as an ideal for the wise to aspire to in their study, one characterized by timing, restraint, accuracy, and eloquence. Israelite sages, too, recognized the importance of knowing when to speak and when to be silent; they also praised truthfulness and eloquence. These qualities were not limited to the wise, however, for some people possessed an innate gift of eloquence. Nor was this appreciation for silence limited to Israel and Egypt. Alexander Di Lella cites the following extrabiblical aphorisms: "A sage thing is timely silence, and better than any speech" (Plutarch, c. 100 CE); "Let a fool hold his tongue and he will pass for a sage" (Publilius Syrus, 1st cent. BCE); "Let your speech be better than silence, or be silent" (Dionysius the Elder, 4th cent. BCE).[182] Apparently, many thinkers prized silence as golden.

Matters were not quite so simple, as the contrasting sayings in Prov 26:4-5 reveal. In some situations, neither speech nor silence is unambiguous, for responding to a stupid remark bestows more dignity on it than the comment deserves, and failing to answer may appear to indicate ineptness, an inability to offer better counsel than that given by the fool. Ben Sira knows the tradition represented by this attempt to point out the difficulty in interpreting silence, and he acknowledges that refraining from speech does not always demonstrate wisdom. Some people merely have nothing worthwhile to say.

The analogy in v. 4, although graphic, is not entirely clear. Ben Sira pictures a eunuch being overwhelmed by lust for a young woman, passion that by the very nature of his condition will lead the eunuch nowhere. To that scene, Ben Sira compares the attempt to force an individual devoid of moral formation to behave ethically. Lacking inner motivation, the person can make no progress in doing the right thing.

20:9-17. These verses interrupt the discussion of speech and offer some observations on various oddities of existence: an unexpected windfall that costs much more than its value, honorable losses, so-called bargains that actually amount to a drain on one's finances, and a lender who repeatedly demands repayment before its due date. Anyone who has purchased a used automobile at a "good price," only to discover its actual condition and the expense involved in repairing it, can under-

stand Ben Sira's point. His allusion to persons who rose from humble circumstances to positions of power represents a literary topos in the ancient world, as the story about Joseph demonstrates.

20:18-20. The original topic of this unit returns in v. 18; this "better saying" about the greater damage inflicted by slander than by falling down is widespread.[183] The image in the Greek of v. 19 is lost on modern readers who do not realize that the fatty tail of a sheep was considered a delicacy in the ancient Near East. The saying in v. 20 serves as an instance when timing rather than content renders a remark worthless. Everyone who has suffered in silence, only later to think of an appropriate response, appreciates the significance of timing. The observation in v. 21 that absence of sin does not necessarily indicate virtue resembles an Egyptian saying that only a man's purse prevents him from satisfying his insatiable lust.[184]

20:21-26. These verses take up the matter of shame, especially that resulting from misstating the truth. The stakes in honor and shame are high; one's reputation and life hang in the balance. Persons whose humble circumstances evoke embarrassment and cause them to make promises they cannot keep (v. 23) and liars earn the same reputation as a thief. All three suffer disgrace.

20:27-31. The final unit consists of traditional teachings about the scribal profession—the sages will serve rulers (like Daniel, Ahiqar, Mordecai, and Joseph)—and about special temptations they encounter, such as bribes and unpredictable anger. The concluding couplet states that, like hidden treasure, concealed wisdom is worthless and that hiding one's ignorance is superior to hiding one's intelligence.

---

182. Patrick W. Skehan and Alexander A. Di Lella, *The Wisdom of Ben Sira,* AB 39 (New York: Doubleday, 1987) 300-301.

183. Cf. Zeno's remark, "Better to slip with the foot than with the tongue." Cited in Diogenes Laërtius *Lives and Opinions of Eminent Phyilosophers* vii.26.

184. "Man is more eager to copulate than a donkey; his purse is what restrains him" (*Ankhsheshanky* 24:10).

SIRACH 21:1-10, SIN'S SMOOTH PATH

NAB

21 My son, if you have sinned, do so no more,
and for your past sins pray to be forgiven.
2 Flee from sin as from a serpent
that will bite you if you go near it;
Its teeth are lion's teeth,
destroying the souls of men.
3 Every offense is a two-edged sword;
when it cuts, there can be no healing.
4 Violence and arrogance wipe out wealth;
so too a proud man's home is destroyed.
5 Prayer from a poor man's lips is heard at once,
and justice is quickly granted him.
6 He who hates correction walks the sinner's
path,
but he who fears the Lord repents in his
heart.
7 Widely known is the boastful speaker,
but the wise man knows his own faults.
8 He who builds his house with another's
money
is collecting stones for his funeral mound.
9 A band of criminals is like a bundle of tow;
they will end in a flaming fire.
10 The path of sinners is smooth stones
that end in the depths of the nether world.

21, 5a: *l*^{e} *'oznê yhwh* for *l*^{e} *'oznāyw* (= '*eōs ōtiōn autou*).

NRSV

21 Have you sinned, my child? Do so no
more,
but ask forgiveness for your past sins.
2 Flee from sin as from a snake;
for if you approach sin, it will bite you.
Its teeth are lion's teeth,
and can destroy human lives.
3 All lawlessness is like a two-edged sword;
there is no healing for the wound it inflicts.

4 Panic and insolence will waste away riches;
thus the house of the proud will be laid
waste.^{a}
5 The prayer of the poor goes from their lips to
the ears of God,^{b}
and his judgment comes speedily.
6 Those who hate reproof walk in the sinner's
steps,
but those who fear the Lord repent in their
heart.
7 The mighty in speech are widely known;
when they slip, the sensible person knows
it.

8 Whoever builds his house with other people's
money
is like one who gathers stones for his burial
mound.^{c}
9 An assembly of the wicked is like a bundle of
tow,
and their end is a blazing fire.
10 The way of sinners is paved with smooth
stones,
but at its end is the pit of Hades.

^{a}Other ancient authorities read *uprooted* ^{b}Gk *his ears*
^{c}Other ancient authorities read *for the winter*

COMMENTARY

Three images conjure up the horror of sinful action for Ben Sira's audience, here addressed as "my child." They consist of two threats from the realm of nature—the serpent's bite (cf. Gen 3:1-5; Prov 23:32, which likens the sting of strong drink to that of a snake) and a lion's teeth (cf. 27:10

and Joel 1:6 for the same language)—and one threat from the human domain—a dreaded two-edged sword in the agile hands of someone bent on destruction.

The allusion to the prayer of the poor in v. 5 demonstrates Ben Sira's positive attitude toward

God's rule of the world. As affirmed in ancient religious tradition, God hears the cries of persons in need; the doubts expressed in the book of Job and in Ecclesiastes have not dampened Ben Sira's spirit in the least. The point of v. 8 varies with the manuscript traditions; the Septuagint has "for the winter" (εἰς χειμῶνα *eis cheimōna*), whereas the important MS 248 has "for a tomb" (εἰς χῶμα *eis chōma*). The former implies that one gathers stones instead of wood in preparation for cold weather; the latter reading may suggest that payment on the loan becomes due before the burial mound is complete. The audial pun in v. 9 in the Greek, "a bundle of tow is like a band of lawless ones" (στιππύον συνηγμένον συναγωγὴ ἀνόμων *stippuon synēgmenon synagōgē anomōn*) and the probable reference to techniques employed by the later Romans in the construction of roads in v. 10 bring this brief unit to a close.

REFLECTIONS

In 1 Pet 5:8 the description of the devil evokes all three of the horrors cited in Sir 21:2-3 by combining the old notion of the serpent with that of Satan who resembles a raging lion ready to devour, the usual language for the sword's activity in the OT.

SIRACH 21:11–22:18, THE WISE AND THE FOOLISH

NAB	NRSV
11 He who keeps the law controls his impulses; he who is perfect in fear of the LORD has wisdom.	11 Whoever keeps the law controls his thoughts, and the fulfillment of the fear of the Lord is wisdom.
12 He can never be taught who is not shrewd, but one form of shrewdness is thoroughly bitter.	12 The one who is not clever cannot be taught, but there is a cleverness that increases bitterness.
13 A wise man's knowledge wells up in a flood, and his counsel, like a living spring;	13 The knowledge of the wise will increase like a flood, and their counsel like a life-giving spring.
14 A fool's mind is like a broken jar— no knowledge at all can it hold.	14 The mind*a* of a fool is like a broken jar; it can hold no knowledge.
15 When an intelligent man hears words of wisdom, he approves them and adds to them; The wanton hears them with scorn and casts them behind his back.	15 When an intelligent person hears a wise saying, he praises it and adds to it; when a fool*b* hears it, he laughs at*c* it and throws it behind his back.
16 A fool's chatter is like a load on a journey, but there is charm to be found upon the lips of the wise.	16 A fool's chatter is like a burden on a journey, but delight is found in the speech of the intelligent.
17 The views of a prudent man are sought in an assembly, and his words are considered with care.	17 The utterance of a sensible person is sought in the assembly, and they ponder his words in their minds.
18 Like a house in ruins is wisdom to a fool;	

21, 15c: (*kai*) *epēreasen* (*autō*): so P.
21, 17b: *dianoēthēsontai*: so LXX[S, A, C].

*a*Syr Lat: Gk *entrails*   *b*Syr: Gk *reveler*   *c*Syr: Gk *dislikes*

NAB

the stupid man knows it only as
inscrutable words.
19 Like fetters on the legs is learning to a fool,
like a manacle on his right hand.
20 A fool raises his voice in laughter,
but a prudent man at the most smiles
gently.
21 Like a chain of gold is learning to a wise
man,
like a bracelet on his right arm.

22 The fool steps boldly into a house,
while the well-bred man remains outside;
23 A boor peeps through the doorway of a
house,
but a cultured man keeps his glance cast
down.
24 It is rude for one to listen at a door;
a cultured man would be overwhelmed by
the disgrace of it.
25 The lips of the impious talk of what is not
their concern,
but the words of the prudent are carefully
weighed.
26 Fools' thoughts are in their mouths,
wise men's words are in their hearts.
27 When a godless man curses his adversary,
he really curses himself.
28 A slanderer besmirches himself,
and is hated by his neighbors.

22 The sluggard is like a stone in the mud;
everyone hisses at his disgrace.
2 The sluggard is like a lump of dung;
whoever touches him wipes his hands.
3 An unruly child is a disgrace to its father;
if it be a daughter, she brings him to
poverty.
4 A thoughtful daughter becomes a treasure to
her husband,
a shameless one is her father's grief.
5 A hussy shames her father and her husband;
by both she is despised.
6 Like a song in time of mourning is
inopportune talk,

21, 22b.23b: Trsp *regel nābāl mᵉhērâ ʾel bāyit wᵉʾîš nôsār bahûṣ yaʿămod; ʾĕwîl mippetaḥ yabbîṭ ʾel bāyit, wᵉʾîš mᵉzimmôt yaknîaʿ pānîm;* cf Heb as quoted in *pirqāʾ dᵉrabbēnû haqqādôš* (JQR 1891, p. 695).

NRSV

18 Like a house in ruins is wisdom to a fool,
and to the ignorant, knowledge is talk that
has no meaning.
19 To a senseless person education is fetters on
his feet,
and like manacles on his right hand.
20 A fool raises his voice when he laughs,
but the wise[a] smile quietly.
21 To the sensible person education is like a
golden ornament,
and like a bracelet on the right arm.

22 The foot of a fool rushes into a house,
but an experienced person waits respectfully
outside.
23 A boor peers into the house from the door,
but a cultivated person remains outside.
24 It is ill-mannered for a person to listen at a
door;
the discreet would be grieved by the
disgrace.

25 The lips of babblers speak of what is not their
concern,[b]
but the words of the prudent are weighed
in the balance.
26 The mind of fools is in their mouth,
but the mouth of the wise is in[c] their mind.
27 When an ungodly person curses an adversary,[d]
he curses himself.
28 A whisperer degrades himself
and is hated in his neighborhood.

22 The idler is like a filthy stone,
and every one hisses at his disgrace.
2 The idler is like the filth of dunghills;
anyone that picks it up will shake it off his
hand.

3 It is a disgrace to be the father of an
undisciplined son,
and the birth of a daughter is a loss.
4 A sensible daughter obtains a husband of her
own,
but one who acts shamefully is a grief to
her father.

[a] Syr Lat: Gk *clever* [b] Other ancient authorities read *of strangers speak of these things* [c] Other ancient authorities omit *in* [d] Or *curses Satan*

NAB

but lashes and discipline are at all times
wisdom.

7 Teaching a fool is like gluing a broken pot,
or like disturbing a man in the depths of
sleep;

8 He talks with a slumberer who talks with a
fool,
for when it is over, he will say, "What was
that?"

9 Weep over the dead man, for his light has
gone out;
weep over the fool, for sense has left him.

10 Weep but a little over the dead man, for he
is at rest;
but worse than death is the life of a fool.

11 Seven days of mourning for the dead,
but for the wicked fool a whole lifetime.

12 Speak but seldom with the stupid man,
be not the companion of a brute;

13 Beware of him lest you have trouble
and be spattered when he shakes himself;
Turn away from him and you will find rest
and not be wearied by his lack of sense.

14 What is heavier than lead,
and what is its name but "Fool"?

15 Sand and salt and an iron mass
are easier to bear than a stupid man.

16 Masonry bonded with wooden beams
is not loosened by an earthquake;
Neither is a resolve constructed with careful
deliberation
shaken in a moment of fear.

17 A resolve that is backed by prudent
understanding
is like the polished surface of a smooth
wall.

18 Small stones lying on an open height
will not remain when the wind blows;
Neither can a timid resolve based on foolish
plans
withstand fear of any kind.

21, 25a: *śiptê zēdîm* (for *zārîm=allotriōn*) *lōʾ lāhem* (=*ta ouk autōn*:
LXX^{MSS}; for *bᵉʾ ēlleh*=LXX^B) *yāśîḥû* (=*diēgēsontai*: LXX^S, P, V).

NRSV

5 An impudent daughter disgraces father and
husband,
and is despised by both.

6 Like music in time of mourning is ill-timed
conversation,
but a thrashing and discipline are at all times
wisdom.[a]

9 Whoever teaches a fool is like one who glues
potsherds together,
or who rouses a sleeper from deep slumber.

10 Whoever tells a story to a fool tells it to a
drowsy man;
and at the end he will say, "What is it?"

11 Weep for the dead, for he has left the light
behind;
and weep for the fool, for he has left
intelligence behind.
Weep less bitterly for the dead, for he is at
rest;
but the life of the fool is worse than death.

12 Mourning for the dead lasts seven days,
but for the foolish or the ungodly it lasts all
the days of their lives.

13 Do not talk much with a senseless person
or visit an unintelligent person.[b]
Stay clear of him, or you may have trouble,
and be spattered when he shakes himself off.
Avoid him and you will find rest,
and you will never be wearied by his lack
of sense.

14 What is heavier than lead?
And what is its name except "Fool"?

15 Sand, salt, and a piece of iron
are easier to bear than a stupid person.

16 A wooden beam firmly bonded into a building
is not loosened by an earthquake;
so the mind firmly resolved after due reflection
will not be afraid in a crisis.

17 A mind settled on an intelligent thought
is like stucco decoration that makes a wall
smooth.

[a]Other ancient authorities add 7 Children who are brought up in a
good life, conceal the lowly birth of their parents. 8 Children who
are disdainfully and boorishly haughty stain the nobility of their kindred.   [b]Other ancient authorities add For being without sense
he will despise everything about you

NRSV

18 Fences*a* set on a high place
   will not stand firm against the wind;
so a timid mind with a fool's resolve
   will not stand firm against any fear.

*a*Other ancient authorities read *Pebbles*

COMMENTARY

21:11–22:2. Ancient sages never tired of drawing a sharp contrast between themselves and ignorant ruffians, whom they called fools. One decisive difference between the two groups concerned the value of education.[185] Because they failed to appreciate the worth of knowledge, fools were impossible to educate, information entering their minds and flowing right through into oblivion. The wise place a value on education like ornaments worn by royalty (v. 21); when they learn something, they promptly add to it (v. 15). Here Ben Sira recognizes the importance of preserving the tradition intact, but he balances that idea with the necessity of contributing to the fund of knowledge. Mere retention of ancestral tradition did not make one wise; that instruction from the past had to be thoroughly adapted to new conditions and to personal experience.

Verse 12 recalls the earlier distinction between wisdom and shrewdness, and v. 13 introduces an image that Ben Sira will use again to signify his own effort to write a second volume of instruction (24:30-34). The same symbolism, knowledge as a mighty stream and a life-giving spring, occurs in *Pirqe 'Abot* 6:1, where one who studies Torah for its own sake is described in this way.[186]

This entire unit characterizes fools more fully than wise persons. Fools hear sensible remarks and toss them aside, behave in altogether uncivilized ways, inspire hatred, resent discipline, and babble incessantly. Ben Sira compares their idle chatter to a heavy burden on a journey (v. 14).

The harsh criticism of sluggards within the book of Proverbs continues in 22:1-2, where Ben Sira uses a coarse image to describe them, that of a smooth rock used in the ancient world after a bowel movement.

22:3-6. Here Ben Sira utters one of his most misogynistic statements;[187] his opinion, regrettably, was shared by many at the time.[188] Precisely what inspired the observation that "the birth of a daughter is a loss" can only be surmised, although the context may suggest that he had in mind the difficulty and cost involved in obtaining a suitable husband for her. Elsewhere his comments about daughters imply suspicion about their morals and show that he did not think highly of them—at least not of a certain kind of daughter. One can see how such an opinion of girls would fit nicely into a society that exposes infant daughters to the elements in order for them to die. Echoes of this horrible practice occur within the OT.[189] In its liturgical practice, later Judaism continued this negative attitude toward women. A daily prayer, recommended for all men, stated: "Blessed are you, O Lord our God, King of the Universe, who have not made me a woman," and every man was urged to thank God daily for not making him a woman or a slave.[190] This sentiment reflects the numerous regulations in Jewish law strictly regulating the life of a woman.[191]

185. The HB has preserved minimal information pertinent to ancient formal education, but that has not prevented extravagant claims about schools throughout the land. For cautious assessments of the evidence, see James L. Crenshaw, "Education in Ancient Israel," *JBL* 104 (1985) 601-15, and a forthcoming volume in the Anchor Bible Reference Library, entitled *Across the Deafening Silence: Education in Ancient Israel;* and Stuart Weeks, *Early Israelite Wisdom,* OTM (Oxford: Clarendon, 1994) 132-56.

186. Cf. also 1QH 8:4-15.

187. Warren C. Trenchard, *Ben Sira's View of Women: A Literary Analysis,* BJS 38 (Chico, Calif.: Scholars Press, 1982), has discussed misogynistic elements in the book, without tempering his criticism in the light of the ancient context.

188. C. E. Carlston, "Proverbs, Maxims, and the Historical Jesus," *JBL* 99 (1980) 87-105.

189. The most obvious instance concerns the old story about Yahweh's discovery of an infant girl in the wilderness and nurturing the child until she had reached a marriageable age, at which time the Lord married her (Ezek 16:1-14). The theological point, God's choice of Israel when it had done nothing to deserve it, turns on Israel's existence as an infant that someone had cast out to die.

190. *Menaḥot* 43*b.*

191. One whole division (out of six) in the Mishnah is devoted to "women."

22:9-15. Ben Sira uses strong images to describe fools in these verses. Teaching them is futile, like gluing the pieces of a broken pot together or communicating with a sleepy person. Long experience with dull students probably taught Ben Sira the accuracy of this analogy; the slow student simply misses the point as if half asleep. No wonder Ben Sira recommends perpetual tears for such fools, as opposed to the more usual seven-day mourning for the dead. The image in v. 13 moves one step further than that of fools as the ancient equivalent of toilet paper. Here they shake themselves like pigs (the Hebrew original probably had "dogs") and spread their filth on all bystanders. The comparison of debt and a foreigner to a heavy load occurs also in *Ahiqar.*[192]

22:16-18. The closing unit praises intelligence as both strong and beautiful. The final thought, that fences (or pebbles) cannot withstand a strong wind, may allude to the practice of placing small rocks on a wall enclosing a vineyard or garden so that when a jackal or a fox invaded a garden, the animal would knock them off and alert the farmer. This entire section, 21:11–22:18, is remarkably free of religious teaching, except for the opening verse.

192. See Sayings 29 and 30 in James M. Lindenberger, *The Aramaic Proverbs of Ahiqar* (Baltimore: Johns Hopkins University Press, 1983) 98-99.

REFLECTIONS

Just as Ben Sira's understanding of women reflected a society in which women were born under a curse, so also some modern views of women relegate them to secondary status. The present disparity in pay between women and men, where it still exists, results from various economic factors, chief of which is the understanding of men as providers for families. The subtle shifting of women to lower-paying jobs and assessing them by standards that more appropriately apply to men place women in a disadvantaged position. Pregnancy and its attendant obligations make it more difficult for females to advance in their workplace. Differences in women's temperament and style strike many males as signs of inferiority or lack of motivation. All this and more fuels misogynistic and chauvinistic sentiments today.

For anyone who values human worth and believes such attitudes should vanish like dinosaurs, one can think of no challenge that, if successfully met, offers more reward. First, men can finally begin to treat women in the same revolutionary manner Jesus did. Second, men can start to learn from women in more ways than imaginable, even if it means radically questioning the very foundations of modern society. Third, women can be elevated to senior leadership roles within the church and its ministry. This move alone holds the potential for revolutionizing the devotional life of God's people.

SIRACH 22:19-26, PRESERVING FRIENDSHIP

NAB	NRSV

19 One who jabs the eye brings tears:
    he who pierces the heart bares its feelings.
 20 He who throws stones at birds drives them away,
    and he who insults a friend breaks up the friendship.
 21 Should you draw a sword against a friend,
    despair not, it can be undone.
	[19] One who pricks the eye brings tears,
	    and one who pricks the heart makes clear its feelings.
	 [20] One who throws a stone at birds scares them away,
	    and one who reviles a friend destroys a friendship.
	 [21] Even if you draw your sword against a friend,

NAB

22 Should you speak sharply to a friend,
   fear not, you can be reconciled.
 But a contemptuous insult, a confidence
   broken,
   or a treacherous attack will drive away any
   friend.

23 Make fast friends with a man while he is
   poor;
   thus will you enjoy his prosperity with
   him.
 In time of trouble remain true to him,
   so as to share in his inheritance when it
   comes.
24 Before flames burst forth an oven smokes;
   so does abuse come before bloodshed.
25 From a friend in need of support
   no one need hide in shame;
26 But from him who brings harm to his friend
   all will stand aloof who hear of it.

22, 22c—23, 9: With LXX; but for Heb cf JQR 1921, pp 238ff.

NRSV

   do not despair, for there is a way back.
22 If you open your mouth against your friend,
   do not worry, for reconciliation is possible.
 But as for reviling, arrogance, disclosure of
   secrets, or a treacherous blow—
   in these cases any friend will take to flight.

23 Gain the trust of your neighbor in his poverty,
   so that you may rejoice with him in his
   prosperity.
 Stand by him in time of distress,
   so that you may share with him in his
   inheritance.[a]
24 The vapor and smoke of the furnace precede
   the fire;
   so insults precede bloodshed.
25 I am not ashamed to shelter a friend,
   and I will not hide from him.
26 But if harm should come to me because of
   him,
   whoever hears of it will beware of him.

[a]Other ancient authorities add *For one should not always despise
restricted circumstances, or admire a rich person who is stupid.*

COMMENTARY

In this short section, Ben Sira returns to the topic of friendship (cf. 6:5-17) and comments on the remarkable resiliency of affections. He understands that the severe strain produced by personal insults can cause genuine friendships to snap. Two clear images for inflicting pain and driving friends away—jabbing one's eye and, by analogy, throwing a rock at birds—draw attention to the harm caused by hurtful words. Nevertheless, he believes the constancy of genuine friendship can stand serious offenses such as threatened physical violence and verbal abuse. Ben Sira does not recommend that one count on this strong bond in all instances of abuse because some things (e.g., divulging secrets and treachery) will drive any friend away.

The test of true friendship comes when one cannot do anything to help those befriending him or her. Ben Sira advises his readers to begin a friendship with someone in difficult circumstances and then take pleasure when that person's financial situation improves. The closing observation in the first-person pledges personal loyalty—in the context of a veiled threat, should harm befall the speaker. That is, others will avoid the person who caused the injury, for they will know that he or she cannot be trusted.

SIRACH 22:27–23:6, A PRAYER FOR SELF-CONTROL

NAB

27 Who will set a guard over my mouth,
   and upon my lips an effective seal,
That I may not fail through them,
   that my tongue may not destroy me?

23 LORD, Father and Master of my life,
   permit me not to fall by them!
2 Who will apply the lash to my thoughts,
   to my mind the rod of discipline,
That my failings may not be spared,
   nor the sins of my heart overlooked;
3 Lest my failings increase,
   and my sins be multiplied;
Lest I succumb to my foes,
   and my enemy rejoice over me?
4 LORD, Father and God of my life,
   abandon me not into their control!
5 A brazen look allow me not;
   ward off passion from my heart,
6 Let not the lustful cravings of the flesh master
      me,
   surrender me not to shameless desires.

22, 27c: (ap) autōn: so V; cf P.
23, 1: Trsp mē egkatalipēs . . . autōn after v 4a: cf P, V.
23, 2b: šēbeṭ mûsar for paideian sophias: so P.

NRSV

27 Who will set a guard over my mouth,
   and an effective seal upon my lips,
so that I may not fall because of them,
   and my tongue may not destroy me?

23 O Lord, Father and Master of my life,
   do not abandon me to their designs,
   and do not let me fall because of them!
2 Who will set whips over my thoughts,
   and the discipline of wisdom over my mind,
so as not to spare me in my errors,
   and not overlook my[a] sins?
3 Otherwise my mistakes may be multiplied,
   and my sins may abound,
and I may fall before my adversaries,
   and my enemy may rejoice over me.[b]
4 O Lord, Father and God of my life,
   do not give me haughty eyes,
5 and remove evil desire from me.
6 Let neither gluttony nor lust overcome me,
   and do not give me over to shameless
      passion.

[a]Gk their   [b]Other ancient authorities add From them the hope
of your mercy is remote

COMMENTARY

This moving prayer[193] for control over wrongful speech and carnal lust introduces the two following units, 23:7-15, 16-26. The final verse (v. 27) sums up this section and, indeed, everything up to this point in the book. Other prayers appear in 36:1-13a, 16-22; 51:1-12.

The opening request for a sentry to be perched on the speaker's lips uses a Hebraic expression, מי יתן (mî yittēn, lit., "who will set?"). Ben Sira's

193. For a discussion of prayer in Ben Sira and the rest of wisdom literature, see James L. Crenshaw, "The Restraint of Reason, the Humility of Prayer," forthcoming in Origins: Early Israel and Christianity in Historical and Ecumenical Perspectives, eds. W. G. Dever and J. Edward Wright, BJS (Brown University, 1994). See also James L. Crenshaw, Urgent Advice and Probing Questions (Macon, Ga.: Mercer University Press, 1995) 206-21.

double request for a sentry and a seal demonstrates the urgency of the need. Anyone with this much protection would not fall into sin through speech. The image of a guard for one's mouth also occurs in Ps 141:3 and Ahiqar 14b-15. In Sir 28:24-26, Ben Sira extends the image considerably, recommending a door and a bolt for the mouth and balances and scales for words.

The threefold address to God in 23:1 includes the tetragrammaton (YHWH), Father, and Master of my life. The OT refers to God as Father of the nation of Israel (1 Chr 29:10; Isa 63:16; Mal 2:10). Ben Sira personalizes that form of address (23:1, 4; 51:1, 10). The third epithet, "Master of my life," gives way to "God of my life" in v. 4.

The expression "our Father, our King" (אבינו מלכנו) 'ābînû malkēnû) became popular in Jewish prayers, for the twin ideas cover the immediacy of parental love and the sovereignty of a transcendent ruler of the universe.

The abrupt reference to "their designs" in 23:1 without a clear antecedent prompted W. O. E. Oesterley to rearrange the prayer in the following sequence:

27   . . . and that my tongue destroy me not,
2   O that scourges were set over my thoughts . . .
3   that mine ignorance be not multiplied . . .
4   O Lord, Father, and God of my life,
1   Abandon me not to their counsel,
      Suffer me not to fall by them.
5   Give me not a proud look,
      and turn away concupiscence from me.[194]

194. W. O. E. Oesterley, *The Wisdom of Jesus the Son of Sirach or Ecclesiasticus* (Cambridge: Cambridge University Press, 1912) 150-51.

The manuscript evidence indicates considerable disarray, with the Syriac and the Vg reading v. 1 *b* after v. 4 *a*. The rearrangement is not necessary, for Hebrew poetry often introduces unanticipated pronouns for which the reader must supply an appropriate antecedent.

Verse 2 asks for whips to subject thoughts to their control. Thus doubly protected—from sins of the tongue and from thought—Ben Sira can avoid becoming the object of ridicule. The prayer now takes up one further danger, which might result from success in avoiding sins of speech and thought. He asks for protection from "giant-like eyes," pride; for good measure, he repeats the request for power over sinful lust.

SIRACH 23:7-15, THE PROPER USE OF LANGUAGE

NAB	NRSV
7 Give heed, my children, to the instruction that I pronounce, for he who keeps it will not be enslaved.	7 Listen, my children, to instruction concerning the mouth; the one who observes it will never be caught.
8 Through his lips is the sinner ensnared; the railer and the arrogant man fall thereby.	8 Sinners are overtaken through their lips; by them the reviler and the arrogant are tripped up.
9 Let not your mouth form the habit of swearing, or becoming too familiar with the Holy Name.	9 Do not accustom your mouth to oaths, nor habitually utter the name of the Holy One;
10 Just as a slave that is constantly under scrutiny will not be without welts, So one who swears continually by the Holy Name will not remain free from sin.	10 for as a servant who is constantly under scrutiny will not lack bruises, so also the person who always swears and utters the Name will never be cleansed[a] from sin.
11 A man who often swears heaps up obligations; the scourge will never be far from his house. If he swears in error, he incurs guilt; if he neglects his obligation, his sin is doubly great.	11 The one who swears many oaths is full of iniquity, and the scourge will not leave his house. If he swears in error, his sin remains on him, and if he disregards it, he sins doubly;

a Syr *be free*

NAB

If he swears without reason he cannot be
found just,
and all his house will suffer affliction.

12 There are words which merit death;
may they never be heard among Jacob's
heirs.
For all such words are foreign to the devout,
who do not wallow in sin.

13 Let not your mouth become used to coarse
talk,
for in it lies sinful matter.

14 Keep your father and mother in mind
when you sit among the mighty,
Lest in their presence you commit a blunder
and disgrace your upbringing,
By wishing you had never been born
or cursing the day of your birth.

15 A man who has the habit of abusive
language
will never mature in character as long as
he lives.

23, 12: (*estin lexis*) *antiparabeblēmenē*: so LXX^MSS, V.
23, 14b: *synedreueis*: so LXX^Bc,A, V. 14c: *tikkāšēt*: so P, for *tiškah*
(=*epilathę*). 14d: *ûbᵉmusār°kā titnabbāt*: so P.

NRSV

if he swears a false oath, he will not be
justified,
for his house will be filled with calamities.

12 There is a manner of speaking comparable to
death;[a]
may it never be found in the inheritance of
Jacob!
Such conduct will be far from the godly,
and they will not wallow in sins.

13 Do not accustom your mouth to coarse, foul
language,
for it involves sinful speech.

14 Remember your father and mother
when you sit among the great,
or you may forget yourself in their presence,
and behave like a fool through bad habit;
then you will wish that you had never been
born,
and you will curse the day of your birth.

15 Those who are accustomed to using abusive
language
will never become disciplined as long as
they live.

[a]Other ancient authorities read *clothed about with death*

COMMENTARY

This section, which many Greek manuscripts label "Instruction Concerning the Mouth," takes up two types of language that get people into deep trouble, the one religious and the other secular. First, Ben Sira discusses the lavish use of oaths, which constantly place one under divine scrutiny just like a slave who requires close watch. The implication is that continual supervision will inevitably reveal flaws in character that demand punishment. Oath-taking alone includes the danger of swearing unknowingly to a lie, using the divine name loosely, and placing oneself in danger through excessive obligations that reduce one to poverty. Second, the person who habitually uses lewd speech will inadvertently slip into this manner of talking in circumstances where it will bring disgrace. Ben Sira thinks that such foul language does not belong in the Jewish community ("the inheritance of Jacob," v. 12). This expression usually refers to the land in which Israel dwelled.

SIRACH 23:16-27, ON FORNICATION AND ADULTERY

NAB

16 Two types of men multiply sins,
  a third draws down wrath;
For burning passion is a blazing fire,
  not to be quenched till it burns itself out:
A man given to sins of the flesh,
  who never stops until the fire breaks forth;
17 The rake to whom all bread is sweet
  and who is never through till he dies;
18 And the man who dishonors his marriage
    bed
  and says to himself, "Who can see me?
Darkness surrounds me, walls hide me;
  no one sees me; why should I fear to sin?"
Of the Most High he is not mindful,
19 fearing only the eyes of men;
He does not understand that the eyes of the
    LORD,
  ten thousand times brighter than the sun,
Observe every step a man takes
  and peer into hidden corners.
20 He who knows all things before they exist
  still knows them all after they are made.
21 Such a man will be punished in the streets
    of the city;
  when he least expects it, he will be
    apprehended.

22 So also with the woman who is unfaithful
    to her husband
  and offers as heir her son by a stranger.
23 First, she has disobeyed the law of the Most
    High;
  secondly, she has wronged her husband;
Thirdly, in her wanton adultery
  she has borne children by another man.
24 Such a woman will be dragged before the
    assembly,
  and her punishment will extend to her
    children;
25 Her children will not take root;
  her branches will not bring forth fruit.

23, 16f: In Heb after 12, 14a.
23, 18d.e: ʾiš lōʾ yirʾēnî mî yimnāʿēnî mēḥaṭōʾ, lō yizkōr ʿelyôn:
cf P.

NRSV

16 Two kinds of individuals multiply sins,
  and a third incurs wrath.
Hot passion that blazes like a fire
  will not be quenched until it burns itself
    out;
one who commits fornication with his near of
    kin
  will never cease until the fire burns him up.
17 To a fornicator all bread is sweet;
  he will never weary until he dies.
18 The one who sins against his marriage bed
  says to himself, "Who can see me?
Darkness surrounds me, the walls hide me,
  and no one sees me. Why should I worry?
  The Most High will not remember sins."
19 His fear is confined to human eyes
  and he does not realize that the eyes of the
    Lord
  are ten thousand times brighter than the
    sun;
  they look upon every aspect of human
    behavior
  and see into hidden corners.
20 Before the universe was created, it was known
    to him,
  and so it is since its completion.
21 This man will be punished in the streets of the
    city,
  and where he least suspects it, he will be
    seized.

22 So it is with a woman who leaves her husband
  and presents him with an heir by another
    man.
23 For first of all, she has disobeyed the law of
    the Most High;
  second, she has committed an offense
    against her husband;
  and third, through her fornication she has
    committed adultery
  and brought forth children by another man.
24 She herself will be brought before the
    assembly,

NAB

26 She will leave an accursed memory;
    her disgrace will never be blotted out.
27 Thus all who dwell on the earth shall know,
    and all who inhabit the world shall
        understand,
    That nothing is better than the fear of the
        LORD,
    nothing more salutary than to obey his
        commandments.

23, 27: *w^eyāde^e û kol yôš^ebê ʾ āreṣ, w^ehēbînû kol niš[,]ārîm battēbēṭ* so P.

NRSV

    and her punishment will extend to her
        children.
25 Her children will not take root,
    and her branches will not bear fruit.
26 She will leave behind an accursed memory
    and her disgrace will never be blotted out.
27 Those who survive her will recognize
    that nothing is better than the fear of the
        Lord,
    and nothing sweeter than to heed the
        commandments of the Lord.ᵃ

ᵃOther ancient authorities add as verse 28, *It is a great honor to follow God, and to be received by him is long life.*

COMMENTARY

Ben Sira adopts a common form in wisdom literature, the numerical proverb, to describe those who give themselves over to sexual sins of various kinds. Elsewhere he uses numerical sayings in 25:1-2, 7-11; 26:5-6, 28; 50:25-26. They are found often in Proverbs (Prov 6:16-19; 30:15b-16, 18-19, 21-23, 29-31) and Job (Job 5:19-22; 13:20-22; 33:14-15), and are also in prophetic literature (Amos 1:3–2:16) and in Ugaritic texts. Like the book of Amos, Sirach does not list the full quota of sins (three here, four in Amos) but pauses to explore a single offense, carnal lust.

The section sparkles with psychological insight as Ben Sira describes the insatiable hunger of fornicators, to whom all bread is sweet (cf. Prov 9:17, where the seductress calls stolen water "sweet" and bread eaten in secret "pleasant"), and the endless rationalizations for surrendering to the primal urge. The feeble excuses for adultery—no one will ever know, and God is forgetful—do not reckon with an all-seeing deity who knows the future intimately. Ben Sira comes perilously close to stating a doctrine of predestination in v. 20, which conflicts with his earlier stress on free will.

Having dealt with adulterers in the first part of this treatise on carnal lust, Ben Sira moves on to talk about adulteresses. Their crime consists of breaking the divine legislation, betraying a marital relationship, and bringing children into the world where they will not be wanted.[195] This threefold offense, arranged to emphasize a descending order of gravity, also applies to the adulterer, but Ben Sira does not explicitly say so. The punishment of adultery, according to Lev 20:10 and Deut 22:21-22, was death, and Talmudic law continued this punishment, at least theoretically. Verse 24 extends the punishment to children, which suggests that the death penalty was no longer in force at this time.

The last verse uses the adjectives "better" and "sweeter" to suggest that faithful service to Yahweh held far greater appeal than surrendering to one's sexual passions. The key word "survive" provides the clue to Ben Sira's reasoning, for loyalty to the Lord brings life, but surrendering to passions issues in death.

195. Children of an adulterous union could not belong to the congregation of Israel, according to *Qiddushin* 78b.

REFLECTIONS

The appeal of sexual satisfaction, even with inappropriate partners, will always characterize human existence, as it certainly did in Ben Sira's time. The difficult task of remaining monogamous when bombarded with temptation on every hand or of refraining from sex until the right time and place tests one and all. The knowledge among advertisers that sex pays rich dividends and the active role of fantasy leave many people in the grip of a destructive force. Children are particularly vulnerable. Increased mobility and privacy make liaisons with an attractive other both tempting and possible.

In such a volatile environment, how do Christians negotiate the waters of change? Perhaps the story in Genesis 39 of Joseph's resistance to a seductive summons from Potiphar's wife offers a starting point. Joseph's reason for saying no to the attractive offer was first and foremost theological: "How then could I do this great wickedness, and sin against God?" (Gen 39:9 NRSV). Admittedly, such an act as sleeping with Potiphar's wife would have represented betrayal of his master's trust and bed, but Joseph's only stated concern was quite different. He did not want to prove false to his relationship with God. Moreover, the adulterous act also affects the partner, in this instance, Potiphar. And such conduct inevitably takes a heavy toll on the offenders, for it undermines integrity and weakens character. This satisfaction of carnal desire becomes habitual, as Ben Sira perceived, and in the end it depersonalizes everyone involved, turning them into objects of pleasure.

How can the church encourage interaction between women and men while discouraging obsessive fascination with obtaining the forbidden and avoiding an attitude of indifference to sexual mores? The old obsession with sex as *the* sin, which occupied the church for centuries, has done far more harm than can be recounted here, but new guidelines are essential to assist young Christians in the never-ending struggle to deal responsibly with sexual desires.

PART V

OVERVIEW

Beginning with an elaborate poem extolling wisdom's virtues and identifying wisdom with divine revelation to Moses, and thus to Israel, this section of Sirach ends on a comparable note affirming divine providence. Between these lofty religious sentiments lie observations and advice from Ben Sira concerning the inner sanctum of the family and the heart of individual character, integrity. He characterizes despicable people in general, as well as wives—both desirable and undesirable. This leads to a broader discussion of offenses against companions, as well as the important, yet potentially devastating, matter of lending money and providing collateral for persons needing it. Ben Sira gives his views on rearing children, etiquette, and wealth; these topics, although traditional within wisdom literature, take on added significance in the Hellenistic environment, with its quite different customs and values where public dining and commerce were concerned.

SIRACH 24:1-34, THE PRAISE OF WISDOM

NAB	NRSV
24 Wisdom sings her own praises, before her own people she proclaims her glory;	**24** Wisdom praises herself, and tells of her glory in the midst of her people.
2 In the assembly of the Most High she opens her mouth, in the presence of his hosts she declares her worth:	2 In the assembly of the Most High she opens her mouth, and in the presence of his hosts she tells of her glory:
3 "From the mouth of the Most High I came forth, and mistlike covered the earth.	3 "I came forth from the mouth of the Most High, and covered the earth like a mist.
4 In the highest heavens did I dwell, my throne on a pillar of cloud.	4 I dwelt in the highest heavens, and my throne was in a pillar of cloud.
5 The vault of heaven I compassed alone, through the deep abyss I wandered.	5 Alone I compassed the vault of heaven and traversed the depths of the abyss.
6 Over waves of the sea, over all the land, over every people and nation I held sway.	6 Over waves of the sea, over all the earth, and over every people and nation I have held sway.[a]
7 Among all these I sought a resting place; in whose inheritance should I abide?	7 Among all these I sought a resting place; in whose territory should I abide?
8 "Then the Creator of all gave me his command, and he who formed me chose the spot for my tent,	8 "Then the Creator of all things gave me a command,

[a]Other ancient authorities read *I have acquired a possession*

NAB

Saying, 'In Jacob make your dwelling,
in Israel your inheritance.'
9 Before all ages, in the beginning, he created
me,
and through all ages I shall not cease to
be.
10 In the holy tent I ministered before him,
and in Zion I fixed my abode.
11 Thus in the chosen city he has given me
rest,
in Jerusalem is my domain.
12 I have struck root among the glorious
people,
in the portion of the LORD, his heritage.

13 "Like a cedar on Lebanon I am raised aloft,
like a cypress on Mount Hermon,
14 Like a palm tree in Engedi,
like a rosebush in Jericho,
Like a fair olive tree in the field,
like a plane tree growing beside the water.
15 Like cinnamon, or fragrant balm, or precious
myrrh,
I give forth perfume;
Like galbanum and onycha and sweet spices,
like the odor of incense in the holy place.
16 I spread out my branches like a terebinth,
my branches so bright and so graceful.
17 I bud forth delights like the vine,
my blossoms become fruit fair and rich.
18 Come to me, all you that yearn for me,
and be filled with my fruits;
19 You will remember me as sweeter than
honey,
better to have than the honeycomb.
20 He who eats of me will hunger still,
he who drinks of me will thirst for more;
21 He who obeys me will not be put to shame,
he who serves me will never fail."

22 All this is true of the book of the Most
High's covenant,
the law which Moses commanded us
as an inheritance for the community of
Jacob.

24, 14a: (*en*) *Engaddois:* so LXX^MSS, P. 14d: (*hōs platanos*) *eph
hydatos:* so LXX^MSS, P, V.
24, 15: Omit *dedōka osmēn* : so LXX^MSS, P.
24, 22c: *synagōgē* : so P; cf V.

NRSV

and my Creator chose the place for my tent.
He said, 'Make your dwelling in Jacob,
and in Israel receive your inheritance.'
9 Before the ages, in the beginning, he created
me,
and for all the ages I shall not cease to be.
10 In the holy tent I ministered before him,
and so I was established in Zion.
11 Thus in the beloved city he gave me a resting
place,
and in Jerusalem was my domain.
12 I took root in an honored people,
in the portion of the Lord, his heritage.

13 "I grew tall like a cedar in Lebanon,
and like a cypress on the heights of Hermon.
14 I grew tall like a palm tree in En-gedi,[a]
and like rosebushes in Jericho;
like a fair olive tree in the field,
and like a plane tree beside water[b] I grew
tall.
15 Like cassia and camel's thorn I gave forth
perfume,
and like choice myrrh I spread my fragrance,
like galbanum, onycha, and stacte,
and like the odor of incense in the tent.
16 Like a terebinth I spread out my branches,
and my branches are glorious and graceful.
17 Like the vine I bud forth delights,
and my blossoms become glorious and
abundant fruit.[c]

19 "Come to me, you who desire me,
and eat your fill of my fruits.
20 For the memory of me is sweeter than honey,
and the possession of me sweeter than the
honeycomb.
21 Those who eat of me will hunger for more,
and those who drink of me will thirst for
more.
22 Whoever obeys me will not be put to shame,
and those who work with me will not sin."

23 All this is the book of the covenant of the Most
High God,

[a]Other ancient authorities read *on the beaches*   [b]Other ancient
authorities omit *beside water*   [c]Other ancient authorities add as
verse 18, *I am the mother of beautiful love, of fear, of knowledge,
and of holy hope; being eternal, I am given to all my children, to
those who are named by him.*

NAB

23 It overflows, like the Pishon, with
    wisdom—
    like the Tigris in the days of the new fruits.
24 It runs over, like the Euphrates, with
    understanding,
    like the Jordan at harvest time.
25 It sparkles like the Nile with knowledge,
    like the Gihon at vintage time.
26 The first man never finished comprehending
    wisdom,
    nor will the last succeed in fathoming her.
27 For deeper than the sea are her thoughts;
    her counsels, than the great abyss.

28 Now I, like a rivulet from her stream,
    channeling the waters into a garden,
29 Said to myself, "I will water my plants,
    my flower bed I will drench";
    And suddenly this rivulet of mine became a
    river,
    then this stream of mine, a sea.
30 Thus do I send my teachings forth shining
    like the dawn,
    to become known afar off.
31 Thus do I pour out instruction like prophecy
    and bestow it on generations to come.

24, 25: *kay⁵ʾ ôr*: cf P; for *kāʾ ôr=hōs phōs*.
24, 31: Omit *idete hoti . . . ekzētousin autēn*: so P; varians

NRSV

    the law that Moses commanded us
    as an inheritance for the congregations of
    Jacob.ᵃ
25 It overflows, like the Pishon, with wisdom,
    and like the Tigris at the time of the first
    fruits.
26 It runs over, like the Euphrates, with
    understanding,
    and like the Jordan at harvest time.
27 It pours forth instruction like the Nile,ᵇ
    like the Gihon at the time of vintage.
28 The first man did not know wisdomᶜ fully,
    nor will the last one fathom her.
29 For her thoughts are more abundant than the
    sea,
    and her counsel deeper than the great abyss.

30 As for me, I was like a canal from a river,
    like a water channel into a garden.
31 I said, "I will water my garden
    and drench my flower-beds."
    And lo, my canal became a river,
    and my river a sea.
32 I will again make instruction shine forth like
    the dawn,
    and I will make it clear from far away.
33 I will again pour out teaching like prophecy,
    and leave it to all future generations.
34 Observe that I have not labored for myself
    alone,
    but for all who seek wisdom.ᵈ

ᵃOther ancient authorities add as verse 24, *"Do not cease to be
strong in the Lord, cling to him so that he may strengthen you;
the Lord Almighty alone is God, and besides him there is no savior."*   ᵇSyr: Gk *It makes instruction shine forth like light*
ᶜGk *her*   ᵈGk *her*

COMMENTARY

Like the four major parts in the first half of the book, this section—the first of four parts—begins with an elegant poem about wisdom in three stanzas, vv. 3-7, 8-12, 13-17. Most Greek manuscripts have the title "The Praise of Wisdom." An introduction to the poem (vv. 1-2) and a conclusion (vv. 19-22) give this poem the same number of lines as letters in the Hebrew alphabet. An identification of wisdom with the Mosaic law

follows in vv. 23-29, and a personal claim for the author's inspiration from wisdom (vv. 30-34) concludes the chapter. Some interpreters (e.g., John Snaith) see chap. 24 as the conclusion to part one of the book, vv. 30-34 justifying Ben Sira's addition of a second part, chaps. 25–43.[196] In Snaith's view, a similar hymn in 42:15–43:33 concludes

196. John G. Snaith, *Ecclesiasticus or The Wisdom of Jesus, Son of Sirach*, CBC, NEB (Cambridge: Cambridge University Press, 1974) 120.

part two, just as a hymn in 51:13-30 concludes a third part and also the whole book.

The praise of wisdom in vv. 1-22 draws freely on Prov 8:1-36 (cf. Job 28; Prov 1:20-33) for its language and ideas, although similar hymns occur in ancient Egypt, primarily in aretalogies associated with the goddess Isis.[197] These texts recite her virtues or accomplishments in the first person, praising Isis as creator and ruler of the universe. These same ideas appear in Ben Sira's praise of wisdom, but they already characterize her in the biblical precedents.

24:1-2. The introductory speech mentions wisdom's people and the assembly of the hosts of the Most High. The natural way to understand these references places them in a heavenly context; they represent the angelic hosts attending God's court. Nevertheless, "her people" subsequently takes on a special sense, the nation Israel, even if in these verses it connotes heavenly companions.

24:3-7. The initial stanza uses images from the Priestly creation account in Gen 1:1–2:4a and from the Israelite sojourn in the wilderness. That wisdom issues from the divine mouth and settles like a mist on the entire earth accords with the claim that God spoke the world into existence and that the Spirit hovered over the chaotic mass from which order evolved. Wisdom identifies herself as the pillar of cloud mentioned in Exod 13:21-22, accompanying the Israelites and confirming for them God's watchful eye. Picturing the universe as a vault with circumscribed limits, wisdom claims to have walked around its entire area in a creative act. The reference to plumbing the depths of Sheol amounts to an assertion of sovereignty over its citizens.

Verse 7 introduces the subject of the second stanza: wisdom's search for a resting place. Other traditions picture her as unable to find a home on earth, whereas iniquity was successful in its quest for a suitable residence there, settling like rain or dew in the desert (cf. *1 Enoch* 42:1-2). These two attitudes to the hiddenness of wisdom represent the tension between particularism and universalism within the community. The author of *1 Enoch* did not grant any people exclusive access to divine knowledge, but Ben Sira attributes true wisdom to the Jews.

24:8-12. The second stanza identifies wisdom's resting place as Jerusalem and suggests that the favorable location encouraged her to grow deep roots. Wisdom's selection of the inheritance of Jacob resulted from a divine decree, not from some accident of time or place. The universe came into existence through a divine word, and wisdom pitched her tent in Israel because of God's command. The possessive pronoun "my" attached to the word "Creator" links up with the notion in Prov 8:22 that Yahweh created wisdom first of all, and the mention of dwelling in a tent recalls the tabernacle, or tent of meeting, in the wilderness. Verse 10 introduces an entirely new concept: Wisdom ministers before God in the Temple at Zion, the ancient name for the city of David. Ben Sira's priestly interests successfully link wisdom with the daily sacrificial service, something no previous sage had been willing to do.

24:13-17. The idea of wisdom's taking root leads immediately to the theme of the third stanza, which describes her as various trees in the land of Israel: durable and majestic like the cedar of Lebanon or tall as the cypress on Mount Hermon; beautiful as the palm in Engedi or oleanders in Jericho; useful as the ever-present olive; rare as the plane tree; fragrant as trees yielding spices, perfumes, and incense; sprawling like the huge terebinth. The choice of these trees suggests wisdom's omnipresence; she dwells in the mountains to the north and in the valleys and gorges to the south.[198] This sensual imagery concludes with a somewhat different, although related, simile: Wisdom grew like a vine and gave forth abundant clusters of grapes.

Ben Sira's choice of cassia and myrrh relates to their function, when mixed with cinnamon and fragrant cane, in preparing an ointment essential for the ritual involving the sacred ark. Similarly, galbanum (an aromatic, though bitter, gum), mastic (an aromatic resin), and onycha (an extraction from a marine mollusk) in combination with frankincense produced incense for use in the liturgy. Despite the frequent association of the terebinth with idolatrous cults and sacred prosti-

---

197. On these aretalogies—i.e., hymns in praise of a god or goddess (in this instance, the Egyptian Isis)—see Hans Conzelmann, "Die Mutter der Weisheit [Sir 24:3-7]," in *Festschrift Rudolph Bultmann* (Tübingen: J. C. B. Mohr, 1964) 2:225-34.

198. Merism is the use of opposites to express completeness. Thus the merism "mountains and valleys" reinforces the sense of wisdom's omnipresence.

tution (e.g., 1 Kgs 14:23; 2 Kgs 17:10; 18:4; 23:14; Isa 17:8; 27:9; Jer 17:2; Mic 5:13[Eng., 5:14]), Ben Sira dares to incorporate the image of this splendid shade tree into his description of wisdom.

24:18-22. The concluding invitation develops the notion of viticulture and its fruit; wisdom summons everyone to a feast, as in Prov 9:1-6. She offers food and drink that makes one return for more, and she promises protection from shame and its cause, missing the mark. Patrick Skehan thinks this (conjectural!) use of the verb יחטאו (yeḥeṭā'û) and חוטאי (ḥôṭě'î) in Prov 8:36 are the only instances in the Bible where חטא (ḥāṭā') has its original meaning of "missing the mark."[199]

24:23-29. With v. 23, a new section begins, momentarily in third-person *narrative,* descending into prose. Ben Sira makes an astonishing statement: that divine wisdom, here described, is identical to Israel's prize possession, the Mosaic law. In other words, access to wisdom comes through reflection on the divine commandments, no longer through studying nature and human experience as maintained in Proverbs, the book of Job, and Ecclesiastes. To convey the immensity of its coverage, Ben Sira evokes the ancient myth of the four rivers flowing through the garden of Eden. The Mosaic law is inexhaustible, like those rivers, ever spilling over their banks with beneficial gifts to those who depend on water for survival. The Pishon, the Tigris, the Euphrates, the Jordan, the Nile, and the Gihon comprise the major rivers with which the Israelites were acquainted in fact and in fiction. According to Gen 2:10-14, four rivers—Pishon, Gihon, Tigris, and Euphrates—watered the whole land. To these, Ben Sira adds the Jordan and the Nile. He alludes to the effort on the part of Adam and Eve to grasp knowledge, labeling the result of that first initiative partial. Like the first couple, all those who follow will also fail to capture wisdom's full con-

tents. First and last constitute a merism here—i.e., opposite parts of something representing the whole. No one can contain a river, and none can comprehend the full extent of Torah. The ABB'A' symmetry of v. 29 is total:

A her thoughts
  B her counsel;
A' more abundant than the sea
  B' deeper than the great abyss.

24:30-34. The final section constitutes Ben Sira's personal claim to having been moved by prophetic and sapiential inspiration to write his book, which also became a mighty river spilling over its banks. At first he resembled an irrigation canal watering a small garden, but later he became a river and, even greater yet, a sea. No longer a derivative body, he now pours forth original teaching like prophecy for all who desire it. The final verse claims a selfless motive for his labor, a desire to share his insights with others worthy of their contents (cf. 33:18, where this verse is repeated). The idea that teaching as a light occurs with respect to the law in Ps 119:105; Prov 4:18; 6:23. The author of the book of Wisdom understands wisdom as light (Wis 7:26, 29). In Ps 19:10, the law is said to be sweeter than honey and drippings from the honeycomb; wisdom takes over this imagery and applies it to herself in v. 20.

Some of the ideas in this chapter found expression in Judaism generally. The Alexandrian philosopher Philo Judaeus (c. 15 BCE–45 CE) identified wisdom with the pillar of cloud, and *m. Pesiqta* 186*a* states that God offered the law to all nations but only Israel was willing to accept its stipulations.[200] Homiletical use of this imagined refusal to accept the Torah naturally appealed to the moral imperative and a sense of ethnic superiority.

199. Patrick Skehan, "Structures in Poems on Wisdom: Proverbs 8 and Sirach 24," *CBQ* 41 (1979) 378.

200. Cf. the similar comment in the Babylonian Talmud, *Abodah Zara* 2*b*.

REFLECTIONS

Ancient peoples developed authenticating stories (or myths) to confirm their own views, thus functioning primarily within closed walls, and only secondarily as a defense of these views directed to outsiders. Some of these stories reinforced ethnic claims comparable to contemporary slogans, such as "the noble savage," "the prostitute with a heart of gold," "the land of the free and the home of the brave," etc. Ordinarily, these myths arise to counter less than complimentary value judgments. Compared to an intellectually vigorous Greek culture, the religious tradition of Israel, represented by its legal transmitters like Ezra, gave an appearance of mental softness. Particularistic claims flew in the face of Greek universalism, and monotheism seemed pitifully restrictive over against a rich pantheon.

Ben Sira's response to potential, if not actual, mockery anchors Jewish ethnicity in a universal context. The Creator of the cosmos chose provincial Judah as the appropriate location for divine instructions in right living, a law that applies equally to every citizen in God's special kingdom. For some unspecified reason, God's *logos* rejected all nations except Judah and took up residence at Jerusalem. The consequences of that claim extend to the present era, when opposing factions vie for that sacred ground. Accompanying features of the myth complicate matters beyond repair, especially the belief that God has given this holy land to the Jews and taken it away from its previous owners, the Canaanites.

Perhaps the primary value of such efforts to justify national and religious convictions is negative. They point to the paucity of really persuasive arguments on behalf of particularistic claims, thus calling all groups to abandon imperialistic notions in favor of humble confession alone. Moreover, the sensual delights and visceral level on which the myth operates summon us all to celebrate the beauty of the natural order and its unending mystery rather than wasting time and energy quarreling over religious dogma.

SIRACH 25:1-12, SOME NUMERICAL PROVERBS

NAB

25 With three things I am delighted,
for they are pleasing to the LORD and to men:
Harmony among brethren, friendship among neighbors,
and the mutual love of husband and wife.
2 Three kinds of men I hate;
their manner of life I loathe indeed:
A proud pauper, a rich dissembler,
and an old man lecherous in his dotage.

3 What you have not saved in your youth,
how will you acquire in your old age?
4 How becoming to the gray-haired is judgment,

NRSV

25 I take pleasure in three things,
and they are beautiful in the sight of God and of mortals:[a]
agreement among brothers and sisters,
friendship among neighbors,
and a wife and a husband who live in harmony.
2 I hate three kinds of people,
and I loathe their manner of life:
a pauper who boasts, a rich person who lies,
and an old fool who commits adultery.

3 If you gathered nothing in your youth,
how can you find anything in your old age?

25, 1: (*en trisin*) *ē rastē tę psychę mou, kai auta estin* (*hō raia*): so V; cf P.

[a]Syr Lat: Gk *In three things I was beautiful and I stood in beauty before the Lord and mortals.*

NAB

and a knowledge of counsel to those on in
years!

5 How becoming to the aged is wisdom,
understanding and prudence to the
venerable!

6 The crown of old men is wide experience;
their glory, the fear of the LORD.

7 There are nine who come to my mind as
blessed,
a tenth whom my tongue proclaims:
The man who finds joy in his children,
and he who lives to see his enemies'
downfall.

8 Happy is he who dwells with a sensible wife,
and he who plows not like a donkey yoked
with an ox.
Happy is he who sins not with his tongue,
and he who serves not his inferior.

9 Happy is he who finds a friend
and he who speaks to attentive ears.

10 He who finds wisdom is great indeed,
but not greater than he who fears the LORD.

11 Fear of the LORD surpasses all else,
its possessor is beyond compare.

NRSV

4 How attractive is sound judgment in the
gray-haired,
and for the aged to possess good counsel!

5 How attractive is wisdom in the aged,
and understanding and counsel in the
venerable!

6 Rich experience is the crown of the aged,
and their boast is the fear of the Lord.

7 I can think of nine whom I would call blessed,
and a tenth my tongue proclaims:
a man who can rejoice in his children;
a man who lives to see the downfall of his
foes.

8 Happy the man who lives with a sensible wife,
and the one who does not plow with ox
and ass together.[a]
Happy is the one who does not sin with the
tongue,
and the one who has not served an inferior.

9 Happy is the one who finds a friend,[b]
and the one who speaks to attentive
listeners.

10 How great is the one who finds wisdom!
But none is superior to the one who fears
the Lord.

11 Fear of the Lord surpasses everything;
to whom can we compare the one who has
it?[c]

[b] Heb Syr: Gk lacks *and the one who does not plow with ox and
ass together*   [c] Lat Syr: Gk *good sense*   [d] Other ancient
authorities add as verse 12, *The fear of the Lord is the beginning of
love for him, and faith is the beginning of clinging to him.*

COMMENTARY

In this brief section, Ben Sira returns to the form introduced in 23:16-17, numerical proverb, varying it in the first of two by omitting the smaller number. Verse 1 refers to three sources of pleasure; all have in common an emotion that creates harmony. The first relates to the larger family, the second to people living in the immediate vicinity, and the third moves into the inner sanctum of the home. The next verse names three loathsome types: the pauper who is too proud to accept help, the rich person who lies (the assumption being that wealthy people have no need to

dissemble), and an old lecher. The following four verses reflect on the responsibility of acting one's age. The comment that one who failed to gather anything during youth cannot reasonably expect to do so in advancing years may apply directly to a lecherous desire to recapture the amorous past with a vengeance. Ben Sira notes that old age should be characterized by signs of wisdom and religious devotion, for the aged have the advantage of wide experience. The folly of old lechers is beautifully illustrated in the book of Susanna, which tells of two men who try to blackmail Susanna into complying with their wishes.

Verses 7-12 deal with ten fortunate types of people. Among these, the second and fourth deserve further comment. The wish to see one's enemies' downfall belonged to the piety of biblical psalms (Pss 18:38-43, 48-49; 54:7; 112:8) and laments generally, although the attitude did not enjoy universal acceptance (Prov 17:5; 24:17-18;

cf. Matt 5:43-44). The allusion to plowing with incompatible animals (cf. Deut 22:10) assumes a polygamous environment, the husband having sexual relations with two wives who cannot get along with each other. Ben Sira's elevation of piety over knowledge goes beyond traditional views, in which fear of the Lord was both the originating force and the essence of wisdom. Verse 11 states that worship *surpasses* wisdom.

SIRACH 25:13–26:27, ON WIVES, BOTH BAD AND GOOD

NAB	NRSV

12 Worst of all wounds is that of the heart,
    worst of all evils is that of a woman.
	13 Any wound, but not a wound of the heart!
	    Any wickedness, but not the wickedness of
	        a woman!

13 Worst of all sufferings is that from one's foes,
    worst of all vengeance is that of one's
        enemies:
	14 Any suffering, but not suffering from those
	        who hate!
	    And any vengeance, but not the vengeance
	        of enemies!

14 No poison worse than that of a serpent,
    no venom greater than that of a woman.
	15 There is no venom[a] worse than a snake's
	        venom,[a]

15 With a dragon or a lion I would rather dwell than live with an evil woman.	and no anger worse than a woman's[b] wrath.

16 Wickedness changes a woman's looks,
    and makes her sullen as a female bear.
	16 I would rather live with a lion and a dragon
	    than live with an evil woman.

17 When her husband sits among his neighbors,
    a bitter sigh escapes him unawares.
	17 A woman's wickedness changes her
	        appearance,
	    and darkens her face like that of a bear.

	18 Her husband sits[c] among the neighbors, and he cannot help sighing[d] bitterly.

18 There is scarce any evil like that in a woman;
    may she fall to the lot of the sinner!
	19 Any iniquity is small compared to a woman's
	        iniquity;

19 Like a sandy hill to aged feet is a railing wife to a quiet man.	may a sinner's lot befall her!

20 Stumble not through woman's beauty,
    nor be greedy for her wealth;
	20 A sandy ascent for the feet of the aged—
	    such is a garrulous wife to a quiet husband.

21 The man is a slave, in disgrace and shame,
    when a wife supports her husband.
	21 Do not be ensnared by a woman's beauty,
	    and do not desire a woman for her
	        possessions.[e]

22 Depressed mind, saddened face,
    broken heart—this from an evil wife.
    Feeble hands and quaking knees—
    from a wife who brings no happiness to
        her husband.
	22 There is wrath and impudence and great
	        disgrace
	    when a wife supports her husband.

23 In woman was sin's beginning,	

25, 14: *kephalē=rō᾽š*="poison." (*wᵉ᾽ên ḥēmâ mēḥàmat*) ᾽*iššâ*: so P, V.

25, 16-21.22c-23: So with Heb.

25, 16: (*yašḥîr*) *marᵉèhā* (*wᵉyaqdîr*) *pā̃nèhā* : so LXX (*arkos* for *sakkon*: so LXX^{S,A}).

[a] Syr: Gk *head*   [b] Other ancient authorities read *an enemy's*   [c] Heb Syr: Gk *loses heart*   [d] Other ancient authorities read *and listening he sighs*   [e] Heb Syr: Other Gk authorities read *for her beauty*

NAB

and because of her we all die.

24 Allow water no outlet,
and be not indulgent to an erring wife.

25 If she walks not by your side,
cut her away from you.

26 Happy the husband of a good wife,
twice-lengthened are his days;

2 A worthy wife brings joy to her husband.
peaceful and full is his life.

3 A good wife is a generous gift
bestowed upon him who fears the LORD;

4 Be he rich or poor, his heart is content,
and a smile is ever on his face.

5 There are three things at which my heart
quakes,
a fourth before which I quail:
Though false charges in public, trial before all
the people,
and lying testimony are harder to bear than
death,

6 A jealous wife is heartache and mourning
and a scourging tongue like the other
three.

7 A bad wife is a chafing yoke;
he who marries her seizes a scorpion.

8 A drunken wife arouses great anger,
for she does not hide her shame.

9 By her eyelids and her haughty stare
an unchaste wife can be recognized.

10 Keep a strict watch over an unruly wife,
lest, finding an opportunity, she make use
of it;

11 Follow close if her eyes are bold,
and be not surprised if she betrays you:

12 As a thirsty traveler with eager mouth
drinks from any water that he finds,
So she settles down before every tent peg
and opens her quiver for every arrow.

13 A gracious wife delights her husband,
her thoughtfulness puts flesh on his bones;

14 A gift from the LORD is her governed speech,
and her firm virtue is of surpassing worth.

25, 21: (kî) ʿăbōdâ: so P.
25, 28: With Heb, but trsp v 7 and v 8 of Heb. 8c: ʾašrê šellōʾ nikšal
bilešônô: cf LXX, P.
26, 5b: (prosōpōˌ) ephobēthēn: so LXXᴹˢˢ, P.
26, 10: epi tēˌ adiatrepōˌ: so P; cf LXXᴹˢˢ. Omit thygatri: gloss from 42,
11.

NRSV

23 Dejected mind, gloomy face,
and wounded heart come from an evil wife.
Drooping hands and weak knees
come from the wife who does not make her
husband happy.

24 From a woman sin had its beginning,
and because of her we all die.

25 Allow no outlet to water,
and no boldness of speech to an evil wife.

26 If she does not go as you direct,
separate her from yourself.

26 Happy is the husband of a good wife;
the number of his days will be doubled.

2 A loyal wife brings joy to her husband,
and he will complete his years in peace.

3 A good wife is a great blessing;
she will be granted among the blessings of
the man who fears the Lord.

4 Whether rich or poor, his heart is content,
and at all times his face is cheerful.

5 Of three things my heart is frightened,
and of a fourth I am in great fear:ᵍ
Slander in the city, the gathering of a mob,
and false accusation—all these are worse
than death.

6 But it is heartache and sorrow when a wife is
jealous of a rival,
and a tongue-lashing makes it known to all.

7 A bad wife is a chafing yoke;
taking hold of her is like grasping a scorpion.

8 A drunken wife arouses great anger;
she cannot hide her shame.

9 The haughty stare betrays an unchaste wife;
her eyelids give her away.

10 Keep strict watch over a headstrong daughter,
or else, when she finds liberty, she will
make use of it.

11 Be on guard against her impudent eye,
and do not be surprised if she sins against you.

12 As a thirsty traveler opens his mouth
and drinks from any water near him,
so she will sit in front of every tent peg
and open her quiver to the arrow.

13 A wife's charm delights her husband,
and her skill puts flesh on his bones.

ᵍSyr: Meaning of Gk uncertain

NAB

15 Choicest of blessings is a modest wife,
   priceless her chaste person.
16 Like the sun rising in the LORD's heavens,
   the beauty of a virtuous wife is the
      radiance of her home.
17 Like the light which shines above the holy
      lampstand,
   are her beauty of face and graceful figure.
18 Golden columns on silver bases
   are her shapely limbs and steady feet.

26, 18b: (epi) pternois eustathmois. so LXX^S; cf P, V.

NRSV

14 A silent wife is a gift from the Lord,
   and nothing is so precious as her
      self-discipline.
15 A modest wife adds charm to charm,
   and no scales can weigh the value of her chastity.
16 Like the sun rising in the heights of the Lord,
   so is the beauty of a good wife in her
      well-ordered home.
17 Like the shining lamp on the holy lampstand,
   so is a beautiful face on a stately figure.
18 Like golden pillars on silver bases,
   so are shapely legs and steadfast feet.

Other ancient authorities add verses 19-27:

19 *My child, keep sound the bloom of your youth,*
   and do not give your strength to strangers.
20 *Seek a fertile field within the whole plain,*
   and sow it with your own seed, trusting in
      your fine stock.
21 *So your offspring will prosper,*
   and, having confidence in their good
      descent, will grow great.
22 *A prostitute is regarded as spittle,*
   and a married woman as a tower of death
      to her lovers.
23 *A godless wife is given as a portion to a*
      lawless man,
   but a pious wife is given to the man who
      fears the Lord.
24 *A shameless woman constantly acts*
      disgracefully,
   but a modest daughter will even be
      embarrassed before her husband.
25 *A headstrong wife is regarded as a dog,*
   but one who has a sense of shame will fear
      the Lord.
26 *A wife honoring her husband will seem wise to all,*
   but if she dishonors him in her pride she
      will be known to all as ungodly.
   Happy is the husband of a good wife;
   for the number of his years will be doubled.
27 *A loud-voiced and garrulous wife is like a*
      trumpet sounding the charge,
   and every person like this lives in the
      anarchy of war.

COMMENTARY

Having momentarily introduced the topic of a good wife in 25:1, Ben Sira now turns to a discussion of virtuous and wicked wives, beginning with the latter (25:13-26) and interrupting this strong censure with a brief section on a good wife (26:1-4), only to return to the less complimentary assessment of wives (26:5-12) before concluding on a positive note (26:13-18). In the cursive MSS 70 and 248, as well as Syriac, a section combining positive and negative comments about wives sums up the discussion, ending with an image of a garrulous wife as the sound of a battle cry (תרועה *tĕrû'â*) and the accompanying confusion.

25:13-26. Hyperbole sets the tone for Ben Sira's treatment of the traditional topic about bad wives, and this fact needs to be taken into account when evaluating his attitude toward women. The unpleasantries—severe blows, villainy, suffering, and revenge—provide a semantic and psychological context within which to view the grief caused by a wicked woman. Thus far the language refers to bad women generally, not just to wives. The association of evil women with snakes and their venom was balanced in the ancient world by a positive celebration of the rejuvenating power and virility of these creatures. The reference to "vengeance of enemies" in v. 14 may actually reflect a polygamous setting in which wives jockey for position and harbor grudges that lead to aggressive acts of vengeance in the same way Jacob's wives, Leah and Rachel, expressed rivalry (Gen 29:31–30:24).

The exaggerated speech continues in v. 16 with the first-person expression of preference. The comparison, absurd in the extreme, for no one could live with a lion or a dragon, calls to mind the unbearable situation of dwelling in the same house with an incorrigible woman. Whereas wisdom brightens the countenance, according to Eccl 8:1, for Ben Sira wickedness has the opposite result, darkening the face. To indicate the full effect of such evil, Ben Sira evokes the thought of a bear, perhaps because lions and bears were often associated (cf. Amos 5:18-19). Driven from his own house, the unfortunate husband hangs out with friends and seeks consolation (v. 18).

The next verse uses the same hyperbole of vv. 13-14, *"any* iniquity," although phrased differently to stress the minuteness.

The image in v. 20 emphasizes the difficulty encountered by old people when the terrain does not permit them to plant their feet firmly. A sandy slope is both slippery and hard to negotiate. Ben Sira thinks a complaining wife makes life equally challenging to that of a sandy hill. The following two verses (vv. 21-22) take up the subject of two different ways by which women trap men, in Ben Sira's view: with their beauty and their wealth. Only the latter attraction provokes further comment, the assertion that a man who depends on his wife's assets for daily survival is also subjected to constant abuse.

The bold claim in v. 24 that sin originated with woman, presumably an allusion to Eve's disobedience of the divine decree, and that all subsequent people die because of Eve's sin represents but one of three different viewpoints in ancient Israel regarding sin and death. The usual explanation for death in Judaism focused on Adam's unrepentant attitude rather than on Eve's original disobedience,[201] when it did not assume that human beings were by nature mortal (41:4). In the ancient story of the fall, Eve's disobedience preceded Adam's chronologically (cf. 2 Cor 11:3; 1 Tim 2:14), but Adam's presence and complicity implicate him equally. John Levison has endeavored to exonerate Eve in Ben Sira's eyes; Levison thinks v. 24 refers to an evil wife and to husbands who die because of such terrible spouses,[202] but the contextual evidence and the fragment from Qumran do not make a strong case for the argument. The third source of evil, along with Eve and Adam, was Satan, at least in popular thought.

Verses 25-26 project a patriarchal worldview completely at odds with the modern one, particularly in the West. Ben Sira advises husbands to suppress evil wives' freedom to express themselves just as one builds a dam to prevent the free flow of water. Failing in that endeavor, husbands can then resort to the ultimate contingency, di-

---

201. *Bemidbar Rabba* 13; cf. Rom 5:12, 14-29; 1 Cor 15:22.
202. John Levison, "Is Eve to Blame? A Contextual Analysis of Sirach 25:24," *CBQ* 47 (1985) 617-23.

vorce (cf. Deut 24:1). The language implies severing her from her husband's flesh, which recalls the statement in Gen 2:24 that husband and wife become one flesh. Within Judaism, two opposing attitudes to divorce vied for acceptance, the one lenient—for something as trivial as burnt bread—and the other quite restrictive, allowing divorce only for instances of adultery or other sexual offense. The lenient view merely acknowledges a fact: If one is prepared to divorce a wife over burnt bread, then the marriage is already dead. Ben Sira's view falls into the former camp; a husband can divorce a wife who refuses to bow down before his wishes.

26:1-4. These extreme comments about wicked wives do not constitute the sum of Ben Sira's remarks about wives, for he knows that good women also exist. The praise of virtuous wives, like the charges against bad ones, represents the view of the husband. Good wives bring longevity, peace, blessing, and happiness that expresses itself openly in their husbands' faces. These gifts resemble those that wisdom bestows on her lovers. One can scarcely imagine higher praise than this. Even poverty loses its sting when a man has a good wife, according to Ben Sira.

26:5-12. Having registered strong appreciation for good wives, Ben Sira reverts to the earlier topic of undesirable wives. Although the Greek of v. 10 refers to a daughter, the Syriac reading ("wife") probably retains the Hebrew original. The entire section bristles with arresting images and obscenities, particularly the references to an ill-fitting yoke that rubs the skin of an ox raw, a dreaded scorpion, and the euphemisms for sexual relations—a thirsty traveler drinking from any available stream, sitting (lying) in front of every tent peg (penis) and opening her quiver (vagina) for every arrow (penis). In addition, allusions to drunken and flirtatious conduct make this litany of undesirable behavior extremely uncomplimentary to *some* wives. In Ben Sira's mind, their harm ranks alongside false accusations leading to mob action; v. 5 refers to slander, gang action, and false charges. The form of this verse—only the first part of a numerical saying—is false, like the behavior itself.

26:13-18. These verses take up the subject of good wives once more, this time using comparisons from the Temple to convey their incomparable beauty. When a virtuous wife also possesses good looks, she resembles a menorah, a seven-branched candelabra, and golden and silver pedestals (or ornaments, if one reads "breasts" with Alexandrinus and Vaticanus instead of "feet"). Ben Sira observes that a good wife fattens her husband up, an indication of good health in the ancient Jewish environment, and that such a woman comes as a divine gift, a view shared by the authors of some sayings in the book of Proverbs. The attributes of a good wife include modesty, self-discipline, and orderliness, but they also embrace physical beauty. Ben Sira shows a remarkable appreciation for the external appearance of a woman, although his comments belong in the larger context of character. The remark that the value of chastity cannot be weighed on existing scales indicates where he really places the emphasis. The notion of weighing virtue or vice was widespread in the ancient Near East (cf. the divine judgment on Belshazzar in Dan 5:27 and the Egyptian concept of weighing the soul against a feather representing justice).

Nothing in the final section demands an understanding of it as secondary, despite its absence in the shorter Greek translation (and Hebrew; it is preserved in the expanded Greek version and in Syriac). Nevertheless, much of the material either repeats what Ben Sira has already said or echoes similar remarks in the book of Proverbs. The reference to a wife as daughter in v. 24 strengthens the understanding of v. 10 as an allusion to a wife. This section warns against squandering one's vitality on foreign women, a common theme in wisdom literature, and advises young men to plow their own fields, sowing worthy seed. This euphemism for sexual relations becomes for Ben Sira a way of assuring patrimony. His disdain for prostitutes and adulteresses, as well as his conviction that men get the sort of wives they deserve, places Ben Sira in the mainstream of wisdom's exponents. The suggestion in v. 24 that a modest daughter always retains an element of embarrassment, even in the presence of her husband, appears to press beyond anything prior to this time, when mutual enjoyment of sex was the rule. At the very least, this ideal of modesty differs radically from the exuberance of the young sister ("lover") in the Song of Songs.

REFLECTIONS

The family lies at the center of society today, just as it did long ago. Ben Sira undercuts this significant institution while endeavoring to strengthen it, for he harbored misogynistic sentiments even while singing women's praises. His comments about wicked women raise a significant question: Can praise ever make amends for damaging criticism?

In fairness to him, one must acknowledge the fact that Ben Sira certainly has strong words of approval for good wives. Nevertheless, the crude remarks and generalizing condemnation of a certain kind of woman, together with his suspicion concerning woman's lascivious nature, make an indelible impression on readers' minds. Like violent images that linger long after the fact, these unfavorable comments leave unwelcome vestiges. Words can hurt even more grievously than do sticks and stones, particularly when directed against persons lacking power and prestige. Here, too, the sensual expressions of delight go a long way toward salvaging Ben Sira's reputation as a sage—but not far enough.

In the light of this, Christians may wish to take inventory of their use of language about groups who lack the authority to challenge unwelcome remarks. Over the centuries, the English language has become freighted with derisive terms and unflattering expressions, each of which brings pain to innocent victims. By consulting compendia that isolate such offensive terms, and by studiously avoiding their use, concerned Christians can make a difference in a society that seems to know no limits where offensive speech is concerned.

SIRACH 26:28–27:15, ON INTEGRITY

NAB

19 These two bring grief to my heart,
    and the third arouses my horror:
A wealthy man reduced to want;
    illustrious men held in contempt;
And the man who passes from justice to sin,
    for whom the LORD makes ready the sword.

20 A merchant can hardly remain upright,
    nor a shopkeeper free from sin;

27 For the sake of profit many sin.
    and the struggle for wealth blinds the eyes.
 2 Like a peg driven between fitted stones,
    between buying and selling sin is wedged in.
 3 Unless you earnestly hold fast to the fear of the LORD,
    suddenly your house will be thrown down.

26, 19: *anēr polemistēs*='*îš* (*gibbôr?*) *ḥayil*="a wealthy man" (cf Ru 2, 1). (*andres*) *ainetoi:* cf P.
27, 1: (*charin*) *diaphorou*: so LXX^S; cf 7, 18.
27, 2: *synthlibēsetai* (*hamartia*): cf P, V.

NRSV

28 At two things my heart is grieved,
    and because of a third anger comes over me:
a warrior in want through poverty,
    intelligent men who are treated contemptuously,
and a man who turns back from righteousness to sin—
    the Lord will prepare him for the sword!

29 A merchant can hardly keep from wrongdoing,
    nor is a tradesman innocent of sin.

27 Many have committed sin for gain,[a]
    and those who seek to get rich will avert their eyes.
 2 As a stake is driven firmly into a fissure between stones,
    so sin is wedged in between selling and buying.
 3 If a person is not steadfast in the fear of the Lord,

[a] Other ancient authorities read *a trifle*

NAB

4 When a sieve is shaken, the husks appear;
   so do a man's faults when he speaks.

5 As the test of what the potter molds is in the furnace,
   so in his conversation is the test of a man.

6 The fruit of a tree shows the care it has had;
   so too does a man's speech disclose the bent of his mind.

7 Praise no man before he speaks,
   for it is then that men are tested.

8 If you strive after justice you will attain it,
   and put it on like a splendid robe.

9 Birds nest with their own kind,
   and fidelity comes to those who live by it.

10 As a lion crouches in wait for prey,
   so do sins for evildoers.

11 Ever wise are the discourses of the devout,
   but the godless man, like the moon, is inconstant.

12 Limit the time you spend among fools,
   but frequent the company of thoughtful men.

13 The conversation of the wicked is offensive,
   their laughter is wanton guilt.

14 Their oath-filled talk makes the hair stand on end,
   their brawls make one stop one's ears.

15 Wrangling among the haughty ends in bloodshed,
   their cursing is painful to hear.

27, 5f: For Heb cf 6, 22; (ʾal yēṣeṛ) ʾādām: so LXX, P.

NRSV

his house will be quickly overthrown.

4 When a sieve is shaken, the refuse appears;
   so do a person's faults when he speaks.

5 The kiln tests the potter's vessels;
   so the test of a person is in his conversation.

6 Its fruit discloses the cultivation of a tree;
   so a person's speech discloses the cultivation of his mind.

7 Do not praise anyone before he speaks,
   for this is the way people are tested.

8 If you pursue justice, you will attain it
   and wear it like a glorious robe.

9 Birds roost with their own kind,
   so honesty comes home to those who practice it.

10 A lion lies in wait for prey;
   so does sin for evildoers.

11 The conversation of the godly is always wise,
   but the fool changes like the moon.

12 Among stupid people limit your time,
   but among thoughtful people linger on.

13 The talk of fools is offensive,
   and their laughter is wantonly sinful.

14 Their cursing and swearing make one's hair stand on end,
   and their quarrels make others stop their ears.

15 The strife of the proud leads to bloodshed,
   and their abuse is grievous to hear.

COMMENTARY

A variety of sayings discusses the general topic of honesty, beginning with a numerical proverb about three problematic instances of persons trapped in the opposite state from the expected one (26:28) and ending with a few comments about offensive speech (27:11-15).

26:28. The initial saying refers to a rich person reduced to poverty, intelligence that fails to elicit respect, and a person who forsakes virtue for its opposite. The Greek text has "warrior" (ἀνὴρ πολεμιστής *anēr polemistēs*) for the first of these, probably through a misunderstanding of an

original איש חיל (*ʾîš ḥayil*) or גבור חיל (*gibbôr ḥayil*), "a wealthy man" or "person of substance." In the HB, גבור *gibbôr* means "a mighty person," "a warrior."

26:29–27:3. Ben Sira's suspicion that commerce by its very nature participates in sin grows out of the fact that the very premise of trading consisted of gain at the buyer's expense. In his day, commerce flourished, taking Jews to many places and reducing their leisure. According to *Erubin* 55 b (cf. *Qiddushin* 82 a, which calls such trading "the handicraft of robbery"), such preoccupation with business adversely affected the study of Torah.

Ben Sira credits merchants with sufficient conscience to necessitate turning the eye, an inability to look their victim in the eye. Such body language was already recognized in the book of Proverbs (cf. Prov 6:12-19; 28:27). The bartering process had led to humorous posturing by the buyer, who would protest the exorbitant price at first but subsequently brag to others about the purchase, but Ben Sira's evaluation of the new merchant class lacks humor. He thinks of sin as an inevitable consequence of selling, one as firmly fixed as a tent peg wedged between two rocks to secure it against the wind. In this view he was not alone, as this quote from the Egyptian "Instruction of Ankhsheshanky" 28.4 reveals: "Do not have a merchant for a friend; [he] lives for taking a slice."

27:4-7. The three images that illustrate the manner in which speech demonstrates the discipline of one's mind derive from ordinary farm life in ancient Palestine. After oxen had threshed grain, it was placed in a sieve that retained the husks and dung while allowing the kernels to pass through for immediate use or temporary storage. The analogy suffers somewhat, for one expects the speech to represent pure grain, whereas Ben Sira observes that talk demonstrates flaws, bringing them to the surface. The second comparison is more apt: Just as a kiln tests a potter's vessels, bringing imperfections into the open, so also conversation reveals faulty logic. The third comparison rests on the assumption that a well-tended vine or fruit tree will produce appropriate fruit, but this principle does not always apply (cf. Isa 5:1-7 for acknowledgment that one cannot count on a positive correlation between effort and result, as any farmer knew well).

27:8-10. These observations about perverse expectations, commerce, and testing through speech assert a principle of divine reward and retribution. That idea comes to expression again in vv. 8-10, where Ben Sira observes that one who practices justice and integrity will succeed royally, just as surely as the wicked will encounter a lion in their path.

27:11-15. This thought leads Ben Sira to deplore the offensive banter of the wicked, which is unstable and anarchic. Naturally, he urges good people to associate with others like them, a principle that gave rise to the proverb in v. 9: "Birds roost with their own kind." The adverse effect of offensive language, "causing the hair to stand on end," is the same as that resulting from a divine revelation in Job 4:15. (See Reflections at 27:16–28:26.)

SIRACH 27:16–28:26, OFFENSES AGAINST COMPANIONS

NAB	NRSV
16 He who betrays a secret cannot be trusted, he will never find an intimate friend.	16 Whoever betrays secrets destroys confidence, and will never find a congenial friend.
17 Cherish your friend, keep faith with him; but if you betray his confidence, follow him not;	17 Love your friend and keep faith with him; but if you betray his secrets, do not follow after him.
18 For as an enemy might kill a man, you have killed your neighbor's friendship.	18 For as a person destroys his enemy, so you have destroyed the friendship of your neighbor.
19 Like a bird released from the hand, you have let your friend go and cannot recapture him;	19 And as you allow a bird to escape from your hand, so you have let your neighbor go, and will not catch him again.
20 Follow him not, for he is far away, he has fled like a gazelle from the trap.	

NAB

21 A wound can be bound up, and an insult
forgiven,
but he who betrays secrets does hopeless
damage.

22 He who has shifty eyes plots mischief
and no one can ward him off;

23 In your presence he uses honeyed talk,
and admires your every word,
But later he changes his tone
and twists your words to your ruin.

24 There is nothing that I hate so much,
and the LORD hates him as well.

25 As a stone falls back on him who throws it
up,
so a blow struck in treachery injures more
than one.

26 As he who digs a pit falls into it,
and he who lays a snare is caught in it,

27 Whoever does harm will be involved in it
without knowing how it came upon him.

28 Mockery and abuse will be the lot of the
proud,
and vengeance lies in wait for them like a
lion.

29 The trap seizes those who rejoice in pitfalls,
and pain will consume them before they
die;

30 Wrath and anger are hateful things,
yet the sinner hugs them tight.

28 The vengeful will suffer the LORD's
vengeance,
for he remembers their sins in detail.

2 Forgive your neighbor's injustice;
then when you pray, your own sins will
be forgiven.

3 Should a man nourish anger against his
fellows
and expect healing from the LORD?

4 Should a man refuse mercy to his fellows,
yet seek pardon for his own sins?

5 If he who is but flesh cherishes wrath,
who will forgive his sins?

27, 23a: (glykanei stoma) autou: so LXX^MSS, V.
27, 24: (ouch) homoiōs (autō): so P.
27, 29: Omit eusebōn: cf P.
28, 1b: (tas hamartias autou) diatērōn diatērēsei: so 1 LXX^MSS, V; cf
P.

NRSV

20 Do not go after him, for he is too far off,
and has escaped like a gazelle from a snare.

21 For a wound may be bandaged,
and there is reconciliation after abuse,
but whoever has betrayed secrets is without
hope.

22 Whoever winks the eye plots mischief,
and those who know him will keep their
distance.

23 In your presence his mouth is all sweetness,
and he admires your words;
but later he will twist his speech
and with your own words he will trip you
up.

24 I have hated many things, but him above all;
even the Lord hates him.

25 Whoever throws a stone straight up throws it
on his own head,
and a treacherous blow opens up many
wounds.

26 Whoever digs a pit will fall into it,
and whoever sets a snare will be caught in
it.

27 If a person does evil, it will roll back upon
him,
and he will not know where it came from.

28 Mockery and abuse issue from the proud,
but vengeance lies in wait for them like a
lion.

29 Those who rejoice in the fall of the godly will
be caught in a snare,
and pain will consume them before their
death.

30 Anger and wrath, these also are abominations,
yet a sinner holds on to them.

28 The vengeful will face the Lord's
vengeance,
for he keeps a strict account of[a] their sins.

2 Forgive your neighbor the wrong he has done,
and then your sins will be pardoned when
you pray.

3 Does anyone harbor anger against another,
and expect healing from the Lord?

4 If one has no mercy toward another like
himself,

[a] Other ancient authorities read for he firmly establishes

NAB

6 Remember your last days, set enmity aside;
   remember death and decay, and cease
      from sin!
7 Think of the commandments, hate not your
      neighbor;
   of the Most High's covenant, and overlook
      faults.

8 Avoid strife and your sins will be fewer,
   for a quarrelsome man kindles disputes,
9 Commits the sin of disrupting friendship
   and sows discord among those at peace.
10 The more wood, the greater the fire,
   the more underlying it, the fiercer the
      fight;
   The greater a man's strength, the sterner his
      anger,
   the greater his power, the greater his
      wrath.
11 Pitch and resin make fires flare up,
   and insistent quarrels provoke bloodshed.

12 If you blow upon a spark, it quickens into
      flame,
   if you spit on it, it dies out;
   yet both you do with your mouth!
13 Cursed be gossips and the double-tongued,
   for they destroy the peace of many.
14 A meddlesome tongue subverts many,
   and makes them refugees among the
      peoples;
   It destroys walled cities,
   and overthrows powerful dynasties.
15 A meddlesome tongue can drive virtuous
      women from their homes
   and rob them of the fruit of their toil;
16 Whoever heeds it has no rest,
   nor can he dwell in peace.

17 A blow from a whip raises a welt,
   but a blow from the tongue smashes bones;
18 Many have fallen by the edge of the sword,
   but not as many as by the tongue.

28, 6b: (šaḥat wāmāwet) ûmᵉnaˑ mēḥaṭōˑ: so P; dittog of following
words.
28, 10: Trsp lines to read a.d.b.c: so LXXᴹˢˢ, P. (tēs machēs)
auxēthēsetai: so a few LXXᴹˢˢ; cf P; dittog.
28, 11a: ṣôrî wālōṭ (yaṣṣîtû ˑ ēš): so P.
28, 13a: katarasthai: so LXXᴹˢˢ; cf P, V.
28, 17: mōlōpa: so LXXᴹˢˢ, V.

NRSV

   can he then seek pardon for his own sins?
5 If a mere mortal harbors wrath,
   who will make an atoning sacrifice for his
      sins?
6 Remember the end of your life, and set enmity
      aside;
   remember corruption and death, and be true
      to the commandments.
7 Remember the commandments, and do not be
      angry with your neighbor;
   remember the covenant of the Most High,
      and overlook faults.

8 Refrain from strife, and your sins will be fewer;
   for the hot-tempered kindle strife,
9 and the sinner disrupts friendships
   and sows discord among those who are at
      peace.
10 In proportion to the fuel, so will the fire burn,
   and in proportion to the obstinacy, so will
      strife increase;[a]
   in proportion to a person's strength will be his
      anger,
   and in proportion to his wealth he will
      increase his wrath.
11 A hasty quarrel kindles a fire,
   and a hasty dispute sheds blood.
12 If you blow on a spark, it will glow;
   if you spit on it, it will be put out;
   yet both come out of your mouth.

13 Curse the gossips and the double-tongued,
   for they destroy the peace of many.
14 Slander[b] has shaken many,
   and scattered them from nation to nation;
   it has destroyed strong cities,
   and overturned the houses of the great.
15 Slander[b] has driven virtuous women from their
      homes,
   and deprived them of the fruit of their toil.
16 Those who pay heed to slander[c] will not find
      rest,
   nor will they settle down in peace.
17 The blow of a whip raises a welt,
   but a blow of the tongue crushes the bones.
18 Many have fallen by the edge of the sword,

ᵃOther ancient authorities read burn   ᵇGk A third tongue
ᶜGk it

NAB

19 Happy he who is sheltered from it,
    and has not endured its wrath;
   Who has not borne its yoke
    nor been fettered with its chains;
20 For its yoke is a yoke of iron
    and its chains are chains of bronze!
21 Dire is the death it inflicts,
    besides which even the nether world is a
      gain;
22 It will not take hold among the just
    nor scorch them in its flame,
23 But those who forsake the LORD will fall
      victims to it,
    as it burns among them unquenchably!
   It will hurl itself against them like a lion;
    like a panther, it will tear them to pieces.
24 As you hedge round your vineyard with
      thorns,
    set barred doors over your mouth;
25 As you seal up your silver and gold,
    so balance and weigh your words.
26 Take care not to slip by your tongue
    and fall victim to your foe waiting in
      ambush.

28, 24f: Trsp to read 24a.25b.24b.25a: so LXX^MSS, P, V.

NRSV

   but not as many as have fallen because of
      the tongue.
19 Happy is the one who is protected from it,
    who has not been exposed to its anger,
   who has not borne its yoke,
    and has not been bound with its fetters.
20 For its yoke is a yoke of iron,
    and its fetters are fetters of bronze;
21 its death is an evil death,
    and Hades is preferable to it.
22 It has no power over the godly;
    they will not be burned in its flame.
23 Those who forsake the Lord will fall into its
      power;
    it will burn among them and will not be
      put out.
   It will be sent out against them like a lion;
    like a leopard it will mangle them.
24a As you fence in your property with thorns,
25b so make a door and a bolt for your mouth.
24b As you lock up your silver and gold,
25a so make balances and scales for your words.
26 Take care not to err with your tongue,[a]
    and fall victim to one lying in wait.

[a] Gk with it

COMMENTARY

This section consists of poems about betraying another's trust (27:16-21), retribution (27:22-29), vengeance (27:30–28:11), and slander (28:12-26).

27:16-21. Two images from hunting, that of a released bird or a gazelle, emphasize the futility of trying to repair the damage resulting from betrayal of trust (cf. Prov 6:5). Once a bird or a gazelle has left its trap, no one can easily recapture it. Ben Sira stresses the ultimate cost of revealing secrets about an intimate friend; nobody will ever trust you again. The introductory clause, "whoever betrays secrets" (v. 16), recurs in the final verse of this poem, forming a neat inclusio (v. 21) bracketing the unit of thought.

27:22-29. The poem about retribution evokes Ben Sira's ire for an individual who feigns friend-

ship to your face but plunges a verbal dagger in your back when out of your range of hearing. The language describing the hypocrite's action is noteworthy; he sweetens his words while in your presence but twists his mouth in other people's midst. Ben Sira shares earlier sages' disdain for the practice of winking, viewing it as malicious (cf. Prov 6:13; 10:10). In this context of discussing someone who uses your own words to condemn you by perverting their original meaning, the first person returns once more; but here Ben Sira aligns himself with God. Both of them hate such dissemblers.

Verses 25-29 cite traditional proverbs that assert a relationship between cause and effect, here focusing on the dire consequences of particular actions: throwing a rock straight up (cf. Prov

26:27b), digging a pit (cf. Prov 26:27a; Eccl 10:8), and setting a trap (Ps 9:15-16). Such wishful thinking characterizes much of wisdom literature, largely because the sages believed that God guaranteed justice in society. As numerous proverbial sayings demonstrate, the sages' faith was not naive. The incisive questions in the books of Job (e.g., Job 10:3-7; 24:1) and Qohelet (Eccl 2:16; 3:21) develop some ideas already present in the earlier sayings.

27:30–28:11. The treatment of vengeance links up with the previous discussion, asserting divine retribution based on an accurate record of sinful deeds. Sirach 28:2-5 insists that anyone who desires forgiveness from the Lord must first exercise that compassion toward human enemies (cf. Matt 6:12, 14-15; 18:32-35; Mark 11:5; Luke 21:4; Jas 2:13). This sentiment also appears in Jewish literature generally. For example, God forgives whoever forgives his or her "neighbor";[203] "So long as we are merciful, God is merciful to us; but if we are not merciful to others, God is not merciful to us";[204] "Whoever has pity on men, to him will God be merciful";[205] "Only the one who is merciful with mankind may expect mercy from Heaven."[206] The concluding verses (28:6-7) appeal to the prospect of death as sufficient reason for extending forgiveness to others and remind readers of the supreme commandment: to love God *and* neighbor (Lev 19:18).

The next section (28:8-11) warns against letting sharp words escalate into blows. It quotes a proverbial saying about the amount of wood to use on a fire (Prov 26:20; cf. Jas 3:5). This citation

leads to a similar one in 28:12, which observes that at a certain point when a coal is glowing one can blow on it and start a fire or spit on it and extinguish the ember.[207] This thought leads naturally into a discussion of gossip, for like breath and spit, words proceed form the mouth. This transitional verse demonstrates the difficulty of dividing Ben Sira's teaching into distinct units (cf. the Vg's title at 28:1, "On the Forgiveness of Sins" (*De remissione peccatorum*).

28:12-26. The most striking feature of the discussion of gossip is the claim that slander has destroyed more people than has the sword (v. 18) and that the verbal lash breaks bones (cf. Prov 25:15). In v. 14, the Greek Codex Alexandrinus has "third tongue," a technical expression in rabbinic literature for slander that, according to 'Arak. 15b, slays three people—the slanderer, the slandered, and the person who believes the slanderer. Ben Sira specifically refers to the rupture of marriages resulting from slanderous allegations about innocent wives (v. 15), and he likens slander to an iron yoke (cf. Jer 28:14). A particular example of slander's effect comes from the time of Herod the Great, who believed such reports on his wife Mariamne and had her executed, only to regret his action to the point of near madness. Returning to the earlier teaching about retribution, Ben Sira claims immunity from slander's power for the godly but asserts that wild animals will pounce on the wicked. As a precaution against falling prey to the temptation to slander others, he advises putting a strong bolt on the door of one's mouth and using accurate scales to weigh every utterance prior to speaking. The images of a yoke and chains also occur in Prov 6:24-25, 29-30 with regard to the discipline of wisdom.

203. *Rosh Ha-shanah* 17a.
204. *Megillah* 28a; cf. also *The Testament of the Twelve Patriarchs,* Gad 6:3-7; Zebulon 5:3.
205. *Erubin* 17:72.
206. *Sifre* 93b. See also W. O. E. Oesterley, *The Wisdom of Jesus the Son of Sirach or Ecclesiasticus* (Cambridge: Cambridge University Press, 1912) 178-79.

207. Cf. *Wayyikra Rabba* 33.

REFLECTIONS

Many observations in this part of Sirach move outside the family structure to the broad realm of economic and social relations. On the basis of what is said, one can legitimately conclude that ancient Israel, like much of the West, was overcome by greed. Ben Sira's indictment of merchants leaves little, if any, room for fair trading practice. In earlier times, when the economy was based on bartering, little opportunity existed for making excessive profits through exchange of goods. With the emergence of currency and speculation in commerce, that situation changed forever. Greed has come to characterize our entire society, and cynicism has replaced trust with each revelation of unchecked lust for money.

In addition, confidences are readily broken, and the social fabric tears a little with every betrayal of trust. People profit from slandering others and from exposing every peccadillo to a curious populace. The rules of polite society have given way as more and more parents shirk their responsibility to train young children in the way they should walk. The church has a rare opportunity to take up the slack, nurturing neglected youth in the art of living. Christians who traditionally promise to assist in bringing up new converts in the family of God need to broaden their understanding of nurturing to include rudimentary matters of etiquette, indeed socialization in every aspect.

SIRACH 29:1-20, ON LENDING AND PROVIDING COLLATERAL

NAB

29 He does a kindness who lends to his neighbor,
  and he fulfills the precepts who holds out a helping hand.

2 Lend to your neighbor in his hour of need,
  and pay back your neighbor when a loan falls due;

3 Keep your promise, be honest with him,
  and you will always come by what you need.

4 Many a man who asks for a loan
  adds to the burdens of those who help him;

5 When he borrows, he kisses the lender's hand
  and speaks with respect of his creditor's wealth;
  But when payment is due he disappoints him
  and says he is helpless to meet the claim.

6 If the lender is able to recover barely half,
  he considers this an achievement;
  If not, he is cheated of his wealth
  and acquires an enemy at no extra charge;
  With curses and insults the borrower pays him back,
  with abuse instead of honor.

7 Many refuse to lend, not out of meanness,

NRSV

29 The merciful lend to their neighbors;
  by holding out a helping hand they keep the commandments.

2 Lend to your neighbor in his time of need;
  repay your neighbor when a loan falls due.

3 Keep your promise and be honest with him,
  and on every occasion you will find what you need.

4 Many regard a loan as a windfall,
  and cause trouble to those who help them.

5 One kisses another's hands until he gets a loan,
  and is deferential in speaking of his neighbor's money;
  but at the time for repayment he delays,
  and pays back with empty promises,
  and finds fault with the time.

6 If he can pay, his creditor[a] will hardly get back half,
  and will regard that as a windfall.
  If he cannot pay, the borrower[a] has robbed the other of his money,
  and he has needlessly made him an enemy;
  he will repay him with curses and reproaches,
  and instead of glory will repay him with dishonor.

7 Many refuse to lend, not because of meanness,
  but from fear[b] of being defrauded needlessly.

29, 4a: With P; LXX=v 6b. 4b: (*kai pareschon*) *kopon* : so LXX^MSS, P, V.

29, 5c: (*ûb^e ̓ēt hāšēb*) *yāpîaḥ napšô* : so P; cf 4, 2; 5d: (*kai*) *kairon aiteitai* (?): cf V (6a).

29, 7a: (*polloi*) *ou* (*charin*): so LXX^MSS, P, V.

[a] Gk *he*   [b] Other ancient authorities read *many refuse to lend, therefore, because of such meanness; they are afraid*

NAB	NRSV
but from fear of being cheated.	

NAB

but from fear of being cheated.

8 To a poor man, however, be generous;
  keep him not waiting for your alms;
9 Because of the precept, help the needy,
  and in their want, do not send them away
    empty-handed.

10 Spend your money for your brother and
    friend,
  and hide it not under a stone to perish;
11 Dispose of your treasure as the Most High
    commands,
  for that will profit you more than the gold.
12 Store up almsgiving in your treasure house,
  and it will save you from every evil;
13 Better than a stout shield and a sturdy spear
  it will fight for you against the foe.

14 A good man goes surety for his neighbor,
  and only the shameless would play him
    false;
15 Forget not the kindness of your backer,
  for he offers his very life for you.
16 The wicked turn a pledge on their behalf
    into misfortune,
  and the ingrate abandons his protector;
 17 Going surety has ruined many prosperous men
    and tossed them about like waves of the sea,
18 Has exiled men of prominence
    and sent them wandering through foreign
      lands.
19 The sinner through surety comes to grief,
  and he who undertakes too much falls into
    lawsuits.
20 Go surety for your neighbor according to
    your means,
  but take care lest you fall thereby.

NRSV

8 Nevertheless, be patient with someone in
    humble circumstances,
  and do not keep him waiting for your alms.
9 Help the poor for the commandment's sake,
  and in their need do not send them away
    empty-handed.
10 Lose your silver for the sake of a brother or a
    friend,
  and do not let it rust under a stone and be
    lost.
11 Lay up your treasure according to the
    commandments of the Most High,
  and it will profit you more than gold.
12 Store up almsgiving in your treasury,
  and it will rescue you from every disaster;
13 better than a stout shield and a sturdy spear,
  it will fight for you against the enemy.

14 A good person will be surety for his neighbor,
  but the one who has lost all sense of shame
    will fail him.
15 Do not forget the kindness of your guarantor,
  for he has given his life for you.
16 A sinner wastes the property of his guarantor,
17   and the ungrateful person abandons his
      rescuer.
18 Being surety has ruined many who were
    prosperous,
  and has tossed them about like waves of the
    sea;
  it has driven the influential into exile,
    and they have wandered among foreign
      nations.
19 The sinner comes to grief through surety;
  his pursuit of gain involves him in lawsuits.
20 Assist your neighbor to the best of your ability,
  but be careful not to fall yourself.

29, 8b: (ep' eleēmosynēn) mē parelkysēs: so LXX^{MSS}, V.
29, 10b: (kai mē) katakrybe auto: so 1 LXX^{MS}, V; cf P; LXX^B influenced
by Mt 6, 19.

COMMENTARY

The book of Proverbs advises strongly against guaranteeing loans for someone else (Prov 6:1-5; 11:15; 17:18; 20:16; 22:26-27; 27:13), but Ben Sira urges the opposite, although in a responsible

manner. His motive for this practice and for lending money to the poor, as well as for almsgiving, derives from religious duty, the commandment to be generous to the needy. In accord with the prohibition against charging Jews interest on loans (Exod 22:24; Lev 25:36-37), it plays no role in this discussion of loans. (In the later Talmudic tractate *B. Bat. 90* it is said that "a userer is comparable to a murderer, for the crimes of both are equally irremediable.") Polonius's counsel to Laertes, "Neither a borrower nor a lender be; for loan oft loses both itself and friend"[208] lacks this theological mandate that drove Ben Sira to risk abuse and loss of money. Nevertheless, he enters into the negotiation with open eyes, knowing that borrowers humbly "kiss profusely" (καταφιλέω *kataphileō*) and feign appreciation before acquiring a loan but become obstinate and abusive when payment comes due. Borrowers either blame hard times for failure to meet the deadline, or they accuse the lender of setting the date too early. Irony fills the observation in v. 6 that by lending money to someone the lender acquires an enemy at no extra charge ("freely" [δωρεά *dōrea*]).

The strong "nevertheless" (πλήν *plēn*) in v. 8 places the poor in a different category from the

unappreciative, abusive borrower. Rather than hiding silver under a rock and letting it rust (cf. Isa 45:3; Matt 25:18), one should, in Ben Sira's opinion, obey the commandments and put the money to good use. In this way, one lays up treasure and attains protection from harm (cf. Matt 6:19; 19:21; Jas 5:3). The Vg has the title "On Compassion" (*De misericordia*) at v. 12.

The cautious remarks on guaranteeing a loan or covering a debt for someone indicate that Ben Sira knows the consequences of covering a bad debt. He acknowledges that some generous people have been driven into penury and forced to travel to distant lands because of extending themselves too far out of compassion. He also recognizes unscrupulous and illegal practices, such as seizing collateral when someone has failed to repay a debt at the appointed time (cf. Exod 22:25; Deut 24:12-13; Amos 2:8). Ben Sira's description of the plight of those who engage in careless surety, tossing like the boisterous sea, offers a sober warning to all who consider standing in for a creditor.

---

208. Wiliam Shakespeare *Hamlet* I.iii.75-76.

SIRACH 29:21-28, ON BEING INDEPENDENT

NAB	NRSV
21 Life's prime needs are water, bread, and clothing, a house, too, for decent privacy.	21 The necessities of life are water, bread, and clothing, and also a house to assure privacy.
22 Better a poor man's fare under the shadow of one's own roof than sumptuous banquets among strangers.	22 Better is the life of the poor under their own crude roof than sumptuous food in the house of others.
23 Be it little or much, be content with what you have, and pay no heed to him who would disparage your home;	23 Be content with little or much, and you will hear no reproach for being a guest.[a]
24 A miserable life it is to go from house to house, for as a guest you dare not open your mouth.	24 It is a miserable life to go from house to house; as a guest you should not open your mouth;
25 The visitor has no thanks for filling the cups; besides, you will hear these bitter words:	25 you will play the host and provide drink without being thanked, and besides this you will hear rude words like these:
26 "Come here, stranger, set the table,	26 "Come here, stranger, prepare the table;

29, 23b: *kai oneidismon oikias sou mē akousēs*: so LXX[MSS]; cf V.

[a] Lat: Gk *reproach from your family*; other ancient authorities lack this line

NAB

give me to eat the food you have!
27 Away, stranger, for one more worthy;
   for my brother's visit I need the room!"
28 Painful things to a sensitive man
   are abuse at home and insults from his
   creditors.

NRSV

let me eat what you have there."
27 "Be off, stranger, for an honored guest is here;
   my brother has come for a visit, and I need
   the guest-room."
28 It is hard for a sensible person to bear
   scolding about lodging[a] and the insults of
   the moneylender.

[a] Or *scolding from the household*

COMMENTARY

This brief unit is best understood against the background of Greco-Roman culture, in which certain individuals stayed in the homes of wealthy people as unpaying guests. These parasitic persons were obliged to do menial chores to earn their food and lodging, and in the process they encountered considerable abuse. Ben Sira urges people to be content with their status, whether prosperous or humble, and thus to keep their independence. The initial verse mentions life's essentials: water, bread, clothing, a house for privacy (cf. 39:26, where a different list occurs). The remark in v. 25 about playing the host is ironic, for abuse instead of gratitude greets the "host's" action, making him a virtual slave. The unexpected reference in v. 28 to a creditor links this unit to the preceding one.

SIRACH 30:1-13, ON REARING CHILDREN

NAB

30 He who loves his son chastises him
   often,
   that he may be his joy when he grows up.
2 He who disciplines his son will benefit from
   him,
   and boast of him among his intimates.
3 He who educates his son makes his enemy
   jealous,
   and shows his delight in him among his
   friends.
4 At the father's death, he will seem not dead,
   since he leaves after him one like
   himself,
5 Whom he looks upon through life with joy,
   and even in death, without regret:
6 The avenger he leaves against his foes,
   and the one to repay his friends with
   kindness.

NRSV

30 He who loves his son will whip him
   often,
   so that he may rejoice at the way he turns
   out.
2 He who disciplines his son will profit by him,
   and will boast of him among acquaintances.
3 He who teaches his son will make his enemies
   envious,
   and will glory in him among his friends.
4 When the father dies he will not seem to be
   dead,
   for he has left behind him one like himself,
5 whom in his life he looked upon with joy
   and at death, without grief.
6 He has left behind him an avenger against his
   enemies,
   and one to repay the kindness of his friends.

NAB

7 He who spoils his son will have wounds to
   bandage,
      and will quake inwardly at every outcry.
8 A colt untamed turns out stubborn;
      a son left to himself grows up unruly.
9 Pamper your child and he will be a terror for
   you,
      indulge him and he will bring you grief.
10 Share not in his frivolity lest you share in
   his sorrow,
      when finally your teeth are clenched in
      remorse.
11 Give him not his own way in his youth,
      and close not your eyes to his follies.
12 Bend him to the yoke when he is young,
      thrash his sides while he is still small,
   Lest he become stubborn, disobey you,
      and leave you disconsolate.
13 Discipline your son, make heavy his yoke,
      lest his folly humiliate you.

30, 7: *peripsēchōn hsyion*: so LXX^MS 248, P.
30, 11–33, 3: With Hebrew.
30, 12: *kôp* (from *kpp*) *rō˒ šô bin*^e ˒*ûrāw, raṣṣēṣ motnāyw*
b^e˒*ôdennû na˓ ar*. Omit the rest before *lāmmâ*: dittog and variant.
(*lāmmâ*) *yaqšeh*: cf LXX. *yit˒ allēl* (?) (*bāk*): cf LXX, P.

NRSV

7 Whoever spoils his son will bind up his
   wounds,
      and will suffer heartache at every cry.
8 An unbroken horse turns out stubborn,
      and an unchecked son turns out headstrong.
9 Pamper a child, and he will terrorize you;
      play with him, and he will grieve you.
10 Do not laugh with him, or you will have
   sorrow with him,
      and in the end you will gnash your teeth.
11 Give him no freedom in his youth,
      and do not ignore his errors.
12 Bow down his neck in his youth,^a
      and beat his sides while he is young,
   or else he will become stubborn and disobey
      you,
      and you will have sorrow of soul from him.^b
13 Discipline your son and make his yoke heavy,^c
      so that you may not be offended by his
      shamelessness.

^aOther ancient authorities lack this line and the preceding line
^bOther ancient authorities lack this line   ^cHeb: Gk *take pains
with him*

COMMENTARY

The essential point to remember in assessing
the harsh discipline of children in ancient Israel
(cf. Prov 13:24; 19:18; 22:15; 23:13-14; 29:15)
is the belief that children provide continuity after
their parents' deaths, both in defending the family's rights and in carrying the name forward into
the next generation. Moreover, the severe treatment of children was common throughout the
ancient Near East; a very old Sumerian school
text, numerous Egyptian school texts from a
somewhat later era, and the Aramaic *Sayings of
Ahiqar* (perhaps seventh century BCE) provide copious evidence of this pedagogical practice over
millennia. Ben Sira offers a curious justification for
avoiding familiarity with one's children: They will
lose respect for you. The reference in v. 10 to a
parent gnashing teeth reverses the proverb in Ezek
18:2 and Jer 31:29, where children's teeth are
set on edge because of their parents' deeds.

Verse 7 suggests that coddling a son will make
a parent vulnerable to grief whenever a cry is
heard in the streets, causing their anxious query,
"Is that my child in pain?" The advice against
playing with children assumes paramount importance in the light of the silence within the Bible
about playful interaction between children and
their parents. The entire section presupposes that
children, like wild horses, must be tamed—one
might even say subdued. The language of a heavy
yoke accords with this understanding of children.
The Hebrew, which is missing from 26:2*a*, resumes again at 30:11. The following verse catches
the spirit of the entire discussion: "As a python
pounces on a wild beast, so crush a son's loins
while he is young." This harsh image probably
suggests severe punishment for all offenses, particularly sexual ones—the reason for referring to
chastising the boy's loins.

SIRACH 30:14-25, ON HEALTH

14 Better a poor man strong and robust,
    than a rich man with wasted frame.

 15 More precious than gold is health and well-being,
    contentment of spirit than coral.

16 No treasure greater than a healthy body;
    no happiness, than a joyful heart!

17 Preferable is death to a bitter life,
    unending sleep to constant illness.

18 Dainties set before one who cannot eat
    are like the offerings placed before a tomb.

19 What good is an offering to an idol
    that can neither taste nor smell?

20 So it is with the afflicted man
    who groans at the good things his eyes
    behold!

21 Do not give in to sadness,
    torment not yourself with brooding;

22 Gladness of heart is the very life of man,
    cheerfulness prolongs his days.

23 Distract yourself, renew your courage,
    drive resentment far away from you;
    For worry has brought death to many,
    nor is there aught to be gained from
    resentment.

24 Envy and anger shorten one's life,
    worry brings on premature old age.

25 One who is cheerful and gay while at table
    benefits from his food.

30, 16: Omit second *'ôšer*: so LXX, P; dittog.
30, 17: *mēḥayyîm mārîm*: so LXX, V. Omit c.d: variant of a.b; cf P.
30, 18: (*lipᵉnê*) *gôlēl*: so LXX, P, V.
30, 19: (*mah*) *yōʿîl ʿōlāh leʾĕlīlîm*: so LXX. Omit 19c.d: so LXX.
30, 20: *kēn hammukkeh* (?: *ekdikoumenos!*) *bᵉyad yhwh, rōʿeh bᵉʿênāyw ûmitʾannēaḥ*: cf LXX, P. Omit the rest: variant of 20, 3.
30, 21: (*ʾal tittēn*) *lᵉdāwôn . . . baʾ ăṣātekā*: so LXX, P.
30, 22: (*haʾărîk*) *yāmāyw*: so LXX, P, V.
30, 23c: (*hārag*) *dāwôn*: so LXX, P, V.
30, 25a: Omit *šᵉnôt*: so LXX, P; gloss on *nûmā* (31, 1).

¹⁴ Better off poor, healthy, and fit
    than rich and afflicted in body.

¹⁵ Health and fitness are better than any gold,
    and a robust body than countless riches.

¹⁶ There is no wealth better than health of body,
    and no gladness above joy of heart.

¹⁷ Death is better than a life of misery,
    and eternal sleep[a] than chronic sickness.

¹⁸ Good things poured out upon a mouth that is
    closed
    are like offerings of food placed upon a
    grave.

¹⁹ Of what use to an idol is a sacrifice?
    For it can neither eat nor smell.
    So is the one punished by the Lord;

²⁰ he sees with his eyes and groans
    as a eunuch groans when embracing a girl.[b]

²¹ Do not give yourself over to sorrow,
    and do not distress yourself deliberately.

²² A joyful heart is life itself,
    and rejoicing lengthens one's life span.

²³ Indulge yourself[c] and take comfort,
    and remove sorrow far from you,
    for sorrow has destroyed many,
    and no advantage ever comes from it.

²⁴ Jealousy and anger shorten life,
    and anxiety brings on premature old age.

²⁵ Those who are cheerful and merry at table
    will benefit from their food.

[a]Other ancient authorities lack *eternal sleep*   [b]Other ancient authorities add *So is the person who does right under compulsion*   [c]Other ancient authorities read *Beguile yourself*

COMMENTARY

Codex Vaticanus has the titles "On Health" above v. 14 and "On Goods" over v. 16. The brief section states a truism that robust health is preferable to wealth accompanied by sickness and momentarily dwells on the futility of giving delicacies to those unable to enjoy them, before concluding with encouragement to enjoy life. Ben Sira considers death, with its grim finality, better than constant illness. The Greek translators shied away from his pessimism with regard to life beyond the grave; accordingly, they omit the phrase "eternal sleep." Verse 18 alludes to the practice of offering food and drink to dead ancestors (cf. Tob 4:17), but an apparent interpretive gloss in v. 19 shifts the thought to another familiar ritual, the giving of sacrifices to idols. Allusions to the latter type of worship occur in Deut 4:28; Ps 115:4-7; Isa 44:9-11; 57:6; Wisdom 13; Bel and the Dragon 3:22; and Letter of Jeremiah 27, while Tob 4:17 possibly refers to the placing of food and the pouring of drink offerings on memorial stones (but cf. the attitude in Deut 26:14).

Biblical authors never appreciated the practice among their neighbors of treating idols as if they were alive—dressing them, feeding them, and taking them for a walk. Like so much in the OT as well as in the NT (cf. John 9:2), verses 19-20 understand sickness as divine punishment. Elsewhere Ben Sira offers a more nuanced interpretation of illness, one informed by Hellenistic attitudes to physicians and medicines rather than responding to criticism of this popular notion by the author of the book of Job (cf. Job 38:1-15, but note the resurgence of the popular view in the Greek text of v. 15, "Let him fall into the hands of a physician." The Hebrew text has "Whoever sins before his Maker will behave proudly before the physician"). The graphic portrayal in v. 20 of a eunuch embracing a young woman and groaning captures the utter futility of combining grievous illness with enjoyment of rich foods (cf. 20:4a).

A healthy attitude toward maintaining beneficial psychological states occurs in vv. 21-25. In recognizing the danger of harboring resentment and nursing grief over a prolonged period, Ben Sira resembles Qohelet (cf. Eccl 11:9-10; Matt 6:34). The rabbinic tractate *Sanh.* 100*b* cites a portion of v. 23: "Do not let sorrow enter your heart, for sorrow has killed mighty men." Many ancient thinkers have registered similar ideas, for example, "Anger would inflict punishment on another; meanwhile, it tortures itself."[209]

The order of the Greek text becomes confused after v. 24; two pairs of leaves containing respectively 30:25–33:13*a* and 33:13*b*–36:12 have been transposed. A more natural order, placing 33:13*b*–36:12 before 30:25–33:13*a*, is retained in the Hebrew, the Vg, and *Peshitta.*

209. Publilius Syrus *Moral Sayings* 1009 (1st cent. CE). Cf. the more recent (16th cent. CE) aphorisms by Baltasar Gracian: "The envious die not once, but as oft as the envied win applause," and by Friedrich Nietzsche: "Nothing on earth consumes a man more quickly than the passion of resentment" (*Ecce Homo*). The last reference cited is from Patrick W. Skehan and Alexander A. Di Lella, *The Wisdom of Ben Sira,* AB 39 (New York: Doubleday, 1987) 382.

SIRACH 31:1-11, ON RICHES

NAB

31 Keeping watch over riches wastes the flesh,
   and the care of wealth drives away rest.
2 Concern for one's livelihood banishes slumber;
   more than a serious illness it disturbs repose.
3 The rich man labors to pile up wealth,

31, 1: *šeqed 'ôšer yimḥeh šā'e' ēr, we da' agātô taprîd te nûmâ*: cf LXX, P.
31, 2: (*da' agat miḥyâ) tāsîr* (=*apostē sei*: V) *šē nâ*. Omit *rē a'* ... *ke nāpeš*: so LXX, P; cf 22, 22; 27, 17.
31, 3: *'āmēl (' āšîr) liqbôš*: so LXX, P.

NRSV

31 Wakefulness over wealth wastes away one's flesh,
   and anxiety about it drives away sleep.
2 Wakeful anxiety prevents slumber,
   and a severe illness carries off sleep.[a]
3 The rich person toils to amass a fortune,
   and when he rests he fills himself with his dainties.
4 The poor person toils to make a meager living,
   and if ever he rests he becomes needy.

[a]Other ancient authorities read *sleep carries off a severe illness*

NAB

and his only rest is wanton pleasure;

4 The poor man toils for a meager subsistence,
and if ever he rests, he finds himself in
want.

5 The lover of gold will not be free from sin,
for he who pursues wealth is led astray by
it.

6 Many have been ensnared by gold,
though destruction lay before their eyes;

7 It is a stumbling block to those who are avid
for it,
a snare for every fool.

8 Happy the rich man found without fault,
who turns not aside after gain!

9 Who is he, that we may praise him?
he, of all his kindred, has done wonders,

10 For he has been tested by gold and come
off safe,
and this remains his glory;
He could have sinned but did not,
could have done evil but would not,

11 So that his possessions are secure,
and the assembly recounts his praises.

31, 4: ʿāmēl ʿānî lᵉḥassēr kôbô, wᵉ·im yānûaḥ yihyeh ṣārîk: so
LXX, P. Omit the rest: variants.

31, 5: ʾôhēb (ḥarûs) . . . wᵉrôdēp (mᵉḥîr): so LXX, P.

31, 6: (zāhāb, wᵉhawwātām(ʿal) pᵉnêhem; and omit the following;
so LXX; gloss.

31, 8: (ʾašrê· ʿāšîr: so LXX, P.

31, 10: mî nibdaq bô wayyišlām, wᵉhāyâ lô lᵉtipʾāret, and omit the
rest: variants: so LXX; cf P.

NRSV

5 One who loves gold will not be justified;
one who pursues money will be led astray[a]
by it.

6 Many have come to ruin because of gold,
and their destruction has met them face to
face.

7 It is a stumbling block to those who are avid
for it,
and every fool will be taken captive by it.

8 Blessed is the rich person who is found
blameless,
and who does not go after gold.

9 Who is he, that we may praise him?
For he has done wonders among his people.

10 Who has been tested by it and been found
perfect?
Let it be for him a ground for boasting.
Who has had the power to transgress and did
not transgress,
and to do evil and did not do it?

11 His prosperity will be established,[b]
and the assembly will proclaim his acts of
charity.

[a] Heb Syr: Gk pursues destruction will be filled   [b] Other ancient
authorities add because of this

COMMENTARY

In this unit about the difficulty of being rich
and also virtuous, Ben Sira uses rhetorical questions and emphatic language that comes close in
meaning to "miracle." The prayer attributed to
Agur in Prov 30:8-9 captures the danger inherent
to the wealthy, a temptation to forget God as a
result of (deceptive) self-sufficiency. Others in ancient Israel shared the sentiment expressed in v.
10. This criticism of wealth was also common
among Hellenistic authors of this time. Ben Sira's
understanding of riches was complicated by contradictory impulses—the destructive effect of pur-

suing money as if it were the ultimate thing in
life and the belief that God commanded the
Israelite people to do works of charity by helping
the needy. Extreme poverty, like excessive
wealth, brought special temptations.

Verses 3-4 contrast rich and poor in terms of
the results of a common activity, "toiling." In the
one instance, toil yields plenty, whereas in the
other the labor only brings need. The first known
use in the Bible of the Aramaic loan word "mammon" (ממון mammôn) occurs in v. 8, although
later texts use it often (cf. Matt 6:24; Luke 16:9,

11, 13; and *Pirqe 'Abot* 2.16, "Rabbi Jose said, 'Let your friend's wealth [*mammôn*] be as precious to you as your own' "). Verse 9 probably expresses irony, following an unlikely blessing, one pronounced on a non-existent entity. The next verse suggests that only one who has withstood the ethical test that comes with a fortune has the right to boast, for others do not know how they would deal with the temptation. The final verse alludes to the practice of proclaiming aloud the names of benefactors in the gathered assembly or in writing on the walls of synagogues.

SIRACH 31:12–32:13, ON PROPER ETIQUETTE

NAB

12 If you are dining with a great man,
  bring not a greedy gullet to his table,
Nor cry out, "How much food there is here?"
13 Remember that gluttony is evil.
  No creature is greedier than the eye:
    therefore it weeps for any cause.
14 Toward what he eyes, do not put out a hand;
    nor reach when he does for the same dish.
15 Recognize that your neighbor feels as you do,
    and keep in mind your own dislikes:
16 Behave at table like a favored guest,
    and be not greedy, lest you be despised.
17 Be the first to stop, as befits good manners;
    gorge not yourself, lest you give offense.
18 If there are many with you at table,
    be not the first to reach out your hand.
19 Does not a little suffice for a well-bred man?
    When he lies down, it is without discomfort.
20 Distress and anguish and loss of sleep,
    and restless tossing for the glutton!
  Moderate eating ensures sound slumber
    and a clear mind next day on rising.
21 If perforce you have eaten too much,
    once you have emptied your stomach, you will have relief.
22 Listen to me, my son, and scorn me not;
    later you will find my advice good.

31, 12: Omit *bᵉnî im*: so LXX.
31, 13: Omit *ra' 'ayin sônē' . . . dim'â tidmā'*, and read at end ('al-kēn) mikkol pānîm tidmā': so LXX.
31, 14f: Trsp v 14 and v 15. (*wᵉal*) *tēḥad.*
31, 16: Omit *da' šerē' āka . . . lᵉpānèkā* : variants.
31, 20: *ûnᵉdūdē šēnā*: cf Jᵇ 7, 4. Omit *wᵉtašnîq*: so LXX: gloss. Omit everything after *'ittô*: so LXX; variants.
31, 21f: Order as in LXX, P. Omit second *šᵉma 'bᵉnî etc*: so LXX; variant.

NRSV

12 Are you seated at the table of the great?ᵃ
  Do not be greedy at it,
    and do not say, "How much food there is here!"
13 Remember that a greedy eye is a bad thing.
  What has been created more greedy than the eye?
    Therefore it sheds tears for any reason.
14 Do not reach out your hand for everything you see,
    and do not crowd your neighborᵇ at the dish.
15 Judge your neighbor's feelings by your own,
    and in every matter be thoughtful.
16 Eat what is set before you like a well brought-up person,ᶜ
    and do not chew greedily, or you will give offense.
17 Be the first to stop, as befits good manners,
    and do not be insatiable, or you will give offense.
18 If you are seated among many persons,
    do not help yourselfᵈ before they do.

19 How ample a little is for a well-disciplined person!
    He does not breathe heavily when in bed.
20 Healthy sleep depends on moderate eating;
    he rises early, and feels fit.
  The distress of sleeplessness and of nausea and colic are with the glutton.
21 If you are overstuffed with food,
    get up to vomit, and you will have relief.
22 Listen to me, my child, and do not disregard me,

ᵃHeb Syr: Gk *at a great table*   ᵇGk *him*   ᶜHeb: Gk *like a human being*   ᵈGk *reach out your hand*

NAB

In whatever you do, be moderate,
and no sickness will befall you.

23 On a man generous with food, blessings are
invoked,
and this testimony to his goodness is
lasting;

24 He who is miserly with food is denounced
in public,
and this testimony to his stinginess is
lasting.

25 Let not wine-drinking be the proof of your
strength,
for wine has been the ruin of many.

26 As the furnace probes the work of the
smith,
so does wine the hearts of the insolent.

27 Wine is very life to man
if taken in moderation.
Does he really live who lacks the wine
which was created for his joy?

28 Joy of heart, good cheer and merriment
are wine drunk freely at the proper time.

29 Headache, bitterness and disgrace
is wine drunk amid anger and strife.

30 More and more wine is a snare for the fool;
it lessens his strength and multiplies his
wounds.

31 Rebuke not your neighbor when wine is
served,
nor put him to shame while he is merry;
Use no harsh words with him
and distress him not in the presence of
others.

32 If you are chosen to preside at dinner,
be not puffed up,
but with the guests be as one of
themselves;
Take care of them first before you sit down;
2 when you have fulfilled your duty, then take
your place,

31, 24: (ra⌐ ⌐al leḥem) yērāḡēn or yᵉruggan: cf LXX. Omit the rest:
so LXX.
31, 26: kᵉkûr(bōḥēn) . . . libbôt(lēṣîm): so LXX. Omit the rest: so LXX,
P; variant.
31, 27: kᵉmê (or kᵉmô; LXX) ḥayyîm hayyayin: so P. (mâ ḥayyîm)
laḥāsar (ḥayyayin), wᵉhû; so LXX.
31, 28: (wᵉśāśôn) wᵉ⌐iddûn. (bᵉ⌐ittô) lirᵉwāyâ(?): cf Ps 23, 5. Omit
ḥayyê . . . mērō⌐š: variant of 27c.d.
31, 31b: wᵉ⌐al tᵉbîšēhû bᵉśimḥātô: so LXX. 31d: wᵉ⌐al ta⌐aṣbēhû
lipᵉnê⌐ ănāšîm: cf LXXᴹˢ ²⁴⁸, P.
32, 1a: With LXX; cf P.

NRSV

and in the end you will appreciate my
words.
In everything you do be moderate,[a]
and no sickness will overtake you.

23 People bless the one who is liberal with food,
and their testimony to his generosity is
trustworthy.

24 The city complains of the one who is stingy
with food,
and their testimony to his stinginess is
accurate.

25 Do not try to prove your strength by
wine-drinking,
for wine has destroyed many.

26 As the furnace tests the work of the smith,[b]
so wine tests hearts when the insolent
quarrel.

27 Wine is very life to human beings
if taken in moderation.
What is life to one who is without wine?
It has been created to make people happy.

28 Wine drunk at the proper time and in
moderation
is rejoicing of heart and gladness of soul.

29 Wine drunk to excess leads to bitterness of
spirit,
to quarrels and stumbling.

30 Drunkenness increases the anger of a fool to
his own hurt,
reducing his strength and adding wounds.

31 Do not reprove your neighbor at a banquet of
wine,
and do not despise him in his merrymaking;
speak no word of reproach to him,
and do not distress him by making demands
of him.

32 If they make you master of the feast, do
not exalt yourself;
be among them as one of their number.
Take care of them first and then sit down;
2 when you have fulfilled all your duties, take
your place,
so that you may be merry along with them
and receive a wreath for your excellent
leadership.

aHeb Syr: Gk industrious   bHeb: Gk tests the hardening of steel
by dipping

NAB

To share in their joy
and win praise for your hospitality.

3 Being older, you may talk; that is only your
right,
but temper your wisdom, not to disturb
the singing.

4 When wine is present, do not pour out
discourse,
and flaunt not your wisdom at the wrong
time.

5 Like a seal of carnelian in a setting of gold
is a concert when wine is served.

6 Like a gold mounting with an emerald seal
is string music with delicious wine.

7 Young man, speak only when necessary,
when they have asked you more than
once;

8 Be brief, but say much in those few words,
be like the wise man, taciturn.

9 When among your elders be not forward,
and with officials be not too insistent.

10 Like the lightning that flashes before a storm
is the esteem that shines on modesty.

11 When it is time to leave, tarry not;
be off for home! There take your ease,

12 And there enjoy doing as you wish,
but without sin or words of pride.

13 Above all, give praise to your Creator,
who showers his favors upon you.

32, 4: Omit *ûbᵉlō'... śîaḥ*: so LXX; variant.
32, 5: Omit a.b: so LXX; variant of c.d.
32, 6: Omit a.b: so LXX; variant of c.d.
32, 10: Omit a.b: so LXX; variant of c.d. *bôš yinṣaḥ*.
32, 11: (*pᵉtar lᵉbêtekā) wᵉšāmè titrā'* (cf Gn 42, 1): so V (omit *mē* of LXX). Omit c.d: so LXX; gloss.
32, 12: With LXX; Heb corrupt.
32, 13: Omit c.d: so LXX; variant of 14a.b.

NRSV

3 Speak, you who are older, for it is your right,
but with accurate knowledge, and do not
interrupt the music.

4 Where there is entertainment, do not pour out
talk;
do not display your cleverness at the wrong
time.

5 A ruby seal in a setting of gold
is a concert of music at a banquet of wine.

6 A seal of emerald in a rich setting of gold
is the melody of music with good wine.

7 Speak, you who are young, if you are obliged
to,
but no more than twice, and only if asked.

8 Be brief; say much in few words;
be as one who knows and can still hold his
tongue.

9 Among the great do not act as their equal;
and when another is speaking, do not
babble.

10 Lightning travels ahead of the thunder,
and approval goes before one who is modest.

11 Leave in good time and do not be the last;
go home quickly and do not linger.

12 Amuse yourself there to your heart's content,
but do not sin through proud speech.

13 But above all bless your Maker,
who fills you with his good gifts.

COMMENTARY

This extensive section consists of three discrete topics dealing with conduct in eating (31:12-24), self-control in drinking wine (31:25-31), and behavior at banquets (32:1-13). Egyptian instructional literature devotes considerable space to these subjects, largely because of its use in preparing young men for life at court. In the book of Proverbs, only the brief section in Prov 22:17–24:33, which depends on the *Instruction of Amenemope,* takes up these matters (cf. Prov 23:1-3). Ben Sira's remarks came at a time when Greco-Roman banquets were notorious occasions for gluttony.

31:12-24. Ben Sira offers advice that falls in

the category of common courtesy. In his culture, the host praised the food and guests exercised restraint, lest they appear greedy. The curious argument about the evil eye—that is, an insatiable appetite—and the appropriateness of tears flowing from this instrument needs to be balanced by recognizing the positive contribution of the eye. Ben Sira bases his advice on courtesy and self-interest, arguing that eating in moderation enables one to sleep. In context, the suggestion that one get up and vomit seems better suited as a relief from indigestion than advice during meals to excuse oneself long enough to vomit so as to continue eating everything provided by the host.

31:25-31. The counsel to drink wine in moderation appears in conjunction with lavish praise for this contributor to human happiness. The rhetorical question in v. 27 implies that life without wine is hardly worth living. Nevertheless, Ben Sira knows how wine, drunk in excess, brings misery beyond comprehension. This description of drunken conduct pales in comparison with that in 1 Esdr 3:17-24, which praises wine as the strongest thing in the world.

32:1-13. Hellenistic banquets (symposia) were governed by a strict set of rules. A banquet master was selected for the occasion and may have worn a wreath of flowers (cf. 2 Macc 2:27). Musical entertainment was provided, and senior guests displayed their wisdom; only occasionally were younger guests expected to speak, and that quite briefly.

In v. 13, Ben Sira manages to combine such Hellenistic partying with his own religious inclination, although Greeks also praised their gods at the end of a feast. He demonstrates astute insights about proper social conduct in the advice to go home promptly, even if out of courtesy the host invites you to stay beyond the appointed hour. Ben Sira's knowledge of natural phenomena—the association of thunder with previous lightning—leads to unsupported claims about popular approval of modest persons. The key to this statement lies in one's support group; Ben Sira's fellow scribes would probably have praised modesty. They certainly would not have approved of drinking contests like those in Greek symposia (cf. Isa 5:22 for similar language), for the perils of drunkenness were well known to the authors of Proverbs (cf. Prov 23:29-35).

SIRACH 32:14–33:19, ON DIVINE PROVIDENCE

NAB	NRSV

14 He who would find God must accept discipline;
  he who seeks him obtains his request.
	[14] The one who seeks God[a] will accept his discipline,
	  and those who rise early to seek him[b] will find favor.

15 He who studies the law masters it,
  but the hypocrite finds it a trap.
	[15] The one who seeks the law will be filled with it,
	  but the hypocrite will stumble at it.

16 His judgment is sound who fears the LORD;
  out of obscurity he draws forth a clear plan.
	[16] Those who fear the Lord will form true judgments,
	  and they will kindle righteous deeds like a light.

17 The sinner turns aside reproof
  and distorts the law to suit his purpose.
	[17] The sinner will shun reproof,
	  and will find a decision according to his liking.

18 The thoughtful man will not neglect direction; the proud and insolent man is deterred by nothing.	

32, 14: Omit c.d: so LXX; variant of a.b.
32, 16: *minnešep* (*yōṣî*): so the facsimile. Omit c.d: so LXX; variant of a.b.
32, 17: (*ʾîš*) *ḥāmās*: so B margin, LXX.
32, 18: Omit a.b: so LXX; variant of c.d. (*ʾîš*) *ʿēṣâ* (*lōʾ*) *yāqēl śekel,* (*zēd wālēṣ lōʾ*) *yēḥat môrāʾ* (?): so LXX.

[a]Heb: Gk *who fears the Lord*   [b]Other ancient authorities lack *to seek him*

NAB

19 Do nothing without counsel,
   and then you need have no regrets.
20 Go not on a way that is set with snares,
   and let not the same thing trip you twice.
21 Be not too sure even of smooth roads,
22 be careful on all your paths.
23 Whatever you do, be on your guard,
   for in this way you will keep the
      commandments.
24 He who keeps the law preserves himself;
   and he who trusts in the LORD shall not be
      put to shame.

33 No evil can harm the man who fears the
      LORD;
   through trials, again and again he is safe.
2 He who hates the law is without wisdom,
   and is tossed about like a boat in a storm.
3 The prudent man trusts in the word of the
      LORD,
   and the law is dependable for him as a
      divine oracle.
4 Prepare your words and you will be listened
      to;
   draw upon your training, and then give
      your answer.

5 Like the wheel of a cart is the mind of a fool;
   his thoughts revolve in circles.
6 A fickle friend is like the stallion
   that neighs, no matter who the rider.
7 Why is one day more important than another,
   when it is the sun that lights up every day?
8 It is due to the LORD's wisdom that they
      differ;
   it is through him the seasons and feasts
      come and go.
9 Some he dignifies and sanctifies,
   and others he lists as ordinary days.
10 So too, all men are of clay,
   for from earth man was formed;
11 Yet with his great knowledge the LORD
      makes men unlike;
   in different paths he has them walk.

32, 22: *ûb*e *' ō r*e *ḥō tèkā* (*hiŝŝā mēr*). Omit the rest: so LXX; variants.
32, 33: Omit a.b: so LXX, P; variant of c.d.
33, 2a: (*ûmitmôṭēṭ*) *k*e *biŝ' ā râ ' ŏniyyâ*: cf LXX.
33, 3: (' *iŝ nā bôn*) *yîḇṭaḥ bid*e *bar yhwh*, (*w*e *tôrā tô*) *kā ' ûrîm
ne' ĕmānâ:* cf LXX.
33, 4–35, 7: With LXX; but for Hebrew of 33, 4–34, 1 cf JQR 21 (1931),
pp 223-240.

NRSV

18 A sensible person will not overlook a
      thoughtful suggestion;
   an insolent[a] and proud person will not be
      deterred by fear.[b]
19 Do nothing without deliberation,
   but when you have acted, do not regret it.
20 Do not go on a path full of hazards,
   and do not stumble at an obstacle twice.[c]
21 Do not be overconfident on a smooth[d] road,
22   and give good heed to your paths.[e]
23 Guard[f] yourself in every act,
   for this is the keeping of the
      commandments.

24 The one who keeps the law preserves himself,[g]
   and the one who trusts the Lord will not
      suffer loss.

33 No evil will befall the one who fears
      the Lord,
   but in trials such a one will be rescued again
      and again.
2 The wise will not hate the law,
   but the one who is hypocritical about it is
      like a boat in a storm.
3 The sensible person will trust in the law;
   for such a one the law is as dependable as
      a divine oracle.

4 Prepare what to say, and then you will be
      listened to;
   draw upon your training, and give your
      answer.
5 The heart of a fool is like a cart wheel,
   and his thoughts like a turning axle.
6 A mocking friend is like a stallion
   that neighs no matter who the rider is.

7 Why is one day more important than another,
   when all the daylight in the year is from the
      sun?
8 By the Lord's wisdom they were distinguished,
   and he appointed the different seasons and
      festivals.
9 Some days he exalted and hallowed,
   and some he made ordinary days.

a Heb: Gk *alien*   *b* Meaning of Gk uncertain. Other ancient authorities add *and after acting, with him, without deliberation*
c Heb: Gk *stumble on stony ground*   *d* Or *an unexplored*
e Heb Syr: Gk *and beware of your children*   *f* Heb Syr: Gk *Trust*
g Heb: Gk *who believes the law heeds the commandments*

NAB

12 Some he blesses and makes great,
    some he sanctifies and draws to himself.
Others he curses and brings low,
    and expels them from their place.
13 Like clay in the hands of a potter,
    to be molded according to his pleasure,
So are men in the hands of their Creator,
    to be assigned by him their function.
14 As evil contrasts with good, and death with
    life,
    so are sinners in contrast with the just;
15 See now all the works of the Most High:
    they come in pairs, the one the opposite
      of the other.

16 Now I am the last to keep vigil,
    like a gleaner after the vintage;
17 Since by the LORD's blessing I have made
    progress
    till like a vintager I have filled my
      winepress,
18 I would inform you that not for myself only
    have I toiled,
    but for every seeker after wisdom.

19 Listen to me, O leaders of the multitude;
    O rulers of the assembly, give ear!

33, 13b: *plasai auto* (*kata tēn eudokian autou*): so 1 LXX[MS], V; cf Heb, P.

NRSV

10 All human beings come from the ground,
    and humankind[a] was created out of the
      dust.
11 In the fullness of his knowledge the Lord
    distinguished them
    and appointed their different ways.
12 Some he blessed and exalted,
    and some he made holy and brought near
      to himself;
but some he cursed and brought low,
    and turned them out of their place.
13 Like clay in the hand of the potter,
    to be molded as he pleases,
so all are in the hand of their Maker,
    to be given whatever he decides.

14 Good is the opposite of evil,
    and life the opposite of death;
    so the sinner is the opposite of the godly.
15 Look at all the works of the Most High;
    they come in pairs, one the opposite of the
      other.

16 Now I was the last to keep vigil;
    I was like a gleaner following the
      grape-pickers;
17 by the blessing of the Lord I arrived first,
    and like a grape-picker I filled my wine
      press.
18 Consider that I have not labored for myself
    alone,
    but for all who seek instruction.
19 Hear me, you who are great among the people,
    and you leaders of the congregation, pay
      heed!

a Heb: Gk *Adam*

COMMENTARY

32:14-18. This section on divine providence deals with the positive role of the law in individual lives and posits a theodicy based on polarities in nature and among humans. Five variants in the Hebrew of v. 14 yield virtually the same idea—that whoever seeks God submits to discipline, and the one rising early to pray (cf. 39:50) enjoys divine favor. Praying at sunrise was an act of piety with enor-mous symbolic power, a sanctioning of each new day. Ever conscious of sinners, Ben Sira acknowledges this vulnerability before the law's curses. Knowing the contents of divine instruction, these reckless persons (the Greek has "hypocrite" [ὑποκρινόμενος *hypokrinomenos*]) refuse to observe them, preferring their own wishes to God's. The image of light in v. 16 does not necessarily indicate Ben Sira's familiarity with the lighthouse of Pharos off Alexandria,[210] for biblical literature abounds in such language (Ps 119:105; Prov 6:23).

32:19-24. Verse 19, at which the Vg has the title "Do Everything with Counsel" (*cum consilio omnia facienda*), uses an old idea but gives it a new twist: Think before acting, and having done so, put an end to second-guessing. Ben Sira recognizes the psychological stress generated by constant anxiety over whether one has made the right decision. At the same time, he warns against a sort of brash confidence that ignores real danger such as that posed by brigands lying in ambush on the open roads, and he expects people to learn from past mistakes. Verses 23-24 apply the verb "to keep," "to observe" (שמר *šāmar*) to the Torah as well as to one's life (נפש *nepeš*). According to v. 23, guarding one's ways (or deeds) is tantamount to observing a statute (מצוה *miṣwâ*), while v. 24 varies the verb with reference to Torah (נצר *nāṣar*) but repeats "watches over himself" (שומר נפשו *šōmēr napšô*).

33:1-3. The assertion in 33:1 flies in the face of reality, although many sages subscribed to this simplistic theology. From a certain perspective, however, even the experience of Job can be harmonized with the claim that God rescues good people from tests. The same cannot be said for Job's children and servants, who perished through no fault of their own. The description of sinners as a boat without a rudder, tossing at sea in a tumultuous storm, occurs widely in ancient ethical teachings (cf. Jas 1:6). The belief that a divine oracle, predictive by nature, is reliable like the priestly throw of dice (Urim and Thummim) indicates that Ben Sira trusted heavily in God's control of such minute details as the way these sacred "rocks" fell.

33:4-6. Two images characterize fools, according to vv. 5-6. They repeat themselves incessantly, like a cart wheel and axle, and they lack any discrimination at all, like a rutting stallion scenting for a mare. In v. 4, the Hebrew MS E advises people to give careful attention to what they wish to say, whereas the Greek verb "gather"

(συνδέω *syndeō*) suggests a colorful image of a person binding up clothes and essential supplies in a bundle before setting out on a journey.[211]

33:7-15. Ben Sira tries to explain why people divide into two distinct groups, which he labels wise and foolish, righteous and wicked. First, he notes that in God's wisdom not all days have the same significance in the liturgical calendar, despite their enjoying a common source of light and warmth. Second, Ben Sira concedes that all people derive from the same source, dust, but the potter decides what value to place on the completed vessel. Some people, like Abraham, receive divine blessing; others, like priests, are brought near to the Holy One; still others, like Canaanites, are cursed. From such comparisons, Ben Sira concludes that God made the whole universe like this, each entity having an opposite—good and evil, life and death.[212] This idea of constitutive pairs goes beyond Qohelet's teaching of a time for everything under the sun (Eccl 3:1-8). In this section, Ben Sira probably responds to Jewish Hellenizers who doubted the special place of Israel in the divine economy.

33:16-19. The last four verses of this unit comprise the second authorial self-reference in the book (cf. 24:30-34; 34:12-13; 39:12-15, 32-35; 41:16; 43:32; 50:25-29; 51:1-30). Ben Sira allies himself with the prophets, using the metaphor of a watcher guarding the people against enemy attack (cf. Ezek 3:17; 33:7; Hab 2:1), and with wisdom teachers (cf. Wis 6:12-20). Conscious of his position at the end of a long line of inspired persons, he seeks to overcome the stigma of being last by excelling in knowledge, thus making the last become first. The image of filling his winepress suggests success in learning Torah. Verse 18 repeats the claim of altruism already made in 24:34, and v. 19 asks influential citizens to reflect on his teaching (cf. Wis 1:1; 6:1-2 for this rhetorical form).

Like their modern counterparts, ancient teachers

---

210. Skehan and Di Lella think Rudolf Smend may be right in seeing an allusion to the lighthouse of Pharos in Sir 32:16. See Patrick W. Skehan and Alexander A. Di Lella, *The Wisdom of Ben Sira,* AB 39 (New York: Doubleday, 1987) 397.

211. Cf. Theodotion's use of this verb in Prov 6:21 and Aquila's in Prov 3:3; 6:21; and 7:3 to translate the Hebrew קשר (*qāšar*, "to bind").

212. Cf. the *Testament of the Twelve Patriarchs,* Asher 1:3-4: "God has granted two ways to the sons of men, two mind-sets, two lines of action, two models, and two goals" (accordingly, everything is in pairs, the one over against the other); 5:1-2: "Children, you see how in everything there are two factors, one against the other, one concealed by the other. . . . Death is successor to life, dishonor to glory, night to day, darkness to light, but all these things lead ultimately to day: righteous actions to life, unjust actions to death since eternal life wards off death."

felt the need to capture the attention of their students; to do so, they made direct appeals to be heard. Both Ben Sira and the unknown author of the book of Wisdom flattered their audience by identifying them as rulers and officials, the impor-

tant decision makers in the community. According to the sages' ideology, their students could look forward to appointment in high office, hence the language here is not simply rhetorical flourish.

REFLECTIONS

1. Doubt about the actual operation of a principle of reward and retribution provoked Ben Sira to affirm divine providential care and to make an audacious claim that tilts perilously close to cosmic dualism. Inherent to ethical monotheism is a perennial problem: how to harmonize belief in a benevolent Creator with the presence of so much evil. A moment's thought suggests that a good God would surely have made things capable of running more smoothly—that is, acting in conformity with the divine will. Ben Sira offers a reasonable answer—namely, free will—but then he places this partial resolution of the problem in jeopardy by insisting on something approaching divine determinism. Modern apologists fare little better, even when profiting from Ben Sira's bold endeavor.

2. Anyone who hopes to persuade others to adopt a certain life-style must be prepared for questions about credentials. What right do you have to offer advice? Where did you acquire insights into the nature of reality? Ben Sira asserts the right to teach others, claiming total immersion in Israel's sacred traditions and exceptional success in that study. The sages' authoritative introduction, "Listen, my son, to your dad's advice," functions precisely like the prophetic oracular formula, "Thus has the Lord spoken." Neither the one nor the other actually required others to pay attention, for successful counsel depends on the disposition of the person to whom it is addressed. Learning, therefore, is a mutual process involving teacher and student, one characterized by trust.

This principle applies at every level of instruction. Parents, relatives, friends, and pastors can no longer assume that the mere assertion of authority commands obedience, for respect of that magnitude must be earned. Even the right to share intimate feelings is not automatic, for privacy needs to be honored. Nevertheless, many individuals desperately long for worthy persons to shatter their wall of isolation and construct a relationship of trust and fidelity. Like Ben Sira, unselfish Christians can bring a ray of hope to such lonely children of God.

3. Perhaps the time has come for Christians to acknowledge a need for lifelong education. In the past, emphasis has fallen on the teaching role, so that whatever learning took place came as a result of preparing to instruct others, often children. Society in general has begun to place greater emphasis on continuing education, with major universities offering stimulating and intellectually demanding classes for persons enjoying longer years of retirement. This opportunity for instruction in later life bodes well for active minds and earnest learners among the aged. The church is beginning to recognize this shift among its members and to encourage lifelong learning about spiritual matters, but more needs to be done in this vein.

The present interest among many Protestants in the spiritual life of mystics and in meditation as practiced by monastics of the Roman Catholic Church offers yet another challenge. The potential for spiritual enrichment is almost unlimited, and the combination of meditation and secular existence opens up new ways of dealing with reality. Those persons who allow the deep spiritual life of meditation to shape their decisions have much to gain.

SIRACH 33:20–39:11

PART VI

OVERVIEW

This section begins with an appeal stressing the advantage of maintaining one's independence until the moment of death. The unit concludes with a lengthy comparison of various vocations to that of professional teachers of wisdom. Between introductory and concluding units, one finds quite distinct treatments of several topics of interest to sages generally and some sentiment specific to Ben Sira's own day, but until then foreign to wisdom literature.

SIRACH 33:20-24, THE ADVANTAGE OF INDEPENDENCE

NAB	NRSV
20 Let neither son nor wife, neither brother nor friend, have power over you as long as you live.	20 To son or wife, to brother or friend, do not give power over yourself, as long as you live; and do not give your property to another, in case you change your mind and must ask for it.
21 While breath of life is still in you, let no man have dominion over you. Give not to another your wealth, lest then you have to plead with him;	21 While you are still alive and have breath in you, do not let anyone take your place.
22 Far better that your children plead with you than that you should look to their generosity.	22 For it is better that your children should ask from you than that you should look to the hand of your children.
23 Keep control over all your affairs; let no one tarnish your glory.	23 Excel in all that you do; bring no stain upon your honor.
24 When your few days reach their limit, at the time of death distribute your inheritance.	24 At the time when you end the days of your life, in the hour of death, distribute your inheritance.

33, 21: Order of lines as in Heb, P.

COMMENTARY

The advice in vv. 20-24 to hold on to one's possessions until just prior to death may have been prompted by pious Jews who gave away their wealth in the interest of acquiring credit with God for performing deeds of kindness (מצוות *miṣwôt*). The unfortunate consequence of such generosity, an impoverishment that placed unnecessary hardships on family members of the charitable individual, carried with it an embarrassing need to request assistance. Ben Sira's silence about daughters in this list of family members stands out, for he mentions son, wife, brother, and friend but says nothing about a daughter. The advice to distribute one's goods just before death implies that the practice of writing a last will and testament had not yet become normative. This literary form came to be an important vehicle for ethical instruction, for in it a revered figure approaching the end of life handed down the insights about life acquired through long experience. The well-known *Testament of the Twelve Patriarchs* demonstrates the usefulness of this literary device in Jewish ethical instruction.

REFLECTIONS

In Jesus' day life's unpredictability prompted many Jews to worry about the future in a way that he considered counterproductive, particularly in the light of human inability to control so many factors that shape destiny. His call to trust the heavenly Father notwithstanding, modern Christians join their secular compatriots in worrying about becoming dependent in their later years. Social Security and Medicare may have reduced people's anxiety somewhat, but many persons approaching that period in life when their earning potential goes down and their expenses for medical care skyrocket find themselves frequently worrying about the future.

This anxiety increases as taxes rise, inflation and medical care eat away at people's savings, and they can see no end to the rising spiral of costs. That worry is further heightened by a sense of vulnerability to numerous forces that seem wholly out of control, particularly violence and crime of all sorts. No longer able-bodied, many elderly persons feel like prisoners in their own homes, unable to venture very far for fear of attack. Moreover, the fast pace of society places them at risk, for failing sight, waning dexterity, and slower reaction time increase their chances of having an accident. In addition, they cannot understand the younger generation's lack of respect for their elders. Time appears to have passed them by as so many cherished values go up in smoke.

Ben Sira understood this type of anxiety and suggested a practical way of dealing with it in his time. The secret as he saw things was to hang on to possessions until death, in that way avoiding the necessity of depending on one's family for primary care. He correctly perceived the blow to personal dignity when one must rely on others' goodwill, even when the care givers belong to one's own family.

The theological conviction that God hears the petition of those in need should not prevent caring individuals from addressing the root causes of such anxiety. Ben Sira's partially humorous remark that one should not make fun of old people for "some of us are growing old" personalizes the problem in precisely the right manner. Everyone has a stake in solving the dilemma, for sooner or later each individual will internalize the feelings that generate such anxiety. In this struggle to find answers to a vexing problem, the first consideration may be, by necessity, the strengthening of familial bonds. Perhaps the time has come to recognize children's responsibility to repay parents for their years of generous care. In this regard, we can learn valuable lessons from other cultures, particularly the Arabs and Asians, both of which honor those who have lived a long time.

SIRACH 33:25-33, ON SLAVES

NAB

25 Fodder and whip and loads for an ass;
  the yoke and harness and the rod of his
  master.
26 Make a slave work and he will look for his
  rest;
  let his hands be idle and he will seek to
  be free.
27 Food, correction and work for a slave;
  and for a wicked slave, punishment in the
  stocks.
28 Force him to work that he be not idle,
  for idleness is an apt teacher of
  mischief.
29 Put him to work, for that is what befits him;
  if he becomes unruly, load him with
  chains.
30 But never lord it over any human being,
  and do nothing unjust.
31 If you have but one slave, treat him like
  yourself,
  for you have acquired him with your life's
  blood;
32 If you have but one slave, deal with him as
  a brother,
  for you need him as you need your life:
33 If you mistreat him and he runs away,
  in what direction will you look for him?

33, 25-27: Trsp to read 25a.27a (ʾôl waʾ ăbôt weḥōṭer tômekô: cf
Heb). 25b.27b.26.
  33, 31a.32a: *heis (estin soi oiketēs)*: so Heb 32a. (*age auton hōs*)
adelphon: so LXX[MSS], Heb, P, L.

NRSV

25 Fodder and a stick and burdens for a donkey;
  bread and discipline and work for a slave.
26 Set your slave to work, and you will find rest;
  leave his hands idle, and he will seek liberty.
27 Yoke and thong will bow the neck,
  and for a wicked slave there are racks and
  tortures.
28 Put him to work, in order that he may not be
  idle,
29   for idleness teaches much evil.
30 Set him to work, as is fitting for him,
  and if he does not obey, make his fetters
  heavy.
  Do not be overbearing toward anyone,
  and do nothing unjust.

31 If you have but one slave, treat him like
  yourself,
  because you have bought him with blood.
  If you have but one slave, treat him like a
  brother,
  for you will need him as you need your life.
32 If you ill-treat him, and he leaves you and runs
  away,
33   which way will you go to seek him?

COMMENTARY

Both religious and social legitimation for slavery existed in the ancient world, and Ben Sira did not question these sanctions. The slaves of Israelites possessed minimal rights; for example, Deut 23:15-16 protects a runaway slave from being returned to an abusive owner; Exod 21:2 states that slaves must be set free in the seventh year (cf. Deut 15:12-18); and Exod 21:26-27 lists compensation for the loss of an eye or a tooth as a result of cruel treatment by an owner. Such laws may never have been obeyed, but at the very least they indicate awareness that slaves were in fact qualitatively different from animals, even if they are mentioned frequently in lists alongside oxen, asses, and other cattle (cf. Exod 20:10, 17). Ben Sira's advice to keep slaves busy assumes that "an idle mind is the devil's workshop." But that principle can be pressed too far, and Ben Sira cautions against harsh treatment—beyond, that is, the demeaning use of stocks and chains for unmanageable slaves.[213]

Ben Sira's concluding advice for those modestly well-to-do owners of only one slave would appear to be self-evident. Because you have but one slave, you should be particularly generous to prevent that slave's displeasure and to assure that he or she will not run away. The remark that the owner

purchased the slave with his own blood must be understood figuratively as representing one's life's savings. The motive underlying this conduct is entirely one of self-interest. Several narratives in the Bible indicate that slaves often rose to high places and contributed greatly to the well-being of households, their loyalty to masters often leading to exceptional behavior (cf. Joseph in Genesis 37–50, Eliezer in Genesis 24, and Naaman's Israelite slave in 2 Kings 5).

213. Similar counsel occurs in Papyrus Insinger 14:6-11.

SIRACH 34:1-8, ON DREAMS

NAB

34 Empty and false are the hopes of the senseless,

and fools are borne aloft by dreams.

2 Like a man who catches at shadows or chases the wind,

is the one who believes in dreams.

3 What is seen in dreams is to reality

what the reflection of a face is to the face itself.

4 Can the unclean produce the clean?

can the liar ever speak the truth?

5 Divination, omens and dreams all are unreal;

what you already expect, the mind depicts.

6 Unless it be a vision specially sent by the Most High,

fix not your heart on it;

7 For dreams have led many astray,

and those who believed in them have perished.

8 The law is fulfilled without fail,

and perfect wisdom is found in the mouth of the faithful man.

34, 5b: tôḥîl for tāḥîl (=ōdinousēs): cf P.

NRSV

34 The senseless have vain and false hopes,

and dreams give wings to fools.

2 As one who catches at a shadow and pursues the wind,

so is anyone who believes in[a] dreams.

3 What is seen in dreams is but a reflection,

the likeness of a face looking at itself.

4 From an unclean thing what can be clean?

And from something false what can be true?

5 Divinations and omens and dreams are unreal,

and like a woman in labor, the mind has fantasies.

6 Unless they are sent by intervention from the Most High,

pay no attention to them.

7 For dreams have deceived many,

and those who put their hope in them have perished.

8 Without such deceptions the law will be fulfilled,

and wisdom is complete in the mouth of the faithful.

a Syr: Gk *pays heed to*

COMMENTARY

Although revelatory dreams are reported favorably in the patriarchal narratives (Genesis 37–50), in the stories about the judges (Judg 7:13-15), in

the book of Job (Job 4:12-21; 33:15-18), and even as late as the period when the popular tales preserved in the first six chapters of the second-century BCE book of Daniel took shape, this means of ascertaining the divine will came under sharp attack from several prophets, most notably Jeremiah (cf. Jer 29:8). Ben Sira concurs in this negative assessment of dreams, but he reserves space for legitimate dreams sent by God (cf. the NT dreams of Joseph, of the magi, and of Pilate's wife, Matt 1:20; 2:12-13, 20; 27:19). Such a judgment begs the question, however, for no means existed for determining which one had its origin in divine revelation as opposed to those arising in human fantasy. The same situation pertained in prophecy, for no adequate criterion for distinguishing true prophetic words from false could be found (cf. Deut 18:15-22).[214]

The basis for rejecting dreams, in Ben Sira's view, was their lack of any foundation in tangible reality. They resemble idols in that they possess no link with the realm to which they supposedly point.[215] Ben Sira uses graphic images of utter futility, trying either to take hold of a shadow or to catch the wind in the palm of a hand (cf. Hos 12:1 and Qohelet's use of the latter image as an apt description of human existence, Eccl 1:14; 2:11, 17, 26; 4:6, 16; 6:9). In addition, Ben Sira compares dreams to looking at oneself in a mirror; the pale reflection in a mirror fashioned from polished metal lacked the qualities intrinsic to life itself. The apostle Paul uses this thought to indicate that what one sees in a mirror is only a partial, and necessarily distorted, although to some extent trustworthy, proclamation of God's promise awaiting Christians (1 Cor 13:12). Ben Sira's further line of argument against dreams calls attention to their adverse effect and unreliability; according to the laws of purity and impurity, something ritually clean cannot come from an unclean object, just as truth cannot derive from lies. Rhetoricians in ancient Greece used a similar

argument with regard to ethos, insisting on moral character as an essential ingredient in persuasive speech.[216]

Verse 5 enlarges the discussion to include two other significant ritual functions in the ancient world, particularly in Mesopotamia and Egypt, but certainly present in Israelite culture as well. These highly valued modes of finding out what lay in store for a person were divination and omens. Considerable literature about omens has survived, and even the OT preserves allusions to a number of different kinds of divination (e.g., casting sacred dice, 1 Sam 14:42; shooting arrows, 2 Kgs 13:15-19; observing the flight of birds, drinking a sacred potion, etc.). The vast number of clay livers discovered in Mesopotamia testifies to the enormous significance of hepatoscopy to the Babylonians. Priests observed the livers of animals sacrificed at altars as a means of discovering the will of the gods as it pertained to the person offering the sacrifice. Whereas a considerable population viewed dreams, omens, and divination as reliable and understood the study of these manipulative practices as "scientific," to use a modern term, Ben Sira thought they merely equipped fools for a wild ride, one characterized by an unchecked imagination.

The last verse states Ben Sira's real reason for discrediting these familiar means of discovering the future. In his view, the Mosaic law contained God's complete revelation to the Israelite people, and such unreliable probings as dreams, omens, and divination prevented the divine legislation from attaining its full scope. The faithful exposition of the Torah by a sage provided everything the people needed, Ben Sira insisted, so that no one need resort to proscribed or fundamentally foreign avenues of inquiring about the unknown.

214. James L. Crenshaw, *Prophetic Conflict,* BZAW 124 (Berlin and New York: Walter de Gruyter, 1971), examines the criteria within the Bible for distinguishing true from false prophets and discusses their inadequacy.

215. Robert K. Gnuse, *The Dream Theophany of Samuel* (Lanham, Md.: University Press of America, 1984), looks at ancient Near Eastern interpretation of dreams. Sigmund Freud's reading of dreams as sexual pathology represents a new departure.

216. George A. Kennedy, *Classical Rhetoric and Its Christian and Secular Tradition from Ancient to Modern Times* (Chapel Hill: University of North Carolina Press, 1980). This resource contains numerous insights into persuasive speech. Alongside ethos, Kennedy posits pathos and logos (passion and logic). For the OT, see James L. Crenshaw, "Wisdom and Authority: Sapiential Rhetoric and Its Warrants" VTSup 32 (Congress Volume, Vienna, 1980) 10-29. See also James L. Crenshaw, *Urgent Advice and Probing Questions* (Macon, Ga.: Mercer University Press, 1995) 326-43.

SIRACH 34:9-20, ON THE DANGERS OF TRAVEL AND GOD'S PROTECTION

NAB	NRSV
9 A man with training gains wide knowledge; a man of experience speaks sense.	9 An educated[a] person knows many things, and one with much experience knows what he is talking about.
10 One never put to the proof knows little, whereas with travel a man adds to his resourcefulness.	10 An inexperienced person knows few things, 11 but he that has traveled acquires much cleverness.
11 I have seen much in my travels, learned more than ever I could say.	12 I have seen many things in my travels, and I understand more than I can express.
12 Often I was in danger of death, but by these attainments I was saved.	13 I have often been in danger of death, but have escaped because of these experiences.
13 Lively is the courage of those who fear the LORD, for they put their hope in their savior;	14 The spirit of those who fear the Lord will live, 15 for their hope is in him who saves them.
14 He who fears the LORD is never alarmed, never afraid; for the LORD is his hope.	16 Those who fear the Lord will not be timid, or play the coward, for he is their hope.
15 Happy the soul that fears the LORD! In whom does he trust, and who is his support?	17 Happy is the soul that fears the Lord! 18 To whom does he look? And who is his support?
16 The eyes of the LORD are upon those who love him; he is their mighty shield and strong support, A shelter from the heat, a shade from the noonday sun, a guard against stumbling, a help against falling.	19 The eyes of the Lord are on those who love him, a mighty shield and strong support, a shelter from scorching wind and a shade from noonday sun, a guard against stumbling and a help against falling.
17 He buoys up the spirits, brings a sparkle to the eyes, gives health and life and blessing.	20 He lifts up the soul and makes the eyes sparkle; he gives health and life and blessing.

34, 16c: *skia* (*apo mesē mbrias*): so V.

[a]Other ancient authorities read *A traveled*

COMMENTARY

Ancient sages recognized the broadening experience of travel to foreign lands, but they also knew the accompanying perils. Resorting to first-person narration, Ben Sira discusses these dangers in the context of God's protective care. Interestingly, Ben Sira does not offer any details about the dangers from which his cleverness delivered him (cf. the account of Paul's shipwreck as told in Acts 27:13-44; 2 Cor 11:24-27, 32-33). The remainder of this unit, vv. 14-20, encourages readers to trust the Lord, presumably in undertaking dangerous journeys where brigands, unfamiliar diet and customs, and countless other obstacles to safe travel await the inexperienced traveler.

SIRACH 34:21–35:26, ON SACRIFICES

NAB	NRSV

NAB

18 Tainted his gifts who offers in sacrifice
  ill-gotten goods!
    Mock presents from the lawless win not
    God's favor.
19 The Most High approves not the gifts of the
  godless,
    nor for their many sacrifices does he
    forgive their sins.
20 Like the man who slays a son in his father's
  presence
    is he who offers sacrifice from the
    possessions of the poor.
21 The bread of charity is life itself for the
  needy;
    he who withholds it is a man of blood.
22 He slays his neighbor who deprives him of
  his living;
    he sheds blood who denies the laborer his
    wages.
23 If one man builds up and another tears
  down,
    what do they gain but trouble?
24 If one man prays and another curses,
    whose voice will the LORD hear?
25 If a man again touches a corpse after he has
  bathed,
    what did he gain by the purification?
26 So with a man who fasts for his sins,
    but then goes and commits them again:
  Who will hear his prayer,
    and what has he gained by his
    mortification?

35 To keep the law is a great oblation,
  and he who observes the commandments
    sacrifices a peace offering.
2 In works of charity one offers fine flour,
    and when he gives alms he presents his
    sacrifice of praise.
3 To refrain from evil pleases the LORD,
    and to avoid injustice is an atonement.
4 Appear not before the LORD empty-handed,
    for all that you offer is in fulfillment of the
    precepts.
5 The just man's offering enriches the altar

NRSV

21 If one sacrifices ill-gotten goods, the offering is
  blemished;[a]
22 the gifts[b] of the lawless are not acceptable.
23 The Most High is not pleased with the
  offerings of the ungodly,
    nor for a multitude of sacrifices does he
    forgive sins.
24 Like one who kills a son before his father's
  eyes
    is the person who offers a sacrifice from the
    property of the poor.
25 The bread of the needy is the life of the poor;
    whoever deprives them of it is a murderer.
26 To take away a neighbor's living is to commit
  murder;
27 to deprive an employee of wages is to shed
    blood.

28 When one builds and another tears down,
    what do they gain but hard work?
29 When one prays and another curses,
    to whose voice will the Lord listen?
30 If one washes after touching a corpse, and
  touches it again,
    what has been gained by washing?
31 So if one fasts for his sins,
    and goes again and does the same things,
  who will listen to his prayer?
    And what has he gained by humbling
    himself?

35 The one who keeps the law makes many
  offerings;
2 one who heeds the commandments makes
    an offering of well-being.
3 The one who returns a kindness offers choice
  flour,
4 and one who gives alms sacrifices a thank
    offering.
5 To keep from wickedness is pleasing to the
  Lord,
    and to forsake unrighteousness is an
    atonement.
6 Do not appear before the Lord empty-handed,

34, 21: ḥesed for ḥeser (=epideomenōn): so P.

[a]Other ancient authorities read *is made in mockery*   [b]Other ancient authorities read *mockeries*

NAB

and rises as a sweet odor before the Most
  High.
6 The just man's sacrifice is most pleasing,
  nor will it ever be forgotten.
7 In generous spirit pay homage to the LORD,
  be not sparing of freewill gifts.
8 With each contribution show a cheerful
  countenance,
  and pay your tithes in a spirit of joy.
9 Give to the Most High as he has given to
  you,
  generously, according to your means.

10 For the LORD is one who always repays,
  and he will give back to you sevenfold.
11 But offer no bribes, these he does not
  accept!
  Trust not in sacrifice of the fruits of
  extortion,
12 For he is a God of justice,
  who knows no favorites.
13 Though not unduly partial toward the weak,
  yet he hears the cry of the oppressed.
14 He is not deaf to the wail of the orphan,
  nor to the widow when she pours out her
  complaint;

15 Do not the tears that stream down her
  cheek
  cry out against him that causes them to
  fall?
16 He who serves God willingly is heard;
  his petition reaches the heavens.
17 The prayer of the lowly pierces the clouds;
  it does not rest till it reaches its goal,
18 Nor will it withdraw till the Most High
  responds,
  judges justly and affirms the right.

19 God indeed will not delay,
  and like a warrior, will not be still
20 Till he breaks the backs of the merciless
  and wreaks vengeance upon the proud;

35, 8: (beⁿkol) maś ʾōtèkā : so LXX, P.
35, 9: (ten) leⁿ ʾelyôn: so LXX, V; cf P. ûkeⁿhaśśāgat.
35, 15: (waʾ ănāhâ ʿal) mórídāh: so LXX, V.
35, 16: meⁿšārēt (?) beⁿrāṣôn yēʾ ātēr (?) weⁿṣaʾ āqātô: so LXX.
35, 17: (šawʾ at dal) ʾābîm ḥālāpâ: so B margin, LXX.

NRSV

7 for all that you offer is in fulfillment of the
  commandment.
8 The offering of the righteous enriches the altar,
  and its pleasing odor rises before the Most
  High.
9 The sacrifice of the righteous is acceptable,
  and it will never be forgotten.
10 Be generous when you worship the Lord,
  and do not stint the first fruits of your hands.
11 With every gift show a cheerful face,
  and dedicate your tithe with gladness.
12 Give to the Most High as he has given to you,
  and as generously as you can afford.
13 For the Lord is the one who repays,
  and he will repay you sevenfold.
14 Do not offer him a bribe, for he will not accept
  it;
15 and do not rely on a dishonest sacrifice;
  for the Lord is the judge,
  and with him there is no partiality.
16 He will not show partiality to the poor;
  but he will listen to the prayer of one who
  is wronged.
17 He will not ignore the supplication of the
  orphan,
  or the widow when she pours out her
  complaint.
18 Do not the tears of the widow run down her
  cheek
19 as she cries out against the one who causes
  them to fall?
20 The one whose service is pleasing to the Lord
  will be accepted,
  and his prayer will reach to the clouds.
21 The prayer of the humble pierces the clouds,
  and it will not rest until it reaches its goal;
  it will not desist until the Most High responds
22 and does justice for the righteous, and
  executes judgment.
  Indeed, the Lord will not delay,
  and like a warrior[a] will not be patient
  until he crushes the loins of the unmerciful
23 and repays vengeance on the nations;
  until he destroys the multitude of the insolent,
  and breaks the scepters of the unrighteous;
24 until he repays mortals according to their
  deeds,

a Heb: Gk and with them

NAB	NRSV

NAB

21 Till he destroys the haughty root and
  branch,
    and smashes the scepter of the wicked;
22 Till he requites mankind according to its
  deeds,
    and repays men according to their
    thoughts;
23 Till he defends the cause of his people,
    and gladdens them by his mercy.
24 Welcome is his mercy in time of distress
    as rain clouds in time of drought.

35, 21: (ʿad) yᵉšā rēš (šē beṭ): cf LXX.
35, 24: kᵉ ʿā bê (ḥăzîzîm): so LXX, P.

NRSV

  and the works of all according to their
    thoughts;
25 until he judges the case of his people
    and makes them rejoice in his mercy.
26 His mercy is as welcome in time of distress
    as clouds of rain in time of drought.

COMMENTARY

Historical necessity taught ancient Israelites to think of other means of atonement than sacrifices on the altar in the Solomonic Temple, for during their stay in captivity and for sometime after their return to Judah, circumstances made it impossible for them to carry out the prescribed offerings. Moreover, a strong prophetic voice beginning with Amos and enduring for many years called into question the entire cultic apparatus, at least as practiced in Jerusalem. A rabbinic anecdote from the late first century CE reveals a similar attitude, for when Joshua ben Hannaniah lamented the destruction of the Temple in 70 CE and simultaneously the disappearance of the place of atonement, Johanan ben Zakkai responded that an equally valid means of forgiveness, deeds of kindness, remained, as acknowledged in Hos 6:6: "For I desire steadfast love and not sacrifice,/ the knowledge of God rather than burnt offerings" (NRSV).

34:21-27. In this section Ben Sira tries to do justice to this revolutionary criticism of the sacrificial cult while at the same time granting the binding authority of earlier laws requiring Israelites to bring specific offerings to the Lord. He begins by reinforcing the prophetic indictment of flawed offerings, using the prohibition against giving a blemished animal to the Lord and applying the principle underlying the law to include gifts obtained at the expense of marginalized citizens.

Such gifts, he says, resemble heinous acts of murder (cf. 2 Kgs 25:6-7, the execution of King Zedekiah's sons in his sight); whoever deprives the poor of food are in reality murderers, and the one who delays payment of wages beyond nightfall is likewise guilty of homicide (cf. Lev 19:13; Deut 24:14-15; *Baba Metzia* 112a, "Everyone who withholds an employee's wages is as though he deprived him of his life").

34:28-31. These verses emphasize the necessity of genuine transformation, a radical reversal of one's conduct, if one expects to receive God's forgiveness. Unless one's actions accord with the inner attitude, the two work at cross-purposes, accomplishing nothing. One builds; another tears down. One prays; another curses—and the result is negligible. Similarly, Ben Sira insists, one who has become impure by touching a corpse and who has undergone ritual lustration has gained nothing unless he or she avoids corpses thereafter. On that principle, Ben Sira boldly insists that only those who forsake their sins obtain forgiveness, for fasting alone has no atoning power.

35:1-13. The next section weaves together this ethical transformation of the sacrificial cult and a literal understanding of the requirements concerning tithes and offerings (cf. Tob 1:6-8). Ben Sira equates charitable deeds with the meal offering and thanksgiving offering. Having insisted on the moral requisite for acceptable offerings, he goes on to recommend generosity toward the Most High, who rewards the faithful much more unstintingly.

35:14-26. These verses describe the Lord as champion of widows and orphans (cf. Ps 68:5; Jas 1:27), but one who stands for impartial justice, and they utter a fervent psalm praising God for crushing the wicked. The latter provides a fine point of transition to the prayer in 36:1-22, which reiterates the sentiment about destroying evildoers, in this instance foreigners. Ben Sira assures his readers that imprecation issuing from the lips of the powerless will reach heaven, calling attention to a widow's tears. Whereas Lam 3:44 accuses God of being wrapped in an impenetrable cloud, Ben Sira asserts that the prayer of humble people pierces the clouds and keeps knocking at the door of the Most High until provoking a favorable response. The rapid rehearsal of divine punishment against guilty humans, unexpected in a text of this sort, may reflect the chaotic political situation under the new Seleucid rulers. According to Isa 55:10-11, Yahweh's Word will not return empty but will accomplish its purpose on earth; Ben Sira applies the same reasoning to the prayer of the lowly.

REFLECTIONS

An interesting feature in studying different religions is the effort to maintain specific regulations, believed to be divinely ordained, when historical circumstances change so drastically as to make them obsolete or questionable at best. Such requirements may once have made sense, but now their arbitrary character stands out. One thinks immediately of Jewish dietary laws and restrictions relating to observing the sabbath. Religious leaders confronted with the question about the permanence of divine laws often look for enduring principles that enable them to salvage the essence of sacred commands while discarding the external trappings.

Naturally, this sort of situation arose in ancient Israel after the Temple in Jerusalem was destroyed, making it impossible to fulfill the laws about sacrificing at the sacred altar. During their stay in Babylonia, exiled Judeans were forced to find other ways of obeying their God; in doing so, they resorted to a spiritualization of divine regulations. Back in Judah, the prophet Jeremiah spoke of circumcizing the heart, along with the actual bodily circumcision. Similarly, Joel pleaded with the people of Judah to rend their hearts rather than their garments, and a poetic Hosea referred to prayer and praise as "the bulls of the mouth" (sacrifices, Hos 14:2).

Such transformation of religious language also occurred in respect to specific offerings intended for the temple cult. Religious leaders gradually realized that sacrifices alone had no redemptive power; without repentant attitudes, even multiple offerings achieved nothing beneficial. By the time of Ben Sira, this novel way of looking at age-old ritual obligations existed alongside strong desire to fulfill the letter of the law, once more possible because of the restored Temple. He held both notions in a delicate balance, insisting that charitable deeds and sacrificial offerings brought divine favor.

Christians face the same issue, although focused differently. Over the years the church has constructed a heavy chain of tradition containing numerous obligations that have been given divine sanction. Tithing, specific observance of the Christian sabbath, and loyalty to orthodoxy and orthopraxy specific to a denomination often assume roles like those occupied by Jewish dietary laws and requirements for offering sacrifices in the Temple. Faced with such externals, many Christians search for the spiritual meaning of these rituals. In this quest, Ben Sira provides sound leadership, for he realized that religious ritual devoid of loving deeds was empty and that people need specific ordinances to remind them that love of fellow human beings becomes complete when that love also directs itself to God.

However profound this spiritualization of legal obligations, it runs the risk of dissolving into pious generalities and vague practice. The orthodox Jewish argument that dietary laws, for example, must be observed because people owe allegiance to God carries considerable force, even if we cannot go further and accept such arbitrary regulations as divine law. Individuals from many different cultures have attributed their laws to a particular deity, perhaps primarily as a means of sanctioning them after the fact. Nevertheless, their willingness to submit to "divine legislation" indicates that they felt constrained to recognize an authority beyond their own, and in that regard they were surely worthy examples for moderns.

SIRACH 36:1-22, A PRAYER FOR NATIONAL DELIVERANCE

NAB	NRSV

NAB

36 Come to our aid, O God of the universe, and put all the nations in dread of you!

2 Raise your hand against the heathen,
   that they may realize your power.

3 As you have used us to show them your
   holiness,
   so now use them to show us your glory.

4 Thus they will know, as we know,
   that there is no God but you.

5 Give new signs and work new wonders;
   show forth the splendor of your right hand
   and arm;

6 Rouse your anger, pour out wrath,
   humble the enemy, scatter the foe.

7 Hasten the day, bring on the time;

9 crush the heads of the hostile rulers.

8 Let raging fire consume the fugitive,
   and your people's oppressors meet
   destruction.

10 Gather all the tribes of Jacob,
   that they may inherit the land as of old.

11 Show mercy to the people called by your
   name;
   Israel, whom you named your firstborn.

12 Take pity on your holy city,
   Jerusalem, your dwelling place.

13 Fill Zion with your majesty,
   your temple with your glory.

14 Give evidence of your deeds of old;
   fulfill the prophecies spoken in your name,

NRSV

36 Have mercy upon us, O God[a]
   of all,

2   and put all the nations in fear of you.

3 Lift up your hand against foreign nations
   and let them see your might.

4 As you have used us to show your holiness to
   them,
   so use them to show your glory to us.

5 Then they will know,[b] as we have known,
   that there is no God but you, O Lord.

6 Give new signs, and work other wonders;

7   make your hand and right arm glorious.

8 Rouse your anger and pour out your wrath;

9   destroy the adversary and wipe out the
   enemy.

10 Hasten the day, and remember the appointed
   time,[c]
   and let people recount your mighty deeds.

11 Let survivors be consumed in the fiery wrath,
   and may those who harm your people meet
   destruction.

12 Crush the heads of hostile rulers
   who say, "There is no one but ourselves."

13 Gather all the tribes of Jacob,[d]

16   and give them their inheritance, as at the
   beginning.

17 Have mercy, O Lord, on the people called by
   your name,
   on Israel, whom you have named[e] your
   firstborn,

18 Have pity on the city of your sanctuary,[f]
   Jerusalem, the place of your dwelling.[g]

36, 2: (*hānēp*) *yād ekā* ('*al* '*am*): so LXX, R; cf margin.

36, 3b: (*hikkā bed*) *bām*: so margin, LXX, P.

36, 7b=9a (12a in Heb, LXX): *šabbēr rā'šê šārê 'ôyēb*: so LXX; cf. margin. Omit *kî . . . ta'āseh*: so LXX; gloss from Jb 9,12b; Eccl 8, 4b. Omit *hā'ômēr 'ên zûlātî*: variant of 4b.

36, 8: So with LXX (v. 11), V; cf P (v 9).

---

[a]Heb: Gk *O Master, the God*   [b]Heb: Gk *And let them know you* [c]Other ancient authorities read *remember your oath*   [d]Owing to a dislocation in the Greek Mss of Sirach, the verse numbers 14 and 15 are not used in chapter 36, though no text is missing. [e]Other ancient authorities read *you have likened to*   [f]Or *on your holy city*   [g]Heb: Gk *your rest*

NAB

15 Reward those who have hoped in you,
  and let your prophets be proved true.
16 Hear the prayer of your servants,
  for you are ever gracious to your people;
17 Thus it will be known to the very ends of
    the earth
  that you are the eternal God.

NRSV

19 Fill Zion with your majesty,[a]
  and your temple[b] with your glory.
20 Bear witness to those whom you created in
    the beginning,
  and fulfill the prophecies spoken in your
    name.
21 Reward those who wait for you
  and let your prophets be found trustworthy.
22 Hear, O Lord, the prayer of your servants,
    according to your goodwill toward[c]
    your people,
  and all who are on the earth will know
    that you are the Lord, the God of the ages.

[a] Heb Syr: Gk *the celebration of your wondrous deeds*   [b]
Heb Syr: Gk Lat *people*   [c] Heb and two Gk witnesses: Lat and
most Gk witnesses read *according to the blessing of Aaron for*

COMMENTARY

This prayer seems entirely foreign to wisdom literature as traditionally understood, for nowhere in the books of Proverbs, Job, and Ecclesiastes do such sentiments appear. Ben Sira prays in the tone of laments within the psalter, with one decisive difference: the absence of any praise of God (e.g., Psalms 12–13, 25–26). There, too, however, some laments stand alone (cf. Psalm 38), and elsewhere the book of Sirach has elaborate expressions of praise for the Creator. This prayer begins with a cry for rescue, especially in the Hebrew ("Save us" [הושיענו *hôšî'ēnû*]) and addresses God as lord of all (cf. 45:23 and 50:22 in the Greek and Rom 9:5); it ends with a similar thought, that everyone will know that Yahweh is God of all time (cf. the Prayer of Azariah). A psalm from Qumran uses a similar expression, "Lord of all" (אדון הכל *'ādôn hakkōl*) and "God of all" (אלה הכל *'ĕlōah hakkōl* [Ps 151:4 = 11QPsª 28:7-8]), which reproduces the title of Baal, "Lord of earth" (אדון ארץ *'ādôn 'ereṣ*) and "Lord of all the earth" (אדון כל הארץ *'ādôn kol hā'āreṣ*), attributed to Yahweh.

The language of the prayer echoes traditional texts from Israel's liturgical repertoire as well as more recent eschatology and apocalyptic. Ben Sira cautiously veils his allusions to Seleucid rulers, perhaps concealing a direct reference to Antiochus III the Great, who, according to Dan 11:18, arrogantly claimed to be unique in power ("There is no one besides me"). The anthological style recalls Ezekiel's oft-used formula about the nations' knowing that Yahweh is God (v. 5), which the prophet Joel also uses more than once (Joel 2:27; 3:17). He, too, spoke of signs and wonders when Yahweh renewed the saving activity heralded by Israel's ancestors (Joel 2:28-32; 3:1-5 in Hebrew). Ben Sira implores God to let the end come quickly, that day when the Lord acts in judgment against all the nations (v. 10, קץ *qēṣ*). Then people will recite Yahweh's mighty deeds, צדקות (*ṣidqôt*), as they did in bygone days.

For the moment, the ethic of forgiveness that Ben Sira taught elsewhere has flown out the window, and desire to see revenge poured out on foreigners dominates. That human wish to see the wicked pay for their crimes reaches a peak in vv. 8-12, after which Ben Sira concentrates on the people of God, some of whom are scattered in other countries, with one minor exception in v. 22 (the formula of acknowledgment). He recalls Israel's unique position in Yahweh's eyes, symbolized above all by Zion, and reminds the Lord that some prophecies have not yet come to fruition. The underlying premise of this argument was that ultimately every divine word would be fulfilled.

This plea for deliverance does not mention a messiah, although the language definitely suggests that the eschatological era is being described. Oesterley has noted that silence with respect to a messiah is not unique to Ben Sira in such contexts.[217]

217. W. O. E. Oesterley, *The Wisdom of Jesus the Son of Sirach or Ecclesiasticus* (Cambridge: Cambridge University Press, 1912) 232. A late first-century CE text, Pss Sol 17:23, gives a prayer for deliverance through the Messiah and identifies this person as the Son of David.

Several features of this prayer resemble the *Shemoneh 'Esreh,* "The Eighteen Benedictions," in the Jewish prayer book. In the first century CE the first three benedictions and the last three praises were recited in every synagogue service.

REFLECTIONS

1. Fear of vulnerability in old age is matched by a xenophobia that feeds on partial truths and prejudices, when ample cause for such hatred does not exist. Citizens of the United States boast that their country has historically welcomed everyone to its shores, intent on creating a single society from the resulting melting pot. In periods of heightened conscience, the doors have been thrown open to receive immigrants from numerous oppressive societies, and at other times greed has prevailed—the desire for cheap workers in agricultural areas during recent decades is one example. Once welfare programs and other entitlements fell to these masses and the costs more and more fell to local governments, some people began to question the advisability of such open policies. In the end, economics reveals itself as the decisive issue.

Ben Sira was heir to a similar struggle, chiefly that between returning exiles from Babylonia and the people who had occupied the land of Judah for the previous seventy years or so. Descendants of Joseph who lived in Samaria also pleaded for inclusion in the new state, to no avail. Both the religious authority, Ezra, and the secular governor, Nehemiah, rebuffed the petition and protest of these foreigners, whose claim on the land certainly had merit. Instead, these two leaders enforced a rigorous policy that excluded everyone except returning exiles. That isolationism appealed to Ben Sira, and in this respect placed him at odds with his predecessors in the wisdom tradition.

Fear of those with different skin color, language, and customs comes easily, even in our moments of prayer. Perhaps if such sentiments must surface, that setting is the best one of all, for the self-examination when communicating with God offers an opportunity to purge such hatred. Like Ben Sira, we are forced to rub shoulders daily with people from many different cultures. That necessity can be taken as an opportunity for broadening one's experience in numerous ways without having to travel to distant lands. Assuming that Christians mean what they say about all creatures being children of God, modern society assists the family of God in getting to know their brothers and sisters. From this perspective, we can transform the source of our fears into cause for rejoicing as we endeavor to be the family of God to others.

2. How should we balance idealism and realism in grasping the nature of the universe? On the one hand, so much evidence in our daily lives seems to confirm a skeptical realism, and at the same time denying that truth and beauty stand a chance in this world. On the other hand, we seem unable to relinquish a conviction that God has something better in store for us all. The biblical prophets gave voice to this optimistic hope of an era when God would establish divine rule, transforming creatures into appropriate subjects for this kingdom.

Realism forced religious thinkers to search for a credible explanation for evil; the most natural one suggested equal powers, good and evil, in charge of the universe. Binary thinking as represented by this sharp opposition of the forces of good to the forces of evil has characterized ancient peoples from various cultures, as anthropologists and literary theorists have demonstrated in great detail.[218] Ben Sira drew on Hellenistic theories about complementary pairs, one of which encouraged virtue and rewarded it, the other functioning similarly by punishing wickedness. In this view, the universe itself assisted the Creator in achieving the divine purpose for creation.

Modern believers will probably stop short of such optimism, although they cling tenaciously to belief in a benevolent God who will ultimately, in some mysterious way, tie all the loose ends together. Ben Sira lived in a time of enormous changes but held tightly to his trust in the God of Israel despite apparent evidence that foreign powers could act with impunity against the chosen people. Christians today live in comparable circumstances, with the evidence seeming to indicate that God has abandoned the church and perhaps even the universe. In such a time, we can learn a valuable lesson from Ben Sira, who refused to give up on God. Here is realism tinged with idealism, no small achievement.

218. Mary Douglas, *In the Wilderness, JSOT* 158 (Sheffield: JSOT, 1993), relies on such thinking, among other things, to open up a fresh way of understanding the structure and context of the book of Numbers. She believes that its author deliberately fashioned a satire on the ruling hierarchy, Ezra and Nehemiah, one held together in a complex manner with parallel interlocking panels.

SIRACH 36:23–37:31, ON MAKING DISCRIMINATING CHOICES

NAB

18 The throat can swallow any food,
  yet some foods are more agreeable than others;

19 As the palate tests meat by its savor,
  so does a keen mind insincere words.

20 A deceitful character causes grief,
  but an experienced man can turn the tables on him.

21 Though any man may be accepted as a husband,
  yet one girl will be more suitable than another:

22 A woman's beauty makes her husband's face light up,
  for it surpasses all else that charms the eye.

23 And if, besides, her speech is kindly,
  his lot is beyond that of mortal men.

24 A wife is her husband's richest treasure,
  a helpmate, a steadying column.

25 A vineyard with no hedge will be overrun;

36, 18: ʾōkelet (*gargeret*).
36, 19-21: Order of vv as in LXX.
36, 19: (*maṭ ʿammê*) *ṣayid* (?): so LXX. (*wᵉ lē b*) *mē bîn*: so the facsimile.
36, 20: Omit c.d: so LXX, P; corrupt variant of v 21 (LXX 26).
36, 24: (ʿ *ezer*) *kᵉ negdô*: so LXX; cf Gn 2, 18.20.

NRSV

23 The stomach will take any food,
  yet one food is better than another.

24 As the palate tastes the kinds of game,
  so an intelligent mind detects false words.

25 A perverse mind will cause grief,
  but a person with experience will pay him back.

26 A woman will accept any man as a husband,
  but one girl is preferable to another.

27 A woman's beauty lights up a man's face,
  and there is nothing he desires more.

28 If kindness and humility mark her speech,
  her husband is more fortunate than other men.

29 He who acquires a wife gets his best possession,[a]
  a helper fit for him and a pillar of support.[b]

30 Where there is no fence, the property will be plundered;
  and where there is no wife, a man will become a fugitive and a wanderer.[c]

31 For who will trust a nimble robber
  that skips from city to city?

a Heb: Gk *enters upon a possession*   *b* Heb: Gk *rest*   *c* Heb: Gk *wander about and sigh*

NAB

a man with no wife becomes a homeless
wanderer.

26 Who will trust an armed band
that shifts from city to city?

27 Or a man who has no nest,
but lodges where night overtakes him?

37 Every friend declares his friendship,
but there are friends who are friends in
name only.

2 Is it not a sorrow unto death
when your bosom companion becomes
your enemy?

3 "Alas, my companion! Why were you created
to blanket the earth with deceit?"

4 A false friend will share your joys,
but in time of trouble he stands afar off.

5 A true friend will fight with you against the
foe,
against your enemies he will be your
shieldbearer.

6 Forget not your comrade during the battle,
and neglect him not when you distribute
your spoils.

7 Every counselor points out a way,
but some counsel ways of their own;

8 Be on the alert when one proffers advice,
find out first of all what he wants.
For he may be thinking of himself alone;
why should the profit fall to him?

9 He may tell you how good your way will be,
and then stand by to watch your
misfortune.

10 Seek no advice from one who regards you
with hostility;
from those who envy you, keep your
intentions hidden.

11 Speak not to a woman about her rival,
nor to a coward about war,
to a merchant about business,
to a buyer about value,
to a miser about generosity,
to a cruel man about mercy,

37, 1.10: So with Heb MS D.
37, 2: (hālō') dāyôn: so LXX.
37, 3: hôî rēa' maddûa' nôṣārtā.
37, 7: (derek) 'ēlāyw: so LXX; cf MS D.
37, 11b: ûmērak 'al milḥāmā: so LXX. 11c: 'al teger. 11d.
ûmiqqônēh: so MS D, margin of MS B. 11h: with MS D. 11i.j: with LXX,
P.

NRSV

So who will trust a man that has no nest,
but lodges wherever night overtakes him?

37 Every friend says, "I too am a friend";
but some friends are friends only in name.

2 Is it not a sorrow like that for death itself
when a dear friend turns into an enemy?

3 O inclination to evil, why were you formed
to cover the land with deceit?

4 Some companions rejoice in the happiness of
a friend,
but in time of trouble they are against him.

5 Some companions help a friend for their
stomachs' sake,
yet in battle they will carry his shield.

6 Do not forget a friend during the battle,[a]
and do not be unmindful of him when you
distribute your spoils.[b]

7 All counselors praise the counsel they give,
but some give counsel in their own interest.

8 Be wary of a counselor,
and learn first what is his interest,
for he will take thought for himself.
He may cast the lot against you

9 and tell you, "Your way is good,"
and then stand aside to see what happens
to you.

10 Do not consult the one who regards you with
suspicion;
hide your intentions from those who are
jealous of you.

11 Do not consult with a woman about her rival
or with a coward about war,
with a merchant about business
or with a buyer about selling,
with a miser about generosity[c]
or with the merciless about kindness,
with an idler about any work
or with a seasonal laborer about completing
his work,
with a lazy servant about a big task—
pay no attention to any advice they give.

12 But associate with a godly person
whom you know to be a keeper of the
commandments,
who is like-minded with yourself,

a Heb: Gk in your heart   b Heb: Gk him in your wealth
c Heb: Gk gratitude

NAB

to a lazy man about work,
to a seasonal laborer about the harvest,
to an idle slave about a great task:
pay no attention to any advice they give.

12 Instead, associate with a religious man,
who you are sure keeps the
commandments;
Who is like-minded with yourself
and will feel for you if you fail.

13 Then, too, heed your own heart's counsel;
for what have you that you can depend on
more?

14 A man's conscience can tell him his
situation
better than seven watchmen in a lofty
tower.

15 Most important of all, pray to God
to set your feet in the path of truth.

16 A word is the source of every deed;
a thought, of every act.

17 The root of all conduct is the mind;
four branches it shoots forth:

18 Good and evil, death and life,
their absolute mistress is the tongue.

19 A man may be wise and benefit many,
yet be of no use to himself.

20 Though a man may be wise, if his words
are rejected
he will be deprived of all enjoyment.

21 When a man is wise to his own advantage,
the fruits of his knowledge are seen in his
own person;

22 When a man is wise to his people's advantage,
the fruits of his knowledge are enduring:

23 Limited are the days of one man's life,
but the life of Israel is days without
number.

24 One wise for himself has full enjoyment,
and all who see him praise him;

25 One wise for his people wins a heritage of
glory,
and his name endures forever.

NRSV

and who will grieve with you if you fail.

13 And heed[a] the counsel of your own heart,
for no one is more faithful to you than it is.

14 For our own mind sometimes keeps us better
informed
than seven sentinels sitting high on a
watchtower.

15 But above all pray to the Most High
that he may direct your way in truth.

16 Discussion is the beginning of every work,
and counsel precedes every undertaking.

17 The mind is the root of all conduct;

18 it sprouts four branches,[b]
good and evil, life and death;
and it is the tongue that continually rules
them.

19 Some people may be clever enough to teach
many,
and yet be useless to themselves.

20 A skillful speaker may be hated;
he will be destitute of all food,

21 for the Lord has withheld the gift of charm,
since he is lacking in all wisdom.

22 If a person is wise to his own advantage,
the fruits of his good sense will be
praiseworthy.[c]

23 A wise person instructs his own people,
and the fruits of his good sense will endure.

24 A wise person will have praise heaped upon
him,
and all who see him will call him happy.

25 The days of a person's life are numbered,
but the days of Israel are without number.

26 One who is wise among his people will inherit
honor,[d]
and his name will live forever.

27 My child, test yourself while you live;
see what is bad for you and do not give in
to it.

28 For not everything is good for everyone,
and no one enjoys everything.

29 Do not be greedy for every delicacy,
and do not eat without restraint;

30 for overeating brings sickness,

37, 12a: ʾak ʾim ʾiš mᵉpaḥēd tatmîd: so LXX, P. 12c: Omit ʾim: so LXX, P.
37, 13b: kî ʾên lekā ʾāmûn mimmennû: cf LXX, P.
37, 17: ʾiqqār taḥbûlôt: so MS D. šebāṭîm.
37, 19: (lerabbîm) yeḥkām . . . (hû) nôʾāl: cf MS D, LXX, P.
37, 22-25: With Heb MS D.
37, 22: (pᵉrî daʿtô) neʾĕmān: so LXX; dittog.

[a] Heb: Gk establish   [b] Heb: Gk As a clue to changes of heart four kinds of destiny appear   [c] Other ancient witnesses read trustworthy   [d] Other ancient authorities read confidence

NAB

26 My son, while you are well, govern your
    appetite
    so that you allow it not what is bad for
      you;
27 For not every food is good for everyone,
    nor is everything suited to every taste.
28 Be not drawn after every enjoyment,
    neither become a glutton for choice foods,
29 For sickness comes with overeating,
    and gluttony brings on biliousness.
30 Through lack of self-control many have
    died,
    but the abstemious man prolongs his life.

37, 27b: *we lō' le kol* (*nepeš*): so MS D.
37, 28: *'al tîzer 'el kol* (*ta' änûg*) (?).
37, 29: (*kî be rōb*) *'ōkel*: so MS D, LXX, P.
37, 30: (*rabbîm*) *gäwä' û; omit we 'iwwe 'û*: so MS D.

NRSV

    and gluttony leads to nausea.
31 Many have died of gluttony,
    but the one who guards against it prolongs
      his life.

COMMENTARY

36:23-31. After the passionate expression of
concern that Yahweh inaugurate the messianic
era, exalting Israel and bringing its foreign rulers
low, Ben Sira returns to deal with mundane affairs
of daily existence. First, he discusses the matter
of choosing a partner in marriage. His initial
remark, grounded in the social restrictions placed
on women—that is, their dependence on arranged
marriages—sounds cruel (v. 26). The limited
choice open to a woman explains her readiness
to accept any man; in contrast, men could be
more selective in choosing a wife. Ben Sira's
opening remarks about a discriminating palate and
foods of different quality illustrate his analogical
thinking.

Although he has already commented on good
and bad wives, in vv. 27-29 Ben Sira lavishes high
praise on beautiful and kind wives. The language
echoes the eulogy of personified wisdom in Prov
8:22-36 and the description in Gen 2:18, 20 of
Eve as Adam's helper.[219] The remark in v. 30 that
a man without a wife wanders about like a
fugitive recalls the exact expression applied to the

219. Carol Meyers, *Discovering Eve* (New York: Oxford University
Press, 1988), offers a stimulating exploration of ancient Israelite women
in cultural context.

first murderer, Cain (Gen 4:12, 14, נע ונד
[*nā' wānād*], "a fugitive and a wanderer"). Ben
Sira credits wives with protecting property and
bestowing credibility on husbands. The allusion to
robbers in v. 31 probably points to mercenary
soldiers who traveled wherever clients wanted
them to engage an enemy in combat; the point
of this reference is the comparison with a "foot-
loose and fancy free" male.

37:1-6. The brief unit about unreliable friends
distinguishes between speech and action. Pledges
of friendship do not necessarily carry conviction,
according to Ben Sira, and former friends sometimes become enemies. Moreover, adversity may
prompt friends to abandon the individual whose
fortunes have shifted, for most people act in their
own self-interest (vv. 4-5). The closing remark
may relate to experience in battle, but the Greek
text makes the more general point that a friend
who merits inner thoughts deserves to enjoy one's
prosperity.

37:7-15. By far the most extraordinary section, these verses consist of Ben Sira's astute
advice about seeking counsel from others. "Be
suspicious of all counselors," he warns, "for they
operate from the standpoint of their own selfish

interests." Above all, do not seek advice from anyone who looks on you with suspicion. Anyone needing that counsel is naive beyond belief. In v. 11, Ben Sira lists nine kinds of people to avoid when soliciting advice; all of them would naturally render biased judgments, whether from self-interest or from character flaws. In vv. 12-15, Ben Sira suggests a hierarchy of advisers, beginning with a reliable observer of the law, then moving to self-reliance and ultimately to divine guidance through prayer. The remark that one's own mind is superior to seven sentinels may debunk Hellenistic astrologers,[220] although the hyperbole probably refers to persons on a watchtower who alert citizens of an approaching army.

37:16-31. Verses 16-26 address the matter of effective speech, with emphasis on God's gift and

popular applause. The national sentiment expressed in the prayer in 36:1-22 recurs in v. 25, which contrasts the limited life span of individual persons with the endless duration of the nation of Israel (cf. 2 Macc 14:15). Just as this brief opening refers back to the preceding discussion of counsel (v. 16), the unit concludes (vv. 27-31) with a comment about sickness, which becomes the topic for the following major section. Ben Sira offers some self-evident advice: Beware of foods that harm you and avoid overeating. The vocative "my child" seems especially appropriate to such banal teaching. As vv. 16-26 imply, teachers differed in their knowledge and its application to life, some divorcing the two and suffering the consequences, others enjoying the grace (charm) that elicits praise, and still others offending through arrogance, unfortunate speech patterns, and choice of words.

---

220. Patrick W. Skehan and Alexander A. Di Lella, *The Wisdom of Ben Sira,* AB 39 (New York: Doubleday, 1987) 433, following Rudolf Smend, *Die Weisheit des Jesus Sirach erklärt* (Berlin: Reimer, 1906) 332.

SIRACH 38:1-15, ON PHYSICIANS

NAB	NRSV
38 Hold the physician in honor, for he is essential to you, and God it was who established his profession.	**38** Honor physicians for their services, for the Lord created them;
2 From God the doctor has his wisdom, and the king provides for his sustenance.	2 for their gift of healing comes from the Most High, and they are rewarded by the king.
3 His knowledge makes the doctor distinguished, and gives him access to those in authority.	3 The skill of physicians makes them distinguished, and in the presence of the great they are admired.
4 God makes the earth yield healing herbs which the prudent man should not neglect;	4 The Lord created medicines out of the earth, and the sensible will not despise them.
5 Was not the water sweetened by a twig that men might learn his power?	5 Was not water made sweet with a tree in order that its[a] power might be known?
6 He endows men with the knowledge to glory in his mighty works,	6 And he gave skill to human beings that he[b] might be glorified in his marvelous works.
7 Through which the doctor eases pain and the druggist prepares his medicines;	7 By them the physician[c] heals and takes away pain;
8 Thus God's creative work continues without cease in its efficacy on the surface of the earth.	8 the pharmacist makes a mixture from them. God's[d] works will never be finished; and from him health[e] spreads over all the earth.
	9 My child, when you are ill, do not delay, but pray to the Lord, and he will heal you.

38, 8: (*wᵉtûšiyyâ*) *mē'al pᵉnê 'ăḏāmâ*: so LXX, P.

aOr *his*   bOr *they*   cHeb: Gk *he*   dGk *His*   eOr *peace*

NAB

9 My son, when you are ill, delay not,
    but pray to God, who will heal you:
10 Flee wickedness; let your hands be just,
    cleanse your heart of every sin;
11 Offer your sweet-smelling oblation and
        petition,
    a rich offering according to your means.
12 Then give the doctor his place
    lest he leave; for you need him too.
13 There are times that give him an advantage,
14 and he too beseeches God
    That his diagnosis may be correct
    and his treatment bring about a cure.
15 He who is a sinner toward his Maker
    will be defiant toward the doctor.

38, 10: *hāsēr ma' al w^{e}habēr kappāyim*: cf LXX, P.

NRSV

10 Give up your faults and direct your hands rightly,
    and cleanse your heart from all sin.
11 Offer a sweet-smelling sacrifice, and a
        memorial portion of choice flour,
    and pour oil on your offering, as much as
        you can afford.[a]
12 Then give the physician his place, for the Lord
        created him;
    do not let him leave you, for you need him.
13 There may come a time when recovery lies in
        the hands of physicians,[b]
14 for they too pray to the Lord
    that he grant them success in diagnosis[c]
    and in healing, for the sake of preserving life.
15 He who sins against his Maker,
    will be defiant toward the physician.[d]

[a] Heb: Lat lacks *as much as you can afford*; Meaning of Gk uncertain
[b] Gk *in their hands*   [c] Heb: Gk *rest*   [d] Heb: Gk *may he fall into the hands of the physician*

COMMENTARY

Because ancient Israelites associated sickness with sin, the place of doctors in society presented a problem to the pious, many of whom understood illness as God's punishment of guilty people. According to 2 Chr 16:12, King Asa had a serious ailment of the foot and consulted physicians for the malady, to no avail. The chronicler condemns him for relying on doctors rather than trusting God to heal him. A weighty tradition identified Israel's Lord as healer (Exod 15:26; cf. Job 5:18; Hos 6:1), conceding at the same time that Yahweh brought disease on the unfortunate Egyptians.

Ben Sira endeavors to hold together both concepts, belief in a deity who punishes violators of the divine will by causing them to become sick and a conviction that God actively works to overcome illness in repentant people. In doing so, Ben Sira draws on religious tradition and practical knowledge. Citing an episode in the story of Israel's wandering in the wilderness when Moses purified dangerous ("bitter") water by throwing wood into it (Exod 15:23-25), Ben Sira attributes healing properties to the branch from an unspecified tree. He also appealed to the best pharma-

ceutical information of the early second century BCE, which untrained (professionally) practictioners of healing arts had accumulated over the years through trial and error. These individuals learned that some roots and herbs have medicinal value, and they transmitted that vital information from generation to generation.

Ben Sira was probably not the first to draw the conclusion that if certain plants possess healing properties, then their Creator must have intended it that way. Carried to its logical conclusion, this line of reasoning indirectly challenges the popular notion that sickness and sin go hand in hand. Ben Sira makes that step hesitantly, and in the end he returns to this former position, perhaps flinching from giving up the powerful motivation for ethical conduct residing in threatened sickness.

In Ben Sira's view, doctors work closely with God and the various remedies the Creator placed at human disposal. Naturally, prayer enters the picture here, the physicians humbly invoking divine sanction on their efforts to bring healing to their clients. In this way, Ben Sira endorsed the exalted social status of physicians in the Hellenistic environment but subjected the medical profession to a humbling ritual at the heart of Jewish piety. Thus tradition sanctioned innovation, and everyone gained something in the process.[221]

In the light of vv. 9-15, it seems likely that some devout Jews spurned physicians and thus jeopardized their own health. Ben Sira gently urges them to combine traditional remedies, specifically prayer and sacrifice, with more modern approaches to sickness. This section reeks with old-fashioned views: confession of sin as a prerequisite for healing, offering generous sacrifices as atonement for fault, and the belief that sinners risk divine punishment in the form of disease. Whereas the Hebrew text emphasizes the divine ordaining of physicians (lit., "to allocate" [חלק *ḥālaq*]) and stresses the deity's activity in handing over sinners to illness, the Greek has "created" (κτίσις *ktisis*), with doctors as objects, and refers to defiance toward physicians by those persons incurring God's anger.

Jewish ambiguity toward physicians persists into later times. The telling allusion in the New Testament to one who had exhausted all funds on physicians with no beneficial results (Luke 8:43) probably reflects more than a sense of monetary loss. A saying in the *Mishnah Kiddushin* 4:14 goes much further: "the best among physicians is destined for Gehenna." In Jewish rabbinic literature, hyperbole is common and is not to be pressed literally. That sentiment has continued into more recent times, as Di Lella's citations from Benjamin Franklin, John Donne, and others demonstrate.[222] On the other hand, a rabbinic comment on Exod 21:19 in *Baba Qamma* 85b gives tacit approval to physicians, for it observes that the law gave permission to the physician to practice his art. The reference in Col 4:4 to greetings from "our dear friend Luke, the physician" reveals a similar appreciation for someone in the profession of healing.

This entire discussion of physicians indicates Ben Sira's skill in diplomacy. He avoids offending pious Jews whose understanding of sickness and its remedy was rooted in popular belief, but he also manages to accept radically new views about the cause of sickness and its cure. In the process he underscores the cooperative efforts of pharmacists, doctors, and God in bringing healing to the patient. This attitude takes into account the enormous energy expended on discovering medicinal value in roots and herbs, which is attested in ancient Egyptian papyri listing over five hundred such plants.[223] Ben Sira acknowledges the necessity for divine instruction in assisting physicians to reach correct diagnoses (cf. v. 14, where the Hebrew has a rare loan word from Aramaic, "interpretation" [פשר *pešer*], also meaning "discovery," "diagnosis," otherwise attested in the Bible only in Eccl 8:1.

---

221. Gerhard von Rad, *Wisdom in Israel* (Nashville: Abingdon, 1972), emphasizes Ben Sira's sophisticated awareness of the complex nature of experience, the fact that very few things in life are unambiguous.

222. Skehan and Di Lella, *The Wisdom of Ben Sira*, 441.
223. C. Spicq, "L'Ecclésiastique," *La Sainte Bible* 6, eds. L. Pirot and A. Clamer (Paris: Letouzey et Ane, 1951) 758.

SIRACH 38:16-23, ON MOURNING

NAB	NRSV
16 My son, shed tears for one who is dead 　　with wailing and bitter lament; 　　As is only proper, prepare the body, 　　　absent not yourself from his burial: 17 Weeping bitterly, mourning fully, 　　pay your tribute of sorrow, as he deserves, 18 One or two days, to prevent gossip;	16 My child, let your tears fall for the dead, 　　and as one in great pain begin the lament. 　Lay out the body with due ceremony, 　　and do not neglect the burial. 17 Let your weeping be bitter and your wailing 　　　fervent; 　　make your mourning worthy of the 　　　departed, 　　for one day, or two, to avoid criticism;

38, 16d: *bigwî ātû* cf LXX, P.

NAB

then compose yourself after your grief,

19 For grief can bring on an extremity
   and heartache destroy one's health.

20 Turn not your thoughts to him again;
   cease to recall him; think rather of the end.

21 Recall him not, for there is no hope of his
      return;
   it will not help him, but will do you harm.

22 Remember that his fate will also be yours;
   for him it was yesterday, for you today.

23 With the departed dead, let memory fade;
   rally your courage, once the soul has left.

38, 18: (ba' ăbûr) dibbâ . . . (ba' ăbûr) dāyôn: so LXX.
38, 19: kî middāwôn (yē ṣē' 'āsôn), wᵉ rō a' (lē bā b) ye 'anneh 'osmâ:
so LXX, cf P.
38, 21f: Trsp v 22 before v 21: so LXX, P.

NRSV

then be comforted for your grief.

18 For grief may result in death,
   and a sorrowful heart saps one's strength.

19 When a person is taken away, sorrow is over;
   but the life of the poor weighs down the
      heart.

20 Do not give your heart to grief;
   drive it away, and remember your own end.

21 Do not forget, there is no coming back;
   you do the dead[a] no good, and you injure
      yourself.

22 Remember his[b] fate, for yours is like it;
   yesterday it was his,[c] and today it is yours.

23 When the dead is at rest, let his remembrance
      rest too,
   and be comforted for him when his spirit
      has departed.

a Gk him   b Heb: Gk my   c Heb: Gk mine

COMMENTARY

Ancient Israelites had no mortuaries in which to prepare corpses for burial. The body was laid out in the home, leading to ritual contamination of those residing there. Custom dictated the length of lamentation for the dead, and special laws regulated purification rites for those who became ritually impure. Ben Sira expresses concern over extended grief, suggesting that one shorten its duration for reasons of health. Excessive grief, he argues, threatens well-being, a thoroughly modern insight into the detrimental effects of psychological states on physical health. Ben Sira urges mourners to practice elemental courtesy for the sake of appearance but to get on with life, letting the memory of the deceased rest. Elsewhere he gives more credence to the traditional notion that one should keep the memory of the dead alive and thus ensure a kind of immortality to that person (44:8).

Ben Sira does not seem to address professional mourners, who, accompanied by the music of the flute, cried aloud in the public display of grief (Amos 5:16; cf. Mark 5:38 // Matt 11:17). Their lament (נגה gînâ) took a distinctive form in He-brew verse, a limping meter characterized by three beats that ensued in two further beats. Originally, the shrill cries and beating of breasts may have aimed at driving away evil spirits associated with the dead. Later rabbinic directives mention three days of weeping, seven days of mourning (cf. 22:12; Gen 50:10; Jdt 16:24), and thirty days of letting the hair and beard grow (Mo ed Katan 27 b). This same text states that "whoever indulges in grief to excess over his dead will weep for another" (i.e., his own).

For this unit the Vulgate has the title De exeguiis ("On Mourning Rites"), just as it designated the previous section with the words De medico ("On Physicians"). Ben Sira's silence with regard to prayers for the dead contrasts with 2 Macc 12:43-45, where praying for the dead is commended. For Ben Sira, death had an element of finality; he mentions one's detiny as a matter-of-fact. What was yours yesterday will be mine today—period (v. 22). Furthermore, the occasion of someone else's demise obliges one to contemplate one's own departure, but not in any debilitating fashion (v. 20).

SIRACH 38:24–39:11, THE SUPERIORITY OF THE SCRIBAL PROFESSION

NAB

24 The scribe's profession increases his wisdom;
     whoever is free from toil can become a
       wise man.
25 How can he become learned who guides
       the plow,
     who thrills in wielding the goad like a
       lance,
     Who guides the ox and urges on the bullock,
       and whose every concern is for cattle?
26 His care is for plowing furrows,
     and he keeps a watch on the beasts in the
       stalls.

27 So with every engraver and designer
     who, laboring night and day,
     Fashions carved seals,
       and whose concern is to vary the pattern.
     His care is to produce a vivid impression,
       and he keeps watch till he finishes his
         design.

28 So with the smith standing near his anvil,
     forging crude iron.
     The heat from the fire sears his flesh,
       yet he toils away in the furnace heat.
     The clang of the hammer deafens his ears,
       His eyes are fixed on the tool he is shaping.
     His care is to finish his work,
       and he keeps watch till he perfects it in
         detail.

29 So with the potter sitting at his labor
     revolving the wheel with his feet.
     He is always concerned for his products,
       and turns them out in quantity.
30 With his hands he molds the clay,
     and with his feet softens it.
     His care is for proper coloring,

38, 25b: (bahānît) mardēa`: cf LXX.
38, 26: Trsp a and b: so LXX, P. l° `eglê (marbēq)?: dittog of vv 27f.28g.
38, 27b: (laylâ) kayyôm yinhāg: so B margin, LXX.
38, 27c–39, 15b: With LXX.
38, 27d: (kaihē) epimonē: so LXX^MSS, V.
38, 28e: yaḥāriš for y° ḥaddēš (=kainiei).
38, 30c: (syntelesai to) chrisma: so LXX^MSS, V. 30d: katharisai=
l° bā` ēr=to fire.

NRSV

24 The wisdom of the scribe depends on the
       opportunity of leisure;
     only the one who has little business can
       become wise.
25 How can one become wise who handles the
       plow,
     and who glories in the shaft of a goad,
     who drives oxen and is occupied with their
       work,
     and whose talk is about bulls?
26 He sets his heart on plowing furrows,
     and he is careful about fodder for the
       heifers.
27 So it is with every artisan and master artisan
     who labors by night as well as by day;
     those who cut the signets of seals,
       each is diligent in making a great variety;
     they set their heart on painting a lifelike image,
       and they are careful to finish their work.
28 So it is with the smith, sitting by the anvil,
     intent on his iron-work;
     the breath of the fire melts his flesh,
       and he struggles with the heat of the
         furnace;
     the sound of the hammer deafens his ears,[a]
       and his eyes are on the pattern of the object.
     He sets his heart on finishing his handiwork,
       and he is careful to complete its decoration.
29 So it is with the potter sitting at his work
     and turning the wheel with his feet;
     he is always deeply concerned over his products,
       and he produces them in quantity.
30 He molds the clay with his arm
     and makes it pliable with his feet;
     he sets his heart to finish the glazing,
       and he takes care in firing[b] the kiln.

31 All these rely on their hands,
     and all are skillful in their own work.
32 Without them no city can be inhabited,
     and wherever they live, they will not go
       hungry.[c]

[a]Cn: Gk renews his ear   [b]Cn: Gk cleaning   [c]Syr: Gk and people can neither live nor walk there

NAB

and he keeps watch on the fire of his kiln.
31 All these men are skilled with their hands,
    each one an expert at his own task;
32 Without them no city could be lived in,
    and wherever they stay, they need not
      hunger.
33 They do not occupy the judge's bench,
    nor are they prominent in the assembly;
    They set forth no decisions or judgments,
    nor are they found among the rulers;
34 Yet they maintain God's ancient handiwork,
    and their concern is for exercise of their
      skill.

39 How different the man who devotes
      himself
    to the study of the law of the Most High!
    He explores the wisdom of the men of old
    and occupies himself with the prophecies;
2 He treasures the discourses of famous men,
    and goes to the heart of involved sayings;
3 He studies obscure parables,
    and is busied with the hidden meanings of
      the sages.
4 He is in attendance on the great,
    and has entrance to the ruler.
5 He travels among the peoples of foreign
      lands
    to learn what is good and evil among men.
6 His care is to seek the LORD, his Maker,
    to petition the Most High,
    To open his lips in prayer,
    to ask pardon for his sins.
    Then, if it pleases the LORD Almighty,
    he will be filled with the spirit of
      understanding;
    He will pour forth his words of wisdom
    and in prayer give thanks to the LORD,
7 Who will direct his knowledge and his
      counsel,
    as he meditates upon his mysteries.
8 He will show the wisdom of what he has
      learned
    and glory in the law of the LORD's
      covenant.

38, 32b: ûbaʾ ăšer (ʿou for ou) yāgûrû lōʾ yirʾābû (for yaʿăbōrû=peripatēsousin): so P.
38, 33: Trsp to read c.a.d.e. Omit b: variant of d. ûbᵉmōšᵉlîm for ûbimᵉšalîm (=kai en parabolais).
38, 34b: (kai hē) diēgēsis: cf v. 25d.

NRSV

Yet they are not sought out for the council of
    the people,[a]
33   nor do they attain eminence in the public
      assembly.
They do not sit in the judge's seat,
    nor do they understand the decisions of the
      courts;
they cannot expound discipline or judgment,
    and they are not found among the rulers.[b]
34 But they maintain the fabric of the world,
    and their concern is for[c] the exercise of their
      trade.

How different the one who devotes himself
    to the study of the law of the Most High!

39 He seeks out the wisdom of all the
      ancients,
    and is concerned with prophecies;
2 he preserves the sayings of the famous
    and penetrates the subtleties of parables;
3 he seeks out the hidden meanings of proverbs
    and is at home with the obscurities of
      parables.
4 He serves among the great
    and appears before rulers;
    he travels in foreign lands
    and learns what is good and evil in the
      human lot.
5 He sets his heart to rise early
    to seek the Lord who made him,
    and to petition the Most High;
    he opens his mouth in prayer
    and asks pardon for his sins.

6 If the great Lord is willing,
    he will be filled with the spirit of
      understanding;
    he will pour forth words of wisdom of his own
    and give thanks to the Lord in prayer.
7 The Lord[d] will direct his counsel and
      knowledge,
    as he meditates on his mysteries.
8 He will show the wisdom of what he has
      learned,
    and will glory in the law of the Lord's
      covenant.
9 Many will praise his understanding;

[a] Most ancient authorities lack this line   [b] Cn: Gk *among parables*
[c] Syr: Gk *prayer is in*   [d] Gk *He himself*

NAB

9 Many will praise his understanding;
 his fame can never be effaced;
Unfading will be his memory,
 through all generations his name will live;
10 Peoples will speak of his wisdom,
 and in assembly sing his praises.
11 While he lives he is one out of a thousand,
 and when he dies his renown will not
  cease.

39, 9b: (*ouk exaleiphthē setai*) *to onoma autou*: so P.
39, 11a: ʾ*im yaʿ ămōd* ʾ *eḥād mē* ʾ*elep*: cf Eccl 7, 28. 11b: (*kai ean anapausē tai*) *onoma kataleipsei* (from 11a of LXX): cf P.

NRSV

 it will never be blotted out.
His memory will not disappear,
 and his name will live through all
  generations.
10 Nations will speak of his wisdom,
 and the congregation will proclaim his
  praise.
11 If he lives long, he will leave a name greater
  than a thousand,
 and if he goes to rest, it is enough[a] for him.

[a] Cn: Meaning of Gk uncertain

COMMENTARY

38:24-34a. This section contrasts four professions—farmer, artisan, smith, and potter—with that of the wise. The opening verse specifies the essential requirement for anyone hoping to become a scribe—namely, leisure time. The four trades other than that of scribe consume the workers' time and energy, making it possible for them to study religious texts and converse with informed persons. Nevertheless, these workers contribute to the well-being of society, even if the various honors of a community regularly fall to others. These honors belong to the scribes, who offer counsel, attain public office, and associate with rulers.

An Egyptian instruction from the Twelfth Dynasty (about 1991–1786 BCE) entitled *The Instruction for Duauf,* written by an otherwise unknown Khety and often copied, ridicules numerous occupations in Egypt so as to exalt the scribal profession. Because of the tone of this text, scholars often call it "The Satire of the Trades." The author belittles all occupations except that of scribes; he characterizes the harsh realities associated with sculptors, smiths, carpenters, jewelsmiths, barbers, merchants, brickmakers, builders, farmers, weavers, arrowmakers, couriers, embalmers, cobblers, launderers, fowlers, and fishers. Khety emphasizes the scribes' freedom from a boss, in contrast to all other workers. If Ben Sira knew of this satire, he completely avoided mockery in his remarks about the four professions

other than that of scribe.[224] Moreover, he credits them with maintaining the fabric of the world, something entirely absent from Khety's ridicule. Consistent with his previously stated view of greedy merchants, Ben Sira omits this occupation from the list to be compared with the scribal profession.

The Hebrew text of v. 25 has the farmer conversing with cattle rather than with the wise, although the Greek suggests that he talks about their pedigree. The emphasis on "being occupied with, setting his heart on, and being careful about" conveys the idea that farmers are totally consumed by their work, so that they can never find time or strength to improve their minds. The same emphasis occurs in the description of the artisan, the smith, and the potter. The expression "set their heart on" appears in all four accounts; other comparable phrases are "labors by night as well as day" (v. 27), "is diligent" (v. 27), and "is always deeply concerned" (v. 29). Manual skill has one advantage, according to v. 32: Those who possess it will never lack adequate food, for society cannot do without their wares. Each of them deals with something that is in great demand because of a principle of obsolescence. Food is consumed, seals and pottery are broken, imple-

224. Jack T. Sanders, *Ben Sira and Demotic Wisdom,* SBLMS 28 (Chico, Calif.: Scholars Press, 1983) 69, writes, "that the 'satire of occupations' in 38:24–39:11 relies on an Egyptian antecedent seems beyond doubt."

ments wear out. Daily routines in towns and villages thus created sufficient need for the services of farmers, artisans, smiths, and potters.

38:34b–39:11. In contrast to these, the scribe concentrates on one thing: study. Interpreters have understood the object of this intellectual curiosity as threefold—the law, wisdom, and prophecy—corresponding to the three divisions of the Hebrew Bible, but in a different order from that of the prologue, which has law, prophecy, and the other books.[225] The two different sequences are represented in the Hebrew Bible (law, prophets, writings) and the Septuagint (law, writings, prophets; cf. the Latin Vulgate also). The context suggests a different interpretation of 39:1-3. Ben Sira indicates that the scribes not only concentrate on the law but also apply their minds to insights from various sources: traditional wisdom, oracles, sayings, similes, and proverbs. The introduction to the initial collection in the book of Proverbs uses the following four terms: "proverb," "simile," "wise saying," and "riddle" (Prov 1:6).

Exalting the scribes as confidants of rulers, Ben Sira mentions their experience, acquired through extensive travel, which informs them about human nature. Above all, he praises the wise for their piety, which evokes divine favor and renown among humans. To communicate the exceptional reward for such devotion to learning and virtue, Ben Sira uses the expression "greater than a thousand" (v. 11), which recalls "one in a thousand" in Job (Job 9:3; 33:23) and Ecclesiastes (Eccl 7:28). The unusual divine epithet in v. 6, "the Great Lord" (cf. 46:5; Jas 4:15) occurs in a context that recalls a phrase in Isa 11:2, the promise that the Davidic ruler would be filled with an understanding spirit.

Ancient Judaism endeavored to hold together a belief in the value of manual labor and a conviction that one was obligated to study Torah. On the one hand, the following observation was attributed to Rabbi Gamaliel: "Excellent is study of the law together with worldly occupation, for toil in them both puts sin out of mind. But all study of the law without (worldly) labor comes to nothing and occasions sin."[226] On the other hand, Rabbi Meir was remembered for a quite different view: "Do little in business and be busy with Torah, and be humble in spirit before all men."[227] In Sir 7:15, 22 Ben Sira implies that the wise should also work at manual labor.

---

225. W. O. E. Oesterley, *The Wisdom of Jesus the Son of Sirach or Ecclesiasticus* (Cambridge: Cambridge University Press, 1912) 256.

226. *Pirqe 'Abot* 2:2.
227. Ibid., 4:12.

REFLECTIONS

Modern technology increasingly reinforces vocational elitism, at the same time elevating professions that require advanced education and sophisticated knowledge. In this process, cerebral occupations such as law, medicine, university teaching, and comparable professions in business are placed in prestigious categories of work, whereas manual labor is demeaned. From the perspective of the elite, the nature of much manual labor contributes to their contempt; moreover, in this elitist view, minimal intelligence, skill, or ambition allows these workers to be content with assembly lines, service employment, and menial chores.

Ben Sira's attitude toward the workers of his own day, and Khety's before him, reveals the early roots of elitism. In Ben Sira's defense, it should be recognized that he was fighting for an elevated understanding of intellectual pursuits in a society that valued expertise in various crafts far more than the acquisition of literary skills. His apologetic was written on behalf of poorly paid and barely respected scribes at a time when society had begun to rely on written documents more and more. Art for art's sake hardly commended itself then any more than today; a utilitarian criterion alone seemed to justify expenditure of great time and effort. Using this measuring stick, the professions Ben Sira considers inferior to that of scribes receive high marks. For him, however, other standards canceled this advantage, particularly access to power and fame.

Contemporary disdain for menial laborers has even less to commend it, for this pejorative understanding of the work of one's hands is based primarily on economic factors. Elitists in contemporary North America consider monetary earnings the significant factor in dismissing many occupations as beneath their dignity. This attitude has been internalized by countless workers who labor in jobs from which they receive no personal satisfaction. Lacking adequate self-respect, they take little or no pride in the finished product of their labor. Consequently, the prophecy by elitists becomes self-fulfilling, and people fall into a kind of "treadmill" existence—living out existentially the myth of Sisyphus.

Although some early Christians succumbed to the seductive lure of pre-eminence, both Jesus and the apostle Paul resisted the disciples' desire to be first in rank. Their arguments in rejecting such efforts to attain honor and authority recommend subservience and emphasize the mutual interdependence of the corporate body, the church. Whoever wishes to be first in rank must serve others, for that kind of pre-eminence alone accords with God's will for Christians. Moreover, just as no part of the body can boast that it is more important than another, so also all vocations in the church are complementary and, therefore, equally important.

This understanding of spiritual calling can be meaningfully applied to the diverse ways by which Christians earn a living. All worthy labor, manual or otherwise, contributes to the body politic. No type of profession has more inherent worth than another, although society still tends to value some types of work more highly than others. Manual labor is just as important as its intellectual counterpart. The important thing is that Christians do their work, whatever its nature, with pride and dignity. Having done so, they need not yield to anyone who insinuates that manual labor lacks worth. Perhaps in this way Christians can resist the debilitating trend to connect earnings and self-worth. It is worth recalling that the apostle Paul boasts that he worked night and day (1 Thess 2:9) so that he could preach the gospel without charge (cf. 1 Corinthians 9).

PART VII

OVERVIEW

A carefully crafted hymn extolling the Creator for a well-ordered universe sits awkwardly alongside a harrowing assessment of life as nightmarish. On the one hand, a smooth-running world would appear to offer no refuge for evil and its woeful consequences. On the other hand, human existence is fraught with ambiguity and outright wickedness. Ben Sira endeavors to provide a rational defense of things along the same lines offered by Hellenistic philosophers of his day. The wretchedness of daily existence was compounded by the possibility of falling into shame, both as a result of one's own failure and as a consequence of conduct by one's daughters. Because of the economic value placed on the virginity of eligible wives and their ability to conceive, any behavior that jeopardized either was condemned by society in the strongest way possible. Ben Sira shared this concern. This topic gives way, however, to more elevated thoughts about the beauty of the created world—its wonderful mystery, the Creator's intimate knowledge of all aspects of creation, and a summons to praise.

SIRACH 39:12-35, IN PRAISE OF THE CREATOR

NAB	NRSV

12 Once more I will set forth my theme
  to shine like the moon in its fullness!
	¹² I have more on my mind to express;
	  I am full like the full moon.

13 Listen, my faithful children: open up your petals,
  like roses planted near running waters;
	¹³ Listen to me, my faithful children, and blossom
	  like a rose growing by a stream of water.

14 Send up the sweet odor of incense,
  break forth in blossoms like the lily.
  Send up the sweet odor of your hymn of praise;
  bless the Lord for all he has done!
	¹⁴ Send out fragrance like incense,
	  and put forth blossoms like a lily.
	  Scatter the fragrance, and sing a hymn of praise;
	  bless the Lord for all his works.

15 Proclaim the greatness of his name,
  loudly sing his praises,
  With music on the harp and all stringed instruments;
  sing out with joy as you proclaim:
	¹⁵ Ascribe majesty to his name
	  and give thanks to him with praise,
	  with songs on your lips, and with harps;
	  this is what you shall say in thanksgiving:

16 The works of God are all of them good;
  in its own time every need is supplied.
	¹⁶ "All the works of the Lord are very good,
	  and whatever he commands will be done at the appointed time.
	¹⁷ No one can say, 'What is this?' or 'Why is that?'—
	  for at the appointed time all such questions will be answered.

39, 13b: (*epí rheumatos*) sygrou: so LXX^MSS; cf V.
39, 15c–51, 30: With Heb.

NAB

17 At his word the waters become still as in a
flask;
he had but to speak and the reservoirs
were made.
18 He has but to command and his will is
done;
nothing can limit his achievement.
19 The works of all mankind are present to
him;
not a thing escapes his eye.
20 His gaze spans all the ages;
to him there is nothing unexpected.
21 No cause then to say: "What is the purpose
of this?"
Everything is chosen to satisfy a need.
22 His blessing overflows like the Nile;
like the Euphrates it enriches the surface
of the earth.
23 Again, his wrath expels the nations
and turns fertile land into a salt marsh.
24 For the virtuous his paths are level,
to the haughty they are steep;
25 Good things for the good he provided from
the beginning,
but for the wicked good things and bad.
26 Chief of all needs for human life
are water and fire, iron and salt,
The heart of the wheat, milk and honey,
the blood of the grape, and oil, and cloth;
27 For the good all these are good,
but for the wicked they turn out evil.
28 There are storm winds created to punish,
which in their fury can dislodge
mountains;
When destruction must be, they hurl all their
force
and appease the anger of their Maker.
29 In his treasury also, kept for the proper
time,
are fire and hail, famine, disease,
30 Ravenous beasts, scorpions, vipers,

39, 17a: *bid^ebārô ya'amedû kanned mayim*: so LXX; cf Ps 33, 7.
17b: '*ôṣ^erôt mayim*: so LXX.
 39, 18: *b^emiṣwātô (reṣônô yaṣlîaḥ)*: cf LXX.
 39, 20: Omit *hāyēš . . .'immô* and *w^eḥāzāq*: so LXX.
 39, 21: Omit c.d: variant of a.b: so LXX.
 39, 22: *bírkātô (kay^e'ōṛ)*: so LXX, P.
 39, 24: '*orḥôtāyw l^etammîm . . . l^ezēdîm*: so LXX; cf P.
 39, 29f: Trsp to read: 30d.29a.30a.b. Omit 29b.30c: variants: cf LXX,
P. *b^e'ôṣārô lā'ēt*. so margin. *rā'āb (wādāber)*: so LXX; cf P.

NRSV

At his word the waters stood in a heap,
and the reservoirs of water at the word of
his mouth.
18 When he commands, his every purpose is fulfilled,
and none can limit his saving power.
19 The works of all are before him,
and nothing can be hidden from his eyes.
20 From the beginning to the end of time he can
see everything,
and nothing is too marvelous for him.
21 No one can say, 'What is this?' or 'Why is
that?'—
for everything has been created for its own
purpose.

22 "His blessing covers the dry land like a river,
and drenches it like a flood.
23 But his wrath drives out the nations,
as when he turned a watered land into salt.
24 To the faithful his ways are straight,
but full of pitfalls for the wicked.
25 From the beginning good things were created
for the good,
but for sinners good things and bad.[a]
26 The basic necessities of human life
are water and fire and iron and salt
and wheat flour and milk and honey,
the blood of the grape and oil and clothing.
27 All these are good for the godly,
but for sinners they turn into evils.

28 "There are winds created for vengeance,
and in their anger they can dislodge
mountains;[b]
on the day of reckoning they will pour out
their strength
and calm the anger of their Maker.
29 Fire and hail and famine and pestilence,
all these have been created for vengeance;
30 the fangs of wild animals and scorpions and
vipers,
and the sword that punishes the ungodly
with destruction.
31 They take delight in doing his bidding,
always ready for his service on earth;
and when their time comes they never
disobey his command."

[a] Heb Lat: Gk *sinners bad things*   [b] Heb Syr: Gk *can scourge
mightily*

NAB

and the avenging sword to exterminate the
wicked;
31 In doing his bidding they rejoice,
    in their assignments they disobey not his
        command.
32 So from the first I took my stand,
    and wrote down as my theme:
33 The works of God are all of them good;
    every need when it comes he fills.
34 No cause then to say: "This is not as good
        as that";
    for each shows its worth at the proper
        time.
35 So now with full joy of heart proclaim
    and bless the name of the Holy One.

39, 32: (mērō'š) hityaṣṣabtî: so LXX.
39, 34: (zeh ra') mizzeh: so B margin, LXX, P.

NRSV

32 So from the beginning I have been convinced
        of all this
    and have thought it out and left it in writing:
33 All the works of the Lord are good,
    and he will supply every need in its time.
34 No one can say, "This is not as good as that,"
    for everything proves good in its appointed
        time.
35 So now sing praise with all your heart and
        voice,
    and bless the name of the Lord.

COMMENTARY

This hymn in praise of the Creator (vv. 16-31), together with its introduction (vv. 12-15) and personal conclusion (vv. 32-35), is essentially a theodicy. The "very academic hymn"[228] addresses the question about apparent anomalies in the world, specifically "What is this or why is that?" (vv. 17, 21). As we have seen, in dealing with the general problem of evil Ben Sira employs traditional arguments; for example, he promises eventual rectification, interprets undeserved suffering as disciplinary, and points out that appearances often deceive. Failing to arrive at a satisfactory answer to theodicy, he insists that God is just despite all evidence to the contrary, and humans should, therefore, acknowledge divine mystery by raising their voices in praise rather than in protest.

In addition to such traditional responses to the problem of theodicy, Ben Sira offers at least two new ways of looking at this vexing issue, one philosophical, the other psychological. He takes up the Greek rational argument that the cosmos consists of complementary pairs, good things that promote virtue and harmful things that punish wickedness. Moreover, Ben Sira insists that inner psychological states determine how people view outer experiences and that wicked persons are afflicted with anxiety. The unknown author of the book of Wisdom develops the latter idea more fully in Wis 16:24–19:22, which describes the manner in which fear transforms ordinary things into frightening sources of terror.[229]

39:12-15. Ben Sira's invitation to sing God's praises mentions "faithful children" (υἱοὶ ὅσιοι *huioi hosioi*), a departure from the usual vocative without a qualifying adjective (v. 13) following an appeal for attention. Furthermore, he actually states that this particular hymn should be recited (v. 15). The admission in v. 12 that the author has not exhausted his teachings echoes the initial remarks at the opening of book two, where Ben Sira describes his renewed effort to deal responsibly with a mighty stream of ideas (24:30-34).

228. Snaith observes that "this learned discussion, typical of the lecture room . . . thus becomes a very academic hymn, with the doctrinal lesson that 'All that the Lord . . . commands will happen in due time' repeated almost like a refrain." See John G. Snaith, *Ecclesiasticus or The Wisdom of Jesus, Son of Sirach,* CBC, NEB (Cambridge: Cambridge University Press, 1974) 195.

229. James L. Crenshaw, "The Problem of Theodicy in Sirach," *JBL* 94 (1975) 47-64, examines the various responses to apparent injustice in Ben Sira's teaching and in the book of Wisdom, where the psychological answer dominates. See also James L. Crenshaw, *Urgent Advice and Probing Questions* (Macon, Ga.: Mercer University Press, 1995) 155-74.

The dominant image there was that of a canal that grew into a river and then into a sea; here the emphasis falls on the full moon and flowers growing alongside a flowing stream. There the imagery was restricted to the author; here he moves a step further to include his students in the circle of praise, recalling in the process the pleasant fragrances of nature and also those associated with worship. He likens hymnody and the accompanying music to the beauty and fragrance of oleanders, lilies, and incense. Just as personified wisdom flourished in 24:13-34, so also the scribe, who in 39:1-11 represents Ben Sira's ideal, thrives in the same way.

39:16-31. The hymn in these verses echoes the refrain in Genesis 1, affirming the goodness of everything that God created. Such an extraordinary claim in the face of so many things that seem out of place in an orderly universe must surely have encountered resistance. In the end, claim and counterclaim seem to cancel each other out, just like Ezekiel and his vocal opponents who insisted that Yahweh was unjust (Ezek 18:25-29). Ben Sira has learned a valuable lesson from Qohelet that everything is good in its time (vv. 16-17; cf. Eccl 3:11). The allusion to waters piling up, usually applied to the story about Yahweh's victory over the pursuing Egyptian army (Exod 15:8), may actually recall the separating of waters in Gen 1:9-10.

The stress on divine power and clarity of sight functions to reinforce Ben Sira's theodicy. Because no one can limit God's ability to reward virtuous people (the actual Hebrew word is תשועתו [těšû'ātô], "his saving deeds") and nothing can obscure God's vision, nothing stands in the way of dispensing accurate justice. To accomplish that end, Ben Sira insists, the Lord looks on human beings in blessing and wrath, depending on which is appropriate at a given moment. The beneficial things, intended for the faithful, consist of ten basic ingredients to a good life—an extension from the four necessities of life mentioned in 29:21 (water, bread, clothing, and a house).[230] The six additional items raise the level of comfort: fire for warmth and cooking; iron (and fire) for the making of tools and weapons; salt for flavor;

milk, honey, wine, and oil to complement bread. Curiously, Ben Sira thinks that even these necessities bring misfortune to the wicked (the Hebrew word הפך [hāpak] implies a total overthrow as at Sodom and Gomorrah or Nineveh).[231] This language links up with v. 23, perhaps an allusion to Gen 19:24-28.

Like the blessings, which manifest themselves as basic necessities and for which Ben Sira uses the image of the Nile and the Euphrates rivers, the wrath of God comes to expression in nine natural elements (vv. 28-31). Powerful sirocco winds, a mighty tempest from the southeast, wreak havoc even on solid mountains; fire, hail, famine, pestilence, wild animals, scorpions, vipers, and the sword do the divine bidding to execute sinners. The last of these alone involves human agents. Ben Sira implies that all of nature stands ready to carry out God's wrathful decrees, as do human armies. A contrast may be implied between an obedient nature and willful human beings. To some extent, this list of natural calamities resembles that found in the account of plagues affecting Egypt in the book of Exodus (Exod 7:14–12:32).

39:32-35. In an epilogue to the hymn, Ben Sira reaffirms his long-held conviction that all of God's works are good, and he reiterates the invitation to praise the Creator. This time, at least in the Greek text, he formulates popular sentiment denying divine justice as a statement, "This is not as good as that," instead of repeating the earlier interrogative form, "What is this? What is that?" Pride of authorship prompts him to boast about leaving a written legacy of his intellectual conclusions. Although the Greek text has "Lord" (κύριος kyrios) in vv. 16 and 33, the Hebrew has "God" (אל 'ēl); in v. 35 a marginal note to the Hebrew has "his holy name" (שם קדשו šēm qodšô; cf. שם הקדוש šēm haqqādôš in the text), while the Greek uses kyrios (the Hebrew text has survived in ms B from 39:15, beginning with the reference to songs, to the end of the book). In the Talmudic tractate Sabb. 77b a similar statement to Ben Sira's affirmation uses the customary rabbinic epithet, "the Holy One." It reads: "Not a single thing of those which the Holy One created in this world has been created in vain, as though it did not fulfil its purpose."

---

230. The effort to discover the fundamental elements of the universe represents a similar concern—e.g., the supposition that the universe consists of earth, air, fire, and water.

231. Jack Sasson, *Jonah,* AB 24B (New York: Doubleday, 1990) 234-35, 267, discusses the ambiguity of the niphal use of this verb and thinks the prophet implied that the city would turn over (reform).

REFLECTIONS

1. The primary basis for lauding the Creator, according to Ben Sira, is the goodness of creation. That optimism does not come easily, for some things seem out of place in an orderly universe. Even persons who believe in the essential harmony of creation occasionally adopt the interrogative mode: Why do bad things happen to decent people? What possible justification for cancer cells can one posit?

The beauty of Ben Sira's position resides in the way he situates doubting questions within the framework of spontaneous praise. This manner of facing up to the anomalies of existence prevents skepticism from becoming counterproductive. Confident that the maladies of existence, which Ben Sira calls curses, are divine instruments for punishing sinners, he assumes that time alone will convey fuller knowledge to doubters who refuse to turn away from their Creator.

2. The familiar phrase from *The Rubáiyát* of Omar Khayyám, "A loaf of bread, a jug of wine, and thou," sums up a famous lover's effort to articulate the bare necessities of life. Perhaps Ben Sira's version of the essentials in terms of bread, water, clothing, and a home (Sir 29:21) is more realistic, although his additional reflection expands this list further still. The move from four necessities to ten (Sir 39:26) speaks volumes about human nature, for it reflects the desire to make life not merely tolerable but to some degree comfortable as well. People who have enjoyed the pleasures of the good life may have moments of nostalgia in thinking about a simpler existence, but rarely do they voluntarily relinquish the comforts they have come to know.

In some ways Ben Sira's list strikes modern readers as somewhat one-sided, for it is slanted entirely toward the needs and desires of the body. For an intellectual, as he surely was, the absence of anything cerebral, spiritual, or aesthetic in this list of essentials for living is surprising. Can one imagine life without a book, worship, or music? Whether one agrees with Ben Sira in this regard or wishes to extend the list even further, religious enthusiasts ought to give him credit for asking an important question: What absolute minimum can one possess and still live? Because many citizens of impoverished countries face this question every day, the issue for them is existential rather than hypothetical. Our pondering of the matter may open up the floodgates of compassion as we grasp the magnitude of the gulf between them and us.

The enormous pressure to buy more and more will undoubtedly continue, for it fuels the international economy. So will pangs of guilt when Christians succumb to its persuasive power. Caught in the middle between external forces and inner compulsion, thoughtful individuals grope for adequate criteria for deciding how to spend their financial assets. Asking Ben Sira's unstated question and reaching a conclusion about the essentials for living will equip them to act morally in this situation.

SIRACH 40:1–41:13, LIFE'S WRETCHEDNESS

NAB	NRSV
40 A great anxiety has God allotted, and a heavy yoke, to the sons of men; From the day one leaves his mother's womb to the day he returns to the mother of all the living,	**40** Hard work was created for everyone, and a heavy yoke is laid on the children of Adam, from the day they come forth from their mother's womb

NAB

2 His thoughts, the fear in his heart,
   and his troubled forebodings till the day he
     dies—
3 Whether he sits on a lofty throne
   or grovels in dust and ashes,
4 Whether he bears a splendid crown
   or is wrapped in the coarsest of cloaks—
5 Are of wrath and envy, trouble and dread,
   terror of death, fury and strife.
  Even when he lies on his bed to rest,
   his cares at night disturb his sleep.
6 So short is his rest it seems like none,
   till in his dreams he struggles as he did by
     day,
  Terrified by what his mind's eye sees,
   like a fugitive being pursued;
7 As he reaches safety, he wakes up
   astonished that there was nothing to fear.
8 So it is with all flesh, with man and with
     beast,
   but for sinners seven times more.
9 Plague and bloodshed, wrath and the sword,
   plunder and ruin, famine and death:
10 For the wicked, these were created evil,
   and it is they who bring on destruction.

11 All that is of earth returns to earth,
   and what is from above returns above.
12 All that comes from bribes or injustice will
     be wiped out,
   but loyalty remains for ages.
13 Wealth out of wickedness is like a wadi in
     spate:
  like a mighty stream with lightning and
     thunder,
14 Which, in its rising, rolls along the stones,
  but suddenly, once and for all, comes to
     an end.
15 The offshoot of violence will not flourish,
   for the root of the godless is on sheer rock;

40, 2: With LXX. 2a: *heōs hēmeran* (*teleutēs*).
40, 3: *wᵉˈad lešaḥ bᵉˈāpār (wāˈēper):* so LXX.
40, 4: (*wᵉˈad) lᵉbûš (śimlat ˈôn):* so LXX; cf P.
40, 5a: ˈap *wᵉqin' ā:* so LXX, P. 5d: *šᵉnôt laylá tᵉšanneh daˈāgātō:?;*
for sense cf 42, 9.
40, 6b: *ûmikkēn baḥălômôt kᵉbayyôm yîga' sso* LXX (*kopia* for *skopias*).
6c: *mᵉtaˈta' (mēḥāzôn):* ?; cf LXX.
40, 7f: With LXX.
40, 9: *rāˈāb (wāmāwet):* so LXX.
40, 10b: *ûbaˈăbûrô tābô' (kālā):* so LXX.
40, 15: *nēṣer ḥāmās lō' yirbēh:* cf M, LXX; (*śen*) *ṣûr:* M.

NRSV

  until the day they return to[a] the mother of
   all the living.[b]
2 Perplexities and fear of heart are theirs,
   and anxious thought of the day of their
     death.
3 From the one who sits on a splendid throne
   to the one who grovels in dust and ashes,
4 from the one who wears purple and a crown
   to the one who is clothed in burlap,
5 there is anger and envy and trouble and unrest,
   and fear of death, and fury and strife.
  And when one rests upon his bed,
   his sleep at night confuses his mind.
6 He gets little or no rest;
   he struggles in his sleep as he did by day.[c]
  He is troubled by the visions of his mind
   like one who has escaped from the
     battlefield.
7 At the moment he reaches safety he wakes up,
   astonished that his fears were groundless.
8 To all creatures, human and animal,
   but to sinners seven times more,
9 come death and bloodshed and strife and
     sword,
   calamities and famine and ruin and plague.
10 All these were created for the wicked,
   and on their account the flood came.
11 All that is of earth returns to earth,
   and what is from above returns above.[d]

12 All bribery and injustice will be blotted out,
   but good faith will last forever.
13 The wealth of the unjust will dry up like a
     river,
   and crash like a loud clap of thunder in a
     storm.
14 As a generous person has cause to rejoice,
   so lawbreakers will utterly fail.
15 The children of the ungodly put out few
     branches;
   they are unhealthy roots on sheer rock.
16 The reeds by any water or river bank
   are plucked up before any grass;
17 but kindness is like a garden of blessings,
   and almsgiving endures forever.

[a]Other Gk and Lat authorities read *are buried in*   [b]Heb: Gk *of
all*   [c]Arm: Meaning of Gk uncertain   [d]Heb Syr: Gk Lat *from
the waters returns to the sea*

NAB

16 Or they are like reeds on the riverbank,
    withered before all other plants.

17 But goodness will never be cut off,
    and justice endures forever.

    Wealth or wages can make life sweet,
    but better than either is finding a treasure.

18 A child or a city will preserve one's name,
    but better than either, attaining wisdom.

19 Sheepfolds and orchards bring flourishing
        health;
    but better than either, a devoted wife;

20 Wine and music delight the soul,
    but better than either, conjugal love.

21 The flute and the harp offer sweet melody,
    but better than either, a voice that is true.

22 Charm and beauty delight the eye,
    but better than either, the flowers of the
        field.

23 A friend, a neighbor, are timely guides,
    but better than either, a prudent wife.

24 A brother, a helper, for times of stress;
    but better than either, charity that rescues.

25 Gold and silver make one's way secure,
    but better than either, sound judgment.

26 Wealth and vigor build up confidence,
    but better than either, fear of God.
    Fear of the LORD leaves nothing wanting;
    he who has it need seek no other support:

27 The fear of God is a paradise of blessings;
    its canopy, all that is glorious.

28 My son, live not the life of a beggar,
    better to die than to beg;

29 When one has to look to another's table,
    his life is not really a life.
    His neighbor's delicacies bring revulsion of spirit
    to one who understands inward feelings:

30 In the mouth of the shameless man begging
        is sweet,
    but within him it burns like fire.

41 O death! how bitter the thought of you
    for the man at peace amid his possessions,

40, 16: *lipnê kol hāṣîr nid' ak*: cf M, LXX.
40, 17: *hôn wᵉśākār yamtîqû hayyîm.*
40, 27: *wᵉ ʿal (kol kābôd)*: so LXX, P; cf Is 4, 5.
40, 28: *bᵉnî (hayyê)*: so B margin, LXX, P.
40, 29c: *mig ʿal nepeš maṭ ammê rēaʿ*: cf LXX.
40, 30: *bᵉpî ʿaz nepeš (tamtîq)*: so M.
41, 1: *hôî (lammāwet)*: so B margin, LXX, P.

NRSV

18 Wealth and wages make life sweet,[a]
    but better than either is finding a treasure.

19 Children and the building of a city establish
        one's name,
    but better than either is the one who finds
        wisdom.
    Cattle and orchards make one prosperous;[b]
    but a blameless wife is accounted better
        than either.

20 Wine and music gladden the heart,
    but the love of friends[c] is better than either.

21 The flute and the harp make sweet melody,
    but a pleasant voice is better than either.

22 The eye desires grace and beauty,
    but the green shoots of grain more than
        either.

23 A friend or companion is always welcome,
    but a sensible wife[d] is better than either.

24 Kindred and helpers are for a time of trouble,
    but almsgiving rescues better than either.

25 Gold and silver make one stand firm,
    but good counsel is esteemed more than
        either.

26 Riches and strength build up confidence,
    but the fear of the Lord is better than either.
    There is no want in the fear of the Lord,
    and with it there is no need to seek for help.

27 The fear of the Lord is like a garden of blessing,
    and covers a person better than any glory.

28 My child, do not lead the life of a beggar;
    it is better to die than to beg.

29 When one looks to the table of another,
    one's way of life cannot be considered a life.
    One loses self-respect with another person's
        food,
    but one who is intelligent and well
        instructed guards against that.

30 In the mouth of the shameless begging is
        sweet,
    but it kindles a fire inside him.

41 O death, how bitter is the thought
        of you
    to the one at peace among possessions,

a Heb: Gk *Life is sweet for the self-reliant worker*   *b* Heb Syr: Gk
lacks *but better . . . prosperous*   *c* Heb: Gk *wisdom*   *d* Heb
Compare Syr: Gk *wife with her husband*

NAB

For the man unruffled and always successful,
   who still can enjoy life's pleasures.
2 O death! how welcome your sentence
   to the weak man of failing strength,
Tottering and always rebuffed,
   with no more sight, with vanished hope.
3 Fear not death's decree for you;
   remember, it embraces those before you,
      and those after.
4 Thus God has ordained for all flesh;
   why then should you reject the will of the
      Most High?
Whether one has lived a thousand years, a
      hundred, or ten,
   in the nether world he has no claim on
      life.

5 A reprobate line are the children of sinners,
   and witless offspring are in the homes of
      the wicked.
6 Their dominion is lost to sinners' children,
   and reproach abides with their
      descendants.
7 Children curse their wicked father,
   for they suffer disgrace through him.
8 Woe to you, O sinful men,
   who forsake the law of the Most High.
9 If you have children, calamity will seize
      them;
   you will beget them only for groaning.
When you stumble, there is lasting joy;
   at death, you become a curse.
10 Whatever is of nought returns to nought,
   so too the godless from void to void.
11 Man's body is a fleeting thing,
   but a virtuous name will never be
      annihilated.
12 Have a care for your name, for it will stand
      by you
   better than precious treasures in the
      thousands;
13 The boon of life is for limited days,
   but a good name, for days without number.

41, 4d: ʼên (tôkᵉḥôt) ḥayyîm (bišᵉʼôl): so B margin, LXX.
41, 5: tôlᵉdôt (rāʼîm); cf M.
41, 8a: ʼôy lākem ʼanšê ʼawlâ cf M.
41, 13: Omit vv 14-15 of Heb and LXX: variant of 20, 29f (20, 30f of LXX).

NRSV

who has nothing to worry about and is
      prosperous in everything,
   and still is vigorous enough to enjoy food!
2 O death, how welcome is your sentence
   to one who is needy and failing in strength,
worn down by age and anxious about
      everything;
   to one who is contrary, and has lost all
      patience!
3 Do not fear death's decree for you;
   remember those who went before you and
      those who will come after.
4 This is the Lord's decree for all flesh;
   why then should you reject the will of the
      Most High?
Whether life lasts for ten years or a hundred
      or a thousand,
   there are no questions asked in Hades.

5 The children of sinners are abominable
      children,
   and they frequent the haunts of the ungodly.
6 The inheritance of the children of sinners will
      perish,
   and on their offspring will be a perpetual
      disgrace.
7 Children will blame an ungodly father,
   for they suffer disgrace because of him.
8 Woe to you, the ungodly,
   who have forsaken the law of the Most High
      God!
9 If you have children, calamity will be theirs;
   you will beget them only for groaning.
When you stumble, there is lasting joy;ᵃ
   and when you die, a curse is your lot.
10 Whatever comes from earth returns to earth;
   so the ungodly go from curse to destruction.
11 The human body is a fleeting thing,
   but a virtuous name will never be blotted
      out.ᵇ
12 Have regard for your name, since it will outlive
      you
   longer than a thousand hoards of gold.
13 The days of a good life are numbered,
   but a good name lasts forever.

ᵃHeb: Meaning of Gk uncertain   ᵇHeb: Gk *People grieve over
the death of the body, but the bad name of sinners will be blotted
out*

COMMENTARY

Ben Sira's description of human bondage to sin and death is broken only by a series of comparisons in which the second-mentioned item is preferred (40:18-27), and to some degree by a brief unit about contrasts in conduct, the second of which brings lasting joy (40:12-17; in 40:14, however, the positive one appears first). This grim depiction of the human situation stands in the shadow of Ben Sira's lofty expression of praise for the goodness of creation.

40:1-11. The initial section depicts the heavy yoke worn by all creatures but felt seven times more severely by the wicked. Ben Sira observes that the yoke cannot be lifted from birth to death; he uses the expression "mother of all the living" with reference to the earth. Naturally, this thought echoes the ancient story about the creation of Adam and Eve from dust and the identification of Eve as the mother of all living persons. The language, now traditional, occurs also in the prologue to the book of Job: "Naked I came from my mother's womb, and naked shall I return there" (Job 1:21 NRSV). In this instance, "there" is probably a euphemism for Sheol, not a reference to the mother's womb. Not only do people endure trouble (this word, עסק ['ōseq] does not occur in the HB) and anxiety during their waking hours, but at night they have dreadful nightmares, waking at their moment of greatest need (reading χρεία [chreia] for σωτηρία [sōtēria], "salvation"). No one escapes this yoke, neither the ruler nor the subject, neither rich nor poor. Ben Sira associates the flood with other calamities that God created especially for the wicked. The only relief comes at death, according to v. 11, when dust returns to dust (Gen 3:19), and lifebreath goes back to its divine source (Eccl 12:7).

The poetic niceties of this poem include interlinear parallelism: "the one who sits on a splendid throne" (v. 3) and "the one who wears purple and a crown" (v. 4); "the one who grovels in the dust and ashes" (v. 3) and "the one who is clothed in burlap" (v. 4); the symbolic reference to seven sources of misery (v. 5), signifying fullness, and the explicit statement in v. 8; the portrayal of inner anxiety and the comparable depiction of external dangers; the reference in v.

3*a* to the civil authority and in v. 4*a* to the religious authority.[232]

In this section Ben Sira borrows ideas from a tradition about the miserable lot entrusted to humans: e.g., the curse on rebellious Adam in Gen 3:17-20; Job's reflections about the awful plight of human beings in Job 7 and 14; and the unflattering opinion about the human imagination in Gen 6:5. Although these ancient texts describe a universal human bondage, Ben Sira qualifies this misfortune by attributing far more trouble to sinners than to good people. For Job, divine watchfulness exacerbated suffering, whereas Ben Sira thinks of God's surveillance as assurance of justice.

40:12-17. These verses reaffirm Ben Sira's belief in the divine ordering of things to benefit the righteous on earth. True to precedent, he employs images from nature to reinforce his point. Wealth unjustly acquired resembles wadis in winter, temporarily filled with water from torrential downpours, only to dry up in summer. Similarly, possessions are like deafening thunder, all sound and fury and soon vanished. Children of evil parents are like trees growing on a rocky precipice, their roots clinging to unsubstantial soil and lacking adequate moisture, or like reeds along a riverbank inviting passersby to pull them up (cf. Job 8:11-12). Deeds of kindness, however, flourish for a long time, like a well-tended garden.

40:18-27. Ben Sira introduces ten comparative sayings that lead up to his favorite concept, fear of the Lord. Ancient sages were fond of this device, which modern interpreters label "better-than proverbs."[233] Each of these sayings juxtaposes two ideas, the second of which is deemed more desirable than the first. Such sayings greatly assist scholars in understanding a relative scale of values in a prominent sage from second-century BCE Judah. The positive valence of good wives, mentioned twice in the superior category (vv. 19, 23), and of friendship (v. 20; cf. the Greek, which has

232. Patrick W. Skehan and Alexander A. Di Lella, *The Wisdom of Ben Sira,* AB 39 (New York: Doubleday, 1987) 470.

233. On the forms of sapiential discourse, see James L. Crenshaw, "Wisdom," in *Old Testament Form Criticism,* ed. John H. Hayes, TUMS 2 (San Antonio: Trinity University Press, 1974) 225-64. See also James L. Crenshaw, *Urgent Advice and Probing Questions* (Macon, Ga.: Mercer University Press, 1995) 45-77.

"wisdom") is noteworthy. Some of the sayings occasion no surprise; the discovery of hidden treasure is better than having to work for one's fortune; help from God (as reward for almsgiving) is superior to assistance from family and friends.

Other sayings make one raise an eyebrow, at least momentarily: Intelligent advice is preferable to wealth; a pleasant voice is better than music; green shoots of grain bring more pleasure than grace and beauty (because they indicate a bountiful harvest); wisdom is preferable to progeny and an honorable reputation, acquired through building a city. Ben Sira may reflect the Greek practice of naming cities after prominent figures in society (e.g., Philippi, named after Philip of Macedon; Alexandria, named after Alexander the Great; Antioch, named after Antiochus III).

The threefold use of the phrase "the fear of the Lord" in the final couplet (vv. 26-27) reinforces the importance of piety to Ben Sira, a note already struck indirectly in v. 24, perhaps also in the initial allusion to wisdom, inasmuch as fear of the Lord both leads to and comprises the essence of wisdom. Ben Sira emphasizes the sufficiency of religious devotion; safe in divine solicitude, the one who fears the Lord flourishes like a garden and basks in honor.

40:28-30. Verse 28 introduces the two subjects of the next section as begging and death. In 29:24-27 Ben Sira discussed the indignity of having to eat at someone else's table. Here he raises that topic again, reiterating the loss of respect associated with such dependence. Verse 30 highlights the hypocrisy involved in begging, the necessary self-effacement that masks a bitter resentment within, aptly likened to a fire. Reduced to such non-life, one would be better off dead (v. 28). Burton Mack has conjectured that Ben Sira may have in mind the Cynic practice of begging as a form of social critique.[234] Even if one assumes that Ben Sira's audience comprised an elite group, it does not follow that he would remain silent about the subject of self-reliance. Advice against begging may simply be a traditional topic in such sapiential advice.

41:1-4. Two different particles in Hebrew, the one (הוי *hôy*) signifying grudging reluctance in the face of an unpleasant decree (חק *ḥōq*) and the other (האח *heʾāḥ*) connoting open arms, contrast reactions to death by people in opposite circumstances. The first interjection refers to a person who has adequate resources, personal and otherwise, to enjoy life, whereas the second indicates someone whose aged body "stumbles and trips," having grown weary of the accompanying aches and privations. Naturally, death appears differently to these persons. One thing they have in common, however, is a date with the Grim Reaper. Ben Sira, therefore, urges acceptance of the divine decree as universal and implies that questioning the wisdom of that statute makes no sense. The Hebrew of this verse in MS A has "individual decree" or "statute" (חק *ḥōq*) and "laws," "instruction" (תורות *tôrôt*), but the scroll from Masada reads "end" (קץ *qēs*), as does the Syriac (MS B has "portion" [חלק *ḥēleq*]). Presumably, he thinks the interrogative mode, so typical of existence on earth, vanishes at death, whether it comes early or late. Ben Sira assumes that all distinctions, and hence inequities, disappear in Sheol.

41:5-13. This disquisition on death prompts Ben Sira to reflect on those left behind, particularly children, in his view a person's only access to a kind of immortality. The emphasis falls on offspring of the wicked who have spurned the Most High God, for to them clings a heavy curse. Ben Sira turns to describe the opposite situation of parents whose virtue endures in memory long after their bodies have returned to dust. True to form, he praises reputation over gold, which disappears long before an honorable name does. The three uses of "memorial" (שם *šēm*, lit., "name") in vv. 11-13 reflect Ben Sira's high assessment of reputation. The contrast between the ungodly and a lasting name could hardly be starker. According to v. 10, the wicked will vanish into nothingness ("waste" [תהו *tōhû*]; cf. Gen 1:2; Isa 40:17 for *tōhû* and אפס [*epes*], "cessation" together as here).

---

234. Burton Mack, "Annotations to Sirach," in *The HarperCollins Study Bible,* ed. Wayne A. Meeks (New York: HarperCollins, 1993) 1595.

REFLECTIONS

1. For Ben Sira the highest priority went to religious devotion, which he called "the fear of the Lord." In two ways he signaled the importance of religion, first by mentioning it three times and, second, by leading up to the subject as a sort of crescendo. Closely behind religious service were wisdom and reliable counsel, which Ben Sira prized more than a lasting memory or wealth respectively.[235] Next came a good wife, followed by love, pleasant speech, and the early signs of a bountiful harvest. This corrective to the essentials of life shows that Ben Sira did not let physical appetites dictate important decisions.

From the items he uses in comparing favored things with less desirable ones, Ben Sira opens a door into his own system of values. None of the less-desirables deserves to be labeled as undesirable, least of all children—the only immortality accessible to Jews in ancient times. Likewise, gold and silver, wine and music, grace and beauty belong to the good things in life.

If one really can be known by what one treasures most dearly, then we would do well to explore Ben Sira's question of priorities for ourselves. Precisely where does our treasure lie? In spiritual things or in material comforts? Once we have settled that question decisively and honestly, we shall be ready to go a step farther and ask how the newly ascertained list of priorities can transform our lives and enrich our spirits.

Ben Sira did not conceal the fact that a religious value system often clashes with the dominant mores of society, but when that occurred he urged people to dare to be different. In Christian terms, that may mean courageously saying no to any number of activities, such as excessive spending, unethical financial dealings, cheating in school, immoderate drinking, casual sex, supporting political candidates who are racist or otherwise corrupt, voting for those who think the United States should traffic in weapons. Positively, daring to be different may mean spending time working at unselfish causes and volunteering to help those members of society who have difficulty fending for themselves.

2. What explanation for this treadmill existence makes the most sense? Ben Sira could not make up his mind. Some of his remarks point toward death and the unpleasantries leading up to it as part and parcel of the human condition from the very beginning, whereas other comments place the blame on Eve for disobeying a divine prohibition. Perhaps his inability to opt for one or the other testifies to Ben Sira's awareness of the complexity of the problem.

In one sense, the failure to resolve this dilemma leaves human beings vulnerable to enormous anxiety about death, when ready acceptance of mortality as the human condition has the potential of reducing such concern greatly. To Ben Sira's credit, he realized that the lion's share of worry is self-generated, like a nightmare. In our time, a decisive shift is taking place in that many people worry more about the manner of death than the fact of death itself. Death with dignity has introduced a new factor into the discussion of one's eventual demise. If a person views death as something other than punishment, then death's stigma disappears.

For Christians, death does not signify the ultimate word, for they place their hope in God's gracious activity aimed at drawing humankind into a kingdom of the redeemed. The last word, according to Christian hope, is one of divine acceptance, symbolized by the story of Jesus' resurrection and the anticipation of a resurrection of believers. If that hope is firmly grounded, Christians have a far better reason than Ben Sira had to lift up their voices in constant praise of the Creator and redeemer.

---

235. This arrangement of priorities is not specifically stated in the text but constitutes Ben Sira's probable scale of values, when seen in the overall context of the book.

SIRACH 41:14–42:8, ON SHAME

NAB

14 My children, heed my instruction about
   shame;
      judge of disgrace only according to my
   rules,
   For it is not always well to be ashamed,
      nor is it always the proper thing to blush:
15 Before father and mother be ashamed of
   immorality,
      before master and mistress, of falsehood;
16 Before prince and ruler, of flattery;
      before the public assembly, of crime;
17 Before friend and companion, of disloyalty,
      and of breaking an oath or agreement.
18 Be ashamed of theft from the people where
   you settle,
      and of stretching out your elbow when you
   dine;
19 Of refusing to give when asked,
      of defrauding another of his appointed
   share,
20 Of failing to return a greeting,
      and of rebuffing a friend;
21 Of gazing at a married woman,
      and of entertaining thoughts about
   another's wife;
   Of trifling with a servant girl you have,
      and of violating her couch;
22 Of using harsh words with friends,
      and of following up your gifts with insults;
23 Of repeating what you hear,
      and of betraying secrets—
24 These are the things you should rightly
   avoid as shameful
      if you would be looked upon by everyone
   with favor.

42 But of these things be not ashamed,
   lest you sin through human respect:
2 Of the law of the Most High and his precepts,
      or of the sentence to be passed upon the
   sinful;
3 Of sharing the expenses of a business or a
   journey,
      or of dividing an inheritance or property;

NRSV

14 My children, be true to your training and be
   at peace;
   hidden wisdom and unseen treasure—
      of what value is either?
15 Better are those who hide their folly
      than those who hide their wisdom.
16 Therefore show respect for my words;
   for it is not good to feel shame in every
   circumstance,
      nor is every kind of abashment to be
   approved.[a]

17 Be ashamed of sexual immorality, before your
   father or mother;
      and of a lie, before a prince or a ruler;
18 of a crime, before a judge or magistrate;
      and of a breach of the law, before the
   congregation and the people;
   of unjust dealing, before your partner or your
   friend;
19   and of theft, in the place where you live.
   Be ashamed of breaking an oath or agreement,[b]
      and of leaning on your elbow at meals;
   of surliness in receiving or giving,
20   and of silence, before those who greet you;
   of looking at a prostitute,
21   and of rejecting the appeal of a relative;
   of taking away someone's portion or gift,
      and of gazing at another man's wife;
22 of meddling with his servant-girl—
      and do not approach her bed;
   of abusive words, before friends—
      and do not be insulting after making a gift.

42 Be ashamed of repeating what you hear,
   and of betraying secrets.
   Then you will show proper shame,
      and will find favor with everyone.

Of the following things do not be ashamed,
      and do not sin to save face:
2 Do not be ashamed of the law of the Most
   High and his covenant,
      and of rendering judgment to acquit the
   ungodly;

41, 15f: M has the order: 15a.16a.15b.16b.
41, 19f: M has the order: 19a.20b.19b.20a.

[a] Heb: Gk *and not everything is confidently esteemed by everyone*
[b] Heb: Gk *before the truth of God and the covenant*

NAB

4 Of accuracy of scales and balances,
  or of tested measures and weights;
5 Of acquiring much or little,
  or of bargaining in dealing with a
    merchant;
Of constant training of children,
  or of beating the sides of a disloyal servant;
6 Of a seal to keep an erring wife at home,
  or of a lock placed where there are many
    hands;
7 Of numbering every deposit,
  or of recording all that is given or received;
8 Of chastisement of the silly and the foolish,
  or of the aged and infirm answering for
    wanton conduct.
Thus you will be truly cautious
  and recognized by all men as discreet.

NRSV

³ of keeping accounts with a partner or with
    traveling companions,
  and of dividing the inheritance of friends;
⁴ of accuracy with scales and weights,
  and of acquiring much or little;
⁵ of profit from dealing with merchants,
  and of frequent disciplining of children,
  and of drawing blood from the back of a
    wicked slave.
⁶ Where there is an untrustworthy wife, a seal
    is a good thing;
  and where there are many hands, lock
    things up.
⁷ When you make a deposit, be sure it is
    counted and weighed,
  and when you give or receive, put it all in
    writing.
⁸ Do not be ashamed to correct the stupid or
    foolish
  or the aged who are guilty of sexual
    immorality.
Then you will show your sound training,
  and will be approved by all.

COMMENTARY

Honor and its negative counterpart, shame, were strong motivating forces in ancient Mediterranean cultures. Ben Sira demonstrates the appeal this ethical system had on the Jewish world, although he seems to represent the minority opinion on several specifics. After underscoring the areas in which Jewish readers ought to feel shame (41:17–42:1*a*), he mentions some types of behavior that, he thinks, should occasion no sense of embarrassment (42:1*b*-8). Some of these may have been disputed because they represent a clash between Hellenistic and Jewish values.

42:1b-8. First and foremost, the Mosaic legislation made demands on Jews that set them apart from their Hellenized compatriots and gave the impression of provincialism. Ben Sira admonishes Jews not to be ashamed of the law and covenantal obligations. In a highly mercenary environment, the temptation to make a profit through unethical means must have overtaken many individuals.

Ben Sira urges them to keep accurate records of expenses and to give honest measures, keeping weights and scales completely free of the slightest particles of dust or grain. This concern for accuracy of weights is reinforced in the *m. B. Bat.* 5:10, where merchants are enjoined to clean their measures twice a week, polish weights every week, and clean their scales after every business transaction.[236] Ben Sira also reinforces traditional sexual mores in an era of free attitudes toward sensuality; moralists, he says, ought not to be ashamed of rebuking even their elders for sexual impropriety.

This section actually treats merchants neutrally, accepts profit as appropriate in dealing with them, and insists on written records for deposits or withdrawals. The Zenon papyri from third-century

---

236. W. O. E. Oesterley, *The Wisdom of Jesus the Son of Sirach or Ecclesiasticus* (Cambridge: Cambridge University Press, 1912) 279, refers to *B. Bat.* 88*a* for the same stipulation.

BCE Egypt furnish exceptional evidence of at least one royal official's obsession with an exact account of all business transactions.[237] Ben Sira's own students were probably literate, but the extent of literacy among average citizens is unclear. If it never exceeded 10 percent in classical Greece,[238] not many Jewish citizens in Ben Sira's day likely would have known how to read and write, for the agrarian economy offered few incentives to literacy.

The remarkable comment in 42:1*b* about sinning to save face reveals the dilemma in which many Jews found themselves at this time. Rather than following Jewish custom and calling attention to their foreignness to Greek culture, those Jews who sought a place of honor in the eyes of Hellenists found themselves breaking the Mosaic law for the sake of appearing to be like their cultured rulers. Ben Sira thinks that such Jews should not be ashamed to be different.

41:17–42:1a. The list of conduct unbecoming to Ben Sira's students contains no surprises, unless it be the paucity of sins mentioned.[239] Ben Sira

includes some observations about social location, specifically the authoritative figures in second-century BCE Judah—parents, rulers, judges, the assembled congregation, friends. The list begins in the family circle and ends there: "the place where you live" (v. 19). As usual in sapiential literature, sexual sins dominate, perhaps because of the youthful age of the students, but not entirely so, because sages also warn against the sexual follies of old men. Even lust—for a prostitute or for another man's wife—is included here, because it leads to unfortunate consequences. Notably, Ben Sira mentions abuse of authority, the use of a slave girl for sexual purposes (v. 22), and poor table manners (v. 19).

The Greek translator seems to have misunderstood v. 19, reading אלה (*'ālâ*, "oath") as אלה (*'ělōâ*, "God") and then rendering the phrase "before the truth of God and the covenant."[240]

41:14-16. The introduction to this section on shame includes two verses that also occur in 20:30-31, except for the vocative and accompanying imperatives with their objects ("My children, be true to your training and be at peace"). The Hebrew text has a title above v. 16, "Instruction Concerning Shame" (מוסר בשת *mûsār bōšet*).

---

237. C. Robert Harrison, Jr., "Qoheleth in Social-Historical Perspective" (Ph.D. diss., Duke University, 1991), uses the Zenon papyri as a partial means of illuminating the context within which Ecclesiastes was written. They preserve in part the returns from landed estates in the Ptolemaic province of Judea that were worked by tenant-farmers.

238. After an exhaustive study of literacy in classical Greece, William V. Harris reaches this conservative conclusion. See Harris, *Ancient Literacy* (Cambridge, Mass.: Harvard University Press, 1989) 65-115.

239. Biblical laws and proverbs are never exhaustive, suggesting that they serve a representative function.

240. Marginal notes in the Hebrew text suggest that an earlier version has been compared to the present MS B and that corrective glosses have been added to the latter. See Oesterley, *Ecclesiasticus,* 279.

SIRACH 42:9-14, ON PROTECTING DAUGHTERS' HONOR

NAB	NRSV
9 A daughter is a treasure that keeps her father wakeful, and worry over her drives away rest: Lest she pass her prime unmarried, or when she is married, lest she be disliked; 10 While unmarried, lest she be seduced, or, as a wife, lest she prove unfaithful;	[9] A daughter is a secret anxiety to her father, and worry over her robs him of sleep; when she is young, for fear she may not marry, or if married, for fear she may be disliked; [10] while a virgin, for fear she may be seduced and become pregnant in her father's house; or having a husband, for fear she may go astray, or, though married, for fear she may be barren. [11] Keep strict watch over a headstrong daughter,
42, 9a: *maṭmôn*) *šāqed*: so LXX. 9b: *ûdā' ăgātāh (taprîd/tanîd nûmâ)*: cf B margin, LXX, M.	

NAB

> Lest she conceive in her father's home,
> or be sterile in that of her husband.
>
> 11 Keep a close watch on your daughter,
> lest she make you the sport of your
> enemies,
> A byword in the city, a reproach among the
> people,
> an object of derision in public gatherings.
> See that there is no lattice in her room,
> no place that overlooks the approaches to
> the house.
>
> 12 Let her not parade her charms before men,
> or spend her time with married women;
>
> 13 For just as moths come from garments,
> so harm to women comes from women:
>
> 14 Better a man's harshness than a woman's
> indulgence,
> and a frightened daughter than any
> disgrace.

42, 11a: Omit *bᵉnî:* so LXX. 11b: *śimḥâ lᵉ'ōyēb:* so LXX. 11d:
wᵉhōbîśatᵉkā: so B margin, LXX, P.
42, 12: *ûbên (nāśîm):* so LXX, P.
42, 14: (*tōb*) *rôa' (' îs) miṭṭōb (' iśśâ):* cf M.

NRSV

> or she may make you a laughingstock to
> your enemies,
> a byword in the city and the assembly of[a] the
> people,
> and put you to shame in public gatherings.[b]
> See that there is no lattice in her room,
> no spot that overlooks the approaches to the
> house.[c]
>
> 12 Do not let her parade her beauty before any
> man,
> or spend her time among married women;[a]
>
> 13 for from garments comes the moth,
> and from a woman comes woman's
> wickedness.
>
> 14 Better is the wickedness of a man than a
> woman who does good;
> it is woman who brings shame and disgrace.

[a] Heb: Meaning of Gk uncertain   [b] Heb: Gk *to shame before the
great multitude*   [c] Heb: Gk lacks *See . . . house*

COMMENTARY

This brief section takes up one additional area in which unwanted shame easily arises: the disgraceful conduct of a young woman. Ben Sira fails to note that a man is also implicated in her offense, and even if one emends the text of v. 14 to read "Better a religious daughter than a shameless son" the misogynism remains nonetheless.[241] In this regard, Ben Sira was by no means alone, as shown by the Jewish prayer thanking God that the male speaking the words is not a Gentile, a slave, or a woman.

Ben Sira's observations grew out of the importance Jewish society attached to virginity, primarily because of its value when young women entered into marriage. Fathers, whose role in selecting husbands for their daughters became precarious in cases of lost virginity, worried prior to the wedding date, and even subsequent to it, lest the bride be either unfaithful or barren. To protect unmarried daughters, Ben Sira advises parents to guard them closely and thus prevent them from becoming known as women of easy morals, a byword. To hide a young daughter from a male's gaze and resulting seduction, Ben Sira urges precautionary measures such as preventing her from looking out a window and enjoying the relative freedom—and conversation—of married women. The well-known ivory carving depicting a woman peering from a window reveals this religious motif as common in the ancient Near East, although its full implications are still unclear (cf. Prov 7:6).[242]

241. Skehan and Di Lella, examine emendations and readings suggested by J. Strugnell and F. M. Cross, the latter of whom translates as follows: "but better a daughter of a religious wife than a son of the shameless one." See Patrick W. Skehan and Alexander A. Di Lella, *The Wisdom of Ben Sira,* AB 39 (New York: Doubleday, 1987) 480.

242. A photograph of an ivory carving of a woman at a window, dating from the first half of the eighth century BCE can be found in James B. Pritchard, *The Ancient Near East in Pictures* (Princeton, N.J.: Princeton University Press, 1954) 39, pl. 131.

The concluding remarks in vv. 13-14, which are textually uncertain, leave no doubt that Ben Sira held a low opinion of women. The analogy of moths may mean that just as garments attract moths, so also wickedness lures women, or that insects fly from one piece of cloth to another and women go from man to man. Ben Sira's comment that a man's wickedness is better than a woman's goodness invites modern readers to suspect that

he has taken leave of his senses at this point. True, some women bring shame and disgrace, but they have not seized a monopoly on such conduct. Many men do the same, as Ben Sira surely knew. Perhaps his extreme remarks reveal how far an ancient Jewish teacher would go to protect ethnic identity in a context of cultural and personal subservience.

SIRACH 42:15–43:33, THE WONDERS OF CREATION

NAB	NRSV
15 Now will I recall God's works; 　what I have seen, I will describe. At God's word were his works brought into being; 　they do his will as he has ordained for them. 16 As the rising sun is clear to all, 　so the glory of the LORD fills all his works; 17 Yet even God's holy ones must fail 　in recounting the wonders of the LORD, Though God has given these, his hosts, the strength 　to stand firm before his glory. 18 He plumbs the depths and penetrates the heart; 　their innermost being he understands. The Most High possesses all knowledge, 　and sees from of old the things that are to come: 19 He makes known the past and the future, 　and reveals the deepest secrets. 20 No understanding does he lack; 　no single thing escapes him. 21 Perennial is his almighty wisdom; 　he is from all eternity one and the same, 22 With nothing added, nothing taken away; 　no need of a counselor for him! 23 How beautiful are all his works! 　even to the spark and fleeting vision!	15 I will now call to mind the works of the Lord, 　and will declare what I have seen. By the word of the Lord his works are made; 　and all his creatures do his will.[a] 16 The sun looks down on everything with its light, 　and the work of the Lord is full of his glory. 17 The Lord has not empowered even his holy ones 　to recount all his marvelous works, which the Lord the Almighty has established 　so that the universe may stand firm in his glory. 18 He searches out the abyss and the human heart; 　he understands their innermost secrets. For the Most High knows all that may be known; 　he sees from of old the things that are to come.[b] 19 He discloses what has been and what is to be, 　and he reveals the traces of hidden things. 20 No thought escapes him, 　and nothing is hidden from him. 21 He has set in order the splendors of his wisdom; 　he is from all eternity one and the same. Nothing can be added or taken away, 　and he needs no one to be his counselor. 22 How desirable are all his works,

42, 15c: (*be' ĕmōr yhwh) hāyû (ma' ăsāyw*): conj; cf M, LXX, P.
42, 15d: *wᵉpō' al rᵉṣōnō lāqāḥû*: cf M.
42, 18c.d: With LXX; but *wᵉʾ ôtiyyôt* for *wᵉʾ ôtôt=sēmeia* (LXX[MS 248]).
42, 19: (*ḥălîpôt) wᵉnihyôt*: so B margin, LXX, P.

[a] Syr Compare Heb: most Gk witnesses lack *and all ... will*
[b] Heb: Gk *he sees the sign(s) of the age*

NAB

24 The universe lives and abides forever;
　　to meet each need, each creature is
　　　　preserved.
25 All of them differ, one from another,
　　yet none of them has he made in vain,
　　For each in turn, as it comes, is good;
　　can one ever see enough of their splendor?

43 The clear vault of the sky shines forth
　　like heaven itself, a vision of glory.
2 The orb of the sun, resplendent at its rising:
　　what a wonderful work of the Most High!
3 At noon it seethes the surface of the earth,
　　and who can bear its fiery heat?
4 Like a blazing furnace of solid metal,
　　it sets the mountains aflame with its rays;
　　By its fiery darts the land is consumed;
　　the eyes are dazzled by its light.
5 Great indeed is the LORD who made it,
　　at whose orders it urges on its steeds.
6 The moon, too, that marks the changing
　　　　times,
　　governing the seasons, their lasting sign,
7 By which we know the feast days and fixed
　　　　dates,
　　this light-giver which wanes in its course:
8 As its name says, each month it renews itself;
　　how wondrous in this change!
9 The beauty, the glory, of the heavens are the
　　　　stars
　　that adorn with their sparkling the heights
　　　　of God,
10 At whose command they keep their place
　　and never relax in their vigils.
　　A weapon against the flood waters stored on
　　　　high,
　　lighting up the firmament by its brilliance,
11 Behold the rainbow! Then bless its Maker,
　　for majestic indeed is its splendor;
12 It spans the heavens with its glory,
　　this bow bent by the mighty hand of God.

42, 25d: ûmî (yiśba'): so B margin, LXX, P.
43, 1: tip'eret mārôm rāqîa' l*tōhar, w*'esem šāmayim mar'eh
hădārô: cf B margin, LXX.
43, 2: ma'āśēh 'elyôn: cf M.
43, 5b: ûbid*bārāyw (y*nassaḥ 'abbîrāyw): cf LXX.
43, 8c.d: Trsp to precede v 11.
43, 10a: (ya'ămōd) b*ḥōq: for k*ḥōq: for k*ḥōq=kata krima.
10c.d=8c.d of Heb.

NRSV

　　and how sparkling they are to see![a]
23 All these things live and remain forever;
　　each creature is preserved to meet a
　　　　particular need.[b]
24 All things come in pairs, one opposite the
　　　　other,
　　and he has made nothing incomplete.
25 Each supplements the virtues of the other.
　　Who could ever tire of seeing his glory?

43 The pride of the higher realms is the clear
　　vault of the sky,
　　as glorious to behold as the sight of the
　　　　heavens.
2 The sun, when it appears, proclaims as it rises
　　what a marvelous instrument it is, the work
　　　　of the Most High.
3 At noon it parches the land,
　　and who can withstand its burning heat?
4 A man tending[c] a furnace works in burning
　　　　heat,
　　but three times as hot is the sun scorching
　　　　the mountains;
　　it breathes out fiery vapors,
　　and its bright rays blind the eyes.
5 Great is the Lord who made it;
　　at his orders it hurries on its course.

6 It is the moon that marks the changing
　　　　seasons,[d]
　　governing the times, their everlasting sign.
7 From the moon comes the sign for festal days,
　　a light that wanes when it completes its
　　　　course.
8 The new moon, as its name suggests, renews
　　　　itself;[e]
　　how marvelous it is in this change,
　　a beacon to the hosts on high,
　　shining in the vault of the heavens!

9 The glory of the stars is the beauty of heaven,
　　a glittering array in the heights of the Lord.
10 On the orders of the Holy One they stand in
　　　　their appointed places;
　　they never relax in their watches.

[a] Meaning of Gk uncertain　[b] Heb: Gk forever for every need,
and all are obedient　[c] Other ancient authorities read blowing
upon　[d] Heb: Meaning of Gk uncertain　[e] Heb: Gk The month
is named after the moon

NAB

13 His rebuke marks out the path for the
lightning,
and speeds the arrows of his judgment to
their goal.
14 At it the storehouse is opened,
and like vultures the clouds hurry forth.
15 In his majesty he gives the storm its power
and breaks off the hailstones.
16 The thunder of his voice makes the earth
writhe;
before his might the mountains quake.
17 A word from him drives on the south wind,
the angry north wind, the hurricane and
the storm.
18 He sprinkles the snow like fluttering birds;
it comes to settle like swarms of locusts.
19 Its shining whiteness blinds the eyes,
the mind is baffled by its steady fall.
20 He scatters frost like so much salt;
it shines like blossoms on the thornbush.
21 Cold northern blasts he sends
that turn the ponds to lumps of ice.
He freezes over every body of water,
and clothes each pool with a coat of mail.
22 When the mountain growth is scorched
with heat,
and the flowering plains as though by
flames,
23 The dripping clouds restore them all,
and the scattered dew enriches the
parched land.
24 His is the plan that calms the deep,
and plants the islands in the sea.
25 Those who go down to the sea tell part of
its story,
and when we hear them we are
thunderstruck;
26 In it are his creatures, stupendous, amazing,
all kinds of life, and the monsters of the
deep.
27 For him each messenger succeeds,
and at his bidding accomplishes his will.
28 More than this we need not add;
let the last word be, he is all in all!

43, 23: (ʿānān), wᵉṭāl (pôrēaʿ) yᵉdaššēn.
43, 24: (maḥăšabtô) mašqît rahab, wᵉyitta' (bitᵉhôm): cf LXX, V.
43, 26: (ûgᵉbûrôt) rahab: cf LXX.
43, 30b: wᵉniplēʾt gᵉbûrātô: so LXX; cf B margin.

NRSV

11 Look at the rainbow, and praise him who made
it;
it is exceedingly beautiful in its brightness.
12 It encircles the sky with its glorious arc;
the hands of the Most High have stretched
it out.

13 By his command he sends the driving snow
and speeds the lightnings of his judgment.
14 Therefore the storehouses are opened,
and the clouds fly out like birds.
15 In his majesty he gives the clouds their
strength,
and the hailstones are broken in pieces.
17a The voice of his thunder rebukes the earth;
16 when he appears, the mountains shake.
At his will the south wind blows;
17b so do the storm from the north and the
whirlwind.
He scatters the snow like birds flying down,
and its descent is like locusts alighting.
18 The eye is dazzled by the beauty of its
whiteness,
and the mind is amazed as it falls.
19 He pours frost over the earth like salt,
and icicles form like pointed thorns.
20 The cold north wind blows,
and ice freezes on the water;
it settles on every pool of water,
and the water puts it on like a breastplate.
21 He consumes the mountains and burns up the
wilderness,
and withers the tender grass like fire.
22 A mist quickly heals all things;
the falling dew gives refreshment from the
heat.

23 By his plan he stilled the deep
and planted islands in it.
24 Those who sail the sea tell of its dangers,
and we marvel at what we hear.
25 In it are strange and marvelous creatures,
all kinds of living things, and huge
sea-monsters.
26 Because of him each of his messengers
succeeds,
and by his word all things hold together.

NAB

29 Let us praise him the more, since we cannot
    fathom him,
    for greater is he than all his works;

30 Awful indeed is the LORD's majesty,
    and wonderful is his power.

31 Lift up your voices to glorify the LORD,
    though he is still beyond your power to
    praise;

32 Extol him with renewed strength,
    and weary not, though you cannot reach
    the end:

33 For who can see him and describe him?
    or who can praise him as he is?

34 Beyond these, many things lie hid;
    only a few of his works have we seen.

35 It is the LORD who has made all things,
    and to those who fear him he gives
    wisdom.

43, 32: With B margin. 32c.d: Trsp here from 44, 2 (Heb).
43, 33: With LXX (v. 31).
43, 34b: (*m*ᵉ ˙*aṭ*) *rā˙înû*: so LXX.

NRSV

27 We could say more but could never say
    enough;
    let the final word be: "He is the all."

28 Where can we find the strength to praise him?
    For he is greater than all his works.

29 Awesome is the Lord and very great,
    and marvelous is his power.

30 Glorify the Lord and exalt him as much as you
    can,
    for he surpasses even that.
    When you exalt him, summon all your
    strength,
    and do not grow weary, for you cannot
    praise him enough.

31 Who has seen him and can describe him?
    Or who can extol him as he is?

32 Many things greater than these lie hidden,
    for Iᵃ have seen but few of his works.

33 For the Lord has made all things,
    and to the godly he has given wisdom.

ᵃ Heb: Gk *we*

COMMENTARY

This majestic hymn about the wonders of creation introduces the much longer praise of famous men in 44:1–50:24, as the probable use of "to the pious" (לחסידים *lĕḥăsîdîm*) in v. 33 (cf. the Greek "to the devout ones" [τοῖς εὐσεβέσιν *tois eusebesin*] and "men of kindness" (= "pious men" [אנשי חסד *'anšê ḥesed*]) in 44:1 makes clear.[243] This hymn consists of a poem on the inscrutable knowledge of the Creator (42:15-21), a long section describing the wonders of nature (42:22–43:26), and a conclusion inviting readers to praise the sovereign Lord (43:27-33). In many respects this hymn resembles Psalms 29; 104–105; and Job 38:1-38, as well as noun lists (onomastica) from Egypt and Mesopotamia, which include, among other things, lists of astrophysical phenomena. Such lists were used in educational circles to teach foreign languages and knowledge about the natural world.

42:15-21. The idea that the universe came into existence as a result of divine utterance recalls Gen 1:1-31, a concept that comes to prominence in Wis 9:1; 2 Esdr 6:38; Jdt 16:14; and in the prologue to the Gospel of John. Ben Sira concedes that the task of declaring the full scope of God's works exceeds the capacity of the angelic hosts, specifically astrophysical phenomena enlisted in divine service (cf. *1 Enoch* 1:9). Even the abyss (תהום *tĕhôm*, "Tiamat," the chaos dragon of the deep) and the depths of the human heart lie open before the Most High's penetrating gaze, Ben Sira asserts, and nothing is hidden. That includes the future, which God knows as intimately as the past, without benefit of counselors (cf. Isa 40:14). This theme echoes a similar one in Deutero-Isaiah. Such bold claims function as a theodicy, one based on the view that the Creator sees everything. The Persian notion of the roving eyes of the deity and the Egyptian concept of the eye of Ra, the sun god, reinforced the belief in a harmonious universe. Believing that the Creator

243. The Hebrew text has only the initial (*lamedh*); the Greek translator seems to have read either *lĕḥăsîdîm* or *l'anse ḥesed*.

is the same yesterday, today, and forever, Ben Sira found reason to trust in divine consistency.

42:22–43:26. The idea of opposites, expressed already in 33:15, recurs in 42:24, in this instance connoting variety and thus contributing to the beauty of the universe. Beginning in 43:1, Ben Sira describes astrophysical phenomena (sun, moon, and stars) before turning to geophysical phenomena, such as the rainbow, lightning, clouds, winds, snow, frost, ice, and dew. Finally, he mentions the ocean, that unexplored abyss in which mythological beings were believed to cavort, according to Job 38:8-11; 40–41 and various mythological texts in Deutero-Isaiah (Isa 51:9-10; cf. Isa 27:1; 30:7; Ezek 29:3) and Psalms.

Although the sun is the first to be introduced, the emphasis falls on the moon, presumably because of its determination of the religious calendar. Biblical precedent observed the solar calendar, as did the community at Qumran, whose opponents observed the lunar calendar. Verse 8 contains a play on the words for "moon" (חדש *ḥōdeš*) and "renew" (חדש *ḥādaš*), while using the analogy of a fire signal indicating an army's beginning to march at night. Ben Sira waxes poetic in comparing snow to the deft and orderly descent of birds and locusts, icicles to thorns, frost to ashes scattered on the ground, and a frozen pond to a warrior's breastplate. He con-

cludes this section by returning to the thought of the creative word, this time extending the idea to its cohesive power (43:26).

43:27-33. The final admission that such praise only touches the surface makes a daring assertion: "Let the final word be: 'He is the all' " (cf. Eccl 12:13). The similarity of this confession to Stoic pantheism is undeniable, although Ben Sira goes on to insist that the Creator is greater than all the wonders of the universe (v. 28). In Ben Sira's view, a single divine principle holds the universe together, but God is not encompassed by that entity (cf. the Vg's *ipse est in omnibus*, "He is in all"). This hymn utilizes both Jewish and Stoic ideas of creation and the ordering of things. According to Stoic philosophy, the *logos* (divine rationality) permeates the cosmos and holds it together. In the ancient world, mythological creatures representing chaos were thought to have threatened the divine order; according to v. 23, the Creator brought these creatures, here called Rahab, under control (cf. Job 9:13; 26:12). The God of such power and exquisite artistry justly deserves Ben Sira's adjective "awesome" (נורא מאד ונפלאות *nôrāʾ měʾōd wěniplāʾôt*, "exceedingly terrifying and wondrous," v. 29; cf. Joel 2:11, ונורא מאד [*wěnôrāʾ měʾōd*, "exceedingly dreadful"]).

REFLECTIONS

Anyone who genuinely cherishes the spiritual dimension of reality finds it impossible to restrain songs of praise, for we are surrounded by signs of grace from our waking moment to the second our eyes close in sleep. Grateful hearts seem capable of bursting if we do not express appreciation for the supreme gift of life.

Traditionally, believers have tried to buttress their faith by using the argument from design, believing that the Creator planted in the created world witnesses to the source of all things. We know today that equally cogent arguments against the existence of God can be mustered from apparent flaws in nature and that adaptability is the very nature of things as they evolve. Nevertheless, believers are encompassed by a vast universe almost as mysterious as the God they worship.

The ancient world, like certain segments of the modern population, believed that the mysteries of the universe were revealed to a small band of initiates, who guarded that knowledge zealously from that time forward. Ben Sira acknowledged no such sect, choosing instead to confess his own ignorance in the face of overwhelming mystery. That lack of knowledge did not rule out personal acquaintance with God in some small way, and he readily claimed to have direct experience of the Holy One. Nevertheless, in the end he confessed that his best effort to praise God only scratched the surface, that the moment he arrived at the end of his song he had merely reached the beginning. That perceptive insight cautions modern worshipers against assuming that we have exhausted what can and should be said about the one who dwells in utter darkness.

Ben Sira's endeavor to provide an easy guide to extolling the Creator unites him with countless writers of hymns that have enriched worship over the years. Poets, theologians, and musicians have collaborated to provide a rich repertoire of hymnody that both instructs and motivates, songs that express the unutterable and lead to noble aspirations and deeds.

SIRACH 44:1–51:30

PART VIII

OVERVIEW

This poetic section praising Israel's ancestors follows naturally from the hymn extolling God's creative activity (39:12–43:33), for Ben Sira emphasizes divine election of the heroes lifted up for memorializing. The long account of past worthies concludes with an encomium of Simeon II, the high priest contemporary with Ben Sira (50:1-21), and a brief personal word from Ben Sira (50:22-24). An introduction (44:1-15) mentions a dozen categories of leaders deserving commendation, which then leads to a selective record of Israel's history, beginning with Enoch. The following names complete the list: Noah; Abraham; Isaac and Jacob; Moses; Aaron; Phinehas; Joshua and Caleb; the judges, with specific reference to Samuel only; Nathan; David; Solomon; Rehoboam and Jeroboam; Elijah; Elisha; Hezekiah; Isaiah; Josiah; Jeremiah; Ezekiel; Job; the Twelve Prophets (unnamed individually); Zerubbabel; Jeshua the son of Josadak; and Nehemiah—with a sort of "lest we forget" Enoch, Joseph, Shem, Seth, Enosh, and Adam.

SIRACH 44:1-15, INTRODUCTION

NAB

44 Now will I praise those godly men,
our ancestors, each in his own time:

2 The abounding glory of the Most High's portion,
his own part, since the days of old.
Subduers of the land in kingly fashion,
men of renown for their might,

3 Or counselors in their prudence,
or seers of all things in prophecy;

4 Resolute princes of the folk,
and governors with their staves;
Authors skilled in composition,
and forgers of epigrams with their spikes;

5 Composers of melodious psalms,
or discoursers on lyric themes;

6 Stalwart men, solidly established
and at peace in their own estates—

7 All these were glorious in their time,
each illustrious in his day.

44, 2: *wᵉgôrālō*: conj; *rōdê* (*ʾereṣ*): so B margin, LXX.
44, 4d: *bᵉmaśmᵉrôtām*: cf Eccl 12, 11.

NRSV

44 Let us now sing the praises of famous men,
our ancestors in their generations.

2 The Lord apportioned to them[a] great glory,
his majesty from the beginning.

3 There were those who ruled in their kingdoms,
and made a name for themselves by their valor;
those who gave counsel because they were intelligent;
those who spoke in prophetic oracles;

4 those who led the people by their counsels
and by their knowledge of the people's lore;
they were wise in their words of instruction;

5 those who composed musical tunes,
or put verses in writing;

6 rich men endowed with resources,
living peacefully in their homes—

7 all these were honored in their generations,
and were the pride of their times.

8 Some of them have left behind a name,

[a] Heb: Gk *created*

NAB

8 Some of them have left behind a name
  and men recount their praiseworthy deeds;

9 But of others there is no memory,
  for when they ceased, they ceased.
  And they are as though they had not lived,
  they and their children after them.

10 Yet these also were godly men
  whose virtues have not been forgotten;

11 Their wealth remains in their families,
  their heritage with their descendants;

12 Through God's covenant with them their
    family endures,
  their posterity for their sake.

13 And for all time their progeny will endure,
  their glory will never be blotted out;

14 Their bodies are peacefully laid away,
  but their name lives on and on.

15 At gatherings their wisdom is retold,
  and the assembly proclaims their praise.

44, 8b: *l*ᵉ*hištā῾ôt t*ᵉ*hillōtam.*

44, 10b: *w*ᵉ*ṣidqātām lō῾ niškaḥat:* so LXX; cf v. 13.

44, 11: ῾*im (zar῾ām):* so with B text.

NRSV

  so that others declare their praise.
9 But of others there is no memory;
  they have perished as though they had never
    existed;
  they have become as though they had never
    been born,
  they and their children after them.
10 But these also were godly men,
  whose righteous deeds have not been
    forgotten;
11 their wealth will remain with their
    descendants,
  and their inheritance with their children's
    children.ᵃ
12 Their descendants stand by the covenants;
  their children also, for their sake.
13 Their offspring will continue forever,
  and their glory will never be blotted out.
14 Their bodies are buried in peace,
  but their name lives on generation after
    generation.
15 The assembly declaresᵇ their wisdom,
  and the congregation proclaims their praise.

ᵇHeb Compare Lat Syr: Meaning of Gk uncertain   ᶜHeb: Gk *Peoples declare*

COMMENTARY

The Hebrew text (MS B) has the title "Praise of the Ancestors of Old"; a shorter title, "Praise of the Ancestors," appears in most Greek, Latin, and Syriac manuscripts. The phrase "in their generations" (v. 1) implies a listing in chronological order. Verses 3-6 specify twelve categories of greatness: rulers, men of valor, counselors, prophets, wise leaders, guardians of tradition ("lawgivers"), instructors, compilers of wise sayings, composers, authors, the rich, and the peaceful. This entire unit has a striking end rhyme, תם (*tām*; except for ם [*ām*] in v. 2 and תב [*tāb*] in v. 5). Ben Sira makes a surprising concession in vv. 8-9 that some pious individuals died without leaving a "name," despite his earlier assurance that good people can count on a living memory. Presumably, he offers this brief introduction as a eulogy to these forgotten and nameless persons, together with all others who will be mentioned

in the body of the epic poem. The latter have received appropriate burial and are called to memory by the assembled congregation.

The choice of the number twelve to indicate classes of people probably derives from its general use to designate completeness, as in twelve tribes of Israel, twelve months, twelve memorial stones, twelve disciples. All of these men are called "devout persons" (אנשי חסד *῾anšê ḥesed*), the legacy of Elyon, the Most High.[244]

The emphasis on sages in vv. 3-5 reflects Ben Sira's particular bias, one that does not manifest itself in the actual selection of heroes that follows. A priestly preference easily surfaces in that portrait of great figures of the past with whom God has

244. The expression "those who lift up a proverb in writing" (v. 5) is peculiar, but an emendation to במכתם (*bemiktam*, "lyric") to restore a conjectured end rhyme *tam* has nothing to commend it. See Patrick W. Skehan and Alexander A. Di Lella, *The Wisdom of Ben Sira,* AB 39 (New York: Doubleday, 1987) 499.

worked, and this sacerdotal interest expresses itself in both content and scope. This type of historical retrospect has remote antecedents in Neh 9:6-37; Psalms 78; 105–106; 135–136; Ezek 20:4-44 (cf. Jdt 5:5-21; 1 Macc 2:51-64), although none of these texts focuses on specific human figures. The closest text is Wis 10:1–12:27, which traces Israel's early history by means of allusions to easily identified persons, beginning with Adam. The other historical surveys differ qualitatively in the manner of extolling God, and any human

being mentioned is incidental. Some interpreters think Hellenistic encomia serve as the model for this historical survey, although conceding that Ben Sira has made many adjustments in the process.[245] (See Reflections at 50:1-24.)

---

245. On the affinities between Sirach 44–50 and encomia, see Burton L. Mack, *Wisdom and the Hebrew Epic* (Chicago: University of Chicago Press, 1985); Thomas R. Lee, *Studies in the Form of Sirach 44–50,* SBLDS 75 (Atlanta: Scholars Press, 1986). Chris A. Rollston challenges this interpretation of the text in Sirach in "The Non-Encomiastic Features of Ben Sira 44–50," (MA thesis, Emmanuel School of Religion, 1992).

SIRACH 44:16–45:26, THE SEVEN COVENANTAL FIGURES

NAB

16 ENOCH walked with the LORD and was taken up,
    that succeeding generations might learn by his example.
17 NOAH, found just and perfect,
    renewed the race in the time of devastation.
    Because of his worth there were survivors,
    and with a sign to him the deluge ended;
18 A lasting agreement was made with him,
    that never should all flesh be destroyed.
19 ABRAHAM, father of many peoples,
    kept his glory without stain:
20 He observed the precepts of the Most High,
    and entered into an agreement with him;
    In his own flesh he incised the ordinance,
    and when tested he was found loyal.
21 For this reason, God promised him with an oath
    that in his descendants the nations would be blessed,
    That he would make him numerous as the grains of dust,
    and exalt his posterity like the stars;
    That he would give them an inheritance from sea to sea,

44, 16: gloss: lacking in M.
44, 17d: *ûbe᾽ ôtô (hādal)*: trsp from v. 18a.
44, 18: *berît (ôlām)*: so LXX; cf v 17d.
44, 21c.d: With LXX; cf P.

NRSV

16 Enoch pleased the Lord and was taken up,
    an example of repentance to all generations.

17 Noah was found perfect and righteous;
    in the time of wrath he kept the race alive;[a]
    therefore a remnant was left on the earth
    when the flood came.
18 Everlasting covenants were made with him
    that all flesh should never again be blotted out by a flood.

19 Abraham was the great father of a multitude of nations,
    and no one has been found like him in glory.
20 He kept the law of the Most High,
    and entered into a covenant with him;
    he certified the covenant in his flesh,
    and when he was tested he proved faithful.
21 Therefore the Lord[b] assured him with an oath
    that the nations would be blessed through his offspring;
    that he would make him as numerous as the dust of the earth,
    and exalt his offspring like the stars,
    and give them an inheritance from sea to sea
    and from the Euphrates[c] to the ends of the earth.
22 To Isaac also he gave the same assurance
    for the sake of his father Abraham.

a Heb: Gk *was taken in exchange*   *b* Gk *he*   *c* Syr: Heb Gk *River*

NAB

and from the River to the ends of the earth.

22 And for ISAAC he renewed the same promise
because of Abraham, his father.
The covenant with all his forebears was
confirmed,
and the blessing rested upon the head of
JACOB.

23 God acknowledged him as the firstborn,
and gave him his inheritance.
He fixed the boundaries for his tribes,
and their division into twelve.

45 From him was to spring the man
who won the favor of all:
Dear to God and men,
MOSES, whose memory is held in
benediction.

2 God's honor devolved upon him,
and the Lord strengthened him with fearful
powers;

3 God wrought swift miracles at his words
and sustained him in the king's presence.
He gave him the commandments for his
people,
and revealed to him his glory.

4 For his trustworthiness and meekness
God selected him from all mankind;

5 He permitted him to hear his voice,
and led him into the cloud,
Where, face to face, he gave him the
commandments,
the law of life and understanding,
That he might teach his precepts to Jacob,
his judgments and decrees to Israel.

6 He raised up also, like Moses in holiness,
his brother AARON, of the tribe of Levi.

7 He made him perpetual in his office
when he bestowed on him the priesthood
of his people;
He established him in honor
and crowned him with lofty majesty;

8 He clothed him with splendid apparel,

44, 22a: (hēqîm) kēn: so LXX. 22c: (kol) rīšônîm: so P.
44, 23a: wayyakkîrēhû bibᵉkôrâ: cf B margin, LXX, P; Dt 21, 17.
45, 2: (wayᵉˈammᵉṣēhû) bᵉmôrāˈîm: so B margin, P; cf LXX.
45, 5c: lô lᵉpānāyw miṣwôt: so LXX; cf B margin, P.
45, 6a: (wayyārem) kāmôhû (qādôš): so P, cf LXX.
45, 7b: With LXX. 7c: wayᵉˈaššᵉrēhû (bikᵉbôdô): so LXX. Omit
wayyalbišēhû paˈˈamônîm: dittog from vv 8a.9a.
45, 8b: (wayᵉpāˈārēhû) bikᵉlî ˈôz: so LXX, P.

NRSV

The blessing of all people and the covenant
23 he made to rest on the head of Jacob;
he acknowledged him with his blessings,
and gave him his inheritance;
he divided his portions,
and distributed them among twelve tribes.

From his descendants the Lordᵃbrought forth
a godly man,
who found favor in the sight of all

45 ¹ and was beloved by God and people,
Moses, whose memory is blessed.
² He made him equal in glory to the holy ones,
and made him great, to the terror of his
enemies.
³ By his words he performed swift miracles;ᵇ
the Lordᵃ glorified him in the presence of
kings.
He gave him commandments for his people,
and revealed to him his glory.
⁴ For his faithfulness and meekness he
consecrated him,
choosing him out of all humankind.
⁵ He allowed him to hear his voice,
and led him into the dark cloud,
and gave him the commandments face to face,
the law of life and knowledge,
so that he might teach Jacob the covenant,
and Israel his decrees.

⁶ He exalted Aaron, a holy man like Mosesᶜ
who was his brother, of the tribe of Levi.
⁷ He made an everlasting covenant with him,
and gave him the priesthood of the people.
He blessed him with stateliness,
and put a glorious robe on him.
⁸ He clothed him in perfect splendor,
and strengthened him with the symbols of
authority,
the linen undergarments, the long robe, and
the ephod.
⁹ And he encircled him with pomegranates,
with many golden bells all around,
to send forth a sound as he walked,
to make their ringing heard in the temple
as a reminder to his people;
¹⁰ with the sacred vestment, of gold and violet

ᵃGk he   ᵇHeb: Gk caused signs to cease   ᶜGk him

NAB

and adorned him with the glorious
    vestments:
Breeches and tunic and robe
    with pomegranates around the hem,
9 And a rustle of bells round about,
    through whose pleasing sound at each step
He would be heard within the sanctuary,
    and the children of his race would be
        remembered;
10 The sacred vestments of gold, of violet,
    and of crimson, wrought with embroidery;
The breastpiece for decision, the ephod and
        cincture
11 with scarlet yarn, the work of the weaver;
    Precious stones with seal engravings
    in golden settings, the work of the jeweler,
To commemorate in incised letters
    each of the tribes of Israel;
12 On his turban the diadem of gold,
    its plate wrought with the insignia of
        holiness,
Majestic, glorious, renowned for splendor,
    a delight to the eyes, beauty supreme.
13 Before him, no one was adorned with these,
    nor may they ever be worn by any
Except his sons and them alone,
    generation after generation, for all time.
14 His cereal offering is wholly burnt
    with the established sacrifice twice each
        day;
15 For Moses ordained him
    and anointed him with the holy oil,
In a lasting covenant with him
    and with his family, as permanent as the
        heavens,
That he should serve God in his priesthood
    and bless his people in his name.
16 He chose him from all mankind
    to offer holocausts and choice offerings,
To burn sacrifices of sweet odor for a
        memorial,
    and to atone for the people of Israel.
17 He gave to him his laws,
    and authority to prescribe and to judge:

45, 8d.9a: Trsp *pa'ămônîm* and *rimmônîm*: so LXX.
    45, 11b: Omit *'al haḥôšen*: so LXX; gloss. 11c: *b*^e*millû'ôt zāhāb*
ma'ăśēh ḥārāš 'eben, and omit *kol 'eben y*^e*qārâ* (gloss): so LXX.
    45, 12: ('*ăṭeret pāz*) *mē 'al miṣnāpet*: so LXX.
    45, 13: With LXX.

NRSV

and purple, the work of an embroiderer;
with the oracle of judgment, Urim and
    Thummim;
11   with twisted crimson, the work of an
    artisan;
with precious stones engraved like seals,
    in a setting of gold, the work of a jeweler,
to commemorate in engraved letters
    each of the tribes of Israel;
12 with a gold crown upon his turban,
    inscribed like a seal with "Holiness,"
a distinction to be prized, the work of an
    expert,
    a delight to the eyes, richly adorned.
13 Before him such beautiful things did not exist.
    No outsider ever put them on,
but only his sons
    and his descendants in perpetuity.
14 His sacrifices shall be wholly burned
    twice every day continually.
15 Moses ordained him,
    and anointed him with holy oil;
it was an everlasting covenant for him
    and for his descendants as long as the
        heavens endure,
to minister to the Lord[a] and serve as priest
    and bless his people in his name.
16 He chose him out of all the living
    to offer sacrifice to the Lord,
incense and a pleasing odor as a memorial
    portion,
    to make atonement for the[b] people.
17 In his commandments he gave him
    authority and statutes and[c] judgments,
to teach Jacob the testimonies,
    and to enlighten Israel with his law.
18 Outsiders conspired against him,
    and envied him in the wilderness,
Dathan and Abiram and their followers
    and the company of Korah, in wrath and
        anger.
19 The Lord saw it and was not pleased,
    and in the heat of his anger they were
        destroyed;
he performed wonders against them
    to consume them in flaming fire.

[a] Gk *him*   [b] Other ancient authorities read *his* or *your*   [c] Heb:
Gk *authority in covenants of*

NAB

To teach the precepts to his people,
and the ritual to the descendants of Israel.

18 Men of other families were inflamed against him,
were jealous of him in the desert,
The followers of Dathan and Abiram,
and the band of Korah in their defiance.

19 But the LORD saw this and became angry,
he destroyed them in his burning wrath.
He brought down upon them a miracle,
and consumed them with his flaming fire.

20 Then he increased the glory of Aaron
and bestowed upon him his inheritance:
The sacred offerings he allotted to him,
with the showbread as his portion;

21 The oblations of the LORD are his food,
a gift to him and his descendants.

22 But he holds no land among the people
nor shares with them their heritage;
For the LORD himself is his portion,
his inheritance in the midst of Israel.

23 PHINEHAS too, the son of Eleazar,
was the courageous third of his line
When, zealous for the God of all,
he met the crisis of his people
And, at the prompting of his noble heart,
atoned for the children of Israel.

24 Therefore on him again God conferred the right,
in a covenant of friendship, to provide for
the sanctuary,
So that he and his descendants
should possess the high priesthood forever.

25 For even his covenant with David,
the son of Jesse of the tribe of Judah,
Was an individual heritage through one son alone;
but the heritage of Aaron is for all his descendants.

26 And now bless the LORD
who has crowned you with glory!
May he grant you wisdom of heart
to govern his people in justice,
Lest their welfare should ever be forgotten,
or your authority, throughout all time.

45, 20c.d: Trsp line with LXX. Omit *leḥem* after *nātan lô*: gloss.
45, 21: ' *iššê yhwh* ' *oklô.*
45, 22c: *kî yhwh hûʾ* (*ḥelqô*): cf LXX, P.
45, 25c: (*naḥălat*) ' *iš libᵉnô lᵉbaddô*: cf LXX.
45, 26a: Omit *ḥaṭṭôʾ*: so P; gloss. 26e: *ṭûbām*: so LXX, P.

NRSV

20 He added glory to Aaron
and gave him a heritage;
he allotted to him the best of the first fruits,
and prepared bread of first fruits in
abundance;

21 for they eat the sacrifices of the Lord,
which he gave to him and his descendants.

22 But in the land of the people he has no
inheritance,
and he has no portion among the people;
for the Lord^a^ himself is his^b^ portion and
inheritance.

23 Phinehas son of Eleazar ranks third in glory
for being zealous in the fear of the Lord,
and standing firm, when the people turned
away,
in the noble courage of his soul;
and he made atonement for Israel.

24 Therefore a covenant of friendship was
established with him,
that he should be leader of the sanctuary
and of his people,
that he and his descendants should have
the dignity of the priesthood forever.

25 Just as a covenant was established with David
son of Jesse of the tribe of Judah,
that the king's heritage passes only from son
to son,
so the heritage of Aaron is for his
descendants alone.

26 And now bless the Lord
who has crowned you with glory.^c^
May the Lord^a^ grant you wisdom of mind
to judge his people with justice,
so that their prosperity may not vanish,
and that their glory may endure through all
their generations.

^a^Gk *he*   ^b^Other ancient authorities read *your*   ^c^Heb: Gk lacks
And . . . glory

COMMENTARY

44:16. Beginning with Noah, seven recipients of covenant promises are praised: Noah, Abraham, Isaac, Jacob, Moses, Aaron, and Phinehas. Actually, the section opens with a brief comment about Enoch, an increasingly popular biblical character because of the implication that he escaped death. Later speculation credited him with heavenly journeys, during which time he received revelations of divine mysteries. Ben Sira ignores all this extra-biblical tradition, contenting himself with repeating biblical language about Enoch's pleasing the Lord and being taken up (cf. Wis 4:10; Heb 11:5). An unusual aspect of this reference to Enoch sets it apart: He is said to be an example of repentance, or knowledge. The Greek text implies that Enoch's acquisition of mysteries led to pride, for which he repented. The other figures are not lifted up as examples for readers in this way. The Hebrew fragments of Sirach from Masada do not refer to Enoch; neither does the Syriac text. This evidence suggests that the remark about him may not derive from Ben Sira, although the comment on Enoch seems rather tame. One expects more lavish praise of the kind found in later speculation about heavenly journeys and remarkable wisdom. Its absence in the text from Masada and the Syriac, therefore, may be accidental.

44:17-18. If the praise really starts with Noah, and if v. 16 constitutes a later addition, the entire section begins and ends with the two founders of civilization, Noah and Adam (v. 17; 49:16). Noah's blameless conduct elicits praise—he is "just" (צדיק ṣaddîq) and "perfect" (תמים tāmîm)—and his name gives rise to a pun on the word "remnant" (נוח nûaḥ). Ben Sira explicitly refers to the covenant in Gen 9:8-17, of which the rainbow served as a perpetual reminder.

44:19-21. Ben Sira cites a phrase from Gen 17:4 describing Abraham as "father of a host of nations" and attributes to him a life of obedience to the law, although God had not yet revealed the Sinaitic legislation. The covenant refers to the act of circumcision (Gen 17:9-14), which was widely practiced in the ancient world. Because the Philistines did not submit to this practice, they received the nickname "the uncircumcised" (1

Sam 17:26, 36). The test that Abraham passed alludes to Gen 22:1-19, which is specifically called a divine test (Gen 22:1). Later traditionists developed various features of this incident, interpreting the binding of Isaac as an atonement for sins. The divine oath, reiterated in Gen 22:15-18, incorporates promissory language from Gen 15:5 (cf. Ps 72:8).

44:22-23a. The observations about Isaac and Jacob derive from Gen 17:19; 28:1-4, as well as the poetic blessing in Gen 49:1-27. The Hebrew text of v. 22 reads "son" (בן bēn), but the margin has "in like manner" (כן kēn), for Isaac did not have a son for Abraham's sake. Curiously, Ben Sira says nothing about Joseph at this juncture (cf. 49:15), and this omission accords with this patriarch's minor role in subsequent tradition. At least one feature of the text applies better to Joseph than to Moses, specifically the acknowledgment that he won everyone's approval (cf. Gen 39:4, 21, but see also Exod 2:5-10; 11:3).

44:23b–45:5. Although Ben Sira uses a variant of the traditional invocation for blessed memory ("Moses of blessed memory," rather than "may his name be blessed"), the nine bicola (five verses), as opposed to thirty-two (17 verses) for Aaron and ten (4 verses) for Phinehas, reveal Ben Sira's preference for priestly matters. The Greek translator weakened the comparison of Moses to God, rendering אלהים ('ĕlōhîm) as "angels" (v. 2; cf. the Greek text of Ps 8:5). Moses' ability to terminate the plagues (cf. Exodus 8–10), his receipt of the Decalogue, indeed the entire Sinaitic legislation, and his unique admittance into the divine presence (Exod 33:18) place in relief the ancient assessment of him as the humblest of men (Num 12:3). The rest of the observations are more general, including direct conversation with the Lord and the commission to instruct Israel from life-giving commandments.

45:6-22. The long section praising the priest Aaron is matched only by that extolling Simeon II in 50:1-24. According to Exod 29:9; 40:15, God established a perpetual covenant of priesthood with Aaron, Moses' brother. Psalm 106:15 calls Aaron a holy man, as Ben Sira does in v. 6. The description of priestly vestments in Exodus

28–29 includes four that were worn by all priests (tunic, trousers, turban, girdle) and four worn exclusively by the high priest (breastplate, apron, the upper garment, and the frontlet). Ben Sira omits the girdle, while emphasizing such decorative features as pomegranates, the golden bell, embroidery of various kinds, precious stones, and a gold crown. He thinks of the bells as a reminder to the people, unless the Hebrew implies that the sound calls God's attention to the people, for whom the high priest makes intercession in the holy of holies. This whole description throws little light on the nature of the ephod, which seems to have been a sort of apron with a pouch for holding the Urim and the Thummim, sacred stones. These garments could not be worn by outsiders (v. 13), although soon after Ben Sira made this claim the office of high priest became a prize to be granted by Antiochus IV to the highest bidder (2 Macc 4:7-8, 23-27).

Verses 14-17 describe the priestly duties, and vv. 18-22 mention the rewards for faithful service. First, Ben Sira refers to the two daily offerings, called Tamid in his time. Second, the priests pronounce blessings on the people (cf. Num 6:23-27). The instructional responsibility comes next (v. 17), and nothing is said of the rendering of judgment by means of the sacred Urim and Thummim. Instead, Ben Sira mentions a heinous conspiracy, the offering of strange fire by Korah, Dathan, and Abiram (Num 16:1–17:15), as a contrast to Aaron's faithfulness. Ben Sira concludes by referring to the legitimate portion of offerings that belong to the priestly functionaries, a kind of compensation for the omission of the tribe of Levi during the allocation of the land to the twelve tribes.

Ben Sira's generous remarks about an everlasting covenant with Aaron (vv. 7, 15) suggest that the earlier rivalry between Zadokites and Aaronites has been settled, with Zadokites now incorporated into the line of Aaron. The HB mentions an eternal covenant with Phinehas, and not with Aaron (Num 25:12-13). Under King David, the Zadokites gained sole control of priestly duties and privileges.

45:23-26. The following section jumps over Aaron's son Eleazar in favor of the grandson Phinehas, as if to settle the dispute over priestly lineage once and for all. The struggle for control of the priesthood by the Oniads and the Tobiads illuminates this particular observation. The Oniads were related to Aaron on the paternal side, but the Tobiads laid claim to Aaronite ancestry through the maternal side. The latter group sought to wrest the priesthood from the Oniads in the early second century BCE. Ben Sira's reference in v. 25 to a covenant with David, though out of place here, nevertheless legitimates priesthood alongside royalty as the important social institutions of the day with divinely ordained succession. The expression "third in glory" alludes to Phinehas's place in a line of succession including Moses and Aaron. His zeal, recorded in Num 25:11, earned Phinehas a covenant of peace. This unusual praise of Phinehas as "third in glory" indicates that he was far more important in certain Jewish circles than among Christians, who hardly recognize the name (cf. Ps 106:30-31, a recollection of his zeal, which earned him righteousness for endless generations). The concluding call to bless the Lord, the "Good" (cf. 2 Chr 30:18), also wishes that divine favor will fall on the kingly figure—namely, the high priest, who in Ben Sira's time had acquired considerable political power. In essence, the high priest had become ethnarch. Verse 25 suggests that Davidic kingship was transmitted by direct succession to a single son, whereas the priestly heritage belonged to all descendants of Aaron. (See Reflections at 50:1-24.)

SIRACH 46:1-20, JOSHUA, CALEB, THE JUDGES, AND SAMUEL

46 Valiant leader was JOSHUA, son of Nun
assistant to Moses in the prophetic office,
Formed to be, as his name implies,
    the great savior of God's chosen ones,
To punish the enemy
    and to win the inheritance for Israel.
2 What glory was his when he raised his arm,
    to brandish his javelin against the city!
3 And who could withstand him
    when he fought the battles of the LORD?
4 Did he not by his power stop the sun,
    so that one day became two?
5 He called upon the Most High God
    when his enemies beset him on all sides,
And God Most High gave answer to him
    in hailstones of tremendous power,
6 Which he rained down upon the hostile army
    till on the slope he destroyed the foe;
That all the doomed nations might know
    that the LORD was watching over his
      people's battles.
And because he was a devoted follower of
    God
7 and in Moses' lifetime showed himself loyal,
He and CALEB, son of Jephunneh,
    when they opposed the rebel assembly,
Averted God's anger from the people
    and suppressed the wicked complaint—
8 Because of this, they were the only two
    spared
    from the six hundred thousand infantry,
To lead the people into their inheritance,
    the land flowing with milk and honey.
9 And the strength he gave to Caleb
    remained with him even in his old age
Till he won his way onto the summits of the
    land;
    his family too received an inheritance,
10 That all the people of Jacob might know

46, 1c: (*lihyôt) kiš^e mô*: so LXX.
46, 5b: *k^e · āk^e pû (lô· ôy^e bîm)*.
46, 8a: (*biš^e nayim) hiṣṣālû*: so LXX, P.
46, 9b: *l^e hadrîkô*: so facsimile, LXX, P.

46 Joshua son of Nun was mighty in war,
    and was the successor of Moses in the
      prophetic office.
He became, as his name implies,
    a great savior of God's[a] elect,
to take vengeance on the enemies that rose
      against them,
    so that he might give Israel its inheritance.
2 How glorious he was when he lifted his hands
    and brandished his sword against the cities!
3 Who before him ever stood so firm?
    For he waged the wars of the Lord.
4 Was it not through him that the sun stood still
    and one day became as long as two?
5 He called upon the Most High, the Mighty
      One,
    when enemies pressed him on every side,
and the great Lord answered him
    with hailstones of mighty power.
6 He overwhelmed that nation in battle,
    and on the slope he destroyed his
      opponents,
so that the nations might know his armament,
    that he was fighting in the sight of the Lord;
    for he was a devoted follower of the Mighty
      One.
7 And in the days of Moses he proved his loyalty,
    he and Caleb son of Jephunneh:
they opposed the congregation,[b]
    restrained the people from sin,
    and stilled their wicked grumbling.
8 And these two alone were spared
    out of six hundred thousand infantry,
to lead the people[c] into their inheritance,
    the land flowing with milk and honey.
9 The Lord gave Caleb strength,
    which remained with him in his old age,
so that he went up to the hill country,
    and his children obtained it for an
      inheritance,
10 so that all the Israelites might see
    how good it is to follow the Lord.

a Gk *his*   b Other ancient authorities read *the enemy*   c Gk *them*

NAB

how good it is to be a devoted follower of
the LORD.

11 The JUDGES, too, each one of them,
whose hearts were not deceived,
Who did not abandon God:
may their memory be ever blessed,

12 Their bones return to life from their resting
place,
and their names receive fresh luster in their
children!

13 Beloved of his people, dear to his Maker,
dedicated from his mother's womb,
Consecrated to the LORD as a prophet,
was SAMUEL, the judge and priest.
At God's word he established the kingdom
and anointed princes to rule the people.

14 By the law of the LORD he judged the nation,
when he visited the encampments of
Jacob.

15 As a trustworthy prophet he was sought out
and his words proved him true as a seer.

16 He, too, called upon God,
and offered him a suckling lamb;

17 Then the LORD thundered forth from
heaven,
and the tremendous roar of his voice was
heard.

18 He brought low the rulers of the enemy
and destroyed all the lords of the
Philistines.

19 When Samuel approached the end of his
life,
he testified before the LORD and his
anointed prince,
"No bribe or secret gift have I taken from
any man!"
and no one dared gainsay him.

20 Even when he lay buried, his guidance was
sought;
he made known to the king his fate,
And from the grave he raised his voice
as a prophet, to put an end to wickedness.

46, 13a: 'ăhûb ('ammô): so LXX, P.
46, 14b: (wayyipqōd) 'ohōlê (ya'ăqōb).
46, 16: Omit k^e akpâ ... missābîb: dittog of v 5b.
46, 19: Omit w^egam 'ad 'ēt ... kol hāy: so LXX, P; gloss.

NRSV

11 The judges also, with their respective names,
whose hearts did not fall into idolatry
and who did not turn away from the Lord—
may their memory be blessed!

12 May their bones send forth new life from
where they lie,
and may the names of those who have been
honored
live again in their children!

13 Samuel was beloved by his Lord;
a prophet of the Lord, he established the
kingdom
and anointed rulers over his people.

14 By the law of the Lord he judged the
congregation,
and the Lord watched over Jacob.

15 By his faithfulness he was proved to be a
prophet,
and by his words he became known as a
trustworthy seer.

16 He called upon the Lord, the Mighty One,
when his enemies pressed him on every
side,
and he offered in sacrifice a suckling lamb.

17 Then the Lord thundered from heaven,
and made his voice heard with a mighty
sound;

18 he subdued the leaders of the enemy[a]
and all the rulers of the Philistines.

19 Before the time of his eternal sleep,
Samuel[b] bore witness before the Lord and
his anointed:
"No property, not so much as a pair of shoes,
have I taken from anyone!"
And no one accused him.

20 Even after he had fallen asleep, he
prophesied
and made known to the king his death,
and lifted up his voice from the ground
in prophecy, to blot out the wickedness of
the people.

[a]Heb: Gk *leaders of the people of Tyre*   [b]Gk *he*

COMMENTARY

This unit divides naturally into vv. 1-10 and vv. 11-20, the former praising Joshua and Caleb, the latter lauding unnamed judges and Samuel. Ben Sira unites both of these with puns on the names "Joshua" and "Samuel": v. 1, "Yahweh is salvation"; v. 13, "obtained by request."

46:1-10. Moses' two lieutenants succeeded in one respect where he failed: Joshua and Caleb were allowed to enter the land of milk and honey. Joshua's expertise in battle consisted of timely signals (Josh 8:18, 26); his intercession caused the sun to pause (Josh 13:13; cf. the LXX, which mistakenly has the sun go backward as the shadow does in Isa 38:8) and brought hailstones upon the enemy (Josh 10:11). Together with Caleb, Joshua brought a favorable report about the land of promise and urged Moses to advance there in the hope of defeating its occupants (Num 14:6-10). The number 600,000 appears in various accounts (cf. 16:10; Num 11:21; 14:38; 26:65; Deut 1:36, 38). Caleb's extraordinary strength in advanced years (Josh 14:7, 10-11) enabled him to gain mastery over his enemies, the meaning of the expression "to tread on the high places of the land" (cf. Deut 33:29).

The epithet for God in v. 5 ("the Most High, the Mighty One") occurs here for the first time in Sirach. The Hebrew אל עליון (*'ēl 'elyôn*) is used in v. 5 (twice); 47:5, 8; 48:20; 50:15 (where the Hebrew is missing, but the Greek has ὕψιστος παμβασιλεύς [*hypsistos pambasileus*, "the Most High,

the king of all"]). The Hebrew title *'Elyôn* occurs nine times by itself in Sirach (41:4; 42:2; 44:20; 50:16; 49:4; 41:8; 44:2; 50:17; 50:14). Before chap. 41, the names יהוה (*Yahweh*) and אלהים (*'ĕlōhîm*) occur, the former usually abbreviated ווי (*yyy*).

46:11-20. The two most prominent judges, Gideon and Samson, probably prompted Ben Sira to discuss the larger group without naming anyone, for these two men certainly succumbed to deceit (v. 11). The remark about their bones flourishing (cf. 49:10) implies that ancient Israelites believed that bones, like roots, could extend themselves vigorously (cf. the vision of dry bones in Ezekiel 37 and the story in 2 Kgs 13:21 about the power of Elisha's bones to revivify a corpse).[246]

Samuel's claim to fame is based on his extraordinary birth, his role in anointing both Saul and David to kingship, his priestly function, his prophetic office, and his unimpeachable integrity. Even his appearance after death to a frightened Saul only confirmed for Ben Sira Samuel's prophetic office, already affirmed by the deuteronomistic criterion of accuracy in predicting future events. The failure to mention Saul by name reveals how little regard Ben Sira had for Israel's first king. (See Reflections at 50:1-24.)

---

246. Cf. the Semitic ritual of pouring water on the bones of ancestors. See W. O. E. Oesterley, *The Wisdom of Jesus the Son of Sirach*, 316.

SIRACH 47:1-25, NATHAN, DAVID, SOLOMON, AND REHOBOAM/JEROBOAM

NAB	NRSV
47 After him came NATHAN who served in the presence of David. 2 Like the choice fat of the sacred offerings, so was DAVID in Israel. 3 He made sport of lions as though they were kids,	**47** After him Nathan rose up to prophesy in the days of David. 2 As the fat is set apart from the offering of well-being, so David was set apart from the Israelites. 3 He played with lions as though they were young goats,

NAB

and of bears, like lambs of the flock.

4 As a youth he slew the giant
   and wiped out the people's disgrace,
When his hand let fly the slingstone
   that crushed the pride of Goliath.
5 Since he called upon the Most High God,
   who gave strength to his right arm
To defeat the skilled warrior
   and raise up the might of his people,
6 Therefore the women sang his praises
   and ascribed to him tens of thousands.
When he assumed the royal crown, he
   battled
7 and subdued the enemy on every side.
   He destroyed the hostile Philistines
   and shattered their power till our own day.
8 With his every deed he offered thanks
   to God Most High, in words of praise.
With his whole being he loved his Maker
   and daily had his praises sung;
9 He added beauty to the feasts
   and solemnized the seasons of each year
With string music before the altar,
   providing sweet melody for the psalms
10 So that when the Holy Name was praised,
   before daybreak the sanctuary would
   resound.
11 The LORD forgave him his sins
   and exalted his strength forever;
He conferred on him the rights of royalty
   and established his throne in Israel.

12 Because of his merits he had as his successor
   a wise son, who lived in security:
13 SOLOMON reigned during an era of peace,
   for God made tranquil all his borders.
He built a house to the name of God,
   and established a lasting sanctuary.
14 How wise you were when you were young,
   overflowing with instruction, like the Nile
   in flood!

47, 3b: (*kib*ᵉ*nê*) *ṣō*ʾ*n*: so LXX.
47, 4b: (*wayyāsar*) *ḥerpâ mē*ʾ*al*ʾ*ām*: so LXX; cf P.
47, 7b: *wayyak* (?) (*bip*ᵉ*lištîm*) *ṣārîm*: so LXX.
47, 8c: ʾ*āhab* (ʾ*ōsēhûs*): so LXX, P. 8d: cf LXX^MSS.
47, 9a.b: Trsp v. 10a.b to beginning of v 9 and read with LXX: *nātan*
*l*ᵉ*ḥaggîm hādār*, *way*ᵉ*taqqēn mô*ʾ*ădêm šānâ b*ᵉ*šānâ*. 9d: *w*ᵉ*qôl mizmôr*
*hin*ʾ*îm*: cf B margin, LXX.
47, 10b: (*yārôn*) *miqdāš*: so B margin, LXX.
47, 11d: (ʾ*al*) *yiśrā*ʾ*ēl* so LXX, cf P.

NRSV

and with bears as though they were lambs
   of the flock.
4 In his youth did he not kill a giant,
   and take away the people's disgrace,
when he whirled the stone in the sling
   and struck down the boasting Goliath?
5 For he called on the Lord, the Most High,
   and he gave strength to his right arm
to strike down a mighty warrior,
   and to exalt the power[a] of his people.
6 So they glorified him for the tens of thousands
   he conquered,
   and praised him for the blessings bestowed
   by the Lord,
   when the glorious diadem was given to him.
7 For he wiped out his enemies on every side,
   and annihilated his adversaries the
   Philistines;
   he crushed their power[a] to our own day.
8 In all that he did he gave thanks
   to the Holy One, the Most High,
   proclaiming his glory;
   he sang praise with all his heart,
   and he loved his Maker.
9 He placed singers before the altar,
   to make sweet melody with their voices.[b]
10 He gave beauty to the festivals,
   and arranged their times throughout the
   year,[c]
while they praised God's[d] holy name,
   and the sanctuary resounded from early
   morning.
11 The Lord took away his sins,
   and exalted his power[a] forever;
he gave him a covenant of kingship
   and a glorious throne in Israel.

12 After him a wise son rose up
   who because of him lived in security:[e]
13 Solomon reigned in an age of peace,
   because God made all his borders tranquil,
so that he might build a house in his name
   and provide a sanctuary to stand forever.
14 How wise you were when you were young!
   You overflowed like the Nile[f] with understanding.

a Gk *horn*   b Other ancient authorities add *and daily they sing his*
praises   c Gk *to completion*   d Gk *his*   e Gk *in a broad place*
f Heb: Gk *a river*

NAB

15 Your understanding covered the whole
earth,
and, like a sea, filled it with knowledge.
16 Your fame reached distant coasts,
and their peoples came to hear you;
17 With song and story and riddle,
and with your answers, you astounded the
nations.
18 You were called by that glorious name
which was conferred upon Israel.
Gold you gathered like so much iron,
you heaped up silver as though it were
lead;
19 But you abandoned yourself to women
and gave them dominion over your body.
20 You brought dishonor upon your reputation,
shame upon your marriage,
Wrath upon your descendants,
and groaning upon your domain;
21 Thus two governments came into being,
when in Ephraim kingship was usurped.
22 But God does not withdraw his mercy,
nor permit even one of his promises to fail.
He does not uproot the posterity of his chosen
one,
nor destroy the offspring of his friend.
So he gave to Jacob a remnant,
to David a root from his own family.
23 Solomon finally slept with his fathers,
and left behind him one of his sons,
Expansive in folly, limited in sense,
REHOBOAM, who by his policy made the
people rebel;
Until one arose who should not be
remembered,
the sinner who led Israel into sin,
Who brought ruin to Ephraim
24 and caused them to be exiled from their land.

Their sinfulness grew more and more,
25 and they lent themselves to every evil,

NRSV

15 Your influence spread throughout the earth,
and you filled it with proverbs having deep
meaning.
16 Your fame reached to far-off islands,
and you were loved for your peaceful reign.
17 Your songs, proverbs, and parables,
and the answers you gave astounded the
nations.
18 In the name of the Lord God,
who is called the God of Israel,
you gathered gold like tin
and amassed silver like lead.
19 But you brought in women to lie at your side,
and through your body you were brought
into subjection.
20 You stained your honor,
and defiled your family line,
so that you brought wrath upon your children,
and they were grieved[a] at your folly,
21 because the sovereignty was divided
and a rebel kingdom arose out of Ephraim.
22 But the Lord will never give up his mercy,
or cause any of his works to perish;
he will never blot out the descendants of his
chosen one,
or destroy the family line of him who loved
him.
So he gave a remnant to Jacob,
and to David a root from his own family.

23 Solomon rested with his ancestors,
and left behind him one of his sons,
broad in[b] folly and lacking in sense,
Rehoboam, whose policy drove the people
to revolt.
Then Jeroboam son of Nebat led Israel into sin
and started Ephraim on its sinful ways.
24 Their sins increased more and more,
until they were exiled from their land.
25 For they sought out every kind of wickedness,
until vengeance came upon them.

a Other ancient authorities read *I was grieved*   *b* Heb (with a play
on the name Rehoboam) Syr: Gk *the people's*

47, 15b: *watt*ᵉ*mallē' kᵉmô yām dēʻâ* (?): cf LXX.
47, 16: *ʻadʻ iyyîm rᵉhôqîm higgîʻ šᵉmekā, wayyābôʻû* (for
*wayᵉʻēhābû=kai ēgapēthēs) lᵉšomʻekā (for bišᵉlômeka=en tē eirēnē
sou*); so P; cf LXX.
47, 20d: (*waʻānāhâ ʻal) memšᵉlātekā (for śiklûtekā=aphrosynē
sou*)?
47, 23a: (*wayyiškab šᵉlômô) ʻim ʻabôtāyw:* so LXX. 23b: (*ʻahărāyw)
mizzarʻô:* so LXX. 23e: Omit *yorobʻām ben nᵉʻbāṭ,* and read: *ʻašer hehēṭî.*

COMMENTARY

47:1-11. Eager to indicate prophetic continuity, Ben Sira briefly refers to Nathan, who served ("stood before") David, according to the Hebrew (the Greek has "prophesied in the days of David"). The description of David, almost entirely favorable, resembles that in 1 Chronicles 11–29, a selective use of available traditions. The opening image in v. 2 derives from the sacrificial cult; David is set apart in the same way the choice fat of an offering was lifted off for priestly consumption (Lev 4:8, 10, 19; cf. Ps 89:19). From the story about David's defeat of Goliath, Ben Sira chooses several incidents, particularly David's skill in killing lions and bears, here euphemistically called "play" (1 Sam 17:34-36); the victory over the Philistine champion (1 Sam 17:32-51); the exuberant song of triumph by local women (1 Sam 18:7); and the suppression of surrounding enemies—Moabites, Aramaeans, Edomites, Ammonites, and Philistines—as recorded in 2 Samuel 5–21. Ben Sira mentions the Philistines as the supreme instance of hostile neighbors, noting that their defeat at David's hands was permanent. That is the function of the traditional expression "until our own day" (v. 7).

Beginning with v. 8, Ben Sira concentrates on David's contribution to religious worship, especially his composition of psalms and his musical interests. The chronicler also credits David with musical instruments associated with the chanting of psalms (1 Chr 23:5; cf. Amos 6:5), as well as solemnizing religious festivals (1 Chr 23:31-32). Not until the final verse does Ben Sira acknowledge David's sins, and then only generally as a recipient of divine pardon. Like the chronicler, who does not even mention David's adultery with Bathsheba and murder of Uriah, Ben Sira prefers to dwell on David's virtues—after all, the genre requires praise rather than blame. The last word, however, remains one of grace, the perpetual covenant of kingship (v. 11; cf. 2 Samuel 7).

47:12-22. Ben Sira attributes Solomon's peaceful reign to his father's influence, although he seizes the opportunity to create a pun on the meaning of Solomon's name ("peace"). The chronicler goes so far as to credit David with making preparations for building the Temple in Jerusalem; Ben Sira merely suggests that peaceful conditions, the result of David's victories, made it possible for Solomon to build the sanctuary. Defying all odds, Solomon is reputed to have received wisdom as a youth—utterly impossible in traditional sapiential texts, which assume that wisdom can be acquired only through wide experience and over a long period.[247] Ben Sira alludes to the traditions pertaining to Solomon's wisdom preserved in 1 Kgs 3:9-12, 16-28; 5:9-11; 10:1-12. The reference to his fame's having reached distant islands probably echoes the story about the queen of Sheba, and the observation about the composition of songs, proverbs, riddles, and answers (v. 17) refers to the ancient tradition that Solomon spoke 3,000 proverbs and composed 1,005 songs (1 Kgs 5:12[Eng. 4:32]). Later traditionists credited Solomon with considerably more compositions: Proverbs, Ecclesiastes, Song of Songs, the book of Wisdom of Solomon, the Odes of Solomon, and the Psalms of Solomon, to name a few.

The legendary traditions in 1 Kings also speak of huge sums of gold and silver that the king amassed from distant lands, and Ben Sira does not overlook this feature of Solomon's fame, despite the condemnation in Deut 17:17 of such royal practice. Only with v. 19 does Ben Sira allow himself to mention Solomon's weakness for women, for which the author of 1 Kgs 11:1-10 faults him (cf. Prov 31:3, "Give not your vigor to women, nor your strength to women who ruin kings"). Curiously, Ben Sira ignores the other complaint in 1 Kgs 11:1-13, 33: the sin of idolatry. Verses 21-22 concede the grief occasioned by Solomon's sins and the ensuing rupture in the kingdom, but not without an emphatic affirmation of the Davidic dynasty. That explains the reference to a remnant of Jacob's descendants and a root from David's own family (v. 22).

47:23-25. These verses describe the division of David and Solomon's kingdom into two national states led by Rehoboam in the south and Jeroboam in the north. Ben Sira plays on the meaning of the name of the former, calling him

---

247. James L. Crenshaw, "Youth and Old Age in Qoheleth," *HAR* 10 (1986) 1-13. See also James L. Crenshaw, *Urgent Advice and Probing Questions* (Macon, Ga.: Mercer University Press, 1995) 535-47.

"great in folly" (from רחב [*rāḥab*, "to be wide"]). The contrast between Solomon's wideness of heart (1 Kgs 5:9[Eng. 4:29]) and his son's arrogance could hardly be greater. In the Hebrew, Ben Sira omits the name "Rehoboam," using instead the adjective for "broad, open place" (*rāḥāb*) plus the noun "people" (עם *'am*) to indicate the king, whose folly consisted of increasing forced labor against the advice of senior statesmen (1 Kgs 12:1-24). Instead of naming Jeroboam, archvil-

lain in the deuteronomistic history, Ben Sira uses a clever formula, "let his name not be mentioned" (אל יהי לו זכר *'al yĕhî lô zēker*). The present Hebrew text has the names of both kings written out. Jeroboam's chief offense was the construction of the two rival sanctuaries at Bethel and Dan, the southernmost and northernmost borders of the new kingdom, each featuring a golden bull. (See Reflections at 50:1-24.)

SIRACH 48:1-16, THE PROPHETS ELIJAH AND ELISHA

NAB

48 Till like a fire there appeared the prophet whose words were as a flaming furnace.

2 Their staff of bread he shattered,
    in his zeal he reduced them to straits;

3 By God's word he shut up the heavens
    and three times brought down fire.

4 How awesome are you, ELIJAH!
    Whose glory is equal to yours?

5 You brought a dead man back to life
    from the nether world, by the will of the
        LORD.

6 You sent kings down to destruction,
    and nobles, from their beds of sickness.

7 You heard threats at Sinai,
    at Horeb avenging judgments.

8 You anointed kings who should inflict
        vengeance,
    and a prophet as your successor.

9 You were taken aloft in a whirlwind,
    in a chariot with fiery horses.

10 You are destined, it is written, in time to
        come
    to put an end to wrath before the day of
        the LORD,
    To turn back the hearts of fathers toward
        their sons,
    and to re-establish the tribes of Jacob.

48, 4b: *ûmî* (*kāmôkā*): so LXX, P.
48, 7f: Trsp vv: so LXX, P; cf 3 Kgs 19. 7a: *haššômēa'*: so LXX. 8a: *malkê* (*tašlûmôt*): so LXX, P.
48, 10b: (*lip^enê*) *yôm yhwh*: cf P.

NRSV

48 Then Elijah arose, a prophet like fire,
    and his word burned like a torch.

2 He brought a famine upon them,
    and by his zeal he made them few in
        number.

3 By the word of the Lord he shut up the
        heavens,
    and also three times brought down fire.

4 How glorious you were, Elijah, in your
        wondrous deeds!
    Whose glory is equal to yours?

5 You raised a corpse from death
    and from Hades, by the word of the Most
        High.

6 You sent kings down to destruction,
    and famous men, from their sickbeds.

7 You heard rebuke at Sinai
    and judgments of vengeance at Horeb.

8 You anointed kings to inflict retribution,
    and prophets to succeed you.[a]

9 You were taken up by a whirlwind of fire,
    in a chariot with horses of fire.

10 At the appointed time, it is written, you are
        destined[b]
    to calm the wrath of God before it breaks
        out in fury,
    to turn the hearts of parents to their children,
    and to restore the tribes of Jacob.

11 Happy are those who saw you

[a] Heb: Gk *him*   [b] Heb: Gk *are for reproofs*

NAB

11 Blessed is he who shall have seen you
  before he dies,
12 O Elijah, enveloped in the whirlwind!

  Then ELISHA, filled with a twofold portion of
    his spirit,
  wrought many marvels by his mere word.
  During his lifetime he feared no one,
    nor was any man able to intimidate his
      will.
13 Nothing was beyond his power;
  beneath him flesh was brought back into
    life.
14 In life he performed wonders,
  and after death, marvelous deeds.

15 Despite all this the people did not repent,
  nor did they give up their sins,
  Until they were rooted out of their land
    and scattered all over the earth.
  But Judah remained, a tiny people,
    with its rulers from the house of David.
16 Some of these did what was right,
  but others were extremely sinful.

48, 11a: ʾašrê rôʾěkā wāmêt: cf LXX, P. 11b: Omit: gloss.
48, 12a: ʾēlîyāhû nistār bisᵉʿārā: cf LXX. 12b: ʾělîšāʿ nimlāʾ rûḥô
pîšᵉnayim. 12c wᵉʾôtôt hirbâ kol môṣāʾ) pîhû.

NRSV

and were adorned[a] with your love!
  For we also shall surely live.[b]

12 When Elijah was enveloped in the whirlwind,
  Elisha was filled with his spirit.
  He performed twice as many signs,
    and marvels with every utterance of his
      mouth.[c]
  Never in his lifetime did he tremble before any
    ruler,
    nor could anyone intimidate him at all.
13 Nothing was too hard for him,
  and when he was dead, his body
    prophesied.
14 In his life he did wonders,
  and in death his deeds were marvelous.

15 Despite all this the people did not repent,
  nor did they forsake their sins,
  until they were carried off as plunder from
    their land,
    and were scattered over all the earth.
  The people were left very few in number,
    but with a ruler from the house of David.
16 Some of them did what was right,
  but others sinned more and more.

aOther ancient authorities read and have died   bText and meaning of Gk uncertain   cHeb: Gk lacks He performed . . . mouth

COMMENTARY

The transition in 47:25 sets the stage for Elijah's appearance. Unlike the chronicler, who virtually ignores the history of the northern kingdom, Ben Sira focuses on the activity of the two prophets from the ninth century, passing over in silence the prophetic ministry of Amos and Hosea a century later.

48:1-11. Verse 1 continues the thought of 47:25. Wickedness ran unchecked "until a prophet arose." Ben Sira withholds the prophet's name until v. 4, once more creating a pun from familiar epithets for Elijah, "man of God" (איש אלהים ʾiš ʾělōhîm), who called down fire from God upon his enemies (אש אלהים ʾēš ʾělōhîm). From Mal 3:19, Ben Sira derives the metaphor for Elijah's word as a hot furnace, but most of the

references come from 1 Kings 17–19 and 2 Kings 1–2. That includes the famine Elijah announced to the Omride ruler Ahab (1 Kgs 18:3); his zeal (1 Kgs 19:10, 14); his summoning of fire three times (1 Kgs 18:38; 2 Kgs 1:10, 12); his resuscitation of the son of the widow from Zarephath (1 Kgs 17:17-22); his condemnation of kings (1 Kgs 21:19-24); the divine rebuke at Horeb (1 Kgs 19:8-18); the anointing of kings (indirectly through Elisha; 2 Kgs 8:7-15; 9:1-13); and his ascension into heaven (2 Kgs 2:1-11). In v. 10, Ben Sira uses the formula for citing Scripture, "it is written," with reference to Mal 3:23-24 (cf. Luke 1:17; Matt 11:10, 14; 17:10-13). The phrase "to reestablish the tribes of Israel" appears in Isa 49:6. In Sir 48:10-11 it gives way to uncertain speculation about people who saw Elijah. Apparently it contains a play on the ancient account of Elisha's persistence in seeing his master ascend to heaven, but in the present form it is confused with a blessing on those who might see Elijah's return to earth. The later popular idea that Elijah would precede the Messiah does not find expression here. The strange gloss in v. 11 shifts away from the unusual form of address, which began in v. 4. This second-person speech has a precedent in 47:14-21, where Ben Sira addresses Solomon directly. In Ben Sira's view, Elijah lived up to his name, "Yahweh is my God," for his deeds were awe-inspiring (v. 4).

48:12-16. Verse 12 serves as a transition from praising Elijah to lauding his successor, but Ben Sira misunderstands the concept of inheriting a double portion to mean twice as much rather than twice one's equal share, the portion received by the oldest son. This confusion leads Ben Sira to say that Elisha performed twice as many signs as did his master (see 2 Kgs 2:9-15 for the idea that Elisha was filled with the Spirit). The story about the extraordinary power of his bones—giving life to a corpse that had come in contact with them—shows once more that Ben Sira understood prophetic activity as miraculous power rather than the communication of the divine word (cf. 2 Kgs 13:20-21). He endorses the earlier explanation for the dispersion of the ten tribes, specifically their refusal to repent (2 Kgs 18:11-12). The Hebrew text states that Judah was left—that is, continued under the rule of a legitimate descendant of David. (See Reflections at 50:1-24.)

SIRACH 48:17-25, HEZEKIAH AND ISAIAH

NAB	NRSV
17 HEZEKIAH fortified his city and had water brought into it; With iron tools he cut through the rock and he built reservoirs for water.	17 Hezekiah fortified his city, and brought water into its midst; he tunneled the rock with iron tools, and built cisterns for the water.
18 During his reign Sennacherib led an invasion, and sent his adjutant; He shook his fist at Zion and blasphemed God in his pride.	18 In his days Sennacherib invaded the country; he sent his commander[a] and departed; he shook his fist against Zion, and made great boasts in his arrogance.
19 The people's hearts melted within them, and they were in anguish like that of childbirth.	19 Then their hearts were shaken and their hands trembled, and they were in anguish, like women in labor.
20 But they called upon the Most High God and lifted up their hands to him; He heard the prayer they uttered, and saved them through ISAIAH.	20 But they called upon the Lord who is merciful, spreading out their hands toward him. The Holy One quickly heard them from heaven, and delivered them through Isaiah.
21 God struck the camp of the Assyrians and routed them with a plague.	21 The Lord[b] struck down the camp of the Assyrians, and his angel wiped them out.
22 For Hezekiah did what was right and held fast to the paths of David, As ordered by the illustrious prophet Isaiah, who saw the truth in visions.	22 For Hezekiah did what was pleasing to the Lord, and he kept firmly to the ways of his ancestor David,

48, 17b: *wayyēṭ(ʾⁿltôkāh)*: cf LXX, P. 17c: *bannⁿḥôšet* (or *babbarzel?*): cf LXX. 17d: *wayyîben lammayim (miqweh)*: so LXX.
48, 19a: (*ʾāz nāmôgû) bām libbām*).
48, 22c.d.23: With LXX and P.

[a] Other ancient authorities add *from Lachish*   [b] Gk *He*

NAB	NRSV

23 In his lifetime he turned back the sun
    and prolonged the life of the king.
24 By his powerful spirit he looked into the
    future
    and consoled the mourners of Zion;
25 He foretold what should be till the end of
    time,
    hidden things yet to be fulfilled.
	as he was commanded by the prophet Isaiah,
	    who was great and trustworthy in his
	    visions.
	23 In Isaiah's[a] days the sun went backward,
	    and he prolonged the life of the king.
	24 By his dauntless spirit he saw the future,
	    and comforted the mourners in Zion.
	25 He revealed what was to occur to the end of
	    time,
	    and the hidden things before they happened.
	
	a Gk *his*

COMMENTARY

48:17-19. Although the deuteronomistic history gives qualified approval to six kings in Judah (Asa, Jehoshaphat, Joash, Azariah, Hezekiah, and Josiah), Ben Sira's less generous assessment restricts itself to Hezekiah and Josiah. A wordplay on the name "Hezekiah" (חזקיהו *ḥizqiyyāhû*) enables Ben Sira to speak about the king's strengthening of the capital city, Jerusalem ("he fortified" [חזק *ḥāzaq*]). To provide water for the inhabitants of the city, Hezekiah ordered workers to dig a tunnel 1,749 feet from the Spring of Gihon to the Pool of Siloam (2 Kgs 20:20; 2 Chr 32:30). In 1880, this tunnel was discovered, along with an inscription describing how this remarkable feat was accomplished.[248]

Ben Sira mentions the legendary account of Sennacherib's invasion of Judah during Hezekiah's reign, one for which three different versions have survived (2 Kgs 18:13-27, retold in 2 Chr 32:1-20; Isa 36:1-22; and the altogether different account in the annals of Sennacherib).[249] Whereas the biblical story attributes Sennacherib's withdrawal and the death of 185,000 of his soldiers to the Lord's angel, Ben Sira states that a plague ravaged the invading camp. The reference in Herodotus to a bubonic plague, often used to support the account in Isa 36:1-22, lacks evidentiary force. Such a plague would not have been restricted to the invading army, assuming that Herodotus recalled the incident. The account in 2 Kgs 18:17-35 and 19:14-19 (cf. Isa 37:15-20) about the arrogance of the Rabshakeh ascribes the prayer to Hezekiah, but Ben Sira credits the people with this invocation.

48:20-25. Spreading the hands was the usual gesture during prayer (v. 20); Ben Sira attributes the deliverance of Zion to Isaiah's mediation. The rare title for God in this verse, "the Holy One," reflects Isaianic terminology; Ben Sira probably used "Most High" (עליון *'elyôn*), as "From heaven" (ἐξ οὐρανοῦ *ex ouranou*) in the Greek suggests. In v. 22, another pun on the name "Hezekiah" occurs: "he kept firmly to the ways of David." The reference to Isaiah's visions (cf. Isa 6:1-13) introduces specific praise of the prophet: the sign that promised an extended life span to the king—namely, the backward movement of the shadow on a stairway (2 Kgs 20:6-11; Isa 38:5-8); the proclamation of comfort (Isa 40:1); and the revelation of future events (Isa 40:3-11; 42:9, 24-27). Various legends about Isaiah arose in later Judaism and survive in *The Ascension of Isaiah* and *The Martyrdom of Isaiah* (cf. Heb 11:37, "they were sawn in two," NRSV).[250] (See Reflections at 50:1-24.)

248. James B. Pritchard gives this inscription in translation. See *Ancient Near Eastern Texts Relating to the Old Testament,* ed. James B. Pritchard, 3rd ed. (Princeton, N.J.: Princeton University Press, 1969) 321.
249. Ibid., 287-88.

250. M. A. Knibb, "Martyrdom and Ascension of Isaiah," in *The Old Testament Pseudepigrapha,* ed. James H. Charlesworth (Garden City, N.Y.: Doubleday, 1985) 143-76.

SIRACH 49:1-16, JOSIAH AND SUBSEQUENT HEROES

NAB

49 The name JOSIAH is like blended incense,
  made lasting by a skilled perfumer.
Precious is his memory, like honey to the taste,
  like music at a banquet.

2 For he grieved over our betrayals
  and destroyed the abominable idols.

3 He turned to God with his whole heart,
  and, though times were evil, he practiced virtue.

4 Except for David, Hezekiah and Josiah,
  they all were wicked;
They abandoned the law of the Most High,
  these kings of Judah, right to the very end.

5 So he gave over their power to others,
  their glory to a foolish foreign nation

6 Who burned the holy city
  and left its streets desolate,
As JEREMIAH had foretold;

7 for they had treated him badly
  who even in the womb had been made a prophet,
To root out, pull down, and destroy,
  and then to build and to plant.

8 EZEKIEL beheld the vision
  and described the different creatures of the chariot;

9 He also referred to JOB,
  who always persevered in the right path.

10 Then, too, the TWELVE PROPHETS—
  may their bones return to life from their resting place!—
Gave new strength to Jacob
  and saved him by their faith and hope.

11 How can we fittingly praise ZERUBBABEL,
  who was like a signet ring on God's right hand,

12 And Jeshua, Jozadak's son?
  In their time they built the house of God;

49, 5: (*wayyittēn qarnām*) *l*e ' *āhēr*: cf LXX, P.
49, 7c: Omit *lahàròs*: so LXX; gloss. Omit *wlh . . .* : so LXX.
49, 10b: Cf LXX.
49, 12a.b: With LXX. *bānû bāyit*.

NRSV

49 The name[a] of Josiah is like blended incense
  prepared by the skill of the perfumer;
his memory[b] is as sweet as honey to every mouth,
  and like music at a banquet of wine.

2 He did what was right by reforming the people,
  and removing the wicked abominations.

3 He kept his heart fixed on the Lord;
  in lawless times he made godliness prevail.

4 Except for David and Hezekiah and Josiah,
  all of them were great sinners, ·
for they abandoned the law of the Most High;
  the kings of Judah came to an end.

5 They[c] gave their power to others,
  and their glory to a foreign nation,

6 who set fire to the chosen city of the sanctuary,
  and made its streets desolate,
as Jeremiah had foretold.[d]

7 For they had mistreated him,
  who even in the womb had been consecrated a prophet,
to pluck up and ruin and destroy,
  and likewise to build and to plant.

8 It was Ezekiel who saw the vision of glory,
  which God[c] showed him above the chariot of the cherubim.

9 For God[e] also mentioned Job
  who held fast to all the ways of justice.[f]

10 May the bones of the Twelve Prophets
  send forth new life from where they lie,
for they comforted the people of Jacob
  and delivered them with confident hope.

11 How shall we magnify Zerubbabel?
  He was like a signet ring on the right hand,

12 and so was Jeshua son of Jozadak;
  in their days they built the house
  and raised a temple[g] holy to the Lord,

[a] Heb: Gk *memory*   [b] Heb: Gk *it*   [c] Heb *He*   [d] Gk *by the hand of Jeremiah*   [e] Gk *he*   [f] Heb Compare Syr: Meaning of Gk uncertain   [g] Other ancient authorities read *people*

NAB

They erected the holy temple,
　　destined for everlasting glory.
13 Extolled be the memory of NEHEMIAH!
　　He rebuilt our ruined walls,
　　Restored our shattered defenses,
　　　and set up gates and bars.

14 Few on earth have been made the equal of
　　　ENOCH,
　　for he was taken up bodily.
15 Was ever a man born like JOSEPH?
　　Even his dead body was provided for.
16 Glorious, too, were SHEM and SETH and ENOS;
　　but beyond that of any living being
　　　was the splendor of ADAM.

49, 16a: *nikbādû:* so LXX.

NRSV

　　destined for everlasting glory.
13 The memory of Nehemiah also is lasting;
　　he raised our fallen walls,
　　and set up gates and bars,
　　and rebuilt our ruined houses.

14 Few have[a] ever been created on earth like
　　　Enoch,
　　for he was taken up from the earth.
15 Nor was anyone ever born like Joseph;[b]
　　even his bones were cared for.
16 Shem and Seth and Enosh were honored,[c]
　　but above every other created living being
　　　was Adam.

a Heb Syr: Gk *No one has*　　*b* Heb Syr: Gk adds *the leader of his brothers, the support of the people*　　*c* Heb: Gk *Shem and Seth were honored by people*

COMMENTARY

49:1-7. A poem consisting of twenty-two bicola concludes Ben Sira's eulogy of Israel's heroes. Josiah's eradication of idolatrous worship throughout Judah earned him the approval of the deuteronomist and the chronicler (2 Kgs 23:4-24; 2 Chr 34:33), and moved Ben Sira to liken Josiah's memory to incense and honey. The remark that he grieved over Judah's betrayals refers to Josiah's reaction upon hearing the contents of the book of the law, reportedly uncovered during repairs to the Temple (2 Kgs 22:10-19). In v. 4, Ben Sira sums up the monarchy as being wicked, with three exceptions: David, Hezekiah, and Josiah. Consequently, God had given the holy city and its inhabitants into the hands of the Babylonians (vv. 4-6), as Jeremiah had prophesied (v. 7). Ben Sira refers specifically to Jeremiah's call and uses the language of the divine commission (Jer 1:5, 10). The designation of Jerusalem as "the holy city" occurs elsewhere in Neh 11:1, 8; Isa 48:2; 52:1; and Dan 9:24.

49:8-10. Ben Sira's allusion to Ezekiel comes from the visionary account in Ezek 1:4-28, which describes a sort of chariot. He mentions Job, whom Ezekiel also refers to as a righteous individual from ancient times, along with Noah and Dan'el. The inclusion of Job among the other great

prophets accords with the loose sense of the word "prophet" in Gen 20:7 with respect to Abraham; with the view of Josephus, who includes the book of Job among the prophets; and with later rabbinic literature.[251] The other prophets appear in Ben Sira's list as a single entity, like the book of the Twelve in the HB. He uses for the second time the formula "May their bones send forth new life from where they lie" (cf. 46:12, with reference to unnamed judges). The assertion that the so-called minor prophets overwhelmingly provided hope places extraordinary weight on such passages as Amos 9:11-15; Joel 3:1-21; and Zech 9:9-17.

49:11-13. Ben Sira mentions only three people from the post-exilic period, all of them associated with restoring the Temple (Zerubbabel and Jeshua) and the walls of Jerusalem (Nehemiah). The designation of Zerubbabel as a signet ring derives from the messianic aspirations reflected in Hag 2:23, which seem to have surfaced in connection with the newly founded community and its cult in 516 BCE.[252] Ben Sira's silence about Ezra

251. E.g., *Baba Bathra* 15*b:* "God raised up seven prophets for the gentiles," one of whom is Job.

252. Carol C. Meyers and Eric M. Meyers, *Haggai, Zechariah 1–8,* AB 25B (Garden City, N.Y.: Doubleday, 1987) 47-84; David L. Petersen, *Haggai and Zechariah 1–8,* OTL (Philadelphia: Westminster, 1984) 96-106.

in v. 13 has occasioned much discussion,[253] although the individuals mentioned here—Zerubbabel, Jeshua, and Nehemiah—actively participated in rebuilding the city of Jerusalem and restoring its cult. Ezra's activity resembled that of Josiah, for he endeavored to purge the worship of everything foreign. That zeal should have earned him honorable mention at least.

49:14-16. To provide transition from the heroes of the past to the high priest during his own time, Ben Sira gives a brief survey of global history. First, he mentions Enoch, that subject of endless speculation; then Joseph, the patriarch

whose body was so painstakingly cared for and transported from Egypt to the land of promise; next Shem, the ancestor of the Semites; Seth, the son of Adam; Enosh, Seth's son in whose day people first began to call on the name of Yahweh (Gen 4:26);[254] and finally Adam. The expression "the splendor of Adam" (תפארת אדם *tip'eret 'ādām*) eventually led to speculation about a second Adam who would appear in the messianic age. In addition, the word translated "splendor" links v. 16 with 50:1, "the splendor of his people" (תפארת עמו *tip'eret 'ammô*). (See Reflections at 50:1-24.)

---

253. Peter Höffken, "Warum schweig Jesus Sirach über Esra? ["Why Was Jesus Sirach Silent About Ezra?"]," *ZAW* 87 (1975) 184-201.

254. Steven D. Fraade, *Enosh and His Generation*, SBLMS 30 (Chico, Calif.: Scholars Press, 1984).

SIRACH 50:1-24, SIMEON THE HIGH PRIEST

NAB

50 The greatest among his brethren, the glory of his people,
  was SIMON the priest, son of Jochanan,
In whose time the house of God was renovated,
  in whose days the temple was reinforced.
2 In his time also the wall was built
  with powerful turrets for the temple precincts;
3 In his time the reservoir was dug,
  the pool with a vastness like the sea's.
4 He protected his people against brigands
  and strengthened his city against the enemy.
5 How splendid he was as he appeared from the tent,
  as he came from within the veil!
6 Like a star shining among the clouds,
  like the full moon at the holyday season;
7 Like the sun shining upon the temple,
  like the rainbow appearing in the cloudy sky;

50, 1c: *nibdaq* (*habbāyit*): so LXX.
50, 2.3: Trsp: so LXX, P. 2b: (*pinnôt*) *mā'ôz*. Omit *melek* or understand it of God. 3b: *kayyām* (*bahāmônô*).
50, 6b: Omit *mibbēn*: so LXX, P; dittog from 6a.
50, 7a: Omit *melek*: so P; cf LXX and v 2b.

NRSV

50 The leader of his brothers and the pride of his people[a]
  was the high priest, Simon son of Onias,
who in his life repaired the house,
  and in his time fortified the temple.
2 He laid the foundations for the high double walls,
  the high retaining walls for the temple enclosure.
3 In his days a water cistern was dug,[b]
  a reservoir like the sea in circumference.
4 He considered how to save his people from ruin,
  and fortified the city against siege.
5 How glorious he was, surrounded by the people,
  as he came out of the house of the curtain.
6 Like the morning star among the clouds,
  like the full moon at the festal season;[b]
7 like the sun shining on the temple of the Most High,
  like the rainbow gleaming in splendid clouds;
8 like roses in the days of first fruits,

a Heb Syr: Gk lacks this line. Compare 49.15 *b* Heb: Meaning of Gk uncertain

NAB

8 Like the blossoms on the branches in
   springtime,
   like a lily on the banks of a stream;
   Like the trees of Lebanon in summer,
9 like the fire of incense at the sacrifice;
   Like a vessel of beaten gold,
   studded with precious stones;
10 Like a luxuriant olive tree thick with fruit,
   like a cypress standing against the clouds;
11 Vested in his magnificent robes,
   and wearing his garments of splendor,
   As he ascended the glorious altar
   and lent majesty to the court of the
   sanctuary.

12 When he received the sundered victims
   from the priests
   while he stood before the sacrificial wood,
   His brethren ringed him about like a garland,
   like a stand of cedars on Lebanon;
13 All the sons of Aaron in their dignity
   clustered around him like poplars,
   With the offerings to the LORD in their hands,
   in the presence of the whole assembly of
   Israel.
14 Once he had completed the services at the
   altar
   with the arranging of the sacrifices for the
   Most High,
15 And had stretched forth his hand for the
   cup,
   to offer blood of the grape,
   And poured it out at the foot of the altar,
   a sweet-smelling odor to the Most High
   God,
16 The sons of Aaron would sound a blast,
   the priests, on their trumpets of beaten
   metal;
   A blast to resound mightily
   as a reminder before the Most High.
17 Then all the people with one accord
   would quickly fall prostrate to the ground
   In adoration before the Most High,

50, 8: (kᵉnēṣ) baʿănāpîm.
50, 9b: (zāhāb) miqšâ?: cf LXX.
50, 10b: wᵉkibrôš mᵉrômam ʿānān: so LXX.
50, 11b: kᵉlîl (tipʾāret): so LXX; cf 45, 8.
50, 12c: (ʿăteret) ʾaḥîm: so LXX; cf P.
50, 15: With LXX; cf P.

NRSV

   like lilies by a spring of water,
   like a green shoot on Lebanon on a summer
   day;
9 like fire and incense in the censer,
   like a vessel of hammered gold
   studded with all kinds of precious stones;
10 like an olive tree laden with fruit,
   and like a cypress towering in the clouds.
11 When he put on his glorious robe
   and clothed himself in perfect splendor,
   when he went up to the holy altar,
   he made the court of the sanctuary glorious.

12 When he received the portions from the hands
   of the priests,
   as he stood by the hearth of the altar
   with a garland of brothers around him,
   he was like a young cedar on Lebanon
   surrounded by the trunks of palm trees.
13 All the sons of Aaron in their splendor
   held the Lord's offering in their hands
   before the whole congregation of Israel.
14 Finishing the service at the altars,ᵃ
   and arranging the offering to the Most High,
   the Almighty,
15 he held out his hand for the cup
   and poured a drink offering of the blood of
   the grape;
   he poured it out at the foot of the altar,
   a pleasing odor to the Most High, the king
   of all.
16 Then the sons of Aaron shouted;
   they blew their trumpets of hammered
   metal;
   they sounded a mighty fanfare
   as a reminder before the Most High.
17 Then all the people together quickly
   fell to the ground on their faces
   to worship their Lord,
   the Almighty, God Most High.

18 Then the singers praised him with their voices
   in sweet and full-toned melody.ᵇ
19 And the people of the Lord Most High offered
   their prayers before the Merciful One,
   until the order of worship of the Lord was ended,
   and they completed his ritual.

ᵃOther ancient authorities read *altar*   ᵇOther ancient authorities
read *in sweet melody throughout the house*

NAB

before the Holy One of Israel.

18 Then hymns would re-echo,
  and over the throng sweet strains of praise
    resound.
19 All the people of the land would shout for
    joy,
  praying to the Merciful One,
  As the high priest completed the services at
    the altar
  by presenting to God the sacrifice due;
20 Then coming down he would raise his
    hands
  over all the congregation of Israel.
  The blessing of the LORD would be upon his
    lips,
  the name of the LORD would be his glory.
21 Then again the people would lie prostrate
  to receive from him the blessing of the
    Most High.

22 And now, bless the God of all,
  who has done wondrous things on earth;
  Who fosters men's growth from their
    mother's womb,
  and fashions them according to his will!
23 May he grant you joy of heart
  and may peace abide among you;
24 May his goodness toward us endure in Israel
  as long as the heavens are above.

50, 18b: (wᵉˈal hāmôn) heˈēribû rinnã: cf LXX.
50, 21b: With LXX.
50, 22a: (bārᵉkû-nāˈ) ˈet-ˈĕlôhê hakkōl: so LXX.
50, 23: śimḥat (lēbāb, wîhî) šālôm: so LXX.
50, 24: (yēˈāmēn) ˈimmānû (ḥasdô), bᵉyiśrāˈēl kîmê šāmāyim; and
omit the rest: cf LXX, P.

NRSV

20 Then Simonᵃ came down and raised his hands
  over the whole congregation of Israelites,
  to pronounce the blessing of the Lord with his
    lips,
  and to glory in his name;
21 and they bowed down in worship a second
    time,
  to receive the blessing from the Most High.

22 And now bless the God of all,
  who everywhere works great wonders,
  who fosters our growth from birth,
  and deals with us according to his mercy.
23 May he give usᵇ gladness of heart,
  and may there be peace in ourᶜ days
  in Israel, as in the days of old.
24 May he entrust to us his mercy,
  and may he deliver us in ourᵈ days!

ᵃGk he   ᵇOther ancient authorities read you   ᶜOther ancient
authorities read your   ᵈOther ancient authorities read his

COMMENTARY

Evidently the last of Israel's heroes whom Ben Sira eulogizes has recently passed from the scene, having served as high priest 219–196 BCE. The language of v. 1 implies that Simeon was deceased (cf. the Greek for "in whose life" [ὅς ἐν ζωῇ αὐτοῦ *hos en zōē autou*]). Simeon II, called "the Just," made an

indelible impression on Ben Sira, which he conveys by means of exquisite similes and sensory language. Verses 1-4 continue the dominant theme of the praise of Hezekiah, Josiah, and Nehemiah—the strengthening of the city and improvement of its supply of water. A similar account of repairs in the early second century appears in Josephus,[255] who quotes a letter attributed to Antiochus III to the governor of Palestine after the Battle of Paneas in 199 BCE. If these reports are trustworthy, they indicate enormous political power resting in the hands of the religious leader at this time. The Hebrew words for "temple," בית (*bayit*) and היכל (*hêkāl*), although often used synonymously, can refer to the Temple and to a house generally. The inner sanctuary was called the דביר (*děbîr*), usually translated "Holy of Holies."

In vv. 5-21, Ben Sira describes Simeon's appearance on a special occasion in the Temple, either on Yom Kippur (the Day of Atonement) or at a celebration of the Daily Whole-Offering. Most interpreters opt for the first of these,[256] largely on the basis of the proclamation of the ineffable name (v. 20). Naturally, this view rests on the assumption that by Ben Sira's day the divine name "Yahweh" had become so holy that no one pronounced it, with a single exception: the high priest on the Day of Atonement. This interpretation has recently been challenged,[257] primarily on the basis of the description of the Tamid offering in the Mishnah tractate *Tamid* 6:3–7:3, but this new understanding of Ben Sira's text makes two major assumptions: (1) that the later tractate accurately describes the sacrificial ritual from the second century BCE and (2) that the differences between the two accounts (the omission of the incense offering and the placing of the blessing last instead of third) derive from an accident (the incense offering) or from an intentional change to achieve dramatic effect. The issue cannot be decided on the basis of the evidence available today, and the description in vv. 5-21 may be purposely general.

The emotional language of vv. 6-10 draws on the realms of nature and religious worship to convey Ben Sira's awe at witnessing the high priest in splendid vestments. Ben Sira's exuberance is contagious, as the similes show. Simeon is like a star, the full moon (which governed the timing of festivals), the sun, the rainbow, blossoms, a lily, the lush growth of Lebanon, incense, gold vessels, precious stones, an olive tree. Verses 11-13 describe the scene when a host of priestly attendants hand Simeon the carcasses and other offerings, reminding Ben Sira of a circle of trees.[258] Verse 14 emphasizes the proper ordering of the sacrifice, and v. 15 mentions the drink offering poured out at the foot of the altar. At a blast of the trumpets, everyone falls to the ground. Verse 18 mentions singing, and shouts of joy follow. Then the high priest, having completed the offerings, blesses the people and utters the name "Yahweh." Martin Rinckart's hymn "Nun danket alle Gott" ("Now Thank We All Our God") captures the religious intensity of this text magnificently.[259]

According to Josephus, "the sacred trumpets were long straight metal tubes of hammered silver . . . about a half a yard long . . . composed of a narrow tube, somewhat thicker than a flute and ended in the form of a bell, like common trumpets."[260] The people's response to hearing the name "Yahweh" is underscored in the Mishnah tractate *Yoma* 6.2: "And the priests and the people, who are standing in the court, when they hear the 'Ineffable Name' proceeding forth out of the mouth of the High-priest, bow down and worship, and fall upon their faces saying: 'Blessed be the Name of the glory of His kingdom for ever and ever.'" The expression "people of the land" (עם הארץ *'am hā'āreṣ*, v. 19) originally referred to persons who had high social standing, but eventually it came to refer to those lacking society's esteem. Here they represent the congregation, singing and praying in the presence of the merciful God.

Ben Sira concludes this eulogy of Simeon with a short personal blessing (vv. 22-24). Because of the gracious gift of life, he calls on God to grant permanent well-being to Simeon and his descendants from the line of Phinehas. That wish was quickly frustrated with the assassination of his son Onias III (cf. 2 Macc 4:34); hence the translator removes this hope entirely from the Greek text, making the specific reference a general one applying to all Israel.

---

255. Josephus *Antiquities of the Jews* 12.138-144.
256. W. O. E. Oesterley, *The Wisdom of Jesus the Son of Sirach or Ecclesiasticus* (Cambridge: Cambridge University Press, 1912) 342-43; John G. Snaith, *Ecclesiasticus or The Wisdom of Jesus, Son of Sirach*, CBC, NEB (Cambridge: Cambridge University Press, 1974) 251-53.
257. O. Fearghail, "Sir 50, 5-21: Yom Kippur or the Daily Whole-Offering?" *Bib* 59 (1978) 301-16.

258. Snaith, *Ecclesiasticus*, 252, thinks of the analogy with students and nurses surrounding a surgeon at the operating table.
259. Oesterley, *Ecclesiasticus*, 343.
260. Ibid., 341.

REFLECTIONS

1. The people whom one admires reveal much about oneself. A nation whose young people choose only celebrities for celebrity's sake—sports heroes, movie stars, and rock musicians—as idols has done a poor job of educating its public to appreciate those who contribute to the improvement of the human race. When the names of people like Jonas Salk, Marie Curie, Mahatma Gandhi, Albert Schweitzer, and countless others do not move young and old to expressions of gratitude for noble actions, something seriously wrong has infected the populace.

The deeper problem rests in the loss of imagination, the failure to seek challenges that inspire conduct of an extraordinary nature borne of discipline, achievement, and courage. Belief that God works in and through those who make significant strides toward nobler lives and who help to eradicate disease, crime, and poverty may require unconventional assumptions, but surely such thoughts merit serious consideration.

In looking around for heroes, we seldom pause long enough at home to reflect on our parents' qualifications in this regard. The obvious reason why is immediacy, the fact that we know their flaws too well as a result of constant exposure to them. Discovery that mothers and fathers have feet of clay often comes as a rude awakening, removing them permanently from the list of potential heroes. Ben Sira's willingness to weigh his heroes' complete lives and to make concessions for momentary lapses, some quite serious, stands as a marvelous example for contemporary readers.

Furthermore, he offers another clue with respect to a valid resource for locating heroes. For him, the written tradition of sacred texts—his Bible—contained the list of persons whom he most admired. Naturally, one must choose persons for such a list with care, and in doing so the operative criterion makes a world of difference. Religious persons who ponder seriously the definitive criteria for selecting heroes, and honestly give thought to various alternative criteria, will gain insight into their own values and character. Such meditation could well become a companion piece to annual reassessments at the turn of the year.

In a very real sense, our choice of heroes becomes a kind of sacred story, a record of temptations overcome, obstacles bypassed, goals achieved, and dreams realized. Together their stories move us to greater resolve, warm our souls, and open our eyes to needs and opportunities.

2. The author of the Epistle to the Hebrews acknowledged the presence of a cloud of witnesses hovering over us, a holy memory that lives on in our minds and evokes feelings of solidarity with the past (Heb 12:1-2). Modern believers also sense a presence of the extended family, persons who have preceded us into the great unknown. Those whom we especially cherish continue to have an important place in our lives.

In trying to link up with representatives of a bygone era, we tend to employ expressions from the past that communicated effectively at that time but may have become dead metaphors over the years. Ben Sira's contrivances, such as alphabetic hymns and ancient titles, certainly evoked an earlier time, while risking the alienation of persons in his own day whose language of discourse had become highly charged with Hellenistic ideas and expressions. Religious leaders almost inevitably face this sort of situation. Wishing to recapture the idyllic past, they use concepts appropriate to that period; at the same time, they hope such language has not lost its capacity to communicate in a new context.

Sometimes conservative by nature, religious people can tend to reject new ideas and expressions, and thus to lose touch with much of the population, particularly the young. Here, too, we need to be ever alert to the reasons for conservatism and to abandon this rejection of new ideas if the basis for refusing to change lacks merit. Knowing what to preserve and what to discard may be one of the most significant achievements in life.

3. What place do pomp and circumstance have in worship? Few people have reached a satisfactory answer to this vexing question. On the one hand, it seems entirely appropriate to honor God in as lavish a manner as possible; that includes a whole range of things, such as majestic cathedrals and places of worship; elaborate and expensive vestments; copious means of enrichment, including incense, intonation, music, dance, and so forth. On the other hand, simplicity has extraordinary appeal too. Combining the two, whenever attempted, has not been particularly successful, and yet we respond to both approaches to the holy.

Then, too, the place of religious fervor and a sense of the numinous come into play. Unless devotion to God gives birth to overwhelming gratitude and reminds one of ultimate dependency, it does not seem sufficiently compelling to deserve one's total allegiance. Ben Sira shamelessly gives voice to his religious passion, ultimately bowing before divine mystery. That degree of self-abandonment in the presence of the living God and celebration of gracious divine character challenges ordinary worshipers to ponder why so many days of worship lack this sense of ultimacy and fail to evoke zeal and awe.

SIRACH 50:25-29, A NUMERICAL PROVERB AND AN EPILOGUE

NAB

25 My whole being loathes two nations,
    the third is not even a people:
26 Those who live in Seir and Philistia,
    and the degenerate folk who dwell in
        Shechem.

27 Wise instruction, appropriate proverbs,
    I have written in this book,
    I, Jesus, son of Eleazar, son of Sirach,
        as they gushed forth from my heart's
        understanding.
28 Happy the man who meditates upon these
        things,
    wise the man who takes them to heart!
29 If he puts them into practice, he can cope
        with anything,
        for the fear of the LORD is his lamp.

50, 27: (*mûsar śēkel*) *ûmišlê ᵓōpānîm, kātabtî bassēper hazzeh, yēšûaᶜ ben ᵓelᶜāzār ben sîrāᵓ, ăšer hibbîᶜâ tᵉbûnat libbî*: cf LXX, P
50, 29a: With LXX. 29b: (*kî yirᵓat yhwh*) *nērōᵓ*: so LXX, *lychnos* for *ichnos?*

NRSV

25 Two nations my soul detests,
    and the third is not even a people:
26 Those who live in Seir,[a] and the Philistines,
    and the foolish people that live in Shechem.

27 Instruction in understanding and knowledge
    I have written in this book,
    Jesus son of Eleazar son of Sirach[b] of Jerusalem,
        whose mind poured forth wisdom.
28 Happy are those who concern themselves with
        these things,
    and those who lay them to heart will
        become wise.
29 For if they put them into practice, they will
        be equal to anything,
        for the fear[c] of the Lord is their path.

[a] Heb Compare Lat: Gk *on the mountain of Samaria*   [b] Heb: Meaning of Gk uncertain   [c] Heb: Other ancient authorities read *light*

COMMENTARY

The internationalism of the sage vanishes in this bitter invective about three of Judah's neighbors: Canaanites, Edomites, and Samaritans, for whom Ben Sira uses ancient designations. The Philistines, who gave their name to the land of Palestine, had vanished long before Ben Sira's time, thus he may be referring to the pro-Hellenistic people dwelling along the seacoast. By Seir he indicates the Idumeans, loathed because of their ancestors' treatment of Jews during the Babylonian conquest of Jerusalem; soon after Ben Sira's time, they were forcibly converted to Judaism by John Hyrcanus. The Samaritans, inhabitants of the area around Shechem, had intermarried with the population settled in the vicinity after the expulsion of the Jewish landowners into Babylonian captivity. In the fourth century BCE, Ezra and Nehemiah rebuffed the Samaritans' offer to help restore the sanctuary at Jerusalem. Hostilities between the two groups increased because of the existence of

a rival temple on Mt. Gerizim near Shechem, exacerbated by their claim to be the legitimate descendants of Phinehas. The extent of the Jews' hatred of the Samaritans can be measured by a comment in *The Testament of the Twelve Patriarchs:* "From this day forward Shechem will be called a city of imbeciles, for as one mocks a fool, so we mocked them" (*Testament of Levi* 7.2; cf. Deut 32:21, "a foolish nation" [גוי נבל *gôy nābāl*]; Luke 9:51-55; John 4:9). Such intense dislike led to the destruction of the temple on Mt. Gerizim in 128 BCE.

The epilogue (vv. 27-29) contains Ben Sira's full name and a sort of summary of the advantages that come to those who study his teachings and embody them in their lives. Both meditation (cf. Ps 1:1) and praxis (cf. Eccl 7:2; 9:1) come into play here, and Ben Sira echoes the introduction to the book of Proverbs (1:1-3) and the epilogue to Ecclesiastes (12:9-10).

REFLECTIONS

Even good people have weak moments and blind spots that lead them into embarrassing situations, for which they genuinely repent. Ben Sira's hatred for three neighboring peoples may have been entirely justified, humanly speaking, by their repeated offenses. Nevertheless, his attitude toward Samaritans, Idumeans, and Hellenists along the coastal strip seriously compromised his teachings, for sages should have been able to rise above such petty hatred. The very context of this sentiment, so terribly out of place, corresponds to its place in Ben Sira's life. It did not belong anywhere if he truly lived up to his teaching.

From this text we easily observe that even great men, and by extension women, at some time will have to rely on others' tolerance. No one need hurl the first stone at Ben Sira, for we all are guilty. Such momentary lapses bring dishonor, to be sure, but they should not destroy one's reputation. In judging Ben Sira's character, one needs to consider the total picture rather than a single moment.

Besides the psychological release and honest confession before God, the positive contribution of such expression of hatred may be found in what it generates in good people, specifically extensive self-examination. Perhaps this soul-searching will enable us all to see the error in judging others by nationality, class, or whatever group they belong to rather than seeing each individual as a person deserving the same respect.

SIRACH 51:1-30, A PRAYER OF THANKSGIVING, A HYMN OF PRAISE, AND AN ACROSTIC POEM ABOUT WISDOM

NAB

51 I give you thanks, O God of my father;
I praise you, O God my savior!
I will make known your name, refuge of my
life;

2 you have been my helper against my
adversaries.
You have saved me from death,
and kept back my body from the pit,
From the clutches of the nether world you
have snatched my feet;

3 you have delivered me, in your great mercy,
From the scourge of a slanderous tongue,
and from lips that went over to falsehood;
From the snare of those who watched for my
downfall,
and from the power of those who sought
my life;
From many a danger you have saved me,

4 from flames that hemmed me in on every
side;
From the midst of unremitting fire,

5 From the deep belly of the nether world;
From deceiving lips and painters of lies,

6 from the arrows of dishonest tongues.
I was at the point of death,
my soul was nearing the depths of the
nether world;

7 I turned every way, but there was no one to
help me,
I looked for one to sustain me, but could
find no one.

8 But then I remembered the mercies of the LORD,
his kindness through ages past;
For he saves those who take refuge in him,
and rescues them from every evil.

9 So I raised my voice from the very earth,

51, 1: Trsp a and b: so LXX, P.
51, 2a: Trsp from 2g: *neged qāmay hāyîtā lî ʿezer.* cf LXX. 2d:
(*hiṣṣaltā*) *raglî.* so P. Trsp rest to v 3.
51, 3a: *pᵉṣîtanî kᵉrōb ḥasdekā.* 3b.c: Omit *middibbat ʿām* (variant)
and trsp *miṣṣôṭ dibbat lāšôn ûmissᵉpat šaṭê kāzāb* from v 2. 3d: (*ṣôpê*)
ṣalʿî.
51, 4b: *millabbôt (ʿēš) weʾ ên mᵉkabbeh (?).*
51, 5a: (*mērehem tᵉhôm*) ʿāmōq: cf LXX.

NRSV

51 I give you thanks, O Lord and King,
and praise you, O God my Savior.
I give thanks to your name,

2 for you have been my protector and helper
and have delivered me from destruction
and from the trap laid by a slanderous
tongue,
from lips that fabricate lies.
In the face of my adversaries
you have been my helper ³and delivered me,
in the greatness of your mercy and of your
name,
from grinding teeth about to devour me,
from the hand of those seeking my life,
from the many troubles I endured,

4 from choking fire on every side,
and from the midst of fire that I had not
kindled,

5 from the deep belly of Hades,
from an unclean tongue and lying words—

6 the slander of an unrighteous tongue to the
king.
My soul drew near to death,
and my life was on the brink of Hades
below.

7 They surrounded me on every side,
and there was no one to help me;
I looked for human assistance,
and there was none.

8 Then I remembered your mercy, O Lord,
and your kindnessᵃ from of old,
for you rescue those who wait for you
and save them from the hand of their
enemies.

9 And I sent up my prayer from the earth,
and begged for rescue from death.

10 I cried out, "Lord, you are my Father;ᵇ
do not forsake me in the days of trouble,
when there is no help against the proud.

11 I will praise your name continually,

ᵃOther ancient authorities read *work*   ᵇHeb: Gk *the Father of
my lord*

NAB

from the gates of the nether world, my cry.

10 I called out: O Lord, you are my father,
    you are my champion and my savior;
Do not abandon me in time of trouble,
    in the midst of storms and dangers.

11 I will ever praise your name
    and be constant in my prayers to you.
Thereupon the LORD heard my voice,
    he listened to my appeal;

12 He saved me from evil of every kind
    and preserved me in time of trouble.
For this reason I thank him and I praise him;
    I bless the name of the LORD.

13 When I was young and innocent,
    I sought wisdom.

14 She came to me in her beauty,
    and until the end I will cultivate her.

15 As the blossoms yielded to ripening grapes,
    the heart's joy,
My feet kept to the level path
    because from earliest youth I was familiar
        with her.

16 In the short time I paid heed,
    I met with great instruction.

17 Since in this way I have profited,
    I will give my teacher grateful praise.

18 I became resolutely devoted to her—
    the good I persistently strove for.

19 I burned with desire for her,
    never turning back.
I became preoccupied with her,
    never weary of extolling her.
My hand opened her gate
    and I came to know her secrets.

20 For her I purified my hands;
    in cleanness I attained to her.
At first acquaintance with her, I gained
        understanding
    such that I will never forsake her.

21 My whole being was stirred as I learned
    about her;

51, 12d: Omit following hymn: so LXX, P; later addition.
51, 17: *hôdô*: Q *hôdāy* (?)
51, 18: *wā᾿eḥš*ᵉ*qā*: Q *w᾿śḥqh*.
51, 19: *tāradtî*: Q *trty*; *ûb erôm*ᵉ*mêbā*: Q *wbrwmyh*.
51, 20: *ûb*ᵉ*niqqāyōn*: cf LXX.
51, 20c-30: the Cairo text here is mainly retroversion: cf LXX, P.
51, 21: Omit *kattannûr*: so LXX.

NRSV

and will sing hymns of thanksgiving."
My prayer was heard,
12 for you saved me from destruction
    and rescued me in time of trouble.
For this reason I thank you and praise you,
    and I bless the name of the Lord.

———————

Give thanks to the LORD, for he is good,
    for his mercy endures forever;

Give thanks to the God of praises,
    for his mercy endures forever;

Give thanks to the guardian of Israel,
    for his mercy endures forever;

Give thanks to him who formed all things,
    for his mercy endures forever;

Give thanks to the redeemer of Israel,
    for his mercy endures forever;

Give thanks to him who gathers the dispersed
        of Israel,
    for his mercy endures forever;

Give thanks to him who rebuilt his city and
        his sanctuary,
    for his mercy endures forever;

Give thanks to him who makes a horn to
        sprout for the house of David,
    for his mercy endures forever;

Give thanks to him who has chosen the sons
        of Zadok to be priests,
    for his mercy endures forever;

Give thanks to the shield of Abraham,
    for his mercy endures forever;

Give thanks to the rock of Isaac,
    for his mercy endures forever;

Give thanks to the mighty one of Jacob,
    for his mercy endures forever;

Give thanks to him who has chosen Zion,
    for his mercy endures forever;

NAB

therefore I have made her my prize
possession.

22 The LORD has granted me my lips as a
reward,
and my tongue will declare his praises.

23 Come aside to me, you untutored,
and take up lodging in the house of
instruction;

24 How long will you be deprived of wisdom's
food,
how long will you endure such bitter
thirst?

25 I open my mouth and speak of her:
gain, at no cost, wisdom for yourselves.

26 Submit your neck to her yoke,
that your mind may accept her teaching.
For she is close to those who seek her,
and the one who is in earnest finds her.

27 See for yourselves! I have labored only a
little,
but have found much.

28 Acquire but a little instruction;
you will win silver and gold through her.

29 Let your spirits rejoice in the mercy of God,
and be not ashamed to give him praise.

30 Work at your tasks in due season,
and in his own time God will give you
your reward.

51, 24a: *m*ᵉˈ*oklāh*: conj.
51, 26: {*ûtᵉqabbēl napšᵉkem leqaḥ*: cf LXX.
51, 27: {*kî*} *m*ᵉˈ*aṭ* ˈ*āmāltî, ûmāṣāˈtî harbēh*: cf LXX; P.
51, 29: {*tišmaḥ*} *napšᵉkem*: so LXX, P.
51, 30: *po*ˈ*ōˈûpo*ˈ*olᵉkem b*ᵉˈ*ittô, w*ᵉ*yitten* {*šᵉkarᵉkem b*ᵉˈ*ittô*}: cf
LXX, P. Omit the following lines of Cairo B: so LXX; later additions.

NRSV

Give thanks to the King of the kings of kings,
for his mercy endures forever;

He has raised up a horn for his people,
praise for all his loyal ones.

For the children of Israel, the people close to
him.
Praise the LORD!

———————

13 While I was still young, before I went on my
travels,
I sought wisdom openly in my prayer.

14 Before the temple I asked for her,
and I will search for her until the end.

15 From the first blossom to the ripening grape
my heart delighted in her;
my foot walked on the straight path;
from my youth I followed her steps.

16 I inclined my ear a little and received her,
and I found for myself much instruction.

17 I made progress in her;
to him who gives wisdom I will give glory.

18 For I resolved to live according to wisdom,[a]
and I was zealous for the good,
and I shall never be disappointed.

19 My soul grappled with wisdom,[a]
and in my conduct I was strict;[b]

I spread out my hands to the heavens,
and lamented my ignorance of her.

20 I directed my soul to her,
and in purity I found her.

With her I gained understanding from the first;
therefore I will never be forsaken.

21 My heart was stirred to seek her;
therefore I have gained a prize possession.

22 The Lord gave me my tongue as a reward,
and I will praise him with it.

23 Draw near to me, you who are uneducated,
and lodge in the house of instruction.

24 Why do you say you are lacking in these things,[c]

[a] Gk *her*   [b] Meaning of Gk uncertain   [c] Cn Compare Heb Syr:
Meaning of Gk uncertain

NRSV

and why do you endure such great thirst?

²⁵ I opened my mouth and said,
Acquire wisdom*a* for yourselves without
money.

²⁶ Put your neck under her*b* yoke,
and let your souls receive instruction;
it is to be found close by.

²⁷ See with your own eyes that I have labored
but little
and found for myself much serenity.
²⁸ Hear but a little of my instruction,
and through me you will acquire silver and
gold.*c*

²⁹ May your soul rejoice in God's*d* mercy,
and may you never be ashamed to praise
him.
³⁰ Do your work in good time,
and in his own time God*e* will give you your
reward.

a Heb: Gk lacks *wisdom*   *b* Heb: other ancient authorities read *the*
c Syr Compare Heb: Gk *Get instruction with a large sum of silver,
and you will gain by it much gold.*   *d* Gk *his*   *e* Gk *he*

COMMENTARY

51:1-12. The first twelve verses of this chapter comprise a prayer in which Ben Sira employs traditional language to give thanks for deliverance from an unspecified threat. The prayer is sufficiently general to be used by almost any worshiper. An anthological style draws on the language of biblical psalms to recount the author's subjection to verbal abuse, his descent into the abyss of despair, and his remembering the Lord's mercy. Addressing Yahweh as "my father" (אבי *'ābî*), Ben Sira begs God not to forsake him. The prayer concludes with the declaration that the Lord listened to the plea and acted on behalf of the supplicant (cf. Pss 17:9; 30:3; 55:9; 116:8). In a study on the poetic structure of this declarative psalm of praise, Di Lella identifies six stanzas and isolates instances of artistic balance or corre-

spondence, inclusion, chiasm, breakup of stereotyped phrases, rhyme, and parallelism.[261]

The dual epithet for God, "Lord and King" (v. 1), together with "Father" (v. 10) recall common expressions in ancient Jewish prayers, e.g., "Our Father, our Sovereign" in the prayer by that name, in "Great Love," and in "The Eighteen Benedictions," where the clauses begin with "Our Father" and "Our King" alternately.[262]

A litany of praise follows this prayer in MS B, but it does not appear in the Greek, the Syriac, or any translations based on them. Moreover, the Greek text has a title for the entire chapter, "The Prayer of Jesus, son of Sirach," which applies only

261. Alexander A. Di Lella, "Sirach 51:1-12: Poetic Structure and Analysis of Ben Sira's Psalm," *CBQ* 48 (1986) 395-407.
262. W. O. E. Oesterley, *The Wisdom of Jesus the Son of Sirach or Ecclesiasticus* (Cambridge: Cambridge University Press, 1912) 346.

to vv. 1-12. Although the litany does not appear to have been written by Ben Sira, it dates from before 152 BCE, when the Hasmonean Jonathan received the high priesthood as a reward for supporting Alexander Balas of Syria (cf. 51:12 ix, which implies that Zadokites are still in control of the priesthood). Di Lella conjectures that a member of the Essene community at Qumran wrote the psalm and inserted it into a copy of Sirach that found its way into a cave near Jericho and eventually into the hands of Qaraites, who made copies that were discovered in the Cairo Geniza between 1896 and 1900.[263]

Like Psalm 136, this psalm contains the refrain "for his mercy endures forever" in fourteen of the sixteen verses (cf. Pss 106:1; 107:1; 118:1, 29 for the same expression). The language is entirely biblical ("the Guardian of Israel" in Ps 121:4; "who fashioned everything" in Jer 10:16; 51:19; "the Redeemer of Israel" in Isa 49:7; "who gathered Israel's dispersed" in Isa 56:8; "who rebuilt his city" in Isa 60:13; "who makes a horn to sprout for David's house" in Ps 132:17; Ezek 29:21). Similarly, the divine epithets in 51:12 x-xii derive from the patriarchal narratives—the Shield of Abraham, Rock of Isaac, Mighty One of Jacob.

51:13-30. An alphabetical poem about wisdom concludes the book of Sirach, as in Prov 31:10-31—even though Ben Sira never uses the noun "wisdom" in the poem. Verses 13-21 describe Ben Sira's search for wisdom, and vv. 22-30 contain a personal appeal to others to follow his example. A copy of this poem has been found in a scroll from Qumran (11QPs^a) containing lines א (aleph) through כ (kaph; ll. 1-20). In the translation by J. A. Sanders, this poem is interpreted as an erotic text,[264] and various scholars have offered alternative readings.[265] An erotic understanding of personified wisdom certainly exists in Proverbs 8 and Wisdom 7, however one views Ben Sira's acrostic.

The poem tells how a young Ben Sira determined to cultivate wisdom from youth to old age and how wisdom gave herself to him as he pursued her paths and set his heart on her. As reward for faithfulness, he received a gift of eloquence (cf. Isa 50:4), which equipped him to teach others. He thus invites people to come to his house of learning (MS B has "into my house of instruction" [בבית מדרשי bĕbêt midrāšî]; Di Lella claims that both the Greek and Syriac texts demand a reading of "into the house of learning" [בבית מוסר bĕbêt mûsār] and sees a play on words based on סור [sûr, "to be remote"]).[266] Ben Sira's language about money, reward, and thirst may be purely metaphorical, like Prov 4:5-7; Isa 55:1-3; Amos 8:11. Too little is known about education in second-century BCE Israel to ascertain whether one should assume that Ben Sira received payment for instructing students.[267]

The final two verses nicely juxtapose the complementary theological concepts of grace and merit. Remembering the Lord's mercy, one ought to do good works and await a reward in God's own time. In this short statement, Ben Sira effectively combines religious and social teachings.

The Hebrew manuscript closes with a long subscript stating that the work has reached its conclusion and identifying its author as Simeon, the son of Jeshua who is called Ben Sira. It adds: "The Wisdom of Simeon, the son of Jeshua, the son of Eleasar, the son of Sira. May Yahweh's name be blessed from now unto the ages" (cf. Ps 113:2).

263. Skehan and Di Lella, *The Wisdom of Ben Sira,* 569.

264. J. A. Sanders, *The Psalms Scroll of Qumran Cave II (11QPs^a),* DJD 4 (Oxford: Clarendon, 1965) 70-85; and *The Dead Sea Psalms Scroll* (Ithaca, N.Y.: Cornell University Press, 1967) 112-17.

265. J. Muraoka, "Sir 51:13-20: An Erotic Hymn to Wisdom?" *JSJ* 10 (1979) 166-78; and C. Deutsch, "The Sirach 51 Acrostic: Confession and Exhortation," *ZAW* 94 (1982) 400-409.

266. See Patrick W. Skehan and Alexander A. Di Lella, *The Wisdom of Ben Sira,* AB 39 (New York: Doubleday, 1987) 578.

267. Cf. *Pirqe 'Abot* 4:9.

TRANSLITERATION SCHEMA

HEBREW AND ARAMAIC TRANSLITERATION

Consonants:

א	=	ʾ	ט	=	*ṭ*	פ or ף	=	*p*
ב	=	*b*	י	=	*y*	צ or ץ	=	*ṣ*
ג	=	*g*	כ or ך	=	*k*	ק	=	*q*
ד	=	*d*	ל	=	*l*	ר	=	*r*
ה	=	*h*	מ or ם	=	*m*	שׂ	=	*ś*
ו	=	*w*	נ or ן	=	*n*	שׁ	=	*š*
ז	=	*z*	ס	=	*s*	ת	=	*t*
ח	=	*ḥ*	ע	=	ʿ			

Masoretic Pointing:

Pure-long			Tone-long			Short			Composite *shewa*		
הָ	=	*â*	ָ	=	*ā*	ַ	=	*a*	ֲ	=	*ă*
ֵי or ֶי	=	*ê*	ֵ	=	*ē*	ֶ	=	*e*	ֱ or ֵ	=	*ĕ*
ִי or ִ	=	*î*				ִ	=	*i*			
ֹ or וֹ	=	*ô*	ֹ	=	*ō*	ָ	=	*o*	ֳ	=	*ŏ*
ֻ or וּ	=	*û*				ֻ	=	*u*			

GREEK TRANSLITERATION

α	=	*a*	ι	=	*i*	ρ	=	*r*
β	=	*b*	κ	=	*k*	σ or ς	=	*s*
γ	=	*g*	λ	=	*l*	τ	=	*t*
δ	=	*d*	μ	=	*m*	υ	=	*y*
ε	=	*e*	ν	=	*n*	φ	=	*ph*
ζ	=	*z*	ξ	=	*x*	χ	=	*ch*
η	=	*ē*	ο	=	*o*	ψ	=	*ps*
θ	=	*th*	π	=	*p*	ω	=	*ō*

INDEX OF CHARTS AND EXCURSUSES

ABBREVIATIONS

BCE	Before the Common Era
CE	Common Era
c.	circa
cf.	compare
chap(s).	chapter(s)
d.	died
esp.	especially
fem.	feminine
lit.	literally
LXX	Septuagint
masc.	masculine
MS(S)	manuscript(s)
MT	Masoretic Text
OL	Old Latin
n.(n.)	note(s)
NT	New Testament
OL	Old Latin
OT	Old Testament
pl(s).	plate(s)
v(v).	verse(s)
Vg	Vulgate

Names of Biblical Books (with the Apocrypha)

Gen	Nah	1–4 Kgdms	John
Exod	Hab	Add Esth	Acts
Lev	Zeph	Bar	Rom
Num	Hag	Bel	1–2 Cor
Deut	Zech	1–2 Esdr	Gal
Josh	Mal	4 Ezra	Eph
Judg	Ps (Pss)	Jdt	Phil
1–2 Sam	Job	Ep Jer	Col
1–2 Kgs	Prov	1–4 Macc	1–2 Thess
Isa	Ruth	Pr Azar	1–2 Tim
Jer	Cant	Pr Man	Titus
Ezek	Eccl	Sir	Phlm
Hos	Lam	Sus	Heb
Joel	Esth	Tob	Jas
Amos	Dan	Wis	1–2 Pet
Obad	Ezra	Matt	1–3 John
Jonah	Neh	Mark	Jude
Mic	1–2 Chr	Luke	Rev

Names of Pseudepigraphical and Early Patristic Books

1, 2, 3 Enoch	Ethiopic, Slavonic, Hebrew *Enoch*

Names of Dead Sea Scrolls and Related Texts

CD	Cairo (Genizah text of the) *Damascus (Document)*
1QH	Hôdāyôt (Thanksgiving Hymns) from Qumran Cave 1
1QM	*Milḥā mā h* (*War Scroll*)
1QS	*Serek hayyaḥad (Rule of the Community, Manual of Discipline)*

'Abot	'Abot
'Arak.	'Arakin
m. B. Bat.	m. Baba Batra
m. Ma'aś	m. Ma'aśerot
Šabb	Šabbat
Sanh.	Sanhedrin
m. Yad m. Yadayim	

AB	Anchor Bible
ABD	Anchor Bible Dictionary
AJSL	American Journal of Semitic Languages and Literature
AnBib	Analecta biblica
ANEP	J. B. Pritchard (ed.), Ancient Near East in Pictures
ANET	J. B. Pritchard (ed.), Ancient Near Eastern Texts
APOT	R. H. Charles (ed.), Apocrypha and Pseudepigrapha of the Old Testament
BBB	Bonner biblische Beiträge
BBET	Beiträge zur biblischen Exegese und Theologie
BETL	Bibliotheca ephemeridum theologicarum lovaniensium
Bib	Biblica
BibOr	Biblica et orientalia
BJS	Brown Judaic Studies
BK	Bibel und Kirche
BLS	Bible and Literature Series
BN	Biblische Notizen
BTB	Biblical Theology Bulletin
BZAW	Beihefte zur ZAW
BZNW	Beihefte zur Zeitschrift für die neutestamentliche Wissenschaft
CBC	Cambridge Bible Commentary
CBOTS	Coniectanea Biblica: Old Testament Series
CBQ	Catholic Biblical Quarterly
CBQMS	Catholic Biblical Quarterly—Monograph Series
DJD	Discoveries in the Judaean Desert
EstBib	Estudios bíblicos
ETL	Ephemerides theologicae lovanienses
ETS	Erfurter theologische Studien
FOTL	Forms of Old Testament Literature
GNB	Good News Bible
HAR	Hebrew Annual Review
HR	History of Religions
HSM	Harvard Semitic Monographs
HTR	Harvard Theological Review
HTS	Harvard Theological Studies
HUCA	Hebrew Union College Annual
ICC	International Critical Commentary
ITC	International Theological Commentary
JAAR	Journal of the American Academy of Religion
JB	Jerusalem Bible
JBL	Journal of Biblical Literature
JNES	Journal of Near Eastern Studies
JSJ	Journal for the Study of Judaism in the Persian, Hellenistic and Roman Period
JSOT	Journal for the Study of the Old Testament
JSOTSup	Journal for the Study of the Old Testament—Supplement Series
KJV	King James (or Authorized) Version
LCL	Loeb Classical Library
NCB	New Century Bible
NEB	New English Bible
NIB	New Interpreter's Bible
NIV	New International Version of the Bible
NJB	New Jerusalem Bible
NJBC	R. E. Brown et al. (eds.), The New Jerome Biblical Commentary
NKJV	New King James Version of the Bible
NRSV	New Revised Standard Version
OBO	Orbis biblicus et orientalis

OTL	Old Testament Library
OTM	Old Testament Message
OTS	*Oudtestamentische Studiën*
RB	*Revue biblique*
REB	Revised English Bible
RevQ	*Revue de Qumran*
RSRel	*Revue des sciences religeuses*
RSV	Revised Standard Version of the Bible
RTL	*Revue théologique de Louvain*
SBLDS	SBL Dissertation Series
SBLMS	SBL Monograph Series
SBS	Stuttgarter Bibelstudien
SBT	Studies in Biblical Theology
SVT	*Supplements to Vetus Testamentum*
TextS	*Texts and Studies*
TNK	Tanakh
TLB	The Living Bible
TOTC	Tyndale Old Testament Commentary
VT	*Vetus Testamentum*
VTSup	Vetus Testamentum, Supplements
WBC	*Word Biblical Commentary*
WTJ	*Westminster Theological Journal*
WMANT	*Wissenschaftliche Monographien zum Alten und Neuen Testament*
WUNT	Wissenschaftliche Untersuchungen zum Neuen Testament
ZAW	*Zeitschrift für die alttestamentliche Wissenschaft*
ZThK	*Zeitschrift für Theologie und Kirche*